JIM MURRAY'S
WHISKY
BIBLE
2013

This 2013 edition is dedicated to
that consummate professional of the blending lab, my old and dear friend
David Stewart
to mark his 50th anniversary year with William Grant;
to celebrate the 50th anniversary of the birth of
Angela D'Orazio
who in a short time has put Scandinavian whisky on the map.
My congratulations and love to you both.
It is also dedicated to the cherished memory of
Barry Kitchener (1947 - 2012)

This edition first published 2012 by Dram Good Books Ltd

10 9 8 7 6 5 4 3 2 1

The "Jim Murray's" logo and the "Whisky Bible" logo are trade marks of Jim Murray.

Text, tasting notes & rankings, artwork, Jim Murray's logo and the Whisky Bible logo copyright © Jim Murray 2012

Design copyright © Dram Good Books Ltd 2012

For information regarding using tasting notes from Jim Murray's Whisky Bible contact: Dram Good Books Ltd, 9 Edison Court, Wellingborough, Northamptonshire, UK, NN8 6AH Tel: 44 (0)117 317 9777. Or contact us via www.whiskybible.com

ISBN: 978-0-9554729-7-8

Printed in England by Stanley L Hunt (Printers) Ltd. Rushden, Northamptonshire www.stanleylhunt.co.uk

Written by: Jim Murray
Edited by: David Rankin
Design: James Murray, Jim Murray
Maps and Cover Design: James Murray
Production: James Murray, Billy Jeffrey, Ally Telfer, Dani Dal Molin
Sample Research: Ally Telfer, Julia Nourney
Cover Photograph: Clive Wagner

Author's Note
I have used the spelling "whiskey" or "whisky" depending on how the individual distillers prefer. All Scotch is "whisky". So is Canadian. All Irish, these days, is "whiskey", though that was not always the case. In Kentucky, bourbon and rye are spelt "whiskey", with the exception of the produce of the early Times/Old Forester Distillery and Maker's Mark which they bottle as "whisky". In Tennessee, it is a 50-50 split: Dickel is "whisky", while Daniel's is "whiskey".

JIM MURRAY'S
WHISKY
BIBLE
2013

DRAM GOOD BOOKS

Contents

Introduction

So here I sit. Looking down at the Rocky Mountains from 30,000 feet with the sun setting in a spectacular blaze of gold. The snow-capped peaks below glint a warm colour not dissimilar to the whisky in the glass rattling beside me.

I am in my favourite seat: a window one upstairs on a British Airways Boeing 747 as it powers away from its town of birth. And, at long last, after four brutal, sensory bombarded months, I can relax. Well, almost.

When the final word to this introduction has been typed the tenth edition of Jim Murray's Whisky Bible will have been completed. I have just spent a period in Victoria, British Columbia, and Portland, Oregon, tasting and writing the last of the North American whiskies. By the time I tasted my last sample a record 1,350 new whiskies had been analysed for this edition.

I would be lying if I said that the sleep I will get on this flight will not be welcome. Such is the character of whisky these days, there is barely such a thing as an easy tasting. Certainly there are far, far fewer than when I worked my way through the original 2,100 whiskies in 2003 which made up the very first edition. Then, the majority of whiskies were at 40% or 43% abv and dulled by caramel. Not anymore. Every other whisky I taste appears to be at cask strength and naturally coloured. Distillers, especially the new guys in the US, have gone out of their way to change the whisky landscape with countless rugged, searching drams which stretch taste buds not just to the limit but at times beyond.

Those are tiring enough. But they are fun and sometimes spectacularly beautiful; on the rarest occasions unique. More exhausting are the whiskies similar to the one served to me by the steward. The aroma immediately reveals, (and, honestly, I couldn't make this up!) that sulphur is present...and that is even without having picked it up to nose. One confirming mouthful and ...oh, dear, oh dear! Here's the double irony: I was about to mention the theme of this year's Bible Thumping. And this morning I was writing for Britain's biggest selling Sunday newspaper, telling that any home whisky cabinet is incomplete without the Whisky Bible multi-award winner I have just been served. Yet, here I am, just 12 hours later, looking at a glass of it as a wife might her husband she had just discovered in bed with her sister. Betrayal does not come any bigger. However, there is an irritating sense of inevitability, too...

Which all goes to underline why, of all the Bible Thumpings I have written, this year's is the most hard-hitting and vital yet. I have warned that we have reached a crisis when it comes to the presence of sulphur in whisky – and not just scotch. The last ten minutes has highlighted that threat in the most dramatic and vivid way possible.

But, equally, it would be wrong to say there are no roses in the garden: quite the contrary. As this year's Whisky Bible confirms, there is an extraordinary number of great whiskies out there to enjoy wherever you may be in the world. Yet check through the scores, taste the whiskies and something will become very apparent. Just like in society, the gap between the rich and poor is widening. Especially with scotch. In other words, the very best whiskies are getting collectively better. And there are more of them, as our Liquid Gold section for whiskies scoring 94 and above will testify. While at the bottom end the worst are of even lower quality. This polarisation can be put down to the most extraordinary choice we have in fine old malts these days which ten years ago simply didn't exist in the market place; as well as the better distillers working harder to ensure excellence alongside Scotland's trailblazers turning the industry's old conservatism on its head to re-draw the boundaries. While the poorer quality is a mix of the widening sulphur problem and unsophisticated bottom end parcels being bought up and bottled as shortage of stocks available to bottlers at the mid-range ages bites deep.

It means that Jim Murray's Whisky Bible is perhaps even more relevant today than it was a decade ago. Because choosing a whisky is becoming a little more of a minefield. So an independent map of where to step becomes invaluable.

Whisky, then, remains a moving target. As if to prove it, 2012 has already seen two giants of the independent whisky distilling world, Cooley in Ireland and Bruichladdich on Islay, snaffled up by the big boys for a combined cost of over £100 million. And by the time the 2014 edition is completed I will be surprised if other distilleries have not changed hands.

The sun may be setting on the writing of this edition. But when I wake up the dawn will break on the next. That's Jim Murray's Whisky Bible for you...

Jim Murray
Seat 63A Flight BA48
Somewhere between Seattle and London
August 2012

How to Read The Bible

The whole point of this book is for the whisky lover – be he or she an experienced connoisseur or, better fun still, simply starting out on the long and joyous path of discovery – to have ready access to easy-to-understand information about as many whiskies as possible. And I mean a lot. Thousands.

This book does not quite include every whisky on the market... just by far and away the vast majority. And those that have been missed this time round – either through accident, logistics or design – will appear in later editions once we can source a sample.

Whisky Scoring

The marking for this book is tailored to the consumer and scores run out just a little higher than I use for my own personal references. But such is the way it has been devised that it has not affected my order of preference.

Each whisky is given a rating out of 100. Twenty-five marks are given to each of four factors: nose (**n**), taste (**t**), finish (**f**), balance and overall complexity (**b**). That means that 50% of the marks are given for flavour alone and 25% for the nose, often an overlooked part of the whisky equation. The area of balance and complexity covers all three previous factors and a usually hidden one besides:

Nose: this is simply the aroma. Often requires more than one inspection as hidden aromas can sometimes reveal themselves after time in the glass, increased contact with air and changes in temperature. The nose very often tells much about a whisky, but – as we shall see – equally can be quite misleading.

Taste: this is the immediate arrival on the palate and involves the flavour profile up to, and including, the time it reaches maximum intensity and complexity.

Finish: often the least understood part of a tasting. This is the tail and flourish of the whisky's signature, often revealing the effects of ageing. The better whiskies tend to finish well and longer without too much oak excess. It is on the finish, also, that certain notes which are detrimental to the whisky may be observed. For instance, a sulphur-tarnished cask may be fully revealed for what it is by a dry, bitter residue on the palate which is hard to shake off. It is often worth waiting a few minutes to get the full picture of the finish before having a second taste of a whisky.

Balance: This is the part it takes a little experience to appreciate but it can be mastered by anyone. For a whisky to work well on the nose and palate, it should not be too one-sided in its character. If you are looking for an older whisky, it should have evidence of oak, but not so much that all other flavours and aromas are drowned out. Likewise, a whisky matured or finished in a sherry butt must offer a lot more than just wine alone and the greatest Islay malts, for instance, revel in depth and complexity beyond the smoky effects of peat.

Each whisky has been analysed by me without adding water or ice. I have taken each whisky as it was poured from the bottle and used no more than warming in an identical glass to extract and discover the character of the whisky. To have added water would have been pointless: it would have been an inconsistent factor as people, when pouring water, add different amounts at varying temperatures. The only constant with the whisky you and I taste will be when it has been poured directly from the bottle.

Even if you and I taste the same whiskies at the same temperature and from identical glasses – and even share the same values in whisky – our scores may still be different. Because a factor that is built into my evaluation is drawn from expectation and experience. When I sample a whisky from a certain distillery at such-and-such an age or from this type of barrel or that, I would expect it to offer me certain qualities. It has taken me 30 years to acquire this knowledge (which I try to add to day by day!) and an enthusiast cannot be expected to learn it overnight. But, hopefully, Jim Murray's Whisky Bible will help...!

Score chart

Within the parentheses () is the overall score out of 100.

0–50.5 Nothing short of absolutely diabolical.
51–64.5 Nasty and well worth avoiding.
65–69.5 Very unimpressive indeed.
70–74.5 Usually drinkable but don't expect the earth to move.
75–79.5 Average and usually pleasant though sometimes flawed.
80–84.5 Good whisky worth trying.
85–89.5 Very good to excellent whiskies definitely worth buying.
90–93.5 Brilliant.
94–97.5 Superstar whiskies that give us all a reason to live.
98–100 Better than anything I've ever tasted!

Key to Abbreviations & Symbols

% Percentage strength of whisky measured as alcohol by volume. **b** Overall balance and complexity. **bott** Date of bottling. **db** Distillery bottling. In other words, an expression brought out by the owners of the distillery. **dist** Date of distillation or spirit first put into cask. **f** Finish. **n** Nose. **nc** Non-coloured. **ncf** Non-chill-filtered. **sc** Single cask. **t** Taste. ⁘ New entry for 2013. ⊙ Retasted – no change. ⊙⊙ Retasted and re-evaluated. **v** Variant

Finding Your Whisky

Worldwide Malts: Whiskies are listed alphabetically throughout the book. In the case of single malts, the distilleries run A–Z style with distillery bottlings appearing at the top of the list in order of age, starting with youngest first. After age comes vintage. After all the "official" distillery bottlings are listed, next come other bottlings, again in alphabetical order. Single malts without a distillery named (or perhaps named after a dead one) are given their own section, as are vatted malts.

Worldwide Blends: These are simply listed alphabetically, irrespective of which company produce them. So "Black Bottle" appears ahead of "White Horse" and Japanese blends begin with "Ajiwai Kakubin" and end with "Za". In the case of brands being named after companies or individuals the first letter of the brand will dictate where it is listed. So William Grant, for instance, will be found under "W" for William rather "G" for Grant.

Bourbon/Rye: One of the most confusing types of whiskey to list because often the name of the brand bears no relation to the name of the distillery that made it. Also, brands may be sold from one company to another, or shortfalls in stock may see companies buying bourbons from another. For that reason all the brands have been listed alphabetically with the name of the bottling distiller being added at the end.

Irish Whiskey: There are four types of Irish whiskey: (i) pure pot still; (ii) single malt, (iii) single grain and (iv) blended. Some whiskies may have "pure pot still" on the label, but are actually single malts. So check both sections.

Bottle Information

As no labels are included in this book I have tried to include all the relevant information you will find on the label to make identification of the brand straightforward. Where known I have included date of distillation and bottling. Also the cask number for further recognition. At the end of the tasting notes I have included the strength and, if known, number of bottles (sometimes abbreviated to btls) released and in which markets.

Price of Whisky

You will notice that Jim Murray's Whisky Bible very rarely refers to the cost of a whisky. This is because the book is a guide to quality and character rather than the price tag attached. Also, the same whiskies are sold in different countries at varying prices due to market forces and variations of tax, so there is a relevance factor to be considered. Equally, much depends on the size of an individual's pocket. What may appear a cheap whisky to one could be an expensive outlay to another. With this in mind prices are rarely given in the Whisky Bible.

How to Taste Whisky

It is of little use buying a great whisky, spending a comparative fortune in doing so, if you don't get the most out of it.

So when giving whisky tastings, no matter how knowledgable the audience may be I take them through a brief training schedule in how to nose and taste as I do for each sample included in the Whisky Bible.

I am aware that many aspects are contrary to what is being taught by distilleries' whisky ambassadors. And for that we should be truly thankful. However, at the end of the day we all find our own way of doing things. If your old tried and trusted technique suits you best, that's fine by me. But I do ask you try out the instructions below at least once to see if you find your whisky is talking to you with a far broader vocabulary and clearer voice than it once did. I strongly suspect you will be pleasantly surprised – amazed, even - by the results.

Amusingly, someone tried to teach me my own tasting technique some years back in an hotel bar. He was not aware who I was and I didn't let on. It transpired that a friend of his had been to one of my tastings a few years earlier and had passed on my words of "wisdom". I'd be lying if I said I didn't smile when he informed me it was called "The Murray Method." It was the first time I had heard the phrase... though certainly not the last!

"The Murray Method"

1. Drink a black, unsweetened, coffee or chew on 90% minimum cocoa chocolate to cleanse the palate, especially of sugars.

2. Find a room free from distracting noises as well as the aromas of cooking, polish, flowers and other things which will affect your understanding and appreciation of the whisky.

3. Make sure you have not recently washed your hands using heavily scented soap or are wearing a strong aftershave or perfume.

4. Use a tulip shaped glass with a stem. This helps contain the alcohols at the bottom yet allows the more delicate whisky aromas you are searching for to escape.

5. Never add ice. This tightens the molecules and prevents flavours and aromas from being released. It also makes your whisky taste bitter. There is no better way to get the least from your whisky than by freezing it.

6. Likewise, ignore any advice given to put the bottle in the fridge before drinking.

7. Don't add water! Whatever anyone tells you. It releases aromas but can mean the whisky falls below 40%...so it is no longer whisky. Also, its ability to release flavours and aromas diminish quite quickly.

8. Warm the undiluted whisky in the glass to body temperature before nosing or tasting. Hence the stem, so you can cradle in your hand the curve of the thin base. This excites the molecules and unravels the whisky in your glass, maximising its sweetness and complexity.

9. Keep an un-perfumed hand over the glass to keep the aromas in while you warm. Only a minute or two after condensation appears at the top of your glass should you extend your arms, lift your covering hand and slowly bring the glass to your nose, so the alcoholic vapours have been released before the glass reaches your face.

10. Never stick your nose in the glass. Or breathe in deeply. Allow glass to gently touch your top lip, leaving a small space below the nose. Move from nostril to nostril, breathing normally. This allows the aromas to break up in the air, helping you find the more complex notes.

11. Take no notice of your first mouthful. This is a marker for your palate.

12. On second, bigger mouthful, close your eyes to concentrate on the flavour and chew the whisky - moving it continuously around the palate. Keep your mouth slightly open to let air in and alcohol out. It helps if your head is tilted back very slightly.

13. Occasionally spit – if you have the willpower! This helps your senses to remain sharp for the longest period of time.

14. Look for the balance of the whisky. That is, which flavours counter others so none is too dominant. Also, watch carefully how the flavours and aromas change in the glass over time.

15. Assess the "shape" and mouth feel of the whisky, its weight and how long its finish. And don't forget to concentrate on the first flavours as intensely as you do the last. Look out for the way the sugars, spices and other characteristics form.

16. Never make your final assessment until you have tasted it a third or fourth time.

17. Be honest with your assessment: don't like a whisky because someone (yes, even me!), or the label, has tried to convince you how good it is.

18. When you cannot discriminate between one whisky and another, stop immediately.

The 10th Edition
Renewing Vows

It must be nearly 15 years since I sat in the office of one of the world's biggest publishing companies and was told that the Whisky Bible would be a flop.

So I vowed on the central London street their door emptied out onto that I would go home, form my own publishers and launch a book which I knew would change the whisky appreciating landscape. It was a bright spring morning, the kind of day where green shoots form and buds begin to bloom: where nature cannot be thwarted. The perfect moment, in fact, for the blossoming of a dream.

In fact, it took until 2003 to at last get Jim Murray's Whisky Bible onto the bookshelf. But, since then, more than a third of a million copies has been sold: an extraordinary number for a book which has only ever appeared in English language. And one now having enough international influence for its last World Whisky of the Year to sell more bottles in the 24 hours after the announcement of the award than it had in the entire previous year....

The reason for the delay of the initial launch was because, as it was to be funded by myself, I had to wait until exactly the right time to strike. When I knew that there were a sufficient number of independent bottlers to ensure that each new annual edition would have enough fresh contents to make it a new book in itself, then I made my move. The first year should have been 2002 for a 2003 edition, but it took too long to get the samples assembled and the marketing curtains were drawn closed on that tiny window of opportunity. Instead, I began again in the spring of 2003, this time with an impressive armada of whiskies already gathered and, after spending the hottest-ever summer in Britain indoors tasting, by the autumn of that year the Whisky Bible, comprising of 2,100 whiskies and 256 pages was being read the world over.

Now Jim Murray's Whisky Bible carries 4,500 whiskies over 384 pages. In total, a fraction under 11,500 different whiskies have now been tasted and rated by me especially for the Whisky Bible. On average, around 1,200 new whiskies are nosed and tasted by me each year. It is a punishing schedule, one my friends have tried to curtail by suggesting I publish once every two years. But that would lose the rhythm, impact and importance of the Whisky Bible: one of its beauties is that it contains all the newest whiskies from around the world that I and my team of researchers can find. Publish every two years and it would be instantly out of date.

From the very first moment, my concept of the Whisky Bible was for it to serve the general public and support the then small number of shops which were at the vanguard of the whisky movement. And the distillers, too, by rewarding those companies in the business of whisky excellence. The only way it could serve the public was by being fearlessly honest and entirely trustworthy: if a whisky was not of the highest quality, then the Bible would say so. It also had to campaign if need be: to be an independent voice.

It has meant that some distillers and bottlers have not been quite as forthcoming with samples as they might. One of the latter even told me a few months back (in front of witnesses, amazingly!) that he would not send me samples as I might give a low score. "Why don't you do what some other writers do," he suggested. "If you don't like it, don't include it."

Such a concept is such anathema to me I refuse to believe anyone could do that. Even so, I can assure you that will never be the way I work. I will, as all my professional and personal instincts and beliefs demand, write as I find...whichever the whisky. And to underscore our independence, we have never and will never carry advertising. The marking of the whiskies will be carried without fear or favour. Not as much as a single half point will be given or subtracted depending on brand or bottler: you don't punish the children because of their parents. And, contrary to what I have read on website forums, we don't take money for awards. Indeed, we don't even charge for whiskies to be included in the Bible. If a whisky gets a high score or an award it is because I, rightly or wrongly, believe it to be of that standard.

And we shall continue to campaign. The first edition carried a withering Bible Thumping on the use of caramel. It was a hard-hitting article which we know led to some independent bottlers discarding colouring altogether and a complete reassessment by many distillers.

This year I make no apology for our stance on sulphur: the only regret is that it had to be written in the first place.

We're proud the way Jim Murray's Whisky Bible has served both the consumer and industry for ten editions. Let's hope my nose and tastebuds can withstand the onslaught of ten more...

Bible Thumping
They Have Ears But Listen Not

You see some astonishing sights when bird watching.

It is 18 years since I witnessed in New Zealand the rarely seen phenomenon of two Tuis diving together head first at break neck speed towards the lake on the inside of a volcano, to pull up only feet from splashdown and flutter slowly back upwards, beak-to-beak, in a stunning synchronised mating ritual. Yet I remember it as vividly as only yesterday.

As I do the Siberian Rubythroat which landed just feet from me as I walked around the back of the King Car Distillery in Taiwan, to display its startlingly gaudy "gushing blood" markings.

Or the barn owl which, in the dead of night and in single-minded pursuit of a rodent supper, swooped at full throttle into the still house at Ardbeg in the very first week of its production under new ownership back in 1997.

And, even while researching this book, finding a mysterious and shy Cinnamon Bittern booming to its mate in a mountain-framed Goan paddy field, just about visible in the very last, rapidly fading rays of the evening's light...

Indelible moments all.

But I have yet to see an ostrich sticking its head in the sand. That is, unless you count the whisky industry in their treatment of the problem engulfing it with sulphur-ruined sherry butts.

Whether the industry likes it or not, the Scotch in particular, we are facing crisis time. This is no longer an occasional problem affecting the odd bottling here and there which you may stumble across if you are particularly unlucky. It is rampant. We have reached the point where the question is less if a sherried whisky has been tainted. But by what degree.

Of course, the majority of casks used in whisky maturation are ex bourbon and suffer no such problem. While some sherry butts have escaped and offer nothing other than clean fruit. So there are, of course, a multitude of great whiskies out there entirely free from the bitter residue of sulphur... just check through this book to see how many. But that is no excuse for any person buying a whisky and finding it tainted. And, on the evidence of my tasting over the last few years, and this in particular - the worst I have ever known - the entirely clean sherry butt has become the exception rather than the rule. The tainted butts offer at very best a distant buzz which does not cause fatal damage to the whisky....or your taste buds, but certainly diminish the experience. A great many, though, either leave enough bitterness on the palate to make a second mouthful less than enjoyable. Or are simply utterly awful: a canker on the great and hallowed name of whisky.

And this is not just a case of the odd single cask here. This affects blends as well as single malt, even those containing a small percentage of sherry. Blenders once told me they would just "blend off" the affected casks so no-one notice. It is not a philosophy I have heard espoused with confidence for some while now. For, as it has now become evident, it needs only one heavily sulphured butt to ruin the excellence of beautifully matured whisky from many non-contaminated casks. Further, there are now simply too many of them. Sadly, it is not a problem restricted to Scotland: defective whisky is found in Ireland, Japan, Canada... anywhere where wine casks have been treated with sulphur to kill bacteria.

So far, the industry and some of its satellite commentators appear to be in a state of denial. Bemusingly, I have heard and read some "experts" say that sherry butts and sulphur are not related.

Really...?

For those silly people I have a simple point to make. Before the use of sulphur candles in sherry butts there was no problem in the industry. Since their deployment, there is. QED.

You see, once upon a time, the sherried whiskies of Scotland and Ireland once graced the palate with a softly textured elegance, full of lush richness and charm. It was probably a Macallen 10-year-old dished out to me by a doctor in the furthest north-western point of Scotland way back in 1975 that turned my love of whisky into something a little more intense. Thirty-seven years on, and I can still smell every atom, taste every nuance of that monumental, silk-couched dram: it was a life-changing moment.

And for another 15 years or so I pursued every sherry-matured whisky I could find: not so easy in those days. Then one day in 1991, at Aberlour, distillery manager Puss Mitchell called me over to a group of sherry butts standing outside a warehouse. He asked me to smell them, but did so without giving any indication through voice or expression of his own views. I recoiled when I thrust my nose inside. They had all the appeal of a recently exploded stink bomb. I was shocked. And appalled.

"I'm sending them back," he said. "The other day a lorry came here full of ones just like these. They were on their way to another distillery and they arrived here by mistake. But I didn't let on and checked them out to see what the others are up to. They were just as rank as these."

A few months later I was in the warehouse of a remote and beautiful distillery where I had known the warehouseman for a decade. He opened a few newly filled sherry butts and asked me my opinion. Again, that familiar stink-bomb/exploding match aroma assailed my nose. I told him in no uncertain terms of my thoughts. "Aye," he replied shaking his head with resignation. "And we now see hundreds of these things". And so I learnt first-hand and in the most unpleasant way possible that seriously sub-standard sherry butts were entering the system. That was over 20 years ago...

The question many people ask me is "why?" For years Scotland and Ireland had enjoyed access to sherry butts shipped to the British Isles full of the fortified Spanish wine, oloroso in particular. These would then be emptied by houses such as Harvey's in Bristol and the freshly emptied butts would be sent on to serve the distilleries.

The problems began when Spain changed their laws to prevent anything bottled outside of Jerez being legally called sherry. Being the part of mainland Europe closest to Africa, the mercury rises fast and high in Jerez. So to stop the butts spoiling and bacteria rendering the casks unusable, sulphur candles were burned inside to prevent bacterialogical contamination. Sometimes it would be a short burst. Other times the candles were left in a whole lot longer. The results have proved devastating: a contamination of an entirely different, self-inflicted kind.

Very soon after discovering those first tainted casks, I tackled a whisky executive responsible for buying wood for his company about this. He denied there was any problem, assuring me that by the time the whisky was fully matured the sulphur would be gone.

Oh! Had there been years of research into this, then, by the whisky industry? Actually, no. It was what the guys in the Spanish bodegas selling the casks had told him...

Since then sulphured whisky has been treated by the industry like the insane family member locked up in the attic. But now it is making too much noise and the neighbours have noticed. Except for the apologists, it seems.

Of course, you might point to the odd 30- to 45-year-old single malt which you paid a good wedge for only to find a dirty nose and that diabolical biting sulphur bitterness on the finish. Well, what you have almost certainly tasted is a whisky which has been "rounded off" or "freshened" in newer sherry in an attempt to give it a fruity shine before bottling. An old whisky tradition today fraught with Russian Roulette danger.

Which then suggests that either there are those in the industry who are still not aware of the problem. Or are simply incapable of detecting the sulphur. The answer, regrettably, is both. Even this year I was explaining to a blender of a pretty decent sized whisky company the potential problems and pitfalls of sherry butts. He stared at me wide-eyed and told me it was something he had never heard or discussed with his colleagues.

Which is, 20 years in, a little frightening. And perhaps explains much.

Another point is that it is believed somewhere between a quarter and third of the world's population is incapable of smelling sulphur. It's a genetic thing. Which means that maybe one in three blenders cannot detect it with the butts they are working with.

That, in itself, is not a problem. You can still be an excellent blender and have a sulphur blind spot. One truly legendary blender used to send me samples to check for special bottlings to ensure the sherry butts were clean as he was aware of his weakness in that direction. A great tactic for life: know your weaknesses and concentrate on your strengths.

However, it is imperative that every whisky company has a programme in place to counter this problem. Essentially, do they have the right team in the lab and quality control? If you are going to win the soccer World Cup you can cram your team full of midfielders full of guile and artistry, as do Spain, ironically. But you still need a centre back to defensively win the danger balls into the box and an outstanding goalkeeper on hand to deal with whatever gets through. And so it should be in the blending lab and bottling hall. The blender, however good he is, no matter what kind of Master This That and Other he may be on the label or at a whisky show, must have someone by his side able to spot potential flaws, to clear the dangers. There is no shame in it. Whisky is far too important to be about ego: it must be about professionalism. If the blender cannot spot sulphur, then his assistant must. Simple as that.

This is not so easy when it comes to the small, Independent bottlers. Many I know are, in effect, business people. They buy whisky and they sell it. No problem with that: many do a fabulous service to the whisky-loving public. But the owning of such a company does not alone make them capable of telling if a cask is flawed or not. And while some Independents are absolutely on the ball with what they bottle, a number are not. Which is why my advice to them would be to steer clear of parcels of sherry butt whisky, unless they have their quality tested by someone they know and trust. And in possession of the right genes.

Perhaps, though, above all the things that rankles most for me is the absolute lack of help the public is getting in this direction, other than my writings in the Whisky Bible and the input of a very small handful of other writers worldwide. Some whisky critics, astonishingly, can't spot sulphur at all. Which makes them about as much use as a linesman with no idea of the off side law, a cricket umpire who is stumped by the rules governing LBW or a tone deaf classical music conductor. People who set themselves up as experts must take into account the responsibility that holds. And if they are not up to the job it would be better for all if they said nothing and stuck to writing about some other aspect of the industry. Or postage stamps. Because the likelihood is, an unsuspecting person new to whisky will be steered towards a heavily-sulphured dram that may put them off for life. Or induced, like a sailor to the rocks by a siren, to pay a lot of money for one very big disappointment. Worse, perhaps, such tasting notes – as well as those making sulphur part and parcel of the whisky – are part of a slow, barely perceptible movement, purposely or otherwise, to make acceptable the completely unacceptable.

Some may also argue, for instance, that The Scotch Whisky Association might have done more. But the SWA is, above all else, an organisation to serve the interest of the industry rather than the consumer, a point too often overlooked by certain fawning and amateurish magazine editors. Again, I have no problem with that: as a journalist I have been dealing with such industry associations for nearly 40 years. It is the nature of the beast: they are what they are. And for that I respect them.

But here, for once, I am not sure the industry's best interests have been served. As vital as it was for the good of whisky to see the SWA bravely doing away with such vile terms as "Vatted Malt", would it not have been even more heartening to hear that they were investing significant resources in weeding out the dodgy butts that is actually undermining an entire industry's reputation?

Because here's the sting in the tail. The nightmare is by no means over. Sulphur-treated butts are being emptied and then refilled, further contaminating the next generation of whisky. Surely, after 20 years, an industry which is bringing in £100 a second worldwide in its sales could collectively find the cash to create a programme which would turn those first generation sulphured butts from Hades into garden centre potting tubs rather than second-fill receptacles again tainting what might have been magnificent whisky.

Even more frighteningly, perhaps, is that I now meeting an entire new generation, not just amongst whisky lovers but those who are now in high positions within the industry, who never knew the time when new sherry butts didn't contain sulphur. That is as depressing as it is worrying. Because these newbies often fail to see the problem or act upon it.

And, if reports coming back to me from the Far East are to be believed, we have now reached the stage where "ambassadors" are being coached to tell people that sulphur in whisky is not just normal, but actually a tradition...!

There is, of course, that third of the world's population which, being genetically unable to smell sulphur, are wondering what the fuss is about. And in some respects these people, many being German and other central Europeans, who usually associate sulphur notes with a smoky tone to the whisky, are to a degree a Get Out of Jail Card. But never should they be regarded as validation.

That is why I am dedicating three pages of the 10th edition of the Whisky Bible to the problem which more seriously damages the name of whisky than any other. Doubtless, the usual fingers will be pointed at me with accusations of my trying sensationalise and engineer a story for publicity. Hardly. The Whisky Bible is already barred from some distillery shops where I have pointed out the sulphur faults to their brands. More likely, it is because it takes your truest and most trustworthy friend to tell you when you have BO...

And one final point. There is a reason why pot stills, those gloriously elegant bulbous kettles of which the industry is so rightly proud, are made out of copper. It is because that metal, above all others, clarifies the spirit of sulphur compounds. Taste any spirit made from stainless steel and you will see the immeasurable difference they make.

So what is the point of banging on about the beautiful copper stills, the dents that are purposely put in new ones to minimise the difference in the spirit, if they then go and put their precious new make into a butt of brimstone....?

Ladies and gentlemen of the malt whisky industry. Whichever country you may be in. It is time to wake up, pull your head out of the sand....and smell the sulphur....

Jim Murray's Whisky Bible Award Winners 2013

Gold and Silver to the USA. And Bronze to Great Britain. Surely another day at the London Olympics. But no. As the closing ceremony was being broadcast around the world, the finest whiskies I had found anywhere on the planet this year were finally selected.

Yet having performed in my own marathon, I felt that after four months and over 1,300 new whiskies added there was something strangely familiar about the cream drams which had risen to the surface.

Remarkably, they were the same brands as those which had grabbed themselves the top three spots back in 2011. I felt a little disappointed about that, as after all this searching, it would have been wonderful to unleash a surprise package upon the world. Like I did last year with the Old Pulteney 21. But that exact bottling has been sold out entirely and later batches, though truly magnificent, fell back behind the 17-year-old as the distillery's finest.

Instead, this year we see a double-whammy for the astonishing Buffalo Trace distillery in Kentucky which underlined the growing belief that nowhere makes better whiskey of differing styles more consistently. A year or two back their CEO, Mark Brown, told me that he had sent his staff on Mission Impossible: he had briefed them to produce the first ever whiskey to score a full 100 in a Jim Murray Whisky Bible. I wished him well with that one. But I suspect even he will be delighted to have scooped World Whisky of the Year 2013 with the sprightly and incomparably mouth-watering Thomas Handy Rye. And to have backed that up by grabbing second place, also, with that three-course meal of a bourbon, the William Larue Weller. I originally tasted it the day before the photo shoot for the front cover of this book: suspecting it might be in for a gong, it became the tastiest prop in the history of publishing.

Such was the excellence of those two Kentuckians, Scotland's very finest, once again the most astonishing blend of them all, Ballantines 17-y-o, was beaten down to third place. It is always difficult to judge contrasting styles like those three against each other. But star quality is just that...

The three other whiskies which made the taste off might easilly have been in the top three in another year. The Ardbeg Day, showing some of the old depth of yesteryear, scored 97 but still fell outside the top spots. Just like in the Olympics Canada and Australia missed out. Masterson's 10-Year-Old Canadian Rye reminded us all of just what masterful whisky is made at Alberta, and how it shines when things aren't added to it. While the Port influenced Sullivans Cove showed Tasmania in a whole new whisky light. It was the Americans, though, who went for - and achieved - glory.

2013 World Whisky of the Year
Thomas H. Handy Sazerac Rye (128.6 proof)

‹∞›

Second Finest Whisky in the World
William Larue Weller (133.5 proof)

‹∞›

Third Finest World Whisky in the World
Ballantine's 17 Years Old

‹∞›

SCOTCH

Scotch Whisky of the Year
Ballantine's 17 Years Old
Single Malt of the Year (Multiple Casks)
Ardbeg Day
Single Malt of the Year (Single Cask)
Balblair 1965
Best Scotch New Brand
Dewar House Experimental Age 17 Years
Scotch Blend of the Year
Ballantine's 17 Years Old
Scotch Grain of the Year
SMWS G5.3 Aged 18 Years (Invergordon)
Scotch Vatted Malt of the Year
The Last Vatted Malt

Single Malt Scotch

No Age Statement (Multiple Casks)
Ardbeg Day
No Age Statement (Runner Up)
Aberlour a'bunadh Batch No. 33
10 Years & Under (Multiple Casks)
Glen Grant Aged 10 Years
10 Years & Under (Single Cask)
SMWS 33.116 Aged 8 Years (Ardbeg)
11-15 Years (Multiple Casks)
Lagavulin 12 Years Old Special Release
11-15 Years (Single Cask)
Berry's Own Selection Macduff 2000
16-21 Years (Multiple Casks)
Old Pulteney Aged 17 Years
16-21 Years (Single Cask)
Old Masters Strathmill 21 Years Old
22-27 Years (Multiple Casks)
Highland Park Aged 25 Years
22-27 Years (Single Cask)
Macallan Masters Of Photography 1989
28-34 Years (Multiple Casks)
Benromach 30 Years Old
28-34 Years (Single Cask)
The Whisky Agency Caol Ila 33 Years Old
35-40 Years (Multiple Casks)
The Balvenie Aged 40 Years Batch 2
35-40 Years (Single Cask)
Berry's Own Selection Glen Grant 1974
41 Years & Over (Multiple Casks)
Highland Park 50 Years Old
41 Years & Over (Single Cask)
Balblair 1965

Blended Scotch

No Age Statement (Standard)
Ballantine's Finest
No Age Statement (Premium)
Johnnie Walker Blue Label Casks Edition
5-12 Years
Johnnie Walker Black Label 12 Years Old
13-18 Years
Ballantine's 17 Years Old
19 - 25 Years
Teacher's Aged 25 Years
26 - 50 Years
The Last Drop 50 Years Old

IRISH WHISKEY

Irish Whiskey of the Year
Redbreast Aged 12 Years Cask Strength
Irish Pot Still Whiskey of the Year
Redbreast Aged 12 Years Cask Strength
Irish Single Malt of the Year
Bushmills Aged 21 Years
Irish Blend of the Year
Jameson
Irish Single Cask of the Year
The Tyrconnell Single Cask 11 Year Old

AMERICAN WHISKEY

Bourbon of the Year
William Larue Weller (133.5 proof)
Rye of the Year
Thomas H. Handy Sazerac (128.6 proof)
US Micro Whisky of the Year
Balcones Brimstone
US Micro Whisky of the Year (Runner Up)
Woodstone Microspirit 5 Grain No. 3

Bourbon

No Age Statement (Multiple Barrels)
William Larue Weller (133.5 proof)
No Age Statement (Single Barrel)
Four Roses 16 Years Old Single Barrel 78-3B
9 Years & Under
Ridgemont Reserve 1792 Aged 8 Years
10-17 Years (Multiple Barrels)
Four Roses Limited Edition Small Batch
2011 Barrel Strength
10-17 Years (Single Barrel)
Willett Family Estate Bottled 14 Years Old
18 Years & Over (Multiple Barrels)
Evan Williams 23 Years Old

Rye

No Age Statement
Thomas Handy Sazerac (128.6 proof)
11 Years & Over
Sazerac Kentucky Straight Rye 18 Years Old

CANADIAN WHISKY

Canadian Whisky of the Year
Masterson's 10 Year Old Straight Rye

JAPANESE WHISKY

Japanese Whisky of the Year
Hanyu Final Vintage 2000

EUROPEAN WHISKY

European Whisky of the Year (Multiple)
Penderyn Portwood Swansea City Special
European Whisky of the Year (Single)
Hicks & Healey Cornish Whiskey 2004

WORLD WHISKIES

Southern Hemisphere Whisky of the Year
Sullivans Cove Single Cask HH0509

*Overall age category winners are presented in bold.

The Whisky Bible Liquid Gold Awards (97.5-94)

Jim Murray's Whisky Bible is delighted to again make a point of celebrating the very finest whiskies you can find in the world. So we salute the distillers who have maintained or even furthered the finest traditions of whisky making and taken their craft to the very highest levels. And the bottlers who have brought some of them to us.

After all, there are over 4,500 different brands and expressions listed in this guide and from every corner of the planet. Those which score 94 and upwards represents only a very small fraction of them. These whiskies are, in my view, the elite: the finest you can currently find on the whisky shelves of the world. Rare and precious, they are Liquid Gold.

So it is our pleasure to announce that all those scoring 94 and upwards automatically qualify for the Jim Murray's Whisky Bible Liquid Gold Award. Congratulations!

97.5
Scottish Single Malt
 Ardbeg Uigeadail
 Old Pulteney Aged 21 Years
Scottish Blends
 Ballantine's 17 Years Old
Bourbon
 George T Stagg
 William Larue Weller
American Straight Rye
 Thomas H Handy Sazerac Straight Rye

97
Scottish Single Malt
 Ardbeg 10 Years Old
 Ardbeg Day Bottling
 Ardbeg Supernova
 Brora 30 Years Old
 Glenfiddich 50 Years Old
 Scott's Selection Highland Park 1981
Scottish Grain
 Clan Denny Cambus 47 Years Old
Scottish Blends
 Johnnie Walker Blue The Casks Edition
 Old Parr Superior 18 Years Old
Bourbon
 Parker's Wheated Mashbill Aged 10 Years
 William Larue Weller
American Straight Rye
 Thomas H. Handy Sazerac Straight Rye
Japanese Single Malt
 Nikka Whisky Single Coffey Malt 12 Years
Indian Single Malt
 Amrut Fusion
Taiwanese Single Malt
 Kavalan Solist Fino Sherry Cask

96.5
Scottish Single Malt
 Ardbeg 2000 Single Cask Lord Robertson of Port Ellen KT
 Ardbeg Corryvreckan
 Balblair 1965
 The Balvenie Aged 40 Years Batch 2
 The BenRiach Single Cask 1971
 Bruichladdich 1991 Valinch Anaerobic

Digestion 19 Years Old
 Octomore Orpheus Aged 5 Years Edition 02.2 PPM 140
 Port Charlotte PC6
 The Whisky Agency Caol Ila 33 Years Old
 Berry's Own Selection Clynelish 1997
 The GlenDronach 18 Years Old
 Glengoyne Single Cask 24 Years Old
 Berry's Own Selection Glen Grant 1974
 Glenmorangie Sonnalta PX
 Highland Park 50 Years Old
 Lagavulin 12 Years Old Special Release
 Laphroaig Aged 25 Years Cask Strength 2011
 The Macallan Masters Of Photography Annie Leibovitz 1989 "The Gallery"
 Old Masters Strathmill 21 Years Old
 Old Malt Cask Speyside's Finest Agd 43 Yrs
Scottish Vatted Malt
 The Last Vatted Malt
Scottish Blends
 The Last Drop
 The Last Drop 50 Years Old
 Teacher's Aged 25 Years
Irish Pure Pot Still
 Powers John's Lane Release Aged 12 Years
 Redbreast Aged 12 Years Cask Strength
Bourbon
 Blanton's Gold Original Single Barrel
 Blanton's Uncut/Unfiltered
 Four Roses Single Barrel
 Four Roses 16 Years Old Single Barrel 78-3B
 George T Stagg
 Virgin Bourbon 7 Years Old
American Straight Rye
 Sazerac Kentucky Straight Rye 18 Years Old
Canadian Blended
 Masterson's 10 Year Old Straight Rye
Swiss Single Malt
 Säntis Swiss Highlander Dreifaltigkeit
Welsh Single Malt
 Penderyn Cask Strength Rich Madeira
 Penderyn Portwood Swansea City Special
Australian Single Malt
 Sullivans Cove Rare Tasmanian Single Cask
Indian Single Malt
 Amrut Intermediate

96

Scottish Single Malt
Aberlour a'Bunadh Batch No. 33
Mo Òr Collection Aberlour 1990 20 Year Old
Ardbeg 1977
Ardbeg Kildalton 1980
Ardbeg Provenance 1974
Scotch Malt Whisky Society Cask 33.116 Aged 8 Years (Ardbeg)
Auchentoshan 1978 Bourbon Cask Matured Limited Edition
Scotch Malt Whisky Society Cask 73.44 Aged 29 Years (Aultmore)
A.D. Rattray Benrinnes 1996
Brora 25 Year Old 7th Release
Chieftain's Brora Aged 30 Years
Octomore 5 Years Old
Scotch Malt Whisky Society Cask 23.70 Aged 9 Years (Bruichladdich)
Duncan Taylor Cardhu 26 Years Old
Rare Old Convalmore 1975
Duncan Taylor Cragganmore 25 Years Old
The Dalmore Candela Aged 50 Years
Gordon & MacPhail Glen Albyn 1976
Scotch Malt Whisky Society Cask 104.13 Aged 36 Years (Glencraig)
The GlenDronach Single Cask 1972
The GlenDronach Single Cask 1978
The GlenDronach Single Cask 1992 Batch 4
The GlenDronach Single Cask 1994
Glenfarclas 1967 Family Casks Release V
Glenfarclas 1981 Family Casks Release VII
Glenfarclas 1989 Family Casks Release IX
Glenfarclas 1993 Family Casks Release IX
Glenfiddich 40 Years Old
Glenglassaugh 40 Year Old
Malts Of Scotland Glen Grant 1972
Peerless Glen Grant 40 Years Old
Gordon & MacPhail Glenlivet 1954
Rarest of the Rare Glenlochy 1980
Glenmorangie Truffle Oak
The Whisky Agency Glen Moray 35 YO
Highland Park Aged 25 Years
Highland Park 1973
The Arran Malt 1996 'The Peacock'
Lagavulin 21 Years Old
Laphroaig PX Cask
Laphroaig Quarter Cask
Old & Rare Laphroaig 21 Years Old
Malts Of Scotland Lochside 1967
The Whisky Agency Longmorn 1965
Berry's Own Selection Macduff 2000
Scotch Malt Whisky Society Cask 64.34 Aged 21 Years (Mannochmore)
Dun Bheagan Miltonduff 24 Years Old
Malts Of Scotland Port Ellen 1982
Rosebank 25 Years Old
Scottish Vatted Malt
Big Peat
Big Peat Batch 20 Xmas 2011

Scottish Grain
Clan Denny Caledonian 45 Years Old
Scottish Blends
Ballantine's Finest
Dewar House Experimental Aged 17 Years
Irish Pure Pot Still
Redbreast 12 Years Old
Redbreast Aged 12 Years Cask Strength
Irish Blends
Jameson Rarest 2007 Vintage Reserve
Bourbon
Ancient Ancient Age 10 Years Old
Buffalo Trace Master Distiller Emeritus
Elmer T Lee Collector's Edition
Old Weller Antique 107
Pappy Van Winkle's Family Reserve 15 YO
Willett Family Estate Bottled 14 Years Old
American Straight Rye
Bulleit 95 Rye
Rittenhouse Very Rare 21 YO Barrel 28
Rittenhouse Rye Aged 25 Years Barrel 19
American Small Batch
Stranahan's Colorado Whiskey Batch #67
Stranahan's Colorado Whiskey Batch #90
Canadian Blended
Alberta Premium bott lott L1317
Crown Royal Special Reserve
Japanese Single Malt
Karuizawa 1967 Vintage
Japanese Blended
Hibiki Aged 21 Years
English Single Malt
Hicks & Healey Cornish Whiskey 2004
Finnish Single Malt
Old Buck Second Release
Swedish Single Malt
Mackmyra Privus 03 Rökning Tillåten
Swiss Single Malt
Langatun Old Bear Châteauneuf-du-Pape
Welsh Single Malt
Penderyn Bourbon Matured Single Cask
Scotch Malt Whisky Society Cask 128.3 Aged 5 Years (Penderyn)
Australian Single Malt
Southern Coast Single Malt Batch 002
Indian Single Malt
Amrut Double Cask

95.5

Scottish Single Malt
Scotch Malt Whisky Society Cask 33.108 Aged 13 Years (Ardbeg)
The BenRiach Aged 12 Years Sherry Wood
The BenRiach Single Cask 1990
Benromach 30 Years Old
The Whisky Broker Bowmore 14 Years Old
Bruichladdich Redder Still 1984
Scotch Malt Whisky Society Cask 127.20 Aged 8 Years (Bruichladdich)
Caol Ila 'Distillery Only'

Caol Ila Special Release 2010 12 Years Old
Duncan Taylor Caol Ila 30 Years Old
Liquid Sun Caol Ila 1981
Old Malt Cask Clynelish Aged 28 Years
Cragganmore Special Release 2010 21 YO
The Dalmore Visitor Centre Exclusive
GlenDronach Single Cask 1972
GlenDronach Single Cask 1978
Cadenhead GlenDronach 21 Years Old
The Whisky Cask Glen Elgin Aged 25 Years
Glenfarclas 105
Glenfarclas 1961 Family Casks Release IX
Glengoyne 1999 Aged 11 Years Single Cask
The Whisky Agency Glen Grant 1973
The Glenlivet Founder's Reserve 21 Yrs Old
Gordon & MacPhail Generations Glenlivet
70 Years Old
Gordon & MacPhail Glenlivet 1974
Scotch Malt Whisky Society Cask 2.80
Aged 15 Years (Glenlivet)
Glenmorangie 25 Years Old
Glen Moray 1995 Port Wood Finish
Scotch Malt Whisky Society Cask 35.54
Aged 11 Years (Glen Moray)
The Whisky Castle Glenrothes 21 Years Old
Highland Park Aged 18 Years
Highland Park Vintage 1978
Archives Laphroaig 1998 13 YO 2nd Release
Malts Of Scotland Laphroaig 1998
Old Malt Cask Laphroaig Aged 15 Years
Scotch Malt Whisky Society Cask 29.106
Aged 13 Years (Laphroaig)
Gordon & MacPhail Longmorn 1968
The Macallan Fine Oak 12 Years Old
The Macallan Oscuro
Gordon & MacPhail Mortlach 1971
Malts Of Scotland Port Ellen 1983
Longrow C.V
Malts Of Scotland Ledaig 1998
Gordon & MacPhail Strathisla 1969
Mo Òr Collection Tomatin 1976 34 Years Old
Tullibardine 1962
Mo Òr Collection Tullibardine 1965 44 YO
Elements of Islay Pe1
Glenbridge 40 Years Old

Scottish Vatted Malt
Compass Box Flaming Hart
Compass Box The Spice Tree

Scottish Grain
Clan Denny Invergordon 44 Years Old
Scotch Malt Whisky Society Cask G5.3 Aged
18 Years (Invergordon)

Scottish Blends
Johnnie Walker Black Label 12 Years Old
Royal Salute "62 Gun Salute"
William Grant's 25 Years Old

Irish Single Malt
The Tyrconnell Single Cask 11 Year Old
Bushmills Aged 21 Years
Sainsbury's Dún Léire Aged 8 Years

Bourbon
Booker's 7 Years 4 Months
Buffalo Trace Single Oak Project Barrel 63
Charter 101
European Bourbon Rye Association
Kentucky Straight Bourbon Whiskey 16 Years
Four Roses Limited Edition Small Batch
2011 Barrel Strength
Willett Pot Still Reserve

American Small Batch
Balcones Brimstone
Balcones True Blue Cask Strength
Stranahan's Snowflake Cab Franc
The Notch Aged 8 Years

Canadian Blended
Alberta Premium
Forty Creek Port Wood Reserve
Gibson's Finest Rare Aged 18 Years

Japanese Single Malt
Golden Horse Chichibu Aged 12 Years
Hakushu Single Malt Whisky Agd 12 Yrs
Ichiro's Card "King of Hearts"
Ichiro's Malt Aged 20 Years

Japanese Single Grain
Kawasaki Single Grain

German Single Malt
Austrasier Single Cask Grain

Swedish Single Malt
Mackmyra Brukswhisky
Mackmyra Moment "Rimfrost"

Australian Single Malt
The Nant 3 Years Old Cask Strength

95

Scottish Single Malt
Ardbeg 10
Ardbeg Mor
Old Malt Cask Aultmore Aged 20 Years
The BenRiach Single Cask 1976
Bruichladdich 16 Years Old
Bruichladdich 1989 Black Art 2nd Edition
Octomore 10
Octomore 3rd Edition Aged 5 Years
Malts Of Scotland Port Charlotte 2001
Bunnahabhain Darach Ùr Batch no. 4
Adelphi Bunnahabhain 31 Years Old
Malts Of Scotland Bunnahabhain 1966
Berry's Own Selection Caol Ila 1984
Berry's Own Selection Caol Ila 2000
Duncan Taylor Caol Ila 28 Years Old
Old Malt Cask Caol Ila Aged 15 Years
Adelphi Clynelish 14 Years Old
The Dalmore Eos Aged 59 Years
The Dalmore 62 Years Old
Dalwhinnie 15 Years Old
Glencadam Aged 10 Years
Glencadam Agd 14 Years Oloroso Finish
The GlenDronach Aged 33 Years
The GlenDronach Single Cask 1989
The GlenDronach Single Cask 1991

The GlenDronach 1991 Aged 20 Years
The GlenDronach 1993 Aged 19 Years
Glenfarclas 1962 Family Casks Release VI
Glenfarclas 1972 Family Casks Release VIII
Glenfarclas 1973 Family Casks Release VI
Glenfiddich 18 Years Old
Glenfiddich 1961 47 Years Old
Glenfiddich Snow Phoenix
Glenglassaugh 1973 Family Silver
Glenglassaugh The Chosen Few 1st Edition
"Ronnie Routledge" 35 Years Old
The Whisky Agency Glengoyne 37 YO
Glen Grant Aged 10 Years
The Glenlivet French Oak Reserve 15 YO
The Glenlivet Nadurra Aged 16 Years
Cadenhead Glenlivet 21 Years Old
Gordon & MacPhail Glenlivet 1966
Berry's Own Selection Glen Moray 1991
Glen Ord 25 Years Old
Fine Malt Selection Glen Ord 12 Years Old
Scotch Malt Whisky Society Cask 16.30
Aged 22 Years (Glenturret)
Dun Bheagan Glenugie 30 Years Old
A.D. Rattray Highland Park 1984
Malts Of Scotland Highland Park 1986
The Arran Malt 1997 Single Cask
Lagavulin Aged 16 Years
Malts of Scotland Laphroaig 1996
Old Malt Cask Linkwood Aged 28 Years
The Warehouse Collection Linkwood 28 YO
Riegger's Selection Littlemill 1990
Gordon & MacPhail Longmorn 1973
The Macallan Lalique III 57 Years Old
Malts Of Scotland Macallan 1990
Mo Ór Collection Macallan 1991 19 YO
Mo Ór Collection Miltonduff 1980 30 YO
Mo Ór Collection Port Ellen 1983 27 YO
Old Pulteney Aged 17 Years
Rosebank Aged 12 Years
Scotch Malt Whisky Society Cask 126.2
Aged 10 Years (Springbank)
Malts Of Scotland Strathisla 1970
Talisker Aged 20 Years
Talisker 57 Degrees North
Old Malt Cask Tamdhu Aged 21 Years
Tomatin 1982
The Perfect Dram Tomatin 34 Years Old
Tomintoul Aged 14 Years
Mo Ór Collection Tomintoul 1967 43 YO
The Whisky Agency Tomintoul 1972
Wemyss 1990 Highland "Tropical Spice"
Auld Reekie Islay Malt
Celtique Connexion Saussignac Double
Matured 1997
Celtique Connexion Sauternes 16 Years Old

Scottish Vatted Malt
Douglas Laing's Double Barrel Highland
Park & Bowmore
Johnnie Walker Green Label 15 Years Old
Norse Cask Selection Vatted Islay 1992

Aged 16 Years
Wild Scotsman Aged 15 Years Vatted Malt

Scottish Grain
Clan Denny Carsebridge Aged 45 Years

Scottish Blends
The Bailie Nicol Jarvie (B.N.J)
Chivas Regal 25 Years Old
Clan Gold 3 Year Old

Irish Pure Pot Still
Midleton 1973 Pure Pot Still

Irish Single Malt
Tyrconnell Aged 11 Years
Bushmills Select Casks Aged 12 Years
Bushmills Rare Aged 21 Years

Irish Blends
Jameson
Midleton Very Rare 2009

Bourbon
Buffalo Trace Single Oak Project Barrel 14
Buffalo Trace Single Oak Project Barrel 132
Cougar Bourbon Aged 5 Years
Maker's 46
Woodford Reserve Master's Four Grain

American Corn Whiskey
Dixie Dew

American Straight Rye
Cougar Rye
High West Rocky Mountain 21 Year Old Rye
Rittenhouse Very Rare 21 YO Barrel 8
Sazerac Kentucky Straight Rye 18 Years Old

American Small Batch
McCarthy's Oregon Single Malt
McCarthy's Aged 3 Years batch W10-01
McCarthy's Aged 3 Years batch W12-01
Stranahan's Colorado Whiskey Batch #83
Woodstone Microspirit 5 Grain Straight
Bourbon Single Barrel No. 3

Other American Whiskey
High West Son of Bourye

Canadian Blended
Alberta Premium 25 Years Old
Danfield's Limited Edition Aged 21 Years
Wiser's Legacy
Wiser's Red Letter

Japanese Single Malt
The Hakushu Aged 15 Years Cask Strength
Hakushu 1984
Ichiro's Card "Four of Spades"
Yoichi Key Malt Agd 12 Yrs "Peaty & Salty"
Yoichi 20 Years Old
Pure Malt Black

Japanese Blended
Royal Aged 15 Years

English Single Malt
The English Whisky Co. Chapter 9 Peated

Finnish Single Malt
Old Buck

French Single Malt
Kornog Single Malt Tourbé (Peated) Whisky
Breton Taourc'h Trived 12BC

German Single Malt
The Alrik Smoked Hercynian 4 Years Old

Swedish Single Malt
Mackmyra Moment "Urberg"
Mackmyra Moment "Skog"

Swiss Single Malt
Interlaken Swiss Highland "Classic"

Welsh Single Malt
Penderyn Madeira bott Jun 11
Penderyn Sherrywood Limited Edition

Australian Single Malt
Overeem Port Cask Matured Cask Strength
Southern Coast Single Malt Batch 006

Indian Single Malt
Amrut Two Continents Limited Edition
Amrut Two Continents 2nd Edition

Taiwanese Single Malt
Kavalan Solist Fino Sherry Cask

94.5

Scottish Single Malt
Aberlour Agd 16 Yrs Double Cask Matured
Aberlour a'bunadh Batch No. 29
Aberlour a'Bunadh Batch No. 37
Scott's Selection Aberlour 1989
Adelphi Aultmore 28 Years Old
Balblair 1969
Balblair 1975
The Balvenie Aged 21 Years Port Wood
The BenRiach Aged 15 Years PX Finish
The BenRiach 30 Years Old
The BenRiach 1976 Aged 35 Years
Benromach Vintage 1968
The Laddie Ten
Bruichladdich 32 Years Old DNA 1977
Bruichladdich Infinity Third Edition
Scotch Malt Whisky Society Cask 127.15
Aged 9 Years (Bruichladdich)
Mo Òr Collection Bunnahabhain 1968 42 YO
Old Malt Cask Bunnahabhain Agd 14 Yrs
Wilson & Morgan Bunnahabhain 42 YO
Wemyss 1989 Speyside "Lemon Grove"
Gordon & MacPhail Dallas Dhu 1979
The GlenDronach Grandeur Aged 31 Years
Malts Of Scotland GlenDronach 2002
Glenfarclas 1984 Family Casks Release VII
Glenfarclas 1990 Family Casks Release V
Glenfarclas 1995 45° Heritage Collection
Glenfiddich 15 Years Old
Archives Glen Grant 1975 36 YO 1st Release
Glen Grant Cellar Reserve 1992
Old Malt Cask Glen Grant Aged 35 Year
The Glenlivet Cellar Collection 1973
The Glenlivet Cellar Collection 1980
Gordon & MacPhail Glenlivet 1961
Scott's Selection Glenlivet 1978
The Whisky Cask Glenlivet Aged 33 Years
Malts Of Scotland Glen Ord 1999
Duncan Taylor Octave Glenrothes 40 YO
Old Malt Cask Glenrothes Aged 21 Years

Glen Spey Special Release 2010 21 YO
The Whisky Agency Glentauchers 1975
Highland Park 1970 Orcadian Vintage
The Whisky Cask Highland Park Agd 24 Yrs
Deoch an Doras Inverleven 36 Years Old
The Arran Malt Amarone Cask Finish
Isle of Jura 1976
AnCnoc 12 Year Old
Lagavulin 12 Years Old (8th Release)
Lagavulin 12 Years Old (10th Release)
Laphroaig 27 Years Old
Old Malt Cask Laphroaig Aged 18 Years
Linkwood 12 Years Old
Hart Brothers Linkwood Aged 13 Years
Old Masters Linkwood Aged 12 Years
Scotch Malt Whisky Society Cask 97.21
Aged 21 Years (Littlemill)
The Macallan Fine Oak 18 Years Old
The Macallan Masters Of Photography
Albert Watson 20 Years Old
Old Malt Cask Macallan Aged 21 Years
Silver Seal Macallan 22 Years Old
Scott's Selection Miltonduff 1990
Old Malt Cask Port Ellen Aged 28 Years
Old Pulteney Aged 17 Years
Old Malt Cask Rosebank Aged 20 Years
Scotch Malt Whisky Society Cask 17.28
Aged 8 Years (Scapa)
Hazelburn Aged 8 Years
Dun Bheagan Teaninich Aged 28 Years
Tomintoul Aged 16 Years
The Whisky Agency Tomintoul 1968
Tullibardine John Black Edition No. 6
Tullibardine 1976
Adelphi Breath Of The Isles 15 Years Old
Clan Sinclair Aged 16 Years

Scottish Vatted Malt
Glen Turner Aged 21 Years Limited Edition
John McDougall's Selection Islay Malt 1993
Old St Andrews Twilight

Scottish Grain
Berry's Own Selection Girvan Agd 46 Yrs
Clan Denny Girvan Aged 46 Years
Scotch Malt Whisky Society Cask G5.5 Aged
18 Years (Invergordon)
Late Lamented North of Scotland 37 YO
Clan Denny Port Dundas Aged 34 Years
Clan Denny Strathclyde 33 Years Old

Scottish Blends
Ballantine's Limited
Clan Gold Blended 18 Years Old
Highland Dream 12 Years Old
Johnnie Walker Double Black
Lochside 1964 Rare Old Single Blend
The Tweeddale Blend Aged 12 Years

Irish Single Malt
Green Spot
The Tyrconnell Aged 18 Years Single Cask

Irish Blends
The Irishman Rare Cask Strength

Bourbon
Ancient Ancient Age 10 Star
Benjamin Prichard's Double Barrelled
Bourbon 9 Years Old
Buffalo Trace Single Oak Project Barrel 33
Buffalo Trace Single Oak Project Barrel 61
Buffalo Trace Single Oak Project Barrel 164
Buffalo Trace Single Oak Project Barrel 191
Elijah Craig 18 Years Old Single Barrel
Kentucky Vintage
Knob Creek Aged 9 Years
Old Grand-Dad Bonded 100 Proof
Ridgemont Reserve 1792 Aged 8 Years

American Straight Rye
Rittenhouse Aged 25 Years Barrel 30
Van Winkle Reserve Rye Aged 13 Years Old

American Small Batch
McCarthy's Single Barrel Cask Strength
Stranahan's Colorado Whiskey Small Batch
Stranahan's Colorado Whiskey Batch 60
Stranahan's Colorado Whiskey Batch 75
Stranahan's Snowflake Desire

Other American Whiskey
Buffalo Trace Experimental Collection 1995
French Oak Barrel Aged

Canadian Blended
Forty Creek Confederation Oak Reserve
Royal Reserve Gold

Japanese Single Malt
Hanyu Final Vintage 2000

Belgian Single Malt
The Belgian Owl Single Malt Age 4 Years

English Single Malt
Hicks & Healey Cornish Malt 2004 Cask 29
Founders Private Cellar

French Single Malt
Kornog Taouarc'h Kentan

German Single Malt
Finch Destillers Edition
Old Fahr Single Cask Malt

Welsh Single Malt
Penderyn Madeira Feb 11

Indian Single Malt
Amrut Fusion
The Ultimate Amrut 2005 Cask Strength

94 (New Entries Only)

Scottish Single Malt
Aberlour a'Bunadh Batch No. 36
Aberlour a'Bunadh Batch No. 39
Auchentoshan 1979
A.D. Rattray Aultmore 1982
Mo Ôr Collection Aultmore 1974 36 Years Ol
The BenRiach "Solstice" 17 YO 2nd Edition
The BenRiach 1984 Aged 27 Years
Malts Of Scotland BenRiach 1991
Director's Cut Bunnahabhain Agd 20 Yrs
Gordon & MacPhail Cask Strength Caol Ila
Old Malt Cask Caol Ila Aged 16 Years
The Warehouse Collection Craigellache

Aged 10 Years
Riegger's Selection Deanston 1992
Glencadam Agd 21 Yrs "The Exceptional"
Glenfarclas 1966 Family Casks Release VIII
Glenfarclas 1982 Family Casks Release VIII
Scott's Selection Glen Grant 1993
The Whisky Agency Glen Grant 1975
Berry's Own Selection Glenlivet 1973
Riegger's Selection Glenlivet 1973
Mo Ôr Collection Glen Mhor 1975 34 YO
Glenmorangie Artein Private Edition
Old Malt Cask Glen Spey Aged 25 Years
Malts Of Scotland Glenturret 1977
Old Malt Cask Imperial Aged 24 Years
Malts Of Scotland Laphroaig 1998
Gordon & MacPhail Longmorn 1967
The Macallan Queen's Diamond Jubilee
The Macallan Masters Of Photography
Annie Leibovitz 1996 "The Skyline"
Scotch Malt Whisky Society Cask 24.119
Aged 26 Years (Macallan)
Rosebank 21 Years Old Special Release
Dà Mhile Lost & Found Springbank Organic
Aged 20 Years
Scott's Selection Strathisla 1989
A.D. Rattray Strathmill 1989
Archives Ledaig 2004 7 YO 1st Release
Malts Of Scotland Tomatin 1966
Old Malt Cask Tomintoul Aged 40 Years
Sainsbury's Single Islay Malt 12 Years Old
Unchillfiltered
Glen Marnoch 24 Years Old
Malts Of Scotland Angel's Choice "1836"
Glenbrynth Ruby 40 Year Old Ltd Edition

Scottish Grain
Clan Denny Caledonian Aged 45 Years
Scott's Selection Invergordon 1964

Scottish Blends
Storm

Bourbon
Buffalo Trace Single Oak Project Barrel #81
Buffalo Trace Single Oak Project Barrel #167
Eagle Rare 17 Years Old
Four Roses Single Barrel
John E. Fitzgerald Larceny

American Small Batch
291 Aspen Stave Finished
Edgefield Hogshead Whisky

Canadian Blended
Alberta Premium bott lott L2150

Danish Single Malt
Stauning 1st Edition Peated

English Single Malt
The English Whisky Co. Chapter 7 Rum
Cask Limited Edition

German Single Malt
Seute Deem Single Cask Malt

Welsh Single Malt
Penderyn Madeira bott Oct 11
Penderyn Sherrywood bott Feb 12

Scottish Malts

For those of you deciding to take the plunge and head off into the labyrinthine world of Scotch malt whisky, a piece of advice. And that is, be careful who you take your advice from. Because, too often, I hear that you should leave the Islays until you have tackled the featherlight Speysiders and the bolder, weightier Highlanders. This is just complete, patronising nonsense. The only time that rings true is if you are tasting a number of whiskies in one day. Then leave the smoky ones to last, so the lighter chaps get a fair hearing.

I know many people who didn't like whisky until they got a Talisker from Skye inside them, or a Lagavulin to swamp their tastebuds with oily iodine. The fact is, you can take your map of malt whisky, start at any point and head in whichever direction you feel. There are no hard and fast rules. Certainly with nearly 3,000 tasting notes for Scottish malts here you should have some help in picking where this journey of a lifetime begins.

It is also worth remembering not always to be seduced by age. It is true that many of the highest scores are given to big-aged whiskies. The truth is that the majority of malts, once they have lived beyond 25 years or so, suffer from oak influence rather than benefit. Part of the fun of discovering whiskies is to see how malts from different distilleries perform to age and type of cask. Happy discovering.

Abhainn Dearg
LEWIS

SKYE
Talisker

Tobermory

MULL
Oban

Islay

Bunnahabhain

Caol Ila

Kilchoman
Bruichladdich
Bowmore

Port Ellen   Ardbeg
Laphroaig   Lagavulin

ISLAY
Isle of
Isle of

Springbank
Glen Scotia
Glengyle

ORKNEY ISLANDS

Highland Park
Scapa

Pultney

Clynelish
Brora

Balblair — Glenmorangie
Dalmore — *Invergordon*
Teaninich

Speyside see page 24

Glenglassaugh

Banff
Macduff

Glen Ord

Royal Brackla
Knockdhu

Glenugie

Inverness
Glen Albyn
Glen Mhor
Millburn

Tomatin

Glendronach

Ardmore

Glen Garioch

The Speyside Distillery

Royal Lochnagar

Aberdeen

Dalwhinnie

Glenury Royal

Fettercairn

Fort William
Ben Nevis
Glenlochy

Blair Athol

Glencadam
North Port

Glenesk

Edradour
Aberfeldy

Lochside

Dundee

Glenturret

Perth

Daftmill

Tullibardine

Deanston

Cameronbridge

Glengoyne
Rosebank
St. Magdelene

Glenkinchie

Edinburgh
North British

Loch Lomond
Dumbarton
Inverleven
Littlemill
Auchentoshan

Glasgow
Strathclyde
Port Dundas
Kinclaith

Girvan
Ailsa Bay
Ladyburn

Bladnoch

Key

● **Major Town or City**
🔺 Single Malt Distillery
🔺 (*Italics*) Grain Distillery
✠ Dead Distillery

Speyside

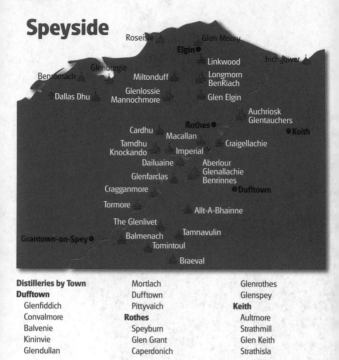

Distilleries by Town

Dufftown
Glenfiddich
Convalmore
Balvenie
Kininvie
Glendullan

Mortlach
Dufftown
Pittyvaich

Rothes
Speyburn
Glen Grant
Caperdonich

Glenrothes
Glenspey

Keith
Aultmore
Strathmill
Glen Keith
Strathisla

Single Malts
ABERFELDY

Highlands (Perthshire), 1898. John Dewar & Sons. Working.

Aberfeldy Aged 12 Years db (83) n22 t21 f19 b21. The nose is superbly enriched by its usual and uniquely nutty depth. The bitter nougat delivery and finish fails to match the expectation. 40% ⊙ ⊙

Aberfeldy Aged 18 Years "Chris Anderson's Cask" db (90) n24 plays the range from bourbon-rich red liquorice right down to diced kumquat; sharp, angular, bold, salty and very enticing; not a single blemish in distillate or wood; t23.5 sharp delivery with a mouth watering malty juiciness, but also weighty, too, with heavy oaks immediately apparent. Any threatening bitterness is seen off by a light dusting of muscovado and dried dates; f21.5 bites deep and caramels out; b22 had the natural caramels just not ticked over a little too exuberantly, this would have headed for a very high score. Aberfeldy in a very unusual light... 54.9%. 248 bottles.

Aberfeldy Aged 21 Years db (92) n24 have I just bitten into a milk cocoa Lubec marzipan? The one which has an orange jam topping the almond paste? I must have. Some sublime bourbon hickory and Demerara on show, too. Superb! t23 uniquely nutty delivery screams "Aberfeldy!"; creamy texture without losing complexity. Out of the oils vanilla rises cleanly; f22 reverts to a fruitiness, including, alas, a slightly furry bitter marmalade drawl from, most probably, just one butt...; b23 a distillery I have long held in very high esteem here gives a pretty clear view as to why... 40% ⊙ ⊙

Aberfeldy Aged 25 Years db (85) n24 t21 f19 b21. Just doesn't live up to the nose. When Tommy Dewar wrote, "We have a great regard for old age when it is bottled," as quoted on the label, I'm not sure he had as many as 25 years in mind. 40%. 150 bottles to mark opening of Dewar's World of Whisky.

⁖ **Berry's Own Selection Aberfeldy 1999** cask no. 27, bott 2012 (86) n21.5 t22 f21 b21.5. A very steady ship is kept as juicy barley struts its stuff on a quite oily base. 46%. nc ncf sc.

⁖ **Gordon & MacPhail Connoisseurs Choice Aberfeldy 1991** (82) n20 t23 f19 b20. Once you'd expect nuts and raisins from this distillery in these kinds of casks, which I strongly suspect includes sherry. Not quite that now, as the finish does little for your next mouthful. But the original delivery shows just how majestic the spirit originally was. 43%

⫶ **James MacArthur Old Masters Aberfeldy 11 Years Old** cask no. 83, dist 2000, bott Oct 11 **(78.5) n18 t22.5 f19 b19.** Delighted to report that the overall tasting experience is very much better than the nose, which is a fabulous example of when cask and spirit are barely on speaking terms. An old cask offering little positive life to the malt is the root cause, as the nose starkly reveals. The mouth-watering freshness of the totally immature malt on delivery is a fillip, though the finish expectedly follows the nose's lead. *55.8%. nc ncf sc.*

⫶ **Mo Ôr Collection Aberfeldy 1994 16 Years Old** first fill bourbon hogshead, cask no. 4016, dist 7 Jun 94, bott 24 Jan 11 **(92) n23** recognised this as Aberfeldy even before I checked the label. Just the right degree of marzipan paste, going easy on the sugars. Also, the vaguest hint of smoke; **t23.5** A fabulous layering of yet more marzipan with acacia honey and diced hazelnut; the malt is firm and even glistens with a degree of flintiness; **f22.5** butterscotch and thickening strands of vanilla; **b23** a typically nutty affair with perhaps an extra dollop of honey: the distillery nutshelled, in fact. When in this natural form, the distillery has the opportunity to reveal itself as a little-known gem of Scotland. *46%. nc ncf sc. Release No. 32. The Whisky Talker. 460 bottles.*

Old Malt Cask Aberfeldy Aged 16 Years refill hogshead, dist Jun 94, bott Dec 10 **(94) n23** heather, lavender and polished leather...; **t24** juicy barley with a beautiful lustre to the thin treacle outlining the vanilla-rich oak; all kinds of spices buzz and fret; **f23** a succession of firm barley-bourbon notes drying towards the very death; **b24** a trademark top range Aberfeldy. Adorable. And quite beautifully constructed. *50%. nc ncf sc. 350 bottles.*

The Whisky Agency Aberfeldy 1983 bott 2010 **(86) n22.5 t23 f19 b21.5.** If Perthshire does boast a honeyed style, this does little to detract from that notion. *49.9%*

ABERLOUR
Speyside, 1826. Chivas Brothers. Working.
Aberlour 10 Years Old db **(87.5) n22.5** plenty of grape, but there is a dry, rough edge to this, too; **t22** the delivery briefly bursts with a grapey welcome which soon gives way to a grating vanilla and toffee; **b21** overly dry with flecks of cocoa; **b22** remains a lusty fellow though here nothing like as sherry-cask faultless as before, nor displaying its usual honeyed twinkle. *43%*

Aberlour 10 Years Old Sherry Cask Finish db **(85) n21 t21 f21 b22.** Bipolar and bittersweet with the firmness of the grain in vivid contrast to the gentle grape. *43%*

Aberlour 12 Years Old Double Cask Matured db **(88.5) n22** pretty unsubtle grape but sweet and attractive; **t22.5** serious juice at first drowns the barley but the oaky-spice heralds its return; **f22** delicate barley remnants; **b22** voluptuous and mouth-watering in some areas, firmer and less expansive in others. Pretty tasty in all of them. *43%*

⫶ **Aberlour 12 Years Old Non Chill-Filtered** db **(87) n22.5** impressive blood orange but a little untidy...and worrying; **t22** superb weight with a surprising degree of barley coming through early on despite the close attention of the fruit; **f21** the fussy finish confirms the fears raised on the nose...; **b21.5** there are many excellent facets to this malt, not least the balance between barley and grape and the politeness of the gristy sugars. But a sulphured butt has crept into this one, taking the edge off the excellence and bringing down the score like a cold front drags down the thermometer. *48%. ncf*

Aberlour 12 Years Old Sherry Cask Matured db **(88) n23** dry sherry and make no mistake; **t22** silky, juicy delivery; cramped slightly by a background bitterness; spices take their time but arrive eventually; **f21** double dry finale thanks to both big oak and the sherry influence; **b22** could do with some very delicate extra balancing sweetness to take it to the next level. Sophisticated nonetheless. *40%*

Aberlour 13 Years Old sherry cask, hand fill db **(84) n21 t22 f20 b21.** Skimps on the complexity. *58.8%*

Aberlour 15 Year Old Double Cask Matured db **(84) n23 t22 f19 b20.** Brilliant nose full of vibrant apples and spiced sultana, but then, after a complex, chewy, malt-enriched kick-off, falls surprisingly flat on its face. *40%*

Aberlour 15 Years Cuvee Marie d'Ecosse db **(91) n22 t24 f22 b23.** This always was a deceptive lightweight, and it's got lighter still. It is sold primarily in France, and one can assume only that this is God's way of making amends for that pretentious, over-rated, caramel-ridden rubbish called Cognac they've had to endure. *43%*

Aberlour 15 Year Old Sherry Finish db **(91) n24** exceptionally clever use of oak to add a drier element to the sharper boiled cooking apple. And a whiff of the fermenting vessel, too; **t22** the sharp fruit of the nose is magnified here ten times; **f23** wave upon wave of malt concentrate; **b22** quite unique: freaky, even. Really a whisky to be discovered and ridden. Once you acclimatize, you'll adore it. *43%*

Aberlour Aged 16 Years Double Cask Matured bott 23 Feb 10 db **(94.5) n24** a magnificent marriage between sweet, juicy fruit and lively spice; sturdy-framed but giving grape, too; **t24** the softest delivery of lightly sugared grape, salivating and sensuous; light spices struggle to free themselves from the gentle oils; **f23** pithy with the vanilla determined to ensure a drier finale; **b23.5** a joyous malt reminding us of just what clean, fresh sherry butts are capable of. A malt of unbridled magnificence. *43%*

Aberlour 18 Years Old db **(91) n22** thick milkshake with various fruits and vanilla; **t22** immediate fresh juice which curdles beautifully as the vanilla is added; **f24** wonderful fruit-chocolate fudge development: long, and guided by a gentle oiliness; **b23** another high performance distillery age-stated bottling. *43%*

Aberlour 100 Proof db **(91) n23 t23 f22 b23.** Stunning, sensational whisky, the most extraordinary Speysider of them all ...which it was when I wrote those official notes for the bottling back in '97, I think. Other malts have superseded it now, but on re-tasting I stand by those original notes, though I disassociate myself entirely with the rubbish: "In order to savour Aberlour 100 at its best add 1/3 to 1/2 pure water. *57.1%*

Aberlour a'bunadh Batch No. 18 db **(93.5) n24.5** textbook oloroso. But what makes this so special is the malt which blasts through: absolutely no chance of the grape dominating for all its massive character; **t23.5** the dryness which catches the mid palate does not lie. But so complete is the delivery you wonder for a brief moment if you are on course for the near perfect malt. Plenty of chocolate orange helps compensate, and some Rolo toffee, too; **f22.5** some inevitable bitterness, but all kinds of toasted fudge notes; **b23** just one butt away from total brilliance. Even so, a dram to cherish. *59.7%. ncf.*

Aberlour a'bunadh Batch No. 27 db **(82) n21 t21.5 f18.5 b21.** More than the odd dud sherry butt. Shame, because some of the intensity of the ginger and Demerara could have made for something ultra special. *60%*

Aberlour a'bunadh Batch No. 28 db **(93.5) n22.5 t24 f23.5 b23.5.** Those of you who like your malts to be quiet in the glass and offer little more than a barley whine, don't even bother. Though there is evidence of a mildly off key sherry butt, such is the uncompromising enormity of all else you cannot be other than blown away. *59.8%*

Aberlour a'bunadh Batch No. 29 db **(94.5) n23.5 t24 f23.5 b23.5.** An indulgent malt lashing on the toffee creams. Not a single false step from beginning to end. World class. *59.9%*

Aberlour a'bunadh Batch No. 30 bott Mar 10 db **(87.5) n23 t23.5 f19 b22.** Though a renegade cask has slipped through the net, some moments are breathtaking. *59.8%*

⋰⋰ **Aberlour a'Bunadh Batch No. 31** db **(93.5) n24** a resounding Jaffa Cake nose, except someone has extracted much of the sugar from the jam. Some big vanillas amid the cocoa, too; **t23.5** a dry delivery with the spices punching hard as the grape unravels; a few maple syrup notes begin to creep in; **f23** long, remains dry as the cocoa levels rise enormously; **b23** chocolate, anyone...? *60.5%. nc ncf.*

⋰⋰ **Aberlour a'Bunadh Batch No. 32** db **(81.5) n20.5 t21 f20 b20.** Decidedly acerbic, and this has nothing to do with the strength. Dries far too violently for any balance to be held. *60.4%. nc ncf.*

⋰⋰ **Aberlour a'Bunadh Batch No. 33** db **(96) n24** now there's an aroma! A good 20 minute nose, this one, as you try to follow the contours of the Demerara sugar and old sherry Dundee cake on one hand and the far drier, dustier vanillas on the other. The peppers are almost akin to those of a wheated bourbon; **t24.5** I think it's the mouth feel that grips the attention first, especially the sheer lusciousness of it. Just as you try to size that up, in pops all kinds of fruit and spice notes, framed by the almost inevitable dark chocolate; those bourbon notes on the nose are backed up by a superb honey-liquorice middle ground; **f23.5** much drier now but the vanillas and other oaky notes show not a degree of bitterness or misalignment; **b24** a masterful dram bubbling over with intense grape....and a whole lot more. Simply gorgeous: the oak involved in this is about as good as it gets. *61.1%. nc ncf.*

⋰⋰ **Aberlour a'Bunadh Batch No. 34** db **(87.5) n21** thick, fruit toffee: rather one dimensional; **t23.5** juicy and warming on delivery and then thickens and sweetens very fast. Again the toffee arrives in thick and chewy fashion, though the peppers offer welcome respite; **f21.5** spiced vanilla toffee; **b21.5** overall, impossible not to enjoy. But a bit of a roly-poly kind of malt in which you feel a little short-changed on the complexity front. *59.6%. nc ncf.*

⋰⋰ **Aberlour a'Bunadh Batch No. 35** db **(90) n22** well spiced and heading into red liquorice bourbon territory; **t22.5** silky and toffee-rich delivery. The sugars build cleverly, with the weight firmly on muscovado before the toffee fudge arrives. A light fruitiness mingles with the growing cocoa; **f23** quite complex with the vanillas and cocoa sure footed and well balanced; **b22.5** from the same school as Batch 34, but avoids being bogged down in sticky toffee; *60.4%. nc ncf.*

⋰⋰ **Aberlour a'Bunadh Batch No. 36** db **(94) n22.5** another Kentucky style nose: the liquorice and spiced vanilla take a vice-like grip and refuse to let go; **t24** big and beefy, the sugars arrive with a near treacle thickness, though it is the enormity of the spice which leaves you gasping; **f23.5** calms down but the oils ensure a more gentle version is played out to maximum complexity; the finish displays some flinty fruitiness, not unlike the crisper rye notes in a very good bourbon; **b24** can you find this year another Speyside whisky come with as much muscle as this...? I doubt it. A malt whisky that appears to have spent as much time in the gym as it did the warehouse... 60.3%. nc ncf.

⁖ **Aberlour a'Bunadh Batch No. 37** db **(94.5) n23** back to a more conventional sherry style here, or seemingly so at first, with what appears to be spiced grape turned up to full volume. However, some powerful bourbon notes are on the prowl and take over proceedings and the fruit effect crumbles...; **t24** spice, as ever, on delivery and as the juiciness grows in intensity, the peppers click up a notch or two; the sugars also arrive early, this time in much lighter mode. Possibly one of the most satisfying deliveries from this brand for some while... which is saying something; **f23.5** vanilla and late molasses interplay superbly; **b24** spice is playing a more central role in a'Bunadh these days and here it is used to excellent effect, putting quite an edge to the fruit. Really beautiful whisky. 59.6%. nc ncf.

⁖ **Aberlour a'Bunadh Batch No. 38** db **(88.5) n22** fruit toffee; **t22** kerpow...!!! the spice thumps you from every direction...hard. Lots more fruit toffee; **f22.5** fruit toffee vindaloo...with a few extra chilli peppers thrown in.; **b22** a heavyweight which maybe overdoes it on the spice. 60.5%. nc ncf.

⁖ **Aberlour a'Bunadh Batch No. 39** db **(94) n22** wonderful fruit ranging from over-ripe apple to succulent date. The spice is straining at the leash; the grape is encrusted in chocolate; **t24** a graceful dance is being choreographed on my tongue. The spices are at the centre, but swirling around them is a dizzying array of juicy grape and salivating barley. The usual big liquorice sub plot is there and the bourbon theme is underlined with honeycomb. Curiously, there is a small still coppery element to this as well. It does no harm at all; **f23.5** a fabulous denouement of Crunchy honeycomb candy and Cadbury's Fruit and Nut...though that is hardly doing justice to the quality of the cocoa...; **b24.5** when they ask for seasoned oak, I am sure the coopers must use pepper. Here, though, as spicy as it may be, everything is under control and weighted superbly. One of the great whiskies of 2012. And confirmation that the best sherry butts on the single malt scene are currently deployed in the a'Bunadh range. 59.8%. nc ncf.

⁖ **Aberlour a'Bunadh Batch No. 40** db **(93.5) n24** one of the freshest fruit noses you could hope for, with a barrow-full of greengages so ripe they are fit to explode...; **t23.5** silky and succulent, the barley and spice make a big impact after the grape skin introduction; inevitable spices lead to a drier butterscotch tart middle; **f22.5** relatively lightweight for an a'Bunadh with the accent firmly on the barley; **b23.5** a shapely malt with no little barley. 61%. nc ncf.

⁖ **Aberlour a'Bunadh Batch No. 41** db **(83) n21 t22 f20 b20.** By normal standards, not too bad a malt, and another with the emphasis on the barley. But as an a'Bunadh, rather lacking...with one or two unattractive tangs too many. 59.7%. nc ncf.

Berry's Own Selection Aberlour 1988 cask no. 5551, bott 2011 **(85.5) n21 t22 f21 b21.5.** The citrus dirt to the honey on delivery is the stuff of dreams. A tired cask does not allow much building upon this early promise. 53.2%. nc ncf sc. Berry Bros & Rudd.

⁖ **Duncan Taylor Dimensions Aberlour 18 Years Old** cask no. 7371, dist 1993 **(86) n21 t22 f21.5 b21.5.** A real steady Eddie cask which efficiently completes its task of dishing out the barley with minimum frills or fuss. 54.3%. nc ncf sc. Duncan Taylor & Co.

⁖ **Mo Òr Collection Aberlour 1990 20 Years Old** first fill bourbon hogshead, cask no. 102107, dist 13 Nov 90, bott 9 Mar 11 **(96) n24.5** as near as damn it perfect: the barley is not only clean and juicy, but tinged with over-ripe pear and sharpened by pear drop. Beyond fantastic! **t24.5** wow! More of the same on the palate. The barley is proud and three dimensional with the spices not even thinking of hanging around and joining the fray from the third or fourth flavour wave. The sugars are crisp and diverse in style, the barley juice flows like a winter stream; **f23** dries out as the first fill cask begins to exert some muscle and the sugars die quite quickly; **b24** a dream cask which celebrates and perhaps even magnifies the magnificence of the classic Speyside style. Not a single note of weakness: extraordinary. Distilled on my 33rd birthday, I might well be putting this to one side to savour on my 55th! 46%. nc ncf sc. Release No. 31. The Whisky Talker. 300 bottles.

Old Malt Cask Aberlour Aged 20 Years refill hogshead, cask no. 6881, dist Oct 90, bott Jan 11 **(85.5) n21 t22 f21 b21.5.** Makes a particular point of saying as little as possible. Just very pleasant with the odd billowing barley moment. But otherwise very shy. 50%. nc ncf sc.

⁖ **Old Malt Cask Aberlour Aged 21 Years** refill sherry butt, cask no. 8230, dist Nov 90, bott Mar 12 **(92) n22.5** lively and loud, the salt bites deep into the candy fruit; **t23** podgy, sweet and chewy there is a fair degree of toffee raisin about this; **f23** love the finale: we are now into Toffo cream toffee style candy with some muscovado sugars softening the finish further; **b23.5** what a fabulous piece of oak the spirit was poured into! Brimming with character: superb! 50%. nc ncf sc. Douglas Laing & Co. 271 bottles.

Provenance Aberlour Over 12 Years refill hogs head, cask no. 6863, dist Autumn 98, bott Winter 2010 **(87) n22** clear honey on toast; **t21.5** some aggressive oak bites. But that honeydew melon barley saves the day; **f22** spices enliven the continuing honey; **b21.5** so delicate, looks as though it could snap at any moment. 46%. Douglas Laing & Co.

⋄ **Riegger's Selection Aberlour 1990** bourbon cask, cask no.16915, dist 30 Oct 90, bott 25 Jan 11 **(87.5) n21.5** walnut and cream cake; **t22** brittle barley with a juicy, crisp sugary coating; **f22** same again, except more accent on the vanilla rather than barley; **b22** shows the firmer side of Aberlour, which was common in the 1980s, rarely seen today. *52.9%. nc ncf sc. Viktor-Rieffer GmbH. 184 bottles.*

⋄ **Scott's Selection Aberlour 1987** bott 2012 **(86.5) n22.5 t22 f21 b21.** Ouch! So oaky it hurts! With some early thick honey to carry out damage limitation it starts off well enough. But then becomes just a little OTT. *54.9%. Speyside Distillers.*

Scott's Selection Aberlour 1989 bott 2011 **(94.5) n24.5** sugared Frosties in milk; the vaguest hint of cinnamon on over-cooked toast; a dab of acacia honey and lime offers the required balance; **t24.5** if you can find a delivery in which the sugars are so perfectly in tune with the drier oaks, please show it to me. The natural caramels build slowly, as do the spices; enough barley to ensure maximum salivation; **f22.5** just a hint of unrequited bitterness but the caramels hold sway; **b23** around this period at Aberlour, the consistency in the quality of production went up a gear or two. Here is fabulous example. *49.8%. Speyside Distillers.*

⋄ **Single Cask Collection Aberlour 17 Years Old** refill sherry hogshead, dist 1996 **(87.5) n22** banana and putty; **t22.5** briefly sharp and barley infested with a massive explosion of spice. But then quietens...and quietens...; **f21.5** whispering vanilla; **b21.5** considering that five of the six Scotch single malts I had tasted today had been tainted by sulphur, this came as something of a relief! Still not the brightest dram you'll ever find, though. *55.9%. sc.*

ABHAINN DEARG
Highlands (Outer Hebrides), 2008. Marko Tayburn. Working.

⋄ **Abhainn Dearg** db **(91) n22** the odd feint when pouring, but let the glass warm for a few minutes and the stronger elements soon burn off. What is left is a soft, pulpy gooseberry note as well as barley sugar and vague spice; **t22.5** intense and chewy, the delivery confirms the wide cut and for a while the flavours are in suspension. Slowly, a meaningful dialogue with the palate begins and it's those gorgeous barley notes which are first to speak up, soon joined by maple syrup and butterscotch tart; the tongue nearly wipes a hole in the roof of your mouth as it tackles the flavour orgy; **f23.5** a wonderful finish, not least because the malt appears to have relaxed into a sugary barleyfest with only a light coppery tang reminding us this is all from a brand new distillery forging its place in island folk lore; **b23** so here we go: the 1,000th new whisky of the 2013 Jim Murray Whisky Bible. And this year I give the honour of that landmark to Abhainn Dearg: the first bottling of a brand new Scotch single malt distillery is that very rarest of species. The fact it comes from Lewis really puts the icing on the cake. Some may remember that a couple of years back I made their new make the 1,001st new whisky for the 2011 edition: I have been keeping a close eye on this, now the most western scotch distillery. And it is strange to think that this is the first malt whisky to come from the Outer Hebrides with a licence attached.... My word, it was worth the wait. For after an unsteady start the quality becomes so clearly touched by angels. I can see everyone on the island having no qualms in tucking into this, even on the Sabbath. Well, maybe not... *46%. nc ncf sc.*

Abhainn Dearg New Make db **(92.5) n23 t23 f23.5 b23.** Exceptionally well made with no feints and no waste, either. Oddly salty – possibly the saltiest new make I have encountered, and can think of no reason why it should be – with excellent weight as some extra copper from the new still takes hold. Given a good cask, no reason this impressive new born son of the Outer Hebrides won't go on to become something significant. *67%*

Abhainn Dearg New Make db **(88) n21.5 t23 f21.5 b22.** OK. I admit that the 1,001st new whisky for the 2011 Bible wasn't whisky at all, but new make. But, as the Isle of Lewis has made it impossible for me not to visit there by now being an official whisky-making island, I thought it was worth celebrating. The new make in this form is rich, clean and malty but with a much heightened metallic feel to it, both on nose and taste, by comparison to other recently-opened distilleries. This is likely to change markedly over time as the stills settle in. So I had better start looking at the Cal-Mac Ferry timetables to go and find out for myself if it does... *Sample from cask at Whiskyfair Limburg 2010*

Abhainn Dearg Spirit Of Lewis PX cask, cask no. 122010 db **(89) n22 t23 f22 b22.** A very brave cask choice, I must say: I can think of no other more likely to throttle the personality out of the embryonic malt. But it does pass on a welcome spiciness which mixes well with the latent saltiness. A vague, distant touch of phenol but can't really tell amid the prune juice. The spirit is standing up to the bullying of the butt rather well... *56.5%. Matured for 2 to 3 months.*

ALLT-Á-BHAINNE
Speyside, 1975. Chivas Brothers. Working.

⋄ **Berry's Own Selection Allt-á-Bhainne 1995** cask no. 125284, bott 2011 **(90.5) n22.5** just so great to find a malt so clean on the nose and allowing the complex barley almost free reign; **t23** a touch oilier and more intense than the nose makes you expect; these waves thump down forcefully on the taste buds offering variation of sweetness and spice only; **f22.5** just a little on the bitter side, though a touch of mocha is welcome; **b22.5** if it's malt you want, it's malt you get...!! Of its type, absolutely wonderful. *53.4%. nc ncf sc. Berry Bros & Rudd.*

Connoisseurs Choice Allt-á-Bhainne 1995 dist 1995 **(88) n21.5 t22 f22.5 b22.** Almost beautiful in its stark simplicity. *43%. Gordon & MacPhail.*

⠿ **James MacArthur Old Masters Allt-á-Bhainne 16 Years Old (89) n22** attractive interplay between newly cut hay and a squeeze or two of lime; **t24** one of those satisfying deliveries where the malt, as this distillery has a tendency to do, appears to multiply in intensity not long after first delivery. The spices in the mid-ground are sublime; **f21** lightens with almost indecent haste, leaving the vanillas to fight on alone; **b22** one of those drams where the delivery is truly irresistible. *54.7%. James MacArthur & Co.*

Malts Of Scotland Allt-á-Bhainne 1992 bourbon hogshead, cask no. 6, dist May 92, bott Feb 11 **(89) n19.5 t24 f22.5 b23.** Such is the purity and depth of the barley it frees itself from its oaky entrapment with glorious results. A real beauty. *56.1%. sc.*

⠿ **Mo Ór Collection Allt-á-Bhainne 1992 18 Years Old** first fill bourbon hogshead, cask no. 12, dist 20 May 92, bott 6 Jan 11 **(88) n22** a tangy, zesty maltfest which goes easy on the sugars; **t23.5** clean with an exceptional emboldening of intense, sturdy malt that shows a just-so degree of give; **f20.5** thins, and lightens with an accent on vanilla; **b22** the nose and delivery is all you could want or ask of this distillery – and perhaps a little more besides. *46%. nc ncf sc. Release No. 33. The Whisky Talker. 460 bottles.*

Old Malt Cask Allt-á-Bhainne Aged 13 Years sherry butt, cask no. 6500, dist Dec 96, bott Jul 10 **(79.5) n18 t21.5 f19.5 b20.** Some sulphur but the enormity of the barley keeps the damage to an absolute minimum. *50%. nc ncf sc. Douglas Laing & Co. 266 bottles.*

⠿ **Old Malt Cask Allt-á-Bhainne Aged 18 Years** refill hogshead, cask no 7610, dist Feb 93, bott Aug 11 **(87) n22** clean malt lightly sweetened with a touch of butterscotch; **t23** soft with the light sugars seeping through ahead of the usual intense malt; **f20** the malt loses ground to the thin vanillas; **b22** easy going with the accent on the Speyside style. *50%. nc ncf sc. Douglas Laing & Co. 290 bottles.*

Old Masters Allt-á-Bhainne 17 Years Old cask no. 40658, dist 1993, bott Nov 10 **(88) n22 t23 f21.5 b21.5.** I am assuming there is no colouring, so the barrel must have given this an enormous jolt of natural caramels. Great fun, all the same. *57.9%. sc. James MacArthur & Co.*

⠿ **Provenance Allt-á-Bhainne Over 11 Years** sherry butt, cask no. 7652, dist Summer 2000, bott Summer 2011 **(82) n19 t21 f21 b21.** The nose may inspire little confidence but the shape on the palate offers a never less than intriguing mix of the rich and the Spartan. *46%. nc ncf sc*

Provenance Allt-á-Bhainne Over 12 Years sherry butt, cask no. 6533, dist Winter 97, bott Autumn 2010 **(83.5) n20 t21 f21.5 b21.** Heavy, heady stuff with a big liquorice middle and late spice. All the hallmarks of a first fill bourbon cask with a little too much to say. *46%. nc ncf sc.*

ARDBEG

Islay, 1815. Glenmorangie Plc. Working.

Ardbeg 10 Years Old db **(97) n24** more complex, citrus-led and sophisticated than recent bottlings, though the peat is no less but now simply displayed in an even greater elegance; a beautiful sea salt strain to this; **t24** gentle oils carry on them a lemon-lime edge, sweetened by barley and a weak solution of golden syrup; the peat is omnipotent, turning up in every crevice and wave, yet never one once overstepping its boundary; **f24** stunningly clean, the oak offers not a bitter trace but rather a vanilla and butterscotch edge to the barley. Again the smoke wafts around in a manner unique in the world of whisky when it comes to sheer élan and adroitness; **b25** like when you usually come across something that goes down so beautifully and with such a nimble touch and disarming allure, just close your eyes and enjoy... *46%*

Ardbeg 10 bottling mark L10 152 db **(95) n24.5** mesmerising: bigger oak kick than normal suggesting some extra age somewhere. But fits comfortably with the undulating peat and dusting of salt; captivating complexity: hard to find a ten year old offering more than this...; **t23.5** a shade oilier than the norm with orange and honey mingling effortlessly with the smoke: more than a hint of icing sugar; melts in the mouth like a prawn cracker...but without the prawns...; **f23.5** drying oak with cocoa powder. The oils help the sugars linger; **b23.5** a bigger than normal version, but still wonderfully delicate. Fabulous and faultless. *46%. Canadian market bottling in English and French dual language label.*

Ardbeg 17 Years Old earlier bottlings db **(92) n23 t22 f23 b24.** OK, I admit I had a big hand in this, creating it with the help of Glenmorangie Plc's John Smith. It was designed to take the weight off the better vintages of Ardbeg whilst ensuring a constant supply around the world. Certainly one of the more subtle expressions you are likely to find, though criticised by some for not being peaty enough. As the whisky's creator, all I can say is they are missing the point. *40%*

Ardbeg 17 Years Old later bottlings db (**90**) n22 t23 f22 b23. The peat has all but vanished and cannot really be compared to the original 17-year-old: it's a bit like tasting a Macallan without the sherry: fascinating to see the naked body underneath, and certainly more of a turn on. Peat or no peat, great whisky by any standards. *40%*

Ardbeg Guaranteed 30 Years Old db (**91**) n24 t23 f21 b23. An unsual beast, one of the last ever bottled by Allied. The charm and complexity early on is enormous, but the fade rate is surprising. That said, still a dram of considerable magnificence. *40%*

Ardbeg 1977 db (**96**) n25 t24 f23 b24. When working through the Ardbeg stocks, I earmarked '77 a special vintage, the sweetest of them all. So it has proved. Only the '74 absorbed that extra oak that gave greater all-round complexity. Either way, the quality of the distillate is beyond measure: simply one of the greatest experiences – whisky or otherwise – of your life. *46%*

Ardbeg 1978 db (**91**) n23 t24 f22 b22. An Ardbeg on the edge of losing it because of encroaching oak, hence the decision made by John Smith and I to bottle this vintage early alongside the 17-year-old. Nearly ten years on, still looks a pretty decent bottling, though slightly under strength! *43%*

Ardbeg 1995 Single Cask No. 2761 2nd fill bourbon, dist Dec 95, bott Mar 10 db (**92.5**) n22.5 t24 f23 b23. Textbook Ardbeg from the point of view that its complexity can be gauged only after five or six mouthfuls. A shifting sands of a dram... *53.3%. 228 bottles. For Feis Ile.*

Ardbeg 1998 Single Cask No. 1275 1st fill bourbon barrel, dist May 98, bott Oct 09 db (**87**) n21 t22 f22 b22. Enjoyable but lacking a bit of the usual Ardbeg charisma and vitality. *55.4%. 252 bottles.*

Ardbeg 1998 Single Cask No. 2763 refill sherry hogshead, dist Sep 98, bott Nov 09 db (**86.5**) n22 t22 f21 b21.5. Ardbeg in a straightjacket. The sherry influence tightens every aspect, restricting the usual effortless grace and complexity. As hard an Ardbeg as you'll ever find. *55.6%. 270 bottles.*

Ardbeg 2000 Single Cask Lord Robertson of Port Ellen KT cask no. 1217, dist Apr 00, bott May 10 db (**96.5**) n24 classic busy but relaxed nose: that delicate squeeze of young lemon dancing with such elegant peat confirms that it can be from no other distillery; t24.5 and there we are: the delivery is at once soft and full of spices which blast you from your chair; again the lemon is quickly in and the phenols melt into cocoa and Demerara...beyond orgasmic; f23.5 exceptionally long even by Ardbeg standards with the lightest oils to assist. Spices, mocha, citrus and smoke stretch into infinity... b24.5 though fun, a number of the distillery bottling casks had left me a little flat. Here though is a cask not just basking in all the finest Ardbegian traditions but taking those unique characteristics and pushing them beyond the distance you thought they might go. And proof, were it needed, that Ardbeg at10 can, as it did one, two and three decades ago, offer something which is the equivalent of a whisky lover's wet dream. Whatever they ask you for this bottling, pay it. Not only is the money going to a great cause. But your experience in whisky will be equally enriched. *53%. For Lord Robertson (proceeds donated to Erskine). 202 bottles.*

Ardbeg Alligator 1st Release db (**94**) n24 delicate: like a bomb aimer...steady, steady, steady...there she goes...and suddenly spices light up the nose; some coriander and cocoa, too; t22.5 surprisingly silky, soft and light; milky chocolate hides some lurking clove in the soothing smoke; f24 hits its stride for a magnificent finale: as long as you could possibly hope for and an-ever gathering intensity of busy, prickly spice. Mocha and a dab of praline see off any potential bitterness to the oaky fight back; b23.5 an alligator happy to play with you for a bit before sinking its teeth in. The spices, though big, are of the usual Ardbegian understatement. *51.2%. ncf. Exclusive for Ardbeg Committee members.*

Ardbeg Alligator 2nd Release db (**93**) n24 clove and black pepper; a degree of bourbony polished leather and liquorice, too; t23 early Demerara sugars and smoke make way for that slow build up of spices again; though perhaps missing the subtlety of the first edition's quietness, it more than has its macho compensations; f23 curiously, a short finale, as though more energy was expended in the delivery. Much drier with the oak having a good deal to say, though the spices nip satisfyingly; b23 something of a different species to the Committee bottling having been matured a little longer, apparently. Well long enough for this to evolve into something just a little less subtle. The nose, though, remains something of striking beauty – even if barely recognisable from the first bottling. *51.2%. ncf.*

Ardbeg Almost There 3rd release dist 1998, bott 2007 db (**93**) n23 t24 f23 b23. Further proof that a whisky doesn't have to reach double figures in age to enter the realms of brilliance... *54.1%*

Ardbeg Blasda db (**90.5**) n23.5 distant kumquat and lime intertwine with gentle butterscotch tart; it's all about the multi-layered barley and the most vague smokiness imaginable which adds a kind of almost invisible weight; the overall clarity is like that found swimming off a Pacific atoll; t22.5 sharp barley hits home to almost mouth-watering effect; again there is the most pathetic hint of something smoky (like the SMWS cask, perhaps from the local water and warehouse air), but it does the trick and adds just the right ballast; **f22** soft spices arrive apologetically, but here it could do with being at 46% just to give it some late lift; **b22.5** a beautiful, if slightly underpowered malt, which shows Ardbeg's naked self to glowing effect. Overshadowed by some degree in its class by the SMWS bottling, but still something to genuinely make the heart flutter. *40%*

Ardbeg Corryvreckan db **(96.5) n23** excellent, thick, not entirely un-penetrable – but close – nascent smoke and a vignette of salty, coastal references save the day; **t24.5** amazing: here we have Ardbeg nutshelled. Just so many layers of almost uncountable personalities with perhaps the citrus leading the way in both tart and sweet form and then meaningful speeches from those saline-based, malty sea-spray refreshed barley notes with the oak, in vanilla form, in close proximity. The peat, almost too dense to be seen on the nose, opens out with a fanfare of phenols. It is slumping-in-the-chair stuff, the enormity of the peat taking on the majesty of Cathedral-esque proportions, the notes reverberating around the hollows and recesses and reaching dizzying heights; such is its confidence, this is a malt which says: "I know where I'm going...!"; **f24** long, outwardly laconic but on further investigation just brimming with complexity. Some brown sugary notes help the barley to come up trumps late on but it's the uniquely salty shield to the mocha which sets this apart. Simply brilliant and unique in its effortless enormity...even by Ardbeg standards; **b25** as famous writers – including the occasional genius film director (stand up wherever you are my heroes Powell and Pressburger) – appear to be attracted to Corryvreckan, the third most violent whirlpool found in the world and just off Islay, to boot, - I selected this as my 1,500th whisky tasted for the historic Jim Murray Whisky Bible 2009. I'm so glad I did because many have told me they thought Blasda ahead of this. To me, it's not even a contest. Currently I have only a sample. Soon I shall have a bottle. I doubt if even the feared whirlpool is this deep and perplexing. *57.1%. 5000 bottles.*

⁘ **Ardbeg Day Bottling** db **(97) n24.5** a dry lead... seemingly. But it's the busy stuff behind the scenes which intrigues. In typical Ardbegian fashion it's what you have to take a little extra time to find which is the real turn on...apart from the rock pool salt, apart from the squeeze of slightly sugared lime, apart from the thinnest layer of honey, apart from the fracturing hickory, apart from the kelp;...; **t24.5** and while the nose at times seems hard and brittle, the delivery moulds itself into the shape of your palate. Soft oils fill the contours; dissolving sugars counter the well-mannered but advancing oak; the phenols take on an earthy form, languid spices and omnipresent smoke; **f23.5** dries again in a vanilla direction with the oak determined to have its say. But it is a gentle speech and one inclusive of the delicate phenols encouraging the growing citrus. The oils remain just higher than the norm and thicken the muscovado-sweetened mocha. The finish, one of the longest you will find this year, carries on beyond what you would normally expect of an Ardbeg. And that is saying something: **b24.5** I left this to be one of the last whiskies I tasted this year. I had an inkling that they might come up with something a little special, especially with the comparative disappointment of the fundamentally flawed Galileo. On first sweep I thought it was pretty ordinary. but I know this distillery a little too well. So I left the glass for some 20 minutes to breathe and compose itself and returned. To find a potential world whisky of the year... *56.8%. Available at distillery and Ardbeg embassies.*

Ardbeg Feis Ile 2011 db **(67) n16 t19 f15 b17.** If anyone asked me what not to do with an Ardbeg, my answer would be: don't put it into a PX cask. And if asked if anything could be worse, I'd day: yeah, a PX Cask reeking of sulphur. To be honest, I am only assuming this is PX, as there is no mention on my sample bottle and I have spoken to them about it. But for something to fail as completely as this my money is on PX. And sulphur. *55.4%*

⁘ **Ardbeg Galileo 1999** db **(87.5) n23** the nose is busy, with a constant criss-crossing of smoke and fruity notes...but takes all the nuances in its stride. Slightly more oak than you might expect of an Ardbeg this age, which seems to give a helping hand to the peat. Thick peaches and apricots absorb the impact of the more weighty bodies; **t23.5** the nose had already told you this was going to be a pretty thick delivery, and so it proves. Anyone old enough to remember original Old Jamaica chocolate from the 1970s (not the nonsense being sold today) will appreciate this as the cocoa and raisins are big with a kumquat sub-layer; the peat is omnipresent yet never overpowering; **f19** crashes back to earth with a fuzzy finish; **b22** today, as I taste this, I am celebrating the first birthday of my grand-daughter Islay-Mae, named after the greatest whisky island in the world. And this was one of half a dozen special whiskies I set aside to mark the event. For it is not often you get the chance to celebrate the first birthday of your first grand-daughter. Nor to taste a malt specially bottled to celebrate some of its fellow Ardbeg whisky that was sent into orbit for experimentation in the Space Station....At least I know a day like this will never be repeated. *49%*

Ardbeg Kildalton 1980 bott 2004 db **(96) n23 t24 f24 b25.** Proof positive that Ardbeg doesn't need peat to bring complexity, balance and Scotch whisky to their highest peaks... *57.6%*

Ardbeg Lord of the Isles bott Autumn 2006 db **(85) n20 t22 f22 b21.** A version of Ardbeg I have never really come to terms with. This bottling is of very low peating levels and shows a degree of Kildalton-style fruitiness. No probs there. But some of the casks are leaching a soft soapy character noticeable on the nose. Enjoyable enough, but a bit frustrating. 46%

Ardbeg Mor db **(95) n24** coastal to the point of sea spray showering you, with the smell of salt all the way home until you reach the peat fire. Evocative, sharp with elements of vinegar to the iodine; **t24** one of the biggest deliveries from Ardbeg for yonks; the peat appears way above the normal 50%, thickset and gloriously bitter-sweet, the steadying vanillas carried on the soft oils; **f23** mocha enters the fray with a raspberry jam fruitiness trying to dampen the continuing smoke onslaught; **b24** quite simply Mor the merrier... 57.5%

Ardbeg Provenance 1974 bott 1999 db **(96) n24 t25 f23 b24.** This is an exercise in subtlety and charisma, the beauty and the beast drawn into one. Until I came across the 25-year-old OMC verson during a thunderstorm in Denmark, this was arguably the finest whisky I had ever tasted: I opened this and drank from it to see in the year 2000. When I went through the Ardbeg warehouse stocks in 1997 I earmarked the '74 and '77 vintages as something special. This bottling has done me proud. 55.6%

Ardbeg Renaissance db **(92) n22.5 t22.5 f23.5 b23.5.** How fitting that the 1,200th (and almost last) new-to-market whisky I had tasted for the 2009 Bible was Renaissance... because that's what I need after tasting that lot...!! This is an Ardbeg that comes on strong, is not afraid to wield a few hefty blows and yet, paradoxically, the heavier it gets the more delicate, sophisticated and better-balanced it becomes. Enigmatically Ardbegian. 55.9%

Ardbeg Rollercoaster db **(90.5) n23** youthful malts dominate; a patchwork of smoke on many different levels from ashy to ethereal: almost dizzying; **t23** again, it's the young Ardbeg which dominates; the delivery is almost painful as you shake your head at the shock of the spices and unfettered peat. A genuine greenness to the malts though some natural caramels do make a smoky surge; **f23** long, buttery in part, limited sweetness; almost a touch of smoked bacon about it; **b21.5** to be honest, it was the end of another long day – and book – when I tasted this and I momentarily forgot the story behind the malt. My reaction to one of my researchers who happened to be in the tasting room was: "Bloody hell! They are sending me kids. If this was any younger I'd just be getting a bag of grist!" This malt may be a fabulous concept. And Rollercoaster is a pretty apt description, as this a dram which appears to have the whisky equivalent of Asperger's. So don't expect the kind of balance that sweeps you into a world that only Ardbeg knows. This, frankly, is not for the Ardbeg purist or snob. But for those determined to bisect the malt in all its forms and guises, it is the stuff of the most rampant hard-ons. 57.3%

Ardbeg Still Young 2nd release dist 1998, bott 2006 db **(93) n24 t24 f22 b23.** A couple of generations back – maybe even less – this would not have been so much "Still Young" as "Getting on a Bit." This is a very good natural age for an Ardbeg as the oak is making a speech, but refuses to let it go on too long. Stylish – as one might expect. And, in my books, should be a regular feature. Go on. Be bold. Be proud say it: Ardbeg Aged 8 Years. Get away from the marketing straightjacket of old age... 56.2%. ncf.

Ardbeg Supernova db **(97) n24.5** moody, atmospheric; hints and threats; Lynchian in its stark black and white forms, its meandering plot, its dark and at times indecipherable message and meaning...; **t24** at first a wall of friendly phenols but only when you stand back and see the overall picture you can get an idea just how mammoth that wall is; there are intense sugary gristy notes, then this cuts away slightly towards something more mouth-fillingly smoky but now with a hickory sweetness; a light oil captures the long, rhythmic waves, a pulse almost; **f24** gentle, sweetening cocoa notes evolve while the peat pulses... again...and again... **b24.5** apparently this was called "Supernova" in tribute of how I once described a very highly peated Ardbeg. This major beast, carrying a phenol level in excess of 100ppm, isn't quite a Supernova...much more of a Black Hole. Because once you get dragged into this one, there really is no escaping... 58.9%

Ardbeg Supernova SN2010 bott 2010 db **(93.5) n24** youthful, punchy and spicy; vanillas and bananas add a sweetness to the molten peat; **t23.5** an explosion of sharp citrus and grassy malt. Not quite what was expected but the smoke and spices cause mayhem as they crash around the palate: eye-watering, safety harness-wearing stuff; **f23** the oak has a bitter-ish surprise but soft sugars compensate. Elsewhere the smoke and spice continues its rampage; **b23** there are Supernovas and there are Supernovas. Some have been going on a bit and have formed a shape and indescribable beauty with the aid of time; others are just starting off and though full of unquantifiable energy and wonder have a distance to travel. By comparison to last year's blockbusting Whisky Bible award winner, this is very much in the latter category. 60.1%

Ardbeg Uigeadail db **(97.5) n25 t24.5 f23.5 b24.5.** Massive yet tiny. Loud yet whispering. Seemingly ordinary from the bottle, yet unforgettable. It is snowing outside my hotel room in

Calgary, yet the sun, in my soul at least, is shining. I came across this bottling while lecturing the Liquor Board of British Columbia in Vancouver on May 6th 2008, so one assumes it is a Canadian market bottling. It was one of those great moments in my whisky life on a par with tasting for the first time the Old Malt Cask 1975 at a tasting in Denmark. There is no masking genius.The only Scotch to come close to this one is another from Ardbeg, Corryvreckan. That has more oomph and lays the beauty and complexity on thick...it could easily have been top dog. But this particular Uigeadail (for I have tasted another bottling this year, without pen or computer to hand and therefore unofficially, which was a couple of points down) offers something far more restrained and cerebral. Believe me: this bottling will be going for thousands at auction in the very near future, I wager. 54.2%

Ardbeg Uigeadail db **(89) n25** awesome package of intense peat reek amid complex fruitcake and leather notes. Everything about this nose is broadside-big yet the massive oak never once oversteps its mark. A whiff of engine oil compliments the kippers. Perfection; **t22** begins with a mind-blowing array of bitter-sweet oaky notes and then a strangely fruity peat entry; real scattergun whisky; **f20** very odd finish with an off-key fruit element that flattens the usual Ardbeg grand finale; **b22** a curious Ardbeg with a nose to die for. Some tinkering - please guys, as the re-taste is not better - regarding the finish may lift this to being a true classic 54.1%

⁘ **Chieftain's Ardbeg Aged 13 Years** barrel, cask no. 1779, dist Jun 98 **(87.5) n22** the most half-hearted phenols you are likely to find after the takeover from Allied; **t22** a gentle stampede of sweet, coffee enriched barley, the smoke takes time to form and intensify...but its getting there; **f21.5** thins out rather too dramatically; **b22** this bottling has gone to America. Get hold of the NYPD – now! Someone has half-inched the peat....!!! In evidence, I'd say the culprit was a certain Ed Dodson, who hadn't yet completely sorted out the non-removal of shell of the barley from the grist... No, honestly, officer, it wasn't me..!! And yes, now you come to mention it, I am a wise guy... 46%. nc ncf sc. Ian Macleod Distillers.

Dun Bheagan Ardbeg 15 Years Old dist Nov 94 **(93) n23** above average phenols even for this distillery marked by a dry, sooty style; **t23** nothing dry about the delivery: almost grist like in its juiciness, **f23** long, with a far better oak accompaniment than you would ever expect from an old Allied distillery; the sugars stay to the far from bitter end; **b24** effortlessly beautiful. Never quite gets out of second gear...never really has to... 53%. nc ncf. Ian Macleod Distillers.

⁘ **Malts Of Scotland Ardbeg 1991** sherry hogshead, cask no. MoS11003, dist Feb 91, bott Oct 11 **(89) n22.5** I think there is more than the standard 50ppm at play here. A lot more. The phenols are enormous...and have to be to keep the crystalline, untainted sherry at bay... **t22** ...though on delivery guess which comes through first loud and clear: almost pure grape juice. This lessens the body and it takes a while for the peat to regroup and build up a significant body of intensity; **f22** so far this has been a battle between peat and pure sherry....and there is no clear winner on the finish, though at last some delicate though molasses-based sugars make a desired and required appearance; **b22.5** bugger me! A sherry butt Ardbeg not fatally torpedoed by sulphur...I don't believe it! 48.4%. nc ncf sc. Malts Of Scotland.

⁘ **Scotch Malt Whisky Society Cask 33.112 Aged 5 Years** second fill sherry butt, cask no. 3965, dist 2005 **(87) n22** astonishing just how dry this nose is; by rights, grist should be coming at you from all angles. But the ash has already formed with a lovely yam sub-plot to ensure the prerequisite sweetness, **t23** again, there is little evidence of its youth. Perhaps a small degree of new make freshness, but it is well hidden behind the confident and full-blooded smoke; **f20** just a little trace of something furry and unwanted takes the edge off the party, **b22** was going along beautifully until a little historic sulphur managed to work its way into the equation. 60.8%. sc. Scotch Malt Whisky Society.

⁘ **Scotch Malt Whisky Society Cask 33.113 Aged 8 Years** first fill barrel, cask no. 1418, dist 2003 **(93.5) n23** dry, ashy, layered smoke...; **t23** dry, ashy, layered delivery...mainly of smoke. But sweetens as red liquorice and Demerara squeeze into the act; a few spicy moments; **f23** long, still retaining the oils and sugars but now extra vanillas and a hint of mocha; **b23.5** seems to go through quite a transformation of styles in a short time. As fascinating as it is delicious..! 60.4%. sc. Scotch Malt Whisky Society.

⁘ **Scotch Malt Whisky Society Cask 33.114 Aged 11 Years** refill butt, cask no. 1553, dist 1999 **(79) n20 t21 f19 f19**. Irrespective as to whether a sherry butt is sound or sulphur-contaminated, the success of a whisky depends on whether a malt achieves an enjoyable degree of balance. This, alas, does not. And further, it also suffers from a slight sulphur taint. This is Ardbeg It should not be so. 56.3%. sc.

⁘ **Scotch Malt Whisky Society Cask 33.115 Aged 11 Years** refill sherry butt, cask no. 1606, dist 1999 **(73.5) n19.5 t20 f16 b18**. Syrupy. Stodgy. Bitter. Tight. Imbalanced. Sulphured. I thought that the SMWS and Ardbeg were part of the same group. All those casks...and they choose this...!!! Following after 33.114, I don't know which I am most: shocked, appalled or angry. Well done, whoever is responsible. You get the world's best distillery. If not, then second only to Buffalo Trace. You have access to its stocks. And then you select, by Ardbegian standards, a complete dud. That, believe me, is some achievement! 55.4%. sc.

⫶⫶⫶ **Scotch Malt Whisky Society Cask 33.116 Aged 8 Years** first fill barrel, cask no. 1422, dist 2003 **(96) n24** the line-up of the sweeter elements hurts the brain: from heather honey to Demerara, they run the gamut. Lavender works in tandem with the heather. And what's the peat doing all this time? Prowling like a proud lion: relaxed but ready for any trouble which might come its way...; **t23.5** hardly surprising the sugars form the vanguard of the delivery, or that soft oils usher in a smoky base. Nor is the degree of complexity, or the way the citrus cuts through the oil like some kind of smoky detergent through grease....; **f24** a succession of bourbon tannins now add a weight that is not peat-related. That said, never for a moment becomes heavy going and delicate notes, even now, abound; **b24.5** Ardbeg at its most amorous. Worth getting 33.113 as a comparison: the difference, though presumably from the same batch, makes the hair stand on end. this is what happens when all the sugars make a countering contribution, rather than being passive a la 113... 60.4%. sc.

Scotch Malt Whisky Society Cask 33.88 Aged 10 Years 1st fill bourbon barrel, cask no. 1792, dist 1999 **(84.5) n22.5 t21 f20 b21.** Big liquorice lilt to the smoke but curiously lacking the usual deft fruitiness. But some evidence that the stills were run a little too keenly on this one. Extremely average by Ardbegian standards. 56.5%. sc. 243 bottles.

Scotch Malt Whisky Society Cask 33.91 Aged 10 Years refill sherry puncheon, cask no. 759093, dist 2000 **(75.5) n19.5 t19.5 f18 b18.5.** A thin, niggardly and hot dram. Proof that a poor cask equals a poor whisky – no matter who makes it. 64.4%. sc. 410 bottles.

Scotch Malt Whisky Society Cask 33.96 Aged 10 Years refill sherry butt, cask no. 1556, dist 1999 **(93) n23** a pretty violent meeting between grape and smoke. And though I abhor violence...gerthcha!!! **t24** knee-buckling stuff! The grapes are simply dripping juice, but the peat will not be outdone. The result is a battle which, had it been in Greek times, would have lived in the classical annals forever; **f23** long, luxurious with persistent fresh grape but also big spice and ever building vanilla; **b23** the grape and toffee from the oak combine to just deflect some of the higher notes of complexity. That said...wow! 56.7%. sc. 668 bottles.

Scotch Malt Whisky Society Cask 33.100 Aged 7 Years 1st fill bourbon barrel, cask no. 1419, dist 2003 **(93.5) n23** one of the delicately peated variety where the smoke hangs by a thread and is easily challenged by citrus for supremacy; a few herbal notes offer greater tread; **t24** mega sweet, but purely from a gristy perspective: virtually no oak sugars I can detect. Just barley-driven ones alone. Because of the tender years this is fabulously juicy; **f23** pretty short by Ardbeg standards. No great oils or oak contribution to lengthen it. But those delicate peats just keep drifting; the only nod to the barrel is a gentle cocoa lilt; **b23.5** in another world, the management at Ardbeg reckoned that, on the rare occasions it was bottled as a single malt, this kind of age suited it best. I don't think bourbon casks were an option for them. But, even so, a memorable, must-have bottling showing the distillery at its most fragile. 60.7%. sc. 254 bottles.

Scotch Malt Whisky Society Cask 33.107 Aged 11 Years refill sherry butt, cask no. 1559, dist 1999 **(91.5) n23.5** trademark big smoke but deceptively lurking in little hideaways to appear not quite as big as it is; still a little grist to be found plus mocha; also a little moist fruitcake popping up here and there; **t22** but it's that grist which shows on delivery followed swiftly by an avalanche of spices; a little cough sweet towards the middle; **f23** enters a wonderful phase of complexity. Vanillas have arrived big time, there is the most distant hint of berry fruit while the peat and spices rumble on...; **b23** Ardbeg at its most charming. 57.8%. sc. 659 bottles.

Scotch Malt Whisky Society Cask 33.108 Aged 13 Years 2nd fill barrel, cask no. 1140, dist 1997 **(95.5) n24** salty, crisp barley with an oily gloss to the smoke; so complex and just about perfectly weighted; **t24** salivating and filled to the brim with juicy lemon notes. The spices kick off early but remain busy if slightly aloof, allowing the smoke full scope to mingle with the vanilla; the sugars are a constant, taking a midline in intensity and remain firmly in the muscovado style; **f23.5** a gentle praline edge to the ever more delicate smoke; **b24** my favourite cask type for Ardbeg. Juicy, elegant... frankly, sublime. 56.6%. sc. 220 bottles.

ARDMORE
Speyside, 1899. Beam Inc. Working.

Ardmore 100th Anniversary 12 Years Old dist 1986, bott 1999 db **(94) n24 t23.5 f22.5 b24.** Brilliant. Absolutely stunning, with the peat almost playing games on the palate. Had they not put caramel in this bottling, it most likely would have been an award winner. So, by this time next year, I fully expect to see every last bottle accounted for... 40%

Ardmore 25 Years Old db **(89.5) n21** decidedly caramel oriented with the smoke thin and crisp; **t23.5** quite brilliant delivery: not only powering, but with an unwavering Demerara and chocolate voice; lightly roasted Blue Mountain benefits from the playful spices; the smoke is little more than a background hum; **f22.5** long with a milky, orangey texture steeling in; **b22.5** a 25-y-o box of chocolates: coffee creams, fudge, orange cream...they are all in there. The nose maybe ordinary: what follows is anything but. *51.4%. ncf.*

Ardmore 30 Years Old Cask Strength db **(94)** n23.5 the first time I have encountered a cough-sweetish aroma on an Ardmore but, like every aspect, it is played down and delicate. Melting sugar on porridge. Citrus notes of varying intensity. Fascinating for its apparent metal hand in velvet glove approach; **t23.5** sweet, gristy delivery even after all these years. And a squeeze of sharp lime, too, and no shortage of spices. Does all in its power to appear half its age. This includes blocking the oaks from over development and satisfying itself with a smoky, mocha middle; the muscovado sugars are, with the smoke, spread evenly; **f23** busy spices and a lazy build up of vanillas; **b24** I remember when the present owners of Ardmore launched their first ever distillery bottling. Over a lunch with the hierarchy there I told them, with a passion, to ease off with the caramel so the world can see just how complex this whisky can be. This brilliant, technically faultless, bottling is far more eloquent and persuasive than I was that or any other day... *53.7%. nc ncf. 1428 bottles.*

Ardmore Fully Peated Quarter Casks db **(89)** n21 t23 f23 b22. This is an astonishingly brave attempt by the new owners of Ardmore who, joy of all joys, are committed to putting this distillery in the public domain. Anyone with a 2004 copy of the Whisky Bible will see that my prayers have at last been answered. However, this bottling is for Duty Free and, due to the enormous learning curve associated with this technique, a work in progress. They have used the Quarter Cask process which has been such a spectacular success at its sister distillery Laphroaig. Here I think they have had the odd slight teething problem. Firstly, Ardmore has rarely been filled in ex-bourbon and that oak type is having an effect on the balance and smoke weight; also they have unwisely added caramel, which has flattened things further. I don't expect the caramel to be in later bottlings and, likewise, I think the bourbon edge might be purposely blunted a little. But for a first attempt this is seriously big whisky that shows enormous promise. When they get this right, it could – and should – be a superstar. Now I await the more traditional vintage bottlings... *46%. ncf.*

Ardmore Traditional Cask db **(88.5)** n21.5 t22 f23 b22. Not quite what I expected. "Jim. Any ideas on improving the flavour profile?" asked the nice man from Ardmore distillery when they were originally launching the thing. "Yes. Cut out the caramel." "Ah, right..." So what do I find when the next bottling comes along? More caramel. It's good to have Influence... Actually, I can't quite tell if this is a result of natural caramelization from the quarter casking or just an extra dollop of the stuff in the bottling hall. The result is pretty similar: some of the finer complexity is lost. My guess, due to an extra fraction of sweetness and spice, is that it is the former. All that said, the overall experience remains quite beautiful. And this remains one of my top ten distilleries in the world *46%. ncf.*

❖ **Teacher's Highland Single Malt** quarter cask finish db **(09)** n22.5 a uniquely floral twist to the un-Ardmorish peat. Of course, there is always peat on Ardmore...but this displays an unusual salty coarseness above the usual 9ppm phenols which suits, lots of toffee vanilla notes, but patted down by elegant kumquat; **t23** they like silk in India, so this should be appreciated. Cream toffee with a two-pronged peat attack – both smoky and spicy; an interesting coppery tang in the mid-ground, as if a still had recently undergone remedial work; **f21.5** just a little too heavy on the buttery toffee fudge, **b22** This is Ardmore at its very peatiest. And had not the colouring levels been heavily tweaked to meet the flawed perceptions of what some markets believe makes a good whisky, this malt would have been better still. As it is: superb. With the potential of achieving greatness if only they have the confidence and courage... *40%. India/Far East Travel Retail exclusive.*

Chieftain's Ardmore Aged 18 Years dist Jun 92, bott 2011 **(93)** n23 soft, slightly dry peat drifts over the relaxed oak-barley mix; **t23** silky body wrapped in a deftly smoky, oak-caramel-rich shroud; **f24** very long finale helped by the cleverly ingratiating smoke and those sugar-coated oils. About as soft a finish as you'll ever find – even after when the spice attack is made; **b23** over the last 30-odd years it has been my good fortune to taste samples from the contents of an enormous number of Ardmore barrels. Which is why I was probably the most vociferous advocate they had ever enjoyed right up until the time the first commercial distillery bottling was launched. This gives you some idea why: it is absolutely typical of the malt for its age: not a single off note, not overly spectacular, yet effortlessly ticks every single positive box in its own delicately peaty way. *46%. nc ncf. Ian Macleod Distillers. USA release.*

❖ **Dun Bheagan Ardmore 12 Years Old** St Etienne rum finish, dist Jun 99 **(87)** n22.5 astonishingly complex aroma – all shadows and whispers. Perhaps a little smoke here, maybe a touch of lime peel there; **t22** the barley heads the parade of delicate soft, almost guarded notes; the fruit is inconsistent though fine; **f20.5** warm and a little bitter; **b22** must admit: I hadn't read the label and was scratching my head wondering when I'd encountered an Ardmore like this before. Believe me: I hadn't. *46%. nc ncf sc. Ian Macleod Distillers.*

L'Esprit Single Cask Collection Ardmore refill bourbon barrel, cask no. 6487, dist Sep 03, bott Oct 10 **(80) n22 t21 f18 b19**. The nose is full of the usual Ardmore understated smoky promise which is never quite fulfilled due to the trademark bitterness of a less than brilliant ex-Allied cask. *46%. nc ncf sc. Whisky & Rhum. 121 bottles.*

L'Esprit Single Cask Collection Ardmore Cask Strength refill bourbon barrel, cask no. 6487, dist Sep 03, bott Oct 10 **(85.5) n22.5 t22 f20 b21.** This is very much better than the 46% version. The reason is quite simple: the intensity of the sugars on the malt, fatally weakened in the other version, have enough about them to see off all but the worst of flaws in the cask. Further proof that whisky and water don't go... *56.2%. nc ncf sc. Whisky & Rhum. 60 bottles.*

❖ **Liquid Sun Ardmore 19 Years Old** bourbon cask, dist 1992, bott 2011 **(91.5) n22.5** as though a kipper has been smoked after being marinated in orange juice...; **t23.5** beautiful in both texture and weight, it is not long before it becomes evident this is a more heavily peated Ardmore than the norm; the layering of phenols and liquorice is glorious; **f22.5** long with a slow melting of molassed sugars and more liquorice; the smoke bounds along beautifully; **b23** someone upped the peat smoke big time. This bottling effortlessly accentuates the greatness of this distillery. *49.9%. sc. The Whisky Agency.*

Malts Of Scotland Ardmore 1992 bourbon barrel, cask no. 5014, dist, Jun 92, bott Dec 10 **(92.5) n22.5** smoky bacon and a distinct peppery nip to the citrus; **t23.5** still some juice in the barley and the peat gathers in light layers; a gorgeous mocha middle is carefully sweetened before the drier vanillas arrive; **f23** the smoky chocolate theme continues, aided by the most choice degree of oil; **b23.5** weighty but with a very deft touch. High quality malt with sublime marbelling. *49.4%. nc ncf sc. Malts Of Scotland. 185 bottles.*

❖ **Mo Òr Collection Ardmore 1992 18 Years Old** first fill bourbon barrel, cask no. 5013, dist 24 Jun 92, bott 21 Jan 11 **(85.5) n21 t23 f20 b21.5**. Behaves absolutely nothing like a first-fill bourbon barrel. The oak interface is barely discernible, other than a slight soapiness much more associated with a clapped out third fill. Still a malt with some outstanding moments, especially as the sugars and smoke merge into a glorious spiciness. *46%. nc ncf sc. Release No. 34. The Whisky Talker. 286 bottles.*

Old Malt Cask Ardmore Aged 15 Years refill hogshead, cask no. 7044, dist Feb 96, bott Mar 11 **(88) n23 t23 f20 b22**. Had the cask been just a little kinder, we would have had a superdram on our hands. As it is, one to hunt down and explore. *50%. nc ncf sc. 212 bottles.*

❖ **Provenance Ardmore Over 7 Years** refill hogshead, cask no. 6959, dist Autumn 2003, bott Winter 2011 **(86) n22 t22.5 f20.5 b21.** Here's a little known fact: when I am working on a blend, it is not unknown for me to take home some Ardmore aged between three and seven to drink while relaxing, so entertaining can it be. This, though, comes from a cask which is pretty well used, so that the interplay between spirit and oak doesn't trouble you too much. *46%. nc ncf sc.*

❖ **Provenance Ardmore Over 8 Years** barrel, cask no. 7928, dist Autumn 2003, bott Winter 2011 **(89.5) n24** one of the most delightful experiences in Scotland is being in the mash room at Ardmore when the boiling water strikes the grist. Here you get a semblance of the aroma; a little background noise states for certain a slightly bitter finish...; **t22.5** just enough oil to stretch every last barley-peat sinew the maximum distance; **f20.5** butterscotch and citrus, then...errr...bitterish; **b22** go on, I dare you to grab a bottle of this and NOT fall in love with the aroma... *46%. nc ncf sc. Douglas Laing & Co.*

❖ **Scotch Malt Whisky Society Cask 66.35 Age 9 Years** refill butt, cask no. 1064, dist 2002 **(88.5) n22** grape with all the give of a coat of armour...; the smoke rattles around somewhere inside; **t23** even the smoke feels it might splinter into a million pieces at any moment; the grape is crunchy and burnt; **f21.5** the small degree of bitterness doesn't come softly; **b22** have not been supplied with details of cask type yet, but probably refill sherry. Whichever, it certainly puts the 'ard into Ardmore.... *58.2%. sc.*

❖ **Single Malts Of Scotland Ardmore 1992 (90.5) n23** remember those guns which used to fire caps...? **t23.5** soft grapefruit, a sprinkle of salt and growing acacia honey; the barley is clean and confident throughout; the smoke hovers rather than dives in; **f21.5** vanilla, cocoa and spice; **b22.5** a very lightly peated version it may be. But it certainly doesn't stint on complexity. A delight. *49.3%. ncf sc. Speciality Drinks. 207 bottles.*

The Whisky Agency Ardmore 1992 bott. 2010 **(86) n22.5 t22 f19.5 b22.** Appears a lot younger than its near 20 years. Gristy, lightly smoked and fresh. *49.9%*

AUCHENTOSHAN

Lowlands, 1800. Morrison Bowmore. Working.

Auchentoshan 10 Years Old db **(81) n22 t21 f19 b19**. Much better, maltier, cleaner nose than before. But after the initial barley surge on the palate it shows a much thinner character. *40%*

Auchentoshan 12 Years Old db **(91.5) n22.5** sexy fruit element – citrus and apples in particular – perfectly lightens the rich, oily barley; **t23.5** oily and buttery; intense barley carrying delicate marzipan and vanilla; **f22.5** simplistic, but the oils keep matters lush and the delicate sugars do the rest; **b23** a delicious malt very much happier with itself than it has been for a while. 40% ⊙ ⊙

⠿ **Auchentoshan 14 Years Old Cooper's Reserve** db **(83.5) n20 t21.5 f21 b21.** Malty, a little nutty and juicy in part. 46%. ncf.

Auchentoshan 18 Years Old bourbon cask, batch no. L092458 db **(87) n21.5** retains its light frame, but bolstered by a new-found bourbon-honey sweetness; **t22.5** the oak shows up early, as you might expect from a 'Toshan of this age. But a thick strata of barley and vanilla sponge in syrup sweetness give it an enjoyable polish; **f21.5** dries with a wobble, but the late spices come up trumps; plenty of chewy toffee to finish with; **b21.5** a much happier soul than previous years, celebrating with an extra dollop of honey. The citrus and almonds promised on the label never quite materialise. 43%

Auchentoshan 21 Years Old db **(93) n23.5** a sprig of mint buried in barely warmed peat, all with an undercoat of the most delicate honeys; **t23** velvety and waif-like, the barley-honey theme is played out in hushed tones and unspoiled elegance; **f23** the smoke deftly returns as the vanillas and citrus slowly rise but the gentle honey-barley plays to the end, despite the shy introduction of cocoa; **b23.5** one of the finest Lowland distillery bottlings of our time. A near faultless masterpiece of astonishing complexity to be cherished and discussed with deserved reverence. So delicate, you fear that sniffing too hard will break the poor thing...! 43%

Auchentoshan 1977 Sherry Cask Matured oloroso sherry cask db **(89) n23 t22 f22 b22.** Rich, creamy and spicy. Almost a digestive biscuit mealiness with a sharp marmalade spread. 49%. sc. Morrison Bowmore. 240 bottles.

Auchentoshan 1978 Bourbon Cask Matured Limited Edition db **(96) n24.5** a nose which stops you in your tracks: Taiwanese green tea sweetened with a brave and enthralling mix of muscovado sugar and manuka honey. There is essence of Kentucky, too, with a bourbony-liquorice trait while the vanillas head at you with two or three different degrees of intensity. How subtle. How complex. So beguiling, you almost forget to drink the stuff... **t24** wonderful strands of sweetness of varying types and levels, from the lighter, fragile citrus notes to something sturdier and more honeyed; the middle ground has a few oily moments which allow all the elements to mix without bias or domination: a near perfectly balanced harmony; **f23.5** long, lush with the barley now having the confidence to reveal itself while the toasted fudge ensures an attractive and fitting bitter-sweet finale; **b24** if there was a Lowlander of the Year, this'd probably wipe the floor with the rest. It's as though someone was in a warehouse, stumbled across this gem and protected it with his life to ensure it was not lost in some blend or other. Whoever is responsible should be given a gold medal, or a Dumbarton season ticket. Ensure you taste this one at body temperature for full blow-away results. 53.4%. 480 bottles.

⠿ **Auchentoshan 1979** db **(94) n23.5** very well aged Christmas fruit cake. With an extra thick layer of top quality marzipan; **t24** sumptuous delivery with the burnt raisin biting deep; bursting with juicy barley; **f23** long with the emphasis on the dryness of the sherry; **b23.5** wow! I'd almost forgotten this distillery was capable of such greatness. It's amazing what a near faultless sherry butt can do. 50.1%

Auchentoshan 1998 Sherry Cask Matured fino sherry cask db **(81.5) n21 t22 f18.5 b20.** A genuine shame. Before these casks were treated in Jerez, I imagine they were spectacular. Even with the obvious faults apparent, the nuttiness is profound and milks every last atom of the oils at work to maximum effect. The sugars, also, are delicate and gorgeously weighted. There is still much which is excellent to concentrate on here. 54.6%. ncf. 6000 bottles.

Auchentoshan Classic db **(80) n19 t20 f21 b20.** Classic what exactly...? Some really decent barley, but goes little further. 40%

Auchentoshan Select db **(85) n20 t21.5 f22 b21.5.** Has changed shape of late, if not quality. Much more emphasis on the enjoyable juicy barley sharpness these days. 40%

⠿ **Auchentoshan Solera** db **(88) n23** a tidal wave of highly attractive, lightly spiced medium sweet sherry; **t22** again it is all grape though there is the faintest echo of barley; **f22** late spices and drier vanilla; now in cream sherry land; **b21** enormous grape input and enjoyable for all its single mindedness. Will benefit when a better balance with the malt is struck. 48%. ncf.

Auchentoshan Three Wood db **(76) n20 t18 f20 b18.** Takes you directly into the rough. Refuses to harmonise, except maybe for some late molassed sugar. 43%

⠿ **Duncan Taylor Dimensions Auchentoshan 13 Years Old** dist Dec 98, bott Jan 12 **(82) n21 t21 f19.5 b20.5.** Good sugars. but the distillate is sloppy and the cask is a little tired. 46%. nc ncf sc. Duncan Taylor & Co.

Hart Brothers Auchentoshan Aged 11 Years dist Jun 99, bott Nov 10 **(84.5) n22 t22 f19 b21.5.** Clean, delicate, displaying a surprising degree of oil and no shortage of sweet barley. 46%. sc.

⁘ **Malts Of Scotland Auchentoshan 1999** sherry hogshead, cask no. 155, bott 2011 **(85.5) n22.5 t22.5 f21.5 b20.** The good news: not a single atom of sulphur to be had. The bad news; an outrageously OTT barrel which so drowns the whisky in sherry that there are no malty survivors. That said, the spices do delight. *57.9%. nc ncf sc. Malts Of Scotland.*

⁘ **Old Malt Cask Auchentoshan Aged 13 Years** refill hogshead, cask no. 6865, dist Dec 97, bott Jan 11 **(83.5) n19 t22 f21 b21.5.** Get past the indifferent nose and some malty little treasures are there to be had. *50%. nc ncf sc. Douglas Laing & Co. 308 bottles.*

⁘ **Old Malt Cask Auchentoshan Aged 14 Years** refill hogshead, cask no. 8257, dist Dec 97, bott Mar 12 **(88.5) n22** lemon and lime cordial; **t23.5** superbly intense malt-citrus melody; **f21** dries a little, as it must. But decent late cocoa; **b22** possibly the ultimate morning dram: few come more refreshing! *50%. nc ncf sc. Douglas Laing & Co. 303 bottles.*

Old Malt Cask Auchentoshan Aged 20 Years refill hogshead, cask no. 6479, dist Aug 90, bott Aug 10 **(91) n22.5** obviously Auchentoshan is in Kentucky: almost pure bourbon...but with some extra walnut oil; **t23** yee-ha! Here we go again: a ridiculous amount of liquorice and tannin bolsters the busy barley; **f22.5** lush, copper-rich and still a light honeyed Kentuckian feel; **b23** a decided Blue Grass tint to this Lowland gold...; *50%. nc ncf sc. 298 bottles.*

Old Masters Auchentoshan 12 Years Old cask no. 102338, dist 1998, bott Jun 11 **(86) n21 t22 f21.5 b21.5.** Freshly cut grass...and makes hay but giving the barley a massively juicy role. Lots of Toffo candy on the finale. *62.9%. sc. James MacArthur & Co.*

⁘ **Premier Barrel Auchentoshan Aged 11 Years** **(85.5) n20.5 t22.5 f21 b21.5.** Light, sugary and mouth-watering with the barley flickering in intensity. Some attractive spices ramp up the interest. *46%. nc ncf sc. Douglas Laing & Co. 182 bottles.*

Premier Barrel Auchentoshan 12 Years Old **(83) n20 t22 f20 b21.** Simplistic big barley. *46%. nc ncf sc. Douglas Laing & Co. 319 bottles.*

Provenance Auchentoshan Over 9 Years refill hogshead, cask no. 6291, dist Autumn 00, bott Summer 2010 **(77) n19 t21 f18 b19.** Clean, juicy but undercooked. *46%. nc ncf sc.*

Provenance Auchentoshan Over 12 Years refill hogshead, cask no. 6862, dist Winter 98, bott Winter 2010 **(86) n21 t22.5 f21 b21.5.** Outwardly thin, but closer examination reveals a malt bristling with barley and at times a sensuously juicy demeanour. *46%. nc ncf sc.*

Vom Fass Auchentoshan 12 Years Old **(79) n20 t21 f18 b20.** Gooseberries on the nose and intense malt on the delivery. But ultimately betrayed by an old, expiring cask. *40%*

⁘ **Wemyss 1998 Single Lowland Auchentoshan "Lemon Sorbet"** bott 2012 **(87.5) n22** busy with a twist of citrus, lime especially; **t22** big malty surge in this distillery's own inimitable juicy style: a real barley fest; **f21.5** back to the lime marmalade, but just a little heavy on the bittering; **b22** could this really be anything other than a 'Toshan? *46%. sc. 314 bottles.*

AUCHROISK
Speyside, 1974. Diageo. Working.

Auchroisk Aged 10 Years db **(84) n20 t22 f21 b21.** Tangy orange on the nose, the malt amplified by a curious saltiness on the palate. *43%. Flora and Fauna.*

Auchroisk Special Release 2010 20 Years Old American and European oak db **(89) n22.5** no little mocha and praline to this; some attractive herbal notes, too; **t22** lively malt is buffeted around the palate by a spicy attack; light oils offer suspension; **f22.5** back to a big, soft death by chocolate finale; **b22** can't say I have ever seen Auchroisk quite in this mood before. Some excellent cask selection here. *58.1%. nc ncf. Diageo. Fewer than 6000 bottles.*

Auchroisk The Manager's Choice bodega sherry European oak, cask no. 11323, dist 1999, bott 2009 db **(84.5) n19 t21.5 f22.5 b21.5.** The astringent nose offers little hope but an entirely different story on delivery. An odd spirity weakness on arrival, but thumping barley and light mocha ensures a pleasant few minutes with the glass. *60.6%. 622 bottles.*

⁘ **Boisdale Auchroisk 1998** cask no. 13423, bott 2012 **(84.5) n21.5 t22 f20 b21.** A pleasant, barley-accented malt which looks pretty but has little to say. *46%. nc ncf sc.*

⁘ **Mo Òr Collection Auchroisk 1991 19 Years Old** first fill bourbon hogshead, cask no. 2560, dist 14 Feb 91, bott 28 Jan 11 **(86) n22.5 t21.5 f20.5 b21.5.** Solid if simplistic stuff. Even so, the malt holds firm and allows the better-than-average oak to stir up some spices. The gooseberry on the nose is a little treat. *46%. nc ncf sc. Release No. 36. 329 bottles.*

Old Malt Cask Auchroisk Aged 21 Years refill hogshead, cask no. 7045, dist Feb 90, bott Mar 11 **(85.5) n21 t21 f22 b21.5.** For such a light distillate the malt is stretched to impressive lengths. Surprisingly fresh and juicy. *50%. nc ncf sc. Douglas Laing & Co. 244 bottles.*

Old Malt Cask Auchroisk Aged 35 Years refill bourbon barrel, cask no. 6703, dist Apr 75, bott Oct 10 **(88) n21.5 t21.5 f23 b22.** I remember receiving from a wine store in Manchester the first ever bottling of this, a 12-year-old in the mid 80s. God, I'm getting old! *47.2%. nc ncf sc.*

⁘ **Provenance Auchroisk Over 10 Years** refill hogshead, cask no. 8198, dist Spring 2002, ott Spring 2012 **(82.5) n21 t21.5 f20 b20.** Hard to imagine a whisky to be more malt-mplistic. *46%. nc ncf sc. Douglas Laing & Co.*

AULTMORE

Speyside, 1896. John Dewar & Sons. Working.

Aultmore 12 Years Old db **(86) n22 t22 f20 b22.** Do any of you remember the old DCL distillery bottling of this from, what, 25 years ago? Well, this is nothing like it. 40%

⁖ **A.D. Rattray Aultmore 1982** cask no. 2215, dist 25 May 82, bott Jun 12 **(94) n22.5** quite a heavyweight with hints of cucumber lightening the honey-vanilla theme; some spiced chocolate lurks...; **t23.5** sweet and spicy kick off with a mix of molasses and fudge thickening the barley; the build up of chocolate turns into mocha with a complex liquorice/hickory backbone and dryness; **f24.5** the liquorice and mocha thread thickens and binds tightly. Even so, the chocolate reinvents itself and to delicious effect; **b24** a malt of exceptionally high quality. 53.8%. sc. A.D. Rattray Ltd.

Adelphi Aultmore 28 Years Old cask no. 2233, dist 1982, bott 2011 **(94.5) n24** the crystalline Demerara attached to the light cinnamon on cooking apple is simply to die for; **t23.5** brilliantly bright delivery: the barley is virtually granite-like while the oak and fruit orbit; the sugars are pure and entirely unrefined; **f23** long with still a wonderfully juicy element complementing the complex spices; **b24** people from Adelphi: I salute you. 57.6%. sc. Adelphi Distillery. 179 bottles.

Berry's Own Selection Aultmore 1991 cask no. 7432, bott 2011 **(86) n21.5 t22 f21 b21.5.** Unmistakably Aultmore in its crunchy barley guise. But a massive attack of natural oak-generated caramels has kept the usual complexity under wraps. Demands a refill, though. 52.8%. nc ncf sc. Berry Bros & Rudd.

Chieftain's Aultmore Aged 13 Years German oak finish, dist May 97, bott 2011 **(84) n20.5 t21.5 f21 b21.** Sweet, malty and very proudly Speyside. 54.9%. nc ncf. Ian Macleod Distillers.

Gordon & MacPhail Connoisseurs Choice Aultmore 1997 (92) n23 lively, lithesome barley seemingly bubbling in the glass. Dangerously alluring...; **t22.5** prickly, tingly malt at first closed and then opens out so the sugars bring the barley into full grassy play; **f23.5** heads at first down a mocha route, but decides instead to go honeycomb; **b23** tender Speyside malt in full spate. It's what G&M do so naturally... 43%. Gordon & MacPhail.

⁖ **James MacArthur Old Masters Aultmore 15 Years Old** cask no. 3592, dist 1997, bott Feb 12 **(85.5) n22.5 t22 f20 b21.** The busy, juicy delivery sees the barley dominating early on. But very little weight with the delicate smoke just apparent on the nose absent on the palate. The finish is thin and short. 54.8%. nc ncf sc. James MacArthur & Co.

⁖ **Mo Òr Collection Aultmore 1974 36 Years Old** first fill bourbon hogshead, cask no. 3740, dist 29 Apr 74, bott 2 Dec 10 **(94) n22** aged, exotic fruit, but a slightly salty version. A few signs of wear...; **t24.5** gorgeously complex delivery: salivating with fabulous texture to the malt, which displays a pitch-perfect harmony between sugars and spices; **f23.5** some late toffee caramel; the spices linger; **b24** a few frayed edges on the nose are repaired by the colourful tapestry on the palate. 46%. nc ncf sc. Release No. 23. The Whisky Talker. 264 bottles.

⁖ **Mo Òr Collection Aultmore 1982 28 Years Old** first fill bourbon hogshead, cask no. 2219, dist 25 May 82, bott 14 Mar 11 **(89.5) n22.5** spotted dog pudding; a real suet and raisin mix with an extra spoonful of spices; **t24** complex delivery, not just in flavours but texture. Malt but with a background of soft fruit and harder liquorice and mocha; **f21** bitters out slightly and becomes just too much the tough guy; **b22** you don't need a TV when you have a malt like this to get into. A psychological thriller all the way. 46%. nc ncf sc. Release No. 30. 300 bottles.

Old Malt Cask Aultmore Aged 20 Years refill hogshead, cask no. 6839, dist Sep 90, bott Nov 10 **(95) n22.5** sweet and crusty like an old bakery. And a bit dusty, too; **t24.5** this must be one of the most intense barley deliveries I have come across in the last four or five years. This is concentrated barley: the sugars have almost a syrupy quality, but the clarity of the barley leaves you almost nonplussed; **f24** long, lightly oiled and softly spiced. A slow descent from the barley mountain of before; **b24** this distillery is quite capable of greatness. But I have never expected to see it in quite this form. A malt you will remember all your born days. 50%. nc ncf sc. Douglas Laing & Co. 274 bottles.

⁖ **Old Malt Cask Aultmore Aged 30 Years** refill hogshead, cask no. 8533, dist May 82 bott May 12 **(88.5) n22.5** busy, a little nippy but excellent fruit custard sweetness; **t22** fre sweet and a little bite to the barley juice early on. But soon settles into a comfortable va elegance befitting its vintage; **f22** Horlicks, with a healthy dollop of vanilla; **b22** spot distillery and age. 50%. nc ncf sc. Douglas Laing & Co. 238 bottles.

Old Malt Cask Aultmore Aged 36 Years refill hogshead, cask no. 3741, dist Apr 7 10 **(83) n21 t20 f21 b21.** Stretches out the barley and spice the best it can. But the a little too advanced... 50%. nc ncf sc. Douglas Laing & Co. 168 bottles.

Premier Barrel Aultmore Aged 12 Years (78) n19 t20 f20 b19. Intense intense and oily what? This is never quite fully answered. 46%. nc ncf sc. 449

⁖ **Provenance Aultmore Over 11 Years** refill butt, cask no. 7772, dist A Autumn 2011 **(83.5) n21 t22 f19 b21.5.** A pleasant, well-weighted if plodd big buzz to liven things up. 46%. nc ncf sc. Douglas Laing & Co.

Provenance Aultmore Over 12 Years refill hogshead, cask no. 7477, dist Autumn 2000, b̶ Summer 2011 **(86) n21.5 t22 f21.5 b21.** When I nosed this without seeing what I had in the glass, I thought some new make was before me. For all the input of the oak, it might as well be. You will find some citrus if you look hard enough! But no off notes and, all in all, sweet, refreshing and entirely enjoyable. Not a bad word to say against it. *46%. nc ncf sc.*

Scotch Malt Whisky Society Cask 73.42 Aged 28 Years refill butt, cask no. 1673, dist 1982 **(92.5) n22.5** subtly fruit driven. Diced greengage with a squeeze of kumquat all embedded in a spotted dog pudding, complete with an over-ripe physalis on top; **t23.5** salivating barley offers a crisp and delicious skeleton; lighter sultana notes do nothing to soften the impact; **f23** a pleasing denouement of mildly puckering fruit aids the lightly sweetened vanillas and persistent barley; **b23.5** a class act without even breaking sweat. *51.1%. sc. 181 bottles.*

⁖ **Scotch Malt Whisky Society Cask 73.44 Aged 29 Years** refill sherry butt, cask no. 1672, dist 1982 **(96) n23** highly evocative mix of powering tannins and rich fruit, though this is more bourbony-oak enriched than previous bottlings I can remember from the same period; the kumquat-sharp vanillas constantly pound; **t24** an immediate avalanche of plain chocolate mousse with diced black cherry and Demerara sugar; **f25** I doubt if I have ever tasted a richer chocolate finale in any whisky: the oils are thick and irresistible and the weight is perfect.; **b24** THE single malt for hard-line chocoholics. A malt you will remember for a lifetime, this is close to being a chocolate liqueur but without all the sickly sweet stuff. Simply, and quite literally, fantastic. *53.7%. sc.*

⁖ **Scotch Malt Whisky Society Cask 73.45 Aged 19 Years** refill sherry butt, cask no. 1391, dist 1992 **(91.5) n22.5** laden with natural caramels and bulky tannins, this is no lightweight; **t23** big mix of fat, oily barley and crisp sugars, the vanilla is a good focal point to chew on; **f23** the enormous oils lengthen the experience while the sugars maintain balance as the drier, spicier notes begin to make a stand; **b23** the SMWS appear to have hit a rich seam of magnificent Aultmores... *56.1%. sc. Scotch Malt Whisky Society.*

⁖ **Scotch Malt Whisky Society Cask 73.46 Aged 12 Years** refill barrel, cask no. 304291, dist 1999 **(89) n21.5** a touch of lime punctuates the barley oak dominance; **t23** salivating with the barley again going into overdrive. The sugars are wonderfully weighted; **f22** long with the accent still on barley and vanilla. Not a hint of bitterness or unease. Impressive...; **b22.5** simplistic, but forgivably so seeing the powering intensity. *576%. sc.*

⁖ **Scotch Malt Whisky Society Cask 73.48 Aged 9 Years** refill hogshead, cask no. 305712, dist 2002 **(90) n23** no half measures with the oak, though the barley clings to the citrus for grim death; **t23** big, chewy vanilla-malt delivery. Excellent sharpness to the barley with the crisper sugars keeping a respectable distance; **f21.5** the odd more bitter element of the oak bares its teeth; **b22.5** peddles hard to keep up its early promise. *60.2%. sc.*

BALBLAIR

Highlands (Northern), 1872. Inver House Distillers. Working.

Balblair 10 Years Old db **(86) n21 t22 f22 b21.** Such an improved dram away from the clutches of caramel. *40%*

Balblair Aged 16 Years db **(84) n22 t22 f20 b20.** Definitely gone up a notch in the last year. The lime on the nose has been replaced by dim Seville oranges; the once boring finish reveals elements of fruit and spice. It's the barley- rich middle that shines, though, and some more work will belt this up into the high 90s where this great distillery belongs. *40%*

⁖ **Balblair 1965** db **(96.5) n23** any more Kentuckian and I do declare that I'd swear this'd been matured in a log cabin with racoons for guards...; a lovely procession of manicured bourbon notes, with semi-peeled kumquats at the van; **t24.5** you will not find a more superbly complex delivery, with this seemingly possessing two bodies in one: the first is a little oily and soft but carrying the darker oaky notes, while simultaneously the mouth fills with juices from both barley and fruit; **f24.5** a mix of peach and melon yogurt mixed in with chocolate mousse, a rare but delightful concoction; light liquorice and hickory dusted with muscovado sugars reminds one of Kentucky again; **b24.5** many malts of this age have the ▪t hanging on in there for grim life. This is an exception: the malt is in joint control and for a moment allows the oak to dominate. It is almost too beautiful for words. *52.3%*

▪alblair 1969 db **(94.5) n22.5** marmalade and pencil shavings; **t23.5** just so salivating ▪ed orange juice intermingles with a glorious array of delicate caramel and vanilla ▪▪ding off with honey; **f24** honey still, now stirred into a bowl of rice pudding; **b24.5** ▪on't even think about touching this until it has stood in the glass for ten minutes. ▪▪e not prepared to give each glass a minimum half hour of your time (and ▪ater), then don't bother getting it for, to be honest, you don't deserve it... *41.4%*

▪▪▪ db **(94.5) n24.5** one of the most complex noses in the Highlands with just ▪▪ou can think of making a starring, or at least guest, appearance at some ▪ster's get-out. Nose it and then defy me...For starters, watch the clever bourbon edge alongside the crème brulee and ground cherry topping...hunt the smoke down, also... **t23.5** the barley descends in the most gentle manner possible but this does not detract from the intensity: wave upon wave of barley melts upon the tastebuds, varying only in their degree of sweetness; **f23** a few more bitter oak noises, but it remains barley all the way, even at this age. Amazing...; **b23.5** essential Balblair. 46%

Balblair 1978 db **(94) n24** evidence of great antiquity hangs all over this nose, not least in the exotic fruit so typical of such vast aging; there is smoke, too: a delicate peat more common at the distillery in those days is evident and most welcome; **t24** the lush delivery offers up an improbably malty juiciness. But this is almost immediately countered by a spicy oakiness which offsets with great charm the salivating barley chorus and layers of delicate fruit and almost nutty vanilla: not for a second is elegance compromised; **f23** those of you with a passion for older Ballantine's will not be much surprised that this was, in its Allied days, once a vital ingredient: such is the clarity of the vanilla-led silkiness. Again, great age is never in doubt. Towards the very death the wisps of smoke found on the nose make a lingering reappearance; **b23** just one of those drams that exudes greatness and charm in equal measures. Some malts fall apart when hitting thirty: this one is totally intact and in command. A glorious malt underlining the greatness of this mostly under-appreciated distillery. 46%

Balblair 1989 db **(91) n23 t23 f22.5 b22.5.** Don't expect gymnastics on the palate or the pyrotechnics of the Cadenhead 18: in many ways a simple malt, but one beautifully told. Almost Cardhu-esque in the barley department. 43%

⠢ **Balblair 1989** db **(88) n21.5** sharp barley untroubled by too much else; **t22** crisp sugars in tandem with no less crunchy barley; **f22.5** moves, at last, away from barley and offers a degree of vanilla-caramel complexity; **b22** a clean, pleasing malt, though hardly one that will induce anyone to plan a night raid on any shop stocking it... 46%

Balblair 1990 db **(92.5) n24 t23.5 f22 b23.** Tangy in the great Balblair tradition. Except here this is warts and all with the complexity and true greatness of the distillery left in no doubt. 46%

Balblair 2000 db **(87.5) n21.5** gristy and grassy; **t22.5** the freshness on the nose is fully accentuated by a juicy, clean barley delivery; **f21.5** dries markedly towards powdery cocoa; **b22** no toffee yet still a clever degree of chewy weight for all the apparent lightness. 43%

Balblair 2001 db **(90.5) n23.5** gooseberries at varying stages of ripeness; barley so clean it must be freshly scrubbed; the kind of delicate spice prickle that is a must; **t23.5** majestic delivery: hard to imagine barley making a more clean, intense and profound entrance than that. The malt forms many layers, each one sugar accompanied but taking on a little more oak; **f21.5** dries, spices up but bitters a little; **b22.5** a typically high quality whisky from this outrageously underestimated distillery. 46%

⠢ **Cadenhead Balblair 20 Years Old** bott 2009 **(88) n21.5** salty malt. Just a few tight wrinkles; **t23** originally sharp, it slowly evolves into a majestic malt fest; **f21.5** slightly tart, as is often the house style. But the malt is unmoved and the sugars are pretty sexy...; **b22** massively malty with the sugars almost grist concentrate. 53%. sc. WM Cadenhead Ltd.

Gordon & MacPhail Rare Vintage Balblair 1979 (88.5) n22 t22.5 f22 b22. A glorious old manor house suffering from woodworm: not entirely sound but still an object of beauty. 43%

⠢ **Gordon & MacPhail Private Collection Balblair 1991 (79.5) n20 t21.5 f20 b18.** An interesting experiment. But, as so many have been through the ages, a failure. Love the juicy delivery. But, overall, way too fussy and tart for its own good. 45%

Old Malt Cask Balblair Aged 20 Years refill sherry butt, cask no. 6340, dist Jun 90, bott Jul 10 **(85.5) n23.5 t21 f20 b21.** The nose announced a stunning cask, the oaky battering on the taste buds told of a malt prematurely aged. Worth finding for the nose alone: the balance of salt, pepper and butterscotch-barley is wonderful. 50%. nc ncf sc. Douglas Laing & Co. 637 bottles.

BALMENACH
Speyside, 1824. Inver House Distillers. Working.

Balmenach Aged 25 Years Golden Jubilee db **(89) n21 t23 f22 b23.** What a glorious old charmer this is! An essay in balance despite the bludgeoning nature of the beast ear' on. Takes a little time to get to know and appreciate: persevere with this belter because i' classic stuff for its age. 58%. Around 800 decanters.

Gordon & MacPhail Connoisseurs Choice Balmenach 1999 (85) n21 t21.5 f21 b' Those with a soft spot for spicy suet pudding will find this irresistible. 43%

⠢ **Mo Ór Collection Balmenach 1988 23 Years Old** first fill bourbon hogshead, 1150, dist 4 Apr 88, bott 25 May 11 **(89) n23.5** subtlety and elegance take all the lead' here. Palma violets dovetail with delicate vanillas and a fleck here and there of ki soft barley sugar heralds in the far brisker peppered oaky notes; lightly oiled, sugars and spices to mix with waves of barley calming matters; **f21** bitters out a gorgeously busy dram. 46%. nc ncf sc. Release No. 51. The Whisky Talker. 44

Old Malt Cask Balmenach Aged 27 Years refill hogshead, cask no. 7148, dist Sep 83, bott Apr 11 **(82) n22 t22 f18 b20.** A real mish-mash. On the nose, green and a little sharp. On the finish, vivid signs of a flailing cask. But elsewhere juicy, malty and fun. Never for a moment, though, does it ever act its 27 years... 50%. nc ncf sc. Douglas Laing & Co. 268 bottles.

⁖ **Provenance Balmenach Over 9 Years** refill hogshead, cask no. 8496, dist Winter 2002, bott Spring 2012 **(79) n19 t21 f19 b20.** A seriously malty cove. But the cask injects a tang. 46%. nc ncf sc. Douglas Laing & Co.

⁖ **Provenance Balmenach Over 11 Years** refill hogshead, cask no. 7827, dist Autumn 2000, bott Autumn 2011 **(71.5) n17.5 t19 f16.5 b17.5.** Juicy delivery but over influenced by wood which may have seen better days. 46%. nc ncf sc. Douglas Laing & Co.

Scotch Malt Whisky Society Cask 48.24 Aged 22 Years refill hogshead, cask no. 1118, dist 1988 **(84) n21.5 t21 f20.5 b21.** A bit of nag: the sharp barley and vivid oak overstates the case just a little too tartly. 49.3%. sc. 265 bottles.

Scotch Malt Whisky Society Cask 48.25 Aged 22 Years refill butt, cask no. 1080, dist. 1989 **(86.5) n22 t22.5 f21 b21.** Clean and mouthwatering, there is an engaging and dogged persistence to this one. Good sugar-spice balance. 56.2%. sc. 268 bottles.

⁖ **Scotch Malt Whisky Society Cask 48.26 Aged 23 Years** refill butt, cask no. 1124, dist 1988 **(91) n23** like when you open up a tin and you find an old dried up fruit cake where the nuts and molasses dominate on the nose and there is a toasty dryness from the shrivelled raisins; **t23** silky barley with a labyrinthine complexity to the suety sugars; **f22** that distant fruit on the nose now begins to show; the sugars remain consistent; **b23** far from a usual bottling, there is much here to surprise and delight. 50.5%. sc.

⁖ **Scotch Malt Whisky Society Cask 48.29 Aged 12 Years** first fill barrel, cask no. 800531, dist 1999 **(89) n21.5** straight as a die vanilla and malt; **t23.5** wow! Where did that salty, tangy, explosive malt come from? Fabulous malt middle and seasoned with effective salt and pepper; fudge and raisin fills the middle; **f22** comparatively bland caramel; **b22** the brightness on the palate makes a mockery of the relatively dull nose and finish. 61%. sc.

⁖ **Scotch Malt Whisky Society Cask 48.30 Aged 12 Years** first fill barrel, cask no. 800533, dist 1999 **(93) n23.5** I defy you not to be turned on by this most delicate and clean of citrus and barley noses; sponge cake with an orange jam filling; physalis about to burst; **t23.5** stunning delivery: almost perfect weight and the interplay between those delicate citrus notes and that barley is priceless. Retains that lovely light sponge cake feel; **f23** the oaks finally come into action, but merely add light liquorice gravitas. Oddly tangy at the death; **b23** an essay in poise...and what happens when you have a near faultless cask. 56.9%. sc.

⁖ **The Whisky Agency Balmenach 33 Years Old** dist 1979 **(89) n23** superb oak presence, conjuring up spiced cocoa and walnuts; **t22** teasing salts tickle the taste buds before a wave of oily sugars move us into vanilla-rich grounds; **f22** long, sweet and as oily as a second-hand car salesman...; **b22** a typically fat lad from this distillery. 52.8%. sc.

THE BALVENIE
Speyside, 1892. William Grant & Sons. Working.

The Balvenie Aged 10 Years Founders Reserve db **(90) n23** astonishing complexity: the fruit is relaxed, crushed sultanas and malty suet. A sliver of smoke and no more: everything is hinted and nudged at rather than stated. Superb; **t24** here we go again: threads of malt binding together barely detectable nuances. Thin liquorice here, grape there, smoke and vanilla somewhere else; **f20** Light muscovado-toffee flattens out the earlier complexity. The bitter-sweet balance remains brilliant to the end; **b23** just one of those all-time-great standard 10-year-olds from a great distillery – pity they've decided to kill it off. 40%

The Balvenie Double Wood Aged 12 Years db **(80.5) n22 t20.5 f19 b19.** OK. So here's the score: Balvenie is one of my favourite distilleries in the world, I confess. I admit it. The original Balvenie 10 is a whisky I would go to war for. It is what Scotch malt whisky is all about. It invented complexity; or at least properly introduced me to it. But I knew that it was going to die, sacrificed on the altar of ageism. So I have tried to get to love Double Wood. And I have tasted and/or drunk it every month for the last couple of years to get to know it and, hopefully fall in love. But still I find it rather boring company. We may have kissed and canoodled. But there is no spark. No romance whatsoever. 40%

Balvenie Signature Aged 12 Years batch 001 db **(93) n25 t23 f21 b24.** This whisky [cre]ated by Grant's blender David Stewart and bottled to mark his 45 years in the industry. [...m]oney, he's now the best in the business and has been for a little while. But it is a [...sha]me that the marketing guys didn't insist on this being an apposite 45% because, for [...th]e wizardry going on here and the fact that the nose should immediately become [... a] whisky legend, this is dreadfully underpowered. 40%

[Balvenie Si]gnature Aged 12 Years batch 003 db **(89) n24** nothing like as rich as the first [...aro]ma is about innuendo and strands. Where once there was powering, fresh-

...out-of-the-oven fruitcake, now there is more of the mixing bowl with the emphasis on the flour rather than the dried fruit. Even so, there is sufficient orange peel to freshen things up; **t23.5** against the odds the barley shows first, only briefly, mind, before a dizzying welter of fruity blows knocks it from the scene. The mouthfeel is silky but roughens up towards the middle ground; **f19** a hint of discord and fluffy dryness; **b22.5** if you don't taste this at body temperature you are doing both yourself and this whisky a huge disservice. One of the great benefits of Balvenie is that it can shine at virtually any age: at 10 it is truly magnificent – though sadly you'll rarely get the chance to discover this these days – and when a couple of years old still the barley has enough charisma to talk a beautiful game. The fruits have a bitter-sweet effect – literally – by helping to map out a wonderful nose but lessening the value of the finish. Enjoyable whisky all the same and what a pity it isn't at 47%... *40%*

The Balvenie Signature Aged 12 Years batch 004 db **(92) n23.5** back to its dried dates origins, helped along by some muscovado sugars keeping a lightness to the vanilla; the spices are little more than a whisper; **t23.5** soft, but with an early noise of some bitterish oak...the price often paid by breaking down the oils by adding too much water. But the reinstatement of the dates and a doughy plum pudding restores the balance; **f22** the vague bitterness returns, predictably, as but there is a double helping of Cornish vanilla ice cream... without the ice; **b23** it is a relief to know that the unparalleled talent in the scotch whisky industry that is David Stewart has not been entirely lost to us, with the legendary blender still working on the Balvenie brand. Next time I see him, I will still insist on knowing why this wonderful whisky, so cleverly complex, remains so woefully underpowered. *40%*

The Balvenie 14 Years Old Cuban Selection db **(86) n20 t22 f22.5 b21.5.** Unusual malt. No great fan of the nose but the roughness of the delivery grows on you; there is a jarring, tongue-drying quality which actually works quite well and the development of the inherent sweetness is almost in slow motion. Some sophistication here, but also the odd note which, on the nose especially, is a little out of tune. *43%*

The Balvenie 14 Years Old Golden Cask db **(91) n23.5** mildly tart: rhubarb and custard, with a vague sprinkling of brown sugar; bourbon notes, too; **t23** mouth-watering and zingy spice offer up a big delivery, but settles towards the middle towards a more metallic barley-rich sharpness; **f22** soft spices peddle towards the finish and a wave or three of gathering oak links well with the sweetened barley strands; **b22.5** a confident, elegant malt which doesn't stint one iota on complexity. Worth raiding the Duty Free shops for this little gem alone. *47.5%*

The Balvenie Roasted Malt Aged 14 Years (90) n21 t23 f22 b24. Balvenie very much as you've never seen it before. An absolute, mouth-filling cracker! *47.1%*

The Balvenie Rum Wood Aged 14 Years db **(88) n22 t23 f21 b22.** Tasted blind I would never have recognized the distillery: I'm not sure if that's a good thing. *47.1%*

Balvenie 17 Years Old Rum Cask db **(88.5) n22** green bananas and oak: curious... **t22.5** initially dry with the oak elbowing in first; several levels of barley battle back while some fudge enters the middle ground; **f22** remains fudgy, with a touch of oily butterscotch tart, but the emphasis is on the dryer, flaky tart; **b22** for all the best attentions of the rum cask at times this feels all its 17 years, and perhaps a few Summers more. Impossible not to love, however. *43%*

Balvenie New Wood Aged 17 Years db **(85) n23 t22 f19 b21.** A naturally good age for Balvenie; the nose is lucid and exciting, the early delivery is thick with rich malt. This, though, has sucked out lots of caramel from the wood to leave an annoyingly flat finish. *40%*

The Balvenie 17 Year Old Madeira Cask Madeira finish, bott 2009 db **(93.5) n24** classically two-toned, with a pair of contrasting tales being told simultaneously yet in complete harmony. One is fruity (especially apple) and ripe and blended with the weighty oak; the other is barley-sweet and refreshing; **t23.5** the juicy grape takes the higher ground, joining forces with the juicier barley; some distance below the oak throbs contentedly; **f23** an oak prickle and a hint of sweet mocha on the vanilla; **b23** an essay in deportment. Every aspect appears to have been measured and weighed. Hurry this imperious whisky at your peril. *43%*

The Balvenie 17 Year Old Sherry Oak db **(88) n23 t22.5 f21 b21.5.** Clean as a nut. H... class sherry it may be but the price to pay is a flattening out of the astonishing com... one normally finds from this distillery. Bitter-sweet in every respect. *43%*

The Balvenie Aged 21 Years Port Wood db **(94.5) n24** chocolate marzipan w... sugar-plum centre; deft, clean and delicate; **t24** hard to imagine a delivery m... weighted: a rich tapestry of fruit and nut plus malt melts on the palate with a ... pithy, grape skin balancing the vanillas and barley oils; **f23** delicately dry wit... buttered fruitcake ensuring balance; **b23.5** what a magnificently improved ... I struggled to detect the fruit. Here, there's no escaping. *40%*

The Balvenie Thirty Aged 30 Years db **(92) n24** has kept its charac... real mixture of varied fruits. Again the smoke is apparent, as is the p... thet the style should have been kept so similar to previous bottli... first of enigmatic, thick barley, then a gentle eruption of controlled...

more oaky involvement but such is the steadiness of the barley, its extraordinary confidence no damage is done and the harmony remains; **b23** rarely have I come across a bottling of a whisky of these advanced years which is so true to previous ones. Amazing. *473%*

The Balvenie Aged 40 Years Batch 1 bott 2010 db **(79)** **n22** **t20** **f18** **b19**. The makings of a great nose: a real nutty Dundee cake special. But a bitter let down on the palate. *48.5%*

The Balvenie Aged 40 Years Batch 2 db **(96.5)** **n25** sit back and experience something just a little special... eyes closed, you might fancy the odd, playful, peek-a-boo atom of peat. You'd be right..it is there. Likewise, for a moment you will be drifting off to Kentucky and breathing in the honeyed charms of a very old bourbon. A hint of cucumber...? Tick. Coconut? Yes. Sultana? Maybe. If so, as voluptuous as a female opera singer. Ah, Greengages! Spilling out their over-ripened juices. And lychee! Does it need a shake of salt to embolden the aromas? No, thanks to the oak, it is already there. Hang on: the oak? What is that up to, exactly? Well, apart from the salt, it is adding some weight. Not so it will drag the whisky down. But rather so it holds all else in place. How do I locate it exactly...? Try looking for those delicate herbs singing apart from the spice; **t24** could never quite live up to the nose and the early, roaring oak is bolder on delivery than it ever was on aroma. But this works, too. Because, against all the odds, there is a juicy barley lustre to this guy which sits comfortably with those big tannins. The sugars are deep and meaningful and magically in sync with all else around it. The spices are deft but build in weight; **f23.5** shows just a few late cracks, as it has every right to do. The light sugars still see off the more militant of the oaky notes; **b24** gets it so right in every department where Batch 1 got it so lamentably wrong. My only sorrow was that I could give the nose only 25 points... A near faultless glass of honour to one of the great distilleries of the world. *48.5%*

The Balvenie 1993 Port Wood db **(89)** **n21** **t23** **f22** **b23**. Oozes class without getting too flash about it: the secret is in the balance. *40%*

⁙ **The Balvenie TUN 1401** batch 1 db **(91)** **n22.5** one of the crispier Balvenie aromas from over the years: as though the barley has a new sugary husk; **t23** indeed, it is those sugars which arrive first on delivery, and they don't even try to be cute about it. The barley trails in behind almost as an afterthought; **f22.5** now a more composed and relaxed period, though there is a weak residual (presumably sherry butt) buzz; **b23** I have definitely experienced Balvenie a lot more complex than this. But there is no faulting the feel good factor... *48.3%. nc ncf.*

⁙ **The Balvenie TUN 1401** batch 2 db **(89.5)** **n23** single plantation Santo Domingo cocoa, draped by Demerara sugar, wafts around the barley and juicy dates with ease and elegance; **t23** a more overt sherry character by comparison to batch 1 on arrival and even forms the framework for the juicy mouth feel; those Demerara sugars intercede as promised; **f21.5** the finish doesn't work along the same creaseless lines and a degree of bitterness points accusingly at a sherry butt; **b22** the odd moment here hits high notes from this distillery I only ever before experienced with the old 10-years-old some quarter of a century ago. *50.6%. nc ncf.*

⁙ **The Balvenie TUN 1401** batch 3 db **(91)** **n22** perhaps a little tight on the nose in part, but there is also a big Kentucky feel to this, too: some of the casks have bitten deep into the American oak and extracted a chunk of toasted honeycomb and Demerara; lots of creamy toffee and raisin; **t23.5** stunning delivery: unlikely you will encounter many better mouth feels for a Speysider this year. Again, that big bourbon oak resonance makes no attempt to hide its macho character. A procession of liquorice and ulmo/manuka honey blend; **f22** some bitter marmalade takes a vaguely furry turn; **b23.5** one of those bottlings which again hits some magnificent heights; it is as though David Stewart is taking his beloved distillery through its repertoire. Still much prefer if he'd keep sherry off the programme, though. *50.3%. nc ncf.*

⁙ **The Balvenie TUN 1401** batch 4 db **(80.5)** **n21.5** **t23** **f17** **b19**. The finish has all the quality of an Andy Murray line call challenge. In this case it is unacceptably bitter, nowhere ar matching up with the utter brilliance of the delivery. *50.4%. nc ncf.*

⁙ **The Balvenie TUN 1401** batch 5 db **(87.5)** **n22** the most honey-rich of the five batches absolutely dripping with acacia and heather honey; no shortage of cream toffee, either; k stream of natural caramels put a gooey lid on some other notes which think about challenge; prickly spices do make it through, though, and even a few citrus notes e stand. Plenty of Toffee to chew on; **f21.5** a little dull and that well known bout as heavy duty a Balvenie as I can remember. Hardly surprising as the appear to have had all their natural caramels dredged from them and this whammy with the sherry. *50.1%. nc ncf.*

R. Diageo. Demolished.

Banff 1975 bourbon barrel, cask no. MoS12015, dist Nov 75, bott Apr nilla and malt fare; **t22** soft body; profound growth in maltiness;

some late nougat and praline; **b22** very pleasant and malt mad, but absolutely refuses to ■ anything which celebrates its longevity. *43.8%. nc ncf sc. Malts Of Scotland.*

Rarest Of The Rare Banff 35 Years Old dist 1975, cask no. 3352 **(86.5) n21 t22 f22.5 b21.** The over enthusiastic oaks do some damage, but also ultimately save the day by carrying out the required repairs offering a fantastic degree of milky chocolate, sweetened by muscovado sugars, along the way. Somehow, it is a triumph! *42.5%. sc. Duncan Taylor & Co.*

BEN NEVIS
Highlands (Western), 1825. Nikka. Working.

Ben Nevis 10 Years Old db **(88) n21** enormously chunky and weighty: for a 10-y-o the oak is thick, but sweetened medley of ripe fruits; **t22** an almost syrupy mouth feel: a tad cloying but the malt is something you can so get your teeth into; **f23** long with traces of liquorice and hickory; **b22** a massive malt that has steadied itself in recent bottlings, but keep those knives and forks to hand! *46%*

Ben Nevis 1984 Single Cask double wood matured cask no. 98/35/1, dist Dec 84, bott Jan 10 db **(73.5) n18.5 t19 f17 b19.** Formidable sherry and some early grape. But once the sulphur gets hold, it refuses to let go. *56%. ncf.*

Ben Nevis 1996 Single Cask bourbon cask, dist May 96, bott Jan 09 db **(90) n22 t23 f23 b22.** A thick-set little gem of a whisky. *56.8%. For Swedish Whisky Society TKS.*

Ben Nevis 1998 Single Cask sherry butt no. 358, dist Jun 05, bott Oct 09 db **(67) n16 t17 f17 b17.** Uncompromising sulphur. *46%. ncf. For Swedish Whisky Society TKS.*

❖ **Cadenhead Ben Nevis 20 Years Old** bott Apr 12 **(82) n19 t20.5 f22 b20.5.** A brooding, bustling malt which overcomes its untidy start with impressive late panache. *56.2%. sc.*

❖ **The Clan Denny Ben Nevis 42 Years Old** dist 1969 **(89.5) n22** thick and heavy with some hefty barley and oak, yet citrus bursts forth like a ray of sunlight...; plenty of mint, too; **t23** compact and intense barley with impressive muscovado sugars; **f22** certainly some clunking unimpressive oak at the death, but the path leading to it was strewn with delicious fudge: it carries its age well; **b22.5** a malt which needs a little time to compose itself in the glass... *47.8%. sc. The Whisky Agency joint bottling with Douglas Laing for Limburg Whisky Fair.*

❖ **Companions of the Quaich Ben Nevis 1996 (88) n23.5** the kind of aroma which makes my nose twitch and my toes curl: the weight between the ultra clean, fizzy barley and the oak is near perfection; the faintest touch of something phenolic; **t23** superb adaptation from nose the delivery, with those barleys really belting out their fullest intensity and the spices and sugars ganging together with magnificent depth; **f20** unravels somewhat as the soft oils cannot quite overcome a late biting austerity; **b21.5** the delivery is unforgettable, displaying a very rare and compelling juiciness. *55.4%*

Kingsbury Finest and Rarest Ben Nevis 44 Years Old dist 1966 **(92) n23.5** a herb garden bordered by lavender; **t23** softly oiled barley delicately lined with honey. Charming degrees of hickory and vanilla tick all the age boxes; **f22.5** reverts back to a malty colossus. Very usual, and highly attractive, way of ending a 44 year sojourn; **b23** at times plays the part of a bourbon with more gusto than it does a malt. However, the late malty revelation at the finale dispels any doubts. An unusual and wonderfully gifted malt. *40.7%. nc ncf sc. Japan Import Systems.*

❖ **The Maltman Ben Nevis Aged 45 Years** sherry cask, cask no. 1801, dist Mar 66 **(89) n22** a surprising amount of butterscotch for ex-sherry; **t22** chocolate Munchies plus some big time vanilla pods; the bourbon trail is an easy one to follow; **f23** remains soft with a quite charming alloy of vanilla and barley; **b22** though ex-sherry, the fruit influence is close to nil. Delicious, untaxing malt. *40.6%. nc ncf sc. Meadowside Blending Co.*

Old Malt Cask Ben Nevis Aged 40 Years refill hogshead, cask no. 6991, dist Mar 71, bott Mar 11 **(94) n23.5** nosed blind, this is almost identical to the oldest whiskeys stored at the old Tom Moore distillery. Almost rabid, yet wonderfully alluring, red liquorice emboldened by spice and a small grain pithiness: complex to the point of intriguing; **t23.5** a busy mixture of oak and barley pepper the palate. Virtually no oil present, which makes for a profound intensity; the sweetness of the barley is lightly sugar coated and suits the drier oaks to a tee; **f23** long despite the lack of the usual creamy oils you associate with this distillery, and doubles up on the vanillas; **b24** all kinds of bourbon fingerprints on this, which means it has survived for decades with aplomb. Fabulous. *45.8%. nc ncf sc. Douglas Laing & Co. 188 bottles.*

Provenance Ben Nevis Over 11 Years refill hogshead, cask no. 6922, dist Autumn 99, Winter 2011 **(77.5) n18 t22 f18.5 b19.** Huge, delicious, richly-flavoured malt does all it ■ clamber over some unfriendly oak. *46%. nc ncf sc. Douglas Laing & Co.*

Provenance Ben Nevis Over 12 Years sherry finished hogshead, cask no. ■ Autumn 98, bott Spring 2011 **(85.5) n19.5 t23 f21.5 b21.5.** This distillery does a h■ and Demerara sugar mix better than most. Here it is in top gear, but the engine mis■ due to some unturned oak. A scintillating, sparks flying ride, nonetheless! *46%.*

∵ **Provenance Ben Nevis Over 12 Years** refill hogshead, cask no. 7432, dist Autur 1998, bott Summer 2011 **(87) n20.5** floral and gristy. Delicate. But has just enough in reserv to see off some of the more unfriendly oak notes; **t22** has that familiar Ben Nevis weighty rumble of thick, almost gelled barley. But the unfriendly fire from the cask fails to materialise, leaving the sugars to happily placate the palate; **f22.5** attractively sweet with some real malty chewability; **b22** the nose suggests a potential problem but on the palate it just gets better and better. *46%. nc ncf sc. Douglas Laing & Co.*

∵ **Provenance Ben Nevis Over 14 Years** refill hogshead, cask no. 8008, dist Autumn 1997, bott Winter 2012 **(86.5) n20 t22.5 f22 b21** A thick, lumbering malt with the sugars, plummy fruit and opaque barley laid on with a trowel. Have to say I find it great fun. *46%. nc ncf sc.*

Vom Fass Ben Nevis 12 Years Old (80) n19 t21.5 f19.5 b20. Juicy barley aplenty. And an almost jammy creaminess, note unlike a Swiss roll. *40%*

The Whisky Agency Ben Nevis 1968 bott 2010 **(80.5) n21 t20 f19.5 b20.** The oaks have got their hooks into this one just a little too vehemently, though the honey peddles flat out to make up for the lost ground. *40%*

BENRIACH
Speyside, 1898. The BenRiach Distillery Co. Working.

The BenRiach db **(86) n21 t22 f21.5 b21.5.** The kind of soft malt you could wean nippers on, as opposed to Curiositas, which would be kippers. Unusually for a BenRiach there is a distinct toffee-fudge air to this one late on, but not enough to spoil that butterscotch-malt charm. No colouring added, so a case of the oak being a bit naughty. *40%*

The BenRiach Curiositas Aged 10 Years Single Peated Malt db **(90.5) n23** the thin smoke is losing out to the honey-fudge; **t23** the peat takes a little time to gather its speech, but when it comes it is fine and softly delivered. In the meantime soft barley and that delicious but curiously dampening sweet fudge struts its stuff; **f22** chalky vanillas and a squirt of chocolate like that found on ice cream cones; **b22.5** "Hmmmm. Why have my research team marked this down as a 'new' whisky I wondered to myself. Then immediately on nosing and tasting I discovered the reason without having to ask: the pulse was weaker, the smoke more apologetic...it had been watered down from the original 46% to 40%. This is excellent malt. But can we have our truly great whisky back, please? As lovely as it is, this is a bit of an imposter. As Emperor Hadrian might once have said: "ifus itus aintus brokus..." *40%*

The BenRiach Aged 12 Years db **(82.5) n21 t20 f21 b20.5.** More enjoyable than the 43% I last tasted. But still an entirely inoffensive malt determined to offer minimal complexity. *40%*

The BenRiach Aged 12 Years db **(78.5) n21.5 t20 f18 b19.** White peppers on the nose, then goes uncharacteristically quiet and shapeless. *43%*

The BenRiach Aged 12 Years Dark Rum Wood Finish db **(85.5) n21 t22 f21 b21.5.** More than a decade ago, long before it ever became fashionable, I carried out an extensive programme of whisky maturation in old dark rum casks. So, if someone asked me now what would happen if you rounded off a decently peated whisky in a rum cask, I'd say – depending on time given for the finish and type of rum – the smoke would be contained and there would be a ramrod straight, steel-hard sweetness ensuring the most clipped whisky you can possibly imagine. And this here is exactly what we have... *46%*

The BenRiach Aged 12 Years Matured In Sherry Wood db **(95.5) n23.5** big, juicy, compelling grape. Absolutely clean and stupendous in its multi-layering; **t24** quite magnificent! How I pray whiskies to be on delivery, but find they so rarely are. Some caramels are caught up in the genteel squabble between the grape juice and the rich barley; **f24** long, faultless and ushering in a chocolate raisin depth; late vanilla and any amount of spice; **b24** since I last tasted this the number of instances of sampling a sherry wood whisky and not finding my taste buds caked in sulphur has nosedived dramatically. Therefore, to start my tasting day at 7am with something as honest as this propels one with myriad reasons to continue the day. A celebration of a malt whisky in more ways than you could believe. *46%. nc ncf.*

The BenRiach Aged Over 12 Years "Arumaticus Fumosus" richly peated style, ex-dark um barrels db **(91) n23 t23 f22 b23.** Very often finishing in rum can sharpen the mouthfeel t at the same time add a sugary sheen. This little gem is no exception. *46%*

The BenRiach Aged Over 12 Years "Heredotus Fumosus" peated PX finish db **(92.5) n23** eat is so thick you could grow a grape vine in it; **t23** the sweetness of the grape arrives y waves, comfortably supported by the thick, oily peat; **f23** long, more sugared smoke oa; **b23.5** at last a PX-peat marriage not on the rocks. What an improvement on the ing. Smokograpus Miraculus. *46%. nc ncf.*

nRiach Aged Over 12 Years "Importanticus Fumosus"** richly peated style, ex-port b **(87) n22 t22 f21 b22.** Hardicus asius Nailsus. *46%*

iach Aged 12 Years "Importanticus Fumosus"** Tawny port wood finish db matter here had it been finished in Short-eared, Long-eared, Little, Barn or

...ny Port, the peat would have come out tops. The smoke is enormous: owl do they do it...? **2.5** a peaty custard pie in the mush: enormous impact with more early vanilla than fruit; **t23.5** now the grape begins to get its head above the smoky parapet; a beautiful balance with the smoke, vanilla and minor spices; **b22.5** you'd be a twit not to buy two of 'em. 46%

The BenRiach Aged 13 Years "Maderensis Fumosus" peated madeira finish db **(85.5) n20 t23.5 f21 b21.** Never a shrinking violet, this still enjoys some pretty off the wall moments. But for a brief success on delivery where the richness of the sugars and smoke work in astonishing harmony, the remainder of the journey is one of vivid disagreement. 46%. nc ncf.

The BenRiach Aged 15 Years Dark Rum Finish db **(86) n20 t22 f22 b22.** Drier, spicier than before. Old Jamaica chocolate candy. 46%. nc ncf.

The BenRiach Aged 15 Years Madeira Wood Finish db **(89.5) n22.5** fascinating dry farmhouse cider gives a deliciously unusual edge; **t21.5** as sharp and tangy as they come: the first three or four waves are all about the grape finish, then the barley has a clear run; **f23** settles rather beautifully with the barley and cocoa-dusted oak offering an excellent exit; **b22.5** very much drier than most Madeira finishes you will find around. Once the scramble on delivery is over, this bottling simply exudes excellence. A collector's must have. 46%

The BenRiach Aged 15 Years Pedro Ximénez Sherry Wood Finish db **(94.5) n25** astonishing layering, each one delicate and fragile: vanilla and lime; gooseberry; barley; grape...a buzz of spice. Not a single bitter or off note. This is one of the world whisky noses of the year: absolute perfection; **t23.5** mouth-filling barley then a spreading of a sugary but fruity theme, especially to the roof of the mouth where it sticks on a light oil; in the meantime there is a slow burn of increasing spice; **f22.5** long, absolutely thick with butterscotch barley, framed by a constant drone of spicy, sugared grape; **b23.5** some of the strangest Scotch malts I have tasted in the last decade have been fashioned in PX casks. And few have been particularly enjoyable creations. This one, though, bucks the trend thanks principally to the most subtle of spice imprints. All the hallmarks of some kind of award-winner. 46%

The BenRiach Aged 15 Years Tawny Port Wood Finish db **(89.5) n21.5** confused and heavy. The fruit has little give; **t23** comes together on the palate with a rare degree of grace. The kicking expected from the fruit never materialises and instead there is a soft malt and firm fruit double whammy; the fruit and nut chocolate arrives earlier than expected; **f22.5** long, with a sustained gracefulness as the malt continues to have an impressive say; a soupçon of furry bitterness at the death; **b22.5** now that really is the perfect late night dram. 46%

The BenRiach Aged 16 Years db **(83.5) n21.5 t21 f20 b21.** Although maltily enjoyable, if over dependent on caramel flavours, you get the feeling that a full works 46% version would offer something more gripping and true to this great distillery. 40%

The BenRiach Aged 16 Years db **(83.5) n21.5 t21 f20 b21.** Pleasant malt but now without the dab of peat which gave it weight; also a marked reduction of the complexity that once gave this such a commanding presence. 43%. nc ncf.

The BenRiach Aged 16 Years Sauternes Wood Finish db **(85) n19.5 t23 f21.5 b21.** One of the problems with cask finishing is that there is nothing like an exact science of knowing when the matured whisky and introduced wood gel to their fullest potential. BenRiach enjoy a reputation of getting it right more often than most other distillers and bottlers. But here it hasn't come off to quite the same effect as previous, quite sensational, versions I have tasted of the 16-y-o Sauternes finish. No denying the sheer joy of the carpet bombing of the taste buds on delivery, though, so rich is the combination of fresh grape and delicate smoke. 46%

❖ **The BenRiach Aged 17 Years "Septendecim" Peated Malt** db **(93.5) n24** easily one of the most complex of all the new peaty noses of the year. Both sweet and dry, with an ashy feel to the peat fire mingling with dangerous complexity. Almost perfectly weighted and balanced; **t24.5** the delivery reveals a light oiliness which is entirely absent from the nose. This in turn maximises the intensity of both the sugars and smoke. When the spices arrive, the harmony is just about complete; **f23** just a dash of oaky bitterness reveals a degree of discord. But the Demerara sugars are so crisp and painstaking in their efforts to ensur balance that all can be forgiven....; **b24** proof, not that it is now needed, that Islay is not alc in producing phenomenal phenols... 46%. nc ncf.

❖ **The BenRiach "Solstice" 17 Years Old 2nd Edition** port finish, heavily peat **(94) n23.5** a touch of the Bowmores with this: definitely a hint of Fisherman's Frie also creamy celery soup; **t23** big and thick, coating the palate superbly, first with then with a rich molassed fruitiness, especially with juicy dates to the fore; f2 back to a Fisherman's Friend stance with the fruit now vanished and some spices enlivening the delicate late sugars; **b24** well, it's the 21st June 201 solstice. And, naturally, pouring down with rain outside. So what better t whisky? With all that heart-warming, comforting peat as thick as a woo the perfect dram for a bitterly cold winter's day the world over. Or n England... 50%. nc ncf.

The BenRiach Aged 18 Years Gaja Barolo Wood Finish db **(89) n22** a bag of sweet w.. gums and gristy barley sub-plot; **t23** brilliant delivery. The taste buds are washed in something approaching grape juice and barley water; **f21.5** bitters and spices out as the oak gets a foothold; **b22.5** the delivery gives one of the most salivating experiences of the year. 46%

The BenRiach Aged 18 Years Moscatel Wood Finish db **(92.5) n23.5** one of those sublime noses where everything is understated: the fresh apples and grape, the most delicate of smoke, the jam on toast, the vanilla...; **t23.5** textbook delivery: every note clean and clear, especially the juicy fruits melting into the lush barley. A buzz of distant background smoke all helped along by the most subtle of oils; **f22** leans towards the vanilla; **b23.5** one of those rare whiskies which renews and upholds any belief I have for cask finishing. Superb. 46%

The BenRiach Aged 20 Years db **(85.5) n21.5 t23 f19 b22.** A much more attractive version than the American Release 46%. The barley offers a disarming intensity and sweetness which makes the most of the light oils. Only a bittering finish shuts the gate on excellence. 43%. nc ncf.

The BenRiach Aged 20 Years db **(78) n19 t20 f19 b20.** This is big, but not necessarily for the right reasons or in the right places. A big cut of oiliness combines with some surging sugars for a most un-BenRiachy ride. 46%. US Market.

The BenRiach Aged 21 Years "Authenticus" Peated Malt (85.5) **n22 t21.5 f21 b21.** A heavy malt, though the smoke only adds a small degree to its weight. The barley is thick and chewy but the oak has a very big say. 46%

The BenRiach 25 Years Old db **(87.5) n21.5** sharp and intense: a fruitcake with extra sultanas but the oak bites...; **t23** not the most subtle of deliveries: the oak rushes in for an eye-wateringly tart and juicy start, but simmers down with hazelnuts and walnut cream cake; on a higher level there is a far more relaxed fruitcake theme pepped up by subtle spice; **f21** the spice continues but there is a furry, chalky dryness; **b22** the tranquillity and excellent balance of the middle is the highlight by far. 50%

The BenRiach 30 Years Old db **(94.5) n24** the fruit, though very ripe and rich, remains uncluttered and clean and is helped along the way by a superb injection of sweetened cloves and Parma Violets; the oak is present and correct offering an egg custard sub-plot; **t24** how ridiculously deft is that? There is total equilibrium in the barley and fruit as it massages the palate in one of the softest deliveries of a 30-y-o around; the middle ground is creamy and leans towards the vanilla; even so, there are some amazingly juicy moments to savour; **f23** very lightly oiled and mixing light grist and rich vanilla; **b23.5** it's spent 30 years in the cask: give one glass of this at least half an hour of your time: seal the room, no sounds, no distractions. It's worth it...for as hard as I try, I can barely find a single fault with this. 50%

The BenRiach Single Cask 1970 PX finish, cask no. 1035 **(93.5) n23 t24 f23 b23.5.** Admission time: I was wholly sceptical that a malt like Benriach at this age would have what was needed to carry the load of something so hefty and uncompromising as a PX cask. I suspect the blender probably thought the same thing. But, against the odds I would say, this has worked...and with aplomb. 49.1%. 250 bottles.

The BenRiach Single Cask 1971 batch 8, hogshead, cask no. 1947, dist 21 Apr 71, bott 2011 db **(96.5) n23.5** gooseberry tart and mint; a slice or two of lime breaks up the honeyed-tannin background; **t25** the delivery is nearly impossible to properly read: not only are the notes delicate but they are myriad and short-lived. There is a hint of sweetened cocoa, but that's only after the taste buds have been confused, seduced and then made near perfect love to by at least a dozen tantalising flavours. Being a mere human, perhaps it is best described as a wondrous bourbon style with a big accent on the small grains. It is hard to tell exactly which are fruit notes and which are sugars. For sure, though, delicate spices play a significant role. This is an absolutely perfect whisky experience. **f23.5** like some kind of whisky orgasm, hard to know where the middle and ending is exactly. A late flourish of chocolate ice cream ensures a happy ending with not a single off note to be detected; **b24.5** a cask of unreconstituted magnificence. I have tasted some astonishing whiskies this year: this, so far, tops the lot. 49.8%. nc ncf sc.

The BenRiach Single Cask 1972 batch 8, hogshead, cask no. 802, dist 18 Feb 72, bott 2011 db **(90.5) n23** plenty of natural vanilla. But it is the blend of near black banana, physalis and ...eberry which takes the plaudits; **t23** the unmistakable sharpness of a malt on the edge ...oak burrows into the taste buds. But that lasts no more than a moment: the layering ...s and fudge rescue the situation and builds a platform for those exotic fruits to re- ...**f22** sweetened lemon and lime amid the vanilla; **b22.5** from the exotic fruit school ...picked just in the nick of time... 40.1%. nc ncf sc.

...ch Single Cask 1975 Tawny port finish, cask no. 4450 db **(83) n20.5 t22.5 f19** ...grape is clean, it is a sweet thing of wonder. But there is a dull note in there ...down 52.2%. 648 bottles.

...ingle Cask 1976 batch 8, butt, cask no. 6942, dist 14 Oct 76, bott 2011 db ...s but leading fruitcake brimming with cherry and molasses; **t24** mouth- ...y beyond – or below? – its years. The sharpness of the fruit appears have a salty bite as the superior oak make its presence felt; the spices have almost perfect impact; **f23.5** long, entirely without a blemish and fading with molasses on toast; **b24** strikingly beautiful. *57.8%. nc ncf sc.*

⸫ **The BenRiach Single Cask 1976 Aged 35 Years** batch 9, cask no. 6967, dist 14 Oct 76, bott 2012 db **(94.5) n23** creaky old leather and dusty libraries...I feel quite at home; some spiced up juicy dates, too; **t24** an engrossing experience: the grape is almost as fresh as it must have been way back in the days when Abba were topping the charts. The inevitable spices hold firm, setting into a rich fudge and mocha middle; **f23.5** some vanillas and tannins peel off from the grape and it is the popping vanilla pods which have the very last say; **b24** it is impossible to ask any more of an old sherry cask from Benriach than this: quite magnificent. *59%. nc ncf sc.*

⸫ **The BenRiach Single Cask 1976 Aged 35 Years** batch 9, Pedro Ximenez sherry finish, cask no. 5317, dist 11 Oct 76, bott 2012 db **(86.5) n21.5 t20.5 f23 b21.5.** An exceptionally sticky beast on the palate and the grape works wonders to overcome some obviously exhausted oak. The mint is a bit of a give-away so far as the state of the cask is concerned. But the injection of the treacle and spice makes for an, ultimately, lovely experience. *54.1%. nc ncf sc.*

⸫ **The BenRiach Single Cask 1976 Aged 35 Years** batch 9, peated, cask no. 8804, dist 6 Dec 76, bott 2012 db **(91.5) n22** the peat is shadowy and the oak just a little too laid back. Dry with some polished wooden floorboard; **t23.5** mouth-watering and what was a dormant whisky has suddenly erupted. The barley is intense and crisp sugar cranks up the salivation levels; the spices arrive pretty early and refuse to err; **f23** long, with a strange garibaldi biscuit sweetness; the spices and sugars are now in perfect rhythm; **b23** yet another cask which makes the BenRiach tasting days one of the highlights of my Whisky Bible writing year. This one shrugs aside the no-show nose and emerges as a Superwhisky, in much the same way Clark Kent finds new life each time he enters a phone box...; *54.9%. nc ncf sc.*

The BenRiach Single Cask 1977 virgin American oak, cask no. 3798 db **(76.5) n21 t19 f18 b18.5.** Proof that there is only so much fun you can have with an old virgin. *43.2%. 292 bottles.*

The BenRiach Single Cask 1977 batch 8, PX hogshead, cask no. 1034, dist 15 Apr 77, bott 2011 db **(80.5) n20.5 t20.5 f19 b19.5.** Huge grape: struggles manfully but unsuccessfully to find a second dimension... *54.3%. nc ncf sc.*

⸫ **The BenRiach Single Cask 1977 Aged 34 Years** batch 9, Sauternes finish, cask no. 2598, dist 18 Aug 77, bott 2012 db **(77) n20 t19 f19 b19.** A real shame, as the usual rich, complex physalis and honey thread is there for all to see. Those who can't pick up sulphur will adore this one, especially as the staining is only light. *44.2%. nc ncf sc.*

⸫ **The BenRiach Single Cask 1977 Aged 34 Years** batch 9, Rioja finish, cask no. 2588, dist 18 Aug 77, bott 2012 db **(90) n23** an intriguing head-on meeting of fruit salad and barley sugar...with some spiced vanilla thrown in to remind you of the age; **t22** silky yet strangely well mannered for a malt which has plenty of spices just bursting to escape; **f22.5** creamy textured, long and deliciously chewable. Some of those spices finally make it into general play; **b22.5** clean, sweet and quietly understated. *44.1%. nc ncf sc.*

The BenRiach Single Cask 1978 Gaja Barolo finish, cask no. 4414 db **(88) n22 t22.5 f22 b21.5.** A bit leaden footed at times, but where it works it does so splendidly. *51.2%*

The BenRiach Single Cask 1978 batch 8, virgin oak hogshead, cask no. 4387, dist 15 Dec 78, bott 2011 db **(86.5) n22 t22 f21 b21.5.** The flavours virtually scream at you. After the carpet bombing by toasty sugars comes a surprising degree of bitterness. *50.9%. nc ncf sc.*

The BenRiach Single Cask 1979 batch 8, ASB cask no. 11195, dist 14 Dec 79, dist 14 Dec 79, bott 2011 db **(86.5) n21.5 t23 f21 b21.** Pleasing: the sugars and spices are a treat on the fabulous delivery. Between the massive oils and light peat almost everything else vanishes. *50.3%. nc ncf sc. Heavily peated.*

The BenRiach Single Cask 1980 batch 8, virgin oak hogshead, cask no. 2531, dist 28 May 80, bott 2011 db **(92) n24** fans of bourbon will appreciate this: red liquorice, old waxed leather, honey comb...all the big, aged Kentucky regulars in there big time; **t23** this is one yielding virgin, believe me. Rare that such a dynamic nose is followed up by such a docile delivery: layer upon layer of light, sometimes vaguely molassed sugars...but where is the skeleton? A touch of hickory meets the middle; **f22.5** stays on its blancmange style course, though the late rays of honey are magnificent; **b22.5** to say it melts in the mouth implies it had some substance in the first place. That is never the case: this is always about flavour rather than structure. Of all the fluids found in this malt, none of it is spinal... *49.8%. nc ncf*

⸫ **The BenRiach Single Cask 1983 Aged 29 Years** batch 9, cask no. 291, dist 6 N 83, bott 2012 db **(93) n24** a supremely stylish mix of sugars used in the '50s and '60 candy cigarettes and playful lime...all topped with custard; **t23** firm barley captures early ground on delivery, slowly allowing the tannins to gather and form a dry, spic **f22.5** surprisingly oily, allowing the barley back into circulation; **b23.5** a really comp showing not a single degree of tiredness. Can't make up its mind to be a hard softie. *43.1%. nc ncf sc.*

The BenRiach Single Cask 1984 PX finish, cask no. 1048 db **(90.5) n23.5 t22.5 f22 b22.** At first just reminded me too much of the Lagavulin PX finish. Enjoyable, but feeling that the peat and sweet grape refuse to be on quite the same wavelength. Massive and enjoyable whisky without a doubt, but a bit like watching your football team winning a game by a decent score without really ever getting into their normal rhythm. In many ways, the 15-y-o version worked far better, I thought. Then remembered that this kind of malt was a mood thing. So held back for another time. Only on a second tasting when in a little darker frame of mind did it all come together... (score on first mood: n22 t21.5 f21.5 b21) 49.2%. 279 bottles.

The BenRiach Single Cask 1984 batch 8, virgin oak hogshead, cask no. 7193, dist 03 Oct 84, bott 2011 db **(88.5) n23.5** the peat is oiled on but has some major molasses to contend with; **t22** the smoke and liquorice notes trip over each other in a jumbled display on the palate. Great fun...and you never quite know what is going to happen next; **f21.5** back to the smoked molasses; **b21.5** a perverse whisky: a kind of peated bourbon... 54.3%. nc ncf sc. Richly peated.

✣ **The BenRiach Single Cask 1984 Aged 27 Years** batch 9, Pedro Ximenez sherry finish, cask no. 1052, dist 19 Sep 84, bott 2012 db **(71) n19 t19 f15 b18.** Ungainly and falls flat on its face. 50.7%. nc ncf sc.

✣ **The BenRiach Single Cask 1984 Aged 27 Years** batch 9, peated, Tawny port finish, cask no. 4050, dist 10 Oct 84, bott 2012 db **(94) n23** a briny, as well as smoky, aspect to the big fruit; thick and heady; hard to believe this is not from a Hebridean island... **t23.5** we can be grateful to the spice-assisted sugary grape for coming alive first, as this means a lovely juiciness thins the rampant smoke; **f24** tangy, spicy...and smoky, of course...; some excellent mocha towards the end; **b23.5** a quite beautiful whisky with much to admire and adore. Yet for all its greatness and undeniable charm you cannot help thinking that certain aspects of the two styles may have cancelled each other out. But that's me just being greedy... 52.5%. nc ncf sc.

✣ **The BenRiach Single Cask 1985 Aged 26 Years** batch 9, Pedro Ximenez sherry finish, cask no. 7190, dist 13 Nov 85, bott 2012 db **(85) n21 t22 f21 b21.** A clean cask with no off notes. But, as is so often the case when this ultra sweet grape and big smoke get together, the picture on the palate is pretty but there is very little to look at. 48.7%. nc ncf sc.

The BenRiach Single Cask 1988 Gaja Barolo finish, cask no. 4424 db **(93.5) n23.5 t24 f22.5 b23.** Superficially, a very similar re-run of the 18-y-o Gaja Barolo. But in reality, much more complex and complete, with the finish intact and the smoke more telling. Another all-round stunner from the wonderful distillery. 54.3%. 322 bottles.

The BenRiach Single Cask 1989 Sauternes hogshead, cask no. 4813, dist 25 Jan 89, bott 2011 db **(74.5) n19 t19 f18 b18.5.** Never gets the chance to open out. 49.1%. nc ncf sc.

The BenRiach Single Cask 1989 virgin oak hogshead, cask no. 5620, dist 21 Apr 89, bott 2011 db **(91.5) n23** telling, almost bolshie but the firm layering of sugars make it less of an ogre; **t24** fabulous, eye-rolling delivery: the barley explodes like a mushroom cloud on the palate. The sugars become particularly noticeable in the fallout but are then immediately toughened by a backbone of drier, intense tannin; **f22** more tannin on the fade; **b22.5** at times like sucking a malt whisky candy... 50.6%. nc ncf sc.

The BenRiach Single Cask 1990 cask no. 970 db **(89.5) n21.5 t23 f22 b22.5.** Another mind-blowing ultra clean maltfest from this distillery. With Cardhu, Glen Moray and Tomatin, no-one can do malt quite like this. 57.1%. 195 bottles.

✣ **The BenRiach Single Cask 1990 Aged 22 Years** batch 9, Tawny port finish, cask no. 2596, dist 24 Jan 90, bott 2012 db **(95.5) n25** there is such aplomb to the almost wafer-brittle thinness of the strand of grape which defines the nose of this whisky, one is almost tempted to put down the glass and applaud. The barley and vanilla attaches itself to the grape with a deftness which defies belief; elsewhere no less delicate stratum of aged dates, faint smoke and manuka honey add to the perfection; **t23.5** stunningly salivating and fresh on delivery, there is a busy jauntiness to this which offers great contrast to the nose. The barley really shines and it takes a little while for the grape to finally emerge. When it does, we are back to a slower, more thoughtful building and dispersal of flavours; **f23.5** all vibrancy now spent, you need about ten minutes to pick your way through the fruity finish. The peat, which you could swear was on the nose, makes a very late reprise...and stays when it gets there; **b23.5** s it happens, just a couple of days back I found a stunning 43-year-old Tawny Port being ⁃rved onboard a Qatar Airlines flight. How an Arab airline got hold of something quite so ⁃gnificent I'd like to know. But I doubted if I would find any Tawny-related drink which would ⁃r it on the nose for the remainder of the year at least. How wrong I was... 53.4%. nc ncf sc.

⁃ BenRiach Single Cask 1992 batch 8, Tawny Port hogshead, cask no. 972, dist 19 Feb ⁃t 2011 db **(93) n24** beautiful, clean and sparkling exuberance to the grape: rather ⁃e I expected their Sauternes to be; **t23.5** more of the same but now with a puckering ⁃s and some real needle in the spice; **f22.5** a few controlled bitter notes headed off ⁃f fruitcake washed down with creamy mocha; **b23** yet another delight from this distillery. 55.6%. nc ncf sc.

The BenRiach Single Cask 1993 batch 8, Barolo hogshead, cask no. 7415, dist 27 May 93, bott 2011 db **(92.5) n23.5** a rare display of tight, almost paranoidly intense fruit with almost paranoidly intense oak. The combination is sweet, intense bliss; **t23.5** the silky arrival does nothing to prepare you for the barrage of white hot spices which sear the palate; like the nose, so thick you could carve the distillery's name into it; **f23** concentrates on the tannins. But no off notes, no bitterness of any kind...just an elegant, roast fudge fade; **b23** unique flavour profile: there is no other offering anything quite like this in the world, trust me... *56.1%. nc ncf sc.*

The BenRiach 1994 Limited Release Madeira Finish Aged 15 Years cask no. 4810, bott Sep 09 db **(87) n23 t22 f20.5 b21.5.** Gives the impression of having been distilled from granite. *57.1%. Exclusive to Kensington Wine Market.*

The BenRiach "Heart of Speyside" db **(85.5) n21.5 t22 f21 b21.** A decent, non-fussy malt where the emphasis is on biscuity barley. At times juicy and sharp. Just a tease of very distant smoke here and there adds weight. *40%*

The BenRiach "Horizons" db **(87) n22** a plethora of natural caramel notes; **t22.5** a simple barley/caramel weight and counterweight; the sugars are even and toasty; **f21** heads off along one very long, straight caramel-vanilla path as far as the eye can see...; **b21.5** few mountains or even hills on this horizon. But the view is still an agreeable one. *50%. nc ncf.*

The BenRiach "Solstice" db **(94) n23.5** gorgeous non-coastal peat. By which I mean, intense smoke, but none of the brine and rock pools which sometimes accompanies it. This is simply clean, lumbering phenols, thickened still further by a good dollop of lascivious fruit...; **t24** a barrage of firm brown sugars are first to show, followed soon after by a cream sundae fruitiness. The smoke is all pervasive and intensifies as the flavours play out; there is also a decent showing of peppery spice pulsing in its intensity; **f23** an enormously long fade, a bit like a midsummer sunset. No surprises, bitterness or off notes whatsoever. Just a slow dimming of all that has gone on before; **b23.5** on midsummer's day 2011, the summer solstice, I took a rare day off from writing this book. With the maximum light available in my part of the world for the day I set off at daybreak to see how many miles I could walk along remote country paths stopping, naturally, only at a few remote pubs on the way. It was a fraction under 28 miles. Had this spellbinding whisky been waiting for me just a little further down the road, I am sure, despite my troubled left knee and blistered right foot, I would have made it 30. *50%. nc ncf.*

Birnie Moss Intensely Peated db **(90) n22** youthful, full of fresh barley and lively, clean smoke; **t23.5** juicy, fabulously smoked, wet-behind the ears gristy sugars; **f22** some vanillas try to enter a degree of complexity; **b22.5** before Birnie Moss started shaving... or even possibly toddling. Young and stunning. *48%. nc ncf.*

Hart Brothers Benriach Aged 14 Years dist Mar 96, bott Jan 11 **(86.5) n21 t22 f22 b21.5.** Doesn't even bother to play the complexity card. Just big, sweet barley all the way. *46% sc.*

⸪ **Liquid Sun BenRiach 15 Years Old** bourbon cask, dist 1996, bott 2011 **(82.5) n20 t22 f20 b20.5.** Perhaps one more for the whisky pathologists than lovers as the lack of meaningful oak means you can work out something about what made this malt tick before it met its demise from vanilla starvation. On the subject of pathologists, I raise this dram as a toast to Jack Klugman, Quincy, who proved that being ugly and 54, like me, was no bar to pulling some highly intelligent and stunningly beautiful women. And any man who sues a big company over contractual rights is a hero in my book. To you, sir! *46%. The Whisky Agency.*

⸪ **Malts Of Scotland BenRiach 1991** bourbon barrel, cask no. 32283, dist Mar 91, bott Jul 11 **(94) n23** thumping malt, but met its match in a lively liquorice and coconut oakiness which refuses to be bullied; **t23.5** exemplary delivery with just the right degree of oil to maximise the limited sugars; **f23.5** the oils stretch and the waves continue to lap, but now we enter a pretty sophisticated phase of dryness. A little cocoa and red liquorice endorse the quality of the oak; **b24** a classy, complex cask. *51.6%. nc ncf sc. Malts Of Scotland.*

⸪ **Mo Ôr Collection BenRiach 1991 19 Years Old** first fill bourbon hogshead, cask no. 110681, dist 24 Sep 91, bott 9 Mar 11 **(81) n21 t21 f19 b20.** Bold barley. But the bitterness from the oak is a little severe. *46%. nc ncf sc. Release No. 37. The Whisky Talker. 300 bottles.*

Old Malt Cask Benriach Aged 15 Years refill hogshead, cask no. 6990, dist Mar 96, bott Mar 11 **(93) n22** mildly shallow but oozing a brassy saltiness; **t24** intense with the juicy malt and vanilla intact and in harmony. Those briny notes remain, but some surprising honeycomb and hickory prop up the middle ground; **f23** loads of toffee and milk chocolate and a few embers of warming spice; **b23.5** one of those malts that doesn't shout its greatness at you. You have to possess a bit of cunning and understanding to discover the hidden gems here. *50%. nc ncf sc. Douglas Laing & Co. 332 bottles.*

Old Masters Benriach 14 Years Old cask no. 43219, dist 1996, bott Feb 11 **(72) n17 t19 f17.5 b18.5.** Not quite the greatest cask in the world, Mr MacArthur! *54%. sc. James MacArthur & Co.*

Provenance Benriach Over 11 Years refill hogshead, cask no. 6821, dist Spring 99, bott Autumn 2010 **(86.5) n22 t22 f21 b21.5.** An intense, compact and natural caramel spined maltfest. *46%. nc ncf sc. Douglas Laing & Co.*

⁖ **Single Cask Collection BenRiach 15 Years Old** bourbon hogshead, dist 1996 **(74) n17 t18 f19 b18.** Malty but thin, hot and aggressively vapourish. *54.3%. sc. Single Cask Collection.*

The Whisky Agency Benriach 1975 bott 2010 **(93) n23** entirely intact with coconut dipped in syrup. The tannins are present but muscovado sugars pepper it with purpose; **t23.5** toasty with sweet oak notes scrambling around the palate; the lightness of touch of the honey is commendable; the spices need locating, but once found play a very clever role; **f23** a real custard pie of a finale with the vanillas in the ascendency; the spices persist to the end; **b23.5** the secret of this malt's success is the alliance between the oils and rich sugars. Fabulous. *50.6%*

The Whisky Agency Benriach 1985 bott 2010 **(86.5) n21 t22 f21 b21.5.** Plenty of malty juices flowing, but feels the oak perhaps just a little too keenly. *48.1%*

BENRINNES
Speyside, 1826. Diageo. Working.

Benrinnes Aged 15 Years db **(70) n16 t19 f17 b18.** What a shame that in the year the independent bottlers at last get it right for Benrinnes, the actual owners of the distillery make such a pig's ear of it. Sulphured and sicklysweet, this bottling has little to do with the very good whisky made there day in day out by its talented team. Depressing. *43%. Flora and Fauna.*

Benrinnes The Manager's Choice refill American oak, cask no. 8994, dist 1996, bott 2009 db **(89.5) n21.5 t23.5 f22 b22.5.** Great to see the distillery in this kind of outstanding form. *59.7%*

A.D. Rattray Benrinnes 1996 cask no. 6463 **(96) n25** absolutely terrifying degree of sherry: a butt from the old school – 100% sulphur free and dripping with toasted raisin and voluptuous dates. Malt, layered with Demerara and soft spice. This is perfection...; **t24** a controlled, slow-motion explosion of spices and a fanning out into all directions of the palate of chestnuts, liquorice, burnt fudge and even barley...; **f23** dries towards a big vanilla exit but with a pithy quality to the fruit. Here a triple-distilled malt does not quite have the body to take the finale on that extra few notches; **b24** if you ever hear some self invented, industry toadying "whisky expert" saying that today's average sherry butt is fine, and no different to how they used to be, just get them to investigate a bottle of this. This is oloroso enriched malt the way I was first weaned on it nearly 40 years ago. The butt is devoid of a single off note: it is clean and could be easily mistaken for a Macallan bottling of the 70s and 80s. This is the way the majority of fresh sherry butts used to be: the industry norm by which I still, to the chagrin of certain others, measure today's malt. I fear that there may now be an entire generation of whisky lovers who have yet to experience anything quite like this mahogany-coloured masterpiece. For there is not a single molecule giving you trouble on the nose and, as that indicates, the entire experience is free from any pressing of the self destruct button. A dram which certain people in, or on the periphery of, today's Scotch whisky industry who deceive themselves and others into thinking they know something about this game should taste...and, if they are capable (which in many cases I doubt), learn from. And it is a bottle I would love to ram up their collective rear ends to stop them talking the absolute drivel which ultimately does the industry – and you the consumer – such a massive disservice. *56.1%. sc.*

⁖ **A.D. Rattray Benrinnes 1998** butt, cask no. 6850, dist 2 Sep 98, bott Feb 12 **(85) n21 t23 f20 b21.** A Spanish sherry butt which isn't quite as pure as the football of the country's national side. But shows some outstanding touches without doubt. *53.5%. sc. A.D. Rattray Ltd.*

⁖ **Hart Brothers Benrinnes Aged 14 Years** cask no. 82, dist 25 Nov 97, bott 15 Apr 12 **(86) n22 t22 f21 b21.** Always fascinated by this distillery: you never know quite what awaits in the glass. This is a thoroughly enjoyable version. Distinctly single minded and complexity free. But a really enjoyable exhibition of barley at its most impervious. *46%. sc.*

Old Malt Cask Benrinnes Aged 19 Years sherry butt, cask no. 7232, dist Jan 92, bott May 11 **(71) n16 t20 f18 b19.** After the horror nose, the malty, chocolate-infested story told on the palate is a comparative treat. *50%. nc ncf sc. Douglas Laing & Co. 286 bottles.*

Provenance Benrinnes Over 12 Years sherry butt, cask no. 6506, dist Winter 97, bott Summer 2010 **(67) n18 t18 f15 b16.** Starts badly. And gets a lot worse... *46%. nc ncf sc.*

⁖ **Riegger's Selection Benrinnes 1998** first fill sherry butt, cask no. 6844, dist 2 Sep 98, bott 7 Feb 12 **(77) n19 t20 f19 b19.** Forceful and unsubtle. The barley and sugars work hard to overcome some major shortcoming. *55.3%. nc ncf sc. Viktor-Riegger GmbH. 420 bottles.*

Robert Graham's Dancing Stag Benrinnes 1988 hogshead, dist 10 Mar 88, bott 09 Jun 11 **(77.5) n20.5 t20 f18 b19.** Big, single tracked malt early on. But almost a collectors' item to find a whisky with so little taste on the finish. *46%. nc ncf sc. 277 bottles.*

⁖ **Scotch Malt Whisky Society Cask 36.56 Aged 22 Years** refill hogshead, cask no. 801, dist 1989 **(91.5) n23** delicate with excellent vanilla-barley balance; a welcome touch of salt; **t23** the nose suggests a big, salivating barley fanfare...and it is deafening...; **f22.5** the barley continues its slightly salty course while the spices make a late noise; **b23** when you find a good Benrinnes, it can charm the barley from its husk... *53.6%. sc. Scotch Malt Whisky Society.*

Vom Fass Benrinnes 11 Years Old (83.5) n22 t22 f20.5 b19. For those who like their barley in fresh, clean concentrated form...and to rip directly into their taste buds. And, some cocoa on the finale apart, not much else besides! Delicious! *57.8%*

BENROMACH
Speyside, 1898. Gordon & MacPhail. Working.

Benromach 10 Years Old matured in hand selected oak casks db **(87.5) n22** how you might expect a chocolate peat bar to be when grated. The odd blood orange note, too; **t22** a gristy sweetness imparts a delicate smoke which mingles with the vanilla; **f21.5** surprising degrees of sugars see off the worst of a bitter oakiness; **b22** for a relatively small still using peat, the experience is an unexpected and delicately light one. *43%*

Benromach 21 Years Old db **(91.5) n22** some exotic fruit and green banana is topped off with a splodge of maple syrup; **t23.5** excellent interplay between the sweeter, barley-rich components and the elegant, spiced oaky backbone; virtually no bite and softened further by an unfurling of vanilla on the middle; **f23** long, oak-edged with a slow, tapering dryness which does nothing to confront the sugared backnotes or even the suggesting of the most delicate smoke; **b23** an entirely different, indeed lost, style of malt from the old, now gone, big stills. The result is an airier whisky which has embraced such good age with a touch of panache and grace. *43%*

Benromach 22 Years Old Finished in Port Pipes db **(86) n22 t23 f20 b21.** Slightly Jekyll and Hyde. *45%. 3500 bottles.*

Benromach 25 Years Old db **(92) n24** seriously sexy with spices interplaying with tactile malt: the bitter-sweet balance is just so. There is even the faintest flicker of peat-smoke to underscore the pedigree; **t22** an early, surprising, delivery of caramel amongst the juicy barley; **f23** lots of gentle spices warm the enriched barley and ice-creamy vanilla, **b23** a classic old-age Speysider, showing all the quality you'd hope for. *43%*

Benromach 30 Years Old db **(95.5) n23.5** spiced sultana, walnuts and polished bookcases; **t24** no malt has the right to be anything near so silky. The sugars are a cunning mix of molasses and muscovado; the honey is thinned manuka. Still the barley gets through, though the vanilla is right behind; **f24** drier, but never fully dries and has enough spotted dog in reserve to make for a moist, lightly spiced finish. And finally a thin strata of sweet, Venezualan cocoa; **b24** you will struggle to find a 30-year-old with less wrinkles than this.. Magnificent: one of the outstanding malts of the year. *43%*

Benromach Cask Strength 1981 db **(91) n21.5 t23 f23.5 b23.** Really unusual with that seaweedy aroma awash with salt: stunningly delicious stuff. *54.2%*

Benromach Cask Strength 2001 db **(89) n21.5** a pretty closed road: the peat stands by a blockage and allows little else to pass; **t23** an amalgamation of soft oil, big alcohol and venomous spice allows the taste buds to be truly duffed up in a splendidly macho manner; **f22** yet more layers of smoky vanilla and sugar, **b22.5** just fun whisky which has been very well made and matured with total sympathy to the style. Go get. *59.9%*

⸭ **Benromach 2002 Cask Strength** db **(88.5) n22** clean, sweet, gristy smoke; **t22.5** big and intense peat on delivery. Soon begins soothing and stroking the taste buds with the softest barley sugar imaginable; **f22** clean and simple with the vanillas showing no more inclination to aggression than the smoke; **b22** most peaty malts frighten those who aren't turned on by smoky whisky. This might be an exception: they just don't come any friendlier. *60.3%*

Benromach 2002 Sassicaia Wood Finish db **(86) n21 t22 f21 b22.** Again this entirely idiosyncratic wood-type comes crashing head to head with the smoke to form a whisky style like nothing else. Dense, breathless and crushed, there is little room for much else to get a word in, other than some oak-extracted sugars. A must experience dram. *45%*

⸭ **Benromach 2005 Sassicaia Finish** db **(92.5) n22.5** lightly smoked, well weighted and boasting a delicate degree of Turkish Delight; **t24** the delivery is just a little special with a silky texture to die for and phenols and fruit that dissolve like candy; **f23** an injection of vanillas stiffen things up. But the weight remains impressive; **b23** a sassy dram in every way... *45%*

Benromach Latitude 57° cask no. 580 db **(73.5) n18.5 t19 f18 b18.** I'm afraid with that sulphur evident it shows the wrong kind of latitude altogether... *57%. 330 bottles.*

Benromach Madeira Wood db **(92) n22** some rolling smoke and chunky dried fruits almost cancel each other out; **t24** voluptuous body displaying soft oils which coat the mouth with a spot on peat which is at once full and chewy yet light enough to allow the layered fruits full reign; the bitter-sweet balance just couldn't be better; **f23** some touches of almost Jack Daniel hickory amid the circling smoke and juiced up fruit; mind-boggling complexity to this for so long; **b23** if you want a boring, safe, timid malt, stay well away from this one. Fabulous: you are getting the feeling that the real Benromach is now beginning to stand up. *45%*

Benromach Marsala Wood db **(86.5) n21.5 t22 f22 b21.** Solid, well made, enjoyable malt, which in some ways is too solid: the imperviousness of both the peat and grape appears not to allow much else get through. Not a dram to say no to, however, and the spices in particular are a delight. *45%*

Benromach Organic db **(91) n23** massive oak input and the freshest oak imaginable. But sits comfortably with the young pulsing malts. Wow!!; **t23** oak arrives first again, but has enough deftness of touch to allow the rich, mouthwatering malts to prosper; **f22** plenty of vanillins and natural, sweet toffee; **b23** young and matured in possibly first fill bourbon or, more likely, European (even Scottish) oak; you cannot do other than sit up and take notice of this guns-blazing big 'un. An absolute treat! *43%. nc ncf.*

Benromach Organic Special Edition db **(85.5) n22 t21 f21.5 b21.** The smoky bacon crisp aroma underscores the obvious youth. Also, one of the driest malts of the year. Overall, pretty. But pretty pre-pubescent, too... *43%*

Benromach Origins db **(84.5) n20 t22 f21 b21.5.** You'd think after tasting over 1,250 whiskies in the space of a few months you'd have nosed and tasted it all. But no: here is something very different. Discordant noises from nose to finish, it is saved by the extraordinary richness of the coppery input and a vague smoky richness finishing with cold latte. *50%*

Benromach Origins Batch 1 "Golden Promise" dist 1999 db **(69.5) n17 t17.5 f17.5 b17.5.** The nose is less than promising. And with good reason. *50%*

Benromach Origins Batch 2 "Port Pipe" dist 1999 db **(86) n22 t20.5 f23 b20.5.** Dense whisky with huge spice. But it is as if in concentrate form with little room for complexity to develop into its full potential. Some charming chocolate and toffee on the finish. *50%*

Benromach Origins Batch 3 "Optic" dist 2000 db **(83.5) n21 t20 f21.5 b21.** Another chunky, tight malt from the new Benromach. Some serious chewing, but a few feints on which to chew... *50%*

Benromach Peat Smoke Batch 3 db **(90.5) n22** excellent nose: pretty decent levels of peak reek evident but dried, rather than cured...; **t23** now that is impressive: the dry peat builds in intensity, though not after the clean and powering barley makes the first speech; **f22.5** dry, chalky and compact; damn it – this is very good, indeed! **b23** an excellent malt that has been beautifully made. Had it been bottled at 46 we would have seen it offer an extra degree of richness. *40%*

Benromach Traditional db **(86) n22 t21 f21.5 b21.5.** Deliciously clean and smoky. But very raw and simplistic, too. 40%

Benromach Wood Finish Hermitage dist 2001 db **(84) n19 t23 f21 b21.** A sweet, tight dram with all the shape crushed out of it. It does have its moment of greatness, though: about three or four seconds after arrival when it zooms into the stratosphere on a massively fruity, sensuously spiced rocket. Then it just fades away... *45%*

Benromach Wood Finish Pedro Ximénez dist 2002 db **(85.5) n21 t22.5 f21 b21.** Combining PX with peated whisky is still probably the hardest ask in the maturation lexicon. Lagavulin are still to get it right. And they have not quite managed it here, either. It's a bumpy old ride, though some of the early chewing moments are fun. Not a bad attempt, at all. Just the learning curve is still on the rise... *45%*

Benromach Vintage 1968 db **(94.5) n23** theoretically way over the top oak. But the sherry acts as a sponge...or, to be more precise, a very well aged fruit cake; some mega juicy plums and figs; **t23** can't fault the marbelling with the fruit running thickly into the spicier, almost bourbony meat. Again the oak is over the top, yet, thanks to the depth of the cocoa and juicy grape, somehow gets away with some outrageous splinters; **f24.5** now completely dazzles as all the more militant elements of the oak have been pacified and we are left with not only a sherry trifle/fruitcake mix, but chocolate cream/raspberry roll for good measure... **b24** a 40 year plus whisky of astonishing quality...? A piece of cake... *45.4%*

⁙ **Benromach Vintage 1969** db **(92) n22** a slightly tired, sappy aroma; honeycomb offers the perfect antidote; **t24** the sugars are queuing to deliver and do so with a barley-rich gentleness. Some milk chocolate arrives, and then a succession of much drier, more assertive oak; **f23** hangs on well and the seasoning is at times both complex and challenging; finishes with coconut shreds dunked in Golden Syrup; **b23** the odd branch of the old oak too many. But still has many magical mahogany moments. *42.6%*

BLADNOCH
Lowlands, 1817. Armstrong Brothers. Working.

Bladnoch Aged 6 Years Bourbon Matured db **(91) n21.5** young, yes. But the soft feints have nothing to do with that; **t22.5** a youthful, oily delivery, not exactly a picture of harmony, gives way to a brutal coup d'etat of ultra intense prisoner-slaughtering barley; **f24** intense barley-concentrate oils offer a perplexing array of sweet, grassy tones; you simply chew and chew until the jaw aches. Cocoa at last arrives, all with a spiced buzz and a smearing of vanillas. Meanwhile your tongue explores the mouth, wondering what the hell is going on; **b23** the fun starts with the late middle, where those extra oils congregate and the taste buds are sent rocking. Great to see a Lowlander bottled at an age nearer its natural best and even the smaller cut, in a roundabout way, ensures a mind-blowing dram. 57.3%

Bladnoch Aged 6 Years Lightly Peated db **(93) n23** a peat fire just bursting into life; **t23** firm, bitter-sweet; the layering of the peat is awesome, with the youth of the malt adding an extra dimension; some citrus notes help lighten the load; **f23.5** smoky hickory; the vanillas make a feeble entry, a gentle oiliness persists; **b23.5** the peat has nothing to do with the overall score here: this is a much better-made whisky with not a single off-note and the cut is spot on. And although it claims to be lightly peated, that is not exactly true: such is the gentle nature of the distillate, the smoke comes through imperiously and on several levels. "Spirit of the Lowlands" drones the label. Since when has outstanding peated malt been associated with that part of the whisky world...?? 58.5%

Bladnoch Aged 6 Years Sherry Matured db **(73.5) n18 t19 f18.5 b18.** A sticky, lop-sided malt where something, or a group of somethings, conjures up a very unattractive overture. Feints on the palate but no excellent bourbon cask to the rescue here. 56.9%

Bladnoch Aged 10 Years db **(94) n23** lemon and lime, marmalade on fresh-sliced flour-topped crusty bread; **t24** immensely fruity and chewy, lush and mouthwatering and then the most beguiling build-up of spices: the mouthfeel is full and faultless; **f23** long, remains mildly peppery and then a dryer advance of oak. The line between bitter and sweet is not once crossed; **b24** this is probably the ultimate Bladnoch, certainly the best I have tasted in over 25 years. This Flora and Fauna bottling by then owners United Distillers should be regarded as the must-get-at-all-costs Bladnoch. If the new owner can create something even to hang on to this one's coat-tails then he has excelled himself. For those few of us lucky enough to experience this, this dram is nothing short of a piece of Lowland legend and folklore. 43%.

Bladnoch Aged 15 Years db **(91) n22.5** remnants of zest and barley sit comfortably with the gentle oaks; **t22.5** excellent delivery and soon gets into classic Bladnoch citric stride; **f23** wonderfully clean barley belies the age and lowers the curtain so delicately you hardly notice; **b23** quite outstanding Lowland whisky which, I must admit, is far better than I would have thought possible at this age. 55%

Bladnoch Aged 16 Years "Spirit of the Lowlands" db **(88) n22 t22 f22 b22.** Really lovely whisky and unusual to see a Lowlander quite this comfortable at such advanced age. 46%. ncf.

Bladnoch 18 Years Old db **(88.5) n21** dulled with oak; **t23.5** fabulous balance between juicy fruit and juicy barley. The gooseberries are green, fat and splitting at the sides...; **f22** vanilla and a trail of light oil allows the barley an extended stay **b22** the juiciness and clarity to the barley, and especially the big gooseberry kick, early on makes this a dram well worth finding. 55%

Berry's Own Selection Bladnoch 1990 cask no. 2462, bott 2011 **(75) n18 t20 f18 b19.** Malty but persists with a strangely off key, mouldy hay persona. 51.2%. nc ncf sc.

⁜ Berry's Own Selection Bladnoch 1992 cask no. 2159, bott 2011 **(91.5) n23** a Lowlander with a thin strata of smoke...intriguing! The barley, though, is as clean and intense as you are likely to find this year; **t23.5** just a splendid exhibition of barley: the type that blenders purr about as the clean, uncluttered intensity travels a long, long way; **f22** ....errr....barley... **b23** almost too simplistic and one dimensional, except for that most tantalizing hint of smoke. Except it is not too simplistic as the barley is so sexily shaped and nubile that you are not sure whether to drink it or sing soppy love songs to it... 46%. nc ncf sc. Berry Bros & Rudd.

⁜ Chieftain's Bladnoch Aged 18 Years hogshead, cask no. 4195, dist Nov 92 **(82.5) n21 t22.5 f19 b20.** Made during an interesting, and uncertain, part of the distillery's history, this malt is slightly out of kilter with the standard style though the barley at full pelt is very attractive. 55.3%. nc ncf sc. Ian Macleod Distillers. USA exclusive.

⁜ Malts Of Scotland Bladnoch 1990 bourbon barrel, cask no. MoS12019, dist Jul 90, bott Apr 12 **(90.5) n22** big citrus; polished school floors; **t23** just as well I can type: I am salivating too much to speak...; **f22.5** the juicy barley withdraws slightly to allow a liquorice-chocolate fudge finale; **b23** when this was distilled I never expected to see this distillery bottled at this kind of age. Or looking quite as shapely as this. 54.4%. nc ncf sc. Malts Of Scotland.

Old Malt Cask Bladnoch Aged 18 Years refill hogshead, cask no. 6909, dist Nov 92, bott Jan 11 **(73.5) n19.5 t19 f17 b18.** More Major Bloodnok, I'm afraid... 50%. nc ncf sc. 187 bottles.

⁜ Old Malt Cask Bladnoch Aged 18 Years sherry finished butt, cask no. 7162, dist. Nov 92, bott Jun 11 **(76.5) n18.5 t21 f18 b19.** Probably a malt which would have done better without the sherry interference. 50%. nc ncf sc. 389 bottles.

Scotch Malt Whisky Society Cask 50.41 Aged 20 Years refill hogshead, cask no. 30538, dist 1990 **(92) n23** attractive flecks of fruit appear to conflict with an almost bourbon-style oakiness. Well measured and weighted: delicate and complex; **t23** charming delivery which fulfils the promise of complexity on the nose. Again, there is a discreet honey-liquorice sweetness which points in a Kentucky-ish direction while elsewhere the barley and vaguely fruity sugars ensure a massive degree of small talk; **f22.5** spices up as the barley levels go down; **b23.5** one of those outstanding drams which keeps you guessing and entertained forever. *54.5%. sc. 162 bottles.*

Scotch Malt Whisky Society Cask 50.44 Aged 18 Years refill hogshead, cask no. 3835, dist 1992 **(82) n19 t21.5 f20.5 b21.** A big, malty fellow, short on finesse. *56.5%. sc. 282 bottles.*

⫸ **Scotch Malt Whisky Society Cask 50.49 Aged 21 Years** refill barrel, cask no. 303511, dist 1990 **(83.5) n20 t21.5 f21 b21.** Hangs on grimly for life, literally. The oak is too aggressive and only some stunning chocolate-orange notes save the day. *55.8%. sc.*

⫸ **Sestante Collection Bladnoch 21 Years Old** dist 1990, bott 2011 **(82) n21 t21 f20 b20** barley aplenty. But all a little hot and harsh. *58.7%. sc. Silver Seal Whisky Company.*

Single Cask Collection Bladnoch Aged 21 Years bourbon hogshead, cask no. 134, dist Jan 90, bott Feb 11 **(83) n18 t23 f20.5 b21.5.** Recovers after a less than promising start on the nose. The clean intensity of the barley is a stark contrast and with its citrus sub-plot gives a good showing of the malt at its most simplistic self. *51.9%. nc ncf sc. 288 bottles.*

BLAIR ATHOL
Highlands (Perthshire), 1798. Diageo. Working.

Blair Athol Aged 12 Years db **(77) n18 t19 f21 b19.** Thick, fruity, syrupy and a little sulphury and heavy. The finish has some attractive complexity among the chunkyness. *43%. Flora and Fauna.*

⫸ **A Fine Cigar's Pleasure Blair Athol Aged 12 Years** sherry butt **(63) n16 t18 f13 b16.** If chewing on a fat cigar is a way of not tasting sulphur-wrecked whisky, I might just think about taking up smoking for the first time in my life.... *50%. Douglas Laing & Co. 443 bottles.*

⫸ **Duthies Blair Athol 13 Years Old** bott 2012 **(86) n21.5 t23 f20.5 b21.** An absolutely typical new style Blair Athol big juicy barley affair - a couple of decades back this was a much dirtier kind of malt unrecognisable from this. Here everything is clean and very sweet. And rather well oiled, too. *46%. sc. WM Cadenhead Ltd.*

⫸ **John Milroy Selection Blair Athol 1998** cask no. 2753, bott 2012 **(84.5) n21 t21.5 f21 b21.** A grassy, malty thirst-slaker. *46%. nc ncf sc. Berry Bros & Rudd.*

Old Malt Cask Blair Athol Aged 15 Years sherry butt, cask no. 6814, dist Nov 95, bott Nov 10 **(77) n19 t21 f18 b19.** Appears terrified to get going. Malty but refuses to find any complexity. *50%. nc ncf sc. Douglas Laing & Co. 545 bottles.*

⫸ **Old Malt Cask Blair Athol Aged 21 Years** refill hogshead, cask no. 7561, dist Aug 90, bott Aug 11 **(88) n21** outwardly pleasant enough. But a bit of a failure on the soapy barrel front...; **t23.5** what the f...? This is whisky? Reminds me, vividly, of a strange concoction many years back I did regarding rum, cognac, vanilla and saffron; **f21.5** after that initial explosion of delicious weirdness we return to earth...and mostly a pretty boring part of it; **b22** there was I shaking my head at the nose, thinking how 21 years ago the malt made at Blair Athol was not quite of the same standard as that made a dozen years back. Then I tasted and was blasted back into my seat. This is the whisky equivalent of a slap around the chops. The finish confirms the faults. But...oh, my word....! *50%. nc ncf sc. Douglas Laing & Co. 268 bottles.*

Premier Barrel Blair Athol Aged 10 Years sherry cask **(86.5) n21.5 t22 f21.5 b21.5.** Any more baby bum-soft casks like this and I might start really warming to this distillery. The grape really is a treat. *46%. nc ncf sc. Douglas Laing & Co. 330 bottles.*

⫸ **Premier Barrel Blair Athol Aged 12 Years** **(90.5) n23** love the unsullied fruit and malt mix; just a hint of spice amid the diced apple; **t23.5** sublime delivery: a teasing, chewable, mouth-watering hurrah is extended about the palate by the deftest of oils; **f21.5** thins just a little too enthusiastically but the vanillas are a treat; **b22.5** Blair Athol at its most seductive. *46%. nc ncf sc. Douglas Laing & Co. 302 bottles.*

Premier Barrel Blair Athol Aged 13 Years **(87) n21** vanilla and barley; **t23** melt-in-the-mouth malt with a delightful cocoa subplot; the barley intensifies beautifully for the middle; **f21** thins to allow in the oak; **b22** soft, malty and easy going. *46%. nc ncf sc. 468 bottles.*

Provenance Blair Athol Over 11 Years refill hogshead, cask no. 7508, dist Winter 99, bott Summer 2011 **(85) n21 t22 f21 b21.** Similar to an Aultmore I tasted yesterday, matured for a similar time in relatively inert casks. Also decently sweet and pleasant with no off notes, but this is oilier and more barley intense. *46%. nc ncf sc. Douglas Laing & Co.*

⫸ **Provenance Blair Athol Over 11 Years** sherry butt, cask no. 7695, dist Winter 1999, bott Summer 2011 **(90) n23.5** clean, subtle and with the faintest echo of grape; an equally distant sound of smoke makes for a perfect accompaniment; **t23** salivating, gentle malt is rounded off in the middle ground by buttered sultana; **f21.5** thins and warms somewhat; **b22** a steady ship which plots a course for calmer waters yet still heads into unfamiliar seas for this distillery. *46%. nc ncf sc. Douglas Laing & Co.*

⫸ **Provenance Blair Athol Over 12 Years** sherry butt, cask no. 6000, dist Winter 1999, bott Winter 2011 **(84.5) n21 t21.5 f21 b21.** A bottling by no means short on charm. But the butt has done little to enhance either the malt or complexity. *46%. nc ncf sc. Douglas Laing & Co.*

Single Cask Collection Blair Athol Aged 12 Years bourbon hogshead, cask no. 2767, dist Apr 98, bott Feb 11 (92.5) n23.5 a sublime mix of delicate lavender and crushed toasted almond; t3 a smattering of honey on the intense barley; f23 a few spices melt into the bourbony fade; gorgeously layered; b23 a superb cask showing the distillery at its very best. Sophisticated and makes a mockery of its strength. 60.3%. nc ncf sc. 337 bottles.

BOWMORE
Islay, 1779. Morrison Bowmore. Working.

Bowmore Aged 12 Years db (91) n22.5 light peats, the air of a room with a man sucking cough sweets; sweet pipe smoke; t23.5 soft, beautiful delivery of multi-layered peats; lots of effervescent spices and molassed sugars; spices abound; f22.5 much drier with sharper berries and barley; the peat still rumbles onwards, but has no problems with the light, sawdusty oaks; b23.5 this new bottling still proudly carries the Fisherman's Friend cough sweet character, but the coastal, saline properties here are a notch or three up: far more representative of Islay and the old distillery style. Easily by far the truest Bowmore I have tasted in a long while with myriad complexity. Even going back more than a quarter of a century, the malt at this age rarely showed such relaxed elegance. Most enjoyable. 40% ⊙

Bowmore "Enigma" Aged 12 Years db (82) n19 t22 f20 b21. Sweet, molassed and with that tell-tale Fisherman's Friend tang representing the light smoke. This Enigma hasn't quite cracked it, though. 40%. Duty Free.

Bowmore "Darkest" Aged 15 Years db (83) n20 t23 f19 b21. In recent years a dram you tasted with glass in one hand and a revolver in the other. No more. But for the sulphur present, this would have been a much higher score. 43%

Bowmore "Mariner" Aged 15 Years db (79) n19 t21 f19 b20. There are two ways of looking at this. As a Bowmore. Which is how I have marked it. Or a something to throw down your neck for pure fun. Which is probably worth another seven or eight points. Either way, there is something not entirely right here. 43%. Duty Free.

Bowmore Aged 17 Years db (77) n18 t22 f18 b19. For all the attractiveness of the sweet fruit on delivery, the combination of burt and rough sweet makes for pretty hard going. 43%

Bowmore Aged 18 Years db (79) n20 t21 f19 b19. Pleasant, drinkable Fisherman's Friend style – like every Bowmore it appears around this age. But why so toffee-dull? 43%

Bowmore Aged 25 Years db (86) n21 t22 f21 b22. Not the big, chunky guy of yore: the age would surprise you if tasted blind. 43%

Bowmore Aged 30 Years db (94) n23 intense burnt raisin amid the intense burnt peat; a deft rummy sweetness strikes an improbable chord with the sweetened lime; the oak is backward coming forward but binds beautifully with both peat and fruit; t24 near flawless delivery showing a glimpse of Bowmore in a form similar to how I remember it some 25 years ago. The peat, though intense does have a hint of the Fisherman's Friend about it, but not so upfront as today. For all the peat, this is clean whisky, moulded by a craftsman into how a truly great Islay should be; f23 dries sublimely as the oak contains the peat and adds a touch of coffee to it in unsugared form. Gentle oils cling tightly to the roof of the mouth; b24 a Bowmore that no Islay scholar should be without. Shows the distillery at its most intense yet delicate; an essay in balance and how great oak, peat and fruit can combine for those special moments in life. Unquestionably one of the best Bowmores bottled this century. 43%

⋅∵⋅ Bowmore 1985 db (89) n21.5 Fisherman's Friend with a mix of muscovado and lightly molassed sugars as ballast; t24 still not technically right. But you have to be a miserable sod not to enjoy the counter-balance between the sugars and the outrageous, weirdly off key peat; f22 stays the course as a bit of a punch-drunk liquorice-sodden Fisherman's Friend addict but its sheer individuality has you in a trance of enjoyment; b21.5 I may have tasted a sweeter Islay. Just not sure when. This whisky is so wrong..it's fantastically right...! 52.6%

⋅∵⋅ Bowmore 100 Degrees Proof db (90.5) n22 low key smoke. Anyone who has been to Arbroath looking for where the Smokies are cured and homed in on the spot by nose alone will recognise this aroma...; t23 delicate in all departments, including the peat. The barley is sweet but it is the tenderness of the oils which stars; f22.5 long with a tapering muscovado finale; b23 proof positive! A real charmer. 57.1%. ncf.

⋅∵⋅ Bowmore Laimrig III db (92) n23.5 so delicate is the ultra clean grape, I am assuming this is a sherry cask finish. Not usually a fan of smoke and grape, but when it is this delicate, what isn't there to like?; t23.5 the softness found on the nose is continued on the palate. The sweetness is cleverly controlled and when the Fisherman's Friend personality arrives, it is quietly muffled, if not smothered to death, by a combination of silky grape, teasing spice and melting muscovado sugars; f22.5 the oak now raises its profile, the deep vanillas and hint of honeycomb underlining a reasonable age; b23 I must ask my research team; where the hell are Laimrigs I and II....? 53.7%

Bowmore Legend db **(88) n22** big peat fire; dry, but really attractively so; **t22.5** Ok, Fisherman's Friend cough sweet maybe, but the countering barley and brown sugar sweetness appears to dissipate the worst of the effect: the result is big peat, very evenly spread; **f22** gentle finale with a vanilla flourish; **b22.5** not sure what has happened here, but it has gone through the gears dramatically to offer a substantial dram with both big peat and excellent balancing molasses. Major stuff. *40%*

⁘ **Bowmore Small Batch Reserve** db **(80.5) n20 t21 f19 b20.5.** With a name like "Small Batch Reserve" I was expecting a marriage between intense Kentucky and Islay. Alas, this falls well short of the mark. *46%*

Bowmore Tempest Aged 10 Years Small Batch Release No.1 db first fill bourbon, bott 2009 **(87) n22.5 t22 f21 b21.5.** Perhaps too dependent on the fudgy character. When given a chance, its coastal attributes are set off to excellent effect. *55.3%*

Bowmore Tempest Aged 10 Years Small Batch Release No.2 1st fill bourbon, bott 2010 db **(93) n23.5** a rousing and strangely subtle mixture of dusty, bone-dry phenols not uncommon to non-island peated malts and a sweeter, tangier smoke, much more reminiscent of lums reeking their winter warmth; all this charged and emboldened by sly degrees of golden syrup and juicy figs; **t23.5** sturdy delivery. Just a light introduction of oils help the easy passage of a more fulsome earthiness, like the nose assisted by sugars, much more gristy this time. There is also a youthful citrus tone to this, though the dissolving vanilla and icing sugars do much good work; **f23** a hint of bitterness from the oak, but the smoke and spices bombard the taste buds. Some muscovado sugars and even the most playful hint of molasses ensures the salty, coastal notes don't take too great a hold...; **b23.5** just turned the bottle round to find some tasting notes banging on about "lemon pepper" here there and everywhere. That is only part of the tale: this is one of the better distillery bottlings to be found at Bowmore in recent years and does much to restore a slightly jaded reputation. Less a tempest than a glide across the Sound of Islay on a sunny day, cheese and tomato sandwich in hand.. But a massive statement by Bowmore, nonetheless. *56%. ncf.*

⁘ **Bowmore Tempest Aged 10 Years Small Batch Release No. 4** db **(89) n22** even by Bowmore standards the peat is light with barely a breeze to alter the course of the smoke. A few renegade spices ping around the citrus vanilla; **t23** if my taste buds were massaged any more softly by the light smoke and spices they might doze off; **f22** lightly smoked vanilla all the way; **b22** a much tamer version than the last Tempest I tasted. Then, there was a crescendo. This one sweeps gently across the palate without kicking up anything like a storm. *55.1%. ncf.*

⁘ **A.D. Rattray Bowmore 1998** cask no. 800005, dist 9 Mar 98, bott Jun 12 **(89) n22** smoked Digestive biscuit...with a fair bit of salt, too; **t23** excellent oils and top rate molasses give the smoke some substance; even the spices fit in seamlessly; **f22** dries, but elegantly; remains smoky and sweet to the very end; **b22** an understated little island treasure. *46%. sc.*

Berry Brothers Bowmore 2000 cask no. 800271, bott 2010 **(85.5) n21 t22 f21 b21.5.** Lightly toasted wholemeal bread on the gently smoked nose. The light oils and roasted almonds give a good account of themselves. *58.2%. nc ncf sc. For The Vintage House. 240 bottles.*

Berry's Own Selection Bowmore 1989 cask no. 7619, bott 2010 **(88.5) n21.5 t22.5 f22.5 b22.** This guy rips into you like a lion into the throat of a wildebeest. Bracing, uncompromising and actually quite a treat...in a brutal kind of way... *50.9%. nc ncf sc. Berry Bros & Rudd.*

⁘ **Berry's Own Selection Bowmore 1994** cask no. 1714, bott 2011 **(83.5) n21 t22 f20 b20.5.** Puts most of its emphasis on the muscular spice kick. Pleasant, but doesn't hang together with too much charm or style. *54.2%. nc ncf sc. Berry Bros & Rudd.*

⁘ **Berry's Own Selection Bowmore 1996** cask no. 1378, bott 2011 **(93.5) n23** two-toned peat offering soft and spiky varieties; salty, too; **t23** juicy and clean: the sugars are muscovado style and are crystal clear; **f23.5** some oily Venezuelan chocolate joins the medium roast Mysore coffee...with brown sugar, of course; **b24** doesn't try to be overtly spectacular: just does what it's meant to very well indeed. *55.9%. 55.9%. nc ncf sc. Berry Bros & Rudd.*

Berry's Own Selection Bowmore 1999 cask no. 800348, bott 2010 **(86) n20 t22.5 f21.5 b22.** Fisherman's Friend meets Liquorice Allsorts. The finish, though, is pure kipper. Not sure if I should be drinking or eating this one... *56.4%. nc ncf sc. Berry Bros & Rudd.*

Berry's Own Selection Bowmore 2002 cask no. 800420, bott 2011 **(84) n20.5 t21.5 f21 b21.** A sweet, seaweedy, earthiness as well as a vaguely spiciness. Curiously, appears to be missing a little bit of copper in the mix. *46%. nc ncf sc. Berry Bros & Rudd.*

⁘ **Berry's Own Selection Bowmore 2003** cask no. 20059, bott 2012 **(91.5) n21.5** the smoke plays little more than peek-a-boo; **t23.5** some light orange notes drift into the peat and vanilla chorus; the sugars leave a malty residue; **f23** the complexity continues, though the phenols rarely raise their voice above a hoarse whisper; **b23.5** its understated and delicate qualities certainly do grow on you. A little gem. *57.9%. nc ncf sc. Berry Bros & Rudd.*

⁘ **Boisdale Bowmore 2000** cask no. 800113, bott 2012 **(83.5) n21.5 t21 f20 b21.** A lazy, frankly boring, beggar that really does deserve a kick up the arse. *46%. nc ncf sc.*

Duncan Taylor NC² Bowmore 1998 (85.5) n22 t21 f21.5 b21. Lightly smoked, softly oiled, delicately oaked and as though any excess sweetness has been extracted from it. *46%. nc ncf. Duncan Taylor & Co.*

⠶ **Duncan Taylor Rare Auld Bowmore 28 Years Old** cask no. 85161, bott 1982 **(86) n20 t22.5 f21.5 b22.** Can't help thinking that this spirit was pumped through the stills at a rare old rate of knots. At times, thin and fiery but at others, the vanilla and smoke offers enough sweetness to genuinely charm. *51.6%. sc. Duncan Taylor & Co.*

⠶ **Duncan Taylor Rare Auld Bowmore 29 Years Old** cask no. 85212, bott 1982 **(89.5) n22.5** a unique signature: Fisherman's Friend wrapped in bourbon and topped with strawberry...not something you experience every day...; **t21.5** a misfit of a delivery with the varied and contrasting flavours and weights finding difficulty in hitting a groove; **f23** a majestic finale; more bourbon and smoke but now some gorgeous vanilla and late exotic fruit; **b22.5** a malt which handsomely pays back on your invested patience. *50.1%. sc.*

Fine Malt Selection Bowmore 10 Years Old (76.5) n19 t21 f18 b19.5. Lightly smoked, liberally sugared but bitterly oaked. *45%. sc. James MacArthur & Co.*

Fortnum & Mason Bowmore Aged 9 Years (88) n22.5 t22.5 f21.5 b22. About 20 years ago I became the first person to give a series of whisky tastings at Fortnum and Mason. I advised then not to add water. On the label of this whisky they do: I shall remind them...add water to this, and it simply is no longer whisky...!! *40%. nc ncf. Fortnum & Mason.*

⠶ **Kingsbury Single Cask Series Bowmore Aged 14 Years** Trois Riviers rum finish **(85.5) n21.5 t22 f21 b21.** You have to be very careful with rum casks: few ever make perfect finishes for a whisky as the sugars have a tendency to constrict the complexity. As pleasant as this virtually smokeless malt is, it is no exception. *46%. sc. Japan Import Systems.*

⠶ **Liquid Sun Bowmore 11 Years Old** bourbon cask, dist 2000, bott 2011 **(88.5) n22** a hint of mocha to the powdery peat; **t22** a short sweet blast of brown sugars quickly followed by a much drier dose of vanilla; **f22.5** an untaxing but entertaining intertwining of those sweet and dry notes; **b22** straight as a die. *46%. sc. The Whisky Agency.*

⠶ **Liquid Sun Bowmore 22 Years Old** bourbon cask, dist 1989, bott 2011 **(84) n20 t22 f20.5 b21.5.** Pleasant and attractively sweet for the first four or five big flavour waves directly after delivery. Thins dramatically on the finish. *50.7%. sc. The Whisky Agency.*

⠶ **Liquid Sun Bowmore 1998** bott 2011 **(84.5) n21 t21.5 f21 b21.** From the Fisherman's Friend school of Bowmore bottlings. Perhaps a little extra sugar than the norm, though this dissolves by the very dry finish. *53.6%. nc ncf sc. The Whisky Agency.*

Malts Of Scotland Amazing Casks Bowmore 1995 bourbon barrel, cask no. 177, dist May 95, bott Sep 10 **(89.5) n22 t24.5 f20.5 b22.5.** Every single aspect of this whisky is instantly recognisable to those few of us who have dealt with this malt in all its varied forms over the last 30 years. Where it takes the breath away is how everything fits together for a minute or two on delivery and just beyond. The finish is a let down by comparison. The star may have shone for only a short while. But while it did, it did so very brightly, indeed. *56.4%. nc ncf sc. 222 bottles.*

⠶ **Malts Of Scotland Bowmore 1989** bourbon hogshead, cask no. MoS11004, dist Oct 89, bott Oct 11 **(86.5) n21 t22 f21.5 b22** Very sweet and quietly smoky. The oils are pleasant but the spices do bite a little. *51.2%. nc ncf sc. Malts Of Scotland.*

⠶ **Malts Of Scotland Bowmore 1995** sherry hogshead, cask no. 111, bott 2011 **(85) n21 t22 f20.5 b21.5.** Perhaps just too much of a soup with grape thrown into the smoky mix, rather than carefully measured first. *56.5%. nc ncf sc. Malts Of Scotland.*

⠶ **Malts Of Scotland Bowmore 1995** sherry hogshead, cask no. MoS12018, dist May 95, bott Apr 12 **(85) n21 t22 f20 b21.5.** Thought I'd tasted a whisky like this some weeks back. Then spotted my notes for MOS 1985 cask 11. Peas in a pod, save the lesser finish on this one. *56.8%. nc ncf sc. Malts Of Scotland.*

⠶ **Malts Of Scotland Bowmore 1999** bourbon hogshead, cask no. MoS110014, dist 22 Sep 99, bott Oct 11 **(88) n22.5** teasing floral notes interact beautifully with the delicate smoke; **t21** perhaps a little thin on delivery but fattens out as light oils seep in with peaty vanilla; **f22.5** almost cocoa oil dryness to this. The chewability climbs dramatically; **b22** for all the alcoholic strength, Bowmore's lightness of touch with its peat is in full evidence. *61.2%. nc ncf sc.*

⠶ **Mo Ór Collection Bowmore 1968 42 Years Old** first fill bourbon hogshead, cask no. 3825, dist 8 Oct 68, bott 3 Nov 10 **(82) n21.5 t21.5 f19 b20.** Without doubt, the Mo Ór collection has been one of the highlights of the whisky year. So there is no little irony that their collector's edition pales in quality to what was to follow. This guy is too old and over oaked. Still has its moments, especially when the sugars get a brief foothold and is allowed to lift the peat and above the oaky swamp. *42.4%. nc ncf sc. Release No. 1. 184 bottles.*

⠶ **Mo Ór Collection Bowmore 1996 13 Years Old** first fill bourbon hogshead, cask no. DL6464, dist 31 Dec 96, bott 9 Sep 10 **(90.5) n21.5** pleasant, lightly smoked but don't hunt too hard for complexity; **t24** a hugely satisfying delivery with a Jammy Dodger gloss to the delivery and a few layers of honey man-marking the phenols; **f22** smoky vanilla; soft with delicate oils; **b23** worth experiencing for the sublime delivery alone. A much better experience than the nose heralds. *46%. nc ncf sc. Release No. 38. The Whisky Talker. 360 bottles.*

·:·:· **Old Malt Cask Bowmore Aged 11 Years** sherry butt, cask no. 7791, dist Sep 00, bott Nov 11 **(88.5) n23** the peat remains attractively defined. Something akin to a rum and raisin sweetness; **t23.5** the thickness on the nose is recreated on the lightly oiled palate; some liquorice blends in beautifully with the smoked grape; **f20** just a little too dry; **b22** at times an exceptional sherry butt which, early on, took me back some 30-odd years when casks like this were not uncommon at Bowmore. A soupy treat. *50%. nc ncf sc. 451 bottles.*

Old Malt Cask Bowmore Aged 14 Years refill hogshead, cask no. 6837, dist Dec 96, bott Jan 11 **(84.5) n21 t21 f21.5 b21.** The type of sweet, lightly smoked malt which adds ballast to a blend. *50%. nc ncf sc. Douglas Laing & Co. 277 bottles.*

Old Malt Cask Bowmore Aged 21 Years refill butt, cask no. 7460, dist Nov 89, bott Jun 11 **(84) n20 t22 f21 b21.** It may be 21, but it would never be served in the USA, so immature is it for its age. Even so, lightly smoked and very tasty... *50%. nc ncf sc. 298 bottles.*

Premier Barrel Bowmore Aged 12 Years (62) n15 t16 f15 b16. Not even peat stands a snowflake's chance in this kind of sherry butt... *46%. nc ncf sc. Douglas Laing & Co. 451 bottles.*

Premier Barrel Bowmore Aged 13 Years (90.5) n23 wonderfully layered smoke entwined with chocolate mint; **t23** textbook interweaving between light smoke and rich barley. The mocha is a delight; **f22** the smoke effect virtually vanished but the sweet malt rumbles on; **b22.5** a sexy, beautifully shaped little belter. *46%. nc ncf sc. 174 bottles.*

Provenance Bowmore Over 10 Years refill hogshead, cask no. 6818, dist Autumn 00, bott Autumn 2010 **(78) n19 t21 f19 b19.** A pleasant, gristy countenance. But the ancient cask adds nothing positive. *46%. nc ncf sc. Douglas Laing & Co.*

·:·:· **Provenance Bowmore Over 10 Years** refill hogshead, cask no. 7594, dist Autumn 2000, bott Summer 2011 **(86.5) n22 t21 f22 b21.5.** An enjoyable malt, though it appears lacking in the usual coastal qualities. *46%. nc ncf sc. Douglas Laing & Co.*

·:·:· **Riegger's Selection Bowmore 1996** bourbon cask, cask no. 1334, dist 7 May 96, bott 2 Mar 12 **(91.5) n22** tight in part, but enough movement to allow the saltiness of the sweet smoke a free hand; **t23** soft and very sweet. The delivery is less about the smoke than the intensity of the bourbon-style sugars; **f23** long, with something of the Maryland cookie about it; **b23.5** sheer entertainment. *55.7%. nc ncf sc. Viktor-Riegger GmbH. 340 bottles.*

·:·:· **Robert Graham's Dancing Stag Bowmore 1990** cask no. 17520, bott Jan 12 **(73.5) n18.5 t19 f17 b18.** Entirely off key, this one gets into a rut. *46%. nc ncf sc. 257 bottles.*

Scotch Malt Whisky Society Cask 3.164 Aged 17 Years 2nd fill hogshead, cask no. 4177, dist 1992 **(94) n23** a slight hint of Victory V. But the molasses and the Palma Violet offer superb depth to the excellent oaks; **t23.5** the vanillas offer both a degree of sweetness and dryness; the smoke offers depth and spice; the sugars also offer unusual ballast as well as balance; **f23.5** plays out the same way as the delivery and middle, but just a notch drier; **b24** I need not have checked the age of this one. For some reason 17 years so often appears to agree with this distillery... especially when in wood as good as this. *54%. sc. 195 bottles.*

Scotch Malt Whisky Society Cask 3.168 Aged 11 Years 1st fill sherry butt, cask no. 390008, dist 1999 **(84) n22 t21 f21 b20.** The deluge of dripping oloroso combines lopsidedly with the smoke to make for a clean, chewy, but, ultimately, ungainly dram. *60.4%. sc. 269 bottles.*

Scotch Malt Whisky Society Cask 3.169 Aged 16 Years refill sherry butt, cask no. 562, dist 1994 **(83.5) n21 t21 f20.5 b21.** Fails to hit a rhythm so even its usual cough sweet persona is only partially developed. As Ed Reardon might observe: less a Fisherman's Friend, more a holiday acquaintance. *56.6%. sc. 589 bottles.*

Scotch Malt Whisky Society Cask 3.176 Aged 20 Years refill barrel, cask no. 1181, dist 1990 **(87.5) n22 t20 f23.5 b22.** An unusual malt which takes a great amount of time to come to terms with its age. But when it gets there, it makes every moment count. *49.4%. sc. 51 bottles.*

Scotch Malt Whisky Society Cask 3.177 Aged 9 Years 1st fill barrel, cask no. 800538, dist. 2001 **(92.5) n22.5** lazy but somehow stirring layers of smoke. Charmingly gristy; **t23.5** excellent balance between the sugars and burgeoning spicy phenols; outstanding mouthfeel and a degree of oil; **f23** a surprising injection of late oak ramps up the vanilla and confirms the 1st fill pedigree; some citrus clings to the gorgeously weighted smoke; **b23.5** Bowmore at its most benign and beautifully made and matured. *61.3%. sc. 223 bottles.*

·:·:· **Scotch Malt Whisky Society Cask 3.179 Aged 21 Years** refill hogshead, cask no. 2808, dist 1990 **(88) n21.5** untidy, higgledy-piggledy nose which refuses to find a rhythm; **t22.5** a bigger delivery than expected and wonderfully juicy, too; the mid ground goes mocha while the smoke begins upping the ante; **f22** now pure cocoa...with very indulgent smoke for a Bowmore; **b22** you just can't beat a glass of smoked chocolate! *50.3%. sc.*

·:·:· **Scotch Malt Whisky Society Cask 3.181 Aged 15 Years** refill hogshead, cask no. 2773, dist 1996 **(86) n22 t22 f20 b22.** Well made, but for all the rich sugars embedded in the smoke, it is let down by a less than wonderful piece of oak. *60.5%. sc.*

⊹ **Scotch Malt Whisky Society Cask 3.185 Aged 16 Years** refill hogshead, cask no. 803, dist 1995 **(92) n23** much friskier smoke than the norm from Bowmore: a charming crispness is laced with gooseberry jam and orange segment; **t24** mmmm! No less sexy on delivery and is aided with a perfect degree of oil; the smoke is now less up front but delicate spices and those sweet gooseberry and sharper citrus notes cover the mid ground well; **f22** loses momentum as the oak digs deep; **b23** now that is rather good... *57.3%. sc.*

⊹ **Scotch Malt Whisky Society Cask 3.189 Aged 14 Years** refill butt, cask no. 2407, dist 1997 **(63) n15 t17 f14 b15.** How such a fatally sulphured malt got anywhere near bottling is beyond me. *58.4%. sc.*

⊹ **Scott's Selection Bowmore 1991** bott 2012 **(89.5) n22** no Bowmore from this period is complete without at least a hint of Fisherman's Friend and here it can be detected alongside the crisp sugars; **t23** lovely delivery with a texture to die for. The mid ground offers a charming nuttiness which adds to the sweet barley and drier phenol complexity; **f22** a surprising degree of standard vanilla, though some smoke lasts the course alongside the spice; **b22.5** a lovely bottling very true and sympathetic to the distillery style. *54.6%. Speyside Distillers.*

⊹ **Silver Seal Bowmore Over 16 Years Old** dist 1995 **(88.5) n22** a few primroses and bluebells in the earthy lead; **t23** early sugars, some of them distinctly molassed and toasty; **f21.5** attractive vanillas come out to play; some late salt; **b22** never an easy distillery to get the measure of, this is a pretty steady ship. *54%. sc. Silver Seal Whisky Company.*

Vom Fass Bowmore 13 Years Old (91.5) n23 delicate, sugar-shrouded smoke; **t23** one of the most mouth-watering peaty malts you are likely to encounter this year. Fabulous barley has no problem being heard while the peat adds both a light anchoring role and something to get your teeth into; **f22** a touch of tired cask bitterness evident but the sugars cock a sweetening snook; **b23.5** it is probably near impossible to locate a Bowmore more true to the distillery than this. A gem of its type. *40%*

The Whisky Agency Bowmore 1993 (87.5) n22 clean with oak having surprisingly little impact on the higher-than-usual peat; **t22.5** all kinds of citrus amid the smoky embers; **f21.5** the sugars recede exposing the vanilla; **b22** makes a mockery of its age by acting only half its years. And that's no bad thing... *53.8%. The Whisky Agency*

The Whisky Agency Bowmore 1995 bott 2010 **(76) n18 t21 f18 b19.** An unfortunate cask, whose faults will, to some, be obscured by the swirling smoke. *54.1%.*

The Whisky Agency Bowmore 1998 bott 2010 **(77.5) n18.5 t21 f19 b19.** Sugary sweet, smoky and virtually colourless for its age. No perceivable complexity. Throw a whisky into an inert cask and you'll get an inert dram. *51.8%. The Whisky Agency.*

⊹ **The Whisky Broker Bowmore 14 Years Old** refill bourbon barrel, cask no. 800229, dist 23 Jun 97, bott 20 Oct 11 **(95.5) n23.5** if it wasn't for a dash of chocolate, the delicate smoke and honey would point me to another island; **t24** the delivery offers sublime balance: all kinds of acacia and clear honey tones brought down to earth by a light nimble of smoke. Do we have the right distillery here? **f24** remains lush and the citrus notes move from an original lemony deftness to a heavier kumquat. This is all encased in gorgeous Venezuelan chocolate to turn the finale into a high quality, lightly spiced candy bar; **b24** what it misses in smoke it makes up for in honey! Almost an HP in disguise. A must have malt! *55%. nc ncf sc. 183 bottles.*

Wilson & Morgan Barrel Selection Bowmore Twenty Years Old cask no. 72555/56, dist 1989, bott 2010 **(86) n22 t22 f21 b21.** Distilled from smoked granite... *46%*

BRAEVAL

Speyside, 1974. Chivas Brothers. Working.

Chieftain's Braeval Aged 13 Years petrus gaia finish, dist Nov 98, bott 2011 **(71.5) n18 t18 f17 b17.5.** In the whisky game, you wine finish at your peril. *43%. nc ncf. Ian Macleod.*

⊹ **Duncan Taylor Dimensions Braes Of Glenlivet 22 Years Old** cask no. 979, dist May 89, bott Dec 11 **(90.5) n22** Speyside in a sniff...; **t23.5** ...and on the palate, too, so clean and vivid is the grassy barley; plenty of light chewing thanks to the sugared vanilla; **f22** a continuation of the same mega clean notes...; **b23** the kind of just-right dram which brings tears of joy to the eye. *55.4%. nc ncf sc. Duncan Taylor & Co.*

Fortnum & Mason Braeval Aged 9 Years (91) n23.5 magnificent: the ginger also appears to have a distant hint of juniper attached. But the butterscotch barley shines brightest; **t23** effortlessly elegant. The barley makes a carefree entrance and appears to pick up some oils and sugared vanilla along the way; **f22** the oaks begin to make a noise; **b22.5** another touch of understated class in Piccadilly. *40%. nc ncf. Fortnum & Mason.*

⊹ **Mo Ór Collection Braeval 1995 15 Years Old** first fill bourbon hogshead, cask no. 186019, dist 12 Dec 95, bott 5 Apr 11 **(84.5) n20.5 t22 f20.5 b21.5.** Surprisingly "milky" in style which belies its first fill pedigree. Huge barley statement on both nose and especially on delivery. But that oak... *46%. nc ncf sc. Release No. 39. The Whisky Talker. 480 bottles.*

Old Malt Cask Braes Of Glenlivet Aged 20 Years refill hogshead, cask no. 6383, dist May 90, Jul 10 **(80) n19.5 t19 f22 b19.5.** Struggles early on. But the stupendous malt present, aided by some sterling cocoa, makes a pleasant experience of it. *50%. nc ncf sc. 329 bottles.*

Premier Barrel Braeval Aged 11 Years sherry cask **(89.5) n22.5 t23 f21.5 b22.5.** A deceptively complex and weighty Speysider. *46%. nc ncf sc. 298 bottles.*

Provenance Braeval Over 11 Years refill hogshead, cask no. 6293, dist Spring 99, bott Summer 2010 **(81) n20 t20 f20.5 b20.5.** The mocha from the middle through to the finish emphasises the surprising lack of meat on the bone. *46%. nc ncf sc. Douglas Laing & Co.*

Provenance Braeval Over 11 Years sherry butt, cask no. 6886, dist Autumn 99, bott Winter 2010 **(75.5) n19 t19 f18.5 b19.** Thin but with some biscuity barley: never quite gets off the ground. *46%. nc ncf sc. Douglas Laing & Co.*

⠿ **Provenance Braeval Over 11 Years** refill butt, cask no. 7596, dist Autumn 1999, bott Summer 2011 **(85) n21.5 t21 f21.5 b21.** Pleasant and biscuity. A kind of 52 proof Ovaltine. *46%. nc ncf sc. Douglas Laing & Co.*

⠿ **Provenance Braeval Over 12 Years** sherry butt, cask no. 8011, dist Autumn 1999, bott Winter 2012 **(84.5) n21.5 t22 f20 b21.** One of the weightiest Braevals ever bottled. Thick, malty and with plenty of chewy fudge. *46%. nc ncf sc. Douglas Laing & Co.*

Vom Fass Braeval 11 Years Old (86) n22 t22 f21 b21. Excellent ginger and butterscotch mix with light spices and a buttery body. Tasty. *40%*

The Whisky Castle Distilled in the Park Braeval "Cairngorm's Dew" (92) n23 marmalade on toast intertwining with walnut oil; **t23.5** ultra soft delivery with the barley in fresh, creamy form melting alongside a light coating of Golden Syrup; **f22.5** long thanks to the oils with the barley, alongside the vanilla, proud to the end; **b23** this distillery is capable of producing a cracking malt: here's proof. *46%. nc ncf sc. Douglas Laing & Co for The Whisky Castle.*

BRORA
Highlands (Northern), 1819–1983. Diageo. Closed.

Brora 25 Year Old 7th Release bott 2008 db **(96) n24** even with the lowest peating levels you ever have nosed from this distillery, the aura of beauty is unmistakable: the soft phenol molecules appears to be perfectly matched with the oak ones. Meanwhile fragile citrus ensures a youthful charm; somewhere there is a hint of bourbon; **t24.5** superb barley kick off, absolute waves of juices running about the palate, and still the smoke holds back, no more than a background murmur; as the middle fills, that bourbon on the nose become more pronounced with shades of honeyed liquorice; **f23.5** long, with the sugars hanging in there allowing the vanillas to form very slowly; **b24** as the distillery closed in March 1983, if memory serves me correctly, this must be coming to the end of the road for the true 25-year-old. Those looking for the usual big peat show might be disappointed. Others, in search of majesty, sophistication and timeless grace, will be blown away. *56.3%*

Brora 30 Years Old db **(97) n24 t25 f24 b24.** Here we go again! Just like last year's bottling, we have something of near unbelievable beauty with the weight perfectly pitched and the barley-oak interaction the stuff of dreams. And as for the peat: an entirely unique species, a giant that is so gentle. Last year's bottling was one of the whiskies of the year. This even better version is the perfect follow-up. *56.4%*

Brora 30 Years Old Special Release refill American and European oak db **(89) n22** the smoke is receding like a balding pate and exotic fruit is taking its place...; **t23.5** the juiciest of juicy barley; the most exotic of exotic fruits; the most delicate of delicate spices, the most non-existent of smoke; **f21.5** practically yawning, so tired is it. But the custard sweetness mixes beautifully with the spice; **b22** seeing as I was the guy who proudly discovered this whisky over 20 years ago, I take more than a keen interest. But like a loved and cherished old relative, you can still adore its personality and unique independence but be aware that it is slowly fading away... *54.3%. nc ncf. Diageo. 2958 bottles.*

⠿ **Brora 32 Years Old Special Release 2011** db **(89) n22** toffee and orange peel; **t23** a delicate smoke creeps in through the back door of the delivery, which concentrates mainly on the same caramels which dominate the nose; the sawdusty vanilla leaves little doubt to the oak's powers; **f22** strained ulmo honey; **b22** a strange bottling containing more natural caramels from a Brora than I have ever before seen. Obviously a dumbing down effect is inevitable but enough of the original beauty remains to enthral. *54.7%. nc ncf.*

⠿ **Chieftain's Brora Aged 30 Years** sherry butt, cask no. 1523, dist Dec 81 **(88.5) n22** relaxed smoke lets in the fruit cocktail; **t23** the delivery surprises: far more caramel than the nose suggests, though this soon melts and helps along the golden syrup and over-ripe greengage for the softest of experiences; **f21.5** just becomes a tad bland as the caramels take too great a stranglehold; **b22** when the oak decides to go on the attack, even the world's greatest spirits can offer so much resistance. But as one of the world's great spirits you can be assured of some masterful complexity along the way, if only fleetingly. *54.6%. nc ncf sc. USA exclusive.*

⁙ **Chieftain's Brora Aged 30 Years** sherry butt, dist Dec 81, bott 2012 **(96) n24** when you find a near perfect sherry butt these days it is a moment for almost lump in the throat joy. The way the apricot and unripe peach and juicy mango intermingles with the spicy yet earthy peat: we are talking faultless weight and major complexity here; **t24.5** no letting up of complexity here either. There is a blend of honeys – orange blossom and thyme – which link fingers and dance around the phenols which slowly transform into praline and walnut...wow! **f23.5** long, with those walnut oils lingering and softening the late phenolic glow; **b24** a malt of a lifetime which barely puts a foot wrong. Magnificent. *50%. nc ncf sc. Ian Macleod Distillers.*

BRUICHLADDICH
Islay, 1881. Rémy Cointreau. Working.

Bruichladdich 10 Years Old db **(90) n22** beautifully clean and zesty, the malt is almost juvenile; **t23** sweet, fruity then malty charge along the tastebuds that geets the mouth salivating; **f23** the usual soft vanilla and custard but a bigger barley kick in the latter stages; **b22** more oomph than previous bottlings, yet still retaining its fragile personality. Truly great stuff for a standard bottling. *46%*

Bruichladdich 12 Years Old 2nd Edition db **(88) n23** big barrage of fruit; crisp barley beautifully integrates with oak; **t22** an uneven, mildly uncertain, delivery due to the grape being out of sync with the big barley; give it about eight-ten seconds and they have found a delicious degree of harmony; **f22** long with the intense, chiselled flavours still slightly at odds, but calming down with some oils; **b21** a similar type of wine involvement to "Waves", but this is oilier in the old-fashioned 'Laddie style and lacks a little of the sparkle. The fruit on the finish is outstanding, though, and I don't think you or I would turn down a third glass... *46%*

Bruichladdich 15 Years Old 2nd Edition db **(86) n22 t23 f20 b21.** Delicious, as usual, but something, possibly fruity, appears to be holding back the show. *46%*

Bruichladdich 16 Years Old bourbon cask db **(89) n22.5** sweet barley hangs from sturdy oak beams; **t22.5** remains firm yet sweet with a charming honeyed streak; again the oak plays a major role but its obvious dry input remains contained; **f22** dries further, with vanilla replacing the honey; some superb spices; **b22** plucked from the cask in the nick of time. In this state rather charming, but another Summer or two might have seen the oak take a more sinister turn. *46%*

Bruichladdich 16 Years Old bourbon/Chateau d'Yquem cask db **(95) n24** if you've got a good half an hour to spend, try using it intelligently by sticking your nose in this for a while: the grape is sweet and sultana juicy; the understated spices somehow hit just the right point to satisfy grape, oak and barley in one hit: some achievement... **t23.5** sweet, as the nose suggests, but the arrival is not all about grape. That sweetness also contains pristine barley... **f23.5** just so soft and subtle with the vanillas offering a discreet escort to the barley-grape marriage; **b24** possibly the most delicate and understated of all the truly great whiskies of the year. Not one for the ice and water brigade. *46%*

Bruichladdich 16 Years Old bourbon/Chateau Haut Brion cask db **(81.5) n21 t21.5 f19 b20.** fruity and busy for sure. But just not the kind of wine barrel effect that does much for me. I'm afraid, not least because of the background buzz on the palate. *46%*

Bruichladdich 16 Years Old bourbon/Chateau Lafite cask db **(89) n24 t22.5 f21.5 b21.5.** Ridiculously soft. Could just do with an injection of something to propel it into greatness. *46%*

Bruichladdich 16 Years Old bourbon/Chateau Lafleur cask db **(92.5) n23 t23.5 f23 b23.** So luminous on the palate, it's positively Lafleurescent... *46%*

Bruichladdich 16 Years Old bourbon/Chateau Latour cask db **(84.5) n21 t21.5 f21 b21.** Enjoyable. But there is a strange aggression to the spice which doesn't altogether sit as comfortably as it might. The fruit heads off into not just grapey but citrus territory, but there is a always a but about the direction it takes... *46%*

Bruichladdich 16 Years Old bourbon/Chateau Margaux cask db **(78.5) n20.5 t20 f19 b19.** Not 1st Cru Bruichladdich, I'm afraid. *46%*

Bruichladdich XVII Aged 17 Years bourbon/renegade rum db **(92) n23** typical rum "clipped" nose; this one with just a shade of soft, dry rubber typical of certain Guyana (especially Enmore) or Barbados marks; a rather lovely lemon tint to the vanilla works a treat; **t23.5** super dry delivery, too, with the sugars taking time to arrive. When they do, they weld with the barley attractively; formidable balance between the barley and spices while a light sprinkling of salt seems to up the spicy oak input to counter the sugars; **f22** mainly dry and attractively layered with short, sweet bands; **b23.5** always good to see the casks of drier, more complexly structured rums being put to such intelligent use. My sample doesn't tell me which rum casks were used, but I was getting vivid flashbacks here of Ruby-Topaz Hummingbirds flitting from flower to flower in the gardens of the now closed Eigflucht distillery in Guyana in the long gone days when I used to scramble around the warehouses there. That distinctive dryness though is pure Enmore, though some Barbadian rum can offer a similar effect. Something very different and a top quality experience. *46%. nc ncf.*

Bruichladdich 18 Years Old bourbon/cognac cask db **(84.5) n23.5 t21 f20 b20.** Big oak-spice buzz but thin. Sublime grapey nose, for sure, but pays a certain price, ultimately, for associating with such an inferior spirit... 46%

Bruichladdich 18 Years Old bourbon/opitz cask db **(80.5) n19 t22 f19.5 b20.** Dry, complex; at times oak-stretched. 46%

Bruichladdich 18 Years Old 2nd Edition bourbon/jurancon db **(86) n22 t21.5 f21 b21.5.** Plenty of fruit, including medium ripe greengages and slightly under-ripe grape. Juicy and sweet in the right places. 46%

Bruichladdich Flirtation Aged 20 Years 2nd Edition db **(86) n21 t22 f22 b21.** Hi sugar! A Laddie for those with a sweet tooth. 46%

Bruichladdich 21 Years Old oloroso cask db **(76.5) n18.5 t21 f18 b19.** Oops! 46%

⫶⫶⫶ **Bruichladdich Black Art 3rd Edition Aged 22 Years** db **(83) n22 t21.5 f20 b20.5.** Where last year' Black Art II managed to get away with the odd slight off note due to its brain-exploding enormity, this year it just hasn't got what it takes to get over the hurdles. Some sumptuous fruit through the middle, but it just ain't enough... 48.7%. nc ncf.

Bruichladdich 32 Years Old DNA 1977 bourbon cask db **(94.5) n23** there are so many bourbon tags on this, especially the waxiness to the honey, that just for a fleeting, off-guard moment I thought I was back nosing Kentucky whisky again. Then a giveaway salty tang coupled with a delicate hint of barley reminded me that I was in the land where the bagpipe abounds...; **t24** ridiculous! I mean, bloody outrageous! No whisky has the right to a delivery that perfect with the lightly oiled texture seemingly holding both oak and grain in equal measures. Buttery and rich, it then pans out back towards Kentucky with some liquorice and threads of honey. Then propels back to Scotland with a uniquely salty toffee middle; **f23.5** relatively easy going and simplistic. But the cream toffee hangs in there and then a late breakdown of almost clichéd bourbon notes from honey to hickory...; **b24** absolutely top of the range, profound and virtually faultless whisky which makes you remember the reason why you fell so deeply in love with this stuff all those many years ago. How fitting that when this was made Laddie was the Scotch distillery closest to America. For this is as much a bourbon in style as Scotch. But who cares? It doesn't matter: great whisky is great whisky. Full stop. 474%

Bruichladdich 37 Years Old DNA 80% bourbon/20% sherry cask, aged in Le Pin wine casks db **(87) n23.5** a beautiful, if potentially dodgy, counter between some gray-haired oak and pre-pubescent grape; **t22** nothing is settled with this one: the oak charges about in one direction, grapey waves soothes in another. A real flavour factory, especially with some light mocha in the middle ground, but don't look for a story here; **f20.5** a bit bitter, furry and nibbling; **b21** balance..? What balance...? Actually, somehow, this crazy thing does find some kind of equilibrium... 41%

Bruichladdich 1984 Golder Still bourbon cask, db **(88.5) n22 t23 f22 b21.5.** A huge amount of natural caramels leached from the oak does the joint job of ensuring extraordinary softness and eroding the higher notes. Still, there is enough eye-rolling honey and spice to keep anyone happy and the rich bourbony character on delivery really is dreamy stuff. 51%

Bruichladdich 1984 Redder Still db **(95.5) n23.5 t24 f23.5 b24.5.** Now it's finding whiskies like this that I became the world's first-full time whisky for. I dreamed of discovering drams which stretched my tastebuds and spoke to me with eloquence, charisma and unmistakable class. This is one such whisky: the style is highly unusual; the cleverness of the layering almost unique. This is the kind of near flawless whisky for which we were given tastebuds. Oh, and a nose... 50.4%

Bruichladdich 1989 db **(75.5) n20 t19 f17.5 b19.** Ouch! 52.9%. Special bottling for Alberta.

Bruichladdich 1989 Black Art 2nd Edition bourbon cask db **(95) n24** a thick fruit composite of probably the juiciest dates you'll find south of the Sahara and a dense hickory and honey strain of bourbon... Not just compelling. But absolutely magnificent...and just so right!!! Sulphur? Can it be? Yes, no...? Can't quite make it out...; **t24** how many deliveries allow the spice ahead of the main thrust? Perhaps more accurately, alongside. Still pretty rare and the way in which the chocolate fruit and nut melts in with the honey and liquorice bourbon notes, you feel anything can happen; **f23** some wonderful oils helping those dates and now walnuts, too, all embedded in light cocoa, to their final spicy farewell; **b24** Bourbon cask, it says. Right. But how did those lush dates get in there? Also, there even appears to be the very faintest (and I mean the odd molecule) of sulphur. But so miniscule it does no damage whatsoever. This is a whisky that asks ten times more questions than it answers. Time, though, not to wonder why, but just bloody well enjoy, for this is one of the great whiskies of the year. 49.7%

Bruichladdich 1990 Aged 18 Years db **(85.5) n22.5 t21 f21 b21.** Enlivened by citrus and emboldened by soft salt. 46%

Bruichladdich 1990 Aged 18 Years cognac cask db **(81.5) n20.5 t21 f20 b20.** Wouldn't be a far greater benefit to the spirit world if Cognac was matured in a Bruichladdich cask...? 46%

Bruichladdich 1991 Aged 16 Years Chat Margaux finish db **(94) n23 t25 f22.5 b23.5.** A true Premier Cru malt...I have been almost certainly the most outspoken critic of whisky finishes: trust me, if they were all like this, you would never hear the merest clack of a dissenting typing key from me again... 46%

Bruichladdich 1991 Valinch Anaerobic Digestion 19 Years Old bourbon & madeira casks db **(96.5) n24.5** huge, yet cleverly weighted fruit with spiced boiled greengages oozing from the glass but very happy to allow golden syrup to share some of its limelight; **t24** if the nose was excellent, the delivery is of no less quality. A light, oily bed allows the grape and sugars to land gently, then a light spicy layer forms another level entirely. All the hallmarks of a juicy first fill Madeira cask at work here...and working well; **f24** perhaps drier than all else before with the spices chipping away and a burnt raisin sharpness mingling with the latent honey; virtually a never ending tale...; **b24** about 20 minutes ago I could name you 250 excellent reasons to go and visit this distillery. I can now name you 251...A potential world whisky of the year that manages to do just about everything right...!!! 52.5% ncf sc. Only available at distillery.

Bruichladdich 1992 Sherry Edition "Fino" Aged 17 Years bourbon/fino sherry db **(94) n23.5** dry, suety, spotted dick; in the background, dried dates lurk deliciously; wonderful balance; **t24** fabulously subtle malt-generated sweetness sits comfortably with a much drier, juicier sub-plot; the mouthfeel hovers around perfection with just enough light oil to grease the roof of the mouth and keep the barley in the ascendancy; **f23** lots to chew here as the vanillas offer a custardy edge, though sugars – whilst present - are at a premium. Again we are back to the dregs of dried dates; **b23.5** exceptionally good: a rare showing of Fino at its most sophisticated and unblemished. 46%. nc ncf.

Bruichladdich 1992 Sherry Edition Pedro Ximénez Aged 17 Years bourbon/PX db **(83) n22 t22 f18.5 b20.5.** My word, that grape really does fly relentlessly at the taste buds. Probably the hardest sherry type to get right and here it works pretty well for the most part. 46%. nc ncf.

Bruichladdich 1993 14 Years Old Bolgheri French oak db **(85.5) n23 t21 f21.5 b20.** The fabulous nose doesn't quite translate once on the palate The natural caramels and barley combo never quite gets it together with the grape. Now the nose: that's a different matter! 46%

Bruichladdich 1993 14 Years Old Sassicaia French oak db **(83) n20 t21 f20.5 b21.** From a too tight nose to a too limp body. Just not my sac... 46%

Bruichladdich 1994 Valinch Blandola bourbon/Chateau d'Yquem casks, dist Sep 94 db **(87) n21.5 t22.5 f21 b22.** A bit muddled here and there but, like the distillery and staff, no shortage of personality. 55.3%. Available only from Bruichladdich's distillery shop.

Bruichladdich 1994 "Kosher" Aged 12 Years db **(85.5) n22 t21 f21 b21.5.** Clean. What else, my dear? 46%

Bruichladdich 1998 db **(89) n22 t22.5 f22.5 b22.** A truly unique signature to this but absolute class in a glass. 46%

Bruichladdich 1998 bourbon/oloroso cask, dist 1998 db **(87.5) n22.5 t22.5 f21 b21.5** Surprisingly conservative. But, joy of joys, not an atom of sulphur to be found...!! 46%

Bruichladdich 1998 bourbon/Manzanilla cask, dist 1998 db **(82.5) n21 t21 f20 b20.5.** Fruity. But bitter where it should be sweet. 46%

Bruichladdich 1998 Ancien Regime db **(84.5) n22 t21.5 f20 b21** An easy, slightly plodding celebration of all things malty, caramelly, oily and vanillay... 46%

Bruichladdich 2001 Renaissance db **(91) n23** lively with the smoke and oak in particular going hammer and tongs; **t23** brilliant delivery! Varying fruit tones hit the palate running but there is a bit of barley reinforcement flexing some considerable muscle. But the star is the ubiquitous smoke which shows a gentle iron fist; **f22.5** a big surge of natural caramels but the spices make a scene; **b22.5** a Big Laddie. 46%

Bruichladdich 2001 The Resurrection Dram 23.10.01 bourbon cask, dist 2001, bott 2009 db **(90.5) n23** so subtle! Spiced sultana on malt, laced with golden syrup; **t23** grist dissolves in the mouth: molten (fruitless) barley again with a sugary sheen. Simplistic, but beautifully effective; **f21.5** long, vanilla-led, spiced and a little bitter; **b23** now, be honest. How can you not have a first class Resurrection in the Bible...? 46%. 24,000 bottles.

Bruichladdich 2004 Islay Barley Valinch fresh sherry butt db **(89.5) n22.5 t24 f21 b22.** Yet another quite fabulous bottling form Bruichladdich, this one really cranking up the flavours to maximum effect. Having said all that, call me mad if you will...but seeing as this is Islay barley, would it not have been a good idea to shove it into a bourbon barrel, so we could see exactly what it tastes like? Hopefully that is on its way... 57.5%

Bruichladdich Infinity Second Edition bourbon/rioja db **(94) n24 t24 f23 b23.** Wasn't it Daffy Duck who used to put on his cape and shout: "Infinity and Beyond" ? Oh, no... it was Buzz Lightyear. Anyways, he must have been thinking of this. And there's certainly nothing dethspicable about this one... 52.5%

Bruichladdich Infinity Third Edition refill cherry tempranillo db **(94.5) n24** the smokiness appears to have a life of its own: still cured bacon, as in previous Infinities (actually can there be such a thing...?) but perhaps a touch of Bavarian smoked cheese, perhaps, as a side dish, next to a freshly diced apple? I adore the lack of oils on the nose; the teasing dryness compensated by a distant fruit freshness; **t24** and its more of the same: just so dry, the palate is parched in seconds. The smoke is ashy, the vanilla is powdery, the malt gristy...just flakes of flavour wafting into every crevice like snow falling on a silent day; **f23** long, with the inevitable build up of dry, powdery spices which match the vanilla for weight and impact; **b23.5** I dare anybody who says they don't like smoky whisky not to be blown away by this. Go on...I dare you... *50%*

⠿⠿ **Bruichladdich Islay Barley Aged 5 Years** db **(86) n21 t22.5 f21.5 b21.** The nose suggests a trainee has been let loose at the stills. But it makes amends with an almost debauched degree of barley on delivery which lasts the entirety of the experience. Heavens! This is different. But I have to say: it's bloody fun, too! *50%. nc ncf.*

Bruichladdich Laddie Classic Edition 1 db **(89.5) n23** salt-lashed and coastal, the barley is shimmering in the glass; **t23** a big barley delivery, but also enjoying a thick, almost fruit-cakey sub-plot, with dark, molassed depth. The piquancy seems to be maximised by the lingering salt; **f21** a degree of bitterness amid the barley caramels; **b22.5** you probably have to be a certain vintage yourself to fully appreciate this one. Hard to believe, but I can remember the days when the most popular malt among those actually living on Islay was the Laddie 10. That was a staunchly unpeated dram offering a breezy complexity. Not sure of the age on this Retroladdich, but the similarities almost bring a lump to the throat... *46%*

Bruichladdich Legacy Series 3 Aged 35 Years db **(91) n22 t22.5 f23.5 b23.** So they managed to find a whisky exactly the same age as Ladie distiller Jim. *40.7%*

Bruichladdich Links "Carnoustie" 14 Years Old db **(78) n19 t20 f19 b20.** Hits some unexpected rough. *46%*

Bruichladdich Links K Club Ireland "16th Hole" 14 Years Old bourbon/syrah, dist 1992, bott 2007 db **(93) n23 t23 f23 b24.** I quite like this, though as hard as I try I can't quite love it. The spices offer great entertainment value and the juiciness on delivery is astonishing, but... My tongue is investigating every crevice in my mouth with some urgency, so I know it's complex – and very unusual, but... It's gossamer light. It kind of teases you. It's playful. But it's not beautiful. Is it...? Third mouthful in and I'm getting hooked. Oh, sod it! I've just upped it from a 86 to 93. What can I do? I'm in love... *46%. nc ncf. 12,000 bottles.*

Bruichladdich Links "Torrey Pines" 15 Years Old db **(89.5) n23 t22.5 f22 b22.** As clean as the perfect tee shot from the 15th... *46%*

Bruichladdich Organic 2003 Anns An T-Seann Doigh bourbon db **(84.5) n22 t22 f20 b20.5.** Thick barley carrying a soft smoke. A slight bitterness threads in and out of the proceedings. *46%. nc ncf. 100% Scottish barley.*

Bruichladdich Organic Multi Vintage bourbon cask db **(87.5) n22** subtle smoke; elements of grist; delicate citrus; **t22** sweet delivery but an immediate bitter-ish back up; coffee ice cream fills the middle; **f20.5** soft oils develop, as does the bitter tang; **b22** genteel. *46%*

Bruichladdich Peat db **(89.5) n23** peat; **t22.5** peat; **f22** peat; **b22** peaty. *46%*

Bruichladdich Rocks db **(82) n19 t22 f20 b21.** Perhaps softer than you'd imagine something called "rocks"! Beautiful little malty charge on entry. *46%*

Bruichladdich Sherry Classic Fusion: Fernando de Castilla bourbon/Jerez de la Frontera db **(91) n23 t23 f22 b23.** What a fantastically stylish piece of work! I had an overwhelming urge to sing Noel Coward songs while tasting this: for the Dry Martini drinkers out there who have never thought of moving on to Scotch... *46%*

Bruichladdich Waves db **(81.5) n20.5 t21.5 f19.5 b20.** Not sure if the tide is coming in or out on this one. Got various sugar and spice aspects which appeals, but there is something lurking in the depth that makes me a little uneasy... *46%*

Bruichladdich WMD II - The Yellow Submarine 1991 db **(75) n20 t19 f18 b18.** This one just doesn't have the balance and sinks. *46%*

Bruichladdich X4 db **(82) n18 t22 f21 b21.** Frankly, like no new make I have ever come across in Scotland before. Thankfully, the taste is sweet, malty and compact: far, far better than the grim, cabbage water nose. Doesn't really have the X-Factor yet, though. *50%*

Bruichladdich X4 +3 Quadruple Distilled 3 Aged Years bourbon db **(86) n21.5 t22 f21 b21.5.** It is as if the sugars in the barley have been reduced to their most intense form: this is all about huge barley of eye-watering intensity. A novel and not unattractive experience. *63.5%. nc ncf. 15,000 bottles.*

⠿⠿ **The Laddie Ten** American oak db **(94.5) n24** a stunning balance between sea spray, the most delicate liquorice and hickory imaginable and blemish-free barley; **t23.5** no let down on delivery with the barley and delicate sugars hand in hand for the first three or four very big flavour waves; the middle has an oaky richness that is not a single hint of weary dryness: gorgeously weighted and rich without over sweetening; **f23** at last the salts form, as do the vanillins and slightly coarser oaky notes. Retains that distinctly coastal feel; **b24** this, I assume, is the 2012 full strength version of an Islay classic which was the preferred choice of the people of Islay throughout the 70s, 80s and early 90s. And I have to say that this is already a classic in its own right.... *46%. nc ncf.*

Octomore 5 Years Old db (96) n23.5 seeing how Octomore is actually a farm on Islay, it is rather fitting that the massive peat here yields a distinctly farm-yardy aroma. Yet this is curiously low on peat reek for a dram boasting phenomenal phenols at 131 parts per million – Ardbeg is about 50; the much smokier PC7 is just 40. That said, obviously peaty, yet an age-related lemon lightness, too...and a herd of cattle...; t24.5 the oils are absolutely perfect, as is the slow unfurling of the myriad strata of peat; those youthful, zesty, citrus notes have been enriched with a perfect degree of golden syrup; a near-perfect sprinkling of spice enriches further...; f24 a wonderful array of vanillas lighten not just the peat but the sweetened mocha which is now making its mark. Long, relaxed and very assured for a malt so young... b24 forget about the age. Don't be frightened by the phenol levels. Great whisky is not about numbers. It is about excellent distillation and careful maturation. And here you have a memorable combination of both... *63.5%*

Octomore Edition 2.1 Aged 5 Years (140 ppm) bourbon cask, bott Jun 09 db (94) n23 a snug nose of tight, thick peat: needs a chainsaw to cut through it; t24 surprisingly sweet delivery with more than a hint of citrus: a massive gristy surge which is about as mouth-watering as heavily peated malt ever gets; the smoke is all enveloping; f23 long with some vanilla at last getting into the act; some excellent late mocha and marzipan thins the smoke; b23 talk about a gentle giant: as though your taste buds are being clubbed to death by a ton of smoky feathers. *62.5%. nc ncf. 15,000 bottles.*

Octomore Edition 2.2 "Orpheus" Aged 5 Years (140 ppm) bourbon/chateau Petrus, bott 2009 db (96.5) n24 when you clean out the ashes of fire that had been fed 100% by peat, that morning after the night before task, this is what you get. Well, partially. You will have to have one hand in the grate, the other around a glass of Petrus...; t24.5 let's get this right: 140ppm phenols? Check. 61% abv? Check. How then, can the landing on the palate be like jumping onto a bed of feathers? The Demerara-gristy sweetness helps. So does the smoke, which envelopes the mouth. But the peat is also dry and that means a magnificent balance with those gristy sugars, so all seems to be in harmony. Brilliant! f23.5 long, and just a gentle wind down of all before. Maybe a bit of extra fruit visible later on, as well as some Liquorice Allsorts; b24.5 a standing ovation for this massive performance...the quite perfect way to bring up my 900th new whisky for the 2011 Bible. Everything works; the age and freshness of the barley, the controlled enormity of the smoke...even the entirely sulphur-free wine barrel. For those with a lot of hair on their chest...and want even more. *61%. 15,000 bottles.*

Octomore 3rd Edition Aged 5 Years bourbon cask db (95) n24.5 as someone who grew up in the countryside and, to this day, spends as much of what little spare time I get traipsing around fields and farmsteads, this is an aroma I know too well...cowsheds! Except here there is that extra element of peat, but that intense sweetness is unmistakable: It may only be a young 'un, and the youth is noticeable, but it remains one of the most distinguished and most flawless of all Scotland's whisky aromas...; t24 as soft to the palate as a view of the sea from Port Charlotte is to the eye... The peat does not compromise, yet nor does it bully, allowing any amount of Demerara sugars to form and intensify with the vanilla and natural caramels from, I suspect, from first fill oak; f23 much quieter than you might expect from the nose, but there is a touch of the Horlicks about the finale; b23.5 I usually taste this late on in the Bible writing cycle: it is so important to be rewarded at the end of a long journey. This hasn't let me down and here's the rub: how something which looms so large be made from so many traits so small...? *59%*

Octomore 4th Edition Aged 5 Years (167 ppm) db (92) n21.5 hardly believable as an Octomore: the smoke appears locked in a caramel bubble...; t23.5 sheer power seems to allow the smoke to burst away from its shackles, but it has to work hard. But there is none of the normal peaty dryness. Instead we are directed towards a delicious praline thread with the nut oils building and a non-specific fruitiness offering little more than a hint; f23.5 80% cocoa smoked chocolate...outrageous! b23.5 Choctomore, surely? *62.5%*

⁙ **Octomore 10** db (95) n24 have I ever mentioned cowsheds? This is David and Ruth Archer's threatened milking parlour...but without the milk...awww nawooo..! t24 as ever, smoke...like someone's set fire to the barn...awww nawooo!; f23 the most intense of all finishes, as though the excess of the cowshed has been drained by marauding badgers... awww nawoooo! b24 when I am tasting an Octomore, it means I am in the home straight inside the stadium after running (or should I say nosing and tasting) a marathon. After this, there is barely another 20 more Scotch malts to go and I am closing in on completing my 1,200 new whiskies for the year. So how does this fair? It is Octomore. It is what I expect and demand. It gives me the sustenance and willpower to get to that crossing line. For to tell you guys about a whisky like this is always worth it...whatever the pain and price. Because honesty and doing the right thing is beyond value. Just ask David Archer... *50%. nc ncf.*

Port Charlotte An Turas Mor Multi Vintage bourbon cask db **(85.5) n23 t22 f20 b20.5** Does much right, especially the intriguing bullying of the colossal peat over what probably passes for grape. But bitters out and struggles to find a balance or plot line to keep you wanting to discover more. *46%*

Port Charlotte PC6 db **(96.5) n24.5** ohhhhhh... arrrrrrrhh... mmmmmmmmmm... oh, the peat, the peat... yesssss... oh my god... mmmmmmm... ohhhhhhh... **t24** first you get the smoky... ooooohhhhhhh... arrrrrrrrr... then the sweeter... mmmmmmmm... arrrrooohhhh... **f24** it finishes with a more gentle arghoooo... mmmmmmm... oooophhhhhh... arrrrrrrrr... **24** not many whiskies have a truly unmistakable nose... and... but this is, this... is... this... mmmmmmmm..., arrrrrhh. Ohhhhhhhh... *61.6%*

Port Charlotte PC7 dist 2001 db **(93.5) n24** dry. The most profound peat fire ashes: not for peaty amateurs... **t24** a few drops of sweetness added; a liquorice/molassed melt to the massive smoke: the phenols seems a lot higher than the 40ppm they talk about; **f22** drops down a gear or two as some bitterness creeps in, as does a secondary fizz to the spice; **b22.5** not quite as orgasmic as last year, sadly. But should still be pretty stimulating... *60.5%*

Port Charlotte PC8 bourbon, dist 2001, bott 2009 db **(88) n22** the bourbon and smoke appear to be rather too in cahoots; **t23** beautifully rounded with the smoke taking off. But the oak is very caramel-centric and lacks complexity; **f21** cartloads of natural caramel; some injury time spice; **b22** enjoyable, but muted by PC standards... *60.5%. 30,000 bottles.*

Berry's Own Selection Bruichladdich 1991 cask no. 2996, bott 2011 **(78) n20 t21 f18 b19.** Malty, but the nose accurately foretells the bitter oak influence which is to follow later. *50.1%. nc ncf sc. Berry Bros & Rudd.*

⁙ **Cadenhead Bruichladdich 20 Years Old** bott Mar 12 **(91) n23** light and lithesome. Unbelievably grassy barley, seasoned with gorgeous sea salt; **t23.5** much oilier than can be detected on the nose. But that barley stays sharp and fresh and brimming with salty vanilla; **f22** does little to shift shape or tack. Just a thin layer of cocoa acknowledges the age; **b22.5** hard to imagine a whisky that outwardly does so little, yet says so much. Beautiful! *52.2%. sc.*

⁙ **Chieftain's Bruichladdich Aged 22 Years** hogshead, dist Apr 89 **(83) n21 t22 f20 b20.** Anyone who remembers the original old Bruichladdich 10-year-old will recognise the contours here. Except this has taken on far too much oak, especially towards the austere finale. *46%. nc ncf sc. Ian Macleod Distillers.*

⁙ **John Milroy Selection Bruichladdich 1992** cask no. 3791, bott 2012 **(88.5) n22** a seaside freshness to the clean barley; **t23** not just vivid barley but you can almost hear the gulls mewing: salty, tangy and as refreshing as a face-full of sea spray; **f21.5** calms down as natural caramels and fudge smother the natural fire; **b22** 'Laddie, old-fashioned style! *54.6%. nc ncf sc. Berry Bros & Rudd.*

⁙ **Liquid Sun Port Charlotte 2002** bott 2011 **(93) n23** beautifully distilled, the peat appears happy to take a back seat to the resplendent citrus notes; **t23.5** as though someone has distilled this from pure lemon juice and maple syrup, with a big chunk of peat tossed into the spirit still...; **f23** some residual spices add topsoil to the smoke and extraordinary citrus; **b23.5** I have never come across any whisky so bursting forth with such sexy citrus. Oh, the zest....the zest...yes...yesssss...oh, my God...!!! *53.5%. nc ncf sc. The Whisky Agency.*

Malts Of Scotland Port Charlotte 2001 zinfandel barrel, cask no. 969, dist Dec 01, bott May 10 **(95) n24 t24.5 f23.5 b24.** It didn't take long, but my taste buds soon hoisted the white flag on this one. Insane amounts of peat, a faultless wine barrel churning out thick fruit. Not the easiest experience to make sense of. But give the whisky time – and yourself to acclimatise – and it begins to make sense. Then it becomes truly unforgettable: an outrageous whisky which pays off...and with interest. *60.6%. nc ncf sc. Malts Of Scotland. Exclusive bottling for Whisky Fair Limburg 2010. 212 bottles.*

⁙ **Malts Of Scotland Port Charlotte 2001** white Rioja hogshead, cask no. MoS11017, dist Dec 01, bott Oct 11 **(88) n22** don't bother to look for harmony. The grape does its thing while the peat goes its own merry way...; **t23** now the two clash head on: at times it is spectacular! The sugars pulse, the smoke explodes, the grape whines...; **f21** not a great finale with the more volatile oily elements having the biggest say; **b22** It so doesn't work in so many ways... yet just so does in others...typical PC!! *66.3%. nc ncf sc.*

Malts Of Scotland Port Charlotte 2002 bourbon barrel, cask no. 77, dist May 02, bott Oct 10 **(93.5) n23 t24 f23 b23.5.** Some might say this one is for x-rated peat whisky lovers only. My message would be: if you don't like smoky whisky, see what you think when taking it to the max... Superb! *61.1%. nc ncf sc. Malts Of Scotland. 218 bottles.*

Malts Of Scotland Port Charlotte 2002 bourbon hogshead, cask no. 1172, dist Nov 02, bott Sep 09 **(85.5) n21.5 t21 f21.5 b21.5.** Heavily smoked cream toffee. *64.2%. nc ncf sc. Malts Of Scotland. 306 bottles.*

Old Malt Cask Bruichladdich 16 Years Old refill hogshead, cask no. 6384, dist Nov 93, bott Jul 10 **(84) n22 t22 f19 b21.** Charmingly light, gristy and simple. *50%. nc ncf sc. 346 bottles.*

Old Malt Cask Bruichladdich 20 Years Old refill hogshead, cask no. 6307, dist Nov 89, bott Jun 10 **(85.5) n23 t22 f19.5 b21.** Big malt statement with some salient saline. *50%. nc ncf sc. Douglas Laing & Co. 289 bottles.*

Old Masters Bruichladdich 20 Years Old cask no. 2493, dist 1991, bott Jun 11 **(90.5) n22.5 t23 f22.5 b22.5.** Faultlessly clean, simplistic malt which has been excellently distilled and matured. A treat. *51.5%. sc. James MacArthur & Co.*

Scotch Malt Whisky Society Cask 23.66 Aged 17 Years refill bourbon hogshead, cask no. 34, dist 1993 **(80) n20 t21 f19 b20.** Lots of malt and caramel. But steadfastly refuses to go anywhere interesting. *53.5%. sc. 217 bottles.*

Scotch Malt Whisky Society Cask 23.67 Aged 8 Years refill barrel, cask no. 520, dist 2002 **(86) n22 t21.5 f21 b21.5.** Sweet, moderately peated and has taken a surprisingly hefty amount of caramel from the oak. *62.5%. sc. 259 bottles.*

Scotch Malt Whisky Society Cask 23.69 Aged 17 Years 2nd fill hogshead, cask no. 1552, dist 1993 **(86.5) n20.5 t22.5 f21.5 b22.** A much happier malt than 23.66, having lived for 17 years in much classier surroundings. However, the view is quite similar and although the sugars make a healthy contribution to the wellbeing of the whisky, it is still frustratingly limited in its self expectation. *53.8%. sc. 270 bottles.*

⸪ **Scotch Malt Whisky Society Cask 23.70 Aged 9 Years** refill barrel, cask no. 755, dist 2001 **(96) n24** classically complex in the distillery's style with a bevy of varied salty notes adding a rich hue to the already beautifully structured liquorice and hickory tones. Somehow the barley manages to make a statement amid all this with commanding eloquence; **t24.5** the mouth doesn't so much water as flood: the barley is pristine and multi-dimensional while the oak makes impressive shapes of varying weight and intensity; **f23.5** long, and with the noticeable lack of oils. Both the barley and oak are given the most free reign possible to continue their complex and delightfully entertaining discussion...; **b24** stunning. Simply stunning...! And proof, not that it was ever needed, that you don't need peat to make an Islay whisky of truly world class stature. *66%. sc.*

Scotch Malt Whisky Society Cask 127.1 Aged 8 Years refill bourbon barrel, cask no 947, dist 2001 **(88.5) n21.5 t23 f21.5 b22.5.** Really enjoyable dramming. But you get the feeling the malt is working overtime to overcome a pretty average cask. *66.5%. sc. 231 bottles.*

Scotch Malt Whisky Society Cask 127.6 Aged 8 Years refill bourbon barrel, cask no. 842, dist 2001 **(82.5) n22 t21 f19.5 b20.** Compared to 127.1, just shows what a sluggish cask can do. Even the complex peat can't overcome the more bitter notes. *65.2%. sc. 231 bottles.*

Scotch Malt Whisky Society Cask 127.12 Aged 8 Years refill barrel, cask no. 383, dist 2002 **(86.5) n22 t22 f21 b21.5.** An enjoyable malt. But an excess of caramel makes it a little sluggish. *66.2%. sc. 160 bottles.*

⸪ **Scotch Malt Whisky Society Cask 127.15 Aged 9 Years** refill barrel, cask no. 388, dist 2002 **(94.5) n23** floral as well as peaty with evening primroses having an unusually telling say. Delicate, for all its obvious oily enormity; **t24** Those oils really do make an early impact. But when that dies down, an explosion of spiced sugars makes one almost groan in delight; **f23.5** long, almost ridiculously so, with the emphasis now on molten Mars bars, with the nougat and natural caramels blending in with the cocoa; **b24** there are a few seconds right in the middle of this which are as close to perfection as I have tasted this year... *65.9% sc*

⸪ **Scotch Malt Whisky Society Cask 127.10 Aged 9 Years** refill barrel, cask no. 374, dist 2002 **(89.5) n23** weighty, with a succession of bigger dark sugar notes, especially Demerara, having a major input; really excellent spice, too...; **t22.5** dry, bordering on the austere as the oils so prevalent in 127.15 surprisingly go AWOL. The sugars are crisper, the spices a little more blatant and warming; **f22** now generally spice dependent; **b22** a most curious bottling which concentrates on solo performances rather than the entire work. *66.1%. sc.*

⸪ **Scotch Malt Whisky Society Cask 127.19 Aged 9 Years** refill barrel, cask no. 384, dist 2002 **(89) n22.5** natural caramels have caught up with this and have made surprising inroads into the apparently shocked phenols; **t23** even on delivery, the tannins race ahead. The mid ground makes amends with a burst of frightening complexity as the sugars, phenols and tannins each claim higher ground; **f21.5** dulls with a smoked fudgy finale; **b22** a malt which peaks and troughs but always has something to keep the taste buds on full alert. *66%. sc.*

⸪ **Scotch Malt Whisky Society Cask 127.20 Aged 8 Years** refill barrel, cask no. 848, dist 2003 **(95.5) n23.5** coal dust mixes in readily with the peaty phenols; far more spices than is the norm ensure a degree of major complexity; **t24.5** the enormity of the nose prepares you for what is coming next. The delivery is something akin to an explosion in a munitions factory: the pyrotechnics leave you gasping as the spices dazzle to an almost blinding degree. As for the amalgam between the vanillas and sugars...well, if you wondered why we were ever given taste buds, now you know... **f24** the spices never less than pulse; the vanillas are always adding a custardy or butterscotch note here and there; the barley even at the death injects a juicy, gristy quality; **b23.5** back in the 1930s, the distillers at Ardbeg always claimed their malt was at peak perfection when it reached eight years of age. There is evidence here that the new regime at Bruichladdich can reasonably make the very same claim... 64.2%. sc.

Vom Fass Bruichladdich 20 Years Old (87.5) n22.5 t22 f21.5 b21.5. Best left in the glass for a while for the honeys to develop. 46%. sc.

Whisky Doris Port Charlotte 7 Year Old hogshead, cask no. 1171, dist Nov 02, bott Sep 10 **(82.5) n20 t21 f20.5 b21.** A crazy mixed up kid: the peats and caramels lurch drunkenly all over the palate. 63.5%. Whisky Doris.

BUNNAHABHAIN

Islay, 1881. Burn Stewart Distillers. Working.

Bunnahabhain 12 Years Old (Older Bottling) db **(80) n19 t21 f20 b20.** Pleasant in its own clumsily sweet, smoky way. But unrecognisable to the masterful, salty Bunna 12 of old. 43.3%. nc ncf.

Bunnahabhain Aged 12 Years db **(85.5) n20 t23 f21 b21.5.** Lovers of Cadbury's Fruit and Nut will adore this. There is, incongruously, a big bourbony kick alongside some smoke, too. A lusty fellow who is perhaps a bit too much of a bruiser for his own good. Some outstanding moments, though. But, as before, still a long way removed from the magnificent Bunna 12 of old... 46.3%. nc ncf.

Bunnahabhain Aged 16 Years Manzanilla Sherry Wood Finish db **(87) n20.5 t23 f21.5 b22.** The kind of undisciplined but fun malt which just makes it up as it goes along... 53.2%

Bunnahabhain Aged 18 Years (Older Bottling) db **(94) n24.5** chestnut colour and, fittingly, roast chestnut on the fruitcake nose: the health-conscious might say there is too much salt in the mix, but it works perfectly here...; **t24** outstanding oloroso with the clean, faultless grape dripping of the salty barley; the oak again offers a nutty background, while Demerara sugars form a crisp counter to the invading salt; burnt raisin underscores the fruitcake character; **f22.5** light mocha, as a very slight bitterness steels its way in; **b23** a triumph for the sherry cask and a reminder of just how good this distillery can be. It's been a long time since I've enjoyed a distillery bottling to this extent. 43%

Bunnahabhain Aged 18 Years db **(93.5) n24** a sumptuous amalgam of lightly salted roasted hazelnut shimmering within its own oil. Oloroso bulging with toasted, slightly singed currants, a sliver of kumquat and topped by thick vanilla. Irresistible... **t24.5** almost impossible to fault: the oloroso grandly, almost pompously, leads the way exuding thick, Christmas pudding depth; a light muscovado sugar top dressing counters the deeper, lightly salted vanillas which begin to emerge; **f22** a very slight sulphury note sullies the tone somewhat, but there is still enough rich vanilla and spotted dick for some enjoyable afters; **b23** only an odd cask has dropped this from being a potential award winner to something that is merely magnificent... 46.3%. nc ncf.

Bunnahabhain XXV Aged 25 Years (Older Bottling) db **(91.5) n23** hard to imagine a more coastal aroma than this: the grape tries to get a word in edgeways but the salt has formed a crusty doorway; what fruit does get through is top quality; **t23** excellent arrival, the grape forcing the pace but with a tell-tale tang of saltiness; busy with a sneaky arrival of malt through the middle; **f22.5** chocolate fruit and nut... and salt; **b23** an intense and fun-packed malt for those who like a fine sherry and a sea breeze. 43%

Bunnahabhain XXV Aged 25 Years db **(94) n23** you almost need a blow torch to cut through the oloroso, so thick is it. A little tight thanks to a minor distortion to a butt, but I am being picky. Salty and seaweedy, the ocean hangs in the air...; **t24** glorious weight and sheen to the delivery. The early balance is nearly perfect as the thick fruit is thinned by the proud barley. The early, contemplative sweetness, buttressed by a wonderful mixture of sultana and Demerara, gives way to the drier oaks and the tingly, chalky signs of a mildly treated butt; **f23** despite the winding down of the sugars the residual fruit manages to overcome the small obstacles placed before it; **b24** no major blemishes here at all. Carefully selected sherry butts of the highest quality (well, except maybe one) and a malt with enough personality to still gets its character across after 25 years. Who could ask for more...? 46.3%. nc ncf.

Bunnahabhain Cruach-Mhòna batch no.1 db **(83) n17.5 t24.5 f21 b20.** It appears that there is a new house style of being strangely and at times spectacularly off balance and less than brilliantly made, but making amends by offering a blistering maltiness which leaves one almost speechless. The delivery alone, with its light smokiness mixing in with the Demerara sugars and Grenadine spices, is the stuff of Islay legend. All else is bizarrely skewed and out of sync. Unique, for sure. 50% nc ncf.

Bunnahabhain Darach Ùr Batch no. 1 db **(87) n21.5 t22.5 f21 b22.** Almost milkshake thick. Not exactly a technical triumph but high marks for entertainment value! 46.3%

Bunnahabhain Darach Ùr Batch no. 4 db **(95) n24** good grief; as though matured in a barrel full of plump sultanas... but from the depth of sweetness, rather than the fruit...if you get my drift. Just a hint of spice as well as coconut and honey. Fabulous in a bourbon kind of salty, Hebridean way...; **t24.5** as thick and richly-textured as any malt you'll find this year. Intense, lightly salted barley is a match for the brimming, fruit-like sweetness; with a salivation factor which disappears through the roof, wonderful bourbon over- and undertones link wonderfully to the mega sugars attached to the vanilla; **f23** much drier with a tangy, kumquat fade but plenty of vigorous spice; **b23.5** because of my deep love for this distillery, with my association with it spanning some 30 years, I have been its harshest critic in recent times. This, though, is a stunner.. *46.3%. nc ncf.*

Bunnahabhain Toiteach db **(78) n19 t21 f19 b19.** Cloying, sweet, oily, disjointedly smoky. Had you put me in a time capsule at the distillery 30 years ago, whizzed me forward to the present day and given me this, it would have needed some serious convincing for me to believe this to be a Bunna. *46%*

Bunnahabhain Toiteach Un-Chillfiltered db **(75.5) n18 t21 f17.5 b19.** A big gristy, peaty confrontation on the palate doesn't hide the technical fault lines of the actual whisky. *46%. ncf.*

Adelphi Bunnahabhain 11 Years Old cask no. 6037, dist 1998, bott 2010 **(81) n19 t22 f20 b20.** Perhaps an interesting way to look at this whisky is how we might the condition of the average present day chap compared to his counterpart of a generation ago. It is agreed that, in the western world, there is a higher percentage of flabby individuals now than in the 1980s, where their condition is far from conducive to good health. Where there was once muscle and tone there is now fat and paunch. That somehow sums up this malt: Bunna, once upon a time, was an impressively taught individual, on whom the malt and salt was found in perfect proportion on its firm frame. Not of late. And though the sherried clothes it wears may well be Saville Row, what lies underneath could do with a major workout. *53.4%. sc. 538 bottles.*

Adelphi Bunnahabhain 31 Years Old cask no. 8893, dist 1979, bott 2011 **(95) n23.5** a classic oloroso butt, dripping with the juices of fat sultana over burnt raisin...the Demerara sugars help reinforce the Melton Hunt cake style. Barley at a premium but decent salt injection; **t24** wow! A volley of black cherry helps dissipate the bulging oak. Good aged bitterness – as opposed to negative, shagged out cask bitterness – goes alongside oloroso dryness and the whole chewy, mature fruitcake theme; as for the spices, the nutty layering, the glorious juiciness...where do I start...? **f23.5** even more black cherry, were that possible...! Those toasted raisins don't give up without a fight, either. **b24** as you know, I am not one for matching food with whisky. But this is already like a frazzled piece of Melton Hunt cake once might have originally found in Dickinson and Morris' Nottingham Street shop and left at the back of a cupboard for a few years. By which I mean...bloody scrummy! *46.5%. sc. 516 bottles.*

Berry's Own Selection Bunnahabhain 1990 cask no. 20, dist 2011 **(67) n17 t18 f16 b16.** Some of the sherry butts taken in at Bunna during these Highland Distillers days of the late 80s and early 90s were among some the most heavily sulphured in Scotland. You will find worse, but this is a fair example... *54.1%. nc ncf sc. Berry Bros & Rudd.*

Director's Cut Bunnahabhain Aged 20 Years refill hogshead, cask no. 7957, dist Dec 91, bott Dec 11 **(94) n22.5** clean but very still for a Bunna. Very light salt and citrus, but otherwise all is quiet on the Sound of Islay... **t24** as though some honey from its then sister distillery of Highland Park has crept into the barrel. No smoke but plenty of heather; big, big harley...; **f23.5** beautifully textured with a wonderful fade of lightly salted honeyed butterscotch; that huge barley hangs on to the very death; **b24** an almost emotional reminder as to exactly why this was once one of my favourite distilleries in the world... *49.6%. Douglas Laing & Co.*

Duncan Taylor Rare Auld Bunnahabhain 24 Years Old cask no. 1598, dist 1987 **(90) n22** some semblance of bourbon at work: a touch of red liquorice amid the florid oak; **t24** at first the oak is a little too aggressive. Then the malt fights back with as much bloody mindedness as aplomb; spiced, busy and, frankly, delicious; there is even a banana and custard moment to savour; **f21.5** dries every bit as expected; **b22.5** holds on grimly for life as the oak does all it can to prise any grip the malt may have on proceedings. A fascinating battle to the death in the glass and on your palate.. *55.7%. nc ncf sc. Duncan Taylor & Co.*

Duncan Taylor Rare Auld Bunnahabhain 32 Years Old cask no. 38408, dist 1979 **(86.5) n22 t23.5 f20 b21.** Bunna rarely sees out the years comfortably. This, though, has done better than I expected and though the finish shows the ravages of time clearly enough, the heady mix of oaky spices and intense, salty malt and exotic fruit on delivery is a treat worth discovering. The early body ain't too bad, either. *47.1%. nc ncf sc. Duncan Taylor & Co.*

Kingsbury "The Selection" Bunnahabhain 9 Years Old puncheons, 1266 & 3694, dist Oct & Dec 11, bott Apr 11 **(89) n22** lack of salt for a Bunna but the barley makes amends; **t23** the malt hits the taste buds like rain crashes against the Paps; **f22** a tad bitter but the rich malt shake compensates; **b22** one of the better young Bunnas for a while even though few of the usual distillery characteristics are present. *43%. nc ncf. Japan Import Systems. 1,611 bottles.*

Liquid Sun Bunnahabhain 1968 refill sherry, bott 2011 **(83.5) n21 t20.5 f21 b21.** Salty and buttery... perhaps overdoes the age, but an attractive number for those who like butter on an over toasted current bun. *47.8% The Whisky Agency.*

⋄⋄ **The MacPhail's Collection Bunnahabhain 2001 (78) n19 t22 f18 b19.** Technically less than impressive. But the barley shines early on. *43%. Gordon & MacPhail.*

⋄⋄ **Malts Of Scotland Bunnahabhain 1966** bourbon hogshead, cask no. MoS11020, bott Nov 11 **(95) n23.5** bares quite a few oaky scars. But there are little tell-tale signs of green shoots...; salt and then the big physalis-led exotic fruit as it opens in the glass; **t24** silky and mesmeric on delivery, the oak tries to rudely lay down a few basic laws, only to be usurped by the gathering fruit which not only softens and sweetens the experience, but creates a path for the mocha and praline; the body, though, is the equal of any lithe being half this whisky's age...; **f23.5** Mars Bars; certainly not fried as only the Scots know how, though there are oils which intensify the experience; **b24** to be honest, I feared the worst when I nosed this. But about 20 minutes of oxidisation in the glass brought forth the desired fruit elements, and we were away... *41.4%. nc ncf sc. Malts Of Scotland.*

Malts Of Scotland Bunnahabhain 1967 bourbon hogshead, cask no. 3315, dist Mar 67, bott Jun 10 **(90) n22.5** guava and salty kiwi fruit abound **t23** the delivery is a barrage of oak. But a flotilla of sugars sail to the rescue, most of them of the muscovado variety. Spices ting randomly around the palate with increasing intensity; **f22** the spices rage long and remorselessly. Creamy butterscotch creates balance; **b22.5** An improbably enjoyable Bunna displaying a rare degree of old age exotic fruit. No shortage of brine amid the oak, either, and some lovely juiciness here and there. *41.1%. nc ncf sc. 147 bottles.*

Malts Of Scotland Bunnahabhain 1968 bourbon hogshead, cask no. 12291, dist Dec 68, bott Jun 10 **(82.5) n21.5 t21 f20 b20.** Fascinating that the 12-y-o I first tasted at the distillery would have come from similar stock to this. Those were in the days before then owners, Highland Distillers, ran amok with sherry butts in the warehouse...the percentage ratio was far greater on the bourbon barrel side than now. Of course, those bourbon casks were filled for early blending or, just maybe, the single malt. They were certainly not laid down to last over 30 years, and this one is showing multiple signs of age distress. Teaming with character and history. But a good dozen summers beyond greatness... *40%. nc ncf sc. Malts Of Scotland.*

Malts Of Scotland Bunnahabhain 1970 "Thomas Ewers" 40 Years Old bourbon hogshead, cask no. 4066, dist Jun 70, bott Jun 10 **(92.5) n23.5** some sawdust is scattered over a sweet coconut and exotically fruity theme. As if distilled on some exotic island...other than Islay! **t22** improbably silky beginning and then a massive kick of OTT oak. Just when you think this has killed this one off, it returns from the dead with a wonderful mix of honey and red liquorice; **f24** the hints of bourbon that can be heard towards the middle now come into full view. A fabulous recovery where the barley and oak defy all the odds to speak as one; **b23** this one has escaped the clutches of old Father Time just enough to tell a beautifully honeyed life story... *40.5%. nc ncf sc. Malts Of Scotland. 299 bottles.*

⋄⋄ **Malts Of Scotland Bunnahabhain 1973** sherry butt, cask no. 3463, dist 26 Mar 73, bott May 11 **(79) n19 t21 f19 b20.** Just a little furry and bitter at the wrong times. *50.2%. nc ncf sc.*

⋄⋄ **Malts Of Scotland Angel's Choice Bunnahabhain 1976** sherry hogshead, cask no. MoS12005, bott Jan 12 **(87.5) n22** one assumes a fino cask as the dryness of the grape almost demands an olive; **t22** ramps itself up for maximum fruity richness but the bite of the vanilla ensures the barley juiciness also has a say; **f21.5** a bit of a scratchy finale with the spirit having a surprising amount to say so late on; **b22** you know when you are in a classic vintage car and the ancient engine is misfiring a bit...? *56.3%. nc ncf sc. Malts Of Scotland.*

⋄⋄ **Malts Of Scotland Bunnahabhain 1997** sherry hogshead, cask no. 3258, bott 2011 **(77) n18.5 t20 f19 b19.5.** Now here's a Pavlovian thing: I set this up as my last tasting of the day without thinking, so traumatised over recent years have I become by sherry butts from Bunna. Not very much sulphur here (though some), I'm relatively delighted to report. But, nonetheless, there is a nihilistic element to this with the spirit not being exactly of the highest quality, the grape being as subtle as an egg custard pie in the mush and the peat fired at you, seemingly, from a paintball gun. *52.9%. nc ncf sc. Malts Of Scotland.*

Malts Of Scotland Bunnahabhain 2005 oloroso barrel, cask no. 3990, dist Dec 05, bott Oct 10 **(86) n22 t22 f21 b21.** An aggressive example of the new, lightly smoked but intense Bunna style. Thick bodied delivery: almost malt concentrate. *55.9%. nc ncf sc. 242 bottles.*

⋄⋄ **Mo Òr Collection Bunnahabhain 1968 42 Years Old** first fill sherry butt, dist 11109, dist 2 Dec 68, bott 14 Jan 11 **(94.5) n24** double-checked the label: the grapes are far too clean and crystalline to be over 30 years, surely. A refined noble rot sweetness, beautifully interlaced with a brief shake of salt, adds to the unexpected lustre and controlled depth; **t23.5** ridiculous! No less than 42-years-old and it makes you salivate. What a magnificent combination of crisp, clean barley and juicy grape. And then the vanillas and spices begin to roll in like a sea mist...; **f23** long, playing happily off the spices as the oak begins to build a head of steam. But never does it cross that fine line between adding and overwhelming....; **b24** a surprise package: knowing Bunna as I do, and having tasted many of their sherry butts from this era over the years, I was expecting a dose of splinters. Instead, I was treated to a malt very comfortable with its old age: fit, healthy and exercising fully yet strictly within its limitations. What a treat! *46%. nc ncf sc. Release No. 13. The Whisky Talker. 254 bottles.*

⸭ **Old Malt Cask Bunnahabhain Aged 10 Years** sherry butt, cask no. 7861, dist Dec 01, bott Dec 11 **(86) n20 t22.5 f21.5 b22.** Takes a little time to hit its rhythm. Certainly the nose waves the white flag with the oak offering a touch too much astringency. After the indifferent delivery, an explosion of spices shocks the malt to its senses and the juicy story is a pleasant malty and fruity one from then onwards. *50%. nc ncf sc. Douglas Laing & Co. 280 bottles.*

⸭ **Old Malt Cask Bunnahabhain Aged 14 Years** refill hogshead, cask no. 7233, dist Aug 97, bott Aug 11 **(94.5) n22.5** a coal, anthracite and peat-mix smokiness is generously smeared with salted butter; **t24.5** there is a dreamy beauty to this one; the malt dissolves on delivery leaving myriad smoky layers; **f23.5** the complexity continues, though now the drying vanillas dig deep into the sugars. The diaphanous smoke continues to tease; **b24** a classy act entirely worthy of Bunnahabhain's great name. *50%. nc ncf sc. Douglas Laing & Co. 333 bottles.*

⸭ **Old Malt Cask Bunnahabhain Aged 14 Years** refill hogshead, cask no. 8616, dist Dec 97, bott Feb 12 **(90) n22** very light smoke drifts across the simplistic barley-oak mix; **t22** early emphasis on the girsty, salivating barley. The smoke arrives later, becoming surprisingly weighty; **f23** a wonderful finish thanks to a decent oak input. Love the almost Indian style spiced nuts as well as the Horlicks which help play down the smoky intensity; **b23** so delicate, you are almost frightened to chew it too hard...a charming and, actually, quite cracking whisky. *50%. nc ncf sc. Douglas Laing & Co. 335 bottles.*

⸭ **Old Malt Cask Bunnahabhain Aged 21 Years** refill hogshead, cask no. 7597, dist Feb 90, bott Aug 11 **(92.5) n22** some celery chopped into the nut and raisin toffee; **t24** gorgeously soft delivery with just enough spice prickle to prevent you from becoming too comfortable. An impressive array of dark sugars amid the bourbony liquorice; **f23** those spices prove persistent blighters, as do the sugars, thus guaranteeing little or no age wear; **b23.5** a compelling malt beautifully made and matured. *50%. nc ncf sc. Douglas Laing & Co. 218 bottles.*

⸭ **The Perfect Dram Bunnahabhain 35 Years Old** dist 1976 **(89.5) n23.5** probes elegantly at the exotic fruit stall...so charmingly well behaved and delicate! **t22.5** soft and lacking the usual Bunna salty explosion for a malt of this age; concentrates nimbly on the barley; **f21.5** runs out of puff on the complexity front and is content with overly simplistic vanilla; **b22** a perfectly charming malt which disguises its coastal roots. One for a very late evening when the brain needs little to tax it. *48.8%. sc. The Whisky Agency.*

Provenance Bunnahabhain Over 9 Years sherry butt, cask no. 6940, dist Autumn 01, bott Spring 2011 **(76.5) n18 t20.5 f19 b19.** Soupy, sweet and sour. And thick. Not sure if the cut on this spirit could have been any wider had they tried... *46%. nc ncf sc.*

⸭ **Provenance Bunnahabhain Over 9 Years** sherry butt, cask no. 7599, dist Autumn 2001, bott Summer 2011 **(84) n21 t22 f20 b21.** Something of jammy Swiss role to this one. The copiously oily delivery is a contrast to the grindingly dry finale. The very vaguest puff of smoke disappears after a brief appearance on the nose. *46%. nc ncf sc. Douglas Laing & Co.*

⸭ **Provenance Bunnahabhain Over 9 Years** sherry butt, cask no. 7860, dist Winter 2001, bott Autumn 2011 **(85) n21 t21.5 f21 b21.5.** Another curiously oiled Bunna. But it is the smoke evident here (hardly at all in its sister sherry cask 7599) which is most baffling. *46%. nc ncf sc. Douglas Laing & Co.*

Provenance Bunnahabhain Over 10 Years refill hogshead, cask no. 6305, dist Winter 99, bott Summer 2010 **(85) n22 t21.5 f20.5 b21.** Thumping malt. But this is as puckeringly dry as they come. *46%. nc ncf sc. Douglas Laing & Co.*

⸭ **Riegger's Selection Bunnahabhain 1977** bourbon cask, cask no. 7865 **(87.5) n23** a 35-year-old malt going on 65. Some major age issues here but the honeycomb and hickory keep this on an attractive course; **t22** beautifully sexy delivery with the barley enjoying a near silk quality. Again, the oak is on the attack and doesn't hold back. But the honeycomb on the nose does the business yet again, though now with far more salt at play; **f21** the oak finally wins through for a very toasty finale; **b21.5** just hangs on to enough honey to see off the encroaching age. *49.7%. nc ncf sc. Viktor-Riegger GmbH.*

Scotch Malt Whisky Society Cask 10.73 Aged 12 Years refill hogshead, cask no. 5410, dist 1997 **(85) n21 t22 f21 b21.** Violently sugary and hot. Engenders some major entertainment value while the peat is ladled on to overflowing. But something, due I think to the indolent posture of the body, naggingly second class about the whole affair. *55.8%. sc. 311 bottles.*

⸭ **Scotch Malt Whisky Society Cask 10.74 Aged 13 Years** refill hogshead, cask no. 5408, dist 1997 **(74) n17 t21 f18 b18.** Sweet and lightly smoked. But the cuts on the stills are all wrong and the oils unacceptable for a distillery so great. *54.8%. sc. Scotch Malt Whisky Society.*

⸭ **Scotch Single Malt Circle Bunnahabhain 1991** cask no. 5447, dist 2 Dec 91, bott 22 Oct 10 **(81) n20 t22 f19 b20.** A jumbled message on both nose and palate as this malt struggles to find either a coherent style or rhythm. Some attractive coppery notes, but all else is a bit of a mess. *54%. sc.*

❖ **Sestante Collection Bunnahabhain 38 Years Old** dist 1972, bott 2011 **(88.5) n23** how salty can a whisky get? Lightly sugared grape preserved in a saline solution; **t22.5** again, early sugars reinforced by fruit and then an almost frightening tidal wave of salt; **f21.5** lovely oils develop, but so too does the oak which has been battering the proceedings throughout; **b21.5** what might have been had only this cask been plucked from the warehouse a decade earlier. This is a malt haunted by the ghost of greatness past. There is the most delicate of fruit notes which shows an unforced class; the type of oak intrusion underlines that the quality of the barrel was exceptional. In fact, it was too good and someone in the company owning this should have spotted its majesty long before it was allowed to lose its defining shape and composure. *46%. sc. Silver Seal Whisky Company.*

Vom Fass Bunnahabhain 12 Years Old (86.5) n21.5 t22.5 f21 b21.5. Competent if simplistic peated Bunna which is rather youthful for its years. *40%*

❖ **The Warehouse Collection Bunnahabhain Aged 14 Years** bourbon hogshead, cask no. 5426, dist 8 Dec 97, bott 13 Apr 12 **(87.5) n22** the resounding sea-breezy peat is not entirely put off course by the wide, oily cut; **t23.5** the oils need a tanker to carry them. The smoke seems to be intensified while the muscovado sugars lighten the molasses. This is big, big whisky...; **f20** long, with that wide cut buzzing at the back of the throat; **b22** technically imperfect. But when the smoke signals are this friendly, who cares...? *58.5%. sc. Whisky Warehouse No. 8. 279 bottles.*

❖ **Wemyss 1991 Single Islay "Honey Spice"** butt, dist 1991, bott 2011 **(86.5) n22 t23.5 f19 b21.5.** A pretty big whisky, one which at times appears to belie its strength. The finale, alas, has a degree of furriness amid the cocoa. But this is all about the delivery and aftermath: honey spice hardly does this justice. Almost a dessert of a malt... delicious! *46%. sc. 743 bottles.*

❖ **Wemyss 1997 Single Islay "Driftwood"** hogshead, bott 2012 **(78) n21.5 t21 f17 b18.5.** To quote from the label: "This Hogshead has a peaty nose, reminiscent of a walk in the bracing sea air." What? I have walked beside many oceanic masses, this year alone involving the Arabian Sea, The Dead Sea, the Red Sea, The Pacific, the Mediterranean, the North Sea, the Irish Sea, the Baltic and probably one or two others besides. And I have to admit the one thing they had in common was a general lack of a peat in the air. Come on guys, please!!! Drop the amateurish, nonsensical and pretentious prose and concentrate instead on getting good whisky bottled, as I know you can, away from the poor cask which offers up an unpleasantly lingering, biting bitterness like this! *46%. sc. 374 bottles.*

❖ **Wemyss 1997 Single Islay "The Malt Barn"** hogshead, bott 2011 **(86) n22 t22 f20.5 b21.5.** A very acceptable example of the new style Bunna showing a charming smokiness to the gristy barley. Thins out just a little too energetically but the early delivery enjoys some excellent moments. *46%. sc. Wemyss Malts. 343 bottles.*

The Whisky Agency Bunnahabhain 8 Years Old sherry cask, dist 2001 **(89) n22 t23 f22 b22.** Swamped with grape, be assured there is not a single off note. A real rarity. *54%*

❖ **The Whisky Agency Bunnahabhain 43 Years Old** bourbon cask, dist 1968, bott 2011 **(85.5) n21 t21 f22 b21.5.** I have tasted a few 40+ Bunnas over the years, some actually in their warehouse. Most were fit for blending only. This has escaped that fate and deserves to. The nose is tired though boosted by orange blossom and the delivery is shudderingly course with oak. But as the oils gel, the malt settles into a more comfortable stance so the interplay between the vanillas and molassed sugars intrigue. *45.7%. sc. The Whisky Agency for 3 Rivers.*

The Whisky Agency Bunnahabhain 1965 refill hogshead, bott 2010 **(78) n20 t19 f20 b19.** Recovers with a welcoming degree of lime. But the oak is uncompromising. *40%. Germany.*

The Whisky Agency Bunnahabhain 1968 bott 2010 **(86) n22 t22 f21 b21.** Sets me in mind of the Liquid Sun bottling from the same company. Similar traits, but moved around in position slightly. More citrus on the nose and much more fat to the body. *47.8%. The Whisky Agency.*

The Whisky Agency Bunnahabhain 1974 (89) n23.5 t21.5 t22.5 b21.5. A malt which should have died but somehow defies the odds by showing some fabulous signs of life. They say salt is a good preservative... *47.3%*

❖ **Whisky Antique Bunnahabhain 42 Years Old Special Bottling** dist 1968, bott 2011 **(92.5) n23** the earliest Bunna in which I have ever picked up trace elements of smoke (though this did happen from time to time when they had to buy malt in from Port Ellen during storm-induced stock shortages); but there is also a touch of citrus, ultra-ripe banana and barley by the bushel; **t23.5** soft bodied yet deliciously intense and yielding barley massaged by luxurious cream toffee; **f23** some light embers of peat find their way to the finale, though now the caramels are pretty rampant; **b23** possibly not matured at the distillery, as there is far less brine apparent than would normally be the case. But a fabulous malt absolutely teeming with life even after all these years. *45.2%. sc. Silver Seal Whisky Company.*

❖ **The Whisky Broker Bunnahabhain 20 Years Old** hogshead, cask no. 5469, dist 2 Dec 91, bott 10 Jan 12 **(89) n22.5** almost like a malty breakfast cereal, only with some polished oak floor for extras; **t22.5** and again! Barley all the way in the most pristine salivating form;

f22 a few spices buzz past, the late fudge-like sugars salute; **b22** a curious Bunna. In many ways of the old school, yet sans the usual coastal qualities. I assume it has spent 20 years maturing inland. *49.7%. nc ncf sc. 286 bottles.*

Wilson & Morgan Barrel Selection Bunnahabhain 42 Years Old cask no. 12408, dist 1968, bott 2011 **(94.5) n24.5** excellent oak intermingles with the barley to truly sophisticated effect. You get this only with ancient malt. But ancient malt which has been fortunate enough to find a first class home for in excess of 35 years. The added saltiness is just too good to be true; **t24** gorgeously lithe with barley forming a lightly sugared sheen and the soft spices adding a mild degree of attitude to the juicinesss. The oak could not be better behaved, or more elegant; **f22.5** a bitter marmalade edge creeps into the fruit and vanilla yoghurt finale; **b23.5** if you don't have a couple of hours to spare, don't even think about pouring a glass. *44.1%. sc. 436 bottles.*

Wilson & Morgan Barrel Selection Bunnahabhain 1997 Heavy Peat cask no. 5376/77, bott 2010 **(85.5) n21 t22 f21 b21.5.** Big, unwieldy and were it not for the enormous chunkiness of the body, it would collapse under the weight of smoke and sugar. Something to seriously chew upon. *46%. Wilson & Morgan.*

CAOL ILA
Islay, 1846. Diageo. Working.

Caol Ila Aged 8 Years Unpeated Style dist 1999, bott 2007 db **(93.5) n23 t24 f23 b23.5.** Oh well, here goes my reputation...honest opinion: on this evidence (backed by other samples over the years) Caol Ila makes better straight malt than it does the peated stuff. Sorry, peat lovers. This should be a, if not the, mainstay of the official Caol Ila portfolio. *64.9%*

Caol Ila Aged 8 Years Unpeated Style 1st fill bourbon, dist 2000, bott 2008 db **(91.5) n23** a touch maltier than the previous bottling; salty digestive biscuit; **t23** beautifully refreshing with a real puckering, salty tartness to the barley; I seem to remember citrus here last year. But this time we have butterscotch and toffee; **f22.5** long, very delicately oiled with the vanillas and toffee in decent harmony; **b23** a bit more of a pudding than last year's offering, but delicious dramming all the way. *64.2%*

Caol Ila Aged 10 Years "Unpeated Style" bott Aug 09 db **(93.5) n24** a beautiful medley of pear and lime with a thin spread of peanut butter for good measure not exactly what one might expect...!!! **t23.5** the barley is just so juicy from the kickoff: the citrus on the nose reappears, though any hopes of pear vanishes; the barley, so rarely heard in a Caol-Ila grows in confidence and intensity as the delivery develops; **f23** not as oily as you might expect, allowing extra oak to emerge; **b23** always fascinating to see a traditional peaty Islay stripped bare and in full naked form. Shapely and very high class indeed. *65.4%. Only available at the Distillery.*

Caol Ila Aged 12 Years db **(89) n23** a coastal, salty biting tang (please don't tell me this has been matured on the mainland!) with hints of rockpools and visions of rock pipits and oystercatchers among the seaweed; **t25** enormously oily, coating the palate with a mildly subdued smokiness and then a burst of gristy malt; **f21** caramel and oil; **b22** a telling improvement on the old 12-y-o with much greater expression and width. *43%*

Caol Ila 12 Years Old Special Release 2010 1st fill bourbon oak cask, dist 1997 db **(95.5) n23** the smoke is almost an afterthought to the red liquorice lead. Bracing, tangy, full of energy...; **t24** to die for. The trademark oils arrive only as an apologetic afterthought to the delivery which takes at least six mouthfuls to get the measure of. Uniquely, the lead characteristic is sweetened cocoa, something of a bourbon front which is further backed by toasted honeycomb. The smoke offers no more than ballast and refuses to assert any authority on the salivating malt; **f24** now the limited oils have arrived they are put to excellent use by lengthening the finale. The vanillas are sweetened; the barley is galvanised by a curiously fruity earthiness and the most delicate spices imaginable tiptoe across the taste buds...; finally, a discreet muscavado sugar fanfare pipes the experience to its majestic close... **b24.5** the peat more or less takes a back seat in what is a masterful display of force and diplomacy on the palate. Most probably the best Caol Ila I have tasted in recent years. And this in a year of magnificent Caol Ilas. *576%. nc ncf. Diageo. Unpeated, fewer than 6000 bottles.*

⋄ **Caol Ila 12 Years Old Special Release 2011** db **(89) n21.5** stretched and surprisingly thin, the bourbony vanillas are just a little too cocky; **t23.5** more at home on the palate where the vanillas continue to screech but now harmonise with the crisp sugars and peek-a-boo peat; **f22** long with some lengthy tannin-enriched speeches. The oak holds sway even as the smoke tries to muscle back into the frame late on; **b22** a sideways look at a big distillery allowing the casks to have the loudest say over the malt: not at all common with this Islay. *64%. nc ncf.*

Caol Ila Aged 18 Years db **(80) n21 t20 f19 b20.** Another improvement on the last bottling, especially with the comfortable integration of citrus. But still too much oil spoils the dram, particularly at the death. *43%*

Caol Ila 1979 db **(74) n20 t19 f17 b18.** Disappointing. I could go on about tropical fruit yada, yada, yada. Truth is, it just conks out under the weight of the oak. Too old. Simple as that. *58.6%*

Caol Ila 1997 The Manager's Choice db **(93.5) n24** dry, ashy peat sweetened less by grist but mango chutney; **t23.5** the grist arrives and sharpens up quickly: a barley juiciness sets in as Lincoln biscuit/garibaldi dunked in peat hogs the middle ground; hickory and liquorice begin to form; **f23** dusty, but the liquorice and smoke hold sway; **b23** when this malt is not enveloped in taste bud-clogging oil, it really can be a little special. Here's further proof. *58%*

Caol Ila 'Distillery Only' bott 2007 db **(95.5) n24 t24 f23.5 b24.** Caol Ila is the third hardest distillery to get to in Scotland: however should you do so some time soon you can reward yourself by picking up a bottle of this. I can say honestly that the journey will be very much worthwhile... *58.4%. 5,000 bottles. Available only from the Caol Ila Distillery shop.*

Caol Ila Moch db **(87) n22** dry. Ground roast coffee which is decently smoked; **t22** a green barley delivery: sharp, juicy and a slow build up of oil and cocoa; **f21** vanilla but with a touch of bittering oak; **b22** easy drinking Islay. Though I think they mean "Mocha"... *43%*

⠶⠶ **Archives Caol Ila 2000 10 Years Old Inaugural Release** barrel, cask no. 3309899, dist Nov 00, bott Aug 11 **(86.5) n22 t22 f22 f21 b21.5.** Dry nose and delivery, then sweetens with a sugary injection and heads into the realms of pleasant nuttiness. *59.1%. nc ncf sc. Whiskybase B.V. 220 bottles.*

Berry's Own Selection Caol Ila 1980 cask no. 4938, bott 2011 **(90) n22.5** clean, almost hock-like in its delicate sweetness...except for the rumbling smoke; there is also a curious juniper/rye sharpness... **t23** mouth-watering, the barley is stretched and the smoke sweet and all-encompassing; the usual oils fill the middle ground alongside a brief array of brown sugars; **f22** good length with a distinct build up of spice and cocoa; **b22.5** charming and elegant throughout. *55.6%. nc ncf sc. Berry Bros & Rudd.*

⠶⠶ **Berry's Own Selection Caol Ila 1982** cask no. 6514, bott 2011 **(77) n19 t19 f20 b19.** An uncouth dram. First it shows rather too much of the seedier side of the cask on the nose. Then the puckering spice leaves little to the imagination. *56.4%. nc ncf sc. Berry Bros & Rudd.*

⠶⠶ **Berry's Own Selection Caol Ila 1983** cask no. 4825, bott 2011 **(91) n22.5** like a middle-aged sailor: salty with the peat showing distinct signs of thinning; **t23** oily and spicy with the malt punching through rather impressively; **f23** barely any peat makes it through to the end. But the mocha finale is rather charming; the sugars are a delight: a wonderful mix of acacia honey, burned fudge and maple syrup; **b23.5** this is a malt which has battled against all the odds to present to you absolutely top class fayre from this distillery, stretching itself as far as it can go without the unwelcome interruption of tired oak to do so. *54.9%. nc ncf sc. Berry Bros & Rudd.*

Berry's Own Selection Caol Ila 1984 cask no. 5389, bott 2010 **(95) n23** mesmerising. A gentle citrus flourish to the nutty smoke; coal dust; **t24** fabulous. The delivery is a near perfect arrival of orange-dusted barley, all in an understated soup of liquorice and smoke; **f24** delicate. More of the same, but at half the voltage; **b24** spellbinding! Another Caol Ila which shows its brilliance thanks to the lack of the usual oils. *53.7%. nc ncf sc. Berry Bros & Rudd.*

Berry's Own Selection Caol Ila 2000 cask no. 309878, bott 2011 **(95) n23.5** quite stunning, lilting, hugely smoked grist. Hard to imagine a more balanced interplay between light sugars and drier oak; Palma violets, the most distant hint of juniper, and even a touch of honey on butter; the peat is far more weighty than is the norm for this distillery, though it may not be obvious due to the beautiful balance; **t23.5** eschewing the usual oiliness, the whisky celebrates its high peat personality (appears, as does the nose, a distance above the 35ppm norm) with an uninterrupted view of the dissolving sugars and the layering of the phenols and cocoa; the pace of the spice makes one purr...; **f24** wow! How elegant is that? Really long, as should be expected from such a major degree of smoke and a slow unravelling of the light sugars, delicate spices and vanillas. Sublime...; **b24** I think it would be hard to find a better cask of Caol Ila at this age if you spent all year trying. Also, if this doesn't confirm that this has to be around the distillery's best age, I don't know what does. *576%. nc ncf sc.*

⠶⠶ **Cadenhead Caol Ila 21 Years Old** Apr 12 **(88) n22** age has shorn the malt of some of its smoke intensity, allowing the barley much greater say than normal; **t22** big, big barley on delivery with some pretty major oak nearby. The sugars and smoke arrive almost as an afterthought... **f22** some salt and spice intensify what had been a low key affair... **b22** I doubt if an old Islay comes more steady or sober than this... *51.9%. sc. WM Cadenhead Ltd.*

⠶⠶ **Duncan Taylor Dimensions Caol Ila 28 Years Old** cask no. 3625, dist 1983, bott Jan 12 **(95) n24.5** just about the perfect nose for such an oldie: salt leads the way, closely followed by an outwardly thick yet uber-complex interplay of fat raisin and marmalade. The smoke is deft, cleverly thickening here to fill in gaps, thinning there to allow the vanillas and molassed sugars ample scope to play. There appears to be almost a rum element to this, so happily in tandem are the spices and sugars; **t24.5** absolutely dissolves on the palate with a perfect combination of spiced smoke and juicy yet oak-tinged sugars. Very little oil beyond that needed for essential maintenance work and spreading the sweet, smoky word; the spices tease and tingle, the vanillas trumpet their quality; **f22.5** despite the lack of usual oils from this distillery, the length doesn't appear compromised. A light treacle touch to the growing liquorice but the subtly spiced smoke keeps all in order; **b23.5** it is well known that Caol Ila doesn't rate as my favourite Islay. But Duncan Taylor have unearthed a stunner here. Seemingly from a sherry butt, there are so many sugar and spice elements at work it now gives the impression of having spent a life in a Demerara cask. Unique and truly unforgettable. *54.3%. sc.*

⟐ **Duncan Taylor Dimensions Caol Ila 30 Years Old** cask no. 2929, dist Nov 81, bott Feb 12 **(88) n22** expecting something along the lines of cask 2928, but this heads much more into Bowmore-ish territory with a light Fisherman's Friend character tagging onto the molasses; **t22** sharp, though buttery delivery with a delicious smoked sugar edge; the barley unifies with the citrus vanilla; **f22** a delicate spice buzz sees this unusual Caol Ila to a close; **b22** it may be next in line to the magnificent cask 2928, but they are very different animals. *54.4%. nc ncf sc. Duncan Taylor & Co.*

Duncan Taylor Octave Caol Ila 28 Years Old cask no. 400926, dist 1983 **(93.5) n23** the peat is lazy and distinctly of the farm yard variety: cows are definitely offering a pastoral symphony...; **t23** beautiful delivery of early sugars. The standard Caol Ila oiliness here works to good effect by intensifying the scraps of flavours offered. The peat begins deftly but builds momentum; **f(23.5** even some flecks of barley added to the worty sugars. Excellent control from the oak while the peat continues to insist on adding the backing only; **b24** if you are ever to have one whisky over the eight, you could do worse than this very complex Caol Ila. A dram which after a slow starts builds to a moving crescendo. *51.7%. sc.*

⟐ **Duncan Taylor Rare Auld Caol Ila 30 Years Old** cask no. 2928, dist 1981 **(95.5) n24** complex with an astonishing array of attractive vegetable and earthy notes entirely in kilter with subtle spiced honey and a dab of maple syrup. The peat appears to be mixed with a degree of gun smoke; **t24.5** deliveries rarely come better than this either in terms of weight or mouth feel. The smoke has riches and depth but is both supported by the oak and particularly hushed by it. The sugars are diverse and no less rich and the maple syrup suspected on the nose is now proved; **f23** long thanks to its oils which assist rather than overkill as this distillery has the propensity of doing. Back to an attractive vegetable element to the earthiness and the oils are happy to play themselves out; **b24** what can you say? The bourbon casks were better in those days, of course, and here is a rare chance to see the oak stand up to some near bullying tactics with aplomb. Huge, absolutely top class, whisky with the cask giving as good as it gets and an object lesson for the new generation of blenders and "experts" in the field to learn....and weep. *54.8%. sc. Duncan Taylor & Co.*

Fine Malt Selection Caol Ila 10 Years Old dist 2000, bott May 11 **(90) n22** eschewing the usual oils, the peat is in clean and beautifully defined form: mildly gristy but with some invigorating citrus; **t23** you won't find a cleaner Islay delivery this year: the delicate oils ramp up the sugars, lightly dulling the smoke but ensuring a wonderful whole...; **t22** smoked molten icing sugar with a gradual build up of vanilla and kumquat; **b23** an absolutely typical, on the money bottling from James MacArthur. *45%. sc. James MacArthur & Co. USA release.*

⟐ **Gordon & MacPhail Cask Strength Caol Ila 1999 (94) n22.5** rugged stuff: some rough and tumble to the peat with the oak no less inclined to stick the boot in; **t24.5** superb delivery! Like the nose, it is a bruiser, only here we have the extra dimension of chocolate Swiss Roll and molassed fruitcake combined. Don't look for soothing silkiness. this is about controlled aggression and power; **f23** that chocolate spins itself out to the very end; the fruit and cream accompaniment is superb; **b24** a warlord of the isles... *61.6%. Gordon & MacPhail.*

Kingsbury Celtic Caol Ila 24 Years Old dist 1984 **(89.5) n22.5 t23 f21.5 b22.5.** Catches the essence of the distillery remarkably well. Delightful. *53.2%. nc ncf sc. 229 bottles.*

⟐ **Liquid Library Caol Ila 11 Years Old** dist 2000, bott 2011 **(87) n22** somewhere under all that oil you know there is some major peat smoke lurking....; **t22.5** clean, malty, oily and very smoky though the peat reveals itself by degree; **f21** a tiring cask bitters matters out slightly; **b21.5** a Caol Ila in its oiliest livery. Delicious but don't go in search of complexity. *46%. sc. The Whisky Agency*

Liquid Library Caol Ila 1984 bourbon hogshead, bott 2010 **(86) n21 t22 f21.5 b21.5.** A rare occasion when oil quenches the fire. At times tight and very hot with an over abundance of sugar. But brought under control by the oils for quite a memorable experience. *59%*

⟐ **Liquid Sun Caol Ila 1981** bott 2011 **(95.5) n24** a wonderful and quite charming compilation of delicate peaty and sooty notes: a blending of old steam trains and distant peat fires on the salty wind; **t24** like the nose, this is all about hint and delicacy. There is no doubting the salt. Nor the gooseberry jam. Nor the thin spreading of honey on golden toast. What is remarkable is the deftness of touch of the smoke...; **f23** remains long by virtue of the light oils which leads a train of varying sugar and honey notes. All understated, of course...; **b24.5** has withstood the inquisition of time with an exhibition of great elegance A must experience whisky. *52.9%. nc ncf sc. The Whisky Agency.*

⊰⊱ **Malts Of Scotland Caol Ila 1979** bourbon hogshead, cask no. MoS12022, dist Mar 79, bott Apr 12 **(84.5) n21.5 t22 f20 b21.0.** You know when a malt is getting just a little ripe when the oak actually outperforms the peaty input of a Caol Ila... *52.3%. nc ncf sc.*

Malts Of Scotland Caol Ila 1981 bourbon hogshead, cask no. 4807, Mar 81, Sep 10 **(85.5) n21 t22 f21 b21.5.** Some fabulously violent, alcoholic aggression helps paper over some cracks in the oak. Absolutely nothing wrong with the peat involvement, though! *59.8%. nc ncf sc. Malts Of Scotland. 216 bottles.*

⊰⊱ **Malts Of Scotland Caol Ila 1981** bourbon hogshead, cask no. MoS11009, dist May 81, bott Aug 11 **(83) n20 t22.5 f20 b20.5.** For a few brief moments this malt positively beams and glistens on the palate, its enormity writ large in spice. But the overall effect leaves you with the feeling that this would have done a better job in a 30-year-old blend, rather than standing alone with its oaky exhaustion fully exposed. *59.2%. nc ncf sc. Malts Of Scotland.*

⊰⊱ **Malts Of Scotland Caol Ila 1995** bourbon hogshead, cask no. 9805, dist Aug 95, bott May 11 **(88.5) n21** the oak almost outweighs the smoke; **t23** a gorgeous liquorice injection on the delivery mingles almost perfectly with the expanding peat; **f22** a much drier send off, but the vanillas play their part well; **b22.5** an impressive exhibition of controlled, cleverly smoked aggression. *54.1%. nc ncf sc. Malts Of Scotland.*

⊰⊱ **Malts Of Scotland Caol Ila 2000** bourbon hogshead, cask no. 309876, dist Nov 00, bott May 11 **(86) n22 t22 f21 b21.** Absolutely classic blending fodder, except perhaps missing the usual degree of oiliness. Juicy, lightly sugared, smoky and makes no unreasonable demands on either nose or palate. *54.6%. nc ncf sc. Malts Of Scotland.*

Master Of Malt Caol Ila 30 Year Old refill hogshead, dist 1980, bott 2010 **(88.5) n22.5 t23 f21 b22.** Gains dramatically from the intensity of the strength. A real fun experience with a malt which wears its age with aplomb. *57.4%. nc ncf sc. Master Of Malt. 154 bottles.*

⊰⊱ **Mo Òr Collection Caol Ila 1980 30 Years Old** first fill bourbon hogshead, cask no. 2570, dist 19 Mar 80, bott 4 Feb 11 **(81.5) n20.5 t22 f19 b20.** An over-aged cask with the oak dominating intrusively. *46%. nc ncf sc. Release No. 15. The Whisky Talker. 300 bottles.*

⊰⊱ **Mo Òr Collection Caol Ila 1983 27 Years Old** first fill bourbon hogshead, cask no. 4824, dist 12 Oct 82, bott 11 Mar 11 **(89.5) n22** butterscotch tart and mixed fruit; a few honeyed notes hover. The smoke is conspicuous by its absence; **t23.5** the lack of peat allows the oils to reveal their intensity to the fullest. Salty barley to the fore...; **f22** dries as the salt bites a little deeper; **b22** if you are looking for a smoky Islay, give this a swerve. But if you want to inspect the skeleton of the malt... *46%. nc ncf sc. Release No. 48. The Whisky Talker. 400 bottles.*

Old Malt Cask Caol Ila Aged 14 Years refill hogshead, cask no. 6535, dist Sep 96, bott Sep 10 **(90) n22.5** dry, old lum peat reek; **t23** no such dryness on delivery: various degrees of sugar help balance the smoky impact; **f22** lightly smoked butterscotch and bread and butter pudding; **b22.5** unusually sweet without displaying a gristy complexion. Another Caol Ila making the most of a lack of oil. *50%. nc ncf sc. Douglas Laing & Co. 329 bottles.*

⊰⊱ **Old Malt Cask Caol Ila Aged 14 Years** refill hogshead, cask no. 6898, dist Sep 96, bott Jan 11 **(89.5) n2.52** dry and ashy top layer, the gristy sugars lurk no great distance below; **t23.5** sensual delicacy: soft and delicately oiled and brimming full of light barley- and oaky-induced sugars; the peat knows exactly where not to go to allow maximum complexity; **f21.5** a little on the bitter side; **b22** soothingly sweet and carries its considerable smoky weight lightly. *50%. nc ncf sc. Douglas Laing & Co. 180 bottles.*

⊰⊱ **Old Malt Cask Caol Ila Aged 15 Years** refill hogshead, cask no. 8003, dist Sep 96, bott Jan 12 **(95) n23** crisp barley for a Caol Ila with the smoke offering a specific, toasty shape rather than its usual oily generalisation; **t24** the weight and texture are quite sublime and here we have the smoke playing a dual role: both as a lightly oiled purveyor of sweetness and as a sterner, slightly spicy lead. A gristy barley sweetness adorns the lighter vanillas; **f24** long, thanks to that most subtle oil, with a light cocoa depth; **b24** an unforgettable cask: this distillery rarely displays so well. *50%. nc ncf sc. Douglas Laing & Co. 299 bottles.*

⊰⊱ **Old Malt Cask Caol Ila Aged 16 Years** refill hogshead, cask no. 7931, dist May 95, bott Dec 11 **(94) n24** smoked Swiss cheese on a plate of salted celery and spiced liquorice. As intriguing as it is sublimely aromatic and balanced; **t23.5** unusual for a Caol Ila but the lively sugars surge ahead of the oils; the lightly smoked barley still retains a gristy quality; **f23** an excellent sweet-dry finale which gathers the cocoa and spices and play them out to full effect. The smoke now offers its full worth; **b24** a Caol Ila showing a style rarely seen since the 1980s. Of its type, a classic. *50%. nc ncf sc. Douglas Laing & Co. 189 bottles.*

Old Malt Cask Caol Ila Aged 21 Years refill hogshead, cask no. 6912, dist Mar 90, bott Mar 11 **(80) n20.5 t20.5 f19 b20.** Extremely tight with the oak in confrontational mood. *50%. nc ncf sc. Douglas Laing & Co. 148 bottles.*

Old Malt Cask Caol Ila Aged 30 Years refill hogshead, cask no. 7182, dist Sep 80, bott May 11 **(86.5) n23 t21 f21.5 b21.** A fascinating bottling which held up my early start to the day as I took extra time to try and figure this one out. The peat is only in trace form and instead we are treated to a display of candy store fruits. The lack of smoke, however, means the age of the cask is felt at times profoundly. Even so, the sort of dram that deserves time and respect. *50%. nc ncf sc. Douglas Laing & Co. 270 bottles.*

Old Malt Cask Caol Ila Aged 30 Years refill hogshead, cask no. 6858, dist Nov 80, bott Jan 11 **(79) n21 t21 f18 b19.** Some serious bitterness at play here. *50%. nc ncf sc. 318 bottles.*

Provenance Caol Ila Over 9 Years refill hogshead, cask no. 6802, dist Winter 01, bott Autumn 2010 **(78.5) n20 t19 f20 b19.5.** Oily, sweet, pleasant yet a few cylinders have packed in. *46%. nc ncf sc. Douglas Laing & Co.*

Provenance Caol Ila Over 10 Years refill hogshead, cask no. 7237, dist Winter 01, bott Summer 2011 **(84.5) n22.5 t21 f21 b20.** After the initial gristy big peat burst, quietens down to little more than a near oakless whisper... *46%. nc ncf sc. Douglas Laing & Co.*

⫶⫶ **Provenance Caol Ila Young & Feisty Small Batch Bottling** cask no. 7767 & 7768, bott Autumn 2011 **(84) n21 t22.5 f19.5 b21.** Not so much young and feisty as infantile and spoilt. A fun whisky full of smoky rhetoric. But the bitter-ish finish deserves a smacked bum. *46%. nc ncf. Douglas Laing & Co.*

⫶⫶ **Provenance Caol Ila Young & Feisty Small Batch Bottling** refill hogshead, bott Spring 2012 **(91) n23** sound, clean peat enjoying excellent sweet and dry undertones; **t23.5** fine delivery: the smoke is to the fore, but the delicate sugars soon guide the overall shape: hugely satisfying; **f22** a little disapproval from the oak but those lightly smoked sugars handle the situation well; **b22.5** does most of what you hope from a Caol Ila. *46%. nc ncf sc. Douglas Laing & Co.*

⫶⫶ **Provenance Caol Ila Young & Feisty Small Batch Bottling** refill hogshead, cask no. 8010 & 8124, bott Winter 2012 **(82) n19 t22 f20 b21.** The limitations of the cask put a muzzle on what must have been some very decent spirit. *46%. nc ncf. Douglas Laing & Co.*

Rare Auld Caol Ila 27 Years Old dist 1983, cask no. 3620 **(88) n22 t23 f21 b22.** Not sure the cask was designed for this kind of age. But the malt certainly was... *52.7%. sc.*

⫶⫶ **Scotch Single Malt Circle Caol Ila 1999** cask no. 310808, dist 23 Sep 99, bott 5 Oct 11 **(89.5) n23** the peat is spray-painted on: thick, dry and salty; **t22.5** beautifully clean barley makes a pleasant start, then it's peat, muscovado sugars and oaky spices all the way; **f22** simplifies down to the very basics. Not a trace of bitterness or an off note, though; **b22** about as subtle as a one tonne bomb. But what good clean fun! Love it!! *61.4%. sc.*

Scotch Malt Whisky Society Cask 53.142 Aged 20 Years refill hogshead, cask no. 5427, dist 1989 **(89.5) n22 t22.5 f22.5 b22.5.** A relaxed bottling which wears its 20 years with ease. Attractively delicate throughout. *55.9%. sc. 209 bottles.*

Scotch Malt Whisky Society Cask 53.146 Aged 17 Years refill sherry butt, cask no. 10904, dist 1993 **(85) n21 t22 f21 b21.** The barley is pugnacious and juicy. But shows minimal complexity and development for its age. *60.9%. sc. 553 bottles.*

Scotch Malt Whisky Society Cask 53.148 Aged 10 Years refill hogshead, cask no. 310827, dist 1999 **(84.5) n22 t21.5 f20 b21.** Big on alcohol, limited on depth and development. *66.1%. sc. 271 bottles.*

Scotch Malt Whisky Society Cask 53.152 Aged 14 Years refill hogshead, cask no. 2757, dist 1997 **(89) n22 t22.5 f22.5 b22.** Almost purifies the palate: not something said too often about a Caol Ila... *577%. sc. 291 bottles.*

⫶⫶ **Scotch Malt Whisky Society Cask 53.154 Aged 17 Years** refill hogshead, cask no. 10905, dist 1993 **(77) n20 19 f19 b19.** How ordinary can a Caol Ila be? Surely there were better casks than this to choose from? Very poor oak. *59.8%. sc. Scotch Malt Whisky Society.*

⫶⫶ **Scotch Malt Whisky Society Cask 53.156 Aged 10 Years** refill hogshead, cask no. 312007, dist 2000 **(89.5) n21.5** this kipper can still bite; **t22.5** a dry nip to the smoke; mildly ashy and devoid of the usual oily coating; **f23** now really goes into complexity overdrive as the warming spices hit a perfect crescendo with the gathering muscovado sugars; **b22.5** a lovely little essay in complexity. *57.6%. sc. Scotch Malt Whisky Society.*

⫶⫶ **Scotch Malt Whisky Society Cask 53.157 Aged 10 Years** refill hogshead, cask no. 312008, dist 2000 **(91.5) n22.5** clean, gristy and mildly simplistic, the peat is much starker than usual for a Caol Ila; **t22.5** the delivery concentrates on the smoke ahead of the oil... hang on...what oil? Unusually crisp and almost gristy; light spices bob and weave; **f23.5** a few vanilla notes confirm some oak is involved and now the delicate sugars enter the fray and continue the salivating theme; **b23** lacking the usual oils, this is almost like seeing all the distillery's charms for a change instead of with three layers of clothing... *58%. sc.*

⫶⫶ **Scotch Malt Whisky Society Cask 53.158 Aged 15 Years** refill hogshead, cask no. 14551, dist 1996 **(84.5) n21 t21.5 f21 b21.** Dry yet firmly sugared. Just annoyingly underdeveloped for its age. *58.6%. sc. Scotch Malt Whisky Society.*

⫶⫶ **Scotch Malt Whisky Society Cask 53.166 Aged 15 Years** refill ex-bourbon hogshead, cask no. 12557, dist 1996 **(90) n22** anyone who has ever crushed a parched, fried grain of peated malt in their fingers will recognise the aroma immediately; **t24** superb delivery tasting tall to show every single one of its 35ppm phenol; some Demerara sugars rumble elsewhere while the lack of usual oils help elevate the honeycomb middle; **f21.5** falls away as the oak fails to live up to the quality of the spirit; **b22.5** a slightly better cask would have rendered this a mini classic. A real experience, though. *58.1%. sc.*

Scott's Selection Caol Ila 1981 bott 2011 **(74) n19 t19 f18 b18.** The huge smoke does all in its power to overcome the weakness of the oak. In the end, an unequal struggle. *61.7%. Speyside Distillers.*

Single Cask Collection Caol Ila Aged 10 Years bourbon hogshead, cask no. 309889, dist Nov 00, bott Feb 11 **(94) n23.5** fizzing, thick peat. But enough grist and top spin to make for something stirring; the oak engineers a surprising early cocoa and liquorice sub plot. Wow!! **t24** superb delivery. Helped monumentally by the usual lack of oil, allowing the peat and rich sugars unrestricted access to the taste buds; **f23** some natural caramels dull things slightly. But the smoke and spices roll on; **b23.5** a quite superb, beautifully above average bottling which works on countless levels. *58.5%. nc ncf sc. Single Cask Collection. 235 bottles.*

Single Cask Collection Caol Ila Aged 27 Years sherry butt, cask no. 3623, dist May 83, bott Sep 10 **(88.5) n22.5 t23 f20.5 b22.5.** Overall, a sound butt allowing the grape to cohabit comfortably with the peat: not the most common of phenomena. *51.5%. nc ncf sc. 64 bottles.*

⁓ **Wemyss 1996 Single Islay "Smokehouse"** hogshead, bott 2011 **(88.5) n21.5** a squeeze of grapefruit on an Arbroath Smokie....; **t23** satisfying amalgam of fruit and smoke but with the grist still standing tallest; **f21.5** a tad bitter as the oak cuts in but still a good smoky send off; **b22.5** plays its drier and juicier personalities against each other with aplomb. *46%. sc. Wemyss Malts. 363 bottles.*

⁓ **The Whisky Agency Caol Ila 33 Years Old** dist 1979 **(96.5) n24.5** for the age, pretty close to perfect. You fear that time will have thinned the peat to a mere shell. Not a bit: delicately powered, ashy and very much alive...; **t24** so beautiful with its molten sugars dragging along a multitude of peaty notes. The sugars head towards more molassed pastures as the experience unfolds; **f24** very late in the day, citrus pops up from somewhere. The lightly oiled phenols now carry mocha. This is dreamy stuff; **b24** when you open a bottle of 33-year-old Islay, you are looking for one of the times of your life. This happily obliges. *53.7%. sc.*

The Whisky Agency Caol Ila 1979 bourbon hogshead, bott 2011 **(89.5) n22.5 t23.5 f21.5 b22.** Shows many a sign of great age. But worth finding for the astonishing delivery alone. *52%. The Whisky Agency.*

⁓ **The Whisky Agency Caol Ila 1992** bott 2011 **(87.5) n22.5** a nose that makes you sit up and take notice: a smattering of white pepper causes chaos in the smoky lines; the citrus is a delightful distraction; **t22.5** soft and melt-in-the mouth delivery with the malt cranking up the sugars and smoke in equal degrees; the spices begin their bombardment; **f20.5** annoyingly bitter as the oak takes a wrong turn; **b22** puckering and busy, this is less about the smoke and more about how the spices assert themselves. *50.5%. nc ncf sc. The Whisky Agency.*

⁓ **The Whisky Agency Caol Ila 1993** bott 2012 **(85.5) n22 t21.5 f21 b21.** A pleasant, good looking but, ultimately, lazy dram which you feel deserves a good whipping for its indolence. *56.1%. nc ncf sc. The Whisky Agency.*

⁓ **Whisky Antique Caol Ila 28 Years Old Special Bottling** dist 1983, bott 2011 **(84.5) n21 t22 f20.5 b21.** A curious Caol ila with plenty of pepper, minimal smoke and no shortage of toffee, especially on the finale. *46%. sc. Silver Seal Whisky Company.*

Wilson & Morgan Barrel Selection Caol Ila 1998 Limited Edition cask no. 10729-38, dist 2010 **(79) n19 t21.5 f18.5 b20.** From the stridently oily school of Caol Ilas. Some profound bitterness evident. *48%. Wilson & Morgan.*

CAPERDONICH

Speyside, 1898. Chivas Brothers. Closed.

Duncan Taylor Caperdonich 1972 bott Sep 10, cask no. 6735 **(78) n19 t19 f20 b20.** Puckering... *51.4%. Duncan Taylor & Co.*

⁓ **Gordon & MacPhail Connoisseurs Choice Caperdonich 1998 (82) n19 t22 f20.5 b20.5.** A thin, pleasant though entirely underwhelming malt which, for all its barley theme, gives another clue as to why it was decided the distillery wasn't worth saving. *46%.*

Malts Of Scotland Caperdonich 1972 sherry hogshead, cask no. 1144, dist Oct 72, bott Mar 11 **(91) n21** a bit of a train wreck; oaky splinters everywhere and some hybrid bourbon notes despite the fruity undertone; **t22.5** at first the taste buds are rushed head on by a bizarre legion of kamikaze oak. The fuss ends and a clearer picture of salivating honey and barley emerges. As this comes more into focus, a very soft smokiness drifts over the scene and butterscotch fills the middle ground; **f24** no OTT oak now. A beautifully serene fade of butterscotch tart and light honey and even some traces of Melton Mowbray Hunt cake; **b23.5** at times looks as though done for by the oak. But salvaged in impressive fashion by the steady input of honey and raisin. Just gets better and better as it goes along. *57.4%. sc. Malts Of Scotland.*

Malts Of Scotland Caperdonich 1972 sherry hogshead, cask no. 1145, dist Oct 72, bott Mar 11 **(81.5) n20.5 t19 f21 b21.** Never comes close to matching the brilliance of its sister cask, 1144. Goes into the same oaky dive, but is unable to pull out in sufficient time. *52.4%. sc.*

·:·: **Malts Of Scotland Caperdonich 1994** bourbon hogshead, cask no. 625, dist Mar 94, bott May 11 **(79) n21 t20 f19 b19.** A good example of why the distillery was closed down and dismantled, though some attractive cocoa and barley sugar manage to dodge the ruthlessly searing heat of the spirit. *53.3%. nc ncf sc. Malts Of Scotland.*

·:·: **Mo Ór Collection Caperdonich 1972 38 Years Old** first fill bourbon hogshead, cask no. 7437, dist 7 Nov 72, bott 25 Jan 11 **(87.5) 22** huge oak impact, but the fruit is more kumquat rather than the desired mixed exotic; **t22** soft delivery with the barley building a platform on the oily ground. Again the oak has a big say, but levels off with a cocoa dryness; **f21.5** chocolate sponge, though with little sugar; **b22** makes a bold attempt to recreate the great old Capers of six or seven years ago. But this has absorbed too much oak for any form of greatness, though it is always enjoyable. *46%. nc ncf sc. Release No. 9. The Whisky Talker. 162 bottles.*

Octave Caperdonich 38 Years Old dist 1972, cask no. 414293 **(94) n23.5** spellbinding blend of medium roast Java and kumquat. Here, though, salt appears to be added, rather than sugar; **t24** the delivery has the unusual distinction of being both firm and oily at once. The levels of tannin, leavened by hickory and molasses, are as complex as they are impressive; some bite despite the lightness of touch to the biscuit barley; **f23** takes a more genteel spiced vanilla route back home; **b23.5** an unusual old Caper, as this one has not gone down the famous exotic route it usually prefers to take. Instead, a high dose of extra high-quality oak has moved it along a more cocoa enriched path which suits it well. Not a single shred of evidence pointing towards degenerative aging, despite the oak having a big say... *52.5%. sc. Duncan Taylor & Co.*

Old Malt Cask Caperdonich 28 Years Old refill hogshead, cask no. 6623, dist Jun 82, bott Sep 10 **(69) n18 t18 f16 b17.** Had all this late distillery's output been this bad, I would have turned up with a ball and chain myself... Curious that an anagram of the letters found between the C and the H in Caperdonich is: "I Done Crap". *50%. nc ncf sc. 310 bottles.*

Rarest Of The Rare Caperdonich 38 Years Old dist 1972, cask no. 7461 **(91.5) n22** plenty of red liquorice and hickory sets this on a bourbon footing; **t23** the oak certainly makes an early song and dance, but the light honeycomb and golden syrup completes an excellent balancing job; **f23** again the oak is profound..and yet again there is sugars enough to ensure equilibrium... and even allow a few juicy barley notes to be heard at the very end: impressive; **b23.5** plenty of feel good factor. One for the sweet toothed amongst us. *54.6%. sc. Duncan Taylor & Co.*

Scotch Malt Whisky Society Cask 38.20 Aged 16 Years refill hogshead, cask no. 64211, dist 1994 **(83) n20 t22 f20.5 b20.5.** Huge, clean juicy barley distilled in a bit of a rush. Hot, intense and invigorating, it is fascinating as a Caper but does little to set the pulse racing in the Great Whisky Scheme of things. *57.4%. sc. 254 bottles.*

·:·: **The Whisky Agency Caperdonich 18 Years Old** dist 1994 **(81) n22 t19 f20 b20.** Sweet. But ouch!! It's hotter than the sun...! (That's for you, Armando) *52.2%. sc.*

CARDHU
Speyside, 1824. Diageo. Working.

Cardhu 12 Years Old db **(83) n22 t22 f18 b71.** What appears to be a small change in the wood profile has resulted in a big shift in personality. What was once a guaranteed malt love-in is now a drier, oakier, fruitier affair. Sadly, though, with more than a touch of something furry. *40%*

·:·: **Duncan Taylor Rare Auld Cardhu 26 Years Old** cask no. 2873, dist 1984 **(96) n25** I'm in love: if I didn't have a deadline, this is a nose I could wallow in all day. What's ringing my bells? Well the absolutely perfect - and I mean faultless - weight balance between an allspice (almost bread pudding) richness mixing in with the diced kumquat zest. The sugars are subtle and varied but edge towards muscovado depth; this is as long, labyrinthine and mysterious as a Brazilian rain forest..; **t24.5** fabulous delivery with the silky oils attached to the body grabbing the attention at first. Then a confident, striding display of bourbon oak, liquorice and tannins. But the sugars keep pace effortlessly; **f23.5** at last the malt thins and the oaks encroach a little too keenly. Busy and a little biting around the tongue; the malt offers a last, sugary hurrah...; **b24** a real rarity. And one worth waiting for: an essay of weighty Speyside complexity. But, please. Spend at least half an hour on the nose before you taste: no water, just body temperature. You will thank me – and Cardhu - forever. Notably, I tasted this on February 29th. I expect it'll be another four years before I find such a cask from Cardhu again... *54.4%. nc ncf sc. Duncan Taylor & Co.*

·:·: **Scotch Malt Whisky Society Cask 106.18 Aged 27 Years** refill hogshead, cask no. 2882, dist 1984 **(91) n23** a busy entanglement between soft oak and delicate orange blossom honey; **t23** for all the background oak, the delivery is surprisingly light with almost a whipped cream consistency; the Jamaican Blue Mountain coffee ensures a subtle middle ground;

the sugars are little more than bystanders but, as ever, it is the barley which quietly steels the show; **f22** a thin spreading of marmalade on granary toast; **b23** beautiful complexity throughout from this under-rated distillery. *52.6%. sc.*

⋙ **The Whisky Agency Cardhu 1984** bott 2011 **(92) n22.5** as SMWS 106.18 above but with a little extra oak, or is that manuka in with the orange blossom? **t23** very similar to above but more oil to the whipped cream and the orange blossom honey produces the goods a fraction earlier than before; **f23** extra oak weight on the finish, balanced by a slightly sweeter mocha and praline finale; **b23.5** this one has had me scratching my head. Two whiskies side by side, poured from different bottles. Yet like two peas in a pod, the second showing only a marginal degree of extra oak encroachment and fractionally better balance. On checking, I spotted they were the same age and the same strength. Take your eye off the ball and you'd easily think it was the same cask. *52.6%. nc ncf sc. The Whisky Agency.*

CLYNELISH
Highlands (Northern), 1968. Diageo. Working.

Clynelish Aged 15 Years "The Distillers Edition" double matured in oloroso-seco casks Cl-Br: 169-1f, bott code L6264CM000 03847665, dist 1991, bott 2006 db **(79) n20 t20 f19 b20.** Big in places, distinctly oily in others but the overall feel is of a potentially brilliant whisky matured in unsympathetic barrels. *46%*

Clynelish The Manager's Choice first fill bourbon American oak, cask no. 4341, dist 1997, bott 2009 db **(90.5) n22.5 t23 f22.5 b22.5.** Excellent cask selection. Everything is geared towards accentuation the untarnished richness of the malt. *58.5%. 232 bottles.*

Adelphi Clynelish 14 Years Old cask no. 4715, dist 1997, bott 2011 **(95) n24.5** imagine concentrated butterscotch on a slightly overcooked pastry; you then find a lime, a kiwifruit and a physalis...you mix the juices together and pour onto the tart. And then, just to send your senses to another plane, take the richer elements of the kind of honeycomb and hickory found in the finest bourbons...and stir in gently...oh...my...god...!!! **t24.5** so many whiskies with a great nose are a let down on delivery: not this one, buster! Near perfect weight and oil involvement makes for an entrance which borders on the sublime. A cross section of Demerara and muscovado sugar combine with watered-down dark treacle to take on the spices head to head. It is a near perfect match, though elsewhere the barley even manages to say a juicy 'hullo' and the honeycomb shines; **f22** huge vanilla. But the spices keep warbling; **b24** Adelphi are impressing me with a number of their bottlings right now. And this is another that is to be hunted down at all costs. *59.5%. sc. Adelphi Distillery. 247 bottles.*

⋙ **Archives Clynelish 1997 14 Years Old Inaugural Release** bourbon hogshead, cask no. 4634, dist Jul 97, bott Jul 11 **(89.5) n22.5** the oak takes a back seat and allows the malt to dazzle...; incredible young and lemon drop-like; **t22.5** mouth-watering barley pulses out more and more beautifully sweetened citrus; **f22** the barley is left to itself; **b22.5** it is a rare event when a bourbon cask on perhaps its third time round does not interfere with a minor degree of negativity. Of its type, quite gorgeous. *53.9%. nc ncf sc. Whiskybase B.V. 160 bottles.*

Berry's Own Selection Clynelish 1997 cask no. 4706, bott 2010 **(96.5) n24** a fruit shop on a warm day in southern France. You almost expect to hear wasps in the background...; bananas and exploding greengages abound. But rather than wasps, you get spicy bees, as a little spiced honey goes a long way...; **t24** perhaps only a layer of caramel, blunting some of the more complex notes, prevents a perfect score here. Instead, you have to deal with enough spices to keep a Moroccan market going for a month, and a whiole string of varying honey and barley notes which ying and yang from one side of the palate to the other; **f23.5** downgrades to merely brilliant on the finale with a disappointing number of fabulous oak and fruit notes turning into a banana and custard dessert from heaven. Blast! I was hoping for so much more...; **b24** absolutely everything you can ask from this distillery at this age and from this type of cask. Taste this without sighing...I challenge you..! One of the whiskies of this and many a year. *56.8%. nc ncf sc. Berry Bros & Rudd.*

⋙ **Berry's Own Selection Clynelish 1997** cask no. 6864, bott 2012 **(92.5) n22** an enticing melody of light citrus, heavier toasty oak and the very vaguest puff of smoke; **t23.5** delicate delivery with a lighter body than normal. The barley is juicy but the spices are quite astonishing, yet next out of context with the mashed banana and light honey; **f23** long with a light oil forming and lengthening the egg custard tart...with no little sugar and cocoa sprinkled on top; **b24** like so often from this great distillery, an absolute treat for the taste buds. *46%. nc ncf sc.*

⋙ **Boisdale Clynelish 1997** cask no. 6467, bott 2012 **(93.5) n23** artful barley at work: delicate, fragile yet bold enough to inject a degree of fruit; there is something in the wind to watch carefully late on; **t24.5** you are probably wondering where I have docked the half mark. "I mean", you will say, "where the hell can you find fault with that?" For the weight, somewhere between bantam and fly, is perfect. So too is the slow motion development of the barley. The introduction of the gristy sugars is faultless and the intertwining with some

...skier oak notes is beyond reproach. The answer is just a frisson of bitterness, noticeable only because the malt is just so delicate; **f22.5** the mildly sub-standard bitter oak makes only limited impact as the sugars, picking up something of a fruity theme, do an excellent damage limitation job; **b23.5** Clynelish, in all its finery, makes one of the best deliveries on the palate this year... *46%. nc ncf sc. Berry Bros & Rudd.*

⋅⋗ **Chieftain's Clynelish Aged 14 Years** hogshead, cask no. 4717, dist Apr 97 **(91) n22.5** fascinating nose which never seems to settle: each sniff offers a slightly different view of the lightly smoked bananas and custard; **t24** one of those divine deliveries where delicate oils thrust the multi-layered lightly sugared barley directly at the more deadpan oak; mocha and caramel fills the middle; **f22** thins out somewhat as the vanilla gets a little chalkier; **b23** slightly more oaky vanilla than usual. But doesn't impact too badly on the usual high complexity. *46%. nc ncf sc. Ian Macleod Distillers. USA exclusive.*

⋅⋗ **Duncan Taylor Dimensions Clynelish 21 Years Old** cask no. 3229, dist May 90, bott Feb 12 **(89.5) n22** wow! is this 21 years old only? Has the heavy fruit and tannins of a malt almost twice that age...; **t23** rich delivery: the oak is profound but kept in check by some fabulous fudge and liquorice notes; the body is always thick, the mid-ground creaks with oak; **f22** still no need to put the Zimmer frame away...; **b22.5** fruity enough, and pretty sexy in part. But prematurely aged. Discover what many top 35-40-year-old malts taste like for only half the price...! *51.4%. nc ncf sc. Duncan Taylor & Co.*

⋅⋗ **Duthies Clynelish 16 Years Old** sherrywood, bott 2012 **(90) n22** fruitcake with plenty of warmed nuts...; **t23.5** salivating delivery despite the burnt raisins and a buoyant follow through full of dark cherries and muscovado sugar; **f22.5** late spices jazz up the butterscotch; **b23** get spirit from one of Scotland's finest distilleries, put it into a decent, untainted sherry cask...and you are unlikely to go too far wrong. *46%. sc. WM Cadenhead Ltd.*

⋅⋗ **Hart Brothers Clynelish Aged 14 Years** cask no. 5743, dist 21 May 97, bott 30 Apr 12 **(92) n23.5** quite brilliant: some candy shop fruitiness mixed in the most delicate stem ginger imaginable plus golden syrup. Some peaches and mangoes up the fruity sweetness further; **t23** soft and silky, the malt displays a degree of gristy sweetness which appears to ramp up the juice levels without the fruit on the nose being present; **f22.5** now some spices offer late extra complexity and depth; a wave of natural caramels make for a slightly subdued finale; **b23.5** a hugely complex Clynelish, as they so very often are.... *46%. sc.*

⋅⋗ **Malts Of Scotland Clynelish 1982** bourbon hogshead, cask no. MoS11015, dist 15 Dec 82, bott Oct 11 **(93) n23** a wonderful mix of herbs and freshly diced celery; the sweetness is supplied by telling vanillins – complete with spice – and coconut. **t23.5** the big oaky thrust is softened by a further build up of mega juicy barley sugar notes; complex and wonderfully structured, as usual; **f23** a saline drip is fed into the lightly spiced finale. The continuing sugars enrich the texture; **b23.5** such a dependable distillery! *53.7%. nc ncf sc. Malts Of Scotland.*

⋅⋗ **Malts Of Scotland Clynelish 1989** bourbon hogshead, cask no. MoS12012, dist 29 Sep 89, bott Jan 12 **(90.5) n22.5** anyone who has tasted spirits in Eastern Europe will recognise this distinctive slivovitz, crushed pip style: astonishing! **t23** more of the same with the barley swamped by the juiciest light fruitiness imaginable. The sugars, distinctly of the white, icing sugar variety, are sublime; **f22.5** long with sweetened vanilla and still a fruity twist to the barley; **b22.5** quite bizarre, considering this is from a bourbon cask: has all the attributes of one that has spent some time alongside a dry grape... *53.2%. nc ncf sc. Malts Of Scotland.*

⋅⋗ **Malts Of Scotland Clynelish 1998** bourbon hogshead, cask no. MoS12025, bott 2012 **(85) n21 t22 f21 b21.** A thick, sweetened malt milkshake of a dram though undermined by a cask which ensures a degree of tartness. *50.7%. nc ncf sc. Malts Of Scotland.*

Old Malt Cask Clynelish 13 Years Old refill hogshead, cask no. 6055, dist Apr 97, bott Apr 10 **(86.5) n21 t22 f22 b21.5.** Surprisingly simplistic for a Clynelish. But what little it does, it does with effortless charm. *50%. nc ncf sc. Douglas Laing & Co. 343 bottles.*

⋅⋗ **Old Malt Cask Clynelish Aged 16 Years** refill hogshead, cask no. 7920, dist Jun 95, bott Nov 11 **(91.5) n22.5** a thin, if unique, blend of gooseberry and kiwifruit; **t23.5** the usual Clynelish elegance fuses the malt and spices together with aplomb; elsewhere light fruit and spice dally with intent; the intensity of the juices defies belief; **f22.5** still juicy and intensely malty but now more of a cocoa theme; **b23** effortlessly superb. *50%. nc ncf sc. 287 bottles.*

Old Malt Cask Clynelish Aged 21 Years refill hogshead, cask no. 6939, dist Jan 90, bott Feb 11 **(90.5) n22.5** teasing citrus and vanilla with the lightest smattering of spice and a even more deft hint of smoke; **t23.5** juicy lime and tangerine blend; the middle confirms t spicy smoke on the nose; **f22** light oils plus a touch of caramel-chocolate; **b22.5** delicate delicious. *50%. nc ncf sc. Douglas Laing & Co. 265 bottles.*

⋅⋗ **Old Malt Cask Clynelish Aged 28 Years** refill hogshead, cask no. 7553, dist D bott Aug 11 **(95.5) n24** the odd puff of peat is met with equal pathetic force by juicy pe clinker-rich coal dust; no shortage of sweet barley; **t24.5** a near perfect delivery. Th is intense and juicy. This comes and goes in five or six waves which get steadily arriving at the same time is an ever-enlivening spiciness; black peppers squabbling an fighting or space against the ever encroaching, thickening malt; **f23** much thinner now with perhaps an odd hint of smoke here and there; the occasional bite of pepper but a constant of delicate malt. It is the vanilla which has the big final say; **b24** it is bottlings like this which help confirm my suspicion that this is the fairest of all the Diageo distilleries... 50%. nc ncf sc.

Old Masters Clynelish 13 Years Old cask no. 4643, dist 1997, bott Sep 10 **(92) n23** zesty and packed with honey notes. A hint of bigger oak than usual for the age; a molecule or two of smoke, too; **t23.5** gorgeously fresh honey but again the oak has an essence of pine feel; the malt is powerful enough to bounce back; the smoke thinks it's got away without being spotted. It hasn't; **f22.5** milky cocoa topped with icing sugar; **b23** brimming with all the honeyed beauty you might expect from this sublime distillery. 52.1%. sc. James MacArthur & Co.

⠿ **The Perfect Dram Clynelish 23 Years Old** dist 1989 **(87) n22** lightly smoked; broad honey-spice waves; **t22.5** typical Clynelish delivery, busting with a honeyed complexity; **f20.5** a slightly unyielding cask injects a little bitterness; **b22** frustrating! 49.7%. sc.

⠿ **Robert Graham's Dancing Stag Clynelish 1995** hogshead, cask no. 8658, dist 22 Sep 95, bott Sep 11 **(81) n19 t22 f19 b21.** A far better experience than the nose will lead you to believe. The moist ginger bread on delivery is a lovely touch. But the limitations of the oak take this malt only so far. 46%. nc ncf sc. Robert Graham. 461 bottles.

Scotch Malt Whisky Society Cask 26.69 Aged 10 Years refill bourbon hogshead, cask no. 51, dist 2000 **(84) n20 t22.5 f20.5 b21.** Clean, juicy barley but strictly limited. Even for a great distillery such as Clynelish, you need good oak to flourish. 57%. sc. 252 bottles.

Scotch Malt Whisky Society Cask 26.73 Aged 15 Years refill sherry butt, cask no. 6117, dist 1995 **(74.5) n18 t18 f19 b18.5.** Weird. At times shows outlines of the Fisherman's Friend character better known at Bowmore...but without the peat. Really would like to know why this was bottled. 55%. sc. 283 bottles.

Scotch Malt Whisky Society Cask 26.77 Aged 27 Years 2nd fill hogshead, cask no. 2584, dist 1983 **(86.5) n22 t22 f21 b21.5.** Lots of ticks, but few gold stars. A sound dram with a touch of nip and aggression. But the oak is a little lopsided and the resulting caramels are laid on thick. 55.1%. sc. 204 bottles.

Scotch Malt Whisky Society Cask 26.80 Aged 19 Years 2nd fill hogshead, cask no. 4435, dist 1992 **(90.5) n22** a major injection of oak sits comfortably with the sturdy barley. Usually there is some honey around, though here it is in delicate amounts outweighed by the citrus; **t22.5** fabulous tannins add instant spice while a tart, mildly eye-watering and shrill honey-sugar note rips into any drier vanillas; **f23** settles impressively with those spices still radiating and the tannins heading towards Kentucky. But it is the clever interplay with those sugars which really hit the high spots; **b23** I was beginning to wonder if the SMWS were losing their touch slightly with distillery 26. But, at last, a sample which is busy and challenging and absolutely brimming with all the right stuff. Hurrah! 53%. sc. 97 bottles.

⠿ **Scotch Malt Whisky Society Cask 26.82 Aged 15 Years** refill sherry butt, cask no. 6119, dist 1995 **(68) n17 t18 f16 b17.** A sulphur-riddled offering. 57.9%. sc.

⠿ **Scotch Malt Whisky Society Cask 26.86 Aged 21 Years** refill barrel, cask no. 7923, dist 1990 **(88.5) n23.5** the distillery's standard – and highly desirable – honeyed signature; **t23.5** busy delivery with minimal viscosity but maximum honeyed lubrication; a few butterscotch and Lubec marzipan notes massage the taste buds further; **f20** sinks a little as the oak catches up to offer a countering bitterness; **b21.5** shame about the late failure of the oak: until then things had motored along beautifully. 50.5%. sc.

⠿ **Scotch Single Malt Circle Clynelish 1989** cask no. 3843, dist 7 Jun 89, bott 12 Feb 12 **(88.5) n22.5** a dab of something superficially fruity lightens the malty load; a real toasty, bourbon liquorice base note; **t22** superb weight and surprise package of early vanillins cranking up the early intensity; the usual honeyed suspects begin to appear as matters calm; **f22** a light finish, not entirely unlike porridge with a dollop of molten honey; **b22** the first whisky of yet another long tasting day. And it is important to start it with one which is a safe bet to get your taste buds off to a flying start. Not quite as flowing and complex as one might hope due to the big oak, but no disappointments either. 51.8%. sc. Scotch Single Malt Circle.

⠿ **Single Cask Collection Clynelish 14 Years Old** refill sherry hogshead, dist 1997 **(76) n18 t22 f17 b19.** Stunning delivery...which is saying something under the circumstances. Of ⠿e ten Scotch whiskies I have tasted today, this is the fifth tainted by sulphur. 56.8%. sc.

⠿ **Wemyss 1997 Single Highland Clynelish "Fresh Fruit Sorbet"** hogshead, bott ⠿2 **(92) n23.5** not so sure about the fresh fruitsorbet. Unless barley is now a fruit. From ⠿distillery you'd expect a salad bowl on the nose. Instead we are treated to wonderful ⠿directional grassy notes augmented with thin maple syrup; **t23** it's all about the barley ⠿. And this gives it to you in a Speysidey Tomatin kind of way with the malt just ⠿hicker by the second; **f22.5** dries as the vanillas assemble; **b23** this distillery is just ⠿y good. How simultaneously bold yet subtle can a whisky get? 46%. sc. 331 bottles.

The Whisky Agency Clynelish 1972 sherry cask **(86) n21 t23.5 f20 b21.5.** In over 30-odd years, I can count the number of times I have seen Clynelish in this ultra sherry state on one hand. Pretty shagged out, but worth finding to extend your whisky knowledge, alone. *45.8%*

⁖ **The Whisky Broker Clynelish 14 Years Old** refill sherry hogshead, cask no. 6884, dist 14 Jul 97, bott 28 Sep 11 **(89.5) n22.5** classic fruit cake, though this one tends to have more moist high quality marzipan than most; **t24** this distillery can't help making you swoon on delivery whichever type of sound cask it has been matured in: a magnificent almost Christmas pudding richness to this...just lacking the silver thruppencies; **f21** the big burnt raisins fight on valiantly and make light of the few late sulphur notes; **b22** my usual twitch which appeared when I read this was from refill sherry disappeared once it hit my glass. Not perfect, but some cracking moments along the way. *53.7%. nc ncf sc. 285 bottles.*

Wilson & Morgan Barrel Selection Clynelish 1995 Sherry Finish bott 2010 **(73.5) n17 t21.5 f17 b18.** Here's a good example why the two words "finish" and "sherry" make me shudder when rearranged and placed side-by-side. The tragedy is that this was obviously a sublime cask before its fate was sealed in the sherry butt. *46%. Wilson & Morgan.*

COLEBURN
Speyside, 1897–1985. Diageo. Closed.

The Whisky Agency Coleburn 26 Year Old dist 1983, bott 2009 **(88.5) n22 t23 f21.5 b22.** Coleburn is a rare whisky. A thoroughly enjoyable Coleburn is rarer still. So here's one you've just got to go and track down... *49.5%. The Whisky Agency, Germany.*

CONVALMORE
Speyside, 1894–1985. William Grant & Sons. Closed.

Convalmore 1977 bott 2005 db **(91) n23 t23 f22 b23.** Must be blended with Botox, as there is no detrimental ageing to either nose or delivery. A quite lovely and charming whisky to remember this lost – and extremely rare - distillery by. *57.9%. 3900 bottles.*

Rare Old Convalmore 1975 (96) n24.5 t24 f23 b24.5. A caressing, ambient dram: certainly shows great age but does it in a style and manner which demands total respect. A true classic and yet another example of a distillery lost to us hitting heights of which other can only dream. *43%. Gordon & MacPhail.*

CRAGGANMORE
Speyside, 1870. Diageo. Working.

Cragganmore Aged 12 Years db **(81.5) n20 t21 f20 b20.5.** I have a dozen bottles of Cragganmore in my personal cellar dating from the early 90s when the distillery was first bottled as a Classic Malt. Their astonishing dexterity and charm, their naked celebration of all things Speyside, casts a sad shadow over this drinkable but drab and instantly forgettable expression. *40%*

Cragganmore Aged 14 Years The Distillers Edition finished in port casks, dist 1993, bott 2007 db **(85) n22 t21 f21 b21.** The tightly closed fruit on the palate doesn't quite match the more expansive and complex nose. *40%*

Cragganmore Special Release 2010 21 Years Old refill American oak, dist 1989 db **(95.5) n23.5** huge age, but the close knitted nature of the clean barley ensures all the strength required to keep the oak in check; the odd pine-laden tannin and even a touch of pineapple and honeydew melon gives the nod towards something a little exotic; **t24** you can ask little more from a Speyside-style delivery at this age and from bourbon. The barley is so wholesome and well integrated that the palate goes into immediate barley-juice overdrive; the oaks offer up some half-hearted cocoa but some full blown molasses. The result is a single malt of unstinting enormity, yet unambiguous magnificence; **f23.5** some light liquorice joins forces with the cocoa and molasses to underline the bourbon credentials. Massive age, the odd creak here and there. But never for a second is the quality breeched; **b24.5** what a fascinating, awe-inspiring dram. More or less at the very time this malt was being made, I remember talking to the manager at the then barely known Speyside distillery. He told me that the new Classic Malt 12-year-old was selected at that age because it was felt that, as a singleton (though not for blending), Cragganmore did not give its best over that age. I still tend to agree, in general. But here is a bottling which is making me look at this distillery is a new light...and that light is a beacon. I think the manager and I would have stood in amazement if we knew just how fine that young spirit would be when entering its 21st year. 112 per cent proof that you should never say never... *56%. nc ncf. Diageo. Fewer than 6000 bottles.*

⁖ **A.D. Rattray Cragganmore 1997** cask no. 1494, dist 28 Mar 97, bott Jun 12 **(84.5) n21 t22 f20.5 b21.** Concentrated barley, but the oak offers an unwelcome tang. *46%. sc.*

Berry's Own Selection Cragganmore 1989 cask no. 2880, bott 2010 **(86.5) n22 t21.5 f21.5 b21.5.** A grassy, hay loft kind of malt which is happy to explore its own cereal roots. As a single malt, enjoyable but perhaps a little limited. For a blend, this would have done one hell of a job upping the malt signature. 53.5%. nc ncf sc. Berry Bros & Rudd.

Berry's Own Selection Cragganmore 1997 cask no. 1513, bott 2010 **(87) n21.5 t21.5 f22 b22.** One very aggressive Speysider with limited conversation. 58.3%. nc ncf sc.

Berry's Own Selection Cragganmore 2000 cask no. 3673, bott 2011 **(86.5) n21 t22 f22 b21.5.** Craggymalt, more like...! Technically less than perfect from a distillation perspective, as the nose and finish testifies. But my word! It is hard not to be impressed by the almost Glen Grant-esque, granite-faced barley which assails the taste buds! Hard and juicy. 56.8%. nc ncf sc. Berry Bros & Rudd.

Duncan Taylor Dimensions Cragganmore 25 Years Old dist 1986 **(96) n24.5** earthy without being smoky; sweet yet no trace of sugars; bourbony yet with no overpowering liquorice; fruity but with little sign of grape; spicy yet without aggression: enigmatic, ultra complex and magnificent; **t24.5** rarely does a single mouthful last so long or take you on a journey seemingly without end: the spices hanging around the nose here gather in nibbling, tantalising squadrons; the sugars form and reform at regular intervals, each time moving towards a honeycomb weightiness; throughout the barley perches juicily on the taste buds and the dates move from old and dry to ripe and lush; **f23** the spices hint at something of the vaguest smokiness; the oak takes on new cask form; **b24** just track down a bottle and be prepared to give up two or three days of your life for a journey you'll never forget. Wondrously beautiful: the very reason why I can never fall out of love with whisky. 54.6%. sc.

Duncan Taylor Rare Auld Cragganmore 18 Years Old cask no. 1385, dist 1993 **(83) n20 t21 f22 b20.** Not a spoiled sherry butt by any means. In fact, astonishingly clean. But one which swamps all else with mushy grape and allows little else to survive. Fantastically spiced, juicy but heavier than a sumo wrestler drowned in a vat of oloroso: OTT. 55.3%. sc.

Duncan Taylor Rare Auld Cragganmore 23 Years Old cask no. 1964, dist 1987 **(86.5) n22 t22 f21 b21.5.** An exceptionally warming malt with a tendency to overplay its floral hand, which includes no shrinking violets. Spicy and dries with intent. 55.3%. sc.

Duthies Cragganmore 18 Years Old bott Mar 12 **(88.5) n22** if the barley was any sharper it'd cut your nose off; **t23** gorgeously mouth-watering barley where age has been eschewed for almost three-dimensional malt: intense yet with the weight of the average soufflé...; **f21** thin vanilla; **b22.5** a flighty little hussy. 46%. sc. WM Cadenhead Ltd.

Malts Of Scotland Cragganmore 1999 bourbon hogshead, cask no. MoS110012, dist 11 Dec 99, bott Oct 11 **(92) n23** some neo Kentuckian notes with a serious bourbon edge to every aspect of the sweetness. There are peppery spices, but far out-battled by a stupendous orangey-liquorice note more usually associated with Wild Turkey...; **t23.5** magnificent weight from the off...or should that be oof!! Because this fair takes the breath away, the shards of manuka honey in perfect sync with the thick vanilla and persistent liquorice; **f22.5** long, with the oaks still having a major say, though the sugars last the pace longest; **b23** a relentless tide of vanilla and barley. For the bourbon lovers among the malt connoisseurs. 55.1%. nc ncf sc.

Master Of Malt Cragganmore 20 Year Old cask no. 1146, dist 1991 **(87) n22** an attractive, slightly unusual nuttiness as found in a west coast salad; lively liquorice; **t22** a thick bourbon richness to the intense barely; **f21.5** big, a little unwieldy and some bittering oak; **b21.5** no shortage of character and class, but perhaps on the wane. 53.5%. sc. Master Of Malt.

Mo Ôr Collection Cragganmore 1989 21 Years Old first fill bourbon hogshead, cask no. 2840, dist 14 Nov 89, bott 14 Mar 11 **(87.5) n21.5** Almost like salt and lime on a tequila. Only without the tequila; **t22.5** big, big age though the barley is trimming off the grey hairs. A salty tightness to the butterscotch and vanilla cream biscuit; somewhere some juicy barley is found to breathe the required life into the malt; **f21.5** dry, tired but pleasantly spiced; **b22** It is unlikely you will ever come across a saltier Cragganmore. Perhaps just a shade too much age for its own good, there is easily enough sugar to make a telling contribution and ramp up the complexity. 46%. nc ncf sc. Release No. 27. The Whisky Talker. 395 bottles.

Old Malt Cask Cragganmore Aged 13 Years refill hogshead, cask no. 6497, dist 1997, bott Aug 10 **(70.5) n18 t18 f17 b18.5.** Faltering and never hits its stride. More a case of Craggan-less... 50%. nc ncf sc. Douglas Laing & Co. 349 bottles.

Old Malt Cask Cragganmore Aged 19 Years refill hogshead, cask no. 6547, dist Mar 91, bott Sep 10 **(86) n21 t21.5 f22 b21.5.** Not the most sympathetic cask. But here is another journey down memory lane. Soon after turning the world's first full time whisky writer back in 1992, I managed to get a whole bunch of new male samples from the previous 12 months. And I remember a very lightly smoked Cragganmore which both surprised me and caught my eye. Now here it is as a strapping 19 year-old...or would be had it been in a cask that did it full justice. Even so, a real sweet, earthy charmer. 50% nc ncf sc. Douglas Laing & Co. 308 bottles.

Provenance Cragganmore Over 11 Years refill hogshead, cask no. 7189, dist Summer 00, bott Summer 2011 **(87.5) n21.5 t22 f22 b22.** Even from what is probably a third fill cask, the quality sparkles. 46%. nc ncf sc. Douglas Laing & Co.

Scotch Malt Whisky Society Cask 37.47 Aged 23 Years refill butt, cask no. 179, dist 1988 **(83.5) n21.5 t21 f20.5 b20.5.** Plenty of citrus and juicy barley but rather overbearing oak. Decent enough, but would have done a better job in a blend. *54.9%. sc. 148 bottles.*

⋅⋅⋅ **Scotch Malt Whisky Society Cask 37.49 Aged 12 Years** refill hogshead, cask no. 840, dist 1999 **(89.5) n22.5** exemplary Speyside: big barley with a slight grassy edge but enough oak from the cask to ensure a balancing dryness and weight; **t23** just love that delivery: absolutely maxes out on the barley and clean enough to make your teeth sparkle; **f22** long and malty but dispenses with complexity; **b22** yummy! *54.2%. sc. Scotch Malt Whisky Society.*

⋅⋅⋅ **Scotch Malt Whisky Society Cask 37.51 Aged 18 Years** first fill sherry butt, cask no. 1379, dist 1993 **(92) n23** faultless sherry butt: clean grape with no off notes and generous enough to allow a barley-bourbon thread for added complexity; **t23** dry delivery with the oloroso showing its colours – literally! But soon the oak injects a spicy edge and the barley adds a fabulous salivating quality; **f23** long with chocolate fruit and nut. Yet still the barley keeps coming...; **b23** always great to find a malt which can stand up to a massive, clean sherry butt and offer a devastating return volley. *60%. sc. Scotch Malt Whisky Society.*

⋅⋅⋅ **Wemyss 1989 Single Speyside "Lemon Grove"** hogshead, dist 1989, bott 2011 **(94.5) n24** delicate citrus caress the nose from all angles. A very fine dusting of grist ensures the sugars and barley notes meld effortlessly; the lightest throb of smoke offers a degree of backbone; **t24** textbook delivery: clean but by no means neutral as the immediate intensity of the barley is not only apparent, but so too is the fabulous growth in flavour: juicy with a sprinkling of icing sugar melting in the mouth with the grist; the citrus notes dovetail without ever gaining control; **f23** light vanillas remind you of the good age to this; **b23.5** the citrus and sugars have a much bigger say than the distillery usually allows. Sublime. *46%. sc. 371 bottles.*

CRAIGELLACHIE
Speyside, 1891. John Dewar & Sons. Working.

⋅⋅⋅ **Berry's Own Selection Craigellachie 1991** cask no. 2715, bott 2011 **(83) n21 t22 f20 b20.5.** An oily, eye-watering barley-fest. *55.8%. nc ncf sc. Berry Bros & Rudd.*

⋅⋅⋅ **Chieftain's Craigellachie Aged 13 Years** Oloroso finish, dist Mar 99, bott 2012 **(89) n22** an excellent light smoke backdrop to the honey and citrus lead; **t23** quietly aggressive as the barley displays little subtlety; some jammy fruitiness as well; **f22.5** a tad bitter but good vanilla; **b22.5** seriously satisfying. *43%. nc ncf sc. Ian Macleod Distillers.*

Duncan Taylor Octave Craigellachie 11 Years Old cask no. 752330, dist 1999 **(73.5) n17 t19 f19 b18.5.** A score of wrong notes. *54.8%. sc.*

⋅⋅⋅ **Duncan Taylor Dimensions Craigellachie 21 Years Old** cask no. 5399, dist Aug 90, bott Jan 12 **(89) n22** charming exotic and citrus fruit combo; **t23** ethereal barley though the vanilla is more earthbound; very attractive spice; **f22** lengthened by just so oils. Excellent barley finale. **b22** Craigellachie in very fine fettle. *52%. nc ncf sc. Duncan Taylor & Co.*

Hart Brothers Craigellachie Aged 14 Years dist Nov 96, bott Jan 11 **(86) n21.5 t22 f21 b21.5.** Just a little oak interference at the finish. Nothing too serious, gladly. For this is a busy little creature with a curious salty sharpness to its big malt chorus. *46%. sc.*

⋅⋅⋅ **Kingsbury "The Selection" Craigellachie 8 Years Old** butt, cask no. 900085 & 900086, dist Aug 02, bott Apr 11 **(69.5) n17 t18 f17 b17.5.** Sad to say, but someone has selected a very poor cask. *43%. nc ncf. Japan Import Systems. 1,651 bottles.*

Old Malt Cask Craigellachie 14 Years Old hogshead & claret barrels, cask no. 6278, dist Feb 96, bott Jun 10 **(79) n19 t20.5 f19 b20.** Does its best to raise its game despite an obvious light flaw. The rich malty oils are impressive. *50%. nc ncf sc. Douglas Laing & Co. 275 bottles.*

⋅⋅⋅ **Old Malt Cask Craigellachie Aged 14 Years** refill hogshead, cask no. 8185, dist Dec 97, bott Feb 12 **(87) n21.5** light, though busy, malt; **t23** much bigger on delivery: the barley offers a big, slightly oily surge. Spices and vanilla back up pleasantly; **f21** vanilla and cocoa; **b21.5** a very simple malt, but attractive. *50%. nc ncf sc. Douglas Laing & Co. 354 bottles.*

Premier Barrel Craigellachie Aged 11 Years sherry cask **(91.5) n23.5** a beautiful summer garden perfume to add to the clean ripe fruit; **t23** lush and juicy with a swooning degree of spice; **f22** a very light bitter fuzz, but the grape is so beautifully drawn there is no damage done; **b23** dangerous malt; the kind of stuff that can be drunk all day, every day... *46%. nc ncf sc.*

⋅⋅⋅ **Premier Barrel Craigellachie Aged 12 Years** **(75.5) n18 t20 f18.5 b19.** Not even a tidal wave of barley can entirely overcome the limitations of the cask. *46%. nc ncf sc.*

Provenance Craigellachie Over 12 Years sherry butt, cask no. 7507, dist Summer 99, bott Summer 2011 **(82.5) n19 t21 f21.5 b21.** Better than the nose suggests and even tries to the game with a late injection of salty cocoa. *46%. nc ncf sc.*

⋅⋅⋅ **Provenance Craigellachie Over 12 Years** sherry butt, cask no. 8444, dist 1999, bott Spring 2012 **(84.5) n21 t21.5 f21 b21.** An attractive malt which concentrat malty simplicity, but is not beyond adding a degree of sweetened seasoning to get flowing. *46%. nc ncf sc. Douglas Laing & Co.*

⚗️ **Provenance Craigellachie Over 12 Years** sherry butt, cask no. 7607, dist Summer 199? bott Summer 2011 **(76.3) n18 t19 f20 b19.5.** Worth tasting alongside the provenance cask 7974 just so you can see the difference between decent and very indifferent oak. 46%. nc ncf sc.

⚗️ **Provenance Craigellachie Over 12 Years** sherry butt, cask no. 7974, dist Autumn 1999, bott Winter 2011 **(88.5) n21** dusty, but flecks of fruit fight through; **t23** superb delivery full of understated power and barley at its most vibrant; **f22** attractively long with the spices fading then returning; **b22.5** a lovely dram swimming in personality. 46%. nc ncf sc.

⚗️ **Scotch Malt Whisky Society Cask 44.50 Aged 18 Years** refill barrel, cask no. 5793, dist 1993 **(89) n21.5** sharp and tangy, the barley appears to have been steeped in sea water...; **t23** good grief! the salty tang to the malt almost brings a tear to the eye; the thumping bourbon vanillas are no less saline intense; the middle has a light Walnut Whip feel; **f22** a little sweetened walnut oil creeps in to soften things a little; **b22.5** love to know where this cask has been kept: one of the most coastal Speyside whiskies you'll taste this year... 58.3%. sc.

⚗️ **Scotch Malt Whisky Society Cask 44.51 Aged 22 Years** refill hogshead, cask no. 3876, dist 1989 **(90) n22** a blender's treat: clean, playful barley offering just a little salt to the surviving grist; **t23** a beautiful delivery which draws the best out of both the barley and cask. The sugars are intact and err towards the standard white side; the barley is more complex and fill out to the full as the oils gather; **f22.5** exactly the butterscotch and vanilla style you'd expect. Though the return of the salt is a bit of a surprise; **b22.5** great to find the distillery in excellent form both in production and cask choice. Unostentatiously gorgeous. 53.7%. sc.

⚗️ **The Warehouse Collection Craigellache Aged 10 Years** bourbon hogshead, cask no. 212, dist 30 Aug 99, bott 15 Dec 09 **(94) n23.5** punchy barley: a little salt adding zest and zip; elsewhere, outstanding crushed young walnut and hazel notes are topped by a distant and surprising strawberry jam sweetness; **t24** one of the most juicy deliveries of the year. The barley is as clean as you can get without even beginning to bore. This is partly because of the complexity of the crisp sugars, as well as the fabulous marriage between the malt and Danish marzipan. Again, though, it is the delicate salt which seems to arouse the complexity into a state of juicy excitement; **f23** long, still a multitude of barley notes but now late spices buzz in; **b23.5** my favourite age and cask type for this distillery. Rarely is Craigellachie these days displayed in better profile. This will be considered the bar all future 10-year-old Craigellachies will have to clear for years to come. 59%. sc. Whisky Warehouse No. 8. 311 bottles.

DAILUAINE
Speyside, 1854. Diageo. Working.
Dailuaine 1997 The Manager's Choice db **(87.5) n21.5** intriguing... **t23** wow!!! Well, what do you know: a Dailuaine going on a charm offensive. On one hand the big malty body thumps into the taste buds, then several layers of honey wash over the wounds. Superb...; **f21** tails off rather too quickly towards the bittering oak; **b22** one of the most enjoyable (unpeated!!) Dailuaines I've come across in an age. There is the usual distillery biff to this, but not without a honeyed sarley net. Great fun. 58.6%

Dailuaine Aged 16 Years bott lot no. L4334 db **(79) n19 t21 f20 b19.** Syrupy, almost grotesquely heavy at times; the lighter, more considered notes of previous bottlings have been lost under an avalanche of sugary, over-ripe tomatoes. Definitely one for those who want a massive dram. 43%

Adelphi Dailuaine 27 Years Old cask no. 4319, dist 1983, bott 2011 **(81.5) n20 t20 f21 b20.5.** Good grief...! I found fingernail scratches in my chair after tasting this. They came from me, I assume, as I gripped for grim life as spasms passed. Walnut and dates. With a spectacularly vicious kick in the walnuts... 58.1%. sc. Adelphi Distillery. 219 bottles.

⚗️ **Archives Dailuaine 1983 28 Years Old First Release** hogshead, cask no. 865, dist 23 Feb 83, bott 4 Jan 12 **(85.5) n21 t22 f21 b21.5.** Talk about déjà vu! For a moment I thought I had tasted this before, or at least a more emboldened version of this thin but pleasant offering. Then spotted my Mo Ór 1983 notes....!! 47.3%. nc ncf sc. Whiskybase B.V. 265 bottles.

Berry's Own Selection Dailuaine 1973 cask no. 10418, bott 2010 **(83) n22 t21 f20 b20.** Very rarely do you find a whisky with so much age and so little give. Outwardly juicy, but absolutely hard as granite. 50.6%. nc ncf sc. Berry Bros & Rudd.

Chieftain's Dailuaine Aged 12 Years French oak finish, dist Mar 99, bott 2011 **(69.5) n17 ⦚.5 f17 b17.** Just occasionally, and I mean very occasionally, you find a cracking French oak ⦚hed malt. This isn't it. 46%. nc ncf. Ian Macleod Distillers.

Mo Ór Collection Dailuaine 1983 27 Years Old first fill bourbon hogshead, cask no. ⦚st 23 Feb 83, bott 2 Dec 10 **(87.5) n21** thin and vaguely apple-fruity but with the barley ⦚ing a say; **t22.5** clean, salivating with a butterscotch lid to the gooseberry pie; **f22** ⦚re plaintiff calls of apple but now the vanilla grips like a vice; **b22** a rough and ready ⦚ bite is more young cider brandy than malt. But the overall effect shimmers with ⦚other-one allure... 46%. nc ncf sc. Release No. 20. The Whisky Talker. 407 bottles.

Old Malt Cask Dailuaine Aged 14 Years bourbon barrel, cask no. 6995, dist Apr 97, bott Apr 11 **(80) n19 t20.5 f20 b20.5.** Pleasant, malty but somewhat featureless blending fodder. *50%. nc ncf sc. Douglas Laing & Co. 265 bottles.*

⋄ **Old Malt Cask Dailuaine Aged 15 Years** refill barrel, cask no. 8240, dist Apr 97, bott Apr 12 **(86) n21 t21.5 f22 b21.5.** A thumping malt which eschews subtlety. The nose is a bit like an old paperback, but the sharpness of the barley is a page turner. *50%. nc ncf sc. 268 bottles.*

The Perfect Dram Dailuaine 1971 bourbon hogshead, bott 2010 **(78.5) n19.5 t19 f20 b20.** Pleasant and engaging in its own limited way, though shows a piney, creosotey tendency as it embraces old age. Memo to the powers that be at The Whisky Agency: if you are in search of The Perfect Dram, Dailuaine isn't the place to start... *46.6%. The Whisky Agency.*

⋄ **Provenance Dailuaine Over 11 Years** sherry butt, cask no. 8012, dist Spring 2000, bott Winter 2012 **(84) n21 t21 f21 b21.** A pleasant malt in a mildly fruity, juicy nondescript kind of way. *46%. nc ncf sc. Douglas Laing & Co.*

⋄ **Provenance Dailuaine Over 12 Years** sherry butt, cask no. 8434, dist Autumn 1999, bott Spring 2012 **(84.5) n21.5 t20.5 f21.5 b21.** A warming malt where you feel the stills were going at some lick when this was distilled. Attractive mint chocolate on the finish. *46%. nc ncf sc.*

⋄ **Riegger's Selection Dailuaine 1998** bourbon cask, cask no. 3396, dist 31 Mar 98, bott 6 May 12 **(79.5) n20 t19 f20.5 b20.** A distillery known to have its odd off day when distilling. This salty and salivating effort came from one of them. *58.5%. nc ncf sc. 298 bottles.*

Scotch Malt Whisky Society Cask 41.47 Aged 7 Years 1st fill bourbon barrel, cask no. 800243, dist 2003 **(86) n22 t21 f21.5 b21.5.** There you go. All those old Dailuaines letting you down time and time again. When its forte was being bottled at what I think is always a fascinating age in Scotland when the malt gets a chance to say its piece, especially when in first fill cask. Can't escape the fire, but you must have a heart of steel not to enjoy the oak-barley tapestry. *61.2%. sc.*

Scotch Malt Whisky Society Cask 41.49 Aged 30 Years 2nd fill sherry butt, cask no. 9137, dist 1980 **(83) n21.5 t21 f20 b20.5.** A tart monster of a dram which has you thumping the back of your own head to restore you to life. The sherry offers a lot more refinement on the nose than the palate where it fails to cope with the distillery's, rolled-sleeve, aggressive style. *50.9%. sc. 51 bottles.*

⋄ **Scotch Malt Whisky Society Cask 41.50 Aged 30 Years** refill hogshead, cask no. 9135, dist 1980 **(86) n21.5 t21 f22 b21.5.** By no means a shy character and brimming with chocolate nut. Always tangy, a little honeycomb towards the finish, too. *53.5%. sc.*

⋄ **Scott's Selection Dailuaine 1983** bott 2011 **(84) n21 t23 f20 b20.** Marked with all the usual ticks and crosses. But a few extra ticks, and even the odd gold star, for the gorgeous exuberance of the honey-sweetened barley on delivery. *57.9%. Speyside Distillers.*

DALLAS DHU
Speyside, 1899–1983. Closed. Now a museum.

Duncan Taylor Collection Dallas Dhu 1981 cask no. 389 **(90) n21.5 t21.5 f24 b23.** Until the finale, it's difficult to know where this one is going. Or even that it is Dallas Dhu, as this is a much wilder, kick ass version than most... *55.1%*

⋄ **Gordon & MacPhail Rare Vintage Dallas Dhu 1979 (94.5) n23** marginally earthy but probably only there for the fruit and nuts to grow in; green banana and toasted yam lead, pecan pie follows behind; **t23.5** how can barley melt in the mouth after 32 years? It defies logic and description. What makes it work so well, is that the base and baritone sugars from the oak never for a moment attempt to drown the tenor from the grist. Often that is the key to a whisky's success and here it is demonstrated perfectly: it means the complexity levels remain high at all times and the depth of oak controlled; **f23.5** long, with the vanilla enjoying a nutty depth, moving into a more deliciously praline oiliness. The tannins are firm enough to remind us that 1979 was a long time ago now but not a single hint of oaky degradation. Clear, confident, strident notes from first to last; **b24** good ol' Gordon and MacPhail! I can hardly recall the last time a bottling from this distillery popped along – depressing to think I am old enough to remember when they were so relatively common they were being sold on special offer...!! It was always a class act; it's closure an act of whisky vandalism, whether it be preserved as a museum or not. This, even after all these years, shows the extraordinary quality we are missing day in, day out... *43%*

DALMORE
Highands (Northern), 1839. Whyte and Mackay. Working.

The Dalmore 12 Years Old db **(90) n22** mixed dates: both dry and juicy; **t23** fat, rich delivery with a wonderful dovetailing of juicy barley and thick, rumbling fruit; **f22.5** lots of toffee on the finish, but gets away with it thanks to the sheer depth to the barley and the busy sherry sub-plot; **b22.5** has changed character of late yet remains underpowered and with a shade too much toffee. But such is the quality of the malt in its own right it can overcome any hurdles placed before it to ensure a real mouth-filling, rumbustious dram. 40%

The Dalmore Dee Dram 12 Years Old db (63.5) n15.5 t17 f14 b16. Words fail me...40%

The Dalmore 15 Years Old db (83.5) n21 t21 f20.5 b21. Another pleasant Dalmore that coasts along the runway but simply fails to get off the ground. The odd off note here and there, but it's the blood orange which shines brightest. 40%

The Dalmore 18 Years Old db (76.5) n19 t21 f18 b18.5. Heaps of caramel and the cask choice might have been better. 43%

The Dalmore 21 Years Old db (87) n22 just how many citrus notes can we find here? Answers on a postcard... on second thoughts, don't. Just beautifully light and effervescent for its age: a genuine delight; t23 again, wonderfully fruity though this time the malt pushes through confidently to create its own chewy island: fabulous texture; f20 simplifies towards toffee slightly too much in the interests of great balance. A lovely coffee flourish late on; b22 bottled elegance. 43%

The Dalmore Forty Years Old db (82) n23 t20 f19 b20. Doubtless my dear friend Richard Paterson will question whether I have the ability to spot a good whisky if it ran me over in a ten ton truck. But I have to say here that we have a disappointing malt: I had left this too late on in writing this year's (2008) Bible as a treat. But it wasn't to be. A soft delivery: but of what? Hard to exactly pin down what's going on here as there is so much toffee and fruit that the oak and barley have been overwhelmed. Pleasant, perhaps, but it's all rather dull and passionless. Like going through the motions with an old lover. Adore the sherry-trifle/toffee mousse nose, though... 40%

The Dalmore Astrum Aged 40 Years db (89) n23.5 I think this is as far as you can take oak and still be on the credit side: a rich saltiness seems to inject life and extra sharpness to the blackcurrants, dates, plums and stewed cooking apples which abound. The very lightest dusting of allspice furthers the piquancy; t21 for a moment the fruit – and even stratum of barley - looks intact, but soon the oak arrives with a brutal vengeance. The middle ground becomes puckeringly tight; f22 relaxes as sugars are released and some vanillas arrive but at the very death the bitter oaks dominate; meanwhile a fruity sub-note rumbles...; b22.5 this guy is all about the nose. The oak is too big for the overall framework and the balance hangs by a thread. Yet somehow the overall effect is impressive. Another summer and you suspect the whole thing would have snapped... 42%

The Dalmore Aurora Aged 45 Years db (90.5) n25 unquestionably an intriguing and engaging nose, full of subtleties and quirky side streets. Initially, all these sub plots and intrigues are to do with oak and very little else. However, the spices once located are a treat and open the door to the delicate boiled fruit which, after making a tentative entrance, begins to inject the required sweetness; give ten minutes in the glass to discover something quite sublime and faultless... t22 rounded on delivery but again it's all about the oak which piles up untidily on the palate, though the odd exotic fruit note can be detected. Salt dovetails with that fruit but it is heading downhill... f21.5 some vaguely malty vanilla but the oak is now dominating though some mocha does come to the rescue; b22 sophisticated for sure. But so huge is the oak on the palate, it cannot hope to match the freakish brilliance of the nose. 45%

The Dalmore 50 Years Old db (88) n21 buxom and bourbony, the oak makes no secret of the antiquity; t19 oak again arrives first and without apology, some salty malt creaking in later. Ripe cherries offer a mouthwatering backdrop; f25 comes into its own as harmony is achieved as the oak quietens to allow a beautiful malt-cherry interplay. Spices arrive for good measure in an absolutely has-it-all, faultless finish: really as much a privilege to taste as a delight; b23 takes a while to warm up, but when it does becomes a genuinely classy and memorable dram befitting one of the world's great and undervalued distilleries. 52%

The Dalmore Candela Aged 50 Years db (96) n25 there you go: that's the next half hour to 45 minutes taken up...trying to unravel this one. Fresh fruity frame, but the picture in the middle is far more difficult to understand. Dates – both dried and juicy – mingle with finest quality Lubec marzipan paste (sans chocolate) while a few spices nip in to say 'hullo'; clean, relaxed...and very sprightly for its age; t24 immediate onrush of oaks, offset by a cherry sauce and later plain chocolate fondant to ensure any bitterness is kept in check; elsewhere an improbable layering of barley juice and fruit again makes a mockery of the age; f23.5 for a whisky reaching half a century, curiously reserved with the oaks now really starting to get a degree of bitterness generated; a thin line of chocolate and raisin helps keep that bitterness at acceptable levels; b23.5 just one of those whiskies which you come across only a handful of times in your life. All because a malt makes it to 50 does not mean it will automatically be great. This, however, is a masterpiece, the end of which seemingly has never been written... 50% (bottled at 45%). Whyte & Mackay. 77 bottles.

The Dalmore Selene 58 Years Old cask no. 1781/1782 dist Jun 51 db (87.5) n23 t22 f21 b21.5. A fascinating experience, but in terms of quality, though very good indeed for its range alone, not in the same league as the Dalmore 50 or 60-y-o. A great present for anyone born in 1951, or supporters of Queen of the South marking the 60th anniversary of their winning the Scottish Div 2 title. But as a whisky spectacle: great nose, decent delivery and then after that... you are on your own. *44%. Whyte & Mackay. 30 bottles.*

The Dalmore Eos Aged 59 Years db **(95) n24.5** extraordinary pulsing of rich, dry sherry notes: nutty and polished oak in one of the finer Mayfair antique shops or clubs. The moistest, choicest Lubeck marzipan with a thread of Jaffa jam and, as the whisky settles into its stride, this moves to Jaffa cakes with heavy dark chocolate; very limited spice, but the salt levels grow..; **t24** ultra dry delivery despite the juices flowing from the very first moment: the grape is beautifully firm and holds together light oils and burgeoning oak which threaten to inject a weighty toastiness; the mid ground though is a triumph of glorious lightly molassed vanilla notes with strands of barley; spices buzz and fizz and add even further life; **f22.5** a light off-key bitterness knocks off a mark or two, but the cocoa and burnt raisin charge to the rescue; **b24** for those of you who thought this was a camera, let me put you in the picture. This is one well developed whisky, but by no means over exposed, as it would have every right to be after nearly 60 years. Indeed: it is one of those drams which utterly confounds and amazes. I specially chose this as the 1001st new whisky for the 2012 Bible, and those of us old enough to be young when most of its sister casks were hauled off for blending, there was an advert in the '60s which said: "1,001 cleans a big, big carpet...for less than half a crown." Well this 1001 cleans a big, big palate. But I can't see a bottle of this majestic malt going for as little as that... *44%*

The Dalmore 62 Years Old db **(95) n23** PM or REV marked demerara potstill rum, surely? Massive coffee presence, clean and enormous, stunning, topdrawer peat just to round things off; **t25** this is brilliant: pure silk wrapping fabulous moist fruitcake soaked in finest oloroso sherry and then weighed with peat which somehow has defied nature and survived in cask all these years. I really cannot fault this: I sit here stunned and in awe; **f24** perfect spices with flocks of ginger and lemon rind; **b24** if I am just half as beautiful, elegant and fascinating as this by the time I reach 62, I'll be a happy man. Somehow I doubt it. A once in a lifetime whisky – something that comes around every 62 years, in fact. Forget Dalmore Cigar Malt – even I might be tempted to start smoking just to get a full bottle of this. *40.5%*

The Dalmore 1263 King Alexander III db **(86) n22 t22.5 f20 b21.5.** Starts brightly with all kinds of barley sugar, fruit and decent age and oak combinations, plus some excellent spice prickle. So far, so good...and obviously thoughtfully and complexly structured. But then vanishes without trace on finish. *40%*

The Dalmore 1978 db **(89.5) n23.5** moist sponge cake with a generous layer of golden syrup; a few delicate citrus notes lighten further but a plumy counterweight excels; **t22** juicy delivery with a fine array of early barley and fruit. But there is a big oaky surge, though never to an overall detriment; **f21.5** finishes as a coffee cake with the odd bitter bean; **b22.5** a seriously lovely old dram which is much weightier on the palate than nose. *47.1%. 477 bottles.*

The Dalmore 1979 db **(84) n21 t21.5 f20 b21.5.** Hard to find a more rounded malt. Strangely earthy, though. *42%. 487 bottles.*

The Dalmore 1980 db **(81.5) n19 t21 f20.5 b21.** Wonderful barley intensity on delivery does its best to overcome the so-so nose and finale. *40%*

The Dalmore Matusalem 1981 db **(91.5) n23** muscular and beautifully primed with soft herbs amid the fruit; marmalade at the bottom of an old jar; **t23.5** now, do I love that delivery! Waxy and thick in a uniquely Whyte and Mackay style, there is a clever muscovado-molasses mix which not just ramps up the sugars but the weight and depth, also; **f22.5** some tangy notes while the sugars fight a rearguard action with the bittering oak; **b22.5** had someone tied me to a rack and kept pulling until I said this could be something other than a W&M production, I would have defied them to the bitter end... *44%. 497 bottles.*

The Dalmore 1981 Amoroso Sherry Finesse amoroso sherry wood cask db **(85.5) n21 t22 f21.5 b21.** A very tight, fruity, dram which gives away its secrets with all the enthusiasm of an agent under torture. Enjoyable to a degree... but bloody hard work. *42%*

The Dalmore Mackenzie 1992 American oak/port pipes, bott 2009 db **(88.5) n23 t22 f21 b22.5.** I suppose you could say that such is the influence of the grape that this is a tad one dimensional. But such is the grim state of wine casks in the industry today, one is forgiven for falling on bended knee and kissing the bottle. Though even this isn't without its sulphury failings... *46%*

The Dalmore Vintage 2001 Limited Edition db **(84.5) n21 t22 f20.5 b21.** Ah... a Dalmore of straw colour displaying such delicate intricacies with the barley...complex, especially with the varying degrees of malt to the oils... What???? I was asleep? I was dreaming...? What do we have here? Oh. Yet another mahogany-coloured Dalmore. Another Dalmore so thick, nutty-toffeed and chewy you can hardly tell where the story starts and ends. Or exactly what the story is that differs from the others... Yes, overall a generally pleasant experience but the feeling of déjà vu and underachievement is depressingly overwhelming. *48%*

The Dalmore Rivers Collection Dee Dram Season 2011 db **(81.5) n20 t22.5 f19 b20.** Where the previous bottling was a complete disaster, this one is friendly and approachable. Still don't expect anything two dimensional on the finish as the caramel attack and a strand of bitterness dries your taste buds to squeaking point. But the delivery is a very pleasant, chewy affair for sure. 40%

The Dalmore Rivers Collection Tweed Dram Season 2011 db **(86) n21 t22 f21.5 b21.5.** Silky and slinky, a real soup of a malt in which the barley occasionally rises high to deliciously juicy effect. 40%

The Dalmore Rivers Collection Tay Dram Season 2011 db **(86.5) n22.5 t23 f20 b21.** Despite the house toffee-neutered finale and the odd but obvious cask-related off note, there is still plenty to enjoy here. 40%

The Dalmore Cabernet Sauvignon db **(79) n22 t19 f19 b19.** Too intense and soupy for its own good. 45%

The Dalmore Castle Leod db **(77) n18.5 t21 f18.5 b19.** Thumpingly big and soupy. More fruit than you can wave a wasp at. But, sadly, the sting comes with the slightly obvious off note. 46%

⁙ **The Dalmore Ceti** db **(91.5) n24** a nose for fruitcake lovers everywhere: ripe cherries and blood orange abound and work most attractively with the slightly suety, muscovado enriched body...; **t23.5** the nose demands a silky delivery and that's exactly what you get. Rich fruit notes form the principle flavour profile but the backing salivating barley and spice is spot on; the mid ground becomes a little saltier and more coastal...; **f21.5** a vague bitterness to the rapidly thinning finale, almost a pithy element, which is slightly out of sync with the joys of before; **b22.5** a Ceti which warbles rather well... 44.7%

The Dalmore Cigar Malt Reserve Limited Edition db **(73.5) n19 t19.5 f17 b18.** One assumes this off key sugarfest is for the cigar that explodes in your face... 44%

⁙ **The Dalmore Cromartie** dist 1996 db **(78.5) n20 t22 f17.5 b19.** Always hard to forecast what these type of bottlings may be like. Sadly there is a sulphur-induced bitterness and tightness to this guy which undermines the more attractive marmalade notes. 45%

The Dalmore Gran Reserva sherry wood and American white oak casks db **(82.5) n22 t21.5 f19 b20.** An improvement on the near nonentity this once was. But still the middle and finish are basic and lacking sophistication or substance outside a broad sweet of oaky chocolate toffee. Delightful mixture of blood orange and nuts on the approach, though. 40%

The Dalmore Visitor Centre Exclusive db **(95.5) n25** this isn't just about fruit: this is a lesson in a nosing glass in how the marriage and equilibrium between salt, sugars, barley and delicate fruit juices should be arranged. There is not an off note; no party dominates; the complexity is beguiling as the picture shifts and changes in the glass every few seconds. Also, how the weight of the whisky is essential to balance. It is, frankly, the perfect malt whisky nose... **t24** so off we go on a journey around about fifteen fruit levels, half that number of sugar intensities and a fabulous salty counter. Close your eyes and be seduced...; **f22.5** a minor blemish as a vaguely bitter note from the oak creeps in. Luckily, the thick barley sugar is in there to repair the damage; remains salty to the very end; **b24** not exactly the easiest distillery to find but a bottle of this is worth the journey alone. I have tasted some sumptuous Dalmores over the last 30-odd years. But this one stands among the very finest. 46%

⁙ **Master Of Malt Dalmore 14 Year Old** dist 1996 **(90) n21.5** Digestive biscuit which needs to cut down on the salt content slightly; **t24** oh, yes! The lack of caramel means you can see with breathtaking clarity the most fabulous complexity to a delivery: intense, ultra-clean barley with vivid, almost eye-watering salt and sugars opening the way for the zesty praline middle...my God! You want to kiss its very beauty...!! **f22** soft vanillas tame the salty fire, alas, but the late cocoa compensates pleasantly; **b22.5** always wonderful to meet a exquisitely naked Dalmore, as so often it is wrapped in an opaque gown of caramel. 55.5%. sc.

Old Malt Cask Dalmore Aged 12 Years refill butt, cask no. 7096, dist Apr 99, bott Apr 11 **(86) n22 t22 f22.5 b22.5.** An endearing malt which grips your attention the further along the track it travels. The barley and light citrus are superb. 50%. nc ncf sc. 429 bottles.

Old Malt Cask Dalmore Aged 20 Years refill butt finished in amontillado sherry butt, cask no. 6838, dist Apr 90, bott Nov 10 **(90) n23** dense, almost impenetrable fruit; mainly blood orange, but some freshly grilled liver, too...talk about meaty...; **t23.5** thicker than a medieval castle wall, but with a lot more yield. Salivating as the onrush of barley carries with it traces of lemon and brown sugars; **f21.5** bitters as we are back to that meaty strata; lots of vague feinty notes; **b22** knife and fork required... 50%. nc ncf sc. Douglas Laing & Co. 224 bottles.

Old Malt Cask Dalmore Aged 33 Years rum finished hogshead, cask no. 6632, dist Dec 76, bott Oct 10 **(70) n18 t18 f17 b17.** That's odd. I always associated butyric with something a lot younger than this! 50%. nc ncf sc. Douglas Laing & Co. 98 bottles.

Premier Barrel Dalmore 12 Years Old **(85.5) n19.5 t22 f22 b22.** Great fun with this characterful malt taking your taste buds on a rollercoaster ride. The nose isn't exactly great, but there is a gorgeously spiced fruit cake quality to this...without the grapes being present. Forget about an evening of romance and sophistication: this is a lovely bit of rough. *46%. nc ncf sc. Douglas Laing & Co. 146 bottles.*

❖ **Provenance Dalmore Over 10 Years** refill hogshead, cask no. 7645, Spring 2001, Summer 2011 **(84.5) n21 t21.5 f21 b21.** Malty, gristy sweet and very tame. *46%. nc ncf sc.*

Provenance Dalmore Over 11 Years refill butt, cask no. 6566, Spring 99, Autumn 2010 **(87.5) n23 t22 f21 b21.5.** Dalmore as it should be, but is so rarely seen: in all its meaty nakedness. The cut here is much wider than you might expect a mainstream pot still single malt, but it ensures character abounds. *46%. nc ncf sc. Douglas Laing & Co.*

DALWHINNIE
Highlands (Central), 1898. Diageo. Working.

Dalwhinnie 15 Years Old db **(95) n24** sublime stuff: a curious mixture of coke smoke and peat-reek wafts teasingly over the gently honied malt. A hint of melon offers some fruit but the caressing malt stars; **t24** that rarest of combinations: at once silky and malt intense, yet at the same time peppery and tin-hat time for the tastebuds, but the silk wins out and a sheen of barley sugar coats everything, soft peat included; **f23** some cocoa and coffee notes, yet the pervading slightly honied sweetness means that there is no bitterness that cannot be controlled; **b24** a malt it is hard to decide whether to drink or bath in: I suggest you do both. One of the most complete mainland malts of them all. Know anyone who reckons they don't like whisky? Give them a glass of this – that's them cured. Oh, if only the average masterpiece could be this good. *43%*

DEANSTON
Highlands (Perthshire), 1966. Burn Stewart Distillers. Working.

Deanston 6 Years Old db **(83) n20 t21 f22 b20.** Great news for those who remember how good Deanston was a decade or two ago: it's on its way back. A delightfully clean dram with its trademark honey character restored. A little beauty slightly undermined by caramel. *40%*

Deanston 12 Years Old db **(74) n18 t19 f18.5 b18.5.** It is quite bizarre how you can interchange this with Tobermory in style; or, rather, at least the faults are the same. *46%. ncf.*

Deanston Aged 12 Years db **(75) n18 t21.5 f17.5 b18.** The delivery is, for a brief moment, a malty/orangey delight. But the nose is painfully out of sync and finish is full of bitter, undesirable elements. A lot of work still required to get this up to a second grade malt, let alone a top flight one. *46.3%. ncf. Burn Stewart.*

Deanston 1967 casks 1051-2, filled Friday 31st Mar 67 db **(90) n23 t23 f21 b23.** The oak is full on but there is so much class around that cannot gain control. A Perthshire beauty. *50.7%*

Deanston Virgin Oak db **(90) n22.3** does exactly what it says on the tin: absolutely brimming with virgin oak. To the cost of all other characteristics. And don't expect a bourbon style for a second: this is sharp-end tannins where the sugars have their own syrupy point of entry; **t23** now those sugars dissolve with some major oak attached: many years back, I tasted a paste made from roasted acorns and brown sugar...not entirely dissimilar; **f22.5** continues to rumble contentedly in the oakiest possible manner...but now with some fizzy spice; **b22** quirky. Don't expect this to taste anything like Scotch... *46.3%*

Marks & Spencer Deanston Aged 12 Years db **(84.5) n20.5 t22 f21 b21.** It's been a while since I found so much honeyed malt in a Deanston. Echoes of 20 years ago. *40%. UK.*

Marks & Spencer Deanston Aged 17 Years Limited Edition db **(88.5) n20 t23.5 f22.5 b22.5.** Overcomes a taught, off-key nose to open into something full of juice, fruity intrigue. Really enjoyed this one. *46.3%. ncf. 979 bottles.*

❖ **Mo Òr Collection Deanston 1995 15 Years Old** first fill bourbon hogshead, cask no. 382, dist 3 Feb 95, bott 28 Jan 11 **(74.5) n18 t20 f18.5 b19.** Fights back from a dreadful nose and at times offers a compensating sweetness to the distinct barley. But not very good whisky is not very good whisky. *46%. nc ncf sc. Release No. 40. The Whisky Talker. 506 bottles.*

❖ **Riegger's Selection Deanston 1992** bourbon cask, cask no. 11, dist 16 Dec 92, bott 11 Feb 11 **(94) n23** intricate citrus bolsters the delicate barley tones. The vanillas are clean and supportive; cocoa lurks somewhere in the background; **t24** the salivating barley and sugars engage in the most comfortable harmony; the odd mocha note gives way to a growing display of delicate spices; the overall weight and pace nears perfection...; **f23** drier, but those excellent mildly gristy sugars still hold the upper hand; the mocha returns now for a more dominating role; **b24** easily one of the best Deanstons I have tasted for a very long time. Worth finding! *57.2%. nc ncf sc. Viktor-Riegger GmbH. 178 bottles.*

Robert Graham's Dancing Stag Deanston 1995 hogshead, dist 14 Jul 95, bott Oct 10 **(86) n21.5 t22 f21.5 b21.** An enjoyable maltfest if you can cope with the sugars. And the fact that a 15-year-old malt has the sophistication of a whisky half that age... *46%. nc ncf sc. 186 bottles.*

⁘ **The Whisky Agency Deanston 35 Years Old** dist 1977 **(78) n21 t20 f18 b19.** A little unlucky. What was clearly good spirit to start off with has gone through the wood. Some decent moments, but doesn't gel. *40.4%. sc.*

DUFFTOWN
Speyside, 1898. Diageo. Working.

⁘ **Director's Cut Dufftown Aged 30 Years** sherry butt, cask no. 8232, dist Mar 82, bott Mar 12 **(92) n22.5** near impenetrable nutty sherry which binds and gags the barley like a thief does a bank manager before running off with the loot; **t24** a bulldozer of a slightly dirty malt meets the express train of concentrated sherry head on. The result is almost mesmeric; the taste buds witness some of the biggest flavours of the year crash over them in random fashion. Walnut oil softens the blow...but only by minimal amounts; **f23.5** as the dust settles some spices replace the earlier sugars; **b22** displays all the subtlety of a kick in the nuts. But is strangely and compellingly delicious. *51.7%. nc ncf sc. Douglas Laing & Co. 189 bottles.*

⁘ **Gordon & MacPhail Connoisseurs Choice Dufftown 1999 (85.5) n20.5 t22.5 f21 b21.5.** If you are going to find a very drinkable Dufftown, you have to trust Gordon and MacPhail – as usual. Even so, a workmanlike rather than spectacular malt, though the surprise tang of gooseberry amid the barley is more than attractive. *43%*

Kingsbury Finest and Rarest Dufftown 34 Years Old dist 1975 **(74) n19 t19 f18 b18.** Stodgy, podgy and totally bereft of finesse. But probably the only place where the words "Finest" and "Dufftown" will be found on the same line... *45.9%. nc ncf sc. Japan Import Systems.*

Old Malt Cask Dufftown Aged 28 Years refill hogshead, cask no. 7147, dist Nov 82, bott Apr 11 **(78.5) n18.5 t19.5 f21 b19.** Overly sweet and overly fiery, though the milky mocha on the finale works hard to compensate. Overall, though, ordinary whisky from a distinctly ordinary distillery. *50%. nc ncf sc. Douglas Laing & Co. 247 bottles.*

⁘ **Scott's Selection Dufftown 1988** bott 2011 **(76) n20 t19 f18 b19.** Despite the score, this isn't too bad a mark for this distillery during this era. The trouble was, they were producing a syrupy type of malt, devoid of anything approaching subtlety and displaying a "dirtiness" to the finish in particular (to quote someone who worked there at the time, and who took me through the make back in about 88/89). Even after 23 years in the cask, you can see things have little changed. The sugars, quite simply, are out of control. *58.3%. Speyside Distillers.*

⁘ **Silver Seal Dufftown Over 28 Years Old** dist 1983, bott Dec 11 **(88.5) n22** light with an attractive mealy composition. Biscuity in a fruit shortcake kind of way; only the odd glimpse of the usual dirtiness; **t23.5** wow! An enormous delivery with the barley in near concentrate form; the mixed sugars are of the molassed and aged maple syrup variety; **f21** dirty and spiced; **b22** always brave to bottle from this distillery. And, for once, it has paid off. Somehow manages to convert its failings into its strengths. *54.2%. sc. Silver Seal Whisky Company.*

Singleton of Dufftown 12 Years Old db **(71) n18 t18 f17 b18.** A roughhouse malt that's finesse-free. For those who like their tastebuds Dufft up a bit... *40%*

EDRADOUR
Highlands (Perthshire), 1837. Signatory Vintage. Working.

Edradour Aged 10 Years db **(79) n18 t20 f22 b19.** A dense, fat malt that tries offer something along the sherry front but succeeds mainly in producing a whisky cloyingly sweet and unfathomable. Some complexity to the finish compensates. *43%*

Edradour Ballachin #1 The Burgundy Casks db **(63) n17 t16 f15 b15.** A bitter disappointment in every sense. Were the Burgundy casks sulphur treated? I'd say so. Something completely off-key here. A shocker. *46%*

Edradour Ballachin #2 Madeira Matured db **(89) n22 t22 f23 b22.** On the nose and entry I didn't quite get the point here: putting a massively peated malt like this in a Madeira cask is a bit like putting Stan Laural into bed with Marylyn Munro. Thankfully doesn't come out a fine mess and the Madeira certainly has a vital say towards the beautifully structured finale. It works! I feel the hand of a former Laphroaig man at work here. *46%*

FETTERCAIRN
Highland (Eastern), 1824. Whyte and Mackay. Working.

Fettercairn 12 Year Old db **(66) n14 t19 f16 b17.** If the nose doesn't get you, what follows probably will...Grim doesn't quite cover it. *40%*

Fettercairn 30 Years Old db **(73) n19 t18 f18 b18.** A bitter disappointment. Literally. *46.3%*

Fettercairn 40 Years Old db **(92) n23** technically, not exactly how you want a 40-y-o to be: a bit like your old silver-haired granny knitting in her rocking chair...and sporting tattoos. But I also have to say there is no shortage of charm, too...and like some old tattooed granny, you know it is full of personality and has a tale to tell... **t24** I was expecting dates and walnuts... and I have not been let down. A veritable date and walnut pie you can chew on until your jaw is numb; the sharp raisiny notes, too, plus a metallic sheen which reminds you of its provenance...; **f22** those burned raisins get just a little more burned...; **b23** yes, everyone knows my views on this distillery. But I'll have to call this spade a wonderfully big, old shovel you can't help loving...just like the memory of me tattooed ol' granny... 40%. 463 bottles.

Fettercairn 1824 db **(69) n17 t19 f16 b17.** By Fettercairn standards, not a bad offering. Relatively free from its inherent sulphury and rubbery qualities, this displays a sweet nutty character not altogther unattractive – though caramel plays a calming role here. Need my arm twisting for a second glass, though. *40%*

Fettercairn Fior Limited Release (80) n18.5 t22 f19.5 b20. Fat, sweet and relatively shapeless on the palate, bitter on the finish and very dark in the glass. No more than you might expect. But by about the sixth mouthful it does grow on you a bit, and you begin to relish that short-lived but excellent malt juiciness backed by spice and myriad rough edges. *42%*

⫶⫶ **Old Malt Cask Fettercairn Aged 16 Years** refill hogshead, cask no. 7725, dist Nov 95, bott Nov 11 **(71.5) n18 t18.5 f17 b18.** Hot, thin and superficially malty. *50%. nc ncf sc. Douglas Laing & Co. 314 bottles*

Old Malt Cask Fettercairn Aged 19 Years refill hogshead, cask no. 6382, dist Dec 90, bott Jul 10 **(82) n20.5 t23 f18.5 b20.** Refreshing delivery with a very attractive crispness to the barley. *50%. nc ncf sc. Douglas Laing & Co. 318 bottles.*

Provenance Fettercairn Over 9 Years refill hogshead, cask no. 5434, dist Autumn 00, bott Summer 2010 **(68) n16 t18 f17 b17.** Grimly ordinary for all the big malt. *46%. nc ncf sc.*

Provenance Fettercairn Over 10 Years refill hogshead, cask no. 6919, dist Autumn 00, bott Winter 2011 **(67.5) n15.5 t18 f17 b17.** The next time Fettercairn blender Richard Paterson tells me how great this distillery is, he'll get a pie full of shaving foam in his face. It will be a lot kinder than making him drink this nonsense. *46%. nc ncf sc. Douglas Laing & Co.*

GLEN ALBYN
Highlands (Northern) 1846–1983. Diageo. Demolished.

⫶⫶ **Gordon & MacPhail Rare Vintage Glen Albyn 1976 (96) n22.5** salty and nippy. And the theme thunders into an early Kentuckian drawl, with red liquorice and hickory prominent, **t24.5** I am shaking my head in disbelief. Not through disappointment, but wonder! How can something of this antiquity still fill your mouth with so much juice? The barley still offers a degree of grassiness, though this is camouflaged by the softest bourbon characters I have seen in a long time. The honeycomb is in molten form, as is the vanilla which appears to carry with it a fabulous blend of avocado pear and ulmo honey; **f24.5** a pathetic degree of oaky bitterness tries to interrupt, but it is swept aside by the residual and very complex sugars. There remains some spicy activity and even some Kentuckian red liquorice and hickory, but that South American honey really does the business **b24.5** wow! My eyes nearly popped out of my head when I spotted this in my sample room. Glen Albyns come round as rarely as Scotsman winning Wimbledon. Well, almost. When I used to buy this (from Gordon and MacPhail in their early Connoisseur's Choice range, as it happens) when the distillery was still alive (just) I always found it an interesting if occasionally aggressive dram. This masterpiece, though, is something else entirely. And the delivery really does take us to places where only the truly great whiskies go... *43%*

Old Malt Cask Glen Albyn 35 Years Old dist 26 Sep 69, bott Jul 05 **(90) n24 t23 f21 b22.** Understandable signs of longevity, but overall this is simply wonderful. *50%. 229 bottles.*

Rarest of the Rare Glen Albyn 1979 cask no. 3960, dist Dec 79, bott Mar 06 **(91) n23 t23 f22 b23.** Of Scotland's disappearing malts, this is going with flourish. *57.3%. 244 bottles.*

GLENALLACHIE
Speyside, 1968. Chivas Brothers. Working.

Glenallachie 15 Years Old Distillery Edition db **(81) n20 t21 f19 b19.** Real battle between nature and nurture: an exceptional sherry butt has silk gloves and honied marzipan, while a hot-tempered bruiser lurks beneath. *58%*

Glenallachie Aged 35 Years Anniversary Selection first fill sherry, bott 2010 **(84.5) n21 t21 f22.5 b20.** OTT... No doubting the high quality of the sherry butt. But for the alchemy to work, it must combine with the malt to magical effect. Sadly, it doesn't, mainly because the malt just doesn't have the wherewithal to engage. *46.9%. nc. Speciality Drinks Ltd.*

⫶⫶ **Director's Cut Glenallachie Aged 40 Years** sherry butt, cask no. 8217, dist Mar 72, bott Mar 12 **(88) n23** big sherry; **t22.5** big spiced sherry; **f22.5** big sweet sherry; **b20** Glenallachie 40 years ago made one of Scotland's invisible whiskies. Not because it hardly ever saw the light of day as a single malt – a rare foray in the European market was the best it achieved – but, rather, the spirit was so lacking in personality that blenders told me it was put into blends to cheaply bulk up the malt content rather than give character. So for Glenallachie to shine as a single malt, a good cask is essential. Here we have a clean, uncontaminated sherry butt that is in very fine form. However, any trace of the malt it once contained has entirely vanished. *56.8%. nc ncf sc. Douglas Laing & Co. 146 bottles.*

⋄ **Gordon & MacPhail Connoisseurs Choice Glenallachie 1999 (85) n22 t22 f20 b21.** Ingratiatingly clean, monosyllabically malty and in its very finest blending regalia. *43%*

⋄ **Malts Of Scotland Glenallachie 1973** bourbon hogshead, cask no. MoS11018, dist Mar 73, bott Oct 11 **(86.5) n21 t22.5 f21.5 b21.5.** Unusually rich for a Glenallachie and even appears to boast a sultana-fruit sweetness despite its bourbon heritage. The middle ground, when the mocha arrives, is particularly attractive. *44%. nc ncf sc. Malts Of Scotland.*

Malts Of Scotland Glenallachie 1995 bourbon hogshead, cask no. 1257, dist Mar 95, bott Apr 11 **(81.5) n20 t21 f20.5 b20.** Hot and painfully thin in the distillery style. But some delightful mouth-watering malt and late chocolate, too. Surprisingly attractive. *53%. sc.*

⋄ **Mo Òr Collection Glenallachie 1973 37 Years Old** first fill bourbon hogshead, cask no. DL6746, dist 31 Mar 73, bott 3 Nov 10 **(82) n22 t21.5 f19 b19.5.** Even after nearly four decades, a malt which still has the propensity to cut through the taste buds like a blow torch. Has filled out since its younger days and is especially attractive on the nose and early delivery. But the rest is a battle. *46%. nc ncf sc. Release No. 25. The Whisky Talker. 266 bottles.*

⋄ **Old Malt Cask Glenallachie Aged 16 Years** refill hogshead, cask no. 7932, dist May 95, bott Dec 11 **(82.5) n20 t22 f20 b20.5.** Clean, malty, but miserly: with a touch of the new makes about it, more of a 16 month than a 16 year whisky... Even so, there is something crystalline and compellingly attractive about the delivery. *50%. nc ncf sc. 295 bottles.*

Old Malt Cask Glenallachie Aged 38 Years refill butt, cask no. 6498, dist Mar 72, bott Aug 10 **(83.5) n23.5 t20.5 f19.5 b20.** Fabulous aroma, full of bright barley. But the severe limitations of the distillery become more apparent once you get to taste it. *50%. nc ncf sc. 384 bottles.*

Old Malt Cask Glenallachie Aged 38 Years sherry butt, cask no. 6880, dist Mar 72, bott Jan 11 **(92.5) n24** potentially the sherry butt of the year: not even the vaguest hint of an off-sulphury note. Just juicy grape and pith, fortified by the trademark big Glenallachie malt swirl; **t23** a juicy tour de force of spiced grape and vivid barley; **f22.5** grape and vanilla; **b23** all reference points to the distillery have been obliterated by a stonkingly beautiful, and quite faultless sherry butt. You just can't go wrong with a bottle like this. *50%. nc ncf sc. 302 bottles.*

Robert Graham's Dancing Stag Glenallachie 1995 hogshead, dist 10 Nov 95, bott Sep 10 **(82) n21 t21 f20 b20.** A very good example of this distillery at its usual malt in a straight jacket self. *46%. nc ncf sc. Robert Graham. 168 bottles.*

⋄ **Scott's Selection Glenallachie 1993** bott 2012 **(82) n21 t21 f20 b20.** Sweet and malty. But as tight as the arse of one of the ducks I used to feed at the distillery... *55.6%.*

The Whisky Agency Glenallachie 1971 bott 2010 **(86.5) n21 t22 f22 b21.5.** Back in the early 80s, this would not have been much of a success as a 10 to 12 years-old, so emaciated would it have been. However, it has progressed with time, even somehow adopting a slight citrusy poise. Quite charming, if still a little undercooked. *51.2%. The Whisky Agency.*

The Whisky Agency Glenallachie 1972 bott 2010 **(73) n19 t19 f17 b18.** Soapy rocket fuel. *49.9%. The Whisky Agency.*

⋄ **The Whisky Agency Glenallachie 1973** bott 2011 **(85.5) n22 t22 f20 b21.5.** Heavily perfumed on the nose and laden with barley on delivery. But for all the usual fire midway through and thin finish, you cannot help but enjoy its clean simplicity. *50.4%. nc ncf sc.*

GLENBURGIE
Speyside, 1810. Chivas Brothers. Working.

Glenburgie Aged 15 Years bott code L00/129 db **(84) n22 t23 f19 b20.** Doing so well until the spectacularly flat, bitter finish. Orangey citrus and liquorice had abounded. *46%*

⋄ **Berry's Own Selection Glenburgie 1983** cask no. 9806, bott 2011 **(92.5) n23** blazes a spectacularly malty trail. The barley is almost in concentrated form; the sugars seem to be both on the periphery, yet somehow attached...thrillingly rich and complex; **t23.5** not just a case of the taste following the nose but even embellishing upon it. The malt seems to arrive in one huge mass and then radiates beautiful, lightly sweetened barley around the palate; **f23** the usual Burgie natural caramel...and barley...; **b23** confident, competent, beautifully distilled and matured. And if there were a Richter Scale of maltiness, this would come flying off the gauge... *56.3%. nc ncf sc. Berry Bros & Rudd.*

⋄ **Chieftain's Glenburgie Aged 12 Years** hogsheads, dist Nov 98, bott Sep 11 **(88) n23.5** exemplary combination of light, playful aromas mixing up rather beautifully with some delicate citrus and even juicier barley. The Middle-Eastern touch of lemon and mint adds a lovely flourish; **t22** a much more workaday aspect to the warming, vaguely biting, delivery with the vanillas making the most of a surprisingly thin body; **f20** spices blossom as it thins and bites further; **b22** one of those malts which is chiefly about the nose. *43%. nc ncf.*

Dun Bheagan Glenburgie 11 Years Old bourbon hogshead, dist Nov 98 **(86.5) n22 t22 f21 b21.5** A pretty accurate and attractive account of a Burgie at this age in ex-bourbon: on one hand massive barley drive, on the other natural caramels and delicate bourbony notes come in to play. 43%. nc ncf. Ian Macleod Distillers.

⁘ **Gordon & MacPhail Rare Vintage Glenburgie 1966 (90) n22.5** distinctly floral: a real midsummer's night garden job...complete with creosoted fences; **t22** much softer on delivery with cream toffee dominant; there is also a big barley juiciness, too; **f23** the Rolo effect clings and expands, complete with milk chocolate which builds its shares. The final moments are quite dry with chalky vanilla seeping in with raw hazelnuts for depth; **b22.5** a malt which has reached a point in its life where it is not exactly sure where it is going. You get the feeling the most of the successes are by luck rather than design. But it doesn't really matter: after giving it at least 15 minutes in the glass, simply enjoy! 43%

⁘ **Kingsbury "The Selection" Glenburgie 17 Years Old** hogshead, cask no. 100 & 101, dist Feb 04, bott Apr 11 **(79.5) n18.5 t21 f20 b20.** Sweet and sugary, the sheer brilliance of the original spirit works minor miracles to make the most, and overcome the limitations, of some very ordinary oak. 43%. nc ncf. Japan Import Systems. 852 bottles.

⁘ **Old Malt Cask Glenburgie Aged 16 Years** refill hogshead, cask no. 8005, dist Apt 95, bott Jan 12 **(88.5) n22** big, very lightly sweetened malt but mainly grassy; **t22** salivating, mouth cleansing and bursting with barley; **f22** a very polite introduction of drier vanilla and the faintest hint of red liquorice and butterscotch; **b22.5** if I was giving a lecture, I could unveil this malt and reveal exactly why Burgie is such a spot-on blending malt: here the barley is true, clean and persistent....very much in the distillery style. 50%. nc ncf sc. 304 bottles.

⁘ **Provenance Glenburgie Over 11 Years** refill hogshead, cask no. 7653, dist Autumn 1999, bott Summer 2011 **(92.5) n23** green, under-ripe gooseberry; the very vaguest puff of smoke; **t23** juicy, clean malt attack; slow diffusion of sugars towards the middle; **f23** surprisingly lengthy where just a little phenolic spice tacks on to the vanilla; **b23.5** a quite gorgeous bottling: a whispering, understated gem of no little complexity. 46%. nc ncf sc.

⁘ **Scotch Malt Whisky Society Cask 71.34 Aged 13 Years** refill gorda, cask no. 1580, dist 1998 **(82) n18 t23 f20 b21.** Gorda Bennett!! OK, this whisky does have its charms and the big chocolate fruit and nut explosion is a joy. But the cask is faulty. If you can live with the sub standard nose and finish, give it a go. 56.8%. sc. Scotch Malt Whisky Society.

⁘ **Whisky Antique Glenburgie 26 Years Old Special Bottling** dist 1983, bott 2009 **(89.5) n22.5** attractive suet, spotted dog pudding; crispened with Demerara sugar; **t23.5** soft, juicy delivery soon backed up with some stinging spices. The fruit arrives early too, making for a gorgeous first half dozen waves; **f21.5** dries a little as the cocoa and mildly burned toast arrives; **b22** a metallic hand in a silky glove... 57.7%. sc. Silver Seal Whisky Company.

GLENCADAM

Highlands (Eastern), 1825. Angus Dundee. Working.

Glencadam Aged 10 Years db **(95) n24** crystal clarity to the sharp, ultra fresh barley. Clean, uncluttered by excessive oak, the apparent lightness is deceptive; the intensity of the malt carries its own impressive weight and the citrus note compliments rather than thins. Enticing; **t24** immediately zingy and eye-wateringly salivating with a fabulous layering of sweet barley. Equally delicate oak chimes in to ensure a lightly spiced balance and a degree of attitude; **f23** longer than the early barley freshness would have you expecting, with soft oils ensuring an extended, tapering, malty edge to the gentle, clean oak; **b24** sophisticated, sensual, salivating and seemingly serene, this malt is all about juicy barley and balance. Just bristles with character and about as puckeringly elegant as single malt gets...and even thirst-quenching. My God: the guy who put this one together must be a genius, or something... 46%

Glencadam Aged 12 Years Portwood Finish db **(89.5) n22.5** oaky vanillas manage to shape this attractively while delicate, clean grape bends this towards a subtle fruit and custard effect: soft, playful and teasing; **t22.5** attractive marriage of those drier vanillas promised on the nose with that fragile fruit; for all the softness there is a playful nip to be had, too; a youngish barley flashes keenly about the taste buds; **f22** a rumble of prickly spice and cocoa but that clean fruit, as light as it is, lasts the distance; **b22.5** after coming across a few disappointing Port finishes in recent weeks, just wonderful to experience one as you would hope and expect it to be. 46%

Glencadam Aged 14 Years Oloroso Sherry Cask Finish bott May 10 db **(95) n24** pinch me: I'm dreaming. Oloroso exactly how it should be: classically clean with a dovetailing of dry and sweeter grape notes which are weighty, but not heavy enough to crush the lighter barley and vanillas from adding to the sumptuous and elegant mix; **t23.5** mouth-filling with firstly fat grape then a second flavour round of spices and custardy vanillas; **f24** much drier now with the accent on the barley but still that light spice persists, actually increasing in weight and effect as it goes along; **b23.5** what a total treat. Restores one's faith in Oloroso whilst offering more than a glimpse of the most charming infusion of fruit imaginable. 46%

Glencadam Aged 15 Years db **(90.5) n22.5** soft kumquats mingle with the even softer barley. A trace of drier mint and chalk dust points towards the shy oak. Harmonious and dovetails beautifully; **t23** sharp, juicy barley - almost fruity - fuses with sharper oak. The mouth-watering house style appears to fatten out as gentle oils emerge and then give way for a spicy middle; **f22** long, with those teasing, playful spices pepping up the continued barley theme. Dries as a 15 year old ought but the usual bitterness is kept in check by the prevailing malt; **b23** the spices keep the taste buds on full alert but the richness and depth of the barley defies the years. Another exhibition of Glencadam's understated elegance. Some more genius malt creation... *46%*

Glencadam Aged 21 Years "The Exceptional" bott May 10 db **(81) n21.5 t22 f17.5 b20.** For a little distillery with a reputation for producing a more delicate malt this is one big whisky. Sadly, the finish is out of kilter, for the delivery is a knife and fork job, offering some extraordinary variations on a fudgy-maple syrup theme which promises much. *46%*

⸬ **Glencadam Aged 21 Years "The Exceptional"** bott Oct 11 db **(94) n23.5** oh, just so sexy!! The sugars have a sparkle in their eye while the malt carries a lemon sharpness which breaks up the heavier aromas. A nose to take a good 10 to 15 minutes with, as the clarity allows you to see a long way...; **t24** just like the nose, the sugars show first. But here there is more complexity: almost a step ladder of intensity. As it climbs, it gets a little heavier in oils, eventually taking on a barley-themed fudge; the whole show is in slow motion, with the odd, shortly-lived burst of spice, and a very lightweight fruitcake richness; **f23** long, now surprising spice-free and sugar-softened and with the accent very much on the vanilla; **b23.5** this distillery is emerging out of the shadows from its bad old Allied days as one of the great Scottish single malt distilleries. So good is some of their whisky, this "exceptional" bottling is almost becoming the norm. *46%. nc ncf.*

Glencadam Single Cask 1978 sherry cask, cask no. 2332, dist Apr 78, bott Sep 10 db **(88) n21.5** about as dry a fruitiness as you are ever likely to find: borders on tight, perhaps through, amongst other things, a little pine seeping in. Fruit cake baked with minimum sugars; **t22.5** the delivery is also a shy, conservative affair but at least with a build up of increasingly strident molasses; **f22** again, heads back towards a dry, toasty fruitiness with a little bitterness battling the fading sugars; **b22** what to make of a malt like this? Absolutely refuses to open itself up, yet so much is quietly said...or not. Intriguing. *46%. nc ncf sc. 405 bottles.*

Glencadam Single Cask 1978 cask no. 2335, bott no. 554, dist Apr 78, bott Mar 09 db **(93.5) n24 t24 f22.5 b23.5.** A fabulous distillery which is coming out of the shadows since its confidence-sapping Allied days and is now putting Brechin on the map. Its secret is that the malt is of a consistently high standard; one willing and able to get the best out of any cask type used. Some malts can't handle sherry, failing to get their personality across. This one appears able to do just that without batting an eyelid. *46%. nc ncf. 615 bottles.*

Berry's Own Selection Glencadam 1990 cask no. 5982, bott 2011 **(85.5) n22 t21 f21 b21.5** Bright and pulsing in the Glencadam style. But just a little more hot and aggressive than should be expected. Can't not delight in the barley, though. And the chocolate dessert on the finale. *56.6%. nc ncf sc. Berry Bros & Rudd.*

Malts Of Scotland Glencadam 1985 bourbon hogshead, cask no. 3990, dist Jun 85, bott Nov 10 **(89) n21.5 t22.5 f22.5 b22.5.** Not for the lily-livered. Bursting from the glass with controlled aggression and attitude. *55.4%. nc ncf sc. Exclusive bottling for Interwhisky 2010.*

⸬ **Mo Òr Collection Glencadam 1985 25 Years Old** first fill bourbon hogshead, cask no. 3997, dist 26 Jun 85, bott 2 Dec 10 **(91) n22** pretty thick with oak; nose blind and you'd be tempted to think bourbon, so intense is the vanilla; **t24** absolutely stunning mouth-feel: perfect weight and oiliness and then a slow, sexy dissolving of honey and sugar into the ever-building oak; **f22** the rapid drying offers a startling contrast to the delivery; **b23** Glencadam is not overrun with first fill bourbon casks. Always good to see a fine example hit the shelves. *46%. nc ncf sc. Release No. 19. The Whisky Talker. 341 bottles.*

⸬ **Old Malt Cask Glencadam Aged 21 Years** refill hogshead, cask no. 8167, dist Oct 90, bott Feb 12 **(91) n22** wonderfully clean, powdery malt...though not in a gristy way; **t23.5** full blooded, unadulterated, gorgeously concentrated...malt; **f22.5** a little spice mixed in with the Horlicks; **b23** if you have a soft spot for Maltesers grab two bottles if you can. A real gent of a bottling. *50%. nc ncf sc. Douglas Laing & Co. 304 bottles.*

⸬ **Provenance Glencadam Over 12 Years** refill butt, cask no. 7656, dist Winter 1998, bott Summer 2011 **(87) n22** soft fruits and vanilla; very distant smoke; **t22** a blizzard of delicate spices counter the gentle malt arrival; **f21** a slight harshness to the vanilla; **b22** enticingly delicate despite the limitations of the cask. *46%. nc ncf sc. Douglas Laing & Co.*

⸬ **Scotch Malt Whisky Society Cask 82.19 Aged 13 Years** refill puncheon, cask no. 1322, dist 1998 **(76.5) n19.5 t20 f18 b19.** Eye-watering. *55.7%. sc. Scotch Malt Whisky Society.*

⸬ **Wemyss 1990 Single Highland "Caribbean Fruit"** hogshead, dist 1990, bott 2011 **(90.5) n22.5** unusually dry for a Glencadam. But there is spot-on harmonisation between the floral tones and the ever-burrowing oak; **t23** a typical Glencadam in that the mouth-feel to the delivery is about as good as it gets. The barley takes some enticing but eventually displays in full juiciness; **f22** a light sugaring to the vanilla; the pace to the finish is mesmerising; **b23** perhaps the oak has rung the malt a little too dry to over celebrate the fruitiness. But a sophisticated, high quality dram without doubt. *46%. sc. Wemyss Malts. 320 bottles.*

GLENCRAIG
Speyside, 1958. Chivas Brothers. Silent.
Scotch Malt Whisky Society Cask 104.13 Aged 36 Years refill barrel, cask no. 7825, dist 1974 **(96) n24** wonderful aroma: heavyweight stuff with all the characters playing at full throttle but within a seemingly confined space. So the bananas and ripe oranges would explode from the glass, except the thick bourbon is holding them by the lapels. Massive, magnificent... and very different...; **t24** the first oak notes to burn off are over the top and spent. But after about the third wave it settles down with the introduction of telling muscovado sugars and a seemingly roasty maltiness; spices dovetail with an almost cooing gentleness while slowly, but unmistakably, the barley builds up enough intensity to make a salivating contribution; **f23.5** the spices persist while the bourbon characteristics hold sway. The dryness of the sawdusty oak never hints at bitterness while the kumquats and figs ensure a distant softness; **b24.5** don't get many of these guys to the dozen. What a relief this one's a cracker! If you are to buy only one major whisky this year, make it this. *50.6%. sc. 179 bottles.*

GLENDRONACH
Highlands, 1826. The BenRiach Distillery Co. Working.
The GlenDronach Aged 8 Years "Octarine" db **(86.5) n23.5 t23 f19 b21.** Juicy yet bitter: a bipolar malt offering two contrasting characters in one glass. *46%. nc ncf.*

The GlenDronach 12 Years Old db **(92) n22** some pretty juicy grape in there; **t24** silky delivery with the grape teaming with the barley to produce the sharpest delivery and follow through you can imagine: exceptionally good weight with just enough oils to make full use of the delicate sweetness and the build towards spices and cocoa in the middle ground is a wonderful tease; **f22.5** dries and heads into bitter marmalade country; **b23.5** an astonishingly beautiful malt despite the fact that a rogue sherry butt has come in under the radar. But for that, this would have been a mega scorer: potentially an award-winner. Fault or no fault, seriously worth discovering this bottling of this too long undiscovered great distillery *43%*

The GlenDronach Aged 12 Years "Original" db **(86.5) n21 t22 f22 b21.5.** One of the more bizarre moments of the year: thought I'd got this one mixed up with a German malt whisky I had tasted earlier in the day. There is a light drying tobacco feel to this and the exact same corresponding delivery on the palate. That German version is distilled in a different type of still; this is made in probably the most classic stillhouse on mainland Scotland. Good, enjoyable whisky. But I see a long debate with distillery owner Billy Walker on the near horizon, though it was in Allied's hands when this was produced. *43%*

⁂ **The GlenDronach Aged 12 Years "Revival"** db **(83) n20 t22.5 f20.5 b20.** Glendronach at 12 is a whisky which has long intrigued me...for the last three decades, in fact. Always felt Allied had problems dealing with it, though when it was right it was sumptuous. Here it is a distance from being right: odd tobacco notes creeping into the fray, though that rings a bell with this distillery as I'm sure the old "Original" showed a similar trait. A very decent malty middle but elsewhere it flounders somewhat. *43%. nc ncf.*

The GlenDronach Original Aged 12 Years Double Matured db **(88) n23 t21 f22 b22.** Vastly improved from the sulphur-tainted bottling of last year. In fact, their most enjoyable standard distillery bottling I've had for many years. But forget about the whisky: the blurb on the back is among the most interesting you are likely to find anywhere. And I quote: "Founder James Allardice called the original Glendronach, 'The Guid Glendronach'. But there's no need to imitate his marketing methods. The first converts to his malt were the 'ladies of the night' in Edinburgh's Canongate!" Fascinating. And as a professional whisky taster I am left wondering: did they swallow or spit... *40%*

The GlenDronach 14 Years Old Sauternes Finish db **(78.5) n18 t22 f19 b19.5.** That unique Sauternes three dimensional spiced fruit is there sure enough...and some awesome oils. But, with so much out of key bitterness around, not quite I had hoped for. *46%. nc ncf.*

The GlenDronach 14 Years Old Virgin Oak db **(87) n22.5** what a naughty virgin! All kinds of tempting vanilla and butterscotch notes... and spice, of course...; **t22** a little flat-chested with the barley vanishing under a sea of oily, natural caramel; **f21** caramel and vanilla; **b21.5** charming, pretty, but perhaps lacking in passion... *46%. nc ncf.*

The GlenDronach 15 Years Old db **(77.5) n19 t18.5 f20 b20.** The really frustrating thing is, you can hear those amazingly brilliant sherry butts screaming to be heard in their purest voice. Those alone, and you could, like the 12-y-o, have a score cruising over the 95 mark. I can't wait for the next bottling. *46%*

The Glendronach 15 Years Old db (83) n20 t22 f20 b21. Chocolate fudge and grape juice to start then tails off towards a slightly bitter, dry finish. 40%

The GlenDronach 15 Years Old Moscatel Finish db (84) n19 t22.5 f21.5 b21. Such is the intensity of the grape, its force of life, it makes a truly remarkable recovery from such a limited start. But it is hard to be yourself when shackled... 46%. nc ncf.

The GlenDronach 15 Years Old Tawny Port Finish db (84.5) n21 t22 f20.5 b21.5. Quite a tight fit for the most part. But when it does relax, especially a few beats after delivery, the clean fruit fairly drips onto the palate. 46%. nc ncf.

The GlenDronach Aged 15 Years "Revival" db (88.5) n22 almost impenetrably thick malt, further strengthened by an oak-muscovado exoskeleton; t23 again the malt takes on massive form; the fruit marches along as a sub-plot; f21.5 vanilla and malt, a slightly bitter finale; b22 unambiguously Scottish... A fantastically malty dram. 46%

The GlenDronach 18 Years Old db (96.5) n24 groaning under the weight of sublime, faultless sherry and peppers; t24 puckering enormity as the saltiness thumps home. Black forest Gateaux complete with cherries and blended with sherry trifle. The spices have to be tasted to be believed. The sugars range from Demerara to light molasses; f24 again the sugars are in perfect position to ramp up the sweetness, but the grape, vanilla and spices are the perfect foil; b24.5 the ultimate sherry cask whisky. Faultless and truly astounding! 46%. nc ncf.

The GlenDronach Aged 18 Years "Allardice" db (83.5) n19 t22 f21 b21.5. Huge fruit. But a long-running bitter edge to the toffee and raisin sits awkwardly on the palate. 46%

The GlenDronach 21 Years Old db (91.5) n23.5 thumping sherry of the old fruitcake school; a serious number of toasty notes including hickory of a bourbon style; t23.5 no less lush delivery than the nose portends; the follow up layerings of burnt raisin and cremated fudge are pretty entertaining; f22 like burnt toast, a touch of bitterness at the death; b22.5 a quite unique slant on a 21-year-old malt: some aspects appear very much older, but some elements of the grape occasionally reveal a welcome youth. Memorable stuff. 48%. nc ncf.

The GlenDronach Grandeur Aged 31 Years db (94.5) n23.5 dry, mildly peppery vanilla; crushed golden raisin counter-plot; t24 spice-dusted grapes explode on the palate on entry; the mouth-feel plays a key role as the early lushness carries the fruit only so far before it begins to break up, allowing a fabulous spicy complexity to develop; f23.5 beautiful intertwining between those golden raisins and coffee. The spices are never far away...; b23.5 just one hell of an alpha sherry butt. 45.8%

The GlenDronach Aged 33 Years oloroso db (95) n24 t24 f23 b24. Want to know what sherry should really nose like: invest in a bottle of this. This is a vivid malt boasting spellbinding clarity and charm. A golden nugget of a dram, which would have been better still at 46%. 40%

The GlenDronach Single Cask 1971 oloroso cask no. 483 (80) n20 t22 f19 b19. Plenty of marmalade to be getting on with here. But the finish is tight and bitter. 49.4%. 544 bottles.

The GlenDronach Single Cask 1971 batch 4, PX puncheon, cask no. 1436, dist 25 Feb 71, bott 2011 db (89) n22.5 big peppery grape; t22 mint humbug complete with toffee; f22.5 a thread of barley and vanilla adds an extra dimension; b22 silky, fresh, never less than delicious but maybe not the most complex 40-year-old on the market. 48.5%. nc ncf sc.

⋅∷⋅ **The GlenDronach Single Cask 1971 Aged 41 Years** batch 6, Pedro Ximenez sherry puncheon, cask no. 1247, dist 25 Feb 71, bott 2012 db (87) n21 all is so intense that the higher notes are flattened, leaving the duller, over-tired notes too big a say; t22 syrupy and at first sweet though the spices soon enter like drunken cowboys bursting into the saloon looking for a fight. The salty bite thins out some of the fatter notes; f22 salty and oaky, the grape begins to take a much sturdier direction but leads us only unto a very milky coffee; b22 a lovely whisky, but one which has been worked too hard to tell a coherent story. A malt desperate to find its rhythm though, for all the high class fun, never quite gets there. 47.9%. nc ncf.

The GlenDronach Single Cask 1972 batch 4, oloroso cask no. 712, dist 02 Mar 72, bott 2011 db (95.5) n24.5 the rare beauty of an entirely faultless sherry butt. The grape is heavily cratered by oak and some beautiful spices, dried orange pith and floral notes (especially lilacs) ensure the complexity is never less than astonishing...; t24 for a brief second the grape puffs out its chest like a proud wood pigeon, but the oak is not very far behind; a fabulous, very delicately oiled ensemble of impressive molassed notes and other earthy, roasty controlled honey moments; f23 the oak, inevitably, takes command and bitters out the buttery notes; b24 if you can head back in time to the late 80s, the Glendronach 12 had a nose not dissimilar to this: absolutely faultless sherry. Then it was too faultless and quite drowned out anything the barley had to say. The barley is still silent. But the oak has the megaphone towards the end... However, the overall play is one of the finest veteran actors squeezing every nuance out of their lines and, taking the pathos to just bearable proportions, reminding us of what we will be missing in the years to come due to the near wiping out of sherry butts like these... 49.9%. nc ncf sc.

The GlenDronach Single Cask 1972 batch 5, oloroso cask no. 716, dist 02 Mar 72, bott 2011 db (88) n23 a tight, dense nose, lacking many of the intricacies of its sister cask but winning over the heart with its studied portrayal of both elegant grape and oak. Intriguingly, the lack of grape reveals a trace of smoke that is not at all apparent on Batch 4; **t22.5** much juicier on delivery with an impressive early volley of cracked grape and gooseberries. When the oak arrives, it does so with maximum impact; **f20.5** oaky...; **b22** unmistakably related to cask 712, though this does not enjoy quite so much swirling grape. This was bottled at a time when it was unlikely ever to improve in the barrel and just one more summer might have allowed the oak to have spoiled the party. As it is: a delight! 54.4%. nc ncf sc.

⁘ **The GlenDronach Single Cask 1972 Aged 40 Years** batch 7, Oloroso sherry butt, cask no. 710, dist 2 Mar 72, bott 2012 db **(96) n23** countless strands of aged malt here: so old, the oak could well have woodworm. But the richness of the sherry is almost the stuff of make-believe....though instantly recognisable to those of us who tasted the sherry version of the distillery at 12 years in the 1980s and 90s....; **t24.5** the delivery is of oak crashing in a forest... mighty and all consuming. For a while it is almost eye-watering, if somehow juicy. But, slowly, the more delicate shards of grape appear while the spices blossom and sugars emerge unscathed and celebrating their usual high performance Demerara style; the middle ground is one of both dried and juicy dates and some pretty high class Jamaican blue mountain coffee. Wow...this is like a big succulent bourbon matured in a top class sherry butt!! **f24** dries again for a while as the oaks regroup like dazed Triffids. A wonderful briny element appears to soften rather than embolden the oak's impact and allows both the spices and sugars to dampen the work of the vanilla. The fruit remains, even offering black cherry at times; **b24.5** on delivery, there is a puckering of the taste buds which makes you fear that age has done its worst. The recovery is as remarkable as it is magnificent. This is a malt which if you should ever chance upon, you give the guy your coat if you have not money enough; even your under garments if it does the trick! For this is a whisky so complex, so complete, it is almost exhausting... 49%. nc ncf sc.

The GlenDronach Single Cask 1978 batch 5, oloroso puncheon, cask no 1067, dist 29 Dec 78, bott 2011 db **(95.5) n24** good god...! Not just sulphur free (well, 99.25%!). But not even the vaguest hint of tired oak or gratuitous sweetness. What we have is a spotless assembly of grape, of at least six different sweetness and intensity values I could count. Some spice spills, inevitably, into the picture. But the big surprise is the shadow of barley spotted moving slowly beneath it all...; **t24** a fabulous arrival on the palate: all shimmering yet somehow puckering grape, both fresh and burnt to a crisp. The oak notes are firm and bulging with vanilla; various blackberries and weeping, over-ripe cherries fill in the middle; **f23.5** that .75% comes back to haunt, but such is the integrity of the grape, it is barely noticeable; **b24** when I first visited this distillery under its new management, its owner, Billy Walker, told me that he had found some of the best sherry casks he had ever encountered in his long career. I would not be remotely surprised if this is one of them... This is, as nigh as damn it, faultless... 50.1%. nc ncf sc.

⁘ **The GlenDronach Single Cask 1978 Aged 33 Years** batch 6, Oloroso sherry puncheon, cask no. 1068, dist 29 Dec 78, bott 2012 db **(96) n23.5** ever been in a high quality antique shop specialising in 18th century furniture...? **t24.5** from the nose you'd expect an oaky salute. Not a bit of it: the grape juices set you off salivating instead. There are many kinds of old pot still Demerara rum notes to enjoy, especially those with a touch of coffee; and the Demerara sugars there in abundance, too; **f24** a wonderful saltiness begins to make itself felt, at first distantly and then more stridently. But it never offers more than is required...the spices and dark, lengthy sugars see to that; **b24.5** when this distillery gets it right, your taste buds don't stand a chance. Almost brain-explodingly complex... 52.9% nc ncf sc.

The GlenDronach Single Cask 1989 batch 4, PX puncheon, cask no. 2917, dist 07 Dec 89, bott 2011 db **(86) n22 t21.5 f21 b21.5.** Lashings of sugar candy grape: it is like a high alcohol boiled sweet. But a little bit of interference in Jerez has stunted the development somewhat. 54.1%. nc ncf sc.

The GlenDronach Single Cask 1989 batch 5, PX puncheon, cask no. 3314, dist 09 Nov 89, bott 2011 db **(95) n24.5** if my life were not dictated by deadlines, it would be tempting to take a morning off and just spend a blissful few hours nosing this: you are unlikely ever to find a more relaxed and magnificent balance between sultry grape and scandalous spice...; **t24** almost disappointingly well behaved on the palate: the sherry has too much to say and at first overwhelms all else. Even the spices retreat for cover after the briefest of early flourishes, But I say "almost": further exploration reveals a plumy depth and a slow build up of quite unexpected barley notes on oil; **f23** clean, if mildly uninspired grape; the spices regroup for a late, delicious, rally; **b23.5** what do make of a cove like this? The nose suggests a potential whisky of the year. Though the experience on the palate is a lot more urbane, given time it reveals itself as a pretty complex piece of work. Always a treat (and bloody rare), though, to find a sherry cask entirely free of sulphur. 53.5%. nc ncf sc.

⁘ **The GlenDronach Single Cask 1989 Aged 22 Years** batch 7, Pedro Ximenez sherry puncheon, cask no. 5475, dist 30 Nov 89, bott 2012 db **(92) n22.5** pithy and dry, the nose is almost the complete opposite of what you might expect; **t23** sensational delivery! The sugars are tight and intense and not free to roam over the big vanilla and spice. The fruit is almost pure grape skin. When a sweetness does evolve there is a touch of the honeycombs about it; **f23** long, with a wonderful interweaving of lightly fruited vanillas and crisp, Demerara crusted barley; **b23.5** a malt which becomes spellbinding as the tale unfolds. *51.6%. nc ncf sc.*

⬩⬩⬩ **The GlenDronach Single Cask 1989 Aged 23 Years** batch 6, Moscatel barrel, cask no. 4885, dist 18 Jan 89, bott 2012 db **(80.5) n19.5 t21 f20 b20.** The muscatel gives a generous injection of fruit. But there is the nagging feeling (and not for the only time with a Glendronach) that, a long time ago, a cask has waited a long while to be filled. *53.9%. nc ncf sc.*

The GlenDronach Single Cask 1990 batch 4, PX puncheon, cask no. 1032, dist 29 Aug 90, bott 2011 db **(81) n21.5 t20 f19.5 b20.** Plenty of fruit juice. But the furry bitterness tells its own tale. I predict this to be a knockout in mainland Europe, however. *53.3% nc ncf sc.*

⬩⬩⬩ **The GlenDronach Single Cask 1990 Aged 22 Years** batch 6, Pedro Ximenez sherry puncheon, cask no. 2966, dist 30 May 90, bott 2012 db **(77.5) n20 t20 f18.5 b19.** Tangy...and for all the wrong reasons. Sulphur free, though. *55.1%. nc ncf sc.*

The GlenDronach Single Cask 1991 batch 5, oloroso cask no. 2406, dist 01 Nov 91, bott 2011 db **(95) n24** an absolutely honest aroma showing the style of sherry at its healthiest and most confident: dry with the grape sharing equal billing with the oak; **t24** the delivery of your dreams: the grape is firm yet juicy, the sugars are nearby but controlled. Charismatic and elegant from the off, the dry sherry style is endearing; **f23.5** dries towards burnt raisin as the oaks impact; **b23.5** of its type, dry oloroso, you cannot find finer. *55.4%. nc ncf sc.*

⬩⬩⬩ **The GlenDronach Single Cask 1991 Aged 20 Years** batch 7, Pedro Ximenez sherry puncheon, cask no. 3183, dist 15 Nov 91, bott 2012 db **(95) n23** of the mocha and Demerara rum school of Glendronach though this time with extra tight sugars; **t24** thick on delivery and thickens further as the flavours pan out. Almost a coffee cake and Swiss roll marriage with grape jam for filling; **f24** long, thick-bodied until almost the very last moment and a few fudge and mocha-flavoured Lubec marzipan notes sidle in delightfully. The light spices pulse...; **b24** tries to be syrupy and overbearing but fails miserably. Has to settle for being brilliant. *51.3%. nc ncf sc.*

The GlenDronach Single Cask 1992 batch 4, oloroso cask no. 161, dist 22 May 92, bott 2011 db **(96) n24.5** anyone into Basset's Liquorice Allsorts will recognise this one: chocolate and liquorice (the brown and black ones) squashed in the fingers, while elsewhere a glass of oloroso fills the room with rich grapey notes. Of course, spices abound, as they must... or do I mean Musto...? **t25** Is it sweet? Is it sour? Does it have the fruity pungency of Granny's Voice Cough drops? Does is radiate toffee apple recently bitten into? Does it somehow posses a bourbony rich, old honeyed depth? Yes, it does...and so much more...; **f22.5** a degree of taught bitterness creeps in, though it would be churlish to begrudge its presence. The oils up their game, too. But it makes for a very long, toasty, burnt hot-cross bun finale...; **b24** this was distilled almost to the week that I became the world's first full-time whisky writer. Perhaps I should buy a cask as good as this to bottle in celebration...now there's an idea... Because it would be hard to find a whisky of even more of the magnitude than this to represent all that I stand for...This just has to be the Single Cask of the Year... *59.2%. nc ncf sc.*

⬩⬩⬩ **The GlenDronach Single Cask 1992 Aged 19 Years** batch 7, Oloroso sherry butt, dist 27 Nov 92, bott 2012 db **(85) n22 t21.5 f20 b21.5.** Distinctly nutty, with walnuts shining on the nose. Very dry and oaky throughout with the grape helped along with some busy spice. *57.8%. nc ncf sc.*

The GlenDronach Single Cask 1993 oloroso butt no. 523 db **(94) n23.5 t24.5 f22.5 b23.5.** Sulphur-less. Sophististicated. Sensational. *60.4%. 634 bottles.*

The GlenDronach Single Cask 1993 batch 5, oloroso cask no. 1, dist 15 Jan 93, bott 2011 db **(78) n21 t20 f18 b19.** It would be hard to find a juicier butt than this. But a sulphur candles has the ability to strangle so many things at birth. *54.9%. nc ncf sc.*

⬩⬩⬩ **The GlenDronach Single Cask 1993 Aged 18 Years** Oloroso sherry butt, cask no. 1607, dist 24 Sep 93, bott 2012 db **(78) n18.5 t21 f19.5 b19.** A sulphured butt that despite its grapey riches is off key thanks to sub-standard wood. *56.1%. nc ncf sc. Distillery exclusive.*

⬩⬩⬩ **The GlenDronach Single Cask 1993 Aged 19 Years** batch 6, Oloroso sherry butt, cask no. 536, dist 26 Feb 93, bott 2012 db **(95) n23.5** a degree of breakfast business here: some mid roast Java coffee appears to have been sweetened with grape jelly; **t24.5** supremely sweet with the sugars arriving in a rush...just ahead of the pounding spice. The mid ground is an explosion of complexity, and just about perfectly weighted and very lightly oiled. Again coffee at play, but some major bourbon and Demerara rum notes also have a big say; absolutely huge, yet carries itself off with rare grace; **f23** plenty of mocha sweetened with...Demerara, of course...; **b24** another ultra complex gem from this magnificent distillery. *59.4%. nc ncf sc.*

The GlenDronach Single Cask 1994 batch 4, oloroso cask no. 97, dist 28 Jan 94, bott 2011 db **(90) n22.5** wonderfully nutty, with walnut oil mixing with crushed toasted hazelnuts;

apples and oranges dilute the thick, sweet grape; just a mild discordant note at the back; **t24** top quality mouth feel and body: minimum oils, maximum lushness. The middle could almost be a bourbon with its honeycomb and liquorice theme; **f21** a little tight, burnt out bitterness; **b22.5** like a flower in the sun, leave in the glass for a good 20 minutes for it to open properly. 60.1%. nc ncf sc.

⁖ **The GlenDronach Single Cask 1994 Aged 18 Years** batch 7, Oloroso sherry butt, cask no. 98, dist 28 Jan 94, bott 2012 db **(96) n24** absolutely huge grape: a real Dundee cake dripping with oloroso and Demerara. The spices are profound but sit comfortably with the richness of the fruit; **t24** enormous yet somehow fresh and mouth-watering. For all the fruit and spice the barley is clearly visible and offers a more deft sweetness; the fudgy vanilla heads towards a hickory-style bourbon character; **f23.5** long with a slight sprinkling of salt. Otherwise it rumbles just like the delivery and middle, but now with far more humbleness; **b24.5** a faultless sherry butt. The malt offers an almost perfect accompaniment. As it happens, I had this sample in my hand as the Queen gave her 6pm address on June 5th to round off her 60th anniversary celebrations: I could hardly have had a more fitting dram with which to toast her with...which I gladly did. Congratulations, your Majesty. And thank you. 58.2%. nc ncf sc.

The GlenDronach Single Cask 1996 oloroso butt, cask no. 193 db **(88.5) n22 t23.5 f21 b22.** An almost frightening whisky. The ferocity of the sherry might have some hiding behind their sofas. 59.4%. 399 bottles.

⁖ **Cadenhead GlenDronach 21 Years Old** bott 2012 **(95.5) n24** this promises to be something special: stewed apple with a little clove seasoning; **t24** I sit here purring. This is exactly what I demand of a 21-year-old from a distillery of this stature and it delivers with frightening ease. The barley may be precise and salivating, but the busying of the plot by fragile fruits, quarrelsome spices and multi-toned oils and sugars is mesmerising; **f23.5** settles into something a little more simplistic, with a malt-nougat and rich barley fade of the highest order; **b24** an effortless essay in magnificence. 51.1%. sc. WM Cadenhead Ltd

⁖ **Malts Of Scotland Glendronach 2002** sherry hogshead, cask no. MoS12004, bott 2012 **(94.5) n23** an enormous, quarrelsome marriage between very fresh oak and dripping, unspoiled sherry. The vanillins actually square up with the grape, neither staring the other down; a highland equivalent of a Mexican Standoff ensues; **t24** the sherry is actually too big and bold for a perfect delivery, crowding out the barley entirely. Slowly the oak gets a toehold and as the spices spread, things become fabulously interesting; **f24** chocolate and jam spread on burnt toast; **b23.5** not even a hint of a fault on this cask. The sherry might be just a little bit of a bully, but you can't but admire the muscle. Not so much a dram as a statement. A bruising whisky experience. And not a single sulphur atom in sight. 54.8%. nc ncf sc.

Old Malt Cask GlenDronach Aged 18 Years refill hogshead, cask no. 6910, dist May 95, bott Jan 11 **(84.5) n21 t21 f21.5 b21.** Enjoyably simplistic: dense, malty and quietly satisfying. 50%. nc ncf sc. Douglas Laing & Co. 346 bottles.

GLENDULLAN (see also below)
Speyside, 1972. Diageo. Working.

Glendullan Aged 8 Years db **(89) n20** fresh, gingery, zesty; **t22** distinctly mealy and malty. **f24** brilliant – really stunning grassy malt powers through. Speyside in a glass – and a nutshell; **b23** this is just how I like my Speysiders: young fresh and uplifting. A truly charming malt. 40%

Glendullan The Manager's Choice European oak, cask no. 12718, dist 1995, bott 2009 db **(93.5) n24.5** just a near flawless nose: an absolute perfection of balance between purring barley and fresh fruit, especially apples. Just love the new-mown hay... in fact, everything about this, especially that mix of old and new characteristics ...; **t23.5** intriguing combination of ripening fruit and young-ish make: has a suet pudding feel but with the extra addition of thick sultana and reduced plum sauce; **f23** a long, leviathan of rich fruit, dappled with barley and vanilla; **b22.5** a bit like finding a perfectly preserved old Merc with low mileage: performs as beautifully as it does effortlessly and offers a priceless symmetry between simplicity and style. Whoever chose these casks deserves a medal struck. And take this one at body temp only. 58.7%. 635 bottles.

Singleton of Glendullan 12 Years Old db **(87) n22** significant oak hides some of the Jamaican ginger; **t22** a gutsier barley character with stifled honey and the oak dives in again; **f21** dry with a slight return of ginger; **b22** much more age than is comfortable for a 12-y-o. 40%

Fine Malt Selection Glendullan 14 Years Old dist 1997, bott May 11 **(86) n23.5 t23.5 f18 b21.** A disappointingly bitter ending to a lively story full of delightful surprises 45%. sc. James MacArthur & Co. USA release.

⁖ **Gordon & MacPhail Connoisseurs Choice Glendullan 1997 (85) n22 t21 f21 b21.** Tries hard to impress, and the hayrick nose makes a success of getting the Speyside message across. But a little too syrupy sweet for its own good. 43%. Gordon & MacPhail.

Provenance Glendullan Over 11 Years refill hogshead, cask no. 7191, dist Autumn 99, bott Spring 2011 **(86) n22 t22 f21 b21.** Soft, sweet, ultra malty blending fodder which is low on complexity but high on charm. *46%. nc ncf sc. Douglas Laing & Co.*

⁙ **Provenance Glendullan Over 12 Years** refill hogshead, cask no. 8013, dist Autumn 1999, bott Winter 2012 **(82.5) n22 t21 f19 b20.5.** One of those skinny chaps: all barley, no meat. *46%. nc ncf sc. Douglas Laing & Co.*

⁙ **Royal British Legion Glendullan 1999** cask no. 16546, bott 2012 **(85.5) n20.5 t23 f21 b21.** The nose leaves you in little doubt what kind of rough ride awaits. But the shimmering intensity of the barley, especially on delivery, is a delicious wonder to behold. *58.8%. nc ncf sc.*

GLENDULLAN *(see also above)*
Speyside, 1898–1985. Closed.

Glendullan 1978 Rare Malt db **(88) n23** exceptional piquancy to this with the quietness of the oak shattered by a lemon-citrus shrill. Genuinely wonderful; **t22** a lovely, tart start with that citrus making a crashing entry but the oak barges in soon after and coffee is soon on the menu; **f21** more coffee and lemon cake, though it by now a very small slice; **b22** Sherlock Holmes would have loved this one: he would have found it lemon-entry. *56.8%*

GLEN ELGIN
Speyside, 1900. Diageo. Working.

Glen Elgin Aged 12 Years db **(89) n23** blistering, mouthwatering fruit of unspecified origin. The intensity of the malt is breathtaking; **t24** stunning fresh malt arrival, salivating barley that is both crisp and lush: then a big round of spice amid some squashed, over-ripe plums. Faultless mouthfeel; **f20** the spice continues as does the intense malt but is devalued dramatically by a bitter-toffee effect; **b22** absolutely murders Cragganmore as Diageo's top dog bottled Speysider. The marks would be several points further north if one didn't get the feeling that some caramel was weaving a derogatory spell. Brilliant stuff nonetheless. States Pot Still on label – not to be confused with Irish Pot Still. This is 100% malt... and it shows! *43%*

⁙ **Liquid Sun Glen Elgin 1984** bott 2011 **(85) n21.5 t22 f20.5 b21.** By no means the first cask I have tasted this year where age has got the better of the obvious honey theme. Nor will it be the last. Enjoyable, but obviously not at its zenith. *45.1%. nc ncf sc. The Whisky Agency.*

⁙ **Malts Of Scotland Glen Elgin 1975** bourbon hogshead, cask no. MoS11024, bott Nov 11 **(91.5) n22.5** pretty tired oak. But beyond that a massive salt and honey mix; some lovely lime jam amid the Jaffa Cake; **t23.5** creaks, cracks and leaks oak in every way thinkable. And yet the acacia honey mixing with toasty honeycomb, Demerara sugar and the oils of Venezuelan cocoa ensure a very special experience; **f22.5** long, and more of the same, but with more spice and less sugars; **b23** despite the biting oak, there is little doubting the once greatness of this cask. A decade ago this would have been a world beater. *46.8%. nc ncf sc.*

⁙ **The Perfect Dram Glen Elgin 36 Years Old** bourbon cask, dist 1975, bott 2011 **(88.5) n22** a close relation to the Malts of Scotland bottling. A little extra salt this time round; **t22.5** eye-watering oak, but just enough sugars and honey to make for a delicious counter; Jaffa cake but now no lime; **f22** salty; **b22** fascinating. It is as though the Malt of Scotland cask has had some of its sugars removed to be replaced by extra salt... *48.2%. sc. The Whisky Agency.*

⁙ **Scott's Selection Glen Elgin 1995** bott 2011 **(89) n22.5** freshly baled straw sweetened with a honey and lime-marmalade freshness; a hint of smoke; **t23** and again on the delivery, which combines those sweet, fluting fruity notes with a sumptuous texture to match; **f21.5** over enthusiastic bitterness at the death, but only after a vanilla custard fade; **b22** excellent malt which in an even better cask might really have meant business. *571%. Speyside Distillers.*

The Whisky Agency Glen Elgin 1975 bourbon hogshead, bott 2011 **(83.5) n22 t21 f20 b20.5.** Competent whisky showing just a little too much oak than it requires for greatness. Puckeringly tart in part, but there is still a depth to the barley which endears. *51.5%*

⁙ **The Whisky Cask Glen Elgin Aged 25 Years** bourbon cask, dist 1984, bott 2009 **(95.5) n23** a finely tuned mix of traditional heavy bourbon notes sweetened with Golden Syrup and lightweight fruit including glazed cherries; **t24** a magnificent delivery with the emphasis on the sugars, but inclusive of complex malt and vanilla; the middle ground is also a riot of light Golden Syrup melting into a toasted fruit loaf; **f23.5** vanilla and butterscotch until it comes out of your ears; **b24** so many strands of Golden Syrup, the dentist might be called in. A superb experience from a superb distillery. *49%. sc. The Whisky Cask.*

GLENESK
Highlands (Eastern), 1897–1985. Diageo. Demolished.

Duncan Taylor Collection Glenesk 1983 cask no. 4930 **(89.5) n22 t23 f22 b22.5.** By far the best Glen Esk I've tasted in years. Perhaps not the most complex, but the liveliness and clarity are a treat. *52.1%*

GLENFARCLAS
Speyside, 1836. J&G Grant. Working.

Glenfarclas 8 Years Old db (86) n21 t22 f22 b21. Less intense sherry allows the youth of this malt to stand out. Mildly quirky as a Glenfarclas and enormous entertainment. 40%

Glenfarclas 10 Years Old db (80) n19 t20 f22 b19. Always an enjoyable malt, but for some reason this version never seems to fire on all cylinders. There is a vague honey sheen which works well with the barley, but struggles for balance and the nose is a bit sweaty. Still has distinctly impressive elements but an odd fish. 40%

Glenfarclas 12 Years Old db (94) n23.5 a wonderfully fresh mix of grape and mint; t24 light, youthful, playful, mouthwatering. Less plodding honey, more vibrant Demerara and juiced-up butterscotch; f23 long, with soft almost ice-cream style vanillas with a grapey topping; b23.5 a superb re-working of an always trustworthy malt. This dramatic change in shape works a treat and suits the malt perfectly. What a sensational success!! 43%

Glenfarclas 15 Years Old db (85.5) n21.5 t23 f20 b21. One thing is for certain: working with sherry butts these days is a bit like working with ACME dynamite....you are never sure when it is about to blow up in your face. There is only minimal sulphur here, but enough to take the edge off a normally magnificent whisky, at the death. Instead it is now merely, in part, quite lovely. The talent at Glenfarclas is unquestionably among the highest in the industry: I'll be surprised to see the same weaknesses with the next bottling. 46%

Glenfarclas 17 Years Old db (93) n23 just so light and playful: custard powder lightens and sweetens, sultana softens, barley moistens, spice threatens...; t23 the relaxed sherry influence really lets the honey deliver; delightfully roasty and well spiced towards the middle; f23 when I was a kid there was a candy – pretend tobacco, no less! – made from strands of coconut and sweetened with a Demerara syrup. My, this takes me back...; b24 an excellent age for this distillery, allowing just enough oak in to stir up the complexity. A stupendous addition to the range. 40%

Glenfarclas 21 Years Old db (83) n20 t23 f19 b21. A chorus of sweet, honied malt and mildly spiced, teasing fruit on the fabulous mouth arrival and middle compensates for the few blips. 43%

Glenfarclas 25 Years Old db (84) n20 t22 f20 b22. A curious old bat: by no means free from imperfect sherry but compensating with some staggering age – seemingly way beyond the 25-year statement. Enjoys the deportment of a doddering old classics master from a family of good means and breeding. 43%

Glenfarclas 30 Years Old db (85) n20 t22 f21 b22. Flawed yet juicy. 43%

Glenfarclas 40 Years Old db (94) n23 old Demerara rum laced with well aged oloroso. Spicy, deep though checked by vanilla; t23 toasty fruitcake with just the right degree of burnt raisin; again the spices are central to the plot though now a Jamaican Blue Mountain/ Mysore medium roast mix makes an impressive entrance; t24 long, with the oak not just ticking every box, but doing so with a flourish. The Melton Hunt cake finale is divine... b24 couldn't help but laugh: this sample was sent by the guys at Glenfarclas after they spotted that I had last year called their disappointing 40-year-old a "freak". I think we have both proved a point... 46%

Glenfarclas 40 Years Old Millennium Edition db (92) n23 t23 f23 b23. An almost immaculate portrayal of an old-fashioned, high-quality malt with unblemished sherry freshness and depth. The hallmark of quality is the sherry's refusal to dominate the spicy, softly peated malt. The oak offers a bourbony sweetness but ensures a rich depth throughout. Quite outstanding for its age. 54.7%. nc ncf.

Glenfarclas 50 Years Old db (92) n24 Unique. Almost a marriage between 20-y-o bourbon and intense, old-fashioned sherry. Earthy, weighty stuff that repays time in the glass and oxidization because only then does the subtlety become apparent and a soft peat-reek reveal itself; t23 an unexpected sweet – even mouthwatering - arrival, again with a touch of peat to add counter ballast to the intense richness of the sherry. The oak is intense from the middle onwards, but of such high quality that it merely accompanies rather then dominates; f22 warming black peppers ping around the palate; some lovely cocoa oils coat the mouth for a bitter-sweet, warming and very long finish; b23 Most whiskies cannot survive such great age. This one really does bloom in the glass and the earthy, peaty aspect makes it all the more memorable. It has taken 50 years to reach this state. Give a glass of this at least an hour's inquisition, as I have. Your patience will be rewarded many times over. 44.4%

Glenfarclas 105 db (95.5) n23.5 the youthful grape comes in clean, juicy bunches; the herbs and spices on a rack on the kitchen wall; t24 any lovers of the old Jennings books will here do a Mr Wilkins explosive snort as the magnificent barley-grape mix is propelled with the force of dynamite into the taste buds; survivors of this experience still able to speak may mention something about cocoa notes forming; f24 long, luxurious, with a pulsing vanilla-grape mix and a build up of spices; light oils intensify and elongate; b24 I doubt if any restorative on the planet works quite as well as this one does. Or if any sherry cask whisky is so clean and full of the joys of Jerez. A classic malt which has upped a gear or two and has become exactly what it is: a whisky of pure brilliance... 60%

⁙ **Glenfarclas 1953 Aged 58 Years** first fill sherry butt, cask no. 1674, dist 20 Nov 53, bott 13 Feb 12 db **(91) n24** if you could draw in your mind's eye just how the great old sherry butts of yesteryear nosed at their most complex, you would find facets of that picture here. The grape makes its statement but does not dwell or boast. It allows so many other aroma profiles to the dais: the vanilla is coated in lemon, the dryer hickory accompanied by sweeter blackjacks; a slice of apple, a whiff of bluebell...it is almost an aromatic tapestry of all the things that can make a whisky great; **t23** the delivery is sherry coated and the bold molassed sugars hold out for a while, though the strain shows as the creamy mocha forms. But when the oaks break through, age is writ large; **f21** a creaking finale, though the timber never quite cracks under the strain of nigh on 60 years. Busy spices make a defiant and heroic late charge; **b23** sections of the nose are outstanding. The passing years, though, have crept up with the body. Yet, once you acclimatise, it is a dram you are unlikely to forget. Majestic. Literally. 47.2%. nc ncf sc. 400 bottles.

Glenfarclas 1960 The Family Casks Release VI sherry hogshead, cask no. 1772 db **(94) n25** I remember having some Melton Hunt cake once which lay forgotten in a kitchen cupboard for about four years. This really does remind me of it: fruity, thick, raisins not so much toasted as charred, dripping with molasses and yet showing a spicy defiance. A nose of such complexity it commands an absolute minimum of 30 minutes attention...At about 20 minutes in it announces its perfection... **t24** you actually laugh to yourself at the delivery: it is so outrageously good! Where does such juiciness come from after half a century of being cooped up in a cask? Lots of toasted fruit but the honeycomb and Danish marzipan do a magnificent job of keeping the balance; **f21.5** inevitably a price has to be paid and it comes on the exhausted, bitter finale. But it is entirely forgiven... **b23.5** this is the 999th whisky tasted for Whisky Bible 2012. And what a choice – what a whisky! Let's just say that the 1960 is drinking well... 47%. sc.

Glenfarclas 1961 The Family Casks Release VI sherry hogshead, cask no. 1326 db **(91) n25** it is ridiculous! How is any human supposed to describe this? Like the 1960 Release VI, it is faultless: different, but faultless. Here we have blackberries in both juicy and jam form, the latter spread over slightly burnt toast, of course. There is a swirl of salted butter in there, too. Nearby a slightly more roasted than the norm cup of Jamaican Blue Mountain coffee gently steams...; **t23** hickory and molasses link with the most toasty raisins imaginable; toasted honeycomb...which becomes toastier by the moment...; **f20** bitters out like a coffee struck by water too far on the boil; **b23** up until the bitterness forming towards the middle, this was on course for World Whisky of the Year... I need say no more. 54.4%. sc.

⁙ **Glenfarclas 1961 The Family Casks Release VII** sherry hogshead, cask no. 1325 db **(87.5) n23.5** the sherry has taken on a formidable thickness of character, absorbing a degree of creosote from the ancient oak; **t23** the delivery is exactly as the nose promises: big, juicy, salivating grape and then a gravy of oaky tones; dried dates and walnuts abound; **f19** bitters out dramatically; **b22** earlier this year I officially opened an allotment for very young children suffering from cancer (anyone wishing to contribute to this touching cause please contact 0844 879 4247 or visit www.nctlctrust.com). I mention this because one of the most magical aspects of being able to nose, is that it can take you on a journey when you least expect it. I nosed this, and suddenly I was in my dad's wheelbarrow being carried to his old allotment in Surrey. I remember him liberally painting his little shed there in creosote. And the mildly creosoteish nose to this took me back, involuntarily, to that warm Sunday afternoon, probably back in 1961, when, as coincidence will have it, this was made. 47%. sc. 108 bottles.

⁙ **Glenfarclas 1961 The Family Casks Release IX** sherry hogshead, cask no. 3050 db **(95.5) n23.5** a busy junction where many of the darker sugar types meet, though the tannins act like traffic lights to stop them crashing into each other. Surprisingly well ordered and beautifully balanced; the toffee apple is a lovely distraction; **t24** and again on delivery we have those huge tannins and impressive sugars doing the perfect job of cancelling out each others' excesses; almost like a malty porridge with molten muscovado sugar and juicy sultanas; **f24** long and not a hint of bitterness as those dark sugars radiate deeply; the oaks do pop up with a spicy, coconut, treacle edge. Ridiculously yummy for its age.... **b24** where this succeeds and cask 1325 struggles, is that this maintains the sugars and balance throughout: a rare trick for a cask some 50 years of age! 48%. sc. 133 bottles.

Glenfarclas 1962 The Family Casks Release VI sherry hogshead, cask no. 2649 db **(95) n22.5** hardly usual to find a whisky this age...and even more unusual to find one with a nose like this: unique, I'd say. Not often an aroma comes up that I don't recognise or can't pigeonhole. But there is one here! I would say it was from the wine influence, rather than the actual oak, but I could be wrong. It is dry, halfway to being vaguely vegetable but seems to keep the grape grounded and allow the spices to fly; **t24.5** And do those spices fly!!!! A magnificent delivery with the grape now out of its shackles and accompanied by some muscular sugars, too. Lots of juicy plum jam and toasted raisin, but no bitterness at all; **f24** a brilliant finale which somehow flips from a fruit influence to a more bourbon style with honeycomb, liquorice and a hint of molasses doing an outstanding job; **b24** a quite unique whisky with countless twists and turns and displaying a personality the like of which I have never seen before. Might be a bit scary early on, but stick with it. You will be rewarded more than handsomely. *55.7%. sc.*

⁘ **Glenfarclas 1962 The Family Casks Release VIII** sherry hogshead, cask no. 2648 db **(85.5) n21.5 t22 f21 b21.** Just strays outside the area of comfort once or twice. The delivery is sublime, but the beauty is fleeting. Plenty still to savour from a clean butt...but just a little too bitter from wear and tear. *49.2%. sc. 135 bottles.*

⁘ **Glenfarclas 1963 The Family Casks Release VIII** sherry hogshead, cask no. 179 db **(89.5) n21.5** of that tomato soup variety of sherry; **t22** a big, eye-watering whack of oak, but the taste buds are kissed better by a juicy grape follow through; **f23.5** at last finds a welcome degree of balance, with the more vigorous elements of the oak now having backed off completely. The mocha is distinctly more high roast Mysore than chocolate; late on some major heavy duty fruitcake; **b22.5** goes round the houses a bit to get to where it wants to go. But we can all celebrate when it finally arrives. *50.4%. sc. 194 bottles.*

⁘ **Glenfarclas 1964 The Family Casks Release VII** sherry butt, cask no. 4719 db **(86) n22.5 t23.5 f19 b21.** Time has played some peculiar tricks on this old dram. Both the nose and delivery are draped with a mixture of hugely delicious fresh and ancient grape notes, as well as spice, giving a distinctive two-tone effect. This finish, though, bitters out too violently. *48.5%. sc. 377 bottles.*

Glenfarclas 1965 The Family Casks Release V cask no. 4362, bott May 10 db **(91.5) n24 t23.5 f21.5 b22.5.** As silky a whisky as you might ever find. Needs a minimum half hour in the glass to open properly. *51.9%*

⁘ **Glenfarclas 1965 The Family Casks Release IX** sherry butt, cask no. 4502 db **(73.5) n18 t22 f15 b18.5.** A silky assassin. *53.7%. sc. 509 bottles.*

⁘ **Glenfarclas 1966 The Family Casks Release VIII** sherry butt, cask no. 4186 db **(94) n23** it's the bottled aroma of Wembley. Brylcreem. Woodbines. The oak of 100,000 rattles Of Booby Moore leading the team onto the pitch...of sweat...; **t23.5** a dram that's perfect to experience from a table at home...or off the bar...; **f23.5** as sweet as a devastating shot from Geoff Hurst... mmm... I think it's all over...; **b24** ...it is now..! *51.1%. sc. 461 bottles.*

Glenfarclas 1967 The Family Casks Release V cask no. 5110, bott May 10 db **(96) n24** cuts a nutty dash to seriously underscore the big fruitcake quality here; no shortage of bourbon, orange peel and liquorice characteristics, either; **t24.5** like sneezing, tasting this is something it's impossible to do with your eyes open...helped by an extraordinary alcohol kick of its age, the soupy intense kumquat, over-ripened banana and sherry (as it is sherry you get here, not grape...!!) form an indestructible alliance, refusing to allow even 40 years of oak to make any kind of telling impact, other than to offer a tame and friendly vanilla frame in which the fruit can take centre stage; elsewhere brown sugars and spices adorn the picture and the odd little liquorice bourbon feature makes a cameo appearance; **f23.5** the milky cocoa makes a much later start than you'd expect, thanks to the bullying fruit, tangy orange peel and banana milkshake sticks to the very end; **b24** one of those whiskies once tasted, never forgotten. A malt which hasn't grown old gracefully. it has simply become a fruity Lothario, seducing every taste bud in sight. And taking it by force if it has to... *60.8%*

Glenfarclas 1968 The Family Casks Release VI sherry hogshead, cask no. 534 db **(86.5) n22.5 t21 f21.5 b21.5.** Some milky mocha softens the impact but the oak is very keenly felt. *49.5%. sc.*

Glenfarclas 1969 The Family Casks Release VI sherry hogshead, cask no. 3187 db **(89.5) n23.5** the oak takes first, second and third positions in dominance here with burned raisin and cherry fruitcake hanging on for dear life; some exemplary spice; **t22.5** fruit takes first and third place; oak second. Massively chewy with a mocha subplot and the burned raisin becoming more intense by the moment; **f21.5** tires and bitters as caramel begins to increase; **b22** nothing shy about the oak here. *56.2%. sc.*

⁘ **Glenfarclas 1970 The Family Casks Release VII** sherry hogshead, cask no. 6778 db **(90.5) n23** thick grape: the oak punches through, but a cleanly bitten, crunchy toffee apple injects surprising vigour; **t22** the oak arrives in puckering fashion; major league Demerara sugars required to ensure a balance; **f23** settles comfortably with the grapes back on track and a chocolate fudge finale...along with some late warming spice; **b22.5** I think I remember a previous '70 vintage which was among the best I have ever tasted from this distillery. This is big and bold, but the oak now has a much bigger say. *51.7%. sc.*

⁘ **Glenfarclas 1971 The Family Casks Release VII** sherry butt, cask no. 150 db **(77) n20 t22 f17 b18.** Starts on the palate with a pretty spectacular display of old style sherry and then, as the nose threatens, tightens and bitters dramatically. *51%. sc. 468 bottles.*

⫶ **Glenfarclas 1972 The Family Casks Release VIII** sherry butt, cask no. 3547 db **(95)** **n23.5** if you have a thing for sticky, over-ripe dates and juicy prunes then this could be your lucky day...! **t24.5** sublime delivery with a texture to die for! Absolute bliss as a fabulous, magnificently even-handed grape shimmies its way around the palate offering some manuka honey here, a little mocha there; the spices are almost too laid back to notice; **f23** as if tired of dispensing various grapey tones, it now concentrates on a semi-bourbony oak depth, even with a touch of liquorice and hickory on display; **b24** class in the glass! *47.4%. 608 bottles.*

Glenfarclas 1973 The Family Casks Release VI sherry hogshead, cask no. 2567 db **(95)** **n(24.5)** there are fruitcakes of varying intensity of flavour. This portrays the finest type, those that cost an arm and a leg at Christmas. This is rocking under its own weight in heavily toasted raisin. Big molasses and chunky almonds still sizzling in their own oils; distant hint of freshly ground high roast Java; teasing clove and other vague, lesser spices...; a little orange peel and maple syrup joins the fray as the whisky oxidises; **t24** the weight is exceptional, it's vitality and intensity thrilling; perfect balance of sweeter honeys and drier, more bitter raisin and then a slow lift off of spices which reach great heights; a wave of natural caramels slightly oil the wheels further; **f22.5** the caramel tends to take over, though a bitterness from the oak persists; a little treacle helps counter this; **b24** a whisky which speaks for itself and with spellbinding eloquence. A portrait of just how a sherried whisky should be. If you are lucky enough ever to see this, take a hammer to the piggy bank. *51.4%. sc.*

⫶ **Glenfarclas 1973 The Family Casks Release VIII** sherry butt, cask no. 2598 db **(84)** **n21 t22 f20 b21.** Clean-ish, massively spiced in part but very loose with the grape. Quite bubble gummy on the nose and finish. *56.5%. sc. 456 bottles.*

⫶ **Glenfarclas 1975 The Family Casks Release IX** refill butt, cask no. 1 db **(92.5) n23** green banana...after over 35 years! Deliciously ridiculous! Putty and golden syrup; **t23.5** tart delivery, concentrating on the under-ripe fruits; big barley bite; **f23** long with vanillas worming a way in but the golden syrup staying firm; just a little furry; **b23** mmmmm! *54.7%. sc. 344 bottles.*

⫶ **Glenfarclas 1978 The Family Casks Release VII** refill hogshead, cask no. 590 db **(86.5) n22 t22 f21 b21.5.** Never quite hits what I would get when I used to tell a joke to a late old friend of mine, Doris Stokes: a happy medium. Either swimming in supercharged sugars or a little on the sharp and astringent side. *46.3%. sc. 240 bottles.*

Glenfarclas 1981 The Family Casks Release V cask no. 58, bott May 10 db **(88.5) n22.5 t23 f21 b22.** As cluttered and intricate as a Victorian sitting room. And in its own way, just as classically beautiful, too. *50.9%*

⫶ **Glenfarclas 1981 The Family Casks Release VII** plain hogshead, cask no. 57 db **(96)** **n24** orange blossom honey. But that is merely the enticing finger, drawing you in to where red liquorice, glace cherries, treacle sponge cake and delicate shades of hickory await...; **t25** that's it. That is absolute perfection on delivery. I cannot find a fault as the oak is of exquisite quality: seasoned to the very highest standard. Never have I found a whisky which just sits and melts on the tongue quite like this: a meringue made from a mix of ulmo honey, butterscotch, walnut oil, icing sugar and barley grist. With the liberal dosage of citrus and the underlying bourbon-style liquorice depth, not for a moment is it a tad too sweet; **f23.5** just bitters a little as the sweeter elements wear off, but the weight and body remain spot on; **b24** when you find a Glenfarclas in this fettle, it makes you wonder why they don't move away from their sherry bias more often. This is Speyside malt at its zenith. *50.8%. sc. 183 bottles.*

Glenfarclas 1982 The Family Casks Release V cask no. 633, bott May 10 db **(87) n23 t22.5 f20 b21.5.** A long way from the Glenfarclas norm, but an enjoyable diversion! *54.2%*

⫶ **Glenfarclas 1982 The Family Casks Release VIII** sherry hogshead, cask no. 4568 db **(94) n23** if you are into sugared stewed gooseberries, this is the malt for you...; **t23.5** the gooseberries have been lost on delivery, but the sugars – full of lively acidity – are in full flow. A wonderful marriage of gristy barley juice and a grape; **f24** the vanillas ensure that a certain decorum controls the naked exuberance of the sugars; **b23.5** possibly one of the sweetest whiskies I have ever seen extracted from the sherry cask....! *54.9%. sc. 233 bottles.*

⫶ **Glenfarclas 1983 The Family Casks Release IX** refill hogshead, cask no. 43 db **(92)** **n22.5** needs a few minutes in glass to settle. Then a complex citrus dance is performed...; **t24** hi honey! Oh my word: I could chew on this all day. The orange blossom honey sets up camp but allows all kinds of spicy friends along. The buttery vanilla is a welcome guest, not least because it refuses to stay too long; **f22.5** simplifies with those vanillas returning and even appears to offer the vaguest and most tiny of smoky adieus; **b23** just one of those gorgeous drams which stylishly entrances. *51%. sc. 273 bottles.*

⫶ **Glenfarclas 1984 The Family Casks Release VII** plain hogshead, cask no. 6030 db **(94.5) n23** surprisingly fresh, even to the extent of a new makey fingerprint, which barely seems possible. But this is helped by the house-style citrus: a fresh zestiness, this time in tandem with a lemon drop sharpness; **t24** I feel that my taste buds are sitting in the most soothing pool of citrusy malt, slowly having their nerve endings massaged and manicured;

any cracks found are filled in with honey and marzipan; **f23.5** the barley juices appear to stretch into the distance, enough to carry the most sublime butterscotch and vanilla; **b24** Glenfarclas does mind-blowing citrus like no other Speyside distillery. *51%. sc. 264 bottles.*

⁙ **Glenfarclas 1986 The Family Casks Release IX** refill sherry butt, cask no. 4336 db **(68)** **n17 t19 f15 b17.** Oh, Lordy... *58.4%. sc. 574 bottles.*

Glenfarclas 1988 Quarter Casks cask no. 251-261, dist Jan 88, bott Feb 08 db **(91) n23 t23.5 f22 b22.5.** Chocolate fruit and nut bar lovers will be happy with this one, as will devotees of unspoiled sherry casks. *46.1%. German market. 1,478 bottles.*

⁙ **Glenfarclas 1989 The Family Casks Release IX** sherry butt, cask no. 12989 db **(96) n24** probably the most moist Melton Hunt Cake you'll ever find; **t24** a stunning delivery: the oloroso is dripping with greengages and dates, all backed up by lush spiced treacle; **f24** a classy fruity fade concentrating on the burnt raisin especially; **b24** oh, if only all sherry matured malts in Scotland from this era could be as faultless as this... *55.9%. sc. 622 bottles.*

Glenfarclas 1990 The Family Casks Release V cask no. 5095, bott May 10 db **(94.5) n23.5** big clean grape, but the coffee aspect hints of dark rum, too; **t24.5** juicy, beautifully sweetened and structured grape; strata of Lubec marzipan and elsewhere a butterscotch-barley intrigue; **f23** long with the fruit mingling confidently with a busy, peppery spice; always Demerara sugars keep the spices and vanillas in very good shape; **b23.5** you will dream of dusty bodegas if you drink this late at night. Massive sherry, but excellent balance and complexity, too. The delivery and early complexity ranks among the best whisky moments of the year. Strikingly gorgeous. *56.5%. 459 bottles.*

⁙ **Glenfarclas 1990 The Family Casks Release VIII** sherry butt, cask no. 5099 db **(83.5) n21.5 t23 f19 b20.** Oh, so many grapey gold medals and a wonderful thread of golden syrup. But the finish is too dry for all the wrong reasons. *56.5%. sc. 615 bottles.*

⁙ **Glenfarclas 1991 The Family Casks Release IX** sherry butt, cask no. 5669 db **(87) n23** toffee apple on speed...; **t22** an enormous delivery of thick caramel and thicker grape; **f21.5** salty and delightfully aggressive; **b20.5** never seems to form a meaningful narrative; just a succession of round or angular shapes pitched together at random. *57.1%. sc. 624 bottles.*

⁙ **Glenfarclas 1992 The Family Casks Release VIII** sherry butt, cask no. 861 db **(81.5) n22 t22.5 f17 b20.** Lands rather beautifully with a late furry nibble; *59.5%. sc. 550 bottles.*

Glenfarclas 1993 The Family Casks Release V cask no. 3942, bott Apr 10 db **(72) n17.5 t19.5 f18 b18.** All over the place. The black sheep of the family... *59.7%. 566 bottles.*

⁙ **Glenfarclas 1993 The Family Casks Release IX** sherry butt, cask no. 74 db **(96) n24** I am not sure if sherry gets any more intense than this without shutting out all other degrees of complexity. But the wonderful drip-feeding of both spice and herbs, ulmo honey and cracked leather really does take this up a few notches; **t24** presumably oloroso: the body is thick and dripping with intense, spiced grape. The vanillas are a perfect foil; **f24** the stunning ulmo honey continues to the very end where it stays arm in arm with the roasted nuts and drying grape skins; **b24** I am on my knees with my head bowed towards this bottle; a cask which would have been very much at home in the 60s and 70s...this offers us something which has now almost entirely been lost to the whisky world. *58.7%. sc. 627 bottles.*

Glenfarclas 1994 The Family Casks Release V cask no. 3629, bott Apr 10 db **(86) n22 t21 f22 b21.** So dripping in clean, rich sherry that all barley traces have been expunged. Eye-watering, lightly spiced, entirely sulphur-free, and, even if a little heavy-handed here and there, in its more lucid moments of a style now almost unique to this distillery. *59.3%. 609 bottles.*

⁙ **Glenfarclas 1994 The Family Casks Release IX** sherry butt, cask no. 2950 db **(93.5) n24** if this was any more sherry-ish it would be...a sherry...; thankfully, given time a whole complex gamut of oaky notes begin to wander in and out; **t23** the clean, unblemished grape on the nose stands the delivery in the highest stead; nutty, lively, full of dates and dried prunes in a molassed setting; **f23.5** my word, how can you say no to that rich chocolate mousse stuffed with walnuts...? **b23** takes me back to the 1970s when you could frolic with unblemished sherry butts to your heart's desire... *57.9%. sc. 629 bottles.*

Glenfarclas 1995 The Family Casks Release VI sherry hogshead, cask no. 6778 db **(71) n17.5 t18.5 f17 b18.** Tarnished family silver. *60.1%. sc.*

⁙ **Glenfarclas 1995 The Family Casks Release IX** sherry butt, cask no. 6612 db **(76.5) n18 t21.5 f18 b19.** As bright as a 2012 British summer's day... *52.5%. sc. 650 bottles.*

Glenfarclas 1995 45° The Heritage Malt Collection sherry cask, dist Nov 95, bott Sep 06 db **(94.5) n24 t23.5 f23.5 b23.5.** Exceptional. Absolutely everything you could demand from a sherried malt of this age. Not a single off note and the freshness of comparative youth and complexity of years in the cask are in perfect harmony. *45%. Spain.*

⁙ **Glenfarclas 1996 The Family Casks Release VII** sherry butt, cask no. 1306 db **(80.5) n19 t22.5 f19 b20.** Not exactly perfect. But the sugars hit the heights. *55.6%. sc. 593 bottles.*

Glenfarclas 1997 Cask Strength Premium Edition matured in sherry casks, cask no. 642-648, dist Feb 97, bott Mar 09 db **(77.5) n18.5 t20 f19.5 b19.5.** In their defence, the quality of some of the casks that have gone into this are so good, it may have been possible to have missed the obvious problem. But it is there, and unmistakably so *55.5%. German market.*

Glenfarclas 175th Anniversary 2011 db (**94**) n23.5 crisp and precise fruit: clean and hedging towards bon bons. The very vaguest hint of smoke adds extra depth; vanilla and spice fly the other way; t24 fabulous delivery: every aspect dissolves on impact. The fruits are again subtle yet lush, the sweetness initially from gristy icing sugar, though towards the middle more muscovado. Again, the lightest imaginable wisps of smoke and more profound spices; f23 cream toffee; burnt raisin; b23.5 hard to imagine an experience more gentle than this where alcohol is concerned. No slam bam stuff here. Every moment is about whispers and brushes of the nerve endings. Sensual whisky. *43%. nc. J&G Grant. 6000 bottles.*

⋯⋯ **Cadenhead Glenfarclas 21 Years Old** dist 1990, bott 2011 (**89.5**) n22.5 vanilla, marmalade and a shake of salt; t22.5 clean, sharp delivery; citrussy with major tang factor; f22 allows the vanillas a bigger role on the creamy fade; b22.5 charming. Never stops entertaining. *54.3%. sc. WM Cadenhead Ltd. 222 bottles.*

Luvians Open Bottle 2010 Glenfarclas 17 Years Old sherry butt (**90**) n22 light fruitcake with a honey middle; t23 soft delivery with an unusual vanilla arrival ahead of the fruit. The middle reverts to vanilla and butterscotch with an attractive chalky feel; f22.5 a hint of burnt raisin but there is the late honeycomb, too; b22.5 underplays the fruit and homes in on the honey. Deliciously different. *43%. Luvians Bottle Shop.*

Scotch Malt Whisky Society Cask 1.158 Aged 11 Years 1st fill barrel, cask no. 800062, dist 1999 (**91.5**) n23 charmingly gristy, despite life in a first fill cask! Surprisingly delicate, though there are some curious vanilla explosions with the spice; t23.5 fabulously sharp malt is thrown forwards by a secondary surge of oak; in the wake is a highly complex ebbing and flowing of varying bourbon notes, with slivers of honeycomb and peppered hickory noticeable; f22 a burned toast bitterness on the fudge; those complex bourbon notes just keep on going; b23 complexity is the key but most impressive is the intensity: a dram I could enjoy all night. Not that it was ever needed, but what a way to prove that the excellence of this distillery has nothing to do with sherry... *61.8%. sc. 231 bottles.*

⋯⋯ **Scotch Malt Whisky Society Cask 1.160 Aged 11 Years** first fill barrel, cask no. 800150, dist 2000 (**88.5**) n21.5 dry with a saline lead; t22 big delivery with no shortage of tannins; the sugars arrive quite late but in good numbers; f23.5 easily the best part: first milky cocoa and then coffee before the two merge...; b21.5 A solid malt making the most of the salty tannins dredged from a very fresh cask. Just love the late mocha. *55.6%. sc.*

GLENFIDDICH
Speyside, 1887. William Grant & Sons. Working.

Glenfiddich 12 Years Old db (**85.5**) n21 t22 f21 b21.5. A malt now showing a bit of zap and spark. Even displays a flicker of attractive muscovado sugars. Simple, untaxing and safe. *40%*

Glenfiddich 12 Years Old Toasted Oak Reserve db (**92.5**) n22.5 t23.5 f22.5 b24. Another bottling to confound the critics of Glenfiddich. This is as fine an essay in balance, charm and sophistication as you are likely to find in the whole of Speyside this year. Crack open a bottle... but only when you have a good hour to spend. *40%*

Glenfiddich Caoran Reserve Aged 12 Years db (**89**) n22.5 t22 f21.5 b23. Has fizzed up a little in the last year or so with some salivating charm from the barley and a touch of cocoa from the oak. A complex little number. *40%*

Glenfiddich Rich Oak Over 14 Years Old new American & new Spanish oak finish db (**90.5**) n23 fascinating: there is a nod towards Japanese oak in the naked wood profile here. Toned down, though, by a huge pithy kumquat presence. That this is virgin oak there can be no doubt, so don't expect an easy ride; t22 soft oils help for a quiet landing: like lonely oaks falling in a forest...there is a brief sensation of passing barley. Then it returns again to a number of oak-laden notes, especially the spices which move towards a creamy mocha territory; f23.5 possibly the best phase of the experience. The vivid, surging oak has cooled and some barley oils mingle in a relaxed fashion with the sweetening, very mildly sugared mocha; b22 from the moment you nose this, there is absolutely no doubting its virgin oak background. It pulls towards bourbon, but never gets there. Apparently European oak is used, too. The result is something curiously hinting at Japanese, but without the crushing intensity. Delicious, thoughtful whisky and one to tick off on your journey of malt whisky discovery. Though a pity we don't see it at 46% and in full voluptuous nudity: you get the feeling that this would have been something really exceptional to conjure with. *40%. William Grant.*

Glenfiddich 15 Years Old db (**94.5**) n23 such a deft intermingling of the softer fruits and bourbon notes...with barley in there to remind you of the distillery; t23 intense and big yet all the time appearing delicate and light; the most apologetic of spices help spotlight the barley sweetness and delicate fruits; f24.5 just so long and complex; something of the old fashioned fruit salad candy about this but with a small degree of toffee just rounding off the edges; **b24** if an award were to be given for the most consistently beautiful dram in Scotland, this would win more often than not. This under-rated distillery has won more friends with this masterpiece than probably any other brand. *40%*

Glenfiddich Aged 15 Years Cask Strength db (85.5) **n20 t23 f21 b21.5.** Improved upon the surprisingly bland bottlings of old, especially on the fabulously juicy delivery. Still off the pace due to an annoying toffee-ness towards the middle and at the death. *51%*

Glenfiddich Distillery Edition 15 Years Old db (93.5) **n24.5** banana skins, but there is no slip up here as the aroma spectrum moves from ultra fat sultanas on one side to dried coconut on the other. You'll find countless other reference points, including lightly salted celery and even molten candle wax. Quite astonishing and, even with its spice nip, one of the great whisky noses of 2010; **t24** my word!! Just so lively...enormous complexity from the very first mouthful. The mouthfeel is two-toned with heavier fruit not quite outstripping the flightier barley. All kinds of vanilla – both dry and sweet – and a dusty spiciness, too; **f22** tones down rather too dramatically, hedging much more towards the more docile banana-vanilla elements; **b23** had this exceptional whisky been able to maintain the pace through to the finish, this would have been a single malt of the year contender - at least. *51%. ncf.*

Glenfiddich Aged 15 Years Solera Reserve *(see Glenfiddich 15 Years Old)*

Glenfiddich 18 Years Old db (95) **n23.5** the smoke, which for long marked this aroma, appears to have vanished. But the usual suspects of blood orange and various other fruit appear to thrive in the lightly salted complexity; **t24.5** how long are you allowed to actually keep the whisky held on the palate before you damage your teeth? One to really close your eyes and study because here we have one of the most complex deliveries Speyside can conjour: the peat may have gone, but there is coal smoke around as the juicy barley embeds with big fat sultanas, plums, dates and grapes. Despite the distinct lack of oil, the mouthfeel is entirely yielding to present one of the softest and most complete essays on the palate you can imagine, especially when you take the bitter-sweet ratio and spice into balance; **f23** long, despite the miserly 40% offered, with plenty of banana custard and a touch of peat; **b24** at the moment, the ace in the Glenfiddich pack. If this was bottled at 46%, unchilfiltered etc, I dread to think what the score might be... *40%*

⋄ **Glenfiddich Age Of Discovery Aged 19 Years Bourbon Cask Reserve** db (92) **n23.5** not just complex, but so delicate one is almost afraid to nose too deeply incase you break the poor thing into a million pieces. The barley skits around like a highly strung actress on the edge of a breakdown; **t24** of such butterfly qualities, it wanders at random around the palate, touching down here and there to offer a barely legible malty weight; the sugars are no less constrained, a thin heather honey style feebly patting away the encroaching oak: the whole thing, like the nose, is wonderfully neurotic; **f22** melts away with limited grace and tact for far too short a finale; **b22.5** for my money Glenfiddich turns from something quite workaday to a malt extraordinaire between the ages of 15 and 18. So, depending on the casks chosen, a year the other side of that golden age shouldn't make too much difference. The jury is still out on whether it was helped by being at 40%, which means the natural oils have been broken down somewhat, allowing the intensity and richness only an outside chance of fully forming. *40%*

Glenfiddich Age Of Discovery Aged 19 Years Madeira Cask Finish db (88.5) **n22.5** mixed fruit but emboldened by gentle, oak-enriched spices. Delicate yet confident and, as the drier elements take hold, one is reminded of gooseberry jam on mildly burnt toast; **t22.5** soft, lightweight delivery... maybe too gentle due to the lack of strength. The fruits are again evident with a touch of physalis adding piquancy to the more obvious grape; juicy and well-balanced; **f21** flattened by an onslaught of caramels and vanilla; **b22.5** oddly enough, almost a breakfast malt: it is uncommonly soft and light yet carries a real jam and marmalade character. *40%*

Glenfiddich 21 Years Old db (86) **n21 t23 f21 b21.** A much more uninhibited bottling with loads of fun as the mouth-watering barley comes rolling in. But still falls short on taking the hair-raisingly rich delivery forward and simply peters out. *40%*

Glenfiddich 30 Years Old db (93.5) **n23** always expect sherry trifle with this: here is some sherry not to be trifled with... salty, too; **t23.5** the juiciest 30-y-o I can remember from this distillery for a while: both the grape and barley are contributing to the salivation factor...; the mid ground if filled with light cocoa, soft oils and a delicate hickory-demerara bourbon-style sweetness; **f23.5** here usually the malt ends all too briefly. Not this time: chunky grape carries on its chattering with the ever-increasing bourbon-honeycomb notes; a vague furry finale...; **b23.5** a 'Fiddich which has changed its spots. Much more voluptuous than of old and happy to mine to a grapey seam while digging at the sweeter bourbon elements for all it is worth. Just one less than magnificent butt away from near perfection and a certain Bible Award... *40%*

Glenfiddich 40 Years Old batch 7 db (96) **n24** it's the spices which win hands down here. Yes, there is all kinds of juicy, voluptuous fruit...this nose is dripping with it. But the spices are the rudder steering a path through spectacular scenery...; **t24** ...so no surprises it is the eloquent spices which speak first on delivery. Nothing brash. No violence. Just considered and balanced, bringing the most from the oak and allowing a juicy degree of salt to enliven things further; to work properly sugars are required and sublime traces of muscovado sugars appear to bring the fat sultanas to bursting; **f23.5** now we get to the burnt raisin bit of the fruit cake effect. That's just how it should be...; oh, and did I mention the spices...? **b24.5** for the 750th New Whisky for the 2012 Bible, I decided to select a distillery close to my heart... and the age I'll be next birthday... Believe me: this guy didn't let me down. Full frontal fruit and spice. Perfectly toned and all the curves in all the right places. Rrrrr!!! *45.8%. 600 bottles.*

Glenfiddich Rare Collection 40 Years Old db **(86.5) n22.5 t23 f20 b21.** A quite different version to the last with the smoke having all but vanished, allowing the finish to show the full weight of its considerable age. The nose and delivery are superb, though. The barley sheen on arrival really deserves better support. *43.5%*

Glenfiddich 50 Years Old db **(97) n25** we are talking 50 years, and yet we are still talking fresh barley, freshly peeled grape and honey. Not ordinary honey. Not the stuff you find in jars. But the pollen that attracts the bees to the petunia: and not any old petunia: not the white or the red or pink or yellow. But the two-toned purple ones. For on the nose at least this is perfection; this is nectar... **t24** a silky delivery: silky barley with silky, watered down maple syrup. The middle ground, in some previous Glenfiddich 50-year-olds a forest of pine and oak, is this time filled with soft, grassy barley and the vaguest hint of a distant smoke spice; **f24** long, long, long, with the very faintest snatch of something most delicately smoked: a distant puff of peat reek carried off on the persistent Speyside winds, then a winding-down of vanillas, dropping through the gears of sweetness until the very last traces are chalky dry; **b24** for the record, my actual words, after tasting my first significant mouthful, were: "fuck! This is brilliant." It was an ejaculation of genuine surprise, as any fly on the wall of my Tasting Room at 1:17am on Tuesday 4th August would testify. Because I have tasted many 50-year-old whiskies over the years, quite possibly as many as anyone currently drawing breath. For not only have I tasted those which have made it onto the whisky shelves, but, privately, or as a consultant, an untold number which didn't: the heroic but doomed oak-laden failures. This, however, is a quite different animal. We were on the cusp of going to press when this was released, so we hung back. William Grant blender David Stewart, whom I rank above all other blenders on this planet, has known me long and well enough to realise that the surrounding hype, with this being the most expensive whisky ever bottled at £10,000 a go or a sobering £360 a pour, would bounce off me like a pebble from a boulder. "Honestly, David," he told my chief researcher with a timorous insistence, "please tell Jim I really think this isn't too oaky." He offered almost an apology for bringing into the world this 50-year-old babe. Well, as usual David Stewart, doyen of the blending lab and Ayr United season ticket holders, was absolutely spot on. And, as is his want, he was rather understating his case. For the record, David, next time someone asks you how good this whisky is, just for once do away with the Ayeshire niceness installed by generations of very nice members of the Stewart family and tell them: "Actually, it's bloody brilliant if I say so myself! And I don't give a rat's bollocks what Murray thinks." *46.1%*

Glenfiddich 1961 47 Years Old cask no. 9016 db **(95) n24.5** massive bourbon flourish: all kinds of liquorice, hickory and dates, over toasted honeycomb. All this topped by molten chocolate caramel. The massive oak is outwardly OTT, but those sweeter bourbon notes and a number of herbal and ginger strands compensate: lots of what might be construed as negatives make one very big positive; **t24.5** some dark sugars and salivating prune juice sweeten the way and allow a lush cushion for the oaky explosion you just know is about to happen; it arrives in the middle ground. But by now the chocolate and caramel evident on the nose has already formed a welcoming committee, backed by those dates and burgeoning fudge; **f22** annoyingly tired with the oak claiming early victory, but still the depth of so many enormous facets strike back with not just style but with an imperious inevitability; **b24** taste this whisky within a few minutes of opening the bottle and judge at your peril. Leave for a good half hour and then the full portrait is unveiled. For all its excellence, the oak is far too rampant for true greatness to be achieved. Or so you might reasonably think. The truth, however, must be revealed: this makes for a stunningly fine whisky experience. *43.8%. sc.*

⁘ **Glenfiddich Malt Master's Edition** double matured in oak and sherry butts db **(84) n21 t22 f20 b21.** I would have preferred to have seen this double matured in bourbon barrels and bourbon barrels... The sherry has done this no great favours. *43%*

⁘ **Glenfiddich Millennium Vintage** dist 2000, bott 2012 db **(83.5) n21.5 t22 f20 b20.** Short and not very sweet. Good juicy delivery though, reminiscent of the much missed original old bottling. *40%*

Glenfiddich Snow Phoenix bott 2010 db **(95) n23.5** graceful and delicate, there is obviously some age lurking, lord-like, in the background. But it is the younger malts, reminiscent of the long-lost, original, no-age statement version that steals the show, imprinting the unique grassy, tingly signature into the glass; **t24** a time machine has taken me back 25 years: it is like the original Glenfiddich at its juicy, ultra-salivating youthful finest but now with a honey enriched backbone and some real belief in the oaky spices, where they were once half-hearted a generation ago; **f23** long, with that honeyed sheen remaining impressively attached to the dynamic barley; **b24.5** it is no easy task for blender Brian Kinsman to emerge from the considerable shadow of the now retired David Stewart, the world's finest blender of the last 20 years. But here he has stepped up to the plate to create something which captures the very essence of the distillery. It is almost a deluxe version of the original Glenfiddich: something that is so far advanced of the dull 12-year-old, it is scary. This is sophisticated whisky, have no doubt. And the first clear, impressive statement declaring that Glenfiddich appears to remain in very safe hands. Whatever Brian did from those casks, exposed to the bleak Speyside winter, he should do again. But to a far wider audience. *47.6%. ncf.*

GLEN GARIOCH
Highlands (Eastern), 1798. Morrison Bowmore. Working.

Glen Garioch 8 Years Old db **(85.5) n21 t22 f21 b21.5.** A soft, gummy, malt – not something one would often write about a dram of this or any age from Geary! However, this may have something to do with the copious toffee which swamps the light fruits which try to emerge. *40%*

Glen Garioch 10 Years Old db **(80) n19 t22 f19 b20.** Chunky and charming, this is a malt that once would have ripped your tonsils out. Much more sedate and even a touch of honey to the rich body. Toffeed at the finish. *40%*

Glen Garioch 12 Years Old db **(88.5) n22** gooseberries and fudge...and a touch of smoke...!!!!; **t23** mouth filling with a delicious degree of sharp maltiness; **f21.5** toffees out, though a little smoke drifts back in; **b22** a significant improvement on the complexity front. The return of the smoke after a while away was a surprise and treat. *43%*

Glen Garioch 12 Years Old db **(88) n22.5** rich, and full bodied. Fudge with the vaguest hint of fruit. A little earthy; **t22.5** big, bold delivery again with that earthiness working well alongside a big toffee-fudged barley juiciness; **f21.5** thins a little, but still enjoyably earthy; boosted by late spice; **b22** sticks, broadly, to the winning course of the original 43% version, though here there is a fraction more toffee at the expense of the smoke. *48%. ncf.*

Glen Garioch 15 Years Old db **(86.5) n20.5 t22 f22 b22.** In the a bottling I sampled last year the peat definitely vanished. Now it's back again, though in tiny, if entertaining, amounts. *43%*

Glen Garioch 21 Years Old db **(91) n21** a few wood shavings interrupt the toasty barley; **t23** really good bitter-sweet balance with honeycomb and butterscotch leading the line; pretty juicy, busy stuff; **f24** dries as it should with some vague spices adding to the vanilla and hickory; **b23** an entirely re-worked, now smokeless, malt that has little in common with its predecessors. Quite lovely, though. *43%*

Glen Garioch 1797 Founders Reserve db **(87.5) n21** fruit toffee fudge; **t22** some fizz on delivery followed by a rampaging barley juiciness; much lighter and softer than the strength indicates, **f22.5** excellent mocha accompanies the fruit with aplomb; **b22** impressively fruity and chewy: some serious flavour profiles in there. *48%* ☺

◌ **Glen Garioch 1958** db **(90) n24 t21 f23 b22.** The distillery in its old smoky clothes: and quite splendid it looks! *43%. 328 bottles.*

◌ **Glen Garioch 1995** db **(86) n21 t22 f21.5 b21.5.** Typically noisy on the palate, even though the malty core is quite thin. Some big natural caramels, though. *55.3%. ncf.*

◌ **Glen Garioch 1997** db **(89.5) n22** lively barley bolstered by what appears to be a generous but perfectly acceptable cut on the stills; **t23** huge delivery which makes the most of the 48% abv. This doesn't need water, just time and a strong jaw to chew it. That wide cut on the nose is confirmed on the palate with a feisty oiliness which drags every last nuance from the barley; **f22** long with those oils now intensifying around a cocoa glow; **b22.5** I have to say: I have long been a bit of a voice in the wilderness among whisky professionals as to regards this distillery. This not so subtly muscled malt does my case no harm whatsoever. *56.7%. ncf.*

Adelphi Glen Garioch 20 Years Old cask no. 2691, dist 1990, bott 2010 **(85.5) n21 t22.5 f21 b21.** A pleasant alpha barley experience. But the massive sugars make matters a little one dimensional. *54.9%. sc. Adelphi Distillery. 234 bottles.*

◌ **Archives Glen Garioch 1990 21 Years Old First Release** hogshead, cask no. 252, dist 28 Dec 90, bott 5 Jan 12 **(77) n19 t21 f19 b19.** Any sweeter and my teeth will drop out. Never gives the impression of high quality malt. *54%. nc ncf sc. Whiskybase B.V. 267 bottles.*

◌ **Liquid Sun Glen Garioch 21 Years Old** dist 1991 **(88) n21.5** a little bit of distillery nip on the nose; thin barley; **t22.5** fattens up on delivery and surges with a gorgeous and satisfying vanilla and barley oily combo; **f22** warms with an intriguing mix of distillery bite and quite separate spices, the cocoa rounds matters off; **b22** the distillery on its best behaviour for that period. A very even malt. *52.8%. sc. The Whisky Agency.*

Liquid Sun Glen Garioch 1990 bourbon hogshead, bott 2011 **(85) n21 t22.5 f20.5 b21.** Lovely, juicy barley but very few trimmings. *54%. The Whisky Agency.*

Malts Of Scotland Glen Garioch 1991 bourbon hogshead, cask no. 3175, dist May 91, bott Jul 10 **(86) n21.5 t23 f20 b21.5.** Some marvellous sugars adds lustre to the juicy malt before it tapers out. *50.1%. nc ncf sc. Malts Of Scotland. 142 bottles.*

⋅⋅⋅⋅ **Old Malt Cask Glen Garioch Aged 25 Years** refill hogshead, cask no. 7866, dist May 86, bott Nov 11 **(88.5) n22** chunky with an almost Bowmore-style Fisherman's Friend edge to the quagmire malt: curious, seeing they are from the same company....; at times it is like a vaguely peated bourbon; **t22.5** again, Fisherman's Friend...but without any great peat residue, though there is definitely a smokiness. The barley is juicy and brimming with muscovado sugars. Plus more bourbony liquorice and hickory; **f22** long and attractive; **b22** uniquely Geery. And an impressive attempt to unite Scotland with Kentucky. *50%. nc ncf sc. 174 bottles.*

Provenance Glen Garioch Over 9 Years refill hogshead, cask no. 6299, dist Autumn 00, bott Summer 2010 **(87.5) n21.5 t22 f22 b22.** A Geary with fascinating echoes of its past. *46%. nc ncf sc. Douglas Laing & Co.*

Rare Auld Glen Garioch 19 Years Old dist 1991, cask no. 3855 **(90) n22** a fine balance between the peppery oak and crisp malt; **t23.5** superb arrival with excellent intensity to the clean, beautifully-layered barley; **f22** a flicker of gooseberry to the malt; **b22.5** a sophisticated, wonderfully complex dram worth hunting down. *51.1%. sc. Duncan Taylor & Co.*

⋅⋅⋅⋅ **The Whisky Agency Glen Garioch 20 Years Old** bourbon cask, dist 1991, bott 2011 **(85.5) n21.5 t23 f20 b21.** An attractive malt making the most of an intense barley simplicity. Some muscovado sugars balance out the spices. *54.4%. sc.*

GLENGLASSAUGH
Speyside, 1875. Scaent Group. Working.

Glenglassaugh 21 Year Old db **(94) n23.5** elegant and adroit, the lightness of touch between the citrus and barley is nigh on mesmeric: conflicting messages of age in that it appears younger and yet you feel something has to be this kind of vintage to hit this degree of aloofness. Delicate and charming...; **t24.5** again we have all kinds of messages on delivery: the spices fizz around announcing oaky intentions and then the barley sooths and sweetens even with a degree of youthful juiciness. The tastebuds are never more than caressed, the sugar-sweetened citrus ensuring neither the barley or oak form any kind of advantage; impeccably weighted, a near perfect treat for the palate; **f22.5** white chocolate and vanilla lead the way as the oak begins to offer a degree of comparative austerity; **b23.5** a malt which simply sings on the palate and a fabulous benchmark for the new owners to try to achieve in 2030...!! *46%*

Glenglassaugh 26 Years Old db **(78.5) n19 t21.5 f18.5 b19.5.** Industrial amounts of cream toffee here. Also some odd and off key fruit notes winging in from somewhere. Not quite the gem I had hoped for. *46%*

⋅⋅⋅⋅ **Glenglassaugh Master Distillers' `Selection Aged 28 Years** dist 1983 db **(93) n23** seville orange and vanilla. But not quite that simple...don't get me started on the antique leather...; **t24** the body is of the type you might see on a Scandinavian beach in high summer: beautiful tone and delicate curves in all the right places. The barley myriad juices; the oak conjures several layers of vanillas, including a light covering of ulmo honey; **f22.5** just bitters out slightly, though remains busy; **b23.5** knowing Norway as I do, glad to see these lovely people are getting their money's worth! *49.8%. nc ncf sc. Norway exclusive. 400 bottles.*

Glenglassaugh 30 Year Old db **(89) n23** the grape of noble rot stands haughtily beside the oak without blot; **t23** fruity, silky, if in some places a little flat. Lots of dried dates, demerara, chocolate raisins, a little of this, a little of that... **f21** against every wish, drifts away incoherently, mumbling something coffee-ish; **b22** sheer poetry. Or not... *43.1%*

⋅⋅⋅⋅ **Glenglassaugh Rare Casks Aged Over 30 Years** db **(86) n22 t21 f21.5 b21.5.** Nearly four decades in an oak cask has resulted in a huge eruption of caramels. Soft oils and citrus abounds but it is the oak which dominates. *43%. nc ncf sc. Actual age 36 years. 280 bottles.*

⋅⋅⋅⋅ **Glenglassaugh The Chosen Few 1st Edition "Ronnie Routledge" 35 Years Old** sherry butt, dist May 76 db **(95) n24** lacking the over enthusiastic oak which might have been expected, it enjoys the freedom with a wonderful display of its trademark orange blossom honey but with extra butterscotch, red liquorice and glace cherries. Very bourbony, but this time with a distinctive barley lilt; **t24** the strength is almost perfect for the degree of intensity proffered by the complex early sugars. The natural caramel forms a medium-depthed layer, but one easily penetrated by myriad further bourbon signatures, the spiced liquorice not being the least of them; **f23.5** long with a near perfect weight to the oil and oaky background. Busy spices and busier sugars, all done with panache; egg custard tart, improbably sprinkled with a little hickory and allspice; **b23.5** I had no idea Ronnie Routledge was 35 years old. Thought he was much younger... *49.6%. 654 bottles.*

Glenglassaugh Aged 37 Years db **(92) n23.5** honeycomb and hickory; burnt (or with the vaguest hint of smoke, is that burning?) date and walnut cake with liberal helpings of Demerara sugar; a hint of spice on the ever thickening vanilla. Not a single off note, or hint of over exertion...; **t23** excellent honey and spice delivery. First-class oils and beeswax ensure the sugars glide around the palate as if on skates; a curious subplot of glazed cherry ups the salivation factor even further; **f22** more vanillas and a little (smoky?) praline for a finale flourish; **b23.5** after all those years, dementia has set in: it thinks it's a bourbon... And not any old bourbon, believe me... 54.8%. nc ncf.

⋯⋯ **Glenglassaugh Master Distillers' Selection Aged 37 Years** dist 1974 db **(90.5) n23** a complex smattering of oaky tones, almost all of them recognisable in well matured bourbon: the most attractive is the interplay between the orange blossom honey and much drier hickory; **t23** the honey tries to carry on from the nose. But brought to a halt a far more aggressive toasty oak, though a brief early kumquat injection restores balance; **f22** sugar-free mocha; **b22.5** for the US market only, one assumes it was sent to Oakland. And I have just spotted the tasting notes I did for their 37-year-old bottled last year...the characteristics almost identical! Oh well, it is personally reassuring that even with over 1,000 tasting notes completed for the next Bible, my poor old palate is still registering! 56%. nc ncf sc. USA exclusive. 470 bottles.

Glenglassaugh 40 Year Old db **(96) n24.5** the kind of oak you'd expect at this age – if you are uncommonly lucky or have access to some of the most glorious-nosing ancient casks in all Scotland - but there is so much else on the fruity front besides: grape, over-ripe yam, fat cherries...And then there is a bourbony element with molassed hickory and sweetened vanilla: wake me, I must be dreaming...on second thoughts, don't; **t24.5** pure silk on delivery. All the flavours arrive in one rich wave of consummate sweetness, a tapestry celebrating the enormity of both the fruit and oak, yet condensed into a few inches rather than feet; plenty of soft medium roast Jamaican Blue Mountain and then at times mocha; on the fruity front there is juicy dates mulched with burned raisin; **f23** the relative Achilles heel as the more bitter, nutty parts of the oak gather, **b24** it is as if this malt has gone through a 40-year marrying process: the interlinking of flavours and styles is truly beyond belief. 44.6%.

Glenglassaugh Aged 43 Years db **(91) n23.5** a nose of rare clarity for its age. Or it is once it has been in the glass for a good 15 minutes. Then the wrinkles vanish and we are left with a vibrant, juicy nose offering a sweetness that runs the full gamut from fruit to biscuit... Not surprisingly there is a death by chocolate feel to this one, too. And even a little smoke; not entire free of the odd gremlin, but not too much damage done; **t24** you really don't spit this kind of whisky, however professional you are. Not sure if the silkworm has been bred yet that can produce something as silky as this guy. A few random spices here, a splash of walnut oil there; **f21** a slight Achilles heel: some weaknesses show as a mild bitterness leaks in. But I am not quibbling; **b22.5** another ridiculously magnificent malt from a distillery which should never have been closed in the first place. 48.7%. nc ncf.

Glenglassaugh Andrea Cammineci 1972 refill butt db **(92.5) n23.5** spiced bonbons, with some black cherry for good measure; the sweetness is dull, of the liquorice variety as well as toasty raisin; **t24** those looking for a big sherry statement are in for a shock: the delivery is nearer Kentucky with tidal waves of waxy honeycomb and natural caramels; the odd piece of fruitcake can be spotted bobbing around; **f72** enters a no-man's-land for a while where there is a lack of anything much. Then, slowly, a fruitcake toasty dryness emerges, along with walnut oil; **b23** one of those rare hybrids that manages to get the best of both worlds; will appeal to high quality bourbon lovers every bit as those looking for sumptuous sherried drams... 59.1%. nc ncf sc. For German distribution.

Glenglassaugh 1973 Family Silver db **(95) n23 t24 f24 b24.** From first to last this whisky caresses and teases. It is old but shows no over-ageing. It offers what appears a malt veneer but is complexity itself. Brilliant. And now, sadly, almost impossible to find. Except, possibly, at the Mansefield Hotel, Elgin. 40%

Glenglassaugh The Manager's Legacy No.1 Jim Cryle 1974 refill sherry hogshead db **(90.5) n21.5** citrus and various salty, herbal notes try to prop up a crumbling castle as an incoming tide of oak begins to wash it away...; **t23.5** where did that come from? Early oak, but then a magnificent recovery in the form of sharp old orange peel and a salty, mega malty thrust. Some dried fruit, mainly old dates and plums, build further bridges and as the saline quality intensifies, the juicier it all becomes; **f22.5** long with spices and plenty of cream toffee; **b23** talk about blowing away the cobwebs! The nose trumpets all the hallmarks of a tired old malt in decline. What follows on the palate could not be more opposite. Don't you just love a surprise! 52.9%. nc ncf sc. 200 bottles.

Glenglassaugh The Manager's Legacy No.2 Dod Cameron 1986 refill sherry butt, dist Dec 86 db **(92) n23.5** the sherry residue must have been as thick as tar when they billed this butt: an enormous welter of pithy and juicy grape married with the aroma one might expect at a Fruitcake Fest. The odd roasty bitter note counters the sweeter Demerara tones. Wow!

115

t24 a near perfect delivery with that thick grape arriving hand-in-hand with sublime spices; again a burnt toast bitterness battles it out with some macho sugars; **f22** back to a more Dundee cake style, with a few natural caramels thrown in; **b22.5** did anyone mention this was from a sherry butt...? A vague, mildly out of kilter, bitterness knocks the odd mark off here and there, but a dram to kick the shoes off to and savour. *45.3%. nc ncf sc. 500 bottles.*

Glenglassaugh The Manager's Legacy No.3 Bert Forsyth 1968 refill sherry butt, dist Dec 68 db **(89) n22** almost Amazonian amounts of oak but there is enough black cherry and dried dates to offer charm and complexity. A twist of salt doesn't hurt, either; **t23** the oak has most of its own way on delivery. But there is a slow clawing back of vital ground as juices begin the flow and sugars come out of hiding; the odd exotic fruit moment, too; **f22** any residual bitterness is absorbed by the mocha; **b22** a kind of upside down whisky: usually the big oaks arrive at the death. Here they are all upfront... An excellent whisky that, by rights, should never be... *44.9%. nc ncf sc. 300 bottles.*

Glenglassaugh The Manager's Legacy No.4 Walter Grant 1967 refill sherry hogshead, dist May 67 db **(86.5) n19.5 t22 f23 b22.** Despite the oaky wounds to the nose, the palate is far more open and somehow reaches a degree of depth and complexity which makes for an excellent and unexpected experience. *40.4%. nc ncf sc. 200 bottles.*

⋰⋰ **Glenglassaugh Revival** new, refill and Oloroso sherry casks db **(75) n19 t20 f17 b19.** Rule number one: if you are going to spend a lot of money to rebuild a distillery and make great whisky, then ensure you put the spirit into excellent oak. Which is why it is best avoiding present day sherry butts at all costs as the chances of running into sulphur is high. There is some stonkingly good malt included in this bottling, and the fabulous chocolate raisin is there to see. But I look forward to seeing a bottling from 100% ex-bourbon. *46%. nc ncf.*

Glenglassaugh The Spirit Drink db **(85) n20 t22 f21.5 b21.5.** A pretty wide margin taken on the cut here, it seems, so there is plenty to chew over. Richly flavoured and a tad oily, as is to be expected, which helps the barley to assert itself in midstream. The usual new make chocolaty element at work here, too, late on. Just great to see this distillery back in harness after all these years. And a great idea to get the new spirit out to the public, something I have been encouraging distilleries to do since my beard was still blue. Look forward to seeing another version where a narrower cut has been made. *50%. 8,160 bottles.*

Glenglassaugh The Spirit Drink Fledgling XB db **(91) n22 t23.5 f22.5 b23.** The barley arrives unblemished and makes a proud, juicy stand. A surprising degree of early natural caramel. Prefer this over the peat, to be honest, and augers well for the distillery's future. *50%*

Glenglassaugh The Spirit Drink Peated db **(89.5) n22 t23 f22 b22.5.** Enjoyable and doesn't appear close to its 50%abv. But it's not about the bite, for there is a welcome citrus freshness to this, helped along the way by a peatiness which is big but by no means out to be the only important voice. *50%*

Glenglassaugh The Spirit Drink That Blushes to Speak Its Name db **(85) n22 t21.5 f21 b21.** Not whisky, of course. New make matured for a few months in wine barrels. The result is a Rose-looking spirit. Actually takes me back to my early childhood – no, not the tasting of new make spirit. But the redcurrant aroma which does its best to calm the new make ruggedness. Tasty and fascinating, though the wine tries to minimalise the usual sweetness you find in malt spirit. *50%*

⋰⋰ **Mo Ôr Collection Glenglassaugh 1983 26 Years Old** first fill Oloroso sherry butt, cask no. 171, dist 17 Jun 83, bott 8 Oct 09 **(72) n19 t20 f15 b18.** Despite the blood orange, this is a dry and nutty affair. But gets drier, and unacceptably so, as the sulphur candle takes hold. *50.4%. nc ncf sc. Release No. 6. The Whisky Talker. 885 bottles.*

GLENGOYNE
Highlands (Southwest), 1833. Ian Macleod Distillers. Working.

Glengoyne 10 Years Old db **(90) n22** beautifully clean despite coal-gas bite. The barley is almost in concentrate form with a marmalade sweetness adding richness; **t23** crisp, firm arrival with massive barley surge, seriously chewy and textbook bitter-sweet balance; but now some oils have tucked in to intensify and lengthen; **f22** incredibly long and refined for such a light malt. The oak, which made soft noises in the middle now intensifies, but harmonises with the intense barley; an added touch of coffee signals some extra oak in recent bottlings; **b23** proof that to create balance you do not have to have peat at work. The secret is the intensity of barley intermingling with oak. Not a single negative note from first to last and now a touch of oil and coffee has upped the intensity further. *40%*

Glengoyne 12 Years Old db **(91.5) n22.5** salty, sweet, lightly fruity; **t23** one of the softest deliveries on the market: the fruit, gristy sugars and malt combine to melt in the mouth: there is not a single hint of firmness; **f23** a graduation of spices and vanilla. Delicate and delightful...; **b23** the nose has a curiously intimate feel but the tasting experience is a wonderful surprise. *43%*

Glengoyne 12 Years Old Cask Strength db **(79) n18 t22 f19 b20.** Not quite the happiest Glengoyne I've ever come across with the better notes compromised. *57.2%. nc ncf.*

Glengoyne 12 Years Old Scottish Merchant's Choice 1996 sherry hogshead no. 3447 db **(88.5) n22 t23 f21.5 b22.** High quality sherry influence. *57.8%*

Glengoyne 13 Years Old Single Cask 1995 European oak sherry hogshead no. 2082, dist Oct 95 db **(94) n24 t24 f23 b23.** For those of you wandering what a 1990s non sulphured sherry butt tastes like – and I am sure some of your still don't know for certain – grab some of this. And just jump into that glass: it's safe and wonderful! *56.1%. Ian Macleod.*

Glengoyne Aged 14 Years Limited Edition oloroso cask **(77) n19 t20 f19 b19.** A vague sulphur taint. But rather underpowered anyway. *40%. nc. Marks & Spencer UK.*

⋆ **Glengoyne Single Cask 14 Years Old** bourbon hogshead, cask no. 1546, dist 1 May 97 db **(91.5) n22** outwardly dull thanks to a big natural caramel injection but there is some honeyed promise; **t23** among the rich spiced tannins is a sumptuous honey middle, lightened by a soft citrus edge; **f23.5** mocha enters to give a drying Jaffa Cake feel; **b23** those lucky Swedes. Not only do they get all those stunning women, but this as well. *57.8%. nc ncf sc. Swedish exclusive.*

⋆ **Glengoyne 15 Years Old** db **(73.5) n18 t19 f18 b18.5.** Some sub-standard, left-out-in-the-rain oak crept in from somewhere. Ouch. *40%. Travel Retail exclusive.*

Glengoyne 16 Years Old Single Cask 1993 American oak sherry hogshead no. 899 db **(86) n22 t22 f21 b21.** Hold the front page, for here's the amazingly good news: sherry hogshead used...no sulphur. The not quite such good news is that the grape is so dominant, not much else gets a look in. Some lovely coffee notes to cling on to, and all-in-all a dram worthy of a second glass. *53.9%. For Dr Jekyll's Pub, Oslo.*

Glengoyne 17 Years Old db **(86) n21 t23 f21 b21.** Some of the guys at Glengoyne think I'm nuts. They couldn't get their head around the 79 I gave it last time. And they will be shaking my neck not my hand when they see the score here...Vastly improved but there is an off sherry tang which points to a naughty butt or two somewhere. Elsewhere mouth-watering and at times fabulously intense. *43%*

Glengoyne 18 Years Old Ambassador's Choice 1990 bourbon cask no. 2850, dist Nov 90 db **(92) n23** thick natural caramels offer clean barley, oranges and a number of delicate sugars; **t23.5** excellent barley layering on delivery: sweet despite some prickle and nip. Mouthwatering yet creamy...this is a complex hombre; **f23** remains big and returns to those caramels on the nose; **b22.5** I am assuming that the Ambassador who chose this isn't Scotland's Ambassador to England. No, I think they mean the guy who turns up wearing a kilt at some whisky festival or other and tells you Glengoyne/ Talisker/ Glenmorangie, or whoever he (or she) is representing, is the dog's. Well, take a bow Mr Glengoyne Ambassador: you obviously know your casks. This is a charmer with hobnail boots. *59.9%*

Glengoyne 21 Years Old db **(90) n21** closed and tight for the most part as Glengoyne sometimes has a tendency to be nose-wise, with the emphasis very much on coal gas; **t22** slow to start with a few barley heads popping up to be seen; then spices arrive with the oak for a slightly bourbony feel. Gentle butterscotch and honey add a mouth-watering edge to the drier oaks; **f24** a stupendous honey thread is cross-stitched through the developing oak to deliver near perfect poise and balance at finish; **b23** a vastly improved dram where the caramel has vanished and the tastebuds are constantly assailed and questioned. A malt which builds in pace and passion to delivery a final, wonderful coup-de-grace. Moments of being quite cerebral stuff. *43%*

Glengoyne 21 Years Old Sherry Edition db **(93) n22 t24 f23 b24.** The nose at first is not overly promising, but it settles at it warms and what follows on the palate is at times glorious. Few whiskies will match this for its bitter-sweet depth which is pure textbook. Glengoyne as few will have seen it before. *43%*

Glengoyne 23 Years Old Single Cask 1986 European oak sherry butt no. 399 db **(85) n22 t22 f21 b21.** Though from a sherry cask, fascinating just how many bourbon attributes sneak onto the nose. An enjoyable malt, but not without the odd flaw. *53.6%*

⋆ **Glengoyne Single Cask 24 Years Old** European oak sherry butt, cask no. 354, dist 14 May 87 **(96.5) n24** I could almost weep as this is the way a sherry butt should be on the nose: CLEAN and full of rich tannins, pith, spice and complex sugars; **t24.5** oh, yes.....YES!!! Brilliant. Exactly how it should be for the age: the barley, oak and grape are all at the very points you would expect them to be. As for the spices: this is swoonable stuff... **f24** and again, confirmation that this cask is clean without a single off note. No bitterness, no puckering of the tongue. The juicy grape, bolstered by honey melon and spice, embraces the rich slightly bourbony tannins with relish...; **b24** Glengoyne in full pomp. Magnificent. *54.8%. nc ncf sc.*

Glengoyne 40 Years Old db **(83) n23 t21 f19 b20.** Thick fruit intermittently pads around the nose and palate but the oak is pretty colossal. Apparent attempts to reinvigorate it appear to have backfired. *45.9%*

Glengoyne 1990 Aged 19 Years Single Cask bourbon hogshead, cask no. 2848, dist 28 Nov 90 db **(94) n22** slightly meaty: pan fried calf's liver. With a celery side dish. Don't believe me? Try it and then let me know... **t24** we are now in a world of honeycomb barley. The spices at first tip toe slowly, then run; the juices flow while the sugars punctuate at the right time in the right place; **f24** quite magnificent. The spices are virile and peppery. The vanillas have a go at trying to dominate...but fail miserably. Still those barley notes keep on coming; **b24** could there be a more eloquent example of just why every Glengoyne should be matured in ex-bourbon cask? *59.6%. nc ncf sc. Exclusively available on the Whisky Exchange.*

Glengoyne 1990 Single Cask Ambassador's Choice bourbon hogshead, cask no. 2850, dist 28 Nov 90 db **(91.5) n22** a vigorous examination by vanilla and butterscotch; **t23.5** absolutely no faulting the magnificent parity between the honey and the toffee. Spices abound and the barley is fresh and salivating; **f22.5** more toffee vanilla, but the sugars are pretty consistent; **b23.5** don't expect this Ambassador to be expelled in a hurry... *59.9%. nc ncf sc. German release.*

Glengoyne 1995 Aged 15 Years Single Cask European oak sherry hogshead, cask no. 2093, dist 26 Oct 95 db **(91.5) n22.5** crushed walnuts and dates; **t23.5** the big spice explosion on delivery is unexpected given the relatively dormant nature of the nose; the fruit is thick and abiding, showing big fat sultana amid confident oak; **f22.5** heads towards a big mocha finale and a style much older than its years; **b23** positively yodels in gorgeous integrity. *56.1%. nc ncf sc. Swiss release.*

Glengoyne Port Cask Finish 1996 db **(74) n17 t20 f18.5 b18.5.** Decent fruit on delivery, but elsewhere proof that in whisky there is no such thing as any port cask in a storm... *46%. Ian Macleod.*

Glengoyne Vintage 1996 db **(70) n16 t18 f18 b18.** Creamy, but off key. *43%. nc ncf. USA.*

Glengoyne 1997 Single Cask English Merchant's Choice sherry hogshead, cask no. 2716, dist 17 Jun 97 db **(89) n22** burned fruit cake...in which someone has forgotten to add the dough...; **t23** sherry trifle...in which someone forgot to add the sponge...; **f22** grapey, spiced barley...in which someone forgot to add the barley...; **b22** a young fogey of a malt. Elsewhere in the Bible I have lamented this virtually lost style of sherried whisky: something akin to a size 46 overcoat placed on a five year old lad, who vanishes under the cloth. The malt may have been similarly swamped by the grape, but it does offer a degree of entertainment...and not an atom of sulphur to be had! *54.6%. nc ncf sc.*

Glengoyne Vintage 1997 db **(68) n16 t18 f17 b17.** The "S" word strikes. And with a vengeance. *43%. nc ncf. German release.*

Glengoyne 1999 Aged 11 Years Old Single Cask sherry hogshead, cask no. 2163, dist 22 Sep 99 db **(95.5) n23.5** thumping, clean grape. Some lovely candy shop notes, especially of the old granny cough sweet variety; **t24** not just voluptuous, but absolutely mouth-watering to the point of having to salivate like a rabies victim. The spices swill about the palate as though they own the place. The layering of green apples and greener peach is astonishing; **f24** softens, though the spices continue to maraud. The analogy to a cough sweet becomes even more pertinent; **b24** entirely impressed. One of the best sherry butts for its tender years for a good while. Time to start looking for Easyjet tickets... *57.4%. nc ncf sc. German release.*

Glengoyne 'Glen Guin' 16 Year Old Shiraz Finish db **(79) n18.5 t20 f19.5 b20.** Some oily depth here. *48%*

Glengoyne Burnfoot db **(84) n21 t21 f21.5 b21.** A clodhopping bruiser of a malt. Good honey, though. *40%. Duty Free Market.*

⁙ **Glengoyne Teapot Dram** db **(86.5) n23 t22 f20.5 b21.** The nose, for its obvious fault, still has a truly classic oloroso-style depth. However, the light sulphur stain is not so easily covered up once tasted. A slightly cracked teapot, I'm afraid. *58.8%. nc ncf. Distillery exclusive.*

Kingsbury "The Selection" Glengoyne 9 Years Old butt, cask no. 389, dist Mar 01, bott Aug 10 **(72) n18 t18 f18 b18.** Mr. Tanaka, my dear old friend. Let us dine at your favourite restaurant, Claridges. Or at my Club next door. Either way, I'll pay. Providing, that is, you give sherry butts the widest possible berth when bottling for Kingsbury... *43%. nc ncf sc. Japan Import Systems. 822 bottles.*

Malts Of Scotland Glengoyne 1973 bourbon barrel, cask no. 678, dist Feb 73, bott Mar 10 **(87.5) n21.5 t22 f22 b22.** Knife-edge malt, saved by natural sugars. *50.4%. nc ncf sc. Malts Of Scotland. 97 bottles.*

Malts Of Scotland Clubs Glengoyne 1998 sherry hogshead, cask no. 1135, dist Apr 98, bott Oct 10 **(85.5) n21 t22 f21 b21.5.** A sulphur-free, clean sherry hoggy, for sure. But the enormity of the grape drowns out much chance to see the malt develop beyond a spicy mocha theme. *52.9%. nc ncf sc. Malts Of Scotland. 280 bottles.*

⁙ **Malts Of Scotland Glengoyne 1998** sherry hogshead, cask no. MoS12003, dist 1 Apr 98, bott Jan 12 **(90.5) n23** simplistic oloroso trademark; weighty, distinctly Dundee fruitcake in style, complete with toasted almonds; **t23** mouth-filling with excellent black pepper bite to the toasty raisin; limited complexity development, but some late vanilla; **f22** more vanilla as it dries; **b22.5** a clean, untainted sherry butt offering pure silk. *52.7%. nc ncf sc.*

❖ **Malts Of Scotland Glengoyne 1998** sherry hogshead, cask no. MoS11006, dist May 98, bott Aug 11 **(63) n17 t16 f15 b15.** The MOS12003 above thankfully dodged the sulphur bullet. This, alas, did not. *53.7%. nc ncf sc. Malts Of Scotland.*

❖ **Malts Of Scotland Glengoyne 1998** sherry hogshead, cask no. MoS12024, dist Apr 98, bott Apr 12 **(66) n17 t17 f16 b16.** Opening a sherry butt Glengoyne is the equivalent of tackling an UXB. This one has exploded in my face... *54.8%. nc ncf sc. Malts Of Scotland.*

❖ **Old Malt Cask Glengoyne Aged 14 Years** refill hogshead, cask no. 7661, dist Sep 97, bott Sep 11 **(83) n21 t21 f20 b21.** A dry guy with a spicy clout. 50%. nc ncf sc. 307 bottles.

The Perfect Dram Glengoyne 1972 bott 2011 **(86) n20 t22 f22 b22.** Makes up for the so-so nose with a well mannered display of sharp but lively barley. Tasted blind, hard to believe this is almost reaching the big 4-0. But the minimalist impact from the lazy oak has certainly allowed the barley to sparkle. *46.3%. The Whisky Agency.*

❖ **Provenance Glengoyne Over 11 Years** refill hogshead, cask no. 7604, dist Winter 1999, bott Summer 2011 **(89) n22.5** top class barley with controlled dusting of sugar; **t22** fabulous clarity to the malt: crisp, precise and very comfortable as the oak gathers; some delicate citrus fizz; **f22** a hint of medium roast Mysore coffee amid the natural caramel; **b22.5** crystalline and beautifully clean. 46%. nc ncf sc. Douglas Laing & Co.

Provenance Glengoyne Over 12 Years refill hogshead, cask no. 6859, dist Autumn 98, bott Winter 2010 **(81) n21 t21 f19 b20.** A spotty-faced youth by Glengoyne standards. Malty, sweet but limited in scope. *46%. nc ncf sc. Douglas Laing & Co.*

❖ **Provenance Glengoyne Over 12 Years** refill hogshead, cask no. 7962, dist Winter 1999, bott Winter 2011 **(81.5) n21 t20 f20 b20.5.** Structurally, the malty weight is very similar to their new 11-year old. But an inferior cask means far less positive development. 46%. nc ncf sc.

The Whisky Agency Glengoyne 37 Years Old sherry cask, dist 1972, bott 2010 **(95) n24** a sherry trifle – though mainly of custard – is splattered into your face...; all kinds of crushed nut, too plus the unmistakable sweetness of biscoito de polvilho doce; **t24** now that is pretty classy. a crisp, malty delivery sweetened by grape-flecked sugars. The spices are a side dish wanting main course exposure. But a beautiful butterscotch middle bugles in the oak; **f23** how many different types of vanilla are there...? **b24** this is the year of the great old malt. Few, though, offer the evenly-loaded complexity found here. A 37 year old whisky, which might take just as many years to get to the bottom of... *57%. The Whisky Agency.*

❖ **The Whisky Cask Glengoyne Aged 37 Years** bourbon cask, dist 1972, bott 2010 **(92.5) n23** we have entered exotic fruit territory here, but there is much more: almost like sniffing at the herb rack; **t23.5** bold sugars see off the bigger tannins. We get back to those dry herbs again, though vanilla pods are in biggest demand; wonderful kumquat and lemon notes; **f23** long with a pretty standard vanilla and butterscotch fade, chalky oak gives a dry send off; **b23** about as busy a malt as you'll find. Full of herb and spicy intent. *51.8%. sc. The Whisky Cask.*

GLEN GRANT
Speyside, 1840. Campari. Working.

Glen Grant db **(87) n21.5** young barley, new-mown grass and a smudge of toffee; **t23** huge flavour explosion led by juicy, young malt. Soft spices reveal an oaky interest, too; **f21** over-laced with caramel; **b21.5** this is a collector's malt for the back label alone: truly one of the most bizarre I have ever seen. "James Grant, 'The Major'" it cheerfully chirrups, "was only 25 when he set about achieving his vision of a single malt with a clear colour. The unique flavour and appearance was due to the purifiers and the tall slender stills he designed and the decision to retain its natural colour..." Then underneath is written: "Farven Justeter Med Karamel/Mit Farbstoff"" Doh! Or, as they say in German: "Doh!" Need any more be said about the nonsense, the pure insanity, of adding colouring to whisky. 40%

Glen Grant 5 Years Old db **(89) n22.5** dry and herbal with crushed celery, grist, agave, a sprinkle of pepper; **t22** crisp, firm barley with the sweetness handcuffed by a quick spurt of vanilla; semi-serious spice; **f21.5** clean, late oils and warming peppers; **b23** elegant malt which has noticeably grown in stature and complexity of late. 40%

Glen Grant Aged 10 Years db **(95) n23.5** OK: let's take turns in counting the rungs on the barley ladder here....the usual crisp aroma, but softened by deft, if unspecific fruitiness (maybe the distant aroma of a very old orange and by no means unpleasant!), myriad vanilla and butterscotch notes can do without the toffee one; **t24** magnificent! A malty delivery which simultaneously melts in the mouth, yet offers granite-like barley that crashes into your teeth; the star, perhaps are the sugars which vary from caster, through golden syrup and pans out somewhere in the muscovado range – curiously honey-free, though; **f23** a tad tangy, though the caramel returns to turn out the lights after the butterscotch and marzipan say goodnight..; **b23.5** unquestionably the best official 10-y-o distillery bottling I have tasted from this distillery. Absolutely nails it! Oh, and had they bottled this at 46% abv and without the trimmings...my word! Might well have been a contender for Scotch of the Year. It won't be long before word finally gets around about just how bloody good this distillery is. 40% ⊙⊙

Glen Grant Aged 16 Years bott Mar 10 db **(91.5) n23** a lovely under-ripe banana sharpness to this while the malt snuggles up to the crunchy green apple; a playful molecule of smoke wafts around; **t23.5** salivating, fresh, slightly green ...and that's just the first few nano-seconds of the delivery! Next comes a lengthy, relaxed wave of oilier barley, with a coppery, honeyed depth; tangy vanilla fills the middle ground; **f21.5** medium length, more oils and barley but with a degree of bitterness; **b22** again the finish doesn't do justice to the earlier jousting on the nose and palate. The label talks about orchard fruits, and they are absolutely spot on. Apples are order of the day, but not sure about the ripe bit: they appear slightly green to me... and that suits the nature of the crisp malt. A gorgeous whisky I fully expect to see improve over coming batches: it's one that has potential to hit superstar status. 43%

Glen Grant Cask Strength Limited Edition Aged 17 Years cask no. 17152, dist Feb 92, bott May 09 db **(94) n23.5 t24 f23.5 b23**. The nose suggests there maybe some added caramel; the whopping bourbon notes suggests it could be natural. Either way, strip a little toffee away and you might be left with what would have been a contender for Scotch single malt of the year. The balance and artistry beggars belief. Glen Grant distillery really is capable of producing some of the most monumental malt moments you can find on the whisky shelves today. 58.8%. 360 bottles.

⋙ **Glen Grant Distillery Edition Aged 19 Years** cask no. 17161, dist 12 Feb 92, bott 6 Jan 12 db **(92) n22.5** not the usual brusque nose; much softer than normal with ingratiating chocolate fudge notes tacked to the lemon barley theme; **t23.5** various medium weight tannins try to dampen the onslaught (or rather, not) but a soft molasses and burnt raisin sharpness does nothing to stifle the complexity; **f23** any longer and it'd be like waiting in a Post Office queue. Heads into the delicious direction of the chocolate and coconut side of liquorice allsorts; **b23.5** curiously, it seems I was at the distillery the week (possibly the day) this was distilled! Manager Denis Malcolm was there then, just (thankfully!) as he is today. Wonderful to see there are some consistencies in the changing whisky world... 52.4%. ncf sc. 222 bottles.

Glen Grant Cellar Reserve 1992 bottled 08 db **(94.5) n23** a beguiling array of crisp barley and crystalised sugary notes; if a nose can be crunchy and brittle, then this really is it; **t24** the tastebuds virtually swoon under this glorious bathing of barley and sugar; unbelievably juicy and mouth-watering for its age, the oak is there to ensure backbone and fair play and does nothing to subtract from the most graceful notes, except perhaps to pep up slightly with a teasing spiciness; **f24** more playful spices and a chocolate fudge lending weight to the glassy barley edge; one to close the eyes to and be consumed by; **b23.5** one of the great world distilleries being revealed to the us in its very finest colours. They tend to be natural, with no colourings added, therefore allowing the extraordinary kaleidoscope of subtle sweetnesses to be deployed and enjoyed to their fullest. I defy you not to be blown away by this one, especially when you realise there is not a single big base note to be heard... 46%. nc ncf.

Glen Grant 170th Anniversary db **(89) n23.5 t23.5 f20 b22**. The odd mildly sulphured cask has slipped through the net here to reduce what was shaping to be something magnificent. Still enjoyable, though. 46%

Glen Grant The Major's Reserve bott Mar 10 db **(85.5) n21.5 t23 f20 b21**. Forget about the so-so nose and finish. This is one of those drams that demands you melt into your chair on delivery, such is the fresh beauty of the malt and stunning honeycomb threads which tie themselves around every taste bud. Pity about the ultra dry, caramel-rich finish, but apparently nearly all the sherry butts have now been used up at the distillery. Thank gawd for that. 40%

⋙ **Archives Glen Grant 1975 36 Years Old First Release** hogshead, cask no. 5476, dist 18 Apr 75, bott 4 Jan 12 **(94.5) n25** only this distillery and Caperdonich produce fruit as exotic as this...and usually from casks of this vintage; **t23** silky delivery as required by the nose, though these days the oak can nip a bit; **f23.5** tires slightly, hence the light tang. The custardy vanilla and the fruit makes for a superb dessert **b23** I had expected the exotic fruit treatment. But not this Fortnum and Masonesque fruit basket... 46.6%. nc ncf sc. Whiskybase B.V. 81 bottles.

⋙ **Berry's Own Selection Glen Grant 1974** cask no. 7643, bott 2012 **(96.5) n25** at 54, am I too old to swoon? That near perfection of thick grape infused with essence of barley malt. The sugars are mere hints: grist here, honeydew melon there. And all emboldened by a smattering of herb and not overly antagonistic spice; **t24** the spices are more upfront now. But before they get a chance to really soar, molten honey fills the palate and dispenses grape in its cleanest form; the middle is a marvellous mix of coconut and raisin chocolate; **f23.5** maybe suffering from not quite knowing where the middle ends and the end begins. But there is no bitterness, no oak trying to have the last say at the cost of all else. Just a slow denouement, perhaps with a sprig of mint attached, of all else that has gone before; **b24** when I come across an unspoiled nugget like this, a malt of timeless magnificence, then the whisky world seems such a wonderful place in which to live. Those responsible for Scotland's whisky future could do worse than invest in a bottle and see what steps have to be taken to continue this glittering tradition. Certainly, the casks which have gone into this bottling represent a high water – or is it grape juice? – mark for Scotch single malt whisky. 47.8%. nc ncf sc.

- **Berry's Own Selection Glen Grant 1974** cask no. 7646, bott 2012 **(79) n20.5 t22 f17.5 b19.** A fascinating and dramatic contrast with Berry's other Glen Grant offering this year. A kind of bottled proof that more is less. Plenty of wonderful spiced orangey-grape notes to get on with and thoroughly enjoy. But the failings are stark. 49.3%. nc ncf sc.

- **Duncan Taylor Dimensions Glen Grant 21 Years Old** cask no. 16973, dist Aug 90, bott Jan 12 **(85) n21 t22.5 f21.5 b20.** A weirdo whisky. First we start with, if not unattractive, then certainly a fuddled and uncomfortable noise. This is followed with, outside the "Malts of Scotland Whisky Liqueur", one of the sweetest deliveries I've experienced, with your teeth wondering if permanent damage has been done. 55.5%. nc ncf sc.

Duncan Taylor Glen Grant 1972 cask no. 446483, bott Sep 10 **(86) n19 t22 f23 b22.** A much better whisky than the out of sorts nose suggests. Builds not just in confidence but fruity aggression for a decent late night dram. 54.8%. Duncan Taylor & Co.

- **Duncan Taylor Rare Auld Glen Grant 16 Years Old** cask no. 85090, dist 1995 **(88) n22.5** solid malt; a wall of the stuff offers at first a sharp crack across the bows before some sugary notes seep out almost shyly; **t22.5** intense barley; busy spices arrive just as the vanilla begins to be heard; **f21** the malt vanishes quickly leaving the vanilla and spices to fight it out alone; **b22** not a malt for the squeamish: the intensity is sometimes challenging. 54.9%. sc.

- **First Cask Glen Grant 23 Years Old** bourbon hogshead, cask no. 10182, dist 12 Jul 85, bott 28 Aug 08 **(92.5) n23** barley concentrate with several charming layers of peek-a-boo bourbon; red liquorice and black cherry; **t23.5** lightly oiled barley with just enough attitude from the sugars and spices to crank up the complexity levels; **f22.5** reverts back to a genteel maltiness though with enough spice to confirm it still has a pulse; **b23.5** a serenely malty yet complex dram which has been around for a while, but there are still stocks left in Holland, apparently! Don't ask me how!! 55.8%. nc ncf sc. Whisky Import Nederland. 187 bottles.

- **Gordon & MacPhail Distillery Label Glen Grant 1996** (87) n22.5 fragile, with the barley any moment about to give way to the vanilla; **t22** a reversal on the nose with the vanillas in early control, but now it's those delicate barley notes which fight back. Just a slight degree of acacia honey, too; **f21** and finally the vanilla holds sway...; **b21.5** without G&M, it is unlikely Glen Grant would be as well loved as it is today: they carried its torch for decades. However, as lovely as this malt may be, they are doing a slight disservice. This really should be at 46%, as the quality would be increased significantly. 40%. Gordon & MacPhail.

- **Gordon & MacPhail The Queen's Diamond Jubilee Glen Grant 60** first fill sherry hogshead, cask no. 465, dist 2 Feb 56, bott 2 Feb 12 **(92.5) n24.5** stunning smorgasbord of diced aged citrus and other fruit peel sets this off to a delicate and fresh start; the smoothness is supplied by a blend of heather and orange blossom honey; a tantalising trail of distant peat smoke; **t23** light, delicate delivery offering early barley and thin, juicy grape. But the oak has a lot to say and makes a resounding vanilla custard statement; **f22** thins out as the oaks take sharp command. Enough residual sugars to make for a pleasant if oaky landing; **b23** how interesting to see a '52 Glen Grant picked for the Jubilee Celebrations. Back in 1992 I bought my then wife a bottle of Gordon and MacPhail 1952 for her 40th birthday. And I have to say that that bottling, still bristling with vibrancy, is better than this, which for all its charm is feeling the years. How do I know for sure? I still have that bottle. But ssshh! Don't tell my ex....!! 42.3%. sc. Gordon & MacPhail. 85 bottles.

- **Malts Of Scotland Glen Grant 1972** sherry hogshead, cask no. 8235, dist Nov 72, bott Jun 11 **(96) n23** liberal degrees of manuka honey dovetail with the vanilla and fruitcake; **t25** textbook! A near perfection of malt and fruit interlinking and then offering up a heady mix of nuts and spices; **f23.5** the nuttiness intensifies and adds a degree of salt; the vanillas buzz and glow; a little late malty flourish towards the finale; **b24.5** Glen Grant boasted some of the finest sherry butts of the 1970s. This is one of them. 48.2%. nc ncf sc. Malts Of Scotland.

- **Malts Of Scotland Angel's Choice Glen Grant 1972** sherry hogshead, cask no. MoS12006, dist 1972, bott Jan 12 **(89) n23** gloriously weighted grape, at times heading off towards a fruitcake complexity, but more happy in being the base of a sherry trifle; **t24** thickly knotted oak radiates warm spices; the sugars and grapes are huddled together to form an intense core; **f20** the spices continue to pulse while the vanillas, sugars and fruits untangle; furry finale; **b22** the surprising slight tang on the nose and finish means that it is not quite in the same class as the Malts of Scotland version. 54.1%. nc ncf sc. Malts Of Scotland.

- **Mo Òr Collection Glen Grant 1972 38 Years Old** first fill bourbon hogshead, cask no. 16568, dist 31 May 72, bott 25 Jan 11 **(88) n23** some pretty hefty layers of tannin, but a light hickory surge softens the attack and appears to underline the sugars; **t22** a big oak and sugar battle heads off into creamy mocha and spices; **f21** dries just a little too violently, though the spices are fine; **b22** a white knuckle ride of a dram. One fears it is going to disintegrate into old age at any moment, but it just manages to keep the wheels on the tracks. 46%. nc ncf sc. Release No. 16. The Whisky Talker. 210 bottles.

⋙ **Mo Ôr Collection Glen Grant 1985 25 Years Old** first fill bourbon hogshead, cask no. 10187, dist 12 Jul 85, bott 2 Dec 10 **(83) n23 t21.5 f19 b19.5**. Great nose, full of pithy crushed grape seeds despite its bourbon cask heritage. But for all its light sugar coating, simply cannot cope with the overwhelming dry oak. 46%. nc ncf sc. Release No. 53. 310 bottles.

⋙ **Old Malt Cask Glen Grant Aged 18 Years** refill hogshead, cask no. 8006, dist Oct 93, bott Jan 12 **(80) n19 t21 f19.5 b20.5**. Huge, delicious malt. But the cask just isn't up to snuff. 50%. nc ncf sc. Douglas Laing & Co. 311 bottles.

Old Malt Cask Glen Grant Aged 35 Years brandy butt, cask no. 6279, dist Apr 75, bott Jun 10 **(94.5) n23.5** one of the most Summery noses I have encountered this year: ripe greengages falling off the tree − I could be in France (eating their fruit, not drinking their brandy). I don't think the spices could be better paced or the combined oak/fruit depth more in tune to receive; **t23** silk body with the fruit and barley ridiculously well matched; **f24** improbably long, the vaguest hint of oil and a slow rolling out of the icing sugars and delicate sultanas; **b24** I absolutely guarantee that whatever brandy was originally in this butt, it wasn't a patch on the whisky in this bottle... 50%. nc ncf sc. Douglas Laing & Co. 371 bottles.

⋙ **Old Malt Cask Glen Grant Aged 36 Years** brandy finished butt, cask no. 7820, dist Apr 75, bott Nov 11 **(87) n22** a huge and by no means unattractive pithy grape presence: it is as though the malt has been substituted for crushed grape pips; some lovely spices intervene; **t22** soft and immediately salivating and moderately sweet with the spices galloping in at the double; the dry middle of spice, more grape pip and oaky vanilla is almost inevitable; **f21.5** dry and enclosed; **b21.5** Glen Grant is probably the crispest, the most staccato, of all the malt produced in Scotland. And if I was asked how to enclose a malt and give it the tightest finish possible, my answer might be to finish it in a Cognac or brandy cask. So when I saw the label... 50%. nc ncf sc. Douglas Laing & Co. 268 bottles.

Old Masters Glen Grant 19 Years Old cask no. 35955, dist 1992, bott Mar 11 **(87.5) n22 t22 f21.5 b22**. Never for a moment thinks about letting up in its intensity. 59.4%. sc.

Peerless Glen Grant 40 Years Old dist 1970, cask no. 3497 **(96) n24** almost defies belief as the barley absolutely sparkles; gooseberries punctuated with oak; nothing is out of place... it is almost too perfect... **t24** nigh on perfect weight on delivery. There is a stunningly crisp sheen to the barley, which appears coated by Demerara sugar crystals. The oak offers a deep, semi-earthy Java coffee background...and is probably behind the slow swelling of spice that sits so comfortably in the nougat-vanilla middle; **f24** confirms itself as a malt of the rarest quality: the barley continues its sugar-led path, the spices beet out their delicate tattoo, the oaks weave a vanilla-butterscotch tapestry and various random fruit notes pop up here and there...; **b24** more Cary Grant...just how sophisticated is this...? A whisky which I found almost impossible to spit and shows just why the very greatest whiskies you ever taste are things of not just unique beauty, but experiences never to be forgotton. 48.5%. sc. Duncan Taylor & Co.

⋙ **The Perfect Dram Glen Grant 39 Years Old** sherry cask, dist 1972, bott 2011 **(86) n21 t21.5 f22 b21.5**. A dram which will doubtless make some weak at the knees. But, for me, an example of a malt that shows faded greatness but with just not enough sugars present to make a must-have malt. Even so, once you get past the eye-watering oak, there is enough mocha and black pepper to make for a long and entertaining experience. 51.1%. sc.

Premier Barrel Glen Grant Aged 12 Years (88) n22 t23 f21.5 b21.5. If this were a steak, it'd be red raw. But try and find one juicier than this... 46%. nc ncf sc. 324 bottles.

⋙ **Provenance Glen Grant Over 8 Years** refill barrel, cask no. 7611, dist Summer 2003, bott Summer 2011 **(88) n22** a squirt of lemon zest in the crisp barley; **t22.5** beautiful delivery: barley sugar on a yielding, lightly oiled platform of vanilla; **f21.5** light, with spiced custard; **b22** a good example of the distillery showing its lilting maltiness when at that curious age between youth and maturity. 46%. nc ncf sc. Douglas Laing & Co.

⋙ **Provenance Glen Grant Over 12 Years** refill hogshead, cask no. 7649, dist Autumn 1998, bott Summer 2011 **(83.5) n21 t22 f20 b20.5**. A volley of juicy grains does all it can to overcome the unflattering oak. 46%. nc ncf sc. Douglas Laing & Co.

⋙ **Scotch Malt Whisky Society Cask 9.63 Aged 8 Years** first fill barrel, cask no. 800547, dist 2002 **(93) n23.5** absolutely brimming with malty promise. Sweet and sharp, the closest commercial nose to this used to be the old non-age statement Glenfiddich; **t24** few whiskies force you into such rabid salivation. Fresh, clean and the barley simply exploding with lusty juices; **f22.5** the oak finally gets a word in edgeways. It arrives with a spicy butterscotch signature; **b23** this is a distillery very well suited to comparatively young malt. You will not find a more compelling case for a distillery bottling 8-year-old at cask strength than this. 60.9%. sc.

⋙ **Scott's Selection Glen Grant 1993** bott 2011 **(94) n22** the usual tight barley and a very well behaved cask means a technical triumph but the complexity, beyond the simplest green apple tones, is relatively limited. My word, though: what you could do with this in a top class blend...; **t25** there may be relative inactivity on the nose. But it makes amends in scary fashion by going ballistic on the palate. One of the deliveries of the year as the taste buds are flooded under a deluge of the most profoundly clear and juicy barley notes you are ever likely to experience; **f23** cannot match the delivery, and doesn't try. Settles, instead, for a simplistic but very effective vanilla fade...with clean and crisp barley for company to the very end; **b24** a lesson in magnificent Speyside-style malt. The nose is a blender's many Christmases coming at once ...but the delivery is something else altogether. *53.7%. Speyside Distillers.*

⋅⋅⋙⋅⋅ **The Whisky Agency Glen Grant 1972** bott 2011 **(84) n22 t21 f20 b21.** The softness on the mocha towards the end somewhat glosses over the oaky strain this malt is under from first to last. *52.3%. nc ncf sc. The Whisky Agency.*

The Whisky Agency Glen Grant 1972 refill sherry, bott 2011 **(89) n23 t22 f22 b22.** An old speysider just about on the edge, but the quality is glorious! *52.8%*

The Whisky Agency Glen Grant 1973 (95.5) n24.5 wow! By which I mean: fruitcake concentrate, but in the cleanest, almost Sauternes-sweet/spicy way. Actually, more of a cor-blimey...wow-wow-wow..., bordering on the f**me sideways..!!! **t24** the oak is every bit as big as it should be. Yet so sublimely well structured and weighted in the fruit and barley interplay, it makes absolutely no negative impact. The secret, though, is the fabulous weight to the oil, which does a great job of carrying the spices and spreading the sugars, but heroically refuses to deaden the value. Wondrous...; **f23.5** just the vaguest hint of oak weariness, but no more than an aged film star panting at the end of a long chase. But it is a distant cry of bitterness which can barely be heard amid the contended and very long afterglow of the fruit-spice-barley orgy of before...; **b24** knocking on the door of being the finest single cask I have tasted this year...Pity it was up against the Peerless Glen Grant 38... *52.4%*

⋅⋅⋙⋅⋅ **The Whisky Agency Glen Grant 1975** bott 2011 **(94) n23.5** diced apple...this could almost be a brandy; just a jot of cinnamon and allspice. Age. and lots of it. Not taking the exotic fruit route. but something much more like home cooking; **t24** silky barley delivery... then there we go again: we are back to the cider brandy. Has that degree of fruity firmness and crisp sugars, coupled with a real small still- styled metallic tang ; **f22.5** the oak kicks in for sure, but does so with more than a degree of good manners, allowing all the fruit, copper and barley to say their piece before leaving; **b24** wonderful whisky: it's as simple as that... *50.7%. nc ncf sc.*

Whisky Doris Glen Grant 38 Years Old refill sherry, cask no. 1650, dist Feb 72, bott Mar 10 **(86.5) n21 t22 f22 b21.5.** Exceptionally oily for a Glen Grant. Even so, pleasingly rough enough to give you a good punch in the kisser where you might have hoped for something a little more delicate and fruity. *53.6%*

GLENGYLE
Campbeltown, 2004. J&A Mitchell & Co. Working.

Kilkerran Single Malt db **(80) n19** very young, slightly Shredded Wheaty, a touch of tobacco leaf, mint and some heavy oils; **t20** ungainly arrival with big barley, big oils, big natural caramel; **f21** settles towards a light, slightly sweeter and gristier fade, **b20** Glyngyle's first offering doesn't rip up any trees. And maybe the odd flaw to its character that you won't see when the distillery is fine-tuned. But this is the first-ever bottling from this brand new Campbeltown distillery and therefore its chances of being a worldbeater as an untried and untested 3-y-o were pretty slim. I will be watching its development with relish And with heart pounding... *46%. Available exclusively from distillery direct from cask.*

Kilkerran Single Malt bott 22 May 07 db **(84) n20 t21 f22 b21.** Sadly, I was out of the country and couldn't attend the Coming of Age of Kilkerran, when its first casks turned three and became whisky. Very kindly, they sent me a bottle as if I was there and, therefore, these are the notes of the very first bottling handed out to visitors. Interestingly, there is a marked similarity in distillery style to the 46% bottling in that the malt offers a crescendo of quality. This is only three year old whisky, of course, and its fingerprints will alter as it spends longer in the cask. *62%. nc ncf.*

Kilkerran 'Work in Progress' db **(88) n22.5** youthful, malty and a pinch of salt creeping into this one.. **t22** a simple malty delivery is the prologue to a simple, barley-rich tale. Dries to a surprising degree after the initial quick burst of barley sugar with the vanillas kicking hard, followed even by some spice; **f21.5** lots of natural caramel with the malt; **b22** doing very well. *46%*

GLEN KEITH
Speyside, 1957. Chivas Brothers. Silent.

Glen Keith 10 Years Old db **(80) n22 t21 f18 b19.** A malty if thin dram that finishes with a whimper after an impressively refreshing, grassy start. *43%*

❖❖ **Berry's Own Selection Glen Keith 1993** cask no. 97100, bott 2012 **(88) n22** ultra grassy and salivating: as refreshing as a malt of this age dare hope to be; **t22.5** ridiculously gristy for a malt of this age; the sugars are so clean, you could clean your teeth with them...; **f21.5** dulls out slightly as the creaking vanilla gets a toe-hold; **b22** if someone asked me to imagine an 18 or 19-y-o Glen Keith in a well-used but very serviceable bourbon cask and distilled to a slightly above average standard, it would be almost exactly like this. *53.8%. nc ncf sc.*

❖❖ **Cadenhead Glen Keith 13 Years Old** bott 2011 **(83) n20 t21.5 f21 b20.5.** Pretty one dimensional. But if your preferred dimension happens to be clean, intense, semi-new makey barley then this offers all you need. *54.2%. sc. WM Cadenhead Ltd.*

❖❖ **Cadenhead Glen Keith 18 Years Old** bott 2012 **(89) n22.5** the grassiest, most juicy barley you'll ever find; **t22.5** the nose is untroubled by oak, and there is little in evidence on delivery as that juicy barley enjoys supremacy; **f22** the lightest hint of praline shows the cask does offer something quite positive after all; **b22** Glen Keith raising the Speyside colours with singular pride. Quietly adorable. *54.3%. sc. WM Cadenhead Ltd.*

❖❖ **John Milroy Selection Glen Keith 1993** cask no. 97101, bott 2012 **(86.5) n21.5 t22 f21.5 b21.5.** Not entirely dissimilar to the Berry's Own cask 97100, but with more spice and less sparkle. *55.3%. nc ncf sc. Berry Bros & Rudd.*

❖❖ **Liquid Sun Glen Keith 21 Years Old** dist 1991 **(82.5) n21 t21 f20 b20.5.** Pleasant. No off notes. But tends to just sit in the glass doing very little other than radiating malt. *51.7%. sc.*

Malts Of Scotland Glen Keith 1970 bourbon hogshead, cask no. 6042, dist Sep 70, bott Feb 11 **(92) n24** classic oak-induced exotic fruit with pineapple and crushed physalis to the fore plus some pleasing spices on the vanilla. Creaking with great age, but complex and classy; **t22** perhaps slightly too active on the oak front early on, but soon settles and the fruits return with the delicate, lemon sheen; **f23** back to full complexity with a touch of spice to the mocha; **b23** it's extraordinary how often a malt renowned for being average at best in its early and mid life somehow achieves a degree of exotic fruity greatness in its dotage. *49.1%. sc.*

❖❖ **Old Malt Cask Glen Keith Aged 18 Years** refill hogshead, cask no. 7671, dist Sep 93, bott Sep 11 **(90.5) n23** the oak plays second lead to the barley, but through its understated gravitas steals the show; the bourbon undercurrent allures; **t23** excellent weight with a touch of honeycomb and delicate bourbon-style liquorice ensuring that the salivating barley dominates only up to a point; **f22** long with the vanillas now in control; a late chocolate coffee bean flourish; **b22.5** an impressive bottling. *50%. nc ncf sc. Douglas Laing & Co. 311 bottles.*

❖❖ **Old Malt Cask Glen Keith Aged 18 Years** refill hogshead, cask no. 7963, dist Sep 93, bott Dec 11 **(77) n19.5 t20 f18.5 b19.** Worth buying both this and cask 7671 above: just astonishing the difference the quality of a cask can make. *50%. nc ncf sc. 320 bottles.*

❖❖ **Scott's Selection Glen Keith 1996** bott 2011 **(90.5) n23** busy, busy, busy! Barley nipping and fluttering about in the most vivid terms with that uniquely toffee apple sharpness as well as white pepper pepping up the celery; **t23** not often GK gets into its stride so confidently and so early. The barley is pinging around with a bullet hardness and the salivation levels fly off the scale. As the mocha begins to descend and the sugars transform from grist to Demerara, there are signs that the cask is beginning to play up; **f22** vanilla and mocha. The late bitterness, though unwelcome, isn't mean enough to spoil the party; **b22.5** magnificent spirit, showing Glen Keith at its very best. Just a shame about the cask, which just fails to last the course. Still, for the most part a fabulous whisky experience. *57.6%. Speyside Distillers.*

❖❖ **Sestante Collection Glen Keith 18 Years Old** dist 1991, bott 2009 **(77) n21 t19 f18 b19.** Hardly recognisable as a Scotch and has all the bizarre and in-your-face characteristics of a malt matured in a barrel made from something other than oak. More likely to find this style in Germany or Austria. Several layers of kumquat save the day. *46%. sc.*

❖❖ **Sestante Collection Glen Keith 40 Years Old** dist 1970, bott 2011 **(87.5) n22** nutty; almost an antique furniture feel to this, complete with some old polish! **t22.5** the delivery spells in every way imaginable, o-l-d-a-g-e. Yet enough sugars, tinged by pretty eye-watering zest, help get it through the oaky onslaught; **f21** a little spice at the death...but it creaks its way to the finishing line; **b22** thought by mistake that this was their 1991 bottling, as I was unaware they had a much older version. Relieved on discovering my mistake, as I wondered what the hell had happened to this to make it age so drastically. *46.1%. sc. Silver Seal Whisky Company.*

The Whisky Agency Glen Keith 1970 bott 2010 **(81) n21 t19 f20.5 b20.5.** Yet another bottling from the Whisky Agency displaying more oak than Henry VIII's Compass Rose...and is close to befalling a similar fate. *45.1%. The Whisky Agency.*

The Whisky Agency Glen Keith 1970 (92) n21.5 déjà oak...; **t23.5** didn't expect that! Fabulous!! Not only is the barley intact, but it pulses out giggawatts of sharp sugars and bourbon honeycomb and liquorice; **f23.5** a massive orangey tang at the back of my palate. All topped by spiced dark Columbian cocoa; light oils work a form of magic; **b24** a real livewire of a dram that offers little on the nose but takes you into new worlds once it hits the palate. Sensational. *54.2%. The Whisky Agency.*

GLENKINCHIE
Lowlands, 1837. Diageo. Working.

Glenkinchie 12 Years Old db **(85) n19 t22.5 f21.5 b22.** The last 'Kinchie 12 I encountered was beyond woeful. This is anything but. Still not firing on all cylinders and can definitely do better. But there is a fabulous vibrancy to this which nearly all the bottlings I have tasted in the last few years have sadly lacked. Impressive. 43%

Glenkinchie Aged 15 Years The Distillers Edition Amontillado finished, dist 1992, bott 2007 db **(94) n23.5 t24 f23 b23.5.** Now this is absolutely top class wine cask finishing. One of my last whiskies of the night, and one to take home with me. Sophisticated, intelligent and classy. 46%

Glenkinchie 20 Years Old db **(85.5) n21 t22 f21.5 b21.** When I sampled this, I thought: "hang on, haven't I tasted this one before?" When I checked with my tasting notes for one or two independents who bottled around this age a year or two ago, I found they were nigh identical to what I was going to say here. Well, you can't say its not a consistent dram. The battle of the citrus-barley against the welling oak is a rich and entertaining one. 58.4%

Glenkinchie Special Release 2010 20 Years Old refill American oak, dist 1990 **(86.5) n23 t22 f21 b21.5.** Workhorse malts like Kinchie were hardly designed for 20 years in the cask. So although this one is hemmed in by oak from all sides, what a treat to see the nose, at least, offer a malty sparkle and fruity, mildly herbal depth of complexity. Some juiciness and residual sugars on the delivery, too. 55.1%. nc ncf. Diageo. Fewer than 6000 bottles.

Glenkinchie 1992 The Manager's Choice db **(78) n19 t22 f18 b19.** Has a lot going for it on delivery with a barley explosion which rocks you back in your chair and has you salivating like a rabies victim. But the rest of It is just too off key. 58.1%. Diageo.

THE GLENLIVET
Speyside, 1824. Chivas Brothers. Working.

The Glenlivet Aged 12 Years db **(79.5) n22 t21 f18 b18.5.** Wonderful nose and very early development but then flattens out towards the kind of caramel finish you just wouldn't traditionally associate with this malt, and further weakened by a bitter, furry finale. 40%

The Glenlivet Aged 12 Years Old First Fill Matured db **(91) n22.5 t22.5 f23 b23.** A quite wonderful whisky, far truer to The Glenlivet than the standard 12 and one which every malt whisky lover should try once in their journey through the amber stuff. Forget the tasting notes on the bottle, which bear little relation to what is inside. A gem of a dram. 40%

⠿ **The Glenlivet Excellence 12 Year Old** db **(87) n22** clean, gristy barley; slightly chalky and tart; so clean, you fancy you can even detect the very faintest of phenols; **t21.5** almost too delicate as the barley tries, but fails, to keep its toothold; some big vanilla, **f22** more comfortable and balanced towards the finish as a few sugars and spices step aboard; **b21.5** low key but very clean. The emphasis is on delicate. 40%. Visitor Centre and Asian exclusive.

The Glenlivet 15 Years of Age db **(80) n19 t21 f20 b20.** Undeniable charm to the countless waves of malt and oak. But don't expect much in the way of complexity or charisma. 40%

The Glenlivet French Oak Reserve 15 Years of Age Limousin oak casks db **(95) n22.5** oo la la citrus; aver spice, **t23** comme ci comme ca caramels rescued by an uplifting injection of sweet barley; the juicy, salivating qualities are quite startling if not profound; **f22.5** long, with a fabulous butterscotch fade and a slow dissolving of dark sugars; **b23** I have to say that after tasting nearly 800 cask strength whiskies, to come across something at the ancient 40% is a shock to the system. My taste buds say merci... And, what is more, a bottle of this shall remain in my dining room for guests. Having, a lifetime ago, lived with a wonderful French girl for three years I suspect I know how her country folk will regard that... Oh, and forgive a personal message to a literary friend: Bobby-Ann...keep a bottle of this beside the Ancient Age... 40%

The Glenlivet Nadurra Aged 16 Years American oak bourbon, bott code LR10039 db **(94) n23.5 t24 f23 b23.5.** How curious: when I first nosed this one I thought: "hmmmm, stem ginger". Then looking up my previous entry saw ginger was included there, too. This time, though, the chocolate is conspicuous by its absence and a more bourbon character prevails. Remains the "must have" official Glenlivet for me to pour guests. 48%

⠿ **The Glenlivet Nadurra Aged 16 Years** batch no. 0911P, bott Sep 11 db **(95) n23.5** one of those teasing noses which revels in its own complexity. The Glenlivet bright barley style is there in abundance, but the layering of the tannins and the sharpness this creates fair makes the heart skip a beat; **t24** puckeringly tart on delivery, those rich tannins are softened by the sugars of the barley; barley sugar candy sucked simultaneously with lemon drops; **f23.5** more vanilla dependent with an almost inevitable butterscotch subplot. A few weightier cough sweets slip in at the end...; **b24** this remains by far and away the finest and most consistent style from this historic distillery. A Speyside must-have for any single malt lover. 53%. ncf.

The Glenlivet Nadurra Aged 16 Natural Cask Strength batch no. 0808F, bott Aug 08 **(94) n23.5** Glenlivet in concentrate. literally. Delicate, juicy barley with the oak offering little more than a dais for the malt to make its lilting speech; **t24** every bit as salivating as the nose suggests. A fabulous brittleness and just a light puff of smoke helps soften things. Strands of citrus everywhere but it's the mouth-feel that has you whimpering with pleasure; **f23** dries at full pelt but that massive malt sees it through the turbulence; **b23.5** Glenlivet in its purest and most delicious form. Truly classic Speyside. *576% Canada market.*

The Glenlivet Aged 18 Years bott Feb 10 db **(91) n22** attractive mixture of honeycombed bourbon and fruitcake; **t23.5** oh...just didn't expect that...!! Fabulous, honey-sweet and slightly sharp edge to the barley: excellent weight and mouthfeel with the honeycomb on the nose making slow but decisive incursions; **f23** a very slight technical flaw drops it half a point, but there is no taking away from the improbable length of the dissolving honey and barley...some gentle chewing is required, especially with the late juices and vanilla arriving; **b23** a hugely improved bottling seriously worth discovering in this form. Appears to have thrown off its old shackles and offers up an intensity that leaves you giving a little groan of pleasure. *43%*

The Glenlivet Archive 21 Years Old batch no. 0508B bott Nov 08 db **(87.5) n22 t23.5 f20 b22.** Forget the nondescript finish: just settle down and be royally entertained by the enormity and panache of the big honey arrival. *43%*

The Glenlivet Archive 21 Years Old batch no. 1109D, bott Dec 09 db **(86.5) n22.5 t23 f20 b21.** Against the undisputed glory of a 60-second purple patch on delivery when the thick fruit, honey, spice and weight are in total harmony, the rest is comparatively humdrum with a very slight flaw helping to restrict the development to take this to where it belongs. *43%*

The Glenlivet Founder's Reserve 21 Years Old db **(95.5) n23.5** initially tight and, even after 20 minutes in the glass, allows the grape to unfurl in the most niggardly fashion. Thing is: the few notes, in tandem with some gorgeous Columbian cocoa, spices, orange peel and rich dates, reveals that much is to come on the palate... **t24.5** those spices are the first to flee the confines of the thick grape, but so many layers of grape skin and mocha follow that you can sit there for a good five minutes and still not entirely work out what is going on; the spices are not just persistent but simply magnificent; **f23.5** long, with (milky) cocoa and dates (of the juicy rather than dried variety) leading the way; a light sulphur note detracts half a mark, but it is testament to the malt that it barely detracts from the moment; **b24** on this evidence, one of the whiskies of the year for sure. I really don't think my 800th new single malt of the year could have been a more inspired – or lucky - choice. *55.6%. ncf. 1824 bottles.*

The Glenlivet XXV 25 Years Old batch no. 50416, bott Oct 08 db **(91) n23 t24 f21.5 b22.5.** Possibly the ultimate non-peated late night dram. One cask away from a massive score and a certain award... *43%*

The Glenlivet 1973 Cellar Collection bott Oct 09 db **(94.5) n24** luxurious stewed sultanas in a custard tart; yet for a malt heading towards 40, improbable grist, too: clean, complex, thick and simply spellbinding... **t24** just melts into the taste buds with the freshest, cleanest, juiciest charm you could possibly imagine, yet always with a nibbling spice darting around the side of the tongue; **f23** a touch of oaky bitterness, but a mere detail: the late oils are sympathetic and contain a surprising degree of vanilla; **b23.5** for Glenlivet lovers, I point you towards something a little special... *49%. Chivas.*

❖ **The Glenlivet Cellar Collection 1980** bott Aug 11 db **(94.5) n23** no shortage of chalky oak creating almost a bloom to the fruit. There is citrus, but that fruit has slightly more tropical shades, especially green banana; **t24** one of those deliveries where the mouth-feel actually outpoints the flavours – not that there is anything wrong there. Soft and yielding, even with an early puff of distant smoke, but just enough fibre to ensure a chewy element to those fruits which are now extolling the virtues of grassy barley; **f23.5** it would be easy just to concentrate on the big peppery spices. But then you would be missing the mocha, not to mention the vanilla ice cream with a physalis topping; **b24** some of you in the know will have been expecting exotic fruit from this...and you won't be disappointed! *43.3%. ncf. 500 bottles.*

The Glenlivet Nadurra 1991 batch no. 0809A, bott Aug 09 db **(89) n22.5 t23 f21 b22.5.** Ah, had they only been a little more circumspect with the caramel... *48%*

The Glenlivet Nadurra 1991 batch no. 0310B, bott Mar 10 db **(78) n19 t22 f18 b19.** A sulphurous sherry butt or two leaves you wondering what might have been. *48%. Chivas.*

The Glenlivet Master Distiller's Reserve db **(86.5) n22.5 t22 f20.5 b21.5.** I chose this as my 800th whisky to taste for the 2012 Bible against the Founder's Reserve on the strength of the nose over the first 30 seconds. Oh, well. Shows you the pricelessness of time when evaluating a whisky... *40%*

❖ **Berry's Own Selection Glenlivet 1973** cask no. 10658, bott 2012 **(94) n23.5** despite the fact it pulses antiquity this remains sprightly and nubile, the barley absolutely fizzing on the nose. A few shards of honey offer weight and resonance to the citrus; **t24** demands a mouth-watering delivery after that nose, and that is exactly what you get. The spices flock to the scene so the taste buds are at once drowned, caressed and burnt alive...; **f23** long, with a slow devaluation of the sugars as the vanillas take command; **b23.5** about as salivating a near 40-year-old you are likely to find! *48.6%. nc ncf sc. Berry Bros & Rudd.*

⟐ **Berry's Own Selection Glenlivet 1973** cask no. 10822, bott 2012 **(84.5) n22 t22.5 f19 b21.** The barley and the expected spices do all in their power to enliven, enrich and entertain. But the deeper oak renders it at times a bit of a maudlin dullard. 47.6%. nc ncf sc.

⟐ **Berry's Own Selection Glenlivet 1974** cask no. 5247, bott 2012 **(83.5) n20.5 t22 f21 b20.** Sharp, with plenty of malt to go around. But just a little too tangy and off balance for its own good. 46%. nc ncf sc. Berry Bros & Rudd.

Berry's Own Selection Glenlivet 1976 cask no. 18081, bott 2010 **(80.5) n20 t21.5 f19 b20.** No particular faults and shows a disarming sweetness early on. Just an exhausted malt at the end of a very long life, I'm afraid. 46%. nc ncf sc. Berry Bros & Rudd.

Berry's Own Selection Glenlivet 1994 cask no. 58453, bott 2011 **(71) n18 t18.5 f17 b17.5** Thank you. Next...! 58.9%. nc ncf sc. Berry Bros & Rudd.

⟐ **Cadenhead Glenlivet 21 Years Old** bott 2011 **(95) n23.5** what a darling of a nose: the oaks lead the way with a fabulous French toast sweetness, but there is a babbling undercurrent of spice and barley, too.; **t24.5** this is the way a Glenlivet of this age should behave: plenty of barley and all kinds of salivating properties. But the sheer delight is in the puckering sharpness of the spiced apple and semi-bourbony honeycomb. The vanillas enter butterscotch territory and a lemon zesty gristiness still has something to say; even the oak is a little different; **f23** settles into a more subtle denouement where the barley sugars and citrus sit comfortably with a less intense oakiness; **b24** really not the easiest whisky I have ever had to spit out! Absolutely overflowing with flavours. A classic! 55.7%. sc. WM Cadenhead Ltd.

⟐ **Duncan Taylor Octave Glenlivet 21 Years Old** cask no. 470899, dist 1970 **(86) n22 t22 f21 b21.** Hate to say it, but for all its wealth of intense barley riches, the oak forces this a little out of tune. If you like to pick a few splinters from between your teeth, then go get, for there is much to enjoy! But for all its compensating blood orange and ribald barley, the oak is just a little too uncouth for where you might prefer it to be. 46.1%. sc. Duncan Taylor & Co.

Gordon & MacPhail Generations Glenlivet 70 Years Old dist 1940 **(95.5) n24.5** the very first notes have a diced ginger quality to it: understated, but there. As that fades, a recognisable trait of great age begins to creep in: something akin to exotic fruit. This variety is a little dryer than some, perhaps with banana skins trying to inject a vanilla element. Slowly, spices begin to emerge – never rabid but a buzzing heard above the general murmur. Is it the ancient remnants of smoke? Or just some oaky attitude? Difficult to say at first, but then a clue: as the whisky oxidizes the oak has a more vociferous note and the drying process begins in earnest. 20 minutes in and the gingers and exotic fruits have been replaced by earthier oak notes and a touch of clove, too and very late on...could it be? Is that the odd (non-spiced) molecule of peat...? Actually, leave the empty glass to dry of its own accord (when it hits 25/25), and you will be left in little doubt; **t23.5** if tasted early, the oaks are slightly OTT. So don't! Leave for about 15 minutes, then start tasting: a thick amalgamation of natural caramels and barley; shows almost a nougat quality at times with the toffee carrying with it a squeeze of sultana; actually becomes juicier in the middle for a while; the spices nibble and buzz, but no more viciously than your partner around your neck...; **f24** long. Not a threat of bitterness: just magnificent oak Moves into a mocha mode. And as it oxidises, the creamier it becomes, helped along the way by an extra quarter spoonful of Demerara every now and again...; **b24** you may not be too surprised that I selected this as the 1,000th whisky to be officially tasted for the Whisky Bible 2012. Like an ancient glacier, it is a malt on the move: so slowly, it is imperceptible. I have tried to capture the path it takes over time and the scores are the average ones over a good hour. This is nothing like G&M's previous 70-year-old. It does have something in common, though: the kind of oak influence that, were it possible to return in 70 years time, I would be surprised if today's casks could come even close to matching. This whisky seemingly defies nature. It absolutely refuses to seek shelter under a honeyed umbrella and somehow plots a course from its hushed hello as it is poured to its exquisitely elegant denouement by taking us through a journey of hints, might-bes, and whispers. For the lucky ones amongst us, it is a unique journey of a lifetime. 45.9%

Gordon & MacPhail Private Collection Glenlivet 1954 (96) Bassett's chocolate liquorice. An outline of earthy smoke plus toffee apple with a surprising degree of Golden Delicious. I really have no idea how a whisky this old can be so devoid of any off notes – well, apart from the fact the oak was so much better in those days; **t23.5** first up come some oak-led spices, but all very civil. A charming soft oil lubricates the taste buds without them really noticing; there is a very brief puckering sharpness of the oak, but a wave of barley-tinged fruitcake fills the middle; **f24.5** such a wonderfully weighted finale it borders on the ridiculous. Understated but evident layers of chocolate sponge, walnut cake (with cream) and a liberal smattering of dates makes for a finish bordering on perfection. Especially if you can pick up on that delicate smoke which re-enters the picture and seems like the glow from a swallowed and well matured Melton Hunt cake... **b24** if there is a heaven, I think I have just entered it. For no company in the world does this kind of veteran whisky better than Gordan and MacPhail and here they have exceeded even themselves. Guessed this would be an outstanding whisky to mark my 700th specifically tasted for the Bible 2012, and 600th new entry. My word: was I right...! 50.6%

⋅⋅⋅ **Gordon & MacPhail Rare Vintage Glenlivet 1961 (94.5) n24** nutty: hazelnut and almonds to the fore, including hints of marzipan. A mix of salted butter and Demerara sugar fills the gaps, long with a a thin spreading of lime jelly; **t23.5** the oak shows a dark, threatening side. But the star quality of the dark, roasty sugars beats back the ravages of time and positively laughs in its face; **f23** the oak, earlier, had threatened to spoil the party. But now it has been tamed and offers a meek contribution to the slow unwinding of the vanillas and surprisingly intact barley, plus the toasted fudge and dried dates. A few pecans and walnuts offer extra oiliness, and all is carried out in slow motion; **b24** a very dear friend and colleague told me today that his mother was diagnosed with Alzheimer's. It was terribly sad news, and something she understood and accepted with fortitude, magnanimity and a courage which came so natural I doubt if she realised she even had it. "They are a different breed" said my friend with unaffected reverence, referring to the generation which survived a World War, so would take whatever low card fate was dealing them with the same innate stoicism. I have a mother who was 91 last week, is mentally sharp as a knife but unable to walk unaided, and a final remaining blood uncle also with Alzheimer's whom I visit whenever in London. So I knew exactly what he meant. And in a far, far less important way, I feel something similar regarding the whiskies of yesteryear and today. I cannot see that many whiskies reaching 50 years with the kind of resilience that this whisky shows me here. The casks of today, both sherry and bourbon, are so much more inferior – weaker - that we can only look upon this vanishing generation of malts, like the one in my glass before me, as we do our own kinfolk. So easily taken for granted. So dreadfully under- appreciated when with us. And to be painfully and immeasurably missed when they are gone. 43%

Gordon & MacPhail Private Collection Glenlivet 1963 (88) n23 t21.5 f21.5 b22. Defies the odds to stay together. A malt that feels its age, but can still get around. 40.6%

⋅⋅⋅ **Gordon & MacPhail Rare Vintage Glenlivet 1966 (95) n24** spices drill into the nostrils and explode; yams sit steaming on a plate; celery is being salted and freshly chopped; plasticine is being kneaded by a child; casks of apple brandy sit 100 yards away in a dank cellar; a cracked old chesterfield is being pushed into an antique showroom; a conker has just split in your hand....; **t23.5** obviously, the oak makes the first play as the body is so thin. But the cask is made of magnificent stuff because it still allows the barley the stage for a while; **f23.5** dries and spices up. The vanillas are brief, quickly replaced by sturdier liquorice and Demerara sugars; **b24** I have never quite understood how whisky from this distillery gets past a dozen years, let alone makes it to such antiquity. Yet when it does, it carries its stardom with the grace of a movie star who understands the value of stage-managed humbleness. 43%

⋅⋅⋅ **Gordon & MacPhail Rare Vintage Glenlivet 1967 (83) n21 t20 f21 b21.** You should get a free white flag with every bottle: this is a whisky which, for all its salty enormity, has surrendered to the oak. 43%. Gordon & MacPhail.

Gordon & MacPhail Private Collection Glenlivet 1974 (95.5) n24.5 this is ridiculous. How, with a mere human nose (albeit a pretty fine-tuned one, apparently), am I supposed to work out all that is going on here? Well, let's start with the grape: hard to begin anywhere else. A distinct musto quality to this, alongside the usual Melton Hunt cake mature fruitiness. Nuts, too: brazils and pecans in abundance; and just don't get me started on the molasses...; **t23.5** this time the sugars kick off the proceedings: naturally they tend to be dark in character with molasses leading the way. The grape is thick and wonderfully overcooked; **f24** normally, bitterness on a finish is the kiss of death for a whisky: not here. This is not from exhausted oak. It is, as it should be, an amalgam of big tannin and even bigger grape. And all coated with virtually flawless molasses and toasty natural caramel. There is some sharp marmalade, too, just to finish it – and you - off...; **b24** I have been seriously thinking about investing in an MG Roadster 1974 vintage. One reason is because I remember at school discussing with next desk buddy, Legin Reltub (aka Nigel Butler) and my long ago tragically lost amigo Ian Lovell the merits of this then newly released car which featured prominently in Playboy. I told them, one day, when I had made my pile, I would be the proud owner of the babe magnet which radiated from the glossy pages before us. I owe it to my loyal sidekick Ian at least to keep to my word. Why am I thinking of that now? Well, because this whisky just reminded me of it. All sleek lines, elegant oomph and come-to-bed classicism. This one, dear, much missed Ian, is to you, mate... 50.1%

⋅⋅⋅ **Gordon & MacPhail Rare Vintage Glenlivet 1977 (86) n22.5 t22.5 f20 b21.** A delicate dram with improbable degrees of citrus for its age. Sadly, the weak strength helps break up the oils and give the bittering oak a much larger say than it deserves. 43%

Gordon & MacPhail Private Collection Glenlivet 1980 (85.5) n21 t23.5 f20 b21. A subdued, slightly soapy number which enjoys its best, toasty moments on delivery and with some honey comb soon after. 48.5%

Gordon & MacPhail Private Collection Glenlivet 1991 (93) n23 apple and pear stew, sweetened only by a thin sprinkling of Demerara sugar; vanilla ice cream with raspberry sauce...; a light but telling oaky spiciness; **t23** mouth-watering malt on delivery enjoying just about perfect weight. The oaks are raring to go, but a light butterscotch and burnt honeycomb middle set up the mocha middle; **f23.5** a ridiculously elegant fade involving gentle nuances of mocha and Demerara...and still some barley...! **b23.5** a faultless bottling, allowing the malt an uninterrupted speech. Probably an independent bottling by which others from this distillery should be measured for the age. *54.5%*

⁘ **Kingsbury Single Cask Series Glenlivet Aged 17 Years** Trois Riviers rum finish **(87.5) n22** almost a Glen Grant brittleness to this with sugar encrusting the bright barley; **t22** pretty sweet delivery with a lovely degree of grassy, salivating sharpness. Again, the sugars are profound; **f21.5** stays on its malty track with the vanillas at last adding weight and a degree of gravitas; **b22** sweet and simplistic, but works rather well. *46%. sc. Japan Import Systems.*

⁘ **Mo Òr Collection Glenlivet 1977 33 Years Old** first fill bourbon hogshead, cask no. 13141, dist 29 Jun 71, bott 2 Dec 10 **(87.5) n20.5** somewhat grizzled with oaky oak. An injection of kumquat keeps the circulation going; **t22** the oak needs no second invitation to shove its wooden foot in the door. Slowly the barley battles back, with a little bit of oil here and fudge there; **f23** at last all the pieces fit together and, with a light chocolate and mint flourish, seems to live happily ever after; **b22** you know when a friendly dog jumps slobberingly all over you? Well it's like that, but with the oak... *46%. nc ncf sc. Release No. 28. 274 bottles.*

⁘ **Old Malt Cask Glenlivet Aged 10 Years** sherry butt, cask no. 8191, dist Sep 01, bott Feb 12 **(89.5) n21.5** an excellent clean sherry butt...but where is the malt? The vanilla whipped ice cream isn't it! **t23** soft and satisfying, the grape enters the fray first and, finally, the barley shows its head, injecting a juicy element alongside the more chewy oak; **f22.5** very late spice and fruity mocha; **b22.5** the kind of malt which, even for its lack of major complexity, makes you inwardly purr... *50%. nc ncf sc. Douglas Laing & Co. 387 bottles.*

⁘ **Old Malt Cask Glenlivet Aged 16 Years** refill butt, cask no. 8214, dist Sep 95, bott Mar 12 **(73.5) n18.5 t19 f18 b18.** The nose tells you what is to come and you won't be disappointed. Or, rather, you will... *50%. nc ncf sc. Douglas Laing & Co. 299 bottles.*

⁘ **Old Malt Cask Glenlivet Aged 19 Years** refill hogshead, cask no. 7609, dist Apr 92, bott Aug 11 **(92) n23.5** the banana and cherry drop aroma is as delightful as it is invigorating; **t23** mouth-watering with those cherries showing early then giving way to spices and vanilla; the barley is always on the prowl; **f22.5** remains chewy forever; the vanilla really doesn't want to leave the stage; **b23** a right little smasher. *50%. nc ncf sc. Douglas Laing & Co. 283 bottles.*

Old Malt Cask Glenlivet Aged 34 Years refill hogshead, cask no. 7192, dist Jun 77, bott Jun 11 **(90.1) n23** honey and citrus ladled into the vanilla. Excellent weight; **t23** the delivery hangs on the richness of the oils. Again honey at the foreground though an undertow of mildly bitter oaks ensures parity. Spices bounce with abandon; **f22** now those peppery spices take command, warming the palate. Still the honey lingers, though: impressive! **b22.5** rarely does a Glenlivet show this degree of honey and spice. Superb. *50%. nc ncf sc. 210 bottles.*

⁘ **Old Malt Cask Glenlivet Aged 34 Years** refill hogshead, cask no. 7734, dist Jun 77, bott Sep 11 **(87) n21.5** a sharp fruity note is dulled by a little distant mustiness; the barley displays a thick core; **t22** the big age is apparent as the oak burrows deep on arrival; tangy and juicy with a refreshing liveliness to the barley; the spices have some major nip and bite; **f21.5** creamy barley and tired oak; **b22** the integrity of the barley has not been breached, but the failing oak ran it close. Still plenty of life left, though. *50%. nc ncf sc. 232 bottles.*

⁘ **Riegger's Selection Glenlivet 1973** bourbon cask, cask no. 10474, dist 10 Dec 73, bott 6 Apr 10 **(94) n24** those who love marmalade on your toast will flock to this one. The barley remains crisp and intact but the citrus, coupled with the light liquorice and hickory, will steal your heart; **t23.5** silky delivery where the barley offers a naked show of its pristine self; the fruits are slower to emerge than on the nose, but do finally make a bow, replaced by creamy mocha; **f23** shy spices confirm the age of the cask yet the barley still offers a juicy freshness; **b23.5** get onto the next flight to Germany. Fast! *475%. nc ncf sc. 127 bottles.*

⁘ **Scotch Malt Whisky Society Cask 2.80 Aged 15 Years** first fill sherry butt, cask no. 71354, dist 1996 **(95.5) n24.5** it is like entering a high class bakers: treacle tart, rhubarb crumble, well-aged fruitcake fortified with sherry and molasses, cinnamon scones...this whisky should be a few thousand calories if the nose is anything to go by; **t23.5** spice on delivery and moving into overdrive in the mid section, but perhaps with not quite the body to match. This is Glenlivet, so it is bound to be juicy one way or another; **f23.5** the weight collects at the finish where those spices dissipate among the black cherry and vanillas; **b24** like the most voluptuous company you prefer to spend an evening with, this has a faultless butt... *60.1%. sc.*

⁘ **Scott's Selection Glenlivet 1977** bott 2012 **(89) n21.5** tired...; some chopped roast hazelnut offers something positive, **t22** just enough sugars left in the tank to soften the spicy, oaky blows; a quick, sharp burst of tangy orange before the oak closes in; **f23** vanilla and Horlicks make for a relaxing finale; **b22.5** teetering on the brink of oaky extinction but somehow finds the personality and complexity to make for an enjoyable dram. *43.8%*

⁙ **Scott's Selection Glenlivet 1978** bott 2012 **(94.5) n23** exotic fruit on cue...; **t24.5** plenty of action on the palate from the very first moment. A beguiling mix of almost clichéd oak notes for the age and region, again putting its weight behind the rich fruit element. But what works so well is this intermingling with fabulous texture and toffee shortcake butteriness; **f23** settles into a much steadier stream of vanilla; **b24** the kind of malt which leaves your taste buds in a state of exhaustion. Perennial motion on the palate. *51.1%. Speyside Distillers.*

Scott's Selection Glenlivet 1980 bott 2011 **(91) n22.5** crystal ginger; some evidence of tired oak, but the barley has a juicy edge, backed up by some serious sugar; **t23** throw back your head and chew for a good five minutes. The spices are spot on, though the oak still has a distinctly aggressive stance. But hints of mocha and butterscotch help settle matters while proud barley thrusts a jutting jaw of muscovado; **f22** pretty long considering the distinct lack of oils; the spices persist; the barley remains governing and almost aloof; **b23.5** I must admit; the nose had me worried. But there was enough sweetness lurking in there somewhere for hope. And my wishes were granted. A charmer which takes you seemingly day by day through every one of its 30 years... *45.5%. Speyside Distillers.*

⁙ **The Whisky Cask Glenlivet Aged 33 Years** bourbon cask, dist 1977, bott 2010 **(94.5) n23.5** a genuine surprise with a distant hint of Arbroath Smokies hanging around the more voluptuous barley notes; the fruity notes are pastel shaded and vulnerable; **t24** mouth-watering barley, but every malt atom carries with it two from the oak cask. There is enough muscovado sugar on hand to smooth out any wrinkles, though; **f23** dries out in time and allows the spices to develop beautifully; long and remains lush for all the oak's best work; **b24** there are some excellent old Glenlivets doing the rounds right now. And this is up there amongst the very best. *56.7%. sc. The Whisky Cask.*

GLENLOCHY
Highlands (Western), 1898–1983. Diageo. Closed.
Rarest of the Rare Glenlochy 1980 cask no. 2454 **(96) n24 t24.5 f23.5 b24.** This does what it says on the tin: this really is the rarest of the rare. I do not often see this stuff either in bottled form or privately through a whisky year. It makes hen's teeth look pretty two-a-penny. But then one must ask the question: why? Any distillery capable of making malt this good should still be working, rather than being turned into a small hotel. (Jim Murray and all at Dram Good Books Ltd would like to assure readers of a nervous disposition that no whisky was spat out during the tasting of this sample.) *54.8%. Duncan Taylor.*

GLENLOSSIE
Speyside, 1876. Diageo. Working.
Glenlossie The Manager's Choice first fill bourbon American oak, cask no. 14098, dist 1999, bott 2009 db **(92.5) n23.5 t23.5 f23 b22.5.** One of the most impressive examples of Speyside malt, apparently not even out of nappies but treating you to a spectacular display of barley in all its beauty. Confirmation, barely needed, that with Clynelish, this has to be Diageo's most under-rated distillery. *59.1%. 207 bottles.*

Berry's Own Selection Glenlossie 1975 cask no. 5951, bott 2010 **(87.5) n22 t22 f22 b21.5.** Worth some serious time to enjoy. But please accept the wrinkles of great age. *49.7%. nc ncf sc.*

Hart Brothers Glenlossie Aged 11 Years dist Nov 98, bott Oct 10 **(88.5) n22.5 t22 f22 b22.** A beautiful vehicle for the distillery to show its elegance. *46%. sc.*

⁙ **Liquid Sun Glenlossie 36 Years Old** refill sherry cask, dist 1975, bott 2011 **(86) n22.5 t22 f20.5 b21.** The line between greatness and just very good is a pretty fine one in whisky. Just a single summer can represent the border. This, though, has crossed four or five. The charm of the orange and lime aroma and delivery is there for all to see; the excellence of the oils is also a triumph. And the spices, layered with praline, really do delight. But the over-aging takes its toll somewhat on the finish and balance. *48.3%. sc. The Whisky Agency.*

⁙ **The Maltman Glenlossie Aged 19 Years** bourbon cask, cask no. 18232, dist Jul 78, bott Jun 97 **(84) n21 t22 f20 b21.** Time warp whisky: this has taken an age to get onto the shelves, having been bottled back in 1997 but just released from bond. Was it worth the wait? Well, don't expect a rip-roaring Lossie: this is pretty tame stuff and, though non-coloured I'm told, there is a bit of old-fashioned toffee here - in this case obviously from the cask. *43%. nc ncf sc. Meadowside Blending Co.*

⁙ **Malts Of Scotland Glenlossie 1975** bourbon hogshead, cask no. MoS11022, bott Nov 11 **(91.5) n22.5** dank stinging nettles, earthy, a hint of pine yet enlivened by acacia honey and suet pudding; **t23.5** much sweeter on the palate. The spices bombard from the first moment, then sugars re-establish themselves with the lazy muscovado weight; **f22.5** dries as those spices continue to attack; the vanilla retains a light citrus edge; just a few waves of mocha

...ompletes the experience; **b23** intense and busy, the quality of the whisky is never in doubt. All this fun and aggro and undisguised brilliance without a single peaty particle in sight. There are those out there who will refuse to believe it. 49.8%. nc ncf sc. Malts Of Scotland.

⁘ **Old Malt Cask Glenlossie Aged 18 Years** refill butt, cask no. 7789, dist Sep 93, bott Jan 12 **(91)** n22 one fancies one can almost detect a distant hint of smoke...no doubting the spice and less than brilliant oak, though...; **t23** much more clarity on the delivery where the barley rings through as clear as the ring on a crystal tasting glass; **f23** remains mouth-watering and beautifully sweet; **b23** outrageously juicy. 50%. Douglas Laing & Co. 416 bottles.

⁘ **Scotch Single Malt Circle Glenlossie 1984** cask no. 2534, dist 4 Oct 84, bott 24 Feb 10 **(88.5)** n23 it is though the cask has been left to lie in the Dead Sea for a few years; some bourbony tannins; **t22.5** when next in my kitchen I will blend some honey and salt together and see if I can recreate this; tart yet strangely attractive; **f21** a long wind-down of various honey and salt residues...; **b22** forget about the strength. The abruptness of this whisky stems from its extraordinary reliance on all things salty. 60%. sc. Scotch Single Malt Circle.

GLEN MHOR
Highlands (Northern), 1892–1983. Diageo. Demolished.
Glen Mhor 1976 Rare Malt db **(92.5)** n23 **t24** f22 **b23.5**. You just dream of truly great whisky sitting in your glass from time to time. But you don't expect it, especially from such an old cask. This was the best example from this distillery I've tasted in 30 years...until the Glenkeir version was unleashed! If you ever want to see a scotch that has stretched the use of oak as far it will go without detriment, here it is. What a pity the distillery has gone because the Mhor the merrier... 52.2%

Glen Mhor Private Collection 1966 (91) n23.5 thick, toasty oak seasoned further by a touch of salt; not quite piny, but thinking about it. There is a pretty impressive marmalade on burnt toast in the next room quality about it and, as it oxidises, the natural caramels begin to have a presence; very late on into oxidisation we enter sumptuous date and walnut territory; **t23** sharp, juicy delivery then massive amounts of silky caramels keep an oaky undertow at bay; relatively simplistic but a few dates and walnuts to be had relatively early on; **f22** some residual bitterness, but still the caramels dominate; **b22.5** the trick with any very old whisky is that you must give them time to be themselves. After being cooped up for years in oak and then glass, it takes time for them to come fully alive: a classic case in point here. Virtually undrinkable upon opening the bottle to being a treat, if of limited complexity, after 20 minutes in the glass. These guys are so rare I don't honestly expect to come across another one distilled in the 60s that will give me much more than this. Sad, as one of my first experiences in the Scottish whisky shop, in the mid 70s, involved a guy trying to sell me a bottle of G&M Glen Mhor. The Glen Mhor are getting less. And lesser... 45%. Gordon & MacPhail.

⁘ **Mo Òr Collection Glen Mhor 1975 34 Years Old** first fill bourbon hogshead, cask no. 4036, dist 31 Dec 85, bott 3 Nov 10 **(94)** n23.5 not sure what I love most: the happy integration of the barley and oaky vanilla after all these years. Or the playful, now you see it, now you don't, nature of the peat. Add to that the oranges and nutty cocoa and you really have something of rare beauty; **t23.5** so soft and silky: the barley and muscovado sugars form a procession and serene enough to embrace the intense yet never burdensome oak; the spices are little more than an afterthought; **f23** butterscotch sprinkled with a lightly salted oakiness and mildly sugared barley; the mouth-feel remains almost glass-like while the mocha is little more than a very delicious whisper; **b24** it has been a very long time since I have found a Glen Mhor in such fine fettle and so in tune with itself. I suspect there are very few like these remaining... 43.3%. nc ncf sc. Release No. 10. The Whisky Talker. 170 bottles.

GLENMORANGIE
Highlands (Northern), 1843. Glenmorangie Plc. Working.
Glenmorangie 10 Years Old db **(94)** n24 perhaps the most enigmatic aroma of them all: delicate yet assertive, sweet yet dry, young yet oaky: a malty tone poem; **t22** flaky oakiness throughout but there is an impossibly complex toastiness to the barley which seems to suggest the lightest hint of smoke; **f24** amazingly long for such a light dram, drying from the initial sweetness but with flaked almonds amid the oakier, rich cocoa notes; **b24** you might find the occasional "orange variant", where the extra degree of oak, usually from a few too many first-fill casks, has flattened out the more extreme peaks and toughs of complexity (scores abou 89). But these are pretty rare – almost a collector's item – and overall this remains one of t' great single malts: a whisky of uncompromising aesthetic beauty from the first enigmatic w to the last teasing and tantalising gulp. Complexity at its most complex. 40%

Glenmorangie 15 Years Old db **(90.5)** n23 chunky and fruity: something distinctly candy about this one; the barley's no slouch, either; and, just to raise the eyebrows, j' faintest waft of something smoky...; **t23** silky, a tad sultry, and serious interplay betw‹

and barley; a real, satisfying juiciness to this one; **f22** dries towards the oaky side of things, but just a faint squeeze of liquorice adds extra weight; **b22.5** exudes quality. *43%*

Glenmorangie 15 Years Old Sauternes Wood Finish db (68) n16 t18 f17 b17. I had hoped – and expected – an improvement on the sulphured version I came across last time. Oh, whisky! Why are you such a cruel mistress...? *46%*

Glenmorangie 18 Years Old db (91) **n22** pleasant if unconvincing spotted dick; **t23** sharp, eye-watering mix of fruit and mainly honeyed barley; nutty and, with the confident vanillas, forming a breakfast cereal completeness; **f23** Cocoa Krispies; **b23** having thrown off some previous gremlins, now a perfect start to the day whisky... *43%*

Glenmorangie 25 Years Old db (95.5) **n24** it's strap yourself in time: this is a massive nose with more layers, twists and turns than you can shake a thief at. Soft, mildly lush Lubec marzipan is sandwiched between fruit bonbons and myriad barley tones. Worth taking half an hour over this one, and no kidding... **t24** the clarity on the nose is matched here. Every single wave of flavour is there in crystal form, starting, naturally, with the barley but this is soon paired with various unidentified fruits. The result is salivation. Towards the middle the oak shows form and does so in various cocoa-tinged ways; every nuance is delicately carved, almost fragile, but the overall picture is one of strength; **f23.5** medium length with the cocoa heading towards medium roast Java **b24** every bit as statesmanlike and elegant as a whisky of this age from such a blinding distillery should be. Ticks every single box for a 25-year-old and is Morangie's most improved malt by the distance of Tain to Wellingborough. There is a hint of genius with each unfolding wave of flavours with this one: a whisky that will go in 99/100 whisky lover's top 50 malts of all time. And that includes the Peatheads. *43%*

Glenmorangie 30 Years Old db (72) **n17** t18 f19 b18. From the evidence in the glass the jury is out on whether it has been spruced up a little in a poor sherry cask – and spruce is the operative word: lots of pine on this wrinkly. *44.1%*

Glenmorangie Vintage 1975 db (89) **n23** clementines! It must be Christmas...; **t23** improbably clean malt for something so aged, then a layer or three of fruit and spiced vanilla; **f21** bitters out as an oaky trench is found; **b22** a charming, fruity and beautifully spiced oldie. *43%*

Glenmorangie 1977 db (92) **n24 t23 f22 b23.** Excellent, but a trifle underpowered...what would this have been like at 46%...??? Shows little of its great age as the oak is always subservient to the sweet barley and citrus. *43%. Exclusively at Harrods.*

Glenmorangie Pride 1981 dist Oct 81, bott 2010, Sauternes barrique db (77.5) **n18 t22 f18 b19.5.** The Pride before a fall...? I know that gifted blender Bill Lumsden feels that a touch of sulphur can sometimes bring good to a dram. He and I share many similar views on whisky. But here we very much part company. For me, sulphur is a fault. Nothing more. Nothing less. The entire reason for stills to be made from copper is so sulphur compounds can be removed. So by adding them back in, as they obviously have here via the barriques, can be nothing other than a negative step. Perhaps I am at fault for having a zero tolerance on sulphur. But when, for me, it spoils the nose, muddies the middle and bitters the finish, how can I do anything other than judge accordingly? The tragedy here is that it is obvious that some astonishing elements are at play. Even through the bitter haze I could detect some gorgeous honey and glazed fruits and stems; so excellent, in fact, that for a few brief moments the faults are silenced. But that is only a respite. Those unable to spot sulphur, through smoking or their DNA, will doubtless find much to enjoy and wonder why I have marked this down. But I cannot join the general back-slapping on this whisky. I have been told that someone has suggested the sulphur on this soon goes away. It doesn't: it never does – that is absolutely ridiculous. And why some whisky critics can't nose sulphur is beyond me. About as useful as a wine writer unable to spot a corked wine; or a music critic unable to hear the cello playing in entirely the wrong key. Sorry. But I have to be the sole dissenting voice on this one. *56.7%*

⋰ **Glenmorangie Artein Private Edition** db (94) **n24** it's the spices that get you: at first you don't quite notice them. Then you realise there is a background buzz, like peppers slyly added to a gazpacho soup, and there is a slight tomato fruitiness, too; the sweetness is a subtle combination of maple syrup and molten Mars Bars; **t23.5** that sweetness arrives early but in very diluted form and refuses to overtake the barley sugar and chocolate raisin; **f23** the spices on the nose return for the finale which sit deliciously with the malt-nougat fade; **b23.5** if someone has gone out of their way to create probably the softest Scotch single malt of the year, then they have succeeded. *46%. ncf.*

Glenmorangie Artisan Casks db (93) **n23 t23.5 f23 b23.5.** If whisky could be sexed, this ▊uld be a woman. Every time I encounter Morangie Artisan, it pops up with a new look, ▊fferent perfume. And mood. It appears not to be able to make up its mind. But does it ▊w how to pout, seduce and win your heart...? Oh yes. *46%*

▊nmorangie Astar** db (88) **n21 t23 f22.5 b22.** Decidedly strange malt: for quite a while ▊ if someone has extracted the barley and left everything else behind. A star is born? perhaps. But perhaps a new breed of single malt. *571%*

Glenmorangie Burgundy Wood Finish db **(72) n17.5 t19.5 f18 b18.** Sulphured whisky de table. 43%

Glenmorangie Burr Oak Reserve db **(92) n24 t24 f22 b22.** Fades on the finish as a slightly spent force, but nose and arrival are simply breathtaking. Wouldn't be out of place in Kentucky. 56.3%

Glenmorangie Cellar 13 Ten Years Old db **(88.5) n22 t22.5 f22 b22** oh, if only I could lose weight as efficiently as this appears to have done... oh, I have! My love and thanks to Nancy, Nigel and Ann Marie. 43%

Glenmorangie Elegance db **(92) n22** quite herbal and soothing; **t24** the thinnest layer of icing sugar coats the silk-soft malt; every bit as gentle as the nose suggests; **f22** medium to short with some attractive rolling vanilla; **b24** a surprise package that is not entirely dissimilar to the Golden Rum, only a tad sweeter. 43%

Glemorangie Finealta db **(84.5) n21 t22 f20.5 b21.** Plump and thick, one of the creamiest malts around. For what it lacks in fine detail it makes up for in effect, especially the perky oaky spices. 46%

Glenmorangie Lasanta sherry casks db **(68.5) n16 t19 f16 b17.5.** The sherry problem has increased dramatically rather than being solved. 46%

Glenmorangie Madeira Wood Finish db **(78) n19.5 t20.5 f19 b19.** One of the real problems with wine finishes is getting the point of balance right when the fruit, barley and oak are in harmony. Here it is on a par with me singing in the shower, though frankly my aroma would be a notch or two up. 43%

Glenmorangie Margaux Cask Finish db **(88) n22 t22 f22 b22.** Even taking every whisky with an open mind, I admit this was better than my subconscious might have considered. Certainly better than the near undrinkable Ch. Margaux '57 I used to bring out for my birthday each year some 20-odd years ago... 46%

Glenmorangie Nectar D'or Sauternes Finish db **(94) n23** delicate cinnamon on toast and a drizzle of greengage and sultana; **t24** refreshing and dense on the palate as the bitter sweet battle goes into overdrive; excellent weight and body; **f23** remains clean and precise, allowing some custard onto the apple strudel finale; **b24** great to see French casks that actually complement a whisky – so rare! This has replaced the Madeira finish. But there are some similar sweet-fruit characteristics. An exercise in outrageously good sweet-dry balancing 46%

Glenmorangie Quinta Ruban Port Finish db **(92) n24** typical Morangie complexity, the grape notes added act almost like a prism to show their varied hues; **t23** fruit and spice about as the oak goes in search of glory: barley stands in its way; **f22** light, deftly sweetened and juicy to the end; **b23** this replacement of the original Port finish shows a genuine understanding of the importance of grape-oak balance. Both are portrayed with clarity and confidence. This is a form of cask finishing that has progressed from experimentation to certainty. 46%

Glenmorangie Sherry Wood Finish db **(84) n23 t21 f20 b20.** Stupendous clean sherry nose, then disappoints with a somewhat bland display on the palate. 43%

Glenmorangie Signet db **(80.5) n20 t21.5 f19 b20.** A great whisky holed below the waterline by oak of unsatisfactory quality. Tragic. 46%

Glenmorangie Sonnalta PX db **(96.5) n24** now this works: has that heavy-handed feel of a sweet sherry butt (or five) at work here, usually the kiss of death for so many whiskies. But an adroit praline sub-plot really does the trick. So with the malt evident, too, we have a three-pronged attack which somehow meshes in to one. And not even the merest hint of an off-note...goodness gracious· a new experience...!!! **t24** Neanderthal grape drags its knuckles along the big vanilla floor before a really subtle light Columbian coffee kick puts us back on course; sharper vanillas from some awkward oak threatens to send us off course again but somehow it finds a settled, common ground; **f24.5** now goes into orgasmic overdrive as Demerara sugar is tipped into some gorgeous, cream-lightened mocha. This is obviously to wash down the Melton Hunt cake which is resplendent in its grape and roast nut finery. It is the perfect whisky finish... **b24** remains a giant among the tall stills. A mesmeric whisky... 46%

Glenmorangie Traditional db **(90.5) n22** orange blossom, barley sugar and chalk dust; **t23** delicate delivery revelling in gentle complexity: really playful young-ish malt makes for a clean start and middle; **f22.5** soft mocha notes play out a quiet finish; **b23** an improved dram with much more to say, but does so quietly. 57.1%

Glenmorangie Truffle Oak db **(96) n24 t24 f25 b23.** The Glenmorangie of all Glenmorangies. I really have to work hard and deep into the night to find fault with it. If I am going to be hyper-critical, I'll dock it a mark for being so constantly sweet, though in its defence I have to say that the degree of sweetness alters with astonishing dexterity. Go on, it's Truffle oak: make a pig of yourself...!! 60.5%

Scotch Malt Whisky Society Cask 125.43 Aged 18 Years 1st fill bourbon hogshead, cask no. 10895, dist 1991 **(88) n24 t23 f19 b22.** The barrel type is never in dispute: more bourbon notes than Scotch ones... 54.6%. sc. 140 bottles.

Scotch Malt Whisky Society Cask 125.47 Aged 15 Years 1st fill hogshead, cask no. 13230, dist 1995 **(91) n23.5** a sharp barley edge pierces the natural caramels; a number of pre-bourbon notes become pure bourbon as it oxidises..; **t22.5** mouth-watering, as that sharpness on the nose foretells; a lovely build up of spices dazzle; **f22.5** remains spicy despite the chewy vanilla and light hickory; **b22.5** a delightful malt that may also impress diehard Kentuckians. *56.1%. sc. 310 bottles.*

Scotch Malt Whisky Society Cask 125.49 Aged 9 Years refill Burgundy barrique, cask no. 12210, dist 2001 **(84) n21.5 t21 f20.5 b21.** A bitter-sweet affair. *60.8%. sc. 282 bottles.*

⊹⊱ **Scotch Malt Whisky Society Cask 125.50 Aged 12 Years** dechar/toasted hogshead, cask no. 13056, dist 1998 **(92) n22.5** heavy with bourbony sugars and vanillas; **t24** deliciously sweet delivery and much thicker bodied than the norm for this distillery. The slow spice development works in harmony with the budding vanilla; **f22.5** soft vanilla ice cream...with a dry wafer...; **b23** well, that extracted most of the sugars out of that cask! *50.5%. sc.*

⊹⊱ **Scotch Malt Whisky Society Cask 125.52 Aged 10 Years** first fill hogshead, cask no. 2948, dist 2001 **(89) n22** nutty; some drier wafer, too; **t23** what a distillery this is: hardly gets out of second gear, withsheer simplicity and magnificent texture to the barley; **f22** vanilla and mocha; **b22** for a first fill 'Morangie, a real easy goer. *60%. sc. Scotch Malt Whisky Society.*

⊹⊱ **Scotch Malt Whisky Society Cask 125.53 Aged 14 Years** first fill designer hogshead, cask no. 8093, dist 1997 **(84.5) n22.5 t22 f20 b21.** One of those noses which evolves slowly and takes time to unravel. But also one of those malts where the cask just does no favours to the development on the palate. *55.3%. sc. Scotch Malt Whisky Society.*

⊹⊱ **Scotch Malt Whisky Society Cask 125.54 Aged 9 Years** refill hogshead, cask no. 12209, dist 2001 **(85.5) n21.5 t22 f21 b21.** Fruity. And fat. But, for all its power, a long way from firing on all cylinders. *61.4%. sc. Scotch Malt Whisky Society.*

⊹⊱ **Scotch Malt Whisky Society Cask 125.56 Aged 8 Years** first fill barrel, cask no. 1703, dist 2003 **(86) n21.5 t22 f21 b21.5.** You roll with the spicy punches with this one. A fascinating look at a Morangie under ten years trying to cope with the richness of a first fill barrel. A slightly unequal battle, as the barley is swamped. *60.8%. sc.*

⊹⊱ **Scotch Malt Whisky Society Cask 125.57 Aged 11 Years** first fill barrel, cask no. 1396, dist 2000 **(84) n21 t22 f20 b21.** Not surprised by the late bitterness which throws a wobbly on the overall balance as the nose foretold of this malt. *55.4%. sc. Scotch Malt Whisky Society.*

⊹⊱ **Scotch Malt Whisky Society Cask 125.61 Aged 10 Years** refill hogshead, cask no. 12207, dist 2001 **(88) n22** a big wave of curiously tight sugars, some of which take different paths into mildly fruity territory; **t23** the enormity of the sugars on delivery almost pin you back in your chair; a vague fruitiness hovers; **f21** a degree of blood orange bitterness; **b22** a real mixed bag of a malt very far removed from the classic 10-year-old distillery bottling. *61%. sc.*

GLEN MORAY
Speyside, 1897. La Martiniquaise. Working.

Glen Moray Classic 8 Years Old db **(86) n20 t22 f21 b23.** A vast improvement on previous bottlings with the sluggish fatness replaced by a thinner, barley-rich, slightly sweeter and more precise mouthfeel. *40%*

Glen Moray 10 Years Old Chardonnay Matured db **(73.5) n18.5 t19 f18 b18.** Tighter than a wine cork. *40%*

Glen Moray 12 Years Old db **(90) n22.5** gentle malt of varying pitch and intensity; **t22** a duller start than it should be with the vanilla diving in almost before the barley but the juicy, grassy notes arrive in good time; **f23** long, back on track with intense malt and the custardy oak is almost apologetic but enlivened with a dash of lime: mmmmm... pure Glen Moray! **b22.5** I have always regarded this as the measuring stick by which all other malty and clean Speysiders should be tried and tested. It is still a fabulous whisky, full of malty intricacies. Something has fallen off the edge, perhaps, but minutely so. Still think a trick or two is being missed by bottling this at 40%: the natural timbre of this malt demands 46% and no less.... *40%*

Glen Moray 16 Years Old db **(74) n19 t19 f18 b19.** A serious dip in form. Drab. *40%*

Glen Moray 16 Years Old Chenin Blanc Mellowed in Wine Barrels db **(85) n20 t22 f22 b21.** A fruity, oak-shaded dram just brimming with complexity. *40%*

Glen Moray 20 Years Old db **(80) n22 t22 f18 b18.** With so much natural cream toffee, it is hard to believe that this has so many years on it. After a quick, refreshing start it pans out, if anything, a little dull. *40%*

Glen Moray 30 Years Old db **(92.5) n23.5** it's probably the deftness of the old-fashioned Speyside smoke in tandem with the structured fruits that makes this so special; **t23.5** for a light Speysider, the degree of barley to oak is remarkable: soft, oil-gilde d barley is met by a wonderful, if brief, spice prickle; **f22.5** deft layering of vanilla and cocoa; a sprinkle of muscovado sugar repels any darker oak notes; **b23** for all its years, this is comfortable malt, untroubled by time. There is no mistaking quality. *43%*

Glen Moray 1959 Rare Vintage db **(91) n25 t23 f21 b22.** They must have been keeping their eyes on this one for a long time: a stunning malt that just about defies nature. The nose reaches absolute perfection. *50.9%*

Glen Moray 1962 Very Rare Vintage Aged 42 Years db **(94) n23 t24 f23 b24.** The first temptation is to think that this has succumbed to age, but a second and a third tasting reveal that there is much more complexity, integrity and balance to this than first meets the tastebuds. The last cask chosen by the legendary Ed Dodson before his retirement from the distillery: a pretty perceptive choice. A corker! *50.9%. sc.*

Glen Moray 1984 db **(83) n20 t22 f20 b21.** Mouthwatering and incredibly refreshing malt for its age. *40%*

Glen Moray 1989 db **(86) n23 t22 f20 b21.** Doesn't quite live up to the fruit smoothie nose but I'm being a little picky here. *40%*

Glen Moray 1992 Single Cask No 1441 sherry butt db **(74) n17 t21 f18 b18.** Oops! Didn't anyone spot the sulphur...? *59.6%*

Glen Moray 1995 Port Wood Finish bott Dec 09 db **(95.5) n23** a surprising liquorice base to the healthy spiced fruit; **t24** vivid grape: clean, intense and, for a while, dominant. The oak surges back with a few tricks of its own, the most impressive being a liquorice-hickory thrust and a soothing custardy topping. Meanwhile, the grape offers spice and a sheen; **f24.5** a wonderful array of spicy chocolate and raisin notes that appear to continue indefinitely. Needs to be tasted to be believed. **b24** possibly the most satisfying wine finish of the year. *56.7%*

Glen Moray 1995 Single Sherry Cask sherry butt db **(56) n15 t14 f13 b14.** So stunned was I about the abject quality of this bottling, I even looked on the Glen Moray website to see if they had said anything about it. Apparently, if you add water you find on the nose "the lingering soft sulphury smoke of a struck match." Well, here's the news: you don't need water. Just open the bottle and there's Rotorua in all it's stink bomb finery. And errr,..hullo, guys... some further news: that means it's a bloody faulty, useless cask. And has no right to be put anywhere near a bottling hall let alone set loose in a single bottling. This, quite frankly, is absolutely rank whisky, the type of which makes my blood boil. I mean, is this really the best cask that could be found in the entire and considerable estate of Glen Moray..???? Am I, or is it the whisky world going mad...? *59.6%*

Glen Moray 2001 Single Chenin Blanc Cask cask no. 1839 db **(74.5) n19 t19 f18 b18.5.** I have to be honest: if I was going to mature a malt in a French wine cask, I would be a little - no, make that very - nervous. And here's why. A real battle between stupendous grape which boasts almost a perfection of sugars and a barrel which is typically flawed. People in different parts of the world may view this whisky with enormous fluctuation in the results. *60.7%. sc.*

Glen Moray Classic db **(86.5) n22 t21.5 f21.5 b21.5.** The nose is the star with a wonderful, clean barley-fruit tandem, but what follows cannot quite match its sure-footed wit. *40%*

Glen Moray Wine Cask Edition bott Sep 09 db **(83.5) n20 t23 f20 b20.5.** When in full flow this is just bursting with some of the juiciest fruit you are likely to encounter. But a familiar bitter buzz brings down the value. How sad. *59.7%*

⬩⬩ **Berry's Own Selection Glen Moray 1991** cask no. 5654, bott 2012 **(95) n23** a lovely intertwining of polished oaky floors and muscovado-polished barley; **t24.5** deliveries on the palate rarely come more delicious than this: Glen Moray, when on form, is in the true malty elite of Scotland and here it tops the Premier League. The blend of sugars, some honeyed, spices and cocoa make you groan with pleasure; **f23.5** the vanilla and butterscotch kick in as you suspect they might. But the barley remains steadfast and clean; **b24** I have long regarded Berry's whisky buyer Dougie McIvor one of the genuinely understated gems of the industry and the best whisky writer we never had. Here he demonstrates his understanding of clean, barley-rich malts which has made this year's crop of Berry's Own Selection arguably their best yet. When you taste this you can see why I exploded in rage at the deficiencies of the official "Distillery Manager" bottling a few years back... *573%. nc ncf sc. Berry Bros & Rudd.*

⬩⬩ **Duncan Taylor Dimensions Glen Moray 20 Years Old** cask no. 9408, dist 1991 **(88.5) n22.5** finely balanced with the saltiness bringing just enough out of the oak to lighten the weight; **t22.5** the sugars show few inhibitions here; juicy despite some obvious age; **f22** the oak catches up again; **b22** an understated dram. *54.8%. sc. Duncan Taylor & Co.*

⬩⬩ **Duncan Taylor Dimensions Glen Moray 24 Years Old** cask no. 2311, dist Sep 86, bott Dec 11 **(90.5) n23** huge bourbon footprint; that's if you get footprints on the nose; **t23** brown sugar notes swamp the taste buds. The spices appear to have a muscovado edge. The chocolate liquorice is sublime, as is the salivating lime; usually barley is prevalent with Glen Moray: here it is peripheral; **f22** custard tart and icing sugar carries out the farewells; **b22.5** Glen Moray at its most confident and forceful. *51.6%. nc ncf sc. Duncan Taylor & Co.*

⬩⬩ **Duncan Taylor Octave Glen Moray 24 Years Old** cask no. 701120, dist 1986 **(93) n23.5** astonishing esters: a degree of Jamaican pot still rum sweetness to this, especially so far as those spiced honeys are concerned; **t23** rum again! I am in a Jamaican warehouse...actually I'm not: I am in England and hailstones are thumping against my window. Those spices, just like on the nose, infuse with fabulous evenness; **f23** that coppery edge lasts to the very end; **b23.5** I have tasted many Glen Morays in my time: indeed, this was the first distillery I took my son, James, to in 1987 when he was just six months old. But I have never quite experienced one with such a feel of the West Indies. The Octave in question must have been penned by Bob Marley. *50.2%. sc. Duncan Taylor & Co.*

⁙ **Duncan Taylor Rare Auld Glen Moray 24 Years Old** cask no. 2306, dist 1986 **(90.5) n23.5** a lovely cross between butterscotch and bluebells, aided by a delicate earthiness softened by a light spreading of honey; **t23** spot-on weight with the barley displaying a dual role of softness and crispness while a tiny dollop of maple syrup goes a long way; **f21.5** fades just a little too quickly as the vanillas offer a burnt toast finale; **b22.5** a deluxe and hugely enjoyable blueprint for the better Glen Morays distilled during this period. *51.7%. sc.*

⁙ **Malts Of Scotland Glen Morey 1977** bourbon hogshead, cask no. MoS12021, dist Oct 77, bott Apr 12 **(91.5) n23.5** the highlight of the experience: ripe peaches and some underlying avocado; big, big age on the oak, but so deftly done!; **t23** and this underlined on the lime, fig and black cherry delivery. The latter note is normally associated with sherry, but not here. The mid ground lessens in puckering intensity and is happy to concentrate on the intense malt and butterscotch; **f22.5** more lightly oiled malt. And vanilla; **b22.5** now listen guys. As a Murray, whose name most probably originated from this region a great many centuries ago, may I just ask that you spell Moray correctly on your labels?! Anyway, while your spelling may be crap, your ability to pick a superb cask is not in doubt. *52.1%. nc ncf sc. Malts Of Scotland.*

⁙ **Mo Òr Collection Glen Moray 1971 39 Years Old** first fill bourbon hogshead, cask no. 5, dist 11 Oct 71, bott 21 Jan 11 **(93) n24** varying layers of citrus and a surprising dash of apple. There is also a quite beautiful date and walnut sponge here, too. The barley keeps its integrity despite a tendency to veer off in a Kentucky direction; the oak isn't exactly of a retiring nature; **t23** fingers of sugar-coated liquorice tease the taste buds as thickening oils inject a full barley personality; **f23** even and benefits from the late butterscotch; **b23** so teasingly bourbony, they could re-name it Knob Moray... *46%. nc ncf sc. Release No. 11. The Whisky Talker. 429 bottles.*

⁙ **Mo Òr Collection Glen Moray 1989 21 Years Old** first fill bourbon hogshead, cask no. 7277, dist 24 Oct 89, bott 24 Oct 10 **(82.5) n21 t21 f20.5 b20.** The barley sugar is eclipsed by a dull but persistent bitterness. *46%. nc ncf sc. Release No. 49. The Whisky Talker. 419 bottles.*

Old Malt Cask Glen Moray Aged 19 Years refill hogshead, cask no. 6637, dist Oct 91, bott Oct 10 **(87) n21.5 t22.5 f21 b22.** This malt and I have a lot in common. Firstly, it is where us Murrays get our name. And it also appears a lot younger than it actually is... *50%. nc ncf sc.*

⁙ **Provenance Glen Moray Over 11 Years** refill hogshead, cask no. 6816, dist Autumn 99, bott Autumn 2010 **(89) n22 t23 f22 b22.** Don't bother looking for meaningful mouthfuls and hidden depth. This is simply rollicking malt, of the very simplest kind. Fabulous quality eschewing complexity for effect. Lively and luscious...love it!! *46%. nc ncf sc.*

⁙ **Provenance Glen Moray Over 11 Years** refill hogshead, cask no. 7603, dist Spring 2000, bott Summer 2011 **(85.5) n22.5 t21 f21 b21.** Clean, youthful and with a few spices up its sleeve. *46%. nc ncf sc. Douglas Laing & Co.*

Rare Auld Glen Moray 24 Years Old cask no. 2858, dist 1986 **(91.5) n22** excellent marriage between lively salts and wonderfully grassy, invigorating barley; **t23** puckering sharpness on delivery, then a slow striptease of the barley, slowly revealing its naked self; **f23.5** long, with the saline nose returning for a big but beautifully proportioned finale. The barley remains clean and profound; **b23** brimming with juicy life: a sheer joy! *55.6%. sc. Duncan Taylor & Co.*

Rare Auld Glen Moray 37 Years Old dist 1973, cask no. 7050 **(92) n23.5.** any grapier and you would have to buy the whisky by the bunch... just love the cinnamon swirl on the apple crumble; **t24** the grape plasters itself around the palate and clings to it like a tart to a millionaire; a beautiful, if slightly furtive, blood orange injection causes a welcome degree of salivation; **f21.5** spent oak and burnt fruitcake going back into the oven... **b23** technically, so many things not quite right. But bollocks to that: sometimes you have to let your hair get blown in the wind and savour the rough with the smooth. A minor Speyside gem...for those who can see it. Oh, and a classic for nosing the empty glass first thing in the morning... The 500th whisky tasted for the 2012 Bible and it was a fitting choice. *49.3%. sc. Duncan Taylor & Co.*

Scotch Malt Whisky Society Cask 35.44 Aged 35 Years refill hogshead, cask no. 84, dist 1975 **(82) n19 t21 f20 b21.** Ancient, impenetrable forests of oak on the nose; some pleasing sugars fight a rearguard action. I doubt if the people who made this whisky saw it being bottled as a 34-year-old single malt, simply as I know they never felt it had the legs. For all its big neo-bourbon mannerisms and crude attempts towards a sugary-citrussy greatness, you can perhaps see why. *55%. sc. 167 bottles.*

Scotch Malt Whisky Society Cask 35.50 Aged 47 Years refill hogshead, cask no. 174, dist 1962 **(92.5) n23** some shy barley notes pop their head above the oaky parapet. If anyone remembers their wooden school floors being sandpapered and then polished (probably at exactly the same time this whisky was being made) will recognise the effect...; **t24** a pretty polished performance on delivery, too: heads towards a beautiful light honeycomb status but the toastiness is delayed by the slow dissolving of a mixing of icing and muscovado sugars; the vanilla filling the midground is acceptably sawdusty; **f22.5** surprisingly long, given the distinct lack of oils. Hints of bitterness remain just that while the vanilla intensity is turned up a notch; **b23** not often the SMWS come up with something quite as old as this and pretty unusual for a Glen Moray to remain intact after so many Elgin winters. Not exactly unscathed, but it wears its oaky scars with pride: an Elgin Marvel... *40%. sc. 201 bottles.*

Scotch Malt Whisky Society Cask 35.52 Aged 34 Years refill hogshead, cask no. 1259/3, dist 1976 **(93.5) n22.5** some heavyweight citrus sometimes appears crushed under the weight of the oak. Some oxidization though manages to help forge a fragile balance; **t24** rare for a Glen Moray to show this degree of juiciness at such age; the barley flexes its muscles but the butterscotch and vanillas reveal equal stamina; the spices and light, granular honey tones embark on a journey of setting right some oaky wrongs; **f23.5** long, some excellent late oils, and the return of some eye-watering citrus notes to thin the vanillas; **b23.5** there is a lightness of touch here which manages to keep the greatest excesses of the oak at bay and actually formulates a surprisingly well structured dram. Requires at least 20 minutes in the glass to open and relax, though, before drinking. Not a distillery which openly embraces great age. But when it gets it right, has the ability to totally astonish. *52.3%. sc. 110 bottles.*

Scotch Malt Whisky Society Cask 35.54 Aged 11 Years 1st fill bourbon barrel, cask no. 4474, dist 1999 **(95.5) n23.5** lovely sandalwood plus light spices; someone appears to come up with just the right degree of salt to add to malt; **t24** several layers of barley with varying degree of maple syrup; the star quality is ensured by the near perfection to the weight and oils; the spicing could not be bettered while the light saline quality draws out and amplifies the considerable complexity to the midground; **f24** long and makes every atom of oak count; honey spread over digestive biscuit **b24** such a bottling shows exactly why for the last quarter of a century I have greatly prized this malt... Flawless. *57%. sc. 245 bottles.*

Scotch Malt Whisky Society Cask 35.55 Aged 39 Years refill hogshead, cask no. 1163/1, dist 1971 **(82) n20 t21 f20.5 b20.5.** Hangs on with grim death to the last vestiges of life. The over-oaked nose is clear statement of intent and just enough natural sugars from the hoggy survive, though its overall balance and integrity suffers. *50.3%. sc. 278 bottles.*

Scotch Malt Whisky Society Cask 35.58 Aged 26 Years refill butt, cask no. 31091, dist 1984 **(93.5) n24** dreamy complexity: the lightness of touch of the lime and tangerine notes takes some believing. All the delicacy of the very lightest of fruit sponge cakes; **t24** so no surprise that the delivery should be equally as deft: the malt merely kisses the taste buds while the even lighter, powdered sugars land like snowflakes; **f22.5** just slightly heavy with the vanilla by comparison and the faintest degree of bitterness; **b23** effortless elegance. *41%. sc.*

Scotch Malt Whisky Society Cask 35.59 Aged 39 Years refill hogshead, cask no. 1571, dist 1971 **(87) n22** kumquats and dry marmalade spread over burnt toast; **t22.5** the delivery is the high point of the experience as the barley simply melts into the palate taking with it myriad sugar notes: for a while the over-aged oak is too stunned to take action... **f21**...though it finally does towards the finish; **b21.5** in reality, over-the-top oak from a cask aged maybe five or six years too many. But some of the jewels on display are quite dazzling. *40.9%. sc.*

Scotch Malt Whisky Society Cask 35.60 Aged 39 Years refill hogshead, cask no. 8942, dist 19/1 **(84.5) n22 t21.5 f20.5 b20.5.** Always a shame when you find that the oak has got to the whisky before you... *42.3%. sc. Scotch Malt Whisky Society.*

Scotch Malt Whisky Society Cask 35.65 Aged 10 Years refill Chardonnay hogshead, cask no. 7222, dist 2001 **(84.5) n22 t22 f20.5 b20.** Big oak toastiness with some major buttery elements and a tidal wave of seemingly teeth-rotting sugars. Suspect this was a beauty maybe three or four years back but now almost too much of a good thing. *60.3%. sc.*

Single Cask Collection Glen Moray 21 Years Old bourbon hogshead, dist 1990 **(89) n22** just a little tart, if you know what I mean, though there is something of a jam tart to this, too! That sharpness steadies as the barley makes a stand; **t22** the oak is far too aggressive early on, leaving the malt in the shade; exotic fruit and manuka honey do the trick; **f23** reverts to serious oakiness then goes into complexity overdrive; **b22** at times, the simplicity of Glen Moray means that it struggles to comfortably wear its age. That's how this one starts, but gradually eases into its antiquity. Look closely, around about the time the jam and Venezuelan cocoa arrives at the back end, and there is great complexity to be enjoyed. *55%. sc.*

The Whisky Agency Glen Moray 35 Years Old dist 1977 **(96) n23.5** brags about its age with an engaging, exotic fruit-rich display. The chalkier elements suggest that the oak has gone as far as it can, but there are no breaches in excellence; **t24** soft delivery with an immediate mouth-watering barley thrust. Those exotic fruits pop up around the palate with a delightful randomness; light oils amplify the delicate sugars; **f24** fears of oak dominance are never realised. Instead we have a lovely minty cocoa finish with just the right sprinkling of spice; **b24.5** a highly accomplished, absolutely top dollar antique whisky. *51.8%. sc.*

GLEN ORD
Highlands (Northern), 1838. Diageo. Working.

Glen Ord Aged 12 Years db **(81) n20 t23 f18 b20.** Just when you thought it safe to go back...for a while Diageo ditched the sherry-style Ord. It has returned. Better than some years ago, when it was an unhappy shadow of its once-great self, but without the sparkle of the vaguely-smoked bottling of a year or two back. Nothing wrong with the rich arrival, but the finish is a mess. I'll open the next bottling with trepidation... *43%*

Glen Ord 25 Years Old dist 1978 db **(95) n24 t24 f23 b24.** Some stupendous vatting here: cask selection at its very highest to display Ord in all its far too rarely seen magnificence. *58.3%*

Glen Ord 28 Years Old db **(90) n22 t23 f22 b23.** This is mega whisky showing slight traces of sap, especially on the nose, but otherwise a concentrate of many of the qualities I remember from this distillery before it was bottled in a much ruined form. Blisteringly beautiful. *58.3%*

Glen Ord 30 Years Old db **(87) n22 t21 f23 b21.** Creaking with oak, but such is the polish to the barley some serious class is on show. *58.8%*

Glen Ord 1997 The Manager's Choice db **(93.5) n24** oh my word...what have we here...? Just the most enticing little fruit pastel number you could ask for, and all played out on the softest malty field imaginable. Genuinely complex and enticing with the nose being teasingly caressed; **t23.5** then, just to shock, a real injection of bite and nip on delivery with a tangy blood orange thread which follows from the nose; **f23** custard powder oakiness with some late hickory and toffee; **b23** when given the chance, Glen Ord offers one of the fruitiest drams on the market. Here it is in its full blood orange element. A beauty! *59.2%*

Singleton of Glen Ord 12 Years Old db **(89) n22.5** no-one does blood orange quite like Glen Ord...; **t22.5** salivating arrival with the malt elbowing its way past the persistent fruit; **f22** vanilla and some clever spices; **b22** a fabulous improvement on the last bottling I encountered. Still possesses blood oranges to die for, but greatly enhanced by some sublime spices and a magnificent juiciness. *40%*

Singleton of Glen Ord 32 Year Old db **(91) n23.5 t23 f22 b22.5.** Delicious. But if ever a malt has screamed out to be at 46%, this is it. *40%*

⠿ **Cadenhead Ord 15 Years Old** bott 2012 **(89.5) n22** pulsing barley; **t23** a riot of flavour on delivery. The salt and barley mix before the sugars arrive is awesome; a super-salivating sample...; **f22** much more sanguine with butterscotch dominant; **b22.5** the spectacular delivery is far from ORDinary... *57.3%. sc. WM Cadenhead Ltd.*

Fine Malt Selection Glen Ord 12 Years Old dist 1998, bott May 11 **(95) n23.5** the delicate smoke threads its way between light honey and juicy green grass. The barely noticeable oak offers only so much weight. Not a single off note, or character out of line...; **t23.5** melt-in-the-mouth barley is followed home by that playful smoke promised on the nose. The sweetness is identical to that found in cake mix you lick from your mum's bowl...; **f24** citrus darts around the more stubborn vanillas. The smoke dovetails with the muscovado and glazed cherries; **b24** if you are looking for a Glen Ord which shows all its characters in a very bright light, look no further. A classic in every sense. An irresistible tour de force for this magnificent distillery. *45%. sc. James MacArthur & Co. USA release.*

Liquid Sun Glen Ord 1996 bourbon hogshead, bott 2011 **(87) n22 t22.5 f21 b21.5.** Naggingly pleasant. *53%. The Whisky Agency.*

Malts Of Scotland Glen Ord 1996 bourbon hogshead, cask no. 2171, dist Mar 96, bott Apr 11 **(86.5) n21 t22 f22 b21.5.** The intense sweetness – and puckering sharpness - of the barley is not even slightly bothered by the oak. This is from a pretty spent cask, but at least one gets the opportunity to see the malt, warts and all... Also, a surprising degree of smoke to be found. Lovely stuff. *53.3%. sc. Malts Of Scotland.*

Malts Of Scotland Glen Ord 1999 bourbon hogshead, cask no. 31212, dist Mar 99, bott Mar 10 **(94.5) n23.5** for a bourbon hoggy, there is a strange semi-grapey depth to this; **t24** fantastic spice attack on delivery. Followed by strata of honey of varying intensity; **f23.5** a curious burnt raisin fruit cake intensity which flies in the face of the bourbon liquorice and honey doing the rounds elsewhere. The spices congregate and accelerate in their effect; **b23.5** further proof that the owners of this distillery appear to not quite realise the goldmine they are sitting on. Beautiful! *54.5%. nc ncf sc. Malts Of Scotland. 289 bottles.*

⠿ **Malts Of Scotland Glen Ord 1999** bourbon hogshead, cask no. MoS110013, dist 9 Mar 99, bott Oct 11 **(88.5) n21.5** typical Ordie fruit and spice; **t23** those of a nervous disposition unable to withstand a malt-spice onslaught should withdraw now. A greengage and boiled apple middle, but the barley and its juices run through with ease; **f22** simplifies back to oak, barley and spice basics; **b22** a long way from perfection, but a dram to keep your senses on alert all night long. 54.4%. nc ncf sc. Malts Of Scotland.

Old Malt Cask Glen Ord Aged 14 Years refill hogshead, cask no. 7478, dist Apr 97, bott Jul 11 **(85) n21.5 t22 f21 b21.5.** Juicy, spicy, still wet behind the ears. A Peter Pan of a malt. 50%. nc ncf sc. Douglas Laing & Co. 149 bottles.

Old Malt Cask Glen Ord Aged 21 Years refill butt, cask no.6538, dist Jan 89, bott Sep 10 **(86) n20.5 t22 f22 b22.** Juicy, teeming with barley, spicy; coconut and cocoa anchored yet somehow younger than its years. Would never have quite recognised this as a Glen Ord, had I not known. But some golden nugget moments here, make no mistake. 50%. nc ncf sc. Douglas Laing & Co. 361 bottles.

❖ **Provenance Glen Ord Over 7 Years** refill hogshead, cask no. 7644, dist Autumn 2004, bott Autumn 2011 **(82.5) n20 t22 f20 b20.5.** A little celebration of all things citrusy. 46%. nc ncf sc. Douglas Laing & Co.

Provenance Glen Ord Over 11 Years refill hogshead, cask no. 6725, dist Spring 99, bott Autumn 2010 **(94) n23** a potpourri of dried flowers and herbs; **t24** heather-honey almost of a Highland Park style, complete with a squirt of something smoky; **f23.5** golden syrup with a heathery dryness; **b23.5** if Diageo want to compete head to head with Highland Park, they had better grab a bottle of this and send it to the lab... One of the must have whiskies of the year. 46%. nc ncf sc. Douglas Laing & Co.

❖ **Provenance Glen Ord Over 11 Years** refill hogshead, cask no. 9008, dist Spring 2000, bott Winter 2012 **(89) n23** a style this distillery does so well: a light fruit salad emboldened by citrus-stained barley with only the most distant rumbles of peat offering weight; **t22.5** mouth-watering, clean and then a fabulous cascade of barley in varying degrees of sweetness; **f21.5** thins slightly but peppery spice compensates; **b22** another cask that is too easy to overlook. Take your time with this and just let it melt in the mouth... 46%. nc ncf sc. Douglas Laing & Co.

Scotch Malt Whisky Society 77.21 Aged 23 Years refill hogshead, cask no. 3367, dist 1987 **(86) n20.5 t20.5 f23 b22.** As charming as this very well might be, one wonders why this isn't making magic in a 21-year-old blend where its orangey notes would make whoopee. As a singleton, languid to start then finally finds its voice and balance to magnificent effect. Certainly, the spices and fruit towards the finish make for a malt to enjoy late in the evening when patience is a virtue and contemplation comes naturally. 57.2%. sc. 237 bottles.

Scotch Malt Whisky Society 77.23 Aged 23 Years 2nd fill hogshead, cask no. 3370, dist 1987 **(86) n22 t22.5 f20.5 b21.** An initially mouth-watering suet and sawdust merchant that lives as long on the palate as it does the memory. 56.8% sc. 226 bottles.

❖ **Scotch Malt Whisky Society Cask 77.26 Aged 23 Years** refill hogshead, cask no. 3368, dist 1987 **(92.5) n23** lightly fried yam, with a slightly yolky, salty background. The vanillas are deft and complex; **t23.5** soft oils ensure the barley yields at all the right points. Excellent salt and sugar mix. The middle ground is vanilla concentrate with a touch of nougat; **f73** remains juicy and barley rich to the very end, despite the increased oaky weight; a light sprinkling of honeycomb helps; **b23** a Highland malt refusing to accept its age and still showing an almost imperious vigour. Superb! 55.6%. sc. Scotch Malt Whisky Society.

❖ **Scotch Malt Whisky Society Cask 77.27 Aged 11 Years** refill hogshead, cask no. 4, dist 2000 **(86) n21.5 t22 f21.5 b21.** Overflowing with intense barley. Well made and matured. But, though deliciously simplistic, could do with stretching the complexity a little. 55.2% sc.

❖ **The Warehouse Collection Glen Ord Aged 22 Years** refill sherry butt, cask no. 30, dist 19 Jan 90, bott 12 Apr 12 **(84.5) n21.5 t22 f20 b21.** The delivery delights; the finish frustrates. 53.2%. sc. Whisky Warehouse No. 8. 535 bottles.

GLENROTHES
Speyside, 1878. Edrington. Working.

The Glenrothes 1978 dist Nov 78, bott 2008 db **(90.5) n23** over-ripe gooseberries mixed with dry tobacco; suet pudding and vanilla pods: attractively intriguing; **t23** relaxed, lush barley coats the mouth with a muscovado sugar edge; **f22** mushy sultana and toasty oak; **b22.5** sheer – and delicious – entertainment. 43%

The Glenrothes 1988 Vintage dist 16 Dec 88, bott 04 Nov 08 db **(93) n22** stunning toasted honeycomb **t24.5** exceptional delivery. Not only is the mouth feel quite perfect, the deft marriage of honey, honeycomb, treacle and maple syrup has to be tasted to be believed...; **f23** dries and spices up as the oaks grab hold; **b23.5** a gorgeous bottling still doing the rounds... and should be hunted down and polished off. 43%

The Glenrothes 1988 Vintage bott 2010 db **(74) n18.5 t19 f18 b18.5.** For all the obvious high quality sugars present, it still can't overcome the Spanish imposition. 43%

The Glenrothes 1994 dist Oct 94, bott 2007 db **(77) n19 t20 f19 b19.** The citrus appears as promised on the label, but sadly a few unadvertised sulphured butt-related gremlins are present also. 43%

The Glenrothes 1995 Vintage dist 26 Oct 95, bott 06 Sep 10 db **(87.5) n20** distilled vanilla...? **t22** one of the laziest deliveries you'll find: a pretty nondescript malt-oak job with a mouth feel which lies there like a doormat. Slowly, though, there is a twitching of spices, a little liquorice and the odd fruity yoghurt note; **f23** carries on in the same delicate and now complex and vaguely toasty manner: rather wonderful; **b22.5** like an old grump that takes its time to wake and finally has to be kicked out of bed. Once up, certainly does the biz. *43%*

The Glenrothes 1998 Vintage dist Dec 98, bott Feb 09 db **(66) n16 t20 f14 b16.** Really would have thought they would have got the hang of this sulphur lark by now... *43%*

The Glenrothes 1998 Vintage bott 2010 db **(73.5) n20 t19 f16 b18.5.** Talk about bitter-sweet...!!! *43%*

The Glenrothes Alba Reserve db **(87.5) n22** muted honey and spice rising from the flattish nosescape; **t22** silky, malty delivery with some toffee turning up in the middle ground; **f21.5** decent length with more of the same and just a hint of a liquorice flourish; **b22** you know that smartly groomed, polite but rather dull chap you invariable get at dinner parties? *40%*

The Glenrothes John Ramsay bott 2009 db **(89.5) n22.5 t23.5 f21.5 b22.** Elegant and charming. What else did you expect...? *46.7%. 1400 bottles.*

The Glenrothes Robur Reserve db **(81.5) n20.5 t22 f19 b20.** With the youthful barley prominent early on, one of the sweetest distillery bottling from Glenrothes I've come across. Bitter cask fade, though. *40%*

The Glenrothes Select Reserve db **(80) n17.5 t22 f20.5 b21.** Flawed in the usual Glenrothes sherry places, but the brilliance of the sharp barley wins your heart. *40%*

The Glenrothes Three Decades bott 2009 db **(90.5) n23.5 t24 f21.5 b22.5.** Not without a minor blemish here and there, but the overall magnitude of this allows you to forgive quite easily. The distant sulphur apart, a stunner. *43%. Duty Free exclusive.*

Adelphi Glenrothes 20 Years Old cask no. 12898, dist 1990, bott 2011 **(86) n21.5 t20 f23 b21.5.** An enjoyably clean sherry butt, but it's a hard slog through the gears. *58.6%. sc.*

⁘ **Archives Glenrothes 1988 23 Years Old Third Release** refill sherry hogshead, cask no. 7318, dist 6 Jun 88, bott 4 Jan 12 **(79) n19 t21 f19 b20.** Tight, dry and short of couth. *53.4%. nc ncf sc. Whiskybase B.V. 80 bottles.*

⁘ **Cadenhead Glenrothes 15 Years Old (88) n22** it's as though someone has moved the distillery to the seaside...very salty; **t23** no less sharp on delivery with those tangy salty malt notes giving way to mocha – seriously tasty! **f21** a caramel overdose: a boring end to a lovely dram; **b22** from an ex-bourbon cask...thank heavens! *53.8%. sc. WM Cadenhead Ltd.*

⁘ **Duncan Taylor Dimensions Glenrothes 20 Years Old** cask no. 5154, dist Mar 91, bott Dec 11 **(85.5) n21.5 t22 f21 b21.** For all its liveliness and thrust, there is a slight tangy blight to the cask which relegates this to a lower whisky division. *49.6%. nc ncf sc. Duncan Taylor & Co.*

Duncan Taylor Octave Glenrothes 40 Years Old cask no. 495777, dist 1970 **(94.5) n23** elegant and deft, a soft peach note sits prettily with the vanilla and, one almost fancies, the most delicate hint of smoke imaginable; **t23.5** the oaks arrive hurriedly, but mainly carrying with it caramels. The barley still has enough freshness to offer a juicy diversion; **f24** spices arrive late but entirely in keeping with the understated nuances of all the other characteristics; the softness is concluded by melt-in-the-mouth chocolate ice cream... **b24** quite fantastic malt which is unerringly subtle. *40.6%. sc.*

Duncan Taylor Octave Glenrothes 40 Years Old cask no. 495780, dist 1970 **(86) n21.5 t22.5 f20.5 b21.5.** A Braveheart of a dram. Creaking here and there and obviously feeling its age, somehow it has the sheer willpower and class to cobble together a bunch of vivid barley-mocha notes to go down guns blazing. *40.9%. sc.*

Malts Of Scotland Glenrothes 1968 bourbon hogshead, cask no. 13509, dist Nov 68, bott Feb 11 **(86) n21 t22 f21.5 b21.5.** Enough honey and spice to fend off some hairy oak. At times looks as though the years have taken too great a toll...but there is no denying the life force is strong. *45.2%. sc. Malts Of Scotland.*

⁘ **Malts Of Scotland Angel's Choice Glenrothes 1970** bourbon hogshead, cask no. MoS11026, bott Nov 11 **(86.5) n21.5 t22 f21.5 b21.5.** If you don't mind getting a splintered tongue, tuck in! Some wonderful honeycomb moments which soothe and amaze. But the massive oaky imprint is just a little too fierce for greatness. *44.5%. nc ncf sc. Malts Of Scotland.*

⁘ **Mo Ór Collection Glenrothes 1988 22 Years Old** first fill bourbon hogshead, cask no. 7321, dist 6 Jun 88, bott 2 Dec 10 **(87) n23.5** Marmalade on pretty well scorched toast; no shortage of lemon and lime, either...; **t22** for all the fruit on the nose, the barley is first to break through and makes for a succulent dish; **f19.5** overzealously bitter; **b22** doesn't quite live up to its early expectation. The nose, though, has you setting the table for breakfast... *46%. nc ncf sc. Release No. 42. The Whisky Talker. 403 bottles.*

⁘ **Old Malt Cask Glenrothes Aged 21 Years** refill butt, cask no. 7532, dist Jun 90, bott Sep 11 **(94.5) n22** nougat and raisin; elsewhere there are slightly bizarre hints of marmite and liquorice; **t24** excellent delivery sporting a silky sheen to the barley and then a powering spice-bite to the sherry; some beautiful oils attempt to confuse the two camps but there is enough tension between the juicy barley and ever-thickening fruit to ensure the taste buds are kept working overtime; **f24.5** sheer Melton Hunt Cake roastiness to the fruit. The spices fizz around the palate with abandon. The oils intensify and ensure the molassed sugars carry on for an almost ridiculous amount of time. Drying vanillas soon arrive; **b24** a sulphur-free spicefest. Wonderful! *50%. nc ncf sc. Douglas Laing & Co. 328 bottles.*

Peerless Glenrothes 41 Years Old cask no. 12881, dist 1969 **(85) n20 t21.5 f22 b21.5.** Peerless. But not ageless... *44.2%. sc. Duncan Taylor & Co.*

⋄ **Provenance Glenrothes Over 10 Years** refill barrel, cask no. 7917, dist Summer 2001, bott Autumn 2011 **(84) n20 t21.5 f21.5 b21.** A well-made, malty and vaguely spicy individual enjoying scant help from the cask. *46%. nc ncf sc. Douglas Laing & Co.*

Provenance Glenrothes Aged 11 Years (86) n21 t22 f21.5 b21.5. A pithy little number seemingly distilled and matured in an orangery. *46%*

⋄ **Riegger's Selection Glenrothes 1986** bourbon cask, cask no. 2, dist 15 Dec 86, bott 30 Nov 10 **(86.5) n21.5 t22.5 f21 b21.5.** Slaps on the sweet, thick barley with abandon. Decent spices, too. *53.3%. nc ncf sc. Viktor-Riegger GmbH. 369 bottles.*

Scotch Malt Whisky Society Cask 30.64 Aged 18 Years 2nd fill hogshead, cask no. 8601, dist 1992 **(88.5) n23 t22 f21.5 b22.** Always great to see this get the chance to strut its malty stuff away from a sherry butt. *55.7%. sc. 244 bottles.*

Scott's Selection Glenrothes 1986 bott 2011 **(88.5) n21.5 t21.5 f23.5 b22.** A rollercoaster of a dram, at times heading for oaky oblivion but pulls out of the dip with a dramatic late winner. Phew! Probably the most complicated and hardest malt to judge this year: like a fabulous lover with a crap personality. One minute you love her...then you hate her...then you love her... *51.7%. Speyside Distillers.*

⋄ **Scott's Selection Glenrothes 1990** bott 2011 **(90.5) n22.5** excellent depth to the chalky, liquorice and leathery bourbon theme; **t23** superb balance to the sugar involvement as the barley and muscovado melt in unison; more bourbon tones as the spice bites deep and the chocolate is smothered liberally around; **f22.5** long and sugary; thins out for a papery finish; **b22.5** the kind of Scotch that would be dearly loved in Kentucky. *58.3%. Speyside Distillers.*

The Whisky Agency Glenrothes 39 Years Old dist 1970, bott 2009 **(90.5) n22.5** surely a bourbon in disguise... **t23** a teasing, semi-spiced array of red liquorice, hickory and other delicious bourbon notes, especially honey; **f22.5** long, lightly oiled and magnificently spiced; **b22.5** a malt to be celebrated and one more happy to wear the flag of Kentucky than The Saltire *48.1%. The Whisky Agency.*

The Whisky Agency Glenrothes 1980 (92.5) n23.5 gentle measures of barley, ginger, lime and kumquat bound together by the very softest smoke; **t24** quite brilliant delivery: the sugars are crisp and beautifully defined, strengthened by a rod of oak. The spices are in tandem and build into something meaningful; **f22** flattens as the vanillas and higher tannins arrive; **b23** a genuine Speyside gem. *50.9%. The Whisky Agency.*

The Whisky Castle Raw Cask Glenrothes 21 Years Old sherry butt, cask no. 7471, dist 07 May 89, bott Oct 10 **(95.5) n23** dripping with fat sultanas and sublimely spiced; **t24.5** near enough the perfect delivery: the fruit is sweet, but immediately balanced by some pulsing spices and cocoa and a fabulous and unexpected puff of smoke; the subsequent layers talk up the spices and allow a gorgeous butterscotch and light honey thread... wow! **f24** long with spotted dick and the most extraordinary trail of diminishing but gorgeous honey; **b24** it this doesn't get people beating a path to the shop, nothing will... sublime whisky: one of the finest casks of the year. *54%. nc ncf sc. Blackadder for The Whisky Castle.*

GLEN SCOTIA
Campbeltown, 1832. Loch Lomond Distillers. Working.

Glen Scotia 12 Years Old db **(73.5) n18 t19 f18 b18.5.** Ooops! I once said you could write a book about this called "Murder by Caramel." Now it would be a short story called "Murder by Flavours Unknown." What is happening here? Well, a dozen years ago Glen Scotia was not quite the place to be for consistent whisky, unlike now. Here, the caramel is the only constant as the constituent parts disintegrate. *40%*

Glen Scotia 2000 bourbon barrel, cask no. 087, dist 06 Jun 00, bott 28 Jul 11 db **(87) n22** tight but very malty; **t22** juicy barley punches through a wall of caramel; **f21** slightly bitter as the oak ups the ante; **b22** similar to cask 627 from year 2001. Only here the barley and oak have combined to add a degree of attitude and the barrel is less helpful. *45%. nc ncf sc. 320 bottles.*

Glen Scotia 2001 bourbon barrel, cask no. 627, dist 05 Nov 01, bott 28 Jul 11 db **(91.5) n22.5** gristy clean malt allowing the sugars unrestricted access; **t23** huge amount of natural caramels, but for those who like Maltesers candy...beware! **f23** long, with the malt stretching out forever and a day; **b23** dangerous: the kind of seemingly simple and undemonstrative whisky that you could end up spending all day, every day drinking. *45%. nc ncf sc. 330 bottles.*

Glen Scotia 2002 American oak hogshead, cask no. 164, dist 22 Apr 02, bott 28 Jul 02 db **(77.5) n19 t21.5 f18 b19.** I know the maturing casks from this distillery quite well and this is not representative of what is sitting in their warehouse. This is a rather feeble effort, for all its big barley. And in a sub-standard cask, too. 45%. nc ncf sc. 410 bottles.

Glen Scotia 2007 bourbon barrel, cask no. 225, dist 23 Apr 07, bott 28 Jul 11 db **(86.5) n22 t22 f21 b21.5.** Huge clouds of natural caramels drift around the palate. But the sugars are secure and the odd molecule of smoke adds a curious balance. Very different. 45%. nc ncf sc.

Hart Brothers Glen Scotia Aged 18 Years dist Feb 92, bott Jan 11 **(66) n15.5 t18 f15.5 b17.** Dear, oh dear, oh dear... 46%. sc.

❖ **Kingsbury Single Cask Series Glen Scotia Aged 19 Years** Trois Riviers rum finish **(86) n21.5 t22 f21.5 b21.5.** Pretty tight in places and in others has a problem to breathe. But the salivating nip and tang to the crisp sugars and insistent barley makes for an interesting dram. 46%. sc. Japan Import Systems.

Malts Of Scotland Glen Scotia 1972 bourbon hogshead, cask no. 1926, dist Sep 72, bott May 10 **(88) n21.5 t22.5 f22 b22.** Creaks more than a haunted house. But hangs on in there determined to entertain. And succeeds. 45.1%. nc ncf sc. Malts Of Scotland.

Malts Of Scotland Glen Scotia 1972 bourbon hogshead, cask no. 1931, dist Sep 72, bott May 10 **(89) n22 t22 f23 b22.** The malt disappears under an avalanche of oak-extracted sugar. But the bourbon effect, combined with the never-say-die oak, rescues this dramatically. 45.7%. nc ncf sc. Malts Of Scotland.

❖ **Malts Of Scotland Glen Scotia 1991** bourbon hogshead, cask no. MoS12009, dist 22 May 91, bott Jan 12 **(84) n22 t21 f20 b21.** A very high quality cask, injecting molassed tannins, ensures some depth and quality to some very ordinary original spirit. 54.5%. nc ncf sc. Malts Of Scotland.

❖ **Mo Ôr Collection Glen Scotia 1992 18 Years Old** first fill sherry cask, cask no. 6, dist 25 Mar 92, bott 2 Dec 10 **(61) n17 t18 f12 b14.** Grim degrees of sulphur. 46%. nc ncf sc. Release No. 41. The Whisky Talker. 1076 bottles.

Old Malt Cask Glen Scotia Aged 18 Years bourbon barrel, cask no. 6481, dist Mar 92, bott Aug 10 **(85.5) n20.5 t22 f21.5 b21.5.** Sugary enough to rot your teeth. Enjoyable, though, I must admit! 50%. nc ncf sc. Douglas Laing & Co. 312 bottles.

Scotch Malt Whisky Society Cask 93.44 Aged 11 Years refill barrel, cask no. 505, dist 1999 **(93) n22.5** clean, even peating with more of a crofter's fireside than a sea shore...; **t(23)** molassed liquorice keeps apace with the full blown peat; surprisingly juicy with the barley occasionally visible; **f(24)** a stunning finish: a slow injection of butterscotch and vanilla helps the peat to unravel. The manner in which it slowly dries and breaks down into its complex, constituent parts is a revelation...; **b(23.5)** Campbeltown has obviously drifted on a tectonic plate out to sea to Islay... 61.8%. sc. 220 bottles.

❖ **Scotch Malt Whisky Society Cask 93.47 Aged 9 Years** refill barrel, cask no. 152, dist 2002 **(92.5) n22.5** youthful phenols lightened by some major citrus; **t24** melt-in-the-mouth peat which is about as soft as any peaty whisky gets. Milky chocolate also softens the proceedings; **f23** a lovely build up of salt and vanilla; the smoke wafts around with a feather-light touch; **b23** Scotia confirming it does peat with aplomb. An excellent age to enjoy this, too, as the oak has made little more than a guest appearance. 59.7%. sc.

❖ **Scotch Malt Whisky Society Cask 93.48 Aged 12 Years** refill barrel, cask no. 510, dist 1999 **(87.5) n22** remember Merlin's Brew ice lollies? The one with the outrageously delicious chocolate mint theme? This is like a lightly peated version of that...; **t22** after the big, spicy, biting peat comes...Merlin's Brew yet again. There appears to be a theme here...; **f21.5** a little on the hot side, but that cocoa and peat finale make amends; **b22** an attractive, minty bottling of the new malty Scotia. 62%. sc. Scotch Malt Whisky Society.

❖ **Scotch Malt Whisky Society Cask 93.49 Aged 19 Years** refill butt, cask no. 226, dist 1992 **(61) n15 t16 f14 b16.** Dreadful and substandard to an almost legendary degree. 57.8%. sc.

❖ **Scotch Malt Whisky Society Cask 93.52 Aged 9 Years** refill barrel, cask no. 153, dist 2002 **(88.5) n22** attractive Victoria sponge nose, complete with powdered sugar. The barley is unusual, though...; **t23** big, clean, bounding barley showing excellent weight yet not being lost in oils; **f21.5** slightly bitters but those persistent malt and sugar notes hang on in; **b22** thick and syrupy but the barley does a good job. 58.4%. sc.

❖ **Scott's Selection Glen Scotia 1991** bott 2010 **(81.5) n19 t20 f21.5 b21.** Just looking for a mirror to see if there is any enamel left on my teeth. Violent. 58.7%. Speyside Distillers.

❖ **Scott's Selection Glen Scotia 1991** bott 2012 **(84.5) n21 t21 f21.5 b21.** Resounding oak makes this an eye-watering one...; some trace mocha makes life easier towards the end. 53.8%. Speyside Distillers.

❖ **The Warehouse Collection Glen Scotia Aged 20 Years** first fill sherry butt, cask no. 5, dist 25 Mar 92, bott 8 Aug 12 **(86) n22 t24 f19 b21.** Delighted to report sulphur didn't explode in my face. But this has been treated, alas, and the bitterness gathers slowly but surely at the death. Until it gets there, enjoy the chocolate raisin ride! *59.5%. sc. Whisky Warehouse No. 8. 470 bottles.*

⁘ **Wemyss 1991 Single Campbeltown Glen Scotia "Strawberry Ganache"** butt, bott 2012 **(83.5) n20 t22 f20 b21.5.** In the US, the film "Whisky Galore" was called "Tight Little Island". This would have starred: it is a tight little whisky...there is plenty of grape and chewability. But there is enough sulphur candle influence to limit the fun. *46%. sc. 833 bottles.*

The Whisky Agency Glen Scotia 1972 bott 2010 **(79) n20 t19 f20 b20.** Even exotic fruit has a sell by date... *40.1%. The Whisky Agency.*

GLEN SPEY
Speyside, 1885. Diageo. Working.

Glen Spey Aged 12 Years db **(90) n23** the kind of firm, busy malt you expect from this distillery plus some lovely spice; **t22** mouthwatering and fresh, a layer of honey makes for an easy three or four minutes; **f22** drier vanilla, but the pulsing oak is controlled and stylish; **b23** very similar to the first Glen Spey I can remember in this range, the one before the over-toffeed effort of two years ago. Great to see it back to its more natural, stunningly beautiful self. *43%*

Glen Spey Special Release 2010 21 Years Old sherry American oak cask, dist 1988 db **(94.5) n23** a huge nose by this distillery's standards. There are elements of fruit, but more delicious are the controlled oaky bourbony offerings. Honeydew melon, vanilla and red liquorice abounds...telling you something about the variation of weight; **t24** the delivery is silky and positively melts into the taste buds, making a mockery of the strength. The honey is stupendously well proportioned and carries spices which prickle as much as the sugars sparkle; **f23.5** long, with a wonderful butterscotch/lemon curd tart ensemble. There is a distant fruitiness, burned raisin more associated with aging oak than grape; **b24** Glen Speys of this age tended to find their way into blends where they would beef up the sweeter malt content. Sometimes they were used to impart clean sherry or at least fruit, but otherwise give nothing of themselves. This bottling tends to take both strands and then ties them up in a complex and compelling fashion. Wonderful. *50.4%. nc ncf. Diageo. Fewer than 6000 bottles.*

Old Malt Cask Glen Spey Aged 14 Years refill hogshead, cask no. 6955, dist Feb 97, bott Feb 11 **(89) n22 t22 f23 b22.** Probably as true to the house style as you are likely to find. *50%. nc ncf sc. Douglas Laing & Co. 338 bottles.*

⁘ **Old Malt Cask Glen Spey Aged 25 Years** refill hogshead, cask no. 8196, dist Nov 86, bott Feb 12 **(94) n23.5** how evocative! A stroll through bluebell woods; slightly earthy without the smoke and floral without the pungency. Fresh and allows the barley to display a wonderful citrus edge; **t24** mouth-watering delivery with the malt growing in intensity by the second...amazing! **f23** slackens in pace as the vanillas move in; **b23.5** Rarely have I found a Glen Spey so self-assured and intense. Bravo! *50%. nc ncf sc. Douglas Laing & Co. 299 bottles.*

Provenance Glen Spey Over 12 Years refill hogshead, cask no. 7190, dist Spring 99, bott Spring 2011 **(78.5) n19 t20 f19 b19.5.** A pleasant enough malt. But always a little tight, sweet and nutty... *46%. nc ncf sc. Douglas Laing & Co.*

GLENTAUCHERS
Speyside, 1898. Chivas Brothers. Working.

⁘ **Duncan Taylor Dimensions Glentauchers 15 Years Old** dist May 96, bott Dec 11 **(92) n23** classic for the distillery: crisp barley, softened by much more rounded citrus and vanilla notes. Exactly what you should expect at this age; **t23.5** the clarity is magnificent. Barley, sugar and vanilla sounds simple enough, but when in this uncluttered, sumptuous form,,,,oh, my word! **f22.5** a light degree of oak bitterness is compensated by some late, prickly spices. The barley remains compact and unmolested; **b23** I would say this is about as definitive 'Tauchers as you are ever likely to find in bottled form for the age and oak. *46%. nc ncf sc.*

Provenance Glentauchers Over 10 Years refill butt, cask no. 6522, Mar 83, Jul 10 **(91) n23** a light caress of peat is almost lost amid the sharpness of the barley; **t24** beautifully structured; the degree of oils is close to perfection while that strand of delicate smoke gives extra earthiness and depth to the clear, grassy malt; **f21.5** still light enough for the vanillas to show; **b22.5** a slightly beefier 'Tauchers than the norm, even sporting the faintest degree of smoke. The malt intensity to the delivery is a rare treat. A chance to see why this malt is a consistent blender's delight. *46%. nc ncf sc. Douglas Laing & Co.*

⁘ **Provenance Glentauchers Over 12 Years** refill hogshead, cask no. 8014, dist Autumn 1999, bott Winter 2012 **(88.5) n22** lively barley and enlivened further by a stem of ginger; **t22.5** some agreeable diced apple gives the already juicy malt a welcome boost and fits snugly with the lightly honeyed oil; **f22** where did those spices spring from...? **b22** a typical understated 'tauchers offering much more than first meets the eye. Or palate. *46%. nc ncf sc.*

Scotch Malt Whisky Society Cask 63.26 Aged 21 Years 2nd fill hogshead, cask no. 5626, dist 1989 **(92.5) n23** a very equal balance between the oak and barley; clean and showing a delightful Malteser candy quality; **t23** firm, sound barley which makes the most of the sharp maltiness. The oak offers light salt to balance the delicate sugars; **f22.5** back to the Maltesers...; **b24** high quality Speyside of limited complexity but showing just why this is prized for its sincere malty qualities in older blends. Quietly superb. *52.6%. sc. 161 bottles.*

The Whisky Agency Glentauchers 1975 bott 2010 **(94.5) n23** the oak is trying to crush all the life out of this one, but some old banana takes on the challenge; **t23.5** beautifully soft and you fancy some barley melts in the mouth along with the vanilla concentrate. Gorgeously refined; **f24** a stupendous essay of vanilla and chocolate ice cream...I don't think I have ever tasted a malt softer on the palate than this... **b24** at first it seems the clock has ticked once too many times for this Tauchers. However, a little oxidisation in the glass brings some barely believable life into the Old Timer. Indeed, these notes are taken at its imperious height at about 12 minutes. Then, it hits extraordinary greatness and a lightness of touch which I have rarely encountered before: it is as though it has been distilled from feathers. But don't leave it too long in there: it soon fades away... *47.3%. The Whisky Agency.*

GLENTURRET
Highlands (Perthshire), 1775. Edrington. Working.

Glenturret Aged 8 Years db **(88) n21** some sma' still randomness; **t22** silky honey, a few feinty oils perhaps, but attractive; **f23** honey overdrive with spice; **b22** technically no prizewinner. But the dexterity of the honey is charming, as this distillery has a tendency sometimes to be. *40%*

The Glenturret Aged 10 Years db **(76) n19 t18 f20 b19**. Lots of trademark honey but some less than impressive contributions from both cask and the stillman. *40%*

The Glenturret Aged 15 Years db **(87) n21 t22 f22 b22**. A beautifully clean, small-still style dram that would have benefitted from being bottled at a fuller strength. A discontinued bottling now: if you see it, it is worth the small investment. *40%*

Glenturret 1991 Aged 15 Years cask no. 638 db **(82) n20 t21 f21 b20**. Honeycomb and chocolate: liquid fruit jelly. Heavyweight stuff and at times a little stodgy. *55.3%*

Glenturret 1992 Aged 14 Years cask no. 855 db **(72) n18 t19 f17 b18**. A tad feinty and never quite finds the right key despite the best efforts of the honey and spice. *59.7%*

Glenturret 1993 cask no. 840 db **(83.5) n21 t20 f21.5 b21**. I'm afraid the heat on this one isn't simply down to the giant strength. This is hot whisky but with some attractively sharp notes. *59.5%*

❖ **Cadenhead Glenturret 15 Years Old** bott 2011 **(83) n20 t22 f20 b21**. The cut from this distillate is pretty wide, so there is plenty of oil and buzz on the palate. Some honey, too, as well as the usual coppery sharpness. *53%. sc. WM Cadenhead Ltd.*

The MacPhail's Collection Glenturret 1998 (85) n19 t21.5 f22.5 b22. Always a delight to come across a rare bottling like this. Technically, not quite Premier League. But the honeycomb and forceful barley are a source of joy. *40%*

❖ **Malts Of Scotland Glenturret 1977** bourbon hogshead, cask no. MoS12007, dist 28 Oct 77, bott Feb 12 **(94) n22.5** the oaks are bit on the heavy side with mint, natural caramels and sap evident. But such is the high quality of malt, and so rich its body, that the citrus-honey still powers through after all this time; **t23.5** wow! Gorgeously silky, with the old trademark acacia honey arriving at the double. There is a coppery thread, but in comfortable balance with the intact, juicy malt; **f24** lengthens with the oils and now the complexity, helped along the way with a delicate touch of Lubec marzipan, goes into overdrive; **b24** finding truly great Glen Turret these days is a bit of an ask. I have just found one. *47.4%. nc ncf sc.*

❖ **Malts Of Scotland Glenturret 1980** bourbon hogshead, cask no. MoS12008, dist 14 May 80, bott Feb 12 **(89.5) n23** so much lemon, I thought some washing up liquid had got onto my hands. It hadn't...; **t22** lemon curd tart...and going easy on the tart.... **f22** ...until now with some late, dry crusty vanilla. Slight spice, too; **b22.5** always great to find a faultlessly made Turret in excellent form. *42.5%. nc ncf sc. Malts Of Scotland.*

❖ **Old Malt Cask Glenturret Aged 17 Years** sherry butt, cask no. 7972, dist Sep 94, bott Dec 11 **(82) n19 t22 f20 b21**. The odd flaw, as might be expected. But gets away with it and celebrates with some half decent honey. *50%. nc ncf sc. Douglas Laing & Co. 298 bottles.*

Scotch Malt Whisky Society Cask 16.30 Aged 22 Years 2nd fill hogshead, cask no. 829, dist 1988 **(95) n23.5** polished leather and beeswax; a vague hint of molasses but rather distant and the pollen has a bigger say; **t24** a wonderful sheen gives a polished effect to the barley. Honey is a Glenturret trait and here it builds up to wonderful levels, offset splendidly by busy spices; **f23.5** the oak behaves (or is that beehives?) with great aplomb, offering little more than a wooden crutch for the vanilla, honey and spice to perform its magic; the late balance between the dry vanilla oak and the light honeyed barley is worth buying the bottle for alone; **b24** a notoriously temperamental whisky, not least because of the small stills. However, this shows the distillery to advantage from just about every angle...a

Perthshire classic and, remarkable to relate, better than anything I have ever seen bottled by the proprietors themselves. *51.6%. sc. 206 bottles.*

The Whisky Agency Glenturret 1980 bott 2010 **(90) n22** tries to be honeyed. But the vanilla has the bigger say; there is even an unusual fresh cabbage note; **t23.5** excellent delivery and early follow through. Distinct signs of tiredness. But the waxiness of the honey seems to fill in the cracks; some liquorice arrives in the middle ground; **f22** the beeswax is waning...; **b22.5** a really superb whisky which makes light of a few age problems not least thanks to the most attractive mouthfeel. Lovely stuff. *50.9%. The Whisky Agency.*

⠴⠶ **The Whisky Agency Glenturret 35 Years Old** dist 1977 **(84) n21.5 t21 f21 b20.5.** having just tasted this alongside their 1977 Glen Moray, it is fascinating to see how one bottling shows where the oak has been embraced and allowed to be part of the all-round development of nose and flavours, while the other struggles to keep its balance as the wood becomes a little too astringent. I'll let you guess which one this is. *46.7%. sc.*

GLENUGIE
Highlands (Eastern). 1834–1983. Whitbread. Closed.

Deoch an Doras Glenugie 30 Years Old dist 1980, bott 2011 db **(87) n22** marzipan and oranges offer some controlled sweetness. A thread of recognisable bitterness is apparent but remains attractive and even slightly aloof; **t23.5** the delivery is a technical dream as far as sherry butts are concerned. A combination of rich, juicy fruit sharpened by the feel of a coppery zestiness (not something I often past associated with this distillery) and then a middle ground of intense caramels; **f19.5** grinds out a bitter finale; **b22** now there's something I didn't expect to see again: a distillery bottling of Glenugie. Well, technically, anyway, as Glenugie was part of the Chivas group when it died in the 1980s. As far as I can remember they only brought it out once, either as a seven- or five-year-old. I think that went to Italy, so when I walked around the old site just after it closed, it was a Gordon and MacPhail bottling I drank from and it tasted nothing like this! Just a shame there is a very slight flaw in the sherry butt, but just great to see it in bottle again. *52.13%. nc nct. Chivas.*

Dun Bheagan Glenugie 30 Years Old butt, cask no. 5375, dist Sep 80 **(95) n23.5** a rare clarity of clean grape, with minimal barley or oak interference. And of sulphur...not a single atom at all...; sometimes you fancy there is a little swell of smoke in there...no, surely not..., **t23.5** the delivery concentrates on the unusually clean grape and a backbone of crisp sugars; there is a mild and strangely welcome bite to the spirit but this heralds a soft vanilla entry; **f24** what an outstanding finish: a stunning display of sugars at varying levels of intensity backed by a marzipan depth and a gooseberry flourish; **b24** I am old and ugly enough to have bought Glenugie from a shop in Peterhead for a matter of less than ten quid. These days it is near enough impossible to find. But I can probably count on my two hands the number of times I have encountered a sherried version. If this is the cask I am thinking of, I have encountered it many times in the warehouses of Ian MacLeod over the years and occasionally tested its progress. I think they have bottled at probably the optimum time. What sets this guy apart from even the very high quality bottlings of the last five years is the extraordinary integration of the parts. Hot as Hades when a youngster, it now has the ability to bring every single nuance into play. Astonishing: for my money the best from this distillery I have encountered in some 30 years. Oh, and for the avoidance of doubt; I didn't spit a drop... *50%. sc. Ian Macleod Distillers.*

⠴⠶ **Scotch Malt Whisky Society Cask 99.13 Aged 31 Years** refill hogshead, cask no. 3102, dist 1980 **(92.5) n22.5** some of the old Glenugie traits: brittle, uncompromising barley with limited yield. New, though, are the softer shades of exotic fruit, some recognisable as fruit salad candy; **t23** you could almost use this as a sugar training platform: the common theme is the gristy barley which has defied logic to last years. But it runs through crystallised maple syrup efficiently enough and even hints at molasses; spices begin to articulate; **f23** excellent mocha doesn't drown out the spice, but the dark sugars ensure balance; **b24** like Littlemill, in its day Glenugie produced a spirit the better blenders treated with caution: a malt you added into blends sparingly. But from unpromising beginnings it has matured in old age into something high class and entertaining. To be savoured. *43.8%. sc. Scotch Malt Whisky Society.*

GLENURY ROYAL
Highlands (Eastern), 1868–1985. Diageo. Demolished.

Glenury Royal 36 Years Old db **(89) n22 t23.5 f21.5 b22** With so much dark, threatening oak around, the delivery defies belief or logic. Cracking stuff!! *579%*

Glenury Royal 36 Years Old db **(89) n21 t23 f22 b23.** An undulating dram, hitting highs and lows. The finish, in particular, is impressive: just when it looks on its last legs, it revives delightfully. The whole package, though far from perfect, is pretty astounding. *50.2%*

⠴⠶ **Glenury Royal 40 Year Old Limited Edition** dist 1970, bott 2011 db **(84) n20.5 t20 f22 b21.5.** Glenury is these days so rare I kept this back as a treat to savour as I neared the end of the book. The finale throws up a number of interesting citrus equations. But the oak, for the most part, is too rampant here and makes for a puckering experience. *59.4%. 1,500 bottles.*

Glenury Royal 50 Years Old dist 1953 db **(91) n23** marvellous freshness to the sherry butt; this had obviously been a high quality cask in its day and the intensity of the fruit sweetened slightly by the most delicate marzipan and old leather oozes class; a little mint reveals some worry lines; **t24** the early arrival is sweet and nimble with the barley, against the odds, still having the major say after all these years. The oak is waiting in the wings and with a burst of soft liquorice and velvety, understated spice beginning to make an impression; the sweetness is very similar to a traditional British child's candy of "tobacco" made from strands of coconut and sugar; **f22** masses of oak yet, somehow, refuses to go over the top and that slightly molassed sweetness sits very comfortably with the mildly oily body; **b22** I am always touched when sampling a whisky like this from a now departed distillery. *42.8%*

The Whisky Agency Glenury Royal 1973 bourbon hogshead, bott 2011 **(84.5) n19 t22.5 f21.5 b21.5.** An absolutely creaking old Royal very much at the end of its reign. Yet it has enough regal know-how to somehow play down the worst excesses of the oak and maximise every last nuance of its majesty. Here we can still locate some sumptuous honey threads and the odd vanilla pod to die for. *43%. The Whisky Agency.*

HAZELBURN *(see Springbank)*

HIGHLAND PARK
Highlands (Island–Orkney), 1795. Edrington. Working.

Highland Park 8 Years Old db **(87) n22 t22 f22 b21.** A journey back in time for some of us: this is the orginal distillery bottling of the 70s and 80s, bottles of which are still doing the rounds in obscure Japanese bars and specialist outlets such as the Whisky Exchange. *40%*

Highland Park Aged 12 Years db **(78) n19 t21 f19 b19.** Let's just hope that the choice of casks for this bottling was a freak. To be honest, this was one of my favourite whiskies of all time, one of my desert island drams, and I could weep. *40%*

Highland Park Saint Magnus Aged 12 Years 2nd edition db **(76.5) n18.5 t21 f19 b19.** Tight and bitter 2nd edition. *55%*

Highland Park Aged 15 Years db **(85) n21 t22 f21 b21.** Had to re-taste this several times, surprised as I was by just how relatively flat this was. A hill of honey forms the early delivery, but then... *40%*

Highland Park Earl Magnus Aged 15 Years 1st edition db **(76.5) n20 t21 f17.5 b18.** Tight and bitter. *52.6%. 5976 bottles.*

Highland Park 16 Years Old db **(88) n23** softly softly strains of oranges, honey and vanilla; **t23** mouthwatering and delightfully weighted barley with soft nuances of liquorice and smoke; **f20** toffee-vanilla: just a little too quiet; **b22** I tasted this the day it first came out at one of the Heathrow whisky shops. I thought it a bit flat and uninspiring. This sample, maybe from another bottling, is more impressive and showing true Highland Park colours, the finish apart. *40%. Exclusively available in Duty Free/Travel Retail.*

⋅❈⋅ **Highland Park Thor Aged 16 Years** db **(87.5) n22.5** very difficult to pick an easy path through this dense offering: the fruitcake is dank and full of pith, the toffee fudge thick. However, the peat is delicate, allowing full view of a stray cask which will probably cause problems elsewhere; **t23.5** the usual HP silk mouth-feel on delivery. But the spices are far more upfront than normal and the layered cocoa backing is quite sublime; the vague smoke fills up the middle ground; **f19** a disappointing, un-godlike, truly mortal finale. Tangy and off key; **b22.5** now, from what I remember of my Norse gods, Thor was the God of Thunder. Which is a bit spooky seeing as hailstones are crashing down outside as I write this and lightning is striking overhead. Certainly a whisky built on power. Even taking into account the glitch in one or two of the casks, a dram to be savoured on delivery. *52.1%. 23,000 bottles.*

Highland Park Aged 18 Years db **(95.5) n23.5** a thick dollop of honey spread across a layer of salted butter; in the background the ashes of a peat fire are emptied; **t24** eye closing beauty: immediate glossy impact of rich, vaguely metallic honey but upped in the complexity stakes by the subtle intense marbling of peat; the muscular richness, aided by the softness of the oil ensures that maximum intensity is not only reached but maintained; **f24** long continuation of those elements found in the delivery but now radiating soft spices and hints of marzipan; **b24** if familiarity breeds contempt, then it has yet to happen between myself and HP 18. This is a must-have dram. I show it to ladies the world over to win their hearts, minds and tastebuds when it comes to whisky. And the more time I spend with it, the more I become aware and appreciative of its extraordinary consistency. The very latest bottlings have been astonishing, possibly because colouring has now been dropped, and wisely so. Why in any way reduce what is one of the world's great whisky experiences? Such has been the staggering consistency of this dram I have thought of late of promoting the distillery into the world's top three: only Ardbeg and Buffalo Trace have been bottling whisk(e)y of such quality over a wide range of ages in such metronomic fashion. Anyway, enough: a glass of something honeyed and dazzling calls... *43%*

Highland Park Aged 21 Years db (82.5) n20.5 t22 f19 b21. Good news and bad news. The good news is that they appear to have done away with the insane notion of reducing this to 40% abv. The bad news: a sulphured sherry butt has found its way into this bottling. *47.5%*

Highland Park Aged 25 Years db (96) n24 big aged oak amid the smoke and honey: it appears something a lot older has got in here...; uniquely complex and back to its very best; t24 silky and confident, every usual box is ticked – or even double ticked. Much more honey and smoke than I have seen here for a while and it's not all about quantity. What quality! f24 long with amazing degrees of oil, almost of the bourbony-corn variety! Helps keep those mind-bending honeys coming! b24 I am a relieved man: the finest HP 25 for a number of years which displays the distillery's unmistakable fingerprints with a pride bordering on arrogance. One of the most improved bottlings of the year: an emperor of a dram. *48.1%*

Highland Park Aged 30 Years db (90) n22 a fascinating balancing act between juicy fruit and very tired, splintered oak; t22.5 the age waters the eye, so powerful is the oak. But it settles into an oily sweetness displaying both a lazy smokiness and burnt raisin; f23 some real complexity here with oils filling in the drier vanilla moments; b22.5 a very dramatic shift from the last bottling I tasted; this has taken a fruitier route. Sheer quality, though. *48.1%*

Highland Park 40 Years Old db (90.5) n20.5 tired and over-oaked but the usual HP traits are there in just enough force to save it from failing with an extra puff of something smoky diving in to be on the safe side; t22.5 even after 40 years, pure silk. Like a 40-year-old woman who has kept her figure and looks, and now only satin stands in the way between you and so much beauty and experience.. and believe me: she's spicy...; f24 amazing layering of peat caresses you at every level; the oak has receded and now barley and traces of golden syrup balance things; b23.5 I have to admit to picking splinters from my nose with this one. Some of the casks used here have obviously choked on oak, and I feared the worst. But such is the brilliance of the resilience by being on the money with the honey, you can say only that it has pulled off an amazing feat with the peat. Sheer poetry... *48.3%*

Highland Park 50 Years Old dist Jan 60 db (96.5) n24.5 mint, cloves and a thin coat of creosote usurp the usual deft heather and smoke to loudly announce this whisky's enormous age. Don't bother looking for honey, either. Well, not at first... However, there is a growling sweetness from the start. deep and giving up its part molten Demerara-part treacle character with miserly contempt, as though outraged by being awoken from a 50-year slumber. Of course, as the whisky oxidises there is a shift in pattern. And after about ten minutes a wine effect – and we are talking something much more akin to a First Growth Bordeaux than sherry - begins to make a statement. Then the sugars transmogrify from treacle to molasses to manuka honey; t24 certain sugars present on the delivery, though at first hard to quite make out which Some surprising oil ensures suppleness to the oak; there is also a wonderful marriage, or perhaps it is a threesome, between old nutty fruitcake, tangy orange-enriched high quality north European marzipan, and ancient bourbon...; f24 silky with some wonderful caramels and toasted fudge forming a really chewy finale. As well as ensuring any possible old-age holes are plugged; b24 old whiskies tend to react to unchartered territory as far as time in the oak is concerned in quite different ways. This grey beard has certainly given us a new slant Nothing unique about the nose. But when one is usually confronted with those characteristics on the nose, what follows on the palate moves towards a reasonably predictable path. Not here. Truly unique – as it should be after all this time. *44.8%. sc. 275 bottles.*

Highland Park 1964 Orcadian Vintage refill hogshead, bott 2009 db (90.5) n23 t22 f23 b22.5. At times you think the old oak is going to sink without trace, taking the whisky with it. But such is the pedigree of the HP make, that it not only fights back but regains control. An honour to experience. *42.2%. 290 bottles.*

Highland Park 1968 Orcadian Vintage refill casks, bott 2009 db (88.5) n20 t23.5 f23 b22. The spicy oak has taken too firm a grip for true greatness. But some of the passages offer wonderful moments of contemplation. *45.6%. 1550 bottles.*

Highland Park 1970 Orcadian Vintage db (94.5) n23.5 much smokier than present day HP..would love to have nosed the new make 40 years ago: it would have been massive; helped along here with a squeeze of blood orange; t24 splinters on delivery – in both senses - but the silky malt-honey body is able to absorb everything thrown at it; the degrees of sweetness run from honey, through light sugars to subtle Lubec marzipan: sublime; f23.5 long, again with a distinctive orangey note clinging to the sweet, lightly smoked barley: elegant...; b23.5 most other malts would have disintegrated under the weight of the oak. This takes it in its stride, and actually uses the extra vanilla to excellent effect. Memorable. *48%*

Highland Park 1973 bott 2010 db (96) n24 what could be better than a standard HP nose, complete with all that delicate smoke and honey? An HP nose with a decent smidgeon of high quality bourbon! Well that's what those extra years in the cask has gone and given you; **t25** mouth-watering barley enters the arena hand-in-hand with the most pristine acacia honey. Directly behind is two-tone smoke: one firm, lightly peated and spiced, the other a softer, billowing safety net; the middle ground concerns molten manuka honey and muscovado sugar thickened with vanilla...and then the lightest hint of mocha...frankly, perfect...; **f23** lighter, lengthy with toffee and liquorice; **b24** now that, folks, is Highland Park and make no mistake! *50.6%*

Highland Park Vintage 1978 db **(95.5) n24** some thumping oak is of such high quality it only adds to the mix, rather than detracts. The smoke level is pretty high considering it's had so long in the cask and this helps fend off any oaky excess. Elsewhere tangy kumquats mix with physalis and greengages. The usual honey has given way to soft molasses; **t24** I hope the flight is a long one if you have bought this Duty Free: you really need a good hour alone with this guy to begin to understand his foibles and complexities. The delivery offers a surprising degree of sharpness and life, in which those citrus notes formulate. Then a gentle mixing of delicate, vaguely weary smoke and an almost bourbony red liquorice and light honeycomb mix...; **f23.5** a very light oiliness has formed and provides all that is required to give an extra polish to those soft oaky tones. An equally understated mocha and molasses creamy sweetness ties up the loose ends; **b24** if you are buying this in Duty Free, a tip: get it for yourself...it's too good for a gift!! This purrs quality from first to last. And is quite unmistakably Highland Park. A noble malt. *478%. Available in Global Travel Retail.*

Highland Park 1990 bott 2010 db **(90) n23** a sprig of lavender (probably in lieu of standard heather) dovetails jauntily with ubiquitous honey and a puff of smoke; **t23** sublime delivery: an almost perfect degree of oil to help the honey slither into its rightful place at the head of the flavour queue with some toffee vanilla not far behind. Just a hint of soapiness; **f22** long, with a buzzing smokiness...and late toffee pudding; **b22** much more like it...!! *40%*

Highland Park 1994 bott 2010 db **(87) n23** ah-ha!! Recognisable light smoke and honey sparked by that uniquely enigmatic sweetness...; **t22** a toffee-raisin thread to the honey; **f20.5** inexplicably vanishes off radar; **b21.5** I am not sure what is happening here. HPs of this vintage should be soaring into the comfortable 90s. But again the finish is dull and the usual complexity of the malt is vanishing behind a murky veil. *40%*

Highland Park 1997 "The Sword" db **(79.5) n19 t23 f18 b19.5.** Shows its cutting edge for only a brief while on delivery – when it is quite spectacular. Otherwise, painfully blunted. *43%. Available in Taiwan.*

Highland Park 1998 bott 2010 db **(85) n22 t22 f20 b21.** They must have special Orcadian spiders to spin a silk this fine. But, though pleasant, disappointing by HP standards as it never gets to spread its wings. The whisky, that is: not the spider. *40%*

Highland Park Earl Haakon db **(92) n22.5** the smoke is unusually fishy – something of the Arbroath Smokie. But there are massive tracts of oak waiting in the wings – fresh, red-blooded and happy to keep the honey company; **t24** even by HP's extraordinary standards, the mouth feel on this guy makes the knees tremble. Aided by spices which shimmy and contort all over the palate, the first five or six waves are as good as any malt I have tasted this year; heads towards a surprisingly lightweight butterscotch middle; **f22.5** caramels are happy to lead the fade; **b23** a fabulous malt offering some of the best individual moments of the year. But appears to run out of steam about two thirds in. *54.9%. 3,300 bottles.*

Highland Park Hjärta db **(79.5) n18.5 t22 f19 b20.** In part, really does celebrate the honeycomb character of Highland Park to the full. But obviously a major blemish or two in there as well. *58.1%. 3924 bottles.*

Highland Park Leif Eriksson bourbon and American oak db **(86) n22 t22 f21 b21.** The usual distillery traits have gone AWOL while all kinds of caramel notes have usurped them. That said, this has to be one of the softest drams you'll find. *40%. Edrington.*

Highland Park New Make Spirit Drink dist Feb 10, bott Mar 10 db **(85.5) n21 t22 f21 b21.5.** Doesn't boast the usual degree of ultra rich texture of new make HP – even when reduced – and though sweet, malty and enjoyable, with its few extra metallic molecules not exactly how I recently tasted new make HP in a blending lab. A curious choice. *50%. Venture Whisky Ltd.*

⋰∴⋱ **A.D. Rattray Highland Park 1984** cask no. 1753, dist 17 Dec 84, bott Jun 11 **(95) n23** light smoke: tick. Heather: half a tick. Honey: three ticks...; **t24** delicate spice: tick. Light smoke: tick. Juicy barley: two ticks. Honey: three ticks. Perfect weight and body: how many ticks can you find in the box?; **f24** repeat procedure for taste. Except find a tick from somewhere for the vanilla and butterscotch; **b24** this is probably the closest thing to a model HP you will ever come across. For its age, it does everything asked and expected of it in just the right proportions. If you ever see this bottle and don't grab it...give yourself a ticking off...! *58.6%. sc.*

Adelphi Highland Park 12 Years Old cask no. 714, dist 1998, bott 2011 **(87.5) n20.5 t23 f21.5 b21.5.** Fascinating: an unusual, forthright, more Kentucky than Kirkwell signature to this one. *58.2%. sc. 95 bottles.*

⫶⫶⫶ **Archives Highland Park 2000 11 Years Old Second Release** bourbon hogshead, cask no. 800005, dist 2 Jun 00, bott Jan 12 **(85) n22 t21 f21 b21.** Quite smoky. But even the famous HP honey, which is quite abundant here, fails to entirely get to grips with an oak-driven bitterness. *50.9%. nc ncf sc. Whiskybase B.V. 129 bottles.*

⫶⫶⫶ **Duthies Highland Park 19 Years Old** sherrywood **(69) n17 t19 f16 b17.** Very sweet on delivery. But very sulphured elsewhere. *62.6%. sc. WM Cadenhead Ltd.*

⫶⫶⫶ **Hart Brothers Highland Park Aged 22 Years** cask no. 3961, dist 23 Apr 90, bott 30 Apr 12 **(92.5) n23** light smoke, honey etc.: the essence of Highland Park in every respect; **t23** irresistible combination of juicy barley and then those signature smoke and honey notes; **f23** a 22 gun salute of spices; a few light sugars, a little firmer than honey, form to balance superbly; **b23.5** excellent quality and unmistakably HP. *46%. sc.*

Hart Brothers Highland Park Aged 32 Years dist Nov 77, bott Aug 10 **(93.5) n23** bananas and custard and a few other notes displaying dotage; **t24** that is a quite beautiful delivery: entirely unexpected from the nose. The very softest vanillas imaginable on a lightly oiled base plus sublime sugars nesting amid something approaching a lightly smoked gristiness; they say we return to childhood as we get older...; **f22.5** hard to find more gentle vanillas if you searched every cask in Scotland... **b24** even though grey haired and stooping somewhat, the elegance and good breeding is unmistakable. A beautiful whisky experience. *46%. sc.*

⫶⫶⫶ **James MacArthur Old Masters Highland Park 13 Years Old** cask no. 5790, dist 1998, bott Feb 12 **(88) n22** spices prickle the honey; **t23** salivating and attractively tart barley as the salt bites deep. The honey is always around to soothe; **f21** burned coffee; **b22** perhaps not quite matured in the finest oak Scotland has seen, but there is certainly nought wrong with the spirit. *57.5%. nc ncf sc. James MacArthur & Co.*

The MacPhail's Collection Highland Park 1987 (84.5) n22 t23 f18.5 b21. For all its obvious brilliance on the nose and delivery, helped along by a much higher degree of smoke than is the norm, it doesn't quite make it as an all round success story. The delivery is fabulous with its massive honey and peat. But the finish falls flat on its face by offering a bitterness entirely out of place with its early prospects. Of course the smoke on the nose papered over the cracks in the oak, but the degree of tightness did make you wonder... *43%*

Malts Of Scotland Highland Park 1986 bourbon hogshead, cask no. 2296, dist Jun 86, bott Feb 11 **(95) n24.5** If there is a nose that encapsulates HP at its most delicate and understated, then this must be it: all the trademark flourishes, but seemingly in miniature. Perhaps the lightness of it all is emphasised by the lemon-citrus slant. Whatever, it is a thing of beauty; **t24** the nose and taste are an exact match: the citrus is plentiful and dilutes the honey and smoke into flavours which tantalise rather than dominate; there are soft vanillas, too, plus spice and barley juice. A little bitterness creeps into the late middle; **f22.5** even though the cask is showing the odd sign of fatigue at this point, there is still enough of the delicate sugars to ensure a charming glow, not unlike the effect of the sunset at midnight on June 30th at HP. **b24** curses! Tasting this just a couple of days after the 75th anniversary being distilled: had I known, I would have shifted my tasting schedule to mark the occasion especially. And, believe me: with a malt like this, there is a lot to celebrate. *50.7%. nc ncf sc. 234 bottles.*

Master Of Malt Highland Park 13 Year Old refill bourbon hogshead, dist 1997, bott 2010 **(91) n23** waxy smoke: clever spices and Palma violets seriously up the intensity levels; a touch of physalis helps lighten them a little; **t23.5** those spices are first out of the blocks and some heavy duty honey, backed by a ridge of natural caramel ensures all stays on the plump side; **f21.5** plenty of vanilla and caramel; **b23** everything you would expect from a sound HP cask. *57%. nc ncf sc. Master Of Malt. 281 bottles.*

⫶⫶⫶ **Mo Òr Collection Highland Park 1986 24 Years Old** first fill bourbon hogshead, cask no. 2275, 27 Jun 86, bott 29 Oct 10 **(92) n23** slightly more butterscotch than honey this time, though the delicate floral notes star; **t24** the smoke is barely noticeable on the nose, but it arrives here on about the fifth or sixth wave to complete an impressive opening; the maple sugars are fragile and very clean; the spices are as gentle as they come; **f22** back to butterscotch with the inevitable vanilla whirl; **b23** hints and shadows about: as deft as they come. *46%. nc ncf sc. Release No. 8. The Whisky Talker. 300 bottles.*

⫶⫶⫶ **Mo Òr Collection Highland Park 1996 14 Years Old** first fill bourbon barrel, cask no. DL6457, dist 13 Sep 96, bott 14 Sep 10 **(86.5) n21 t22.5 f21 b22.** The limitations of oak only partially block the delicately-smoked complexity. The even-handed sweetness on delivery really is sublime. *46%. nc ncf sc. Release No. 50. The Whisky Talker. 475 bottles.*

Old Malt Cask Highland Park Aged 13 Years refill hogshead, cask no. 6398, dist Sep 96, bott Jul 10 **(90) n22.5** intense with the barley prominent and the honey of the slightly forgotten in the jar variety; **t23** lovely delivery with decent body: like honey on porridge; **f22** long, with waxy vanilla fade; **b22.5** clean as a whistle: no scars from the cask at all (well, maybe the very faintest, almost negligible trace of later bitterness) and all the usual HP characteristics in perfect working order. *50%. nc ncf sc. Douglas Laing & Co. 388 bottles.*

⁙ **Old Malt Cask Highland Park Aged 14 Years** sherry butt, cask no. 7234, dist Sep 96, bott Jun 11 **(90) n22** vanilla and perhaps a very distant degree of smoke; **t22.5** almost identical to cask 7865, but with a little extra cocoa; **f22.5** peat, honey and cocoa; **b23** virtually a re-run on the taste buds of another HP OMC: real peas in a pod! That said, this has a little extra complexity and better use of the sweeter elements. *50%. nc ncf sc. 300 bottles.*

⁙ **Old Malt Cask Highland Park Aged 15 Years** sherry hogshead, cask no. 7865, dist Sep 96, bott Nov 11 **(88.5) n21.5** the closest to fruit on this is under-ripe tomatoes; a few shards of vanilla; **t22.5** lovely spiced honey and even a degree of hickory on hand; lightly oiled; the smoke shows itself subtly through the middle ground; **f22** still the peat and honey continues; **b22.5** the fruit hangs back allowing the complexity to gather pace. *50%. nc ncf sc. 394 bottles.*

Old Malt Cask Highland Park Aged 27 Years refill sherry hogshead, cask no. 6377, dist Mar 83, Jul 10 **(89) n23 t23 f21 b22.** Old Beer cask, more like... *50%. nc ncf sc. 247 bottles.*

Premier Barrel Highland Park Aged 12 Years (82.5) n20 t22 f20 b20.5. Plenty of Golden Syrup and attractive, almost coppery metallic sharpness. But never settles or feels particularly happy with itself by HP standards. *46%. nc ncf sc. Douglas Laing & Co. 182 bottles.*

Premier Barrel Highland Park Aged 12 Years (85.5) n21.5 t22.5 f20 b21.5. A slight bitter edge cannot entirely disturb the well entrenched honey and kumquat. *46%. nc ncf sc. Douglas Laing & Co. 370 bottles.*

Premier Barrel Highland Park Aged 13 Years (87.5) n22.5 t23 f20.5 b21.5. Wonderful nose and delivery combo. *46%. nc ncf sc. 319 bottles.*

Provenance Highland Park Over 11 Years refill hogshead, cask no. 7086, dist Autumn 99, bott Spring 2011 **(88) n22.5 t22 f21.5 b22.** HP at its most simple and easy going. *46%. nc ncf sc. Douglas Laing & Co.*

Provenance Highland Park Over 12 Years refill hogshead, cask no. 6822, dist Autumn 98, bott Autumn 2010 **(77) n18.5 t21.5 f18 b19.** An OK-ish whisky. But by HP's mega-high standards, thin and less than convincing. *46%. nc ncf sc. Douglas Laing & Co.*

Provenance Highland Park Over 13 Years refill hogshead, cask no. 7479, dist Autumn 97, bott Summer 2011 **(87) n20.5 t23 f21.5 b21.5.** A curious HP, this. Seems to splutter like a plane with a dodgy engine and just as it appears to be heading to earth, it starts up again and soars off to offer wonderful views. *46%. nc ncf sc. Douglas Laing & Co.*

Scotch Malt Whisky Society Cask 4.148 Aged 10 Years 1st fill bourbon barrel, cask no. 800271, dist 2000 **(86) n21.5 t22.5 f21 b21.** Plenty of sweet, juicy character and spice. But you get the feeling the whole thing is half cooked. Indeed: if this is from a first fill bourbon barrel, then either it has been maturing in a snow drift for the last 10 years, or the cask had matured a bourbon for about 20 years... *59.9%. sc. 206 bottles.*

Scotch Malt Whisky Society Cask 4.151 Aged 26 Years refill sherry butt, cask no. 1751, dist 1984 **(93) n23** plums and dates as well as grape here: pretty weighty for an HP; **t23** the impact is like being hit by a ton of grapey feathers; an appealing mix of natural caramels and fruit... shouldn't work, but just does, though it needs a generous dose of spices to inject a biting balance; **f23.5** long and highly impressive. Still there is no aggression, just continuing waves of fruit and nut chocolate; **b23.5** the distillery has a silky character at the best of times. Here it somehow marries substance with near weightlessness: some trick! *53%. sc. 226 bottles.*

⁙ **Scotch Malt Whisky Society Cask 4.155 Aged 11 Years** first fill barrel, cask no. 800158, dist 1999 **(93) n22** relatively light for an HP of this age: someone forgot to add the peat to the kiln, or at least get it to smoke; **t23.5** they certainly did forget to add the barley which comes through in the juiciest terms; **f24** from somewhere the vaguest hint of spice and smoke arrive...better late than never; **b23.5** just a beautifully made malt, even if all the usual HP characteristics take a bit of time to evolve. *58.6%. sc. Scotch Malt Whisky Society.*

Scott's Selection Highland Park 1981 bott 2011 **(97) n24** all the usual HP characteristics are here in almost clichéd amounts: the smoke, the heather, the honey... but this has an added extra: a delicate degree of jelly baby fruitiness, mainly lime but with the strains of a raspberry tartness to counter the sweeter honey, as well; I would use the word delicate, but that hardly begins to do it justice... **t25** a faultless delivery. The honey and maple syrup are diluted so not to overwhelm the Rich Tea barley; the spices dissolve on impact while the vanillas carry just enough oaky dryness to balance the sugars: this is a force of nature...; **f24** here you might reasonably expect a bittering from the oak to break the spell you are by now under. But it never arrives. Instead, we have yet more and more layering of honey and now natural caramels, but with the sugars and spices still dancing together in the background...; **b24** perhaps the most remarkable thing about this particular bottling, is that it is almost a distillation of the great Highland Park distillery itself. Absolutely nothing jumps out at you as being extra special. Conversely, I cannot find a single fault with it, either. It is as if this whisky in my glass is making a very simple statement: "This is why I have been one of the world's top five most consistent whiskies." It is quite impossible to even attempt to contradict it. Indeed, had it even gone further and told you that it is one of the top ten single cask whiskies you are likely to taste in your lifetime, I am not sure where the materials required for a counter argument could be found. This, ladies and gentlemen, is near as damn it as good as it gets... *48.5%. Speyside Distillers.*

⁘ **Scott's Selection Highland Park 1989** bott 2012 **(84.5) n22 t20.5 f21.5 b20.5.** Unusual for a HP of this age in that the honey has been outflanked by the oak. *51.4%. Speyside Distillers.*

⁘ **The Whisky Agency Highland Park 27 Years Old** bourbon cask, dist 1984, bott 2011 **(93) n24** complex with a fascinating smattering of peat and coal dust. Bigger than usual citrus for this distillery, giving the feeling of a room newly cleaned after a visit from the chimney sweep; the spices and soft red liquorice offer just the right weight; **t23.5** distinctive tangerine notes ensure a controlled sweetness to balance against the spices and dusty smoke; the midground is thick with vanilla and barley; **f22** relatively shy and retiring and dependent on the clean barley; **b23.5** soft and satisfying. Pushes all the right buttons. *52.5%. sc.*

The Whisky Agency Highland Park 1977 bott 2010 **(88.5) n23.5 t22 f21 b22.** The shape of the whisky has been weathered by time. But its innate beauty remains fully recognisable. *52.3%. The Whisky Agency.*

⁘ **The Whisky Agency Highland Park 2000** bott 2012 **(86) n22 t22 f20.5 b21.5.** Some classic honey and light peat moments here ensure a familiar tune on both nose and palate. Thins just a little too enthusiastically. *53.3%. nc ncf sc. The Whisky Agency.*

⁘ **Whisky Antique Highland Park 22 Years Old Special Bottling** dist 1988, bott 2011 **(85) n20 t23 f20.5 b21.5.** The streaks of honeyed greatness here more than compensate for the failings of the over exposed, milky oak. The gorgeous high notes really can shatter the crystal most impressively, though. *53.4%. sc. Silver Seal Whisky Company.*

⁘ **The Whisky Cask Highland Park Aged 24 Years** bourbon cask, dist 1986, bott 2010 **(94.5) n24.5** heather: tick. Peat: tick. Honey: tick. Barley: tick. All in perfect rhythm and order and offering crotch-bulging complexity; **t24** quite superb interplay between the smoke and juicier, fruitier notes, especially the Jaffa Cake and lemon zest; excellent spice in the middle ground; **f22.5** an annoying degree of late cask bitterness. But the light smoke won't be denied, nor the honey and sugars. **b23.5** you're unlikely to find a more Highland Parky Highland Park this year. So much pollen with this honey, I've just had a sneezing fit! *52%. sc.*

Whisky Doris Highland Park 1995 bourbon hogshead, cask no. 1468, dist Jul 95, bott May 10 **(89.5) n23 t23.5 f21 b22.** HP = Honeyed Perfectly... *55.8%. Whisky Doris.*

IMPERIAL

Speyside, 1897. Chivas Brothers. Silent.

Imperial Aged 15 Years "Special Distillery Bottling" db **(69) n17 t18 f17 b17.** At least one very poor cask, hot spirit and overly sweet. Apart from that it's wonderful. *46%*

⁘ **Archives Imperial 1995 16 Years Old Third Release** bourbon cask, cask no. 50035, dist May 95, bott Apr 12 **(89) n72** sharp, clean, lively barley; just a murmur of bourbon-style liquorice; **t23** salivating, quite brittle in a Glen Grant style maltiness with some citrus sticking to the light oils; **f22** good oak offers just the right degree of clean vanilla; **b22** even, quite simplistic, yet always a delight. *51.7%. nc ncf sc. Whiskybase B.V. 60 bottles.*

⁘ **Glen Karadag** dist 1997, bott 2011, Crimean Madeira cask **(90) n22.5** a mildly tight nose, and not immediately recognisable within the normal Imperial family of characteristics. But I have just noticed this is a Crimean Madeira, so it is not something this distillery sees every day. Most intriguing is the light gooseberry fruitiness tied in with vaguely spiced barley; **t23** much firmer and more confident. The crisp barley surge is superb, the deft almost gristy sweetness a perfect foil for the bubbling spices; **f22** thins as the vanilla takes charge. A thread of pithy fruit, marrying even more spice, reminds you of the Madeira link; **b22.5** after taking three of us two days to open the sample bottle, this needed to be worth waiting for...As it happens, it really was! *46%. Duncan Taylor & Co. Ukraine exclusive. 414 bottles.*

Gordon & MacPhail Distillery Label Imperial 1993 (88.5) n23 t22 f21.5 b22. Enjoyable whisky, not least because you are never quite sure the direction it is taking next. *43%*

Old Malt Cask Imperial Aged 16 Years refill hogshead, cask no. 7018, dist Apr 95, bott Apr 11 **(85) n21 t21 f21.5 b21.5.** Untaxing mega-malty Imperial showing all its blending colours. *50%. nc ncf sc. Douglas Laing & Co. 271 bottles.*

⁘ **Old Malt Cask Imperial Aged 35 Years** refill butt, cask no. 7431, dist Oct 76, bott Oct 11 **(90) n22** how do you get so many citrus notes on a malt so old...? **t23.5** improbably refreshing for its age with the delivery all about the barley and lime hinted at on the nose; **f22** quite sublime cocoa: almost something of the chocolate liqueur about the finale...; **b22.5** Don't know why. But a bar in Lexington, Virginia, flashed into my mind while tasting this. I must have tasted a malt that evening very close to this in style to cause the flashback. Well, this one certainly doesn't Stonewall... *50%. nc ncf sc. 443 bottles.*

⁘ **Scotch Single Malt Circle Imperial 1995** cask no. 512690, dist 24 Jan 95, bott 15 Feb 12 **(92) n23** a touch of fizzing perry with a sprig of mint; **t24** gorgeous delivery with the barley revelling in its freedom to expand in the juiciest of directions; just about perfect degree of oils and the spice-sugar mix in mid-ground is faultless; **f22** the vanilla and butterscotch which forms is soon lost behind a degree of Allied-style barrel-bitterness; **b23** another imperious stunner from this underestimated distillery. *50%. sc. Scotch Single Malt Circle.*

⋮ **Sestante Collection Imperial 19 Years Old** dist 1991, bott 2011 **(85.5) n22 t21 f21 b21.5.** A very firm malt with limited lateral movement on the palate. But the upfront barley plus cinnamon on the delicate fruit is good enough. *55.3%. sc. Silver Seal Whisky Company.*

⋮ **The Whisky Agency Imperial 1995** bott 2011 **(78) n21 t20 f18 b19.** Juicy and delicate to start, but the light spirit is no match for the bitterness of the poor quality and unforgiving cask. *46%. nc ncf sc. The Whisky Agency.*

INCHGOWER
Speyside, 1872. Diageo. Working.

Inchgower 1993 The Manager's Choice db **(84.5) n21 t21.5 f21 b21.** Like your malts subtle, delicate, clean and sophisticated? Don't bother with this one if you do. This has all the feel of a malt that's been spray painted onto the taste buds: thick, chewy and resilient. Can't help but like that mix of hazelnut and Demerara, though. You can stand a spoon in it. *61.9%*

⋮ **Berry's Own Selection Inchgower 1982** cask no. 6967, bott 2011 **(80) n21.5 t21 f18.5 b19.** An oil-slicked monster reminding us of Inchgower's excesses from its last days at Bell's. Fun, if you want your taste buds to have the crap kicked out of them. *54.5%. nc ncf sc.*

Berry's Own Selection Inchgower 1982 cask no. 6968, bott 2010 **(84.5) n21.5 t22 f20 b21.** A knife and fork job with masses of dark sugars and spice. Fun, but bitters out and lacks the usual complexity. *56.2%. nc ncf sc. Berry Bros & Rudd.*

⋮ **Dun Bheagan Inchgower 29 Years Old** hogshead, dist Jun 82 **(91) n22.5** the complex balance between the honey and latent fruitiness is a treat; **t23.5** this distillery usually offers a clunking heavyweight of a start. Here we have a light acacia honey lead, then a full barley-rich juice fest. Spices towards the middle are fabulous; **f22** settles for a more sedate honey-barley finale; **b23** rarely the most gainly of whiskies, this Inchgower overcomes its trademark indelicacies with a dizzying degree of spiced honey. *54.3%. nc ncf sc. Ian Macleod Distillers.*

⋮ **Duncan Taylor Rare Auld Inchgower 29 Years Old** cask no. 6975, dist 1982 **(87.5) n22** as salty as a sailor's armpit; **t21.5** a thudding delivery which biffs the taste buds. Somehow the sugars and barley find common ground amid the mayhem; **f22** settles into a chunky, barley-filled finish; **b22** a macho dram which is reassuringly aggressive. *54.8%. sc. Duncan Taylor & Co.*

⋮ **Gordon & MacPhail Connoisseurs Choice Inchgower 1997** (84.5) **n21 t21.5 f21 b21.** A plodding malt which does its best to do as little as possible. Yet the cask is good and as enjoyable as a corner shop cheese sandwich. *43%*

Malts Of Scotland Inchgower 1982 bourbon hogshead, cask no. 6969, dist Jun 82, bott Feb 11 **(91.5) n23** leafy and dry, the oaks make their mark without offering the expected bourbony sugars; **t24** gazooks! The taste buds are absolutely over-run by the magnificence of the brilliantly spiced barley which is bolstered by a natural burned fudge; loads of custard topped by molten muscovado sugars... stunning; **f21.5** slightly too vigorously drying; **b22.5** this whisky happened to be made on the very same day as my chief researcher, Ally Telfer, was born. It is obvious which malt has matured more magnificently over the years... *57.2%. nc ncf sc. 212 bottles.*

Old Malt Cask Inchgower Aged 28 Years refill hogshead, cask no. 6455, dist Jun 82, bott Aug 10 **(91) n23.5** a fabulous battle between big, bourbon sweetness, freshly squeezed orange and sliced cucumber...; **t23.5** the barley beats its chest on arrival but, not surprisingly, those bourbon incantations on the nose can be heard again; sharp kumquat and deft marzipan complete the job; **f21.5** drying custard vanilla; **b22.5** a typically lusty Inchgower which revels in its bawdy brute force. But there is real quality here, too. A fabulous example of this distillery's finer moments. *50%. nc ncf sc. Douglas Laing & Co. 165 bottles.*

⋮ **Provenance Inchgower Over 12 Years** sherry butt, cask no. 7654, dist Spring 1999, bott Spring 2011 **(85) n22 t21 f21 b21.** Ticks all the malty boxes, the nose conjures up a marvellous kumquat and gooseberry combo and the oak is top quality. The spirit, however, is a little stretched. *46%. nc ncf sc. Douglas Laing & Co.*

⋮ **Provenance Inchgower Over 12 Years** sherry butt, cask no. 7937, dist Spring 1999, bott Winter 2011 **(86) n21 t22 f21.5 b21.5.** Limited in its range across the palate perhaps, but there is no denying its clean, mouth-watering properties. An enjoyable dram. *46%. nc ncf sc.*

The Whisky Agency Inchgower 1974 bott 2010 **(89) n21.5 t23.5 f22 b22.** An unusual malt for its age, having a dark, mysterious nature rather than one that has opened up over time. Compellingly different. *50.4%. The Whisky Agency.*

The Whisky Castle Cask Collection No. 15 Inchgower 20 Years American oak, cask no. 6987, dist 1990, bott 2011 **(89) n22 t23 f22 b22.** I have to say that this distillery as often as not comes up with a malt with an almost eccentric character. Here's another one. *46%. nc ncf sc. Angus Dundee for The Whisky Castle. 264 bottles.*

INVERLEVEN
Lowland, 1938–1991. Demolished.

❖ **Deoch an Doras Inverleven 36 Years Old** dist 1973 **(94.5) n24** just one of those noses where you think twice about tasting: not because it is bad, but quite the opposite...you really don't want the experience to end. Exotic fruit sitting comfortably with bigger oak notes and the juiciest of grassy malt; **t23.5** a slightly ungainly delivery but after the first three or four flavour waves settles into a more rhythmic pulsing of light golden syrup, fresh barley, cocoa and spices; a bourbon sub text is deliciously fascinating; **f23** exemplary dovetailing of the finer details of the malt, with the spices now showing a little more keenly; **b24** as light on the palate as a morning mist. This distillery just wasn't designed to make a malt of this antiquity, yet this is to the manor born. 48.85%. nc ncf. Chivas Brothers. 500 bottles.

Gordon & MacPhail Distillery Label Inverleven 1991 (93.5) n24 t23.5 f22.5 b23.5. Handled the aging process with an accomplished performance. Surprisingly suave: one of the surprise packages of the year. 40%

ISLE OF ARRAN
Highlands (Island–Arran), 1995. Isle of Arran Distillers. Working.

The Arran Malt 8 Years Old Pinot Noir Finish db **(79.5) n19 t21 f19.5 b20.** Pleasant enough. But just seems to lack the trademark Arran balance and has a few lopsided moments to boot, especially at the death. 50%. Isle of Arran Distillers.

The Arran Malt 8 Years Old Pomerol Wine Finish db **(87) n19** another Arran which strains against a fruity muzzle; **t23.5** that's much more like it!! All the harmony missing on the nose arrives in buckets as the trademark thickness of body takes on the spiced grape without missing a beat. Beautiful...; **f22** much drier, as it should be, but the chalkiness of the oak hardly makes a dent on the barley-grape surface. Just a slight wobble on the finish; **b22.5** Full bodied and lush. 50%. Isle of Arran Distillers.

The Arran Malt Under 10 Years Old db **(89) n22** limp, lush barley of the butterscotch variety; **t23** those stunning soft oils are working overtime to spread the sweet barley, **f22** long, biscuity and balanced; **b22** this one's kicked its shoes and socks off . 43%

The Arran Malt 10 Year Old db **(87) n22.5** sharp and lively with an unusual (and unwelcome) fruity nip; no shortage of polished oak floors and big vanilla; **t22.5** juicy with a number of lighter sugars in attendance; the barley forms the main thrust, but still a vague fruit character presses itself; **f20** surprisingly dull with the vanilla working hard for attention; **b22** it has been a while since I last officially tasted this. If they are wiling to accept some friendly advice, I think the blenders should tone down on raising any fruit profile and concentrate on the malt, which is amongst the best in the business. 46%. nc ncf.

The Arran Malt 12 Years Old db **(83) n21.5 t22 f20.5 b21** Hmmmm. Surprise one, this. There must be more than one bottling already of this. The first I tasted was perhaps slightly on the oaky side but otherwise intact and salt-honeyed where need be. This one has a bit of a tang: very drinkable, but definitely a less than brilliant cask around. 46%

❖ **The Arran Malt 12 Years Old Cask Strength Batch 1** bott Sep 11 db **(78) n21 t22 f17 b18.** There is no questioning that Arran is now one of Scotland's Premier League quality malts. But the strength of their whisky is in their bourbon casks, not so much their sherry. And to create a batch like this was tempting fate. The sulphur present is by no means huge, but it takes only a single off butt to spoil the party. 54.1%. nc ncf. 12,000 bottles.

The Arran Malt Aged 14 Years db **(89.5) n22** light dusting of cumquat and physalis does not form quite a big enough umbrella to cope with the oaky storm clouds; **t23.5** usual sublime weight to the body, but the oak makes its pitch several beats earlier than the norm. Fortunately there is still enough Demerara sugar and barley sugar to make for a massively juicy experience; **f21.5** dries profoundly with the oak offering a chalky farewell; **b22.5** a superb whisky, but the evidence that there has been a subtle shift in emphasis, with the oak now taking too keen an interest, is easily attained. 46%. ncf.

❖ **The Arran Malt 1995 Bourbon Single Cask Distillery Festival Release 2012** cask no. 128 db **(92.5) n23.5** packs quite an oaky punch for one so relatively young: chunky, chocolaty and brimming with spiced nougat; **t23** doesn't do anything to lessen the pace on delivery: the spices virtually shriek at you as the liquorice takes on an almost fruity edge; **f23** toasty and sharp; the sugars babble and squabble on the big oaky fade which enjoys a wonderful Jaffa Cake finale; **b23** now that really is one profound Isle of Arran... 54.7%. nc ncf sc.

The Arran Malt 1996 'The Peacock' Icons of Arran bott 2009 **(96) n24.5** oh my word: what a shame I have only three or four months to write this book: the degree of complexity will take that time to unravel. Both floral and fruity in almost perfect doses, the white pepper perfectly balances the light saltiness. The big weight is deceptive as the delicate sultana and perry sub plot appears to give more air and space to the overall picture. Outstanding...; **t24.5** what a delicate creature this is: the juicy grape appears to be apparent on a couple of levels, sandwiching the honey and hickory bourbon notes between them; **f23** long, now with that hint of pear on the nose re-surfacing as the finish nestles somewhere between butterscotch tart and buttered toast; **b24** yet again this outstanding distillery delivers the goods: one of the most outstanding malts of the year and certainly one of the most complex. I've not yet spoken to the Arran guys about this, but would happily bet my house that this is a sublime mix of top bourbon cask and faultless sherry. As fabulous as this distillery unquestionably is, they will be hard pressed to keep this standard going... *46%*

The Arran Malt 1996 Single Cask sherry butt, cask no. 1596, bott 2009 db **(88.5) n22 t23 f21 b22.5.** Excellent whisky. But no doubt the oak is a tad too domineering and the points here would have been higher if bottled a couple of years earlier. *54.4%*

The Arran Malt Single Sherry Cask 1996 cask no. 1973, dist 11 Dec 96, bott 31 Mar 11 db **(91.5) n23** crystalline fruit, including a hint of banana to soften matters. Clean and, for those capable of sherried whisky hard-ons, about as arousing as it gets. I suspect... **t24.5** rock solid barley wrapped in juicy grape. Spices arrive on demand and stay the course. The sugars are the stuff of future sugar hero worship... I doubt if those with the sherried hard-ons have made it to this point...; **f21.5** crumbles slightly as it dries. Bitterness creeps in, but those sugars and spices do a pretty impressive job; **b22.5** a rare case of a great whisky being let down slightly by the quality of the European oak itself, rather than any sulphur treatment. For the most part, glorious. *54.1%. nc ncf sc. UK exclusive. 264 bottles.*

⁘ **The Arran Malt 1996 Bourbon Single Cask** cask no. 400 db **(93) n24** a sawdusty dryness slowly gives way to ultra-delicate maple syrup and coconut notes. But it's all whispers and hints, making it all the sexier; look out for the Mars bars with a sprinkling of salt. When the honey and kumquat starts to weave itself into the picture...wow! **t23** much silkier delivery than the full on and sometimes sparky nose testifies to. Barley resounds first and foremost with the sugars inching their way in alongside the ever darkening oaky tones. There's the familiar chocolate and spice theme towards the middle; **f22.5** much more strait laced and vanilla happy; **b23.5** high quality, complex and rewarding. *46.8%. nc ncf. Distillery exclusive.*

The Arran Malt Sherry Single Cask 1997 ex-sherry hogshead no. 410 db **(88.5) n23 t22 f21.5 b22.** Elegant. *52.2%*

The Arran Malt Sherry Single Cask 1997 ex-sherry hogshead no. 435 db **(89) n22.5 t23 f21.5 b22.** Lively and showing a pleasing edginess. *52.5%*

The Arran Malt Sherry Single Cask 1997 ex-sherry hogshead no. 517 db **(86.5) n22 t22 f21 b21.5.** The occasional clap of thundering, salty malt, but the fruitiness tones the intensity down towards the middle and finish. *53.5%*

The Arran Malt Sherry Single Cask cask no. 819, dist Jun 98, bott Jun 09 db **(91) n23 t24 f22 b22.** A thumpingly good sherry cask with not a single off note detectable. *57.7%*

The Arran Malt 1997 Single Cask sherry hogshead no. 965, bott 2010 db **(93.5) n24 t24 f22.5 b23.** For those who like their grape a little seasoned. A celebration of what a good, untarnished sherry butt should be all about. What a star...!! *55%. Belgium.*

The Arran Malt 1997 Single Cask sherry hogshead no. 1318, bott 2009 db **(95) n24 t24.5 f23 b23.5.** The kind of sophisticated malt you could drop an olive into...but don't..!! *52.5% Japan.*

The Arran Malt 1997 'The Rown Tree' Icons of Arran bott 2010 db **(77.5) n18.5 t22 f18 b19.** The key here is balance and harmony. And this, unusually for an Arran, possesses little of either. The bitter finish confirms the unhappiness hinted at on the nose. Someone was barking up the wrong tree when putting this one together and the malt, in this form, even for all the sweet, bright moments on delivery, is ready for the chop. *46% Isle of Arran Distillers*

The Arran Malt 1998 Single Cask sherry butt no. 452, bott 2009 db **(93.5) n23.5 t24 f23 b23.** Wonderfully assertive yet always pays respect to the salty sub-plot. Complex, elegant and never short of character. A charmer bordering on the old school. *56.3% USA.*

The Arran Malt 1998 Single Cask bourbon cask no. 650, bott 2009 db **(89) n21.5 t23 f22 b22.5.** Lacking the usual weight and showing signs of an impatient stillman, still this malt turns cartwheels on the taste buds. An entertainer. *576% USA.*

The Arran Malt 1998 Single Cask bourbon cask no. 673, bott 2009 db **(87.5) n21 t22 f22.2 b22.** Many of the same attributes as cask 650; and my suspicion about some rapid distillation has been confirmed. *55.7% Norway.*

The Arran Malt 1998 "The Westie" Icons Of Arran oloroso cask, bott 2011 **(85) n20.5 t22.5 f21 b21.** Pleasant but, frankly, dull fayre, despite the spicy teasing on delivery. Such an oloroso cask may be fine for a commoner, but hardly fit for an emperor... *46%. nc ncf. 6000 bottles.*

⁘ **The Arran Malt 1999 "The Eagle" Icons Of Arran** bourbon barrels & sherry hogsheads, bott 2012 db **(77) n19.5 t20.5 f18 b19.** Don't know about the eagle having landed: this one never took off...the wings have been clipped by sulphur. *46%. nc ncf. 6,000 bottles.*

The Arran Malt 1999 Vintage 15th Anniversary Edition finished in amontillado, bott 2010 db **(92.5) n24** sherry as you demand it shows on the nose. Clean, confident, a hint of sultana only as this is dry, yet always with enough finesse for the barley to come through loud and clear: an absolute treat...; **t23.5** salivating from the off with a glittering delivery of fresh grape and spice. Waves of vanilla punch through and there is a fabulous malty flourish towards the middle. But those spices continue to pulse...; **f22.5** drier, with vanilla pods and a buttery residue; **b22.5** there is no mistaking excellence. And here it appears to flow freely. 54.6%

The Arran Malt Open Day Single Bourbon Cask Bottling 2011 db (94) **n23.5** unbelievable degree of fruit sitting alongside the rich barley and muscovado-enriched bourbon notes; **t24** a match of spice and sugared barley made in heaven; **f23.5** the earlier juiciness evaporates as the vanillas lay claim. But enough spices – and fruit – remain for the finale to be anything but standard; **b23.5** to me, Arran in a high class bourbon cask shows the distillery to its very finest advantage: my case rests... 52%. nc ncf sc. Sold at distillery during 2011 Open Day.

The Arran Malt 2005 Single Cask "The Peated Arran" bourbon cask no. 116, bott 2009 db (89) **n22.5 t22 f21.5 b22.** For its tender years, it works uncommonly well. 57.7%

The Arran Malt Ambassador's Choice db (87.5) **n22 t22 f21.5 b22.** So heavy with oak I was amazed I could pick the nosing glass up... 46%

The Arran Malt Amarone Cask Finish db (94.5) **n23** the buzzing black peppers leave you in no doubt what is to follow. As does the stunning clarity of the grape and crisp, business-like manner of the barley: stirring! **t24** and so it is played out on the palate: the grape is juicy and sweet, the barley is firm and forms the perfect skeleton, the spices pop busily around the palate. No great age evident, but the oak also chimes in with a few choice cocoa notes; **f23** a shard of bitterness, but nothing which subtracts from the gloss; **b23.5** as cask finishes go, this one is just about perfect. 50%. nc ncf.

The Arran Malt Bourgogne Finish db (74) **n18 t19 f18 b19.** Arran Malt Vinegar more like... 56.4%

The Arran Malt Chianti Classico Riserva Cask Finish db (85) **n19 t23 f21 b22.** Mamma mia. there eeza poco zolfo ina mia malto!! Butta chicco d'uva. ee eez eccellente! 55%

⟐ **The Arran Malt Devil's Punch Bowl Chapter No. 1** db (72) **n17.5 t22.5 f15 b17.** For a few brief moments the delivery shows why Arran can rightly be considered one of the best distilleries in Scotland. But the finish, following on from the faulty nose, suggests they are in danger of blowing their reputation. I don't know what's happened in the last year but there appears to be a new policy of involving sherry butts at every turn. Sadly, they are not weeding out the sulphured ones and the result here is ruinous brimstone for the Devil's Punch Bowl. If you are going to dance with the devil – present era sherry butts – you had better know exactly what you are doing. Otherwise you're be playing with fire 52.3%. nc ncf. 6,600 bottles.

The Arran Malt Fino Sherry Cask Finish db (82.5) **n21 t20 f21 b20.5.** Pretty tight with the bitterness not being properly compensated for 50%

The Arran Malt Fontalloro Wine Cask Finish db (84.5) **n20 t22 f21.5 b21.** For a wine cask, the malt really does sing. 55%

The Arran Malt Lepanto PX Brandy Finish db (85) **n22 t22 f20 b21.** Tight, unusually thin for an Arran, but some lovely sweet fruit amid the confusion. Pretty oaky, too. 59%

The Arran Malt Madeira Wine Cask Finish db (77.5) **n19 t21 f18.5 b19.** The odd exultant moment but generally flat, flaky and bitter. 50%

The Arran Malt Moscatel Cask Finish db (87) **n22 t21.5 f22 b21.5.** Arran is pretty full bodied stuff when just left to its own devices. In this kind of finish it heads towards an almost syrupy texture. Luckily, the grape effect works fine. 55%

The Arran Malt 'Original' db (80.5) **n19 t22 f19.5 b20.** Not the greatest bourbon casks used here 43%

The Arran Malt Pineau des Charentes Cask Finish db (94) **n22.5** wispy barley clouds in a bright, sweet-grapey sky; **t24** succulent and spicy. Delivery is first class, allowing full weight to the grassy barley before those fuller, fruitier notes close in. The spices are fabulously subtle and mildly puckering; **f23.5** a real chocolate dessert helped by the slow build up of soft oils; **b24** I may not be the greatest fan of cask finishes, but when one comes along like this, exhibiting such excellence, I'll be the first to doff my hat. 55%

The Arran Malt Pinot Noir Cask Finish db (73.5) **n18 t19 f18 b18.5.** A less than efficient cask from the Germans who produced it. Plenty of off key moments on nose and taste, but it does enjoy a too brief, barely redeeming Bird's Angel Delight chocolatey moment. 50%

The Arran Malt Pomerol Cask Finish Bordeux wine casks db (86.5) **n20 t23 f22 b21.5.** Although the cask is very marginally flawed, the relentlessness of the sweet, juicy grape and barley is a sheer delight. The odd cocoa note does no harm either. 50%

The Arran Malt Port Cask Finish db (85.5) **n21 t22.5 f22 b20.** One of the real problems with cask finishes is that there is no real or straightforward reference point to knowing exactly when the host flavours and the guest ones are in maximum alignment. For all this one's obvious charms. I get the feeling it was bottled when the balance was pretty low on the graph... 58.3%. nc ncf.

The Arran Malt Premier Cru Bourgogne Cask Finish db **(86) n21 t22 f21 b22.** An entertaining dram which some would do somersaults for, but marks docked because we have lost the unique Arran character. 56.4%

The Arran Malt Robert Burns 250 Years Anniversary Edition db **(91.5) n22.5** mainly floral with just a light touch from the barley; **t23.5** unusually light and flighty in body. A dusting of caster sugar softens the vanilla even further: juicy, a touch spicy and quite wonderful; **f22.5** a few oils had formed towards the middle and follow through to the end. Again it is barley dominant with a squeeze of something citrussy; **b23** curiously, not that far away from the light Lowland style of malt produced in the 60s and 70s in Burns' native Lowlands. Not the usual Arran, but shows that it can change personality now and again and still be a total charmer. 43%

The Arran Malt St. Emilion Cask Finish Grand Cru Classé wine casks db **(89) n24** huge aroma: thick grape and big fruitcake. The vanillas have a toasted feel to them; crisped hazelnut, too; **t22** almost too big and busy as the intensity of the grape and the roastiness of the oak clash. But a fabulous river of sweet barley flows freely enough once it gets past the early dam; **f21.5** muscovado and grapey sugars see off some threatening bitterness but it is still a bit on the heavy side; **b21.5** not the best balanced whisky you'll ever pour. But such is the sheer force of flavours, you have to doff your beret... 50%

The Arran Malt Sassicaia Wine Cask Finish db **(92.5) n22.5 t23.5 f23 b23.5.** Unquestionably one of Arran's better wine finishes. 55%

The Arran Malt Sauternes Cask Finish db **(86) n21 t23 f21 b21.** Plenty of sugars and allure. But natural caramels bring an abrupt halt to the complexity. 50%. nc ncf.

The Arran Malt Sauternes Finish db **(84) n21 t22 f20 b21.** Strap yourself in for this one: eye-watering sultana and 240 volts of spice. Choked with oak, though. 56%

The Arran Malt "The Sleeping Warrior" bott 2011 db **(84.5) n19 t22.5 f21.5 b21.5.** Zzzzzzzz. 54.9%. nc ncf. 6000 bottles.

The Arran Malt Tokaji Aszu Wine Cask Finish db **(83) n20 t21.5 f21 b20.5.** Pleasant enough, but the wine dulls the more interesting edges. 55%

Isle of Arran 'Jons Utvalgte' Aged 7 Years db **(87) n22** intense malt with trace vanilla; t21.5 tangy malt thickens; **f22** a touch of spiced butterscotch and vanilla adds relief to the full on barley; **b21.5** The clean intensity of the malt is soup-like. 46%. Norway.

The Peated Arran "Machrie Moor" 1st release db **(86.5) n22 t22 f21 b21.5.** A bit of a surprise package: I have tasted many peated Arrans over recent years, the majority voluptuous and generous in their giving. Yet this one is strangely aloof. The flavours and nuances have to be sought rather than presented for inspection and there is a hardness throughout which makes for a very solid dram. That said, it has many fine qualities, too. And the mouth-watering unravelling of its slightly cough-sweetish intensity is great entertainment. A fascinating, mixed bag. 46%. nc ncf. 9000 bottles.

⁘ **Cadenhead Arran 15 Years Old** bott Apr 12 **(88.5) n21.5** just a little tightness from the cask; **t23** the limitation of the oak is shrugged aside by the zingy, eye-watering salty barley. The sugars dissolve beautifully; **f21.5** the cask constricts but the salty and spiced custard still has much to offer; **b22.5** Arran heading into virtually unknown territory at this age. Perhaps not quite the complete deal but plenty going on here to delight. 56.9%. sc. WM Cadenhead Ltd.

Connoisseurs Choice Arran 1999 (90) n23 clean barley offers a squeeze of citrus in just the right spots; **t22.5** fresh barley and newly cut grass; the oak takes a meandering course, offering the odd touch of natural caramels; **f22** butterscotch and delicate spice; **b22.5** outwardly simple malt. But spend a little time with it and drink in the understated complexity. 43%

⁘ **Duncan Taylor Dimensions Isle Of Arran 15 Years Old** dist Dec 96, bott Feb 12 **(84.5) n21 t22 f20 b21.5.** Plenty of fizz and citrus to the barley. But probably not quite the best cask Arran has ever been filled into. 46%. nc ncf sc. Duncan Taylor & Co.

⁘ **Hart Brothers Isle Of Arran Aged 15 Years** sherry wood, cask no. 1312, dist 24 Sep 96, bott 30 Apr 12 **(86) n21 t23.5 f20 b21.5.** As present day sherry butts go, not a bad one. But, then, not a great one either. The finish is dull and a little fuzzy but at least the delivery and follow through gives us a delicious Swiss Roll cream and jam middle to enjoy. 46%. sc.

McCulloch Arran 8 Years Old oloroso hogshead, cask no. 772, bott Sep 10 **(86) n21.5 t23 f20 b21.5.** Those happy souls unable to detect sulphur should make a bee-line for this: before being treated in Jerez this probably would have qualified as one of the sherry butts of the year. 49%. nc ncf sc. Chester Whisky & Liquors. 305 bottles.

⁘ **Mo Òr Collection Isle Of Arran 1996 14 Years Old** first fill bourbon hogshead, cask no. 96/868, dist 5 Aug 96, bott 2 Dec 10 **(87) n22.5** almost something of a leek and celery broth with plenty of salt added; there is also juicier and floral undertones, too; **t22.5** the big juicy barley arrival is no surprise. Nor is the fabulous complexity between the sugars and salts which follow; **f20.5** the bitter finish is unusual for a first fill cask; **b21.5** an excellent spirit undone slightly by a disappointingly tight cask. 46%. nc ncf sc. Release no 35. 475 bottles.

Old Malt Cask Arran Aged 15 Years refill hogshead, cask no. 7504, dist Jul 96, bott Jul 11 **(93) n24** spellbinding: so delicate, subtle and sophisticated it almost seems a shame to go on and taste: the barley is fresh but seemingly sharpened by a single shake of salt; the citrus notes are alive and alluring, hedging towards orange pith; the sugars refuse to be buttonholed: neither honey or dark brown, or a syrup. Or maybe a touch of all three...; **t23.5** mouth-watering from the off. A cascade of intense barley is followed by a thrilling delivery of massive spice. Again there is a shaft of sweetness that falls into no immediate category...perhaps nearer a gristy style; **f22.5** dips slightly as a little bitterness from the oak makes an entrance. But the spices stay buzzing and the barley continues its refreshing course; **b23** in some respects the best old Arran above ten years I have encountered. Friendly memo to my friends at Arran: please note... this is not a cask finish... *50%. nc ncf sc. Douglas Laing & Co. 321 bottles.*

Provenance Arran Over 12 Years refill hogshead, cask no. 6418, dist Autumn 97, bott Summer 2010 **(89) n21.5 t23 f22 b22.5.** Can't say I have ever encountered an Arran displaying this kind of personality before. But have to say: I like it! *46%. nc ncf sc. Douglas Laing & Co.*

Provenance Arran Over 12 Years refill hogshead, cask no. 6824, dist Summer 98, bott Autumn 2010 **(80) n20 t21 f19 b20.** Along similar lines to cask 6418, but the missing sweetness and less meaningful spice exposes the oak's weaknesses. *46%. nc ncf sc.*

Provenance Arran Over 12 Years refill hogshead, cask no. 7163, dist Summer 98, bott Spring 2011 **(89) n22 t23.5 f21.5 b22.** Fruity, fresh and frisky. *46%. nc ncf sc.*

-:- **Provenance Arran Over 13 Years** refill butt, cask no. 7680, dist Winter 1997, bott Autumn 2011 **(84.5) n21 t22 f20 b21.5.** An attractively made dram but unusual for this distillery by not spreading its wings beyond some charming barley notes. *46%. nc ncf sc. Douglas Laing & Co.*

Scotch Malt Whisky Society Cask 121.38 Aged 7 Years refill sherry butt, cask no. 800397, dist 2002 **(69.5) n18.5 t19 f15.5 b16.5.** I could weep. All those magnificent casks of Arran out there and the judging panel, in their combined "wisdom", choose this sulphured dross. Astonishing. A great distillery, the Society's outstanding reputation and its members have all been done no favours whatsoever. *61.6%. sc. 668 bottles.*

-:- **Scotch Malt Whisky Society Cask 121.51 Aged 9 Years** refill butt, cask no. 800399, dist 2002 **(90) n22** clean grape: juicy yet just enough vanilla weight for a satisfying depth; **t22** shades of new make on the delivery but this is quickly trampled upon by intense grape and spice; **f23.5** remains mouth-watering, with now far less of a combative feel between barley and fruit. There is even a dusting of cocoa as the spices settle into a more relaxed state; **b22.5** a charming, fresh-faced version brimming with youth and vitality. *61.3%. sc.*

-:- **Scotch Single Malt Circle Arran 1998** cask no. 98/652, dist 11 Jun 98, bott 9 Dec 10 **(89.5) n23.5** more than a single pinch of salt brings out the sharper aspects of the barley. A wonderful marriage of sweet, fresh grist and the creakier resonance of aged oak; the butterscotch topped with diced physalis is a bonus; **t23** invigorating delivery with the taste buds standing to attention, puckering under the onslaught of the salt and spiced honey malt; a lovely sheen thanks to delicate copper notes; **f21** cocoa and vanilla; **b22** the whisky equivalent of a bracing shower under a waterfall to liven you up. *54.9%. sc.*

-:- **The Whisky Agency Arran 1995** bott 2012 **(76) n18 t21 f18 b19.** no matter how good the spirit, if the cask isn't up to the mark. It is a testament to Arran's excellence that some gorgeous honey notes can still be heard through the tart noise. *52.3%. nc ncf sc.*

ISLE OF JURA

Highlands (Island–Jura), 1810. Whyte and Mackay. Working.

Isle of Jura 5 Years Old 1999 db **(83) n19 t23 f21 b20.** Absolutely enormously peated, but has reached that awkward time in its life when it is massively sweet and as well balanced as a two-hour-old foal. *46% The Whisky Exchange*

Isle Of Jura Aged 10 Years db **(79.5) n19 t22 f19 b19.5.** Perhaps a little livelier than before, but still miles short of where you might hope it to be. *40%*

-:- **Jura Elixir Aged 12 Years Fruity & Spicy** db **(77) n18 t21 f18 b20.** Fruity, spicy and a little sulphury, I'm afraid. Those who can't spot sulphur will love the caramel-fruitcake enormity. *40%*

Isle of Jura Mountain of Gold 15 Years Old Pinot Noir cask finish db **(67.5) n15 t18 f17 b17.5.** Not for the first time a Jura seriously hamstrung by sulphur - for all its honeyed sweetness and promise: there are some amazingly brilliant casks in there tragically wasted. And my tastebuds partially crocked because of it. Depressing. *46%. 1366 bottles.*

Isle of Jura Mountain of Sound 15 Years Old Cabernet Sauvignon finish db **(81) n20 t21.5 f19.5 b20.** Pretty quiet. *43%*

Isle of Jura The Sacred Mountain 15 Years Old Barolo finish db **(89.5) n21.5 t24 f21.5 b22.5** Hoo-bloody-rah! One of the three from this series has actually managed to raise my pulse. Not, it must be said, without the odd fault here and there. But there really is a stunning interaction between the grape and barley that sets the nerves twitching: at its height this is about as entertaining a malt as I've come across for some time and should be on everyone's list for a jolly jaunt for the taste buds. Just when I was beginning to lose faith in this distillery... *43%*

Isle Of Jura Aged 16 Years db **(90.5) n21.5** salty, coastal, seaweedy, but with an injection of honey; **t23.5** carries on from the nose perfectly and then ups the stakes. The delivery is malt dependent and rich, the salty tang a true delight; **f23** all kinds of vanillas and honeys carried on a salty wind; **b23** a massive improvement, this time celebrating its salty, earthy heritage to good effect. The odd strange, less than harmonious note. But by far and away the most improved Jura for a long, long while. *40%*

Isle of Jura Aged 21 Years 200th Anniversary db **(74) n19 t19 f18 b18.** Don't know what to say. Actually, I do. But what's the point...? *44%*

Isle of Jura 21 Years Old Cask Strength db **(92) n22 t24 f23 b23.** Every mouthful exudes class and quality. A must-have for Scottish Island collector... or those who know how to appreciate a damn fine malt *58.1%*

Isle of Jura 30 Years Old db **(89) n22.5** a touch of orange peel and mildly overcooked yam: soft, intriguing and pepped up further by the beginnings of a few sweet bourbony notes; **t22.5** the delivery flutters onto the palate. It's a pretty delicate encounter, perhaps softened by a touch of cream toffee but there is enough life in the juicy citrus and layered barley to get the tongue exploring; spices soon begin to pop around the palate as some vanilla encroaches; **f22** chewy, toffeed, fat and still a touch of spicy feistiness; **b22** a relaxed dram with the caramel dousing the higher notes just as they started to get very interesting. If there is a way of bringing down these presumably natural caramels – it is a 30 years old, so who in their right mind would add colouring? – this would score very highly, indeed. *40%*

Isle of Jura 40 Years Old finished in oloroso wood db **(90) n23** a different species of Jura from anything you are likely to have seen before: swamped in sherry, there is a vague, rather odd smokiness to this. Not to mention salty, sea-side rockpools. As a pairing (sherry and smoke), the odd couple... which works and doesn't work at the same time. Strange... **t22** syrupy sweet delivery with thick waves of fruit and then an apologetic 'ahem' from the smoke, which drifts in nervously. Again, everything is awkward... **f22** remains soft and velvety, though now strands of bitter, salty oak and molasses drift in and out; **b23** throw the Jura textbooks away. This is something very different. Completely out of sync in so many ways, but... *40%*

Isle of Jura 1974 db **(87.5) n23 t22.5 f20.5 b21.5.** Stick your nose in this and enjoy those very first outstanding moments on delivery. *42%*

Isle Of Jura 1974 db **(85.5) n22 t23 f18.5 b22.** A case where the unhappy, bitter ending is broadcast on the nose. Talk about warts 'n all...!! *44.5%*

Isle of Jura 1976 db **(94.5) n24.5** a fascinating wisp of smoke acts almost like a thread which stitches together myriad complex, barely discernable facets which make for a nose to be treasured. We are talking pastel shades here, nothing brash or vivid. Vanilla shapes the background but the light herbal notes, marrying with the deft, crushed between the fingers berries makes for the most teasing of experiences. Look out for gooseberries and a butterscotch/honey mix in particular; **t24** works with rare magnificence from the go simply because the barley leads the way with such ease and there is neither OTT oils or oaks to blur the picture; varying types of sugars follow behind and spices are also in close attendance, again with a marvellous hint of smoke lingering; **f22.5** shows an acceptable and understandable degree of oaky bitterness but the spices and barley still ride high; **b23.5** absolutely beautiful whisky which carries its age with unfeigned elegance. *46.1%*

Jura Boutique Barrels Vintage 1995 bourbon Jo finish db **(89.5) n24.5 t23.5 f20 b21.5.** There are moments when you wonder if you have a possible malt of the year on your hands. Then the slip shows... Even so, one of the more memorable whiskies of the 2011 Bible. *56.5%*

Jura Boutique Barrels 1996 db **(78) n21 t21.5 f17.5 b18.** A clumsy whisky in which the fruit fits the malt in the same way a size 46 jacket fits a guy with a 40 inch chest. Either too cloyingly sweet or just too viciously bitter. *54%. 493 bottles.*

Jura Boutique Barrels Vintage 1999 heavily peated, bourbon Xu finish db **(84) n21.5 t21 f20.5 b21.** Pretty peat. But not in the same league as the Prophecy, simply because the base spirit is nowhere near as good. *55%*

Jura Elements "Air" db **(76) n19.5 t19 f18.5 b19.** Initially, I thought this was earth: there is something strangely dirty and flat about both nose and delivery. Plenty of fruits here and there but just doesn't get the pulse racing at all. *45%*

Jura Elements "Earth" db **(89) n23.5 t22 f21.5 b22.** I haven't spoken to blender Richard Paterson about these whiskies yet. No doubt I'll be greeted with a knee on the nuts for declaring two of these as duds. My guess is that this is the youngest of the quartet by a distance and that it is probably why it is the best. The peat profile is very different and challenging. I'd still love to see this in its natural plumage as the caramel really does put the brakes on the complexity and development. Otherwise we could have had an elementary classic. *45%*

Jura Elements "Fire" db **(86.5) n22.5 t21.5 f21 b21.5.** Pleasant fare, the highlight coming with the vaguely Canadian-style nose thanks to a classic toffee-oak mix well known east of the Rockies. Some botanicals also there to be sniffed at while a few busy oaky notes pep up the barley-juiced delivery, too. Sadly, just a shade too toffee dependent. 45%

Jura Elements "Water" db **(73.5) n18.5 t19 f18 b18.** Oranges by the box-full trying to get out but the mouth is sent into puckering spasm by the same sulphur which spoils the nose. 50%

Jura Prophecy profoundly peated db **(90.5) n23.5** something almost akin to birchwood in there with the peat and salt; there is a wonderful natural floral note as well as coastal elements to this one; **t23** impressively two-toned: on one side is the sharper, active barley and peat offering an almost puckering youthfulness and zest; on the other, a sweeter, lightly oiled buzz...a treat; **f22** thins as the vanillas enter; **b22** youthful, well made and I prophesize this will be one of Jura's top scorers of 2011... 46%

Jura Superstition db **(73.5) n17 t19 f18 b18.5.** I thought this could only improve. I was wrong. One to superstitiously avoid. 43%

⋰ **Archives Isle Of Jura 1988 24 Years Old Third Release** bourbon cask, cask no. 752, dist May 98, bott May 12 **(87) n22.5** interesting balance between sharp, grassy barley and minty old oak; **t22** excellent delivery full of juice, then fattens out enormously to a semi-syrupy constitution; **f20.5** inelegant oils and oak; **b22** a heavy malt resplendent early on in its sugary frock. 51.3%. nc ncf sc. Whiskybase B.V. 60 bottles.

⋰ **Dun Bheagan Isle Of Jura 11 Years Old** St Etienne rum finish, dist May 00 **(82) n20 t22 f19 b21.** I'm not sure if the rum finish has smoothed out the usual rougher edges form this distillery or dumbed down what appears to be a charming maltiness. A little bit of the chewing gum about this. 46%. nc ncf sc Ian Macleod Distillers.

⋰ **Mo Òr Collection Isle Of Jura 1988 22 Years Old** first fill bourbon hogshead, cask no. 756, dist 19 Apr 88, bott 15 Dec 10 **(87) n20.5** the vague, distant smoke is a surprise package. Not particularly brilliant, but displays an attractive, salty character; **t22** the softness of the delivery is yet another surprise; the richness of the malt isn't. A pleasant tang of blood orange; **f22.5** soft cocoa, leading into mocha. The vanilla is firm and shuts the gate on further development; **b22** a real Jaffa Cake of a dram. 46%. nc ncf sc. Release No. 52. 352 bottles.

⋰ **Old Malt Cask Isle Of Jura Aged 16 Years** refill hogshead, cask no. 7739, dist Apr 95, bott Oct 11 **(74.5) n19 t19 f18 b18.5.** It may be 16 years old, but it looks nowhere near the age of consent. A gristy, wet behind the ears offering. 50%. nc ncf sc. 207 bottles.

⋰ **Provenance Jura Over 9 Years** refill hogshead, cask no. 8510, dist Spring 2003, bott Spring 2012 **(85.5) n21.5 t22 f21 b21.** Chunky, ribald barley with a good dollop of maple syrup. If you are looking for poise or subtlety, move on... 46%. nc ncf sc. Douglas Laing & Co.

Planeta Jura 12 Year Old Finished in Planeta Syrah Cask (86) n21.5 t23 f20 b21.5. Some excellent finishing has allowed the malt to magnify all the juicy elements. Very rich and attractive whisky: impressed. 46%. sc. Enotria.

Provenance Jura Over 11 Years refill hogshead, cask no. 6827, dist Summer 00, bott Autumn 2010 **(77) n19 t20 f18.5 b19.5.** An extraordinary projection of great age is somehow made: so pine-like is it in its resonance. Some decent juicy malt but is all about sows ears and silk purses. 46%. nc ncf sc. Douglas Laing & Co.

Provenance Jura Over 11 Years refill hogshead, cask no. 6994, dist Summer 99, bott Winter 2011 **(73) n18.5 t19 f17 b18.5.** Takes time to get off the ground...and soon crashes. 46%. nc ncf sc. Douglas Laing & Co.

⋰ **The Whisky Agency Jura 24 Years Old** dist 1988 **(85) n21 t22 f21 b21.** A big, thick lump of a malt with major barley juiciness and over oakiness. Never quite sits right, though it does have its fleeting moments of charm. 51.3%. sc.

KILCHOMAN
Islay, 2005. Kilchoman Distillery Co. Working.

Kilchoman Autumn 09 Release db **(85) n21 t22.5 f20 b21.5.** Still to completely find it's legs: a youthful malt is trying desperately hard to hit the high notes, but falling short. Or perhaps I should say flat as the fruit here is acting like caramel in dumbing down the more complex notes you know are in there somewhere...especially in the final third. Like the Inaugeral Release there is a feinty element to this, not all of it bad, but certainly marks the nose and finish. Also a charming gristiness: you feel as though you are standing there watching the barley being dried. But as yet doesn't quite have the early excellence that Arran, for instance, boasted. But these are early days in the distillery's life. And, for me, anything drinkable at all is a bonus... 46%

Kilchoman Winter 2010 Release fresh and refill bourbon db **(88) n23** peat with the kind of thickness one associates with the walls of Scottish castles...; a bit of dry pepper, too; **t22** sweet delivery: well oiled with a surprising degree of early oak caramels; the smoke is big though not to sure of the role it is supposed to play; **f21** a tad bitter; **b22** size doesn't really matter, apparently. Well that is certainly the case here. This may be a big boy, displaying a stonking

50ppm phenols, but its fails to match the overall elegance of the Kilchoman Inaugural 100% Islay...which is a p-challenged 15ppm. The Inaugural showed great purpose throughout. This is a big crash, bang wallop merchant. That said, fully enjoyable stuff! *46%. nc ncf.*

Kilchoman Spring 2011 Release oloroso finish db **(93.5) n23.5** there is no doubting the enormity of the smoke, but that is matched by the deftness of the lightly molassed grape. What a surprisingly well suited marriage; **t24** and there we go again: juicy yet dry at the same time. The delivery offers outstanding early balance and control. Also, very hard to believe this is just three years old: behaves something nearer ten or twelve. Excellent soft oils which act as a reservoir for the melting muscovado sugar; **f22.5** garibaldi biscuit and coffee; the smoke does not act much like a 50ppm giant; **b23.5** have to admit: when I this was a 50ppm phenol malt finished in oloroso, my head was in my hands and my heart was filled with trepidation. This is a story that normally ends in tears... But what a surprise! A faultlessly clean butt helped, but the grape is by no means overplayed and its main function, apart from balance, appears to be to generate a feeling of extra age and tranquillity in the glass. A lovely and genuinely unexpected Islay experience. On this evidence, Kilchoman has well and truly arrived and can hold its head as high as the other Islay distilleries... *46%. nc ncf.*

Kilchoman Inaugural Release db **(87.5) n21** the smoke lurks around like a detective under a streetlamp: trying to look casual but can be easily seen. A distant but distinct feintiness gives a mildly off kilter oiliness, but things are lightened by an effusive citrus note; **t23** the coppery evidence of a new still soon makes its mark but the fanning out of the phenols towards a vaguely hickory style, all underscored by sultry fruit notes, makes for a gentler experience than might have been earlier predicted on arrival; **f21.5** bitters out slightly as both the effect of the feints and stills combine; some very late spice has the last word; **b22** not by any means perfect but what could have been something of a bumpy ride has been helped along by some very good casks: like an excellent football referee, you don't notice it, but not only is it there, it makes the best of what is on offer. Not a great whisky. But a very promising start. *46%. nc ncf.*

Kilchoman Inaugural 100% Islay 1st fill bourbon db **91.5 n23.5** a superb nose which takes full advantage of some excellent oak to give weight to the soft gristiness. Young, but no hint of a Bambi here: this has found its feet already...; **t24** fabulous delivery. Soft, genteel peats melt into a light citrus sweetness and then several waves of red-liquorice oak add just the right anchor; **f21.5** pleasant and vanilla-driven though slightly untidy, as one might reasonably expect; **b22.5** in a quite different world to the first two bottlings. Those, falteringly, gave reason for hope. But a slight degree of concern, too. This is unerringly fine: clean and purposeful and making a very clear and eloquent statement. *50%. nc ncf.*

⁙ **Kilchoman Machir Bay** bott 2012 db **(93) n23** fireside peat ash wrapped in sherry; **t23.5** beautifully distilled barley and grist – both youthful and some weighed down with a little vanilla – tapping out some major peaty notes; just a little bitter as it appears the oak has been forced slightly. The sultana fruit maximises the juiciness; **f23** long with a wonderful ulmo honey depth and the now restrained peat taking a support role rather than the lead; **b23.5** it is over 30 years since I first tried to play football on the sands of Machir Bay. I did it because with the winds never ceasing, it was, like a latter day Canute, an attempt at the impossible. A bit like trying to get to the bottom of this malt, in fact. In some respects it works, in others I feel a degree of sherry may just have knocked out some of the more complex characters in an attempt to soften. It is, however, much more successful than my failed attempts at playing "Keepie Uppie" against the perennial winds of Machir Bay... *46%. nc ncf.*

⁙ **Kilchoman Sherry Cask Release** bott 2011 db **(83) n21.5 t21.5 f19 b21.** The thumping peat and at times almost syrupy sherry is just too much of a good thing. *46%. nc ncf.*

⁙ **Kilchoman Vintage 2006** bott 2012 db **(93.5) n24** I close my eyes and allow myself to be consumed by the aroma which takes me away from a freezing, rain-soaked summer in England, to a freezing, rain-soaked summer on Islay, with gulls screeching from a distance, peat on the wind from Port Ellen and midges biting hard with an uncanny accuracy for the most sensitive nerve endings. You are unlikely to find an aroma which so perfectly embodies maritime Islay; **t23.5** the sugars seemingly so tied up with the phenols on the nose appear to have momentarily escaped the smoky masters to make the delivery a sweet one. But the smoke is on its trail and soon has the caster sugar and maple syrup back in custody allowing vanilla to make its presence felt; **f22.5** bitters very slightly; the peat now has the density of an Arbroath smoky while spice rattles in late on; **b23** a sweetly peated triumph. *46%. nc ncf.*

KINCLAITH
Lowlands, 1957–1975. Closed / Dismantled.

⁙ **Mo Ör Collection Kinclaith 1969 41 Years Old** first fill bourbon hogshead, cask no. 301453A, dist 28 May 69, bott 29 Oct 10 **(85.5) n22 t22 f20.5 b21.** Hangs on gamely to the last vestiges of life, though the oak, without being overtly aggressive, is squeezing all the breath out of out it. *46%. nc ncf sc. Release No. 2. The Whisky Talker. 164 bottles.*

KNOCKANDO

Speyside, 1898. Diageo. Working.

Knockando Aged 12 Years dist 1994 db **(86) n22 t22 f21 b21.** An usually light bottling for Diageo. Here you get full exploration of the attractive, malty skeleton. But Knockando has a tendency towards dryness and the casks here oblige rather too well. A delicate dram all the same. *43%*

Knockando Aged 12 Years dist 1995 db **(71.5) n16 t19 f18 b18.5.** If there was an award for Worst Nose of the Year, this must be somewhere in the running. *43%*

Knockando Aged 12 Years dist 1996 db **(76) n18 t20.5 f18.5 b19.** Disappointing. As someone who knows this distillery perhaps as well as anyone working for its current owners, I had hoped for a dry, sophisticated dram to send me into various degrees of ecstasy. Instead, I am left lamenting a few poor casks which have distorted what this distillery stands for. *43%*

Knockando Aged 18 Years sherry casks, dist 1987 db **(77) n19 t21 f18 b19.** Bland and docile. Someone wake me up. *43%*

⁖ **Knockando 25 Years Old Special Release 2011** db **(77) n20 t22 f16 b19.** One or two renegade sherry butts away from what would have been a memorable whisky. *43%. nc ncf.*

Knockando 1990 db **(83) n21 t22 f20 b20.** The most fruity Knockando I've come across with some attractive salty notes. Dry, but a little extra malty sweetness these days. *40%*

Knockando The Manager's Choice Spanish sherry European oak, cask no. 800790, dist 1996, bott 2009 db **(94) n23.5** I think my staff have poured me the wrong stuff: they've opened up some pot still Demerara, right...? Wrong. No, definitely from the Knockando sample. Well, well, well...let's just say it's a fruity, sugary, rich start on the nose...; **t25** actually, I don't care if this is rum or whisky. When you get flavours this beautifully defined, a body this sublimely structured...it really doesn't much matter. Oozes fruity, beautifully natural sweetened quality and complexity; **f22** a slight bitterness on the finish where, for the first time, there is a very minor blemish, but the array of sugars still make for something memorable...and absolutely 100% nothing like I have ever tasted from any previous Knockando...; **b23** I have been in the Demerara region Guyana, crawled around a rum warehouse at a rum distillery and opened a cask of rum which has less rum characteristics than this rumbustuous chappie. Quite a rum do. *58.6% 599 bottles.*

⁖ **Old Malt Cask Knockando Aged 17 Years** refill hogshead, cask no 7762, dist Aug 94, bott Oct 11 **(86.5) n22 t23 f20 b21.5.** The wonderful depth and complexity to the textbook sharp Knockando style barley is undermined slightly by the bitterness on the finish. *50%. nc ncf sc. Douglas Laing & Co. 175 bottles.*

KNOCKDHU

Speyside, 1894. Inver House Distillers. Working.

AnCnoc 12 Year Old db **(94.5) n24** so complex it is frightening: delicate barley; delicate spices; delicate butterscotch-vanilla, delicate citrus... and all the while the lightest discernible sugars melt into the malt; **t23** it had to be salivating... and is! Yet there is enough oaky-vanilla roughage to ensure the citrus and barley don't get their own way; **f23.5** a slow but tingling arrival of spices fit hand in glove with the complex cocoa-barley tones; **b24.5** a more complete or confident Speyside-style malt you are unlikely to find. Shimmers with everything that is great about Scotch whisky... always a reliable dram, but this is stupendous. *40%*

AnCnoc 13 Year Old Highland Selection db **(85) n21 t23 f20 b21.** A big Knockdhu, but something is dulling the complexity. *46%*

AnCnoc 16 Years Old db **(91.5) n22** sharp, pithy, salty, busy...; **t23.5** those salts crash headlong into the taste buds and then give way to massive spice and barley; soft sugars and vanilla follow at a distance; **f23** salted mocha and spice; **b23** unquestionably the spiciest AnCnoc of all time. Has this distillery been moved to the coast..? *46%*

AnCnoc 26 Years Old Highland Selection db **(89) n23 t22 f23 b21.** There is a little flat moment between the middle and finish for which I have chipped off a point or two. That apart, superb. *48.2%*

AnCnoc 30 Years Old db **(85) n21** pipe smoke, old leather armchairs and a sprig of mint: this seems older than its years; **t23** wonderfully thick malt, beefed up in intensity by drawing in as much oak as it comfortably can; the honeycomb and molassed sweetness adds a lovely touch; **f19** big natural caramel and some pretty rough-stuff oak; **b22** seat-of-the-pants whisky that is just on the turn. Still has a twinkle in the eye, though. *49%*

AnCnoc 35 Years Old db **(86) n21 t21 f22.5 b21.5.** Tries to take the exotic fruit route to antiquity but headed off at the pass by a massive dollop of natural caramels. The slow burn on the spice is an unexpected extra treat, though. *43%*

⁖ **AnCnoc 35 Years Old** bourbon and sherry casks db **(88) n22.5** any saltier and you expect the odd barnacle to be attached...; **t22** dry thanks to the oak and for the same reas evolved into a complex malt with the butterscotch providing the sweetness covering a multitude of subtle spice notes; **f21.5** barley and vanilla; **b22** the usual big barley sheen has dulled with time here. Some attractive cocoa notes do compensate. *44.3%. nc ncf.*

An Cnoc 1993 db **(89) n22 t21 f24 b22.** Quite an odd one this. I have tasted it a couple of times with different samples and there is a variance. This one takes an oakier path and then invites the barley to do its stuff. Delicious, but underscores the deft touch of the standard 12-year-old. *46%*

AnCnoc 1994 db **(88.5) n22.5 t22.5 f21.5 b22.** Coasts through effortlessly, showing the odd flash of brilliance here and there. Just get the feeling that it never quite gets out of third gear... *46%. ncf.*

AnCnoc 1995 db **(84.5) n21 t22 f20.5 b21.** Very plump for a Knockdhu with caramel notes on a par with the citrus and burgeoning bourbon. Some barley juice escapes on delivery but the finish is peculiarly dry for the distillery. *46%*

⁘ **AnCnoc Peter Arkle** first fill sherry casks db **(67) n17 t17.5 f16.5 b17.** Unattractive and grimly off key. *46%. nc ncf.*

Knockdhu 23 Years Old db **(94) n23 t24 f23 b24.** Pass the smelling salts. This is whisky to knock you out. A malt that confirms Knockdhu as not simply one of the great Speysiders, but unquestionably among the world's elite. *57.4%.*

Harrods Knockdhu Aged 12 Years (84) n19 t23 f21 b21. One can assume only that caramel (or an exceptional dull sherry cask) has been added here because it is otherwise impossible to find such a flat nose from a Knockdhu. However, the arrival on the palate is bliss, with dates combining with glossy honey and marzipan, but again the finish is only a dull echo of what it should be. Shackled greatness. *40%.*

LADYBURN
Lowlands, 1966–2000. William Grant & Sons. Closed.

⁘ **Mo Òr Collection Rare Ayrshire 1974 36 Years Old** first fill bourbon barrel, cask no. 2608, dist 10 May 74, bott 1 Nov 11 **(89.5) n22** a battering of unpretentious oak. But there is a light sweetened salted butter halo which offers something else; **t23.5** the delivery concentrates on those sugars, the first to arrive being not much more complex than basic icing sugar. But the map changes as a wonderfully complex portfolio of spices make their mark; **f22** virtually croaks on the spot, with, initially, not much more than oak-strewn vanilla. But like Lazarus it rises, with a red liquorice and chalky citrus glint in its once dead eye; **b22.5** I had a feeling it'd be this distillery when I saw the title on the label... it couldn't be much else! Fascinating to think that I was in final countdown for my 'O' levels when this was made. It appears to have dealt with the passing years better than I have. Even so, I had not been prepared for this. For years during the very early 1990s Grant's blender David Stewart sent me samples of this stuff and it was, to put it mildly, not great. Some were the oakiest malt I ever tasted in my life. And, to compound matters further, the distillery's own bottling was truly awful. But this cask has re-written history. *46%. nc ncf sc. Release No. 4. The Whisky Talker. 261 bottles.*

LAGAVULIN
Islay, 1816. Diageo. Working.

Lagavulin 12 Years Old 7th release, bott 2007 db **(92.5) n23 t23 f23 b23.5.** Brooding, enigmatic and just pulsing with quiet sophistication. A dram to drink quietly so all can be heard in the glass... *56.4%*

Lagavulin 12 Years Old 8th release, bott 2008 db **(94.5) n24** heady mixture of coal dust and peat reek, quite dry but not without some fried banana sweetness in the most delicate terms possible; **t24.5** a lightly oiled landing allows the peats to glide around the palate with minimal friction; a light dusting of hickory powder works well with the big, but by no means brooding phenols; the sweetness levels are just about perfect; **f22.5** surprisingly short with a dull toffee flourish to the smoke; **b23.5** sensational malt: simply by doing all the simple things rather brilliantly. *56.4%*

Lagavulin 12 Years Old 10th release, bott 2010 db **(94.5) n23.5** a dusty, gristy combination. As though someone has swept up the remnants of an anthracite pile and mixed it in with powdered peat and grist. And then sprinkled liberally with hickory. Dry with sugars at a premium; **t24** the arrival offers a surprising amount of juice: still enough rich barley still not under the influence of oak. The sugars, so shy on the nose, show all the bashfulness of a teenage wannabe on a TV talent show. Except these sugars do have talent...; all the while the smoke hangs around like reek on a windless winter morn; **f23.5** long with a touch of melted molasses spread over a butterscotch tart; the peat could hardly be more gentile; **b23.5** keeps on track with previous Releases. Though this is the first where the lowering of the ppms from to 35 really do seem noticeable. Quite beautiful, nonetheless. *56.5%*

Lagavulin 12 Years Old Special Release 2011 db (96.5) n24.5 the kind of perfectly weighted aroma which makes your hairs stand on end and your taste buds salivate. The peat takes neither ashy nor oily form, or maybe it takes both....you decide. And the light mintiness to the lemon....extraordinary! t24 the oils form with limited density on delivery. Not only do they usher in the controlled peat, but also a milky mocha thread which perfectly absorbs the percussion of most explosive spices; f23.5 softens out with the deft sugars now in command over the vanilla; the thin, creamy mocha continues; b24.5 so the peat may not pound as it did when the Whisky Bible began life in 2003: the phenols are noticeably lighter here. But it is not all about size: balance and complexity still reign supreme. 57.5%. nc ncf.

Lagavulin 16 Years Old db (95) n24 morning cinders of peat from the fire of the night before: dry, ashy, improbably delicate. Just a hint of Demerara sweetness caught on the edge; t24 that dryness is perfectly encapsulated on the delivery with the light sugars eclipsed by those countless waves of ash. A tame spiciness generates a degree of hostility on the palate, but the mid-ground sticks to a smoky, coffee-vanilla theme; f23 light spicy waves in a gentle sea of smoke; b24 although i have enjoyed this whisky countless times socially, it is the first time for a while I have dragged it into the Tasting Room for professional analysis for the Bible. If anyone has noticed a slight change in Lagavulin, they would be right. The peat remains profound but much more delicate than before, while the oils appear to have receded. A different shape and weight dispersal for sure. But the sky-high quality remains just the same. 43%

Lagavulin Aged 16 Years The Distillers Edition PX cask, dist 1991, bott 2007 db (83) n22 t21 f20 b20. I have oft stated that peat and sherry are uncomfortable bed-fellows. Here, the two, both obviously from fine stock and not without some individual attraction, manage to successfully cancel each other out. One is hard pressed to imagine any Lagavulin this dull. 43%

Lagavulin 21 Years Old bott 2007 db (96) n24.5 t24 f23 b24.5. Big peat and grape rarely work comfortably together and here we a have malt which struggles from the nose to finish to make some kind of sense of itself. There will be some Islayphiles who will doubtless drool at this and while certain aspects of the finish are quite excellent the balance never appears to come into focus. 56.5%

Lagavulin Special Release 2010 12 Years Old refill American oak db (94) n24.5 unambiguously Lagavulin: the mixture of chalkiness to the gristy peat, all ringed by light oil, is unmistakable. Clean, wonderfully shaped and disciplined in its use of spice; t24 the same can be said here as the nose: it absolutely screams Lagavulin and is bolstered by a clever injection of muscovado sugars which actually boosts rather than relieves the intensity. The oils are so soft, they could come from Leeds...; f22 just a shade of disappointing bitterness as tired cask cocks a snook at the continuing spices and forming cocoa; b23.5 Bloody hell! This is some whisky...! 56.5%. nc ncf. Diageo.

Lagavulin The Manager's Choice bodega sherry European oak cask no. 4446, dist 1993, bott 2009 (4th and final release) db (91) n24 t22.5 f22.5 b22. A lot more toffee and oil than I expected. But the quality is beyond question: tastes like it's from the days when Lagavulin was a 50ppm merchant. 54.7% 597 bottles

LAPHROAIG
Islay, 1815. Beam Inc. Working.

Laphroaig 10 Years Old db (90) n24 impossible not to nose this and think of Islay: no other aroma so perfectly encapsulates the island – clean despite the rampaging peat-reek and soft oak, raggy coast-scapes and screeching gulls – all in a glass; t23 one of the crispiest peaty malts of them all, the barley standing out alone, brittle and unbowed, before the peat comes rushing in like the tide: iodine and soft salty tones; f20.5 the nagging bitterness of many ex-Allied bourbon casks filled during this period is annoyingly apparent here... b22.5 has reverted back slightly towards a heavier style in more recent bottling, though I would like to see that old oomph at the very death. Even so, this is, indisputably, a classic whisky. The favourite of Prince Charles apparently: he will make a wise king... 40%

Laphroaig 10 Years Old Cask Strength batch no. 001 bott Feb 09 db (91.5) n22.5 like a throbbing 6 litre engine below a still bonnet, you are aware of the peaty power waiting to be unleashed; t23.5 a stunningly sublime, slightly watered muscovado sugar coating ensures the dry, phenolic explosion conjures myriad variances on a theme; f23 a quite milky chocolate quality dovetails to excellent effect with the smoke; b22.5 a Groundhog Day of a malt with the waves of smoke starting identically but always panning out a little differently each time. Fascinating and fun. 57.8%

Laphroaig 10 Years Old Original Cask Strength (with UK Government's Sensible Drinki Limits boxed on back label) db (92) n22 a duller nose than usual: caramel reducing normal iodine kick; t24 recovers supremely for the early delivery with some stunning b peppers exploding all over the palate leaving behind a trail of peat smoke; the contr sweetness to the barley is sublime; f23 again there is a caramel edge to the finish, b does not entirely prevent a fizzing finale; **b23** caramel apart, this is much truer to form than one or two or more recent bottlings, aided by the fresh, gristy sweetness and explosive spices. Wonderful! *55.7%*

Laphroaig Aged 15 Years db **(79)** n20 t20 f19 b20. A hugely disappointing, lacklustre dram that is oily and woefully short on complexity. Not what one comes to expect either from this distillery or age. *43%*

Laphroaig 18 Years Old db **(94)** n24 multi-layered smokiness: there are soft, flightier, sweeter notes and a duller, earthier peat ingrained with salt and leather; **t23.5** perhaps it's the big leg-up from the rampant hickory, but the peat here offers a vague Fisherman's Friend cough sweet quality far more usually associated with Bowmore, except here it comes in a milder, Demerara-sweetened form with a few strands of liquorice helping that hickory to a gentler level; **f23** soft oils help keep some late, slightly juicy barley notes on track while the peat dances off with some spices to niggle the roof of the mouth and a few odd areas of the tongue; **b23.5** this is Laphroaig's replacement to the woefully inadequate and gutless 15-year-old. And talk about taking a giant step in the right direction. Absolutely brimming with character and panache, from the first molecules escaping the bottle as you pour to the very final ember dying on the middle of your tongue. *48%*

Laphroaig Aged 25 Years db **(94)** n23 the clean - almost prim and proper - fruit appears to have somehow given a lift to the iodine character and accentuated it to maximum effect. The result is something much younger than the label demands and not immediately recognisable as Islay, either. But no less dangerously enticing... **t24** the grapes ensure the peat is met by a salivating palate; particularly impressive is the way the sweet peat slowly finds its footing and spreads beautifully; **f23.5** no shortage of cocoa: a kind of peaty fruit and nut chocolate bar... **b23.5** like the 27-y-o, an Islay which doesn't suffer for sherry involvement. Very different from a standard, bourbon barrel-aged Laphroaig with much of the usually complexity reined in, though its development is first class. This one's all about effect - and it works a treat! *40%*

Laphroaig Aged 25 Years Cask Strength 2011 Edition oloroso and American oak casks db **(96.5)** n24 an immense nose with fruit and smoke dished out in equal measure: rarely have I located so much marmalade on a Laphroaig nose. An extraordinary degree of black pepper, too. The smoke, though intense, enjoys a wonderful degree of layering; **t24.5** the peat is, as is so often the case with this distillery, the first to show. But it does so with such a suave sophistication that one is tempted to bow at its majesty. The backdrop to this is a molassed cocoa depth. But it is the light oils bringing in the distinctive vanilla followed by the Jaffa cake orange...; **f24** lengthened by those most delicate oils, the vanilla still has a presence while the smoke forms circular patterns of almost feather-like substance; **b24** quite possibly the finest bottling of Laphroaig I have ever encountered. And over the last 35 years there have been a great many bottles... *48.6%*

Laphroaig 27 Years Old sherry cask, dist 1980, bott 2007 db **(94.5)** n24 t23.5 f23 b24. One of the better examples of big sherry and big peat working in close harmony without the usual bristling stand off. A real class act. *574%*. nc. *972 bottles.*

Laphroaig Aged 30 Years db **(94)** n24 t23 f23 b24. The best Laphroaig of all time? Nope, because the 40-y-o is perhaps better still... just. However, Laphroaig of this subtlety and charm gives even the very finest Ardbeg a run for its money. A sheer treat that should be bottled at greater strength. *43%*

Laphroaig Aged 40 Years db **(94)** n23 t24 f23 b24. Mind-blowing. A malt that defies all logic and theory to be in this kind of shape at such age. The Jane Fonda of Islay whisky. *43%*

Laphroaig Càirdeas Ileach Edition ex bourbon Maker's Mark casks, bott 2011 db **(90)** n23 a beautiful grist theme with spice and floral tones; **t22.5** lounges around the palate as though it owns the place. Just stretches out, brings a few brown sugar notes absent-mindedly into play and dozes off into a toffee-enriched land of nod; **f22** a few bitter oak notes, but the natural caramels and peaty spices tip toe around determined not to cause a scene; **b22.5** the name of the whisky means "friendship". And it is unlikely you will ever find a Laphraoig 101 any friendlier than this... *50.5%*

⁖ **Laphroaig Càirdeas Origin** quarter casks, bott 2012 db **(89)** n24 the kind of nose that will send hardcore Islayphiles into near ecstasy: some real iodine clinging to the phenols and a sharp-toothed bite to the oak; something on the nose does worry me for later down the line...; **t22.5** gorgeous mouth-feel with muscovado sugars climbing aboard the smoky train. Barley is evident, as well as a few green apple notes, suggesting something youthful in there; the mid ground starts getting a little rough; **f20.5** irritatingly bitters out: what a shame; **b22** started like a train and hit the buffers for the finish. Still, early on it is quite superb. *51.2%*. ncf.

⁖ **Laphroaig PX Cask** bourbon, quarter and Pedro Ximenez casks db **(96)** n23.5 a hugely coal dusty element to this: anthracite, to be precise. The grape effect is a little thin and monosyllabic. But there is an extra sturdiness to the oak which injects the required complexity and helps identify the figs and physalis against the clearer red liquorice-bourbony background; **t24.5** the delivery is at first muddled, though the texture and shape of the body is never less than superb; the smoke bounces contentedly around the firmer oaks; even a touch of lightly smoked mocha here and there. A harder sugar edge from the PX tries to quieten matters a little too forcefully, but there is enough left in the peaty tank to allow spices to quash any chance of that; **f24** long, perhaps restricted by some uncompromisingly firm sugars, but there is both barley and smoke enough for a satisfying finale which includes some high quality cocoa; **b24** I get the feeling that this is a breathtaking success despite the inclusion of Pedro Ximenez casks. This ultra sweet wine is often paired with smoky malt, often with disastrous consequences. Here it has worked, but only because the PX has been controlled itself by absolutely outstanding oak. And the ability of the smoke to take on several roles and personas simultaneously. A quite beautiful whisky and unquestionably one of the great malts of the year...in spite of itself. 48%. *Travel Retail exclusive.*

Laphroaig Quarter Cask db **(96) n23** burning embers of peat in a crofter's fireplace; sweet intense malt and lovely, refreshing citrus as well; **t24** mouthwatering, mouth-filling and mouth-astounding: the perfect weight of the smoke has no problems filling every crevice of the palate; builds towards a sensationally sweet maltiness at the middle; **f24** really long, and dries appropriately with smoke and spice. Classic Laphroaig; **b25** a great distillery back to its awesome, if a little sweet, self. Layer upon layer of sexed-up peatiness. The previous bottling just needed a little extra complexity on the nose for this to hit mega malt status. Now it has been achieved... 48%

Laphroaig Triple Wood ex-bourbon, quarter and European oak casks db **(86) n21 t21.5 f21.5 b21.** A pleasing and formidable dram. But one where the peat takes perhaps just too much of a back seat. Or, rather, is somewhat neutralised to the point of directional loss. The sugars, driven home by the heavy weight of oak, help give the whisky a gloss almost unrecognisable for this distillery. Even so, an attractive whisky in many ways. 48%. *ncf.*

⋘ **A Fine Cigar's Pleasure Laphroaig Aged 10 Years** refill hogshead **(88) n21** minimal oak impact; something of an Arbroath Smoky to this; **t22.5** much more lush on delivery with soft oils transporting the big sugars far and wide; the smoke is delicate and even; **f22.5** at last a touch of vanilla; the smoke is delicate, almost aloof; **b22** enjoyable even to a strict non-smoker like myself.. 50%. nc ncf sc. *Douglas Laing & Co.* 210 bottles.

A.D. Rattray Laphroaig '86 dist Feb 86, cask no. 2123 **(88) n21.5 t23 f22 b22.5.** It's amazing how 60% abv can focus what matters in a malt when at first the paths have vanished. 60.6%. sc.

⋘ **Archives Laphroaig 1998 13 Years Old Second Release** bourbon hogshead, cask no. 700228, dist 14 May 98, bott Dec 11 **(95.5) n24** the peat is worn much the way a Visa by Robert Plant is carried by a lady for whom expense and prestige is a right rather than a privilege. Just so delicate and natural....and very high class...; **t24** the delivery is every bit as chic and understated. The peat never for a moment tries to upstage the well sugared and beautifully clear barley, **f23.5** a light injection of nutty nougat and vanilla adds a slightly drier and weightier feel to what remains a classy act; **b24** Laphroaig at its most effortlessly sublime from the first sniff to the final, smoky pulse. 54.2%. nc ncf sc, *Whiskybase B.V.* 80 bottles.

Berry's Own Selection Laphroaig 1998 cask no. 700223, bott 2010 **(94) n24** Laphroaig showing that, given a good cask and the right number of years, it is the most iodiney of all the Islays. ; **t23.5** a grippingly dry delivery where the peat smoke appears to soak up all the moisture on the palate; this is wonderfully countered by mere outlines of sugar adding balance; **f23** steadfastly remains dry but with attractive vanilla joining the powdery throng; **b23.5** another Berry's bottling with the unnerving ability to buttonhole the distillery's innate house style. 58.7%. nc ncf sc. *Berry Bros & Rudd.*

Berry's Own Selection Laphroaig 1998 cask no. 700254, bott 2010 **(82.5) n20 t22 f20 b20.5.** A pleasant, peaty experience for the most part. But that it will come to a vaguely bitter, muddled finish is foretold on the nose. 58.9%. nc ncf sc. *Berry Bros & Rudd.*

⋘ **Chieftain's Laphroaig Aged 14 Years** hogsheads, dist May 97, bott Sep 11 **(85) n21.5 t21 f21.5 b21.** Smoky, but never quite relaxes. The dryness overpowers the sweetness just a little too astringently perhaps. 43.3%. nc ncf. *Ian Macleod Distillers.*

⋘ **Director's Cut Laphroaig Aged 15 Years** refill hogshead, cask no. 8255, dist Oct 96, bott Mar 12 **(89) n22** dry phenols bolstered by citrus; **t23** superb delivery with a sweet liquorice wave easily coping with the smoke; **f22** silky vanilla and mocha; **b22** the soft oil smears the sugars and phenols into all the right places... 57.2%. nc ncf sc. *Douglas Laing & Co.* 193 bottles.

⋘ **Dun Bheagan Laphroaig 17 Years Old** hogshead, dist May 94 **(82) n20 t21 f20.5 b20.5.** A familiar experience of excellent distillate let down by a cask which doesn't match the malt's quality. 49.2% nc ncf sc. *Ian Macleod Distillers.*

⋘ **First Cask Laphroaig 21 Years Old** refill hogshead, cask no. 5936, dist 8 Jun 90, bott 8 Mar 12 **(91.5) n22.5** predominantly dry with a coastal ash to the phenols; **t23.5** big, resounding smoke though this time with a few huge waves of fudgy sugars to ram home the weight; **f22.5** lightens slowly as the peat turns from smoke to spice; the sugars stay in top gear; **b23** with old Allied casks, you actually breathe a sigh of relief when you get to the end and bitterness from a poor barrel doesn't spoil things. Big thumbs up here! *52.6%. nc ncf sc. Whisky Import Nederland. 280 bottles.*

⋙ **Hart Brothers Laphroaig Aged 22 Years** cask no. 3688, dist 26 Apr 90, bott 30 Apr 12 **(88) n22** about as thick and oily as Laphroaig gets: there is almost a buttery quality to the smoke; **t22.5** chewy from the off with that creamy texture coating the peat on thickly; lots of natural cream toffee insuring excellent sweetness; **f21.5** relatively lazy and simplistic but the outline of some spice welcome; **b22** pleasing and enjoyable without tearing up trees. Other than the ones it had been sitting in for the last 22 years, of course... *46%. sc.*

⋙ **James MacArthur Old Masters Laphroaig 13 Years Old** cask no. 700234, dist 1998, bott Feb 12 **(83) n21 t23 f19 b20.** A beauty with a bit of a limp... The delivery of soft, dissolving sugars is mesmeric, especially as the smoke begins to take a grip. However the nose reveals an oaky tightness which predicts bitterness on the finish. *56.2%. nc ncf sc.*

⋙ **Kingsbury Single Cask Series Laphroaig Aged 12 Years** Trois Riviers rum finish **(89) n21.5** seriously needing balance: the smoke and sugars are barely on speaking terms; **t23** but now they do! The sugars act as a friendly field while the smoke thickens. Intriguing; **f22** now dry and the smoke takes a chewy turn; **b22.5** a less than promising nose but the big sugars actually do a job. Genuinely complex. *46%. sc. Japan Import Systems.*

Liquid Library Laphroaig 1998 bourbon hogshead, bott 2011 **(84.5) n21 t21 f21 b21.5.** Straightforward smoke fest. The tired cask means a relative silence in this library. *53.3%*

⋙ **Liquid Sun Laphroaig 13 Years Old** refill sherry cask, dist 1998, bott 2011 **(58) n15 t17 f12 b14.** For all its thick sugars and smoke, the sulphur dictates grimly. Technically dreadful, but there will be some in Germany who will set up a new religion to worship it... That's my taste buds wrecked for the day...and it's only 9.42am... *56.6%. sc. The Whisky Agency.*

Liquid Sun Laphroaig 1991 sherry hogshead, bott 2011 **(91.5) n22.5** the strands of peat and sherry refuse to meet; **t24** sweet, viscous, ultra smoked fruitcake; even for those of us who are not great fans of this style, this is some experience... **f22.5** dries and bitters slightly but neither the grape or phenols let up; **b22.5** a battle of egos between smoke and sherry with each wielding mighty blows upon the other. Huge. *53.3%. The Whisky Agency.*

Liquid Sun Laphroaig 1998 bourbon hogshead, bott 2011 **(83) n20 t21 f21 b21.** Very similar in style to the Liquid Library '98 bottling due to a relatively inert cask. More spice evident here, though. *52.9%. The Whisky Agency.*

Malts Of Scotland Laphroaig 1990 bourbon hogshead, cask no. 2229, dist Mar 90, bott Feb 11 **(91.5) n23** the unmistakable call of buttered kippers...unless you mistake it for a Laphroaig...; **t23** you might as well use the knife and fork you had prepared for the kippers for this: thick with a fabulous deft molassed depth; an attractive wholemeal biscuit background; **f22.5** a touch toasty and the last oils spreading the smoke as far as it can; **b23** putting Laphroaig into a decent cask makes a huge difference. Here's one that was. *52.6%. nc ncf sc. 178 bottles.*

Malts Of Scotland Clubs Laphroaig 1996 bourbon hogshead, cask no. 7313, dist Oct 96, bott Apr 10 **(86) n21.5 t23 f20. b21.5.** Not perhaps the greatest oak at work, but the massive sugar compensates. *57.3%. nc ncf sc. Malts Of Scotland. 255 bottles.*

Malts Of Scotland Laphroaig 1998 bourbon hogshead, cask no. 700272, dist Jun 98, bott Jan 11 **(95.5) n23.5** a stunningly beautiful portrait of smoke embers and liquorice; **t24** at first compact, but then the molasses and smoke start to do their stuff. A playful butterscotch note begins to sing, but is almost immediately overcome by the gathering smoke; **f23.5** remains guardedly intense but still those sugars keep searching for the whites of your eyes, carried on a wave of almost erotic oils; **b24.5** "hang on", I thought. "Have I tasted this whisky twice this year? Is age catching up on me as much as these malts?" Panic over. This is a very close approximation of the Old Master's 12, and on closer inspection I discover they are just a few casks apart... And the Old Master's ain't a bad whisky by any stretch of the imagination! However, this is even better ...much better: it is what the other might have been had not that slight oak interference. For scholars of whisky, you could do worse than buy both bottles and taste one beside the other. One excellent, the other bordering on one of the Islays of the Year. It is on two whiskies like this that you can cut your clinical teeth. *59.6%. nc ncf sc. 152 bottles.*

⋙ **Malts Of Scotland Laphroaig 1998** bourbon hogshead, cask no. MoS11002, dist Mar 98, bott Jul 11 **(88.5) n22** light and citrusy; the smoke offers both sweetness and weight; **t22.5** bounding sugars ensure the smoke melts on the tongue; chocolate sponge cake fills the middle; a decent variety of spices; **f22** dry, stubbornly spicy and ashy; **b22** oak takes a back seat to some simplistic smoke. *56.4%. nc ncf sc. Malts Of Scotland for Aquavitae 2011.*

⋙ **Malts Of Scotland Laphroaig 1998** bourbon hogshead, cask no. MoS11001, dist Mar 98, bott Aug 11 **(70.5) n18 t19 f16.5 b17.** Pretty raw and off key. *53.4%. nc ncf sc.*

⋙ **Malts Of Scotland Laphroaig 1998** bourbon hogshead, cask no. 5920, dist May 98, bott May 11 **(94) n24** classic dry smoke; a mix of both peat and soot; **t24** again dry from the off but just enough sugars to first soften the peaty impact, then a few waves of vanilla and walnut oil to add almost perfect weight and depth; **f22.5** simplifies considerably and finishes in a surprisingly tame manner, though the salt hanging onto the peaty embers is very attractive; **b23.5** the distillery in a nutshell. Well, in a bourbon hogshead... *53.4%. nc ncf sc.*

⸭ **Malts Of Scotland Laphroaig 1998** bourbon hogshead, cask no. 5921, dist May 98, bott May 11 **(88) n23.5** an Islayphile's dream: wonderful salt and spices attached to the dry peat...just paints a picture of that beautiful distillery in the glass; a little, well-hidden edge which makes me worry for the finish...; **t22** plenty of golden syrup really makes the big peat an easy catch to land: chewy and juicy; **f20.5** the smoke carries the full length, but a little bitterness arrives as promised by the nose; **b22** overcomes the usual Allied cask problem to deliver a rousing and classic Laphroaig. *52.9%. nc ncf sc. Malts Of Scotland.*

⸭ **Malts Of Scotland Laphroaig 1998** sherry hogshead, cask no. MoS11007, dist Mar 98, bott Sep 11 **(50) n13 t14 f10 b13** Absolutely reeking of sulphur. A shocker. So this should double the price in Germany.... *52.5%. nc ncf sc. Malts Of Scotland.*

⸭ **Malts Of Scotland Laphroaig 1998** bourbon hogshead, cask no. 5922, bott 2011 **(81) n21.5 t22 f18 b19.5.** A more lightly smoked version than the norm for this distillery. A shame, as it allows the bitterness of the poor cask to carry far too much weight. *59.8%. nc ncf sc.*

⸭ **Mo Ór Collection Laphroaig 1990 20 Years Old** first fill bourbon hogshead, cask no. 5941, dist 8 Jun 90, bott 1 Dec 10 **(89) n22.5** dry peat soot lightly sprinkled with Demerara sugar; something of the farmyards about this; **t22.5** those sugars on the nose arrive without hesitation: much sweeter and juicier than you could possibly expect; **f22** reverts back to a smoky sootiness again, though those sugars persist; **b22** a real sweetie; literally! *46%. nc ncf sc. Release No. 21. The Whisky Talker. 449 bottles.*

Old & Rare Laphroaig 21 Years Old refill sherry hogshead, dist Mar 89, bott Jun 10 **(96) n24** Man sherry!! The most masculine sherry aroma imaginable with sultana fit to explode integrating with smoke fit to suffocate, fruitcake at its raunchiest; sherry trifle at its juiciest... and not even the hint of a hint of the feared "s" word... **t24** a to die for delivery: one of those massive moments that is so well controlled that it somehow momentarily seems smaller than it actually is. But close your eyes and feed into that wine and spine interplay – the smoky backbone will not be dominated by the juicy grape and vice versa; the spices sparkle while the sweeter barley shine; **f24** a long burn for the spice guarantees an even longer fade; the grape remains clean, confirming that this is one of those most rare phenomena - a quite faultless sherry butt - and juicy and between them butterscotch, hickory and tannin ply their considerable trade...; **b24** don't let this whisky deceive you: for all its finesse and faultlessness, for all its rounded edges, for all its good manners...this is a beast. This, one of the great whiskies of 2011, is a vixen dressed as a kitten; a vamp as the high school prefect. Not so much old and rare. But Old and Raring... *56.9%. nc ncf sc. 212 bottles.*

⸭ **Old Malt Cask Laphroaig Aged 11 Years** refill hogshead, cask no. 8315, dist Feb 01, bott Apr 12 **(89) n22.5** trademark Laphroaig dry, salty smoke; **t23** early muscovado sugars make an excellent platform for the vanilla and peat to make a complex middle, **f21.5** bitters out slightly; **b22** does what it says on the tin. *50%. nc ncf sc. Douglas Laing & Co. 289 bottles.*

Old Malt Cask Laphroaig Aged 12 Years refill butt, cask no. 7458, dist Mar 99, bott Jun 11 **(90.5) n22** thick, dense...not for the Islay amateur...; **t22.5** excellent delivery: a distinct molasses and liquorice heart with veins of honey. The ubiquitous smoke is both soft and firm; **f23** more of the same but now a little more butterscotch and a tinge of honeycomb; **b23** a superb cask, bipolar in personality, seemingly of smoked molasses... *50%. nc ncf sc. Douglas Laing & Co. 303 bottles.*

Old Malt Cask Laphroaig Aged 12 Years refill hogshead, cask no. 6539, dist May 98, bott Sep 10 **(79.5) n20 t21 f19 b19.5.** Dense smoke but weighed down further by bitter oak. *50%. nc ncf sc. Douglas Laing & Co. 262 bottles.*

Old Malt Cask Laphroaig Aged 12 Years refill hogshead, cask no. 6704, dist Apr 98, bott Oct 10 **(83.5) n22 t21.5 f19 b21.** Tries hard to find a rhythm despite the cask. Some milky cocoa helps. *50%. nc ncf sc. Douglas Laing & Co. 318 bottles.*

⸭ **Old Malt Cask Laphroaig Aged 12 Years** refill hogshead, cask no. 7806, dist Aug 99, bott Oct 11 **(87.5) n22** a touch Fisherman's Friend mixes in with the mint and sugars; **t22.5** deft smoke intertwines with muscovado sugars; **f21** a long fade of vanilla and peat; less dries than shrivels as its bulk is lost unevenly; **b22** warts and all Laphroaig which employs enough old tricks to keep anyone entertained. *50%. nc ncf sc. Douglas Laing & Co. 188 bottles.*

Old Malt Cask Laphroaig Aged 15 Years refill hogshead, cask no. 7492, dist Jul 96, bott Jul 11 **(86.5) n22 t22 f21 b21.5.** Enjoyable and no slouch on the smoke front. A slight cough sweet character raises the eyebrows a little. *50%. nc ncf sc. Douglas Laing & Co. 308 bottles.*

⸭ **Old Malt Cask Laphroaig Aged 15 Years** refill hogshead, cask no. 7966, dist Oct 96, bott Dec 11 **(95.5) n24** Barratt's chocolate liquorice meets gristy smoke: a real complex number where a subtle dexterity is the key despite the obvious enormity; **t24.5** textbook delivery of soft oils and mixed sugars, including maple syrup. The smoke offers a dual role of offering caressing weight and a punchy spiciness; the middle ground is a fabulous mix of praline, vanilla and honeydew melon.....wow!!; **f23** long with the cocoa playing out with the multi-layered smoke; **b24** pure class. *50%. nc ncf sc. Douglas Laing & Co. 321 bottles.*

Old Malt Cask Laphroaig Aged 17 Years refill hogshead, cask no. 6630, dist Mar 93, bott Oct 10 **(82) n19 t22.5 f20 b21.5.** The trouble is, this is an old malt cask. Much older than the 17-y-o malt it contained. So the slight off key finale is foretold by the nose, as usual. The good news is that the delivery is a busy and delicious peat-spiced splendour with an admirable degree of sweetness. *48.2%. nc ncf sc. Douglas Laing & Co. 150 bottles.*

Old Malt Cask Laphroaig Aged 18 Years refill hogshead, cask no. 7120, dist Mar 93, bott Mar 11 **(94.5) n23.5** sensuous, sexy, salty...not sure if it is one's panting partner or a Laphroaig at its most alluring vivacious...; **t24.5** the low levels of smoke detected on the nose begin with the same laziness on delivery. However, with a minute or two the peat has not just built up a head of steam, but now there are spices buzzing in every direction; the light sugars also play an important part in bringing the oak into play; wonderful bourbony liquorice and raisin ensures the malt enters new levels of intensity and complexity; **f22.5** delicate traces of spice remain; burnt fudge and friendly oils do the rest; **b24** at times the balance and complexity between the outstanding bourbony oak and smoke cannot be bettered. Occasionally even strays into the world of pot still Demerara rum. What a quite magnificent experience. *50%. nc ncf sc. Douglas Laing & Co. 121 bottles.*

⠿ **Old Malt Cask Laphroaig Aged 18 Years** refill hogshead, cask no. 7992, dist Sep 93, bott Dec 11 **(84.5) n21.5 t22 f20 b21.** Unusually sweet for a Laphroaig yet struggles against a very tight cask determined to add a bitter edge. *50%. nc ncf sc. 271 bottles.*

Old Malt Cask Laphroaig Aged 21 Years refill hogshead, cask no. 7459, dist Mar 90, bott Jun 11 **(90) n22.5** pleasantly farmyardy, but they must be growing mint...; **t22.5** ...there we go: a flavour I've not enjoyed for a while – a Merlin's Brew mint and chocolate ice lolly. Which kind of fits in neatly with the mint on the nose... **f22.5** and the chocolate caramel on the finish...; **b22.5** deceptively smoky: a lot less peat on the palate than the nose suggests. *50%. nc ncf sc. Douglas Laing & Co. 122 bottles.*

Old Masters Laphroaig 12 Years Old cask no. 700233, dist 1998, bott Feb 11 **(93) n23** Laphroaig, quite literally, in essence; a milky note which lives below ground, docks it a point; **t23.5** clean-cut peat. Big, bold, yet refreshing and delicate; **f22.5** vanillas and the return of the milk fog up the previous clarity, but the smoke drifts to the end; **b23** a near exemplary cask. *57.2%. sc. James MacArthur & Co.*

The Perfect Dram Laphroaig 1990 bott 2011 **(86.5) n21.5 t22.5 f20.5 b22.** Counters its slight nip and bite with an impressive interplay between the smoke, liquorice and mild molasses. A bit of bitterness creeps in at the death. An enjoyable dram. But "perfect"...? *56.3%*

Premier Barrel Laphroaig Aged 11 Years (78) n19.5 t21 f18.5 b19. Lightly smoked with not quite enough about it to entirely overcome the bitter oak *46%. nc ncf sc. 264 bottles.*

⠿ **Premier Barrel Laphroaig Aged 11 Years (89) n22** a real spike to the smoke despite some oils trying to add a sugary weight; **t23.5** zips around the palate with youthful abandon. Little oak present to prevent the barley, smoke and sugars crash into the taste buds like joyriders wrapping themselves into lamp-posts and doing a runner; **f22** relatively short, but full of zesty smoke; **b22** when they say "premier barrel" I think they mean here one that is least likely to alter the course of the spirit. Youthful and delicious! *46%. nc ncf sc. 328 bottles.*

Provenance Laphroaig Over 9 Years refill hogshead, cask no. 6421, dist Winter 01, bott Summer 2010 **(85.5) n22 t22 f20 b21.5.** A very gentle, almost non-committal, farmyardy version which treads wearily with the oak and boosts the vanilla to high levels. *46%. nc ncf nsc.*

Provenance Laphroaig Over 10 Years refill hogshead, cask no. 7161, dist Spring 01, bott Spring 2011 **(89) n23 t22 f22 b22.** Excellent Laphroaig which differs from the distillery bottling by its relaxed simplicity, distinct lightness and an extra injection of sugars. *46%. nc ncf sc.*

Provenance Laphroaig Over 10 Years refill hogshead, cask no. 6921, dist Winter 01, bott Winter 2011 **(80) n21 t20 f19 b20.** The usual problem of over-used old Allied casks is responsible for a degree of bitterness. But the high quality of the smoky distillate can still be marvelled at. *46%. nc ncf sc. Douglas Laing & Co.*

⠿ **Provenance Laphroaig Over 10 Years** refill hogshead, cask no. 7566, dist Winter 2001, bott Summer 2011 **(91) n23.5** dry, sooty smoke over a vanilla base; **t22.5** the sugars appear under protest; the smoke bathes the taste buds with subtlety; **f22.5** the lack of oils here is reflected by the medium length finish. The dry, dusty smoke never lets up; **b22.5** almost a blueprint for a classic Laphroaig 10-y-o of the very driest variety...!! *46%. nc ncf sc.*

⠿ **Provenance Laphroaig Over 10 Years** refill hogshead, cask no. 7841, dist Winter 2001, bott Autumn 2011 **(81.5) n20 t22 f19 b20.5.** The miserly cask does little to enhance the crusty peat. Worth buying alongside cask 7566 to show just what oak can do in just ten years to a malt as distinctive as Laphroaig. *46%. nc ncf sc. Douglas Laing & Co.*

Provenance Laphroaig Over 11 Years refill butt, cask no. 6629, dist Winter 99, bott Autumn 2010 **(91) n22.5** hard to imagine a more zesty Laphroaig than this; **t23** silky delivery offering first a wave of juicy, peatless barley, then several squeezes of lemon and, finally, several oily layers of smoke **f22.5** long, with a lovely manuka honey edge to the citrus and smoke; the oils seize every last complex opportunity; **b23** obviously distilled from smoked lemons...and with no little success. Brilliantly different. *46%. nc ncf sc. Douglas Laing & Co.*

Scotch Malt Whisky Society Cask 29.88 Aged 9 Years refill butt, cask no. 334, dist 2001 **(75.5) n18.5 t20.5 f18 b18.5.** The nose tells you there is trouble down the line with a poor cask. What follows doesn't disappoint. Or does, depending on your viewpoint. *60.9%. sc. 653 bottles.*

Scotch Malt Whisky Society Cask 29.89 Aged 20 Years refill butt, cask no. 12629, dist 1989 **(84.5) n20.5 t21.5 f21.5 b21.** Massive contribution from some granite-like muscovado sugar, aided by deft spice, saves the day against an uncompromising cask. *54.3%. sc. 605 bottles.*

Scotch Malt Whisky Society Cask 29.92 Aged 10 Years refill sherry butt, cask no. 700062, dist 2000 **(91.5) n23** when the richness of the grape can be heard above the tinnitus of the peat, you really take note...; **t23** lush grape and even a juicy barley blast. The peat is less than dominant; **f22.5** long, with some fruit candy amid the hickory and smoke; **b23.5** a rare marriage between grape and peat which appears blessed. *63.2%. sc. 584 bottles.*

Scotch Malt Whisky Society Cask 29.94 Aged 11 Years refill sherry butt, cask no. 2748, dist 1999 **(94) n23** the nose is almost a replay of 29.92 but somehow manages to get the grape across with even greater clarity. What makes this even more remarkable is that the peat seems a whole lot heftier; **t24** the delivery is one huge battle for supremacy between squelching grape and thumping peat; **f23** some real spice to the fade which now includes some major vanilla; **b24** simply beautiful whisky. *58.8%. sc. 610 bottles.*

Scotch Malt Whisky Society Cask 29.97 Aged 20 Years refill butt, cask no. 10835, dist 1990 **(79) n20 t21 f19 b19.** Sweet. But another less than stupendous piece of oak making a poor contribution. *59.1%. sc. 608 bottles.*

Scotch Malt Whisky Society Cask 29.103 Aged 13 Years refill hogshead, cask no. 700064, dist 1998 **(87.5) n21.5 t22 f22 b22.** Grade A blending fodder. *57.5%. sc. 247 bottles.*

⁘ **Scotch Malt Whisky Society Cask 29.106 Aged 13 Years** refill hogshead, cask no. 700066, dist 1998 **(95.5) n23.5** a sparkling trade off between light yet lively peat and wonderful citrus; **t24** gloriously weighted; the barley and delicate fruits offer a surprising lightness while the peats act as the expected anchor; **f24** long with a dry, ashy finale in perfect harmony to the juicy, sugar-studded barley; a slight, late, bitterness to the oak is the only fly in the ointment; **b24** for what has been a disappointing year for independent bottlings of Laphroaig, this classic bottling has been very badly needed. *57.3%. sc. Scotch Malt Whisky Society.*

⁘ **Scotch Malt Whisky Society Cask 29.109 Aged 20 Years** refill butt, cask no. 10837, dist 1990 **(91.5) n23** No off-notes. Very few other notes other than grape....and peat trying to get a word in edgewise; **t23** silky grape on delivery...followed by less silky grape. The peat is found in a chocolate fudge middle; **f22.5** lots more chocolate fudge. With spiced raisins....; **b23** some may regard this as their whisky of the year, so enormous is the sherry input. For me, balance has been compromised, though there is no denying that this is great fun. *59.2%. sc.*

⁘ **Scotch Malt Whisky Society Cask 29.110 Aged 10 Years** refill hogshead, cask no. 398, dist 2001 **(86.5) n22 t22 f21 b21.5.** A very tight cask where the salt squeezes the living daylights out of all else. Big, eye-watering flavours, uncompromising peat but, eschewing restraint, simply too much of a good thing. *57.2%. sc. Scotch Malt Whisky Society.*

⁘ **Scotch Malt Whisky Society Cask 29.111 Aged 10 Years** refill hogshead, cask no. 400, dist 2001 **(86) n21.5 t22 f21 b21.5.** As soft and soothing a malt as cask 29.110 is a vixen. But the oak is not quite up to scratch, so the bitter lines apparent cannot be outmanoeuvred by the malty talent on show. The softness of delivery is a treat, though. *57.3%. sc.*

⁘ **Single Cask Collection Laphroaig Aged 13 Years** bourbon hogshead, cask no. 1998 **(92.5) n23** a superb combination of sweet gristy barley and citrus-tinted smoke. Even a hint of gooseberry there, too; **t23** salivating and succulent, the barley is oozing with beautifully peated juice; **f23.5** the vanillas arrive to combine with the smoke for a drier finale; **b23** a cracking cask full of lusty intent but showing a great deal of craft, too. *60.8%. sc.*

Vom Fass Laphroaig 12 Years Old (90.5) n22 a healthy, clean cask does little to interrupt the gentle, mildly salty smoky pulse; **t22** how gentle is that? The smoke, the sugars, the butterscotch, even the oils...every element in a seemingly deliberate rhythm; **f23.5** now I'm really hooked: the peat remains on best behaviour, but the rich liquorice melting into it is almost cruel...; **b23** creeps up and seduces you like a young temptress in a smoky bar... *43%. sc.*

The Whisky Agency Laphroaig 11 Years Old (75.5) n20 t19 f16 b17.5. Sadly, a malt of promise has been torpedoed by oak that has given way and now offers a milky note, which leads to a vivid bitterness. At a tasting recently, someone in the audience informed me they had been told that if you leave it in the glass, it goes away. If only! Yet more drivel spouted by so called experts, I'm afraid... *54.5%. The Whisky Agency.*

⸭ **The Whisky Agency Laphroaig 21 Years Old** bourbon cask, dist 1990, bott 2011 **(84.5)** **n22 t22.5 f19 b21.** A curious malt: enjoyable and sweet early on but little helped by at times appearing weirdly thin with a touch of smoky acetate. *56.8%. sc. The Whisky Agency.*

⸭ **Whisky Antique Laphroaig 21 Years Old Special Bottling** dist 1990, bott 2011 **(91.5)** **n22** has much to say, yet does so in a confined space where any amount of peat and fruit are crushed together; **t23** the delivery is equally condensed and it is not until the fourth or fifth layer that those gargantuan notes begin to find breathing space; most impressive is the juicy fruit; **f23.5** dries with all kinds of coal and peat dust clogging the palate; **b23** hardly one for the squeamish. Light Speyside lovers beware! *57.7%. sc. Silver Seal Whisky Company.*

The Whisky Agency Laphroaig 1990 bott 2010 **(81)** **n19 t21 f20 b21.** Some anthracite in with the peat. Niggardly and thin for the most part; expansive and sweet on the rare occasions it has the mind. *52.8%. The Whisky Agency.*

The Whisky Agency Laphroaig 1990 bourbon hogshead, bott 2010 **(94)** **n23** thumping iodine attached to butter spread on to a slightly burned piece of toast; **t24** much sweeter delivery than expected: a light, sugary sheen coating the fomenting peat. Dries impressively in the middle phase while the peppers get to work; **f23** dries exactly how it should, with the peat almost taking a powdery form but brown sugars ensuring balance and length; **b24** an attractively shaped, slightly buttery version. Absolutely gorgeous, in fact. *56.1%*

The Whisky Castle Collection No. 12 Laphroaig 12 Years sherry butt, cask no. 80017, dist 1998, bott 2011 **(74)** **n18.5 t19 f18.5 b18.** Imagine both the Berlin and London Symphony Orchestras being assembled to play Tod und Verklarung. One starts in C Major and the other in D flat... I could weep. Without the sulphur, this might well have been the best single cask of the year. Lovely people bottling a potentially stupendous whisky to be sold in probably the best whisky shop in Scotland... Like Strauss, what a story I might have told... *63.9%. nc ncf sc. A.D. Rattray for The Whisky Castle. 324 bottles.*

Whisky Doris Laphroaig 2000 bourbon hogshead, bott 2010 **(80)** **n22 t21 f18 b19.** Tries to spin an attractive, honeyed tale despite the remorselessly bittering oak. *59.1%*

Wilson & Morgan Barrel Selection Laphroaig Twenty Years Old cask no. 2348/49, dist 1990, bott 2010 **(87.5)** **n22 t22 f21.5 b22.** Almost impossible to believe this is 20 years old: at times you feel you can still spot the odd feinty note. *46%. Wilson & Morgan.*

LINKWOOD
Speyside, 1820. Diageo. Working.

Linkwood 12 Years Old db **(94.5)** **n23.5** gorgeous malt absolutely bursting at the seems with barley-rich vitality; citrus and anthracite abound; **t24** a quite stunning delivery with some of the clearest, cleanest, most crystalline malt on the market. The sugars are angular and decidedly Demerara; **f23** a long play out of sharp barley which refuses to be embattled by the oaky vanillas; light spices compliment the persistent sugars; **b24** possibly the most improved distillery bottling in recent times. Having gone through a period of dreadful casks, it appears to have come through to the other side very much on top and close to how some of us remember it a quarter of a century ago. Sublime malt: one of the most glittering gems in the Diageo crown. *43%*

Linkwood 26 Year Old port finish dist 1981, bott 2008 db **(85)** **n20 t24 f20.5 b20.5.** Can't say that either nose or finish do it for me. But the delivery is brilliant: the enormity and luxurious sweetness of the grape leaves you simply purring and rolling your eyes in delight. *56.9%*

Linkwood 26 Year Old rum finish, dist 1981, bott 2008 db **(89.5)** **n23.5** sharp, flinty; enticing nose prickle; **t23.5** lots of juice, then a touch of spruce as the oak kicks in; the sweetness is delicate and softer on development than many rum finishes; **f21** becomes dependent on cream toffee; **b21.5** a real touch of the rum toffee raisin candy to this one. *56.5%*

Linkwood 26 Year Old sweet red wine, dist 1981, bott 2008 db **(89)** **n22.5** punchy, salty and lively; distinct sherry-custard trifle; wine and oak together spin out the spice; **t23** perky delivery, again with spice to the fore; juicy grape and a lively layering of oak; **f21** dulls out slightly as it sweetens, again with a cream toffee softness; **b22** juicy, spicy: doesn't stint on complexity. *56.5%*

Linkwood 1974 Rare Malt db **(79)** **n20 t21 f19 b19.** Wobbles about the palate in search of a story and balance. Finds neither but some of the early moments, though warming, offer very decent malt. The best bit follows a couple of seconds after – and lasts as long. *55%*

Adelphi Linkwood 26 Years Old cask no. 5266, dist 1984, bott 2011 **(94)** **n23.5** full on blood orange and rhubarb is fortified with wild spices; **t23.5** textbook mouth-feel followed by x-rated spices which rip relentlessly into you. Some accommodating brown sugars dab a welcome degree of relief...; **f23** a fabulous mixture of dark and brown chocolate (to be a little more precise a typical central American style with central German), while those peppers continue their assault; **b24** Linkwood is one of those malts that is akin to going out on a blind date. You have no idea whether you are about to come face to face with something you wish not only to get to know intimately, but enjoy a night of joy without end. Or it might just be a characterless, vacuous ratbag you want to shove into a taxi and send home within the first ten minutes. Here's one I wouldn't mind spending a night alone with... and expect a bleeding back in the morning...576%. sc. Adelphi Distillery. 113 bottles.

꙳ **Boisdale Linkwood 1991** cask no. 10344, bott 2012 **(88) n22** ginger and clove has been squeezed into a mildly rummy aroma, broadcasting the good age; **t21.5** the nose suggests the potential for a spiced up delivery and it doesn't disappoint. The oak really does bite deep, but soon soothing thick barley is on hand; **f22.5** a far more comfortable finish with the excesses now dampened down and extra sugars in for balance; **b22** a malt aged as far as it can comfortably go. 46%. nc ncf sc. Berry Bros & Rudd.

Chieftain's Linkwood Aged 11 Years German oak finish, dist Jun 99, bott 2011 **(70) n20 t22 f19 b19**. Before I read the details, I was on to them: "ha-ha!", I thought. "It's one of those sneaky German cask things, with all its tannin and sugars." But before those thoughts were set in stone, some slightly off-key bitter notes on the finish began to appear and I began to wonder. But I was right the first time, apparently. Always trust your instincts, I say... 571%. nc ncf.

꙳ **Duncan Taylor Rare Auld Linkwood 20 Years Old** cask no. 8323, dist 1990 **(90) n24** fabulous and something bordering original! A real mix of lively fruit, chopped aubergine and salted celery; some black peppers and cocoa-vanilla in there, too...; **t23.5** beautifully weighted delivery, then a surprising degree of clean, mouth-watering barley; the sugars early on show a textbook degree of poise; **f20** fades severely as the vanilla becomes just a little too dominant and tart; **b22.5** doesn't quite live up to the promise on the nose and delivery, though remains a hugely enjoyable dram, never short of surprises. 48.3%. sc. Duncan Taylor & Co.

Gordon & MacPhail Distillery Label Linkwood 25 Years Old (91) n23 tangy, lively and refusing to admit its old age: a fabulous marriage of Palma violets and something much fruitier; **t23.5** fabulously refreshing with a continuous retracing of its malty steps. A little curious salt sits comfortably with the oak; **f22** much drier and vanillin pronounced; **b22.5** if anyone is capable of making a Linkwood tick, it is G&M: wonderful! 43%

꙳ **Gordon & MacPhail Private Collection Linkwood 1991** Cote Rotie finish **(72) n19 t18 f18 b17**. Certainly fruity. But just too many faults from the cask. 45%. Gordon & MacPhail.

꙳ **Gordon & MacPhail Rare Vintage Linkwood 1973 (87) n23** caramelised biscuit meets Garibaldi; there are some serious bourbon style kumquat notes amid the big oak kick; **t22** enough barley sugars and vague chocolate notes are dredged up to make for a pleasantly chewy experience; **f20.5** dries out until your eyes water; **b21.5** outrageous, as it is simply over the hill. Or should be. But it gathers enough charisma from somewhere to make for an intriguing battle between the malty remnants and the massive oak. 43%. Gordon & MacPhail.

Hart Brothers Linkwood Aged 13 Years dist Apr 97, bott Jan 11 **(94.5) n23.5** thick barley riddled with sublime citrus and vanilla. Light oils add weight to the new mown grass; **t24** silky and salivating as it had to be. Brilliant display of brown sugars and the most delicate hint of glazed ginger possible as the butterscotch mounts; **f23** a long fade of all those previous characters and hardly a hint of oak bitterness but some spices for sure; **b24** how much more of a Speysider can this be...? Of its style, just about perfect. 46%. sc.

꙳ **Hart Brothers Linkwood Aged 14 Years** cask no. 4144, dist 17 Apr 97, bott 15 Apr 12 **(87) n21.5** thin, with everything pointing to grassy, clean barley; **t22** mouth-watering with the barley dominating all aspects of delivery and follow through; **f22** a spiced vanilla buzz, but the malt retains control; **b21.5** very simple whisky. But attractive all the same. 46%. sc.

Hart Brothers Linkwood Aged 19 Years dist May 91, bott Jan 11 **(94) n22.5** despite a mild flaw, a beautiful mix of Dundee cake, apple pie with cinnamon and vanilla sponge... **t23.5** full bodied delivery with the juicy grape and liquorice making an unlikely alliance; some spices and little honey are found in the chunky middle ground; **f22.5** medium length with a pleasing pithy dryness; **b23** maybe Hart's should buy Linkwood: they certainly know how to make it sing, even from a less than perfect cask... 46%. sc.

Kingsbury Single Cask Series Linkwood 20 Years Old Valdespino's PX **(86.5) n23 t21.5 f21 b21**. While I would usually drink a PX aged 20 years in a whisky cask over a 20-y-o malt matured in a PX barrel at least 99 times out of 100, I must admit that this guy has some outstanding attributes. Especially the nose which offers just the right degree of spice to the rambling grapey sugar. The delivery is of the right stuff, too. But then, as is so often the case, enormity of the wine tends to befuddle all else. 46%. nc ncf sc. Japan Import Systems.

꙳ **Liquid Sun Linkwood 27 Years Old** bourbon cask, dist 1984, bott 2011 **(91.5) n22.5** gristy, for all its years, and lightly dappled with smoke; **t23** beautifully weighted, fabulously juicy and the smoke leads into a complex array of spices; **f23** long, thanks to the smoke, but the cocoa confirms the antiquity; **b23** this has been a vintage year for decent Linkwood releases and this smoky offering is by no means cowed by its company. 53.2%. sc.

꙳ **Malts Of Scotland Linkwood Peated 1987** bourbon hogshead, cask no. MoS11008, dist Sep 87, bott Sep 11 **(91) n22.5** Arbroath Smokies and diced apple; **t23** smoky and spiced from the off, but nothing too heavy and the sugars stay until the midway point. Certainly the malt is tangible until the cocoa arrives; **f22.5** dries as the oak takes hold. But the Smokies still have something to say; **b23** an attractive malt unusual for its playful smokiness. *51.4%. nc ncf sc. Malts Of Scotland.*

⫶⫶⫶ **Mo Ór Collection Linkwood 1983 27 Years Old** first fill bourbon hogshead, cask no. 5714, dist 17 Nov 83, bott 14 Jan 11 **(92) n22.5** anyone who used to invest in a Wagon Wheel biscuit from their school tuck shop will have memories flooding back from the chocolate and spice combo here: this one is of the jammy variety; **t24** one of the great deliveries of the year: the sweetness accompanying the lightly honeyed barley acts only as the perfect foil for the light peppers and crisp vanilla which descends; the lightest of sheens suggests a sugary glaze to the barley; **f22** pans out with delicate vanillas and almost indelicate butterscotch; **b23.5** clean, bold, purposeful and beautifully weighted, this does slightly more than can be expected of it. *46%. nc ncf sc. Release No. 29. The Whisky Talker. 352 bottles.*

Old Malt Cask Linkwood Aged 21 Years refill butt, cask no. 6302, dist May 89, bott Jun 10 **(62) n15 t17 f15 b15.** Sulphur tainted. *50%. nc ncf sc. Douglas Laing & Co. 484 bottles.*

⫶⫶⫶ **Old Malt Cask Linkwood Aged 21 Years** refill butt, cask no. 7102, dist May 90, bott Mar 12 **(64) n16 t18 f14 b16.** Riddled with you-know-what... *50%. nc ncf sc. 450 bottles.*

Old Malt Cask Linkwood Aged 26 Years refill hogshead, cask no. 6627, dist Jan 84, bott Oct 10 **(92.5) n23** pronounced grassy barley top dresses the milky oak; **t23.5** every bit as juicy as the nose suggests but even displaying an extra degree of icing sugar; just a playful hint of spice and twist of citrus; **f22.5** soft oils allow the same song to be repeated; **b23.5** simplistic but everything it does is completed with a flourish and a touch of class. *50%. nc ncf sc. Douglas Laing & Co. 126 bottles.*

Old Malt Cask Linkwood Aged 28 Years refill hogshead, cask no. 6499, dist Aug 82, bott Aug 10 **(95) n24** excellent oak lead which fully celebrates the barley-rich freshness; more than a hint of freshly squeezed carrot juice underlines an earthy depth; **t24** beautifully oiled, the forceful sugars cling to the barley as the spices make an impact; juicy and chewy with massive liquorice and hickory notes which would not be out of place in the very finest bourbons; **f23.5** dries as the oak and vanilla dominate but still so much to explore; **b23.5** a memorable Linkwood which revels in its vivid beauty. *50%. nc ncf sc. Douglas Laing & Co. 152 bottles.*

Old Masters Linkwood Aged 12 Years cask no. 11650, dist 1998, bott Feb 11 **(94.5) n23** wonderful sprinkling of allspice and bluebells on the big barley lead; **t24.5** just so intact and composed as the malt forms a thick train of sharp and juicy barley which takes you into mega salivation mode; the weight nears perfection; **f23.5** a fabulous display of spicy zestiness; **b23.5** a quite masterful cask from the Old Master... *54.6%. sc. James MacArthur & Co.*

Provenance Linkwood Over 12 Years refill hogshead, cask no. 6823, dist Spring 98, bott Autumn 2010 **(84.5) n21 t21.5 f21 b21.** Clean, lightly juiced, mega-simplistic malt designed to bulk up any decent blend. *46%. nc ncf sc. Douglas Laing & Co.*

⫶⫶⫶ **Provenance Linkwood Over 12 Years** bourbon barrel, cask no. 8242, dist Summer 1999, bott Spring 2012 **(88) n21.5** thin barley bolstered with cooked apple; **t22.5** mega-salivating barley with the sugars offering just the right degree of crispness; **f22** light vanilla and the sugars persist; **b22** clean, attractive and simplistic. *46%. nc ncf sc.*

⫶⫶⫶ **Scotch Malt Whisky Society Cask 39.83 Aged 28 Years** refill hogshead, cask no. 5412, dist 1982 **(85.5) n21 t21.5 f21.5 b21.5.** Looking for a docile malt? Back off! Vague fish paste to the aroma but every other nuance clings to something with a barley theme. *53.9%. sc.*

⫶⫶⫶ **Scotch Malt Whisky Society Cask 39.84 Aged 21 Years** refill hogshead, cask no. 8314, dist 1990 **(88.5) n23** unusual to find an exotic fruit touch to a malt which has reached only its early 20s. But it is there, as is a light red liquorice bourbon trait and a touch of hickory; **t22** for all the age on the nose, initially a salivating delivery with a malty theme. It is not long before the oak takes command, however; **f21.5** dry and overworked oak; **b22** have you ever seen a grey and balding 21-year-old bloke...? *48%. sc. Scotch Malt Whisky Society.*

⫶⫶⫶ **Scott's Selection Linkwood 1991** bott 2011 **(87.5) n21.5** the creaky oak out performs the malt; **t22** a sharp delivery of petulant oak slowly cut down to size by the juicy barley; well spiced throughout; **f22** from the vanilla and butterscotch school with a late malty flourish; **b22** takes a while to find its feet but is pretty well balanced when it does. *59.3%. Speyside Distillers.*

⫶⫶⫶ **Single Cask Collection Linkwood 27 Years Old** bourbon hogshead, dist 1984 **(92.5) n22.5** a tight nose flaked with oak and linseed. Some red liquorice and cinnamon-apple; **t23.5** big oils on delivery help the maple syrup cover a wider area but are reduced in effect as the spices begin to up the complexity, again cinnamon having an input; **f23** long, with the vanillas showing cleanly and keenly; **b23.5** not just a bourbon hogshead. But gives all the indications of a first-fill because some real Kentucky character leaks into this one, yes-sir-ee! A very decent spirit has spent 27 years in a top cask. *57%. sc. Single Cask Collection.*

⫶⫶⫶ **The Warehouse Collection Linkwood Aged 11 Years** bourbon barrel, dist May 97, bott Jun 08 **(89) n22.5** superb citrus and salt nose; the clean barley links with tingling peppers to provide a complex punch; **t22.5** salivating and crisp, the barley goes steady on the sugars and provide enough muscovado to balance the grapefruit sharpness; **f22** softens towards vanilla and butterscotch with a twinge of spice, too; **b22** apparently still quite a few bottles of this are still around. They shouldn't be for much longer. *46%. sc. Whisky Warehouse No. 8. 271 bottles.*

⁖ **The Warehouse Collection Linkwood Aged 28 Years** bourbon hogshead, cask no. 1620, dist 15 Mar 84, bott 8 Aug 12 **(95) n24.5** Bourbon hoggy it may be, but the prevailing kumquat is the key. Wonderfully coastal, with a sea-breeze saltiness cleansing both the barley and light, dry coconut-oak. Some serious floral note and did I mention the fruit?; **t24** the nose is a hard act to follow, but the fabulous combo of mega-sweetened puckering oak gives it a pretty good shot. The spices in the middle ground are as complex and busy as you'll find with any Speysider this year; **f22.5** dips slightly as the more astringent aspects of the oak are briefly exposed. But still a delicious meal; **b24** rare to start a new tasting day with a treat such as this. Beautiful whisky. *56.7%. sc. Whisky Warehouse No. 8. 171 bottles.*

⁖ **Wemyss 2000 Single Speyside "Vanilla Zest"** butt, bott 2011 **(88.5) n21** sherbet lemon and zest; very clean and a little new makey...) **t23** delivers exactly as expected; clean and fresh with a barley juiciness and zesty bite; **f22** a slow unveiling of vanilla but remains clean and true; **b22.5** the word "zest" had formed in my mind when nosing even before I knew the full name of the brand! Does what it says on the tin... *46%. sc. 792 bottles.*

LITTLEMILL
Lowland, 1772. Loch Lomond Distillers. Demolished.
Littlemill Aged 8 Years db **(84) n20 t22 f21 b21.** Aged 8 Years, claims the neck of the dumpy bottle, which shows a drawing of a distillery that no longer exists, as it has done for the last quarter of a century. Well, double that and you'll be a lot closer to the real age of this deliciously sweet, chewy and increasingly spicy chap. And it is about as far removed from the original 8-y-o fire-water it once was as is imaginable. *40%.*

Littlemill 1964 db **(82) n21 t20 f21 b20.** A soft-natured, bourbony chap that shows little of the manic tendencies that made this one of Scotland's most-feared malts. Talk about mellowing with age... *40%*

⁖ **Archives Littlemill 1988 23 Years Old Third Release** cask no. 08/1077, dist 7 Nov 88, bott May 12 **(75.5) n18.5 t20 f18 b19.** Much closer in style to a not particularly great slivovitz than a malt. *49.3%. nc ncf sc. Whiskybase B.V. 48 bottles.*

⁖ **Archives Littlemill 1989 22 Years Old Inaugural Release** cask no. RTN-11-238, dist May 89, bott Jul 11 **(80) n20 t21 f19 b20.** Begins ungracefully and moves into a much maltier theme later on before falling away again. *48.3%. nc ncf sc. Whiskybase B.V. 120 bottles.*

⁖ **First Cask Littlemill 20 Years Old** bourbon barrel, cask no. 726, dist 7 Mar 90, bott 14 Oct 10 **(87) n20.5** sharp, a touch of tobacco, by no means in tune; but saved by a vague nutty-nougat theme not uncommon in Kentucky; **t23** salivating barley. Followed by...more barley! Gosh this is one malty beast...; **f21.5** the nip and bite of a slightly hot spirit, and some unwelcome oaky tang, too. But the intense malt saves the day; **b22** you get a lot of barley to each pour... *56.2%. nc ncf sc. Whisky Import Nederland. 225 bottles.*

⁖ **Hart Brothers Littlemill Aged 20 Years** cask no. 19, dist 27 Feb 92, bott Mar 12 **(88.5) n23.5** peppery and attractively floral – in a dank forest kind of a way; some bourbon theme, too; **t22** thin, sweet barley; watered down barley sugar; **f21.5** papery and increasingly warming; **b21.5** the palate makes no attempt to hide that slightly gluey side to its personality but a bit of an entertainer, especially on the characterful nose. *46%. sc.*

⁖ **Malts Of Scotland Littlemill 1989** sherry butt, cask no. 2511, dist 28 Mar 89, bott May 11 **(84) n20 t22 f20.5 b21.5.** Littlemill....in a late 1980s sherry butt! That is like playing Russian Roulette with five loaded chambers.... Yet, this one is a decent cask with no sulphur. Even so, the grape has its work cut out to douse the flames of this napalm malt. Hot doesn't quite do it justice. Though this is a mere vindaloo of a whisky: without the sherry one suspects this would have been a Littlemill Phall! *52.8%. nc ncf sc. Malts Of Scotland.*

⁖ **Old Malt Cask Littlemill Aged 19 Years** refill hogshead, cask no. 6552, dist Nov 91, bott Nov 10 **(74) n20 t19 f17 b18.** Malty and juicy in part. But otherwise like chewing glass. *50%. nc ncf sc. Douglas Laing & Co. 340 bottles.*

⁖ **Old Malt Cask Littlemill Aged 20 Years** refill hogshead, cask no. 7099, dist Nov 91, bott Nov 11 **(88) n22** you know those fruit-scented soap bars...; **t22.5** lush and surprisingly sweet on entry. Then a short burst of the flame thrower before all kinds of Malteser notes beckon; **f21.5** those strange, slightly soapy off notes on the nose re-appear; **b22** a distillery that never fails to amaze – one way or another. Overly perfumed. As fiery as a five-foot nothing flamed-haired Scottish midfielder. *50%. nc ncf sc. 121 bottles.*

⁖ **Riegger's Selection Littlemill 1990** first fill sherry butt, cask no. 2, dist 20 Dec 90, bott 24 Nov 10 **(95) n24** a truly faultless sherry butt of the very highest order. Not just from the copious dates and walnut richness but because it allows the barley to make a fabulously malty contribution; **t24** silky beyond words. The spices arrive early but in outstanding shape allowing as much grape and malt as required to fill the middle, complex ground. Softly nutty and chewy, we now head in Melton Hunt Cake direction with a little lardy cake on the side; **f23** much vanilla and barley, but a hint of burnt raisin lurks. The oils work deftly and to excellent effect; **f24** if 25 years ago you had told me I would one day taste a Littlemill as good as this, I would have laughed in your face... *53.6%. nc ncf sc. Viktor-Riegger GmbH. 198 bottles.*

⋄ **Scotch Malt Whisky Society Cask 97.21 Aged 21 Years** first fill barrel, cask no. 732, dist 1990 **(94.5) n23** malt breakfast cereal complete with creamy milk...and a sprinkling of muscovado sugar; a curious – and decidedly attractive – blend of Demerara rum and bourbon whiskey; **t24** you'd expect something Kentuckian maybe but, no, it's intense barley first out of the traps. And then bourbon honeycomb catches up and overtakes; chocolate is not far behind...; **f23.5** long, with a wonderful trailing of diverse sugars, not least coconut syrup; lots of mocha with a dab of vanilla; **b24** what a shame this distillery is so much better dead than when alive...this is Littlemill at its zenith. *54.7%. sc. Scotch Malt Whisky Society.*

⋄ **Scott's Selection Littlemill 1992** bott 2012 **(90) n22** some of the distillery's traditional nip and aggression is still at large, though now works well with so much vanilla to hand; **t22** silky mouth-feel while the barley appears to have the teeth of a crocodile...; **f23** settles down for a friendlier, more sugar-coated finale....topped off with bang on spice; **b23** the recent bottlings of Littlemill have been remarkable for their consistency. And they don't get any more consistent than this...An adorable rogue. *55.6%. Speyside Distillers.*

⋄ **Sestante Collection Littlemill 19 Years Old** dist 1990 **(85) n20 t22.5 f21 b21.5.** A fiery little number where the barley pierces the taste buds like an exocet. The resulting explosion, though, is sugar-rich and by no means unpleasant. *57%. sc. Silver Seal Whisky Company.*

⋄ **Single Malts Of Scotland Littlemill 1989** refill sherry cask **(89) n22** just the first nosing of this tells you that life is about to get interesting: some controlled nip and bite with some many things wrong it almost seems right; **t22** fruity and fluting delivery and then promptly rips into your taste buds. Make sure you have a chair with arms attached...; **f22.5** steadies as the sugars and barley finally make an entrance; **b22.5** a bone shaker of a whisky experience; a thuggish bouncer in a £500 whistle and flute. It's rough, tough....and bloody great fun! *55.7%. ncf sc. Speciality Drinks. 183 bottles.*

⋄ **Silver Seal Littlemill Over 20 Years Old** dist 1990 **(84.5) n21.5 t22.5 f19.5 b21.** Time has tamed the bad boy of the Lowlands. No ripping your throat out here. A pleasant, simple malt awaits. Though the bitter finish does knee one in the nuts, somewhat. *46%. sc.*

The Whisky Agency Littlemill 1989 sherry wood, bott 2011 **(89) n22.5 t22.5 f21.5 b22.5.** Wow! A Littlemill not showing its usual vampire tendencies. The right kind of sherry butt really can sooth the savage beast. If you see it, add to your collection! *47.1%*

LOCH LOMOND

Highlands (Southwestern), 1966. Loch Lomond Distillers. Working.

Craiglodge sherry wood cask 139, dist 26 Mar 98 db **(72) n17 t19 f18 b18.** Cloying, off-key, rough...and they're the good points. The nose of sherry and smoke don't gel and it never recovers. *45%*

Croftengea cask no. 24, dist 22 Jan 97 db **(87) n22** pungent young peat, bracing, clean and even mildly salty; **t22** refreshing barley with coffee/smoke double act; **f21** vanilla and dry toast; **b22** what a difference a cask makes: entirely together and charming. *45%*

Inchmurrin 12 Years Old db **(86.5) n21.5 t22 f21.5 b21.5.** A significantly improved dram which is a bit of a malt soup. Love the Demerara injection. *40%*

Loch Lomond 18 Years Old db **(78.5) n19 t21 f19 b19.5.** A demanding, oily malt which is a long way from technical excellence but is no slouch on the chocolate nougat front. *43%*

Loch Lomond 21 Years Old db **(89.5) n22.5** a real chunky fella with all kinds of melted fruit and chocolate bar properties; a few oily nuts, too...; **t23** the usual fruitcake feel to this, plus the Demerara sugar topping; **f22** light oils carry vanilla and cocoa; **b22** a little while since I last tasted this, and pretty close to exactly how I remember it. Seems to revel in its own enormity! *43%*

Loch Lomond Copper Pot Still 1966 db **(92) n23 t23.5 f23 b22.5.** Shows remarkably little wear and tear for its great age. A gentleman of a whisky. *45%*

Loch Lomond Gavin's Single Highland Malt dist 1996, bott 2007 db **(90.5) n23 t23 f22.5 b22.** Ester-fuelled and fabulous. *45%. nc ncf.*

Loch Lomond No Age Statement db **(74.5) n18 t20 f18 b18.5.** Still feinty and out of sync, though the lively sugars try to compensate. *40%*

Loch Lomond Single Highland Peated Malt db **(74) n16.5 t20 f19 b18.5.** Feints and peat simultaneously: not something you happen upon very often. Thankfully. *46%*

⋄ **Scott's Selection Inchmurrin 1997** bott 2012 **(83.5) n20 t23 f20 b20.5.** All about the delivery. Want to know what malted barley tastes like? Look no further. *55.3%. Speyside Distillers.*

LOCHSIDE
Highlands (Eastern), 1957–1992. Chivas Brothers. Demolished.

Berry's Own Selection Lochside 1981 cask no. 777, bott 2011 **(90) n23** vaguely molassed (dry rather than moist) a hint of burnt raisin...Garibaldi biscuits, really, with an extra dose of salt; **t22.5** silky delivery with an immediate juicy flourish. Again dark sugars formulate, but now we have little fruit but charismatic barley and wave upon wave of vanilla; **f22** melt-in-the-mouth vanilla and toffee; **b22.5** the almost unerring palate of Mr Douglas McIvor has struck bull's-eye again...not a single off note to be had. *46%. nc ncf sc. Berry Bros & Rudd.*

Berry's Own Selection Lochside 1981 cask no. 808, bott 2011 **(85) n21.5 t22 f20.5 b21.** In some ways as aggressive as cask 777 is gentle. Much more roasty and bitter. The extra drama on the palate entertains but the odd note that doesn't quite harmonise. *46%. nc ncf sc. Berry Bros & Rudd.*

⁘ **The Cooper's Choice Lochside 1967 Aged 44 Years** cask no. 807 **(96.5) n24.5** yep. Pretty close to perfection. At first it is the softest of smoke which gets you primed. Then the pastel-shaded fruit begins to take shape, perhaps drawing from the honey blossom honey which is weighted by the butterscotch oak and Nice biscuits; **t24.5** again the smoke makes a very early foray, but it is a ghostly one and does a masterful job of keeping anchored the lighter fruit tones. Astonishingly after all these years the barley is still capable of a big juicy volley. While the oak, though arriving early, is of the most benign type offering a seemingly impossible layering of delicate tannins which emboldens and enriches; **f23.5** just a little thinner here with the oat now showing a slightly more austere trait. However, that priceless and ultra complex smoke ensures the finale is one of quiet dignity; **b24** it is amazing that I had to travel 6,000 miles to find this in British Columbia. But, this is the kind of whisky you would travel four times that kind of distance to experience. Easily one of the top ten single casks I have tasted in the last five years. *41.5%. 354 bottles.*

⁘ **First Cask Lochside 46 Years Old 5th Anniversary Bottling** refill sherry cask, dist Nov 63, bott Mar 10 **(91) n24** an unashamed fruitcake aroma, absolutely reeking of moist molassed sugar and glazed cherries; the sherry trifle goes easy on the custard but instead we get polished antique furniture and a mild bourbon-style toasted honeycomb; **t23** after all that on the nose, a real softy. The custard missing from the trifle has turned up here and anyone who has tasted melted sugar on their porridge will also recognise a flavour profile here; much less sherry influence than expected, save the inevitable rich oloroso delivery; **f21** fades a little too quickly and a surprising tangy bitterness begins to take hold; **b23** a rare view of Lochside from a sherry butt. And one that will get rarer by the day... *46.6%. nc ncf sc. 71 bottles.*

⁘ **Malts Of Scotland Lochside 1967** bourbon hogshead, cask no. MoS12016, bott Mar 12 **(96) n24.5** I could keep my beak in the glass forever. A Jamaican medium ester pot still sweetness to this; the oak interweaves majestically. A series of delicate lemon notes remind me of pancakes, thanks probably to the sugars which sweeten it; **t24** not so much melts in the mouth but dissolves and hides in every crevice: the oak tries to make a big play but the mix of three vital ingredients – golden syrup, Greek honey and heather honey – ensures that all we hear from the cask is a buttery, vanilla squeak; **f23.5** a hint of tangy marmalade and blood orange and still that unsalted butter; some late, pernickety spices buzz around the tongue late on; **b24** the Spanish may be the possessors of the World and European Cups through their beautiful football. But why did they have to close a distillery which offered a malt with every bit as much flair and movement? *41.7%. nc ncf sc. Malts Of Scotland.*

Old Malt Cask Lochside Aged 19 Years refill hogshead, cask no. 6653, dist Oct 91, bott Oct 10 **(90) n21.5** something of the dank malting about this; a little mossy but sweet, also; **t23.5** barley concentrate: about as intense malt as you are ever likely to find. Some salivating citrus and muscovado sugars ensure complexity; **f22.5** simple malt and vanillas; **b22.5** beautifully structured and deeply satisfying malt. Adorable. *50%. nc ncf sc. 315 bottles.*

Old Malt Cask Lochside Aged 21 Years refill barrel, cask no. 6953, dist, Apr 89, bott Feb 11 **(74) n17 t22 f17 b18.** What a strange beast... I know there will be many who will swoon at this one. But there is something about it to me that is just a little uncouth. It has the front of a dandy, yet beneath the veneer we find the chancer flattering to deceive. It is the Mr Hyde to the 19-year-old's Jekyll. *48.2%. nc ncf sc. Douglas Laing & Co. 126 bottles.*

LONGMORN
Speyside, 1895. Chivas Brothers. Working.

Longmorn 15 Years Old db **(93) n23** curiously salty and coastal for a Speysider, really beautifully structured oak but the malt offers both African violets and barley sugar; **t24** your mouth aches from the enormity of the complexity, while your tongue wipes grooves into the roof of your mouth. Just about flawless bitter-sweet balance, the intensity of the malt is enormous, yet – even after 15 years – it maintains a cut-grass Speyside character; **f22** long, acceptably sappy and salty with chewy malt and oak. Just refuses to end; **b24** these latest bottlings are the best yet: previous ones had shown just a little too much oak but this has hit a perfect compromise. An all-time Speyside great. *45%*

Longmorn 16 Years Old db **(84.5) n20.5 t22 f21 b21.** This was one of the disappointments of the 2008 edition, thanks to the lacklustre nose and finish. This time we see a cautious nudge in the right direction: the colour has been dropped fractionally and the nose celebrates with a sharper barley kick with a peppery accompaniment. The non-existent (caramel apart) finale of yore now offers a distinct wave of butterscotch and thinned honey...and still some spice. Only the delivery has dropped a tad...but a price worth paying for the overall improvement. Still a way to go before the real Longmorn 16 shines in our glasses for all to see and fall deeply in love with. Come on lads in the Chivas lab: we know you can do it... *48%*

⁝⁝ **A.D. Rattray Longmorn 1992** cask no. 71783, dist 25 May 92, bott Jun 12 **(86.5) n21.5 t23 f21 b21** Decent enough dram, the best of the 1992 bunch, with good salt and sugar drive on delivery. *58.1%. sc. A.D. Rattray Ltd.*

⁝⁝ **Archives Longmorn 1992 19 Years Old Third Release** bourbon cask, cask no. 86607, dist Oct 92, bott May 12 **(88.5) n22** busily floral and herbal; **t22.5** not quite so busily malty and sugary; **f22** puts its feet up and enjoys the spice; **b22** a hard-working malt. *48.5%. nc ncf sc. Whiskybase B.V. 60 bottles.*

⁝⁝ **Boisdale Longmorn 1992** cask no. 71762, bott 2012 **(82.5) n21 t21 f20 b20.5.** The perfect dram before going to bed: that's if it doesn't send you to sleep before you even reach the stairs. Bland. *46%. nc ncf sc. Berry Bros & Rudd.*

⁝⁝ **Cadenhead Longmorn 16 Years Old** dist 2011 **(91) n22** lively malt: sharp and pungent...the aroma of a cask being dumped; **t23.5** barley comes neither fresher nor more mouth-watering than this. The oak has added a degree of lemon and vanilla; **f23** fine dust icing sugars stretch the finish and ensure the improbably salivating gristiness sees us through to the end; **b22.5** Longmorn at 16 exactly how it should be, yet is so rarely seen! A personal favourite of its type: sheer uncomplicated but highly effective fun; a malt showing the kind of clarity you find when gazing into the distance after a refreshing rain shower. *53.5%. sc.*

⁝⁝ **Duncan Taylor Dimensions Longmorn 19 Years Old** cask no. 71738, dist May 92, bott Feb 12 **(85.5) n21.5 t22 f21 b21.** In keeping with this particular batch of '92 Longmorns, pleasant but falls under the spell of the natural caramels. *53.7%. nc ncf sc. Duncan Taylor & Co.*

⁝⁝ **First Cask Longmorn 23 Years Old** refill sherry hogshead, cask no. 14379, dist 13 Oct 88, bott 9 Jan 12 **(79) n20.5 t20 f19 b19.5.** I'll let you guess....Not ruinously bad, though, and the grape certainly pounds through for a while. *52.6%. nc ncf sc. 259 bottles.*

Gordon & MacPhail Private Collection Longmorn 1964 (86) n22 t23.5 f21.5 b19 [That's on opening and tasting within first 15 minutes. Now leave for 45 mins minimum in warm room and this is what you get: (90.5) n24 t23 f22.5 b21...] I have been shot back 25 years to my days in Fleet Street. Now and then, as I did the rounds of the famous hostelries there, I would end up in El Vinos. And they would have their own single malt bottling, usually dripping in a sherry not so much sumptuous as pompous. And I would hate it. Today, after nearly 20 years of battling, often it appears single-handedly, against appalling sulphur-fucked casks, I tend to view these types of malt with a little more latitude than I once might. There is absolutely no sulphur at all; sadly, little sign of the whisky, either, which has been entirely lost under the mountainous weight of the lavish grape. But, nonetheless, I now wholeheartedly commend this whisky to you, where once I would have counselled a wide berth. Not for its greatness, but, rather, for its touching adherence to an ancient whisky style close to extinction and that is unlikely ever to be repeated. *51.9%*

⁝⁝ **Gordon & MacPhail Rare Vintage Longmorn 1964 (93.5) n23** half an hour's worth of testing out cracked yet highly polished old chesterfields...; **t23.5** the integrity of the sherry has lasted almost 50 years and here offers the most attractive dark cherry you will find; sweetened by molasses and burnt fudge; **f23.5** when first poured, the finale is pretty oaky aggressive. Leave a while to oxidise and that oak begins to put a protective arm around the surprisingly juicy fruit; the dark sugars and marzipan also join forces and become a little special...; **b23.5** it's waited some 47 years to come out and have a chat with you. So leave it in the glass a good 20 minutes before listening to what it has to say. *43%*

⁝⁝ **Gordon & MacPhail Rare Vintage Longmorn 1967 (94) n23** I've entered a world of expensive polished Victorian wooden artefacts; **t23.5** a delicate yield of honey allows in far more bourbon liquorice notes and overdone toast; complexity and delicacy are sky high; **f23.5** a layer of Chilean honey is soothingly spread on the toast; **b24** an antique whisky with the aroma of a Dorking antique shop. The notes should be written by Arthur Negus. But he'll tell you it's the residual honey effect that goes for the sweetest song. *43%*

Gordon & MacPhail Longmorn 1968 (95.5) n23.5 marzipan with a fleck of ginger and thick cut marmalade: additional sugars of the honeycomb variety; **t24** exceptional delivery: the oak-blooded spices arrive at the same moment as the honeyed barley for one memorable rush; stupendous grassy malt cleans the palate to make way for a slow cocoa-enriched burn...; **f24** confirmation of a brilliant cask comes with this finale which is entirely free of any element of bitterness. Instead, the spices play a subdued role in keeping with the buttered coconut cake exit; a wondrous degree of cocoa and soft oil make it almost too good to be true; **b24** a fabulous malt which goes to prove just how good a preservative alcohol is. The higher strength does this malt no harm at all; indeed, it helps form a Longmorn of as high a quality for its age as you are ever likely to encounter. 60.5%

Gordon & MacPhail Longmorn 1971 (90) n21 an over-tired bourbon...? **t23** the sugars work overtime to keep the forest of oak grounded. The very mildest puff of smoke still detectable and some cocoa, too. The result, aided by soft barley oil, is a surprisingly well adjusted Longmorn; **f22.5** the oaks creep back into play, but the spices team up with those gorgeous sugars to do the trick; **b23.5** a much more integrated whisky than the G&M Rare Vintage version. In fact, knowing the distillery and the frighteningly advanced age of the malt, this is very much an old dog showing new tricks... 43%

Gordon & MacPhail Rare Vintage Longmorn 1971 (86.5) n21 t22.5 f21 b21.5. A pleasing old chap which is puffing a bit with all that oak it has to carry. But a moderate injection of maple syrup gives him the energy to carry on. 47.4%. Exclusive bottling for The Whisky Agency.

❖ **Gordon & MacPhail Rare Vintage Longmorn 1973 (95) n24.5** thinks about heading into fruitcake territory but hangs back: the sherry is just a little too clean, the vanillas a little too sweet...it opts for a trifle, instead...; complex, almost perfectly weighted and a reminder of what a real, untainted sherry butt should smell like; **t24** no spring chicken for sure, but somehow the grape feels as though its juices first flowed only yesterday. The oak, though, does underscore the age with an impressive array of dry toasty notes with hazelnut puree. Remarkably, the barley remains fresh and intact; **f23** dries according to the rules with a vague molasses note to the starchy vanillas; a buttery edge offers a degree of oil; **b23.5** Longmorn has long been a staple of Gordon and MacPhail. Here you can see exactly why. 43%

❖ **Hart Brothers Longmorn Aged 19 Years** cask no. 110933, dist 11 Sep 92, bott 30 Apr 12 **(80.5) n21 t22 f18.5 b19.** Sticky toffee and then curiously bitters out. 46%. sc

❖ **Malts Of Scotland Longmorn 1975** bourbon hogshead, cask no. 3977, dist Mar 75, bott May 11 **(81.5) n20 t21 f20.5 b20.** For all the spice and almost Mr Whippy-style vanilla, there appears to be a conspiracy to bottle Longmorn older than it should be. It starts with the distillers themselves, and is carried on by the independents. Sure, the citrus and bourbon notes are to be applauded. But it is too old and OTT. Something younger, please! 46.4%. nc ncf sc.

Malts Of Scotland Longmorn 1976 bourbon hogshead, cask no. 5892, dist May 76, bott Jan 11 **(80) n19 t20 f21 b20.** Pleasant, but rather one dimensional after extracting all the natural caramels the cask possessed. 51.5%. nc ncf sc. Malts Of Scotland. 132 bottles.

❖ **Malts Of Scotland Longmorn 1992** bourbon hogshead, cask no. MoS12011, idst 22 May 92, bott Jan 12 **(86) n22 t22 f21 b21.** At first very good juicy malt then becomes bogged down in natural caramels. Attractive buzz, though. 52.6%. nc ncf sc. Malts Of Scotland.

Masterpieces Longmorn 1978 bourbon cask **(86) n22.5 t22.5 f20 b21.** This has many things going for it – except maybe its age. I have never understood why Longmorn is not launched more often in something around the 8 to 14 years range, when it is at its most effervescent. Here we have another example of the malt hanging on to the cliff face by its finger nails. All the fun and complexity is found on the nose and delivery where the sugar and barley are still in play. Just 58%. nc ncf sc. Speciality Drinks Ltd. 135 bottles.

❖ **Mo Òr Collection Longmorn 1988 22 Years Old** first fill bourbon hogshead, cask no. 14378, dist 13 Oct 88, bott 21 Jan 11 **(65.5) n16.5 t18 f15 b16.** Probably the most un first fill, bourbon-esque cask I have come across from this distillery. Unimpressive in so many ways I don't quite know where to start... 46%. nc ncf sc. Release No. 44. The Whisky Talker. 411 bottles.

❖ **Old Malt Cask Longmorn Aged 21 Years** refill hogshead, cask no. 8256, dist Feb 91, bott Mar 12 **(88.5) n22** a touch opaque with the sharp barley of jungle-like density; **t22.5** like the nose, the barley is so thick it takes time for much else to come into focus. At last some relatively delicate sugars emerge, as do the big oils which reduce chances of further complexity; **f22** just a little hot and thins out with pretty standard vanilla; **b22** a huge whisky which hides itself well. Quite a trick. 50%. nc ncf sc. 303 bottles.

Provenance Longmorn Over 8 Years refill hogshead, cask no. 6830, dist Autumn 02, bott Autumn 2010 **(93) n23** the lightest possible strata of smoke shoehorns in a biscuit-like maltiness; **t24** deft barley showing a surreal number of different sugar notes is happy to embrace the growing vanilla and butterscotch; light spice enters the fray; **f23** a surprise hint of gooseberry does nothing to shake this off its intensely malty course...; **b23** who gives a toss that this is an eight year old? Great whisky is just that...however old it may be. Adorable and, frankly, must have. 46%. nc ncf sc. Douglas Laing & Co.

Scotch Malt Whisky Society Cask 7.65 Aged 21 Years 2nd fill sherry butt, cask no. 18573, dist 1989 **(76) n18 t21 f18 b19.** I adore the defiant glow of honey and marmalade as another sherry butt bites the dust. 55.2%. sc. 164 bottles.

Scotch Malt Whisky Society Cask 7.66 Aged 18 Years refill hogshead, cask no. 48422, dist 1992 **(83)** n22 t21.5 f19.5 b20. A good example of a well made, firmly structured malt suffering somewhat at the hands of a cask not quite up to the task. *49.4%. sc. 215 bottles.*

⠿ **Scotch Malt Whisky Society Cask 7.69 Aged 8 Years** first fill barrel, cask no. 800279, dist 2003 **(89.5)** n21.5 obviously youthful, and equally obviously of a high standard though in an underdeveloped state; t23.5 age counts for little as the palate is packed with highly charged barley and sugars sporting a caramelised, oaky tint which is not to be found on the nose; quite sharp, almost aggressive in its flavour distribution....but bloody delicious! f23 falls back into the safer zones of muscovado sugar sweetened cocoa and quite rich liquorice. Certainly begins to take a bourbon shape..; b23 the nose may struggle to find its balance, but the delivery spins as many plates as you like. *61.6%. sc. Scotch Malt Whisky Society.*

⠿ **Scotch Malt Whisky Society Cask 7.70 Aged 19 Years** refill hogshead, cask no. 48420, dist **(88.5)** n22 powerful oaky caramels make for a flattish though Kentuckian aroma; t22 explosive delivery with some viperish pepper; after a few waves the natural caramels begin leaving their tide mark; f22.5 plenty of recognisable bourbon characteristics on the long tail; b22 when you get this degree of caramel occurring naturally and the effect it has, you can see why it is suicide to add any to the official bottling. *51.1%. sc.*

⠿ **Scotch Malt Whisky Society Cask 7.71 Aged 19 Years** refill hogshead, cask no. 48423, dist 1992 **(91)** n22.5 less bourbon than 7.70 with the weightier elements broken up by a succession of clean citrus notes; t23 soft and malty delivery, becoming chewier. Excellent medium roast Java offers delicate bitterness which works perfectly with the sweeter malt; f22.5 the barley remains slightly gristy and juicy while the mocha rounds matters off pleasantly; b23 the lack of natural caramels make for a jauntier malt. *53%. sc.*

⠿ **Scott's Selection Longmorn 1992** bott 2012 **(90.5)** n22 superb hazelnut spread on toast: creamy yet busy; dank barley offers a very green aspect; t23.5 beautiful delivery: the nuttiness turns up as expected and there is a degree of bite to the oak, but all very acceptable. Stewed apples then a kind of sweet, barley crumble tart fills the mid ground rather deliciously; f22 the sugars stay loyal as the barley goes a surprising distance; b23 simply delicious; one of the better Independent Longmorns, SMWS apart. *58.1%. Speyside Distillers.*

⠿ **The Whisky Agency Longmorn 1965** bott 2011 **(96)** n25 oh, it's one of those!! Longmorn and Glen Grant had gifted upon them 40 to 50 years ago some of the finest sherry butts that those living today can remember. Just one inhalation of this reveals this to be one. Even after all this time the grape is not only intact but radiating equal measures of delicate sugars and spices, especially the white peppers. The oak degredation is zero. Anything less than 25 minutes nosing this is a crime against whisky: to add water – even a teaspoonful deserves - being taken outside and shot...; t24 the oak is definitely more up to the challenge here and makes sure you know it's around. But, again, so rich is the grape, so confident the sugars attached, that the oak offers little more than a growl before backing off; a wonderful fruitcake, seemingly encased in chocolate pampers the middle ground, luxuriating in a delicate oiliness; f23 just for a moment the oak catches all else off guard and strikes a slightly bitter note. But it is short lived as wave upon wave of dry dates and liquorice engulf the palate; b24 this could well be, after all these years, The Fat Lady of Limburg singing for... I looked at the samples that were sent and furrowed my brow. You would never believe that I'd tasted royalty and fame if you saw me now. But my sense of taste is such that I'll distinguish with my tongue the subtleties a spectrograph would miss. And announce my decision, while demanding my reward: a bottle of this. (With thanks and apologies to Brian Eno) *51.8%. nc ncf sc. The Whisky Agency. Joint bottling with Gordon & MacPhail for Limburg Whisky Festival.*

⠿ **Whisky Antique Longmorn 22 Years Old Special Bottling** dist 1988, bott 2011 **(87)** n21 salted peanut spread on burnt toast; a twist of lemon; t22 early on, as barley-biased as you might expect. But there is a real bite in there, also, while the oak shouts rather than whispers its presence; f22 the sugars begin to make an effort and calm the growing excesses of the oak; b22 Antique by nature, this one. Seems a great deal older than its 22 years and another summer in the cask will have done some serious damage. *54.4%. sc.*

THE MACALLAN
Speyside, 1824. Edrington. Working.

The Macallan 7 Years Old db **(89)** n23 beautifully clean sherry, lively, salty, gentle peppers; t23 mouth-filling and slightly oily. Some coffee tones intertwine with deep barley and fruit; f21 unravels to reveal very soft oak and lingering fruity spice; b22 an outstanding dram that underlines just how good young malts can be. Fun, fabulous and in recent bottlings has upped the clarity of the sherry intensity to profound new heights. *40%*

The Macallan Fine Oak 8 Years Old db **(82.5)** n20.5 t22 f20 b20. A slight flaw has entered the mix here. Even so, the barley fights to create a distinctive sharpness. However, a rogue sherry butt has put paid to any hopes the honey and spice normally found in this brand. *40%*

The Macallan 10 Years Old db **(91) n23** oloroso appears to be the big noise here, but clever, almost meaty, incursions of spice offer an extra dimension; fruity, yet bitter-sweet: dense yet teasingly light in places; **t23** chewy fruit and the old Macallan silk is back: creamy cherries and mildly under-ripe plum ensures a sweet-sour style; **f21.5** traces of vanilla and barley remind us of the oak and barley, but the fruit reverberates for some while, as does some annoying caramel; **b23.5** for a great many of us, it is with the Mac 10 our great Speyside odyssey began. It has to be said that in recent years it has been something of a shadow of its former great self. However, this is the best version I have come across for a while. Not perhaps in the same league as those bottlings in the 1970s which made us re-evaluate the possibilities of single malt. But fine enough to show just how great this whisky can be when the butts have not been tainted and, towards the end, the balance between barley and grape is a relatively equal one. *40%*

The Macallan 10 Years Old Cask Strength db **(85) n20 t22 f22 b21.** Enjoyable and a would give chewing gum a run for its money. But over-egged the sherry here and not a patch on the previous bottling. *58.8%. Duty Free.*

The Macallan Fine Oak 10 Years Old db **(90) n23** finely tuned and balanced: everything on a nudge-nudge basis with neither fruit nor barley willing to come out and lead: really take your time over this to maximise the entertainment; **t22.5** brimming with tiny, delicate oak notes which just brush gently, almost erotically, against the clean barley; **f21.5** drier, chewier and no less laid-back; **b22** much more on the ball than the last bottling of this I came across. Malts really come as understated or clever than this. *40%*

The Macallan Sherry Oak 12 Years Old db **(93) n24** thick, almost concentrated grape with a stunning degree of light spices. Topped with boiled greengage; **t23.5** clean sherry is heralded not just by vanilla-thickened grape but a deft muscovado sweetening and a light seasoning of spice; **f22.5** cocoa, vanilla and fudge. Remains clean and beautifully layered; **b23** I have to say that some Macallan 12 I have tasted on the road has let me down in the last year or so. This is virtually faultless. Virtually a time machine back to another era... *40%*

The Macallan 12 Years Old Sherry Oak Elegancia db **(86) n23 t22 f20 b21.** Promises, but delivers only to an extent. *40%*

The Macallan Fine Oak 12 Years Old db **(95.5) n24** faultless, intense sherry light enough to allow the fabulous apple and cinnamon to blend in with the greengage and grape, **t24** a near perfect entry: firm, rummy sugars are thinned by a barley-grape double act; juicy yet enough vanilla to ensure structure and layering; **f23.5** delicate spice keeps the finish going and refuses to let the muscovado-grape take control; **b24** a whisky whose quality has hit the stratosphere since I last tasted it. I encountered a disappointing one early in the year. This has restored my faith to the point of being a disciple... *40%*

Macallan Gran Reserva Aged 12 Years db **(92) n23** massive cream sherry background with well matured fruit cake to the fore: big, clean, luxurious in a wonderfully old-fashioned way. Oh, and a sprinkling of crushed sultana just in case the grapey message didn't get across... **t24** a startlingly unusual combination on delivery: dry yet juicy! The ultra fruity lushness is dappled with soft spices; oak arriving early-ish does little to alter the path of the sweetening fruit; just a hint of hickory reveals the oak's handiwork towards the middle; **f22** dry, as oloroso does, with a vaguely sweeter edge sparked by notes of dried date; the delicate but busy spices battle through to the toffeed end; **b23** well, you don't get many of these to the pound. A real throwback. The oloroso threatens to overwhelm but there is enough intrigue to make for a quite lovely dram which, as all good whiskies should, never quite tells the story the same way twice. Not entirely without blemish, but I'm being picky. A Macallan soaked in oloroso which traditionalists will swoon over. *45.6%*

The Macallan Fine Oak 15 Years Old db **(79.5) n19 t21.5 f19 b20.** As the stock of the Fine oak 12 rises, so its 15-y-o brother, once one of my favourite drams, falls. Plenty to enjoy, but a few sulphur stains remove the gloss. *43%*

The Macallan Fine Oak 17 Years Old db **(82) n19.5 t22 f19.5 b21.** Where once it couldn't quite make up its mind on just where to sit, it has now gone across to the sherry benches. Sadly, there are a few dissenters. *43%*

The Macallan Sherry Oak 18 Years Old db **(87) n24 t22 f20 b21.** Underpowered. The body doesn't even come close to matching the nose which builds up the expectancy to enormous levels and, by comparison to the Independents, at 43% appears weak and unrepresentative. Why this isn't at 46% at the very least and unambiguously uncoloured, I have no idea. *43%*

The Macallan 18 Years Old dist 1991 db **(87) n22 t22.5 f21 b21.5** Honestly: I could weep. Some of the sherry notes aren't just textbook...they go back to the Macallan manuals of the early 1970s. But the achievable greatness is thwarted by the odd butt of you know what... *43%*

The Macallan Fine Oak 18 Years Old db **(94.5) n23.5** classic cream sherry aroma: thick, sweet but enlivened by a distinct barley sharpness; **t24** juicy, chewy, clean and intense delivery. Strands of honey and syrup help pave the way for vanillas and spices to get a grip;

the complexity levels are startling and the weight just about spot on; **f23** a degree of blood orange bitterness amid the cocoa and raisin; the spices remain lazy, the texture creamy; **b24** is this the new Fine Oak 15 in terms of complexity? That original bottling thrived on the balance between casks types. This is much more accentuated on a cream sherry persona. But this sample is sulphur-free and quite fabulous. 43%

The Macallan Masters Of Photography Albert Watson 20 Years Old db (94.5) **n24** if there is such a thing as a seismograph for measuring sherry, this would be bouncing from wall to wall. Concentrated noble rot, with a few roasted almonds and spices tossed in; **t24.5** as soft as a 20-year-old sherry... without the whisky. It works beautifully as the required balance between sugars and spice is there in bundles; and as well as sherry trifle, there is blackcurrant on butterscotch, too; **f22.5** just a hint of bitterness but plenty of over-ripe greengage and toasty vanilla to see you off; **b23.5** it's one of those! (Bizarrely, as I wrote that, Milton Jones said exactly the same words on the radio...spooky!) Once I would have marked this down as being simply too sherry drowned. But since clean sherry butts are now at a premium, I am seeing whiskies like this in a very different light: certainly not in the negative... It can still be argued that this is far too sherry driven, with too much else overpowered. And maybe just a little too bitter on the finish. But of its once thought extinct type, staggering. 46.5%. Edrington.

The Macallan Fine Oak 21 Years Old db (84) **n21 t22 f20 b21.** An improvement on the characterless dullard I last encountered. But the peaks aren't quite high enough to counter the sulphur notes and make this a great malt. 43%

The Macallan 25 Years Old db (84.5) **n22 t21 f20.5 b21.** Dry with an even drier oloroso residue; blood orange adds to the fruity mix. Something, though, is not entirely right about this and one fears from the bitter tang at the death that a rogue butt has gained entry to what should be the most hallowed of dumping troughs. 43%

The Macallan Fine Oak 25 Years Old db (90) **n22** coal dusty: the plate of old steam engines; a speckle of raisin and fruitcake; **t23.5** despite the early signs of juicy grape, it takes only a nanosecond or two for a much drier oak-spiced spine to take shape; the weight is never less than ounce perfect, however; **f22** puckering, aged oak leaves little doubt that this is a malt of advanced years, but a few liquorice notes ensure a degree of balance; **b22.5** the first time I tasted this brand a few years back I was knocked off my perch by the peat reek which wafted about with cheerful abandon. Here the smoke is tighter, more shy and of a distinctly more anthracitic quality. Even so, the sweet juiciness of the grape juxtaposes gamely with the obvious age to create a malt of obvious class. 43%

The Macallan Fine Oak 25 Years Old db (89) **n23** cream soda meets cream sherry... but where is the smoke that was always apparent? Are the remnants tucked away in those spices? Lubeck marzipan makes a surprise appearance; **t23** almost a drier version of the Fine Oak 18, with a little extra tannin; a distinctive honey and marmalade thread; **f21** bitters to furry blood oranges; **b22** very similar to the Fine Oak 18. However, the signature smoke has vanished, as I suppose over time it must. Not entirely clean sherry, but much remains to enjoy. 43%

The Macallan Fine Oak 30 Years Old db (81.5) **n22 t22 f18 b19.5.** For all its many riches on delivery, especially those moments of great bourbon-honey glory, it has been comprehensively bowled middle stump by the sherry. Gutted. 43%

The Macallan 40 Years Old dist 10 May 61, bott 09 Sep 05 db (90) **n23** no shortage of oak, as you might expect. But nutty, too (chestnut pure, to be precise). The scope is broadened with a distracted smokiness while oak maximizes the longer it stays in the glass; **t23** soft and yielding, with a lovely dovetailing of vanillins and delicate sherry. The grape appears to gain control with a sweet barley sidekick before the oak recovers; **f22** soft oils formulate with some laite and slightly salted, Digestive-style biscuit. Gentle spices delight; **b22** very well-rounded dram that sees off advancing years with a touch of grace and humour. So often you think the oak will take control, but each time an element intervenes to win back the balance. It is as if the dram is teasing you. Wonderful entertainment. 43%

The Macallan 50 Years Old dist 29 Mar 52, bott 21 Sep 05 db (90) **n25** we all have pictures in our minds of the perfect grandmother: perhaps grey-haired and knitting in her rocking-chair. Or grandfather: kindly, gentle, quietly wise, pottering about in the shed with some gadget he has just made for you. This, then, is the cliched nose of the perfect 50-year-old malt: time-defying intensity and clarity; attractive demerara (rum and sugar!) sweetened coffee, a tantalizing glimpse at something smoky and sensationally rich grape and old fruit cake. So that the sweetness and dryness don't cancel each other out, but complement each other and between them tell a thousand tales. Basically, there's not much missing here... and absolutely all you could wish to find in such an ancient Speysider...; **t23** dry delivery with the oak making the early running. But slowly the grape and grain fights back to gain more than just a foot-hold; again telling wisps of smoke appear to lay down a sound base and some oily barley; **f19** now the oak has taken over. There is a burnt-toast and burnt raisin bitterness, lessened in effect marginally by a sweeter vanilla add-on; **b23** loses it at the end, which is entirely excusable. But until then, a fabulous experience full of passion and complexity. I nosed and tasted this for over an hour. It was one very rewarding, almost touching, experience. 46%

The Macallan Millennium 50 Years Old (1949) db (90) n23 t22 f22 b23. Magnificent finesse and charm despite some big oak makes this another Macallan to die for. 40%

The Macallan Lalique III 57 Years Old db (95) n24.5 coffee and walnut cake. That's the simple way of looking at this one: but give yourself maybe half an hour and a slightly more detailed picture forms. The fruit conjures dates and walnuts – so walnuts and walnut oil is a pretty common thread here. And truffle oil, amazingly. The oak is toasty liquorice and overcooked fudge. But the delicate smoke I was expecting is conspicuous by its absence...until very late on. Only after a major degree of oxidisation does it add that extra delicate dimension; t23 a soft landing in the canopy of the oaky trees with those coffee notes noticeable on the nose now really making a stir. Most beautiful, perhaps, is the lightness of touch of the Demerara and muscovado sugar blend, damped in intensity by a sprinkling of vanilla. Some surprising oils form and make for a silky middle ground; f23.5 some late spices, no more than a smattering, underline the oak without overstating the case while the sugars do their almost invisible job of keeping the dryer notes under control; like on the nose, a little smoke drifts in from seemingly nowhere; b24 I chose this as my 1,000th new whisky tasted for the 2012 Bible not just because of my long-standing deep love affair with this distillery, but also because I honestly felt it had perhaps the best chance to offer not just a glimpse at the past but also the possibility of a whisky experience that sets the hairs on the back of my neck on end. I really wasn't disappointed. It is almost scary to think that this was from a vintage that would have supplied the whiskies I tasted when getting to first discover their 21-year-old. Then, I remember, I thought the malt almost too comfortable for its age. I expected a bit more of a struggle in the glass. No less than 36 years on, the same thing crosses the mind: how does this whisky find it so easy to fit into such enormous shoes? No experience with this whisky under an hour pays sufficient tribute to what it is all about. Checking my watch, I am writing this just two minutes under two hours after first nosing this malt. The score started at 88.5. With time, warmth, oxidation and understanding that score has risen to 95. It has spent 57 years in the cask; it deserves two hours to be heard. It takes that time, at least, to not just hear what it has to say to interpret it, but to put it into context. And for certain notes, once locked away and forgotten, to be slowly released. The last Lalique was good. But simply not this good. 48.5%

The Macallan 1824 db (88) n24 t23.5 f19 b21.5. Absolutely magnificent whisky, in part. But there are times my job is depressing...and this is one of them.. 48%

The Macallan 1824 Estate Reserve db (90.5) n22 excellent clean grape with an intriguing dusting of mint; t23 almost a Jamaican pot still rum sheen and sweetness; beautiful weight and even some barley present; f22.5 satisfying, gorgeously clean with very good vanilla-grape balance; b23 don't know about Reserve: definitely good enough for the First Team. 45.7%

The Macallan 1874 Select Oak db (82) n19 t22 f20 b21. Soft, silky, sometimes sugary... and tangy. Not convinced every oak selected was quite the right one. 40%

The Macallan 1851 Inspiration db (77) n19.5 t19.5 f19 b19. Flat and uninspirational in 2008. 41%

The Macallan 1937 bott 1969 db (92) n23 an outline of barley can eventually be made in the oaky mist; more defined as a honeyed sweetness cuts in. Fingers of smoke tease. When nosing in the glass hours later the fresh, smoky gristiness is to die for ... and takes you back to the mill room 67 years ago; t22 pleasantly sweet start as the barley piles in – even a touch of melon in there; this time the oak takes second place and acts as a perfect counter; f24 excellent weight with soft peat softening the oak; b23 subtle if not overly complex whisky where there are few characters but each play its part exceptionally well. One to get out with a DVD of Will Hay's sublime Oh Mr Porter which was being made in Britain at the same time as this whisky and as Laurel and Hardy were singing about a Lonesome Pine on the other side of the pond; or any Pathe film of Millwall's FA Cup semi-final with Sunderland. 43%

The Macallan Gran Reserva 1981 db (90) n23 t22 f22 b23. Macallan in a nutshell. Brilliant. But could do with being at 46% for full effect. 40%

The Macallan Gran Reserva 1982 db (82) n21 t22 f20 b19. Big, clean, sweet sherry influence from first to last but doesn't open up and sing like the '81 vintage. 40%

⁘ **The Macallan Masters Of Photography Annie Leibovitz 1989 "The Gallery"** sherry butt, cask no. 12251 db (96.5) n24.5 just love those pulsing spices and the cloves which gee up the ample grape and apple. Clean, fresh and almost perfectly structured and weighted. Sherry butts of the old school, so very rarely seen these days; t24 there we go: an almost perfect reflection on the palate of the beautiful aroma. The grape does what all fruit should do in a whisky: lead but not dominate to the cost of all else. Like the nose, there is no sulphur evident: a pristine cask. The barley comes through in tandem with the oak, offering almost a chocolate malt style depth. The spices do as spices should: they simply add resonance and piquancy: they do not scold or burn, or detract from all other complex machinations! f24 long, chewy and now dried dates inject a sublime fruit and toffee richness; still the barley returns for more; **b24** like that ace photo sitting on a newsroom picture desk, this stands out above all the other Speysiders I have tasted so far this year...Colin Gower, the Richard Paterson of the national newspaper picture desks, grab a bottle, my old friend....!! *56.6%. sc. 285 bottles.*

⠿ **The Macallan Masters Of Photography Annie Leibovitz 1991 "The Bar"** sherry oak puncheon, cask no. 7023 db **(87)** **n22** heavy duty, one dimensional though enjoyable clean grape; **t22** sweet, with enough spice to entertain; **f22** chocolate fruit and nut; **b21** enjoyable but astonishingly simple as malt and complexity has been cropped. *50.8%. sc. 285 bottles.*

⠿ **The Macallan Masters Of Photography Annie Leibovitz 1995 "The Library"** sherry oak hogshead, cask no. 14007 db **(82.5)** **n21.5 t21 f20 b20.** A clean, unsulphured cask. But the soupy grape is entirely over exposed. Frankly, boring as no meaningful shape or form can be seen. *59.6%. sc. 145 bottles. Exclusive to distillery, Global Travel Retail and private sale.*

⠿ **The Macallan Masters Of Photography Annie Leibovitz 1996 "The Skyline"** American oak butt, cask no. 10019 db **(94)** **n23.5** top grade input from the oak with a colourful array of darker sugars working alongside brooding tannins; **t24** the nose cranks up the expectation, the delivery delivers! Those muscovado sugars saturate the taste buds alongside just the right degree of spice to counter; the tannins pulse and head towards a mocha middle but veer off towards a more banana custard sweetness; **f22.5** not as long as might be hoped, but the quality remains to the end; **b24** quite outstanding cask composition. *55.5%. sc. 285 bottles.*

Macallan Cask Strength db **(94)** **n22 t24 f24 b24.** One of those big sherry babies; it's like surfacing a massive wave of barley-sweetened sherry. Go for the ride. *58.6%. USA.*

The Macallan Easter Elchies Seasonal Cask Selection Winter Choice 14 Years Old db **(94)** **n24 t24 f23 b23.** From a faultless cask and one big enough to have its own Postcode... *54%. Exclusive to visitor centre.*

The Macallan Estate Reserve db **(84)** **n22 t22 f20 b20.** Doh! So much juice lurking about, but so much bitterness, too. ...grrrrr!!!! *45.7%*

The Macallan Fine Oak Master's Edition db **(91)** **n23** one of the most delicate of all Macallan's house noses, depending on a floral scented theme with a sweetish malty tinge to the dank bracken and bluebells; **t23** so salivating and sensual! The tastebuds are caressed with sugar-coated oaky notes that have a devilish buzz about them; **f22** more malt and now vanilla with a bitter cocoa death... **b23** adorable. *42.8%*

The Macallan Fine Oak Whisky Maker's Selection db **(92)** **n22 t23 f23 b24.** This is a dram of exquisite sophistication. Coy, mildly cocoaed dryness, set against just enough barley and fruit sweetness here and there to see off any hints of austerity. Some great work has gone on in the lab to make this happen: fabulous stuff! *42.8%. Duty Free.*

The Macallan Oscuro db **(95.5)** **n24.5** the cleanest, most juicy grape dripping into a puddle of molten muscovado sugar: amazed I have not been attacked by wasps while nosing this; it would be too much on its own, but there is a sprinkling of spice to balance things beautifully; **t24** golden sultanas, ripe fig, exploding greengages and that muscovado sugar and spice again...unreal...; **f23** a little bitter, probably from the oak which until now had hardly got a look in; some toasty vanilla makes a late entry but that juicy, lightly spiced fruit just keeps on going; **b24** oh, if all sherried whiskies could be that kind - and taste bud-blowingly fabulous! *46.5%*

⠿ **The Macallan The Queen's Diamond Jubilee** sherry cask matured **(94)** **n23.5** heavy duty grape, but clean as a whistle. Damsons and dates abound; **t23** it's one of those amazingly full, slightly uncouth, types of sherry malts, where the grape is piled on thick and only the fittest barley and oak notes manage to make their way through – and there are few. Tasty, though! **f24.5** now it moves into overdrive. The overbearing grape on delivery has vanished and we are left with a really complex fade, full of massive chocolate which sits atop a plum pudding sweetened by molasses; **b23** a wonderful, high quality sulphur-free zone where Macallan unashamedly nails its sherried credentials to the union flag. *52%. 2012 bottles. UK exclusive.*

The Macallan Royal Marriage db **(89)** **n23.5** unusually salty, with another happy marriage – this time between oak and grape. Tries to head off into the world of blissful, silky evenness, but that salty-liquorice character is like a dog with a bone - thankfully; **t22.5** black cherries make a fabulous statement on delivery, and right behind is that salty tang you just knew would be there; also a big caramel surge; **f21** bitters and dries annoyingly: just like I am sure the marriage won't...; **b22** some amazing moments to remember. *46.8%*

The Macallan Select Oak db **(83)** **n23 t21 f19 b20.** Exceptionally dry and tight; and a little furry despite the early fruitiness. *40%*

The Macallan Whisky Makers Edition db **(76)** **n19 t20 f18 b19.** Distorted and embittered by the horrific "S" element... *42.8%*

The Macallan Woodlands Limited Edition Estate Bottling db **(86)** **n21 t23 f21 b21.** Toffee towards the finish brings a premature halt to a wonderfully mollased early delivery. *40%*

Alchemist Macallan 18 Years Old **(73)** **n18 t19 f18 b18.** Ah, the alchemy of turning liquid gold into sulphur. A trick many a German palate will cherish... *46%. nc ncf. Alchemist.*

Gordon & MacPhail Speymalt from Macallan 1990 (71) n18 t19 f16 b18. S is for Speyside. And, alas, sulphur... *43%. Gordon & MacPhail.*

⁙ Hart Brothers Macallan Aged 14 Years cask no. 84, dist 26 Feb 98, bott 15 Apr 12 **(89.5)** n23 light traces of almonds and nougat work excellently with the subtle spices; t21.5 the complexity on the nose is lost under the intense presence of sweet barley; f22.5 returns to a more symphonic work with trace cocoa elements working with a return of the nougat and bolstered by delicate honey; b22.5 almost too delicate and understated. You have to listen very carefully and with great patience to hear the full beauty of this malt. *46%. sc.*

Hart Brothers Macallan Aged 19 Years dist May 91, bott Jan 11 **(69)** n17 t19 f16 b17. sweet grapes by the bunch full. Sadly, sulphured. *46%. sc.*

Hart Brothers Macallan Aged 19 Years dist May 91, bott Jan 11 **(69)** n18 t18 f16 b17. Identical to the 46% but the profile coming from slightly different angles. *55%. sc.*

Heiko Thieme's 1974 Macallan 65th Birthday Bottling cask no. 16807 dist 25 Nov 74 bott Jul 08 **(94)** n23 the clarity of the sherry takes some believing: this malt has obviously been in a good clean home for the last 34 years: not a single off note and the balance between grape, oak, spice and sweetened tomato puree is exceptional...; t23 the arrival is sharp, both in terms of barley and grape. At first it looks shocked to have escaped the cask, or is hunting around for the alcohol to tie it together. But soon it finds harmony, helped along the way by a stunning chocolate and raisin middle which leads to some sweetening molasses; f24 now enters into a class of its own. We all know about the fruitcake cliché well here it is in glorious roasted raisin brilliance. Melton Hunt cake and trifle combined; the length makes a mockery of the strength. And it looks as though someone forgot to go easy on the burnt cherry. The vanillas are deft, the coffees are medium roast, b24 this is not whisky because it is 38%abv. It is Scottish spirit. However, this is more of a whisky than a great many samples I have tasted this year. Ageism is outlawed. So is sexism. But alcoholism isn't....!! Try and become a friend of Herr Thieme and grab hold of something a little special. *38% 238 bottles.*

⁙ Malts Of Scotland Macallan 1990 Oloroso sherry hogshead, cask no. 1134, dist 24 Jan 90, bott 27 May 11 **(95)** n24 dense: like stickling your nose inside a Macallan cask at the distillery in the early '80s. Just a hint of salt, but mainly it's moist fruitcake, ripe and ready to explode greengages, a leaf or two of mint , a touch of lavender and a vague hint of spotted dog pudding; t24 where does one begin? With the almost perfect spices? The ineffective shackles on the sweetness? The measuring of the intensity of the cocoa against the rich fruits? Which kind of fruit cake it reminds you of most...? f23 just a whisky where you run out of superlatives, your brain is over-run with ultra pleasant sensations and the only words which form are '...cor, bugger me !!' b24 if I could take you back 30 years, you'd find every Macallan 21 tasted something rather similar to this, though not always quite so well appointed in the complexity stakes. Flawless, not a sulphur atom in sight: stunningly made and matured and a malt you spend a very quiet night alone with. For even silk isn't this silky... *49.1%. nc ncf sc. Malts Of Scotland.*

⁙ Malts Of Scotland Macallan 1990 Fino sherry hogshead, cask no. 1135, dist 24 Jan 90, bott 27 May 11 **(82)** n21 t22 f19 b20. I have spoken and written much about the detrimental effect of sulphur on sherry butts and the resulting spoiling of the whisky it later contains. And have hacked off a number of people in the whisky industry because of it, one or two who, in denial, claim the problem is a figment of my imagination. Nothing I have written, though, has been as eloquent as the unambiguous statement made by these two sister casks. One has been very mildly treated with sulphur. The other, almost certainly, escaped any treatment whatsoever. Try each whisky side by side and I'll let you decide which... *51.5%. nc ncf sc.*

⁙ Mo Òr Collection Macallan 1991 19 Years Old first fill bourbon hogshead, cask no. 21436, dist 21 Feb 91, bott 24 Nov 10 **(95)** n23.5 a wonderful mix of mocha and Seville orange; a lovely salty tidemark, too; t24 doesn't so much caress the taste buds as pamper them to death; the sugars are a dream, as crunchy as the barley is molten; f23.5 back to the mocha, though pepper has now replaced the salt; b24 a Macallan with no baggage can be a very beautiful thing. *46%. nc ncf sc. Release No. 12. The Whisky Talker. 429 bottles.*

⁙ Old Malt Cask Macallan Aged 14 Years refill hogshead, cask no. 7738. dist Oct 97, bott Oct 11 **(89.5)** n23 diaphanous citrus; the barley shows remarkable clarity; t23 mouth-watering gristy barley helped along by lush muscovado notes; f21.5 vanilla and a little oak weariness; b22 Macallan for the most part at its most sprightly. *50%. nc ncf sc. 365 bottles.*

Old Malt Cask Macallan Aged 15 Years refill butt, cask no. 6540, dist Oct 95, bott Oct 10 **(83.5)** n21 t22.5 f18.5 b21.5. Unusual for a Macallan in that the sherry offers a tangy sweetness for the main course as well as a bitter marmalade finish. *50%. nc ncf sc. 410 bottles.*

Old Malt Cask Macallan Aged 18 Years refill hogshead, cask no. 7246, dist Jun 93, bott May 11 **(86.5)** n22.5 t22.5 f20 b21.5. One of those big natural caramel-laden jobbies that roars along the runway but is never quite able to take off. A delicious journey nonetheless. *50%. nc ncf sc. Douglas Laing & Co. 288 bottles.*

⁘ **Old Malt Cask Macallan Aged 18 Years** bourbon barrel, cask no. 7700, dist Jun 93, bott Nov 11 **(84.5) n21 t22 f21 b20.5.** Exceptionally sweet and has no pretentions as to balance. *50%. nc ncf sc. Douglas Laing & Co. 192 bottles.*

⁘ **Old Malt Cask Macallan Aged 18 Years** refill butt, cask no. 8210, dist Nov 93, bott Feb 12 **(79) n18 t21 f19.5 b20.5.** For all its obvious failings, has plenty of barley backbone to make for an decent-ish dram. Nose apart, that is. *50%. nc ncf sc. Douglas Laing & Co. 412 bottles.*

Old Malt Cask Macallan Aged 20 Years wine finished barrel, cask no. 5069, dist Aug 90, bott Jan 11 **(85.5) n22 t21 f21.5 b21.** Reminds me of a lady of loose morals who tests soap: amazingly clean, but still a little tart. *50%. nc ncf sc. Douglas Laing & Co. 318 bottles.*

Old Malt Cask Macallan Aged 21 Years refill hogshead, cask no. 7090, dist May 90, bott May 11 **(94.5) n23.5** a stunning amalgam of sultana and sweeter bourbon notes; the fruit also heads towards spiced yam and caramel; **t24** perfect delivery: the barley leaps from the first note and the juiciness just keeps on developing; the middle ground begins hinting of muscovado-sweetened mocha: outrageously refreshing for its age; **f23** long and more and more bourbon tones flex their muscles...with wonderfully good grace; **b24** looking for a magnificent, fault-free Macallan 21? Look no further... *50%. nc ncf sc. 160 bottles.*

Premier Barrel Macallan Aged 8 Years (89) n22.5 t22 f22 b22.5. If someone asked me to draw you a picture of a clean Macallan at eight showing all its usual intense attributes, this would be it...; *46%. nc ncf sc. Douglas Laing & Co. 150 bottles.*

Provenance Macallan Over 12 Years refill hogshead, cask no. 6983, dist Autumn 98, bott Winter 2011 **(90) n22.5** beautiful barley, clean, sharp and vaguely fruity; **t22** wave upon wave of gorgeous barley; **f22** carries on its simple course, but with an extra injection of chalky vanilla and citrus; **b22.5** not overly taxing. But what it does, it does quite beautifully. *46%. nc ncf sc.*

Provenance Macallan Over 12 Years refill hogshead, cask no. 7087, dist Autumn 98, bott Spring 2011 **(91) n22.5** crushed sultanas; **t23** big spiced barley take off: the oak is prodigious for its age and chips in with a chewy mixture of fruit and bourbon honeycomb; **f22.5** sugared almonds; **b23** a quality cask offering a surprising degree of fruit. *46%. nc ncf sc.*

Provenance Macallan Over 13 Years refill hogshead, cask no. 7201, dist Autumn 97, bott Summer 2011 **(85.5) n21.5 t22 f21 b21.** Sweet, mildly spicy and scarily easy going. *46%. nc ncf sc. Douglas Laing & Co.*

Scotch Malt Whisky Society Cask 24.114 Aged 21 Years refill butt, cask no. 16520, dist 1989 **(86) n21.5 t22 f21 b21.5.** Thoroughly enjoyable whisky which perhaps just overdoes the sugary caramel to take it into the next level of excellence. *52.3%. sc. 165 bottles.*

Scotch Malt Whisky Society Cask 24.116 Aged 20 Years 1st fill sherry hogshead, cask no. 278057, dist 1990 **(91.5) n22.5** huge spiced sultana; the odd "s" atom, but those peppers are the promise of thick juice is pretty damn sexy; **t23** an early puckering "s" note is blasted into the sidings by a staggering degree of explodingly fat sultana; the grape arrives in layers, as does a rich coffee note; **f23** coffee cake complete with walnuts. A few dates thrown in for good measure; **b23** not quite 100% free of impurity, but still a stonking cask! *55.8%. sc. 202 bottles.*

⁘ **Scotch Malt Whisky Society Cask 24.117 Aged 20 Years** first fill sherry hogshead, cask no. 278046, dist 1990 **(87) n21** grape but very tight with limited growth; **t22.5** surprisingly active with the spices grappling liquorice and barley; **f21.5** a slight off-note buzz, but not enough to spoil the oaky fun; **b22** not quite the perfect cask but clean enough for the grape to make a mouth-watering contribution and the spices to form a delightful backing. *55.4%. sc.*

⁘ **Scotch Malt Whisky Society Cask 24.118 Aged 20 Years** first fill sherry hogshead, cask no. 278047, dist 1990 **(67) n17 t17 f16 b17.** A gruesome tale of dire sulphur. On nosing I held this back to be my last whisky of the day... and with very good reason. *50.7%. sc.*

⁘ **Scotch Malt Whisky Society Cask 24.119 Aged 26 Years** refill hogshead, cask no. 2612, dist 1985 **(94) n23** rich, with the barley, sharp and slightly fruity, interwoven with a light coppery thread; **t23.5** a brain-explodingly complex delivery with all kinds of small flavours popping up here and there, with a light coppery sharpness multiplying the intensity: it's as if a new still or two was being put through its paces; **f23.5** long and now with a fabulous, salivating fruitiness giving the big vanilla and butterscotch a run for its money; **b24** a bottling which captures the small still style of the distillery perfectly. *51.7%. sc. Scotch Malt Whisky Society.*

⁘ **Scotch Malt Whisky Society Cask 24.120 Aged 20 Years** first fill sherry butt, cask no. 278059, dist 1990 **(70) n19 t18 f16 b17.** The sulphury knife cuts deep enough... *56.3%. sc.*

⁘ **Scott's Selection Macallan 1989** bott 2012 **(88) n21** a few oak shavings amid the barley; **t22** the delivery again shows its full age but the barley digs deep to find the sugars to compliment the peek-a-boo butterscotch; **f23** much happier finish, with soft oils helping the malt form an intense finish; **b22** wobbles around a bit, but the quality and complexity are always there. Just have to be patient and hunt them out a bit... *50.1%. Speyside Distillers.*

⁘ **Scott's Selection Macallan 1990** bott 2012 **(85.5) n21.5 t21 f21.5 b21.5.** Shows some bright honey touches at times, as well as a distinctive small still richness. Able and pleasant without setting the pulse racing. *46.1%. Speyside Distillers.*

⋯ **Silver Seal Macallan 22 Years Old** dist 1988 **(94.5) n23.5** not quite classic Macallan: certainly has the intense grape and it's untainted, too. But here there is an extra degree of must and spice; **t24.5** for a moment the taste buds reach out and touch Macallan perfection. It lasts but a few seconds, but long enough for you to appreciate the astonishing density and balance to this. Again, the juice and spice are in near perfect accord; **f23** a huge cocoa backlash as the grape dissipates, offering a Cadbury Fruit and Nut finale... **b23.5** if you don't reach some form of ecstasy with this, you might as well stick to vodka. *56.7%. Whisky Antique.*

The Whisky Castle Old Malt Cask Macallan Aged 13 Years refill hogshead, cask no. 7195, dist Oct 97, bott May 11 **(86) n21 t22.5 f21 b21.5.** Huge barley theme. And sweet enough to rot your teeth. Liqueur lovers will drag this off the shelf... *55.3%. nc ncf sc. Douglas Laing & Co for The Whisky Castle.*

MACDUFF

Speyside, 1963. John Dewar & Sons. Working.

Glen Deveron Aged 10 Years dist 1995 db **(86) n19 t23 f23 b21.** The enormity of the third and fourth waves on delivery give some idea of the greatness this distillery could achieve perhaps with a little more care with cask selection, upping the strength to 46% and banning caramel. We'd have a malt scoring in the low to mid 90s every time. At the moment we must remain frustrated. *40%*

Glen Deveron Aged 15 Years db **(88.5) n22** the vaguest hint of smoke curls around the foot of the honey; **t22.5** one of the most delightful signatures of a Macduff is the softness of textures and a hint of honey lurking somewhere in close proximity. No disappointments here; **f22** more lush, light sweetness but more than a hint of toffee; **b22** for those who like whisky to caress rather than attack their taste buds. *40%*

⋯ **Berry's Own Selection Macduff 2000** cask no. 5774, bott 2011 **(96) n24** pounding and gorgeously clean oloroso-style grape. A really stunning mixture of dried fruit and sweet honey...and a fascinating degree of bourbony liquorice; **t24** just as mouth-filling as the nose promises, though the spices flood in from all directions and pack quite a sting. The remainder is like chewing through ultra moist fruitcake laden with cherries; **f24** so long you could almost doze off counting the flavour waves. The vanilla takes time to get a foothold, but manages in the end. Though the spices remain...; **b24** nuttier and juicier than a fruitcake...and, my word, what a delicious cherry to chew on... Fizzing, fruity and, frankly, fantastic! *60%. nc ncf sc.*

⋯ **Duncan Taylor Dimensions Macduff 17 Years Old** dist Jun 94, bott Nov 11 **(67) n17 t19 f15 b16.** Sweet, but Macduffed up by sulphur. *46%. nc ncf sc. Duncan Taylor & Co.*

⋯ **Gordon & MacPhail Connoisseurs Choice Macduff 1997 (91.5) n23** a soft nougat and honey interplay; pick any citrus note you like...; **t24** hazelnut and honey: the texture is exceptional; mocha and natural caramel fills things out beautifully; **f21.5** a degree of late barley even offers a juicy richness; a hint of praline and walnut whip; **b23** so delicate, so damned beautiful, you just want this Macduff to carry on. *43%. Gordon & MacPhail.*

⋯ **Kingsbury "The Selection" Macduff 8 Years Old** butt, cask no. 900265 & 900266, dist Aug 02, bott Apr 11 **(71.5) n18.5 t19 f16 b17.** Puts the duff in Macduff... *43%. nc ncf. Japan Import Systems. 1,666 bottles.*

L'Esprit Single Cask Collection Macduff 2000 first fill sherry butt, cask no. 5778, dist 15 Nov 00, bott 19 Oct 10 **(75) n18 t22 f17 b18.** Natural colour. Un-natural sulphur. *46%. nc ncf sc. Whisky & Rhum. 298 bottles.*

L'Esprit Single Cask Collection Macduff 2000 Cask Strength first fill sherry butt, cask no. 5778, dist 15 Nov 00, bott 19 Oct 10 **(76) n18 t23 f17.5 b18.5.** I can only imagine the faultless, wondrous beauty of what would have been one of the finest oloroso casks in the entire bodega before its fateful encounter with that lighted candle. The fact that so many mountainous points of magnificent grape can still be seen above the sulphur clouds is astonishing: a lesser butt would have lost its identity entirely. *61.1%. nc ncf sc. Whisky & Rhum. 60 bottles.*

Malts Of Scotland Macduff 1980 bourbon hogshead, cask no. 6107, dist Oct 80, bott Mar 11 **(85) n21.5 t22.5 f20 b21.** Tighter than a pair of 1980 disco trousers. Some eye-watering sweetness and an attractive nuttiness, too. But bitters out. *54.1%. sc.*

⋯ **Mo Òr Collection Macduff 1973 37 Years Old** first fill bourbon hogshead, cask no. 20, dist 30 Nov 73, bott 2 Dec 10 **(89.5) n23** drifts towards Kentucky like a moth towards a flame, so telling is the big orange on the liquorice; **t22** big oaky beating of the chest, then a slow diffusion of kumquat notes; **f22** light vanilla, a mounting of spices and citrusy barley sign off; the confident sugars save the day; **b22.5** magnificently complex, but tries to hang onto its youth unconvincingly. *46%. nc ncf sc. Release No. 22. The Whisky Talker. 281 bottles.*

Old Malt Cask For A Fine Cigar's Pleasure Macduff Aged 10 Years sherry butt **(85.5) n21 t22 f21 b21.5** MacPuff, surely... Sweet, syrupy and a real meal of a dram. But at least a sherried Macduff not showing signs of debilitating sulphur... give that whisky a cigar... *50%. nc ncf sc. Douglas Laing & Co. 319 bottles.*

Old Malt Cask Macduff Aged 21 Years refill hogshead, cask no. 7149, dist Mar 90, bott Apr 11 (68) n16.5 t18.5 f16 b17. A Macduff not to carry on with. Some of the whisky from this distillery from '89 and 90 were shockers. *50%. nc ncf sc. Douglas Laing & Co. 252 bottles.*

⁖ **Old Malt Cask Macduff Aged 21 Years** refill hogshead, cask no. 8002, dist Dec 90, bott Jan 12 (90) n22 soft, with varying butterscotch tones; t23.5 beautifully sharp delivery with some wonderful fragments of honey amid the sublime barley; f22 long and hangs on to a long honeycomb note; b22.5 now there's a thing! I absent-mindedly nosed and tasted this without taking note of what whisky exactly I had before me. And images of the old William Lawson 12-year-old blend of maybe two decades ago came flooding into my mind. Imagine my astonishment when I realised just what I had in the glass. For this was the major malt used in that blend... *50%. nc ncf sc. Douglas Laing & Co. 272 bottles.*

Provenance Macduff Over 10 Years refill hogshead, cask no. 6541, dist Winter 99, bott Autumn 2010 (81.5) n22 t21 f19 b19.5. Coppery sharpness blunted by oils. *46%. nc ncf sc.*

Provenance Macduff Over 10 Years sherry butt, cask no. 6966, dist Autumn 00, bott Winter 2011 (84) n19 t22.5 f21 b21.5. Recovers with great panache from the slight flaw evident on the sherry butt. The levels of juicy fruit are delightful. *46%. nc ncf sc.*

⁖ **Scotch Single Malt Circle Macduff 1980** cask no. 6865, dist 28 Nov 80, bott 1 Sep 11 (86.5) n21.5 t22.5 f21 b21.5. The oak has taken a few prisoners. And some quite excellent chocolate orange and honey notes do manage to escape. *52.8%. sc. Scotch Single Malt Circle.*

⁖ **Vom Fass Macduff 28 Years Old** (88.5) n23 t22 f21.5 b22. A cask on the edge of tiredness has rolled out a wonderfully impressive malt full of delicate fruit. *40%*

⁖ **The Whisky Agency Macduff 38 Years Old** bourbon cask, dist 1973, bott 2011 (83) n21.5 t21 f20 b20.5. Another of a batch of '73s doing the rounds. That was like a moth to the flame with its aging. This one well and truly got its wings singed... *47%. sc.*

MANNOCHMORE
Speyside. 1971. Diageo. Working.

Mannochmore Aged 12 Years db (84) n22 t21 f20 b21. As usual the mouth arrival fails to live up to the great nose. Quite a greasy dram with sweet malt and bitter oak. *43%.*

Mannochmore 1998 The Manager's Choice db (71.5) n18 t18 f17.5 b18. A very bad cask day... *59.1%*

⁖ **Cadenhead Mannochmore 15 Years Old** dist 1996, bott Apr 12 (93.5) n24 one of those all evening noses that takes an hour or so to fully appreciate: in particular, just love the Bakewell tart and the toasted almonds; the very faintest dab of phenol adds both spice and weight; t23 my palate feels as though it has just slid into a lovely warm bath after a hard day's tasting: luxurious mouth-feel with plenty of barley on the menu and a near perfect salty-sharp/gristy sweet balance; f23 the late, light tang is not from a poor cask but from further manoeuvrings between the saline and sugary, though some Maryland Cookie dough offers further complexity; b23.5 a beautifully crafted malt. *56.4%. sc. WM Cadenhead Ltd.*

Chieftain's Mannochmore Aged 28 Years hogshead, dist Aug 82, bott 2011 (93) n23 gorgeous interplay between liquorice-honey bourbon notes and prime barley; t23 the honey remains but picks up some butterscotch along the way. A degree of toffee makes for a chewy middle ground; f23.5 you might have thought after 28 years the finish might just be getting a little tired. But no hint of it: even a degree of copper to ensure length and backbone to the fade; b23.5 ridiculously rich and lively. *474%. nc ncf. Ian Macleod Distillers.*

Gordon & MacPhail Connoisseurs Choice Mannochmore 1991 (88.5) n22 t22 f22 b22.5. Understatedly ticks the right boxes. *46%*

Old Malt Cask Mannochmore Aged 13 Years refill hogshead, cask no. 6567, dist Jun 97, bott Sep 10 (89) n21.5 t22 f23 b22.5. If you are looking for a light, malty number which has juiciness and spice in equal proportion...here it is! *50%. nc ncf sc. 228 bottles.*

Old Malt Cask Mannochmore Aged 20 Years refill hogshead, cask no. 6306, dist Feb 90, bott Jun 10 (91) n23.5 beautifully complex: freshly sliced runner beans, dank north-facing gardens, tannin and a hint of salt...; t23 at last some sweetness: the delivery shows an unexpected gristy quality and then a developing vanilla theme of varying depth; f22 long, with the salt returning but the confident oils spread the remaining sugars thickly; b22.5 on its day, Mannochmore can be an impressive malt. This is its day... *50%. nc ncf sc. 345 bottles.*

Provenance Mannochmore Aged 12 Years (80) n20 t20 f20 b20. The perfect blending malt: virtually no character... just heaps of barley and some soft oil to big it up. *50%. nc ncf sc.*

⁖ **Provenance Mannochmore Over 12 Years** refill hogshead, cask no. 8189, dist Spring 1999, bott Winter 2012 (86.5) n22 t22 f21.5 b21. Refreshing with intense grist and juicy barley. But just a little on the hot but non-spicy side. *46%. nc ncf sc.*

Scotch Malt Whisky Society Cask 64.28 Aged 9 Years 1st fill barrel, cask no. 1906, dist 2001 (81) n21.5 t21 f18.5 b20. Has much to say for itself and, though mainly inarticulate, proves pretty sharp-tongued and bitter. *58.3%. sc. 240 bottles.*

Scotch Malt Whisky Society Cask 64.30 Aged 22 Years refill hogshead, cask no. 219079, dist 1988 **(85.5) n20 t21.5 f22.5 b21.5.** Crunchy sugars work well with the salty oak. Tries to be unimpressive, but just can't help showing some old world charm. *49.5%. sc. 260 bottles.*

⁘ **Scotch Malt Whisky Society Cask 64.34 Aged 21 Years** refill barrel, cask no. 1510, dist 1990 **(96) n24** just how many variations on a honey theme can you spot? I'm at about five, though some are heavily disguised amid the hickory and butterscotch; if that wasn't complex enough, we also have a vivid floral edge with bluebells leading the way; **t24** an almost perfect degree of oil accentuates the sugars but allows the vanillas to do their own thing unimpeded; some crushed nuts, dry dates and spices make for a super-rich middle ground; **f23.5** long and big on the mocha; back to the honeycomb towards the finale; **b24.5** outwardly an understated malt in so many ways, but don't be fooled: this is pure star quality! *56%. sc.*

⁘ **The Warehouse Collection Mannochmore Aged 19 Years** bourbon hogshead, cask no. 6606, dist 5 May 92, bott 11 Nov 11 **(87) n22.5** clean, teasing barley with a curious vanilla depth; the sugars and salts seem a little compartmentalised...; **t22** ...yet it is they which show first before an outbreak of brittle barley; **f20.5** tangy citrus; late natural caramel; **b22** from the crunchy school of Speysiders.. *49.5%. sc. Whisky Warehouse No. 8. 118 bottles.*

The Whisky Agency Mannochmore 1982 bott 2010 **(86.5) n21.5 t22 f21.5 b21.5.** Requires time to settle and relax in the glass. When it does, the barley shows to a far greater extent than you might expect from a malt of almost 30 years. *49.9%. The Whisky Agency*

MILLBURN
Highlands (Northern), 1807–1985. Diageo. Demolished.
Millburn 1969 Rare Malt db **(77) n19 t21 f18 b19.** Some lovely bourbon-honey touches but sadly over the hill and declining fast. Nothing like as interesting or entertaining as the massage parlour that was firebombed a few yards from my office twenty minutes ago. Or as smoky... *51.3%*

MILTONDUFF
Speyside, 1824. Chivas Brothers. Working.
Miltonduff Aged 15 Years bott code L00/123 db **(86) n23 t22 f20 b21.** Some casks beyond their many years have crept in and unsettled this one. But some real big salty moments to savour, too. *46%*

Berry's Own Selection Miltonduff 1998 cask no. 3604, bott 2010 **(87.5) n22 t22 f21.5 b22.** A very close approximation of the official 12 year old distillery version brought out by Allied In the days when they had no idea whatsoever what they were doing with their malts: a very decent, confident and well made Speysider. *46%. nc ncf sc.*

Berry's Own Selection Miltonduff 1998 cask no. 3605, bott 2011 **(86) n21 t22 f21.5 b21.5.** As solid as cask 3605 but with its barley juiciness limited by what seems a fruitcake let loose with a flame thrower... Entertaining, to put it mildly... *57%. nc ncf sc. Berry Bros & Rudd.*

⁘ **Dun Bheagan Miltonduff 24 Years Old** hogshead, dist May 87 **(96) n24** teasing fruity notes of wavering intensity; well matured fruit cake but there are sumptuous greengages and runny honey, too; the spices are perfectly well behaved and the vanillas are graceful **t24** like the nose, the delivery is a fabulous amalgam of all faiths. There are both bourbon honey and liquorice notes harmonising with fruity notes to die for. The spices are almost too perfect in weight; **f23.5** content to move down the old fruitcake washed down with mocha scenario; **b24.5** yet another bottling which makes one wonder why this has never been a malt which has received the backing as a singleton it deserved. Once you've had a glass of this stuff you know it: in many ways the complete dram. *55%. nc ncf sc. Ian Macleod Distillers.*

Malts Of Scotland Miltonduff 1980 bourbon hogshead, cask no. 12429, dist Sep 80, bott Jan 11 **(82) n19 t22.5 f19.5 b21.** A fine example of the distillery in all its blending finery: a few milky notes denoting a cask at the end of its tether but the enormity of the barley is there to be admired. *44.7%. nc ncf sc. Malts Of Scotland. 259 bottles.*

⁘ **Mo Ór Collection Miltonduff 1980 30 Years Old** first fill bourbon hogshead, cask no. 12431, dist 12 Sep 80, bott 24 Nov 10 **(95) n24** a superlative, zesty nose which shows you why blenders prize this as a malt which speaks so much more eloquently than many others: especially with the higher, honeyed notes, perfectly balanced with the earthier tones of salty, lightly peppered bacon: the perfect whisky to return home to and call to your partner: high honey, I'm ham...; **t24** there is no faulting the weight, shape and balance of the delivery; when you get a mouthful of this, the barley seemingly acts like a 19th century native American before fighting the cowboys: it grows in a tent city...; **f23** now it teases you with its roundness, maltiness and chocolate; oh, no that's a malt teaser...; **b24** a whisky which religiously, and quite literally, gets the wrong meaning with any potentially ambiguous tasting note. Oh, no: that's Milton Jones... *46%. nc ncf sc. Release No. 18. 321 bottles.*

⁘ **Old Malt Cask Miltonduff Aged 21 Years** refill hogshead, cask no. 7921, dist May 90, bott Nov 11 **(89.5) n23** superb nose with roasted peanuts on toast and a cup of mocha sitting nearby. The subtlety of the sugars borders perfection; **t22.5** soft barley delivery but there is a firm backbone to this, allowing a crunchy feel to the proceedings. Sharp, almost eye-watering in part with a lightly salted sub-plot; **f22** the creamy mocha on the nose returns; **b22** this distillery doesn't have to work hard to produce excellent whisky. And though this one is relatively simple, it's complex enough... *50%. nc ncf sc. Douglas Laing & Co. 183 bottles.*

⁘ **Scott's Selection Miltonduff 1990** bott 2011 **(94.5) n23.5** displays its usual pastel shaded sugars: everything understated and delicate, though this time with a not quite so usual element of dried dates; **t24.5** almost a nonchalance bordering on arrogance to the way in which the perfectly weighted barley moves across the palate; the sugars are a little fudge-like and thick, the spices are present but shy. The layering of kumquat and milky mocha borders the sensational; **f23** a thin muscovado-molassed mix sets the tone for the long finish, in which oak gets some kind of dry toe hold but can barely hang on; the complexity and layering remains exceptional; **b23.5** this distillery must, surely, one day be publicly outed by their owners as one of the world's finest, let alone Scotland's... *59.2%. Speyside Distillers.*

⁘ **Scott's Selection Miltonduff 1990** bott 2012 **(86) n21 t22 f21.5 b21.5.** A lazy, chewy offering with too much toffee dampening down the excellent work of the juicy barley and busy oak. *55.3%. Speyside Distillers.*

⁘ **Wemyss 1987 Single Speyside Miltonduff "Wild Berry Spice"** barrel, bott 2012 **(87) n21.5** the oak threatens darkly but enough malt and liquorice bubbles through...; **t22** certainly spiced, though at first it is calmed by an oily wave of simplistic but attractively sugared barley; a hint of Swiss roll style raspberry jam and cream; **f21.5** the oils and slightly one dimensional spice continue, but complexity is sketchy; **b22** as someone who spends as much spare time as possible rambling in the country, my autumns are spent picking wild berries. And you've got me here, guys...never yet found a wild spiced Swiss Roll...! *46%. sc. 169 bottles.*

⁘ **The Whisky Agency Miltonduff 1989** bott 2011 **(90.5) n22** leathery and dry without the oak getting any kind of meaningful grip; some freshly baked bread, though lacking the subtle sweetness; **t23** lovely soft oil heralds the dawn of some stunning muscovado sugars; the middle ground offers a subtle mid-roast Java coffee note; **f22.5** a plethora of spices ensure a busy finale; **b23** a malt to take your time with. It will be very well rewarded. *50%. nc ncf sc. The Whisky Agency.*

MORTLACH
Speyside, 1824. Diageo. Working.
Mortlach Aged 16 Years db **(87) n20** big, big sherry, but not exactly without a blemish or two; **t23** sumptuous fruit and then a really outstanding malt and melon mouthwatering rush; **f22** returns to heavier duty with a touch of spice, too; **b22** once it gets past the bold if very mildly sulphured nose, the rest of the journey is superb. Earlier Mortlachs in this range had a slightly unclean feel to them and the nose here doesn't inspire confidence. But from arrival on the palate onwards, it's sure-footed, fruity and even refreshing ... and always delicious. *43%*

Mortlach 32 Years Old dist 1971 db **(88) n22 t22 f22 b22.** Big and with attitude... *50.1%*

⁘ **Berry's Own Selection Mortlach 1998** cask no. 3798, bott 2012 **(87) n19** a little dirty – in the house style; **t24** the taste buds are blanketed by one of the most impenetrable barley experiences known to mankind. It is as though you are sucking on a boiled malt whisky sweet which takes forever to dissolve; **f22** the imperfections on the nose pan out at the very death. But there are some spices to contend with; **b22** a typical knife and fork merchant from Mortlach where the puffy nose wins little for beauty, but is compensated with big personality on delivery. Impossible not to fall in love a little. *56.8%. nc ncf sc. Berry Bros & Rudd.*

⁘ **Chieftain's Mortlach Aged 18 Years** sherry butt, dist May 93, bott Sep 11 **(80) n19 t23 f19 b19.** A shame. The nuttiness and molassed sweetness to the sherry is truly superb. But the darker, drier forces at work drag the overall quality down. *57.2%. nc ncf sc. Ian Macleod.*

⁘ **Dun Bheagan Mortlach 12 Years Old** hogshead, dist Aug 98 **(90) n22** a surprising, slightly plumy fruitiness to this. The weight of the malt impresses; **t23** now that is a lovely delivery: the sweetness of the barley breaks down in almost orchestrated moves: the peeling of a malty onion. Clean, soft yet compact and exuding excellence; **f22.5** long with the softest of malty oils. The oaky balance shows no dodgy cask bitterness whatsoever; **b22.5** something of a workhorse malt, but in this form is showing there is more to it than the one dimensional thug we've had to endure for the last decade. This, from time to time, actually radiates some real charm. To see Mortlach as it hasn't been viewed for some while, go fetch! *43%. nc ncf.*

⁘ **Gordon & MacPhail Rare Vintage Mortlach 1971 (95.5) n25** as solid and clean a sherry as you are likely to find: mangos, salted lime, grape pith, kumquat peel, thinned molasses, physalis, exploding gooseberry, Crunchie bar,...it's as though someone has taken the lot, crushed them in a mortar and pestle and added ancient oloroso: perfection! **t24** black cherries, which don't appear on the nose, most certainly do here. Along with a soft volley of spice and muscovado and molassed sugars; the middle is molten Milky Way topped off with even more honeycomb; **f22** it tires somewhat and even the odd degree of bitter oak assembles. But there are still many positives to behold; **b24.5** if you don't like a whisky like this, then you should give up. The kind of dram I spend my life searching for... *43%. Gordon & MacPhail.*

⁙ **Gordon & MacPhail Rare Vintage Mortlach 1976 (84.5) n22.5 t21.5 f20 b20.5.** An underpowered dram which begins with a magnificently dextrous, if sawdusty, nose but falls away slightly as the weakened oils fail to hold honeyed but chalky excesses of the oak. *43%*

⁙ **Hart Brothers Mortlach Aged 14 Years** cask no. 12843, dist 15 Oct 97, bott 15 Apr 12 **(86) n22 t22.5 f20 b21.5.** Creamily textured and impressively intense especially towards the start. *46%. sc.*

Old Malt Cask Mortlach Aged 13 Years refill butt, cask no. 6574, dist Sep 97, bott Sep 10 **(80) n20 t19.5 f20.5 b20.** The technical flaws are outweighed by the vivid sharpness and intensity of the barley. Fun. *50%. nc ncf sc. Douglas Laing & Co. 424 bottles.*

⁙ **Old Malt Cask Mortlach Aged 15 Years** refill hogshead, cask no. 7647, dist Aug 96, bott Aug 11 **(81.5) n18 t22.5 f20 b21.** Sweet, buttery and spicy. *50%. nc ncf sc. 350 bottles.*

⁙ **Old Malt Cask Mortlach Aged 21 Years** refill puncheon, cask no. 7489, dist Sep 90, bott Sep 11 **(87) n19** perhaps not the ideal blueprint for a Speyside nose as there is some tired oak in there. But enough sugars to give hope: **t23.5** Much juicier and more compact than the nose would lead you to believe. After the initial barley blast, opens out superbly to allow in the spices and begin a breath-taking series of complex waves involving toasty, fudgy notes, myriad spices and even a hint of manuka honey and liquorice; **f22.5** the tannins kick in but add just the right degree of dryness; oily and long; **b23** from such an unpromising nose, there is much to celebrate afterwards. *50%. nc ncf sc. 271 bottles.*

Planeta Mortlach 18 Year Old planeta nero d'avola cask **(86) n21 t21.5 f22 b21.5.** A thick, soupy Mortlach showing all the refinement of a tattooed arm-wrestler. But though the grapey, sherryed fruit is all over this like a rash, there is not a single off note. The perfect malt for those who think style is a four-letter word. *46%. sc. Enotria.*

Premier Barrel Mortlach Aged 12 Years (89) n22.5 t23 f21.5 b22. Shows what an above average barrel can do to a below average distillery... *46%. nc ncf sc. 175 bottles.*

Premier Barrel Mortlach Aged 14 Years (84) n21 t22 f20 b21. Teaming with natural caramels. Clean and vanilla-rich, too. *46%. nc ncf sc. Douglas Laing & Co. 180 bottles.*

⁙ **Premier Barrel Mortlach Aged 14 Years (83.5) n21 t22.5 f19 b21.** An intense malt. A character on the nose suggests this might be heading for a fall further on down the line. But the big malt delivery is a treat. *46%. nc ncf sc. Douglas Laing & Co. 178 bottles.*

⁙ **Premier Barrel Mortlach Aged 14 Years (92) n23** a subtle and unexpected pinch of peat to this. Chimes well with the sugary malt; **t23.5** soft layers of peat intertwine effortlessly with the barley-vanilla theme. The odd squeeze of something citrusy ensures a clean, salivating experience; **f22.5** vanillas offer a drying component but the light sugars persist deliciously while the smoke breaks down to something spicier; **b23** elements in the makeup of this remind me of when I first tasted Mortlach over 30 years ago and has been lost for something approaching the last two decades. *46%. nc ncf sc. Douglas Laing & Co.*

Provenance Mortlach Over 8 Years montilla finish butt, cask no. 6929, dist Spring 01, bott Spring 2011 **(85) n20 t22 f21.5 b21.5.** A thoroughly enjoyable Speysider which shows the density of a black hole and the dexterity of a Saudi Arabian thief. I, for one, would still come back for a second glass, though. *46%. nc ncf sc. Douglas Laing & Co.*

Provenance Mortlach Over 8 Years sherry finished butt, cask no. 7265, dist Spring 03, bott Summer 2011 **(88) n21 t22.5 f22 b22.5.** An enjoyable heavyweight. *46%. nc ncf sc.*

⁙ **Provenance Mortlach Over 8 Years** Montilla butt, cask no. 7679, dist Spring 2003, bott Autumn 2011 **(88.5) n22** spotted dog pudding with a layer of molten sugar; **t22** thickly coated in malt and fruit, the middle ground fizzes with spice and is not shy in coming forward with the oak; **f22.5** more spice, then a superb late dawning of delicate brown sugars; a smattering of cocoa powder tops things off delightfully; **b22** a dense malt in which evidence of youth is far from easy to trace. Chunky and chewy from first to last. *46%. nc ncf sc. 163 bottles.*

Provenance Mortlach Over 12 Years refill butt, cask no. 6372, dist Autumn 97, bott Summer 2010 **(76) n18 t20 f18 b19.** Some lovely barley on impact, but does not possess the wherewithal to see off the off-colour oak. *46%. nc ncf sc. Douglas Laing & Co.*

Scotch Malt Whisky Society Cask 76.71 Aged 20 Years 1st fill sherry butt, dist Aug 89 **(59) n15 t15 f14 b15.** One assumes this was bottled by the Society only to give its members an idea of what sulphured, truly awful whisky tastes like. *60.1% 606 bottles.*

Scotch Malt Whisky Society Cask 76.72 Aged 20 Years 1st fill sherry butt, cask no. 3677, dist 1989 **(63) n17 t16 f14 b16.** That's my taste buds comprehensively screwed for another day... *59.2%. sc. 565 bottles.*

Scotch Malt Whisky Society Cask 76.77 Aged 16 Years 1st fill sherry butt, cask no. 4848, dist 1994 **(61) n17 t15 f14 b15.** Bloody awful doesn't cover it. Another example of that well known whisky equation: Sherry + Mortlach = Disaster. *58%. sc. 604 bottles.*

Scotch Malt Whisky Society Cask 76.79 Aged 14 Years 1st fill sherry butt, cask no. 7273, dist 1995 **(89) n22 t22 f23 b22.** Enough all round grapey complexity to set the taste buds salivating. *56.3%. sc. 551 bottles.*

❖ **Scotch Malt Whisky Society Cask 76.85 Aged 15 Years** first fill sherry butt, cask no. 4393, dist 1995 **(79) n19 t21 f19 b20.** No major off notes, other than the inevitable tang on the finish which matches the off-colour nose. Just stupefyingly dull. *55.2%. sc.*

❖ **Scotch Malt Whisky Society Cask 76.87 Aged 9 Years** first fill barrel, cask no. 4532, dist 2002 **(85.5) n21 t21.5 f22 b21.** Massively malty, gristy and fresh. The spices make do for the complexity interest. *59.5%. sc. Scotch Malt Whisky Society.*

❖ **Silver Seal Mortlach Over 13 Years Old** dist 1997 **(74) n19 t20 f17 b18.** Subtlety, charm, charisma, complexity, class...yes, it has none of those whatsoever. Lumpy, hot and less than brilliantly made whisky: ideal for the persistent visitor who comes to your home to help themselves to your best malt. *46%. sc. Silver Seal Whisky Company.*

❖ **Silver Seal Mortlach Over 22 Years Old** dist 1989, bott Dec 11 **(83) n21 t20 f21 b21.** A wholesome malt despite its propensity to want to pick fights with all your taste buds. Enough peppered sugar character and walnut oil to make for a pleasant-ish, if warming, experience. *58.2%. sc. Silver Seal Whisky Company.*

Vom Fass Mortlach 21 Years Old (74) n18.5 t19 f18 b18.5. Syrupy, heavy-handed and not for a moment finds a happy rhythm. A dud on many levels, yet I know many who will prostrate themselves before it... *43%*

❖ **The Warehouse Collection Mortlach Aged 11 Years** bourbon hogshead, cask no. 9052, dist 29 Jun 00, bott 3 Aug 11 **(88) n21.5** a little dirty in the Mortlach style, but a little pineapple to the honey cleanses things somewhat; **t23** big, pulsing oily malt with the emphasis on spiced barley. The trick, though, is the kaleidoscopic sugars which twist from an early Demerara style to a later muscovado, taking in the odd golden syrup note at points between. This, though, is beautifully underscored by spice; **f21.5** much more simplistic vanilla; **b22** hats off to these German bottlers. Mortlach is not an easy distillery from which to locate an entertaining cask. The chaps have achieved it. *59.9%. sc. Whisky Warehouse No. 8. 271 bottles.*

The Whisky Castle Old Malt Cask Mortlach Aged 13 Years refill hogshead, cask no. 7196, dist Sep 97, bott May 11 **(83) n21 t21.5 f20 b20.5.** Any more syrupy and it would have serious pretensions of being a liqueur...Some lovely bold and mouth-watering moments, though. *56.9%. nc ncf sc. Douglas Laing & Co for The Whisky Castle. 120 bottles.*

Wilson & Morgan Barrel Selection Mortlach 20 Years Old cask no. 4412, dist 1990, bott 2010 **(71) n18 t17 f19 b17.** Such an over-the-top, grizzly Mortlach, it is almost classic for the style. Some delightful mocha makes a game of it against the sulphur very late on. *56.5%. sc.*

MOSSTOWIE
Speyside, 1964–1981. Chivas Brothers. Closed.

Rare Old Mosstowie 1979 (84.5) n21.5 t21 f21 b21. Edging inextricably well beyond its sell by date. But there is a lovely walnut cream cake (topped off with brown sugar and spices) to this which warms the cockles. Bless... *43%. Gordon & MacPhail.*

NORTH PORT
Highlands (Eastern), 1820–1983. Diageo. Demolished.

Brechin 1977 db **(78) n19 t21 f18 b20.** Fire and brimstone was never an unknown quantity with the whisky from this doomed distillery. Some soothing oils are poured on this troubled – and sometimes attractively honeyed – water of life. *54.2%*

OBAN
Highlands (Western), 1794. Diageo. Working.

Oban 14 Years Old db **(79) n19 t22 f18 b20.** Absolutely all over the place. The cask selection sits very uncomfortably with the malt. I look forward to the resumption of normality to this great but ill-served distillery. *43%*

Oban Aged 15 Years The Distiller's Edition db finished in Montilla Fino casks, dist 1992, bott 2007 **(90) n22.5 t23 f22.5 b22.** This isn't all about complexity and layering. It's about style and effect. And it pulls it off brilliantly. *43%*

Oban Aged 15 Years The Distiller's Edition db finished in Montilla Fino casks, dist 1993, bott 2008 **(91.5) n22** nutty, tight, a little musty; **t24** much more assured: the dryness of the grape sports beautifully against the obviously more outgoing and sweeter barley: excellent balance between the two; **f22.5** perhaps the Fino wins, as it dries and embraces the oak quite happily; **b23** delicate and sophisticated whisky. *43%*

PITTYVAICH

Speyside, 1975–1993. Diageo. Demolished.

Pittyvaich Aged 12 Years db (64) n16 t18 f15 b15. It was hard to imagine this whisky getting worse. But somehow it has achieved it. From fire-water to cloying undrinkability. What amazes me is not that this is such bad whisky: we have long known that Pittyvaich can be as grim as it gets. It's the fact they bother bottling it and inflicting it on the public. Vat this with malt from Fettercairn and neighbouring Dufftown and you'll have the perfect dram for masochists. Or those who have entirely lost the will to live. Jesus... *43%. Flora and Fauna.*

PORT ELLEN

Islay, 1825–1983. Diageo. Closed.

Port Ellen 1979 db (93) n22 mousy and retiring; a degree of oak fade and fruit on the delicate smoke t23 non-committal delivery but bursts into stride with a series of sublime, peat-liquorice waves and a few rounds of spices; f24 a surprising gathering of oils rounds up the last traces of sweet barley and ensures an improbably long – and refined – finish; b24 takes so long to get out of the traps, you wonder if anything is going to happen. But when it does, my word...it's glorious! *57.5%*

Port Ellen 29 Year Old 8th Release, dist 1978, bott 2008 db (90.5) n23 t22.5 f22.5 b22.5. The glory and charisma is still there to cast you under its spell, but some high notes are missed, the timing not quite what it was, yet still we stand and applaud because we recognise it exactly for what it is: beauty and genius still, but fading beauty; receding genius. Something which only those of us of a certain vintage, can remember as being that unique, almost naked, celebration of Islay malt whisky it once so beautifully and so gloriously was. *55.3%*

Port Ellen 31 Years Old Special Release refill American & European oak, dist 1978, bott 2010 db (88.5) n22 borderline OTT oak, perhaps to be expected: the vague hint of juniper wasn't. A twist of lemon seems to accentuate the gin nature, though the most delicate smoke possible coaxes you back to Scotland again; t23 oak is pile-driven into the taste buds, molasses and hickory work well while the cocoa and peat are carried on the oils, f22 long with plenty of spices zipping around and cocoa on the warm fade; b21.5 shows some serious cracks now, though that can't be helped; this whisky was never made for this type of age. Still some moments to close the eyes and simply cherish, however; *54.6%. nc ncf. Diageo. Fewer than 3000 bottles.*

❖ **Port Ellen 32 Years Old Special Release 2011** db (88.5) n22.5 PE at its drowsiest: not so much the normal ashy notes of old age, but dust. The phenols hang on in there; t22.5 a burst of gristy sugars has been infiltrated by some muscly oak but surprisingly virile lemon; f22 any drier and you could use this for a smoky martini. Actually, anyone found putting anything into a PE, other than more PE, will have to be brought to me for the most severe sentencing. b22 really feeling its age, though there are many superb passages of play. *53.9%. nc ncf.*

Dun Bheagan Port Ellen 28 Years Old hogshead, dist May 82 (86) n22 t22 f20 b22. Some beautiful moments, especially with the lightness of touch with the smoke – and the unusual citrus notes for a malt so old – is fabulous. But the oak lets the side down somewhat. *50%. nc ncf. Ian Macleod Distillers.*

❖ **Malts Of Scotland Port Ellen 1982** sherry hogshead, cask no. MoS12017, dist Feb 82, bott Apr 12 (96) n24 the sultanas are so juicy, the smoke for a moment has a problem competing; a degree of harmony is contrived, though a chunk of hickory tries to intervene; the smokiness is meaty, not dissimilar to certain sausages I have found in Bavaria; even a hint of Rupp cheese; t24.5 massive delivery, helped along by the surprising strength for its age; with the phenols powering through while they have the chance. Several layers of seriously overcooked Christmas pudding tries to have its cake, so to speak...; the barley flows, the fruit juices flow...spices bombard...; f23.5 long, with the burnt cherries and raisins coming back with a vengeance; the smoke is now much more ethereal; b24 stunning whisky. The sherry, even though this time from a faultless butt, dumbs down to a degree and takes the edge off the complexity. But it doesn't matter: this is one very big dram to savour from the very top drawer of Islay malts. *58.6%. nc ncf sc. Malts Of Scotland.*

Malts Of Scotland Port Ellen 1983 refill sherry butt, cask no. MoS66, dist Mar 83, bott Sep 10 (95.5) n23 low res citrus helps break up the bigger smoke notes. Some serious anthracite amid the peat reek; t23.5 light delivery, though not dull. The contrary as juicy barley lets rip with juicier grape. Mocha and praline combine for the middle, with a hint of Jaffa Cake; f24.5 long with the mocha becoming more milky and spices now hitting home but with supreme sophistication; b24.5 quietly magnificent with much to shout about. *56%. nc ncf sc. 322 bottles.*

❖ **Malts Of Scotland Port Ellen 1983** bourbon hogshead, cask no. MoS11011, dist Feb 83, bott Oct 11 (91) n22 dry and ashy like the other '83 vintages out this year. But this offers a bit more tart aggression; t23 the sugars gang up fast and true; the smoke helps deflect some of the harder strikes especially from the early spice; f23 the spices linger, but otherwise calms beautifully, again with the delicate smoke seemingly pulling all the strings; **b23** comes out a snarling fighter, ends a buttercup-sniffing pacifist. *58.9%. nc ncf sc. Malts Of Scotland.*

Mo Òr Collection Port Ellen 1983 27 Years Old first fill bourbon hogshead, cask no. 627A, dist 16 Mar 83, bott 29 Oct 10 **(95) n25** blows you away...or would, if it was vicious enough. But, no, this whisky is all about calmness and elegance. Astonishingly, it has lost none of its 35ppm phenols in the passing 27 years, which makes one suspect that this cask started off somewhere a little higher. The still gristy sugars are in complete harmony with both the still peat and sympathetic oak; delicate kumquat pops up here and there, as well as sugared mint; **t23.5** there's those grists again! How does it do that after so many years in the cask. The mint on the nose appears now as minted tea, though it would be a little wide of the mark to call it Lapsang Souchong; the mid ground is a busy affair of muscovado sugars and vanillas trying to retain their identities; **f23** even paced and helped by a total lack of oils. There is a very mild degree of bitterness, but the remnants of the grist and oakier sugars do their best to nip that in the bud; **b23.5** I had a bit of a feeling about this guy: the age, the colour...let's call it instinct. So I opened this as the 750th new whisky tasted for the 2013 Bible....and it's good to know that little man inside me, as Edward G Robinson described it in Double Indemnity, is still alive and kicking.... *46%. nc ncf sc. Release No. 5. The Whisky Talker. 164 bottles.*

Old Malt Cask Port Ellen 27 Years Old refill hogshead, cask no. 6397, dist Mar 83, bott Jul 10 **(92.5) n23.5** a leaf or two of mint adds further joy to the salty light smoke; **t23.5** excellent interplay between busy spice and smoky vanilla. Excellent deftness to the oil; **f22.5** the lingering smoke compensates for late tiredness; **b23** in wonderful nick. *50%. nc ncf sc. Douglas Laing & Co. 199 bottles.*

Old Malt Cask Port Ellen 27 Years Old refill hogshead, cask no. 6588, dist Feb 83, bott Sep 10 **(85.5) n22 t21.5 f21 b21.** A little hot and aggressive. Some unusual cough sweet tendencies to this one. *50%. nc ncf sc. Douglas Laing & Co. 225 bottles.*

Old Malt Cask Port Ellen 27 Years Old refill hogshead, cask no. 6702, dist Mar 83, bott Nov 10 **(89) n23 t22 f21 b23.** A genteel Islay. *50%. nc ncf sc. Douglas Laing & Co. 230 bottles.*

Old Malt Cask Port Ellen 27 Years Old refill hogshead, cask no. 6708, dist Mar 83, bott Oct 10 **(95) n24.5** probably the most delicate, complex and sublimely weighted peat aroma this year. The interplay between the smoke, citrus and vanilla is truly the stuff of whisky legend. Frankly, impossible to ask for more; **t23** nearly 30 years old and yet the delivery is that of melting grist! How the hell does that happen? Again, the peat is so deft you can barely measure it. The citrus notes have dissolved sugars... The oaks equally dissolve, showing just enough weight to count but doing nothing to dominate; **f23.5** medium length due to lack of oils, but the fade is a beautiful dimming of the early glory; **b24** I could do with a full bottle of this stuff. Not a single off note: what a way to visit a lost gem. *50%. nc ncf sc. Douglas Laing & Co. 217 bottles.*

⁘ **Old Malt Cask Port Ellen Aged 28 Years** refill hogshead, cask no. 7244, dist Feb 83, bott Jun 11 **(94.5) n23** an ashy dryness is countered by molten liquorice-muscovado; **t24** grist! How does it do that after all this time. I thought that old Port Ellen trademark was a thing of the past; the sugars and smoke in rhapsodic harmony; **f23.5** the gristy effect continues with a degree of lemon now sharpening the smoky barley; **b24** after 28 years not a single blemish. Spectacular! And not least for its understated elegance. *50%. nc ncf sc. Douglas Laing & Co. 292 bottles.*

⁘ **Whisky Antique Port Ellen 26 Years Old** dist 1983, bott 2009 **(89) n22** as dry as port Ellen ever get. Not just ashy, but that stringent nose burn that sometimes comes along with embers; a light hint of creosote; **t22.5** sugars at last! A sprinkling of caster sugar melts immediately on the palate; as soon as that has dissolved, a smoky-liquorice substitute dives in; **f22** long, reverting back to that dry ashy persona; a late barley juiciness breaks out only to be replaced by butterscotch; **b22.5** a fascinating dram, at a stage of its life where it cannot sit comfortably for more than a few moments. *53.5%. sc. Silver Seal Whisky Company.*

⁘ **Whisky Antique Port Ellen 28 Years Old** dist 1983, bott 2011 **(91) n22** obviously a twin cask to their 2009 bottling: very similar but a few extra softening vanillas here; **t23** sugars aplenty but this time not of the superfine variety: much weightier and a little more molassed, heading in a muscovado direction. The smoke eschews the ashy route and joins the oils to form a more voluptuous peatiness, again with caramels at play; **f23** much softer on the finish than its twin with the smoke gliding home, even sporting a degree of citrus, rather than crash-landing; late smoky mocha; **b23** displays the kind of softness of touch that could convert many who think they don't like peaty whisky. *55.5%. sc. Silver Seal Whisky Company.*

PULTENEY

Highlands (Northern), 1826. Inver House Distillers. Working.

Old Pulteney Aged 12 Years db **(90.5) n22** pungent, busy and full of zesty zap. Enough salt to get your blood pressure up; **t23** beautifully clean barley, again showing little shortage of saltiness, but thriving in its zesty environment; **f22.5** the vanillas and cocoa carry out an excellent drying operation. The sea-breeze saltiness continues to hang on the taste buds...;

b23 a cleaner, zestier more joyous composition than the old 43%, though that has less to do with strength than overall construction. A dramatic whisky which, with further care, could get even closer to the truth of this distillery. *40%*

Old Pulteney Aged 12 Years db (85) **n22 t23 f19 b21.** There are few malts whose finish dies as spectacularly as this. The nose and delivery are spot on with a real buzz and panache. The delivery in particular just bowls you over with its sharp barley integrity: real pulse-racing stuff! Then... toffee...!!! Grrrr!!! If it is caramel causing this, then it can be easily remedied. And in the process we'd have a malt absolutely basking in the low 90s...! *43%*

Old Pulteney Aged 15 Years db (91) **n21** pretty harsh and thin at first but some defter barley notes can be detected; **t24** an attention-grabbing, eye-wateringly sharp delivery with the barley in roasty mood and biting immediately with a salty incision; the barley-sugar effect is mesmerising and the clarity astonishing for its age; **f23** long, with those barley sugars working overtime; a slight salty edge there but the oak behaves impeccably; **b23** only on about the fourth or fifth mouthful do you start getting the picture here: enormously complex with a genuine coastal edge to this. The complexity is awesome. *54.9%*

Old Pulteney Aged 17 Years db (95) **n22** tight but does all that is possible to reveal its salty, fruity complexity with pears and lemons to the fore; **t25** one of the softest, most beautifully crafted deliveries in the whisky world. Absolutely faultless as it picks the most fabulous course among the honeyed vanilla and barley which is so delicate words simply cannot do justice, **f24** near perfect balance between the vanillas and delicate honeys; **b24** the nose confirms that some of the casks at work here are not A1. Even so, the whisky performs to the kind of levels some distillers could only dream of. *46%*

Old Pulteney Aged 21 Years db (97.5) **n25** if you had the formula to perfectly transform salt, citrus, the most delicate smoke imaginable, sharp barley, more gristy barley, light vanilla, toasty vanilla, roasted hazelnut, thinned manuka honey, lavender honey, arbutus blossom and cherry blossom, light hickory, liquorice and the softest demerera sugar into the aroma of a whisky, you still wouldn't quite be able to recreate this perfection...; **t24** the sugars arrive: first gristy and malt-laden, then Demerara. This is followed by a salty, nerve-tingling journey of barley at varying intensity and then a slow but magnificently complete delivery of spice...; **f24** those spices continue to buzz, the vanillas dovetail with the malt and the fruit displaying a puckering, lively intensity. Ridiculously long fade for a malt so seemingly light, the salts and spices kiss the taste buds goodnight...; **b24.5** by far and away one of the great whiskies of 2012, absolutely exploding from the glass with vitality, charisma and class. One of Scotland's great undiscovered distilleries about to become discovered, I think... and rightly so! *46%*

⁑ **Old Pulteney Aged 30 Years** db (93.5) **n23** magnificent spectrum of exotic fruits; leave no doubts about its age: plenty of mango, especially, while the odd tinned peach appears to have been tossed into the dainty salad; **t24** melts-in-the-mouth, aided by the strength. But that means the richer flavours grab only half a hold and soon slip away; the mid-ground has the feel of a chocolate fruit liqueur, except the liqueur might have more attitude; **f23** medium length but we are back into exotic fruits territory: an unusual development for a malt. Maybe it is a mixture of the subtle salt and delicate, semi-drowned orange blossom honey which is raising the fruity profile; **b23.5** I know there is not too much of this north Scottish nectar, but they would have been better to have brought this out at 46%...if they were able, that is. *40.1%*

Old Pulteney 30 Years Old db (92) **n23.5** fabulous mix of Jaffa cake and bourbon, seasoned by a pinch of salt; **t23.5** an early, unexpected, wave of light smoke and silkier oak gives immediate depth. But stunning, ultra-juicy citrus and barley ensures this doesn't get all big and brooding; **f22** thinner and oakier with a playful oak-spice tingle; plenty of vanilla controls the drier aspects; **b23** I had to laugh when I tasted this: indeed, it had me scrambling for a copy of the 2009 Bible to check for sure what I had written. And there it was: after bemoaning the over oaking I conjectured, "As Pulteney has the fascinating tendency to radically shift style over not too long a period, I can't wait for the next instalment." And barely a year on, here it is. Pretty far removed from last year's offering and an absolute peach of a dram that laughs in the face of its 30 years... *45%*

⁑ **Old Pulteney Aged 40 Years** db (88.5) **n22** on first nose, a little tight: needs time to unloosen. When it does there is enough cloves to stock a dentist's for a month; **t21** the delivery is eye-watering in its oaky intensity: virtually pure tannin. Thankfully the malt is intact, following behind like a faithful St Bernard's dog, dispensing molassed sugars at essential moments; **f23.5** a gorgeous chocolate pecan tart, where the chef has gone a little heavy on the salt; **b22** a malt just waiting to wilt and keel over. However, it's survival instinct is strong, while its complexity at the death is scrumptious! *51.3%*

Old Pulteney Isabella Fortuna cask no. WK499, bott 2010 db (91.5) **n23** reminiscent of a breakfast I had in Grenada some years back: lots of slightly green banana, the lightly sweetened oiliness of mixed diced nuts and a light coastal saltiness in the air: just so wonderfully fresh...; **t23.5** wow! Pulteney rarely comes more unambiguously malty than this.

For all the bite of the salt and oak – which is more a little nip and nibble, to be fair – it is the barley which shines proudest of all; both sweet and sharp in equal measures; **f22.5** a touch tangy; **b22.5** over the 30-odd years I have been tasting whisky from this distillery I have noticed that its quality simply continues rising, unlike a number of other whiskies I could name. Here's further proof. *52%. 18,000 bottles.*

Old Pulteney WK209 db **(71)** n68.5 t18 f16.5 b17. Could well be liked by the Germans. *46%*

⁛ **Old Pulteney WK217** db **(88.5)** **n21** some pretty young notes offer a background "new make" freshness; the salt and delicate, peachy fruits are only half-formed; **t22** the delivery reveals unusual youthfulness, amply balanced by a more impressive saline contour which hits you like sea spray in the face: a rare eruption of flavour in a sensual experience; **f23** the oaks appear to have ganged together to proffer an oily, praline fade; **b22.5** the WK series is named after the old fishing vessels which used to be based in the town's harbour. I suspect old WK217 rarely had a day at sea in waters as calm as this softy of a malt. *46%*

⁛ **Cadenhead Pulteney 20 Years Old** bott 2009 **(91)** **n24** what a nose...! Just so delicate and complex. Very lightly salted and coastal, with a nod towards clear rock pools; there is even a touch of distant Pennan peat fires on the wind. The malt is fresh with the sugars crisp and countering the sharper tones. Complex and, frankly, something of a turn on; **t23** wonderful, crystalline clarity to the early barley with almost a fizz to the salt-malt interaction. Just so juicy....! **f21.5** damn! Typically Allied in the finish, in that a slight bitterness develops, though nothing which, ultimately, undoes the overall enjoyment. Also, a really busy, complex and unusually bitty and peppery spice – something not unknown in bourbons - takes off on full damage limitation; **b22.5** I'm glad I have plenty of this left. For the next time I spend an evening with a beautiful woman, I would like to smear this all over her body... *56.9%. sc.*

Gordon & MacPhail Rare Vintage Old Pulteney 1980 (88.5) n23 t22.5 f21 b22. Rock steady, clean and fulsome. *43%*

⁛ **Gordon & MacPhail Cask Strength Pulteney 1998 (92)** **n22** citrusy, with a powerful kumquat element as well as big vanilla and a surprising rumble of natural caramels; **t23** mmmmmm! What a delivery! Barley concentrate eventually giving way to a tangy saltiness missing on the nose; sharp and eye-watering and wonderfully layered; **f23** the barley plays out until the end, but some cocoa and spice make a near inevitable appearance; the salt also sticks around, though seasons with little less gusto than before, keeping the burgeoning sugars honest; good late oils; **b24** the nose may be missing the normal coastal depth to this malt, but it makes up for it elsewhere! Confirmation of what a cracking distillery this is. *56.9%*

Malts Of Scotland Old Pulteney 1998 bourbon hogshead, cask no. 1217, dist Feb 98, bott Jan 11 **(72)** **n16 t19 f18.5 b18.5.** Sweet malt with a touch of apple and pear. But limited by a flawed cask – unusual for these bottlers. *52.5%. nc ncf sc. Malts of Scotland. 301 bottles.*

The Whisky Castle Exclusive Old Pulteney Aged 14 Years cask no. 1180, dist 1997, bott 2011 **(82.5)** **n21 t22 f19 b20.5.** A confident, impressive individual at times with plenty of kumquat and honey comb. But it's all a bit of a front: there is also a darker, more bitter, side... *58.9%. nc ncf sc. Gordon & MacPhail for The Whisky Castle.*

ROSEBANK
Lowlands, 1840–1993. Diageo. Closed. (But if there is a God will surely one day re-open)
Rosebank Aged 12 Years db **(95)** **n24 t24 f23 b24.** Infinately better than the last F&bottling, this is quite legendary stuff, even better than the old 8-y-o version, though probably a point or two down regarding complexity. The kind of whisky that brings a tear to the eye... for many a reason... *43%. Flora and Fauna.*

⁛ **Rosebank 21 Years Old Special Release** db **(94)** **n24** fabulous interplay between apple and berry fruits, though it's the pear juice which acts as the sweetening agent; a nose to spend a good 20 minutes over; **t23.5** at once fizzing and busy while soft and caressing; natural caramels combine with coconut oil to offer the weightier sheen; **f23** dries but never bitters; healthy vanilla all the way **b23.5** can any Lowland be compared to a fully blossomed Rosebank? This is whisky to both savour and worship for this is nectar in a Rose... *53.8%. nc ncf.*

Rosebank 22 Years Old Rare Malts 2004 db **(85)** **n22 t23 f19 b21.** One or two Rosebank moments of joyous complexity but, hand on heart, this is simply too old. *61.1%*

Rosebank 25 Years Old db **(96)** **n24.5 t23.5 f24 b24.** I had to sit back, take a deep breath and get my head around this. It was like Highland Park but with a huge injection of sweetened chocolate on the finale and weight – and even smoke – from a Rosebank I had never quite seen before. And believe me, as this distillery's greatest champion, I've tasted a few hundred, possibly thousands, of casks of this stuff over the last 25 years. Is this the greatest of all time? I am beginning to wonder. Is it the most extraordinary since the single malt revolution took off? Certainly. Do I endorse it? My god, yes! *61.4%*

⁛ **Chieftain's Rosebank Aged 20 Years** butt, dist Oct 90, bott Sep 11 **(88)** **n22** a little dull with the red liquorice tannins dominating; quite a salty theme to the quiet honey, too;

t22.5 some serious spice prickle injects some major action; a delicate honey thread forms the audience; **f21.5** back to a mildly one-dimensional oaky theme; **b22** a rose with several thorns... 55.7%. nc ncf sc. Ian Macleod Distillers.

Dun Bheagan Rosebank 20 Years Old French oak finish, dist Feb 90 **(90.5) n23.5** can't think of a better way to start the day: honey and orange juice...oh, and some Rosebank...; a few tables away is a kipper...; **t23** tip-top mouth feel with the firm barley offering the skeleton for the much fleshier fruits. The oils also carry a fabulous cracked pepper bite and the slight semblance of smoke that is fleetingly alluded to in the nose; **f21.5** if you expect a degree of bitterness on the home straight of a French oak finish, then you will not be disappointed. Though this is much better than the norm. **b22.5** so good, you could weep. 46%. nc ncf. Ian Macleod Distillers.

Old Malt Cask Rosebank Aged 20 Years refill hogshead, cask no. 6396, dist Feb 90, bott Jul 10 **(93) n22.5** a few flakes of sandalwood help blunt the sharpness of the bourbon lead; over-ripe kumquat, nougat and crushed pistachio; even a very curious touch of gristiness; **t23.5** a surprising depth to the juicy barley balances against the oh schedule spice. The odd citrus note nibbles away; the midpoint is clean and nimble; **f23.5** all kinds of oaky statements: not one of them drab or determined to get the upper hand of the rest; lightly sweetened vanillas keep the balance on track; **b23.5** exquisite. 50%. nc ncf sc. 232 bottles.

Old Malt Cask Rosebank Aged 20 Years refill butt, cask no. 6815, dist Feb 90, bott Nov 10 **(94.5) n23.5** big citrus chorus; **t24.5** initially sweet, friendly and barley-rich. Then the taste buds are at the receiving end of a massive spice kick; it is hard to imagine a Lowlander of this age offering so much; **f23** cools considerably as the vanillas trot to the rescue. But some pulsing spices thankfully remain; **b23.5** obviously from the very same stable as cask 6396, above. But this one revels in a spicy belligerence, perhaps railing against the injustice of being silenced when other distilleries, some of which are not fit to be mentioned in the same breath, continue to have the marketing men lavishing their money upon them. 50%. nc ncf sc. 449 bottles.

∴ **Old Malt Cask Rosebank Aged 21 Years** refill hogshead, cask no. 8227, dist Jun 90, bott Mar 12 **(90.5) n23.5** excellent floral depth to the honey and crisp vanillas; the citrus is a delight; **t23** a light, teasing touch where the barley makes the juiciest impact possible with so much oak present; the vanillas are dry but friendly, the honey moves towards a cocoa-nougat middle; **f21.5** the vanillas dry up – like a salt lake in the desert...! **b22.5** molten chocolate-honey candy. 50%. nc ncf sc. Douglas Laing & Co. 136 bottles.

∴ **Old Malt Cask Rosebank Aged 21 Years** refill butt, dist Feb 90, bott Aug 11 **(89) n23.5** it's a question of counting the different shades of honey: I can spot three without difficulty. And seemingly on a bed of crushed Digestive biscuit...; **t22** an early spice kick is doused by those varied honeys; takes on a surprising degree of oil; **f21** the honey is usurped by a thin vanilla sign off; **b22.5** unusually oily but those honeys are sublime. 50%. nc ncf sc. 268 bottles.

∴ **Old Malt Cask Rosebank Aged 21 Years** refill hogshead, cask no. 8247, dist Jun 90, bott May 12 **(82.5) n21 t21.5 f19 b21**. A seriously bipolar dram. The buttock-clenching tightness on delivery and thereafter is a result of a very tight, uncompromising cask. However, the constant lip-smacking qualities are due to a spirit with more than the ghost of varying shades of honey. 50%. nc ncf sc. Douglas Laing & Co. 116 bottles.

∴ **Scotch Malt Whisky Society Cask 25.59 Aged 20 Years** refill barrel, cask no. 2009, dist 1991 **(86.5) n21.5 t23 f21 b21**. Honey and spice aplenty if you look for it. But this cask is slightly hunged up with natural caramels which give a heavy, restricted feel to the proceedings. A rose which refuses to bloom. 53.8%. sc. Scotch Malt Whisky Society.

∴ **Scotch Malt Whisky Society Cask 25.60 Aged 20 Years** refill barrel, cask no. 2018, dist 1991 **(87.5) n21.5** sluggish and toffee heavy; **t23** superb delivery with a sparkling oak-sharpened tang to juicy barley. The odd honey note surfaces but is countered by chunky caramel; **f21.5** more creamy toffee; **b21.5** similar to 25.59, except here the caramel is marginally less attentive. 51.1%. sc. Scotch Malt Whisky Society.

ROYAL BRACKLA

Speyside, 1812. John Dewar & Sons. Working.

Royal Brackla Aged 10 Years db **(73) n18 t20 f17 b18**. A distinct lowering of the colours since I last tasted this. What on earth is going on? 40%

∴ **Cadenhead Royal Brackla 19 Years Old** Demerara rum cask, bott Apr 12 **(84.5) n22 t22 f19 b21.5**. From the cask type you'd expect a malt as hard as nails. And that's exactly what you get. Enjoys some memorably bold and juicy moments. 55.9%. sc.

∴ **Duncan Taylor NC2 Royal Brackla 12 Years Old** dist 1999 **(86) n21.5 t22 f21 b21.5**. Solid and simplistic with much emphasis on the rigid sugars keeping the barley in place. The spice element works quite beautifully. 46%. Duncan Taylor & Co.

∴ **Duncan Taylor Dimensions Royal Brackla 14 Years Old** dist Sep 97, bott Nov 11 **(84) n21.5 t21.5 f20 b21**. A distillery which is a bit uptight at the best of times shows little inclination for fun here. 46.1%. nc ncf sc. Duncan Taylor & Co.

⫶⫶⫶⫶ **Fortnum & Mason Jubilee Royal Brackla Aged 11 Years** dist 1999 **(89) n21.5** exceptionally light, allowing what little oak influence there is to have a fuller say than you might expect. The barley retains a touch of grist and lemon; **t24** shy it may be on the nose, it sweeps onto the taste buds like a 19th century debutante might fill a grand staircase as she enters the ball. Honey and spice and all things thrice as the flavours pound, pound and pound again. Lightly oiled bourbon notes of a red liquorice and mild hickory hue help fill out the petticoats and gown, all covering a thin vanilla body; **f21.5** content with idle vanilla and barley chatter; **b22** I used to do annual whisky tastings at Fortnum and Mason when this malt was just a twinkle in the distiller's eye. They did not have a house malt this good. They have called it "The Queen's Own Whisky." A charming, elegant, demure princess of a dram. *46%. nc ncf. Fortnum & Mason.*

⫶⫶⫶⫶ **Gordon & MacPhail Connoisseurs Choice Royal Brackla 1995 (88) n22** spotted dog pudding and stewed apple; **t22** silky malt and a riot of dark sugars; some evidence of a wide cut by the stillman; **f22** the extra oils inject spice and mocha to counter the vanilla; **b22** a softer, sweeter and more friendly Brackla than many on the market just now. This one works quite well, though technically not totally sound. *46%. Gordon & MacPhail.*

⫶⫶⫶⫶ **Old Malt Cask Royal Brackla Aged 12 Years (77) n20 t20 f18 b19.** The tang of an unhelpful cask spoils the party somewhat. *50%. nc ncf sc. Douglas Laing & Co. 250 bottles. In celebration of the Queen's Diamond Jubilee.*

Provenance Royal Brackla Over 11 Years refill hogshead, cask no. 6819, dist Autumn 99, bott Autumn 2010 **(84.5) n21 t21.5 f21 b21.** Reminds me of a wartime whisky: all the richer flavours seem strictly rationed. *46%. nc ncf sc. Douglas Laing & Co.*

Scotch Malt Whisky Society Cask 55.20 Aged 12 Years 2nd fill hogshead, cask no. 10656, dist 1998 **(89) n22 t23.5 f21.5 b22.** Had the finish carried on where the main body left off this would have been Royalty, indeed... *58.8%. sc. 202 bottles.*

ROYAL LOCHNAGAR
Highlands (Eastern), 1826. Diageo. Working.
Royal Lochnagar Aged 12 Years db **(84) n21 t22 f20 b21.** More care has been taken with this than some other bottlings from this wonderful distillery. But I still can't understand why it never quite manages to get out of third gear...or is the caramel on the finish the giveaway...? *40%*

Royal Lochnagar 1994 The Manager's Choice db **(89.5) n23** a lovely fruit cocktail containing guava and lychee amid the grapey orange; **t23.5** sensual delivery with the barley at first forming an oily base then a subtle layering of oak and light fruits; **f21.5** mallow and mocha...but the toffee drowns out the higher notes; **b21.5** much more intense and heavyweight than the norm. Also a bit of toffee on the finish brings down the marks slightly. Great stuff, even so. *59.3%*

Royal Lochnagar Selected Reserve db **(89) n23** superb oloroso, clean and spicy with apples and pears; **t23** stupendous spice lift-off which really starts showing the malts to great effect; **f21** the malts fade as the toffee progresses; **b22** quite brilliant sherry influence. The spices are a treat. *43%*

Old Malt Cask Lochnagar Aged 13 Years refill butt no. DL 6290, dist Jun 97, bott Jun 10 **(89) n22.5** perky barley of the most mouth-watering grassy variety...; **t23** ...and exactly the same again on delivery: there is even a big spice injection which is hardly the norm for a Lochnagar; **f21.5** the usual sma' still coppery tang; **b22** an excellent malt with which to check that your taste buds are alive and well... *50% Douglas Laing. 380 bottles.*

⫶⫶⫶⫶ **Old Malt Cask Royal Lochnagar Aged 14 Years** refill butt, cask no. 7595, dist Apr 97, bott Aug 11 **(89.5) n21.5** bizarrely, a vague new make element clings to the barley and citrus; **t23.5** a superb delivery with the grist melting on the palate in the sexiest way possible; like a young virgin falling into your arms and craving love...; **f23** there is the lightest of vanilla touches here, little more than a threat amid the persistent and almost perfectly sugared barley; **b21.5** how can a whisky spend 14 years in a cask, pick up virtually no colour and yet get a very healthy tick of approval from me. Answer: the oak, as well as not imparting too much positive, does nothing negative, either. So there are none of the bitter notes you often find at the tail end of a cask like this to spoil the experience. Just a gorgeously refreshing and bright malt, the like of which you will not find every day... *50%. nc ncf sc. 460 bottles.*

⫶⫶⫶⫶ **Provenance Royal Lochnagar Over 10 Years** refill hogshead, cask no. 7648, dist Winter 2001, bott Summer 2011 **(89.5) n22** fabulously vibrant. The oak has scarcely made an impact, leaving the barley to celebrate both a malty and juicily fruity edge; **t23** even more mouth-watering than you could hope for. Gristy in part, with the sugars dissolving on the palate. Some lovely lemon adds zip and zest. The has a small still feel, not surprisingly, and the copper really has a presence; **f22** mocha with a slice of lime; **b22.5** no wonder Prince Albert used to visit this distillery: this bottling looks like a Riesling! But one can certainly be amused on nose and taste... *46%. nc ncf sc. Douglas Laing & Co.*

Provenance Royal Lochnagar Over 12 Years refill butt, cask no. 6374, dist Summer 98, bott Summer 2010 **(91.5) n23** an intriguing aroma of honey, carrot juice and very distant cordite; **t23.5** what a cracking marriage between barley sugar and busy, ever-growing spice. That cordite nose translates perfectly but it is the overall clarity and yield in delivery which really makes the heart sing; **f22** a little oak bitterness, but the spices do their job; **b23** so often a hit or miss distillery, there is no doubting the sheer quality here. A must have bottling for this tiny and temperamental distillery. 46%. nc ncf sc. Douglas Laing & Co.

⬦ **Provenance Royal Lochnagar Over 12 Years** refill butt, cask no. 8187, dist Summer 1999, bott Winter 2012 **(91) n22** curious mix of honey and stewed, unsalted celery...; some old polished leather, too; **t23** a soufflé-light delivery of watered down acacia honey and an unusual march past of delicate Victoria sponge cake offering varying degrees of vanilla and custard....very different...and delicious! **f23** just more of the same, but with a long fade; **b23** an uncommonly good year for Lochnagar bottlings, and this is the best I have tasted so far. 46%. nc ncf sc. Douglas Laing & Co.

⬦ **The Whisky Broker Royal Lochnagar 9 Years Old Queen's Diamond Jubilee** hogshead, cask no. 644, dist 8 May 02, bott 26 Jan 12 **(90.9) n22.5** lightly stewed apple with delicate vanilla rather than cinnamon; **t22.5** fresh, salivating, crisp and then a fabulous slow motion explosion of intense barley and spice; lacks the normal coppery sharpness; the sugars are precise and a joy; **f23.5** long clean and uncluttered by anything other than even more concentrated barley and a gorgeous maple syrup and spice wind down: **b22** diamond coloured for the Queen Elizabeth's Diamond Jubilee. But it works for, despite the minimalist oak involvement, it never fails to charm. And for this whisky: we are amused. 55.5%. nc ncf sc. 353 bottles.

ST. MAGDALENE
Lowlands, 1798–1983. Diageo. Demolished.

Linlithgow 30 Years Old dist 1973 db **(70) n18 t18 f16 b18.** A brave but ultimately futile effort from a malt that is way past its sell-by date. 59.6%

Hart Brothers St. Magdalene Aged 28 Years dist Sep 82, bott Jan 11 **(91) n22** busy barley with some excellent polished furniture; malt in an antique shop; **t23** gristy barley, at first fresh and then bowing under the weight of big honey and maple syrup; so much oilier than I have seen from this distillery...; **f23** a swatch of vanillas, some enjoying a degree of spiciness; **b23** one of my sons lives next to the site where this distillery used to be: I shall ensure he gets a bottle of this. I never, for one moment, believed all those years back that this distillery was able to stand up to such age so easily. Life never ceases to amaze... 46%. sc.

⬦ **Mo Òr Collection Linlithgow 1982 28 Years Old** first fill bourbon hogshead, cask no. 2203, dist 5 Oct 82, bott 1 Nov 10 **(88) n21.5** a touch of plasticine, but an agreeable degree of fruit and barley, too; **t23** a gristy, juicy sweetness holds its ground and the spices follow in with impressive timing; **f21.5** fades and bitters slightly with minimal development beyond the oak; **b22** way better than I suspected it might be. The finish is thin, but all else is a treat. 46%. nc ncf sc. Release No. 7 The Whisky Talker. 900 bottles.

Old Malt Cask St Magdalene Aged 27 Years refill hogshead, cask no. 6478, dist Dec 82, bott Aug 10 **(92) n23** some black pepper seriously ups the ante. Lemon curd tart, whipped cream and barley sugar completes the attractive nose; **t23.5** beautifully weighted citrus works impressively with the juiciest barley imaginable; **f22.5** the black peppers on the nose were no illusion; **b23** when I used to talk to the guys at this long lost distillery, they told me they saw it as three- and five-year-old fodder for the blends. They would be quite astonished not just that this, like the 28-years-old below, made it this far, but was so damned good at the end of its unlikely journey. 50%. nc ncf sc. 264 bottles.

Old Malt Cask St Magdalene Aged 28 Years refill butt, cask no. 6810, dist Sep 82, bott Nov 10 **(94) n22.5** green olives dull the complexion of the buttery lemon barley; **t23.5** the vivid, mouth-watering barley is at odds with the nose; **f24** lightly oiled, delicately but positively spiced and ridiculously fresh for its age: memorable; **b24** another Lowland hero worthy of some kind of honour of achievement against the odds. This must have been stored in an exceptionally good cask. 50%. nc ncf sc. Douglas Laing & Co. 439 bottles.

⬦ **Old Malt Cask St Magdalene Aged 29 Years** refill butt, cask no. 7662, dist Oct 82, bott Oct 11 **(92) n22.5** busy and perfectly weighted nose even displaying a surprising – no, astonishing! - element of delicate smoke (and I mean no more than the odd atom or two here) to provide the anchor for the cleanest of vanilla-barley mixes; **t23.5** one of the softest deliveries of the year as the gristy malts melt juicily. This leaves a clear run for the lightest of spice and charming of milk chocolate mousses; **f23** vanilla and butterscotch, as one might imagine, but the spices return to lengthen matters to the max; **b23** unfortunately not a malt that turns up often these days. And this little essay in subtle complexity proved to be a great and very pleasant surprise. A go-grab no brainer! 50%. nc ncf sc. Douglas Laing & Co. 288 bottles.

SCAPA

Highlands (Island–Orkney), 1885. Chivas Brothers. Working.

Scapa 12 Years Old db **(88) n23** honeydew melon, soft salt and myriad styles of barley: really complex with a sprinkling of coal dust on the fruit; **t22** brilliant mouth arrival: the most complex display of malt and cocoa, the fruit is ripe figs with a thread of honey; **f21** a slight bitterness with some developing toffee, but the malt stays the distance; **b22** always a joy. 40%

Scapa 14 Years Old db **(88) n22** toasted oak, butterscotch and lime; **t22.5** fresh barley for its age, a few bands of light oak but some fruity notes towards the drying middle **f21.5** chalky but some toffee interferes with the usual sweeter finale; **b22** enormous variation from bottling to bottling. In Canada I have tasted one that I gave 94 to: but don't have notes or sample here. This one is a bit of dis-service due to the over-the-top caramel added which appears to douse the usual honeyed balance. Usually, this is one of the truly great malts of the Chivas empire and a classic islander. 40%

Scapa 16 Years Old db **(81) n21 t20.5 f19.5 b20.** For it to be so tamed and toothless is a crime against a truly great whisky which, handled correctly, would be easily among the finest the world has to offer. 40%

Scapa 'the' Orcadian 16 Years Old db **(87.5) n22** honey offering both density to the body yet a lightness of touch; distant smoke alongside a squeeze of satsuma and shake of salt; **t22** silky and gently spiced on delivery; a citrus and toffee follow through; a hint of honey lurks; **f21.5** the softness of touch persists though one is left waiting for the oak which seems unable to battle through the toffee-honey soup; **b22** a thin wisp of honey is key to the weight and balance of this malt. 40%. For the Swiss market.

Gordon & MacPhail Distillery Label Scapa 2000 (81.5) n21.5 t21 f19 b20. Very strange: Gordon and MacPhail have been bringing out magnificent bottlings of this malt for as long I can remember. Yet this vintage is, though apparently natural coloured and quite pleasant in its own way, not in the same league as previous incarnations. Perhaps a price is being paid for limited wood availability at the distillery during its stop-start days. Or perhaps an inconsistency in the distillate the open-closed policy of Allied was inevitably going to produce. This is a flat Scapa divest of the genius which set this distillery apart. But if anyone can get these bottlings back on track, I'm sure it will be G&M. 43%

Old Malt Cask Scapa Aged 17 Years refill hogshead, cask no. 6560, dist Oct 93, dist Oct 10 **(86.5) n21 t22 f21.5 b22.** A very even marriage between the sharp barley and the slightly briny, toffee oak. 50%. nc ncf sc. Douglas Laing & Co. 314 bottles.

Old Malt Cask Scapa Aged 17 Years refill hogsdhead, cask no. 6925, dist Oct 93, bott Feb 11 **(89) n22 t23 f22 b22.** Enjoyable whisky which would have scored even more highly in a better cask. 50%. nc ncf sc. 333 bottles.

Scotch Malt Whisky Society Cask 17.28 Aged 8 Years 2nd fill hogshead, cask no. 310, dist 2002 **(94.5) n23.5** a wonderful salt and honey tapestry; marvellously refreshing; **t24** quite magnificent. The delivery is another patchwork of honeys of varying intensity and sweetness but with the barley bobbling in and out at regular intervals; the salt and pepper background is sublime; **f23** long with the spices prevailing and the honeys melting into a butterscotch and caramel morass; **b24** worth becoming a member for a bottling like this one alone. Absolutely encapsulates the distillery at an age when it is at its most dynamic and in a cask type which is most sympathetic. An easily overlooked gem. 56.7%. sc. 253 bottles.

⁘ **Scotch Malt Whisky Society Cask 17.33 Aged 9 Years** refill barrel, cask no. 313, dist 2002 **(83.5) n22.5 t22 f19 b20.** Those bitter Allied casks can be heartbreakers. The big honeycomb lead had, until their intervention, been a treat. 57.7%. sc.

SPEYBURN

Speyside, 1897. Inver House Distillers. Working.

Speyburn 10 Year Old db **(82) n20 t21 f20.5 b20.5.** A tight, sharp dram with slightly more emphasis on the citric. A bit of toffee on the finale. 40%

Speyside 12 Years Old db **(85) n22 t22 f20.5 b21.5** Copious honey and malt on delivery. Simplistic, effective but a tad bitter on finish. 40%

Speyburn Aged 25 Years db **(92) n22 t24 f23 b23.** Either they have re-bottled very quickly or I got the diagnosis dreadfully wrong first time round. Previously I wasn't overly impressed; now I'm taken aback by its beauty. Some change. 46%

Speyburn Bradan Orach db **(76.5) n19 t20 f19.5 b18.** Fresh, young, but struggles to find a balance. 40%

⁘ **Provenance Speyburn Over 7 Years** sherry butt, cask no. 8498, dist Winter 2004, bott Spring 2012 **(74) n19 t19 f19 b17.** Had to check for a moment if I was tasting Speyside. The malt and oak are not on speaking terms and hard to find a less harmonious youngster. 46%. nc ncf sc. Douglas Laing & Co.

THE SPEYSIDE DISTILLERY
Speyside, 1990. Speyside Distillers. Working.

The Speyside 10 Years Old db **(81)** n19 t21 f20 b21. Plenty of sharp oranges around; the malt is towering and the bite is deep. A weighty Speysider with no shortage of mouth prickle. 40%

The Speyside Aged 12 Years db **(81)** n19 t22 f19.5 b20.5. Unusual to find feints to this degree after twelve years. Some short-lived honey...but it's hard work! 40% ⊙⊙

The Speyside Aged 15 Years db **(75)** n19 t20 f18 b18. A case of quantity of flavours over quality. 40%

Cú Dhub db **(88)** n22 leopards may not change their spots....but Black Dogs evidently do. Some serious toffee apple at play here helped along by a few zingy spices; t22.5 have to say: I like the delivery. As silky textured as you'll ever find, there is a malt surge doused in burnt fudge. The sugars are delicate and a little bit of a treat; f21.5 wins few prizes for subtlety with its big oily, toffeed finish. But, again, there is enough in the complexity, and late spices especially, to make for an entertaining dram; b22 not exactly a thoroughbred and you won't find it winning any prizes at Cruft's. But a malt which has improved beyond recognition in recent years and now even boasts a degree of enjoyable complexity. And you know something else...not a single sulphur note in sight... 40% ⊙⊙

Drumguish db **(87)** n18 t22 f19 b19. Historically, not one of my favourite drams. But I have to say that this has improved by a considerable degree. Still feinty, and the delivery is not promising. But once it settles, there is a very acceptable degree of honey-led complexity before the feints bite back. 40% ⊙⊙

⫶⫶⫶ **Mo Ór Collection Speyside 1994 16 Years Old** first fill bourbon hogshead, cask no. 34, dist 25 Apr 94, bott 2 Dec 10 **(85.5)** n19 t23 f22.5 b21. They have done well to select one of the better casks from this distillery for this period. Straighter than a Roman road, and perhaps a little broader from the oils. But beyond the barley and most simplistic oak there is little to engage the mind or taste buds. But of all the deliveries I have found in bottled form from this distillery, this ranks among the best. 46%. nc ncf sc. Release No. 45. 385 bottles.

⫶⫶⫶ **Old Malt Cask Speyside Aged 20 Years** sherry butt, cask no. 8472, dist May 92, bott May 12 **(81)** n21 t21 f19 b20. A real glassful of dates and walnuts. But the cut is simply too wide to get away with it comfortably. 50%. nc ncf sc. Douglas Laing & Co. 294 bottles.

⫶⫶⫶ **Scott's Selection Speyside 1993** bott 2011 **(89)** n21.5 maybe slightly feinty but, with the extra nutty oil it provides, easy to forgive; just dig that juicy date, too; t22 fat, oily and brimming with the most intense sugar-laden barley you'll find this year. Again, at times reverting to a date-like thickness of flesh; so juicy and chewy you want to give the bottle a little kiss...; f23 long, with the expected custardy vanillas arriving. But the Demerara sugars absolutely refuse to be cowered. The last tones are those of the kind of wafer cones you find for ice cream...minus the Mr Whippy..; b22.5 now there you go! We can start to re-write the history books regarding the quality of whisky from this distillery. For this is, though it be made up like an old tart you might find along an unlit canal path, uncommonly fine merchandise worthy of a knee trembler whatever your whisky persuasion, whatever your sex... 61.5%. Speyside Distillers.

SPRINGBANK
Campbeltown, 1828. J&A Mitchell & Co. Working.

⫶⫶⫶ **Hazelburn Aged 8 Years** bourbon cask, bott 2011 db **(94.5)** n23 green apple represents the more dashing aspect of the very young barley; t24 fabulously solid barley; intense and complete. The youth shimmers on the palate, the malt mixing contentedly with pleasing early butterscotch; elsewhere there is a real richness seemingly imparted from the stills themselves; f23.5 confirmation of an excellent cask in use here as the lightly spiced vanilla enjoys the odd strand of honey; more light metals breaking into the lengthy barley; b24 a very curious coppery sheen adds extra lustre and does no harm to a very well made spirit filled into top grade oak. For an eight year old malt, something extra special. 46%

Hazelburn Aged 8 Years 3rd Edition (triple distilled) bott 2007 db **(89)** n22 t22.5 f22 b22.5. Somewhat effete by comparison to last year's big malty number. Here there is a shade more accent on fruit. Very light, indeed. 46%

Longrow Aged 10 Years db **(78)** n19 t20 f19 b20. This has completely bemused me: bereft not only of the usual to-die-for smoke, its warts are exposed badly, as this is way too young. Sweet and malty, perhaps, and technically better than the marks I'm giving it – but this is Longrow, dammit! I am astonished. 46%

Longrow Aged 10 Years 100 Proof db **(86)** n20 t23 f22 b21. Still bizarrely smokeless – well, maybe a flicker of smoke as you may find the involuntary twitching of a leg of a dying fly – but the mouthfeel is much better here and although a bit too oily and dense for complexity to get going, a genuinely decent ride heading towards Hazelburn-esque barley intensity. Love it, because this oozes class. But where's the ruddy peat...?! 57%

⁃❀⁃ **Hazelburn Aged 12 Years** fresh sherrywood, bott 2012 db **(85.5) n22 t21 f21.5 b21.** At times nutty. At others, oily. And is that the vaguest hint of phenol I spot bouncing around at one stage...? But overall a malt which does not, at this juncture in its life, seem entirely at ease with either itself or the cask. Some lovely moments of lucidity but for the most part it's an interrupted work in progress. Still, this is the 666th new whisky I have tasted for the 2013 Bible, so it was likely to have a little bit of devil in it.. 46%

Longrow 14 Years Old refill bourbon and sherry casks db **(89) n24** you can count on complexity when it comes to the Longrow 14 nose. The smoke is delicate, always happy to give way to any fruity or oaky notes passing. A bit of a stunner; **t23.5** gorgeous texture on delivery, plus a hint of chocolate mint amid that half-hearted smoke. Burnt raisin fills the mid-ground, alongside some crunchy Demerara sugar; **f19** just a little furry; **b22.5** again, a sherry butt proves the Achilles heel. But until then, a charmer. 46% ☉ ☉

Longrow Aged 18 Years db **(94) n23.5 t23 f24 b23.5.** Tries to hide its light under a bushel... but fails. The most subtle and sophisticated Longrow I've come across in 20 years... 46%

Longrow CV bott 2012 **(91) n24** nippy spices infuse with the dry date; the smoke is delicate with an almost dry tobacco edge; the harder peat teams up with the gentle Demerara; **t24.5** soft and silky, again the fruit notes intermingle and add a banana and mango juiciness to the oils; the smoke again keeps a low profile, happy to accompany the more telling sugars; **f19.5** dries quickly as the furry bitterness from a sherry butt take hold; **b23** for a few moments this is heading onto the shortlist of potential Whisky Bible award winners, but a familiar furry rumble – a bit like the distant thunder currently heard from my tasting room – means vital points are lost. Even so, the nose and delivery are something very special, indeed. 46% ☉ ☉

Longrow Gaja Barola Wood Expression Aged 7 Years db **(91.5) n23.5 t22.5 f23 b22.5.** Taking this on is like running around an asylum claiming you're Napoleon. But I have to admit; it's fun! An accidental classic that is unlikely to be repeated...even if they tried..!! 55.8%

Springbank Society Aged 9 Years Rum Wood bott Mar 07 db **(93.5) n23 t23.5 f23 b24.** A mere pup by Springbank standards. For once its comes through as a real winner in these tender years, doubtless aided by the mercurial charms of the rum and even an unexpected touch of smoke to make for a most complex and entertaining dram. 60.2%

Springbank Aged 10 Years db **(89.5) n22** a surprising hint of peat ash; makes the lemon citrus carry a shade more weight; **t23** that usual Springbank trick at this age of showing oaky depth bouncing off the youthful malt; excellent oil and still a touch of smoke; **f22** thins out with a bitter-ish vanilla tang; **b22.5** although the inherent youthfulness of the 10-y-o has not changed, the depth of body around it has. Keeps the taste buds on full alert. 46% ☉ ☉

Springbank Aged 10 Years (100 Proof) db **(86) n21.5 t22 f21 b21.5.** Trying to map a Springbank demands all the skills required of a young 18th century British naval officer attempting to record the exact form and shape of a newly discovered land just after his sextant had fallen into the sea. There is no exact point on which you can fix...and so it is here. A shifting dram that never quite tastes the same twice, but one constant, sadly, is the bitterness towards the finale. Elsewhere, it's one hell of a journey...! 57%

Springbank 11 Years Old Madeira Wood Expression db **(88) n23 t22.5 f21.5 b21.** Madeira perhaps as you've never seen it before: don't go thinking Glenmorangie or Penderyn with this one. As big as the fruit is, the smoke outguns it. 55.8%

Springbank Aged 15 Years db **(88.5) n22.5** full of chunky, malty promise; **t22** big, oily barley spreads across the palate; dry, a little tart even with limited sweetness; **f22** more oil and huge natural oak caramel; **b22** last time I had one of these, sulphur spoiled the party. Not this time. But the combination of oil and caramel does detract from the complexity a little. 46% ☉ ☉

Springbank Aged 18 Years db **(90.5) n23** busy in the wonderful Springbank way; delicate greengage and date; nippy; **t23** yummy, mouthwatering barley and green banana. Fresh with excellent light acacia honey; **f21.5** fabulous oak layering, including chocolate. A little off-key furriness from a sherry butt late on; **b23** just one so-so butt away from bliss... 46% ☉ ☉

Springbank Vintage 1998 cask no. 08/263, bott Jun 09 db **(92) n24** strewth! You know how generations of Australian batsmen have chipped away single-mindedly at English bowlers for hours on end over the years...well you need that kind of dedication to get through the seemingly impregnable sherry here. When you do, you'll pick up some pretty amazing notes, perhaps the pick of the bunch being a glorious meeting of dried dates, Mysore coffee and molasses. And then you get to the grape itself, which helps form a Melton Hunt cake structure but with some pretty well cooked raisins...but there's plenty more to discover, so I don't see you declaring before the end of the second day on this one...; **t23** how roasty is that...? Grape in both fresh juicy form and more bitter, pleasantly burned. More bite than the 46% abv would have you think is capable of and soothing hickory fills the middle ground; **f22.5** long. Some molassed dregs keep the finish away from anything too bitter; **b22.5** when I started trying to unravel this one my beard was still black... 53.3% 612 bottles

Springbank 2000 cask no. 240, dist Oct 00, bott Apr 09 **(90) n23** a beautiful alloy of concentrated barley and thickish, condensed, oak and a much younger personality: barley still wet behind the ears and, though a little fruity, still waiting for its nuttiness to drop...; **t23.5** again we have a concentrated display with the barley topped by all kinds of molten sugars so the pulses are sweet, vibrant and often; yet another strata offers a degree of bourbon honeycomb and hickory and this is interwoven with a thinner, pre-pubescent barley. Elsewhere are chewy, burnt raisin notes...some mixture...; **f21.5** a little salty tang to this and a tad furry, too; **b22** not your average eight- or nine-year-old Springbank and certainly not your average malt. Tuck in: there's a little bit for everyone in this one...except smoke lovers! 48% Specially bottled for Lia and Koos den Boef Vlaardingen. 110 bottles.

Berry's Own Selection Springbank 1992 cask no. 61, bott 2011 **(88) n22 t23 f21.5 b21.5.** Not often a Springbank fades away. But this one does. 46%. nc ncf sc. Berry Bros & Rudd.

⬩⬩⬩ **Dà Mhìle Lost & Found Springbank Organic Aged 20 Years** cask no. 237, dist 1992, bott 2012 **(94) n23** when first launched as a seven-year-old in 2000 the nose displayed some ungainly feints from where they tried to stretch the unique single run as far they could. Here is proof that time deals with feints in no uncertain manner. And that the casks they filled the historic organic malt in was as good as they get: roast Blue Mountain blended with a medium Java sets the tone and even the mountainous liquorice and Demerara appear dwarfed by the coffee; **t23.5** ever sat down in the morning with the most sublime but heavy roast coffee, the finest natural molassed sugars and beautifully crafted bread baked that morning, freshly toasted and groaning under salted butter...? **f24** absolutely goes into overdrive: the sugars are extraordinary and difficult to translate as there is a criss-crossing of so many styles. Yet late barley juice filters through what appears to be hickory and liquorice. The spices kiss rather than strike. this is wonderful....entirely typical of a Springbank hitting its optimum age between 20 and 25 years. **b23.5** the sun is a circle; the world is a sphere; the greatest fun in existence involves round objects either being kicked or struck by willow. Life, however we look at it, no matter how we try to force to be otherwise, is circular. So how fitting that the very last Scotch whisky to arrive (behind the deadline time!) for this year's 2013 Whisky Bible happens to be the very first whisky I ever wrote about as a professional whisky writer, the first-ever organic malt distilled. It was carried out by award-winning cheese maker John Savage-Onstwedder, who hired Springbank distillery to carry out his dream. And it arrived as I celebrate my 20 years as the world's first full time whisky writer. What goes round, comes round...and here it is again.... re-released 20 years on. 57.3%. sc. J&A Mitchell for Dà Mhìle. 87 bottles.

Hart Brothers Springbank Aged 14 Years dist Nov 96, bott Jan 11 **(90.5) n23** any amount of honey..very limited fruit; **t22.5** again the delivery and middle is all about acacia honey and a little liquorice; some mild sultana; **f22** intense vanilla and custard tart; **b23** thick, almost glutinous barley wins the battle over the grape hands down. Great fun; superb quality 46% sc

Hart Brothers Springbank Aged 14 Years dist Nov 96, bott Jan 11 **(73) n19 t19 f17 b18.** I checked and was told that this was from the same cask as the Springbank 46% I don't know what to say, other than I didn't find any sulphur on that one... 55.2%. sc.

⬩⬩⬩ **Malts Of Scotland Springbank 1998** sherry hogshead, cask no. MoS12014, bott Apr 12 **(85.5) n21 t22 f21.5 b20.5.** Well, you can't say this is a shy dram. Indeed, it has much to say, especially on delivery. Then the barley out performs any input by the grape to a massive margin. But, as is so often the case with malts under 15 from this distillery, structure and format appears to have been lost in a sprawling free-for-all. The nose, tight and helped only by a shallow smokiness, is a good indication of what is to follow. 51.5%. nc ncf sc.

Scotch Malt Whisky Society Cask 27.84 Aged 12 Years refill barrel, cask no. 733, dist 1997 **(93) n23** distilled sea water? The cask has been kept in a sea shore cave? I have very rarely come across a whisky so vividly displaying such a maritime personality; **t23** mouth-watering then a succession of intense barley soup. But beautifully seasoned; **f23.5** after the barley soup comes the dessert of honey; **b23.5** one of the better 12-year-old Springbanks I have tasted in a while, the salty injection helping to break down those thick caramels. 58%. sc. 213 bottles.

Scotch Malt Whisky Society Cask 27.89 Aged 10 Years refill barrel, cask no. 122, dist 2000 **(86) n21 t22 f21.5 b21.5.** Enjoyable. But in so many ways indicative of why this distillery struggles at these relatively low ages to come close to its greatness of later years. A massive onslaught of natural caramels which are pleasant enough, but keeps any complexity in a straightjacket. The salty, sweaty armpit nose is worth discovering, though!! 55.9%. sc. 263 bottles.

⬩⬩⬩ **Scotch Malt Whisky Society Cask 27.93 Aged 11 Years** refill barrel, cask no. 128, dist 2000 **(84.5) n21 t22 f20.5 b21.** Some of the same tobacco characteristics as 27.95...and I see the casks are related: this is most probably from the same distillate. However, the cask here is nowhere near as accommodating. 51.5%. sc. Scotch Malt Whisky Society.

⬩⬩⬩ **Scotch Malt Whisky Society Cask 27.94 Aged 11 Years** first fill sherry hogshead, cask no. 87, dist 2000 **(78) n20.5 t19 f18.5 b19.** Not one to be added to this wonderful distillery's annals of greatness.... 54.6%. sc. Scotch Malt Whisky Society.

⚜ **Scotch Malt Whisky Society Cask 27.95 Aged 11 Years** refill hogshead, cask no. 168, dist 2000 **(90) n22** a little tobacco perhaps and the most distant phenols. Jumbled, fruity and darkly attractive in an off-beat way...; **t23.5** much more clarity on delivery. That tobacco note arrives early before we are treated to a party of busy spices; barley develops healthily and to full juice effect; **f22** a touch bitter, but the barley shines under some late salt; **b22.5** I have long stated that Springbank doesn't really get out of bed until it's about 18 years old. Here, the combination of lively barley and fruit are irresistible. *50.2%. sc. Scotch Malt Whisky Society.*

Scotch Malt Whisky Society Cask 126.2 Aged 10 Years (Hazelburn) refill barrel, cask no. 15, dist 2000 **(95) n23** salty bacon with grits; the sugars are light, the oaks perfectly mannered. A little prickle...this promises something special...; **t24.5** ...and it really doesn't let you down. One of the best deliveries of a 10-year-old malt I have tasted this year, helped by a controlled weight to die for. There are oils, but just enough to help spread the honeyed word; not enough to over-run all other character traits. Some salt sharpens the barley; a nibble of butterscotch hints of age it has not yet achieved; **f23.5** the faintest degree of cask bitterness, but it doesn't stand a chance against the continuing honey theme; **b24** the difference between a Springbank and Hazelburn at exactly the same age can be astonishing. Like this one. *54%. sc. 263 bottles.*

⚜ **Scotch Single Malt Circle Springbank 1996** cask no. 77, dist 10 Oct 96, bott 6 Jan 11 **(63) n16.5 t16.5 f14 b16.** Springbank is a distillery which I feel flies more naturally and elegantly than most other distilleries in the world. This one, though, has crash landed with its wheels up. Accident investigators will hardly know where to start... *53.7%. sc. Scotch Single Malt Circle.*

⚜ **Scotch Single Malt Circle Springbank 1997** cask no. 319, dist 4 Apr 97, bott 7 Jan 11 **(92.5) n23** you have to smile when you nose this: it is the aroma of a dank old warehouse in a glass! Incredibly salty, even slightly musty. Plenty of kumquat notes, too; **t23** a mildly puckering saline delivery is soon giving way to a fabulous build up of citrus and spice; if you find a middle better weighted than this, let me know...; **f23** the oaks take their usual place at the rear but there is also a wonderful, very vaguely metallic, sharpness to the end; **b23.5** as ever, a Springbank with much to say and in a unique voice. *55.1%. sc. Scotch Single Malt Circle.*

STRATHISLA
Speyside, 1786. Chivas Brothers. Working.

Strathisla 12 Years Old db **(87.5) n22.5** the smoke evident on the last few tastings of this has been largely usurped by a heavy fat-sultana grapiness. Back to its old heavyweight self of a few years back, except the malt-fruit balance is kinder to the nose and the merest whiff of smoke is still detectable; **t23.5** thick, sweet barley swamps the tastebuds early on but slowly nudged aside by the trademark sweet sultana; engaging chocolate honeycomb towards the middle; **f20** duller than before with some big caramels kicking in and the unmistakable furry signature of the odd dud sherry butt; **b21.5** still a big, chewy dram which is about as heavy in body as you are likely to find anywhere in Speyside. Very enjoyable, though you know deep down that some fine tuning could take this guy easily into the 90s. *43%*

Strathisla Distillery Edition 15 Years Old db **(94) n23** flawlessly clean and enriched by that silky intensity of fruity malt unique to this distillery; **t23** the malt is lush, sweet and every bit as intense as the nose; a touch of toffeespice does it no harm; **f24** just so long and lingering, again with the malt being of extraordinary enormity: these is simply wave upon wave of pure delight; **b24** what a belter! The distillery is beautiful enough to visit: to take away a bottle of this as well would just be too good to be true! *53.7%*

Gordon & MacPhail Strathisla 1963 1st fill sherry, bott 2011 **(84) n22 t22 f19.5 b20.5.** Like a marathon runner at the end of his endurance, staggers blindly across the finishing line. An exhausted malt, displaying enough salt for a heart attack. But the roasted raisins and burnt molasses still shows some impressive physique. *51.8%. For Limburg Whisky Fair.*

⚜ **Gordon & MacPhail Rare Vintage Strathisla 1969 (95.5) n24** fascinating to nose this beside the 1972 vintage. This has embraced the oak to the advantage of the sherry as the grape now has a slightly weightier partner it can show its more deft tones against; less fruitcake here though no shortage of cooked apples and pears seasoned with a little cinnamon; **t23.5** sublime delivery! Again the sherry has excellent body, enjoying a rich texture which makes the most of the light saltiness present, giving all the flavours present a sharper edge. Amazingly, the barley makes a very juicy appearance. Elsewhere, some hints of sherry trifle, as well as a sherry-chocolate mousse, complete with over-ripe banana-custard. But it is the weight of the Demerara sugars against the rich oaky vanillas which offer the most mesmerising battle; **f23.5** sugars remain calm, collected and comfortably in sync with any of the weightier oak notes which offer much more of a spicy, burnt honeycombed bourbon style than anything the fruit can produce; **b24.5** the kind of magical Speyside oldie which, among the independents, only Gordon and MacPhail can conjure. A true classic. *43%*

Gordon & MacPhail Rare Vintage Strathisla 1970 (77.5) n20 t22 f17 b18.5. Were I a gambling man I would wager that this whisky has been rounded off in a fresh sherry butt somewhere along the line to take out any oaky creases. I may be wrong, of course... 43%

⁘ **Gordon & MacPhail Rare Vintage Strathisla 1972** (88) n23 major fruitcake statement (with old Demerara rum added, not whisky!), with the emphasis on the molassed and toasted glazed cherries and overly burned raisin; t22 much softer body than the nose promises. The sherry shows virtually no backbone. But the initially thin flavours build into something which dominate all else; f22 some vague hint of chocolate raisin. But they've gone heavy on the raisin; b21 a real heavyweight sherry butt. But one that bullies rather than coerces. 43%

Hart Brothers Strathisla Aged 13 Years dist Jun 97, bott Jan 11 (85) n21.5 t21.5 f21 b21. A pretty true to form Strathisla heavyweight with the butterscotch-barley ruling the roost over the lighter citrus. Just a little oak laziness dulls the fun. 46%. sc.

⁘ **Hart Brothers Strathisla Aged 14 Years** cask no. 78924, dist 19 Jun 97, bott 15 Apr 12 (89.5) n22 clean malt with a dash of semi-spiced oak bourbon style; t22 juicy, grassy barley enjoying a good oily body; a hint of Brazil nut oil; f23 now the spices cascade; chocolate arrives late, presumably to go with the Brazils; b22.5 benefits hugely from having matured in very good oak. Has "Speyside" tattooed all over it. But this is adorable stuff. 46%. sc.

Malts Of Scotland Strathisla 1970 sherry hogshead, bott Mar 11 (95) n24.5 the raisins are burned, but not to a crisp, the figs are ripe, but not to exploding point while bourbon oak is present with thick liquorice but not without the balancing honeycomb. For a 40-year-old malt, it really doesn't get much better than this...; t23.5 the alcoholic bite does no harm whatsoever in accentuating the grip of the fruit, its wonderfully integrated depth and yet the ease in which the oak and even strands of barley are brought on board. Light oils help coat the mouth with this complex soup of a dram and even a touch of salt helps bring the flavours to the boil; f23 dries in the manner oloroso should. Keeps closer to the wine style than the delivery and absorbs the mocha oakiness with ease; b24 an absolutely faultless oloroso butt weaves a wonderfully rich tapestry. In many ways a malt by which others of its ilk should be judged. 59.6%. sc.

⁙ **Old Malt Cask Strathisla Aged 16 Years** (85) n21.5 t21.5 f21 b21. A rolling, undulating experience with the barley and spices filling the contours of the palate. A little off key oak flattens things a little. 50%. nc ncf sc. Douglas Laing & Co.

Provenance Strathisla Over 10 Years refill hogshead, cask no. 6301, dist Winter 99, bott Summer 10 (72) n18 t18 f18 b18. Starts off kilter and never corrects itself. 46%. nc ncf sc.

⁘ **Provenance Strathisla Over 12 Years** refill hogshead, cask no. 7658, dist Summer 1999, bott Summer 2011 (81.5) n21 t20.5 f20 b20. A malty Plain Jane. 46%. nc ncf sc. Douglas Laing & Co.

⁘ **Scott's Selection Strathisla 1989** bott 2011 (94) n22 carrot juice with hickory and spice; t24.5 a classic of its kind; the delivery is shimmering with deep oaky spices yet for all the enormity of the obviously top quality cask the barley has its own agenda and comes through vividly; the mid ground settles towards a walnut oil and lightly molassed sweetness: fabulous!; f23 long, soft oils spreading every atom of sweetness as far as they will stretch; b23.5 just shows what this distillery can do when untethered... a sheer delight! 56.5%. Speyside Distillers.

STRATHMILL
Speyside, 1891. Diageo. Working.

⁘ **A.D. Rattray Strathmill 1989** puncheon, cask no. 10310, dist 13 Oct 89, bott Jun 12 (94) n22.5 sparkling barley: a gorgeous mix of grist and golden syrup; t24.5 yes...!! Shows exactly why I regard the output from Strathmill as one of the most malty spirits in Scotland: grassy, juicy, clean and almost too salivating. Yet the star turn is the middle where the spices kick in to counter the pulsing acacia honey...fabulous! f23 not a bitter element to this: the oak acts like a gent and offers untainted butterscotch, though it can hardly be seen for the continuing sweet barley chorus; b24 one of the tastiest Puncheons I have seen since Jason scored a hat-trick for Millwall against Crystal Palace a couple of Christmases back....! 58.6%. sc. A.D. Rattray Ltd.

⁘ **Archives Strathmill 1974 37 Years Old Inaugural Release** bourbon hogshead, cask no. 1231, dist Jun 74, bott Jun 11 (85) n22 t21.5 f21 b21.5. The years have not damaged this dram, but the degree of natural caramels and tannins means that meaningful complexity is out of the question. 44.5%. nc ncf sc. Whiskybase B.V. 180 bottles.

⁘ **James MacArthur Old Masters Strathmill 21 Years Old** cask no. 101112, dist 1990, bott Feb 12 (96.5) n24 fantastically complex: how do you get so many varying sweet notes to work so well together without the nose heavily laden becoming like a candy store? Have fun spotting the differing shades of sweetness, but you should be able to spot the light rum notes, the touch of Irn Bru, the heavy rum notes and the Lubec marzipan complete with cocoa; t24 those rum notes on the nose translate into a light, coppery sheen. Then a plethora of playful spices mingle with the honeycomb....; f23.5 dulls a little as the vanillas take charge. Still enough sugar to go round, though; b24 the old J&B blender Jim Milne always had a special place in his heart for this distillery. Here you can see exactly why. 54.1%. nc ncf sc.

⁖ **Old Malt Cask Strathmill Aged 35 Years** refill hogshead, cask no. 7817, dist Apr 76, bott Feb 12 **(93) n23.5** the erstwhile J&B blender and my very dear friend Jim Milne used to take me to this distillery often and he would guide me through the casks at varying ages, explaining just why he adored its malty charisma. Jim would be purring at this one if he was still with us...and he would especially enjoy the most subtle of citrus counter weights; **t23** again the malt is of the cleanest and most intense style. It has taken on a little oak, but only enough to offer just the right degree of gravitas; **f23.5** maybe a touch of salt now to the tannin, but that lingering malt really does take your breath away...; **b23** hang on to your hats: this is one of the most deliciously malty rides in town...! 47.2%. nc ncf sc. 176 bottles.

Old Malt Cask Strathmill Aged 36 Years refill hogshead, cask no. 7186, dist May 75, bott May 11 **(91) n22.5** lavender and orchid. Powerful, but not overpowering; **t23** sweet, with a build up first of gristy barley and then richer, darker sugars; some spices play ball but vanilla hits the middle earlier than expected; **f23** anyone who spends time in Brazil will appreciate this: the most perfect biscoito de polvilho; **b22.5** I know this distillery's greatest ever advocate saw it as a provider of mainly youngish to mid-range malts. It is one of the great mysteries, as well as one of my profound regrets, that it is not found at ten to a dozen years old. In the meantime, this fabulous bottling shall have to suffice. 44.1%. nc ncf sc. 367 bottles.

TALISKER
Highlands (Island–Skye), 1832. Diageo. Working.
Talisker Aged 10 Years db **(93) n23** Cumberland sausage and kipper side by side; **t23** early wisps of smoke that develop into something a little spicier; lively barley that feels a little oak-dried but sweetens out wonderfully; **f24** still not at full throttle with the signature ka-boom spice, but never less than enlivening. Some wonderful chocolate adds to the smoke; **b23** the deadening caramel that had crept into recent bottlings of the 10-y-o has retreated, and although that extraordinary, that wholly unique finale has still to be re-found in its unblemished, explosive entirety, this is much, much closer to the mark and a quite stupendous malt to be enjoyed at any time. But at night especially. 45.8%

Talisker 12 Years Old Friends of the Classic Malts db **(86) n22 t21.5 f21 b21.5.** Decent, sweet, lightly smoked...but the explosion which made this distillery unique - the old kerpow! - appears kaput. 45.8%

Talisker Aged 14 Years The Distillers Edition Jerez Amoroso cask, dist 1993, bott 2007 db **(90.5) n23 t23 f22 b22.5.** Certainly on the nose, one of the more old-fashioned peppery Taliskers I've come across for a while. Still I mourn the loss of the nuclear effect it once had, but the sheer quality of this compensates. 45.8%

Talisker Aged 20 Years db **(95) n24 t24 f23 b24.** I have been tasting Talisker for 28 years. This is the best bottling ever. Miss this and your life will be incomplete. 62%

⁖ **Talisker 25 Years Old** db **(88) n22.5** a sweeter nose than normal despite the raging oaks; the first from this distillery with Fisherman's Friend qualities..; **t22** the oak pounds in from all directions, this time giving the sugars less room to manoeuvre than on the nose; **f21.5** very distant spiced smoke. But just a little jaded after 25 years of whisky maturation. Mind you, I know how it feels... **b22** pretty taken aback by this one: it has taken a fancy to being a bit of a Bowmore, complete with a bountiful supply of Fisherman's Friends. 45.8%

Talisker 25 Year Old bott 2008 db **(92) n23** lazy smoke drifts over a scene of light citrus and slowly forming ancient oaks; **t23.5** soft vanillas arrive first, then a wave of muted peppers stinging only playfully as the sweet barley unfolds just so charmingly; **f22.5** the oaks really are revving up, but the sweet barley provides the balance; peat and citrus provide an unlikely fade; **b23** busy and creaking but a glass or two of this offers some classy entertainment for the evening. 54.2%

Talisker 25 Years Old db **(88.5) n23** fragile and frugal: the peat leads, but does so tamely. All other elements are likewise shy but with the exotic fruit and treacle just about audible; **t22** sweet delivery with a muscovado-charged cream toffee dominating. Slowly, apologetically the spices begin to emerge; **f21.5** tame toffee and vanilla; **b22** another Talisker almost choked with natural caramels. Chewy and undoubtedly charming. 54.8%

Talisker 25 Years Old db **(92) n23.5 t24 f22.5 b22.5.** Fabulous stuff, even though the finish in particular is strangely well behaved. 58.1%

⁖ **Talisker 30 Years Old** db **(93.5) n23** complex and slightly bitty, lemon-lightened phenols, sitting comfortably atop a pile of buttery egg custard tart. A lot sexier than it sounds...! **t24** the citrus leads the way here, too. It helps intensify the juiciness of the barley, though a countering liquorice and crunchy Demerara sugar sweetness amplifies the age. The smoke is restrained though not beyond offering a spice throb; **f23** just a few shuddering oaky passes, but the smoke, sugar, spice and even a little salted butter ensure the fade is long and satisfying; **b23.5** much fresher and more infinitely entertaining than the 25 year old...!!! 45.8%

Talisker 30 Year Old bott 2008 db **(89) n21** very tired oak; **t23.5** who would have believed it...? The delivery shows no woody failings whatsoever, but silky-soft barley, with a touch of toffee, and a slow-motion deployment of half-hearted smoke: just the right degree of sweetness and chewiness; **f22** remains soft with the toffee-vanilla dominant; **b22.5** this malt seriously defies the nose, which gives every indication of a whisky about to peg it. The softness of the experience is memorable. *49%*

Talisker 30 Years Old db **(84.5) n21 t21.5 f21 b21.** Toffee-rich and pretty one dimensional. Did I ever expect to say that about a Talisker at 30...? *53.1%*

Talisker Special Release 2010 30 Years Old refill American & European oak db **(93) n23** shards of honeycomb pierce the thin cloud of smoke; some bristling spice suggests daddy may be home; **t24** superb delivery: an explosion of rabid spices tear at the taste buds, though some astonishingly refined honey does its best to hold it back; there is a melt-in-the-mouth barley sub plot and the natural caramels one comes to expect from this guy; a late burst of garibaldi biscuit rounds things off efficiently; **f23** relatively docile by comparison and perhaps over dependent on the caramel. But at least the spice keeps buzzing...; **b23** a Talisker with some snap, grunt and attitude. *57.3%. nc ncf. Diageo. Fewer than 3000 bottles.*

Talisker 57 Degrees North db **(95) n24** salty, smoky, coastal, breezy. The distillery's location in a nose... **t24.5** peat encased in a muscovado sugar, in the same way a fly might be enveloped in amber, melts to allow the slow blossoming of a quite beautiful and peaty thing...; **f23** some welcome whip and bite; the smoke and vanillas hang in there and even the odd hint of mocha puffs around a bit; **b23.5** a glowing tribute, I hope, for a glowing whisky... *57%*

Old Malt Cask Talisker 10 Years Old refill hogshead, cask no. 7409, dist Jun 01, bott. Jun 11 **(88) n22 t22 f22 b22.** One of the biggest whisky double takes I have ever made...almost of James Finlayson proportions...Very little discernable peat and arrives only at the finish. Well made, though, and from a pretty decent cask. *50%. nc ncf sc. Douglas Laing & Co. 245 bottles.*

TAMDHU
Speyside, 1897. Ian Macleod Distillers. Mothballed.

Tamdhu db **(84.5) n20 t22.5 f21 b21.** So-so nose, but there is no disputing the fabulous, stylistic honey on delivery. The silkiest Speyside delivery of them all. *40%*

Tamdhu Aged 18 Years bott code L0602G L12 20/08 db **(74.5) n19 t19 f18 b18.5.** Bitterly disappointing. Literally. *43%*

Tamdhu 25 Years Old db **(88) n22** citrus showing now a more orangey based style to the lemon of its youth; **t22** typically fat and intense; the barley eventually escapes the gravitational pull of the oils to offer a barley sweetness, **f21** dried dates vanilla; **b23** radiates quality. *43%*

Chieftain's Tamdhu Aged 16 Years fino sherry butt, dist Mar 94, bott 2011 **(89) n22 t23 f22 b22.** An excellent butt, but the barley fails to make too many waves. Even so, you won't go wrong with this clever wee dram. *46%. nc ncf. Ian Macleod Distillers.*

⚬⚬ **Gordon & MacPhail Cask Strength Tamdhu 2001 (75) n19 t19 f17 b18.** Sweet and fruity but slightly off key. *58%. Gordon & MacPhail.*

Liquid Sun Tamdhu 1990 sherry butt, bott 2011 **(73) n18 t20 f17 b18.** A bit of a tragedy, this. Despite the obvious faults with the butt, the degree of honey and raisin on delivery point to a paradise lost. *48.1%. The Whisky Agency.*

The MacPhail's Collection Tamdhu 1971 (88) n23 t22 f21.5 b21.5. A curious malt, with the palate never quite living up to the promise of the nose. But the fact it has survived intact at all is a miracle. *43%*

Malts Of Scotland Tamdhu 1990 sherry butt, cask no. 8119, dist May 90, bott Mar 11 **(93) n23.5** dates, walnut, toffee and all the other things you demand from a top-notch sherry butt. Only spice is missing...; **t24** but it doesn't take long to arrive on delivery and does much to pep up the blood orange and pithy attack; plenty of mocha filling the middle; **f22.5** the spices and molasses survive to the delicious death; **b23** fabulous sherry butts at Tamdhu are hardly two-a-penny. Savour this rarity. *49.8%. sc. Malts Of Scotland.*

⚬⚬ **Mo Ór Collection Tamdhu 1987 23 Years Old** first fill Oloroso sherry butt, dist 3649, dist 2 Jul 87, bott 2 Dec 10 **(64) n16 t17 f15 b16.** The problem with first fill sherry butts (especially from this distillery) in 1987 is that they were likely to be riddled with sulphur. And this is, believe me. *46%. nc ncf sc. Release No. 17. The Whisky Talker. 656 bottles.*

Old Malt Cask Tamdhu Aged 13 Years wine finished barrel, cask no. 6906, dist Sep 97, bott Jan 11 **(64) n16 t17 f15 b16.** When they say "wine Finished", they really aren't joking... *50%. nc ncf sc. Douglas Laing & Co. 354 bottles.*

Old Malt Cask Tamdhu Aged 21 Years sherry hogshead, cask no. 6956, dist Dec 89, bott Mar 11 **(95) n24.5** you know when you visit an ancient castle and you spot the two-feet thick walls? Well, this has that kind of substance: something from before our time where you know the people responsible knew what they were doing... almost a lost craft. The grape isn't quite impenetrable... it is pierced by a beam mildly acidic sugar. And molasses...; **t24** how many layers of grape? I lost count at six. Each with a varying degree of either fruit, such as juicy, over-ripe greengage or a pulpier, more bitter note... and molasses; **f23** long, layered with the drier, chalky oak tones acting as the cement to the grapey brick. The lasting sweetness is supplied by... the molasses **b23.5** I don't do price: I have no idea what a bottle of this goes for. But, whatever it may be, rip their arms off... *50%. nc ncf sc. Douglas Laing & Co. 154 bottles.*

⋇ **Provenance Tamdhu Over 12 Years** refill hogshead, cask no. 7657, dist Winter 1998, bott Summer 2011 **(84) n21.5 t21.5 f20 b21.** Hard to imagine more single-mindedly gristy blending fodder if you tried...; *46%. nc ncf sc. Douglas Laing & Co.*

⋇ **Provenance Tamdhu Over 12 Years** refill hogshead, cask no. 8166, dist Spring 1999, bott Winter 2012 **(78.5) n19 t21.5 f18.5 b19.5.** I expect the cask holding this underdeveloped malty whisky to turn up at Garden Centre near you soon... *46%. nc ncf sc. Douglas Laing & Co.*

⋇ **Riegger's Selection Tamdhu 1988** bourbon cask, cask no. 417, dist 28 Jan 88, bott 8 Mar 12 **(91.5) n23.5** superb zesty and very moist Lubek marzipan; a fair bit of salt around, too; **t23.5** magnificent spice attack quickly followed by rich honeycomb; the middle thickens with soft oils and lilting lime, coconut and maple syrup sweetness; **f22** thins out a little too fast towards vanilla; **b22.5** reminds me of a heated debate I had with a blender who told me that he thought Tamdhu was a second rate malt and avoided it when possible. I told him I thought he was mistaken: in ex-bourbon it could prove quite bold and had much going for it. He admitted all his limited stock was in sherry, so I certainly understood his point of view. He refused to believe me: wish I had a bottle of this with me at the time! *57.2%. nc ncf sc. 199 bottles.*

⋇ **Scott's Selection Tamdhu 1984** bott 2011 **(88.5) n22** buy a box of mini fruit tart pies, sniff the green one and compare... **t23** lush malt exclusively concentrates on the barley theme at first before switching its attention to a more salty, eye-watering aspect; spices creep up to excellent effect; **f21.5** bitters out a bit too much; **b22** this distillery has often been accused of making sub-standard malt. Poppycock! Nothing wrong with the distillate here, however, a better cask would have made this something to really remember... *49.6%. Speyside Distillers.*

Whisky Doris Tamdhu 25 Years Old refill hogshead, cask no. 2834, dist Oct 84, bott Jul 10 **(83.5) n20 t21 f21.5 b21.** If you are into uncompromising barley, and very tight oak, then this bottle has your name on it. Especially if your name is Doris. *50.1%. Whisky Doris.*

TAMNAVULIN
Speyside. 1966. Whyte and Mackay. Working.

Tamnavulin 1966 Aged 35 Years cream sherry butt db **(91) n24 t22 f23 b22.** For those who love great old sherry, this is an absolute. Perhaps too much sherry to ever make it a true great, but there is no denying such quality. *52.6%*

Gordon & MacPhail Connoisseurs Choice Tamnavulin 1991 (76) n19 t20 f18 b19. Massively malty but just a little tart in the areas which matter most. *43%*

Old Malt Cask Tamnavulin Aged 21 Years refill hogshead, cask no. 7502, dist Oct 89, bott Jul 11 **(88) n22.5 t22.5 f21 b22.** By no means standard fare: at first appears considerably older than its age, then more youthful due to the big oil slick... *50%. nc ncf sc. 206 bottles.*

⋇ **Old Malt Cask Tamnavulin Aged 25 Years** refill butt, cask no. 8432, dist Dec 86, bott Apr 12 **(82.5) n20 t22 f19.5 b21.** If you taste this blind I doubt if any more than five per cent of you would recognise this as a 25 year old malt: I certainly wouldn't. As youthful and juicily gristy as a malt a third of that age, this is the Cliff Richard of Speyside. Amazing what 25 years in a third filled cask at the bottom of warehouse can do...or not! *50%. nc ncf sc. 302 bottles.*

⋇ **Riegger's Selection Tamnavulin 1993** bourbon cask, cask no. 1013, dist 24 Mar 93, bott 24 Mar 11 **(86) n21.5 t22 f21.5 b21.** A bit of a sloppy cask means there is an underlying edge. But the salivation factor of the barley rockets through the roof; the spices are a treat. Love the little hint of mint tagging onto the cocoa, too. *56.9%. nc ncf sc. Viktor-Riegger GmbH. 176 bottles.*

The Whisky Agency Tamnavulin 1967 bott 2010 **(86.5) n22 t22 f21 b21.5.** Plenty of surprisingly youthful, almost zesty charm which, initially, defies the years. But the passing summers – and oak – catch up with it in the end. *41%. The Whisky Agency.*

TEANINICH
Highlands (Northern), 1817. Diageo. Working.

Berry's Own Selection Teaninich 1973 (83.5) n22 t22 t21 f20 b20.5. Even accounting for the strength, thinner than you might expect with the timid malt entirely subservient to the oak. Some lovely leathery-honey notes here and there, though. *41.8%. Berry Bros & Rudd.*

⋇ **Boisdale Teaninich 1973** cask no. 6066, bott 2012 **(85) n22 t21 f21 b21.** The strength of this malt gives some idea of what time has done to this malt. Massively oaky, though there is enough molasses and spice to see it into the next world. *40.1%. nc ncf sc.*

Chieftain's Teaninich Aged 28 Years hogshead, dist Dec 82, bott 2011 **(85) n21 t22 f21.5 b21.5.** A serious oaky infusion boasts enough sugar and salt to make for a complex, if rather over-aged, meal of a dram. Plenty to enjoy for a final nightcap, though. *46.8%. nc ncf.*

⊹ **Dun Bheagan Teaninich Aged 28 Years** hogshead, dist Dec 82, bott Nov 11 (94.5) n23.5 fabulous nip to the barley despite its good age and an enticing interplay between the vaguest of phenol notes and a tannin-fuelled saltiness; the sweetness is catered for by a complex intermingling of maple syrup and thin molasses; t24 those sugars are first at the scene when it comes to delivery though we have excellent barley and vanilla strata as the oak takes a foothold; the spices are only half cocked but the glazed cherry on the sponge cake is adorable; f23 long, with the molasses taking over from the maple and the vanillas glowing beside the barley; not a single hint of bitterness...superb!; b24 I have never shared some blenders' dismal view of this distillery. Here is a vivid example as to why. *51.8%. nc ncf sc. Ian Macleod Distillers.*

⊹ **John Milroy Selection Teaninich 1982** cask no. 7714, bott 2012 (87.5) n22 malty ice cream wafer cones; t21.5 the spice fair pings off the solid barley. Virtually no yield until a little oil arrives carrying sugar; f22 the oils ensure a chewy vanilla finale; b21.5 if the water for this whisky ran over granite, then a lot of granite came with it. *45.4%. nc ncf sc. Berry Bros & Rudd.*

⊹ **Mo Òr Collection Teaninich 1983 27 Years Old** first fill bourbon hogshead, cask no. 7660, dist 29 Nov 83, bott 8 Feb 11 (92.5) n23 lively barley with a fine salt and honey edge; t24 sweet, palate-cleansing, ever-sweetening barley. The spices are sublime: almost faultless for its type; f22 settles down to a contented vanilla-rich and lightly spiced finale; b23.5 a charming, clean, nubile malt displaying a quite vivid Speyside style: a fine example of how regions mean nothing at all. *46%. nc ncf sc. Release No. 26. The Whisky Talker. 391 bottles.*

Old Malt Cask Teaninich Aged 27 Years refill hogshead, cask no. 6454, dist Dec 82, bott Aug 10 (80) n21 t20 f19 b20. Still standing, maltilly, after all these years. Just. *50%. nc ncf sc. Douglas Laing & Co. 239 bottles.*

Scotch Malt Whisky Society Cask 59.40 Aged 27 Years 2nd fill hogshead, cask no. 6758, dist 1983 (86.5) n22 t22 f21 b21.5. Sweet, malty and lusty, this doesn't want for personality. A shade on the hot side, though. *55%. sc. 186 bottles.*

⊹ **Wemyss 1982 Single Highland "Winter Spice"** hogshead, bott 2011 (87.5) n21.5 spiced suet; diced uncooked green vegetables, t22.5 heavy duty malt: really thick and would be quite dull were it not for the effervescence of the spices; f21.5 the inevitable vanilla cannot shake off the peppers; b22 so weighty and plodding your tongue aches! *44.4%. sc. 201 bottles.*

TOBERMORY
Highlands (Island–Mull), 1795. Burn Stewart Distillers. Working.

Ledaig 10 Years Old db (85) n21.5 t22 f20 b21.5. Some gorgeous and beautifully weighted peat at play here, showcased in full glory on the nose and delivery. Has to paper over some cracks towards the finish, though. *46.3%*

Ledaig Aged 10 Years db (85.5) n20 t22.5 f21.5 b21.5. Almost a Bowmore in disguise, such are its distinctive cough sweet qualities. Massive peat: easily one of the highest phenol Ledaigs of all time. But, as usual, a slight hiccup on the technical front. Hard work not to enjoy it, though. *46.3%. nc ncf.*

Ledaig Aged 10 Years db (63) n14 t17 f15 b17. What the hell is going on? Butyric and peat in a ghoulish harmony on nose and palate that is not for the squeamish. *43%*

Ledaig Aged 12 Years db (90) n23 serious farmyard aromas – and as someone who spent three years living on one, believe me...borderline butyric, but somehow gets away with it, or at least turns it to an advantage; t23.5 the staggering peat on the nose is no less remarkable here: chunky, clunking, entirely lacking poise and posture. And it obviously doesn't give a damn...; f21.5 strange gin-type juniper amid the smoke; b22 it has ever been known that there is the finest of lines between genius and madness. A side-by-side comparison of the Ledaig 10 and 12 will probably be one of whisky's best examples of this of all time... *43%*

Tobermory Aged 10 Years db (67.5) n16 t17 f17.5 b17. A less than brilliantly made malt totally bereft of character or charm. I have no idea what has happened here. I must investigate. Frankly, I'm gutted. *40%*

Tobermory 10 Years Old db (73.5) n17.5 t19 f18 b19. The last time I tasted an official Tobermory 10 for the Bible, I was aghast with what I found. And didn't taste again for the remainder of the day, I remember. So I prodded this sample I had before me of the new 46.3% version with all the confidence Wile E Coyote might have with a failed stick of Acme dynamite. No explosions in the glass or on my palate to report. And though this is still a long way short, and I'm talking light years here, of the technical excellence of the old days, the uncomplicated sweet maltiness has a very basic charm. The nose and finish, though, are still very hard going. *46.3%*

Tobermory Aged 10 Years db (85) n20 t22.5 f21 b21.5 Bracing, nutty and malty the oils perhaps overdo it a little but there are enough sugars on hand to steer this one home for an enjoyable experience overall. *46.3%. nc ncf.*

Tobermory Aged 15 Years db (93) n23.5 dripping with fresh, clean, ultra high quality oloroso there remains enough tangy malt to underscore the island location; t23.5 a fabulous marriage of juicy grape and thick, uncompromising malt. It is an arm wrestle for supremacy between the two...but it is the delicate spices which win; **f23** salty chocolate raisin; **b23** a tang to the oils on both nose and finish suggests an over widened middle. But such is the quality of the sherry butts and the intensity of the salt-stained malt, all is forgiven. *46.3%. nc ncf.*

Tobermory Aged 15 Years Limited Edition db **(72.5) n17 t18 f19 b18.5.** Another poorly made whisky: the nose and delivery tells you all you need to know. *46.3%*

⁘ **Archives Ledaig 2004 7 Years Old First Release** cask no. 900009, dist 4 Oct 04, bott 5 Jan 12 **(94) n23.5** exceptionally clean with a limited coastal feel; a beautiful hickory sweetness to the peat; **t24** outstanding delivery with uncanny balance between the sugars, the peat and oak **f22.5** thins a little, though the smoke doesn't; **b24** a whisky entirely at one with itself. *61.9%. nc ncf sc. Whiskybase B.V. 302 bottles.*

⁘ **Gordon & MacPhail Private Collection Ledaig 1993** St Joseph wood finish **(70) n18 t19 f16 b17.** I assume St Joseph is the patron saint of sulphur. *45%*

⁘ **Hart Brothers Tobermory Aged 17 Years** cask no. 987, dist 22 Apr 95, bott 30 Apr 12 **(76.5) n20.5 t19 f18 b19.** Ungainly, though some might enjoy the sweet, nutty nose. *46%. sc.*

⁘ **Kingsbury "The Selection" Ledaig 9 Years Old** hogshead, cask no. 900129 & 800130, dist Oct 01, bott Apr 11 **(87.5) n22.5** gristy smoky bacon...with the emphasis on the grist; **t22** more grist; less smoke than on the nose; **f22** vanilla with the vaguest hint of smoke; **b21.5** one of the sweetest peaty malts you'll find. *43%. nc ncf sc. Japan Import Systems. 805 bottles.*

Malts Of Scotland Ledaig 1997 bourbon hogshead, cask no. 800029, dist Mar 97, bott Oct 10 **(79) n18.5 t23 f18 b19.5.** Usually I am an advocate of bourbon cask over sherry butt any day. But here is a prime example of where it allows the faults created in the distilling process full cry, where it would have been swamped and overcome by a massive sherry, such as the '98 bottling. Even so, the delivery is a beguiling treat. *60.3%. nc ncf sc. 303 bottles.*

Malts Of Scotland Ledaig 1998 sherry butt, cask no. 800025, dist Apr 98, bott Sep 10 **(95.5) n23** no sulphur, no (negative) feints...nothing to do other than bathe in the glow of outstanding oloroso, a praline peatiness and brawny brininess... **t24.5** mesmerising complexity on delivery and the first 20 or 30 flavours which crash into the taste buds. Lively, surprisingly youngish, smoky, salty...yet loads of Demerara and oils to counter anything the drier oloroso and saline notes might throw down... **f23.5** long, with the Demerara and spices dancing together long into the night... **b24.5** it has been many a year since encountering a Ledaig of such magnificence. I am blown away... *61.8%. nc ncf sc. 256 bottles.*

⁘ **Malts Of Scotland Ledaig 1998** sherry butt, cask no. MoS11010, dist Apr 98, bott Aug 11 **(76) n18 t21 f18 b19.** For a brief moment on the palate I thought this one was going to get away with it: the grape had actually fought its way through to show a juicy clarity and it actually chimed pleasantly with the peat. But that was brief and tantalising. The remainder of the story is one of World War Three on the palate. *61.2%. nc ncf sc. Malts Of Scotland.*

⁘ **Mo Òr Collection Tobermory 1995 16 Years Old** first fill bourbon hogshead, cask no. 1646, dist 8 Nov 95, bott 2 Dec 10 **(91) n22** a lovely, lilting edge of lemon curd tart on the barley; **t23** richly textured with some early spices which become quite boisterous later on. The barley remains thick and true; **f23** a light touch of cocoa as the spices and growing sugars engage; **b23** one of the better bottlings – official or otherwise – to have made it out of this distillery for quite a while. *46%. nc ncf sc. Release No. 46. The Whisky Talker. 480 bottles.*

⁘ **Mo Òr Collection Ledaig 1994 16 Years Old** first fill bourbon hogshead, cask no. 228066, dist 5 May 94, bott 24 Jan 11 **(93.5) n23** a few miserly phenols add weight to the more flighty salt and barley sugar; **t23.5** salivating from the off with the emphasis of the barley and spices; there is something like a lemon sherbet zing to the middle; **f23.5** thins out though the vaguely smoked chocolate mint is a pretty novel experience; **b23.5** if you are expecting to be blown away with peat like a Ledaig of old, this will disappoint. This almost has all the classic signs of a peated malt where the husk has been removed. That said, well weighted and complex. Very different and never less than delicious. *46%. nc ncf sc. 330 bottles.*

⁘ **Old Malt Cask Tobermory Aged 15 Years** refill hogshead, cask no. 7933, dist Apr 96, bott Dec 11 **(75) n17 t20 f19 b19.** Weighty whisky. But, alas, singularly unattractive. *50%. nc ncf sc. Douglas Laing & Co. 289 bottles.*

Robert Graham's Dancing Stag Tobermory 1996 hogshead, dist 16 Apr 96, bott Sep 10 **(76) n18 t20 f19 b19.** After tasting five stupendous whiskies in a row the sequence comes to a shuddering halt. The barley here is big and intense and the sugars are impressive. But something in its overall makeup just sits all wrong. *46%. nc ncf sc. 258 bottles.*

Robert Graham's Treasured Selection Tobermory 1996 hogshead **(78) n18 t21 f20 b19.** The treasure chest is not quite empty, but don't expect to find gold, either. The sugars and oils add bearable intensity and lustre. *59.5%. nc ncf sc. Robert Graham. 100 bottles.*

⁘ **The Whisky Agency Ledaig 7 Years Old** dist 2005 **(73) n18.5 t19 f17.5 b18.** Clumsily made malt. Having tasted it beside the 2004 Archive edition, a lesson in good and bad distillation. *52.1%. sc.*

Wilson & Morgan Barrel Selection Tobermory 1995 refill sherry, bott 2011 **(85)** n19 t22.5 f22 b21.5. Strikingly firm for a Tobermory with a light coating of grape softening some of the harder edges. Love the delicate sweetness. *46%. Wilson & Morgan.*

TOMATIN
Speyside, 1897. Takara, Shuzo and Okura & Co. Working.

Tomatin 12 Years Old db **(85.5)** n21 t21.5 f22 b21. Reverted back to a delicately sherried style, or at least shows signs of a touch of fruit, as opposed to the single-minded maltfest it had recently been. So, nudge or two closer to the 18-y-o as a style and shows nothing other than good grace and no shortage of barley, either. *40%*

Tomatin Aged 15 Years ex bourbon cask, bott 2010 db **(86)** n21 t22 f21.5 b21.5. One of the most malty drams on the market today. Perhaps suffers a little from the 43% strength as some of the lesser oak notes get a slightly disruptive foothold. But the intense, juicy barley trademark remains clear and delicious. *43% Tomatin Distillery*

❖ **Tomatin 15 Years Old** bourbon barrels and Spanish Tempranillo wine casks db **(88.5)** n22 the odd rogue note here but it is as if the acacia honey and marmalade are doing all they can to smother them. Red liquorice and barley lend a hand to the good guys; **t23** exceptionally rounded with the malt coming through with that uniquely Tomatin intensity. Jaffa cake orange and cocoa join the ripe figs and muscovado sugars in the middle ground; **f21** dips slightly as the off note detected on the nose resurfaces with a dry austerity Again the sweeter elements come rushing like white blood cells; **b22.5** not free from the odd problem with the Spanish wine casks but gets away with it as the overall complexity and enjoyment levels are high. *52%*

Tomatin Aged 18 Years db **(85)** n22 t21 f21 b21. I have always held a torch for this distillery and it is good to see some of the official older stuff being released. This one has some serious zing to it, leaving your tastebuds to pucker up - especially as the oak hits. *40%*

Tomatin 18 Years Old db **(88)** n22.5 a real clean sherry statement; **t22** a bit of a finoesque kick to this, then the oily malts grab the fruit and slowly assimilate it into a fruity maltshake **f21.5** unbelievably gentle and demure; **b22** what a well-mannered malt. As though it grew up in a loving, caring family and behaves itself impeccably from first nose to last whimpering finale; *43%*

Tomatin Aged 18 Years sherry finish, bott 2010 db **(92.5)** n22.5 busy, thick milkshake maltiness with a touch of fruitcake; **t23.5** cream sherry: creamy + sweet barley + fruity = cream sherry...; **f23** very long with a touch of controlled spicy fizz to the proceedings. But that indomitable barley signature sings to the end; **b23.5** finished in quite superior sherry butts. A malt brimming with character and quality What a treat! *46%. ncf. Tomatin Distillery.*

Tomatin Aged 21 Years created using 6 refill American oak casks and the 7th an ex sherry butt, bott 2009 db **(81)** n22 t22.5 f18.5 b19 A clattering, chattering, cluttering malt never once getting into rhythm to tell a coherent story. The sherry-pitched nose is jumbled but attractive; the delivery is at first rampant and entertaining but the middle and finale fall away, with the odd negative note at the death. A good one to pour your friends while they are blindfolded: this will confuse them. *52% Tomatin Distillery. 2400 bottles.*

Tomatin 25 Years Old db **(89)** n22 the trademark Tomatin 25 citrus nose – plus perhaps a dash of exotic fruit - proudly attacks and teases... **t23** but we have a different lad on the palate: starts gently with the citric, mouth-watering maltiness but where once it famously vanished for a while, now a regiment of spices go on the attack; soft oils ensure a rich presentation; **f21.5** a becalmed finale with the malt having found its voice again; **b22.5** not a nasty bone in its body: understated but significant. *43%*

Tomatin 30 Years Old db **(91)** n22 if there was a hint of the exotics in the 25-y-o, it's here, five years on, by the barrel load. Evidence of grape, but the malt won't be outdone, either; **t23** silky and sultry, there is every suggestion that the oak is thinking of going too far. Yet such is the purity and intensity of the malt, damage has been repaired and/or prevented and even at this age one can only salivate as the soft oils kick in; **f23.5** probably my favourite part of the experience because the sheer deliciousness of the chocolaty finale is awesome; **b22.5** malts of this age rarely maintain such a level of viscosity. Soft oils can often be damaging to a whisky, because they often refuse to allow character to flourish. Yet here we have a whisky that has come to terms with its age with great grace. And no little class. *49.3%*

Tomatin 30 Year Old European & American oak casks db **(85.5)** n21 t21 f22.5 b21. Unusually for an ancient malt, the whisky becomes more comfortable as it wears its aged shoes. The delivery is just a bit too enthusiastic on the oaky front, but the natural caramels soften the journey rather delightfully. *46%. ncf.*

Tomatin 40 Years Old db **(89.5)** n21.5 a few oaky yawns because this old guy's feeling a bit tired; **t22** for all the oak intrusion, for all the burntish honeycomb, for all the old aged spices coming through, for all the first-rate impression of a high-class old bourbon, somehow, eventually, it's the malt which really catches the eye; **f23** still oily after all these years and though the oak tries to get a bit tough, it doesn't stand a chance: the sweet malt, and those oils see to that; **b23** not quite sure how it's done it, but somehow it has made it through all those oaky scares to make for one very impressive 40-y-o!! Often it shows the character of a bourbon on a Zimmer. *42.9%*

Tomatin 1973 refill American oak cask, cask no. 25602 db **(85) n21.5 t21 f21.5 b21** Like an heroic old soldier, mortally wounded, struggling yet determined to complete its mission, this ancient malt defies the odds to make a thoroughly enjoyable experience. Yes, it pegs out in the end, the victim of a thousand too many oaky arrows to the heart. But the juicy, lightly honeycombed big-barleyed battle it rages is worthy of a medal. *44%. ncf sc. 184 bottles.*

Tomatin 1982 refill sherry puncheon, cask no. 92 db **(95) n24** deft spices, grape, oak and assorted sugars in proportions one usually only dreams about; **t24** top marks for the mouth feel and delivery alone. The clarity of grape and spice confirm in the first nanosecond exactly what the nose tells you: no sulphur. And so uncluttered or ruined it carries on imperiously with the spices piling into the molasses and fruit caked bowels; **f23** plum pudding with a superb sugary crust and, finally, some barley join the spices and burgeoning vanilla; **b24** this whisky is something to be savoured. In fact, of its type from this distillery it is peerless. *57%. ncf sc.*

Tomatin 1997 1st fill bourbon, bott 2009 db **(93.5) n23.5 t24 f23 b23.** Another outlandishly beautiful malt from this underrated distillery. Had they mixed in a few second fill casks into this, the complexity would have been fearsome and the stuff of legend. *57.1%. 244 bottles.*

Tomatin 1999 refill American oak, Tempranillo finish, bott 2009 **(92) n22 t23.5 f23 b23.5.** Looking for something different? Give this a whirl around the palate. Fabulous. *57.1%. 302 bottles.*

Tomatin Decades European & American oak casks db **(91) n23** floral and earthy yet equally fruity and vivid: as if nosing in a greenhouse.. **t23** big malt but the strands of toffee become chewier as the oaky theme develops; light, vaguely peaty, spices open out on an increasingly vanilla landscape; **f22.5** big age as the oak, in curiously diverse forms, take control. Just love the sugars of the cream toffee; **b22.5** an intriguing onion of a malt, of which the layers can, with concentration, be stripped away. The light smoke does its job immaculately. A malt for those with an hour to spare... *46%. ncf. Marriage of 1967, 1976, 1984, 1990 and peated 2005 Tomatins.*

⁂ **Berry's Own Selection Tomatin 1991** cask no. 51, bott 2012 **(90.5) n22** strangely breakfast cereal-like in style: some major Malt Shreddies at work here...; **t23** Tomatin, like Glen Moray, is among the malty elite. The mind-blowing intensity here underlines the fact.... wow!!! **f23** not just malty, but some sublime sugars enrich it and fill out the finish... **b22.5** plants the Tomatin flag proudly at the summit of Mount Malt... *54.8%. nc ncf sc.*

Chieftain's Tomatin Aged 13 Years German oak finish, dist Apr 97, bott 2011 **(88) n22 t22 f22.5 b21.5.** Less about balance, more about dramatic effect. A whole bunch of sugary moves you rarely see. *50.2%. nc ncf. Ian Macleod Distillers.*

⁂ **The Clan Denny Tomatin 44 Years Old** dist 1967 **(67.5) n15 t20.5 f15 b17.** A malt which renders me speechless – for all the wrong reasons. Please tell me this was put into a new sherry butt for "freshening" before bottling. Or, rather, please don't... *51.9%. sc. The Whisky Agency joint bottling with Douglas Laing for Limburg Whisky Fair.*

⁂ **Gordon & MacPhail Connoisseurs Choice Tomatin 1989 (91) n23.5** sweet barley concentrate; lovely citrus and the most delicate liquorice weaves in and out of the malty anthem; **t23** here we go again: the nose transferred to the palate, except a little dustier in part in the middle section; **f22** bitters very slightly, but almost like a blood orange amid the barley-vanilla theme; **b22.5** a just about spot on representation of exactly how I would describe the style demographic for this distillery at that age. *43%. Gordon & MacPhail.*

Liquid Sun Tomatin 1976 sherry butt, bott 11 **(82.5) n21 t21 f19.5 b21.** Some of the sherry butt notes you might expect. And a few bitter ones you might not. *48.7%. The Whisky Agency.*

⁂ **Malts Of Scotland Tomatin 1966** sherry butt, cask no. MoS11021, bott Nov 11 **(94) n24** hard to imagine grape could be quite so thick after all this time: spiced up like warm spotted dog; the smell from your lover's bedroom of toast burning in the kitchen: salty, sweaty and just a little acrid...; **t23.5** and while previously on the subject of dogs...a bit of an early dog fight between oak and grape, though it is the lovely lemon curd/chocolate hazelnut spread mix which takes the lead; **f23** pulsing spices rise above the deeper oaks while the late burnt grape skids in on the oils; **b23.5** a miraculous dram with the delicate sugars keeping their heads when it could have been so easy to get lost in an oaky forest. *46.1%. nc ncf sc.*

⁂ **Mo Ór Collection Tomatin 1976 34 Years Old** first fill sherry butt, cask no. 4, dist 31 Dec 76, bott 7 Feb 11 **(95.5) n24** a touch of blackcurrant to the dates and walnut. Over-ripe greengages are added to the Melton Hunt Cake; **t24** the silkiest of deliveries and each of the first seven or eight flavour waves allows grape, both sweet and of a drier crushed pip variety, to lap upon the taste buds; **f23.5** the fruit meanders a long way down the path towards the finish, but as the spices pick up, so does a minty chocolate theme; the weight remains impressive and even; **b24** an exemplary sherry butt of a type seldom found today. A magnificent malt, indisputably classic old stuff. *46%. nc ncf sc. Release No 14. The Whisky Talker. 954 bottles.*

⚜ **Old Malt Cask Tomatin Aged 21 Years** refill hogshead, cask no. 7967, dist May 90, bott Dec 11 **(87) n21.5** a rare example of a 21-y-o malt still showing some new make character: young, fresh, malty clean and lively...; **t22** all kinds of brittle malty sugars crack against the palate as the vanilla takes its time to arrive; even a puff of smoke is detectable; **f22** at last a degree of age as the oak wells and thickens; **b21.5** a 21-year-old whisky going on 21 months. A third fill cask for sure, though of high quality. A few blenders would have killed for this cask...! *50%. nc ncf sc. Douglas Laing & Co. 340 bottles.*

Old Malt Cask Tomatin Aged 40 Years refill hogshead, cask no. 7273, dist Dec 70, bott May 11 **(93) n23** this type of aroma, wallowing in its exotic fruitiness, comes only with a light malt reaching antiquity; **t23.5** luxurious and very comfortable in its fruity skin. The barley is still sound and welcomes the high quality vanillas with equanimity; **f23** the faintest degree of smoke attaches itself to the elegant vanilla fade: very old school; **b23.5** beautiful. Almost a blueprint for a fine old Speyside-style malt. *44.3%. nc ncf sc. Douglas Laing & Co. 168 bottles.*

⚜ **The Perfect Dram Tomatin 34 Years Old** sherry cask, dist 1976, bott 2011 **(95) n24** mmmmm! Just get those sherry trifle meets Melton Hunt Cake notes: fruity, subtly spiced, yet light, playful and complex: a real rarity for its vintage; it's the sultanas though that will blow you away... **t24** this distillery is one of the maltiest in the world and the barley plays its part in interweaving with the heavier oaky notes. But those spices: Where do they come from? Obviously the oak, and possibly partially from the sherry. But they never, for a moment try to dominate and sugars have an easy time of lightening the middle ground which becomes ridiculously juicy with the fresh barley; **f23** the vanillas and liquorice arrive, but the spices pound their merry beat to the last; **b24** any whisky calling itself "The perfect Dram" is setting itself up for a proverbial punch on the kisser and a spectacular fall from grace. However, knowing the distillery, knowing the year and knowing the type of cask, you really could not ask for much more than this. A dram which should take a year to empty. it is for those special, quiet moments only. It is, quite simply, glorious. *51.9%. sc. The Whisky Agency.*

Rare Auld Tomatin 33 Years Old dist 1976, cask no. 6822 **(91) n23** the oak attempts to bludgeon you. But a wonderful sugar-fruit density swings both towards a liquorice-bourbon theme and a grapey-apple freshness; the spice is spot on; **t22.5** mouth-watering barley and sugared fruit and then a massive surge of oaky mocha and blood orange; **f23** calms down so the sugars work a magic spells on the milk chocolate oak; **b22.5** this excellent whisky may be aged 33 years...but it seems considerably older. *51%. sc. Duncan Taylor & Co.*

Scott's Selection Tomatin 1988 bott 2011 **(88) n22 t22.5 f21.5 b22.** One of those really lovely, if non-spectacular, whiskies offering so many key elements to a good dram, you really can't say no to another glass... *50.6%. Speyside Distillers.*

⚜ **Scott's Selection Tomatin 1993** bott 2012 **(86) n21.5 t22.5 f20.5 b21.5.** Intense barley. But where did all that toffee come from? Delicious, but a bit of a mystery. *56%*

⚜ **The Warehouse Collection Tomatin Aged 19 Years** bourbon hogshead, cask no. 16364, dist 24 Sep 90, bott 19 Feb 10 **(90.5) n23** crush some honeycomb candy in your hand, and you get this. Though I doubt you get the dry banana and barley as well; **t23** either this cask has been sitting by the sea somewhere or every last bit of salt in the cask has been extracted. The result is a heightened flavour profile for the balancing manuka honey; **f22** a touch of praline softens the big oaky fade; **b22.5** another summer and that oak would have crossed the border. A fabulous whisky...in the nick of time *57.3%. sc. Whisky Warehouse No. 8. 174 bottles.*

⚜ **The Warehouse Collection Tomatin Aged 28 Years** refill sherry butt, cask no. 29, dist 12 Jan 82, bott 23 Feb 10 **(85) n23 t21 f20 b21.** A shame. A very clean sherry butt with not a single blemish. But the involvement of the oak has turned this into hard work, especially if you have a problem with searing spices. *55.3%. sc. Whisky Warehouse No. 8. 574 bottles.*

The Whisky Agency Tomatin 1966 sherry butt, bott 2011 **(94) n23** at first the aroma seems a touch claustrophobic, but let the air get to this one and the juiciness of the grape is unveiled before your very nose...; **t24** outstanding delivery with a touch of noble rot to the first wave or two, followed by a more traditional degree of fruitcake and then even a degree of oak-puckered barley; the subtle spices do a fabulous job; **f23.5** the big oak at first looks threatening but high quality vanilla sprinkled with sugars ensure a balanced finale; **b23.5** a textbook oldie but with all the twists and turns of a novel... *46.1%. The Whisky Agency.*

The Whisky Agency Tomatin 1976 bott 2010 **(85.5) n22 t22 f20.5 b21.** Plenty of grey whiskers but a charming display of herb on the nose and spice on the palate does the trick. *51.1%*

TOMINTOUL
Speyside, 1965. Angus Dundee. Working.

Tomintoul Aged 10 Years db **(79) n19 t21 f20 b19.** The caramel is less bossy than before but, for all its sharpness and decent oak finale, still doesn't quite click. *40%*

⸭ **Tomintoul Aged 12 Years Oloroso Sherry Cask Finish** db (73.5) n18.5 t19 f18 b18. Tomintoul, with good reason, styles itself as "The Gentle Dram" and you'll hear no argument from me about that one. However, the sherry influence here offers a rough ride. 40%

Tomintoul Aged 12 Years Portwood Finish db (85) n21.5 t22.5 f20 b21. Plenty of tangerines on the nose and a marmalade on burnt toast finish. But the star quality is in the delivery which shows superb early lushness to the malt. 46%. nc ncf.

Tomintoul Aged 14 Years db (95) n24 curiously, there is a sea-weed saltiness attached to this one: not exactly what you expect to find from a malt made and (I think) matured in the centre of the Scottish Highlands. But it adds a compellingly attractive - if eyebrow raising – element to this delicately framed and gently structured, lightly honeyed malt fest. The oak splendidly keeps within the spirit of the style; t24 just how many variations on a honeyed theme can you get? Here I count at least five, each wave coming in after the other with just the odd nip and tuck or expansion of its intensity; the very faintest smoke is detectable and just when the natural caramels appear to be getting too excited, the malt re-establishes itself; f23 medium length, but sheer quality all the way: Bird's custard mixing dreamily with drier, playfully spiced, oaky vanillas. The lightest of oils spreads the grassy, sharper malts to ensure a wonderful lightness of touch; b24 not a single weakness: no bitterness, no off notes, no caramels other than those naturally from the oak, no sulphur. Just magnificent whisky bottled exactly the way it is meant to be. An absolute corker from this little-known but outstanding distillery and one of the most delicately complex distillery bottlings of the year. 46%

Tomintoul Aged 16 Years db (94.5) n24.5 a fruity concoction of apples and pears topped with vanilla ice cream; even the vaguest hint of something smoky...one of the noses of the year; t23.5 every bit as gentle as the label promises, as the light oils coat the palate with a fabulously intense and delicately sweetened barley skin. The skeleton is playful oak; f23 a wonderful, multi-layered interplay between malt and oak-vanillas. Long, curiously spice-free, increasingly dry but hugely sophisticated; b23.5 confirms Tomintoul's ability to dice with greatness. 40%

Tomintoul Aged 21 Years db (93.5) n24 has all the hallmarks of a malt which contains casks a lot older than the stated age: the fruit is of the exotic variety and the manner in which those fruit and defter floral notes effortlessly intertwine confirms not just the magnificence of quality but also familiarity between oak and malt; t24 silky and soft with the balance of the light sugars to barley almost perfect; the vanillas grow, as they should, but the freshness to the barley never diminishes; f22 slightly on the furry side but now the vanillas dance and light spices begin to arrive; b23.5 just how good this whisky would have been at cask strength or even at 46 absolutely terrifies me... 40%

Tomintoul Aged 27 Years db (87) n22 t22.5 21.5 b21. The last time I saw a colour like this was on antique expert David Dickinson's face. Still, lots of charm and character to go round... and on the whisky, too. 40%

Tomintoul Aged 33 Years bott 2009 (90.5) n21 not promising. A little touch of resin, even drying creosote...; some incongruous orange blossom lightens the load; t23.5 improbably juicy delivery. Whisky marmalade and figs melt in with the sweetened vanilla and intense barley; f23 long with barley-thickened molasses. A hint of kumquat at the death; b23 didn't see that coming; thought it was almost dead in the bottle on nosing. A Lazarus of a malt. 43%

Tomintoul With A Peaty Tang db (94) n23 t24 f23 b24. A bit more than a tang, believe me! Faultlessly clean distillate that revels in its unaccustomed peaty role. The age is confusing and appears mixed, with both young and older traits being evident. 40%

⸭ **Archives Tomintoul 1969 42 Years Old Third Release** bourbon cask, cask no. 4266, dist Jun 69, bott Mar 12 (88.5) n22 oaky seeds are sown: has more in common with Kentucky than Keith; t22 big oak but the barley still has enough life to keep control; f22 quiet and happy to snooze in a vanilla-caramel stupa; b22.5 looks like crashing fatally into the oak, but the integrity of the barley performs miracles. Charming. 42.4%. nc ncf sc. Whiskybase B.V. 60 bottles.

⸭ **Liquid Sun Tomintoul Peated 11 Years Old** dist 2001 (86) n22 t21.5 f21 b21.5. A straightforward malt: peaty, clean, a touch of citrus but a shade too sweet for great complexity. 476%. sc. The Whisky Agency.

⸭ **Liquid Sun Tomintoul 43 Years Old** dist 1969 (88.5) n21 aggressive oak; t22 the delivery is none-too promising as splinters of oak are driven into the tongue. But the barley and liquorice notes regroup to find some sugar from somewhere, inevitably molasses; light oils and caramels form to make a softer middle than once seemed possible; f23 mmm! Hard not to love that late citrus which sits with the chocolate very comfortably; b22.5 ever been to a tennis match where the old guy is a set down in a Gland Slam final and being played off the court before switching on the brilliance to storm back to victory....? 476%. The Whisky Agency.

Liquid Sun Tomintoul 1967 bourbon hogshead, bott 2011 (83.5) n21 t22 f20 b20.5 This one would have been magnificent had it been bottled maybe eight or nine years ago. But it still shows the well-worn contours of its greatness and tries its best to see off the encroaching oak with a few defiant rays of honey. 49.8%. The Whisky Agency.

⁘ **Malts Of Scotland Tomintoul 1967** bourbon hogshead, cask no. MoS11023, bott Nov 11 **(86) n22.5 t20.5 f22 b21.** The oak is just a little too dominant. Even so, this is one very complex old beast with some excellent sugars helping to ensure a degree of balance against the marauding salt. *47.5%. nc ncf sc. Malts Of Scotland.*

⁘ **Malts Of Scotland Tomintoul 1967** rum barrel, cask no. MoS12020, bott Mar 12 **(83.5) n22 t21 f20 b20.5.** I would need Dr Frankenstein, not a rum cask, to inject life back into this guy. Some pleasant sugars, but a little cough syrupy in part. *51.3% nc ncf sc.*

⁘ **Malts Of Scotland Tomintoul 2001** bourbon hogshead, cask no. MoS12010, dist 25 Jun 01, bott Jan 12 **(84) n23 t21 f19 b21.** The peat is full on - and quite beautiful on the nose - the barley is rock hard and the barrel is not great, hence the bitter finish. *53.9%. nc ncf sc.*

⁘ **Mo Ór Collection Tomintoul 1967 43 Years Old** first fill bourbon hogshead, cask no. 4691, dist 19 Jun 67, bott 2 Dec 10 **(95) n23.5** from the marmalade on burnt toast school though with a side dollop of lime jelly; **t24** sublime delivery. The oak is right up there, but unlike some others from this distillery it doesn't dominate at any given moment. Instead, it gently persuades the marmalade and sugars to fall into file and then mix gently. The result is a silky, malt driven treat with very well-mannered spices; **f23.5** delicate golden syrup absorbs the vanillas like treacly suspension. No bitterness, no eye-watering oakiness. Just a gorgeous, relaxed fade; **b24** improbably good! *46%. nc ncf sc. Release No. 24. The Whisky Talker. 215 bottles.*

⁘ **Old Malt Cask Tomintoul Aged 40 Years** refill hogshead, cask no. 8007, dist Mar 71, bott Jan 12 **(94) n23** as much exotic fruit as could be wished for. A lovely bourbony red liquorice tang represents the oak with aplomb, perhaps with a hint of creosote; the laziest of light phenols hang in the air; **t24** ridiculously fragile: the barley is waif-like, the vanillas gentle and planting a row of delicate kisses rather than a big smacker on the chops...; **f23.5** long, despite the fragility of the flavours. Against the odds, the sugars seem to gather rather than diminish; **b23.5** majestic and magnificent. *45.6%. nc ncf sc. Douglas Laing & Co. 142 bottles.*

⁘ **Old Malt Cask Tomintoul Aged 40 Years** refill barrel, cask no. 7731, dist Apr 71, bott Sep 11 **(87.5) n21** lemon zesty barley...only a sprinkling of saline vanilla hints at the age; **t23** mouth-watering and fresh, the barley has the juiciness of a malt a fraction of the 40 given years; **f22** tightens rather too quickly as the oak takes command; **b21.5** for a whisky of such antiquity, the story is surprisingly one-dimensional and barley bound... though always enjoyable. *46.8%. nc ncf sc. Douglas Laing & Co. 209 bottles.*

⁘ **Scott's Selection Tomintoul 1989** bott 2011 **(84.5) n21 t22 f20.5 b21.** Exceptionally malty. Wonderfully well sugared. But this is a malt whisky over 21–years-old...it has to move on from there... *53.2%. Speyside Distillers.*

⁘ **The Whisky Agency Tomintoul 1968** bott 2011 **(94.5) n23.5** no doubting the age, but the lack of aggression or bitterness from the oak is unusual. Some slightly overcooked fruit, which almost suggests an old sherry butt, but I suspect this is bourbon thanks to the peaches and apricots; **t23.5** more oak evidence on delivery than nose, but the slow meandering among the dates and assorted brown sugars, Demerara especially, ensures the balance is never compromised; **f23.5** just like the butterscotch tart I had at school in Surrey, except here some late barley gathers and intensifies to mix with the watered down ulmo honey; **b24** you dangerously exotic little thing, you! Defies the years to entice and finally seduce. Let it sit in the glass for 15 minutes before tackling. *43.2%. nc ncf sc. The Whisky Agency.*

⁘ **The Whisky Agency Tomintoul 1969** bott 2011 **(88) n21** no-one at home: dull; **t22.5** the oak shows a few early knots but soft, sweetened mocha soothes the way; a light citrus tang offers much needed complexity; **f22** soft, bereft of great depth, but content in its sugary vanilla fade; **b22.5** makes up for the nothing nose with an electrifying display of delicate sugars and juicy citrus. Although it doesn't ramp up quite the complexity you might hope for a malt this age , its gentle nature is very attractive. *53.1%. nc ncf sc. The Whisky Agency.*

⁘ **The Whisky Agency Tomintoul 1972** bott 2011 **(95) n24** a degree of exotic fruit, except much more sophisticated than that; a drizzle of peat blends beautifully with the mocha. All is understated and with the soft caresses almost as erotic; **t24** the barley is remarkably agile and salivating, though soon thin strands of manuka honey and honeycomb are attaching themselves to a cocoa backbone; the subtlety of sweetness astonishes while the texture makes you purr; **f23** yet more cocoa, getting milkier by the minute: a wonderful finale of Brazilian biscuit; **b24** I have had the good fortune over a great many years to meet quite a few veteran actresses who somehow retained a beauty that the passing of time could not tarnish. This immaculate whisky reminds me of them. *45.7%. nc ncf sc.*

⁘ **The Whisky Agency Tomintoul Peated 2001** bott 2011 **(85) n21.5 t22.5 f20 b21.** A lightly peated, slightly creamy dram which is done few favours by a tired cask which adds little to the table except a late bitterness. The delicate gristy smokiness is a delight, however. *49.7%. nc ncf sc. The Whisky Agency.*

The Whisky Castle Tomintoul Aged 21 Years refill bourbon hogshead, cask no. 6544, dist 1989, bott 2010 **(91.5) n22.5** ridiculously lively barley for its years: crisp, juicily fresh and owning

Scottish Malts

a very unusual Sauternes-sweet quality – especially unusual as this is from bourbon...; **t23.5** oh...I just love it! Again crisp, but well mannered enough to bend in the right places to allow the barley to find all those hidden nooks and crannies on the palate.. **f22.5** vanilla, a slight fudge effect...but those beautiful, remorseless barley notes just carry on delighting...; **b23** on this magnificent evidence, I am celebrating Tomintoul...and The Whisky Castle!! *50%. nc ncf sc. For The Whisky Castle. In celebration of Cairngorm's National Park. 144 bottles.*

TORMORE
Speyside, 1960. Chivas Brothers. Working.

Tormore 12 Years Old db **(75) n19 t19 f19 b18.** For those who like whisky in their caramel. *40%*

Tormore Aged 15 Years "Special Distillery Bottling" db **(71) n17 t18 f19 b17.** even a supposed pick of choice casks can't save this from its fiery fate. *46%*

⫶ **Mo Òr Collection Tormore 1996 14 Years Old** first fill bourbon hogshead, cask no. DL6868, dist 30 Nov 96, bott 9 Feb 11 **(84) n21.5 t21 f21.5 b20.** Malty, pleasant and clean. But puckeringly sharp and limited in overall complexity, except for a surprise twist of a vaguely bourbony sweetness on the finish. *46%. nc ncf sc. Release No. 47. 500 bottles.*

⫶ **Provenance Tormore Over 11 Years** refill hogshead, cask no. 6861, dist Autumn 1999, bott Winter 2011 **(78) n18 t20 f21 b19.** Cumbersome and unexpectedly oily, though the grist on the finale entertains. *46%. nc ncf sc. Douglas Laing & Co.*

⫶ **Scotch Malt Whisky Society Cask 105.16 Aged 28 Years** first fill sherry hogshead, cask no. 900008, dist 1983 **(78.5) n18.5 t21 f19 b19.** Surprised to find a slight sulphury note in a cask from this vintage, but it was there on the nose to the extent that I decided to make this the last one I'd taste before lunch. Disappointing, though those unable to detect sulphur should be able to enjoy with abandon. *54.5%. sc. Scotch Malt Whisky Society.*

⫶ **Scotch Malt Whisky Society Cask 105.17 Aged 28 Years** first fill sherry hogshead, cask no. 900003, dist 1983 **(83) n20 t22 f20 b21.** Rich, voluptuous grape dominates. But a vague, bitterish off note rains on the party. *55.3%. sc. Scotch Malt Whisky Society.*

TULLIBARDINE
Highlands (Perthshire), 1949. Tullibardine Ltd. Working.

Tullibardine 1962 sherry hogshead, cask no. 3185, bott 2011 db **(95.5) n24** an astonishing marriage between faultless oak, firm malt and clean, rich but non-dominating fruit. Hugely unusual because after all these years a negative note is bound to creep in somewhere. However, this is faultless. The fruit candy lead is just so fresh and fabulous...; **t24** the clarity of the grape tells only half the story. What works here is the layered development of the chocolatey oak, the barley sugar malt and the fruitcake mixed spices; **f23.5** vanilla and butterscotch as you might expect, but just the very faintest wisp of smoke hovering above the toasted sultana more than does the trick; **b24** I can scarcely believe a malt of such antiquity has passed through the years so unscathed. There are no sepia tones or scratches to this, however. Simply timeless. *41.8%. sc.*

Tullibardine 1964 sherry hogshead, cask no. 3354, bott 2011 db **(89.5) n21** oak inflamed and a touch of pine. The malts try to redress the balance, but it is a battle; **t22.5** where did that come from? More delicate and salivating than the nose would even come close to admitting. Some heavy duty oak arrives towards the middle ground but there is enough fruit to cushion the blow; **f23** long with any number of sultana and fruitcake notes absorbing the burnt raisin of the oak; **b23** the faltering start on the nose sends false messages for the joy which is to follow. *42.1%. sc.*

Tullibardine 1976 sherry hogshead, cask no. 3161, bott 2011 db **(94.5) n23** dense spotted dog pudding style aroma with a vague farmhouse fruitcake edge; **t24** mouth-watering, the barley and fruit are in happy unison. Surprising degrees of malt detectable given the richness of the grape and the slow but assured development of the spices; **f23.5** tingly spices now excel and the natural caramels from the oak act as an extra harmonious anchor; **b24** voluptuous and tactile, a fruity feast to take a good half hour over. Complex; simply magnificent. *50.2%. sc.*

Tullibardine 1988 John Black Edition 4 bott 2008 db **(91.5) n23.5** gosh!! How about this for ultra ripe figs and greengages? Wonderfully spiced, honeyed - in an intriguingly understated style - and clean for good measure. One of those you leave the empty glass to give any room's aroma a touch of class to for a few days... **t23** the grape cascades onto the taste buds in a thick, dizzying regiment of fruitiness, by no means all grape, either. The spices hinted at on the nose are here ramrod hard and unyielding; **f22.5** the intensity on delivery fades quite dramatically to leave an almost new-makey cocoa residue. Surprising...and delicious...; **b22.5** An altogether superior and much more complex animal to J B's disappointing No 3 Selection. *46%*

Tullibardine 1992 Rum Finish bott 2009 db **(89.5) n22** caramelized...but without the toffee, if you see what I mean...; **t23** crunchy, sugar-coated barley helped along the way with a lovely sheen; **f22.5** a mildly sweetened vanilla flourish; **b22** cracking stuff! *46%*

Tullibardine 1993 bott 2009 db **(91.5) n22 t23.5 f23 b23.** Intrinsically sweet barley. But spellbindingly charming all the way. *40%*

Tullibardine 1993 Moscatel Finish bott 2007 db **(92.5) n23.5 t23.5 f23 b22.5.** This really is how wine casks should integrate. A minor stunner. *46%*

Tullibardine 1993 Oloroso Sherry Finish bott 2008 db **(89) n23 t23 f21 b22.** Almost a trip down Memory Lane: once a pretty standard sherry butt, but now a treat. *46%*

Tullibardine 1993 Pedro Ximénez Sherry Finish bott 2009 db **(87) n21 t23 f20.5 b22.5.** Sticky and enjoyable. *46%*

Tullibardine 1993 Port Finish bott 2008 db **(83.5) n21.5 t21 f20 b21.** A bumbling, weighty kind of dram with indistinct shape and purpose, even to the extent of displaying a more bourbony gait than a fruity one. Enjoyable, decently spiced but limited in scope. *46%*

Tullibardine 1993 Sauternes Finish bott 2008 db **(84.5) n22 t22 f20 b20.5.** Sleepy and soft with the expected major grape input. Yet rather flattens out too early and to too great a degree. Pleasant, but a little disappointing, too. *46%*

Tullibardine Aged Oak bott 2009 db **(86) n21.5 t21 f22 b21.5.** Aged oak maybe. But early on this is all about the malt which is faultless. Major oaky buzz later. *40%*

Tullibardine Aged Oak Edition bott 2010 db **(88) n21** youthful, vaguely gristy and despite a slight vanilla interference the malt is unopposed in its dominance; **t22** a beautiful array of deft sugars and playful spice enriches the charming malt; **f22.5** remains youthful and lively to the end with seemingly fresh battalions of barley arriving from somewhere, **b22.5** beautifully made malt which is full of life. *40%. nc.*

Tullibardine Banyuls Finish bott 2011 db **(68) n16 t18 f17 b17.** I saw the sulphur coming on this. A steaming mug of intense black coffee and a cool glass of taste bud restorative coconut water wait in the wings. *46%. nc ncf.*

⁖ **Tullibardine Banyuls Finish** bott 2012 db **(71) n17 t19 f17 b18.** A minor tragedy: take away the sulphur and you have what would have been a serious Juicefest. Not for the first time with a banyuls cask, I could cry! *46%. nc ncf.*

Tullibardine John Black db **(84.5) n20 t21.5 f22 b22.** Young, clean and bursting with all kinds of delicious maltiness. An almost perfect first dram of the day. *40%. nc.*

Tullibardine John Black Edition No. 5 sherry hogshead, cask no. 15022, dist 1992, bott Nov 10 db **(93.5) n23** toffee apple with some medium roast Java percolating in the background; crushed sultana and very green apple; **t24** a luxurious texture is still crisp enough to allow both the barley and fruit all the space it needs to develop; really does juice out beautifully and as natural caramels form on the middle, some rollicking spices arrive; **f23** long with a delightful sherry trifle finale, topped lightly with cream. **b23.5** the John Black Edition appears to get better year on year. Here there is no doubting the faultless sherry. *63.8%. nc ncf sc. 328 bottles.*

⁖ **Tullibardine John Black Edition No. 6** bourbon barrel, cask no. 10002, dist 1993, bott Dec 11 db **(94.5) n24** wonderful assortment of aromas, all seemingly of perfect weight. The first threads of menthol show a malt aged older than its years and rich liquorice underlines a bourbon theme. But there is fruit, too, especially of the candy variety; there is no skimping on complexity here; **t23** the barley is of the instantly dissolving variety, the craggy oak sticks around longer but is blunted by mouth-watering spices: even so, it goes way beyond normal bourbon notes; **f23.5** a long fade out with echoes of all the previous combinations of flavours; the late, controlled dryness is oaky icing on the cake; **b24** there are very few whiskies which, professionally, I find impossible to spit out. Here is one. *55.1%. nc ncf sc.*

Tullibardine Premier Cru Classé Finish Chateau Lafite casks, dist 1992, bott Nov 10 **(89.5) n21.5** curiously spiky and fractured with the fruit and malt seemingly having their backs to each other. Both factions can be easily spotted; **t22.5** salivating with layers of fresh barley squaring up to the invading fruit; elsewhere spices begin to gather; **f23** long and curiously dry. The spices still prod and nip but the fruit has the greatest impact; **b22.5** a quite fascinating whisky which will keep you entertained for hours. It's like having War Games in a glass. Curiously, I tasted this from the cask when it was a few months younger. At full strength and with the malt having more telling depth and confidence there was more harmonisation. Proof that each of these type of bottlings are truly unique and impossible to replicate. *46%. nc ncf.*

Tullibardine Pure Pot new make db **(90.5) n24 t23 f21.5 b22.** Pure delight! Not whisky, of course, but a great example of how new make malt should be. *69%*

Tullibardine PX Finish dist 1993, bott 2008 db **(85) n23 t22 f20 b20.** A big, at times bone-hard, whisky which, like many which have spent time in Pedro Ximénez casks, have found it difficult to acquire the kind of balance hoped. The nose offers great promise with a real old-fashioned fruitcake flourish but after the melt-in-the-mouth delivery gets past the barley lead, the degree of bitterness outweighs the growing soft fig notes. For equilibrium, needed less – or more – time in cask: we'll never know. *46%*

⁖ **Tullibardine Sauternes Finish** bott 2012 db **(90.5) n22** quite tight with fruit and barley bound together; a mild spearmint sweetness lightens things; **t23** the balance between the juicier grape, diced apple and the keynote light sugars is excellent, as is the soft oils and ever buzzing spices; **f22.5** butterscotch tart with a light chocolate topping; **b23** the spices attached to the richness of the body makes for a very satisfying and quite intriguing malt. *46%. nc ncf.*

Tullibardine Vintage Edition Aged 20 Years dist 1988, bott 2008 db **(86) n22 t22 f21 b21.** The malt sparkles on the nose and delivery. Fades as caramels kick in. *46%*

⁖ **Mo Ór Collection Tullibardine 1965 44 Years Old** Oloroso sherry butt, cask no. 959, dist 23 May 65, bott 26 Nov 09 **(95.5) n23** big fruitcake with burnt raisins, yet the whole seems to have been cooked beautifully; **t23.5** a silk delivery with some pins left in it: the thick grape seems to glide over the palate but the spices ensure it is not plain sailing; there is lush Demerara sugars to ensure stability; other fruits abound in this juicy set up, not least black cherry and dates; **f24** the kind of fade that stretches far into the distance. At last more gentle vanillas emerge while those gorgeous, now molassed sugars thinly coat both the oak and the persistent fruit. You would feel hard done by if cocoa didn't form somewhere, and it dutifully does with a light praline touch late in the day; **b25** a riveting malt which just gets better and better. After the procession of underwhelming Scotch singletons I have been tasting today, it is so good to at last find one of undisputed quality. *48.8%. nc ncf sc. Release No. 3. 197 bottles.*

⁖ **Scott's Selection Tullibardine 1989** bott 2012 **(86.5) n22 t22 f21 b21.5.** An attractive all rounder with a comfortable oak supporting act warming up the big barley lead. Lovely spices, too. *55.7%. Speyside Distillers.*

⁖ **Wemyss 1989 Single Highland "Rum & Raisin"** hogshead, bott 2011 **(87) n22** creamy, with a curious though not unattractive linseed and millet freshness; **t22** immediately lip-smacking barley followed by a slightly top heavy oakiness; the spices both excite and smooth things over; **f21** again the oak is just a touch too active; **b22** a malt which lives dangerously: on the edge so far as the oak involvement is concerned, but enough complexity and fun for a few extra ticks. *46%. sc. Wemyss Malts. 299 bottles.*

UNSPECIFIED SINGLE MALTS (Campbeltown)

Cadenhead's Campbeltown Malt (92) n22 t24 f23 b23. On their home turf you'd expect them to get it right... and, my word, so they do!! *59.5%*

Cadenhead's Classic Campbeltown (92) n23 t24 f22 b23. What a dram! Must be what they gave Lazarus... *50%*

UNSPECIFIED SINGLE MALTS (Highland)

⁖ **Ailein Mor (84) n21 t22 f20 b21.** An ultra soft malt with plenty of chew to it and a honey-caramel sweetness. *40%. Robert Graham.*

Asda Extra Special Highland Single Malt 12 Years Old (79.5) n21.5 t21 f18 b19. Performs well with a chunky body until it bitters dramatically at the finale. *40%*

Cadenhead's Classic Highland (82) n19 t22 f21 b20. The trace of fusel oil on the nose guarantees a big delivery. Highly malty! *50%*

Cadenhead's Highland Malt (90) n22 t23 f22 b23. Does barley come any more pure or intense than this...? *60.2%*

Co-operative Highland Single Malt Aged 12 Years (79) n22 t21 f17.5 b18.5 Guys! You have to tone down the caramel drastically – preferably remove it altogether. It is there in such enormity that after the first ripe cherry delivery on the palate, all else is entirely lost: the whisky vanishes completely. Such a shame, as the nose suggests we might have been in for something rather lovely. *40%. Co-operative UK.*

Deerstalker Aged 10 Years bott 06/05/11 **(87.5) n22** so delicate it feels like it is breaking into a thousand pieces just on the nose. Very intense, though fragile, barley; even a hint of sherbet; **t23** mouth-watering beyond belief. Immeasurable degree of barley that is as juicy as spring grass; some spices and caramels ensure a degree of pastures new and balance; **f21** the danger of an ultra-light dram like this is that you are left prey to any lurking oak bitterness; **b21.5** a 10 year old masquerading as a malt half that age. The deerstalker must belong to Holmes, who has done a pretty fine job tracking down some decent third fill casks. Possibly the most refreshing drams of the year and one of the few that might actually slake a thirst...! *40%. nc*

Duncan Taylor Majesty Single Highland Malt 30 Years Old (93.5) n22.5 t24 f23.5 b23.5. The nose suggests a malt past its sell by date. The reality on the palate is anything but. A thrilling way to mark the 800th new whisky for Bible 2011. *40%*

Glen Burn Single Highland Malt (81) n20 t20 f21 b20. Pleasant, gentle if simplistic pub fodder. *40%. Glen Burn Distillers.*

Glenfinnan Highland Scotch Single Malt Over 12 Years Old (84) n22 t23 f19 b20. Starts beautifully with citrus and rose petals among other delights. But then stops dead just as you pass the middle. Damn!! *40%. Celtic Whisky Compagnie, France.*

Glen Marnoch 12 Years Old dist Mar 98, bott Oct 10 **(83) n21 t21 f20 b21.** Shards of honey try to penetrate the fog of caramel and coffee. *40%. Aldi.*

Glen Marnoch 18 Years Old bott Oct 10 **(84.5) n21 t22.5 f20 b21.** Some delicious dates, walnuts and spices are to be found in there somewhere. But just too thick and shapeless for a malt this age. *40%. Aldi.*

Glen Torran Highland Single Malt 8 Years Old (75) n17 t21 f18 b19. Sparkles briefly on arrival, helped along the way by lovely spice. But the caramel on the nose and finish does it in. *40%. Roderick & Henderson for London & Scottish International.*

⫶⫶⫶ **Glen Turner Aged 21 Years Limited Edition (94.5) n24** gorgeously soft smoke but what is a real turn on is the diced orange and lemon peel spiced up to the hilt; **t23** at first soft sugars form, but these are brushed aside by mountainous waves of spice. Inevitably, citrus forms the base of the body, like leaves in an autumnal park. The smoke is delicate again yet gristy, too; **f23.5** had there not been a caramel finale to this, the score would have been even higher! But we just have to make do with a gorgeously long fade with the spices buzzing and the smoke drifting...; **b24.5** oddly enough I grew up with a name like this involved in my everyday life. Len Turner was my late father's best friend. And as a small boy both he and his wife, Maude, unofficial uncle and aunt, showed me untold kindness. They have both been gone over 30 years now...but it would have been lovely to present them with a bottle of this very beautiful whisky, just to say: "thanks". *53.1%. ncf. La Martiniquaise. 500 bottles.*

The Grangestone Whisky Collection Highland Single Malt 12 Years Old (87) n22 the distant aroma of raspberry jam spread on warm, slightly overcooked toast; but mainly it is big barley; **t22** sweet, sugary delivery; gristy at times; a late juicy surge; **f21** dries as we return to the burnt toast; **b22** a safe bet. *40%. Quality Spirits International.*

⫶⫶⫶ **The Grangestone Whisky Collection Highland Single Malt 21 Years Old (89) n23.5** there is the odd spice lurking about and this teams up magnificently with the most luscious plum and mango fruitiness...gosh! **t22.5** silky textured delivery making big play of its age: the barley and sugars combine for maximum salivation and the spices slowly evolve to, literally, pepper the taste buds; **f21** loses Brownie points with a slightly bitter finish; **b22** what a softie! Not sure whether to drink this or pat and pet it...Think it's one to drink – some aspects are superb. *40%. Quality Spirits International.*

⫶⫶ **Highland Queen Majesty Classic (84.5) n21.5 t21 f21 b21.** The horse on the label somehow perfectly represents the plodding nature of this whisky. A single malt bottling of the old-fashioned school in that it is well made and matured with no off notes at all. But shy coming forward, too, and never quite makes it from a walk to a trot. *40%*

⫶⫶⫶ **Highland Queen Majesty Aged 8 Years (84) n22 t21 f20 b21.** Another soft, silky and safe malt, though complexity is lost under a big toffee theme. Well made and decently matured though. *40%. Highland Queen Scotch Whisky Company*

⫶⫶⫶ **Highland Queen Majesty Aged 12 Years (86.5) n22 t22 f21 b21.5.** The most gentle and easy going malt, though the toffee notes have much to do with that. Even so, some charming characteristics bubble underneath. The nose benefits from its apple and pear fruitiness and the usual silky texture is punctured by some lively spices. *40%*

⫶⫶⫶ **Highland Queen Majesty Aged 16 Years (90.5) n24** the oak provides a complex smorgasbord of tannins and spice notes, as well as the usual butterscotch and delicate liquorice. Buttered toast appears to be on the menu, too, as well as a puree of greengages and elderberries; **t22.5** the heavy watering down of this malt works perhaps to a very limited degree on the very first aspects of the delivery, which celebrates a thin honey sweetness to the clean barley; breaks down slightly in midstream as the oak becomes a little too dry and chalky as the oils holding the intensity together are washed away; **f22** despite the sugars trying to linger on, vanishes very quickly as malt of this inappropriate strength is always likely to do. However, it must be said, the quality of the casks has, like the entire HQM portfolio, been of the very highest standard with not a single off note; **b22** your majesty! I am impressed! Benefits from the toning down of the caramel character and doubtless would benefit further from being at the 46%abv its age warrants. *40%*

⫶⫶⫶ **Highland Queen Majesty Distiller's Selection Limited Edition 1989** ex-bourbon hogsheads, bott 2009 **(87) n22.5** some busy oak prickle; **t22** the barley waves the white flag as some bourbon-oak tones begin to take control; **f21** thin, but well spiced; **b21.5** again, good casks helping out a well-made malt. But, for all the main sugar and spice theme, complexity remains at a premium. *40%. Highland Queen Scotch Whisky Company.*

⫶⫶⫶ **Master Of Malt Highland Single Malt (86.5) n23 t21.5 f21 b21.** Enjoys a distinctly sma' still constitution with copper being as much part of the makeup as the chalky malt. *40%*

Matisse 19 Year Old Highland Single Malt bott Oct 09 **(85) n22 t21.5 f21 b21.5.** Even flavoured and tempered: a safe, malty, lightly fruity dram. *46% Matisse Spirits Co Ltd*

Matisse 1996 Single Cask Highland Malt Special Scottish Parliament Edition bott Apr 10 **(90) n23 t23 f22 b22.** The nose wants to make you run your fingers around the inside of the glass and devour whatever you get...a whisky far too good to be wasted on mere politicians. *58.6%. Matisse Spirits Co Ltd. 222 bottles.*

McClelland's Highland Single Malt (80) n21 t20 f19 b20. Easy going – until the bitter finish kicks in. *40%*

Sainsbury's Single Highland Malt Aged 12 Years (88) n22 playful spices and banana skins; **t22** juicy delivery showing a degree of youth and freshness; **f22** long with plenty of caramel and vanilla. A few spices promised on the nose make a late entry; **b22** hard to imagine a more easy drinking malt than this. What it loses in simplicity of character, it makes up for with a clean, steady degree of rich textures. *40%. UK.*

⋯∷⋯ **Sainsbury's Single Highland Malt 12 Years Old Unchillfiltered (84.5) n20 t22 f21 b21.5.** Love it! Admittedly, not technically the best spirit ever distilled (as the nose confirms rather too proudly), but that extra width of cut ensures a malt you can contentedly chew on for an age. *46%. nc ncf. Ian Macleod for Sainsbury's UK.*

Tantallan 10 Years Old Highland Single Malt (86) n21.5 t22.5 f21 b21. Has kept impressively to its massively malted principles with a squirt here and there of fruit, too. But let down slightly by the bitterness of the odd tired bourbon barrel. *40%*

Tesco Highland Single Malt 12 Years Old (88.5) n23 chunky and alluring with dates and chocolate marzipan starring; **t23.5** superbly textured with magnificent muscovado sugar and light spice balance; still more marzipan dipped in plum brandy; **f20** relatively disappointing despite the vanilla...just a little furry; **b22** the odd flaw cannot undo a really lovely whisky brimming with weight and character. *40%. Tesco.*

⋯∷⋯ **Wemyss Aged 14 Years Single Highland "A Day at the Coast"** hogshead, bott Aug 11 **(90.5) n23** if they mean chocolate topping on vanilla ice cream, I know where they are coming from; **t23** refreshing barley with just the right pinch of salt; the barley positively throbs while the oak sits like a lion awaiting the moment to pounce; **f22** dry, vanilla-led and with those barley-saline sugar notes to the death; **b22.5** the day at the coast certainly wasn't Margate. Worthy of a "wish you were here" postcard! *46%. sc. 354 bottles. USA exclusive.*

⋯∷⋯ **Wemyss Aged 29 Years Single Highland "The Dunes"** hogshead, bott Aug 11 **(75.5) n19 t19.5 f18 b19.** Lost in a burning vanilla desert... *46%. sc. 202 bottles. USA exclusive.*

Wemyss 1989 Single Highland "The Fruit Bowl" refill hogshead, bott Sep 09 **(89.5) n22.5 t23 f22 b22.** Mild mannered and meandering. *46%. Wemyss Malts Ltd. 331 bottles.*

Wemyss 1989 Single Highland "The Herb Garden" bott Apr 09 **(89) n24.5** dry, delicate, naughtily understated. Dried orange and chopped walnuts in groundnut oil. The vanillas are clean and unthreatening; **t24** a malty blast but with featherbed weight. Still nutty but the malts are salivating; the chocolate orange middle is sublime; **f19** hits the buffers by comparison. Just the wrong type of fruit with a sharpness out of sync with the magnificence of before; **b22.5** the nose and early delivery was the stuff of world whisky of the year. Doesn't manage to stay on course, but so worth discovering. *46%. sc. 345 bottles.*

Wemyss 1989 Single Highland "The Orange Tree" hogshead, bott 2011 **(92) n22** tapioca pudding with a blob of jam; **t23.5** sensual and salivating a watered down freshly squeezed orange is sweetened by slightly burned molasses; **f23** soft oils and cocoa; **b23.5** well done to Wemyss: they have unearthed some stunners... and here is another! *46%. sc. 272 bottles.*

Wemyss 1990 Single Highland "Chocolate Plums" bott Apr 09 **(71) n17.5 t19 f17 b17.5.** Plum duff... *46%. sc. Wemyss Malts. 345 bottles.*

Wemyss 1990 Single Highland "Mocha Spice" butt, bott 2011 **(84.5) n20 t23.5 f20 b21.** Not entirely without blemishes. And way too fruity for mocha (which tends to come from bourbon cask) but some juicy delights on offer. *46%. sc. Wemyss Malts. 732 bottles.*

Wemyss 1990 Single Highland "Red Berry Cream" butt, bott 2011 **(71) n17.5 t18.5 f17 b18.** Must have come from a feintyberry bush... *46%. sc. Wemyss Malts. 865 bottles.*

Wemyss 1990 Single Highland "Spiced Plum" bott Apr 09 **(93) n23** a distinctly grapey, almost plum brandy-esque aroma which straddles a degree of thinness with a sharper fruit quite beautifully; **t24** still more of the slivovitz style: sharp, sweet, lightly bodied but fabulously layered with the vanilla arriving with a delicate degree of mocha; **f22.5** the lightness of the structure allows the oak to have a big say but the spices ensure plenty of continuing activity on the palate; **b23.5** forget the "figs". You won't find them as they aren't there. But one thing is certain: this is brilliant whisky! *46%. sc. Wemyss Malts. 345 bottles.*

Wemyss 1990 Single Highland "Tropical Spice" refill butt, bott Sep 09 **(95) n24.5 t24 f23 b23.5.** A peach of a barrel. Highly unusual in character and never seemingly the same any two times you taste it. *59.4%. Wemyss Malts Ltd. 767 bottles.*

Wemyss 1997 Single Highland "Vanilla Summer" hogshead, bott 2011 **(93) n23** big bourbon signature; **t23.5** an imposing flypast of various bourbony mainstays, with red liquorice and a delicate Demerara-vanilla to the fore; **f23** dries elegantly towards a touch of butterscotch and honeycomb; **b23.5** more like a Kentucky Spring... *46%. Wemyss Malts. 363 bottles.*

Wilson & Morgan Sherry Cask Malt "Highland Heart" cask no. 4446, 4448 & 4450, dist 2001, bott 2009 **(75.5) n18 t22 f17 b18.5.** For a while the golden honey flies high and handsomely. Then a familiar sherry off note breaks my lowland heart. *43%*

UNSPECIFIED SINGLE MALTS (Island)

Adelphi's Fascadale Aged 10 Years Batch 2 bourbon hogshead, bott 2010 **(86.5) n22.5 t21.5 f21 b21.5.** Punchy, peaty, and attractively aggressive. *46%. 3746 bottles.*

Dun Bheagan Island Single Malt Aged 8 Years (93) n23 t24 f23 b23. As beautiful as a Scottish isle. *43%. Ian Macleod Distillers.*

Isle Of Mull Aged 10 Years (77) n16.5 t22 f19.5 b19. A balanced Ledaig defined...peat and feints in equal measure. *40%. Marks & Spencer UK.*

Macleod's Island (85) n21 t22 f21 b21. A soft, toffee-fudged affair. Easy drinking. *40%*

⊰⊱ **Master Of Malt Island Single Malt (91.5) n22.5** apparent evidence of age here as we have a big wave of exotic fruit, with passion fruit to the fore; **t23** gorgeous delivery: silky with a delicate degree of honey but an even more melodious stratum of peat; the delicate fruits hang on in there despite the big brush strokes from elsewhere; **f22.5** the smoke heads in to spicier territory, but the underlying fruit remains salivating; **b23.5** don't know about Lord of the Isles. More like Lord of the Flies...Fruit flies, that is...! They would be hard pressed to find even an over-ripe mango any juicier than this gorgeous malt... *40%*

UNSPECIFIED SINGLE MALTS (Islay)

Adelphi Breath Of The Isles 15 Years Old cask no. 1792, dist 1995, bott 2010 **(94.5) n24** excellent honey-smoke combo; floral pollen-like notes; spices take a little time to arrive but when they do, they no more than complete the picture; **t24** sublime honeycomb: actually breaks down honey constituents thanks to a manuka-acacia mix; a liquorice layer; **f22.5** threatens to bitter up, but instead light spices and more honeycomb edge it closer to a bourbon-style finale, **b24** take a breath of this every day and you'd live for ever... *58%. sc. Adelphi Distillery. 245 bottles.*

Adelphi's Liddesdale Aged 18 Years Batch 1 sherry butt, bott 2010 **(94) n23.5 t24 f23 b23.5.** An exceptional Islay where complexity and balance are the key *46%. 2962 bottles.*

Asda Extra Special Islay Single Malt 12 Years Old (91) n23 t23 f22.5 b22.5. A high quality Islay from the old traditional school *40%*

Auld Reekie 10 Years Old (90.5) n22 thumping peat, younger in style than its given age; **t23.5** sweet, gristy, sugary peat which fair cleans the palate. How salivating is that...? **f22.5** so many smoke signals. And every one saying: youthful peat... **b22.5** about as subtle as a Glasgow kiss followed by a knee in the nuts. Just a whole lot more enjoyable... *46%*

Auld Reekie Islay Malt (95) n24 t24 f23 b24. My last whisky of the day and a dram I shall be tasting all the way to when I clean my teeth. On second thoughts... I'll do them in the morning. Only kidding. But this is a must have dram for Islayphiles: true genius. *46%*

Berrys' Reserve Islay (86.5) n21.5 t22.5 f21 b21.5. Fat, sweet, chewy and particularly pleasing on delivery. Decent nip, too. *46%. Berry Bros & Rudd.*

Blackadder Peat Reek (88) n23 t22 f21 b22. A clean, very gentle giant. *46%. Blackadder Int.*

Cadenhead's Classic Islay (91) n23 t23 f22 b23. I admit: totally baffled by this one. Just can't read the distillery at all: a completely different take on any of them: kind of Ardbeigian, but a Labphraogish blast and a hint of Caol Ila's oils. Yet it is all, yet none of them. Oddly enough, it reminds of Port Ellen when about eight years old. But, obviously, can't be. Classic, indeed! *50%*

Cadenhead's Islay Malt (84) n22 t21 f20 b21. Fat, well enough peated but lacks ambition and complexity. *58%*

Classic of Islay Single Malt Cask Strength (81) n20 t22 f19 b20. Fat, smoky, oily, very sweet, tight. Enjoyable, but lacking character development due mainly to the casks. *58%*

Dun Bheagan Islay Vintage 2000 (88) n22 t22.5 f21.5 b22. A plodding malt which reveals its considerable charms in slow motion. *43%. Ian Macleod for Canadian Market.*

Elements of Islay Ar2 (90.5) n22 t23.5 f22.5 b22.5. Sunshine one minute, storms the next...yep: this whisky about sums up the elements of Islay quite succinctly. *60.5%*

Elements Of Islay Br1 (89) n22.5 refreshing, peat-free, vivid citrus and a sprinkle of salt; **t22.5** barley gushes in the salivating delivery and then an immediate blanket of caramel; **f22** caramel, vanilla and a lot of chewing; **b22** absolutely delicious and clean but quietened by what appears to be a massive dose of natural caramels from the oak. Hang on: for an Elements of Islay, shouldn't rain be in there somewhere...? *53.6%. ncf. Speciality Drinks Ltd.*

⊰⊱ **Elements Of Islay Br2 (87.5) n22** how buttery can a peaty nose get? **t22** superb delivery of crisp Demerara sugars; again there is pure, unsalted butter now rubbing up against toasted raisin-loaf and a thin spreading of marmalade; **f21.5** much more simplistic with the smoke lingering and the much drier vanillas being as forceful as possible; **b22** a malt with an identity crisis. Off key in part, absolutely on the ball elsewhere. *49.3%. ncf. Speciality Drinks.*

Elements of Islay Cl1 (85.5) n21 t22.5 f21 b21. Molassed Fisherman's Friend cough sweet. Where have I tasted this style before? Simplistic, but a real meal. *62.9%*

Elements Of Islay Lg2 (77) n19 t20 f19 b19. The storm? *58%. Speciality Drinks Ltd.*

Elements of Islay Lp1 (91) n23 t23.5 f22 b22.5. A big, fruity Islay with few pretensions of subtlety. *58.8%. Speciality Drinks Ltd.*

Elements of Islay Pe1 (95.5) n24 t24.5 f23.5 b23.5. This is a fabulous, nigh faultless, example of the purest element of Islay: its whisky... *58.7%. Speciality Drinks Ltd.*

Finlaggan Islay Single Malt 10 Years Old (82) n21 t21 f20 b20. Beautiful citrus notes mildly tempered with smoke: an enormous improvement from the caramel-ruined previous "Lightly Peated" bottlings. *40%. The Vintage Malt Whisky Co.*

Finlaggan "Old Reserve" Islay Single Malt (79.5) n19 t21 f19 b20.5. A smoky shadow of its once great self. *40%. The Vintage Malt Whisky Co Ltd.*

⁖ **First Cask Isle Of Islay 21 Years Old** first fill sherry butt, cask no. 12, dist 24 Dec 90, bott 9 Jan 12 **(77) n19 t21 f18 b19.** Back in 1990, only one distillery on Islay was filling non-peated spirit into sherry butts as often as not sulphur treated. This one has been, but not so badly affected as others and the grape is still quite profound. *54%. nc ncf sc. Whisky Import Nederland. 360 bottles.*

The Ileach Islay Single Malt (85) n20.5 t22 f21 b21.5. Not the dram it was. Once near faultless, now a highly smoked hotchpotch. Not without its lovely moments, but pray the next bottling is nearer its magnificent old self. *40%*

Islay Storm (76) n19 t20 f19 b18. More of a drizzle. *40%. C.S. James & Sons.*

Islay Storm 12 Years Old (81) n20 t21 f20 b20. Some lovely spice emphasis the seaweed kick. Decent oak weight, too. *40%. C.S. James & Sons.*

McClelland's Islay Single Malt (88) n22 t22 f22 b22. No mistaking which distillery this little beaut is from: Bowmore anyone? *40%*

Macleod's Islay (84.5) n21 t22 f20.5 b21. Considering the raging bull of a malt this used to be, this appears to have been snipped in its prime. Toffee and coffee have as much impact as the peat, which offers more smoke than depth. *40%. Ian Macleod.*

Marks and Spencer Islay Single Malt Aged 12 Years (83) n21.5 t21 f20 b20.5. Entertaining rough-house malt which belies its strength. Cordite on the nose and beyond... *40%*

⁖ **Master Of Malt Islay Single Malt (82) n22 t21 f19 b20.** Pleasant enough, but a bit sweet and soupy at first before the late bitterness tells a tale. *40%*

Port Askaig Aged 30 Years (81.5) n19 t22.5 f20 b20. Some malts make it through to this age unscathed. Some don't. This falls into the latter category. Some exotic notes, but this always appears to work less well for Islays than mainlanders. The odd wonderful malt and caramel moment, even so. *45.8%. Speciality Drinks Ltd.*

Port Askaig Cask Strength (89) n22 t23.5 f21 b22.5. Surprisingly juicy after the nose. Profound. *57.1%. Speciality Drinks Ltd.*

The Queen of the Hebrides Islay Single Malt Whisky (85) n22 t22 f20 b21. Big, rolling fat peats: any fatter and it'd be declared obese. *40%. Wine Shop, Leek; Islay Whisky Shop.*

Robert Graham's The Hoebeg Single Islay Malt (88) n23 t22.5 f21 b21.5. What first appears to be a big, roaring Islay turns out to be a smoky kitten. *40%*

Sainsbury's Single Islay Malt Aged 12 Years (92.5) n23 stupendously coastal with any number of salty shades working in harmony with the refreshing citrus. The smoke massages rather than confronts; **t23.5** light vanillas manage to out manoeuvre the smoke while the juicy barley and fruits build and build; **f22.5** the smoke virtually vanishes as the lightly oiled vanilla and citrus takes us to the close; **b23.5** Islay malt has been Sainsbury's trump card for a little while. And here they have managed to trump themselves. Almost ridiculously delicate. *40%*

⁖ **Sainsbury's Single Islay Malt 12 Years Old Unchillfiltered (94) n24** sublime mix of peat ash from a crofter's hearth and lightly salted Seville orange...; **t23.5** delicate oils go a long, long way. here they maximise the smoke to gently coat the palate while the delicate sugars see off both a drier vanilla upsurge and a slow development of sharpish citrus; **f23** the delicate peat subsides in waves, like the tide departing Loch Gruinart....; **b23.5** I still remember the days when some British supermarkets would use only unpeated Islay whisky for their own label bottlings as they were too terrified that a big peat attack would scare their customers off. Let's just say that the evidence of this is that times have changed... A beast of a bottling! *46%. nc ncf. Ian Macleod for Sainsbury's UK.*

Smokehead Extra Black Aged 18 Years (94) n23 t24 f23.5 b23.5. Doubtless some will prefer the in-your-face standard version. This is for those seeking a bit of grey-templed sophistication. *46%*

Smokehead Islay db (92) n24 t23 f22 b23. This company does this kind of whisky so well. A little gem. *43%. Ian Macleod.*

Tesco Old Islay Single Malt 12 Years Old (80.5) n20 t21 f19.5 b20. Smoky for sure. But somehow thin and a little basic. *40%. Tesco.*

⁖ **Wemyss Aged 15 Years Single Islay "A Matter of Smoke"** hogshead, bott Aug 11 **(84) n22 t21 f20 b21.** Dishes out the peat in spades. Very little yield either from cask or spirit, though. *46%. sc. 337 bottles. USA exclusive.*

Wemyss 1981 Single Islay "Whispering Smoke" hogshead, bott 2011 (94) n23 a beautiful meeting of butterscotch, salt, lemon peel and surprisingly crisp barley; t24 fabulous texture: a real golden syrup and burned fudge sweetness to the barley with busy spices popping around the palate; f23 earthy, chewy and wards off any oaky excess without breaking sweat; b24 just one of those really magnificent malts which cannot be ignored. *46%. Wemyss Malts. 228 bottles.*

Wemyss 1984 Single Islay "Crumpets & Cordite" bott Apr 09 (90) n23.5 playful smoke, sweetened with a touch of banana. Not quite cordite...more anthracite...; t23.5 genuinely complex: the barley is fresh and juicy; the smoke is both thick and lightly spiced but enjoys a lighter sub-plot, too; f20.5 just a slight wobble from the cask but enough spice to see it through; b22.5 I always fancy sophisticated, beautifully-shaped crumpet like this... *46%. sc. Wemyss Malts. 342 bottles.*

Wemyss 1996 Single Islay "Burnt Heather" bott Apr 09 (85.5) n21 t23 f20 b21.5. An array of sugars do a wonderful job in balancing out the spices. Pure, juicy entertainment. *46%. sc. Wemyss Malts. 342 bottles.*

Wemyss 1996 Single Islay "Honey Smoke" hogshead, bott Sep 09 (85) n21.5 t22 f20.5 b21. I was expected to find a smoked out hive. Instead, a rather salty dram where the sweetness is of a more muscovado sugar rather than honey variety. *59.6%. 425 bottles.*

Wemyss 1996 Single Islay "Smoke On The Sea Shore" hogshead, bott 2011 (86) n21.5 t22 f21 b21.5. Smoky, massively salty and with a refreshing twist of lemon. I doubt I have ever come across a malt with such a twee, chintzy name. But it just about does what it says on the tin. *46%. Wemyss Malts. 328 bottles.*

Wemyss 1996 Single Islay "Smoke Stack" hogshead, bott 2011 (88) n22.5 smoky bacon but chunky barley, too; t22 clean, sweet and some molassed smoke; delightful layering of juicy barley; f21.5 light vanilla; b22 sweet and well mannered. *46%. sc. 294 bottles.*

Wemyss 1997 Single Islay "Autumn Leaves" refill bourbon, bott Sep 09 (75) n18 t19 f19 b19. Technically, not quite the greatest whisky: one I will leaf well alone... *46%*

Wemyss 1997 Single Islay "Autumn Warmer" hogshead, bott 2011 (63) n14 t18 f15 b16. Poorly constructed distillate to begin with. *46%. 360 bottles.*

Wemyss 1997 Single Islay "Bonfire Embers" bott Apr 09 (84) n22 t22 f19 b21. As bonfires go, this is a very sugary one. Oh, and peaty... *46%. sc. Wemyss Malts. 342 bottles.*

Wemyss 1997 Single Islay "Sandy Seaweed" bott Apr 09 (84) n22 t22.5 f19 b20.5. In the artificial light of my tasting bunker, on picking this up I thought it was new make. To my astonishment, it's been around longer than the Euro. As is often the case when exhausted old casks are deployed, the nose and delivery are excellent (and new makey/gristy) but the finish is bitter and off key. *46%. Wemyss Malts Ltd. 347 bottles.*

Wemyss 1997 Single Islay "Vanilla Smoke" bott Apr 09 (73.5) n17.5 t21 f17 b18. Smoke. But dodgy wood means it just doesn't fire properly. *46%. sc. 342 bottles.*

Wilson & Morgan House Malt "Born on Islay" cask no. 309928 & 309934, dist 2001, bott 2010 (86) n21.5 t22 f21 b21.5. A curious thick set Islay with a mildly industrial nose, revealing the oiliness of old workshops. The delivery is sweet but a little muted. 43%

Wemyss 1999 Single Islay "Well Mannered Mint" hogshead, bott 2011 (92.5) n23 I say: how awfully delicate the smoke is...; t23 frightfully gentle delivery with a sweet, juicy smokiness which slowly heads towards milky cocoa; f23 frightfully chocolate-minty; b23.5 anyone who remember's Merlin's Brew chocolate mint lolly will have more than a pang of nostalgia here. *46%. Wemyss Malts. 307 bottles.*

⋯ **The Whisky Broker Islay Malt** first fill sherry butt, cask no. 3, dist 17 Dec 90, bott 29 Mar 12 (80) n19 t22 f19 b20. Voluptuous grape and busy spice. Just a little too tight in part, though, for obvious reasons. *54.5%. nc ncf sc. 739 bottles.*

⋯ **The Whisky Broker Islay Malt** first fill sherry butt, cask no. 54, dist 24 Dec 90, bott 9 Jan 11 (85.5) n23 t22 f19.5 b21. A two-toned sherry. Magnificent sultana and cinnamon-rich juicy grape to drool over. But a bitter taint takes away some of the gloss. *54.8%. nc ncf sc.*

Wilson & Morgan House Malt "Born On Islay" dist Aug 02, bott Jan 11 (87.5) n22 big smoke: an interesting marriage of dryish grist and thick oils; t22 a full bodied house with an outbreak of gristy sugars; f21.5 bitters out; coffee and smoke; b22 absolutely presentable, oily-smoked everyday dramming. A still-house malt with a good view... 43%

Wm Morrison Islay Single Malt Aged 10 Years (84) n21 t22 f21 b20. A uniform Islay which, though pleasant and initially sweet, fails to trouble the imagination or pulse. 40%

UNSPECIFIED SINGLE MALTS (Lowland)

Cadenhead's Classic Lowland Bourbon wood (82) n19 t21 f21 b21. Much juicier and fortified with rich barley than the nose suggests. 50%

Cadenhead's Lowland Malt (90) n22 t23 f22 b23. One of the best lowlanders around. Fabulously fresh! 56.4%

Master of Malt 12 Years Old Lowland 2nd Edition (86.5) n22.5 t22 f20.5 b21.5. Lots of joined up aromas, with apple and liquorice character linking with drier elements quite effortlessly while the delivery offers attractive weaving between youthful maltiness and an older, slightly bourbony edge. *40%*

·:·· **Master Of Malt Lowland Single Malt** (86) n22 t21.5 f21 b21.5. If one was to paint in one's mind's eye a delicate, grassy, inoffensive Lowlander, this would just about be it. *40%*

UNSPECIFIED SINGLE MALTS (Speyside)

·:·· **A.D. Rattray Whisky Experience Malt 1** dist 2003 (87.5) n22 complex aroma, semi-full bodied with a floral-apple lightness to the encroaching oaks; t22.5 firm barley with the usual salivating disposition; moves seamlessly towards a spicier attack; f21 simplifies as the vanilla and spice take overall command; b22 well made and richly textured malt. *40%. sc.*

Asda Extra Special Speyside Single Malt 12 Years Old (76) n18.5 t19 f19 b19.5. The last time I tasted this, some thug attacked my office and smashed up neighbouring property. If only there could be some similar violence to my taste buds, as this is as docile and nondescript as it comes. *40%*

·:·· **Ben Bracken Aged 12 Years** (86.5) n22 t22.5 f20.5 b21.5. A classically easy going Speyside with no bumps or surprises. Accentuates its delicate nature attractively and makes the most of its juicy barley core. *40%. Lidl.*

Berrys' Reserve Speyside (88) n21.5 t22.5 f22 b22. Entirely unspectacular, utterly lacking in star quality... and yet... a very pleasant, fault-free dram which hits the spot. *46%*

Celtique Connexion Saussignac Double Matured 1997 bott 2010 (95) n24 the vaguest degree of smoke drops anchor on the fruit. Freshly cleaned mature plums and tangy fruit cubes from the boiled sweet jar; Clean, lively, intense; t24 thrilling delivery full of fresh, spicy grape, salivating barley and meaningful caramel; f23 long with the caramels continuing the cream toffee theme, but with extra spices arriving late... and that irrepressible grape...; b24 dreamy. Faultless. Just bloody fantastic! Displays more life, vitality and reasons to live than the entire main stand at Selhurst Park... *46%. nc ncf sc. Celtic Whisky Compagnie. 381 bottles.*

Cuidich'n Righ 10 Years Old (83.5) n21.5 t22 f20 b20. About as simple as they come: the barley is sharp but the oak offers only so much support. *40%. Gordon & MacPhail.*

·:·· **Glenbridge 40 Years Old** European oak sherry casks (95.5) n24 all the signs of enormous age: exotic fruit, a sweet sheen to the nose and no shortage of crushed fruit stone and pith: almost like opening a bag of caramelised dried fruits; suave and sophisticated; t24 silky and tactile delivery making much of the fruit-barley combination; the oaks inject an almost sawdusty element, allowing somewhere for the richer, juicier notes to drain into; the spices are by no means shy and have much to say; f23.5 more spice and dry vanilla as the fruitier characteristics evaporates; again there is a late oiliness apparent, similar to the 24-year-old; b24 appears to be related in style to the 24-year-old and shows many similar characteristics. This, however, has dried in the extra 15 years and although the spices still rumble, there is slightly less on the sugary front to ensure an exact balance. That said, another malt showing no signs of ill health; obviously beautifully made and whoever put this into wood knew something about buying in good quality casks. *40%. Aldi. 3,000 bottles.*

·:·· **Glenbrynth Twenty One Limited Release** first release, bott 2011 (84) n21 t21 f21 b21. I can understand why it is called 21. Not sure how to say how disappointed I am with this malt. Has the odd lively moment and a few juicy ones, too. But they are too few and far between: this is a whisky which gets into second gear but no further. Just too many blind alleys and, literally, bitter endings. *43%. OTI Africa.*

·:·· **Glen Marnoch 24 Years Old** dist 1987 (94) n23.5 the softest of vanilla-toffee affairs with a thick slice of egg custard tart. Enough delicate spice and sugar to make things pretty interesting and even create a soft Jamaican pot still rum effect; some superb zesty kumquat sharpness ensures impressive complexity; t23.5 a beautiful delivery of juicy malts and immediate playful spice which maintain a presence throughout; the oak also displays early but is too well mannered to interrupt the muscovado sugar development; f23 a long finish thanks to a barely discernible yet vital degree of light oils; the spices and drier oak notes have a bigger say now, as does a charming brushing of cocoa powder; b24 a magnificent malt showing an age greater than its given years but with no off notes or signs of weariness. A malt which keeps the taste buds working hard and long. *40%. Aldi. 3,000 bottles.*

GlenParker Speyside Single Malt (86.5) n21 t22.5 f21.5 b21.5. An enjoyable, bracing malt with plenty of backbone and bite. If you are looking for flavour and personality, you can do a lot worse. *40%. Angus Dundee.*

·:·· **Lidl Speyside Single Malt Aged 18 Years** (84) n21.5 t21.5 f20 b20.5. At first silky sweet but then a dull fellow riddled with caramel character at the cost of most else. *40%. Clydesdale Scotch Whisky Company for Lidl.*

Macleod's Speyside (86) n21.5 t22 f21 b21.5. Friendly, malty and juicy. *40%*

❖ **Malts Of Scotland "1836" 1995** sherry hogshead, cask no. 37, dist Dec 95, bott May 11 (68) n17 t19 f15 b17. Sweet. But badly sulphur stained. *50.5%. nc ncf sc. Malts Of Scotland.*

❖ **Malts Of Scotland Angel's Choice "1836" 1970** sherry hogshead, cask no. MoS11025, bott Nov 11 (94) n23 we are dealt yummy sweet (and very clean!) grape; t23.5 sees the yummy grape. Raises it delicate spice, especially cinnamon; f24 the light vanilla folds allowing the ulmo honey to clean up; b23.5 an ace dram. *53.5%. nc ncf sc. Malts Of Scotland.*

❖ **Malts Of Scotland Whisky Liqueur 20 Years Old** (75) n21 t18 f18 b18. What the hell was THAT.....!!!! At first I thought they meant Liqueur Whisky, having been told this is a single malt. But, no: having tasted it, the word order is right. If this is pure single malt whisky, then it is the sweetest I have ever encountered. As though matured in a cask still dripping with maple syrup when filled. I can see a few women going wild over this. *40%. Malts Of Scotland.*

Master of Malt 40 Year Old Speyside 2nd Edition (92.5) n23 t24 f23 b22.5. Brinkmanship doesn't quite cover it...but the intense and multi-faceted sugars cope with the major splinters in there. *40%*

❖ **Master Of Malt Speyside Single Malt** (82.5) n20.5 t21.5 f20 b20.5. Sweet, lightly oiled but troubled by a bitter finish and wilfully refuses to crank up the complexity. *40%*

McClelland's Speyside (77.5) n20 t19 f18.5 b19. Remains stunningly inert. *40%*

❖ **Muirhead's Silver Seal Aged 8 Years** (75.5) n18.5 t20 f18 b19. Just too lacking in character and complexity to get away with the harshness of the feints. *40%*

❖ **Muirhead's Silver Seal Aged 12 Years** (87) n22 grassy to the point of sniffing dank bales of hay; t22 crisp, precise barley with a lovely gristy sweetness; f21.5 the oak seeps in with the expected vanilla for a clichéd Speyside finale...; b21.5 doesn't try to be flash. Just does Speysidey things very well indeed! *40%. Highland Queen Scotch Whisky Company.*

❖ **Muirhead's Silver Seal Chassagne Montrachet Burgundy Wood Finish** (89) n23 if you are into a little cinnamon in your grape – and when I say grape, I mean grape juice style grape – then this juicy little number will send you mad...; t22.5 voluptuous mouth-feel, though not helped by the measly strength. The oils break up too easily but this gives the grape an opportunity to dominate, which it accepts. The vanillas fight through at the midpoint; f21.5 dusty, chalky over-drying vanilla; b22 oh, guys! Had you only gone at 46%, then you would have had a real winner. As it is, charming, delicate and delicious... *40%. 5,000 bottles.*

❖ **Muirhead's Silver Seal Limited Edition 1987** (86.5) n21.5 t22.5 f21 b21.5. A delicate and characterful malt which pays a price for not finding a cask which could just give a fuller finish more in keeping with what had gone on before. Certainly the use of the bourbony honey and hickory notes are compelling on the nose and delivery. All the same, an attractive any-time-of-the-day malt. *40%. Highland Queen Scotch Whisky Company. 3,500 bottles.*

❖ **Muirhead's Silver Seal Special Edition 1993** (89.5) n23 how elegant! Playful lemon and citrus lay naked beside clean barley....rrrr! t23 soft barley gently laps against the taste buds. It's silky sweetness welcomes in those very same citrus notes found on the nose; f21.5 thins as the oak converts those juicy lemons into slightly more bitter marmalade tones; b22 just so delicate and sexy. *40%. Highland Queen Scotch Whisky Company*

❖ **Old Malt Cask Probably Speyside's Finest Distillery Aged 18 Years** refill hogshead, cask no. 6376, dist Nov 96, bott Jul 10 (73) n18 t20 f17 b18. Maybe arguably the finest distillery. But no disputing it is a long way from being their finest cask...the "s" word has reared its ugly head again. *50%. nc ncf sc. Douglas Laing & Co. 313 bottles.*

Old Malt Cask Speyside's Finest Aged 41 Years sherry butt, cask no. 5515, dist Nov 67, bott Sep 09 (82) n22 t21 f19 b20. Salty biscuit and mocha. But buckles under the weight of oaky expectancy. *50% Douglas Laing & Co Ltd. 456 bottles.*

Old Malt Cask Speyside's Finest Aged 42 Years sherry butt. DL 6245, dist Nov 67, bott Jun 10 (88) n23 t21.5 f22 b21.5. You know the elegant building in your town which is crumbling a bit and someone's tarted it up slightly in not quite the right colours...? *50%. Douglas Laing. 385 bottles.*

Old Malt Cask Speyside's Finest Aged 43 Years sherry butt, dist Jun 66, bott Oct 09 (96.5) n24 t24.5 f24 b24. As near as damn it faultless... *48.2%. For The Whisky Show 2009.*

Sainsbury's Single Speyside Malt Aged 12 Years (89) n22.5 lively, vaguely fruity, orange pithy, with attractive, clean vanillas; t22.5 pure malt and custard delivery with a superb, lightly oiled, ultra soft texture; a light, juicy barley thread works wonders; f22 anyone for a malt milkshake? b22 you will do well to find a softer, more friendly malt. A creamy delight. *40%. UK.*

❖ **Sainsbury's Single Speyside Malt 12 Years Old Unchillfiltered** (91.5) n22.5 a fresh, juiciness in the great Speyside tradition with enough zest to see off a little toffee; t23.5 this translates to the palate perfectly. Fantastic mix of barley grist, acacia honey and the busiest of peppery spices; f22.5 trims down in complexity as the toffee reasserts itself but still plenty of barley to go round; b23 absolutely gorgeous! *46%. nc ncf. Ian Macleod for Sainsbury's UK.*

⁘ **Sansibar Single Speyside Malt 8 Years Old** sherrywood, dist 2003 **(78) n20 t22 f17 b19.** For a few moments on delivery the honey and almost sultana-sweet fruitiness hold together beautifully. The nose also shows some outstanding fruit and nut quality, though usually well hidden. I once interviewed the legendary American comedian and actor Bob Hope. But with the bitter taint hovering around, this is one road to Zanzibar he might not have enjoyed... *52.9%. sc. The Whisky Agency.*

⁘ **Shieldaig Speyside Aged 10 Years (85.5) n21.5 t22 f21 b21.** If this was a dog, it'd be one of those silly ones that'd lie on its back all day awaiting a tickle. Friendly, sweet, bursting with barley. But complexity has gone walkies.... *40%. Booker.*

⁘ **Spey River Eight Years Matured** bourbon oak **(89) n23** heavier on the oak than a normal 8-y-o, though the bourbony red liquorice notes point towards excellent new fill casks; some excellent peppers, too; **t23** so yielding and come-to-me sexy you could give it a kiss. The sugars are sublime, of the light muscovado variety, and herald in the confident barley; **f21** overly dries, partly because of the strength, but also the odd bitter note from a cask; **b22** simplistic, but what it does, it does with genuine panache. *40%. Quality Spirits International.*

Tesco Speyside Single Malt 12 Years Old (88) n22.5 billowing barley: clean, extensive and gorgeously fresh; **t22** absolutely spot on delivery of malt operating on both crisp and oily levels tinged with the lightest of sugar coatings; the middle is attractively vanilla dominant; **f21.5** dryish but with the malt still pounding through; **b22** a lovely whisky entirely devoid of the smoke promised on the label. Not remotely complex but very true to the regional style and thoroughly enjoyable. *40%. Tesco.*

⁘ **Tesco Speyside 18 Year Old (84) n21 t22 f20 b21.** Pleasant, but enough unwelcome tangy notes to ensure this will not be talked about in a decade's time. Chewy, thick-bodied, decent honey and spice here and there though the finish dies a little feebly. *40%. Tesco.*

⁘ **Wemyss Aged 20 Years Single Speyside "Winter Larder"** butt, bott Aug 11 **(63.5) n16 t16.5 f15 b16.** Only for those who seasonally stock up on sulphur. *46%. sc. Wemyss Malts. 654 bottles. USA exclusive.*

Wemyss 1990 Single Speyside "Toffee Apples" dist 1990, bott Apr 09 **(70) n17 t18.5 f17 b17.5.** "Sulphured Casks 1990" *46% Wemyss Malts Ltd. 335 bottles.*

Wemyss 1991 Single Speyside "Ginger Treacle" dist 1991, bott Apr 09 **(63.5) n16 t17.5 f15 b15.** "Sulphured Casks 1991" *46% Wemyss Malts Ltd. 335 bottles.*

Wemyss 1995 Single Speyside "Spiced Apples" refill hogshead, bott Sep 09 **(91) n22.5 t24 f22.5 b22.** A rich, satisfying, high quality dram. *46%. 386 bottles.*

Wemyss 1996 Single Speyside "Ginger Compote" butt, bott 2011 **(69) n16 t18.5 f17 b17.5.** Ginger compost...? *46%. sc. Wemyss Malts. 767 bottles.*

Wemyss 1996 Single Speyside "The Honey Pot" hogshead, bott 2011 **(88.5) n22** butterscotch tart; **t23** big barley signature with more than a hint of honey on toast; **f21.5** dries with vanilla and cocoa dominating; **b22** no so much a honey pot as a thimble full. But a real charmer. *46%. sc. Wemyss Malts. 299 bottles.*

Wemyss 1996 Single Speyside "Vanilla Oak" butt, bott 2011 **(84.5) n21.5 t22 f20 b21.** Totally puzzled by the Vanilla oak tab: the oak plays only a supporting role to the outstanding barley. Not the greatest barrel and offers little positively on oaky front. But the quality of the distillate is exceptional. *46%. Wemyss Malts. 733 bottles.*

⁘ **The Whisky Agency Housemalt Single Speyside 8 Years Old** refill sherrywood, dist 2003 **(91.5) n23** delicate grape and grapefruit blossom beside the Bakewell tart theme; **t23.5** slight saline bite then a resounding sherry and bourbon mix with grape seeming to be taking on several waves of liquorice and hickory: superb!; **f22** layers of chocolate with the odd burnt raisin tossed in; **b23** forget the age: enjoy the charisma. *52.9%. sc.*

The Whisky Agency Speyside Single Malt 1969 bott 2010 **(92.5) n22** at first, appears weighed down with wood. But boiled molassed sweetness is evident, as well as overcooked gooseberry tart; **t24** fabulous delivery: grip tightly to your chair as the spices rip around your palate. But the balancing sugars do a near perfect job and we are back with hint of a fruit pie again...; **f23.5** calms down with a creamy mocha...with an extra sugar; **b23.5** one of the spiciest drams of the year. Delicious! *54.3%. The Whisky Agency.*

UNSPECIFIED SINGLE MALTS (General)

Chieftain's The Cigar Malt Aged 15 Years hogshead, dist Apr 95, bott 2011 **(94) n24** a spicy affair: delicate with fascinating tangy tangerine oak complexity; **t22.5** a muddled delivery, but within a beat or two it has set its course. And that is to the heart of a cocoa bean. Massive waves of milky chocolate; **f23.5** fantastically long finish with deft oak spices piling on those sugars and cocoa; **b24** must be one of those chocolate cigars I used to eat when I was a kid. Seemingly distilled from 100% malted cocoa and matured in a cask coopered by the gods. A gun to the head would never induce me to smoke a cigar or even cigarette (I did once have one put to my head by a weirdo to force me to smoke dope, and I turned that down, too – but that's another story). But just try and stop me drinking this stuff... *46%. nc ncf. Ian Macleod Distillers. USA release.*

⬝ **Clan Sinclair Aged 16 Years (94.5) n23.5** pretty stunning aroma with the smoke heading in three directions: first laying down an ashy base, as well as a soft smoky blanket. And then adds delicate spice for complexity. Dreamy stuff! **t24** a procession of gentle Demerara sugars are soothingly bathed in smoke and a surprising lack of salt (which makes me 99% convinced this isn't an Islay); the caramels cling to the yielding oils while the sugars build up in intensity once more; **f23** delicate, long, beautifully oiled and boasting a delicate, smoky, gristy sweetness to the very end; **b24** I have subsequently learned this is a Speysider, though not mentioned on the bottle. Must surely be Benriach at its most charming...and peaty! *43%. Scotia Blending Co. India exclusive.*

⬝ **The Whisky Agency Housemalt 16 Years Old** sherry cask, dist 1995, bott 2011 **(61) n15 t17 f14 b15.** Ex-sherry maybe. But, alas, there is nothing ex about the sulphur. *46%. sc.*

Scottish Vatted Malts
(also Pure Malts/Blended Malt Scotch)
100 Pipers Aged 8 Years Blended Malt (74) n19 t20 f17 b18. A better nose, perhaps, and some spice on arrival. But when you consider the Speysiders at their disposal, all those mouth-wateringly grassy possibilities, it is such a shame to find something as bland as this. *40%*

Ballantine's Pure Malt Aged 12 Years bott code. LKAC1538 **(88.5) n22.5** spicy mixture of honey, light smoke and added orange; **t23** stupendous mouth-feel with the fruit re-inserted alongside the honey; **f21** pretty thin with almost a grainy feel alongside the bittering oak; **b22** no sign of the peat being reintroduced to major effect, although the orange is a welcome addition. Remains a charmer. *40%. Chivas.*

Barrogill (90) n22.5 t23 f22.5 b22. Prince Charles, who allows the name to be used for this whisky, is said to enjoy this dram. Hardly surprising, as its pretty hard not to: this is wonderful fun. Curiously, I have just read the back label and noticed they use the word "robust" I have employed "lusty". Either way, I think you might get the message. *40%*

Barrogill North Highland Blended Malt Mey Selections bott code P012630 **(79) n18 t21 f20 b20.** Recovers attractively – helped by a mighty dose of concentrated maltiness - from the disappointing nose. *40%. Inver House Distillers for North Highland.*

Bell's Signature Blend Limited Edition bott 2009, bott no. 42515 **(83.5) n19 t22 f21 b21.5.** The front label makes large that this vatted malt has Blair Athol and Inchgower at the heart of it as they are "two fine malts selected for their exceptionally rich character". Kind of like saying you have invited the Kray twins to your knees up as they might liven it up a bit. Well those two distilleries were both part of the original Bell's empire, so fair dos. But to call them both fine malts is perhaps stretching the imagination somewhat. A robust vatting to say the least. And, to be honest, once you get past the nose, good back-slapping fun. *40%. 90,000 bottles.*

Berrys' Best Islay Vatted Malt Aged 8 Years (82) n20 t21 f20 b21. Smoky, raw, sweet, clean and massive fun! *43%. Borry Bros & Rudd.*

Berry's Own Selection Blue Hanger 5th Release bott 2010 **(81) n20 t21 f20 b20.** Not a lot – but enough – sulphur has crept in to take the edge of this one. *45.6%. nc ncf.*

Berry's Own Selection Islay Reserve 2nd Edition (86.5) n22 t22 f21 b21.5. Maybe an Islay reserve but has enough smoky weight and hickory/chocolate charisma to be pushing for the first team squad. *46%. nc ncf. Berry Bros & Rudd.*

Berry's Own Selection Speyside Reserve 2nd Edition (79.5) n21 t21.5 f18 b19. Some excellent early sharpness and honey depth but falters. *46%. nc ncf. Berry Bros & Rudd.*

Big Peat (96) n25 magnificent array of salt and bitty peat; heavy yet light enough for the most delicate of citrus. Hard to find a nose which screams "Islay" at you with such a lack of ambiguity: it is, frankly, perfect. **t24** the delivery is constructed around a fabulous bourbon Demerara sugar and liquorice framework; the peat enters as soon as this is in place and in varying layers of oiliness and depth. The mid ground sees the re-emergence of the more complex Ardbeg and Port Ellen factions, a bourbon style, small grains busyness; **f23.5** long, softly oiled still and then a slow dissolving liquorice and spice; vanillas pop up very late, still accompanied by soft Demerara; **b23.5** I suppose if you put Ardbeg and Port Ellen together there is a chance you might get something rather special. Not guaranteed, but achieved here with the kind of panache that leaves you spellbound. The complexity and balance are virtually off the charts, though had the Caol Ila been reduced slightly, and with it the oils, this might well have been World Whisky of the Year. *46%. ncf Douglas Laing & Co.*

⬝ **Big Peat Batch 20 Xmas 2011 (96) n24** just one of those noses where it takes a tremendous act of will to put the glass down....the interplay between the salts and sugars, the counterweights between the different varieties of phenols themselves; **t23.5** when the delivery strikes home with the oils, phenols and sugars in immediate harmony, you know you are in for an experience. the question is: can it keep this quality to the end? **f24.5** ....indeed it can! In fact, it improves and so complex and tantalising are those astonishing Demerara and peaty riches, it is hard to quite know where the end begins. A number of teasing bourbon tones, on the liquorice and hickory side – perhaps with a hint of honey – stoke the fires of complexity further...; **b24** I haven't got a television these days as my life is simply too busy. And with entertainment like this in the glass to keep you occupied, who needs one...? I doubt if any Christmas Special on the box came remotely close to matching this...! *57.8%. nc ncf.*

❖ **Big Peat Batch 26 (83.5) n21.5 t21.5 f20 b21.** Not quite as big a peat as some, suffering from over-active oils and a bitter rear-guard. Still has the odd powerful puff, though... *46%. nc ncf. Douglas Laing & Co.*

❖ **Big Peat Batch 27 (88) n22** sturdy, confident smoke, yet never over stating its case; **t22** excellent delivery with a wonderfully sexy slow injection of muscovado; **f22** really gets into its stride with the smoke and burgeoning vanillas in happy rhythm; **b22** well weighted sugars and just the right degree of smoked vanilla fade. Just spotted that this, the 888th new whisky for the Bible 2013 scored...88. It had to be ...!! *46%. nc ncf. Douglas Laing & Co.*

❖ **Big Peat Batch 28 (84.5) n22 t22 f20 b20.5.** Pleasant. But appears to possess a bit too much Caol Ila style oiliness to set the peaty pulse racing. *46%. nc ncf. Douglas Laing & Co.*

❖ **Big Peat Batch 29 (89.5) n22.5** excellent coastal feel; pretty decent oil to smoke ratio, too: clean and sits well in the glass; **t23** an impressive number of varying sugar notes, some of a more earthy variety, balance out the drier, chalkier oak tones. The smoke is ungainly, lumbering... but very handsome; **f22** a kind of Laphroaig cask bitterness has a minimal impact thanks to the prevailing oils and sugars; **b22** a peaty massage. *46%. nc ncf.*

❖ **Big Peat Batch 30 (92) n23** lovely hickory and Chocolate Cheerio branch to the main peaty trunk; **t22** I sigh at first with the early delivery of some major oil. But relax as the peat really does begin to stack up and a coastal saltiness intensifies the vanillas; **f23.5** superb finale with the sugars in far better control than some previous bottlings and they only escort the smoke rather than dominate it. The oils have also taken a break, giving a chance for the full complexity – even including a surprise citrus guest appearance – to work its magic; some low key spices offer a brief farewell; **b23.5** that's much more like it! This is far more how I expect this dram to be. *46%. nc ncf. Douglas Laing & Co.*

The Big Smoke 40 (83) n22 t21 f20 b20. Pure grist. *40%*

The Big Smoke 60 (92) n23 clean gristy lead with a freshly toasted bread depth; **t23.5** lovely sprightliness to the barley and zest to the peat; youthful but some impressive age lines, too; **f22.5** some coppery notes to the spicy, smoky finale; **b23** much more delicate and in touch with its more feminine self than was once the case. A real beauty. *60%. Duncan Taylor & Co.*

Black Face 8 Years Old (78.5) n18.5 t22 f19 b19. A huge malt explosion in the kisser on delivery, but otherwise not that pretty to behold. *46%. The Vintage Malt Whisky Co Ltd.*

Burns Nectar (89.5) n22 honeycomb dipped in lime juice; **t22** glorious mouth feel to delivery: a soft, oily platform from which more honey can easily be detected; chewy toffee and vanilla, too; **f23** the lightest sprinkling of spice and some ginger cake to round off beautifully; **b22.5** a delight of a dram and with all that honey around, "Nectar" is about right. *40%*

Carme 10 Years Old (79) n21.5 t20 f18.5 b19. On paper Ardmore and Clynelish should work well together. But vatting is not done on paper and here you have two malts cancelling each other out and some less than great wood sticking its oar in. *43%*

❖ **Cask Islay Vatting No. 1 (89) n23** young: the colour of coconut water, but somewhat smokier to nose... Huge peat of a bold, dry, ashy, slightly biting variety...; **t22** crisp, with a few crunchy sugars doing their best to stave off the peaty attack. It is, inevitably, an unequal battle; **f22** spicy, a little nippy but good late cocoa; **b22** those looking for a soft, smoky, inoffensive little Islay to keep them company had better look elsewhere... *46%. ncf. A.D. Rattray Ltd.*

Castle Rock Aged 12 Years Blended Malt (87) n22.5 grassy, under-ripe gooseberry; **t23** every bit as fresh and juicy as the nose suggests **f19.5** a creeping bitterness; **b22** stupendously refreshing: the finish apart, I just love this style of malt. *40%*

Cearban (79.5) n18 t21.5 f20 b19. The label shows a shark. It should be a whale: this is massive. Sweet with the malts not quite on the same wavelength. *40%. Robert Graham Ltd.*

❖ **Celtique Connexion Sauternes 16 Years Old** dist 1995, bott 2012 **(95) n24** if you're into walnut-studded, Demerara-sweetened three-year-old fruit cake, then get a sniff of this. More sherry than a sherry cask...; **t24** just so intense, just so full of ultra-ripe fruit (with dates and walnut plus greengages and physalis heading the cast) that you cannot be other than filled with wonder. It would all be too much, except when that huge delivery is over, barley at last makes an appearance, also with a nutty theme towards the middle; **f23** I could almost shed a tear; not a single hint of sulphur, no bitterness from a tired cask. Just a long, elegant fade of barley tinged with the remnants of old Dickinson and Morris Melton Hunt Cake...you know; the one that you have had waiting in the back of the cupboard for the last five years...; and the final, lingering note: walnut oil..; **b24** not many whiskies make me cough, and hardly any at all at just 46%abv. But this, though only because the intensity caught me by surprise. And what a pleasant one! This horse chestnut-coloured malt is one you are unlikely to forget in a hurry. As sweetly balanced and beautiful to enjoy as Josh Wright's stunning volley for Millwall at Burnley in February 2012.... *46%. nc ncf. Celtic Whisky Compagnie.*

Clan Campbell 8 Years Old Pure Malt (82) n20 t22 f20 b20. Enjoyable, extremely safe whisky that tries to offend nobody. The star quality is all on the complex delivery, then it's toffee. *40%. Chivas Brothers.*

Clan Denny (Bowmore, Bunnahabhain, Caol Ila and Laphroaig) **(94) n24 t23 f23 b24.** A very different take on Islay with heavy peats somehow having a floating quality. Unique. *40%*

⠢ **Clan Denny Islay (86.5) n21.5 t23 f21 b21.** A curiously bipolar malt with the sweetness and bitterness at times going to extremes. Some niggardly oak has taken the edge of what might have been a sublime malt as the peat and spices at times positively glistens with honey. *46.5%. nc ncf sc. Douglas Laing & Co.*

Clan Denny Speyside (87) n22 big, big malt: exceptionally clean and soft. Oily, too; **t22** a charming sweetness to the barley helps counter the more bitter aspects of the approaching oak; delicate oils help make for an exceptionally soft delivery **f21** no shortage of vanilla as it bitters out; **b22** a Tamdhu-esque oiliness pervades here and slightly detracts from the complexity That said, the early freshness is rather lovely. *46%. Douglas Laing.*

Compass Box Canto Cask 10 bott Jul 07 **(86.5) n20.5 t21 f23.5 b21.5.** One the Canto collection which slipped through my net a few years back, but is still around, I understand. Typical of the race, this one has perhaps an extra dollop of honey which helps keep the over vigorous oaks under some degree of control. Sublime finish. *54.2%. nc ncf 200-250 bottles.*

Compass Box Eleuthera Marriage married for nine months in an American oak Hogshead **(86) n22 t22 f20 b22.** I'm not sure if it's the name that gets me on edge here, but as big and robust as it is I still can't help feeling that the oak has bitten too deep. Any chance of a Compass Box Divorce...? *49.2%. Compass Box for La Maison du Whisky.*

Compass Box Flaming Hart second batch, bottling no. FH16MMVII **(95.5) n23.5 t24.5 f23 b24.5.** The Canto range was, I admit, a huge over-oaked disappointment. This, though, fully underlines Compass Box's ability to come up with something approaching genius. This is a whisky that will be remembered by anyone who drinks it for the rest of their lives as just about the perfect study of full-bodied balance and sophistication. And that is not cheap hyperbole. *48.9%. nc ncf. 4,302 bottles.*

Compass Box Flaming Heart 10th Anniversary bott Sep 10 **(92) n24** earthy, almost rustic in its smouldering stubble smokiness; a number of almost zingy fruity notes ensure the balance; **t23** naturally, the smoke has an important early role and gets its lines away without a hitch; a light sliver of dark chocolate melts into the impressive oils; **f22** lashings of vanilla though the oak may scare some, as might a light tanginess; **b23** this one, as Flaming Heart so often is, is about counterweight and mouth feel. Everything appears just where it should be... *48.9%. nc ncf 4186 bottles*

Compass Box Lady Luck American white oak hogshead, bott Sep 09 **(91) n22** earthy; tree bark; dank woods; an irrigated Taiwanese tomato field; **t24** much lighter than the nose...and sweeter...and spicier...wow!!... **f23** pure chocolate mousse before some bitterness descends; **b22** just a shade too sweet for mega greatness like The Spice Tree, but quite an endearing box of tricks. *46%. Compass Box Whisky Co.*

Compass Box Oak Cross bott May 10 **(92.5) n23** all kinds of bourbony red liquorice notes and drilled, oaky spices. But the butterscotch tart takes me back to my earliest school memories...; **t24** a delivery which makes you gasp out loud: decent weight, but absolutely no pressure on the taste buds as it coats the mouth and the injection of maple syrup is to die for. The bitter-sweet interplay is exceptional, again keeping a big oaky butterscotch shape, but lightened by lemon curd tart; **f22.5** now those oaky vanillas get a clearer sight of goal but the barley still fends off any excess; **b23** the oak often threatens to be just too big a cross to bear. But such is the degree of complexity, and cleverness of weight, the overall brilliance is never dimmed. Overall, a bit of a tart of a whisky... *43%. nc ncf.*

Compass Box The Peat Monster bott May 10 **(82) n21.5 t21.5 f19 b20.** It is as though Victor Frankenstein's creation has met Bambi. Monsters don't come much stranger or more sanitised than this... *46%. nc ncf.*

Compass Box The Peat Monster Reserve (92) n23 t23.5 f22.5 b23. At times a bit of a Sweet Monster...beautiful stuff! *48.9%*

Compass Box The Spice Tree first-fill and refill American oak. Secondary maturation: heavily toasted new French oak **(95.5) n24.5** quite paradoxical. First sniff and you think: "whoa! That's a big-un." Then you nose again, slowly and carefully you realise that whilst the nose does seem superficially big, it is actually made up of dozens of tiny aromas ganging together. The main theme is delicate tangerine and vanilla – almost like tangerine yogurt – but there are weightier spices to note, all of them fragments, especially the watery allspice and ginger...sublime...; **t24.5** and now the palate continues with exactly the same theme: a million little flavour explosions, all timed to go off one after the other, but all on a sweet muscovado sugar bed created by the superb base malt of Clynelish; **f23** thins rapidly into a more basic vanilla, though there is still a spice pulse and glow; just a little bitter at the death; **b23.5** having initially been chopped down by the SWA, who were indignant that extra staves had been inserted into the casks, The Spice Tree is not only back but in full bloom. Indeed, the blossom on this, created by the use of fresh oak barrel heads, is more intoxicating than its predecessor – mainly because there is a more even and less dramatic personality to this. Not just a great malt, but a serious contender for Jim Murray Whisky Bible 2011 World Whisky of the Year. *46%*

Compass Box The Spice Tree Inaugural Batch (93) n23 t23 f23 b24. The map for flavour distribution had to be drawn for the first time here: an entirely different whisky in shape and flavour emphasis. And it is a map that takes a long time to draw... *46%. 4150 bottles.*

Co-operative Group (CWS) Blended Malt Aged 8 Years (86.5) n22 t22 f21 b21.5. Much, much better! Still a little on the sticky and sweet side, but there is some real body and pace to the changes on the palate. Quite rich, complex and charming. *40%*

Cutty Sark Blended Malt (92.5) n22 a salty, sweaty armpit doesn't fill you with confidence at first, but then light smoke descends as well as some prime grassy barley; **t24** magnificent! The mouth feel is close to perfection, as there is a dazzling sheen to this one thanks to a just-so squirt of something a little oily; the vaguest of smoke wrestles with the more clear-cut barley; **f23** thinner, but maintains the malty sheen, though dried now by vanilla; the building of the spices is quite wonderful; **b23.5** sheer quality: as if two styles have been placed in the bottle and told to fight it out between them. What a treat! *40%. Berry Bros & Rudd.*

⬩⬩⬩ **Douglas Laing's Double Barrel Ardbeg & Glenrothes (91)** n23 just about as complex as you'd expect; the peat reveals a peppery trait which seasons the light oak; **t23** soft delivery of intense barley and smoky grist; the phenols are delicate but confident enough to make inroads into the vanilla and malty nougat; **f22** a little oil helps emphasise the smoky acacia honey sweetness; **b23** a feather-light whisky offering subtlety throughout; *46%*

Douglas Laing's Double Barrel Ardbeg & Glenrothes Aged 10 Years product no. MSW2685 **(92)** n22 a salty breeze apart, the curiously inconspicuous Ardbeg allows the Speysider to dominate; **t24** but a different story on delivery where the malts are sharp, jagged and juicy while the smoke and oak, and even some rich dates from somewhere, hover in the background; with a metallic sheen and the nod spurt of honey here and there, this is different...and works a treat; **f23** a deft smoke edge to the vanilla; **b23** not what I was expecting. But a lovely experience nonetheless. *46%. Douglas Laing & Co Ltd.*

Douglas Laing's Double Barrel Ardbeg & Glenrothes Aged 10 Years product no. DBS0003 **(88.5)** n23 great nose: delicate, playful smoke lightened by lime Rowntree's Fruit Gums; **t22** firm barley with virtually no give but a slow unveiling of juicy barley; the smoke is also firm but flighty; **f21.5** an oaky bitterness; **b22** an uncompromising but fun way to bring up New Whisky no. 750 for Bible 2011... *46%. Douglas Laing.*

Douglas Laing's Double Barrel Braeval & Caol Ila Aged 10 Years (78) n18 t21 f20 b19. The Mike and Bernie Winters of double barrelled whisky. *46%. Douglas Laing & Co Ltd.*

Douglas Laing's Double Barrel Caol Ila & Braeval Aged 10 Years (84.5) n21 t22 f20.5 b21. It is probably impossible to find a malt which is more friendly and inoffensive. Or two malts which have done such a first class job of cancelling each other's personalities out. *46%*

⬩⬩⬩ **Douglas Laing's Double Barrel Caol Ila & Tamdhu (89)** n22 light, agreeable grassy barley in a thin peaty mist; **t23** as though someone has added a little cooking oil and muscovado sugar to the big barley delivery; adore the way the smoke edges in...; **f22** long – hardly surprising with the oil – and a delicate, increasingly spicy fade; **b22** put two oily malts together and you get...an oily whisky... *46%*

Douglas Laing's Double Barrel Glenrothes & Ardbeg Aged 10 Years 4th Release (89.5) n21.5 surprisingly angular and sharp; **t23** and on delivery, too, though a soft caress of lightly oiled smoke helps. A few waves of honey hit the middle with some citrus thinning things down; **f22.5** lightly smoked custard; **b22.5** despite the average nose the charmingly effete palate is another matter entirely. *46%. Douglas Laing.*

Douglas Laing's Double Barrel Highland Park & Bowmore (95) n23 pounding spices and dry smoke; **t24.5** a passionate embrace of honeyed peat followed by waves of juicy barley almost gives you the vapours; **f24** long, lip-smacking with the improbable degree of honey lasting the distance; the peat gives way to a stunning array of spices; **b23.5** the vital spark of fury to this one keeps the palate ignited. A standing ovation for such a magnificent performance on the palate. *46%. Douglas Laing & Co Ltd.*

⬩⬩⬩ **Douglas Laing's Double Barrel Ledaig & Bowmore (87)** n22.5 busy phenols, though not as busy as those complex sugars; **t22** gristy and melt-in-the-mouth with the sugars again out-performing the smoke; **f21.5** yet more grist with the smoke hanging on to its sugary coat-tail; the only oak evident is a degree of late bitterness; **b21** about as sweet a marriage as you are likely to find. For some, it may be too sweet! *46%. Douglas Laing & Co.*

Douglas Laing's Double Barrel Macallan & Laphroiag 5th Release (93) **n23.5** rousing barley balances the light, flakey smoke; **t24** the ultra delicate theme continues, with a lovely jam Swiss Roll sweetness mixing it with the gristy peat; juicy with a slow building of oil; **f22.5** long with a sprinkling of grated chocolate in the vanilla and smoke; **b23** as if born to be together. *46%*

Douglas Laing's Double Barrel Macallan & Laphroaig Aged 9 Years (83.5) **n21 t22 f20 b20.5.** Curiously muted. Sweet with the natural caramels outweighing the smoke. *46%*

⁘ **Douglas Laing's Double Barrel Mortlach & Laphroaig** 2nd Release (83.5) **n20 t22 f20.5 b21.** Compared to the Ardbeg/Glenrothes match, about as subtle and delicate as a smoky custard pie in the face. Hot and snarling fare. *46%*

⁘ **Douglas Laing's Double Barrel Talisker & Craigellachie** (73) **n19 t19 f17 b18.** Should be divorced on the grounds of adultery with a poor cask. *46%*

Duncan Taylor Regional Malt Collection Islay 10 Years Old (81) **n21 t22 f19 b19.** Soft citrus cleanses the palate, while gentle peats muddies it up again. *40%*

The Famous Grouse 10 Years Old Malt (77) **n19 t20 f19 b19.** The nose and finish headed south in the last Winter and landed in the sulphur marshes of Jerez. *40%. Edrington Group.*

The Famous Grouse 15 Years Old Malt (86) **n21 t22 f21.5 b21.5.** Salty and smoky with a real sharp twang. *43%. Edrington Group.*

The Famous Grouse 15 Years Old Malt (86) **n19 t24 f22 b21.** There had been a hint of the "s" word on the nose, but it got away with it. Now it has crossed that fine – and fatal – line where the petulance of the sulphur has thrown all else slightly out of kilter. All, that is, apart from the delivery which is a pure symphony of fruit and spice deserving a far better introduction and final movement. Some moving, beautiful moments. Flawed genius or what...? *40%*

The Famous Grouse 18 Years Old Malt (82) **n19 t21.5 f21 b20.5.** Some highly attractive honey outweighs the odd uncomfortable moment. *43%. Edrington Group.*

The Famous Grouse Malt 21 Years Old (91) **n22** candy jar spices, green apple and crisp barley. **t24** spot on oak offers a platform for the myriad rich malty notes and now, in the latest bottlings, enlivened further with an injection of exploding spice... wow! **f22** flattens slightly but muscovado sugar keeps it light and sprightly; **b23** a very dangerous dram: the sort where the third or fourth would slip down without noticing. Wonderful scotch! *43%. Edrington Group.*

The Famous Grouse 30 Years Old Malt (94) **n23.5** brain-implodingly busy and complex: labyrinthine depth within a kind of Highland Park frame with extra emphasis on grape and salt; **t24** yesssss!!!! Just so magnificent with the theme being all about honeycomb...but on so many different levels of intensity and toastiness: so juicy too. **f23** now the spices dive in as the barley resurfaces again; long, layered with spot on bitter-sweet balance; **b23.5** whisky of this sky-high quality is exactly what vatted malt should be all about. Outrageously good. *43%*

Glenalmond 2001 Vintage (82.5) **n22 t21.5 f19 b20.** Glenkumquat, more like: the most citrusy malt I have tasted in a very long time. *40%. The Vintage Malt Whisky Co Ltd.*

Glenalmond "Everyday" (89.5) **n21.5** mainly malt, **t23.5** soft delivery which increases in barley intensity at a remarkably even rate; excellent gristy sugar-vanilla balance; **f22** remains on its malty crusade to the death; **b22.5** they are not joking; this really is an everyday whisky. Glorious malt which is so dangerously easy to drink. *40%*

Glen Brynth Aged 12 Years Blended Malt (87) **n22.5 t23 f19.5 b22.** Deja vu...! Thought I was going mad: identical to the Castle Rock I tasted this morning, right down to the (very) bitter end ..!!! *40%. Quality Spirits International.*

⁘ **Glenbrynth Blended Malt 12 Years** (87.5) **n22.5** deft fruit and always great to find a nose where your senses are caressed rather than attacked; the barley arrives in almost fresh, green, unmalted form; **t22.5** as much honeycomb and coppery sharpness as you could wish for; **f21** thins too rapidly, though some welcome spices hang on to the coattails of the sugars; **b21.5** heavyweight malt which gets off to a rip-roaring start on the delivery but falls away somewhat from the mid ground onwards. *43%. OTI Africa.*

⁘ **Glenbrynth Ruby 40 Year Old Limited Edition** (94) **n23.5** huge nose with as much oak as the buttressing fruit and molasses can withstand; a vague smokiness dips in and out of the slightly burnt Melton Hunt fruit cake; **t24** soft delivery showing the barley to far better effect than the nose manages. The fruit grows in stature, moving from sultana to toasted raisin at a gallop; **f23** the finish positively throbs with old oak and a little smoke. The molassed sugars ensure a wonderful bitter-sweet fade; **b23.5** has all the hallmarks of a completely OTT, far too old sherry butt being brought back to life with the aid of a livelier barrel. A magnificent experience, full of fun and evidence of some top quality vatting at work, too. *43%. OTI Africa.*

Glendower 8 Years Old (84) **n21.5 t21 f20.5 b21** Nutty and spicy. *43%*

⁘ **The Glenfohry Aged 8 Years Special Reserve** (73) **n19 t19 f17 b18.** Some of the malt used here appears to have come from a still where the safe has not so much been broken into, but just broken! Oily and feinty, to say the least. Normally I would glower at anyone who even thought of putting a coke into their malt. Here, I think it might be for the best.. 40%

Glen Turner Pure Malt Aged 8 Years L525956A **(84) n20 t22 f22 b20.** A lush and lively vatting annoyingly over dependent on thick toffee but simply brimming with fabulously mouth-watering barley and over-ripe blood oranges. To those who bottle this, I say: let me into your lab. I can help you bring out something sublime!! 40%

⫸ **Glen Orchy (80.5) n19.5 t21.5 f19.5 b20.** Not exactly the most subtle of vatted malts though when the juicy barley briefly pours through on delivery, enjoyable. 40%. Lidl.

Glen Orrin (68) n16.5 t17.5 f17 b17. In its favour, it doesn't appear to be troubled by caramel. Which means the nose and palate are exposed to the full force of this quite dreadful whisky. 40%. Aldi.

Glen Orrin Six Year Old (88) n22 a bit sweaty but the oranges delight. Some delicate background smoke is a surprising complement; **t23** big, chewy and rugged with outstanding soft-oiled lushness which helps to dissipate the youthfulness; **f21** delicate spice and arousing coffee-cocoa: a bigger age signature than you might expect **b22** a vatting that has improved in the short time it has been around, now displaying some lovely orangey notes on the nose and a genuinely lushness to the body and spice on the finish. You can almost forgive the caramel, this being such a well balanced, full-bodied ride. A quality show for the price. 40%

Hedges and Butler Special Pure Malt (83) n20 t21 f22 b21. Just so laid back: nosed and tasted blind I'd swear this was a blend (you know, a real blend with grains and stuff) because of the biting lightness and youth. Just love the citrus theme and, err...graininess...!! 40%

Imperial Tribute (83) n19.5 t21.5 f21 b21. I am sure – and sincerely hope – the next bottling will be cleaned up and the true Imperial Tribute can be nosed and tasted. Because this is what should be a very fine malt... but just isn't. 46%. Spencer Collings.

Islay Trilogy 1969 (Bruichladdich 1966, Bunnahabhain 1968, Bowmore 1969) Bourbon/ Sherry **(91) n23 t23 f22 b23.** Decided to mark the 700th tasting for the 2007 edition with this highly unusual vatting. And no bad choice. The smoke is as elusive as the Paps of Jura on a dark November morning, but the silky fruits and salty tang tells a story as good as anything you'll hear by a peat fire. Take your time...the whiskies have. 40.3%. Murray McDavid.

J & B Exception Aged 12 Years (80) n20 t23 f18 b19. Very pleasant in so many ways. A charming sweetness develops quickly, with excellent soft honeycomb. But the nose and finish are just so...so...dull...!! For the last 30 years J&B has meant, to me, (and probably within that old company) exceptionally clean, fresh Speysiders offering a crisp, mouth-watering treat. I feel this is off target. 40%. Diageo/Justerini & Brooks.

J & B Nox (89) n23 classy Speyside thrust, youthful and crisp with a wonderful strand of honey. Gentle oak balances pleasingly; **t23** the nose in liquid form: exactly the same characteristics with some extra, gently peppered toast towards the middle; **f21** dries just a little too much as the barley tires; **b22** a teasing, pleasing little number that is unmistakably from the J&B stable. 40%. Diageo.

John Black 8 Years Old Honey (88) n21 vanilla to the fore; **t22.5** the promised honey arrives on delivery couched by fresh barley; **f22.5** light, delicate back to vanilla; **b22** a charming vatting. 40%. Tullibardine Distillery.

John Black 10 Years Old Peaty (91) n23 salty and peaty; **t23** soft and peaty; **f22** delicate and peaty; **b23** classy and er...peaty. 40%. Tullibardine Distillery.

John McDougall's Selection Islay Malt 1993 cask no. 103 **(94.5) n23.5** peek-a-boo peat can barely make itself heard above the honeyed barley and lightly salted oak. 'Delicate' barely covers it... **t24.5** seductive beyond belief: the soft rounding off of the honey with a mint-chocolate peatiness, especially as it fills the middle ground, really is one for the collector's corner: unique and simply breathtaking, and with a Bowmore-ish Fisherman's Friend bite hitting for a couple of nano seconds, pretty intriguing, too; **f22.5** drier with soft peat embers giving way to the milk coffee and vanilla; **b24** complex, superbly weighted and balanced malt which just keeps you wondering what will happen next. 54.7%. House of Macduff.

Johnnie Walker Green Label 15 Years Old (95) n24 kind of reminds me of a true, traditional Cornish Pasty: it is as though the segments have been compartmentalised, with the oak acting as the edible pastry keeping them apart. Sniff and there is a degree of fruit; nose again and there is the Speyside/Clynelish style of intense, slightly sweet maltiness. Sniff a third time and, at last you can detect just a hint of smoke. Wonderful... **t23.5** no compartmentalisation here as the delivery brings all those varying characters together for one magnificently complex maltfest. Weightier than previous Green Label events with the smoke having a bigger say. But the oak really bobs and weaves as the palate is first under a tidal wave of juicy malt and then the fruit and smoke – and no little spice – take hold...; **f23.5** soft smoke and grumbling spice latch on to the fruit-stained oak; plenty of cocoa just to top things off; **b24** god, I love this stuff...this is exactly how a vatted malt should be and one of the best samples I've come across since its launch. 43%. Diageo.

Jon, Mark and Robbo's The Rich Spicy One (89) n22 t23 f22 b22. So much better without the dodgy casks: a real late night dram of distinction though the spices perhaps a little on the subtle side... 40%. Edrington.

Jon, Mark and Robbo's The Smoky Peaty One (92) n23 t22 f23 b24. Genuinely high-class whisky where the peat is full-on yet allows impressive complexity and malt development. A malt for those who appreciate the better, more elegant things in life. 40%. Edrington.

⁕ **The Last Vatted Malt** bott Nov 11 (96.5) n24 the work of both oak and the peat kiln appear to be well matched here. Though perhaps it is the orange blossom and pear fruitiness that really makes the heart skip a beat; t25 a sublime delivery. The Compass Box marque of oakiness is stamped prominently, but couched this time by a stunning mix of cream cocoa, lightly sweetened by Demerara. Improbably, half way in there is a steady stream of juicy barley...about the same time you notice how well balanced the smoke is: like a great football referee, you don't actually notice him being there, but makes all else run beautifully; f23.5 doesn't try to develop. Just allows the elements that make up this complex whisky the space to run their own course...; b24 being an American, Compass Box founder and blender, John Glaser, knows a thing or two about pouring two fingers of whisky. So I join John in raising two fingers to the SWA and toast them in the spirit they deserve to thank them for their single-minded and successful quest to outlaw this ancient whisky term. 53.7%. nc ncf. Compass Box. 1,323 bottles.

Mackinlay's Rare Old Highland Malt (89) n22 mainly a vanilla structure on the nose with a mildly industrial oily heaviness lurking deep in its bowels. There is a hint of a hint of citrus and a more profound barley quality sweetened in the way a small puddle of molten sugar does the trick on porridge; t22 much more weighty on delivery than the nose ever achieves. Back more now to the trademark W&M denseness (though without the usual accompanying toffee) with a thick soup of barley and oak thinned only by a slow development of vanilla. That distant industrial oil on the nose becomes a lot more profound from the early middle ground onwards; f22 chewy with a mocha, vaguely smoked and oily finale; b23 possibly the most delicate malt whisky I can remember coming from the labs of Whyte and Mackay. Thought it still, on the palate, must rank as heavy medium. This is designed as an approximation of the whisky found at Shackleton's camp in the Antarctic. And as a life-long Mackinlay drinker myself, it is great to find a whisky baring its name that, on the nose only, briefly reminds me of the defter touches which won my heart over 30 years ago. That was with a blend: this is a vatted malt. And a delicious one. In case you wondered: I did resist the temptation to use ice. 473%. Whyte & Mackay.

Matisse 12 Year Old Blended Malt (93) n23.5 t23 f22.5 b23. Succulent, clean as a whistle mixture of malts with zero bitterness and not even a whisper of an off note: easily the best form I have ever seen this brand in. Superb. 40%. Matisse Spirits Co Ltd.

Matisse Aged 12 Years (79) n17 t21 f20 b21. Not sure if some finishing or re-casking has been going on here to liven it up. Has some genuine buzz on the palate, but intriguing weirdness, too. Don't bother nosing this one. 40%. The Matisse Spirits Co Ltd.

Milroy's of Soho Finest Blended Malt (76) n18 t19 f20 b19. Full flavoured, nutty, malty but hardly textbook. 40%. Milroy's of Soho.

Mo'land (82) n21 t22 f19 b20. Extra malty but lumbering and on the bitter side. 40%. Master Of Malt.

Monkey Shoulder batch 27 (79.5) n21 t21.5 f18 b19. Been a while since I lasted tasted this one. Though its claims to be Batch 27, I assume all bottlings are Batch 27 seeing as they are from 27 casks. This one, whichever it is, has a distinctive fault found especially at the finale, which is disappointing. Even before hitting that point a big toffeed personality makes for a pleasant if limited experience. 40%. William Grant & Sons.

"No Age Declared" The Unique Pure Malt Very Limited Edition 16-49 Years (85) n22.5 t19.5 f22 b21. Very drinkable. But this is odd stuff: as the ages are as they are, and as it tastes as it does, I can surmise only that the casks were added together as a matter of necessity rather than any great blending thought or planning. Certainly the malt never finds a rhythm but maybe it's the eclectic style on the finish that finally wins through. 45%. Samaroli.

Norse Cask Selection Vatted Islay 1992 Aged 16 Years hogshead cask no. QWVIM3, dist 92, bott 09 (95) n24 t24 f23 b24. The recipe of 60/35/5 Ardbeg/Laphroaig/Bowmore new make matured in one cask is a surprise: the oiliness here suggests a squirt of Caol Ila somewhere. This hybrid is certainly different, showing that the DNA of Ardbeg is unrecognisable when mixed, like The Fly, with others. Drinkable...? Oh, yes...!! Because this, without a single negative note to its name, is easily one of the whiskies of the year and a collector's and/or Islayphile's absolute must have. 56.7%

Norse Cask Selection Vatted Islay 1991 Aged 12 Years (89) n24 t23 f21 b21. Fabulous, but not much going in the way of complexity. But if you're a peat freak, I don't think you either notice...or much care...!! 59.5%. Quality World, Denmark.

Old St Andrews Fireside (88.5) n22 delicate, bright, the faintest hint of distant smoke; t22.5 sharp, clean and full of malty freshness; f21.5 custard creams dunked in spiced milk; b(22.5) beautifully driven... 40%. Old St Andrews Ltd.

Old St Andrews Nightcap (89) n21.5 oak and spice plus the odd atom of smoke amid the Tunnock's caramel wafer...; t24 beautiful weight on delivery and the muscovado sugar edge is a pure delight; salivating and eye-wateringly sharp: a classic vatted malt early flavour profile...; f21 dries quickly amid the vanilla and caramel; b22.5 some delightful weight and mass but perhaps a bit too much toffee takes its toll. 40%. Old St Andrews Ltd.

Old St Andrews Twilight (94.5) n24 fabulous: a classic clean, Speyside-juicy style which is quite irresistible. Not a single harsh or discordant note here...it is almost pure grist; t23.5 mirrors the nose to a tee...; f23 light, flaky vanilla and spice begins to take over; b24 less Twilight as Sunrise as this is full of invigorating freshness which fills the heart with hope and joy: Lip-smacking Scotch malt whisky as it should be. Anyone who thinks the vatted malt served up for golf lovers in these novelty bottles is a load of old balls are a fair way off target... 40%. Old St Andrews Ltd.

Poit Dhubh 8 Bliadhna (90) n22.5 toffee-banana; t23.5 sublime delivery: perfect weight and chewability with light spice mixing with the cocoa-rich barley; f21.5 toffee fudge; b22.5 though the smoke which marked this vatting has vanished, it has more than compensated with a complex beefing up of the core barley tones. Cracking whisky. 43%. ncf. Pràban na Linne.

Poit Dhubh 12 Bliadhna (77) n20 t20 f18 b19. Toffee-apples. Without the apples. 43%. ncf. Pràban na Linne.

Poit Dhubh 21 Bliadhna (86) n22 t22.5 f21 b20.5. Over generous toffee has robbed us of what would have been a very classy malt. 43%. ncf. Pràban na Linne.

The Pot Still Scotch Vatted Malt Over 8 Years Old (90) n22 excellent oak sub plot to the ballsy barley; t24 goes down with all the seductive powers of long fingernails down a chest: the wonderful honey and barley richness is stunning and so beautifully weighted; f22 a lazier finale, allowing the chalky oaky notes to make folly of those tender years; b22 such sophistication: the Charlotte Rampling of Scotch. 43.5%. ncf. Celtic Whisky Compagnie, France.

Prime Blue Pure Malt (83) n21 t21 f21 b20. Steady, with a real chewy toffee middle. Friendly stuff. 40%

Prime Blue 12 Years Old Pure Malt (78) n20 t20 f19 b19. A touch of fruit but tart. 40%

Prime Blue 17 Years Old Pure Malt (88) n23 clever weight and a touch of something fruity and exotic, too; t21 thick malt concentrate; f22 takes a deliciously latte-style route and would be even better but for the toffee; excellent spicing; b22 lovely, lively vatting: something to get your teeth into! 40%

Prime Blue 21 Years Old Pure Malt (77) n21 t20 f18 b18. After the teasing, bourbony nose the remainder disappoints with a caramel-rich flatness. The reprise of a style of whisky I thought had vanished about four of five years ago 40%

·:· **Rattray's Selection Blended Malt 19 Years Old Batch 1** Benrinnes sherry hogsheads **(89.5)** n22 half-hearted fruit but the barley packs a punch; t23.5 magnificent! What a delivery and follow-through. As sharp and biting as one of those eye-watering fruit candies school kids love; fabulous weight between the puckering barley and the vivid fruit; the oak is always pounding away with gusto; f21.5 bitters slightly too enthusiastically though an oaky chocolate mousse does help; b22.5 absolutely love it! Offers just the right degree of mouth-watering complexity. not a malt for those looking for the sit-on-the-fence wishy-washy type. 55.8%. Auchentoshan, Bowmore, Balblair & BenRiach. A.D. Rattray Ltd.

Sainsbury's Malt Whisky Finished in Sherry Casks (70) n18 t19 f16 b17. Never the greatest of the Sainsbury range, it's somehow managed to get worse. Actually, not too difficult when it comes to finishing in sherry, and the odd sulphur butt or three has done its worst here. 40%. UK.

Scottish Collie (86.5) n22 t23 f20.5 b21. A really young pup of a vatting. Full of life and fun but muzzled by toffee at the death. 40%. Quality Spirits International.

Scottish Collie 5 Years Old (90.5) n22.5 teasing interplay between grassy young malts and something just a little more profound and vaguely phenolic; t23 more of the same on delivery; an engaging sharpness keeps the tastebuds puckered; f22 long, with the accent on that wonderfully clean ,sweet and sharp barley; even the soft toffee can't get much of a toe-hold; b23 fabulous mixing here showing just what malt whisky can do at this brilliant and under-rated age. Lively and complex with the malts wonderfully herded and penned. Without colouring and at 50% abv I bet this would have been given a right wolf-whistle. Perfect for one man and his grog. 40%. Quality Spirits International.

Scottish Collie 8 Years Old (85.5) n22 t21.5 f21 b21. A good boy. But just wants to sleep rather than play. 40%. Quality Spirits International.

Scottish Collie 12 Years Old (82) n20 t22 f20 b20. For a malt that's aged 84 in Collie years, it understandably smells a bit funny and refuses to do many tricks. If you want some fun you'll need a younger version. 40%. Quality Spirits International.

Scottish Leader Imperial Blended Malt (77) n20 t20 f18 b19. Now don't be confused here: this isn't Imperial malt from Speyside. And although it says Blended, it is 100% malt. What is clear, though, is that this is pretty average stuff. 40%. Burn Stewart.

Scottish Leader Aged 14 Years (80) n21 t21 f19 b19. A cleaner, less peaty version than the no-age statement vatting, but still fails to entirely ignite the tastebuds 40%. Burn Stewart.

❖ **Scott's Selection Burnside 1994** bott 2012 **(93)** n23.5 for Dundee cake lovers the world over, especially those with a soft spot for toasted almonds; certainly doesn't go easy on the glazed sherries and molasses; a little unwelcome dryness is in the air, too; **t24** the famous integrity of the Balvenie malt shows to sublime effect here: so much fruit and yet the barley has such a big say, too. Toasty, for sure, and eye-wateringly fruity. But a light salty tang brings out the sharper aspects of the honeycomb; **f22.5** tightens a little until the Glenfiddich makes its mark...only joking!! Maybe some evidence of not quite the perfect cask, but its mild failings are easily forgiven; **b23.5** I may well be wrong. But I think this is the first time I have seen a Burnside, which is a cask of Balvenie spoiled as a single malt by having a spoonful of same age Glenfiddich added to it, in a commercial bottling rather than as a sample in my blending lab! Believe me: it was well worth waiting for...! 56.7%. Speyside Distillers.

Sheep Dip (84) n19 t22 f22 b21. Young and sprightly like a new-born lamb, this enjoys a fresh, mouthwatering grassy style wth a touch of spice. Maligned by some, but to me a clever, accomplished vatting of alluring complexity. 40%

Sheep Dip 'Old Hebridean' 1990 dist in or before 1990 **(94)** n23 every aspect has the buoyancy of an anchor, the subtlety of Hebridean Winter winds. Thick peat offering both smoke and a kippery saltiness is embraced by honey; **t24** big, weighty delivery with an immediate spice and honey delivery; a butterscotch barley theme appears and vanishes like a small fishing craft in mountainous waves; **f23.5** that honey keeps the pace and length, while a beautiful bourbon red liquorice beefs up the vanilla; **b23.5** you honey!! Now, that's what I call a whisky...!! 40%. The Spencerfield Spirit Co.

The Six Isles Pomerol Finish Limited Edition French oak Pomerol wine cask no. 90631-90638, dist 2003, bott 2010 **(85.5)** n19 t23 f21.5 b22. What makes the standard Six Isles work as a vatted malt is its freshness and complexity. With these attributes, plus the distinctive distilleries used, we consistently have one the world's great and truly entertaining whiskies. With this version we have just a decent malt. The wine finish has levelled the mountains and valleys and restricted the finish dramatically, while the nose doesn't work at all. Perfectly drinkable and the delivery is extremely enjoyable. But as a Six Isles, delighted it's a Limited Edition. 46%. Ian Macleod. 3266 bottles.

S'Mokey (88) n22.5 playful peat covering three, maybe four, levels of weight and intensity. Lively and opens well with a few citrus notes apparent; **t22** sweet with a light oiliness spreading the weight and smoke efficiently; **f21.5** remains on the light side with the vanilla levels rising as the smoke drops; **b22** delicate, sweet and more lightly smoked than the nose advertises. 40%. Master Of Malt.

Tambowie (84.5) n21.5 t21.5 f20.5 b21. A decent improvement on the nondescript bottling of yore. I have re-included this to both celebrate its newly acquired lightly fruited attractiveness...and to celebrate the 125th anniversary of the long departed Tambowie Distillery whose whisky, I am sure, tasted nothing like this. 40%. The Vintage Malt Whisky Co Ltd.

Treasurer 1874 Reserve Cask (90.5) n23 huge oak: pungent and salty with a soupcon of peat; lightly molassed with a more telling imprint of maple syrup; **t23** dense delivery: the wood is among the leaders, as is a pithy orange. But giant waves of malt break over the taste buds to claim control; the extra complexity is completed with busy spice; **f22.5** toffee fudge and raisin; **b22** some judicious adding has been carried out here in the Robert Graham shop. Amazing for a living cask that I detect no major sulphur faultlines. Excellent! 51%. Robert Graham Ltd. Live casks available in all Robert Graham shops.

Vintner's Choice Speyside 10 Years Old (84) n21.5 t22 f20 b20.5. Pleasant. But considering the quality of the Speysiders Grants have to play with, the dullness is a bit hard to fathom. 40%. Quality Spirits International.

Waitrose Pure Highland Malt (86.5) n22 t22 f20.5 b22. Blood orange by the cartload: amazingly tangy and fresh; bitters out at the finish. This is one highly improved malt and great to see a supermarket bottling showing some serious attitude...as well as taste!! Fun, refreshing and enjoyable. 40%

❖ **Wemyss Malts "The Hive" Aged 8 Years** bott Nov 11 **(85.5)** n21 t23 f20 b21.5. You may get stung on the nose but the delivery is pure nectar. Sadly, the bitter finish lives up to the nose's prediction. 40%. Wemyss Malts.

Wemyss Malts "The Hive" Aged 12 Years (93) n23 a sumptuous combination of various honeys – including Manuka and lavender – which team with citrus and vanilla comfortably. The lightest breeze of smoke adds ballast; **t24** no disappointments on delivery where the honey becomes almost liquid form. Indeed, the texture is divine and carries a ridiculous number of oaky layers, seemingly glued together with beeswax; a heavier liquorice thread works beautifully; **f22.5** a degree of vague bitterness gives the effect of over toasted honeycomb; **b23.5** mixing different malt whiskies is an art form – one that is prone to going horribly wrong. Here, though, whoever is responsible really is the bees-knees... 40%

Wemyss Malts "Peat Chimney" 5 Years Old (82.5) **n**20.5 **t**21 **f**20 **b**21. Rougher than the tongue of a smoking cat. 40%. Wemyss Malts Ltd.

Wemyss Malts "Peat Chimney" 8 Years Old (85) **n**21.5 **t**21.5 **f**21 **b**21. Delightful chocolate amid the attractively course peat. 40%. Wemyss Malts Ltd.

Wemyss Malts "Peat Chimney" Aged 12 Years bott Oct 10 **(90.5) n**22.5 good vanilla depth to the clunking phenols: the peat is positively lashed to the aroma; **t**23 beautifully made malt with an outstanding understanding between the light but silky oils, phenols and sympathetic sugars; **f**22.5 the vanillas return but retain their smoky chaperone; **b**22.5 gorgeous: does what it says on the tin... 40%. Wemyss Malts.

Wemyss "Smooth Gentleman" 5 Years Old (80) **n**20 **t**21 **f**19 **b**20. A bit of a schoolkid with an affectation. 40%. Wemyss Malts Ltd.

Wemyss Malts "Smooth Gentleman" 8 Years Old (89) **n**21 sweet but a little bland; **t**23.5 much better arrival with a gorgeous barley-toffee impact assisted, naturally, by a spoonful of acacia honey; **f**22 returns to a more middle-of-the-road character, but still deliciously soft and rich...and a little juicy; **b**22.5 more of a Kentuckian George Clooney than a Bristolian Cary Grant. 40%. Wemyss Malts Ltd.

Wemyss Malts "Smooth Gentleman" Aged 12 Years 1st fill bourbon cask, bott Oct 10 **(88.5) n**23 honeycomb and chocolate with a dash of ginger; **t**22 big oak early on but the barley keeps it honest; **f**21.5 vanilla and butterscotch...but dries big time; **b**22 a very attractive and competent, vaguely spicy gentleman who has a bit of a penchant for butterscotch and chocolate. 40%. Wemyss Malts.

Wemyss Malts "Spice King" 5 Years Old (76) **n**18.5 **t**20 **f**18.5 **b**19. A little on the mucky, tangy side. 40%. Wemyss Malts Ltd.

Wemyss Malts "Spice King" 8 Years Old (87) **n**22 plenty of butterscotch and fudge; **t**22 chewy toffee with a malty, honeyed strata; **f**21.5 more toffee. Just when you start wondering where the spice is, it appears very late on through the trademen's entrance, though does the best it can not to disturb those at home; **b**21.5 hard to believe this lush malt is in any way related to the 5-y-o...!! 40%. Wemyss Malts Ltd.

Wemyss Malts "Spice King" Aged 12 Years bott Oct 10 (85) **n**22.5 **t**21 **f**21 **b**21. Thoroughly enjoyable sugar edge to the decent smoke. A bit thin on the complexity front, though. 40%. Wemyss Malts.

Wemyss Vintage Malt The Peat Chimney Hand Crafted Blended Malt Whisky (80) **n**19 **t**22 **f**20 **b**19. The balance is askew here, especially on the bone-dry wallpapery finish. Does have some excellent spicy/coffee moments, though. 43%. Wemyss Vintage Malts Ltd.

Wemyss Vintage Malt The Smooth Gentleman Hand Crafted Blended Malt Whisky (83) **n**19 **t**22 **f**21 **b**21. Not sure about the nose: curiously fishy (very gently smoked). But the malts tuck into the tastebuds with aplomb showing some sticky barley sugar along the way. 43%

Wemyss Vintage Malt The Spice King Hand Crafted Blended Malt Whisky (84) **n**22 **t**22 **f**20 **b**20. Funnily enough, I've not a great fan of the word "smooth" when it comes to whisky. But the introduction of oily Caol Ila-style peat here makes it a more of a smooth gentleman than the "Smooth Gentleman." Excellent spices very late on. 43%. Wemyss Vintage Malts.

Wholly Smoke Aged 10 Years (86.5) **n**22.5 **t**22.5 **f**20 **b**21.5. A big, peaty, sweat, rumbustuous number with absolutely no nod towards sophistication or balance and the finish virtually disintegrates. The smoke is slapped on and the whole appears seemingly younger than its 10 years. Massive fun, all the same. 40%. Macdonald & Muir Ltd for Oddbins.

Whyte & Mackay Blended Malt Scotch Whisky (78) **n**19 **t**22 **f**18 **b**19. You know when the engine to your car is sort of misfiring and feels a bit sluggish and rough...? 40%. Waitrose.

Wild Scotsman Scotch Malt Whisky (Black Label) batch no. CBV001 (91) **n**23.5 **t**23.5 **f**21 **b**23. The type of dram you drink from a dirty glass. Formidable and entertaining. 47%

Wild Scotsman Aged 15 Years Vatted Malt (95) **n**23 **t**24 **f**24 **b**24. If anyone wants an object lesson as to why you don't screw your whisky with caramel, here it is. Jeff Topping can feel a justifiable sense of pride in his new whisky: for its age, it is an unreconstituted masterpiece... 46% (92 proof). nc ncf. USA.

Mystery Malts

Chieftain's Limited Edition Aged 40 Years hogshead (78) **n**22 **t**22 **f**16 **b**18. Oak-ravaged and predictably bitter on the death (those of you who enjoy Continental bitters might go for this..!). But the lead up does offer a short, though sublime and intense honey kick. The finish, though... 48.5%. Ian Macleod.

Cu Dhub (see Speyside Distillery)

Scottish Grain

It's a bit weird, really. Many whisky lovers stay clear of blended Scotch, preferring instead single malts. The reason, I am often told, is that the grain included in a blend makes it rough and ready. Yet I wish I had a twenty pound note for each time I have been told in recent years how much someone enjoys a single grain. The ones that the connoisseurs die for are the older versions, usually special independent bottlings displaying great age and more often than not brandishing a lavish Canadian or bourbon style.

Like single malts, grain distilleries produce whisky bearing their own style and signature. And, also, some display characteristics and a richness that can surprise and delight. Most of the grains available in (usually specialist) whisky outlets are pretty elderly. Being made from maize and wheat helps give them either that Canadian or, depending on the freshness of the cask, an unmistakable bourbony style. So older grains display far greater body than is commonly anticipated.

Light whiskies, including some Speysiders, tend to adopt this north American stance when the spirit has absorbed so much oak that the balance has been tipped. So overtly Kentuckian can they be, I once playfully introduced an old single grain Scotch whisky into a bourbon tasting I was conducting and nobody spotted that it was the cuckoo in the nest ... until I revealed all at the end of the evening. And even had to display the bottle to satisfy the disbelievers.

Younger grains may give a hint of oncoming bourbon-ness. But, rather, they tend to celebrate either a softness in taste or, in the case of North British, a certain rigidity. Where many malts have a tendency to pulverise the taste-buds and announce their intent and character at the top of their voice, younger grains are content to stroke and whisper.

Scotch whisky companies have so far had a relaxed attitude to marketing their grains. William Grant had made some inroads with Black Barrel, though with nothing like the enthusiasm they unleash upon us with their blends and malts. And Diageo are apparently content to see their Cameron Brig sell no further than its traditional hunting grounds, just north of Edinburgh, where the locals tend to prefer single grain to any other whisky. And the latest news from that most enormous of distilleries...it is getting bigger. Not only are Diageo planning to up their malt content by building a new Speyside distillery, but Cameronbridge, never a retiring place since the days of the Haigs in the 1820s is set for even grander expansion. Having, with Port Dundas until recently, absorbed the closure of a number of grain distilleries over the last 30 years something had to be done to give it a fighting chance of taking on the expansion into China, Russia and now, most probably, India. It is strange that not more is being done. Cooley in Ireland have in the last year or so forged a healthy following with their introduction of grain whiskies at various ages. They have shown that the interest is there and some fresh thinking and boldness in a marketing department can create niche and often profitable markets. Edrington have entered the market with a vatted grain called Snow Grouse, designed to be consumed chilled and obviously a tilt at the vodka market. The first bottling I received was disappointingly poor and I hope future vattings will be more carefully attended to. All round, then, the news for Scottish grain lovers has not been good of late with the demolition of mighty Dumbarton and now, controversially, closure of Port Dundas itself. With the expansion of Cameronbridge and a 50% stake in North British, Diageo obviously believe they have all the grain capacity they require.

The tastings notes here for grains cover only a few pages, disappointingly, due to their scarcity. However, it is a whisky style growing in stature, helped along the way not just by Cooley but also by more Independent bottlers bringing out a succession of high quality ancient casks. And we can even see an organic grain on the market, distilled at the unfashionable Loch Lomond Distillery. Why, though, it has to be asked does it take the relatively little guys to lead the way? Perhaps the answer is in the growing markets in the east: the big distillers are very likely holding on to their stocks to facilitate their expansion there.

At last the message is getting through that the reaction to oak of this relatively lightweight spirit - and please don't for one moment regard it as neutral, for it is most certainly anything but - can throw up some fascinating and sometimes delicious possibilities. Blenders have known that for a long time. Now public interest is growing. And people are willing to admit that they can enjoy an ancient Cambus, Caledonian or Dumbarton in very much the way they might celebrate a single malt. Even if it does go against the grain...

Single Grain Scotch
CALEDONIAN

Clan Denny Caledonian 45 Years Old bourbon barrel, cask no. HH6294, dist 1965 **(89) n22 t23.5 f21.5 b22.** For all its obvious tiredness, there is plenty of rich character. *46.1%. nc ncf sc.*

Clan Denny Caledonian 45 Years Old refill hogshead, cask no. HH6228, dist 1965 **(96) n23.5** fascinating – and quite stunning – mix of light Canadian and deeper bourbon characteristics; almost a buttery quality to the corn; **t25** that is about as good as you might ever expect the delivery of an ancient grain to be: perfect weight, perfect balance between light sugars, oily corn and drier oak; perfect timing to its slow unveiling of its many complexities...in fact, simply perfect...; **f23.5** simplifies, as a grain really has to but those delicate sugars ensure the oak remains honest; **b24** Super Caley...my prayers have been answered... *476%. nc ncf sc.*

⁘ **Clan Denny Caledonian Aged 45 Years** bourbon barrel, cask no. HH7501, dist 1965 **(94) n23.5** a curious though not unpleasant mix of bourbon whiskey warehouse and my dad's old-train imbued clothes in the early '60s after he got in from work...; **t24** a Kentuckian character from the moment it touches the lips; the sugars are delicate and diverse, the liquorice building in boldness. By the midway point the sugars have moved into fully-fledged honeys; light and brain-explodingly complex; **f23** a wee bitter note from tired oak. But that is outflanked by those oils carrying a gorgeous fruit and nut character and vanilla to die for; **b23.5** anyone who managed to get their hands on the very oldest maturing stocks of Barton bourbon from twenty years ago (and there were very few of us who managed it) would recognise it immediately. The similarities are uncanny. *473%. nc ncf sc. Douglas Laing & Co.*

Scott's Selection Caledonian 1965 bott 2011 **(89.5) n24 t22.5 f20.5 b22.5.** How about that? The nose belongs to Kentucky, the flavours carry a Maple Leaf flag. Aaah, pure Scotch! *45%*

CAMBUS

Clan Denny Cambus Aged 36 Years bourbon barrel, cask no. HH7252, dist 1975 **(89.5) n22 t23.5 f22 b22.** Flawless grain limited only by its simplicity. *52.1%. nc ncf sc.*

Clan Denny Cambus 45 Years Old refill bourbon barrel, cask no. HH5638, dist 1965 **(88.5) n22 t23 f21.5 b22.** A grain which has learned to deal with the impact of age in its very own, sweet way... *45.9%. nc ncf sc. Douglas Laing & Co.*

Clan Denny Cambus 47 Years Old bourbon barrel, cask no. HH7029, dist 1963 **(97) n24.5** a mesmeric blending of classic liquorice-bourbony tones, the vivid vanilla of a great Canadian and the sharp, lively precision of a massive scotch... **t25** if you spent a dozen years of your life trying to create a whisky with absolutely perfect weight on delivery, you'd still fail to match the natural genius of this. The oils have just enough body to coat the palate with a delicate fretwork of the finest light liquorice and honeycomb lustre, but whose fragility is exposed by the orange-citrus sharpness which etches its own, impressive course; the sugars mingle with the spices with 47 years of understanding...; **f23** after almost 50 years in the barrel, there is no surprise that a degree of bitter tightness comes into play. But the compactness of the vanilla keeps damage to a minimum; **b24.5** if this wasn't a Scotch single grain, it might just qualify as Bourbon of the Year. Proof that where a whisky is made, matured, or from makes absolutely no difference: it is the quality which counts. And there will be very few whiskies I taste this year that will outgun this one in the quality stakes... *49.7%. nc ncf sc. Douglas Laing & Co.*

⁘ **Clan Denny Cambus Aged 48 Years** bourbon barrel, cask no. HH 7863, dist 1963 **(93) n24** an old Buffalo Trace from the bottom third of the warehouse? Well it has complexity enough. The clever mixing of the red and black liquorice, that distant, dull rumble of molasses, the teasing spice, the exceptional balance between sweet and dry....; absolutely nothing short of fabulous....; **t23** the tiredness is evident early on, but there is sufficient dark sugars and thumping vanilla to place a delicious sticky plaster over the wounds; a highly unusual oil-led sharpness breathes all the life that is required back into this; **f22.5** dry with the oak gathering pace but thwarted from a full attack by those persistent oils and charming sugars; some diced hazelnut works wonders; **b23.5** no wonder they closed down the Cambus distillery; they must've plain gone and shipped it to Kentucky... *49.5%. nc ncf sc. Douglas Laing & Co.*

Scotch Malt Whisky Society Cask G8.1 Aged 21 Years refill hogshead, cask no. 41759, dist 1989 **(85.5) n22.5 t22 f20 b21.** Decent enough, but a relatively underwhelming way to kick off the Society's account with this legendary grain distillery. A less than endearing piece of oak keeps any chance of the distillery's usual ability to tantalise with clever use of weight and complexity. A few kumquat and delicate clove notes do shake up the caramels on the nose, though. *61.2%. sc. 272 bottles.*

CAMERONBRIDGE

⁘ **Clan Denny Cameronbridge Aged 21 Years** refill butt, cask no. HH7541, dist 1990 **(85.5) n21.5 t22 f20.5 b21.5.** Creamy textured and sweet. Possibly filled into an old – and tired - Islay cask as there is the odd strand of smoke. *58.2%. nc ncf sc. Douglas Laing & Co.*

Clan Denny Cameronbridge 45 Years Old bourbon barrel, cask no. HH6805, dist 1965 **(78)** **n21 t20 f18 b19.** Even grains can feel the cold hand of Father Time on their shoulder... 40.5%. nc ncf sc. Douglas Laing & Co.

Rare Auld Grain Cameronbridge 32 Years Old cask no. 3597, dist 1979 **(92) n23 t23.5 f22.5 b23.** Anything but the norm. 48.8%. sc. Duncan Taylor & Co.

Scott's Selection Cameron Bridge 1973 bott 2010 **(77) n19 t21 f18 b19.** Good grain + poor cask = 77. 41.4%. Speyside Distillers.

⋰⋱ **Scott's Selection Cameron Bridge 1973** bott 2010 **(85) n23.5 t21 f20 b20.5.** Worth getting just for the nose alone, which is top rate Canadian with the corn leaping from the glass. A disappointing bitterness from the oak creeps in to spoil the party somewhat. 44.9%

CARSEBRIDGE

Clan Denny Carsebridge 29 Years Old 1st fill hogshead, cask no. HH6609, dist 1981 **(82) n22 t22 f18 b20.** The intensity of the corn is profound. So too, alas, is the bitter retribution of the tired cask. 53.1%. nc ncf sc. Douglas Laing & Co.

⋰⋱ **Clan Denny Carsebridge Aged 30 Years** refill hogshead, cask no. HH7780, dist 1981 **(91.5) n21.5** light for its age with the odd vegetable note; **t23.5** the astonishing strength for its age does no harm as the mouth-watering grain is driven purposefully into the taste buds; the spices begin midway and show little sign of abating; **f23** good length, though the extended vanillas cannot outrun the spice; **b23.5** is there such a thing as a juicy 30-year-old grain? On this evidence, indubitably. 59.1%. nc ncf sc. Douglas Laing & Co

⋰⋱ **Clan Denny Carsebridge Aged 45 Years** bourbon barrel, cask no. HH7500, dist 1965 **(95) n24** absolutely no doubting the corn used in this whisky: a gently honeyed cross between a Canadian and bourbon, alternating in intensity between the two styles; **t24** the delivery comes down firmly in the bourbon camp; or perhaps I should say softly but decidedly: the oils are sumptuous yet feather-light, the sugars no more than sprinkled; **f23** and now we have the Canadian, with the banana vanillas dominating though the spices warm; **b24** as we have so often seen in Kentucky and Canada, old grains maturing in high quality casks rank among the best whiskies in the world: here is a stunning example. 44.7%. nc ncf sc. Douglas Laing & Co.

DUMBARTON

Clan Denny Dumbarton 45 Years Old refill hogshead, cask no. HH7001, dist 1965 **(89.5) n23 t23 f21.5 b22.** A lovely grain bottled in the nick of time and happy to display the remnants of its zesty vigour 49.5%. nc ncf sc. Douglas Laing & Co.

⋰⋱ **Clan Denny Dumbarton Aged 46 Years** refill hogshead, cask no. HH7542, dist 1964 **(86.5) n22 t23 f20 b21.5.** The tiredness on the finish, confirming the big oaks on the nose, still cannot entirely overcome the beauty of the honey and golden syrup delivery: some of the early moments in the mouth are akin to the soaring strings of a John Barry score. The finish is pure Bay City Rollers. 47.4%. nc ncf sc. Douglas Laing & Co.

Scott's Selection Dumbarton 1986 bott 2011 **(94) n24.5** complex? Doesn't even touch upon what is going on here. Most ungrain like in the manner by which a complex prickle teases the nose. A bit like the small grains working wonders in a bourbon. Not overly sweet, but the cooked molassed sugars do add depth as well as balance; butterscotch in a mildly overcooked tart; **t24** initially a silkier delivery than the nose suggests will happen. But those corn oils are relatively brief and a combination of sugars, of varying degree of intensity, begin to box with the fizzing spices; **f22** some bitterness as one comes to expect from old Allied casks, but the clarity of the grain and now honeyed sugars negates the worst and has a little to spare; **b23.5** when this distillery was closed I was almost beside myself with disappointment...and rage. Following the closure of Cambus, this left Dumbarton as the brightest star in the collapsing grain whisky galaxy. This bottle will give you some insight into just why I treasured it so greatly; certainly more so than the bead counters at Allied who saw its potential as prime real estate over its ability to keep making arguably the best blended Scotch whiskies in the world. My main point of surprise now is why so few bottlings from this giant of a distillery ever see the shelves... 51.5%. Speyside Distillers.

GARNHEATH

Clan Denny Garnheath 43 Years Old refill hogshead, cask no. HH6642, dist 1967 **(94) n24.5** a charming mix of very old Georgian corn whiskey and no less young Demerara column still rum; it would be hard to fine tune the spices to better effect; **t23.5** rare for a grain, the barley is detectable briefly but distinctly early on. It is then lost under a silo of corn but the juiciness never dissipates; **f22.5** fabulously controlled, bristling spice keeps a hint of oaky burnout to a minimum; **b23.5** what a treat: not just a whisky as rare as budgie teeth, but one in tip-top nick for its age. A rare delight. 44.4%. nc ncf sc. Douglas Laing & Co.

GIRVAN

‑:‑ **Berry's Own Selection Girvan Aged 46 Years** cask no. 37532, bott 2011 **(94.5) n24** takes me back to a kitchen in Surrey in the early '60s with my mother boiling the cooking apples from the tree from the back garden, sharp and slightly under-sugared; elsewhere a gallery of spices hang in the air; I may have just broken into a Crunchie bar; **t23.5** silky and magnificent, this is a grain which envelopes the taste buds, caressing them with such delicate oils and oaks, the latter apparent thanks to both a vanilla dryness and a tangier pepper attack; **f23** vanilla ice cream with a dab of honeycomb; the oils keep their shape and weight ensuring the sugars see off any oak attack; **b24** if you have not yet crossed the divide and got into grain whisky, here really is your chance. What a stunner! 46%. nc ncf sc.

Berry's Own Selection Girvan 1989 cask no. 37530/1, bott 2010 **(82.5) n21 t22 f19.5 b20.** Thick, sweet but a little on the tardy side... 45.1%. nc ncf sc. Berry Bros & Rudd.

Clan Denny Girvan 45 Years Old refill hogshead, cask no. HH6276, dist 1965 **(90) n23 t23.5 f21.5 b22.5.** Laid on with a golden trowel. 47.3%. nc ncf sc.

Clan Denny Girvan 45 Years Old refill hogshead, cask no. HH6923, dist 1965 **(88.5) n23 t23 f20.5 b22.** Simplistic, certainly. But as you get older, you learn to appreciate the more simple things in life... 45.3%. nc ncf sc. Douglas Laing & Co.

‑:‑ **Clan Denny Girvan Aged 46 Years** refill hogshead, cask no. HH7669, dist 1965 **(94.5) n23** the tannins sticking to the vanilla lessen the sugars on the acacia honey; liquorice underlines the great age; a small squeeze of lime offers an improbable freshness; **t24** a fabulous delivery which for the first few moments holds a Canadian line of soft corn oil and vanilla. But soon that liquorice on the nose heads the vanguard of the bourbon characteristics, including melt-in-the-mouth manuka honey, which soon take command. The spices fizz but refuse to fully explode; **f23.5** breathtakingly elegant fade with caresses of honeyed vanilla all the way; **b24** sublime. 49.7%. nc ncf sc. Douglas Laing & Co.

‑:‑ **Riegger's Selection Girvan 1964** bourbon cask, cask no. 86, dist 2 Sep 64, bott 7 Feb 11 **(87) n22.5** some evidence of crumbling oak and tiredness but there is enough dry allspice and coriander to inject life and complexity back into the light corn; **t22.5** lightly oiled texture; soft corn oil and delicate muscovado sugars. The vanillas turn from heavy to stark; **f20** just a little bitterness from the fading cask; **b22** lovers of corn whisky will enjoy many aspects of this oldie. 48.7%. nc ncf sc. Viktor-Riegger GmbH. 189 bottles.

Scott's Selection Girvan 1964 bott 2011 **(92.5) n23.5 t24 f22 b23.** Girvan, like Invergordon, is grain which takes full advantage of its sumptuous persona. Here, though, it adds some controlled sharpness. But it's the lordly sugars which really win the day. Superb. 48.8%

INVERGORDON

Berry's Own Selection Invergordon 1971 cask no. 2, bott 2011 **(91.5) n24** more of a high quality column still rum than a whisky...; Demerara in both rum type and sugars evident with the vanillas showing a delicious citrus tinge; some real butterscotch in there, too; **t23** back to being grain whisky now: toffee, toasted fudge and spices; some soft oils glue the busy flavours to the roof of the mouth; **f22** the peppers keep peppering, but the toffee-vanillas dominate; **b22.5** a beautiful experience. 46.7%. nc ncf sc. Berry Bros & Rudd.

Clan Denny Invergordon 44 Years Old refill barrel, cask no. HH4995, dist 1966 **(95.5) n23.5** corn dough and carrot juice; a light smattering of spice ensures some real complexity here; **t24** as soft and sweet as you might imagine an Invergordan to be. But also offers a surprising degree of countering sharpness with a salivating quality of a grain more than half its age **f23.5** a wonderful build up of tingling, busy spice offers an excellent exit; **b24.5** almost quicksand-ish in its softness. But an amazing degree of complexity, too. A true gem of a whisky. 46.8%. nc ncf sc. Douglas Laing & Co.

Clan Denny Invergordon 45 Years Old bourbon barrel, cask no. HH7254, dist 1966 **(88) n22 t22 f22 b22.** Played with an absolutely straight bat: over 45 years every kink appears to have been ironed out. 47.1%. nc ncf sc. Douglas Laing & Co.

‑:‑ **Clan Denny Invergordon Aged 45 Years** bourbon barrel, cask no. HH7864, dist 1966 **(88.5) n22.5** a touch of exotic fruit; **t22** soft and delicately oiled; a huge wave of Canadian-style vanilla tinged with citrus; **f22** more echoes of Canada; the vanilla is curiously sweetening as well as drying; **b22** an unspectacular, well-made and matured grain offering quiet gracefulness. 47.5%. nc ncf sc. Douglas Laing & Co.

‑:‑ **Duncan Taylor Octave Invergordon 38 Years Old** cask no. 520883, dist 1972 **(86.5) n24 t21 f20 b21.5.** Some serious Demerara sugars knit tightly into the intense vanilla. A few bitter notes amid the booming spice. The nose, however, excels and conjures myriad bourbon images. 47.8%. sc. Duncan Taylor & Co.

‑:‑ **First Cask Invergordon 37 Years Old** American oak, cask no. 63641, dist 1 Jul 72, bott 3 Jul 09 **(85) n23.5 t21 f20 b20.5.** A dram which conjures up clearer pictures of ice cracking on the Great Lakes than it does water coursing through the Scottish glens. The corn works beautifully on the nose in particular but the oak bitters from delivery onwards. 44%. nc ncf sc. Whisky Import Nederland. 135 bottles.

Rare Auld Grain Invergordon 38 Years Old cask no. 96251, dist 1972 **(88.5) n22.5 t22.5 f21.5 b22.** Ramrod straight and beyond the nose eschews any grand design of complexity. 44%. sc. Duncan Taylor & Co.

Scotch Malt Whisky Society Cask G5.2 Aged 17 Years virgin toasted oak hogshead, cask no. 53285, dist 1993 **(90.5) n23 t23 f21.5 b23.** Oils apart, barely representative of the distillery at this age but bourbon lovers will be thrilled. 65.3%. sc. 248 bottles.

⁖ **Scotch Malt Whisky Society Cask G5.3 Aged 18 Years** virgin toasted oak, cask no. 53289, dist 1993 **(95.5) n23.5** a fabulous cross between bread pudding and a well-aged Canadian whisky; **t24.5** the delivery may be soft in texture. But there is no holding back on the flavour front as myriad oak notes pour onto the palate with sugars offering varying degrees of intensity and comfort, though all of them sitting very comfortably with the buzzing spice; the main flavour profile constantly hovers between top notch bourbon and ultra fine Canadian; **f23.5** much more simplistic vanilla. But the weight remains almost perfect; **b24** there aren't many grain whiskies so gorgeously influenced by oak to the dozen. Invergordon as you have probably never seen before...and are unlikely to see again... 65.6%. sc. Scotch Malt Whisky Society.

⁖ **Scotch Malt Whisky Society Cask G5.4 Aged 18 Years** virgin toasted oak, cask no. 53288, dist 1993 **(92) n23** you often get Canadian style grains. This is much nearer a Kentuckian with the breakfast marmalade fruitiness jousting with the big oaky liquorice. The sugars are molassed. As heavyweight a nose on a grain as you'll ever find; **t23** the delivery is a kaleidoscope of delicate and indelicate sugars, mostly of the crisp and crunchy variety but offering variations of hues from icing sugar down to Demerara; spices nip and kiss while the vanillas boil up some custard; **f22.5** long with the accent firmly on those darker sugars and bourbony hickory; **b23.5** I must admit I gave the whisky a bit of a quizzical look after both clapping my eyes on its rich colour and breathing in that intense marmalade nose. Only on reading the small print did it all make sense. 65.6%. Scotch Malt Whisky Society.

⁖ **Scotch Malt Whisky Society Cask G5.5 Aged 18 Years** virgin toasted oak hogshead, cask no. 53286, dist 1993 **(94.5) n24** obviously Invergordon has been moved to Kentucky... the diced orange peel and blood orange suggests a bourbon, as does the hickory and spice. How about that manuka, too! Above all, it's like being inside a Victorian or Edwardian cupboard; **t24** there is no distillery in Kentucky which ensures such an oily delivery (mind you, I know one in Tennessee), so Invergordon it must be! But there is no let up to the North American theme, now with various corn notes dominating, Jamaican Blue Mountain coffee taking a stroll through the mid-range and burnt raisin – without the fruit element, if you know what I mean, heading us towards the finale...; **f23** which is a slow switching out of the lights...; **b23.5** a whisky I've had to taste to hit deadline without being supplied with cask details. From the way this is behaving it must be some kind of super first fill or even virgin oak: it is much nearer bourbon than Scotch! 65.3%. sc.

Scott's Selection Invergordon 1964 bott 2011 **(92) n24 t24 f21 b23.** Another which keeps faithfully to the distillery's yielding, melt-in-the-mouth style. But here we have a deep Kentucky drawl and a nose from heaven... 43.8%. Speyside Distillers.

⁖ **Scott's Selection Invergordon 1964** bott 2012 **(94) n22.5** just a little flat with the vanillas having dragged out a few elements from the oak I would preferred not have seen. Even so, there is no denying the virtues of the unusual sugar peanut candy and corn oil also on view; **t24** oooh! Didn't see that coming. After the flat delivery I knew was on its way, several thick waves of lightly salted, melt-in-the-mouth and highly intense barley sugar (in a corn-fuelled grain!!) notes flood through. Next the corn oils themselves burst their banks, an episode those of you who enjoy Corn Whisky will recognise and appreciate; the mid-ground is a matter of coping with the toasty liquorice; **f23.5** silky to the last with the corn and vanilla contentedly holding hands; **b24** when I first nosed this, my instinct was that it would have been better off propping up an ancient old blend. Having now fully tasted it, I am not so sure... 42.3%. Speyside Distillers.

The Whisky Agency Invergordon 1965 bott 2010 **(90) n23.5 t23 f21 b22.5.** A glorious old timer, showing some quality Canadian-style manoeuvres. 44.7%. The Whisky Agency.

LOCH LOMOND

Rhosdhu 2008 Cask No. 2483 re-char bourbon, dist 17/03/08, bott 27/07/11 **(86.5) n22 t22 f21 b21.5.** Delicately clean barley with a touch of lemon and, though engagingly soft, is not beyond showing some sugary teeth. 45%. nc ncf sc.

Rhosdhu 2008 Cask No. 2484 bourbon barrel, dist 17/03/08, bott 27/07/11 **(84) n21.5 t21.5 f20.5 b21.** The barley battles with some aggressive oak, even at this tender age. The spice count is pretty high. 45%. nc ncf sc.

NORTH BRITISH

⠿ **Berry's Own Selection North British 2000** cask no. 4312, bott 2011 **(87.7) n22** gorgeously structured: firm, if understated, sweetness; dank stinging nettles; gooseberry tart; **t22.5** crisp skeleton on which a fatter outer layer of spiced golden syrup hangs; **f21** bitters thanks to some indifferent oak; **b22** neutral whisky....? I don't think so. *46%. nc ncf sc.*

⠿ **Director's Cut North British Aged 50 Years** refill butt, cask no. 8228, dist 1962 **(82.5) n22 t21 f19 b20.5.** How truly bizarre that the whisky waits 50 years to be tasted. And on the day I get round to it, the distillery is closed in the national gaze during a Legionaire's disease outbreak: certainly not what the distiller who made this would have expected two generations ago. I don't think he would have expected this whisky either. Now I may be completely wrong. But I suspect this has been finished in a pretty fresh sherry butt to spruce the dear old thing up before bottling. Sadly, the sherry cask has a light sulphur taint, so the bitterness creeps in. Leave these whiskies well alone, is my motto... *57.1%. nc ncf sc. 222 bottles.*

⠿ **Master Of Malt North British 20 Year Old** cask no. 3228, dist 1991 **(85.5) n22 t22 f20.5 b21.** Some decent, slightly syrupy sugars but bitter at death. *54.1%. sc. Master Of Malt.*

⠿ **Scott's Selection North British 1989** bott 2011 **(86) n21.5 t22.5 f20.5 b21.5.** Threatens to break out and expand on its vanilla-led theme but remains pretty tight throughout. Some puckering saltiness early on. *54%. Speyside Distillers.*

The Whisky Agency North British 1962 (93) n24 t23.5 f22.5 b23. Full of traits and characteristics as rare as this type of whisky. But, above all, absolutely refuses to admit its age. This grain is an inspiration to us all... *47.9%. The Whisky Agency.*

NORTH OF SCOTLAND

Late Lamented North of Scotland 37 Years Old (94.5) n23.5 sweet and nutty, there is a crisp sheen to the more sugary Canadian vanilla notes. Just a slight drizzle of something spicy makes for a beautifully balanced aroma; **t23.5** a sumptuous mouth feel cannot disguise the busy interplay between the weighty vanillas and slicker sugars, which run the range from refined to muscovado; ridiculously clean, allowing a rare clarity on the palate for a whisky of such great age; **f23.5** textbook complexity of an old-fashioned Canadian style. Beautiful corn dots the I and crosses the T, finding the spots still not filled by the sugary vanillas. An almost lazy, apologetic spiciness ramps up the complexity and the expected semi-gluey finale has a surprising mouthwatering quality; **b24** an astonishing whisky completely devoid of the bitterness often found in a whisky of such antiquity, or over the top oakiness. One of the great Scottish Single Grains of recent years and a bottling that Canadian whisky devotees of a near lost style of half a century ago will relish. Monumentally magnificent and, of its type, almost flawless. *44.2%*

⠿ **Scott's Selection North Of Scotland 1971** bott 2012 **(87) n21** a bizarre lightly smoked edge to this. There is relatively little there, but so surprising to find it at all that it is hard to concentrate on much else... **t22** hard as granite. The grains appear to have locked together to allow little to pass or escape. A few sugars do dodge the guards; **f22** maybe a little bitterness to the cask. But vanillas and soft nougat dominate. Until a lightly smoked spiciness makes an entry; **b22** what a weirdo. If grain is filled into an old Islay cask, over 40 years the phenols will vanish. What they are still doing here, though in minor quantities, is open to debate...! *45.1%*

⠿ **Scott's Selection North Of Scotland 1973** bott 2012 **(92) n23.5** black cherries; dripping in molasses and a minty oakiness; muscovado-sweetened Madagascan cocoa of the top order; **t23** huge shape and presence on delivery: thick oils thickened further by oaky vanilla concentrate but enough dark sugars to ensure balance; the mid-ground allows the grain and spice to form comfortably; **f22.5** the oak tires a little but now a few strands of Jaffa cake make for a pleasant finale; **b23** you just know you've had one hell of a big whisky... *48.5%*

PORT DUNDAS

⠿ **Port Dundas 20 Years Old Special Release 2011** db **(90) n21.5** a little nip, but mostly alcohol related. Otherwise a bit of a damp squib, though there is no doubting the overall quality; **t22** pure silk with a few sugars giving a slightly rummy gesture of intense sweetness; the vanillas start forming thickly towards the middle; **f23.5** a sublime finish: varying spices get to grips with the big fruit and tannin and now we have something approaching a blend between pot still Guyana rum and an old bourbon. In its own way, quite brilliant...; **b23** can a whisky be a little too silky. This one tries, especially on the non-committal nose and over friendly delivery. But once the spices rise, things get very interesting... *57.4%. nc ncf sc.*

⠿ **Clan Denny Port Dundas Aged 33 Years** refill hogshead, cask no. HH7543, dist 1978 **(92) n22** simplistic vanilla and toffee; **t23** lazy start then slowly shifts into gear. By the midway point the spices have arrived to keep the growing sugars company; **f23.5** full on complexity and brimming with mocha; shows ever-increasing Canadian tendencies; **b23.5** one of those deliciously rare beasts that just gets better and better as it goes along. 54.2%. nc ncf sc. Douglas Laing & Co.

⁘ **Clan Denny Port Dundas Aged 34 Years** refill hogshead, cask no. HH7543, dist 1978 **(94.5) n23.5** corny Canadian in hyper show off mode: the sugars are bristling and the vanilla almost pulses; **t24** even more silky than the nose suggests with the corn oil ensuring the friendliest of greetings. Excellent "Milky Way" chocolate nougat middle; **f23.5** moves unexpectedly towards a pot still rum character before the corn returns again; **b23.5** not many single malts can match this for sheer deliciousness. 58.6%. nc ncf sc. Douglas Laing & Co.

⁘ **Director's Cut Port Dundas Aged 30 Years** refill hogshead, cask no. 8416, dist 1982 **(87) n21** untidy and tight, the oak constrains just a little too forcefully **t23.5** relaxes on the palate... and how! The slow opening up of the corn oils and accompanying sugars is superb and though complexity is at a premium, the gradual strengthening of the citrus notes is superb; **f20** retracts slightly as the tightness on the nose is repeated at the death; **b22.5** no shortage of action...but, oh! for a better cask!! 58.7%. nc ncf sc. Douglas Laing & Co. 207 bottles.

⁘ **Duncan Taylor Octave Port Dundas 38 Years Old** cask no. 600952, dist 1973 **(86) n23 t21.5 f20.5 b21.5.** One very strange grain whisky. An equal tugging between fruit and bourbon which ensures a fascinating nose. But it never quite gels after the initial rich, biscuity delivery, though always enjoyable and even occasionally juicy, tails off a little. 55.6%. sc.

⁘ **Scotch Malt Whisky Society Cask G6.2 Aged 18 Years** refill barrel, cask no. 20061, dist 1993 **(82) n22 t21 f19 b20.** For all the early sweetness, never quite succeeds in shrugging off an ultimately debilitating bitterness. 55.2%. sc. Scotch Malt Whisky Society.

Scott's Selection Port Dundas 1965 bott 2011 **(91) n24 t23 f21.5 b22.5.** If you ever see a witch's chest in Holland...this is even flatter than that... No peaks or troughs. Just one flavour rolling, seemingly without a second glance, hesitation or join into the next... Not sure whether to adore this incredibly delicate whisky or try to thrash some life into it. Certainly, as I come up to tasting my 1,000th whisky of the year (this is no. 972) I can safely say there has been no other one quite like it. Which must be a good thing. So, upon reflection, one to get to know and love. For it is a thing of rare beauty. Flat chest or not... 43.3%. Speyside Distillers.

STRATHCLYDE

Clan Denny Strathclyde 33 Years Old refill butt, cask no. HH6144, dist 1977, bott 2010 **(94.5) n23.5** pithy grape and pepper; **t23.5** fresh fruit and then an avalanche of pepper and bread pudding spices, complete with a topping of crunchy brown sugars; succulent mouth feel with a superb touch to the delicate oil; **f24** so un-33-year old! No tired oak and the spices still lightly buzz. But more fruity notes now draining away **b23.5** I am not told it has been, but imagine an old grain finished in a lively, fresh and very clean wine cask... A stunner! 57.2%. nc ncf sc. Douglas Laing & Co.

UNSPECIFIED SINGLE GRAIN

⁘ **The Last Vatted Grain** bott Nov 11 **(88.5) n23** some biting fizz to the vanilla; a procession of delicate and indelicate sugars; someone has added some banana and lemon for freshness; **t22** takes a bit of time to find a rhythm on delivery with the softer grains clashing a little with the firmer ones. Settles picturesquely with the sugars dominant and the spices playing along behind; **f21.5** a little bit of tired oak bitterness but the fussing spices, battling with the now muscovado-weighted sugars is a delight; **b22** not just sad that the term "vatted" is now pointlessly outlawed on the bottle. But also that half of the four grain distilleries used in this vatting are equally consigned to history. 46%. nc ncf. Compass Box.

⁘ **Scottish Spirits Single Grain 3 Years Old** (Canned) **(82.5) n21 t21.5 f20 b20.** An absolutely standard, decent quality grain whisky with an attractive sweetness and latent youthful zesty fizz. Ill-served, however, by what I presume is caramel to give it a clichéd scotch look which dulls the finish in particular. In its natural form, this would have scored a lot higher. 40% (80 Proof). USA exclusive.

Vatted Grain

Compass Box Hedonism batch H29MMIX **(91) n22 t23.5 f22.5 b23.** With virtually all the grains launched being older than Zeus' granddad, it is such a relief to find one where you can still just hear the patter of tiny wheat... 43%. nc ncf. 4410 bottles.

Compass Box Hedonism Maximus (93.5) n25 t22.5 f23 b23. Bourbon Maximus... 46%

The Snow Grouse (70.5) n17.5 t18 f17 b18. Served normally, a tedious nonentity of a whisky. What little flavour there is, is toffee-based. On both nose and finish there are distant off notes, but in something so light louder than they might be. Surely...it can't be...? Served chilled as instructed on bottle: (79) n20 t21 f18 b20. Much, much better. Very sweet and the 's' word is confined, especially on the vodka-ish nose. The finish is still a give away though. 40%

Scottish Blends

For the first time in my career, I got a bit of an ear-bashing from a dissatisfied customer at one of my blind whisky tastings. And, of all things, it was because I had not included a blended Scotch in the line-up. My-oh-my! How times change.

Actually the guy was good natured about it, especially when I told him it was because the samples had been lost in transit, but his sense of loss was real. Apparently, he had attended one of my tastings a few years before, arriving as a self-confessed malt snob. He left converted to the blended whisky cause... to the extent it was now his favourite whisky style. As much as it is annoying when things go slightly wrong at an event, I still felt a thrill that more hardcore whisky lovers find experimenting in blends every bit as enjoyable as finding new malts. This implies blended scotch is as good as single malt. And, for my money, that is entirely the case; and if the blender is really doing his or her job, it should often be better. However, that job is getting a little harder each year. Once it was the standard joke that a sulphured sherry butt that had once been marked for a single malt brand would be dumped into a large blend where it would work on BP Chief executive Tony Hayward's "drop in the ocean" principle. However, there is now a lot more than just the odd off sherry butt finding their way in and blenders have to take guard that their blends are not being negatively affected. Certainly, during the course of writing the Whisky Bible I discovered this was becoming a much more common occurrence from the 2010 edition onwards. Indeed, one or two brands which a few years back I would have expected to pick up awards on a regular basis have been hit badly: disappointing and a great loss to whisky lovers.

However, Ballantine's 17 – a blend that has been on a higher plane than most other world whiskies for a very long time – again stood out as the best scotch I had tasted all year, narrowly eclipsing Ardbeg Day. It finally won the Bible's third best whisky in the world award.

Over 90 out of every 100 bottles of Scotch consumed is a blend, and therefore rather common. That has brought about some cold-shouldering from certain elitist whisky lovers who convince themselves a blend must be inferior. Well, not in my books. In fact, perhaps the opposite is true. Until you get to grips with blends you may well be entitled to regard yourself knowledgeable in single malts, but not in Scotch as a whole. Blends should be the best that Scotland can offer, because with a blend you have the ability to create any degree of complexity. And surely balance and complexity are the cornerstones of any great whisky, irrespective of type.

Of course there are some pretty awful blends created simply as a commodity with little thought going into their structure – just young whiskies, sometimes consisting of stock that is of dubious quality and then coloured up to give some impression of age. Yes, you are more likely to find that among blends than malts and for this reason the poorest blends can be pretty nasty. And, yes, they contain grain. Too often, though, grain is regarded as a kind of whisky leper – not to be touched under any circumstances. Some writers dismiss grain as "neutral" and "cheap", thus putting into the minds of the uninitiated the perception of inferiority.

But there really is nothing inferior about blends. In fact, whilst researching The Bible, I have to say that my heart misses more than one beat usually when I received a sample of a blend I have never found before. Why? Well, with single malts each distillery produces a style that can be found within known parameters. With a blend, anything is possible. There are myriad styles of malts to choose from and they will react slightly differently with certain grains.

For that reason, perhaps, I have marked blends a little more strictly and tighter than I have single malts. Because blends, by definition, should offer more.

The most exciting blends, like White Horse 12 (why, oh, why is that, like Old Parr 18, restricted mainly to Japan?) Grant's and the perennially glorious Ballantine's show bite, character and attitude. Silk and charm are to be appreciated. But after a long, hard day is anything better than a blend that is young and confident enough to nip and nibble at your throat on its way down and then throw up an array of flavours and shapes to get your taste-buds round? Certainly, I have always found blends ultimately more satisfying than malts. Especially when the balance, like this year's Bible Scotch of the Year, Ballantine's 17, simply caresses your soul. And they do more: they paint pictures on the palate, flavour-scapes of extraordinary subtlety and texture. No two bottles are ever exactly the same, but they are usually close enough and further illustrate the fascination of a beautifully orchestrated variation on a theme.

With Blended Scotch the range and possibilities are limitless. All it takes is for the drinker not just to use his or her nose and taste-buds. But also an open mind.

Scottish Blends

"10 Years and a Bit" Blended Scotch (84) n21.5 t22 f20 b20.5. Matured in oloroso and finished in a Cognac quartercask. Explains why this blend lurches drunkenly all over the palate. Enough honeycomb, though, for a pleasant few minutes *42%. Qualityworld, Denmark.*

100 Pipers (74) n18.5 t18 f19 b18.5. An improved blend, even with a touch of spice to the finish. I get the feeling the grains are a bit less aggressive than they for so long were. I'd let you know for sure, if only I could get through the caramel. *40%. Chivas.*

Aberdour Piper (88.5) n22 t23 f21.5 b22. Always great to find a blend that appears to have upped the stakes in the quality department. Clean, refreshing with juicy young Speysiders at times simply showing off. *40%. Hayman Distillers.*

Adelphi Private Stock Loyal Old Mature (88) n21 t23 f22 b22. A very attractive number, especially for those with a slightly sweet tooth. *40%*

Antiquary 12 Years Old (92) n23.5 by some distance the smokiest delivery I have seen from this blend since my late dear friend Jim Milne got his hands on it. The last time I had hold of this it was Speyside all the way. Now peat rules; **t23.5** immediate oils and smoke form a thick layer in almost Caol Ila style, but penetrating grains and juicier Speysiders ensure parity of style; **f22** light with vanilla and echoes of peat; **b23** a staggering about turn for a blend which, for a very long time, has flown the Speyside flag. *40%. Tomatin Distillery.*

Antiquary 21 Years Old (93) n23.5 as dense and brooding as an imminent thunderstorm: just a hint of a less than perfect sherry butt costs a point but manuca honey and crushed leaves, all helped along with a delicate peat-reek, ensure something sultry and wonderful; **t23.5** improbably dense with a honeycomb maltiness you have to hack through, the grains offer lighter, bourbony touches; **f23** softer vanillas and toffee, topped with the thinnest layer of molassed sugar and further bourbony notes; **b23** a huge blend, scoring a magnificent 93 points. But I have tasted better, and another sample, direct from the blending lab, came with even greater complexity and less apparent caramel. A top-notch blend of rare distinction. *43%*

Antiquary 30 Years Old (86) n22 t23 f20 b21. Decidedly odd fare but the eccentric nose and early delivery are sublime, with silky complexity tumbling over the palate. *46%*

Antiquary Finest (79.5) n20 t21 f19 b19.5. Pleasantly sweet and plump with the accent on the quick early malt delivery. *40%. Tomatin Distillery.*

Arden House Scotch Whisky (86) n19.5 t22 f22.5 b22. Another great bit of fun from the Co-op. Very closely related to their Finest Blend, though this has, for some reason or other, a trace of a slightly fatter, mildly more earthy style. If only they would ditch the caramel and let those sweet malts and grains breathe! *40%. Co-Operative Group.*

Asda Blended Scotch Whisky (76.5) n19 t21 f17.5 b19. A scattergun approach with sweet, syrupy notes hitting the palate early and hard. Beware the rather bitter finish, though. *40%*

Asda Extra Special 12 Years Old (78) n19 t21 f19 b19. Pleasantish but dragged down by the dreaded S word. *40%. Glenmorangie for Asda.*

The Baillie Nicol Jarvie (B.N.J) (95) n24 the sharpest barley has been taken to a barley-sharpening shop and painstakingly sharpened; this is pretty sharp stuff...the citrus gangs together with the fresh grass to form a dew which is pretty well...er... sharp...; **t24** mouth-watering, eye-closingly, mouth-puckeringly sharp delivery with the barley pinging off the tautest grain you can imagine; **f23** softens with a touch of vanilla and toffee; the late run from the citrus is a masterpiece of whisky closing; **b24** I know my criticism of BNJ, historically one of my favourite blends, over the last year or two has been taken to heart by Glenmorangie. Delighted to report that they have responded: the blend has been fixed and is back to its blisteringly brilliant, ultra-mouth-watering self. Someone's sharpened their ideas up. *40%*

Ballantine's Aged 12 Years (84.5) n22.5 t22 f19 b21. Attractive but odd fellow, this, with a touch of juniper to the nose and furry bitter marmalade on the finish. But some excellent barley-cocoa moments, too. *43%. Chivas.*

Ballantine's 12 Years Old (87) n21 t22 f21 b23. The kind of old-fashioned, mildly moody blend Colonel Farquharson-Smythe (retired) might have recognised when relaxing at the 19th hole back in the early '50s. Too good for a squirt of soda, mind. *40%. Chivas Bros.*

Ballantine's 17 Years Old (97.5) n24.5 deft grain and honey plus teasing salty peat; ultra high quality with bourbon and pear drops offering the thrust; a near unbelievable integration with gooseberry juice offering a touch of sharpness muted by watered golden syrup; **t24** immediately mouthwatering with maltier tones clambering over the graceful cocoa-enriched grain; the degrees of sweetness are varied but near perfection; just hints of smoke here and there; **f24** lashings of vanilla and cocoa on the fade; drier with a faint spicey, vaguely smoky buzz; has become longer with more recent bottlings with the most subtle oiliness imaginable; **b25** now only slightly less weighty than of old. After a change of style direction it has comfortably reverted back to its sophisticated, mildly erotic old self. One of the most beautiful, complex and stunningly structured whiskies ever created. Truly the epitome of great Scotch. *43%. Chivas Bros.* ⊙⊙

Ballantine's Aged 21 Years (93) n24 superbly intrinsic, relying on deft fruit and vanilla notes as the key; **t24** stunningly textured with subtle layers of honey, juicy grasses and refined, slightly subdued, bourbony notes from the grain; **f22** flattens somewhat as the toffee evolves; **b23** one of the reasons I think I have loved the Ballantine's range over the years is because it is a blenders' blend. In other words, you get the feeling that they have made as much, and probably more, as possible from the stocks available and made complexity and balance the keystones to the whisky. That is still the case, except you find now that somehow, although part of a larger concern, it appears that the spectrum of flavours is less wide, though what has been achieved with those available remains absolutely top drawer. This is truly great whisky, but it has changed in style as blends, especially of this age, cannot help but doing. 43%

Ballantine's Aged 30 Years (94) n23.5 satisfying interplay between spiced grape and vanilla-clad smoke; **t24** quite sublime: the delivery simply melts in the mouth. Mainly grain on show early, again with all the attendant vanilla, then a juicier network of sharper barley and fruit. The weight is outstanding; **f23.5** long, with a real grain-malt tug of war. Spices persist and the vanilla ups a gear; **b23.5** quite a different animal to that which I tasted last year...and the year before. Having come across it in three different markets, I each time noted a richer, more balanced product: less a bunch of old casks being brought together but more a sculpted piece from preferred materials. That said, I still get the feeling that this is a work in progress: a Kenny Jackett-style building of a team bit by bit, so that each compartment is improved when it is possible, but not to the detriment of another and, vitally, balance is maintained. 43%

Ballantine's Christmas Reserve (72) n18 t19 f17 b18. Not quite what I asked from Santa. A rare sulphury slip up in the Christmas day snow from the Ballantine's stable. 40%

Ballantine's Finest (96) n24 a playful balance and counter-balance between grains, lighter malts and a gentle smokiness. The upped peat of recent years has given an extra weight and charm that had been missing; **t24** sublime delivery: the mouthfeel couldn't be better had your prayers been answered; velvety and brittle grains combine to get the most out of the juicy malts: a lot of chewing to get through here; **f23.5** soft, gentle, yet retains its weight and shape with a re-emergence of smoke and a gristy sweetness to counter the gentle vanillas and cocoa from the oak **b24.5** as a standard blend this is coming through as a major work of art. Each time I taste this the weight has gone up a notch or two more and the sweetness has increased to balance out with the drier grain elements. Take a mouthful of this and experience the work of a blender very much at the top of his game. 40%. Chivas Bros.

Ballantine's Limited brown bottle, bott code D03518 **(94.5) n23.5** a gentle patchwork quilt of fruit and surprisingly nippy spices. The odd stewed greengage chimes in, as well as toffee apple. And there is something of the early opened bakers too, with that sweet smell of warm cakes and pies...; **t24** obscenely beautiful delivery, perhaps bordering on the delivery of the year. When you taste as many whiskies as I, you sometimes forget that it is, under exceptional circumstances, possible to create a mouth-feel so soft; icing sugars and diluted golden syrup offer moisture to the burnt raisin; **f23** a very slight bitter fade but there are now oaky vanillas to contend with, though they no more than breeze around the palate; **b24** when it comes to Ballantine's I am beginning to run out of superlatives. The last time I tasted Limited, I remember being disappointed by the un-Ballantine's-like bitter finish. Well, from nose to finale, there is a barely perceptible trace of a rogue cask costing half a point from each stage: indeed, it may have cost it World Whisky of the Year. But so magnificent are all those keeping it company there has been no such falling at the last hurdle here. This bottle, rather than finding its way back into my warehouse library, will be living at my home for offering an ethereal quality unmatched by any other whisky in the world. 43%. Chivas.

Ballantine's Limited 75cl royal blue bottle **(89) n22 t24 f21 b22.** Hadn't tasted this for a little while but maintains its early style and quite glorious delivery. 43%

Ballantine's Master's (82) n21 t22 f19 b20. Excellent lively grain and chewy malt, but the always suspect, grain-drizzled finish has become even more nondescript in recent bottlings. 40%

Ballantine's Rare Limited (89.5) n23.5 busy and weighty: light smoke compliments the bananas and raisins; **t22.5** thick and soupy; the delivery and follow through are both lush and viscous and moderately juicy. Again we have bananas in custard plus a more aggressive muscovado-sweetened fruitiness; **f21.5** spices gather as do drier oaks; **b22** a heavier, more mouth watering blend than the "Bluebottle" version. 43%. ncf. Chivas.

⁖ **Barley Barony (83) n21.5 t21 f20 b20.5.** A faintly furry finish follows from a firm, fruity front. 40%. Quality Spirits International.

Bell's Original (91) n23 superb, old fashioned stuff: a few biting grains (as there should be), but kept in good order by a confident, smoky tapestry. Plenty of caramel but still quietly assertive; **t22.5** delivery offers a two-pronged attack of grinding grain and more sumptuous oils and smoke; quick to sweeten though never too far; caramel and vanilla offers a fanfare to a middle spice surge; **f22.5** long with the smoke lengthening the tail further. Usual butterscotch and caramel, but everything charmingly well tailored; **b23** your whisky sleuth came across the new version for the first time in the bar of a London theatre back in December 2009 during the interval of "The 39 Steps". To say I was impressed and pleasantly surprised is putting it mildly. And with the whisky, too, which is a massive improvement on the relatively stagnant 8-year-old especially with the subtle extra smoky weight. If the blender asks me: "Did I get it right, Sir?" then the answer has to be a resounding "yes". 40%

Bells 8 Years Old (85) n21.5 t22.5 f20 b21. Some mixed messages here: on one hand it is telling me that it has been faithful to some of the old Bells distilleries – hence a slight dirty note, especially on the finish. On the other, there are some sublime specks of complexity and weight. Quite literally the rough and the smooth. 40%. Diageo.

Benmore (74) n19 t19 f18 b18. Underwhelming to the point of being nondescript. 40%

Berrys' Blue Hanger 30 Years Old 3rd Release bott 2007 **(90.5) n23** ye olde oake, as one might expect from this olde companye, manifesting itself in sweet exotic fruit; **t22.5** bitter-sweet and tingly, from the very start the blend radiates fruit and big oak; **f22.5** long, spiced, a dash of something vaguely smoky but never tries to disguise its great age; saved at the death by a lush sweetness which sees off any OTT oak; **b22.5** much improved version on the last, closer to the original in every respect. Excellent. 45.6%. Berry Bros & Rudd.

Big "T" 5 Years Old (75) n19 t20 f18 b18. Still doesn't have the finesse of old and clatters about the tastebuds charmlessly. 40%. Tomatin Distillery.

Black & White (91) n22 t23 f22.5 b23.5 This one hasn't gone to the dogs: quite the opposite. I always go a bit misty-eyed when I taste something this traditional: the crisp grains work to maximum effect in reflecting the malts. A classic of its type. 40%. Diageo.

Black Bottle (74.5) n18 t20.5 f17 b18. Barely a shadow of its once masterful, great self. 40%. Burn Stewart.

Black Bottle 10 Years Old (89) n22 so age-weightedly peaty it could almost be a single malt: the grains make little discernible impact; **t23** soft, deft malt and firmer grain. The peat arrives after a short interval; **f22** more vanilla and other oaky tones; **b23** a stupendous blend of weight and poise, but possessing little of the all-round steaming, rampaging sexuality of the younger version...but like the younger version showing a degree less peat: here perhaps even two. Not, I hope, the start of a new trend under the new owners. 40%

Black Dog 12 Years Old (92) n21 t23 f24 b24. Offering genuine sophistication and élan. This minor classic will probably require two or three glass-fulls before you take the bait... 42.8%

Black Dog Century (89) n21 t23 f23 b22. I adore this style of no-nonsense, full bodied bruising blend which amid the muscle offers exemplary dexterity and finesse. What entertainment in every glass!! 42.8%. McDowell & Co Ltd. Blended in Scotland/Bottled in India.

The Black Douglas bott code 340/06/181 **(84) n19 t20 f23 b22.** Don't expect raptures of mind-bending complexity. But on the other hand, enough chewability and spice buzz here to make for a genuinely decent whisky, especially on the excellent finish. Not dissimilar to a bunch of blends you might have found in the 1950s. 40%. Foster's Group, Australia.

The Black Douglas Aged 8 Years bott code 348/06/18/ **(79) n20 t21 f19 b19.** Slightly lacking for an 8 y o: probably duller than its non-age-statement brother because of an extra dollop of caramel. 40%. Foster's Group, Australia.

The Black Douglas Aged 12 Years "The Black Reserve" bott code 347/06/188 **(87) n21 t21 f23 b22.** The toffee does its best to wreck the show – but there are simply too many good things going on to succeed. The slight smoke to the nose delights and the honeycomb middle really does star. 40%. Foster's Group, Australia.

Black Grouse (94) n23 outwardly a hefty nose, but patience is rewarded with a glorious Demerara edge to the malt and oak: superb, understated stature; **t24** again the smoke appears to be at the fore, but it's not. Rather, a silky sweet delivery also covers excellent cocoa and spice **f23** so gentle, with waves of smoke and oak lapping on an oaky shore. Brilliant... **b24** a superb return to a peaty blend for Edrington for the first time since they sold Black Bottle. Not entirely different from that brand, either, from the Highland Distillers days with the smokiness being superbly couched by sweet malts. A real treasure. 40%

⁖ **The Black Grouse Alpha Edition (72.5) n17 t19.5 f17 b18.** Dreadfully sulphured. 40%

Black Knight (85.5) n21 t22 f21 b21.5. More of a White Knight as it peacefully goes about its business. Not many taste buds slain, but just love the juicy charge. 43%. Quality Spirits Int.

Black Ram Aged 12 Years (85) n21 t23 f21 b20. An upfront blend that gives its all in the chewy delivery. Some major oak in there but it's all ultra soft toffee and molasses towards the finish. 40%. Vinprom Peshtera, Bulgaria.

Blend No. 888 (86.5) n20 t21.5 f23 b22. A good old-fashioned, rip-roaring, nippy blend with a fudge-honey style many of a certain age will fondly remember from the 60s and 70s. Love it! 40%. The House of MacDuff.

Broadford (78.5) n19 t19.5 f20 b20. Boringly inoffensive. Toffee anyone? 40%. Burn Stewart.

Buchanan's De Luxe 12 Years Old (82) n18 t21 f22 b21. The nose shows more than just a single fault and the character simply refuses to get out of second gear. Certainly pleasant, and some of the chocolate notes towards the end are gorgeous. But just not the normal brilliant show-stopper! *40%. Diageo.*

Buchanan's Red Seal (90) n22 clean with almost equal portions of grain, malt and oak; **t23** wonderful malt clarity guarantees a rare charm; the grains are crisp and amplify the barley sweetness; **f22** lovely sweet vanilla complements the persistent barley; **b23** exceptional, no-frills blend whose apparent simplicity paradoxically celebrates its complexity. *40%. Diageo.*

Budgen's Scotch Whisky Finely Blended (85) n21 t22 f21 b21. A sweet, chunky blend offering no shortage of dates, walnuts, spice and toffee. A decent one to mull over. *40%*

Callander 12 Years Old (86) n21 t22 f21.5 b21.5. No shortage of malt sparkle and even a touch of tangy salt. Very attractive and enjoyable without ripping up trees. *46.3%. Burn Stewart.*

Campbeltown Loch Aged 15 Years (88) n22.5 deft marzipan and smoke; **t22.5** firm, with ever-increasing oak but never at the cost of the honeyed malt; at times sharp and puckering; **f21** much grainier and firm; dries very slowly; **b22** well weighted with the age in no hurry to arrive. *40%. Springbank Distillers.*

Castle Rock (81) n20 t20.5 f20 b20.5. Clean and juicy entertainment. *40%*

Catto's Aged 25 Years (87.5) n23 t22.5 f20.5 b21.5. A hugely enjoyable yet immensely frustrating dram. The higher fruit and spice notes are a delight, but it all appears to be played out in a padded cell of cream caramel. One assumes the natural oak caramels have gone into overdrive. Had they not, we would have had a supreme blend scoring well into the 90s. *40%*

Catto's Deluxe 12 Years Old (79.5) n20 t21.5 f18 b20. Refreshing and spicy in part, but still a note in there which doesn't quite work. *40%. Inverhouse Distillers.*

Catto's Rare Old Scottish (92) n23.5 the young Speysiders leap from the glass with joyous abandon while the grain looks on benevolently; **t23.5** various shades of citrus and juicy grass make for a mouthwatering experience; a soft honey strand adds the slightest touch of weight and the most delicate of spices chime in; **f22** gentle vanillas balance the sweeter notes; remains refreshing to the death; **b23** currently one of my regular blends to drink at home. Astonishingly old-fashioned with a perfect accent on clean Speyside and crisp grain. In the last year or so it has taken on a sublime sparkle on the nose and palate. An absolutely masterful whisky which both refreshes and relaxes. *40%. James Catto & Co.*

Chequers Deluxe (78.5) n19.5 t20 f19 b20. Charm, elegance, sophistication...not a single sign of any of them. Still if you want a bit of rough and tumble, just the job. *40%. Diageo.*

Chivas Regal Aged 12 Years (83.5) n20.5 t22.5 f20 b20.5. Chewy fruit toffee. Silky grain mouth-feel with a toasty, oaky presence. *40%. Chivas.*

Chivas Regal Aged 18 Years (73.5) n17.5 t20 f17.5 b18.5. The nose is dulled by a whiff of sulphur and confirmation that all is not well comes with the disagreeably dry, bitter finish. Early on in the delivery some apples and spices show promise but it is an unequal battle against the caramel and off notes. *40%*

Chivas Regal 25 Years Old (95) n23 exotic fruit of the first order: some pretty serious age here, seemingly older than the 25 years; **t23.5** mesmerisingly two-toned, with a beautiful delivery of velvety grains contrasting stunningly with the much firmer, cleaner malts. Softly chewable, with a gentle spice fizz as the vanilla begins to mount; unbelievably juicy and mouth-watering despite its advanced age; **f24** long, wonderfully textured and deft; some cocoa underlines the oak involvement, but there is not once a single hint of over-aging; **b24.5** unadulterated class where the grain-malt balance is exemplary and the deft intertwining of well-mannered oak and elegant barley leaves you demanding another glass. Brilliant! *40%*

Clan Campbell (86.5) n21.5 t22.5 f21 b21.5. I'll wager that if I could taste this whisky before the colouring is added it would be scoring into the 90s. Not a single off note; a sublime early array of Speysidey freshness but dulls at the end. *40%. Chivas.*

Clan Gold 3 Year Old (95) n23.5 shimmering elegance; delicate enough to allow both grain and malt a clear voice with a light mintiness and seasoned celery well at home with those gently honeyed vanilla-oaked notes; **t24** an eye closing, mouth-puckering delivery as those fabulous, sharp Speyside-style barley notes get to work. Beyond the obvious malt come several layers of spices of varying intensity and a much drier oak signature; **f23.5** seemingly dry at first but some late crystalised demerara and waves of pristine barley ensure a sublime balance; **b24** a blend-drinkers blend which will also slay the hearts of Speyside single malt lovers. For me, this is love at first sip... *40%*

Clan Gold Blended 15 Years Old (91) n21.5 an intricately delicate fruit style. Soft green banana sweetness borders on sharpness; a wisp of citrus offers a juicy element; effortless complexity with a surprising degree of crispness; **t23** mouth-watering, clean arrival with an early blast of juicy Speyside-style grassy, almost crystalline malt upping the salivation levels on either side of the tongue: a deeply satisfying experience for blend lovers; **f23.5** exceptional. Long with fine strands of controlled spice expertly woven into the malty tapestry. The grains are lush and chewy and add a lustre to the light oaks. A fabulous, almost classical, fade with not a single discordant note to be heard; **b23** an unusual blend for the 21st century, which steadfastly refuses to blast you away with over the top flavour and/or aroma profiles and instead depends on subtlety and poise despite the obvious richness of flavour. The grains make an impact but only by creating the frame in which the more complex notes can be admired. *40%*

Clan Gold Blended 18 Years Old (94.5) n23 a light background coating of dusty oak but the freshness of the barley startles and pleases. Its trademark is the crushed green apple of a whisky almost half its age though the softening custardy sweetness is an unmistakable sign of antiquity; **t24** bristles on the palate: all kinds of peppery spices lead the malty surge. Gloriously mouthwatering: the lushness of the grains make the hairs stand on end as the mouth feel is the stuff of dreams. Apples lead the fruity fray but that intense barley is never far away; a delightful formation of muscovado sugars, then more apples...; **f23.5** chewy, clean and truly rejoicing in the complex dovetailing of the malt and chalk. The oak remains refined throughout, the grains polishing the last of the fading malts. The smattering of light muscovado sugar continues until near the end. Then the slightly drier oaks reintroduce the now intense spices apparent on delivery; **b24** almost the ultimate preprandial whisky with its at once robust yet delicate working over of the taste buds by the carefully muzzled juiciness of the malt. This is the real deal: a truly classy act which at first appears to wallow in a sea of simplicity but then bursts out into something very much more complex and alluring. About as clean and charming an 18-year-old blend as you are likely to find. *40%*

Clan MacGregor (92) n22 superb grains allow the lemon-fruity malt to ping around: clean, crisp and refreshing; **t24** as mouthwatering as the nose suggests with first clean grain then a succession of fruit and increasingly sweet malty notes. A brilliant mouthful, a tad oilier and spicier than of old; **f23** yielding grain; and now, joy of joys, an extra dollop of spice to jolly it along; **b23** just gets better and better. Now a true classic and getting up there with Grant's. *43%*

Clan Murray Rare Old (84) n18 t23 f21 b22. The wonderful malt delivery on the palate is totally incongruous with the weak, nondescript nose. Glorious, mouth-watering complexity on the arrival, though. Maybe it needs a Murray to bring to perfection... *40%. Benriach Distillery.*

Clansman (80.5) n20.5 t21 f19 b20. Sweet, grainy and soft. *40%. Loch Lomond.*

Clansman (78.5) n20 t21.5 f18 b19. Plenty of weight, oil and honey-ginger. Some bitterness, too. *43%. Loch Lomond Distillers.*

The Claymore (85) n19 t22 f22 b22. These days you are run through by spices. The blend is pure Paterson in style with guts etc, which is not something you always like to associate with a Claymore; some delightful muscovado sugar at the death. Get the nose sorted and a very decent and complex whisky is there to be had. *40%. Whyte & Mackay Distillers Ltd.*

Compass Box Asyla 1st fill American oak ex-bourbon, bott May 10 **(93) n24** crisp, complex and crystalline: a fascinating trade off between the granular malts and the vanilla-clad grains; **t24** frighteningly fresh and salivating complexity. Good early weight and texture. Vanillas abound towards the middle; **f22.5** surprisingly rabid grain, but of such excellent quality one can only admire; **b23.5** if you can hear a purring noise, it is me tasting this... *40%. nc ncf.*

Compass Box Asyla Marriage married for nine months in an American oak barrel **(88) n22** a soup of a nose, though slightly over oaked for perfect harmony; **t23** a big, sweet cherry tart kick off with custard and spices galooped on top; **f21** warming, spiced vanilla; **b22** a lovely blend, but can't help feeling that this was one marriage that lasted too long. *43.6%. Compass Box Whisky for La Maison du Whisky in commemoration of their 50th Anniversary.*

Consulate (89) n22 t22 f22.5 b22.5. One assumes this beautifully balanced dram was designed to accompany Passport in the drinks cabinet. I suggest if buying them, use Visa. *40%*

Co-operative Finest Blend (92.5) n23.5 I have been whizzed back to the late 1970s and here's a throwback for even then. Gorse, honey and light, melting oak; the style of grain has changed since then, but that is all; **t23** the trademark velvety grain one immediately associates with this brand is there as a crutch. But rather than being engulfed in delicate peat as before, we are now seduced by the most gorgeous honey-butterscotch; **f22.5** relatively long and still making the most of the very high quality grain. The vanillas are charming; **b23.5** a fabulous and fascinating blend which has divested itself of its peaty backbone and instead packed the core with honey. Not the same heavyweight blend of old, but still one which is to be taken seriously – and straight – by those looking for a classic whisky of the old school. *40%*

Co-operative Premium Scotch 5 Years Old (91.5) n22 perhaps a little on the mucky side, there is enough date and walnut to be getting on with; **t24** wins hands down for its presentation on the palate: silky, fruity, earthy. The smoke has thinned dramatically from its old incarnation. And the caramel has a very big say, too. But those Demerara sugars, the main fingerprint of this blend, are not only still detectable but have upped the oily outline considerably. Real knife and fork stuff; **f22.5** the caramel plays a big part but some vanilla and honey battle gamely through; the grains, though, have the longest and final say...; **b23** from the nose I thought this blend had nosedived emphatically from when I last tasted it. However the delivery remains the stuff of legend. And though it has shifted emphasis and style to marked degree, there is no disputing its overall clout and entertainment value remains very high. *40%*

Craigellachie Hotel Quaich Bar Range (81) n20 t21 f20 b20. A delightful malt delivery early on, but doesn't push on with complexity as perhaps it might. *40%*

Crawford's (83.5) n19 t21 f22 b21.5. A lovely spice display helps overcome the caramel. *40%*

Cutty Black (83) n20 t23 f19 b21. Both nose and finish are dwarfed and flung into the realms of ordinariness by the magnificently substantial delivery. Whilst there is a taint to the nose, its richness augers well for what is to follow; and you won't be disappointed. At times it behaves like a Highland Park with a toffeed spine, such is the richness and depth of the honey and dates and complexity of the grain-vanilla background. But those warning notes on the nose are there for good reason and the finish tells you why. Would not be surprised to see this score into the 90s on a different bottling day. *40%*

Cutty Sark (78) n19 t21 f19 b19. Crisp and juicy. But a nipping furriness, too. *40%*

Cutty Sark Aged 12 Years (92) n22 grain heavy, but crisp and clean; t24 mountainous honey which had been hiding on the nose cascades onto the taste buds. The firm grain gives the honey and accompanying maple syrup a backbone while spices slowly gather; f23 long and lush, toffee begins to absorb the honey; b23 at last! Cutty 12 at full sail...and blended whisky rarely looks any more beautiful! *40%. Edrington.*

Cutty Sark Aged 15 Years (82) n19 t22 f20 b21. Attempts to take the honey route. But seriously dulled by toffee and the odd sulphured cask. *40%. Edrington.*

Cutty Sark Aged 18 Years (88) n22 much oakier output than before with only fragments of sherry; herbal; t22 a safe delivery of yielding grain with out-reaching fingers of juicier malt; decent spice buzz as a bitter-sweet harmony is reached; f22 cream toffee and custard creams; b22 lost the subtle fruitiness which worked so well. Easy-going and attractive. *43%*

Cutty Sark Aged 25 Years (91) n21 a sensational, luxurious, almost erotic but certainly exotic mix of the most delicate peat and juicy sub-Saharan dates. Molten muscovado sugar and light mocha is pelted by spice and you can't escape the sherry trifle-Christmas pudding duet, either... ; t23.5 the usual silkiness is there in layers. But the fruit content has been upped considerably. More sultana and though the normal honey is subdued, the smoky spice more than makes amends; for all its weight, remains impressively juicy; f22.5 the grains come out in force and do a good job of giving a custardy edge to the very light furriness; b23 magnificent, though not quite flawless, this whisky is as elegant and effortlessly powerful as the ship after which the brand was named... *45.7%. Berry Bros & Rudd.*

Demijohn's Finest Blended Scotch Whisky (88) n21 strange, out of shape, but soft; t22 salivating delivery with a wonderful firmness to the grain; the malts eventually mould into the style; f23 remains tangy to the end, even with a touch of marmalade thrown in; b22 a fun, characterful blend that appears to have above the norm malt. Enjoy. *40%. Adelphi.*

Dew of Ben Nevis Blue Label (82) n19 t22 f20 b21. The odd off-key note is handsomely outnumbered by deliciously complex mocha and demerara tones. Ditch the caramel and you'd have a sizzler! *40%. Ben Nevis Distillery. Replacement for Dew of Ben Nevis Millennium Blend.*

Dew of Ben Nevis Special Reserve (85) n19 t21 f23 b22. A much juicier blend than of old, still sporting some bruising and rough patches. But that kind of makes this all the more attractive, with the caramel mixing with some fuller malts to provide a date and nuts effect which makes for a grand finale. *40%. Ben Nevis Distillery.*

Dew of Ben Nevis Supreme Selection (77) n18 t20 f20 b19. Some lovely raspberry jam swiss roll moments here. But the grain could be friendlier, especially on the nose. *40%*

⁖ **Dewar House Experimental Batch No. A39 Age 17 Years** sherry finish, cask no. 001, bott 17 Jul 12 **(96)** n24 faultless grape, but not overly heavy or too sweet. Instead a busy procession of spices, some of them quite peppery and nippy, binds rather beautifully with a delicate vanilla, date and walnut base; t24 you feel you have been flung to the bed and your hands tied while wave upon wave of sensual flavours wash over you, one moment juicy and soft, the next attacking with as much controlled aggression as you can withstand...and all the times the plums and dates and walnuts continue on their ultra-rich fruitcake way; f23.5 you'd expect – demand – a long finish after all that. And you get it thanks to a sublime mix of all those delicate fruits. Alas, a minor build up of sulphur has accumulated, knocking off half a point or so. But if you keep on drinking this stuff, you don't get to the point of noticing...; b24.5 like old Tommy Dewar himself, a unique and classy, classy act. To be honest, when I saw "finished in sherry" on the label I had got to the point this year where I was terrified of opening the bottle. But this shows how it should be done: I'd like to shake the blender by the hand! This was exactly the whisky the scotch industry needed at this precise moment, well that vague residue on the finish apart...(one that probably robbed it of World Whisky of the Year). Even so, unforgettable and truly magnificent. And as experiments go, it knocks the relatively unimportant goings on at Cern into a cocked hat... *58.9%. sc. 30 bottles.*

Dewar's Special Reserve 12 Years Old (84) n20 t23 f19 b22. Some s... you know what... has crept onboard here and duffed up the nose and finish. A shame because elements of the delivery and background balance shows some serious blending went on here. *40%*

Dewar's 18 Years Old (93) n23 confident and complex, the nose makes no secret that its foundations are solid grain. From it hang a succession of nubile malty notes, weighty and not without a minor degree of smoke. The fruit has a strawberry jam presence, and there are spices, of course... **t24** entirely classical in its delivery: firm grain and rich, sweet malt linked arm in arm. Again the grain is bold and firm but tattooed into it is a buzzing busy maltiness, offering varying degrees of weight, sweetness and depth...; **f22.5** a build up of caramel begins to lessen the degree of complexity, though not the body and weight; **b23.5** here is a classic case of where great blends are not all about the malt. The grain plays in many ways the most significant role here, as it is the perfect backdrop to see the complexity of the malt at its clearest. Simply magnificent blending with the use of flawless whisky. *43%. John Dewar & Sons.*

Dewar's 18 Year Old Founders Reserve (86.5) n22.5 t22 f20.5 b21.5. A big, blustering dram which doesn't stint on the fruit. A lovely, thin seam of golden syrup runs through the piece, but the dull, aching finale is somewhat out of character. *40%. John Dewar & Sons.*

Dewar's Signature (93) n24 t23.5 f22 b23.5. A slight departure in style, with the fruit becoming just a little sharper and juicier. Top range blending and if the odd butt could be weeded out, this'd be an award winner for sure. *43%*

Dewar's White Label (78.5) n19 t21.5 f19 b19. When on song, one of my preferred daily blends. But not when like this, with its accentuated bitter-sweet polarisation. *40%*

Dimple 12 Years Old (86.5) n22 t22 f21.5 b21. Lots of sultana while the spice adds aggression. *40%. Diageo.*

Dimple 15 Years Old (87.5) n20 t21 f24 b22.5. Only on the late middle and finish does this particular flower unfurl and to magnificently complex effect. The texture of the grains in particular delight while the strands of barley entwine. A type of treat for the more technically minded of the serious blend drinkers among you. *40%. Diageo.*

Drummer (81) n20 t21 f20 b20. Big toffee. Rolos...? *40%. Inver House Distillers.*

Drummer Aged 5 Years (83) n19 t22.5 f20.5 b21. The nose may beat a retreat but it certainly gets on a roll when those fabulous sharp notes hit the palate. However, it deserves some stick as the boring fudge finishes in a cymbal of too much toffee. *40%. Inver House.*

Duncan Taylor Auld Blended Aged 35 Years dist pre 70 **(93) n23** appears too oaked but time in the glass allows some excellent marmalade and marzipan to appear; **t24** glorious delivery: amazing silk, lots of gentle, natural caramel but topped with honeycomb; **f22** chocolate malt and burnt toast; **b24** an infinitely better dram than previous bottlings, due mainly to the fact that the dangers of old oak appear to have been compensated for. *46%. 131 bottles.*

Duncan Taylor Collection Black Bull 12 Year Old (88.5) n22.5 like many a Black Bull, this is muscular and with no shortage of attitude, it is also a touch oily but the malt is well represented; **t22.5** beautifully chewy with all kinds of natural toffees mixing well with the creaminess and hazelnut; even a light spice to add to the balance; **f21.5** toffee and vanilla; **b22** Black Bulls enjoy a reputation for being dangerous. So does this: once you pour yourself a glass, it is difficult not to have another...and another... *50%. Duncan Taylor & Co Ltd*

Duncan Taylor Collection Black Bull Deluxe Blend Aged 30 Years (93) n24 t24 f22 b23. This pedigree Black Bull doesn't pull its horns in... *50%. Duncan Taylor*

Duncan Taylor Collection Rarest of the Rare Deluxe Blend 33 Years Old (94) n24 a fusion of rich bourbon and old Canadian characteristics beefed up further with diced exotic fruit and a dash of ancient Demerara rum; **t24** the bourbon hits the track running, closely followed by some silky barley couched in velvet grain; invariably some spices pitch in to ramp up the complexity even further; **f22** no great length, but no off notes, either. Instead the oak adds an unsweetened custardy grace; **b23** outstanding and astounding blended whisky. An absolute must for blend lovers...especially those with a bourbony bent. *43.4%*

Duncan Taylor Collection Black Bull 40 Year Old batch 1 **(86.5) n23 t21 f21.5 b21.** Almost certainly whisky which had dipped below 40%abv in the cask has been included in this blend. That would account for the occasional spasm of ultra intense natural caramels, a kind of tell-tale fingerprint indicating this is likely to have been done. The nose is exotic fruit; the delivery is a battle to keep the oak at bay. One which is happily won. *40.2%*

Duncan Taylor Collection Black Bull 40 Years Old batch 2 **(94) n23** a barrel-load of exotic fruitiness that is not unexpected from a whisky of this antiquity; light but with banana and custard the main theme; **t24** ridiculously fresh delivery for its massive age with a brilliant eye-watering quality to the barley. Slightly coppery, too; **f23** virtually no ill effect from the cask, as one might expect from something this delicate. Instead, we are treated to a touch of freshly squeezed orange alongside the lightly creamed mocha; **b24** just sit back and marvel at something so old...yet so young at heart. *41.9%. Duncan Taylor & Co. 957 bottles.*

Duncan Taylor Collection Black Bull Special Reserve batch 1 **(86) n21 t22.5 f21 b21.5.** Juicy in just the right areas. Some charming spice and vanilla, too. *46.6%*

The Famous Grouse (89) n22 a weightier aroma than Grouse once was. Not quite so clean and crisp; now a slight smoke can be detected, while honey threads, once audible, have to fight to be heard; once you get used to it, it is quite lovely...; **t23** a real surprise package for a Grouse, as this is no lightweight on delivery: the flavours come thick and fast – literally – though the intensity makes it hard to pick out individual notes; once acclimatised, there are distinct marmalade and custard qualities, but only after a brooding shadow of smoke moves out of the picture taking some honey with it; **f21.5** lots of mocha and cream toffee with the vanilla adding a dusty quality; **b22.5** it almost seems that Grouse is, by degrees, moving from its traditional position of a light blend to something much closer to Grant's as a middle-weighted dram. Again the colouring has been raised a fraction and now the body and depth have been adjusted to follow suit. Have to say that this is one very complex whisky these days: I had spotted slight changes when drinking it socially, but this was the first time I had a chance to sit down and professionally analyse what was happening in the glass. A fascinating and tasty bird, indeed. *40%. Edrington Group.*

The Famous Grouse Gold Reserve (90) n23.5 ye gods! What an improvement on the last bottle of this I came across!! Really sexy complexity which, though showing decent weight, including delicate smoke, also celebrates the more citrussy things in life. At body temp the complexity of the structure and degree of layering goes through the roof...; **t23** honeyed to start, then an injection of lime and ground cherry; some caramel tries to interfere and to some extent succeeds; **f21.5** the toffee effect immediately curtails further complexity, but there is a slight spice rumble very late on and even a light sprinkling of barley grist; **b22** great to know the value of the Gold Reserve is going up...as should the strength of this blend. The old-fashioned 40% just ain't enough carats. *40%. Edrington Group.*

⁘ **The Famous Jubilee (83.5) n21.5 t22.5 f18.5 b21.** A heavyweight, stodgy, toffee-laden kind of blend a long way from the Grouse tradition. With its ham-fisted date and walnut middle I would have sworn this was the work of another blender entirely. There are redeeming rich honey tones that are a joy. But the dull, pulsing sulphur on the finish has almost an air of inevitability. I promise you this: go back 60 years, and there would have been no blend created with this signature...not only did the style not exist, but it would have been impossible to accomplish. *40%. Edrington.*

The Formidable Jock of Bennachie (82) n19 t22 f21 b20. "Scotland's best kept secret" claims the label. Hardly. But the silky delivery on the palate is worth investigating. Impressive roastiness to the malt and oak, but the caramel needs thinning. *40%. Bennachie Scotch Whisky.*

Fort Glen The Blender's Reserve Aged 12 Years (88.5) n21.5 any British school kid dating back to WW2 will recognise the "Fruit Salad" sweet signature on this. Soft, delicate and evocative; **t23** and no less fruit on delivery as the salivating citrus makes way for a spicier, oilier middle **f21.5** thins out as the grain and vanilla set up camp; **b22.5** an entirely enjoyable blend which is clean and boasting decent complexity and weight. *40%*

Fort Glen The Distiller's Reserve (78) n18 t22 f19 b19. Juicy, salivating delivery as it storms the ramparts. Draws down the portcullis elsewhere. *40%. The Fort Glen Whisky Company.*

Fraser MacDonald (85) n21 t21.5 f21 b21.5. Some fudge towards the middle and end but the journey there is an enjoyable one. *40%. Loch Lomond Distillers.*

Gairloch (79) n19 t20 f20 b20. For those who like their butterscotch at 40% abv. *40%*

Glen Brynth (70.5) n18 t19 f16 b17.5. Bitter and awkward. *43%*

⁘ **Glenbrynth Pearl 30 Year Old Limited Edition (90.5) n22.5** dusty and dry at first; charming diced pear and spice battle through; **t23.5** silky, attractive delivery with excellent grain bite! Complex sweetness offered by heather honey; **f21.5** spicy but fades quickly with caramel; **b23** attractive, beautifully weighted, no off notes...though perhaps quietened by toffee. Still a treat of a blend. *43%. OTI Africa.*

Glen Gray (84.5) n20 t22.5 f21 b21. A knife and fork blend you can stand your spoon in. Plain going for most of the way, but the area between delivery and middle enjoys several waves of rich chocolate honeycomb...and some of the cocoa resurfaces at the finale. *43%*

Glen Lyon (85) n19 t22.5 f22 b21.5. Works a lot better than the nose suggests: seriously chewy with a rabid spice attack and lots of juices. For those who have just retired as dynamite testers. Unpretentious fun. *43%. Diageo.*

⁘ **Golden Piper (86.5) n22 t21 f22 b21.5.** A firm, clean blend with a steady flush through of diverse sugars. The grain does all the steering and therefore complexity is limited. But the overall freshness is a delight. *43%. Whisky Shack.*

Grand Sail (87) n21 nutty and teasingly nibbles; **t22** multi-layered and full of attitude. Spices abound, providing sharp teeth to the cuddly grain; **f22** long, with vanilla and toffee in the starring roles; **b22** a sweet, attractive blend with enough bite to really matter. *40%*

Grand Sail Aged 10 Years (79) n20 t(22.) f18 b19. Pleasant and at times fascinating but with a tang that perhaps the next vatting will benefit from losing. *40%. China market.*

Grand Sail Rare Reserve Aged 18 Years (94) n23 slightly waxy and bourbony; **t24** fabulous silky grain delivery which offers no little early cocoa; as it moulds into the palate, the mix of corn and spice forms a beautifully textured layering to the roof of the mouth; brown sugars slowly form; **f23** long, as the earlier oils suggest, and the chocolate lightly sweetened by brown sugars go into overdrive; a desired degree of late bite, too; **b24** a truly beautiful whisky which cuts effortlessly and elegantly through the taste buds. *40% Angus Dundee. China market.*

Glenross Blended (83) n20 t22 f20 b21. Decent, easy-drinking whisky with a much sharper delivery than the nose suggests. *40%. Speyside Distillers.*

Glen Simon (77) n20 t19 f19 b19. Simple. Lots of caramel. *40%. Quality Spirits International.*

The Gordon Highlanders (86) n21 t22 f21 b22. Lush and juicy, there is a distinctive Speysidey feel to this one with the grains doing their best to accentuate the developing spice. Plenty of feel good factor here. *40%. William Grant & Sons.*

Grand Macnish (79) n19 t21 f19 b20. Welcome back to an old friend...but the years have caught up with it. Still on the feral side, but has exchanged its robust good looks for an unwashed and unkempt appearance on the palate. Will do a great job to bring some life back to you, though. *43%. MacDuff International Ltd.*

Grand Macnish 12 Years Old (86) n21 t22 f21.5 b21.5. A grander Grand Macnich than of old with the wonderful feather pillow delivery maintained and a greater harmonisation of the malt, especially those which contain a honey-copper sheen. *40%. MacDuff.*

Grant's Aged 12 Years bott 30/09/10 **(89.5) n23** vanilla laden and soft. Threads of acacia honey and jam sponge cake, and various other baker's aromas, offer a subdued, delicate and come hither sweetness...; **t23** the delivery is of feather pillow softness with a mildly bracing, slightly salty barley blast and even the most delicate hint of peat; **f21.5** caramels out rather too grandly though the spices stay the course; **b22** can't argue too much with the tasting notes on the label (although I contend that "full, rich and rounded" has more to do with its body than taste, but that is by the by). Beautiful whisky, as can be reasonably expected from a Grant's blend. If only the sharpness could last the distance. *40%. William Grant & Sons.*

Grant's Cask Edition No.1 Ale Cask Finish Edinburgh ale casks **(88.5) n22 t23 f21.5 b22.** always loved this concept: a whisky and chaser in one bottle. This was has plenty of cheer in the complex opening, but gets maudlin towards the end. *40%. William Grant & Sons.*

⬩⬩⬩ **Great King St. Artist's Blend (93) n24** now there's a way to start the day: stunningly enticing with every nuance of the delicate young barley laid bare. A light coating of bourbon oakiness is enhanced by the scrumptious cinnamon apple pie; **t23** even as a hardened pro, I find it is difficult to spit this one. The delivery is firm, juicy and compelling; few blends these days are half so salivating! The grains try not to hide and weigh in with some lovely cocoa and bourbon stratum, allowing the barley to spread the grassy freshness gospel; good weight throughout, **f22.5** just a slight fault here: a little milkiness from a tired bourbon cask, a distant echo on delivery now makes itself heard, but has the good grace to remain in the background as the spices and late Demerara and liquorice notes hold court; **b23.5** the nose of this uncoloured and non-chill filtered whisky is not dissimilar to some better known blends before they have colouring added to do its worst. A beautiful young thing this blend: nubile, naked and dangerously come hither. Compass Box's founder John Glaser has done some memorable work in recent years, though one has always had the feeling that he has still been learning his trade, sometimes forcing the issue a little too enthusiastically. Here, there is absolutely no doubting that he has come of age as a blender. *43%. nc ncf. Compass Box*

Great MacCauley (81) n20 t20.5 f20 b20.5. Reminds me of another whisky I tasted earlier: Castle Rock, I think. Identical profile with toffee and spice adding to the juicy and youthful fun. *40%. Quality Spirits International.*

Green Plaid 12 Years Old (89) n22 the smoke of old has been doused slightly, though mint comes through with the soft barley; **t23** light oils with a gentle sweetness; **f22** vanilla and a hint of smoke; **b22** beautifully constructed and mouth-watering. *40%. Inverhouse Distillers.*

⬩⬩⬩ **Guneagal Aged 12 Years (85.5) n21 t22.5 f20.5 b21.5.** The salty, sweaty armpit nose gives way to an even saltier delivery, helped along by sweet glycerine and a boiled candy fruity sweetness. The finish is a little roughhouse by comparison. *40%. William Grant & Sons.*

Haddington House (85.5) n21 t21.5 f22 b21. Mouth-watering and delicate. *40%*

Haig Gold Label (88) n21 somewhat sparse beyond a vague grapey-graininess; **t23** begins light and unimpressive, but about three flavour waves in begins to offer multi-layered spices and juice aplenty; the sweet-dry ratio as the oak arrives is brilliant; **f22** classy fade with a touch of Cadbury's Fruit and Nut in the mix as the spices persist; **b22** what had before been pretty standard stuff has upped the complexity by an impressive distance. *40%. Diageo.*

Hankey Bannister (84.5) n20.5 t22 f21 b21. Lots of early life and even a malt kick early on. Toffee later. *40%. Inverhouse Distillers.*

Hankey Bannister 12 Years Old (86.5) n22 t21.5 f21 b22. A much improved blend with a nose and early delivery which makes full play of the blending company's Speyside malts. Plenty of toffee on the finish. *40%. Inverhouse Distillers.*

⬩⬩⬩ **Hankey Bannister 21 Years Old (81.5) n21 t22.5 f18 b20.** Exceptionally fruity and soft but the very bitter marmalade on the finish tells a tale. *40%. Inver House Distillers.*

Hankey Bannister 21 Years Old (93.5) n22.5 a fruity ensemble, clean, vibrant and loath to show its age; **t23.5** every bit as juicy as the nose suggests, except here there is the odd rumble of distant smoke; mainly a firm, barley-sugar hardness as the grains keep control; **f23.5** the arrival of the oak adds further weight and for the first time begins to behave like a 21-y-o; long, now with decent spice and with some crusty dryness at the very death; **b24** a beautifully balanced blend that takes you on a series of journeys into varying styles and stories. Does the blend movement a great service. *43%. Inverhouse Distillers.*

Hankey Bannister 25 Years Old (91) n22.5 a slight bourbony honey-hickory edge, to where the 21-y-o has fruit; **t24** a swooning delivery: just about everything in exactly the right place and showing sympathetic weight to the other. The grains are soft, the malts are sturdier and more energetic, the oak docile...for the time being; **f21.5** some bitter cocoa notes reveal the oak to be a little more militant but the light oils help the grains recover the position and balance; **b23** follows on in style and quality to 21-year-old. Gorgeous. *40%*

⫶ **Hankey Bannister 40 Years Old (89.5) n23.5** busy, thick and with hints of Demerara rum. outstanding sugar balance; **t24** stunning delivery, at first a little shy with neither oak nor fruit wanting to go ahead. Then the thick sultana goes for it....and how! Exceptionally oily with soft ulmo honey; **f19.5** spices up but disappointingly bitters out at the death; **b22.5** not sure where the finish came from. But the fruit symphony leading up to it is a thing of beauty. *43.3%. Inver House Distillers.*

Hankey Bannister 40 Years Old (89) n22 t23 f22 b22. This blend has been put together to mark the 250th anniversary of the forging of the business relations between Messrs. Hankey and Bannister. And although the oak creaks like a ship of its day, there is enough verve and viscosity to ensure a rather delicious toast to the gentlemen. Love it! *44%. Inverhouse.*

Hedges & Butler Royal (92) n22.5 curiously salty and coastal, yet peat-free; the grains couldn't get much crisper; **t23.5** sharp, crisp grain working in complete harmony with the sprightly Speyside-style malts; all kinds of citrus, grassy notes; **f23** a lemon zesty liveliness refreshes and cleanses; some chattering, drier cocoa very late on; **b23** massively improved to become a juicy and charming blend of the very highest order. *40%*

High Commissioner (88.5) n22.5 beautiful weight with a touch of the old-fashioned English sweetshop about the subtle sugar input; something lightly rummy about this; **t22.5** star quality delivery and mouth-feel. Chewy with just the right degree of give. Again those sugars have a delightful say in proceedings; **f20.5** shame about the bitter fade; **b22.5** now I admit I had a hand in cleaning this brand up a couple of years back, giving it a good polish and much needed balance complexity. But I don't remember leaving it in quite this good a shape. A bitter semi-off note on the finish, otherwise this guy would have been in the 90s. What a great fun, three-course dram this is... *40%. Loch Lomond Distillers.*

Highland Baron (85.5) n21 t22 f21 b21.5. A very clean, sweet and competent young blend showing admirable weight and depth. *40%. Loch Lomond Distillers.*

Highland Bird (77) n19 t19 f19 b20. I've has a few of these over the years, I admit. But I can't remember one quite as rough and ready as this... *40%. Quality Spirits International.*

Highland Black 8 Years Old Special Reserve (85.5) n22 t22.5 f20 b21. A lovely blend which has significantly improved since my last encounter with it. A touch too much grain on the finish for greatness, perhaps. But the nose and delivery both prosper from a honey-roast almond sweetness. *40%. Aldi.*

Highland Dream 12 Years Old bott Jan 05 **(94.5) n23.5 t24 f23 b24.** Now that is what I call a blend! How comes it has taken me two years to find it? A wet dream, if ever there was one... *43%. J & G Grant. 9000 bottles.*

Highland Dream 18 Years Old bott May 07 **(88.5) n22.5 t22.5 f21.5 b22.** Perhaps doesn't get the marks on balance that a whisky of this quality might expect. This is due to the slight over egging of the sherry which, while offering a beautiful delivery, masks the complexities one might expect. Lovely whisky, and make no mistake. But, technically, doesn't match the 12-year-old for balance and brilliance. *43%. J & G Grant. 3000 bottles.*

Highland Earl (77) n19 t20 f19 b19. Might have marked it higher had it called itself a grain: the malt is silent. *40%. Aldi.*

Highland Gathering Blended Scotch Whisky (78) n19 t20 f19 b20. Attractive, juicy stuff, though caramel wins in the end. *40%. Lombards Brands.*

Highland Glendon (87.5) n21.5 fruity and well rounded; **t22.5** soft, chewy and making the most of some lush grains; **f21.5** toasty but a surprising degree of honey comb at the death; **b22** an honest, simple but effectively attractive blend. *43%. Quality Spirits International.*

Highland Harvest Organic Scotch Whisky (76) n18 t21 f19 b18. A very interesting blend. Great try, but a little bit of a lost opportunity here as I don't think the balance is quite right. But at least I now know what organic caramel tastes like... *40%*

Highland Mist (88.5) n20.5 a tad nutty and bruising; **t23** total transformation on the palate to the nose: bristling with noticeable malt, including a deft smoke, but biting and nipping with glee...; salivating despite the toffee – some achievement! **f22.5** nutty and chewy...but, unlike the nose, very clean and in control; **b22.5** fabulously fun whisky bursting from the bottle with character and mischief. Had to admit, broke all my own rules and just had to have a glass of this after doing the notes... 40%. Loch Lomond Distillers.

Highland Piper (79) n20 t20 f19 b20. Good quaffing blend – if sweet - of sticky toffee and dates. Some gin on the nose – and finish. 40%

Highland Pride (86) n21 t22 f21.5 b21.5. A beefy, weighty thick dram with plenty to chew on. The developing sweetness is a joy. 40%. Whyte & Mackay Distillers Ltd.

Highland Reserve (82) n20 t21 f20 b21. You'll probably find this just off the Highland Way and incorporating Highland Bird and Monarch of the Glen. Floral and muddy. 40%

Highland Reserve Aged 12 Years (87) n21 sweet shop soft fruits and confident toffee plus an attractively sharp nip; **t22** much to chew over. The sugars are well interspersed with lively spice; **f22** beautifully chewy milk toffee pepped up by those light spices; **b22** Anyone who has tasted Monarch of the Glen 12 will appreciate this. Maybe a bit more fizz here, though, despite the big caramel. 43%. Quality Spirits International.

Highland Warrior (77.8) n19 t19 f19.5 b20. Just like his Scottish Chief, he's on the attack armed with some Dufftown, methinks... 40%. Quality Spirits International.

Highland Way (84) n19 t20.5 f22.5 b22. This lovely little number takes the High Road with some beautiful light scenery along the way. The finish takes a charming Speyside path. 40%

Inverarity Limited Edition cask no. 698, dist 1997, bott 2009 **(84.5) n20.5 t22 f21 b21.** A heady, heavy-duty blend where honeycomb rules on the palate and thick dates offer a more intense sweetness. But don't go looking for subtlety or guile: those whose palates have been educated at the Whyte and Mackay school of delicate sophistication will have a ball. 40%

Islay Mist 8 Years Old (84) n20 t22 f21 b21. Turned into one heavy duty dram since last tasting a couple of years back. This appears to absorb everything it touches leaving one chewy, smoky hombre. Just a little tangy at the end. 40%. MacDuff International Ltd.

Islay Mist 12 Years Old (90) n22 Bowmore-style cough sweet dominates over the most gentle of grains; **t23** decent smoke drive, intense at first then feathering out; remains sweet to the house style **f22** long, back to cough sweet and a long fade of gristy, muscovado sugar; **b23** adore it: classic bad cop - good cop stuff with an apparent high malt content. 40%

Islay Mist 17 Years Old (92.5) n22.5 reclusive peat can just be spotted amid the rich vanillas; **t23.5** silky, mouth-watering delivery: a dream of a start for any blend with the light muscovado, semi-bourbony sugars keeping their shape; depth supplied by the shy peat and no less rutiring oak; **f23** long finish with a late spice prickle and sugared almonds. The smoke continues to play a teasing role; **b23.5** always a tracking blend, this has improved of late into a genuine must have. 40%. MacDuff International Ltd.

Islay Mist Delux (85) n21.5 t22 f21.5 b20. Remains a highly unusual blend with the youthful peat now more brilliant than before, though the sugar levels appear to have risen markedly. 40%

Isle of Skye 8 Years Old (94) n23 Isle of Skye? Or Orkney? Honey and smoke play tag; the grain is firm and clean; **t24** just so beautiful. Honeycomb and light fudge form a rich partnership, the smoke is little more than ballast and a shy spice; the grains play a fabulous role in allowing the maltier notes to ping around and increase the salivating qualities, **f23.5** the spice is now pretty warming but the honeycomb and vanilla dominate the finale; **b23.5** where once peat ruled and with its grain ally formed a smoky iron fist, now honey and subtlety reigns. A change of character and pace which may disappoint gung-ho peat freaks but will intrigue and delight those looking for a more sophisticated dram. 40%. Ian Macleod.

Isle of Skye 21 years Old (91) n21 sluggish: trying to work out its own stance; **t23.5** sweet chocolate raisin, sumptuously brushed with a layer of soft smoke and demerara; **f23** wonderfully deft spices nibble at the tastebuds like tiny fish at your feet in a rock pool; grains at last – soft and silky all the way; **b23.5** what an absolute charmer! The malt content appears pretty high, but the overall balance is wonderful. 40%. Ian Macleod.

Isle of Skye 50 Years Old (82.5) n21.5 t21 f20 b20. Drier incarnation than the 50% version. But still the age has yet to be balanced out, towards the end in particular. Early on some distinguished moments involving something vaguely smoked and a sweetened spice. 41.6%

⋰ **The Jacobite (78.5) n18 t18.5 f22 b20.** Neither the nose or delivery are of the cleanest style. But comes into its own towards the finish when the thick soup of a whisky thins to allow an attractive degree of complexity. Not for those with catholic tastes. 40%. Booker.

James Alexander (85.5) n21 t21.5 f21.5 b21.5. Some lovely spices link the grassier Speysiders to the earthier elements. 40%. Quality Spirits International.

James King (76.5) n20 t18 f20 b18.5. Young whiskies of a certain rank take their time to find their feet. The finish, though, does generate some pleasant complexity. 43%

James King Aged 5 Years (85) n21 t21.5 f21 b21.5. Very attractive, old fashioned and well weighted with a pleasing degree of fat and chewy sweetness and chocolate fudge. Refreshingly good quality distillate and oak have been used in this: I'd drink it any day. 40%

James King 8 Years Old (78.5) n18.5 t21.5 f19 b19.5. Charming spices grip at the delivery and fine malt-grain interplay through the middle, even showing a touch of vanilla. But such a delicate blend can't fully survive the caramel. *43%. Quality Spirits International.*

James King 12 Years Old (81) n19 t23 f19 b20. Caramel dulls the nose and finish. But for some time a quite beautiful blend soars about the taste buds offering exemplary complexity and weight. *40%. Quality Spirits International.*

James King 15 Years Old (89) n22 t23 f21.5 b22.5. Now offers extra spice and zip. 43%

James King 21 Years Old (87.5) n20.5 t23.5 f22 b22. Attractive blend, but one that could do with the strength upped to 46% and the caramel reduced if not entirely got rid of. One of those potentially excellent yet underperforming guys I'd love to be let loose on! *43%*

James Martin 20 Years Old (93) n21 t23.5 f24.5 b24. I had always regarded this as something of an untamed beast. No longer: still something of a beast, but a beautiful one that is among the most complex found on today's market. *43%. Glenmorangie.*

James Martin 30 Years Old (86) n21.5 t22 f21 b21.5. Enjoyable for all its exotic fruitiness. But with just too many creaking joints to take it to the same level as the sublime 20-y-o. Even so, a blend worth treating with a touch of respect and allowing time for it to tell some pretty ancient tales... *43%. Glenmorangie.*

J&J Jet (79.5) n19 t20 f20.5 b20. Never quite gets off the ground due to carrying too heavy a load. Unrecognisable to its pomp in the old J&B days: this one is far too weighty and never properly finds either balance or thrust. *40%. Diageo.*

J&B Reserve Aged 15 Years (78) n23 t19 f18 b18. What a crying shame. The sophisticated and demure nose is just so wonderfully seductive but what follows is an open-eyed, passionless embrace. Coarsely grain-dominant and unbalanced, this is frustrating beyond words and not worthy to be mentioned in the same breath as the old, original J&B 15 which, by vivid contrast, was a malty, salivating fruit-fest and minor classic. *40%. Diageo.*

J&B Rare (88.5) n21.5 the most youthful J&B nose ever: young malts and grain integrate well, but those grains really do appear still to have milk teeth; **t22.5** one thing about young whisky: it's packed with flavour. This is salivatory overdrive as the sheer unopposed freshness gives the tastebuds goosebumps; **f22** clean, grain layered with soft vanilla; **b22.5** I have been drinking a lot of J&B from a previous time of late, due to the death of their former blender Jim Milne. I think he would have been pretty taken aback by the youthful zip offered here: whether it is down to a decrease in age or the use of slightly more tired casks – or both – is hard to say. *40%. Diageo.*

Jim McEwan's Blended Whisky (86.5) n20 t22 f22.5 b22. Juicy and eye-watering with clever late spices. *46%. Bruichladdich.*

John Barr (85.5) n20 t22 f21.5 b22. I assume from the big juicy dates to be found that Fettercairn is at work. Outwardly a big bruiser; given time to state its case and it's a bit of a gentle giant. *40%. Whyte & Mackay Distillers Ltd.*

Johnnie Walker Black Label 12 Years Old (95.5) n23.5 pretty sharp grain: hard and buffeting the nose; a buffer of yielding smoke, apple pie and delicate spice cushions the encounter; **t24.5** if there is a silkier delivery on the market today, I have not seen it: this is sublime stuff with the grains singing the sweetest hymns as they go down, taking with them a near perfection of weighty smoke lightened by brilliantly balanced barley which leans towards both soft apple and crème broulee; **f23.5** those reassuringly rigid grains re-emerge and with them the most juicy Speysidey malts imaginable; the lovely sheen to the finish underlines the good age of the whiskies used; **b24** here it is: one of the world's most masterful whiskies back in all its complex glory. A bottle like this is like being visited by an old lover. It just warms the heart and excites. *40%. Diageo.*

Johnnie Walker Blue Label (88) n21 the old, cleverly peated nose has been lost to us and now the accent falls on fruit though this is hardly as cleanly endearing as it might be; **t24** but the magnificence of the mouth arrival is back with a bang with the most sumptuous marriage of over-ripened figs, volumous malt and lightly sprinkled peat all bound together and then expanded by a brilliant use of firm and soft old grains. Spices also sparkle and tease. Magnificent...; **f21** oh, so disappointing again, with the plot played on the arrival and there being insufficient reserve to see off the broodier elements of the slightly bitter oak; **b22** what a frustrating blend! Just so close to brilliance but the nose and finish are slightly out of kilter. Worth the experience of the mouth arrival alone. *43%. Diageo.*

⁘ **Johnnie Walker Blue Label The Casks Edition (97) n24.5** now that is a nose: absolutely brimming with intent and character, this obviously has no designs to just sit there and look pretty. A blend where the malts have a far bigger say than the grains, especially the honeydew melon and red berries. The phenols are surprisingly laconic, but that gives more scope for the duskier notes from the oak to come through, especially the more bourbon-style liquorice and hickory. There is also something there which would be appreciated by lovers of high ester Jamaican pot still rum; **t24.5** the great blends have, traditionally, offered a little nip and bite...and the delivery here shows as many teeth as it does soothing fingers of honey. Wonderful walnut oil and marzipan offer the nuts to go with the delicate fruit and chocolate; the mid range carries on with this high ester, slightly oily sweetness which coats the mouth with kumquats and liquorice; the spices are shallow but offer excellent variance to the vanilla; **f23.5** long, languid, delicately oiled and bowing out with a stunning display of spiced heather honey, mocha, dates, walnuts and the lightest of smoky fades...; **b24.5** this is a triumph of scotch whisky blending. With not as much as a hint of a single off note to be traced from the tip of the nose to tail, this shameless exhibition of complexity and brilliance is the star turn in the Diageo portfolio right now. Indeed, it is the type of blend that every person who genuinely adores whisky must experience for the good of their soul....if only once in their life. *55.8%. Diageo.*

⟴ **Johnnie Walker Double Black (94.5) n23** sweet, distinctly malty and salty (salted celery, to be precise); there is an earthiness to this unlike any other JW. Weighty, but light and aloof enough for hints of honey and orange to blossom; **t23.5** superb mouth-feel on delivery: silky and suave with the malt immediately apparent through the spiced smoke and buttery barley; a string of vanilla notes punctuate the mid ground; the melting of the brown sugars is a dream; **f24** long and confidently spiced. But the trick is in the light oils carried on the smoke (presumably Caol Ila displaying its party piece) and the ambiguity of age: some younger notes play havoc with the more mature tannins. Complex and keeps the palate on full alert from delivery to the very last spice buzz; **b24** double tops! Rolling along the taste buds like distant thunder, this is a welcome and impressive addition to the Johnnie Walker stable. Perhaps not as complete and rounded as the original Johnnie Walker Black...but, then, what is? *40%. Diageo.*

⟴ **Johnnie Walker Gold Label Reserve (91.5) n23** just a little extra weight by comparison to its 18-y-o predecessor. Delicate heather honey, though the higher notes are clipped by caramel. Both are out-performed by the nutty Danish marzipan; a little bitter marmalade also makes a bow; **t24** the star moments of this blend are reserved for the delivery. The texture is the stuff of dreams and the slow opening of the delicate honey tones are sublime, especially as both a juicy Speyside style barley and an enticing vanilla from the grains offer the perfect accompaniments; the spices are reserved, but present; **f22** much duller as the toffee on the nose returns and a light furry bitterness rumbles; **b23** moments of true star quality here, but the finish could do with a polish. *40%. Diageo.*

Johnnie Walker King George V db **(88) n23** delicate smoke and honey with green tea. Unusual, but it works; **t22** good weight and spice buzz on delivery; melting grains help lighten the oak; **f21** gets lost in toffee. Pity. **h22** One assumes that King George V is no relation to King George IV. This has genuine style and breeding, if a tad too much caramel. *43%*

⟴ **Johnnie Walker Platinum Label Aged 18 Years (88) n22** the delicate smoke appears to have as much tobacco as peat; earthy, a sprig of mint and a little nip to the spice; **t23** busy, playfully spiced and gorgeously weighted delivery with excellent orange blossom honey hanging on the oils; the caramels give something else to chew on; **f21** just a bit tight and furry on the finale from the wine cask influence; **b22** this blend might sound like some kind of Airmiles card. Which wouldn't be too inappropriate, though this is more Business than First... *40%. Diageo.*

Johnnie Walker Red Label (87.5) n22 such a crisp delivery of grain; toffee apple, too...with young apples...; **t22** juicy and hard delivery, much in keeping with the nose; toffee arrives early, then a welter of malty blows; **f21.5** crisp grain again and the vaguest hint of smoke joins the vanilla; **b22** the ongoing move through the scales quality-wise appears to suggest we have a work still in progress here. This sample has skimped on the smoke, though not quality. Yet a few months back when I was in the BA Business Lounge at Heathrow's new Terminal Five, I nearly keeled from almost being overcome by peat in the earthiest JW Red I had tasted in decades. I found another bottle and I'm still not sure which represents the real Striding Man. *40%. Diageo.*

Kenmore Special Reserve Aged 5 Years bott code L07285 **(75) n18 t20 f19 b18.** Recovers to a degree from the poor nose. A must-have for those who prefer their Scotch big-flavoured and gawky. *40%*

King Robert II (77) n19 t19 f20 b19. A bustier, more bruising batch than the last 40 per cent version. Handles the OTT caramel much better. Agreeably weighty slugging whisky. *43%.*

Kings Blended 3 Years Old (83) n21 t21.5 f20 b20.5. A young, chunky blend that you can chew forever. *40%. Speyside Distillers.*

King's Crest Scotch Whisky 25 Years Old (83) n22 t22 f19 b20. A silky middle weight. The toffee-flat finish needs some attention because the softly estered nose and delivery is a honey-rich treat and deserves better. *40%. Speyside Distillers.*

Label 5 Aged 18 Years (84.5) n20.5 t22 f21 b21. A big mouthful and mouth-feel. Has changed course since I last had this one. Almost a feel of rum to this with its estery sheen. Sweet, simple, easy dramming. *40%. La Martiniquaise, France.*

Label 5 Classic Black (75) n18 t20 f18 b19. The off-key nose needs some serious re-working. Drop the caramel, though, and you would have a lot more character. Needs some buffing. *40%. The First Blending for La Martiniquaise, France.*

Label 5 Reserve No. 55 Single Cask sherry cask finish, bott code no. E-1067 **(75)** n19 t20 f18 b18. The cordite on the nose suggests fireworks. But somehow we end up with a damp squib. *43%. La Martiniquaise, France.*

Lang's Supreme Aged 5 Years (93.5) n23.5 t23.5 f23 b23.5. Every time I taste this the shape and structure has altered slightly. Here there is a fraction more smoke, installing a deeper confidence all round. This is blended whisky as it should be: Supreme in its ability to create shape and harmony. *40%. Ian Macleod Distillers Ltd.*

The Last Drop (96.5) n24 t25 f23.5 b24. How do you mark a whisky like this? It is scotch. Yet every molecule of flavour and aroma is pure bourbon. I think I'll have to mark for quality, principally, which simply flies off the graph. I'll dock it a point for not being Scotch-like but I feel a pang of guilt for doing so. This, by the way, is a blend that was discovered by accident. It had been put away many years ago for marrying – and then forgotten about in a warehouse. The chances of finding another whisky quite of this ilk are remote, though I'm sure the hunters are now out. It is a one off and anyone who misses this one will kick themselves forever. Astonishing. A freak whisky at its very peak. *52%. The Last Drop Distillers Ltd.*

The Last Drop 50 Years Old (96.5) n25 where once there was bourbon only, now we have a cross fertilisation of aromas. Certainly, once you allow it to breathe, the grape engulfs most else. It is as if the whisky has undergone a fruity polish and shine. On first pouring, the oak has the ability to cause splinters; allow to settle for a while and we are talking a much softer, less senile Drop; and slowly the spices unravel...; **t24.5** perhaps what is so astounding about this, is the way that the balance does not, even for a second, waiver under the occasional oaky onslaught: as it bites, from somewhere a grapey honeycomb flies in to the rescue offering just-so compensatory sugars which perfectly match the most delicate spices imaginable...; **f22.5** now we edge towards a drier finale than before. The original was remarkable for not having a degree of bitterness, though it had every right to be there. Now, alas, there is. The bitterness is slightly furry and dusty, but to make amends we are treated to one very old Melton Hunt cake, indeed; **b24.5** I tend to stick to the old adage: if it isn't broke, don't fix it. However, I do admire what has been done here. Because it was a gamble for the right reasons, which has paid handsomely in many ways, yet has just fallen short in others. Here, they took a magnificent whisky which for no other reason than pure serendipity, like Adam Adament, had awoken in another age but instead of, like our Victorian hero, being lost in a strange new world, found itself in one ready to appreciate and embrace its manifold beauty. This whisky was thrown back for a few extra summers in oak to take it to 50 years. A bold move. And it remains a quite astonishing, for life-remembering dram of labyrinthine complexity. *52%. 198 bottles.*

Lauder's (74) n18 t21 f17 b18. Well, it's consistent: you can say that for it! As usual, fabulous delivery, but as for the rest...oh dear. *40%. MacDuff International Ltd.*

Lauder's Aged 12 Years (93.5) n23 seemingly matured in an orange grove; blossom is everywhere; the grains are clean and crisp, the barley is unmolested and precise; **t24** that is stunning: the most delicate orange delivery melting in with the grassy barley; the grains are bright and act as a sublime mirror to the proceedings; **f23** soft oaky vanillas with some marzipan and Jaffa cake ensuring the controlled sweetness persists to the end; **b23.5** this is every bit as magnificent as the standard Lauder's isn't. *43%*

Loch Lomond Blended Scotch (89) n22 delicate with a simmering weightiness. Mainly grain apparent, but the malt chips in sweetly; **t22.5** excellent double thrust of crispness and velvety yield. The grains lead the way with toffee not far behind but the malt offers soft, barley-sharp contours; **f22** vanilla and caramel but so clean; **b22.5** a fabulously improved blend: clean and precise and though malt is seemingly at a premium, a fine interplay. *40%. Loch Lomond Distillers.*

Lochranza (83.5) n21 t21.5 f21 b20. Pleasant, clean, but, thanks to the caramel, goes easy on the complexity. *40%. Isle of Arran.*

Lochside 1964 Rare Old Single Blend (94.5) n24 sensual citrus: thick cut marmalade thinned by delicate lime. Hints of bourbony liquorice fits the style perfectly; **t23.5** mainly a corn lead: sweet, yielding yet salivating. Momentarily shows signs of wilting under the oak, but responds immediately by slamming the door shut and upping the fruit and vanillas; **f23** remains improbably delicate with the corn and vanilla dovetailing with aplomb; **b24** a unique and entirely fitting tribute to a distillery which should never have been lost. *42.1%. nc ncf. Speciality Drinks Ltd.*

Logan (78.5) n19 t19 f20 b19.5. Entirely drinkable but a bit heavy-handed with the grains and caramel. *40%. Diageo.*

Lombard's Gold Label (88) n22 t22 f22 b22. Excellently weighted with some wonderful honeycomb and spice making their mark. *40%. Lombards Brands.*

Lord Hynett (88.5) n21.5 a bit messy, but there is hope... **t23** which is fully justified by the enormity of the delivery. A bare knuckle fighter of a blend with a sublimely haphazard, random deliciousness; honey and spices don't give shape but purpose; **f22** long, spiced toffee; **b22** just perfect after a shitty day. *40%. Loch Lomond Distillers.*

Lord Scot (77.5) n18.5 t20 f19.5 b19.5. A touch cloying but the mocha fudge ensures a friendly enough ride. *40%. Loch Lomond Distillers.*

Lord Scot (86.5) n20 t22 f22.5 b22. A gorgeously lush honey and liquorice middle. *43%*

Mackessack Premium Aged 8 Years (87.5) n21.5 t23 f21.5 b21.5. Claims a high Speyside content and the early character confirms it. Shoots itself in the foot, rather, by overdoing the caramel and flattening the finish. *40%. Mackessack Giovenetti. Italian Market.*

Mac Na Mara (83) n20 t22.5 f20 b20.5. Absolutely brimming with salty, fruity character. But just a little more toffee and furriness than it needs. Enjoyable, though. *40%*

Mac Na Mara Rum Finish (93) n22 the rum has hardened the aroma; **t24** beautifully crisp with fragile malts clashing with equally crisp barley; the golden syrup works wonders; **f23** serious depth to the malt; the grains soften out with vanilla; **b24** high quality blending, and the usage of the rum appears to have retained the old Mac Na Mara style. *40%. Praban na Linne.*

MacQueens (89) n21.5 t22.5 f22.5 b22.5. I am long enough in the tooth now to remember blends like this found in quiet country hotels in the furthest-flung reaches of the Highlands beyond a generation ago. A wonderfully old-fashioned, traditional one might say, blend of a type that is getting harder and harder to find. *40%. Quality Spirits International.*

Master of Malt 8 Years Old (88) n22.5 t22.5 f21 b22. Understated and refined. *40%*

⋰ **Master Of Malt St Isidore (84) n21 t22 f20 b21.** Sweet, lightly smoked but really struggles to put together a coherent story. Something, somewhere, is not quite right. *41.4%*

⋰ **Master Of Malt World Whisky Day Blend (86) n21.5 t22 f21 b21.5.** Limited complexity and depth but it gets the Orange Aero bit right.... *40.18%. Master Of Malt.*

Matisse 12 Years Old (90.5) n23 vanilla and citrus make comfortable bedfellows; dry Lubeck marzipan perfects the balance; **t23** mouth-watering with little grain evidence. the malt is clear, almost shrill; **f22** gentle vanillas and caramels; the spices arrive late; **b22.5** moved up yet another notch as this brand continues its development. Much more clean-malt oriented with a Speyside-style to the fore. Majestic and charming. *40%. Matisse Spirits Co Ltd.*

Matisse 21 Years Old (86) n23 t22 f20 b21. Begins breathtakingly on the nose, with a full array of exotic fruit showing the older bourbon casks up to max effect. Nothing wrong with the early delivery, which offers a touch of honeycomb on the grain. But the caramel effect on the finish stops everything in its tracks. Soft and alluring, all the same. *40%*

Matisse Old (85.5) n20 t23 f21 b21.5. Appears to improve each time I come across it. The nose is a bit on the grimy side and the finish disappears under a sea of caramel. But the delivery works deliciously, with a chewy weight which highlights the sweeter malts. *40%*

Matisse Royal (81) n19 t22 f20 b20. Pleasant, if a little clumsy. Extra caramel appears to have scuppered the spice. *40%. Matisse Spirits Co Ltd.*

McArthurs (89.5) n22 soft smoke rumbles about like distant thunder on a Summer's day: the grains and light barley are bright; **t22.5** silky delivery with a slow injection of peat as the storm moves overhead; the degree of sweetness to the soft vanillas is sublime; **f22** gentle fade with the smoke rumbling though; **b23** one of the most improved blends on the market. The clever use of the peat is exceptional. *40%. Inverhouse Distillers.*

Michael Jackson Special Memorial Blend bott 2009 **(89) n24 t22.5 f20.5 b22.** Whenever Michael and I had a dram together, his would either be massively sherried or equally well endowed with smoke. This is neither, so an odd tribute. Even so, there is more than enough here for him to savour. *43%. Berry Bros & Rudd. 1000 bottles.*

Mitchell's Glengyle Blend (86.5) n21.5 t22 f21.5 b21.5. A taste of history here, as this is the first blend ever to contain malt from the new Campbeltown distillery, Glengyle. Something of a departure in style from the usual Mitchell blends, which tended to put the accent on a crisper grain. Interestingly, here they have chosen at least one that is soft and voluptuous enough to absorb the sharper malt notes. *40%. Springbank Distillers.*

Monarch Of The Glen Connoisseurs Choice (80) n20 t21 f19 b20. Has changed shape a little. Positively wallows in its fat and sweet personality. *40%. Quality Spirits International.*

Monarch Of The Glen Connoisseurs Choice Aged 8 Years (76.5) n19 t20.5 f18 b19. Leaves no doubt that there are some malts in there... *40%. Quality Spirits International.*

Monarch Of The Glen Connoisseurs Choice Aged 12 Years (88) n21.5 candy store mix of toffee and fruit bonbons; **t22.5** gorgeously silky delivery with barley showing early and then a welter of light fruity punches; **f22** tinned tangerine segments and a slow bitter build; **b22** charming, fruity and a blend to put your feet up with. *40%. Quality Spirits International.*

Monarch Of The Glen Connoisseurs Choice Aged 15 Years (83) n21 t22 f19 b21. Starts off on the very same footing as the 12-y-o, especially with the sumptuous delivery. But fails to build on that due to toffee and bitters at the death. *40%. Quality Spirits International.*

Montrose (74.5) n18 t20 f18 b18.5. A battling performance but bitter defeat in the end. *40%. Burn Stewart.*

Morrisons The Best 8 Years Old (87) n21 t23 f22 b21. Some of the traces of its excellence are still there, it remains highly drinkable, but that greatness has been lost in a tide of caramel. When, oh when, are people going to understand that you can't just tip this stuff into whisky to up the colour without causing a detrimental effect on the product? Is anybody listening? Does anyone care??? Someone has gone to great lengths to create a sublime blend – to see it wasted. Natural colour and this'd be an experience to die for. *40%*

Morrisons Fine Blended Whisky (77) n18.5 t21 f18.5 b19. Sweet, chewy but a few rough edges. *40%. Wm Morrison Supermarket.*

Muirhead's (83) n19 t22 f23 b21. A beautifully compartmentalised dram that integrates superbly, if that makes sense. *40%. MacDonald & Muir.*

⠿ **Muirhead's Blue Seal (83) n21 t21 f20.5 b20.5.** Goes to town quite heavily on the grain. If this is the new version of the old McDonald and Muir dram, then this is a lot oilier, with a silkier mouthfeel. *40%. Highland Queen Scotch Whisky Company.*

The Naked Grouse (76.5) n19 t21 f17.5 b19. Sweet. But reveals too many sulphur tattoos. *40%. Edrington.*

Northern Scot (68) n16 t18 f17 b17. Heading South bigtime. *40%. Bruce and Co. for Tesco.*

Old Crofter Special Old Scotch Whisky (83) n18 t22 f21 b22. A very decent blend, much better than the nose suggests thanks to some outstanding, velvety grain and wonderfully controlled sweetness. *40%. Smith & Henderson for London & Scottish International.*

Old Masters "Freemason Whisky" (92) n24 t23 f22 b23. A high quality blend that doesn't stint on the malt. The nose, in particular, is sublime. *40%. Supplied online. Lombard Brands*

Old McDonald (83.5) n20 t22 f20.5 b21. Attractively tart and bracing where it needs to be with lovely grain bite. Lots of toffee, though. *43.%. The Last Drop Distillers. For India.*

Old Mull (84.5) n22 t21 f20.5 b21. With dates and walnuts clambering all over the nose, very much in the house style. But this one is a shade oilier than most – and certainly on how it used to be – and has dropped a degree or two of complexity. That said, enjoyable stuff with the spices performing well, as does the lingering sweetness. *40%*

Old Parr 12 Years Old (91.5) n21.5 firm and flinty with the grains comfortably in control; **t23.5** no surprise with the mouthwatering juice: the grains help the barley and soft fruit element hit top gear; delicate, light, teasing yet always substantial; **f23** mocha dominates with the vaguest hint of gentle smoke; the weight, length and complexity are stupendous **b23.5** perhaps on about the fourth of fifth mouthful, the penny drops that this is not just exceptionally good whisky: it is blending Parr excellence... *40%. Diageo.*

Old Parr Aged 15 Years (84) n19 t22 f21 b22. Absolutely massive sherry input here. Some of it is of the highest order. The nose, reveals, however, that some isn't... *43%*

Old Parr Classic 18 Years Old (84.5) n21 t21.5 f21 b21. A real jumbled, mixed bag with fruit and barley falling over each other and the grains offering little sympathy. Enough to enjoy, but with Old Parr, one expects a little more... *46%. Diageo.*

Old Parr Superior 18 Years Old batch no. L5171 **(97) n25** here's a nose with just about a touch of everything: especially clever smoke which gives weight but allows apples and bourbon to filter through at will. Perfect weight and harmony while the complexity goes off the scales; **t25** voluptuous body, at times silky but the grains offer enough jagged edges for a degree of bite and bourbon; mouthwatering and spicey with the peats remaining on a slow burner. Toasty and so, so chewy; **f23** the vanilla is gentle and a counter to the firmness of the combined oak and grain. A flinty, almost reedy finish with spices and cocoa very much in evidence; **b24** year in, year out, this blend just gets better and better. This bottling struck me as a possible Whisky of the Year, but perhaps only an outsider. Familiarity, though, bred anything but contempt and over the passing months I have tried to get to the bottom of this truly great whisky. Blended whisky has long needed a champion. This grand old man looks just the chap. This is a worthy, if unexpected (even to me), Jim Murray' Whisky Bible 2007 World Whisky of the Year. *43%. Diageo/MacDonald Greenlees.*

Old Smuggler (85.5) n21 t22 f21 b21.5. A much sharper act than its Allied days with a new honeyed-maple syrup thread which is rather delightful. Could still do with toning down the caramel, though, to brighten the picture further. *40%. Campari, France.*

Old St Andrews Clubhouse (82) n18 t22 f21 b21. Not quite the clean, bright young thing it was many years back. But great to see back in my nosing glass after such a long while and though the nose hits the rough, the delivery is as sweetly struck as you might hope for. *40%*

Old Stag (75.5) n18.5 t20 f18.5 b18.5. Wants shooting. *40%. Loch Lomond Distillers.*

⠿ **The Original Lochlan Aged 8 Years (80.5) n19 t21 f20 b20.5.** Doused in caramel. So much so it's like a toffee and nut bar. One to chew on until your fillings fall out, though the spices compensate on the finish to a degree. Pleasant and sweet, but don't expect great refinement. *40%. Tesco.*

The Original Mackinlay (83) n19 t21 f22 b21. A hard nose to overcome and the toffee remains in force for those addicted to fudge. But now a degree of bite and ballast appears to have been added, giving more of a story to the experience. *40%. Whyte & Mackay Distillers Ltd.*

Passport (83) n22 t19 f21 b21. It looks as though Chivas have decided to take the blend away from its original sophisticated, Business Class J&B/Cutty Sark, style for good now, as they have continued this decently quaffable but steerage quality blend with its big caramel kick and chewy, rather than lithe, body. *40%. Chivas.*

Passport v **(91) n23 23.5 f22 b22.5.** Easily one of the better versions I have come across for a long time and impressively true to its original style. *40%. Bottled in Brazil.*

Passport v **(91) n22.5 t22 f23.5 b23.5.** A lovely version closer to original style with markedly less caramel impact and grittier grain. An old-fashioned treat. *40%. Ecuador.*

Parkers (78) n17 t22 f20 b19. The nose has regressed, disappearing into ever more caramel, yet the mouth-watering lushness on the palate remains and the finish now holds greater complexity and interest. *40%. Angus Dundee.*

Prince Charlie Special Reserve (73) n17 t20 f18 b18. Thankfully not as cloyingly sweet as of old, but remains pretty basic. *40%. Somerfield, UK.*

Prince Charlie Special Reserve 8 Years Old (81) n18 t20 f22 b21. A lumbering bruiser of a dram; keeps its trademark shapelessness but the spices and lush malt ensure an enjoyable experience. *40%. Somerfield, UK.*

⠿ **Queen Margot (86) n21 t22 f21.5 b21.5.** A lovely blend which makes no effort to skimp on a spicy depth. Plenty of cocoa from the grain late on but no shortage of good whiskies put to work. *40%. Wallace and Young for Lidl.*

⠿ **Queen Margot** v **(83.5) n20.5 t22 f20 b21.** Same brand, but a different name on the back label. And certainly a different feel to the whisky with the grains having harsher words than before. *40%. Clydesdale Scotch Whisky Co for Lidl.*

⠿ **Queen Margot Aged 8 Years (89) n22** green banana sits well with the vanilla and gentle citrus; **t22.5** the best blends offer a degree of nip and bite and this doesn't disappoint. A touch of juiciness early on and then the lightest coating of oil soothes - even as the grains gain the upper hand; **f22** a light cocoa element is attractively applied; **b22.5** a satisfying blend with a delicious clarity to the light malts and high class grains. Just the right touch of sweetness, too. *40%. Wallace and Young for Lidl.*

⠿ **Queen Margot Aged 8 Years (84) n20.5 t21 f21.5 b21.** Here's the variant. Darker in colour I notice and a bit of a dullard and simpleton by comparison, though not without an acceptable degree of charm. Much weightier *40%. Clydesdale Scotch Whisky Co for Lidl.*

Real Mackenzie (80) n17 t21 f21 b21. As ever, try and ignore the dreadful nose and get cracking with the unsubtle, big bruising delivery. A thug in a glass. *40%. Diageo.*

Real Mackenzie Extra Smooth (81) n18 t22 f20 b21. Once, the only time the terms "Real Mackenzie" and "Extra Smooth" were ever uttered in the same sentence was if someone was talking about the barman. Now it is a genuine descriptor. Which is odd, because when Diageo sent me a sample of their blend last year it was a snarling beast ripping at the leash. This, by contrast, is a whimpering sop. "Killer? Where are you...???" *40%. Diageo.*

Red Seal 12 Years Old (82) n19 t22 f20 b21. Charming, mouthwatering. But toffee numbs it down towards the finish. *40%. Charles Wells UK.*

Reliance PL (76) n18 t20 f19 b19. Some of the old spiciness evident. But has flattened out noticeably. *43%. Diageo.*

Robert Burns (85) n20 t22.5 f21 b21.5. Skeletal and juicy: very little fat and gets to the mouthwatering point pretty quickly. Genuine fun. *40%. Isle of Arran.*

Robertson's of Pitlochry Rare Old Blended (83) n21 t20 f21 b21. Handsome grain bite with a late malty flourish. Classic light blend available only from Pitlochry's landmark whisky shop. *40%*

The Royal & Ancient (80.5) n20 t21.5 f19 b20. Has thinned out dramatically in the last year or so. Now clean, untaxing, briefly mouth-watering and radiating young grain throughout. *40%*

Royal Castle (84.5) n20 t22 f21 b21.5. From Quality Street, or Quality Spirits? Sweet and very well toffeed! *43%. Quality Spirits International.*

Royal Castle 12 Years Old (84.5) n22 t22 f20 b20.5. Busy nose and delivery with much to chew over. Entirely enjoyable, and seems better each time you taste it. Even so, the finish crumbles a bit. *40%. Quality Spirits International.*

Royal Clan Aged 18 Years (85) n21.5 t21 f21.5 b21. For those giving up gum, here's something to really chew on. Huge degree of cream toffee and toasted fudge which makes for a satin-soft blend, but also one which ensures any big moves towards complexity are nipped in the bud. Very enjoyable, all the same. *40%. Quality Spirits International.*

Royal Household (90.5) n21.5 t23 f23 b23 We are amused. *43%. Diageo.*

⠿ **Royal Park (85) n21.5 t22.5 f20 b21.** Pretty generic with an attractive silky sheen, Demerara sugars and decent late spice swim around in an ocean of caramel. *40%*

Royal Salute 21 Years Old (92.5) n23 has persisted with the gentle, exotic fruit but less lush here with much more punch and poke; it even seems that the smoke which had been missing in recent years has returned, but in shadowy form only; **t23.5** yep! Definitely more bite these days with the grains having a much greater input, for all the juiciness, and the vanilla striking home earlier. Makes for a decent sweet/dry middle, the sweetness supplied by boiled sweet candy; **f23** plenty of cocoa and the very lightest dab of something smoky; **b23.5** if you are looking for the velvety character of yore, forget it. This one comes with some real character and is much the better for it. The grain, in particular, excels. *40%. Chivas.*

Royal Salute 62 Gun Salute (95.5) n24.5 prunes and apples plus a little cinnamon. And grapes, of course. It is in a bed of seemingly natural caramels. It is a smoke-free environment where every oak note is rounded and friendly, where you fancy you can still find the odd mark of barley and yet although being a blend, the grain is refusing to take it down a bourbon path, despite the peek-a-boo honeycomb; **t24** the oak is relatively full on, but early on adds a toasty quality to the marmalade and plum jam. The mid ground casts off any sherry-like clothes and heads for a more honey-rich, vaguely bourbon style without ever reaching Kentucky; **f23** the fade is on the gentle side with sugars dissolving against a slightly bittering background as some of the oak rebels, as you might expect at least one or two of these old timers to do. At the very death comes the one and only sign of smoke...that is some parting shot; **b24** how do you get a bunch of varying whiskies in style, but each obviously growing a grey beard and probably cantankerous to boot, to settle in and harmonise with the others? A kind of Old People's Home for whisky, if you like. Well, here's how...*43%. Chivas.*

Royal Salute The Hundred Cask Selection Limited Release No. 7 (92) n22 a mixture of Caperdonich-esque exotic fruit and slightly over cooked, lactic oak masquerading as rice pudding; **t23.5** the silky glide onto the palate you'd expect from the nose and previous experience; some groaning oak arrives pretty early on; **f23** sweet, muscovado-sprinkled cocoa; **b23.5** as blends go, its entire countenance talks about great age and elegance. And does so with a clipped accent. *40%. Chivas.*

Royal Silk Reserve (93) n22 classically light yet richly bodied under the clear, crisp ethereal grains. The freshly-cut-grass maltiness balances perfectly; **t24** crystal clear grains dovetail with intense, mouthwatering and refreshingly sweet malt to create a perfect pitch while the middle is heavier and livelier than you might expect with the very faintest echo of peat; **f24** delicate oils and wonderful grainy-vanilla ensures improbable length for something so light. Beautiful spices and traces of cocoa offer the last hurrah. Sheer bliss; **b23** I named this the best newcomer of 2001 and it hasn't let me down. A session blend for any time of the day, this just proves that you don't need piles of peat to create a blend of genuine stature. A must have. *40%*

Sainsbury's Basics Blended Scotch Whisky (78.5) n19 t20.5 f19.5 b19.5. "A little less refined, great for mixing," says the label. Frankly, there are a lot of malts out there far less enjoyable than this. Don't be scared to have straight: it's more than decent enough. *40%*

Sainsbury's Scotch Whisky (84.5) n20 t22 f21 b21.5. A surprisingly full bodied, chewy blend allowing a pleasing degree of sweetness to develop. No shortage of toffee at the finish – a marked improvement on recent years. *40%. UK.*

Sainsbury's Finest Old Matured Aged 8 Years (86) n21.5 t21 f22 b21.5. A sweet blend enjoying a melt-in-the-mouth delivery, a silky body and toffee-vanilla character. The spices arriving towards the end are exceptionally pleasing and welcome. *40%. UK.*

Sandy Mac (76) n18 t20 f19 b19. Basic, decent blend that's chunky and raw. *40%. Diageo.*

Scots Earl (76.5) n18 t20 f19 b19.5. It's name is Earl. And it must have upset someone in a previous life. Always thrived on its engaging disharmony. But just a tad too syrupy now. *40%. Loch Lomond Distillers.*

Scottish Chief (77) n19 t19 f19 b20. This is one big-bodied chief, and not given to taking prisoners. *40%. Quality Spirits International.*

Scottish Collie (77) n19 t19 f19 b20. Caramel still, but a Collie with a bit more bite. *40%*

Scottish Collie 12 Years Old (85) n22 t22 f20 b21. On the cusp of a really classy blend here but the bitterness on the finish loses serious Brownie points. *40%. Quality Spirits Int, UK.*

Scottish Collie 18 Years Old (92) n24 t23 f22 b23. This, honey-led beaut would be a winner even at Crufts: an absolute master class of how an old, yet light and unpeated blend should be. No discord whatsoever between the major elements and not a single hint of over-aging. Superb. *40%. Quality Spirits International, UK.*

Scottish Glory dist 2002, bott 2005 **(85) n21 t21 f22 b21.** An improved blend now bursting with vitality. The ability of the grain to lift the barley is very pleasing. *40%. Duncan Taylor.*

Scottish Leader Original (83.5) n17.5 t22.5 f21 b22.5. About as subtle as a poke in the eye with a spirit thief. The nose, it must be said, is not great. But I have to admit I thoroughly enjoy the almost indulgent coarseness from the moment it invades the palate. A real chewathon of a spicy blend with a wicked, in-yer-face attitude. Among all the rough-'n-tumble and slap-'n-tickle, the overall depth, weight, balance and molassed charm ain't half bad. *40%. Burn Stewart.*

Scottish Leader Aged 12 Years (91) n22.5 excellent bourbon notes: honeycomb and liquorice accompanied by light spices and toffee; **t23** big and cream-textured: positively melts on the palate. Huge degree of toffee, but the honeycomb and dates are vibrant enough to be more than heard. Elsewhere the sugars take a positively datey shape and, with a soft nuttiness apparent, there is something about a Dundee cake about this one; **f22** light, milky cocoa and vanilla; **b22.5** absolutely unrecognisable from the Leader 12 I last tasted. This has taken a plumy, fruity route with the weight of a cannonball but the texture of mallow. Big and quite beautiful. *40%. Burn Stewart.*

Scottish Leader 30 Years Old (87) n23.5 stylish: fruit and honey in pretty even measures. Not only is it soft but there is neither spice nor an alcohol prickle to disrupt the silky passage; **t21.5** melt-in-the-mouth delivery with a toffee and raisin theme; **f20.5** too much caramel; a touch of bitterness creeps in; **b21.5** a little too docile ever to be a great whisky, but the nose is something rather special. A bit of attention on the finish and this could be a real corker. *40%. Burn Stewart.*

Scottish Leader Select (91.5) n23 gorgeous honey with a buzzing spice accompaniment; **t23.5** beautiful delivery. Those honeys and spices gang together to make a delightful statement with the grains offering a beautiful custard-rich support; **f22.5** firmer, but the sweetness persists; **b22.5** don't make the mistake of thinking this is just the 40% with three extra percentage points of alcohol. This appears to be an entirely different bottling with an entirely different personality. A delight. *43%. Burn Stewart. For the South African Market.*

Scottish Leader Select (74) n18.5 t19 f18 b18.5. I assume the leader is Major Disharmony. *40%. Burn Stewart.*

Scottish Leader Supreme (72.5) n17 t19 f18 b18.5. Jings! It's like an old-fashioned Gorbals punch-up in the glass – and palate. *40%. Burn Stewart.*

Scottish Piper (80) n20 t20 f20 b20. A light, mildly- raw, sweet blend with lovely late vanilla intonation. *40%*

Scottish Prince (83.5) n21 t22 f20 b20.5. Muscular, but agreeably juicy. *40%*

Scottish Reel (78.5) n19 t19 f20 b19.5. Non fussy with an attractive bite, as all such blends should boast. *40%. London & Scottish International.*

Scottish Rill (85) n20 t20.5 f22.5 b22. Refreshing yet earthy. *40%. Quality Spirits Int.*

⋅∷⋅ **Sheep Dip Amoroso Oloroso 1999** Oloroso sherry casks, bott Mar 12 **(92) n23.5** big toffee apple fanfare and then a slow development of juicy dates and prunes...topped with treacle. A thick aroma, but not too intense for subtlety; **t24** after a nose like that how could it be anything other than lush? Those big sugars are kept in check by an excellent sub-woofer oak; the midground enjoys an outbreak of creamy chocolate, with a little fruit and nut mixed in; **f21** as this matured in Spain, just a touch puzzled by the bitter-ish, furry finale; **b23.5** more like Sherry Dip than Sheep Dip. Actually, chocolate dip wouldn't be too far off the mark, either. To create this, malt which had spent three years maturing in bourbon cask was then shipped to Jerez where it spent a further nine years in presumably fresh sherry. It was worth the trouble... *41.8%. Spencerfield Spirits.*

Something Special (85) n21.5 t22 f20.5 b21. Mollycoddled by toffee, any murderous tendencies seem to have been fudged away, leaving just the odd moment of attractive complexity. You suspect there is a hit man in there somewhere trying to get out. *40%. Chivas.*

Something Special Premium Aged 15 Years (89) n22 a vague, distant smokiness sits prettily with some fruity caramel; **t23** boisterous delivery with unshackled malt adding a wonderful, zesty spiciness amid much more mouth-watering Speyside-style fresh grass; the grain offers the desired cut-glass firmness; **f21** lots of vanilla and too much caramel, but remains busy and entertaining; **b23** fabulous malt thread and some curious raisiny/sultana fruitiness, too. A blend-lover's blend. *40%. Chivas/Hill Thompson, Venezuela.*

Spar Finest Reserve (90.5) n21.5 fabulously clean, young grain offering butterscotch and toffee; elsewhere something earthy rumbles; **t22.5** brilliantly subtle delivery with silky grains ensnared in a sweet shell; towards the middle chocolate fudge and a distinctive smoky rumble forms; **f23.5** one of the best "supermarket" finishes to be found with a stunning array of clean, dapper smoke notes which cling, like softly oiled limpets, to the tastebuds for an improbably long time: lush and beautifully layered, this is masterful blending...; **b23** one of Britain's best value for money blends with an honest charm which revels in the clean high quality grain and earthier malts which work so well together. *40%*

Stewart's Old Blended (93) n22.5 apples and date and walnut cake; clean and more delicate than the early weight suggests; **t24** sublime silky delivery with the slow erection of a fruity platform; the yielding grain cushions the juicy malt aspects; **f23** bitters out as some oak makes its play but firmer malt and molasses compensate superbly; **b23.5** really lovely whisky for those who like to close their eyes, contemplate and have a damned good chew. *40%*

⋅∷⋅ **Storm (94) n23** a clarion call of clean grain amid decimated coconut; **t23.5** superb delivery: the structure is a joy with a lush mouth-feel but the complexity by no means stilted. The odd salty note appears to maximise the oaky depth and that light oiliness ensures the barley-sweetness lasts; superb light spicing begins to intensify towards the middle; **f24** fabulous finale with that spice hanging on in there and acting as the perfect foil for the deft honeycomb and sugars; so clean you feel your teeth are being polished while drinking this; **b23.5** a little gem of a blend that really will take you by storm. 43%. Whisky Shack.

Swords (78) n20 t21 f18 b19. Beefed up somewhat with some early smoke thrusting through and rapier grains to follow. 40%. Morrison Bowmore.

Talisman 5 Years Old (85.5) n22 t22 f20.5 b21. Unquestionably an earthier, weightier version of what was once a Speyside romp. Soft peats also add extra sweetness. 40%

⠴⠶ **Teacher's 50 - 12 Years Old** batch 2-16, bott Sep 11 **(85.5) n20.5 t22.5 f21.5 b21.** Once, before entering the Indian bottling hall, this must have been a strutting peacock of a Scotch blend. But after being doused in a far too liberal amount of caramels it has been reduced to a house sparrow: outwardly common and dull but at least with an engaging personality. The usual Teacher's smoke shows itself only at the death, alas. And all else is a silky honeyed sweetness pleading for an extra degree of complexity. The very complexity, indeed, which was almost certainly there before being coloured to death. If they could sort out the caramel levels in the bottling hall, this would be a blend that would put on a spectacular display.... 42.8%

⠴⠶ **Teacher's Aged 25 Years** batch 1 **(96.5) n24** at first this Teacher's lectures malt to you; not any old malt, but delicately smoked and as light with citrus as it is heavy with phenol. Then slowly the grains emerge, offering weighted consistency to the sweeter, maple syrup elements, until there is a satisfying fusion between the two....; **t24.5** not sure one can quite nose silk, though that's what it appeared to be. But you can certainly spot it on the palate, and that's exactly what we have on delivery: every atom, be it smoky or marmalade orangey, simply melts in the mouth though unusually for a 25-y-o, it does not leave an oaky residue; **f23.5** long, spicy, a little tangy; **b24.5** only 1300 bottles means they will be hard pushed to create this exact style again. Worth a go, chaps: considering this is India bound, it is the karma sutra of blended scotch. 46%. Beam Inc. 1300 bottles. India & Far East Travel Retail exclusive.

Teacher's Highland Cream (90) n23 firm, flinty grain; fruity with gently smoked malt-ensuring weight; **t23** mouth-filling and tenderly sweet; the grains seem softer than the nose suggests; **f22** toffee and lazy smoke; **b22** not yet back to its best but a massive improvement on the 2005 bottlings. Harder grains to accentuate the malt will bring it closer to the classic of old. 40%

Teacher's Highland Cream v **(90) n23** grain dominates, but not the old-fashioned sharp Dumbarton style. This is softer, sweeter with a topping of thick vanilla and butterscotch and delicate barley...where's the famous smoke...??? It's there, but the most distant echo; almost a dull background throb — for some Teacher's diehards, it is too well integrated...; **t22.5** as silky a delivery as the nose promises. Again the grain comes through loud and clear with the playful malts hanging on to its coat-tails. Only towards the middle do the two combine, and rather attractively and with style; **f22** much more spiced with a decided vanilla twirl; still virtually no smoke worthy of the name other than a vague oiliness; **b22.5** a very curious, seriously high grade, variant. Although the Ardmore distillery is on the label, it is the only place it can really be seen. Certainly - the least smoky Teacher's I've come across in 35 years of drinking the stuff: the smoke is there, but adds only ballast rather than taking any form of lead. But the grain is soft and knits with the malts with ease to make for a sweeter, much more lush version than the rest of the world may recognize. 40%

Teacher's Origin (88.5) n22 thick, treacle tart, nose. A pinch of salt ensures a certain piquancy and gentle peat reek on the breeze does no harm, either; **t23.5** thick, soupy and sweet, the delivery is muscular and manful. Toffee takes an early lead, but fabulous spice and several delicate layers of smoke add to the initial beauty; a slightly negative sherry-cask style influence begins to bite in towards the middle and dry things somewhat; **f21** that dryness continues and all other avenues are cut off with toffee; **b22** a fascinating blend which probably ranks as the softest on the market today. That is aided and abetted by the exceptionally high malt content, 65%, which makes this something of an inverted blend, as that, for most established brands, is the average grain content. What appears to be a high level of caramel also makes for a rounding of the edges, as well as evidence of sherry butts. The bad news is that that has resulted in a duller finish than perhaps might have been intended, which is even more pronounced given the impressive speech made on delivery. Lovely whisky, yes. But something, I feel, of a work in progress. Bringing the caramel down by the percentage points of the malt would be a very positive start... 42.8%. ncf. Beam Global.

Té Bheag (86) n22 t21 f21.5 b21.5. Classic style of rich caramels and bite. 40%. ncf. Pràban na Linne.

Tesco Finest Reserve Aged 12 Years (74) n18.5 t19 f18 b18.5. The most astonishing thing about this, apart from the fact it is a 12 year-old, is that it won a Gold "Best in Class" in a 2010 international whisky competition: it surely could not have been from the same batch as the one before me. Frankly, you have to go a long way to find a whisky as bland as this and for a 12-y-o it is monumentally disappointing. 40%.

Tesco Special Reserve Minimum 3 Years Old (78) n18.5 t21.5 f19 b19. Decent early spice on delivery but otherwise anonymous. 40%. Tesco.

Tesco Value Scotch Whisky (83) n19 t21 f22 b21. Young and genuinely refreshing whisky. Without the caramel this really would be a little darling. 40%

Traquair (78) n19 t21 f19 b19. Young, but offering a substantial mouthful including attractive smoke. 46%. Burn Stewart.

The Tweeddale Blend Aged 10 Years (89.5) n22 attractive and well-balanced mix of mint humbug and toffee; **t23.5** beautifully weighted and structured. The non-filtration and 50% malt content combo has paid dividends as the weight and oiliness is highly unusual for a blended scotch. Chewy with an impressive degree of spice development which is in complete harmony with the increased sugar intensity; **f21.5** dries as the oak begins to play its part and the grains begin to bite. Lots of toffee, too; **b22.5** the first bottling of this blend since World War 2, it has been well worth waiting for. 46%. ncf. 50% malt. Stonedean.

⠿ **The Tweeddale Blend Aged 12 Years** bott Jun 11 **(94.5) n23.5** a sumptuous mixture of diced apples with berry fruit. The sugars and honeys are of the lightest variety but complex and perfectly in harmony with the friendly vanillas: a triumph! **t24** boasts that beguiling and entirely disarming mixture of passive aggression, where your taste buds think they are being lulled into an easy, silky ride before being stormed by troops fully armed with spicy vanilla. Always clean, so you get a clear view of the deepening honey in the middle ground; **f23** light oils carry the spices and chewy vanilla the full course. And it is a very long one...; **b24** bravo! A blend which sets out to maximise the (in this case) high quality whiskies used. An engrossing and massively enjoyable celebration of blended scotch. A minor classic, in fact. And not entirely dissimilar, curiously, to a blend I occasionally concoct for my own enjoyment... 46%. ncf. Stonedean.

Ushers Green Stripe (85) n19 t22.5 f21.5 b22. Upped a notch or two in all-round quality. The juicy theme and clever weight is highly impressive and enjoyable. 43%. Diageo.

VAT 69 (84.5) n20 t22 f21 b21.5. Has thickened up in style: weightier, more macho, much more to say and a long way off that old lightweight. A little cleaning up wouldn't go amiss. 40%

White Horse (90.5) n22 busy, with a shade more active grain than normal. But the smoky depth is there, as is a gentle hickory, butterscotch and fruity thread; a few bruising malts can be picked up, too; **t23** the usual sensual delivery, at first almost like a young JW Black, thanks to that soft billowing out towards the gentle honeys and juices; as it reaches the middle the clunking, muddied fist of some volumous malts can be easily detected; **f22.5** playful spices dovetail with vanilla while the smoke reinforces the backbone; **b23** a malt which has subtlety changed shape. Not just the smoke which gives it weight, but you get the feeling that some of Diageo's less delicate malts have been sent in to pack a punch. As long as they are kept in line, as is the case here – just – we can all enjoy a very big blend. 40% Diageo

White Horse Aged 12 Years (86) n21 t23 f21 b21. enjoyable, complex if not always entirely harmonious. For instance, the apples and grapes on the nose appear on a limb from the grain and caramel and nothing like the thoroughbred of old. Lighter, more flaccid and caramel dominated. 40%. Diageo.

Whyte & Mackay 'The Thirteen' 13 Year Old (92) n22.5 t23.5 f23 b23. Try this and your luck'll be in...easily the pick of the W&M blended range. 40%. Whyte & Mackay Distillers Ltd.

Whyte & Mackay Luxury 19 Year Old (84.5) n21 t22 f20 b21.5. A pleasant house style chewathon. Nutty, biting but with a tang. 40%. Whyte & Mackay Distillers Ltd.

Whyte & Mackay Supreme 22 Year Old (87) n21 t23 f20.5 b22.5. Ignore the nose and finish and just enjoy the early ride. 43%

Whyte & Mackay Oldest 30 Year Old (87.5) n23 t23 f20 b21.5. What exasperating whisky this is. So many good things about it, but... 45%

Whyte & Mackay Original Aged Blended 40 Years Old (93) n23 t24 f22 b24. I admit, when I nosed and tasted this at room temp, not a lot happened. Pretty, but closed. But once warmed in the hand up to full body temperature, it was obvious that Richard Paterson had created a quite wonderful monster of a blend offering so many avenues to explore that the mind almost explodes. Well done RP for creating something that further proves, and in such magnitude, just how warmth can make an apparently ordinary whisky something bordering genius. 45%

Whyte & Mackay Special (84.5) n20 t23 f20 b21.5. This has to be the ultimate mood blend. If you are looking for a big-flavoured dram and with something approaching a vicious left uppercut, this might be a useful bottle to have on hand. The nose, I'm afraid, has not improved over the years but there appears to be compensation with the enormity and complexity of the delivery, a veritable orgy of big, oily, juicy, murky flavours and tones if ever there was one. You cannot but like it, in the same way as you may occasionally like rough sex. But if you are looking for a delicate dram to gently kiss you and caress your revered brow, then leave well alone. 40%

William Grant's 12 Years Old Bourbon Cask (90.5) n23 lively and floral. The drier notes suggest chalky oak but the sweet spiciness balances beautifully; **t22.5** flinty textured with both malts and grains pinging around the teeth with abandon; **f22** remains light yet with a clever, crisp sweetness keeping the weightier oaks in check; **b23** very clever blending where balance is the key. *40%*

William Grant's 15 Years Old (85) n21 t23 f20 b21. Grain and, later, caramel dominates but the initial delivery reveals the odd moment of sheer genius and complexity on max revs. *43%*

William Grant's 25 Years Old (95.5) n23.5 some serious oak, but chaperoned by top quality oloroso, itself thinned by firm and graceful grain; **t24** sheer quality: complexity by the shovel-load as juicy fruits interact with darting, crisp barley; again the grain shows elegance both sharpening increasingly mouth-watering malt and softening the oak; **f24** medium length, but not a single sign of fatigue: the sweet barley runs and runs and some jammy fruits charm. Just to cap it all, some wonderful spices dazzle and a touch of low roast Java enriches; **b24** absolutely top-rank blending that appears to maximize every last degree of complexity. Most astonishing, though, is its sprightly countenance: even Scottish footballing genius Ally MacLeod struggled to send out Ayr Utd. sides with this kind of brio. And that's saying something! A gem. *40%*

William Grant's 100 US Proof Superior Strength (92) n23 sublime chocolate lime nose, decent oak; **t24** big mouth arrival, lush and fruity with the excellent extra grain bite you might expect at this strength, just an extra degree of spice takes it into even higher orbit than before; **f22** back to chocolate again with a soft fruit fade; **b23** a fruitier drop now than it was in previous years but no less supremely constructed. *50% (100 US proof)*

William Grant's Ale Cask Reserve (89) n21 t23 f22 b23. A real fun blend that is just jam-packed with jagged malty notes. The hops were around more on earlier bottlings, but watch out for them. Nothing pint-sized about this: this is a big blend and very true in flavour/shape to the original with just a delicious shading of grain to really up the complexity. *40%*

William Grant's Family Reserve (94) n25 this, to me, is the perfect nose to any blend: harmonious and faultless. There is absolutely everything here in just-so proportions: a bit of snap and bite from the grain, teasing sweet malts, the faintest hint of peat for medium weight, strands of oak for dryness, fruit for lustre. Even Ardbeg doesn't pluck my strings like this glass of genius can; **t23** exceptionally firm grain helps balance the rich, multi-layered malty tones. The sub-plot of burnt raisins and peek-a-boo peat add further to the intrigue and complexity (if it doesn't bubble and nip around the mouth you have a rare sub-standard bottling); **f22** a hint of caramel can be detected amid returning grains and soft cocoa tones: just so clean and complex; **b24** there are those puzzled by my obvious love affair with blended whisky - both Scotch and Japanese - at a time when malts are all the rage. But take a glass of this and carefully nurture and savour it for the best part of half an hour and you may begin to see why I believe this to be the finest art form of whisky. For my money, this brand - brilliantly kept in tip-top shape by probably the world's most naturally gifted blender - is the closest thing to the blends of old and, considering it is pretty ubiquitous, it defies the odds for quality. It is a dram with which you can start the day and end it: one to keep you going at low points in between, or to celebrate the victories. It is the daily dram that has everything. *40%*

William Grant's Sherry Cask Reserve (82) n20 t22 f20 b20. Raspberry jam and cream from time to time. Attractive, but somewhat plodding dram that's content in second gear. *40%*

William Lawson's Finest (85) n18.5 t22.5 f22 b22. Not only has the label become more colourful, but so, too, has the whisky. However that has not interfered with the joyous old-fashioned grainy bite. A complex and busy blend from the old charm school. *40%*

William Lawson's Scottish Gold Aged 12 Years (89) n22 t23 f22 b22. For years Lawson's 12 was the best example of the combined wizardry of clean grain, unpeated barley and good bourbon cask that you could find anywhere in the world: a last-request dram before the firing squad. Today it is still excellent, but just another sherried blend. What's that saying about if it's not being broke...? *40%*

Windsor 12 Years Old (81) n20 t21 f20 b20. Thick, walloped-on blend that you can stand a spoon in. Hard at times to get past the caramel. *40%. Diageo.*

Windsor Aged 17 Years Super Premium (89) n23 t22 f22 b22. Still on the safe side for all its charm and quality. An extra dose of complexity would lift this onto another level. *40%*

Windsor 21 Years Old (90) n20 fruity and weighty but something a bit lactic and lethargic from some old bourbon casks has crept in; **t23** excellent oils surround the silk to help amplify the intensity of the fruit and drifting smoke; **f24** some spiciness that shows towards the middle really takes off now as drying vanilla counters the sweet grains; **b23** recovers fabulously from the broken nose and envelopes the palate with a silky-sweet style unique to the Windsor scotch brand. Excellent. *40%. Diageo.*

Ye Monks (86) n20 t23 f21.5 b21.5. Just hope they are praying for less caramel to maximize the complexity. Still, a decent spicy chew and outstanding bite which is great fun and worth finding when in South America. *40%. Diageo.*

Yokozuna Blended 3 Years Old (79.5) n18.5 t20.5 f20 b20.5. It appears the Mongols are gaining a passion for thick, sweet, toffeed, oily, slightly feinty whisky. For a nation breastfed on airag, this'll be a doddle... *40%. Speyside Distillers. Mongolian market.*

Irish Whiskey

Of all the whiskies in the world, it is Irish which probably causes most confusion amongst both established whisk(e)y lovers and the novices.

Ask anyone to define what is unique to Irish Whiskey – apart from it being made in Ireland – and the answers, if my audiences around the world at my tastings are anything to go by, are in this order: i) It is triple distilled; ii) It is never, ever made from peat; iii) They exclusively use sherry casks; iv) It comes from the oldest distillery in the world; v) It is made from a mixture of malted and unmalted barley.

Only one of those answers is true: the fifth. And it is usually the final answer extracted from the audience when the last hand raised sticks to his guns after the previous four responses have been shot down.

There was no shortage of Blarney when the Irish were trying to market their whiskey back in the 1950s and early 60s. Hence the triple distilled/non-peated myth was born. The Irish had had a thin time of it since the 1920s and seen their industry decimated. So the marketing guys got to work.

As much of Ireland is covered in peat, it is hardly surprising that in the 19th century smoky whiskey from inland distilleries was not uncommon. Like Scotland. Some distilleries used two stills, others three. Like Scotland. Sherry butts were ubiquitous in Ireland before World War 2. Just as they were in Scotland. And there are distilleries in Scotland older than Bushmills, which dates from 1784.

However, the practice of using malted and unmalted barley, begun so less tax had to be paid on malted grain, had died out in the Lowlands of Scotland, leaving it for Ireland to carry on alone.

It is hard to believe, then, that when I was researching my Irish Whiskey Almanac way back in 1993, Redbreast had just been discontinued as a brand leaving Green Spot, an ancient gem of a bottling from Mitchell and Son, Dublin's legendary high class wine and spirit merchants, as the sole surviving Pure Irish Pot Still Whiskey. At first Redbreast's owners refused to send me a bottle as they regarded it a pointless exercise, seeing as the brand had gone. After I wrote about it, first in my Almanac and then in newspapers and magazines elsewhere, they had no option other than to reverse their decision: interest had been whetted and people were asking for it once more.

When it was relaunched, the Pot Still came from Midleton. The Redbreast they were discontinuing was Pure Pot Still from the long defunct original Jameson Distillery in Dublin. Jameson may once have been locked in commercial battle with their neighbouring Power's distillery, but they united in the late 19th century when they brought out a book called: "The Truth About Irish Whiskey" in which they together, along with other Dublin distillers, fought against blended and other types of what they considered adulterated whiskey to tell the world that the only true Irish whiskey was Pure Pot Still.

So it was wonderful to see that this year Irish Distillers continued on their course of expanding the number of Pure Pot Still whiskeys available to the public after years of finding only Redbreast and Green Spot... and then only if you were very lucky. Actually, the two newbies are close relations: one being the reintroduction of the long lost brand Yellow Spot. And the other a Redbreast Cask Strength... which shows that it may take some two decades, but are eventually answered.

Another answered prayer came in the shape of Jim Beam's $95 million purchase of Ireland's lone independent distiller, Cooley, in January. The company's founder John Teeling told me soon after opening Cooley that his plan was to one day sell it to Irish Distillers: it was all about business. That sale would have gone through had the Irish Government not stepped in and halted the deal... on the grounds of reduced Competition. It was the only thing John's detailed business plan had not covered. No such problems with the Beam sale. And one thing that has to be said about Beam is that they make outstanding whisk(e)y to both east and west of the Emerald Isle.

However you look at it, it is the end of an era. Cooley makes both excellent grain and malt whiskey. And considering they own a grain plant as well as two malt distilleries, and possess extensive maturing stock, compared to the price paid a few days ago for Bruichladdich Beam have done very well indeed. As for John Teeling and his equally irrepressible son, Jack, they have now left Cooley to set up the Teeling Whiskey Company. Watch this space...

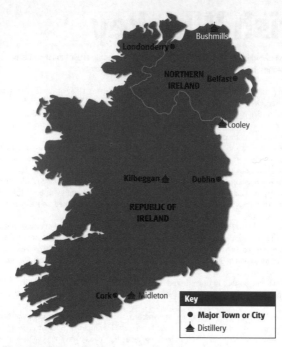

Key
● **Major Town or City**
▲ **Distillery**

Pure Pot Still
MIDLETON (old distillery)

Midleton 25 Years Old Pot Still db **(92) n24 t24 f21 b23.** A really enormous whiskey that is in the truest classic Irish style. The un-malted barley really does make the tastebuds hum and the oak has added fabulous depth. Interesting when tasted against an American rye – the closeness of the character is there to be experienced, but also the differences. A subtle mature whiskey of unquestionable quality. Superb. 43%

Midleton 30 Years Old Pot Still db **(85) n19 t22 f22 b22.** A typically brittle, crunchy Irish pot still where the un-malted grains have a telling say. The oak has travelled as far as it can without having an adverse effect. A chewy whiskey which revels in its bitter-sweet balance. An impressively tasty and fascinating insight into yesteryear. 45%

Midleton 1973 Pure Pot Still db **(95) n24 t24 f23 b24.** The enormous character of true Irish pot still whiskey (a mixture of malted and unmalted barley) appears to absorb age better than most other grain spirits. This one is in its element. But drink at full strength and at body temp (it is pretty closed when cool) for the most startling – and memorable effects. I have no idea how much this costs. But if you can find one and afford it... then buy it!! 56%

MIDLETON (new distillery)

⊰⊱ **Midleton Single Pot Still Single Cask 1994** cask no. 74060, dist 15 Nov 94 db **(93) n23** delicate and clean yet far more happy to trot out the caramels from the oak than the biting grain from the pot still; a few spices carry the unmistakable Irish on the wind, though...; **t23** firms up slightly on delivery, but this is still a softie as IPS goes. Again, the caramel dictates and it takes a little while for the harder grains to force their way through. They arrive in a cocoa-nougat cloak when they do.; **f23.5** some balmy sugar and a slight hint of honey makes this about as silky an IPS as you'll ever come across despite the late oak arrival; **b23.5** probably a mod pot as opposed to a heavy one. A charming bottling, though if only they had been braver and gone for full cask strength... 46%. ncf. Irish Distillers. Exclusive to the Celtic Whiskey Shop.

Midleton Barry Crockett Legacy db **(94) n23.5** spices nip and thrust; delicate fruits form a series of gentle layers; a light bourbon liquorice adds depth...; **t24.5** the delivery provides the sweetness missing from the nose but only after an early surge of oak and soft oils. The middle ground is a battlefield between spices and peachy fruit, with just a touch of honey moving in when it thinks no one is watching...; **f22.5** relatively short and duller than you might expect. The caramels cap the higher points and though spices rumble there is little for it to echo against; **b23.5** another fabulous Pot Still, very unusual for its clever use of the varied ages of the oak to form strata of intensity. One very sophisticated whiskey. *46%. ncf.*

Powers John's Lane Release Aged 12 Years db **(96.5) n24** unmistakable. Unique. Utopian. Irish pure pot still at its most embracing and magnificent. That bizarre bipolar character of rock hard grain so at home in the company of silky, molten honey. Some light, non-specific fruit – a bit like boiled sweets in a candy shop. But a vague menthol note, too...; **t25** as Irish whiskey goes: perfection! The delivery can come only from Irish Pot still – I have encountered it nowhere else. And it is a replay of the nose: soft, dissolve-on-the-palate honey and elsewhere strands of something much firmer – hardening more and more as it moves to the middle ground; **f23.5** wonderful fade: a distant medium roast Java, the Lubec marzipan which you just knew would be coming; a little caramel; some orangey notes... **b24** this is a style of Irish Pot Still I have rarely seen outside the blending lab. I had many times thought of trying to find some of this and bottling it myself. No need now. I think I have just tasted Irish Whiskey of the Year, and certainly one of the top five world whiskies of the year. *46%*

Redbreast 12 Years Old db **(96) n23.5** lively and firm, this one offering a gentle fruity sweetness not too dissimilar to a rye, ironic as there is light bourbony kick off the oak, too; **t24.5** wonderfully clipped and correct in delivery: firm at first - very firm!!! - but slowly the barley melts and light muscovado sugars dovetail with a flinty fruitiness and pillow-soft vanilla; incorrigibly mouthwatering and the build up of spices is just showing off; **f24** remains spicy but clean, allowing a clear view of those varying barley tones drifting away; **b24** Yess...!!! Back to its classically classy, brilliant best. No sulphur casks this time (unlike last year). Just juicy pot still all the way. An old loved one has returned... more gorgeous than ever. *40%. Irish Distillers.*

❖ **Redbreast Aged 12 Years Cask Strength** batch B1/11 db **(96) n24.5** just about the ultimate in Irish whiskey noses. Absolutely rock hard: you feel you could cut diamonds with an aroma like this. It is curiously fruity in that unique Irish Pot Still way, and not just from the obvious sherry involvement, yet shows clearly it's a relation to another whiskey style: American rye. A little hint of mint and lavender goes a long way and offers the only softness in this glorious bitter-sweet aroma; **t24.5** my, oh my, oh my, oh my...one of those deliveries which takes your breath away and it is a few moments before you can compose yourself to think. Or, in my case, to compose myself to compose. The first thing is the sweetness which is never apparent on the nose: here we have the crunchiest Demerara sugar meeting even crunchier muscovado: then a litany of varied fruit and quasi-rye juicy bits...mmmmmm; **f23** majestically long and moves in fabulously mysterious chocolatey ways - chocolate and raisin to be more precise - generating even more salivating moments right until the big chocolate sponge/sherry trifle finale. Late spices, even the faintest possible bitterness of a rogue treated sherry butt, though for once it does no serious damage, other than costing it a possible place in the world's top three. The vanillas come into action for the first time here, too...; **b24** this is Irish pot still on steroids. And sporting an Irish brogue as thick as my great great grandfather John Murray's. To think, had I not included Redbreast in Jim Murray's Irish Whiskey Almanac back in 1994, after it had already been unceremoniously scrapped and discontinued, while championing the then entirely unknown Irish Pot Still cause this brand would no longer have been with us. If I get run over by a bus tomorrow, at least I have that as a tick when St Peter is totting up the plusses and minuses... And with the cask strength, he might even give me two... *57.7%. ncf. Irish Distillers.*

Redbreast 15 Years Old db **(94) n23 t24 f23 b24.** For years I have been pleading for Irish Distillers to launch a pot still at 46%, natural colour and unchillfiltered. Well, I've got two out of three wishes. And what we have here is a truly great Irish whiskey and my pulse races in the certain knowledge it can get better still... *46%. ncf. France.*

Green Spot (94.5) n23.5 mouthwatering and fresh on one level, honey and menthol on another; **t24** crisp, mouthwatering with a fabulous honey burst, alarmingly sensuous; **f23.5** the caramel has receded, leaving the finer, sharper pot still character to battle it out with the honey. The spices are now much clearer too; **b23.5** this honeyed state has remained a few years, and its sharpness has now been regained. Complex throughout. Unquestionably one of the world's greatest branded whiskies. *40%. Irish Distillers for Mitchell & Son, Dublin.*

Green Spot 10 Year Old Single Pot Still dist 1993 **(92) n23 t22 f24 b23.** Launched to celebrate the 200th anniversary of this wonderful Dublin landmark, this is bottled from three mixed bourbon casks of Irish Pot Still. The extra age has detracted slightly from the usual vitality of the standard Green Spot (an 8-y-o) but its quality still must be experienced. *40%*

Green Spot 12 Year Old Single Pot Still dist 1991 **(93) n24 t24 f22 b23.** A single cask restricted to exactly 200 bottles to mark the 200th anniversary of the grand old man of Kildare Street, this is the first Middleton pot still I have seen at this strength outside of a lab. A one-off in every sense. *58%*

❖ **Yellow Spot Aged 12 Years** bourbon, sherry and Malaga casks db **(88.5) n23.5** my nose is sifting through the layers of fruit to get a glimpse of the IPS.... Much has sunk without trace, like a head in an eiderdown pillow. As an archaeologist tenderly scrapping away at a find might, the apricot and orange blossom has to be moved to one side before a degree of brittle grains shows; the spices soon follow...; **t22.5** big initial flavour profile. Enjoyable, fun, lush. But, like the nose, muddled and without a defined structure. Definitely a crispness at work in there late on, but takes its time to arrive; **f20** a little unplanned as bitterness joins in with the apricot, though the complex part of the finale is over quite quickly; **b22.5** if anything, just a shade too many wine casks used which somewhat drowns out the unique IP character. Reminds me of when Barry Walsh was working on the triple maturation theme of the Bushmills 16, probably about 15 years ago. Not until the very last days did all the components click. Just before then, it went through a phase like this (though obviously with malt, not IPS). Knowing current blender Billy Leighton as I do, I can see this whiskey improving in future batches as lessons are learned. not that there isn't already much to enjoy... *46%. Irish Distillers.*

OLD COMBER

Old Comber 30 Years Old Pure Pot Still (88) n23 t24 f20 b21. A classic example of a whiskey spending a few Summers too many in wood: increasing age doesn't equal excellence. That said, always very drinkable and early on positively sparkles with a stunning mouthfeel. Out of respect for the old I have made the markings for taste cover the first seven or eight seconds... *40%*

Single Malt
COOLEY

Connemara bott code L9042 db **(88) n23** a bigger than usual salty, kippery tang; **t22.5** one of the more delicate and mouth-watering deliveries Connemara has given for a while: the peat is at once strident and meek but the subtle gristy sweetness is a constant and first class foil to the vanillas; **f20.5** rather short, toffeed and hurried; **b22** one of the softest smoked whiskies in the world which though quite lovely gives the impression it can't make its mind up about what it wants to be. *40%*

Connemara Aged 8 Years db **(85) n22.5 t21.5 f20 b21.** Another Connemara lacking teeth. The peat charms, especially on the nose, but the complexity needs working on. *46%*

Connemara Aged 12 Years bott code L9024 db **(85.5) n23 t21.5 f20 b21.** The nose, with its beautiful orange, fruity lilt, puts the shy smoke in the shade. *40%*

⁙ **Connemara Bog Oak** bott 26 July 2011, batch V11/07 db **(93) n24** the ancient Bog Oak dug up and fitted to the end of the barrels has definitely made an impact, for there has never been a Connemara nose like this before. It is sweeter for a start, and the iodine character seems more pronounced....a little more concentrated. Just a very different – and hugely enjoyable - twist on a well-known tale...; **t24** again...Connemara, but not quite as we have ever known it. A decidedly molten Mars Bar feel to this, with cocoa and caramel mixing in with the ever-sweetening phenols; **f22.5** silky, but a little tang here, slightly musty... perhaps it needs some new heads...; **b22.5** I guessed with the hand of Cooley blender Noel "Nosher" Sweeney (the man who can put away a roast dinner more quickly than most of us can successfully open a bar of Nutri Grain) behind this it would be anything other than bog standard...And Noel: well done on successfully getting your ancient ends away... *575% (I know from correspondence, some people are interested in this kind of thing: this was distilled on 1/11 (07) and bottled in 2011...and is number 1,111 of the new whiskies tasted for the Bible)*

Connemara Cask Strength bott code L9041 db **(90) n21.5 t23 f22 b22.5.** A juicy negative of the standard bottling: does its talking on the palate rather than nose. Maybe an absence of caramel notes might have something to do with that. *579%*

Connemara Distillers Edition db **(86) n22 t22.5 f20 b21.5.** When I give whisk(e)y tastings around the world, I love to include Connemara. Firstly, people don't expect peated Irish. Secondly, their smoked whisky stock is eclectic and you never quite know what is going to come out of the bottle. This is a particularly tight, sharp style. No prisoners survived... *43%*

⁙ **Connemara Single Cask 18 Years Old Amontillado Sherry Finish** Solera Amontillado sherry cask, cask no. 155, dist 31 Aug 92, bott 12 May 92 db **(70) n18 t19 f16 b17.** Blast! I hoped to finally get through an entire day without sulphur for once. Failed! *46%. sc. Exclusive to the Celtic Whiskey Shop.*

Connemara Turf Mór Limited Edition Small Batch Collection bott code L10215 db **(94) n23.5 t23.5 f23.5 b23.5.** At Burnley FC, the wine served in their boardroom is The Claret's Claret, naturally. I will not be surprised to find this the whiskey on offer... The tasting notes to this just about perfectly match the ones above. *58.2%*

⁙ **Cooley Poitín Origin Edition** dist 26 July 2011, rotation 232/11 db **(92.5) n23.5 t23 f23 b23.** Full bloodied and rumbustious, this is high quality new make Irish that absolutely thumps the salivation button on palate. And, apparently, a mix of malted and unmalted barley in the traditional Irish Pot Still style....though this neither noses nor tastes anything like the new spirit from Midleton. The label waffles on about 1,000 years of Irish tradition. But the use of unmalted barley came into use only when distillers found a way of avoiding tax on the malted stuff. Were there taxes on alcohol in Ireland 1,000 years ago...? 65%

❖ **Irish Turk Beg Maiden Voyage** db **(91.5) n22** punchier and saltier than the normal Cooley malt, this is quite a heavyweight with some Demerara sugars adding to thickening oak; **t23.5** a lot of chewing required, even for the delivery which, though soft, is also a weighty beast; again a saltiness persists bringing out the full flavour of the barley; **f22.5** some shades of fudge and natural caramels; **b22.5** brooding and quite delicious. 44%

Locke's Aged 8 Years bott code L9005 db **(88) n22.5** excellent, rousing citrus; **t22** begins bright fresh and sharp, clouds over slightly with caramel; **f22** barley loses its toffeed marker from time to time to complete a juicy experience; **b21.5** a beautiful malt at probably this distillery's optimum age. 40%

Locke's Aged 8 Years Crock (92) n23 pounding, intense, grassy-sweet barley; **t24** excellent mouth arrival and almost immediately a honey-rich delivery of lush, slightly oily malt: wonderful, wonderful stuff! **f22** soft oak tempers the barley and a degree of toffee digs in and flattens the...; **b23** much, much better cask selection than of old: some real honey casks here. A crock of gold...! 40%

Locke's Aged 9 Years Grand Crew cask no. 700, dist Feb 00, bott Sep 09 db **(91.5) n23 t23.5 f22.5 b22.5**. This took me back a few years. Having the three new Locke's lined up was like the days when I went through the Cooley warehouses looking for casks to put into Knappogue. This wasn't far off the style I was searching for. The right age, too. 58.9%. Cooley for The Irish Whisky Society. 233 bottles.

Locke's Aged 10 Years Premier Crew cask no. 713, dist Feb 00, bott Jul 10 db **(88) n22 t23 f21 b22**. The cask does its best to try and spoil the barley fun. Here's a tip: stick to younger malts. Cooley is brilliant and relatively undiscovered at between seven and nine years. And there is less time for cask to bite back... 46%. Cooley for The Irish Whisky Society. 292 bottles.

Tullamore Dew Single Malt 10 Years Old db **(91.5) n23** when I was a child in the early '60s, an aunt used to bring me the odd bag of toffee. These toffees were studded with crystalised fruit and opening the bag was always a delight: it was something akin to this...; **t23** soft-textured and delicate. Again the toffee is ubiquitous. But the juicy nature of the fruit, coupled with a tingly spice, lifts it above the norm; **f22.5** the caramels and spices play out the medium finish, perhaps with a hint of butterscotch too; **b23** the best whiskey I have ever encountered with a Tullamore label. Furtively complex and daringly delicate. If only they could find a way to minimise the toffee... 40%. William Grant & Sons.

The Tyrconnell bott code L9074 db **(86) n21 t22 f22 b21**. Sweet, soft, chunky and with a finely spice finale. 40%

The Tyrconnell Aged 10 Years Madeira Finish bott code L8136 db **(91) n23 t23 f22 b23**. Not quite the award-winning effort of a few years back, as those lilting high notes which so complimented the baser fruit tones haven't turned up here. But remains in the top echelon and still much here to delight the palate. 46%

The Tyrconnell Aged 10 Years Port Finish bott code L8167 db **(81.5) n21.5 t21 f19 b20**. Toffee all the way. 46%

The Tyrconnell Aged 10 Years Sherry Finish bott code L8168 db **(84) n22 t21 f21 b20**. Like the Port Cask in this present series we have a thick malt that is friendly, toffeed and generally flat. This one, though, does have the odd peak of grapey richness, but you have to travel through a few plateaux to reach them. 46%

Tyrconnell Aged 11 Years sherry cask finish, cask no. V09-10 *#336 db **(95) n23.5** my word! This bodes very well! Black pepper notes ginger up the intense marmalade and honey. Clean and brimming with undisguised intent; **t24** magnificent. The palate is left salivating and, if you are not careful, you are left dribbling as a glorious delivery of rich grape and sweetened orange paste offers the juicy introduction while a slow rumbling of ever-increasing spice shakes you to the core; **f23.5** long with a slow build up of oils and further fruit. Very late on a succession of bourbon-style honeycomb and molassed notes begin to make their mark; **b24** a thrilling virtuoso performance. Those who bought a bottle of this when they had the chance are unlikely to have regretted it. 58.5%. Bottled for Whisky Live 2011.

The Tyrconnell Aged 14 Years cask no. 3179, rotation K92/25 db **(93) n23** apple blossom (no, honestly!), cedar wood and still remnants of ultra clean barley; **t23** refreshingly rich barley offering a shard of golden syrup to its perfectly lush delivery; **f23** long, soft vanilla, a touch of tannin and those continuing gentle oils...sigh, what bliss!! **b24** By rotation, K92 means it was distilled in 1992. Which just proves this distillery really has come of age, because, make no mistake, this is a belter... 46%

❖ **The Tyrconnell Single Cask 11 Year Old** db **(95.5) n23.5** sings the house style with a voice of rare clarity. The thin orange blossom honey is divine; **t25** of the great Irish whiskey malt deliveries for this and many years: perfection. The weight of the barley and oak cannot be bettered while the clarity of the malt and pink grapefruit is faultless; **f23** long, but concentrates purely on winding down the charming complexity of all that has gone before. And not an atom of bitterness from the oak...; **b24** well, if there weren't enough reasons to go to Dublin, you now have this... *46%. sc. Exclusive to the Celtic Whiskey Shop.*

⫸ **The Tyrconnell Single Cask 11 Year Old Anima Negra Mallorcan Wine Cask Finish** db **(86) n21.5 t22 f21 b21.5.** Loads going on here and those who like a boiled fruit candy feel to their malt will appreciate this one. *46%. sc. Exclusive to the Celtic Whiskey Shop.*

The Tyrconnell Aged 15 Years Single Cask cask no. 1854/92 db **(92.5) n24 t23 f22.5 b23.** Infinitely more comfortable in its aging skin a similar malt I tasted in Canada last year. *46%*

The Tyrconnell Aged 17 Years Single Cask cask no. 5306/92 db **(87) n22 t22 f21.5 b21.5.** Attractive barley all the way but barely deviates. *46%*

⫸ **The Tyrconnell Aged 18 Years Single Cask** cask no. 592/93 db **(94.5) n24** wow! What a nose! A half hour aroma, with the myriad variances in the shades of honey and marmalade taking an age to unravel; **t23.5** melt-in-the-mouth delivery, but there is a superb sharpness which really allows the barley to stand out after all these years and those kumquat notes to positively fizz; the complexity quotient increases as the vanilla joins to the spices in beating out an oaky tattoo; **f23** lemon curd tart and marmalade mix now works alongside the spice; **b24** "beautiful in its simplicity" trills the label. Guys: are you kidding? Don't undersell yourselves. This is a very complex dram, indeed! And a fitting swan song to this wonderful distillery's final days of independence... *46%. sc.*

The Tyrconnell Single Cask cask no. 9571/1992 db **(85.5) n23 t21 f20.5 b21.** The wonderful citrus notes on the nose are swamped by the oak further down the line. There is no doubting the age of this Cooley! *46%*

Clonmel Peated Aged 8 Years (86) n22 t23 f20 b21. Take the toffee away and you would have one hell of an Irish. Claims to be "Pure Pot Still". It isn't (in Irish terms): it's malt. *40%*

Craoi na Mona Irish Malt Whiskey (68) n16 t18 f17 b17. I'm afraid my Gaelic is slipping these days: I assume Craoi na Mona means "Feinty, badly made smoky malt"... (that's the end of my tasting for the day...) *40%*

Glen Dimplex (88) n23 solid malt with a hint of honey; charming, blemish-free; **t22** gentle development of the malts over simple dusty vanilla; **f21** quite dry, spiced and a little toffeed; **b22** overall, clean and classically Cooley. *40%*

Knappogue Castle 1990 (91) n22 t23 f22 b24. For a light whiskey this shows enormous complexity and depth. Genuine balance from nose to finish; refreshing and dangerously more-ish. Entirely from bourbon cask and personally selected and vatted by a certain Jim Murray. *40%. nc. Great Spirits.*

Knappogue Castle 1991 (90) n22 t23 f22 b23. Offers rare complexity for such a youthful malt especially in the subtle battles that rage on the palate between sweet and dry, malt and oak and so on. The spiciness is a great foil for the malt. Each cask picked and vatted by the author. *40%. nc. Great Spirits.*

Knappogue Castle 1992 (94) n23 t23 f24 b24. A different Knappogue altogether from the delicate, ultra-refined type. This expression positively revels in its handsome ruggedness and muscular body: a surprisingly bruising yet complex malt that always remains balanced and fresh – the alter-ego of the '90 and '91 vintages. I mean, as the guy who put this whiskey together, what do you expect? But it's not bad if I say so myself and was voted the USA's No. 1 Spirit. Virtually all vanished, but worth getting a bottle if you can find it (I don't receive a penny – I was paid as a consultant!). *40%. nc. Great Spirits.*

Knappogue Castle 1993 *(see Bushmills)*

Knappogue Castle 1994 *(see Bushmills)*

⫸ **Liquid Sun Cooley 1999** bott 2012 **(87) n22** cream toffee raisin...without the raisin...; **t22** peated cream toffee....without the peat... **f21.5** complex cream toffee...with the complexity... **b21.5** awash with natural caramels and enjoyable in a horrible way...without the horrible. *53.2%. nc ncf sc. The Whisky Agency.*

Magillian Cooley Pure Pot Still Single Malt (91) n22 slightly waxy and honeyed: Cooley at its softest; **t22** beautiful arrival of highly intense, spotlessly clean malt. The sweetness level is near perfect; **f24** spiceless – unlike the previous bottling. Now just the longest fade-out of malt concentrate in Irish whiskey...and with a touch of honey for good measure; **b23** ... or maybe not..!! *43%. Ian MacLeod Distillers.*

Magilligan Irish Whiskey Peated Malt 8 Years Old (89) n21 t23 f22 b23. Such a different animal from the docile creature that formally passed as Magilligan peated. Quite lovely...and very classy. *43%. Ian Macleod Distillers.*

Merry's Single Malt (83) n20 t22 f20 b21. Ultra-clean barley rich nose is found on the early palate. The finish is flat, though. *40%*

Michael Collins Irish Whiskey Single Malt db **(68) n17 t18 f17 b16.** Bloody hell, I thought. Didn't anyone get my message from last year? Apparently not – and it's our fault as the

...sting notes above were accidentally edited out before they went in. Sorry. But the caramel in the latest bottling has been upped to take the whisky from deep gold to bronze. Making this among the most over-coloured single malt I have tasted in years. Please guys. For the love of whiskey. Please let us taste exactly what a great malt this could be. 40% (80 proof)

Sainsbury's Single Malt Irish Whiskey bott code L10083/16 **(87.5) n22** a lively nose which makes no disguise of its youth: fresh, with the barley out-punching the oak; more than a squeeze of citrus; **t22** sherbet lemon: sharp, piercing and mouth-watering. The barley again makes the most of the limited oak interference for a charming display of light, clean sugars; **f21.5** a touch of caramel and late spice; **b22** classic Cooley showing its big, malty depth. 40%

Sainsbury's Dún Léire Aged 8 Years Single Malt (95.5) n24 the score for this crept upwards as I investigated the aroma like the thermometer in my back garden on a bright Summer's day. The first thing to throw itself at you is Seville blood orange, backed up by a clever layering of barley at varying intensity and sweetness; the delicate oak acts as no more than a buffer in between; **t24** just about the perfect mouth feel: silky and melting on the palate. Again, it was an orangey citrus first to show, then again followed by some stunning malt. Everything dissolves: you don't have to do anything but close your eyes and enjoy, indeed: marvel...but it is hard work to stop yourself chewing; **f23.5** dries slightly, but the bitterness threatened on the label fails to materialise...thankfully. The fruit and barley ride off into the sunset in tandem; **b24** when I read "notes of bitter orange" on the label I feared the worst and expected a sulphurous whiskey. Well maybe there is a molecule or two hanging around, but so minor is it, it is impossible to tell exactly where it comes from. This is one of the great whiskeys from Cooley, ever. And as a supermarket Irish... unsurpassed. One of the surprise packages of world whisky for 2010. Magnificent. 40%. Cooley for Sainsbury's Supermarket.

Shannahan's (92) n23 beautifully young, fresh and zesty: this distillery's best style; **t22** refreshing, clean barley that tries to be little else; **f24** excellent late complexity as some first-class soft vanilla appears; more citrus cleans the palate; **b23** Cooley natural and unplugged: quite adorable. 40%

Slieve Foy Single Malt Aged 8 Years bott code L9108 **(88) n23** so delicate, you feel it could snap if you sniffed at it too hard: beautiful lemony malt with fudge and advocaat mix; **t22.5** pure silk. Juicy young barley that just keeps you salivating. Fudge and vanilla begin to edge their way into the frame; **f21** tame spices and toffee; **b21.5** never deviates from its delicate touch. 40%. Cooley for Marks & Spencer.

Vom Fass Cooley Irish Single Malt 8 Years Old (88) n22 light, clean barley; **t22.5** refreshing, zesty, delicate sugars and malt; **f21.5** a little bit of a tang but good late spices; **b22** a very decent, if undemonstrative, example of the distillery at an age which well suits. 40%

The Wild Geese Single Malt (85.5) n21.5 t21 f22 b21. "A Rare Blend of Pure Aged Irish Malt Whiskies" says the front label. Yet it is a single malt. Confusing. And very unhelpful to a whisky public already being totally bamboozled by the bizarre and misguided antics of the Scotch Whisky Association. It is not a blend. It is a mixing of Cooley malt whiskey, as I understand it. The back label's "Smoother Because We Distil it Longer" is also a bit of a blarney. It's made in a pot still and whilst it is true that if you distil faster (by higher temperatures) you could well end up with "hot" whiskey, I am not aware of this being distilled at a significantly slower rate than at either Bushmills or Midleton. Or do they mean the cut of the run from the spirit still is longer, which would impart more oils – not all of them great? Just ignore the Wild Goose chase the labels send you on and enjoy the malt, with all its failings, for what it is (and this is pretty enjoyable in an agreeably rough and ready manner, though not exactly the stiff of Irish whiskey purists): which in this case for all its malt, toffee and delicate smoke, also appears to have more than a slight touch of feints – so maybe they were right all along...!!! 43%. Cooley for Avalon.

OLD KILBEGGAN

Kilbeggan Distillery Reserve Malt matured in quarter casks, batch no. 1, bott Jun 10 db **(89) n22.5** wonderfully delicate with a distinctive light nutty sweetness to the malt; the you~ is well camouflaged behind a curious (considering you can't get any more inland than t' distillery) coastal saltiness and a weak, nondescript fruit; **t22.5** a sugary delivery to b the thin malty line; quick vanillas and toffee; **f22** mainly fudgy and flat but a light le postscript; a late spice buzz; **b22** an endearingly soft malt to see Kilbeggan distiller into the whiskey world. Shame it has been reduced to 40%, as this one demanded least 46% – indeed, preferably naked – and allowing those delicate, elegant but ma~ characters a chance to bloom. But welcome back...and I look forward to many a with me tasting you as you blossom, as I am sure you will. It has been nearly 20 I first discovered the beauty of Kilbeggan Distillery and I have countless times si~ of that moment. 40%. 1500 bottles. Available only in the distillery gift shop.

The Spirit of Kilbeggan 1 Month (90.5) n22 t23 f23 b22.5. Wow!! They are really getting to grips with the apparatus. Full bodied and lush small still feel to this but radiating complexity, depth, barley and cocoa in equal measures. The development of the oils really does give this excellent length. Impressed! 65.5%

The Spirit of Kilbeggan 1 Year (85) n20.5 t21 f22 b21.5. A veritable Bambi of a spirit: a typical one year old malt which, as hard as it tries, just can't locate its centre of gravity. Even so, the richness is impressive and some highly sugared chocolate mousse near the end is a treat. 62.7%

The Spirit of Kilbeggan 2 Years (84) n20 t21 f22 b21. A tad raw and a little thin. There is some decent balance between oak and malt, but the overall feeling is that the still has not yet been quite mastered. 60.3%

OLD BUSHMILLS

Bushmills Aged 10 Years matured in two woods db **(92.5) n23** has maintained that big sultana and honey signature; **t23** rich delivery, delicately oiled and beautifully rounded. Slightly more two-toned than previously, with the old-fashioned barley-bourbon oak notes coming through in its traditional flaky manner; **f23** very accomplished finish with a wonderful even-ness between barley and fruit. Much more recognisable as a traditional Bushmills than when they first changed the oak recipe; **b23.5** absolutely superb whiskey showing great balance and the usual Antrim 19th century pace with its favour development. The odd bottle of this I have come across over the last couple of years has been spoiled by the sherry involvement. But, this, as is usually the case, is absolutely spot on. 40% ⊙⊙

Bushmills 12 Years Old Distillery Reserve db **(86) n22.5 t22.5 f20 b21.** This version has gone straight for the ultra lush feel. For those who want to take home some 40% abv fruit fudge from the distillery. 40% ⊙

Bushmills Select Casks Aged 12 Years married with Caribbean rum cask db **(95) n23** unusual moist rum and raisin cake effect: effective and just enough spice to deliver extra complexity. Just the very slightest hint of bourbon, too; **t24** adorable malt richness; biscuity and stupendously seasoned yet always remains fresh and mouthwatering. The sweetness is very cleverly controlled; **f24** there are just so many layers to this: the oak is a growing force, but restricts itself to a vanilla topping; **b24** one of the most complex Bushmills in living memory, and probably since it was established in 1784. 40%

Bushmills Aged 16 Years db **(71) n18 t21 f15 b17.** In my days as a consultant Irish whiskey blender, going through the Bushmills warehouses I found only one or two sulphur-treated butts. Alas, there are many more than that at play here. 40% ⊙⊙

Bushmills Aged 21 Years db **(95.5) n24.5** this remains something of a Chinese puzzle on the nose: just how do all those different notes , sometimes soft and rounded, sometimes hard and angular, many of them fruity, manage to intertwine...yet never clash? And why can you never detach one without another clinging on to it. If Sherlock Holmes tried to solve it, this would be a three pipe conundrum...except the use of tobacco would ruin the experience. Just marvel at the greengage and physalis, the flaked vanilla and liquorice, the ulmo honey and hickory...so much else besides; **t24** as melt-in-the-mouth as a whiskey can be: amazingly juicy barley offers the cutting edge and lead while a plethora of delicate sugars dissolve on impact; the fruit is served as a perpetual mixed salad; **f23.5** this is where I am really impressed. Despite all the complexity of the nose and delivery, at the finish the Bushmills trademark flaky vanilla and delicate barley comes through...a signature unique to one distillery in the world; **b24** an Irish journey as beautiful as the dramatic landscape which borders the distillery. Magnificent. 40% ⊙⊙

Clontarf Single Malt (90.5) n23 barley concentrate with a squeeze of orange and distant juniper; **t23** beautifully fresh barley, almost barley sugar, with light sinews of oak; **f22** long, intense barley but with the vanilla standing tallest at the death as welcome spices finally gather; **b22.5** beautiful in its simplicity, this has eschewed complexity for delicious minimalism; 40%. Clontarf Irish Whiskey Co. ⊙

The Irishman Single Malt bottle no. E2496 **(83) n20 t21 f21 b21.** Highly pleasant malt but coffee and toffee on the finish underline a caramel-style whiskey which may, potentially, so much more. 40%. Hot Irishman Ltd.

Knappogue Castle Aged 12 Years bourbon cask matured **(90) n23.5** the oak has got ngst the barley. It means this is a double edged aroma: on one hand bright and rp, on the other there is a duller, more caramel-rich, almost biscuity base. Hugely though, and the toffee apple sideline is a treat; **t23** this translates perfectly on rd and crisp interior (the closest you'll find to an Irish pot still style!) which really vation factor. Then outside a softer, duller toffee effect; **f21** a touch of crème st too much toffee; **b22.5** the massive toffee influence deflects from the huge here which springs a few surprises. 40%. Castle Brands Group.

⋰⋅ **Knappogue Castle Aged 16 Years** sherry finished, dist 1994, bott 2010 **(84) n23 t23 f18 b20.** The nose: love it! Beautifully spiced, windfall apples piled into a barrow...just wonderful! The delivery: soft, chewy, deftly spiced again, even a sexy touch of Turkish Delight, with the malt having so much to say still....then, the finish. The finish...Oh dear, oh dear.. Let's just say, the perfect malt to have before bedtime, because if this doesn't send you to sleep, nothing will. As flat and lifeless as the nose and delivery are rich with invention. And, to make matters worse, a sulphury sub plot bites with bitterness. What a shame. Someone took their eye off the ball, and a potential award has gone begging... *40%. ncf.*

Knappogue Castle 1990 *(see Cooley)*

Knappogue Castle 1991 *(see Cooley)*

Knappogue Castle 1992 *(see Cooley)*

Knappogue Castle 1993 (91) n22 b22 f23 b24. A malt of exceptional character and charisma. Almost squeaky clean but proudly contains enormous depth and intensity. The chocolate finish is an absolute delight. Quite different and darker than any previous Knappogue but not dwarfed in stature to any of the previous three vintages. Created by yours truly. *40%. nc. Great Spirits.*

Knappogue Castle 1994 lot no. L6 **(89) n23 t24 f20 b22.** A wonderful whiskey in the Knappogue tradition, although this one was not done by its creator. That said, it does have an Achilles heel: the finish. This is the most important bit to get right, especially as this is the oldest Knappogue yet. But not enough attention has been paid to getting rid of the oak-induced bitterness. *40%. Castle Brands.*

Knappogue Castle 1995 bott 2007 **(88) n23 t22 f21 b22.** A charming malt showing Old Bushmills in very unusual colours. Lacking the charisma, clarity and complexity of the first Knappogues simply because they were designed to extol the virtues of young (8-year-old) malt. Naturally, extra oak has crept in here, forcing out – as it must – the sharpness and vitality of the barley. A decent effort, but perhaps more should have been done to keep out the aggressive bitterness. *40%*

Single Grain
COOLEY

Greenore 6 Year Old bott code L9015 db **(89) n23.5** even at such tender age this has more to do with bourbon than Irish: gentle, sweet red liquorice, toffee apple, and not even the slightest hint of bitterness...; **t77.5**...but tastes of pure Canadian, especially with the over-enthusiastic caramels; sweet with an amazingly yielding texture; **f21** lightly burnt toast and more toffee; **b22** very enjoyable whiskey. But two points: cut the caramel and really see the baby sing. And secondly, as a "Small Batch" bottling, how about putting a batch number on the label...? *40%. Cooley.*

Greenore 8 Year Old bott code L8190 db **(86.5) n20 t22 f23 b21.5.** The vague hint of butyric on the nose is more than amply compensated by the gradual build up to something rather larger on the palate than you might have expected (and don't be surprised if the two events are linked). The corn oil is almost a meal in itself and the degree of accompanying sugar and corn flour is a treat. *40%. Cooley.*

Greenore 10 Years Old dist 1997, bott 2007 db **(87.5) n22** pretty standard Canadian style: plenty of corn digging in, a touch of toffee sweetness and a degree of bite; **t22** lightly oiled corn and vanilla; the oak dips in and out; **f21.5** pleasantly sweet at times yet amazingly docile, knowing what this grain is capable of... **b22** well made grain and always enjoyable but perhaps not brought to its fullest potential due to some less than inspired oak. *40%*

Greenore 15 Years Old bott code L8044 **(90) n23** the depth of ingrained oak mixed with corn heads you in the direction of Canada; a few spicy folds and golden syrup edges ensure a lovely simple elegance; **t22.5** just the right dosage of spice to counter the sugars; **f22** oaky bitterness outgunned by those marauding dark sugars; **b22.5** the advent of the Kilbeggan 15 reminded us that there must be some grain of that age around, and here to prove it is a superb bottling of the stuff which, weirdly, is a lot better than the blend. Beautiful. *43%*

Greenore 18 Years Old db **(91) n22.5** like a fine Canadian there is superb harmony between the vanilla and soft oils. A custard tart sweetness; **t22.5** lush, silky, improbably mouth-watering; **f23** a really lovely spice zips around, balancing charmingly with the sugars and oils; **b23** this continuous still at Cooley should be marked by the State as an Irish national treasure. One of the most complex grains you'll ever find, even when heading into uncharted territory like this one. *46%. ncf. 4000 bottles.*

Blends

Bushmills 1608 anniversary edition **(94) n23.5** the grain barely gets a look in as the malt and oak dominates from the first whiff. Toasted oak and bread form a dense background, sweetened by muscovado sugar melting on porridge; **t23.5** now that's different: how many blends do you know kick off with an immediate impact of sweetness that offers about four or five different levels of intensity, and each accompanied by a toasted oakiness? Very, very different, charming, fascinating...and delicious; **f23** long, mocha with the emphasis on the coffee and then, at the very end some firm grains at last get a toe-hold; **b24** this whiskey is talking an entirely different language to any Irish blend I have come across before, or any blend come to that. Indeed, nosed blind you'd not even regard it a blend: the malt calls to you like a Siren. But perhaps it is the crystal malt they have used here which is sending out such unique signals, helping the whiskey to form a thick cloak of roasty, toasty, burnt toffeed, bitter-sweetness which takes your breath away. What a fabulous whiskey! And whether it be a malt or blend, who cares? Genius unique whiskey. *40%*

Bushmills 1608 400th Anniversary (83) n21 t21.5 f20 b20.5. Thin-bodied, hard as nails and sports a peculiarly Canadian feel. *46%. Diageo.*

Bushmills Black Bush (91) n23 a firmer aroma with less evident malt and the spices have also taken a back seat. But the gentle, toffee apple and night garden scent reveal that the malt-grain interaction is still wonderfully alluring; **t23** busy delivery, much softer than the nose indicates with the malt first to show. The oak is no slouch either, offering excellent spices; some burnt, raisiny notes help confirm this is Black Bush on song; **f21.5** still over the top caramel interfering but not before some honeycomb makes a small stand; **b23.5** this famous old blend may be under new management and even blender. But still the high quality, top-notch complexity rolls around the glass and your palate. As beautiful as ever. *40%* ☉

Bushmills Original (80) n19 t21 f20 b20. Remains one of the hardest whiskeys on the circuit with the Midleton grain at its most unflinching. There is a sweeter, faintly maltier edge to this now while the toffee and biscuits qualities remain. *40%*

Cassidy's Distiller's Reserve bott code L8067 **(84.5) n21.5 t22 f20 b21.** Some salivating malt on flavour-exploding delivery, but all else tame and gentle. *40%. Cooley.*

Clancey's bott code L8025 **(87) n22** sweet malt bounces off the firmer grain; young, lively and a touch floral; **t21** early toffeed delivery then a parade of vanilla and varied grains, barley most certainly included; **f22** burnt fudge and some teasing spice; **b22** remains an excellent blend for all the toffee. The spice balance excels. *40%. Cooley for Wm Morrison.*

Clontarf Classic Blend (81) n20 t22 f19.5 b19.5. A hard as nails blend softened only by the heavy use of caramel which, though chewy, tends to obliterate any complexity from elsewhere. Ouch! 40%. Castle Brands Group. ☉☉

Delaney's (85.5) n20 t21.5 f22 b22. Young, clean, citrusy, refreshing and proud. Thoroughly enjoyable and dangerously moreish. *40%. Cooley for Co-operative UK.*

Delaney's Special Reserve (84) n21.5 t20.5 f22 b21. An attractive blend with a big late spicy blast. The toffee dominates for long periods. *40%. Cooley for Co-operative Group.*

Feckin Irish Whiskey (81) n20 t21 f20 b20. Tastes just about exactly the feckin same as the Feckin Strangford Gold... *40%. The Feckin Drinks Co.*

Golden Irish bott code L7064 **(93) n23** do I nose before me spice? And syrup-dripping coconut candy tobacco from childhood days? Yep, that and citrussy vanilla; **t23** near perfect mouthfeel helps stoke up the malt intensity. The grain simply moulds into the palate bringing with it an odd twist of cocoa even by the middle; **f23.5** milky chocolate and Demerara make for a long, pleasing, almost breakfast cereal-type finale; **b23.5** by far one of the most enjoyable Irish blends around. Simple, but what it does, it does deliciously well. *40%. Cooley.*

The Irishman Rare Cask Strength bott 2010 **(81.5) n20 t22.5 f19 b20.** Fabulous crescendo of weighty malt on delivery. But just too much bitterness and toffee hits this one. *53%. Hot Irishman Ltd. 2850 bottles.*

The Irishman Rare Cask Strength bott 2011 **(94.5) n23** flecks of honey intermingle perfectly with the lightest blush of greengage. A touch of bourbon liquorice is sweetened by a hint of molasses; a piquancy is added by a sprinkle of salt; seemingly light, yet weighty...; **t24** excellent body with the soft barley circling around the more rigid middle. This profound gentle-firm balance is the main feature, but those salty sugars also dazzle. Egg custard tart middle makes for a friendlier environment; light honey is threaded throughout; **f23.5** more vanilla and custard, but now some excellent light spices, too; **b24** the back labels of Hot Irishman whiskeys are always entertaining, not least for their unique use of the English language. A free Jim Murray's Whisky Bible 2012 for the first person to e-mail in and tell us what the cock-up is on this label. Back to the whiskey: this blend of malt whisky and Pure Irish Pot still, is a mildly more lilting, more lightly coloured, version of Writer's Tears. And, just like the first bottling, a must-have stunner. *53%. Hot Irishman. 2400 bottles.*

The Irishman Superior Irish Whiskey bott code L6299L059 **(93) n23** chunky caramel perhaps, but the apple is green and inviting; even an inclusion of soft manuka honey and ginger – most un-Irish; **t23** lush, with a distinct malt charge before the caramel and oaky spice arrive; **f23** those spices really tick, accentuated by the contrasting molasses and more honey but doused in vanilla; **b24** what a quite wonderful blend: not of the norm for those that have recently come onto the market and there is much more of the Irish Distillers about this than most. Forget about the smoke promised in the tasting notes on the label...it gives you everything else but. And that is one hell of a lot!! 40%. *Hot Irishman Ltd.*

Jameson (95) n24.5 Swoon...bizarrely shows even more Pot Still character than the Redbreast I tasted yesterday. Flinty to the point of cracking. The sherry is there but on reduced terms, allowing the firm grain to amplify the unmalted barley: truly brilliant; **t24** mouth-watering delivery and then wave upon wave of diamond-hard barley and grain; the odd eclectic layer of something sweetish and honeyed, but this is eye-watering stuff; **f22.5** an annoying touch of caramel creeps in, costing points, but even beyond that you still cannot other than be charmed by the layering of cocoa, barley and light grape; **b24** I thought I had detected in bottlings I had found around the world a very slight reduction in the Pot Still character that defines this truly classic whiskey. So I sat down with a fresh bottle in more controlled conditions...and was blown away as usual. The sharpness of the PS is vivid and unique; the supporting grain of the required crispness. Fear not: this very special whiskey remains in stunning, truly wondrous form. 40%

Jameson 12 Years Old Special Reserve (88) n22 caramel, lazy sherry, musty; enlivened by a splash of sharper pot still; **t23** the grape shows little sign of shyness, aided by a bitter-sweet element; good body and layering; **f21** dulls out as the caramel arrives; dusty, drying; **b22** much more sherry than of late and the pot still makes inroads, too. Just needs to lose some of the caramel effect; 40%

Jameson 18 Years Old Limited Reserve eighth batch bott code JJ18-8 **(91) n23** pure bourbon as oak dispenses myriad honey-leather-hickory notes with the Pot Still doing the job of the fruitier "rye"; **t22.5** firm and juicy, gentle spice but a caramel-trimmed middle; **f22.5** the redoubling of the juicier barley notes cuts through the vanilla and caramel to set up a long, delicately weighted finale; **b22.5** the astonishing degree of bourbon on the nose thankfully doesn't make it to the palate where Ireland rather than Kentucky rules. 40%

⸬ **Jameson Black Barrel (91.5) n23** enticing, with the oaky grain pulsing out a firm spiciness while a subtle almost gristy sweetness balances matters. Curious mint and juniper notes offer a curveball; **t23** the grain again dominates, but the sugars are out in force: on one hand barley-rich, elsewhere much more of a toffee nature. Again, just straying towards something juniper..; **f22.5** softens for the first time as the oily toffee and coffee massage; **b23** here's the problem faced by any Jameson blender: the column still grain from Midleton is the hardest on the palate made anywhere in the world. So how do you get it to mould into what you want? Usually you can't, so you have to make the whiskeys around it reflect and deflect for maximum effect. And that's what's going on here: a brittle whisky where the pot still element is magnified very cleverly indeed. Lovely stuff: New Yorkers are a lucky bunch! 40%. *NY exclusive.*

Jameson Gold Reserve (88) n22 a touch of menthol has crept into this much weightier nose: creaks with age as bourbony elements drift in and out of the grape; **t23** sweet, sexily spiced delivery; hardens towards the middle but the grains are surprisingly lush and softly oiled; **f20** glutinous and plodding; **b22** enjoyable, but so very different: an absolute re-working with all the lighter, more definitively sweeter elements shaved mercilessly while the thicker oak is on a roll. Some distance from the masterpiece it once was. 40%

Jameson Rarest 2007 Vintage Reserve (96) n24.5 the crispest, cleanest, most beautifully defined of all the Jameson family: orange peel, hickory, spotted dog pudding, lavender – they're all there mushed around in and in near-perfect proportions; **t24** ditto the arrival with the mouth puckering under the onslaught of very old Pot Still: the bitter-sweet sharpness one would expect from this is there in spades; oak present and correct and edged in thin muscovado layer; **f23.5** vanilla by the barrel-load, pithy fruit and softly spiced barley **b24** is this the whiskey where we see a blender truly come of age. Tall green hats off to Billy Leighton who has, as all the better blenders did in the past, worked his way from quality-testing barrels on the dumping room floor to the lab. With this stupendous offering we have a blender in clover for he has earned his Golden Shamrocks. If the blending alone wasn't stellar enough, then making this a 46%, non chill-filtered offering really does put the tin hat on it (so Billy: you really have been listening to me over the years...!!!) This is truly great whiskey, among the pantheon of the world's finest. 46%

Jameson Signature Reserve (93) n23.5 adore the sharp citrus notes which bore, shrapnel-like, into the firm, though lighter than normal pure Pot Still: supremely balanced; the degree of honey is exemplary...and enticing; **t23.5** gossamer light delivery despite the obvious Pot Still presence. Some caramel momentarily dulls the middle but the flavours return for a beautifully constructed middle with alternating waves of citrus and pot still, occasionally honeyed, much as the nose predicts; the grains are softer than an Irish bog and simply dissolve without fuss; most un-Midleton **f22.5** beautiful: the vanilla does pulse with acacia honey; the Pot sti stands firm and lightly fruity; **b23.5** be assured that Signature, with its clever structuring delicate and inter-weaving flavours, says far more about the blender, Billy Leighton, tha does John Jameson. 40%. *Irish Distillers.*

Kellan American oak cask **(84) n21 t22 f20 b21.** Safe whisky which is clean, sweet and showing many toffeed attributes. Decent spices, too. 40% (80 Proof). Cooley.

Kilbeggan bott code L7091 **(86) n21 t22 f21.5 b21.5.** A much more confident blend by comparison with that faltering one of the last few years. Here, the malts make a significant drive towards increasing the overall complexity and gentle citrus style. 40%. Cooley.

Kilbeggan 15 Years Old bott code L7048 **(85.5) n21.5 t22 f21 b21.** My word! 15 years, eh? How time flies! And on the subject of flying, surely I have winged my way back to Canada and am tasting a native blend. No, this is Irish albeit in sweet, deliciously rounded form. However, one cannot help feeling that the dark arts have been performed, as in an injection of caramel, which, as well as giving that Canadian feel has also probably shaved off some of the more complex notes to middle and finish. Even so, a sweet, silky experience. 40%. Cooley.

Kilbeggan 18 Year Old db **(89) n23** enough caramel to launch a thousand Mars bars. But beneath it can be found a wonderful Jaffa cake orange/chocolate theme and the most delicate of spices; **t21.5** that caramel does no harm in ensuring a lush texture. A string of light sugary notes deal with any encroaching oak; **f22.5** dries, allowing the spices to return for the excellent vanilla finale; **b22** although the impressive bottle lavishly claims "From the World's Oldest Distillery" I think one can take this as so much Blarney. It certainly had my researcher going, who lined this up for me under the Old Kilbeggan distillery, a forgivable mistake and one I think he will not be alone in making. This, so it appears on the palate, is a blend. From the quite excellent Cooley distillery, and it could be that whiskey used in this matured at Kilbeggan... which is another thing entirely. As for the whiskey: apart from some heavy handedness on the toffee, it really is quite a beautiful and delicate thing. 40%

Kilgeary bott code L8063 **(79) n20 t20 f19 b20.** There has always, and still proudly is, something strange about this blend. Cold tea on the nose and a bitter bite to the finish, sandwiches a brief flirtation with something sweet. 40%. Cooley.

Locke's bott code L8056 **(85.5) n21 t22 f21.5 b21.** Now, there you go!! Since I last really got round to analysing this one it has grown from a half-hearted kind of a waif to something altogether more gutsy and muscular. Sweeter, too, as the malts and grains combine harmoniously. A clean and pleasant experience with some decent malt fingerprints. 40%

Michael Collins A Blend (77) n19 t20 f19 b19. Michael Collins was known as the "big fellow". This pleasant, impressively spiced dram, might have enjoyed the same epithet had it not surrendered to and then been strangled by caramel on the finish. 40% (80 proof). Cooley.

Midleton Distillery Reserve (85) n22 t22 f20 b21. A whiskey which, for all its muscovado sweetness offers some memorable barley moments. 40%. Irish Distillers Midleton Distillery only. Changes character slightly with each new vatting. This one is some departure.

Midleton Very Rare 1984 (70) n19 t18 f17 b16. Disappointing with little backbone or balance. 40%. Irish Distillers.

Midleton Very Rare 1985 (77) n20 t20 f18 b19. Medium-bodied and oily, this is a big improvement on the initial vintage. 40%. Irish Distillers.

Midleton Very Rare 1986 (79) n21 t20 f18 b20. A very malty Midleton richer in character than previous vintages. 40%. Irish Distillers.

Midleton Very Rare 1987 (77) n20 t19 f19 b19. Quite oaky at first until a late surge of excellent pot still. 40%. Irish Distillers.

Midleton Very Rare 1988 (86) n23 t21 f21 b21. A landmark MVR as it is the first vintage to celebrate the Irish pot-still style. 40%. Irish Distillers.

Midleton Very Rare 1989 (87) n22 t22 f22 b21. A real mouthful but has lost balance to achieve the effect. 40%. Irish Distillers.

Midleton Very Rare 1990 (93) n23 carrying on from where the '89 left off. The pot still doesn't drill itself so far into your sinuses, perhaps: more of a firm massage; **t23** solid pot still again. There is a pattern now: pot still first, sweeter, maltier notes second, pleasant grains third and somewhere, imperceptibly, warming spices fill in the gaps; **f24** long and Redbreast-like in character. Spices seep from the bourbon casks; **b23** astounding whiskey: one of the vintages every true Irish whiskey lover should hunt for. 40%. Irish Distillers.

Midleton Very Rare 1991 (76) n19 t20 f19 b18. After the Lord Mayor's Show, relatively dull and uninspiring. 40%. Irish Distillers.

Midleton Very Rare 1992 (84) n20 t20 f23 b21. Superb finish with outstanding use of feisty grain. 40%. Irish Distillers.

Midleton Very Rare 1993 (88) n21 t22 f23 b22. big, brash and beautiful – the perfect way to celebrate the 10th-ever bottling of MVR. 40%. Irish Distillers.

Midleton Very Rare 1994 (87) n22 t22 f21 b22. Another different style of MVR, one of mazing lushness. 40%. Irish Distillers.

Midleton Very Rare 1995 (90) n23 big pot still with fleeting honey; **t24** enormous! Bitter, eet and tart all together for a chewable battle of apple and barley. Brilliant; **b21** some mel calms proceedings, but Java coffee goes a little way to restoring complexity; **b22**

they don't come much bigger than this. Prepare a knife and fork to battle through this one. Fabulous. *40%. Irish Distillers.*

Midleton Very Rare 1996 (82) n21 t22 f19 b20. The grains lead a soft course, hardened by subtle pot still. Just missing a beat on the finish, though. *40%. Irish Distillers.*

Midleton Very Rare 1997 (83) n22 t21 f19 b21. The piercing pot still fruitiness of the nose is met by a countering grain of rare softness on the palate. Just dies on the finish when you want it to make a little speech. Very drinkable. *40%. Irish Distillers.*

Midleton Very Rare 1999 (89) n21 t23 f22 b23. One of the maltiest Midletons of all time: a superb blend. *40%. Irish Distillers.*

Midleton Very Rare 2000 (85) n22 t21 f21 b21. An extraordinary departure even by Midleton's eclectic standards. The pot still is like a distant church spire in an hypnotic Fen landscape. *40%. Irish Distillers.*

Midleton Very Rare 2001 (79) n21 t20 f18 b20. Extremely light but the finish is slightly on the bitter side. *40%. Irish Distillers.*

Midleton Very Rare 2002 (79) n20 t22 f18 b19. The nose is rather subdued and the finish is likewise toffee-quiet and shy. There are some fabulous middle moments, some of flashing genius, when the pot still and grain combine for a spicy kick, but the finish really is lacklustre and disappointing. *40%. Irish Distillers.*

Midleton Very Rare 2003 (84) n22 t22 f19 b21. Beautifully fruity on both nose and palate (even some orange blossom on aroma). But the delicious spicy richness that is in mid launch on the tastebuds is cut short by caramel on the middle and finish. A crying shame, but the best Midleton for a year or two. *40%. Irish Distillers.*

Midleton Very Rare 2004 (82) n21 t21 f19 b21. Yet again caramel is the dominant feature, though some quite wonderful citrus and spice escape the toffeed blitz. *40%.*

Midleton Very Rare 2005 (92) n23 t24 f22 b23. OK, you can take this one only as a rough translation. The sample I have worked from here is from the Irish Distillers blending lab, reduced to 40% in mine but without caramel added. And, as Midleton Very Rares always are at this stage, it's an absolute treat. Never has such a great blend suffered so in the hands of colouring and here the chirpiness of the pot still and élan of the honey (very Jameson Gold Label in part) show just what could be on offer given half the chance. Has wonderful natural colour and surely it is a matter of time before we see this great whiskey in its natural state. *40%*

Midleton Very Rare 2006 (92) n22 real punch to the grain, which is there in force and offering a bourbony match for the pot still; **t24** stupendously crisp, then a welter of spices nip and sting ferociously around the palate; the oaky coffee arrives early and with clarity while the barley helps solidify the rock-hard barley; **f23** usually by now caramel intervenes and spoils, but not this time and again it's the grain which really stars; **b23** as raw as a Dublin rough-house and for once not overly swamped with caramel. An uncut diamond. *40%*

Midleton Very Rare 2007 (83) n20 t22 f20 b21. Annoyingly buffeted from nose to finish by powering caramel. Some sweeter wisps do escape but the aroma suggests Canadian and insufficient Pot Still gets through to make this a Midleton of distinction. *40%. Irish Distillers*

Midleton Very Rare 2008 (88.5) n22 t23 f21.5 b22. A dense bottling which offers considerably more than the 2007 Vintage. Attractive, very drinkable and without the caramel it might really have hit the heights. *40%. Irish Distillers.*

⁙ **Midleton Very Rare 2009 (95) n24** oh, wow! the best post bottling nose I have ever found on a Midleton, though a few pre-bottlings have exceeded it in grace. Just. This is the fruitiest I can remember, for sure, with a wonderful sherry trifle feel, only with the extra firmness of Irish pot still. A little avocado pear creaminess also goes a long way; **t24** it is that creaminess which shows first on delivery, alongside a plethora of crisp, dark sugary notes which appear to shadow the pot still character; the star is the contra deal between the soft oils and the rock hard pot still...stunning **f23** remains clean with far more complexity than a Midleton usually retains; the spices are busy and appear to pulse and vary in intensity; **b24** I've been waiting a few years for one like this to come along. One of the most complex, cleanest and least caramel-spoiled bottlings for a good few years and one which makes the pot still character its centre piece. A genuine celebration of all things Midleton and Barry Crockett's excellence as a distiller in particular. *40%. Irish Distillers.*

⁙ **Midleton Very Rare 2010 (84) n21 t22 f20 b21.** A case of after the Lord Mayor's Show. Chewy and some decent sugars. But hard to make out detail through the fog of caramel. *40%*

⁙ **Midleton Very Rare 2011 (81.5) n22.5 t20 f19 b20** Another disappointing version where the colour of its personality has been compromised for the sake of the colour in the bottle. A dullard of a whiskey, especially after the promising nose. *40%. Irish Distillers.*

Millars Special Reserve bott code L8069 **(86) n21 t22 f21.5 b21.5.** Now that's some improvement on the last bottling of this I found, with spices back with abandon and grains ensuring a fine mouthfeel. Even the chocolate fudge at the death is a treat. *40%. Cooley.*

Morrisons Irish Whiskey bott code L10028 **(78) n19 t20 f19 b20.** Sweet, pleasant and inoffensive. *40%. Wm Morrison Supermarket.*

Paddy (74) **n18.5 t20 f17.5 b18.** Cleaned its act up a little. Even a touch of attractive citrus on the nose and delivery. But where does that cloying sweetness come from? As bland as an Irish peat bog but, sadly, nothing like so potentially tasty. *40%. Irish Distillers.*

Powers (91) **n23** rugged pot still and beefed up by some pretty nippy grain; **t24** brilliant mouth arrival, one of the best in all Ireland: the pot still shrieks and attacks every available tastebud; **f22** pulsing spices and mouthwatering, rock-hard pot still. The sweetness is a bit unusual but you can just chew that barley; **b22** is it any coincidence that in this bottling the influence of the caramel has been significantly reduced and the whiskey is getting back to its old, brilliant self? I think not. Classic stuff. *40%. Irish Distillers.*

Powers Gold Label (87) n22 Powers? Really? I had to look twice and re-pour the sample to ensure this was the right stuff. Where is the clunking pot still? Soft, grainy caramel; **t22** attractively sweet with a distinct candy tobacco golden syrup but a serious departure from the ancient style. It's grain all the way, soft and silky as she goes; **f21** more lightness and caramel; maybe some semblance of pot still but you have to hunt to find it; **b22** the solid pot still, the very DNA of what made Powers, well, Powers is vanishing in front of our very noses. Yes, still some pot still around, but nothing like so pronounced in the way that made this, for decades, a truly one-off Irish and one of the world greats. Still delightful and with many charms but the rock hard pot still effect is sadly missed. What is going on here? *40%. Irish Distillers.*

Redbreast Blend (88) n23 some genuinely telling pot-still hardness sparks like a flint off the no less unyielding grain. Just love this; **t23** very sweet and soft, the grain carrying a massive amount of vanilla. Barley offers some riches, as does spice; **f20** a climbdown from the confrontational beginnings, but pretty delicious all the same; **b22** really impressed with this one-off bottling for Dillons the Irish wine merchants. Must try and get another bottle before they all vanish. *40%. Irish Distillers for Dillone IR (not to be confused with Redbreast 12 Years Old Pure Pot Still)*

Sainsbury's Blended Irish Whiskey (86.5) n22 t22 f21 b21.5. A beautifully relaxed blend showing pretty clearly – literally, thanks to an admirable lack of colouring - just how good the Cooley grain whiskey is even at no great age. Clean with a deceptively busy and intense flavour profile. Far too good for the cola the back label says this should go with... *40%. UK.*

St Patrick bott code L030907 **(77) n19 t20 f19 b19.** Good grief! No prisoners here as we have either a bitter oakiness or mildly cloying sweetness, rarely working in tandem. A few gremlins for the Kremlin. *40%. Cooley for Russia.*

Strangford Gold (81) n20 t21 f20 b20. A simplistic, exceptionally easy drinking blend with high quality grain offering silk to the countering spice but caramel flattens any malt involvement. *40%. The Feckin Drinks Co.*

Tesco Special Reserve Irish Whiskey bott code L8061 **(89.5) n21.5** gentle caramels try – and fail – to intervene as the vivid malts and seductive grains fuse; **t23.5** Irish blends don't come any softer: Cooley grain is as good as it gets anywhere in the word and here embrace and amplify the malts wonderfully; **f22** gentle, soft, sweet and clean; **b22.5** a cracker of a blend which allows the malts full scope to do their juicy bit. Possibly more malt than usual for a Cooley blend, but as they say: every little bit helps. *40%. Cooley.*

Tullamore Dew (85) n22 t21.5 f20.5 b21. The days of the throat being savaged by this one appear to be over. Much more pot still character from nose to finish and the rough edges remain, attractively, just that. *40%. Campbell & Cochrane Group.*

Tullamore Dew 10 Years Old (81.5) n21 t21.5 f19 b20. A bright start from this new kid on the Tullamore block. Soft fruit and harder pot still make some kind of complexity, but peters out at the death. *40%. Campbell & Cochrane Group.*

Tullamore Dew 12 Years Old (84.5) n21.5 t21.5 f20 b21.5. Silky thanks to some excellent Midleton grain: there are mouthwatering qualities here that make the most of the soft spices and gentle fruit. An improved whiskey, if still somewhat meek and shy. *40%. Campbell & Cochrane Group.*

Tullamore Dew Black 43 (85) n19 t22 f22.5 b21.5. "Black". Now there's an original name for a new whiskey. Don't think it'll catch on, personally: after all, who has ever heard of a whisky being called "This or That" Black...?? But the whiskey might. Once you get past the usual Tullamore granite-like nose, here even more unyielding than usual, some rather engaging and complex (and especially spicy) things happen, though the caramel does its best to neuter them. *43%. William Grant & Sons.*

Tullamore Dew Heritage (78) n20 t21 f18 b19. Tedious going with the caramel finish a real turn off. *40.0%. Campbell & Cochrane Group.*

Waitrose Irish Whiskey (86.5) n21.5 t22 f21.5 b21.5. Cooley's grain whiskey, about as good a grain made anywhere in the world, is in fine voice here. Pity some toffee stifles it slightly. *40%*

Walker & Scott Irish Whiskey "Copper Pot Distilled" (83) n20 t22 f20 b21. A collectors' item. This charming, if slightly fudgy-finished blend was made by Cooley as the house Irish for one of Britain's finest breweries. Sadly, someone put "Copper Pot Distilled" on the label, which, as it's a blend, can hardly be the case. And even if it wasn't a blend, would still be confusing in terms of Irish whiskey, there not being any traditional Irish Pot Still, that mixture of malted and unmalted barley. So Sam's, being one of the most traditional brewers in Britain, with the next bottling changed the label by dropping all mention of pot still. Top marks, chaps! The next bottling can be seen below. 40%. Sam Smith's.

Walker & Scott Irish Whiskey (85) n21 t22 f21 b21. Oddly, sharper grain has helped give his some extra edge through the toffee. A very decent blend. 40%

The Wild Geese Classic Blend (80.5) n20 t21 f19.5 b19. Easy going, pretty neutral and conservative. If you are looking for zip, zest and charisma you've picked the wrong goose (see below). 40%. Cooley for Avalon.

The Wild Geese Limited Edition Fourth Centennial (93) n23 sensationally clean and with the citrus really taking a starring role; vanillas abound, but in the soft, playful form; light and just so enticing; t23.5 barley notes peck around the tastebuds entirely unfettered by more tactile and heavier elements; lithe and lean, there is no fat on this goose and the vanilla lives up to its best expectation given on the nose while the mouth is drenched in salivating promises – simply stunning; f23 Just so light, the clarity of the barley sugar and vanilla leaves you purring; b23.5 a limited edition of unlimited beauty. One of the lightest, subtle, intriguing and quite simply disarming Irish whiskeys on the market. As a bird and whiskey lover, this is one goose that I shall be looking out for. 43%. Cooley for Avalon

The Wild Geese Rare Irish (89.5) n22 some toffee, yes, but the excellence of the vanilla is there to behold; just a light layering of barley but the gentle citrus caresses with the more exquisite touch... t23 superb arrival on the palate; the grain displays nothing other than excellence in both weight and control, and while the oaks and caramels are a tad bitter, the sweeter barley compensates wonderfully; f22 a silky, almost metallic sheen to the finale which complements the drying vanillins; b22.5 just love this. The Cooley grain is working sublimely and dovetails with the malt in the same effortless way wild geese fly in perfect formation. A treat. 43%. Cooley for Avalon.

Writers Tears (93) n23.5 a glossy Pot Still character: rather than the usual fruity firmness, the recognisable Pot Still traits are shrouded in soft honey tones which dovetail with lightening kumquat-citrus tones. Quite a curious, but always deliciously appealing animal...; t24 works beautifully well: the arrival is an alternating delivery of hard and soft waves, the former showing a more bitter, almost myopic determination to hammer home its traditional pot still standpoint; the sweeter, more yielding notes dissolve with little or no resistance, leaving an acacia honeyed trail; towards the middle a juicier malt element mingles with soft vanilla but the Pot Still character never goes away; f22 relatively short with perhaps the Pot Still, with an old-fashioned cough sweet fruitiness, lingering longest, though its does retain its honeyed accompaniment for the most part; b23.5 now that really was different. The first mix of pure Pot Still and single malt I have knowingly come across in a commercial bottling, but only because I wasn't aware of the make up of last year's Irishman Blend. The malt, like the Pot Still, is, I understand from proprietor Bernard Walsh, from Midleton, but the two styles mixed shows a remarkably similar character to when I carried out an identical experiment with pure pot still and Bushmills the best part of a decade ago. A success and hopefully not a one off. Which is more than I can say for the label, a whiskey collectors – sorry, collector's – item in its own right. There is a wonderfully Irish irony that a whiskey dedicated to Ireland's extraordinary literary heritage should be represented by a label, even a brand name, so punctually inept; it's almost brilliant. The reason for the Writers (sic) Tears, if from the spirits of James Joyce, Samuel Beckett, George Bernard Shaw, Oscar Wilde and perhaps even Maurice Walsh, whose grandson became a legendary blender at Irish Distillers, will be open to debate: we will never know whether they laughed or cried. As far as the actual whiskey is concerned, though, I am sure they, to a man, would have no hesitation but to pen the most luminous and positive critiques possible. 40%. Writers Tears Whiskey Co.

Writer's Tears Cask Strength bott 2011 **(90.5)** n23 a thick nose with honey and butterscotch, but dulled by caramels; t22 a mouth-watering delivery is mildly out of context with the degree of acceleration of toffee and vanilla f22.5 livens up towards the finish as some world-class spices begin to fizz. More accent on the hard-guy/soft-guy approach the two Pure Irish Pot still and malt whiskey styles evoke; b23 sometimes seems a rabble of whiskey with the flavours and shapes never quite deciding where it wants to go. But the randomness of the style is also a strength as you are entertained from first to last, though the caramels do keep the lid on some of the more honeyed moments. And memo to brand proprietor Bernard Walsh: only one mistake on your back label this time... 53%. Hot Irishman. 1200 bottles.

American Whiskey

Not that long ago American whiskey meant Bourbon. Or perhaps a very close relation called Tennessee. And sometimes it meant rye. Though nothing like often as it did prior to prohibition. Very, very rarely, though, did it ever get called single malt, because virtually none was made on the entire North American continent. That was a specialist - and very expensive - type left to the Scots and, to a lesser extent, the Irish. Or even the Japanese if a soldier or businessman was flying back from Tokyo.

I say "virtually" none was made because, actually, there was the odd batch of malt produced in America and, in my library, I still have some distilled at a rye distillery in Maryland in the early 1970s - indeed, I remember drinking the stuff back in 1974. But it was hardly a serious commercial concern and the American public were never made greatly aware of it.

Now, though, at last count it appears that there are at least 25 distilleries doing their best to make whiskey mainly from malted barley but sometimes from rye and corn, too. Some still have much to learn, others have shown that they are well on their way to possible greatness. One distillery, Stranahan's in Colorado, has in a very short space of time managed to bring out a series of bottlings which left no doubt that they have joined McCarthy's of Oregon and Anchor of California in achieving it with another Portland distiller, Edgefield, not that far behind. Balcones of Waco, Texas, is also now among the micro elite.

As a collective movement it is by far the most exciting in the entire whisky world, despite what is happening in certain parts of Europe, especially Germany, Austria, Switzerland and Scandinavia which is expanding by the day. It appears to me that the better "micro distillers" are just a little more advanced in the US and have a stronger urge to grow. Some new wave American distillers, doubtless, will fall by the wayside while others will take their place. But those at the vanguard are likely to act as the spur to keep the others moving onwards and it is a situation I shall monitor very closely. There are squabbles about whether enzymes should be used for fermentation, a question I have been asked about many times. My view is that they should be avoided, although I can understand the reasons for their employment. However, when you are witnessing the birth of an entirely new whiskey life form it is always fascinating to see how it naturally develops. Usually the strongest live and the weakest die. In this survival of the fittest it will soon become apparent which methods are the ones that will succeed - and they tend to be the ones which have served distillers well over the last couple of centuries.

There is no little irony, however, that as we take a closer look at the alternative distilling world within the United States, it is the old order which has now really caught the eye. As I suspected, my award to Sazerac Rye 18 Years Old as Jim Murray's Whisky Bible 2010 World Whisky of the Year bemused quite a number of whisky lovers because it represents a style of whiskey they never as much seen, let alone tasted. Doubtless Thomas Handy rye being named the World's finest for this 2013 Whisky Bible will cause no less consternation.

However, it is worth remembering something that is too easily overlooked in today's "what's the next trick?" whisky world. There is a very good reason why bourbon and rye whiskey from Kentucky and nearby Indiana is today head and shoulders above all other whisky styles around the globe. It is because the high standards set in distillation are perfectly matched by the high quality of the barrels the spirit is placed into, so maturation techniques are uncompromisingly good. While the Scots in particular reel from the influx of hideously substandard sherry butts, not to mention many a dud from France, the Kentuckians have their own laws as to what makes a bourbon. It means they are so far out ahead quality-wise from the rest, they have yet to believe and understand their extraordinary position. Still, some believe, if the Scots are doing it, it must be right. It is a train of thought at which some of us are in a position to raise a quizzical eyebrow.

So maybe it is no surprise that the worst two bourbons I tasted for this year's Bible was one that had been corked. And the other finished in a Cognac barrel. That is not in line with the great tradition of bourbon, even as a boutique bottling. Because, as I have seen elsewhere over the years, once one company starts, others feel duty-bound that they have to follow. The decision is usually that of the marketeers, who may not entirely understand just how great and unique their whisky is. At the moment, Kentucky holds the aces, but is in danger of handing one or two in for a deuce. Around the world, people are being switching on to the unique beauty of great ryes and bourbons. Don't try and fix what's not broken...

Kentucky & Tennessee

Pernod Ricard Seagram Distillery

KY

Louisville • Frankfort

Wild Turkey
Four Roses

Clermont
Boston
Maker's Mark

Bardstown

Nashville

TN

George Dickel
Jack Daniel

Key
• Major Town or City
▲ Distillery

Bardstown
 Heaven Hill
 Tom Moore
Frankfort
 Buffalo Trace

Woodford Reserve
Louisville
Early Times
Bernheim
Stitzel Weller

Bourbon Distilleries

Bourbon confuses people. Often they don't even realise it is a whiskey, a situation not helped by leading British pub chains, such as Wetherspoon, whose bar menus list "whiskey" and "bourbon" in separate sections. And if I see the liqueur Southern Comfort listed as a bourbon one more time I may not be responsible for my actions.

Bourbon is a whiskey. It is made from grain and matured in oak, so really it can't be much else. To be legally called bourbon it must have been made with a minimum of 51% corn and matured in virgin oak casks for at least two years. Oh, and no colouring can be added other than that which comes naturally from the barrel.

Where it does differ, from, say Scotch, is that the straight whiskey from the distillery may be called by something other than that distillery name. Indeed, the distillery may change its name which has happened to two this year already and two others in the last three or four. So, to make things easy and reference as quick as possible, I shall list the Kentucky-based distilleries first and then their products in alphabetical order along with their owners and operational status.

BUFFALO TRACE Leestown, Frankfort. Sazerac. Operating.

BROWN-FORMAN Shively, Louisville. Brown-Forman. Operating.

FOUR ROSES Lawrenceburg. Kirin. Operating

HEAVEN HILL BERNHEIM DISTILLERY Louisville. Heaven Hill. Operating.

JIM BEAM Boston and Clermont. Fortune Brands. Operating.

MAKER'S MARK Loretto. Fortune Brands. Operating.

TOM MOORE Bardstown. Sazerac. Operating.

WILD TURKEY Lawrenceburg. Campari Group. Operating.

WOODFORD RESERVE Near Millville. Brown-Forman. Operating.

Bourbon

Ancient Age (74.5) n18 t18.5 f19 b19. Basic: no frills and certainly no thrills until some late oils and spices kick in. 40%

Ancient Age 90 Proof (86.5) n21 t23 f21.5 b22. If this is supposed to be the same whiskey as standard AA, but with just extra strength, you wouldn't know it. Here the oils have reduced considerably and in their place a quite beautiful tapestry of lively spice and rich, sweetened tannins arrive from the first moment...and last most of the course. More than just a passing nod to this distillery's glory. 45%

Ancient Ancient Age 10 Star (94.5) n23 no pussyfooting here: an immediate lurch into oranges and a firmer, fruitier rye foundation. Of its type (the quiet and understatedly sophisticated) about as good as it gets, nose-wise; **t24** those fruit tones on the nose hit the taste buds running: fresh but allowing the lightly oiled texture to let the soft corn and strapping rye melt together; plenty of chocolate and fudge to entertain, too; also, the spices - which again attack early - do so with rare chivalry; **f23.5** long, with the emphasis always on the custardy oak but the rye notes refuse to go down without a last hurrah; **b24** a bourbon which has slipped effortlessly through the gears over the last decade. It is now cruising and offers so many nuggets of pure joy this is now a must have for the serious bourbon devotee. Now a truly great bourbon which positively revels in its newfound complexity: a new 10 Star is born... 45%

Ancient Age Bonded (92) n23 showing off big time with a fabulous marriage of iron glove and velvet: pounding rye is the glove, a medley of delicate citrus and even, astoundingly, rose petals represents the velvet...; **t24** sumptuous and mouth-filling, the corn adds first flavours and then the oils. Not far behind comes a beautiful mixture of rye-fruitiness and cocoa and then relaxed but serious pounding of light spices; **f23** loses its depth slightly as the chalkier elements of the oak take hold; even so, just enough time for some blood orange to arrive and mingle with the spiced chocolate; **b23** unmistakably Buffalo Trace bourbon...with balls. 50%

Ancient Ancient Age 10 Years Old (96) n23.5 busy, tangy, sharp, rounded, sweet in part - dry in others...an aroma full of contrasts but sings faultlessly for the duration; **t24** almost impossible to spit...the flavours are just so complex, the weight so astonishingly even. This is a marriage between the AAA 10 of about 20 years ago when the story was all about the subtlety of the delicate oak and the more recent version which is an oilier, more robust rye and weightier tannin...viva la difference...!! viva la sameness...!!!; **f24** lightens with several degrees of custardy vanilla serving to accentuate the power of the juicy rye; the oils act as ballast for the almost mesmeric, butterfly-like flightiness of the smaller grains and accompanying, lightly scorched, Demerara sugars **b24.5** this whiskey is like shifting sands: same score as last time out, but the shape is quite different again. Somehow underlines the genius of the distillery that a world class whiskey can reach the same point of greatness, but by taking two different routes...However, in this case the bourbon actually finds something a little extra to move it on to a point very few whiskeys very rarely reach... 43%

Baker's Aged 7 Years bott no. L1074CLA **(89.5) n23** chocolate orange and honey dew melon... pretty attractive even though the oak is taking no prisoners; **t22.5** much more oak than you might expect from a 7-year-old: high roast coffee lightened by a sprinkling of sugar and vanilla; **f22** the toasty hickory and soft corn oil makes for a slightly bitter but soft landing; **b22** infinitely more intense and complex than a few years back: further proof that Beam whiskey is very much improving. Superb whiskey but, if anything, too old for its age... 53.5%

Basil Hayden's 8 Years Old (78) n20 t20 f19 b19. A thin bourbon which never quite finds anchor. Certainly one of the most citrusy bourbons around, but, overall, more Basil Fawlty as this is a bit of a strange, mildly neurotic character. 40%

Benchmark (86) n21 t22 f21.5 b21.5. Unquestionably a better whiskey than once it was with now an entirely well constructed vanilla-sugar depth adding ballast where once there was none. Lovely unexpected spices, too. A real surprise after not having tasted for a couple of years...as, frankly, it hadn't been worth it. Now it is... 40%

Benchmark No. 8 (79) n20 t21 f19 b19. Thinner in body and character than the standard Benchmark. Papery sweetness, but little of the balancing spice of its stablemate. 40%

Benjamin Prichard's Double Barrelled Bourbon 9 Years Old (94.5) n24.5 double chocolate, it appears... as usual a stunning nose from Prichard. Crisp rye and crisper apple teams with equally firm Demerara and liquorice but that chocolate plus corn and vanilla offers the countering softness required; a mega bourbon nose...; **t24.5** like the nose, absolutely breathtaking intensity which spells bourbon with every atom; spellbinding balance between the maple syrup sweetness and the drier vanillas; the corn really does have a major input in flavour **f22** oils and dries out a fraction and some cocoa returns, but remains chewy; **b23.5** if only they could bottle that nose...oh, they have...!!! Just wonderful whiskey. 40%

Blanton's (92) n21.5 t24 f23 b23.5. If it were not for the sluggish nose this would be a Whisky Bible Liquid Gold award winner for sure. On the palate it shows just why little can touch Buffalo Trace for quality at the moment... 40%

Blanton's Gold Original Single Barrel (96.5) n24 a thumping barrage of old honey forgotten in a jar with lavender and leather; **t24.5** rarely does a flavour profile follow the nose so faithfully. Here it also confirms the weight and texture; this is pure chewability. One of the most honeyed middles on the circuit with liquorice, usually ballast, here actually thinning things down a little; the spices hit an early crescendo and then buzz contentedly; **f24** long and remains absolutely unblemished and on a steady course. The honey remains intact; soft vanillas joins the liquorice while the spices just carry on...and on... **b24** it is improbable that a whiskey this enormous and with so many star turns can glide so effortlessly over the palate. One of the best Blanton's in years, this is true Gold standard... 46.5% (93 Proof)

Blanton's 80 Proof (89) n22 t23 f22 b22. Simplistic, soft and full of water-down honey. I doubt you'd say no to a second one... 40%

Blanton's Takara (91.5) n24.5 fabulous orange blossom mingles delightfully with candyfloss wisps of vanilla and icing sugar. A threat of vanilla, celery and spice add the only weight required. One of the most delicate, sexy noses of the whiskey year... **t23** here we go...as expected, almost so light, the flavours land on the taste buds with all the force of feathers settling on the ground from ripped pillow; it is those soft sugars which lead the way, but dissolving before reaching the middle leaving the vanilla in charge; **f22** a little bitterness creeps in with the marmalade; **b22** not quite how many people might envisage a bourbon: certainly not butch enough to keep the wild west gunslingers happy. No this is a bourbon which searches for your feminine side. And being so light, leaves itself open for any off-key bitter notes which might just happen along the way. 49% (98 proof)

Blanton's Uncut/Unfiltered (96.5) n25 t24 f23.5 b24. Uncut. Unfiltered. Unbelievable. 65.9%

⁘ **Booker's 7 Years 0 Months** batch C03 1 16 **(92.5) n22.5** honey on toast; **t23.5** a rumbling, rambling thickly coated feast of spiced liquorice, handsomely topped with vanilla and a late infusion of molasses; **f23** superb oils ensure a long, classy and silky textured finale. Some burned toast is crumbled into the mix for the finish which shows age well above its years; **b23.5** the alcohol may be big but it hardly makes an impact against the enormity of the huge ok statement. Big, seriously fascinating whiskey. 63.7% (1274 Proof)

Booker's 7 Years 4 Months batch no. C03-1-17 **(95.5) n24 t25 f22.5 b24.** The best Booker's I have tasted for a very long while, probably ever. Absolutely world class whiskey. 64%

⁘ **Booker's 7 Years 4 Months** batch C04-A-28 **(92.5) n23** the usual butch bourbon biffing: meaty, high octane liquorice; manuka honey; **t24** a delivery which sends you flying back against your seat: about as roasty as they come with hickory doused in chilli-spiced Demerara sugar; **f22** perhaps a little too raw with the sugars vanishing quickly; **b23.5** you can always guarantee Booker's to entertain and wow you. No exception here. 63.55% (1281 proof)

Bowman Brother's Virginia Straight Bourbon (90) n21 strangely dry and dusty; **t23** deceptively rich, with a pulsing honey and spice theme, **f23** long. The dark sugars melt impressively into the drier vanillas; **b23** quietly confident and complex: a bit of a gem waiting to be discovered. 45% (90 proof)

Buffalo Trace (92.5) n23 a corn-utopia of lightly sugared oils; plenty of custard, too...; **t23** juicy and salivating delivery then many long, slow waves of corn dashing over the oak; traces of weightier liquorice and muscovado sugars; **f23.5** huge vanilla and a real silkiness to the profound corn; **b23** easily one of the lightest BTs I have tasted in a very long while. The rye has not just taken a back seat, but has fallen off the bus. 45% ⊙⊙

Buffalo Trace Master Distiller Emeritus Elmer T Lee Collector's Edition bott. 06/09/11 **(96) n24.5** no shy rye here with a firm, slightly peppery attack and a honeyed counter balance. Sublime... **t24** the spices grab the taste buds by their throats...and then promptly gives the soft, lightly corn-oiled, delicately honeyed kisses. A few shafts of liquorice confirms there is some very serious bourbon-ness going on here; **f23.5** long, with the accent on dry oaks, a burnt caramel sweetness and a re-entering of the firm rye which seals the deal **b24** simply spellbinding. One of the best BT bottlings I have ever enjoyed for bourbon rarely comes more understatedly complete and complex than this. This is the bottle with a nickel coin glued to it. And each complex character within this whiskey gets more than its five cents worth... 45%

Buffalo Trace Single Oak Project Barrel #132 (r1yKA1 see key below) db **(95) n24** busy rye: at once sharp and fruity while simultaneously displaying impressive layers of caramel and liquorice. Complex, exceptionally well profiled and leaves no ambiguity as to regard its high class status; **t23.5** the delivery, like the nose, appears to enjoy two simultaneous entry levels. At the same moment those sharp rye notes appear to be messages carved in granite; this surrounded by a light caramel fog, seemingly ungraspable yet obviously there and having an effect. The next round of flavour centre on varied cocoa notes as well as a variance of textures, especially as the corn oil seeps in; as usual for this distillery, the sugars are of a crisp Demerara/muscovado type, vivid at first but happily becoming background noise as the complexity levels increase; **f23.5** long, with the vanilla, cocoa and corn now dominating to the fade, the rye little more than a distant echo; **b24** this sample struck me for possessing, among the first batch of bottlings, the classic Buffalo Trace personality. Afterwards they revealed that it was of a profile which perhaps most closely matches their standard 8-year-old BT. Therefore it is this one I shall use as the tasting template. *45% (90 Proof)*

Key to Buffalo Trace Single Oak Project Codes

Mash bill type: r = rye; w = wheat
Tree grain: 1 = course; 2 = average; 3 = tight
Tree cut: x = top half; y = bottom half
Warehouse type: K = rick; L = concrete

Entry strength: A = 125; B = 105
Seasoning: 1 = 6 Months; 2 = 12 Months
Char: All #4 except * = #3

❧ **Buffalo Trace Single Oak Project Barrel #1** (r3xKA1*) db (**90.5**) n22 t23 f23 b22.5. Soft corn oil aroma, buttery, big sugars building, silky texture, long. *45% (90 Proof)*

Buffalo Trace Single Oak Project Barrel #3 (r2xKA1) db (**90.5**) n22.5 t23 f22.5 b22.5. Nutty, dry aroma; apple fruitiness and brown sugars. *45% (90 Proof)*

Buffalo Trace Single Oak Project Barrel #4 (r2yKA1) db (**92**) n23 t23 f23 b23. Exceptionally crisp; sharp rye, honeycomb, big liquorice. *45% (90 Proof)*

❧ **Buffalo Trace Single Oak Project Barrel #8** (r3yLA1) db (**92.5**) n23 t23 f23.5 b23. Crisp rye aroma. Fruity, firm, salivating. Spiced toffee and muscovado; toasty. 45% (90 Proof)

❧ **Buffalo Trace Single Oak Project Barrel #10** (r3yKA2*) db (**93**) n23.5 t23.5 f22.5 b23.5. Rich, delicate rye. Complex, busy body; rye oils, tannins; slow sugar build. Bitters. 45%

❧ **Buffalo Trace Single Oak Project Barrel #14** (r3yLA2*) db (**95**) n24 t24 f23 b24. Chocolate rye nose and body; silky texture; brown sugar and vanilla; rye-rich sweet finish. *45%*

❧ **Buffalo Trace Single Oak Project Barrel #17** (r3xKB1*)db (**88.5**) n21.5 t22.5 f22.5 b22. Liquorice nose; oily body sweetens; big vanilla, caramel; dull spice. *45% (90 Proof)*

❧ **Buffalo Trace Single Oak Project Barrel #24** (r3xLB1) db (**90**) n22 t23 f22.5 b22.5. Big liquorice nose and delivery; toffee raisin; big corn oil; medium spice; even ulmo honey. *45%*

Buffalo Trace Single Oak Project Barrel #29 (r3xLB2*) db (**91**) n23 t22.5 f23 b22.5. Crisp rye nose; more precise grain. Excellent spices. *45% (90 Proof)*

Buffalo Trace Single Oak Project Barrel #31 (r3xLB2) db (**87.5**) n22 t22 f21.5 b22. Dull, rumbling and herbal; oily caramel and sugars. Soft. *45% (90 Proof)*

❧ **Buffalo Trace Single Oak Project Barrel #33** (w3xKA1*) db (**94.5**) n24 t23.5 f23 b24. Huge, busy baking spiced cake; muscovado sugar delivery; remains sweet, silky and spicy; 45%

Buffalo Trace Single Oak Project Barrel #35 (w3xKA1) db (**89.5**) n22 t22 f23 b22.5. Soft mint, yeasty; soft toffee delivery, builds in spice. *45% (90 Proof)*

Buffalo Trace Single Oak Project Barrel #36 (w3yKA1) db (**91.5**) n23 t23 f22.5 b23. Vague rum and toffee; bold, salivating, slow spice. *45% (90 Proof)*

❧ **Buffalo Trace Single Oak Project Barrel #40** (w3xLA1) db (**93**) n23 t23 f23.5 b23.5. Soft, spiced cake, big citrus; silky, oily, bananas and golden syrup; late spice, balancing bitters. *45%*

❧ **Buffalo Trace Single Oak Project Barrel #42** (w3yKA2*) db (**85.5**) n22 t21.5 f21 b21. Tight nose opens slowly; sultana pudding with maple syrup. Sweet, late bitterness; 45%

❧ **Buffalo Trace Single Oak Project Barrel #46** (w3yLA2*) db (**88**) n21.5 t22 f22.5 b22 Doughy aroma. Big corn oils and sugars. Late spice growth. Big vanilla. Quietly complex. *45%*

❧ **Buffalo Trace Single Oak Project Barrel #49** (w3xKB1) db (**93**) n24 t23 f23 b23. Chocolate spice, apples, oaky aroma; treacle pudding, soft oils; banana and custard; bitters. *45%*

❧ **Buffalo Trace Single Oak Project Barrel #56** (w3yLB1) db (**91**) n24 t22.5 f22 b22.5. Chocolate vanilla and tannins; soft, slow build up of spice, oily; bitters. *45% (90 Proof)*

Buffalo Trace Single Oak Project Barrel #61 (w3xLB2*) db (**94.5**) n24 t23 f23.5 b24. Classic spiced wheat; Demerara sugars and spices abound. Big. *45% (90 Proof)*

Buffalo Trace Single Oak Project Barrel #63 (w3xLB2) db (**95.5**) n24 t23 f24 b24.5. Subtle dates, spice, cocoa; gentle, oily, perfect spice build. Ultra complex. *45% (90 Proof)*

❧ **Buffalo Trace Single Oak Project Barrel #65** (r2xKA1) db (**91**) n23.5 t22 f23 b22.5. Small grain nose; crunchy muscovado, corn oil; liquorice, vanilla; late spice. Complex. *45%*

Buffalo Trace Single Oak Project Barrel #67 (r2xKA1) db (**89.5**) n22 t23 f22 b22.5. Blandish nose; tart, tight, sharp, some toffee raisin. *45% (90 Proof)*

Buffalo Trace Single Oak Project Barrel #68 (r2yKA1) db (**92**) n22.5 t23 f23.5 b23. Rye depth; deeper, warmer spices, liquorice and light molasses. *45% (90 Proof)*

❧ **Buffalo Trace Single Oak Project Barrel #72** (r2yLA1) db (**89**) n22.5 t23 f21.5 b22. Floral nose; juicy, tangy, citrus. Liquorice, sugary vanilla. Bitter marmalade finish. *45%*

❧ **Buffalo Trace Single Oak Project Barrel #74** (r2yKA2*) db (**88**) n22 t22 f22 b22. Corny nose; more corn oil early on; syrup, huge rye sure on finish; bitters slightly. *45% (90 Proof)*

❧ **Buffalo Trace Single Oak Project Barrel #78** (r2yLA2*) db (**89**) n22.5 t22 f22.5 b22. Small grain busy nose; light spice to oils; light rye, late sugars; chewy caramels. *45% (90 Proof)*

⁙ **Buffalo Trace Single Oak Project Barrel #81** (r2yKB1*) db **(94) n23 t23 f24 b24.** Candy shop fruitiness; delicate oils and flavour development; big yet subdued brown sugars. 45%

⁙ **Buffalo Trace Single Oak Project Barrel #88** (r2yLB1) db **(89) n23.5 t22 f21.5 b22.** Hickory, rye nose; liquorice delivery big caramel surge; bitters on finish. 45% (90 Proof)

Buffalo Trace Single Oak Project Barrel #93 (r2xLB2*) db **(89) n22.5 t22 f22 b22.5.** Soft rye and sugars; juicy grain, tangy citrus, muscovado. 45% (90 Proof)

Buffalo Trace Single Oak Project Barrel #95 (r2xLB2) db **(94) n23 t23.5 f23.5 b24.** Citrus, banana; soft vanilla, profound rye sharpness, spices. Big. 45% (90 Proof)

⁙ **Buffalo Trace Single Oak Project Barrel #97** (w2xKA1*) db **(87) n22.5 t22 f21.5 b21.5.** Toffee apple nose; heavy corn oil, light muscovado sugar, bitters out; 45% (90 Proof)

Buffalo Trace Single Oak Project Barrel #99 (w2xKA1) db **(86.5) n22 t22 f21 b21.5.** Malty, vanilla; thin maple syrup, caramel. Dull. 45% (90 Proof)

Buffalo Trace Single Oak Project Barrel #100 (w2yKA1) db **(94) n23 t23.5 f23.5 b24.** Busy, green, fresh; big juicy, vanilla, muscovado, spices. 45% (90 Proof)

⁙ **Buffalo Trace Single Oak Project Barrel #104** (w2xLA1) db **(91) n23 t23 f22.5 b22.5.** Apple, cinnamon; light spice; corn oil; vanilla and ulmo honey; spices, bitters out. 45%

⁙ **Buffalo Trace Single Oak Project Barrel #106** (w2yKA2*) db **(92.5) n24 t23 f23 b23.5.** Mega complex nose: busy sugars and spices; silky texture; nougat, caramel. 45%

⁙ **Buffalo Trace Single Oak Project Barrel #110** (w2yLA2*) db **(90) n22 t22.5 f22.5 b23.** Intense caramel; liquorice and toffee middle, citrus and salt; caramel finish. 45% (90 Proof)

⁙ **Buffalo Trace Single Oak Project Barrel #113** (w2xKB1*) db **(88) n22.5 t22 f22 b21.5.** Big vanilla nose; minor spice, oily, buttery vanilla. Simple. 45% (90 Proof)

⁙ **Buffalo Trace Single Oak Project Barrel #120** (w2xLB1) db **(89.5) n23 t22 f22.5 b22.** Controlled oak throughout. Intermittent dry vanilla. Delicate sugars. 45% (90 Proof)

Buffalo Trace Single Oak Project Barrel #125 (w2xLB2*) db **(93) n24 t22 f22.5 b22.5.** Heavy oak, spices; firm, juicy. Softer caramel fade. 45% (90 Proof)

Buffalo Trace Single Oak Project Barrel #127 (w2xLB2) db **(85.5) n21.5 t22 f21 b21.** Off balance, citrus; juicy at first, bitters later. 45% (90 Proof)

⁙ **Buffalo Trace Single Oak Project Barrel #129** (r1xKA1*) db **(88) n22.5 t22 f22 b22.** Firm grainy, tannin nose; nougat, nutty, corn oil; clean but dim vanilla fade. 45% (90 Proof)

⁙ **Buffalo Trace Single Oak Project Barrel #131** (r1xKA1) db **(92.5) n23 t23 f23.5 b23.** Relaxed vanilla, light tannin; corn oily, icing sugars, marzipan. 45% (90 Proof)

Buffalo Trace Single Oak Project Barrel #132 See above.

⁙ **Buffalo Trace Single Oak Project Barrel #136** (r1yLA1) db **(92) n23.5 t22.5 f23 b23.** Liquorice on nose and delivery. Spicy. Richer oils. Demerara. Spice. 45% (90 Proof)

⁙ **Buffalo Trace Single Oak Project Barrel #138** (r1yKA2*) db **(87) n22.5 t21.5 f21.5 b21.5.** Marzipan, citrus nose; dull delivery, slow build of muscovado and vanilla. Soft. 45%

⁙ **Buffalo Trace Single Oak Project Barrel #142** (r1yLA2*) db **(89.5) n22.5 t22.5 f22 b22.5.** Light tannin nose; oils, liquorice, spice bite. More corn oil. Sugars, spicy vanilla. 45%

⁙ **Buffalo Trace Single Oak Project Barrel #145** (r1xKB1*) db **(91) n22.5 t22 f23.5 b23.** Nougat, cocoa; busy small grains; oily corn; spiced chocolate. 45% (90 Proof)

⁙ **Buffalo Trace Single Oak Project Barrel #152** (r1yLB1) db **(81.5) n21 t20.5 f20 b20.5.** Vaguely butyric; harsh, hot fat corn, light rye; bitters out. 45% (90 Proof)

Buffalo Trace Single Oak Project Barrel #157 (r1xLB2*) db **(84.5) n21 t21.5 f20.5 b21.** Vague butyric; sharp, juicy corn with slow rye build. Bitter. 45% (90 Proof)

Buffalo Trace Single Oak Project Barrel #159 (r1xLB2) db **(88) n20.5 t22.5 f22 b22.5.** Vague butyric; firm sugars then watery, confident spices, soft honey. Complex. 45% (90 Proof)

⁙ **Buffalo Trace Single Oak Project Barrel #161** (w1xKA1*) db **(87) n21 t22 f22 b22.** Cream caramel candy; juicy corn, oily; more caramel. Light spice. 45% (90 Proof)

Buffalo Trace Single Oak Project Barrel #163 (w1xKA1) db **(90) n23 t22.5 f22 b22.5.** Citrus, bubble gum; spiced muscovado sugars at first, bitters. 45% (90 Proof)

Buffalo Trace Single Oak Project Barrel #164 (w1yKA1) db **(94.5) n23.5 t23 f24 b24.** Citrus and vanilla; massive spice, building. Demerara. Warm and complex. 45% (90 Proof)

⁙ **Buffalo Trace Single Oak Project Barrel #167** (w1yKA1) db **(94) n23.5 t23.5 f23 b24.** Demerara, rummy; intense liquorice, hickory; dark sugars and big spice. 45% (90 Proof)

⁙ **Buffalo Trace Single Oak Project Barrel #170** (w1yKA2*) db **(92.5) n22.5 t23 f23 b23.5.** Sweet, spiced nose; firm, spicy delivery; Demerara and ulmo honey. 45% (90 Proof)

⁙ **Buffalo Trace Single Oak Project Barrel #174** (w1yLA2*) db **(89) n22 t22.5 f22.5 b22.** Delicate oak; juicy corn, liquorice, light spices, buttery corn. Bitter marmalade. 45% (90 Proof)

⁙ **Buffalo Trace Single Oak Project Barrel #177** (w1xKB1*) db **(87) n21.5 t22 f22 b21.5.** Vaguely spiced corn oil; soft, nutty, marzipan sweetness, citrus. Late mocha. 45% (90 Proof)

⁙ **Buffalo Trace Single Oak Project Barrel #184** (w1yLA1) db **(93) n23.5 t23 f23 b23.5.** Tannins, walnut oil; nutty, corn oils. Light spice, firm Demerara sugar. Late fruity spice. Complex. 45%

Buffalo Trace Single Oak Project Barrel #189 (w1xLB2*) db **(88.5)** n24 t22 f21 b21.5. Complex citrus, delicate yet big; tart, sweet, fresh, strangely off balance. *45% (90 Proof)*

Buffalo Trace Single Oak Project Barrel #191 (w1xLB2) db **(94.5)** n23 t23.5 f24 b24. Big, spicy, classic; firm wheaty spiciness, juicy, thick caramels. Complex. *45% (90 Proof)*

Bulleit Bourbon (89) n23 how subtle is that? A pretty noticeable input from the small grains as the rye chips in with a distinguished degree of firm fruitiness and spice; **t23** and the rye is first to show on delivery, offering a crystallised sugar base which the corn oil is happy to lap around; **f21** custard pie and light cocoa; **b22** a very easy going bourbon which makes the most of any rye in the recipe. Dangerously drinkable. *45%*

Charter 101 (95.5) n23.5 standard Charter 101 evening flowers? Check. Usual spices? Check. Obvious lack of honey on the nose? We have a negative, Frankfort. This is just brimming with all the pollen collected from those evening flowers... **t24.5** the lush mouth feel betrays the strength of this bourbon. Again, this has much to do with the honey which absolutely oozes into every crevice of the mouth it can find. Honey was always around on Charter 101, but never like this. Emboldened, it seems, by beautiful blending of lively liquorice and voluptuous vanilla...all with a softly spoken spiciness. But once that settles – even allowing in a chewy fudge sweetness – those honey notes begin to blow you away...simply adorable stuff; **f23.5** long? How long have you got? A sublime layering of Demerara and muscovado sugars embraced by custardy oak...with a cocoa edge throughout. But once that melts you are back to the soft honeyed centre...; **b24** now here is a whiskey which has changed tack dramatically. In many ways it's like the Charter 101 of a year or two back. But this bottling suggests they have turned a warehouse into a giant beehive. Because few whiskeys offer this degree of honey. You can imagine that after all these years, rarely does a whiskey genuinely surprise me: this one has. No wonder there is such a buzz in the bourbon industry right now... *50.5%*

⬧ **Colonel E H Taylor Barrel Proof (91)** n23.5 a kind of a black hole of bourbon: kumquat notes, as well as greengages, liquorice, juicy dates, manuka honey, caramel...all those myriad things that go to make up the essential Kentucky character....concentrated and seemingly crushed into the one small space of this glass...; **t23** intense though surprisingly dry delivery at first; the oak makes clear intention of thickening out the hickory, then a slow deployment of cream toffee and maple syrup; **f22** remains caramel persistent, though a few herbal notes and burnt toast wander through; **b22.5** a big boy which turns out to be a bit of a softy in the end... *67.25% (134.5 Proof). nc ncf.*

Colonel E. H. Taylor Old Fashioned Sour Mash (94) n24 how can something be so light yet possess such gravitas all at the same moment? The corn offers a wonderful butterscotch-honey blend while the rye and oak, though hardly enormous on their own, combine to strengthen, firm and enrich. One of the most subtle aromas of the year; **t23.5** another dual attack: salivating and puckering at once. And also sweet and bitter. Plus rounded and spicy. The rye ensures a lustre to the sugary corn while the oak offers hickory; the mouth feel and weight are exceptional; **f23** long, a very light layer of corn and several more stratum of cocoa and honey; the spice tingle lasts to the very death; **b23.5** when they say "old fashioned" they really aren't joking. This is a style which takes me back to my first bourbon tasting days of the mid 1970s. And, at the moment, it is hard to name another bourbon offering this unique, technically brilliant style. Outstanding! *50% (100 Proof)*

⬧ **Colonel E H Taylor Single Barrel (93)** n23.5 lots of small grain intricacy on the nose: buzzing yet keeping a tight lid on the peppers as the harder, fruitier notes crisply strike home; **t23** homes in on the sugary side of life very fast and with gusto. Yet more than enough hickory keeps the balance while those peppers on the nose finds a way through the defences to nip; **f23** sweeter liquorice and corn oil form late weight while the chocolate and honeycomb positively pulses with the spice; **b23.5** an exceptionally bright barrel that's a bit of a tease. *50% (100 Proof)*

⬧ **Colonel E H Taylor Warehouse C Tornado Surviving (90)** n22.5 the nose is caressed by a muscovado/physalis/kumquat intensity that, for all its enormity, still manages a soft, slightly caramelised landing; **t23** chewy and juicy on delivery, there is a light spice that thinks about kicking up a tempest but then decides against. Again, the natural caramels light corn oils dictate the pace of the flavour spread across the palate. It is slow...; **f22** gentle toffee and raisin with a hint of oaky bitterness; **b22.5** this must be the eye of the storm: a peaceful bourbon that goes about its business with an endearing gentleness. *50% (100 Proof)*

Colonel Lee (70) n17.5 t18.5 f17 b17. The Colonel and I have known each other for a great many years, though it has been a while since I last spent time in his company. A few minutes of his very limited conversation is all I need to remember why... *40%*

Corner Creek Reserve (86) n22 t22 f21 b21. Honeyed with some striking small grain action. *44%. Corner Creek Distilling Company.*

Cougar Bourbon Aged 5 Years (95) n25 t24 f23 b23. If Karl Kennedy of Neighbours really is the whisky buff he reckons he is, I want to see a bottle of this in his home next to Dahl. By the way: where is Dahl these days...? (And by the way, Karl, the guy who married you and Susan in London is a fan of mine. So you had better listen up...!) *37% (74 proof). Foster's Group, Australia.*

Daniel Stewart 8 Years Old (92.5) n22 t23 f23.5 b24. Stellar sophistication. Real complexity here, and, as 8-year-olds go, probably among the most complex of them all. A deep notch up on the previous bottling I encountered. *45%*

Eagle Rare Aged 10 Years Single Barrel (89) n21.5 attractively floral but with a big signature of corn syrup; **t23** early oils as expected, then a surprising change of gear towards a rye-Demerara mix which firms and then moves towards a much spicier, kumquat inclined middle than the nose suggests; **f22** long, with more corn and a little oak bitterness; **b22.5** a surprising trip, this, with some dramatic changes en route. *45%*

Eagle Rare Kentucky Straight Bourbon 17 Years Old bott Fall 2010 **(92.5) n24 t23.5 f22 b23.** The corn hardly makes itself heard and oils at a premium. But for those who love bourbon in their rye...wow!! Oddly enough, while tasting this I am watching, from my sample room, a pair of black vultures circling a bluff at Frankfort, Ky, a short glide from the distillery where this whiskey was made. They are not exactly eagles, I grant you. But, with its eagle-esque deportment and chunkiness, close enough for the moment not to be lost...The Turkey Vultures, meanwhile, are probably waiting until I start on the samples from Lawrenceburg... *45%*

⁘ **Eagle Rare Kentucky Straight Bourbon Whiskey 17 Years Old** dist Spring 1993, bott Fall 2011 **(94) n23.5** a brisk, crispy muscovado and light rye note, all surrounded in fresh citrus. For a 17-year-old shows the aroma of a whisky half its age; **t24** big delivery, yet controlled. The liquorice needs a pneumatic drill to get through, but it eventually cracks and thick creamy fudge seeps from the fissures, along with ulmo honey; **f23** toasty, roasty, burnt raisin, overcooked fruitcake...you get the idea.. But enough residual sugar for balance; **b23.5** a marked improvement on previous bottlings, this goes out of its way to show some macho Kentuckian muscle. *45% (90 Proof)*

Elijah Craig 12 Years Old (79) n20 t21.5 f18.5 b19. Once upon a time this whiskey was as resolute, dependable, unshakable and constant as the cliffs which guide the mighty Kentucky River. And every bit as impressive and memorable. Those were in the days when the bourbon was made at Bardstown, with its massive copper input from unerringly fine stills. Then came the fire. And the distillery was lost. So 13 years after the event the whiskey had to change: there was no way it could not. This bottling is a considerable distance in style from the original. Superficially, plenty of rye and Demerara sugars. But it is hot and untidy. So unlike Elijah Craig 12... *47%*

Elijah Craig 18 Years Old Single Barrel barrel no. 3328, dist 8/9/91 **(94.5) n25** one of the most complex noses of the year with its busy, light warbling of rye, high quality marzipan and honey notes as well as freshly crushed brazil nut and very lightest Jamaican Blue Mountain coffee: as it oxidizes, delicate citrus and leather notes appear. Incredible...; **t23.5** the oak is upfront, as you might expect at this age, but the ryes immediately counter and very juicily so; outstanding weight and the vanillas go very gently; **f22.5** you would expect some negatives at the death from a whiskey of this age. But, instead, it just rolls out the sugared, lightly creamed mocha; **b23.5** masterful. Don't even bother opening the bottle unless you have an hour to spend... *45%*

Elmer T Lee Single Barrel (91) n22 almost seems like a little smoke on the toffee apple and honey...but that just proves to be the tannins riding high; **t23.5** fabulously rich and fulsome, the early lead is a pleasing hotch-potch of liquorice and cream toffee, a dab of acacia honey here and there while the middle heads very much towards burned fudge; **f(22.5)** long, with a steady stream of honey and fudge; lightly spiced butterscotch steers us home at the death; **b23** a sturdy, dense bourbon with above average sweetness. So effortless, it is hard to immediately realise that greatness has entered your glass. *45%*

⁘ **European Bourbon Rye Association Kentucky Straight Bourbon Whiskey 16 Years** hogshead, cask no. 1.1, dist 1994 **(95.5) n24.5** a Kentucky bourbon offering sublime Danish marzipan coated with Venezuelan cocoa and Demerara sugar. If that isn't enough, there is a touch of New Zealand manuka honey and Chilean ulmo honey. Does a nose really get more international than this...? **t24.5** the delivery is nothing as scary as it seems: keep your mouth open while tasting and the alcohol burns off quickly leaving a stunning residue of fabulously concentrated toasted honeycomb and ulmo honey notes. Next a slow deployment of slightly sweetened marmalade tones. Incredible! **f23** finishes like most 16 years olds...quickly! That is once you get past the enormous middle; **b23.5** mind-blowing whisky; the sort of stuff you can trust good ol' Mr Bourbon in Germany to unearth. A stunner..The whiskey ...not Mr Bourbon... *82.7% (165.4 Proof). sc. EBRA. 77 bottles.*

⁘ **European Bourbon Rye Association Kentucky Straight Bourbon Whiskey 18 Years** hogshead, cask no. 1.2 **(85.5) n21.5 t22 f21 b21.** Just 78.1%abv...pathetic! But whatever the strength, the main difference between this and the 16-y-o is that the younger, more powerful whiskey is still in beautiful nick. This, sadly, is showing too many signs of old age and has allowed the giant oak input to destabilise the experience. That said, there is enough natural caramel and tannin here, all blasted into orbit at ultra high strength, to offer something very rarely experienced. *78.1% (156.2 Proof). sc. EBRA. 84 bottles.*

Evan Williams (76.5) n18 t20 f19 b19.5. Unrelentingly sweet and simplistic. *43.3%*

Evan Williams 12 Years (90) n21.5 a touch of the new HH Character, but compensated by a real old fruitcake kick; **t23.5** brilliant mouth arrival with the spices boldly leading the way. Juicy, fruity rye isn't too far behind and the liquorice notes begin to up the ante at just the right time; **f22.5** varying dark sugar tones are sprinkled over the drier vanillins and chalky oakiness; **b22.5** perhaps not the force it recently was, but enough grunt here to emphasise the important bits. Namely the enormity of the rye and the sharp spices. Much more at home than, say, the 12-year-old Elijah Craig, for so long its match for quality. *50.5%*

Evan Williams 23 Years Old (94) n22 t23.5 f24.5 b24. Struts his stuff, refusing to allow age to slow him or dim the shine from his glowing grains. Now oak has taken its toll. This seems older than its 23 years... Or so I first thought. Then a light shone in my soul and it occurred to me: hang on...I have wines going back to the last century. For the older ones, do I not allow them to breathe? So I let the whiskey breathe. And, behold, it rose from the dead. This Methuselah of a whiskey had come alive once more...and how!! *53.5%*

Evan Williams 1783 (81) n19 t20.5 f21 b20.5. Much improved and now an exceptionally spicy offering. *43%*

Evan Williams Single Barrel Vintage 2001 dist Jul 01, bott Oct 10, barrel no. 001 **(85) n21.5 t21 f21 b21.5.** One thing is for absolute certain: this was not distilled at the long lost Heaven Hill distillery in Bardstown. Those were whiskeys which leapt at you from the glass and pulled your face into its enormity. This, by contrast, is most un-Single Barrel-esque. It is a huge outpouring of cream toffee. Enlivened by some layering of delicate citrus. But all rather sweet and monosyllabic...and soft. *43.3% (86.6 Proof)*

⁘ **Evan Williams Single Barrel Vintage 2002** barrel no 1. barrelled 7 Jun 02 bott 1 Nov 11 **(92.5) n23.5** orange blossom honey on a bed of muscovado-sweetened liquorice..; a few strains of pot still Demerara rum are heard from a distance; **t23.5** playful sugars infuse with the lemon-soaked vanillas; teasing and magnificently delicate; **f22.5** bitters out slightly, but enough Demerara balances matters; **b23** an altogether different animal to the Evan Williams single barrel which came from the original Heaven Hill distillery: that was incapable of making a bourbon as feminine as this... *86.6 Proof.*

Fighting Cock Aged 6 Years (82.5) n21 t21.5 f20 b20. I have just gone straight from Virgin Bourbon to Fighting Cock...such are the vagaries of my life. But while the virgin seduced or, rather, raped me, this old Cock leaves me underwhelmed. With its rich colour I had expected untold layering and depth. Instead, it is all rather corn-led and slightly OTT bitter oak. *51.5%*

Four Roses (Yellow Label) (89) n23 subtlety is the key here: small grains bristling and jostling for position against the softer honeyed vanilla; **t23** steady on, there! The delivery is much weightier and altogether thicker than a couple of years back and that honey note (yes, I do mean honey!) is contrasting vitally against the crisper rye; **f21** the fog of vanilla descends; **b22** seriously impressed: this whiskey was always pleasant but afraid to say boo to a goose. Now a honey injection has actually helped ramp up the rye content and the complexity has benefitted. The nose and delivery are exceptional. *40%* ☉

Four Roses (Black Label) (88) n20 t23 f23 b22. A whiskey which starts falteringly on the nose recovers with a sublime delivery of all things bourbon. *40%*

Four Roses Single Barrel warehouse US cask no. 10-2A **(96.5) n25** the perfect bourbon nose: floral (pansies/daffs) meets spice (ginger/pepper/clove) meets honey (acacia) meets fruit (redcurrant/dates) and at the confluence red liquorice and walnut oil is thrown in for good measure. Simply majestic; **t24.5** there are some rye whiskies which don't show this much of that most startling of grains. Clean delivery, almost like crystallised brown sugar melted by the increasing warmth of the spice. The oak adds a degree of liquorice but absolutely no bitter back chat; **f23** long, continues along the same lines but runs out of steam; **b24** if you have ever wondered if Four Roses has the wherewithal to play amongst the super-elite of the whiskey world, then track down this particular bottling and all will be revealed...For me, the finest Four Roses I have ever come across. *50%*

⁘ **Four Roses Single Barrel** barrel 11-3T **(94) n23.5** gentle, playful vanilla lead with maple syrup and toffee apple in joint pole position; **t23** more aggressive delivery, with a thinness to the oak and brittleness to the grain. But a slow corn oil evolvement softens things allowing the brighter brown sugars to sparkle, with a touch of crème brulee as a side dish..; **f23.5** pure cocoa on caramel....long, wonderful! **b24** in so many ways the quintessential delicate bourbon. But one of the most attractive for chocoholics, too.... *50%*

⁘ **Four Roses 16 Years Old Single Barrel Barrel Strength** barrel 78-3B, bott Nov 11 **(96.5) n24.5** weighty, but with easily enough kumquat-soaked liquorice to get the expectation nerves on edge; as bourbons go, it hits the near perfection button among aromas; **t23.5** initial injection of corn oils, then a bunch of spices. After a pause a soft caramel layer drifts across the taste buds; **f24** now enters overdrive with stunning spices spearheading the now seemingly cocoa and caramel house style. A whiskey without end...; **b24.5** in all honesty, 17 years ago – based on previous experience – if someone had asked if Four Roses had it in it to produce a top-drawer 16-year-old bourbon, I would have said: "probably not". Their whisky, then, was a little on the sparse side and struggled to add body to the oak. This, though, is not of a type that was around back in those days. The mix of fruit and chocolate is sublime. But above all, it's the silky texture and balance that have you scratching your head in amazement. *55.5%*

⚬ **Four Roses 16 Years Old Single Barrel Barrel Strength** barrel 78-5A, bott Dec 12 **(87) n22** dried lemon peel; **t22** plenty of caramel but bite also, and not just from the alcohol; **f21.5** a little one dimensional caramel; **b21.5** enjoyable, but just so tight by comparison to 78-3B and not on the same planet complexity-wise. *61.7%*

⚬ **Four Roses Single Barrel Limited Edition 2012 Aged 12 Years Barrel Strength** barrel 81-2B **(89.5) n23** big yet controlled. Sticks to a caramel theme but a few punchy spices and a hint of ulmo honey work wonders; **t23** fruits not even remotely apparent on the nose line up in big numbers like kittens, especially the dates and crunchy, Skagit valley cherries; the salivating rye effect is superb; **f21.5** just a little rumble of discontent from somewhere and the vanillas get a little frisky; the toffee has a lot to say for itself; **b22** lovely whiskey which takes something of the lazy way out as soon as the caramels grab hold. *52.5%*

Four Roses Small Batch (86) n20.5 t22.5 f21 b21.5. It is odd that while the standard Yellow Label has massively increased its personality, this one has, if anything, moved towards a much more neutral stance thanks to the vanillas dominating the nose and finish. The delivery is by no means so restricted, though. Good spice, too. *45% (90 proof)*

⚬ **Four Roses Limited Edition Small Batch 2011 Barrel Strength** oldest 13-y-o, youngest 11-y-o **(95.5) n23.5** a background rumble of caramel and strawberry cream chocolate...this is the rye talking! **t24** magnificent spices on the juicy delivery fit perfectly with the no less juicy citrus and pears; cherry tart again underscores the rye input; **f24** much more vanilla and butterscotch on the finish; **b24** the bottles of Four Roses I have been working through this year have been some of the most extraordinary treats it has been my privilege to enjoy for a very long time. This, on top of the 16-year-old is simply blowing me away... *55.1%*

⚬ **George T Stagg** dist Winter 1993, bott Fall 2011 **(96.5) n24** Stagg, at its lightest and most embracing. A lack of the normal inclusive oils has changed the gravity of this bourbony world, allowing the lighter notes to float more freely. The oak offers its usual gravitas, complete with myriad liquorice and clove tones. But here we have a little of the rye showing, as well as sliced apple and a crispness to the Demerara sugars...intriguing...and very beautiful; **t25** mouth-watering is not normally a term or experience associated with the delivery of a George T Stagg. But here it is the case. It is an odd sensation: salivating thanks, probably, to the sharper rye tones, yet at the same time reeling from the unmistakable big age-ness of the cloves! Unique! Then, to cap it all, the most intense dark chocolate mousse is unleashed upon us to insert a beautiful dessert sweetness right in the middle of the drier oak elements... wow! Wow! WOW!!! **f24** at last those corn oils get a word in and play a vital part in extending the length, depth and complexity (if that were possible) of the finish. The liquorice and hickory are as if by appointment and dovetail with the crusty Demerara sugars with the usual accomplishment. The improbably long finish underlines that this is a whiskey which deserves no less than an hour of anyone's time. Anything less, and you'll never see the full picture; **b24.5** before the bottling of each George T Stagg, the stirring process can shake the dice somewhat, and the scores can be different. Here we see Stagg with fewer oils than normal. This has shifted its stance very slightly. But you have only to ask an astronomer what happens if a planet changes its orbit by only fractions of a degree... *71.3% (142.6 Proof)*

George T. Stagg (97.5) n24 huge: profound, rich and seemingly distilled in the Blue Mountains of Jamaica; hickory and clove in close harmony, lightened with the merest (and I mean tiniest!) dash of redcurrant jelly; **t25** thick oak, yet so well honed are the molasses and Demerara notes that every aspect just seems to slide into place. Juicy, too, as the sub-plot rye makes some bold, sharp statements. And we haven't even reached in about a third of the way. However, the perfect weight, the magnificence of the corn and the marriage between the corn, its oils and the proud tannins is the stuff of legend...; meanwhile, the Jamaican Blue Mountain (mid and heavy roast mix) percolates sublimely...; **f24** a few dim spices are etched delicately into the vanilla but the coffee stays the course assisted by the big vanillas and fabulous Demerara-hickory combo...; **b24.5** astonishing how so much oak can form and yet have such limited negative impact and so few unpleasant side effects. These tasting notes took nearly four hours to compile. Yet they are still in a simplified form to fit into this book... George T Stagg is once again... staggering. *71.5% (143 Proof). ncf.*

Hancock's Reserve Single Barrel (92) n25 huge corn with rye apparent only if you really look hard; creamed rice pudding with a dollop of acacia honey slapped in the middle; a hint of evening gardens...all sewn together by the thinnest thread of liquorice: to die for... **t23** melts-in-the-mouth with an array of light oak and strands of coconut dipped in treacle; a sudden paroxysm of spice before heading towards a surprisingly dry middle; **f21.5** a disappointing finish with the oak taking a rough-handed control... **b22.5** a slightly quieter example of this consistently fine brand. The nose, though, is the stuff of wet whiskey dreams... 44.45%

Heaven Hill Old Style Bourbon (81) n20 t20 f21 b20. a sweeter, more citrusy number than before. Still a lightweight, but offers much more entertainment and style. 40%

Heaven Hill 6 Years Old (83) n20 t20 f22 b21. An infinitely more satisfying bourbon than its Old Style stable mate at this age. The battle between crisp rye and compact caramel is intriguing and pretty tasty to boot. 40%

Heaven Hill Old Style Bourbon 6 Years Old Bottled in Bond (81.5) n18 t21.5 f21 b21. What a strange beast. Sluggish on the nose and vanilla-bound on the finish it tends to hurtle around the palate without thought. The delivery, though, is sharp and enjoyably mouth-watering. 50%

Heaven Hill Mild and Mellow (90) n22 solid depth with liquorice and honeysuckle; **t23** mouth-filling and oily, the small grains break out with gusto. It's enough to make you dribble, such is the salivating effect of the juicy rye. Pretty big stuff; **f22.5** the oak infuses all the spice this needs and the corn keeps it there; **b22.5** you never know what you are going to get with this one: for that it is consistent. This version is full of colour and vitality and is a real (very pleasant) surprise package. A corker. 43%

Heaven Hill Ultra Deluxe Aged 36 Months (80) n20 t21 f19 b20. I remember a surprising liquorice backbone to this last time out. Not now. Lighter all round with corn dominating but the delicate spices are a treat. 40%

Henry McKenna Aged 10 Years Single Barrel barrel no. 642, dist 11/08/11 **(86) n21 t22.5 f21.5 b21.** Much more interesting than the last bottle of this I sampled. Here, as before, the sugars are king. But there is a charming kumquat note on both nose and delivery which burrow into the ever thickening liquorice. Superficially, appears to have much in common with the Virgin 7. But tasted side by side... Even so, good stuff. 50%

Hogs 3 (86.5) n21.5 t22 f21 b22. Have to say this is above average 3-year-old fare, with generous lashings of honey and red liquorice at regular intervals. A note about the label: the commendable sweetness of the whisky comes from the sugars that have melted into the alcohol from the oak and nothing, as claimed, from the water. But that nonsense apart, top-range for age, high-class daily bourbon. 40% (80 Proof). Quality Spirits International.

Jefferson's Reserve batch no. 84 **(91) n23 t23.5 f22 b23.** Once a 15-year-old, no age statement here. But this has seen off a few Summers, and sweetened with each passing one. 45.1%. 2400 bottles.

Jim Beam (86) n21 t21 f22 b21. After a few years kicking its heals, JB White Label has returned to something closer to how I remember it a couple of decades back. Not just a welcome degree of extra weight, but much more honey intensifying and lengthening: someone has been climbing higher up in the warehouse to find this four-year-old... Impressed. 40%

Jim Beam Black Aged to Perfection (89.5) n22 softer, less pungent than the 8-y-o version; **t23** the accent on the sugars with the usual rye boldness taking a back seat behind the sweeter corn, though by no means invisible; **f22.5** gentle vanilla and more molasses with some puckering liquorice towards the finale; **b22.5** Jim Beam Black. But, teasingly with no age statement! Does it live in the shadow of the sublime 8-years-old? Well, perhaps not quite. Lacks the lushness and the peaks and troughs of complexity. But, though a lot more even in temperament, it never fails to delight, even if the standard rye kick is conspicuous by its absence. As a bourbon, excellent. As a Jim Beam Black, a little disappointing. 43% (86 proof)

Jim Beam Black Double Age Aged 8 Years (93) n23 a fraction lighter than usual with a most un-JB milky mocha note braking up the trademark fruitcake and liquorice fingerprint; a few glazed cherries thrown in for sweetness; **t24** again, the intensity has shifted somewhat. This really is polite fayre compared to the usual Black Label character. But no less beguiling with the rye notes playing peek-a-boo with the building Demerara sugars and juicy dates, and the liquorice arriving in slow motion; the middle is fabulously sumptuous and complex, especially now the spices can be heard; **f22.5** thinner than usual with the liquorice and sugars winding down until the vanilla dominates; **b23.5** rather than the big, noisy, thrill-seeking JB Black, here it is in quiet, reflective, sophisticated mode. Quite a shift. But no less enjoyable. 43% (86 proof)

Jim Beam Choice Aged 5 Years (89) n22 t22 f23 b22. A hugely improved whiskey which is no longer betwixt and between but now strikingly makes its own bold statements. Makes noises on both nose and palate way above its five years. A bourbon to grab whilst in this expansive and impressive mood. 40%

Jim Beam Devil's Cut 90 Proof (89) n22.5 subtle spearmint notes in decent harmony with the hickory and Demerara: deceptively weighty and complex; **t24** dream-like delivery!

The weight is close on perfection as the corn oils steam in ahead with the rye, sharp and bright, close behind. The Demerara sugars also make telling contribution early on, helping to accentuate the middle spices; **f20.5** a bit scruffy and untidy as the vanillas dry a little too rapidly **b22** beautifully thrusting the palate both ran ragged and soothed by a devilish degree of silky complexity and intensity. The finish, though, needs a little attention. *45%*

⫶ **John E. Fitzgerald Larceny (94) n23** a gorgeous marriage of floral tones, mint especially, and toffee – leading to a sweet mint humbug persona – plus a choir of thin liquorice and Demerara; **t23.5** silk-textured with a fabulously understated array of sugar and spice... the spice especially. Cream toffee middle; **f23.5** the corn oils spread invitingly around the palate and refuse to budge. The fade sees them clinging fast and the spices really working overtime as the chocolate notes accumulate; **b24** if this doesn't win a few converts to wheated bourbon, nothing will. A high quality, stunningly adorable whiskey, pulsing with elegance and personality. Every drinks cabinet should have this wonderful new addition to the bourbon lexicon. *46%*

John J Bowman Virginia Straight Bourbon Single Barrel (94) n23 Dense and intense; John J means business...plenty of liquorice to accentuate the oak. Dry and toasty; **t24** the delivery is an essay in deportment: big weight, but so evenly balanced that the burnt honey and spice have no problems in showing to the full...chewy and multi-layered; **f23** long with the drying processes giving the honey all the time it needs to make its exit; **b24** one of the biggest yet most easily relaxed and beautifully balanced bourbons on the market. *50%*

Johnny Drum (Black Label) 12 Years Old (78) n20 t22 f18 b18 Attractive early, crusty sugars. But bitters out and loses balance later on. *43%*

Johnny Drum (Green Label) (87.5) n21.5 thick with over-ripe banana and vanilla with no little liquorice input; **t22** soft and succulent with the middle filling with toasty oak and honeyed hickory; no shortage of corn evident; **f22** long, significantly oiled and a decent bitter sweet fade; **b22** has changed direction since I last tasted this one. Now true as a die. And even outperforms the Johnny Drum Black! *43% (86 proof)*

Johnny Drum Private Stock (90.5) n22.5 another aroma you could stand a spoon in: lots of toffee and vanilla but enough corn oil to bathe in...; **t22.5** excellent early sugars immediately squares up to the threatening liquorice. Where they meet proves a touch tart; the oils arrive just as the nose foretells; **f23** gracefully complex and truly offering weight and that tell-tale touch of quality; **b22.5** one of those bourbons where a single glass is never quite enough. Great stuff! *50.5% (101 proof)*

⫶ **J.T.S Brown (83.5) n21.5 t21.5 f19.5 b21.** Mr Brown has been on a diet. The thin finish doesn't live up to the early muscovado promise. *40%*

⫶ **J.T.S Brown Bottled in Bond (86.5) n22 t22.5 f21 b21.5.** Much busier and fuller than the 40% version, though I tend to think that here the ryes have made a greater impact from a different distillation. Still could do with more oils on the finish though late spices compensate somewhat. *50%*

Kentucky Gentleman (86) n19 t22.5 f22 b22.5. Once you get past the disjointed nose, you are in for a very pleasant surprise. The highlight is the delivery on palate and follow-through: a silky-textured (hazelnut) nutty experience with a delightful honeycomb wake. There is a lovely small grain busyness, too. A minor gem of a gentleman. *40%*

Kentucky Supreme Number 8 Brand (76) n18 t19 f20 b19. Simplistic and undemanding with massive emphasis on a barley sugar-style tartness and sweetness. *40%*

Kentucky Tavern (84) n20 t22 f21 b21. Another juicy little number which appears almost to have a young malt feel to it. Clean, with just the right amount of rye sparkle to offer buzz and complexity. *40%*

Kentucky Vintage batch 08-72 **(94.5) n23.5** delicate to the point of brittle. Playful spice prickles as the small grains dance and tease; beautiful citrus notes are just showing off; **t24.5** the whole thing just melts in the mouth. No grating oak nor rabid spices. No bitter char. Just an intricate and delicate mix of grain and vanilla interweaving...and then melting along with some accompanying butterscotch and muscovado sugar. Quite stunning; **f23** both the bitterness and spices grow. But all is balanced and genteel; **b23.5** staggered! I really didn't quite expect that. Previous bottlings I have enjoyed of this have had hair attached to the muscle. This is a very different Vintage, one that reaches for the feminine side of a macho whiskey. If you want to spend an hour just getting to know how sensitive your taste buds can be, hunt down this batch... *45%*

Knob Creek Aged 9 Years (94.5) n23.5 almost arrogantly consistent: you know pretty well what you are going to get...and there it is. In this classic whiskey's case a whole bunch of honeycomb and vanilla, always more delicate than it first appears...; **t24** salivating delivery with rye and barley absolutely hammering on the palate. The corn oil is there not for flavour but effect – it is a fabulous mixture of dates and Demerara rum having the biggest say; **f23.5** wonderfully long with the oak toastiness now really beginning to bite...; **b23.5** no whiskey in the world has a more macho name, and this is not for the faint-hearted. Big, hard in character and expansive, it drives home its point with gusto, celebrating its explosive finish. *50%*

Knob Creek Aged 9 Years Single Barrel Reserve bottling batch no. L1017CLH **(89) n22.5** thick, almost single layered coffee and fruit cake; **t22.5** huge corn oil and spice; sweet and sticky; **f22** plenty of treacle and oak...chewy to the very last coffee dregs; **b22** the point often overlooked by people, even in the industry, is that a single cask is often a part of the sum. So this bottling just shows a single fragment into what will make up the usual Knob Creek small batch bourbon. This particular barrel – and sadly they don't name which one it is for further comparison (a bit of a marketing mistake that, as there are thousands out there dying to compare different styles) is all about depth and weight. Complexity, therefore, does not play a significant role, especially with the rye taking a back seat. Even so, an impressive ride. *60%*

Maker's Mark (Red Seal) (91) n22.5 the liquorice oak arrives early and with more force than you would expect from a Maker's. A bunch of vanilla notes of mixed sweetness try to dampen down the effect; **t23.5** honey...!!! Even more than usual, but this time winning the battle over the wheated spice. A silky mouthfeel and an attractive walnut subplot fits in pleasantly; **f22** the vanilla returns with a little caramel for a sleepy finale; **b23** the big honey injection has done no harm whatsoever. This sample came from a litre bottle and the whiskey was darker than normal. What you seem to have is the usual steady Maker's with a helping hand of extra weight. In fact this reminds me of the old Maker's Gold wax. *45%*

Maker's 46 (95) n23.5 crushed toasted hazelnuts dappled with honeycomb and delicate hickory; beautifully even and well mannered; **t24.5** quite superb: an initially thick, intense delivery which fans out in directions; excellent weight as those honeycomb notes go into overdrive; a dotting of wheaty and oaky spices but it's the way the softest of silky and highly complex flavours crash feather-like into the taste buds which cranks up the points; **f23** surprisingly light and simplistic with the accent firmly on vanilla; **b24** some people have a problem with oak staves. I don't: whisky, after all, is about the interaction of a grain spirit and oak. This guy is all about the nose and, especially, the delivery. With so much controlled honey on show, it cannot be anything other than a show-stopper. Frankly, magnificent. I think I've met my Maker's... *47% (94 proof)*

Most Wanted Kansas Bourbon Mash Whiskey (83) n18 t20 f23.5 b21.5. A sweaty armpit nose is the unlikely overture for an attractively flavoursome and delicately sweet bourbon. Highly unusual and rather gristy in style, the superb finish offers hugely attractive chocolate. One that really grows on you. *40% (80 proof)*

Noah's Mill batch 10-170 **(93) n23.5** classic big aged bourbon: toasted glazed cherry and liquorice to the fore, significant corn oil offering a vanilla and Demerara sugar balance; outstanding weight and poise; **t23.5** again, everything about this signals significant age. But also style and class. Sweetened hickory, a shed load of tannins but all countered by just so dark sugar reinforcements. Enormous whiskey, but totally in tune; **f23** just a little toasty bitterness on the finale deprives this of supreme greatness. Yet there is just enough sugar in the tank to keep the balance on track; **b23** this monster of a bourbon just rumbles along on the palate like one of the four thunderstorms I have encountered in Kentucky today... *57.15%*

Old 1889 Royal Aged 12 Years (78) n19 t20 f19 b20. A curiously ineffectual and ultimately frustrating bourbon which still needs to feel loved for its small grain complexity but succeeds only in demanding a slap for being so lily-livered. In the end it falls between the delicate and full-blown fruity stools. *43% (86 proof)*

Old Bardstown Black Label (85.5) n20 t22.5 f21.5 b21.5. Lush and overtly simplistic there is enough oiled honey and busy small grains to keep you very pleasantly entertained. *43%*

Old Bardstown Black Label (88) n21.5 t23 f21.5 b22. Forget about the 2% difference in strength. On this showing, a whiskey with a different mindset and a more muscular body and liberal use of spice. I'm a sucker for this style of bourbon: love it! *45%*

Old Bardstown Estate Bottled (86.5) n22.5 t22.5 f21 b20.5. Just a tad too sweet for greatness, though there is plenty to enjoy along the way. Can't help feeling the complexity levels are lost en route. *50.5%*

Old Bardstown Gold Label (83) n20.5 t21.5 f20 b21. Sweet, citrusy, juicy, uncomplicated, session whiskey. *40% (80 proof)*

Old Charter 8 Years Old (78) n19 t22 f18 b19. Sweetened up of late and even has a bit of pulse early on. But the finish is dull. *40% (80 proof)*

Old Charter 10 Years Old (84) n20.5 t23 f19.5 b21. From a dazed Brontosaurus, as I described it previously, to one that's been prodded awake. Still cumbersome, but now attacks those citrus and liquorice leaves with a spicy relish. Dozes off again at the end, though, for all the chocolate. *43% (86 proof)*

Old Crow Reserve Aged 4 Years (86) n21.5 t22.5 f21 b21. Huge colour for a 4-year-old. Loads of mocha and fruit on the nose and plenty of toffee on the finish. But the star attraction is the big, oily, fat delivery full of liquorice and brown-sugared coffee. *43% (86 proof)*

Old Fitzgerald (83.5) n19 t21 f22 b21.5. A greatly improved bourbon that is beginning to feel more at home in its sweet, vaguely spicy surroundings. 43%

Old Fitzgerald's 1849 (85.5) n21 t22 f21 b21.5. That's much more like it! After a time in the doldrums, this bourbon has fought back in style. Still one of the sweetest on the market. But the intensity of the spice and the manner in which it dovetails with the Demerara sugars is most enjoyable. Fitz beautifully... 45% (90 proof)

Old Fitzgerald Very Special 12 Years Old (93) n24 lively and energetic, there is a wonderful interweave between liquorice-led ancient notes and something much younger in style. A real freshness, accentuated by the peppery wheat: wow! **t23.5** the sugars are off running – mostly muscovado. But there is a fruit fudge element, too, with the inevitable peppers popping up almost from the first beat and then continuing unabated; **f22.5** the corn floods back adding a custardy element. The spices cannot be tamed, though; **b23** there is always something that makes the heart sing when you come across a whiskey which appears so relaxed in its excellence. At the moment my heart is in the shower merrily lathering itself... 45% (90 proof)

Old Forester Birthday Bourbon dist Spring 93, bott 2005 **(94) n24 t23 f23 b24** One of the most rye-studded stars in the bourbon firmament and wholly in keeping with the fabulous quality for which this brand has now become a byword. 40%

Old Grand-Dad (90.5) n22 t23 f23 b23.5. This one's all about the small grains. A busy, lively bourbon, this offers little to remind me of the original Old Grand-Dad whiskey made out at Frankfort. That said, this is a whisk(e)y-lover's whiskey: in other words the excellence of the structure and complexity outweighs any historical misgivings. Enormously improved and now very much at home with its own busy style. 43%

Old Grand-Dad Bonded 100 Proof (94.5) n23 light rye spices and citrus fruit pop around the glass. One of those weighty yet delicate bourbons, but here the small grain appear at full throttle; **t24** impossible not to be blown away. Exactly like the nose, you are expecting from first impact thundering, almost bullying oak. Instead your taste buds are mesmerised by a fabulous infusion of busy rye. a thousand tiny, crisp explosions in every quarter of the mouth followed by a layering of coconut strands dipped in lightly charred, molten sugars...; **f23.5** very toasty with the oak now unflinchingly taking the rye on; **b24.5** obviously Old Grand-dad knows a thing or two about classy whiskey: this is a magnificent version, even by its own high standards. It was always a winner and one you could bet your shirt on for showing how the small grains can impact upon complexity. But this appears to go a stage further. The base line is a touch deeper, so there is more ground to cover on the palate. It has been a whiskey-lover's whiskey for a little while and after a few barren years, has been inching itself back to its great Frankfort days. The fact that Beam's quality has risen over the last decade has played no insignificant part in that. 50% (100 proof)

Old Heaven Hill Bottled in Bond (79) n18.5 t20.5 f20 b20. Doesn't have much to choose from flavour-wise. But what it has, it has in spades...especially the maple syrup and vanilla. 50%

Old Heaven Hill Very Rare Old Aged 8 Years (88) n23 such a busy little nose! Rye showing various degrees of weight and some very attractive marmalade notes I wouldn't normally associate with this brand; **t22** a strange interplay between thin rye and a fuller, oiler thrust; **f21** tires towards the end and falls back to a safer vanilla mode; **b22** now that is very different! In fact, I can't say I have ever come across a flavour profile quite like it. Maybe it's all from one distillery. I may be wrong, but I get the feeling that the complexity indicates the influence of more than DSP type. 43%

Old Heaven Hill Very Rare Old Aged 10 Years Bottled In Bond (77.5) n19 t20 f19 b19.5. Good Heavens...!! What happened here? I remember this as the mad dog of the whiskey world, thrashing around my palate like something demented. Now it appears the men in the white coats have injected a sedative. Plenty of goody-two-shoes corn and vanilla...but where's the chemistry? 50% (100 proof)

Old Kentucky Aged 4 Years (84) n22 t22.5 f19 b20.5. Hugely enjoyable, busy bourbon where the small grains run amuck for a while. Perhaps over-sweetens towards the middle and runs out of steam towards the end. But as 4-year-olds go, quite a little treat. 40% (80 proof)

⫶⫶⫶ **Old Pogue Master's Select** batch 6816 **(87.5) n23** lashings of cream toffee with a lemon and vanilla freshness; **t22** cranks up the crème brulee even further with big corn oils for accompaniment; **f21** thin vanilla; **b21.5** pleasant and simplistic, showing good oils and early sweetness. 45.5%

Old Rip Van Winkle 10 Years Old (93) n24 absolutely benchmark 10-y-o bourbon to nose: a kaleidoscope of warmed walnut, a vague hint of juniper, more than a twist of citrus and a friendly corn oil carrying vanillas and liquorice. Glorious...; **t23** soft corn oils here, too. Guarantees a baby's bum softness before the spices kick in to ensure a lively welcome for the more graceful molassed notes; **f23** still those oils persist and hold in place the richer elements of the delivery for a good while with cocoa nudging its way in alongside some late sugars;

b23 a much sharper cookie than it once was. And possibly a Maryland Cookie, too, what with the nuts and chocolate evident. As graceful as it is entertaining. *45% (90 Proof). Buffalo Trace.*

Old Taylor Aged 6 Years (89) n23 marzipan and Seville orange offer a delightful lightness of touch and teasing complexity; **t23** almost a hint of single malt about the lightness of touch to the honey here; the arrival is sweet and busy with just enough oaky depth to add ballast; **f21** almost vanishes off the palate though the rye and spice stick around to impress; **b22** the curiously thin finish is in telling contrast to the superbly honeyed middle that simple dances with small-grain charm. So much lighter than the original Old Taylor *(see below)* of McCracken Pike. But certainly has enough weight and fruit punch to make this better than the cheap brand it is perceived to be. *40% (80 proof)*

Old Virginia Aged 6 Years (79) n20 t21 f18.5 b19.5. Old Virginia because of the drying tobacco leaf on the aroma? Sweet, but a lot flatter than the state... *40%. La Martiniquaise.*

Old Virginia Aged 8 Years L434401A **(85) n22 t21 f21 b21.** Vanilla-rich and never quite lives up to the bold nose. *40%. La Martiniquaise, France.*

Old Weller Antique 107 (96) n24.5 only pour this one if you have a good half hour to spare: the nose absolutely mesmerises as it changes shape and depth continuously. The honeys are soft and graceful, never dominating but rounding edges. The spices are well mannered yet condiment. The fruit takes the direction of apple and mango. Together they create a near faultless harmony; **t24** the wheat is vibrant, pressing bold spices into a honeyed core. The layering accentuated by the liquorice and hickory which balance the sweeter elements with rare panache; **f23.5** long with varying textures of oak. Never dries too much while refusing to allow the bountiful sugars the upper hand. All the time the spices throb... **b24** this almost blew me off my chair. Always thought this was pleasant, if a little underwhelming, in the past. However, this bottling has had a few thousands volts past through it as it now comes alive on the palate with a glorious blending of freshness and debonair aging. One of the surprise packages of 2012. *53.5% (107 proof)*

Pappy Van Winkle's Family Reserve 15 Years Old (96) n24.5 the usual blood oranges by the cartload...the lilting mix of plum juice and white bread kneaded until it has become a sweet, sugary ball. All that plus a shy spiciness and some broad oak. But what makes it all work is the lightness of the mix...so big...yet so delicate...; **t23.5** lush but with those threatening oaks on the nose exploding on impact. For a moment just a little OTT, but then several huge waves of cocoa-lined vanilla and marmalade puts the world to rights again...; **f24** long and back to unbridled elegance. Cocoas flit around, as do those wheated softly, softly spices and layers of thinned manuka honey... stunning...; **b24** at a book signing in Canada earlier this year a Bible enthusiast asked me which well-aged, wheated bourbon he should look for. I told him Pappy 15. He looked at me quizzically and said: "Well, that's what I thought, but in the Bible you have it down as rye-recipe." I told him he was wrong... until I checked there and then. And discovered he was right. Of course, Pappy has always been wheated and the lushness on the palate and spices radiating from it has always confirmed this. I'll put it down to not spitting enough. Or perhaps the speed at which I type whilst tasting. Sometimes you mean one thing – then another word comes out. Like when a member of my staff asks for a pay rise. I mean no. But somehow say yes. So apologies to any other I fooled out there. For not only is this a wheated bourbon. With its improbable degree of deftness for something so big, it has edged up a notch or two into a truly world great whiskey...whatever the recipe. *53.5% (107 proof)*

Pappy Van Winkle's Family Reserve 20 Years Old (85) n19.5 t22 f22 b21.5. Definitely a marked improvement upon recent years with the sugars and spices finding far better synchronisation and harmony than in many previous bottling. And the lushness to the mouth feel has distinctly improved. But the oak remains too powering, thereby upsetting the balance. I know I am a loan voice among commentators here, but... *45.2% (90.4 proof)*

Pappy Van Winkle's Family Reserve 23 Years Old (78) n18 t24 f17 b19. If I remember correctly, the last time I tasted this guy, the nose was a turn on while the body left me pretty cold. Bit of an about face here. Now the aroma shows signs of some of the soapier elements of the oak being exposed (much like a Scotch malt which has lived too long in a third-filled cask), and that in turn has, as is usually the case, a negative knock-on effect with the finish. But the delivery, vibrant with spice and trade mark blood orange, is nothing short of stunning. *47.8% (95.6 proof)*

❖ **Parker's Heritage Collection Fifth Edition 10 Year Old Barrel Finished (84.5) n21.5** Cognac casks do as cognac casks will...and that is give a hard edge and tighten the aromatic experience, especially concerning the sugars. These now are crystalline while the oak casts adrift slightly and more severe than normal; **t23** for a few wonderful moments the corn has complete control and sloshes the oil around; next comes a tight, severe oak bite offering bitter chocolate; **f19.5** harsh, hot, biting and a strange unflattering, tangy residue unlike any bourbon I have previously experienced; **b20.5** before I taste this, my message is simple:

tamper with the casks at your peril. Now I have tasted...and retract not a word. Indeed, I now feel I should underline them. Great bourbon whiskey – especially that holding the Parker Beam (not to mention Heaven Hill!) name – is better than this.... *50% (100 Proof). ncf.*

Parker's Heritage Collection Wheated Mash Bill Bourbon Aged 10 Years (97) n24 a faultless aroma: dried fruits (mainly dates and plums) with crushed pine nuts and a sensual spiciness. The sugars are relaxed and, naturally, of the darkened variety, softening the mocha; **t24** magnificent bite on delivery, showing this is not a showcase whiskey, but a living and breathing bourbon. The muscovado sugars are in molten form; the honey is manuka and no other while the spices set about their task with relish. The oils are light but weighty enough to spread the word with ease; **f24.5** long and now more refined...as a finish should always be. Some evidence of vanilla but the liquorice and honeycomb gang together with purpose and poise; **b24.5** hard to find the words that can do justice. I know Parker will be immensely proud of this. And with every good reason: I am working exceptionally hard to find a fault with this either from a technical distillation viewpoint or a maturation one. Or just for its sheer whiskeyness...A potential World Whisky of the Year. *62.1% (124.2 Proof). ncf.*

Peach Street Bourbon (86) n19 t22 f23 b22. The nose, though the weak link, is not without its charms; the delivery offers excellent spice and a real fruit cake quality, complete with juicy dates. The finish, as the oak finds a home, really is a joy. Impressive stuff from a small batch distiller and a two-year-old bourbon. *43%. Peach Street Distillers, Colorado.*

Pure Kentucky Batch 10-96 (77) n20 t20 f19 b18. Surprisingly fruity but lacks cohesion and direction from first to last. *53.5% (107 proof)*

Ridgemont Reserve 1792 Aged 8 Years (94.5) n23.5 throbbing, pulsing oak is kept comfortably in check with a soft honey and mint restraint. Fabulous depth and even a hint of salt to season the effect; **t24** Barton's unique rye and Demerara combo is in full swing here and contrasts fascinatingly with the deeper, vaguely bitterish oak notes; **f23.5** back to a vanilla and rye thread here, oscillating with the house brown sugars; the pulsing of the spice is sublime; **b23.5** now here is a whiskey which appears to have come to terms with its own strengths and, as with all bourbons and malts, limitations. Rarely did whiskey from Barton reach this level of maturity, so harnessing its charms always involves a bit of a learning curve. Each time I taste this it appears a little better than the last...and this sample is no exception to the rule. Excellent. *46.85% (93.7 Proof)*

Rock Hill Farms Single Barrel (85.5) n22 t22 f20 b21.5. An interesting, but perhaps little known point, is that I never read tasting notes of a brand from previous years until after I have tasted the present whiskey. I can usually remember anyway. But this struck me as being a bit odd, even before I referred back, as it seemed to have an extra summer or two to ramp up the intensity, especially of the sugared-marmalade delivery. But the finish still struck me as typically corn led and stubbornly docile. Pleasant, though, if pretty true to type. *50%*

Rowan's Creek batch 10-109 **(67)** n17.5 t19 f15 b16 Pity: the odd barrel in here should not have got through. Definite soapy quality on the nose is countered by a big maple syrup kick on delivery. But the finish confirms all is not well. Talk about up the creek... *50.05% (100.1 proof)*

Russell's Reserve Small Batch 10 Year Old (92.5) n24.5 in many ways, one of the most beguiling and intriguing of all bourbon noses. As a small batch I had expected my tasting notes to be different from the last. Yet each time I picked out gooseberries present, though here I also spot some high quality Danish marzipan, complete with a light, vaguely milky cocoa note. Raspberries are around, too, while the Demerara sugars so normally prevalent are happy to take a back seat. There is plenty of toffee and vanilla but it never gets in the way of this improbable bourbon story...; **t23** that toffee and vanilla on the nose has a far bigger say on the palate and though bolstered by several shock waves of spice, only occasionally allows some rye to pucker through; **f22** creamy textured, busy spice and so much vanilla...; **b23** had the quality and complexity on the palate followed on from the nose I may well have had the world's No 1 whisky for 2012 in my glass. Just slum it with something quite wonderful, instead. Still waiting for an official explanation as to why this is a miserly 90 proof, when Jimmy Russell's preferred strength is 101, by the way... *45%. Wild Turkey.*

Sainsbury's Kentucky Bourbon 3 Year Old (76.5) n19 t19.5 f19 b19. About the most caramel-flattened bourbon I have tasted in a very long time. *40%. Sainsbury's UK.*

Speakeasy Select dist 28 Jan 93 **(87)** n22 t22.5 f21.5 b21. pleasant, but one or four Summers too long for this barrel. *58.1%. Steelbach Hotel, Louisville, Kentucky.*

⬥ **Temperance Trader** distilled in Indiana, batch 005, released Mar 12 **(89)** n22 happy to stick to a corny theme; liquorice is making an entrance; **t23** amazingly heavy on the corn oil, the delicate, diluted golden syrup goes a long way; **f22** the oils and sugars remain but the corn-laden vanillas dominate; **b22** a soft, easy goer which concentrates on charm over complexity. *41.83%. Bull Run, Portland.*

Ten High (68) n17.5 t16.5 f17 b17. Always one of the lighter bourbons, now sporting a curious sweetness which does little to engage. Still a good mixer, though. *40%*

Tom Moore (85.5) n20 t22 f21.5 b22. An improved and engaging whiskey happy to display its increased fruit and complexity. The babbling on the palate of the small grain is a treat. 40%

Tom Moore 100 Proof (88.5) n21 a beautiful mixing of custard and rye; look out for the citrus, too; t23 superb! Thick on the palate, but it immediately melts down to its constituent small grain and rough oak parts; some cocoa invades the middle ground; f22 mocha, sweetened by Demerara sugar but the late spice attack stars; b22.5 another bourbon showing the inimitable Barton 1792 Distillery house style. The majority entertain but fall short in one department or another. Here, thanks to a little less water added in the bottling hall, we can really see how this whiskey can really tick. 50% (100 Proof)

Van Winkle Special Reserve 12 Years Old lot B (77.5) n18.5 t22 f18 b19. A very curious bottling: the nose and finish are both lacking in substance. But the delivery offers brief, spicy, slightly jammy riches. 45.2% (90.4 proof)

Van Winkle 23 Years Old (89.5) n23 big oak impact but still breathing with some soft coffee notes; a freshly opened bag of Liquorice Allsorts candy; t23 sweet muscovado sugars help the liquorice see off some probing pine notes; pulsing spices and diced, slightly burnt apple pie; f21.5 burnt French toast; b22 more of a Van Wrinkle: this is showing a lot of age. But enough of a pulse for one last enthralling show. 57% (114 proof). Buffalo Trace.

Very Old Barton (85.5) n21 t22 f21 b21.5. A fair slab of vanilla to go with the busy-ish spice. Attractive, but nothing like as complex as the 6-y-o label. 40% (80 proof)

Very Old Barton 90 Proof (94) n23 a bit of mint in the tea this time. And perhaps an extra spoonful of sugar; t24 the rye and small grain have gone into overdrive. One of the busier Kentucky whiskeys with no shortage of layering...and spice; f23.5 tons of vanilla to bring the curtain down on the budding hickory and liquorice; b23.5 one of the most dangerously drinkable whiskeys in the world... 45% (90 proof)

Very Old Barton 100 Proof (86) n22 t22 f21 b21. Enjoyable and well made for sure. But by VOB standards pretty dense and one dimensional with the light liquorice-vanilla note having too big a say. Lacking the usual small grain and rye intensity, this cannot be explained by the extra strength alone. 50% (100 proof)

Very Old Barton 6 Years Old (92) n23 I think this is an aroma in the past I have compared to Sahara's camp fires and green tea. Not surprising, really...because that experience is conjured yet again by the very distinct nose. Here, though, a little extra (brown) sugar is added, which I don't remember last time out...; t23 a slightly oilier delivery than normal, but the usual small grain/rye firmness is soon evident and entertaining; f23 elegant vanilla and spices; b23 one of those seemingly gifted bourbons that, swan-like, appears to glide at the surface but on closer inspection has loads going on underneath. 43%

Virgin Bourbon 7 Years Old (96.5) n24 so Wild Turkey-esque in style it is almost untrue: just loads of honey spilling out of the glass, backed up by big rye and leathery oak; t24.5 hold on to the arm of your seats...the mouth feel is massive with chocolate honeycomb surrounded by juicy dates and figs; liquorice has been piled high with really thick molasses...quite incredible; f24 the corn oils carry the sugars to the very end. But like distant thunder beyond the limestone hills, comes the spices and that liquorice, now with a touch of hickory, rumbling to the last...; b24 this takes me back nearly 40 years to when I first began my love affair with bourbon and was still a bit of a whisky virgin. This was the very style that blew me away: big, uncompromising, rugged...yet with a heart of honeyed gold. It is the type of huge, box-ticking, honest bourbon that makes you get on your hands and knees and kiss Kentucky soil. 50.5% (101 proof)

Virgin Bourbon 15 Years Old (92.5) n23.5 t23 f23.5 b23. The kind of bourbon you want to be left in a room with. 50.5% (101 proof)

Virginia Gentleman (90.5) n22 curiously yeasty yet quite full bodied. Plenty of corn but it is the fruit-oak marriage which wins hands down; t23 the full gamut of delicate citrus notes are eventually overpowered by the increasing cocoa; f23 charming oaks add depth to what might have been an overly-sweet, sugary finish; impressive oils last the course; b23.5 a Gentleman in every sense: and a pretty sophisticated one at that. 40% (80 Proof)

Walker's DeLuxe 3 Years Old (86) n22 t22 f21 b21. Excellent by 3-y-o standards. 40%

Weller Special Reserve 7 Years Old (83) n20 t21 f21 b21. Pleasant stuff which sings a fruity tune and is ably backed by subtle spice. Perhaps a little too sweet, though. 45%

Weller 12 Years Old (93) n24 there always appears to be fruit on the nose of this guy and here it is again: green, crunchy toffee apple, apricot and young melon. A little Swiss milk chocolate yodels its presence while the spices tease and prickle. All rather yummy...; t23.5 silk with attitude: corn oil, honey and a few tongue-withering peppers; f22.5 dries, allowing a full look at the 12 years of oak...and that milk chocolate is back; b23 sheer quality. And an enormous leap in complexity and grace from the 7-y-o. 45%

⫶⫶⫶ **Western Gold (85.5)** n21 t22 f21 b21.5. A young, citrusy, light bourbon which concentrates on the delicate honey side of things. Perfect for those who find full-bodied bourbon not to their style....yet! 40%. Lidl.

Wild Turkey (77) n19 t19 f20 b19. As sweet and simple as bourbon gets. Shows few of the qualities that make it such astonishing whiskey when older. *40% (80 proof)*

Wild Turkey 101 (91) n22 the nose still appears to have a big vanilla cap on it. But now a few traces of sugar and spice can be detected while the orange blossom blooms...a vast improvement; **t23.5** luxurious mouth feel. But those spices really get cracking early on and immediately pepper the shafts of sugary light which try to reach the oaky depth; **f22.5** remains chewy with a big vanilla swirl at the death; **b23** by far the best 101 I have tasted in a decade: you simply can't do anything but go weak at the knees with that spice attack. *55.5% (101 proof)*

Wild Turkey American Spirit Aged 15 Years (92) n24 t22.5 f22.5 b23. A delightful Wild Turkey that appears under par for a 100 proofer but offers much when you search those nooks and crannies of your palate. *50.0% (100 proof)*

Wild Turkey Kentucky Spirit Single Barrel barrel no. 96, bott. 5/13/09, warehouse rick 16 **(86.5) n21.5 t22.5 f21 b21.5.** More dense from nose to finish than the type of forest the real Wild Turkey prefers to inhabit. Lots of delicious butterscotch and mocha on show, but surprisingly little development. *50.0% (100 proof)*

Wild Turkey Rare Breed bott code L0049FH **(94) n22.5** the oak and fruit is of that firm, almost smoky, variety that will be readily recognised and appreciated by devotees of Oregon Pino Noit. However, this is a very different bird to the one I last spotted: the butterscotch and honey are absent leaving beery fruits to dominate. Attractive but very odd; **t24.5** much more like it! The puckering oaks are immediately set upon by pots of acacia honey and slightly overcooked butterscotch tart. Reminiscent of the Rare Breed of the early 2000s with the oak pulling up trees, so to speak. The rye notes kick in at about midpoint and dig in satisfyingly deeply; **f23** very long with the burned elements offering the required gravitas. Also overcooked prunes are lightened by under-ripe dates...; **b24** it is hard to credit that this is the same brand I have been tasting at regular intervals for quite a long while. Certainly nothing like this style has been around for a decade and it is massively far removed from two years ago. The nose threatens a whiskey limited in direction. But the delivery is as profound as it is entertaining. Even on this bottling's singular though fabulous style, not perhaps quite overall the gargantuan whiskey of recent years. But, seeing as it's only the nose which pegs it back a point or two, still one that would leave a big hole in your whiskey experience if you don't get around to trying. *54.1%*

Wild Turkey Tradition Aged 14 Years db **(89) n23 t21.5 f22.5 b22.** Something of a departure in style to a Wild Turkey (which is why it is a little odd it is called "Tradition"): this one makes a point of being an old bird. *50.5% (101 proof)*

⋙ **Willett Family Estate Bottled Single Barrel Bourbon 6 Years Old** white oak barrel, cask no. 672 **(88) n22.5** some beautiful flaked coconut in golden syrup; teasing, nibbling spices; **t21.5** an early delivery of muscovado sugars and then a surge of natural caramels soften; **f22** custard tart all the way...; **b22** never quite matches the nose for all round balance but impossible not to love. *60.5% (121 Proof). sc. Special bottling for "Mr Bourbon" (Heinz Taubenheim). 196 bottles.*

⋙ **Willett Family Estate Bottled Single Barrel Bourbon 7 Years Old** barrel no 3667 **(88.5) n23** a dazzling vanilla and caramel duet; good spice prickle; **t22.5** resounding Demerara sugars show early with busy spices in tip-top form; still it is the vanilla which dominates; **f21** thins out for a finale of austerity; **b22** an Early Times style barrel where spice dominates over complexity. *61.05%. 168 bottles.*

⋙ **Willett Family Estate Bottled Single Barrel Bourbon 14 Years Old** white oak barrel, cask no. 1067 **(96) n24** drier, more liquorice; **t23.5** intense delivery with a superb balance between the drier hickory-liquorice combo and the much more open, wider-reaching sugar. Some serious maple syrup in with the molasses here...; **f24.5** that is brilliant: exactly what bourbon should be about! No off notes, no bitterness. Just a complex but fading massaging of the taste buds, with neither those drier tones nor the sweeter ones – and all with the same characteristics as earlier) dominating...classic stuff...; **b24** if I didn't have a book to write I could taste this all day... *576%. sc. Special bottling for "Mr Bourbon" (Heinz Taubenheim). 72 bottles.*

Willett Pot Still Reserve barrel no. 2421 **(95.5) n24.5 t23 f24 b24.** Another fabulous whiskey from Willett. You can so often trust them to deliver and here they have given us a bourbon showing serious oak injection, yet a sweetness which counters perfectly. *47%. 273 bottles.*

⋙ **William Larue Weller** dist Fall 1998, bott Fall 2011 **(97.5) n24** like last year, oak springs eternal from the nose. This time, though perhaps not quite so startling as the previous bottling, there are hints that it may be a better all-rounder on the palate. The give-away is the sugars surrounding the cloves and apples. Still intense...but there is breathing space; **t24** the delivery suggests I am wrong, dammit! Not only big oak, but a little oil plugging the gaps. Hang on: a chink of light. here comes those sugars. They are not heavy molasses but much brighter muscovado and Demerara, which make inroads into the concentrated liquorice; **f25** brilliant! A whiskey which has relaxed entirely, gives you massive oak to chew without the splinters as it is beautifully accompanied by not only the usual mocha but extra, sharply oiled, Venezuelan cocoa beans and the liquorice, light hickory and dark sugars in complete and total harmony: like the Bee Gees, but without the teeth.; **b24.5** wow! This is becoming a must experience whiskey for hardcore bourbon lovers. Well, whisk(e)y lovers period, really! A bourbon which absolutely takes you to the wire with a "will it or won't it" type brinkmanship taking the flavours as far as they will go in an oaky direction without veering off the road and crashing down the cliff side. Majestic. Or, as it's American, perhaps I should say: Presidential.. *66.75% (133.5 Proof)*

William Larue Weller (97) n24 t24 f25 b24. Among the best wheated mash bill bourbon I have ever encountered. Why some whiskeys work better than others is the stuff of long debate. The reason for this particular bottling is relatively simple: you have an almost breathless intensity, yet somehow the constituent parts of the complexity can be individually identified and savoured. That is quite rare in any whiskey with this degree of weight. *674% (134.8 proof). ncf.*

Winn Dixie Bourbon (84.5) n19 t22 f21.5 b22. An entirely agreeable and more-ish bourbon which makes the most of its delicious kumquat and spicy backbone. *40%*

☼ **Woodford Reserve Distiller's Select** batch 59 **(85) n22 t21.5 f20.5 b21.** Nutty on nose and delivery with plenty to chew on. The sweetness is limited, perhaps by the degree of feints which ensure an oily, slightly bitter finale. *43.2%*

Woodford Reserve Master's Collection Four Grain (95) n24 t24 f23 b24. Sod's law would have it that the moment we removed this from the 2006 Bible, having appeared in the previous two editions without it ever making the shelves, it should at last be belatedly released. But a whiskey worth waiting for, or what? The tasting notes are not a million miles from the original. But this is better bourbon, one that appears to have received a significant polish in the intervening years. Nothing short of magnificent. *46.2%*

Zachariah Harris (89) n22 light, layered oak with a clean, sweet depth; **t23** busy, lots of small grains with a pounding rye and oak contrast; a background hum of honey and a rich oil base; **f22** long, the honey now intensifying with the vanilla; **b22** very good quality, not overly taxing fayre where the spices harmonise comfortably with the generous honey on show. Lovely, every day drinking. *40%*

Tennessee Whiskey
BENJAMIN PRICHARD
Benjamin Prichard's Tennessee Whiskey (83) n21.5 t21 f20 b20.5. Majestic fruity rye notes trill from the glass. Curiously yeasty as well; bounding with all kinds of freshly crushed brown sugar crystals. Pleasant enough, but doesn't gel like Prichard's bourbon. *40%*

GEORGE DICKEL
George Dickel Superior No 12 Brand Whisky (90.5) n22.5 the tannins have been ramped up here and there is no shortage of molasses to compensate; quite floral in part and a touch of green tomato, too! **t23** bigger delivery than a year or so back: again it's all oak and molasses up front forming an impressive, chewy clump. Spices swirl around with the corn oil; the middle is mocha; **f22.5** long, with the mocha finale taking on a slightly creamy texture; **b22.5** a different story told by George from the last one I heard. But certainly no less fascinating. *45%*

JACK DANIEL
Gentleman Jack Rare Tennessee Whiskey (77) n19 t20 f18 b19. A Tennessee that appears to have achieved the impossible: it has got even lighter in character in recent years. A whiskey which wilfully refuses to say anything particularly interesting or go anywhere, this is one for those who prefer their hard liquor soft. *40% (80 proof). Brown-Forman.* ☉

Jack Daniel's (Green Label) (84) n20 t21 f22 b21. A light but lively little gem of a whiskey. Starts as a shrinking violet, finishes as a roaring lion with nimble spices ripping into the developing liquorice. A superb session whiskey. *40% (80 proof)*

Jack Daniel's Old No.7 Brand (Black Label) (92) n23 a lighter blast than of old, offering a stunning candy store aroma, full of sugar and fruit, apples and pineapple cubes especially; **t23** wow! a delicate Jack again going easy with the liquorice and oils and concentrating more on the corn and molasses; **f22.5** vanilla pods bursting and liquorice and sugars joined by late spice; **b23.5** actually taken aback by this guy. The heavier oils have been stripped and the points here are for complexity...but should shock a few old Hell's Angels I know. *40%* ☉ ☉

Jack Daniel's Single Barrel barrel no.7-3915, bott 28 Sep 07 **(87) n21.5 t22 f22 b21.5.** Pleasant, yet perhaps not the most inspiring single cask I have come across from JD. This one refuses to offer up the usual oily weight. *45% (90 proof). Brown-Forman.*

☼ **Jack Daniel's Single Barrel Select** cask no. 11-3758, bott 2 Aug 11 **(86) n21.5 t22 f21.5 b21.** Pleasant, sweet but heavy on the natural caramels. Impedes complexity, but a delight if you're into the sweeter side of Jack. *45% (90 proof)*

⟐ **Jack Daniel's Single Barrel Select** cask no. 11-5065, bott 6 Oct 11 **(89.5) n22** medium weight but with an extra shot of liquorice; **t23** superb molasses and liquorice delivery; a light spreading of manuka honey in the mid ground; **f22** the sugars melt and give way to a more caramel-rich finale; **b22.5** one of those laid back Jacks which does all the good things effortlessly. *45% (90 proof)*

⟐ **Jack Daniel's Single Barrel Select** cask no. 12-0451, bott 31 Jan 12 **(93.5) n23.5** has to be Jack: it can be nothing else with that unique liquorice/hickory combination which bites deep, but with soothing kisses of rich molasses; **t23.5** as the nose...but in delicious liquid form; **f23** some caramels creep out from the oak to soften the finale, though the hickory and molasses shudder through to the finish; **b23.5** absolutely bang on the money. Gets the liquorice bite and sugars in superb combination to create a signature like no other distillery in the world. *45% (90 proof)*

Corn Whiskey

Dixie Dew (95) n22.5 corn whiskey...???? Really...??? The corn oils form a bit of a sweet blob, but elsewhere it is all about graduated degrees of cocoa and hickory...and all rather lovely. **t24** good grief!! Have not tasted a profile such as this: healthy corn oils but then a welter of Columbian Santander Cacao and rye-rich spices interject. Absolutely unique and astonishing...; **f24** the corn plays out its long farewell but the spices don't listen and take up the main ground; a few juicy sultanas fly in...from goodness knows where; **b24.5** I have kept in my previous tasting notes for this whiskey as they serve a valuable purpose. The three matured corn whiskeys I have before me are made by the same distillers. But, this time round, they could not be more different. From Mellow Corn to Dixie we have three whiskeys with very differing hues. This, quite frankly, is the darkest corn whiskey I have ever seen and one of world class stature with characteristics I have never found before in any whiskey. Any true connoisseur of whisk(e)y will make deals with Lucifer to experience this freak whiskey. There is no age statement...but this one has gray hairs attached to the cob... 50%

Georgia Moon Corn Whiskey "Less Than 30 Days Old" (83.5) **n21.5 t22 f20 b20.** If anyone has seen corn whiskey made – either in Georgia or Kentucky – then the unique aroma will be instantly recognisable from the fermenters and still house. Enjoyable stuff which does exactly what it says on the jar. *50%*

J. W. Corn (92.5) n23 I have long associated this brand with sophistication...and still do. The spice and cocoa layering is sublime, the injection of citrus startling; **t23.5** sweet, very graciously oiled; corn leads the charge but the oak backed by vanilla and butterscotch is not far behind; **f23** back to a nutty chocolate number with a clever sub plot of dates and red liquorice; **b23** in another life this could be bourbon. The corn holds the power, for sure. But the complexity and levels are so far advanced that this – again! – qualifies as very high grade whiskey. Wonderful that the normal high standard is being maintained for what is considered by many, quite wrongly, as an inferior spirit. *50%*

Mellow Corn (83) n19 t21 f22 b21. Dull and oily on the nose, though the palate compensates with a scintillating array of sweet and spicy notes. *50%*

Single Malt Rye
ANCHOR DISTILLERY

Old Potrero Single Malt Straight Rye Whiskey Essay 10-SRW-ARM-E (94) n24 t23 f24 b23 The whiskey from this distillery never fails to amaze. With the distillery now under new management it will be fascinating to see what lands in my tasting lab. Even at 75% quality we will still be blessed with astonishing whiskeys. *45% (90 proof)*

Straight Rye

Abraham Bowman Limited Edition dist 4/3/98, bott. 12/15/09 **(85) n21 t22 f21 b21.** For those who like rye with their vanilla. *63.2%*

Bulleit 95 Rye (96) n25 only the rye from the Lawrenceburg Indiana distillery can conjure a perfect rye aroma such as this...and that is exactly where it is from. Cinnamon and crunchy muscovado sugar crystal on green apple...so soft...so rigid...so unique...; **t24.5** exactly as the nose is fashioned, so is the delivery. At once liltingly soft yet absolutely granite hard...the rye offers both fruity and spicy branches...both lead to a salivating trunk; **f22.5** echoes of firm grain and fruit but pretty quick by comparison to what has gone on before...**23.5** this is a style of rye, indeed whiskey, which is unique. Buffalo Trace makes an ultra high-quality rye which lasts the course longer. But nothing compares in nose and delivery to this...in fact few whiskies in the world get even close... 45%. *Straight 95% rye mash whiskey.*

Cougar Rye (95) n25 t24 f23 b23. The Lawrenceburg, Indiana Distillery makes the finest rye I have ever tasted - and that is saying something. Here is a magnificent example of their astonishing capabilities. Good luck hunting the Cougar. *37%. Foster's Group, Australia.*

Devil's Bit Seven-Year-Old Single Barrel (93.5) n22.5 t24 f23 b24. A must-find rye from one of the most impressive small distilleries in the world. *47.7%. Edgefield Distillery.*

Fleischmann's Straight Rye (87.5) n22 a pipette drop of honey goes a long way; **t22.5** straight down the line rye: firm with a vaguely juicy bent while the honey really does begin to shine; **f21.5** pleasant enough, but surprisingly inert and dusty; **b21.5** one of the most spiceless ryes I have come across. But a lovely mouth-watering touch. *40%*

High West 12 Years Old Rye (92.5) n22 oak and citrus appear to douse the higher rye notes; **t24** fabulous! Stunning and frighteningly brittle delivery where the rye is determined at impact every inch of the palate: the spices are contained but perfectly harmonised; **f23** a cocoa sub plot very much plays second fiddle to the insistent rye; some serious tannins make themselves heard; **b23.5** a very clever rye which will hit a chord of appreciation for those who savour this whiskey style. *46%*

❧ **High West Double Rye** a blend of straight rye whiskeys, batch 12G/9 **(76.5) n18 t21 f18.5 b19.** A rye designed for cowboys. I'll get a dirty glass... *46%*

❧ **High West Rendezvous Rye** a blend of straight rye whiskeys, batch 12D0-1 **(82) n22 t22 f19 b19.** You would think that just adding one good whiskey to another would bring straightforward results. But blending a very old rye with a young one is one of the most difficult tricks in the book....as this whiskey demonstrates. Better than previous batches....but a long way to go before the trick is mastered, let alone perfected. *46%*

High West Rocky Mountain 16 Years Old Rye (86.5) n20 t22.5 f22 b22. Here and there, the nose being a good example, the rye and vanilla cancel each other out. But there is enough viperfish spice and juicy fruit to keep you salivating for a good while. *46%*

High West Rocky Mountain 21 Year Old Rye (95) n23 how sexy is that dance between the milky cocoa and the piercing rye...? **t25** just about everything you could wish for: the rye (as is the case in the very best ones) offers a dual role: it both firms up and fruit enriches, and here refuses to overly play either hand. The sugars are pure melt in the mouth; honeydew melon and liquorice dry out towards a toasty butterscotch-hickory middle; **f23** relaxes to let the vanillas (aided by a little cocoa) take charge; **b24** bizarrely, tastes a whole lot younger than the 16-years-old. Lighter in both colour and character, here you get to see the full personality of an absolutely outstanding rye whiskey. *46%*

Jim Beam Rye (89) n22.5 the odd ray of rye pokes through the cloud of vanilla; occasionally the fruity rye builds into fruity clusters, then vanish again...intriguing doesn't quite cover it... **t23** mouth-watering delivery with those firm rye notes of yesteryear making a bold attempt at dominance. But sweetens out quickly and vanishes beneath the vanilla; **f21.5** a pleasant, spicy afterglow; **b22** it seemed that when Beam changed the colour of the label from bright, road-marking, yellow to a wash-out, over milked custard hue, the vividness had also mysteriously – and tragically - vanished from the rye. Still more caramel than the glory days of old, but unquestionably a very welcome, if limited, move back to its sharper old self. Great stuff once more...now let's see what they can do about the label... *40%*

Old Overholt Four Years Old (85) n22 t21 f21 b21. Still little sign of this returning to its old rip-roaring best. Duller and less challenging with a frustrating dustiness to the procedings. *40%*

Pappy Van Winkle's Family Reserve Rye 13 Years Old (94) n24 outwardly, the aroma basks in a crisp rye flourish; scratch below the surface and there are darker, more sinister oaky forces at work; **t23.5** crisp, almost crackling rye offers both the fruity-clean and burned fruitcake options; **f23** dulls out a bit as the liquorice/toffee oak takes hold but remains alluringly spicy and sensual; **b23.5** uncompromising rye that successfully tells two stories simultaneously. A great improvement on the Winkle rye of old. *47.8%*

Pikesville (77.5) n17.5 t21.5 f19 b19. The freshness is absent here and instead we have a grumpy dustiness which limits development. Know when you have left your car lights on all night and you can't start engine next day? Yep...it's that flat... *40%*

(rī)¹ (94) n23 now that's more like it from Beam: the rye is a solid mass, radiating all kinds of fruity notes. But there are intriguing spices, too, ranging from light cloves to varying peppers; **t24** spot on delivery: as stark as a Kentucky cliff face and just as porous, too: the rye is crisp for sure and the citrus-induced salivating levels sublime. There is a slow build up of mildly milky chocolate, occasionally bordering on praline; **f23.5** the cocoa continues all the way, now with vanilla edging its way in but those light citrus notes balancing against the increasing spice presence...just so complex... **b23.5** (rī)ght up my alley. A fabulous meeting of crispy rye and much softer cocoa: an irresistible and ultra high quality addition to Kentucky's rye whiskey cannon. *46%*

Rittenhouse (78.5) n18.5 t21.5 f19 b20. Juice and spice but lacking sharpness. *40%*

❧ **Rittenhouse 100 Proof Rye** db **(83) n22** fruit and veg! **t22.5** chewy delivery with a degree of cocoa. Then crisps out at the rye, with its usual Demerara sugar foot soldiers panning out; more earthiness later on; **f18.5** and now there is a definite buzz and light bitterness; **b20** the nose is so, so fruity. But there is also a curious steaming asparagus vegetable edge. At first this is by no means unpleasant and adds a certain salty earthiness to the crisp rye. However, the finish displays a definite buzz and vegetable edge which I can't believe is unassociated. Partly enjoyable but perhaps the cask is, for some reason, getting a little stale. *50% (100 Proof). sc. Bottled for the Whisky Exchange.*

Rittenhouse 100 Proof Bottled in Bond (86.5) n20 t23 f21.5 b22. The nose labours for a Rittenhouse 100. But the salivating delivery and sweetly fashioned and richly-spiced rye makes a delightful impact on the palate. *50%*

Rittenhouse Very Rare Single Barrel 21 Years Old (91) n25 t23 f21 b22. I may be wrong, but I would wager quite a large amount that no-one living has tasted more rye from around the world than I. So trust me when I tell you this is different, a genuine one-off in style. By rights such telling oak involvement should have killed the whisky stone dead: this is like someone being struck by lightning and then walking off slightly singed and with a limp, but otherwise OK. The closest style of whisky to rye is Irish pot still, a unique type where unmalted barley is used. And the closest whiskey I have tasted to this has been 35 to 50-year-old pot still Irish. What they have in common is a massive fruit base, so big that it can absorb and adapt to the oak input over many years. This has not escaped unscathed. But it has to be said that the nose alone makes this worthy of discovery, as does the glory of the rye as it first melts into the tastebuds. The term flawed genius could have been coined for this whisky alone. Yet, for all its excellence, I can so easily imagine someone, somewhere, claiming to be an expert on whiskey, bleating about the price tag of $150 a bottle. If they do, ignore them. Because, frankly, rye has been sold far too cheaply for far too long and that very cheapness has sculpted a false perception in people's minds about the quality and standing of the spirit. Well, 21 years in Kentucky equates to about 40 years in Scotland. And you try and find a 40-year-old Scotch for £75. If anything, they are giving this stuff away. The quality of the whiskey does vary from barrel to barrel and therefore bottle to bottle. So below I have given a summary of each individual bottling (averaging (91.1). The two with the highest scores show the least oak interference...yet are quite different in style. That's great whiskey for you. *50% (100 proof). ncf. Heaven Hill.*

Barrel no. 1 (91) n25 t23 f21 b22. As above. *50%*
Barrel no. 2 (89) n24 t23 f20 b22. Dryer, oakier. *50%*
Barrel no. 3 (91) n24 t23 f22 b22. Fruity, soft. *50%*
Barrel no. 4 (90) n25 t22 f21 b22. Enormous. *50%*
Barrel no. 5 (93) n25 t23 f22 b23. Early rye surge. *50%*
Barrel no. 6 (87) n23 t22 f20 b22. Juicy, vanilla. *50%*
Barrel no. 7 (90) n23 t23 f22 b22. Even, soft, honeyed. *50%*
Barrel no. 8 (95) n25 t24 f23 b23. The works: massive rye. *50%*
Barrel no. 9 (91) n24 t23 f22 b22. Sharp rye, salivating. *50%*
Barrel no. 10 (93) n25 t24 f22 b22. Complex, sweet. *50%*
Barrel no. 11 (93) n24 t24 f22 b23. Rich, juicy, spicy. *50%*
Barrel no. 12 (91) n25 t23 f21 b22. Near identical to no.1. *50%*
Barrel no. 13 (91) n24 t24 f21 b22. Citrus and toasty. *50%*
Barrel no. 14 (94) n25 t24 f22 b23. Big rye and marzipan. *50%*
Barrel no. 15 (88) n23 t22 f21 b22. Major oak influence. *50%*
Barrel no. 16 (90) n24 t23 f21 b22. Spicy and toffeed. *50%*
Barrel no. 17 (90) n23 t23 f22 b22. Flinty, firm, late rye kick. *50%*
Barrel no. 18 (91) n24 t24 f21 b22. Big rye delivery. *50%*
Barrel no. 19 (87) n23 t22 f21 b21. Major coffee input. *50%*
Barrel no. 20 (91) n23 t24 f22 b22. Spicy sugar candy. *50%*
Barrel no. 21 (94) n24 t23 f24 b23. Subtle, fruity. *50%*
Barrel no. 22 (89) n23 t22 f22 b22. Mollased rye. *50%*
Barrel no. 23 (94) n24 t23 f24 b23. Soft fruit, massive rye. *50%*
Barrel no. 24 (88) n23 t22 f21 b22. Intense oak and caramel. *50%*
Barrel no. 25 (93) n25 t22 f23 b23. Heavy rye and spice. *50%*
Barrel no. 26 (92) n23 t23 f23 b23. Subtle, delicate rye. *50%*
Barrel no. 27 (94) n25 t23 f23 b23. Delicate rye throughout. *50%*
Barrel no. 28 (96) n25 t24 f23 b24. Salivating, roasty, major. *50%*
Barrel no. 29 (88) n23 t22 f21 b22. Hot, fruity. *50%*
Barrel no. 30 (91) n24 t23 f22 b22. Warming cough sweets. *50%*
Barrel no. 31 (90) n25 t22 f21 b22. Aggressive rye. *50%*

Rittenhouse Rye Single Barrel Aged 25 Years bott Nov 09 **(93.5) n24.5** cinnamon on apple crumble. That's perhaps the easy way of describing something which is almost too astonishingly complex for words. Remember how, with very good justification, I was blown away by the 21-year-old a few years back...? Well this has actually upped the game and taken the rye, nose-wise into a new dimension. When you are playing with old whiskies like this it is too easy for the cask to run away with itself; for an off note or a sign of tiredness to begin an unstoppable journey of destruction. It simply hasn't happened here: what we have is one of the ultimate experiences of truly great spirit being filled into entirely compatible top-drawer barrels and time being allowed to coax every last degree of complexity and beauty possible. Beyond that cinnamon, away from that apple crumble, we have so much more. Like ultra high quality Jamaican medium high ester pot still of advanced years from Long Pond; or lighter efforts from Hampden. There is a golden honey and coconut thread to this, a touch of leathery hickory, too. But we keep getting back to that rye-ramped fruitiness, the key to aroma puzzle...it really is a thing of ridiculous complexity and beauty. And, frankly, mystery... **t24** an immediate arm locking of firm, rock-hard rye in the form of a candy-like fruited, crystalline Demerara sugar, and much more aggressive oak with a real thick hickory/camp coffee assertiveness: one heck of a confrontation; **f22** long with a definite oak drawl but still a fruity juiciness fighting off the worst of the aging; **b23** this is principally about the nose: a thing of rare beauty even in the highest peaks of the whiskey world. The story on the palate is much more about damage limitation with the oak going a bit nuts. But remember this: in Scottish years due to the heat in Kentucky, this would be a malt well in excess of 50 years. But even with the signs of fatigue, so crisp is that rye, so beautifully defined are its intrinsic qualities that the quality is still there to be clearly seen. Just don't judge on the first, second or even third mouthful. Your taste buds need time to relax and adjust. Only then will they accommodate and allow you to fully appreciate and enjoy the creaky old ride. At this age, though, always worth remembering that the best nose doesn't always equal the best tasting experience... 50% (100proof). Heaven Hill.

Barrel no. 1 (93.5) n24.5 t24 f22 b23. As above. 50%
Barrel no. 2 (88) n22 t24 f20 b22. Intense. Crisp, juicy; a tad soapy. bitter. 50%
Barrel no. 3 (89.5) n23 t23.5 f21.5 b21.5. Fabulously crisp. Fruity. Mollassed. 50%
Barrel no. 4 (85) n21.5 t21.5 f21 b21. Subdued fruit. Massive oak. 50%
Barrel no. 5 (90.5) n25 t22.5 f21.5 b21.5. Complex. Mega oaked but spiced, fruity. 50%
Barrel no. 6 (91.5) n24.5 t22 f23 b22. Tangy. Honeyed and hot. Spiced marmalade. 50%
Barrel no. 7 (83.5) n20 t22 f20.5 b21. Treacle toffee amid the burnt apple. 50%
Barrel no. 8 (90) n23.5 t23.5 f21 b22. Flinty, teeth-cracking rye. Crème brulee. 50%
Barrel no. 9 (91) n23.5 t23.5 f22 b22. Massive ryefest. Mocha coated. 50%
Barrel no. 10 (86.5) n22 t23 f20 b21.5. Early zip and juice. Tires towards caramel. 50%
Barrel no. 11 (89) n24 t22 f21 b22. Honeycomb. Hickory. Caramel. Oil. 50%
Barrel no. 12 (84.5) n22.5 t21 f20 b21. Delicate. Vanilla and caramel. Light. 50%
Barrel no. 13 (89.5) n22.5 t23 f22 b22. Succulent. Yet rye remains firm. 50%
Barrel no. 14 (88) n22 t23 f21 b22. Very similar to 13 but with extra caramel. 50%
Barrel no. 15 (86) n21 t23 f20.5 b21.5. Lazy grain. Warming but flat. Caramel. 50%
Barrel no. 16 (92) n23 t23 f23 b23. Sculpted rye: sugared fruit; a twist of juniper. 50%
Barrel no. 17 (86.5) n22.5 t21.5 f21 b21.5. Fizzy, fruity spice calmed by caramel. 50%
Barrel no. 18 (91) n23.5 t23.5 f21.5 b22.5. Pristine rye. Spice. Juicy molasses. Crisp. 50%
Barrel no. 19 (96) n24 t23.5 f24.5 b23.5. Concentrated honeycomb and chocolate. 50%
Barrel no. 20 (89.5) n23 t22 f22.5 b22. Cream toffee. Fruit and spice. 50%
Barrel no. 21 (85) n21 t20 f23 b21. Severe oak delivery. Recovers with mocha toffee. 50%
Barrel no. 22 (81) n20 t20 f21 b20. Mild sap. Fruity. Oily. 50%
Barrel no. 23 (94) n23.5 t24 f23.5 b23. Rich. Fruity. Juicy. Clean. Corn oil. Cocoa. 50%
Barrel no. 24 (88.5) n22.5 t22 f21 b22. Huge vanilla. Slow spice. 50%
Barrel no. 25 (88) n22.5 t21.5 f22 b22. Custard and sugared fruit. Sharpens. 50%
Barrel no. 26 (90.5) n22 t23 f23 b22.5. Classic crisp rye. Big, manageable oak. 50%
Barrel no. 27 (88) n23 t22 f21.5 b21.5. Huge, honeyed oak. Oily. Dries at end. 50%
Barrel no. 28 (91) n22.5 t23.5 f22.5 b22.5. Exemplary honeycomb-rye delivery. Spices. 50%
Barrel no. 29 (94) n23.5 t24 f23 b23.5. Juicy rye; crisp sugar-vanilla-hickory fade. 50%
Barrel no. 30 (94.5) n23 t24 f24 b23.5. Thick rye. Cocoa. Spices. 50%
Barrel no. 31 (79) n21 t20 f19 b19. Lethargic. Bitter. 50%
Barrel no. 32 (88) n21.5 t22.5 f22 b22. Relaxed honeycomb. Hint of mint. 50%
Barrel no. 33 (88.5) n22.5 t22 f22 b22. Powering oak-rye battle. 50%
Barrel no. 34 (84) n23 t21 f20 b20. Thick oak throughout. Corn oil. 50%
Barrel no. 35 (93.5) n22.5 t23.5 f24 b23.5. Big rye. Demerara-hickory. Complex. 50%
Barrel no. 36 (77) n21 t19 f18 b19. Bitter oak. 50%

Russell's Reserve Rye 6 Year Old Small Batch bott. code L0194FH) (93.5) n24 superb balance better the hammer-homed firm fruity rye and the mintier, more vanilla defused elements; t23.5 juice and spice equal partners on the impact; more cocoa where there was once honey. But plenty of dark sugars...; f22.5 soft vanilla and spice make for a well behaved exit; b23.5 has lost none of its wit and sharpness: in fact has improved a notch or two in recent times. Wonderful! 45% (90 proof)

Sazerac Kentucky Straight Rye Whiskey 18 Years Old bott Fall 2010 **(95)** n23.5 t24 f23.5 b24. Some ego-driven, know-nothing commentators who for some mysterious reason claim an expertise with whiskey wonder how people can give different scores each year for a rye which has been living in a stainless steel vat. Of course, it would not occur to them that each time the vat is stirred before bottling the mix reveals subtle differences, depending on where the molecules fall. Line up Sazerac 18, one after the other from the last few years, and tell me which one is identical to the other. They are all quite different, and this one appears to have more than its fair share of sawdust and tannin. *45% (90 Proof)*

⁘ **Sazerac Kentucky Straight Rye Whiskey 18 Years Old** dist Spring 1985, bott Fall 2011 **(96.5)** n24.5 really not sure if rye aromas come through any brighter than this: the joint rye fruity effect and Demerara sugar harmonise and yield a note of crystal clarity – entrancing, enchanting and entirely delectable; t24 like this year's Stagg, the oils are down here slightly for some reason allowing a less impeded view of the grain at work. Not just crisp, but the vanillas have a drier sawdusty feel, though enhanced by a string of shimmering Demerara and thyme honey notes; f24 just more of the same in super slow motion. Though very late in the day the spices begin to rise; b24 if you are looking to climb the Everest of rye whiskeys, then good luck in scaling the lofty, jagged peaks. *45% (90 Proof)*

Thomas H. Handy Sazerac Straight Rye Whiskey (97) n24 seriously heavy duty: thick enough to use for armour plating. Takes time, but slowly the notes become identifiable, the dense, obvious rye apart. On hand warming, concentrated cocoa notes emerge, as well as spiced kumquat. But that is only the beginning: light cloves and molasses confirm the oak's impact; t25 massively thick with the oils of rye and corn forming a surprisingly lush field. The cocoa on the nose is re-introduced, this time as molten chocolate while the juicy fruity rye fizzes and forms mini lakes as the salivation factor goes through the roof (of the mouth); massive infusion of Demerara sugar, but these do no more than balance the gathering spice intensity: perfection ; f24 calms down quite dramatically as the natural caramels and vanillas begin to impact. But still those heady chocolate-rye notes continue their delicious seduction of the taste buds; b24 it has taken me over three hours to taste this. Were all whiskies and whiskeys like this, the Bible, quite simply, would never see the light of day. Beyond enormous. A whiskey which located taste buds I had no idea I actually possess. Just like his near namesake, Thomas Hardy, Thomas Handy has come up with a rambling, immortal classic. *64.5% (129 proof). ncf.*

⁘ **Thomas H Handy Sazerac Straight Rye Whiskey** dist Spring 2005, bott Fall 2011 **(97.5)** n24 delicate, elegant, playful though just a little subdued by Handy standards. That said, on hand warming by placing your fingers around this oily beauty the cloves eventually come off...if you know what I mean...; t24.5 a dazzling delivery which makes a lie of the nose. This is enormous, again with the cloves making the big entrance, though this time right in the middle of a chocolate tart; f24.5 cloves coming off, tarts...sounds a bit like a flavour orgy...and it is! The standard liquorice and hickory are there in number, the rye and crisp Demerara sugars send out their resounding cracks, like a leather ball off a willow bat; finally some trailing vanilla frames the picture; b24.5 a real slow burner. Takes a bit of time on the nose to leave the launch pad. But once off the ground it just doesn't stop travelling. Superb! *64.5% (128.6 Proof)*

Van Winkle Reserve Rye Aged 13 Years Old (94.5) n23.5 beautiful amalgamation of floral and fruit; t24.5 juicy, crisp brown sugar laced with hickory and then a storming middle of spice, tannin and toffee-liquorice; so like an ultra first class Jamaican pot still rum...; f23 with so little corn evident the twilight is shortish, but the sunset is nothing but pure dazzling rye; b23.5 magnificent. *45% (90 proof)*

Wild Turkey (80.5) n18 t22.5 f20 b20. Shackled by a dusty, cocoa-vanilla lethargy, breaks out into its sparkling old self only on delivery. Just not in the same league as the current Russell's Reserve... *50.5%*

Willet Family Estate Bottled Rye Barrel Proof Single Barrel 3 Years Old (91.5) n23.5 t24 f21.5 b22.5. What it loses in complexity, it makes up for in bay-faced freshness and charm. Ryes rarely come more juicy or puckering than this...a must locate rye! *57.7% (115.4 proof)*

Straight Wheat Whiskey

Bernheim Original (91.5) n22 smouldering toast from that-day-baked bread. Mealy, too with a little salt added for effect; t23 that peculiar salty tang on the nose transfers with little difficulty to the palate. It joins a citrusy throng and a delightful sharpness which counters the sweeter, oilier nature of the beast; f23 a classy finale where we are back to toast, if a little burned, and dissolving sugars but, mainly, a crackling firmness which appears to be a stand off between the wheat and the oak; b23.5 by far the driest of the Bernheims I have encountered – and this is about the 11th – showing greater age and perhaps substance. Unique and spellbinding. *45%*

American Microdistilleries
ALLTECH Lexington, Kentucky.

Pearse Lyon's Reserve Malt Whiskey (87) n22 the malt appears to be in three or four different layers of intensity and sweetness; a decent twist of lemon for diversity; **t22** had this whiskey come from Speyside I would not have batted an eyelid: the mashing appears to have been extrememly successful, as does the yeast use...it's just pure malt...; **f21** a light smattering of something oaky and spicy and a little bitter, but otherwise short; **b22** one of the maltiest whiskeys produced in the US today. Very much reminds me of an old Maryland single malt from the early 1970s. 40% (80 Proof)

AMERICAN CRAFT WHISKY DISTILLERY Redwood Valley, California.

Low Gap Clear Malted Bavarian Wheat Whiskey batch 2010/3B, dist 30/07/10, aged 357 minutes in oak **(90.5) n23** oh, the oak...the oak!! Way too much...not really: just kidding. Rich, slightly cut on the heavy side but thoroughly acceptable. The wheat chips in monumentally with an attractively sweet spiciness; **t23** frankly, beautiful. Gloriously rich in texture with those oils doing the trick in coating the mouth and ensuring the toffeed cake is fully heard. Chewy and lightly spiced; **f22** just a little bit of bitterness, confirming the wide-ish cut. But now a decent bitter-sweet balance; **b22.5** in 20 years of doing this professionally, I'm pretty sure I have never come across something that has spent so little time in the oak. Very impressed and pray they have set some of this distillate aside for proper maturation. 42.7%

BALCONES DISTILLERY Waco, Texas.

Balcones Baby Blue Corn Whisky batch no. BB10-15, bott 28/06/10 **(78) n18 t20 f19 b19.** Proudly sporting a Double Gold Medal sticker from a Spirits Competition, one can only assume (and sincerely hope!) it wasn't this batch which somehow wowed the judges. Feinty and frugal, I have already tasted enough from this distillery to know that it can do a lot, lot better than this. Proof of just how carefully you have to keep your eye on the ball... 46%

⠿ **Balcones Baby Blue Corn Whisky** batch BB12-7, bott 28 Apr 12 **(76.5) n18 t20 f19 b19.5.** Still their Achilles heel: corn whisky where they are unable to find the right balance to put the feints to use. 46%

Balcones Brimstone Texas Scrub Oak Smoked Corn Whisky batch no. BRM11-2, bott. 1/11/11 **(94) n23 t23.5 f24 b23.5.** If, like me, you begin your tasting very early in the day... then you can't beat a bit of bacon. Smoked bacon lovers, or devotees of Rupp smoked Alpine cheese, will be in their element. 53%

⠿ **Balcones Brimstone Texas Scrub Oak Smoked Corn Whisky** batch BRM 1200, bott 10 July 12 **(95.5) n24** the smoky bacon house style takes little time to arrive, but this time a much richer fruit note is apparent, too, balancing out the sweet and savory very impressively; **t24** this is higher quality distillate than the first rendition I tasted and it shows in the way in which the corn oils alone act as the conductor of the toasted sugars and delicate spice; the mid ground offers a saltier vanilla, more vivid spice to the at first almost Canadian-style pure fruitiness; **f23.5** long...very long! The smoked scrub oak carries on the very end with a smoked chocolate raisin chewiness with those spices keeping busy; a light whipped-cream texture to the finale, complete with an assortment of oaky tones; **b24** when a distillery goes out of its way to offer something different, and then does so on a silver platter, one can only stand back and applaud. Take a bow distiller Chip Tate and the team: you are doing the whisky world a great service. 61.5%

Balcones Single Malt Whisky (87) n21 abstract echoes of their Brimstone smokiness here gives the malt a unique edge. Takes the third or fourth visit to begin to understand and appreciate...should appeal to dentists, or those with toothache as the clove statement is pretty bold; **t22** huge delivery with fills the mouth with an oily glow. Minimum malty sweetness to see off the oak, then it's cocoa all the way; **f22** attractive vanilla and chocolate; **b22** these guys so remind me of Mackmyra in Sweden in their formative days... 46%

⠿ **Balcones Texas Single Malt Whisky Special Release** finished in yard aged American/French oak, batch SM12-3, bott 24 Apr 12 **(91) n22** relatively tight head but crushed hazelnut and nougat; **t23.5** thick-bodied delivery concentrating at first on delicate molasses, then a steady stream of lively-spiced liquorice and mocha notes; the distillery's almost signature chocolate raisin middle is a treat; **f22.5** the usual lengthy sign off, a tapering of the previous characteristics. Bitters a tad as the heavier oils stand unopposed; **b23** a delicious malt that needs a lot of time and chewing. 52.9%. ncf

Balcones True Blue Cask Strength Corn Whisky batch no. TB10-5, bott. 11/05/10 **(93.5) n22 t23.5 f24.5 b23.5.** Made from 100% Blue Corn, you could call this cornagraphic. It is certainly naked and gives you a rough, full-bodied ride...but also seduces you and caresses more tenderly than you could ever believe. A fabulous experience that will have you gasping for more...Believe me: a Texas star is born... 63%

⁘ **Balcones True Blue Cask Strength Corn Whisky** batch TB/6/3 1 date: 10 July 12 **(95.5)** n24 stunning chocolate honeycomb...wow! An attractive slab of hard toffee walnut, too; **t24.5** incredible delivery. I mean...absolutely bloody stunning! There is a hint of the German-style feints...but this is so magnificently controlled and so intensely wrapped in nougat and honey, with the richest chocolate outer sheathing. The oils are deep and intense and crank up the spices big time. The honey appears now to be in concentrated form; **f23** the flavoursome feints are now as formidable as they are forgivable. So much to chew on especially when the corn oils and lighter feints merge; more nuttiness, this time date and walnut, perhaps with a little marzipan thing going on, too; b24 when they get it right, Balcones are unquestionably the masters of big whisky in the USA outside Kentucky and Tennessee. And certainly ahead of the game in the use of feints to positively steer the experience. What a character whisky...! *68.6%*

BENJAMIN PRICHARD'S DISTILLERY Kelso, Tennessee.
Benjamin Prichard's Double Barrelled Bourbon 9 Years Old *(see bourbon section)*
Benjamin Prichard's Lincoln County Lightning Tennessee Corn Whiskey (89) n24 t22.5 **f21 b22.** Another white whiskey. This one is very well made and though surprisingly lacking oils and weight has more than enough charm and riches. *45%*
Benjamin Prichard's Tennessee Whiskey *(see Tennessee whiskey)*

BERKSHIRE MOUNTAIN DISTILLERS Great Barrington, Massachusetts.
Berkshire Bourbon Whiskey (91.5) n23 beautiful marriage of mocha and mint. But it's the shameless exuberance of the rye which wins the heart...; **t23.5** ...and not content in dominating the nose, it's there at the delivery, firm but fair, and ushering in the caramel and butterscotch; **f23** some oaky spice digs in, and the rye has a hand in that, too: what do you expect? **b23** a bourbon bursting with character: I am hooked! Another micro-gem. *43%*
New England Corn Whiskey (73) n18 t19 f18 b18. Not remotely in the same league as their bourbon, either technically or through character. Plenty of corn oil early on in the delivery. *43%*

BRECKENRIDGE DISTILLERY Breckenridge, Colorado.
Breckenridge Colorado Bourbon Whiskey Aged 2 Years (86) n22.5 t22 f20.5 b21. Full of character, big-hearted, chewy, slightly rugged bourbon where honey and cocoa thrives and spices make a telling impact. How apposite that probably the one and only town in Colorado named after a Kentuckian should end up making bourbon. Being close on 10,000 feet above sea level you'd think ice would come naturally with this one. But it does pretty well without it, believe me... *43%*

CATOCTIN CREEK DISTILLERY Loudoun County, Virginia.
⁘ **Catoctin Creek Cask Proof Roundstone Rye Organic Single Barrel Whisky** batch B12E1 **(88.5)** n21 enormous, but about as clumsy a rye as you'll find. Probably an age thing, but the grains and the premature liquorice on the oak notes aren't the greatest bedfellows...; **t23** hold tight: this is one delivery taking no prisoners. A real mishmash of assorted, mildly aggressive tones, but again with that hickory liquorice element coming out on top; the sugars are thick with molasses; the grain is rock solid; **f22** returns to a spicier, more grain dominant feel. The vanillas have the odd moment of glory; **b22.5** a truly huge rye that, from a technical standpoint, fails its exams. But through a combination sheer delicious belligerence and chutzpah has your taste buds swooning. Great fun! *58%. Distilled from 100% rye. 134 bottles.*
⁘ **Catoctin Creek Roundstone Rye Organic Single Barrel Whisky** batch B12-RR-11 **(80)** n19 t21 f20 b20. A degree of butyric doesn't help a rye that is flapping its wings but failing to get off the ground. *43%*
⁘ **Mosby's Spirit Organic 100% Rye** batch B12B7 **(85.5)** n21.5 t22 f20.5 b21.5. Not quite as seamless as the previous White Dog I tasted from these guys and develops something of a tang. But there is no stinting on flavour intensity and the odd burst of citrus here and there does no harm at all. *40%*

CEDAR RIDGE DISTILLERY Swisher, Iowa.
⁘ **Cedar Ridge Iowa Bourbon Whiskey** barrel no. 124 **(87.5)** n21.5 sweetened broad leaf greens; earthy; **t23** hits its stride on delivery with the ryes making the most telling impact. A little fruity with soft vanilla and sugars; **f21** heavy oils from the distillate coats the busy grains, ramping up the spices a little; **b22** intriguing and entertaining, a complex bourbon which really maximizes the input of the small grains. *40%*
⁘ **Cedar Ridge Unaged Whiskey (85.5)** n21 t22 f21.5 b21. Extremely well made with an impressive lushness. But with its distinct juniper edge, would perhaps have scored higher as a gin... *50%*

CHARBAY DISTILLERY Napa Valley, California.
Charbay Hop Flavoured Whiskey release II, barrels 3-7 **(91) n22 t22 f23 b24.** Being distilled from beer which includes hops, it can – and will - be argued that this is not beer at all. However, what cannot be disputed is that this is a rich, full-on spirit that has set out to make a statement and has delivered it. Loudspeaker and all. *55%*

CLEAR CREEK DISTILLERY Portland, Oregon.
❖ **McCarthy's Oregon Single Malt** batch W11-01, bott 20 June 2011 **(95) n23** a youthful beauty bursting with peat, but softened by a sprig of mint; the sweetness of the grist is irresistible, the odd mocha note is intriguing; **t23.5** young whiskey for sure but age here is an irrelevance. Enough oak has been sucked into the piece to make a wonderful stand on which the peat can be hung; darting fingers of spice begin to reach out; **f24.5** now hits its stride with the younger notes having died away and now a thick, rollicking smokiness winging it on the oils. Long and nothing short of sublime; **b24** simply adorable whiskey. Not only consistent – has stayed exactly on course though I hadn't tasted it for a couple of years – but refuses to stint on its complexity. Remains an American institution. *42.5%*

❖ **McCarthy's Oregon Single Malt Single Barrel Cask Strength** cask no. 158, bott 1 Nov 10 **(94.5) n23.5 t24 f23 b24.** Probably the most Islay-style of all the McCarthy offerings. Rather than the trademark smoky bacon, here we get an unmistakable sea-salty edge to this both on nose and delivery. But, above all, it is the evenness of the smoke, its patient building of phenols which impresses most. Attach that to the sublime softness of the mouth feel and you have a single malt cask of almost outrageous elegance. *49%. sc.*

❖ **McCarthy's Oregon Single Malt Aged 3 Years** batch W09-01, bott 3 Aug 09 **(87) n23 t22 f20.5 b21.5.** A real softy of a malt by this distillery's standards, really conjuring up a few fruit notes where few have been seen before. The model train oiliness on the nose is a delight; the thinness of the finish is a disappointment. *42.5%*

❖ **McCarthy's Oregon Single Malt Aged 3 Years** batch W10-01, bott 8 Nov 10 **(95) n23.5 t24 f23.5 b24.** I am not sure any micro whisky distillery in the US can do charm and elegance quite like Clear Creek does with its McCarthy's. Here is another bottling which puffs out far bigger smoke than you at first realize, rather in the way Ardbeg does. And in this non-smoky bacon style, Ardbeg is its closest relation in style. A masterful single malt which keeps you smokily spellbound. *42.5%*

❖ **McCarthy's Oregon Single Malt Aged 3 Years** batch W12-01, bott 7 May 2012 **(95) n24** direct from an English pub: smoky bacon bar snacks. In concentrate. Salty with a sweet edge; **t23** young delivery, even slightly new makey. But this seems to open the door to the grist and a stream of diffused sugars make their entry. Vanilla turns to smoked butterscotch; **f24** astonishingly long and, despite the youth, accomplished and complex. The vanilla is flakey but the spices are on the ball. The sugars are late and lengthen the experience with muscovado and thin molasses; **b24** I doubt if you could find, outside of the tropics, such a relatively young whisky with so vibrant and complex a personality. *42.5%*

COLORADO GOLD DISTILLERY Cedaredge, Colorado.
❖ **Colorado Gold Straight Bourbon Over Two Years Old Single Barrel** bott 8 Oct 11 **(86.5) n21 t23 f21 b21.5.** A bit of a whippersnapper of a bourbon. The nose and finish may lack depth. But it is a whiskey bursting with personality and the delivery is an understated treat. A light mocha thread weaves in and out of the muscovado. Fun. *40%*

COPPER FOX DISTILLERY Sperryville, Virginia.
Copper Fox Rye Whisky Aged 12 Months bott. 02/22/11 **(83) n23.5 t21.5 f19 b19.** Bizarrely, doesn't work as well as the spirit, though seemingly made from the same 66% rye mash bill and smoked with the same applewood/cherrywood combination. The sophisticated nose is the star turn, but the flavours never appear to harmonise, save a brief fruity interlude half way through. Very dry finish. *45%*

Wasmund's Distiller's Art Series Single Malt Spirit dist 03/03/11, less than 30 days old **(92) n23.5 t23 f22.5 b23.** The light smoke of 60% applewood and 40% cherrywood really makes itself count, especially on the quite sexy nose. A beautifully characterful and superbly weighted spirit. *62%*

Wasmund's Distiller's Art Series Rye Spirit dist 15/01/11, less than 30 days old **(85.5) n21 t23.5 f20 b21.** An ugly duckling of a spirit which lurches and crashes around the palate without any indication of where it has just been or is about to go. Love it. *62%*

Wasmund's Single Malt Whisky 14 Months Old Batch No. 52 (91.5) n22 t23 f23 b23. Makes a huge lightly honeyed statement: superb! *48%. ncf.*

Wasmund's Single Malt Whisky 42 Months Old Batch No. √-3 (90) n23 quite honestly, I can say this is a unique aroma: the combination of the smoke and the finish has appeared in no other whisky I have ever found. The fruitiness, along with the chocolate fudge, is a winner...; **t24** salivating and full of vigour, you think you are in for a big ride. But then it relaxes to allow a beautifully spiced grape juice to massage your palate...; **f21** annoyingly bitter and dry... preventing it from true, award-winning greatness; **b22** Rick Wasmund is the chuckling, mad professor of American whisky...always seeing what he can cook up next with his experimentations. This one is an oldie by his standards and as well as getting the usual applewood/cherrywood smoke treatment, has also subjected this to a toasted French oak wine stave finish. If he had a chat with either Doctors Frankenstein or Jekyll, he'll discover that not all experiments are guaranteed to be a success. This one, somehow, and against all probability, is. It seriously helps if you allow the whisky to oxidise in the glass for a good ten minutes to give it a chance to unravel. But then sit back and allow one of the silkiest malt whiskies yet created in the USA to dance nubile and erotically all over your taste buds. Well done, prof... This is the 205th — and last — whisky I have tasted for the Bible while in Kentucky. After tasting this, where can you go from here...? 48%

CORNELIUS PASS ROADHOUSE DISTILLERY Hillsboro, Oregon.
⬧ **McMenamins C.P.R. White Owl Distillery (93) n23.5 t23 f23 b23.5.** Top dollar White Dog. Huge amount of copper helps expose all the honey available, especially on the nose. Superbly distilled and surging with barley and spice. 49.3%

CORSAIR ARTISAN DISTILLERY Nashville, Tennessee.
Corsair Rye Moon (85) n20 t22.5 f21 b21.5. A sweet, well-weighted white dog with surprisingly little bite. The odd intense, crystalline rye moment is a joy. 46% (92 proof)

Corsair Aged Rye (73.5) n18 t18 f19 b18.5. Hot and anarchic, not as well made as the Rye Moon. But has enough playful character to keep you guessing what's coming next. 46%

Corsair Triple Smoke (92.5) n24 just about a unique smoke fingerprint: certainly one of the most delicate in the world with a mixture of wood smoke and Arbroath Smokies...so tantalising... **t23** the sugars melt almost immediately leaving a big malty pool on the palate; those delicate smoke tones keep on shifting; **f22** virtually smoked vanilla with a thread of spice; **b23.5** the odd technical flaw, to pick nits. But, overall, a lovely whiskey with a curiously polite smoke style which refuses to dominate. Teasingly delicate and subtle...and different. 40%

DARK CORNER DISTILLERY Greenville, South Carolina
⬧ **Dark Corner Moonshine Corn Whiskey (77.5) n18.5 t22 f18 b19.** Full blooded sweet corn on delivery. But could do with some extra copper elsewhere. 50%

⬧ **Lewis Redmond Bourbon Aged 10 Months** batch 1, dist Oct 11, bott Jul 17 (76.5) n19 t21 f18 b18.5. Big, almost creamy sugar surge early on. But struggles again without sufficient copper to ensure richness and balance. 43%

DISTILLERY 291 Colorado Springs, Colorado.
⬧ **291 Fresh Colorado Whiskey** distilled from corn **(87.5) n21** clean and citrusy; **t22** young spirit but the sweetness is provided by superfine sugars dampened with pure lime juice; **f22.5** very few finishes are this salivating; a little spiced mocha at the death; **b22** fresh as in refreshing...Surprisingly impressive. 45%

⬧ **291 Colorado Rye Whiskey White Dog** matured for less than one week, batch 1 **(90) n22 t23 f22.5 b22.5.** The way a White dog should be: pulling at the leash and baring its teeth. Excellent spices. 50.8%

⬧ **291 Colorado Rye Whiskey White Dog** matured for less than one week, batch R-120604 **(85.5) n21 t22 f21 b21.5.** Something of a rough ride and dries with rigidity and little sympathy. 50.8%

⬧ **291 Colorado Rye Whiskey White Dog** matured for less than one week, batch R-120315 **(88) n22 t22 f22 b22.** Amazingly eschews the fruitier elements of the rye to concentrate on the citrus and spice in the same way as their 291 Fresh. Softly textured and very attractive. 50.8%

⬧ **291 Colorado Whiskey Aspen Stave Finished** rye malt mash, barrel no. 1 **(83.5) n20 t22 f20.5 b21.** Exceptionally rugged whiskey which hits the taste buds like a steam train ramming into a Rocky Mountain rockslide. Combining the uncompromising rigidity of the grain with powerful oak, it's sheer drama all the way! 50.8%

⬧ **291 Colorado Whiskey Aspen Stave Finished** rye malt mash, barrel no. 2 **(94) n23** stunningly clean rye showing all its inherent fruity and crunchy Demerara notes: beautiful; **t24** all the charismatic, crunchy juiciness you demand from a rye and spices in just the right places and proportions; **f23.5** settles into a more oaky, vanilla phase, though the spices pulse happily; **b23.5** a superb, enigmatic rye whiskey which ticks every box: they are obviously fast learners! 50.8%

DELAWARE PHOENIX DISTILLERY Walton, New York.

Rye Dog Batch 11-1 (78.5) n19 t21.5 f18 b19. Sweet, distinctive rye tang but a little short on copper sheen. *50% (100 proof)*

DOWNSLOPE DISTILLING Centennial, Colorado.

⬩⬩⬩ **Double Diamond Whiskey** French/American oak, batch RV-0062, dist 3 Jan 11, bott 30 June 12 **(89) n21.5** dense grain with some earthy oakiness; **t23** a well-polished complexity on delivery, the rye really ensuring a crunchy sugar coating; **f22** coffee muffins; **b22.5** a much, much more complete version than the last DD I found, this time displaying an impressive degree of complexity all round. Not far away from sparkling... *40%. nc ncf.*

⬩⬩⬩ **Double Diamond Whiskey Limited Edition** French oak, batch MW-001, dist 8 Jan 10, bott 1 Apr 12 **(90) n22** a fairly spicy edge to the distinct malt; **t23.5** juicy with subtle fruity depth to the delivery. Silky textured and a magnificent slow burn to the spiced apple; **f22** the spice takes some prising away, but the vanillas now make a stand; **b22.5** for a young whisky this packs a fabulous degree of complexity and depth. Can't wait until it's a grown up... *43%. 225 bottles.*

⬩⬩⬩ **White Double Diamond** batch RV-151A **(85) n22 t22 f20 b21.** Unique aroma to this White Dog! On checking, discovered it is 65% malt and 35% rye, which goes a way to explaining things. Anyone who knows the smell of the inside of Walnut Whip will recognise this...though this is much sharper. A brittle experience on the palate. *40%. nc ncf.*

EASTSIDE DISTILLING Portland, Oregon

⬩⬩⬩ **Burnside Bourbon 4 Year Barrel-Aged** bott 2012 **(92) n24** beautiful! So complex with the small grains performing somersaults to ensure balance remains the key; **t23.5** delicate muscovado sugars and ulmo honey get this one off to a flyer. Just fades in the middle as the oils come through, though not before a liquorice and honeycomb surge delights; **f22** happy to settle for a vanilla-led finale; **b22.5** "Put some sideburns on your face!" screams the back label. Well, a whiskey far too gracious to put hairs on your chest though it would be a close shave to choose this or a Kentucky 4-y-o as one of the best young bourbon noses of the year...Just bristles with charm. *48%*

EDGEFIELD DISTILLERY Troutdale, Oregon.

⬩⬩⬩ **Edgefield Hogshead Whisky** 100% malted barley, batch 12-B **(94) n23.5** chocolate and Lubec marzipan; honeycomb nougat; a little kumquat accumulates with air; **t24** superb texture with an almost perfect degree of oil. The barley has as much scope as it needs to shine; there is a juicy element as well as a weightier oakiness, inevitably heading towards a heather-honey sweetness; **f23** an elegant fade with more nougat honey and mocha; still heavy on the oils; **b23.5** been a little while since I lasted tasted Edgefield. At that time they were seriously getting their act together. Now they deserve star billing in any bar. This is sheer quality and even though the cut is very fractionally wide, the two years in new oak has ensured something bordering magnificence. *46%*

FINGER LAKES DISTILLING Burdett, New York.

Glen Thunder Corn Whiskey (92.5) n23.5 t23 f23 b23. Beautifully distilled, copper rich, Formula 1 quality, absolutely classic corn white dog. The Scotch Whisky Association in particular will love it... *45% (90 proof)*

McKenzie Wheat Whiskey (82) n20 t22 f19.5 b20.5. A few heads and tails in there certainly up the body and help make the sugar-honey notes sing. *45.5% (91 proof)*

McKenzie Bourbon Whiskey (78) n19 t18 f21 b20. Gets off to an oily, rocky start as it struggles to find its balance. But once it gets going, pretty late on, the compensation is worth the wait as the toffee honey becomes a real chewathon. Good late spice, too. *45.5% (91 proof)*

McKenzie Rye Whiskey (85.5) n18 t23 f22.5 b22. No awards for grace and style. But for sheer content and charisma it is a great whiskey to find. The nose shows a little bit of distilling naivety, but the delivery proffers rye like an old 'un. Big oils, but then a thumping wall of firm, fruity muscovado sugars and light liquorice. Some superb spices and chocolate, too. *45.5% (91 proof)*

GARRISON BROTHERS Hye, Texas.

Garrison Brothers Texas Straight Bourbon Whiskey Aged Two Years dist 2008, bott. Spring 2011 **(88) n21** as is the norm with a new distillery, the feints have a bit too much to say for themselves. But those notes are countered by a gripping oaky red liquorice topped with honeydew melon and a pretty sexy spiciness...it has promise...; **t22.5** big and oily as the nose tell you it will be. The palate is coated with a rich demerara and marzipan mix, balanced by toasty oak. You can chew your tongue off...; **f22** those feints return as is expected, but the sweetness still grips to the corn oils and the sugars become just a little more toffeed and toasty; **b23**...despite the odd technical fault, it is very hard not to love this as you might a Texas steak. Plenty of chewing and flavour and fat. For a first bottling, quite wonderful. Another Texas star is born... *47% (94 proof)*

GOLDEN NORTHWEST DISTILLERY Bow, Washington.

❖ **Golden Samish Bay Single Malt Whiskey (88.5) n22.5** honeyed breakfast cereal with a touch of vanilla; **t22** the light feints delivery gives away its distillation style, but it recovers super-fast with a volley of intense brown sugars and salivating barley grist; **f22** the feints serve up the oils which take the spices and honey a very long way; **b22** a German-style single malt from a distillery located in one of the most beautiful areas of barley growing I have ever seen on the west coast of the US. The garden that is the Skagit Valley, famed for its sumptuous boysenberries and crisp cherries, never looks better than when the sun is glinting off the ripened-golden barley crop. This malt reflects the area rather well. *40%*

❖ **Golden Reserve Samish Bay Single Malt Whiskey (84.5) n22 t20.5 f21 b21.** Travels the same course as their standard bottling above. But the feints are just a little more biting and aggressive. *40%*

GREAT LAKES DISTILLERY Milwaukee, Wisconsin.

KinnicKinnic A Blend of American Whiskies (87) n21.5 honey and nougat; **t22.5** gets away with the obviously wide cut by again conjuring up honey a thousand bees would be proud of; **f21** bitters out, as expected; **b22** pronounced Kin-i-nuh-nik, this is one of the most honey-copper resplendent whiskeys from the USA. Follows a distinctive German-style pattern. *43% (86 proof)*

HIGH WEST DISTILLERY Park City, Utah.

High West Silver Oat (86) n20 t22 f22 b22. A white whiskey which at times struggles to find all the copper it needs. But so delicious is that sweet oat – a style that has enjoyed similar success in Austria – that some of the technical aberrations are forgiven. Soft and friendly. *40%*

KINGS COUNTY DISTILLERY Brooklyn, New York.

❖ **Kings County Moonshine Corn Whisky (92) n23 t23 f23 b23.** Absolutely spot on corn whiskey: sweet, clean, berry-fruity, very well made and does exactly what it says on the tin. *40%*

❖ **Kings County Bourbon** batch 44 **(89) n22.5** crisp Demerara sugar; **t22.5** sumptuous texture, aided by melt-in-the-mouth Demerara and natural caramels; **f22** an excellent outpouring of citrus-tinged vanilla; **b22** for a year-old bourbon the sugars have accumulated most charmingly. *45%*

KOVAL DISTILLERY Chicago, Illinois.

Lion's Pride Millett Whiskey (84) n20 t22 f20.5 b21.5. Now I know what Borat, my budgie used to get all excited about. The nose takes a little getting used to: decidedly green, like sweetened spinach. But the delivery, apart from being a whole new whiskey experience, delivers an oily custard tart sweetness (or is that custard sweet tartness?) which is unconventional and enjoyable. So who's a pretty whiskey, then...? *40%. 100% millett.*

Lion's Pride Dark Millett Whiskey (86) n19 t23 f22 b22. Borat, my late and deeply missed budgie, was occasionally known to stick his beak in a glass of whisky when I was looking... and always tried to come back for more. Well, we'd be fighting over this one. Again the nose is hardly enticing. But this time on the palate we have shards of honeycomb among tangy spices. Much more oil, too, which helps the finish distribute the sugars to the very death. Get the nose cleaned up, and this would be a whiskey worth squawking about. *40%. 100% millett.*

Lion's Pride Spelt Whiskey (77) n19 t22 f17 b19. My experiences with Spelt whiskey, wherever in the world it is made, have rarely been happy ones. Actually, this is better than expected. Certainly no problems with the delivery which positively oozes an oily sugary sheen as a fanfare to a milk chocolate middle. Then it all rather falls away. *40%. 100% spelt.*

Lion's Pride Dark Spelt Whiskey (72.5) n18 t19 f17.5 b18. No shortage of juicy sweetness to locate and for a while enjoy. Sadly it is no match for the bitter theme. *40%. 100% Spelt.*

Lion's Pride Wheat Whiskey (79) n20 t20 f20 b19. Not technically pulling up trees. But proof there is better things to do than make bread with it: the oil-driven layering early on is a delight. Improves in the glass: a warm room helps melt some of the higher alcohols. *40%. 100% wheat.*

Lion's Pride Dark Wheat Whiskey (72) n18 t18 f18 b18. No shortage of sweetness and good mouth feel. An underlying bitterness undoes some of the good work. *40%. 100% wheat.*

Lion's Pride Oat Whiskey (77) n22 t21 f16.5 b17.5. Sugar melting on porridge for the excellent nose. The delivery stands up...then those bitter oils develop, alas... *40%. 100% oat.*

Lion's Pride Dark Oat Whiskey (87.5) n21.5 chocolate and ginger fudge melting on porridge this time **t22** wow! Impressive weight and oils, evenly spreading the molten sugars. The oats interplay with vanilla and make for a relatively complex ride; **f22** long, a very light burst of spice and returns to the elegant porridge and sugar theme; **b22** a pretty sexy way to get your oats. The best I have found in this distillery's range: quite lovely whiskey. 40%. 100% oat.

Lion's Pride Rye (88) n21 only a cursory nod towards the rye; **t23** huge cascade of sugars and it appears malt. The rye notes are as hard to locate as a Kentucky warbler in the thickest of undergrowth... **f22** a lovely wood-spice fade; **b22** a really enjoyable, well distilled whiskey. But you'd never guess it was a rye.. 40% (80 Proof)

Lion's Pride Dark Rye (73) n19 t18 f17 b18. The bitter-sweet element is rather too well accentuated. 40% (80 Proof)

MOYLAN'S DISTILLING COMPANY Petaluma, California.

Moylan's Rye Whiskey (89.5) n22.5 t23.5 f21.5 b22. A beautifully businesslike rye which accentuates the grain's crisper aspects. 49.5% (99 proof)

Moylan's Single Malt (73) n17 t19 f18.5 b18.5. A sweet, spicy but off key affair. 43%

Moylan's Single Malt Cask Strength (86.5) n21 t22.5 f21.5 b21.5. Tangy and entertaining, this appears to harness all the malt's sweeter qualities and offers enough oil to make them stick. A genuine mouthful of a malt. 60.8% (121.6 proof)

Moylan's 2004 Cherry Wood Smoked Single Malt Cask Strength (94) n24 easily one of the most subtle of all America's micro distillery whiskeys and is unusual in not trying to make an early statements of intent. The smoke does no more than furnish a thin, earthy gloss to the delicate array of lightly fruited vanillas: absolutely beguiling; **t23.5** more of the same: a distinctive sharp kumquat note injects life into the vanilla; **f23** long yet without a hint of oil with light spices and cocoa playing happily together; again there is a faint, fruity glass to the finale; **b23.5** a top drawer, quite beautifully distilled and matured, malt which goes much easier on the smoke than you'd expect but is bubbling with personality...and quality. Bravo! 49.5% (99 proof)

Moylan's Bourbon Cask Strength (89.5) n21 t23.5 f21.5 b23. These guys certainly know how to distil: technically an excellent whiskey. Yet another very high quality distillate from this truly promising distillery. 57.25% (114.5 proof)

NEW HOLLAND BREWING COMPANY Holland, Michigan.

Brewers' Whiskey Double Down Barley batch 01, **(83.5) n21 t22 f19.5 b21.** A huge caramel swipe – unquestionably of that sweeter style found from oak. The barley and vanilla quietly fight for the upper hand, but the finish is somewhat suspect. There is no doubt that New Holland's Dennis Downing knows how to distil: this is a marvellous composition. But when I get over to his distillery, hopefully quite soon, I must find out where those hoppy, bitter notes are coming from. 45% (90 Proof)

Zeppelin Bend Straight Malt Whiskey barrel no. 4, 5 & 6, bott Feb 10, **(86.5) n19 t23 f22 b22.5.** The delivery is pure, malty joy with a fabulous caramel-muscovado richness to drive home its depth and makes the most of its increased alcohol. The finish offers additional spice. But, overall, there is a feeling of a hoppy-bitter ghost haunting the proceedings. 45% (90 Proof) 140 bottles.

PEACH STREET DISTILLERS Pallisade, Colorado.

⁂ **Colorado Straight Bourbon Aged More Than 2 Years** batch 21 **(89.5) n22** a soft wave of toffee caramel; diced green hazelnut; **t23** delicate procession of vanilla notes; thin manuka honey and a slow acceleration of traditional bourbon notes such as liquorice and honey; the spices decide to tag along reluctantly at first...then with gusto; **f22** the vanilla thins allowing the spices a free run to the finish line; **b22.5** a gentle, beautifully made bourbon where the characters evolve in super slow-mo. The flavours are a decibel lower than the norm: seemingly a club under par throughout. 46%

RANSON SPIRITS Sheridan, Oregon.

⁂ **Whipper Snapper Oregon Spirit Whisky (86.5) n21.5 t22 f21.5 b21.5.** A curiously thin offering for all the obvious corn apparent. Some walnut oil and light Demerara do offer some meat on the vanilla. 42%

ROCK TOWN DISTILLERY Little Rock, Arkansas.

Arkansas Lightning (89.5) n22 t23 f22.5 b22.5. Superbly made. Clean, oily and very impressive. Intrigued by the vaguest hint of sweet fresh shrimp on the nose. Will make a fine whiskey if placed in high quality oak. 62.5%. New, clear spirit pot distilled from Arkansas corn and wheat mash.

⁙ **Rock Town Arkansas Young Bourbon Whiskey Aged Under 4 Years** batch 7 **(86) n22 t22 f21 b21.** Comprehensively German in style, the nougat and chocolate runs thick and deep. Takes a little acclimatising but keep chewing and you'll find the liquorice is a treat. *46%*

ROUGHSTOCK DISTILLERY Bozeman, Montana.

Roughstock Montana Whiskey (81) n19 t20 f22 b20. A very sweet, almost gristy malt which fairly shakes the taste buds to its foundations with its outrageous oily yet rock solid stance. The spices towards the back end are worth a second glass alone...; *45%*

Roughstock Spring Wheat Whiskey (88.5) n21.5 t22 f23 b22. Mon dieu! What is a rollicking great whiskey like this from Montana doing being finished in French oak cask. Survives the experience...and has a wonderful tale to tell. *45%*

Roughstock Black Label (92.5) n22.5 the sugars are thumping, but is it all oak induced? I don't think so... The barley floats merrily around, threatening. Big but quite manageable...; **t23.5** one suspected this would happen on the palate...and it does...! Fabulous delivery with a silky softness for all the body and strength. Malt concentrate which sends you off to another barley rich universe...; **f23** long, with a fine balance between the sturdy vanillas and profound malt; **b23.5** a very beautiful malt whiskey very well made which underlines the happy marriage between barley and virgin oak. A stunner! *64%*

ST GEORGE SPIRITS Alameda, California.

St George Single Malt Lot 10 (90) n22 a touch oily from a widening cut. But the apples see off any potential negatives. If I didn't know better, I'd have said there was rye in that there glass... **t23** crisp to the point of cracking, those oils really come into play offering a certain chocolate mousse quality. But again it is a fruity rye style that stars and juices up the taste buds mercilessly; **f22.5** long, oily and all the developing spice you need; **b22.5** welcome back, my old friend! One of the grand-daddies of the micro distilling world and sticking to its guns for one of the fruitiest of all the malts out there. Even if not technically perfect, this is a three course meal of a malt. And so fruity, this one will appeal to rye lovers, too. In fact, it'll slay you... *40%*

SAINT JAMES SPIRITS Irwindale, California.

Peregrine Rock (83.5) n21 t20.5 f21.5 b20.5. Fruity and friendly, the wine and smoke combo work well-ish enough but the thumping oak injection highlights that maybe there isn't quite enough body to take in the aging. Perhaps less time in the barrel will reduce the bitter orange finale. *40%*

SANTA FE SPIRITS Santa Fe, New Mexico.

Silver Coyote Pure Malt Whiskey (72.5) n16 t21 f17.5 b18. This is made from malted barley, has never seen the inside of an oak barrel yet is called whiskey. Most probably there is some law I am unaware of regarding definitions of whiskey...especially in New Mexico. Even so, not a bad first attempt and on delivery gives a pretty good account of itself as the oils kick in. But somewhere along the line, to significantly up the quality, they have to, among other things (like sorting out the cut), get the spirit to enjoy a lot more contact with copper. A noble effort and I am sure they will improve as they get to know their distillery. Good luck, guys! *40% (80 Proof)*

STEIN DISTILLERY Joseph, Oregon.

⁙ **Straight Rye Whiskey Aged 2 Years** cask no. 7 **(88) n23** no doubting the grains at work here: big fruity rye at that lovely stage between sharp and sweet; **t22** silky, oily, mildly feinty delivery but the excellence of the rye powers through; **f21** the oils offer a spicy buzz; softening caramels; **b22** a whiskey which offers up the grains to the full spotlight. A little more care with the cut and we have something special on our hands. *40%*

STONE BARN BRANDYWORKS DISTILLERY Portland, Oregon.

⁙ **Hard Eight Unoaked Rye Whiskey (86.5) n22.5 t21.5 f21 b21.5.** The excellent fruity-rye nose does not quite show the width of the cut which creates a buzzing oiliness. Good brown sugar balance. *40%*

STRANAHAN DISTILLERY Denver, Colorado.

Stranahan's Colorado Whiskey Small Batch dist Dec 05, cask no. 225 **(94.5) n24 t23.5 f23 b24.** Absolutely magnificent; a malt which never stays still in the glass. By the way, boys: the message on the label to me brought a lump to my throat. Thank you. *47% (94 Proof). sc.*

Stranahan's Snowflake Cab Franc dist Sep 05 **(95.5) n24 t24.5 f23 b24.** What a quite fabulous way to mark my 1,100th new whisky for the 2012 Bible. Not only is it a celebration of great whiskey, but a profound statement of what the small distilleries of the USA are capable of. *47% (94 Proof). sc.*

⁙ **Stranahan's Snowflake Conumdrum Peak** dist 1 Oct 09 **(86.5) n22 t22 f21 b21.5.** Well made, enjoyable whiskey though perhaps a little too simplistic for greatness. Relies too heavily on the natural caramels. *47%. sc. 330 bottles.*

⁙ **Stranahan's Snowflake Desire** dist 3 Jan 07 **(94.5) n24** celebrates its bourbon style in style with this made-in-heaven marriage between golden syrup and maple syrup with liquorice and molasses providing the base. A few prickly spices, of course! **t24** silky mouth feel with caramel concentrate. How creamy can a whisky get? **f23** the cleanness of the cut is emphasised with the purity of the vanilla; the spice rumbles on...; **b23.5** these guys do know how to pick a good barrel... And, frankly, make an exceptional whiskey... *47%. sc. 306 bottles.*

Stranahan's Snowflake Hungarian White Oak Cask Finish dist Dec 07 **(77) n17.5 t21 f19 b19.5.** Chunky, oily, sugary and about as faultless as a Monty Python Hungarian Phrase Book. *47% (94 Proof). sc.*

⁙ **Stranahan's Snowflake Maroon Bells** dist 21 Feb 10 **(85.5) n21.5 t21 f22 b21.** Hell's bells, more like! Ribald in its fruitiness, it never quite hits the required balance with the intense caramel. A shock to the system for Stranahan lovers. *47%. sc. 552 bottles.*

Stranahan's Snowflake Paladise/Grand Mesa dist Apr 05 **(94) n23 t24 f23 b24.** Seriously impressive. I know this distillery makes something a little special, but this is such a sure footed move away from the norm I am stunned. This is my first-ever Stranahan Snowflake... so named because it simply dissolves on touch...? *47% (94 Proof). sc.*

Stranahan's Snowflake Solitude dist Mar 08 **(93) n23 t23 f23.5 b23.5** I chose this as my 1,111th new whisky of the 2012 Bible, because there is a lot of ones in that. And when you spend the best part of three months on your own, virtually cut off from all others, one is number you get used to. So sampling a whisky called "Solitude" strikes home...whatever it tastes like... *47% (94 Proof). sc. Stranahan's.*

Stranahan's Snowflake Triple Wood dist Dec 07 **(86) n21.5 t21.5 f22 b21.** Pulsing with varying degrees of sugar. Juicy and busy, but never quite settles down. *47% (94 Proof). sc.*

Stranahan's Colorado Whiskey Batch No. 56 dist Dec 07 **(87.5) n22.5 t22.5 f21 b21.5.** Plenty of bees at work here. Chewy, big and spicy but shows a generous cut. *47% (94 Proof)*

Stranahan's Colorado Whiskey Batch No. 57 dist Apr 08 **(87) n21 t22 f22 b22.** Has to be the closest two consecutive batches in style: this is obviously a wanna bee... *47% (94 Proof)*

Stranahan's Colorado Whiskey Batch No. 58 dist Jun 08 **(89) n22 t22 f22.5 b22.5.** Back to its more complete self. *47% (94 Proof)*

Stranahan's Colorado Whiskey Batch No. 59 dist Jul 08 **(92) n21.5 t24 f23 b23.5.** Very complex. Very classy. The interplay of the sugars and spice is utterly world class and the bourbon notes which sing at regular intervals do so with a very clear voice. *47%*

Stranahan's Colorado Whiskey Batch No. 60 dist Jul 08 **(94.5) n23 t24.5 f23 b24.** Two whiskeys obviously distilled on the same day (see Batch 59)...and a fascinating variance... This is Stranahan at its most communicative. And brilliant! *47% (94 Proof)*

Stranahan's Colorado Whiskey Batch No. 61 dist Aug 08 **(90.5) n22 t22.5 f23 b23.** Back to its mega fudge state. Lovely whisky. *47% (94 Proof)*

Stranahan's Colorado Whiskey Batch No. 62 dist Sep 08 **(92) n23 t23.5 f22.5 b23.** They appear to have hit a rich seem of consistency. My word: I love this distillery...! *47% (94 Proof)*

Stranahan's Colorado Whiskey Batch No. 63 dist Sep 08 **(83.5) n21 t21.5 f20 b21.** Spicy, more aggressive than normal; a distant vegetable hit suggests another wider cut. *47%*

Stranahan's Colorado Whiskey Batch No. 64 dist Oct 08 **(85) n21 t22 f20.5 b21.5.** By Colorado standards, this is a straight up and downer. Enjoyable, though limited, malt with the emphasis on caramel. A few toasty sugars and spices stretch the flavour profile out a little. *47%*

⁙ **Stranahan's Colorado Whiskey Batch #65** dist 1 Dec 08 **(87.5) n23 t21.5 f21.5 b21.5.** The superb honeys on the nose fail to fully manifest themselves on the palate. Big and caramel rich, but hot without being spicy. *47%*

⁙ **Stranahan's Colorado Whiskey Batch #66** dist 15 Jan 08 **(87.5) n21 t22.5 f22 b22.** Earthy and offering more vegetables on nose before heading off to gather the honey. *47%*

⁙ **Stranahan's Colorado Whiskey Batch #67** dist 30 Dec 08 **(96) n24** one of the classiest Stranahan's for a while: rich manuka honey spread over toasted vanilla; the liquorice/hickory counter weight is sublime; a pinch of salt and squeeze of kumquat...mmm! **t24.5** arguably the best texture to a Stranahan's yet: certainly evidence of the highest quality distillate. Two honey styles – Greek and light manuka – merge and welcome aboard delicate muscovado sugars. But the malt is still grassy and fresh to ensure a wonderful juiciness; **f23.5** an apologetic spice unravels as the citrus notes intensify. The charming vanilla is lightened further by citrus; **b24** you can tell Colorado is in the mountains: this rocks! *47%*

⁙ **Stranahan's Colorado Whiskey Batch #68** dist 15 Feb 09 **(91) n22 t22 t23 f23 b23.** Mines every last caramel atom from the oak. Soft, sexy, understated and complex. *47%*

⁙ **Stranahan's Colorado Whiskey Batch #69** dist 31 Mar 09 **(79) n18 t22 f19 b20.** Recovers beautifully from an awful nose, thanks to a sugary injection. Relapses, though. *47%*

⋙ **Stranahan's Colorado Whiskey Batch #70** dist 19 Apr 09 **(84) n19.5 t22 f21 b21.5.** Oily: a wide cut dishes out the nougat, slaps on the honeys and spices up. 47%

⋙ **Stranahan's Colorado Whiskey Batch #71** dist 20 Mar 09 **(81.5) n19 t22 f19.5 b21.** Returns to its recent vegetable theme. Honey injection then at times harsh and bitter. 47%

⋙ **Stranahan's Colorado Whiskey Batch #72** dist 20 Mar 09 **(92) n22.5 t23.5 f23 b23.** Honey-nut bar nose and delivery; complex sugars; silky, spiced mocha finish. Superb! 47%

⋙ **Stranahan's Colorado Whiskey Batch #73** dist 7 July 09 **(85) n19 t23 f21 b22.** Lush and loud on delivery: a real depth to the acacia honey and liquorice. Still a tad too earthy on nose and finish. 47%

⋙ **Stranahan's Colorado Whiskey Batch #74** dist 2 Sept 09 **(90.5) n22.5 t23 f22 b23.** Full bodied, mouthwatering and chewy. Celebrates the sugar and spice element to the max. 47%

⋙ **Stranahan's Colorado Whiskey Batch #75** dist 11 Oct 09 **(94.5) n23** complex, coy spice; honeyed breakfast cereal, complete with sweetened milk; a floral sub-strata; **t24** just a fabulous delivery. Those sugars and honey so prevalent on the nose launch into orbit, carried by the most delicate oils. The stunning flypast of molasses, maple syrup and golden syrup would be too much, but the ulmo honey keeps the overall sweetness in vanilla-clad check. Wow! **f23.5** the use of the feints has been very clever here, though their spicy buzz now becomes apparent. Still lots of vanilla and butterscotch; **b24** a striking whiskey which stops you in your tracks. Glorious! 47%

⋙ **Stranahan's Colorado Whiskey Batch #76** dist 2 Nov 09 **(83) n20 t22 f20 b21.** Too much generosity on the cut has upped the buzz on the experience a little too profoundly. 47%

⋙ **Stranahan's Colorado Whiskey Batch #77** dist 11 Nov 09 **(87) n21 t22 f22 b22.** Another Stranahan's that works overtime to maximize the sugars from the oak. Releases the caramels, too. 47%

⋙ **Stranahan's Colorado Whiskey Batch #78** dist 17 Dec 09 **(91.5) n22 t24 f22.5 b23.** Relaxed, softly spoken, classy and brimming with sugary intent. Muscovado sugars meet liquorice and manuka honey head on. 47%

⋙ **Stranahan's Colorado Whiskey Batch #79** dist 7 Jan 10 **(87.5) n21.5 t23 f21 b22.** Earthy and oily, wide cut spice. The sugars are thick, the vanilla deep. Feinty finale. 47%

⋙ **Stranahan's Colorado Whiskey Batch #80** dist 13 Jan 10 **(88.5) n22.5 t22 f22 b22.** Caramel city, Colorado. 47%

⋙ **Stranahan's Colorado Whiskey Batch #81** dist 14 Feb 10 **(82) n19 t21 f21 b21.** Huge whisky with the usual Demerara avalanche down the Rockies. But the feints are just too aggressive. 47%

⋙ **Stranahan's Colorado Whiskey Batch #82** dist 7 Mar 10 **(99) n21 t23.5 f23 b23.5.** Clean, simplistic, sugary and another which concentrates on the oaky caramel. 47%

⋙ **Stranahan's Colorado Whiskey Batch #83** dist 20 Mar 10 **(95) n23.5** unusually tight grains allow a distinctive malty feel to this. A sprinkle of salt suggests Digestive biscuit; **t23.5** exactly the same intensity on delivery: barley grist concentrate melts into the oaky vanillas. The famous Stranahan sugars develop, but cannot outrun the spices; **f24** incredible, bitty, buttery complexity with the grain and oak seemingly outdoing each other at every turn. Extraordinary, **b24** a rare example of where the malt element of the whisky overcomes the bourbon aspect. Magnificent complexity: just shows what a marginally thinner cut can do... 47%

⋙ **Stranahan's Colorado Whiskey Batch #84** dist 4 Apr 10 **(84.5) n21 t22 f20 b21.5.** Lots of liquorice but also on the bitter side. 47%

⋙ **Stranahan's Colorado Whiskey Batch #85** dist 4 Apr 10 **(84.5) n21.5 t22 f20 b21.** Similar to #84, even to the bitter off-key finish. Suggests the problem is not a rogue barrel. 47%

⋙ **Stranahan's Colorado Whiskey Batch #86** dist 10 May 10 **(92.5) n22.5 t24 f23 b23.** Clean, malty with crispy brown sugars which decorate the big vanilla spine. Elegantly intense and complex. 47%

⋙ **Stranahan's Colorado Whiskey Batch #87** dist 16 May 10 **(85.5) n19 t22 f22.5 b22.** All kinds of Maryland Cookie chocolate, sugars and spices to see off a slight roughness around the gills. 47%

⋙ **Stranahan's Colorado Whiskey Batch #88** dist 7 June 10 **(76) n19 t20 f18 b19.** Earthy, cooked spicy vegetables but generally struggling to find its balance. 47%

⋙ **Stranahan's Colorado Whiskey Batch #89** dis 13 June 10 **(88) n22 t22 f22 b22.** Another slightly earthy offering; this time ulmo honey and molasses spring to the rescue. 47%

⋙ **Stranahan's Colorado Whiskey Batch #90** dist 19 Apr 09 **(96) n23.5** superb injection of bourbon red liquorice: the oak has gone into overdrive...this promises something rather special...; **t24** juicy delivery with the spices at the driving wheel; the sugars are more relaxed and in syrupy rather than crisp mode; just about perfectly weighted with precision to the delicate oils; **f24** huge vanilla, butterscotch and moist ginger cake with dreamy amounts of spice; **b24.5** one of those liquid golden nuggets they find now and then in them thar Rocky Mountain hills... 47%

TRIPLE EIGHT DISTILLERY Nantucket, Massachusetts.

The Notch Aged 8 Years dist 2000, bott Aug 08 db **(93) n24 t23.5 f22.5 b23.** Very few distilleries make their international bow with a single malt this sublime and superbly constructed. $888 dollars a bottle it may be, but for a taste of America's very first island malt... well, is there really a price? A head turner of a whisky, and every time it's towards the glass. Do we have a world classic distillery in the making...? 44.4% (88.8 proof)

The Notch Aged 8 Years db **(95.5) n24.5 t24.5 f23 b23.5.** Only six bottles of this were produced for a special dinner at the distillery. It is possible one escaped. I admit I had a hand in putting this one together, selecting samples from about half a dozen casks from the warehouse and blending them to certain percentages. Perhaps the closest it might be compared to is a Cardhu, though with a touch extra fruit. For the doubters, proof that this distillery is quite capable of whisky of the very highest calibre. 40% (80 proof)

Triple Eight Distillery db **(90) n23 t23 f21.5 b22.5.** A beautifully-made malt but keeps very much to a lighter style. Almost classically elegant. 44.4% (88.8 proof)

WILLIE HOWELL SPIRITS

WH32137 (73.5) n15 t21 f18.5 b19. As big and intense as you'd expect from any spirit with a cut as wide as this. Very sweet corn oil ensures an uplifting body. 42.5%

WOODSTONE CREEK DISTILLERY Cincinnati, Ohio.

5 Grain Bourbon White Dog (63) n14 t17 f16 b16. Barking up the wrong tree. 47%

Woodstone Creek Blended Whisky (85) n20 t22.5 f21 b21.5. Pretty sharp and keeps you on your toes. A very different herbal aroma, by the way. 42.5%

Woodstone Creek Barrel Aged Biershnapps (76) n20 t20 f18 b18. Pretty sure this has hops, which rules this out as a whiskey and is marked down accordingly. As distilled hopped beer, pretty decent. 42.5%

Woodstone Creek 5 Grain Bourbon (76.5) n17 t20 f19 b19.5. Hard to get past the municipal swimming pool aroma. This one's taken a high dive... 42.5%

Woodstone Creek 10 Year Old Peated Malt (92) 24 23 22 23. Just read the previous tasting notes. There is nothing I can either add nor subtract. Quite, quite wonderful... 46.25%

⬩⬩⬩ **Woodstone Microspirit 5 Grain Straight Bourbon Single Barrel No. 3 (95) n24** mega complex nose with just the right degree of liquorice and manuka honey to get you in a bourbon mood. The small grains are in dizzying perpetual motion; **t24** small still copper sharpness meets a rye-recipe style small grain juiciness with a wheat-recipe style spice. The oak also digs deep and does nothing to lessen the complexity, chipping in with a molten chocolate filling; **f23** softens as the oils filter through but we are back now to a liquorice/hickory feel, sweetened with orange blossom honey; **b24** you can tell Cincinnati borders Kentucky: of all the micro distillery bourbons I have ever tasted, this comes closest to the original big distiller style. Had I tasted blind, for the odd moment or two I might have called this as well aged stock from the Tom Moore distillery in Bardstown. Astonishing. And delightful! 47%

YAHARA BAY DISTILLERY Madison, Wisconsin.

Sample No 1 (87) n22.5 clean with the accent on a maltshake intensity; a squirt of some citrus lightens the experience; **t22** beautifully soft delivery which coats the mouth without the use of higher alcohols. Lovely array of rich barley sugars on a yielding field of corn; **f20.5** comes to an abrupt halt as the odd bitterness creeps in; **b22** a disarmingly elegant whiskey. 40%

American/Kentucky Whisky Blends

Ancient Age Preferred (73) n16.5 t19 f19.5 b18. A marginal improvement thanks mainly to a re-worked ripe corn-sweet delivery and the cocoa-rich finish. But still preferred, one assumes, by those who probably don't care how good this distillery's whisky can be... 40%

Beam's Eight Star (69.5) n17 t18 f17 b17.5. If you don't expect too much it won't let you down. 40%

Bellows (67) n17 t17.5 f16 b16.5 Just too thin. 40%

Calvert's Extra (79) n19 t20 f20 b20. Sweet and mega-toffeed. Just creaking with caramel but extra marks for the late spice. 40%

Carstair's White Seal (72) n16.5 t18.5 f19.5 b17.5 Possibly the cleanest blend about even offering a cocoa tang on the finale. Pleasant. 40%

Hobble Creek (64) n16 t17 f15 b16. Sweet, soft, easy drinking. Total shortage of complexity. 40%

Kentucky Dale (64) n16 t17 f15 b16. Thin and spineless, though soft and decently sweet on delivery. The grain spirit completely dominates. 40%

Kessler (84.5) n20 t21 f22 b21.5. "Smooth As Silk" claims the label. And the boast is supported by what is in the bottle: a real toffee-mocha charmer with a chewy, spicy depth. 40%

PM Deluxe (75) n18 t18 f19 b18. Pleasant moments as the toffee melts in the mouth. *40%*

Sunny Brook (79.5) n20 t21 f19 b19.5. An entirely agreeable blend with toffee and lightly oiled nuts. Plus a sunny disposition... *40%*

Other American Whiskey

Buffalo Trace Experimental Collection 1989 Barrels Rediscovered white oak with seasoned staves, dist Nov 89, bott Dec 10 **(91.5) n24 t23 f22.5 b22.5.** A whispering bourbon of exceptional subtlety which makes minimum fuss of its antiquity. *45% (90 Proof)*

Buffalo Trace Experimental Collection 1991 Barrels Rediscovered white oak with seasoned staves, dist Oct 91, bott Dec 10 **(93.5) n24 t23.5 f23 b23.** Pretty classic stuff. *45%*

Buffalo Trace Experimental Collection 1993 Barrels Rediscovered white oak with seasoned staves, dist May 93, bott Dec 10 **(89) n24 t22 f21 b22.** A long way from the BT norm. *45%*

⬡ **Buffalo Trace Experimental Collection Made With Oats** white oak, dist 29 April 2002 **(85.5) n20 t22 f21.5 b22.** Oats had been used by the Irish in whiskey making for over 100 years. So it is hard to believe that some early American settler or other didn't use this particular recipe somewhere along the line...This, curiously, has a very similar texture on the palate to Sam Smith's celebrated Oat Stout from Yorkshire, England...though this is much more on the sweet side. The nose is a curious affair being both a little smoky but also vaguely butyric and thick with linseed oil. If it's an acquired nose, I haven't quite got there yet. The oats really come into play with the texture, which is a delight. Just lacks the development hoped for. *45% (90 Proof)*

⬡ **Buffalo Trace Experimental Collection Made With Rice** white oak, dist 29 April 2002 **(85) n21 t21.5 f21 b21.5.** Anyone who has tasted beer made with rice notice they have one thing in common: an appalling lack of flavour. So even if I wasn't over-excited by the prospects of this particular experiment, I was at least intrigued! The results did not overly surprise me. I expected, in theory, a bigger oak say than normal, because of less interference from the grain. And that's exactly what we got. If you want to see how oak comes into play, without it really kicking up much of a storm on the complexity front, have a butcher's at this. Sweet, clean...but limited scope. *45% (90 Proof)*

Buffalo Trace White Dog Mash #1 (93) n23 t23 f24 b23. Exceptionally high quality spirit, fabulously weighted, neither too sweet nor dry and with the distinctive cocoa character of the very best grain distillate. Beats the crap out of vodka. "White Dog" is the name for spirit which has run off the still but not yet been bottled: "New Make" in Scotland. It is not, therefore, whiskey as it has not been in any form of contact with oak. But what the hell... It must be at least 15 years ago that I told the old plant manager, Joe Darmond, that he should bottle this stuff as it would sell fast. BT brought it out initially for their distillery shop...and now it is in demand worldwide. ???? !!!! If you are reading this... what did I tell you... and about rye come to that...!!! *62.5% (125 proof)*

⬡ **Heaven Hill Trybox Series Rye New Make** code 7rl1 **(88) n22 t22.5 f21.5 b22.** A sharp, salivating, very lightly oiled, well spiced white dog bristling with flavour. And one which took me back nearly 20 years when Parker Beam poured me some new make rye at HH's now lost distillery in Bardstown and I told him, after tasting, that a proportion should be bottled before barreling. He thought that wasn't a bad plan, though he wasn't entirely sure of its commercial possibilities. This will do fine. Though the spirit in Bardstown had more copper and all round richness. *62.5%*

High West Bourye (84.5) n21.5 t22 f20 b21. With the caramels dominating, exceptionally soft and sweet with the rye much more shy than one might have imagined. A very late in the day spice helps it along. *46%. A mixing of bourbon and rye whiskey.*

⬡ **High West Son of Bourye** a blend of bourbon and rye **(95) n23** the rye notes are as crunchy as a muscovado sugar driveway; **t24.5** the kind of salivation factor that brings you to your knees in a state of grainy euphoria. The radiating brown sugars are as clean as they are exemplary; **f23.5** only now does the bourbon get a word in edgeways, though can offer only a half-hearted honey, caramel and liquorice mix; the spices are sublime; **b24** this son, presumably called Ryebon, is a stunningly stylish chap which comprehensively eclipses its lackluster parent... *46%*

⬡ **High West Campfire** rye, bourbon & Scotch malt, batch no. 3 **(93) n23.5** busy and beautifully balanced; **t22.5** salivating rye strikes first and hard. An armada of honey and caramel types sail softly into view; **f23.5** at last a hint of smoke begins to unravel and sits beautifully, almost Highland Park style, with the oaked honey; the rye ensures a rigidity is maintained as spices form; **b23.5** an enchanting, hugely complex dram...the sort of thing I conjure up in my tasting room every day, in fact, by mixing differing whisky styles from around the world. Here the rye dominates by some margin, creating the backbone on which the sweeter bourbon tones hang. The peated malt ensures a wonderful rumble. Well blended...and great fun! *46%*

Canadian Whisky

It is becoming hard to believe that Canadian was once a giant among the world whisky nations. Dotted all over its enormous land large distilleries pumped out thousands upon thousands of gallons of spirit that after years in barrel became a clean, gentle whisky.

It was cool to be seen drinking Canadian in cocktail bars on both sides of the pond. Now, sadly, Canadian whisky barely raises a beat on the pulse of the average whisky lover. It would not be beyond argument to now call Canadian the forgotten whisky empire with column inches devoted to their column stills measured now in millimetres. It is an entirely sad, almost heartbreaking, state of affairs though hopefully not an irreversible one. The finest Canadian, for me, is still whisky to be cherished and admired. But outside North America it can be painfully hard to find.

Especially seeing how whiskies containing the permitted 9.09% of non-Canadian whisky (or whisky at all) had been barred from the European market. So just to ensure Jim Murray's Whisky Bible remained on the ball I spent two spells this year in Canada tasting every Canadian whisky I could find on the market. The result, as ever, was illuminating. This latest blitz reconfirmed there was now a clear divergence of styles between traditionalist whisky like Alberta Premium and a more creamy textured, fruit-enhanced product once confined to the USA but now found in Canada itself.

However, there is no doubt that we are seeing a change in the perception of Canadian by drinkers who

BRITISH COLUMBIA

ALBERTA

MANITOBA

● Vancouver

▲ Alberta
● Calgary

▲ Okanagan

▲ Palliser

Gimli ▲

Key

● Major Town or City
▲ Distillery
† Dead Distillery

had previously confined themselves to top quality Scotch malt. Following the award of Jim Murray's Whisky Bible Canadian Whisky of the Year 2006 to Alberta Premium, I had the chance to spend time in television and radio studios around the country talking about the exceptionally high quality of top Canadian whiskies. It led to a string of emails from readers telling me they had since tasted Alberta and been somewhat shocked to find a world classic whisky lurking so unobtrusively - and cheaply - on their shelves. For many, this had led to further exploring of Canadian, and uncovering of further gems. For the Jim Murray's Whisky Bible 2013 the winning Canadian whisky asked many questions of just what is happening at Alberta. In July 2012 a knock out blind tasting of 16 award-winning whiskies from around the world I conducted had the people of Sun Peaks in British Columbia's Rocky Mountains speechless when they discovered they had voted Alberta Premium the finest whisky of the evening. No surprise, then, that it is rye from Alberta that not only won top Canadian billing in the Bible, but got through to the last six taste off for World Whisky of the Year. Yet, Masterson's 10-year-old is a label owned by an independent bottler: Alberta's official own new offering, Dark Horse, was anything but a thoroughbred by comparison.

Perhaps one of the things that makes Canadian whisky compelling is its ever-changing face. Many brands do have a tendency to move around in style slightly more than you might expect. However, there is an interesting development from Kentucky which contradicts that in an unorthodox manner. Buffalo Trace have decided to bottle some casks of Canadian in their inventory as a single barrel product. They sent me and others some samples back in their developmental stage and asked us for our input. Now, contrary to what anyone tells you, or claim they know, a Canadian single cask whisky called Bush Pilot was around some 15 years ago, the product of Canadian Club's Okanagan distillery. And each bottling was natural and fascinatingly different. The same can't quite be said for the new Caribou Crossing, a pleasant enough whisky which sports a thumping degree of unionizing caramel while the Canadian whisky lover, or potential convert, is little helped by every bottle looking identical with no cask details. BT have done little wrong in the last decade; indeed, in that time have become the most consistently excellent and exciting distillers in the world taking both bourbon and rye to new heights in my lifetime, and in Drew Mayville (a Canadian, incidentally) they have a blender at the top of his game. But the usual BT sure-footedness appears to have found a hole in the ice - for you can't help thinking that this perfect chance to win over hearts and minds to Canadian has not been fully grasped. Both Drew and I learned our Canadian from the very same school of past Canadian blending masters – and I use the term carefully – so we tend to have very similar views on matters Canadian/ Canadien. When last in Frankfort I was unable to discuss this with him as we had the small matter of the Single Oak Project to dissect. Next time though I will be locking friendly Caribou horns with him.

ONTARIO

QUEBEC

Glenora

NOVA SCOTIA

Quebec

Valleyfield

Montreal

Canada Mist

Toronto

Kittling Ridge

Walkerville

Canadian Single Malts
GLENORA

Glen Breton db **(81) n19 t21 f20 b21.** Ultra sweet malt, in almost concentrated form with a tantalising whiff of smoke hanging around; mildly spiced and slightly oily, soapy finish. 43%

Glen Breton Ice Aged 10 Years db **(85.5) n21.5 t21 f22 b21.** Tasting both a full strength bottled Canadian, and one that had been matured in Icewine barrels, I was nearly blown through the back of my seat and into the wall. One of the biggest shocks to hit you on the Canadian whisky scene today, there is no denying that this whisky offers sufficient panache and lucidity to genuinely impress. Hardly an exercise in perfect balance, it certainly celebrates the art of surprise and, late on, charm. The cocoa-dusted butterscotch really is a rare treat and, thanks to the fruity world it finds itself in, a truly unique and enjoyable experience. 57.2%

Glen Breton Rare db **(80) n18 t21 f20 b21.** Caramel nose a bit soapy but the buttery, sweet malt, with its vanilla fizz, makes for a pleasant experience. 43%

⋯ **Glen Breton Rare Aged 10 Years** bott 2010 db **(89.5) n22** a slight feintiness is soon blown away by a little warming in the hand. This allows the malt to positively sing in the glass, though the choir contains a fruit toffee bass; **t23** ye Gods! Didn't expect the malt to come through so beautifully clear and embellished by a light creamy texture. Even something of the Cardhus about this. So much to chew; the spices rattle up a good pace as the oaks begin to arrive; **f22** dries and thins with the accent on toffee vanilla; **b22.5** an impressive whisky: one of the best bottlings of this age for some while and showing the malt at full throttle. 43%

⋯ **Glen Breton Rare Aged 14 Years** db **(92) n23.5** probably the most Scottish style of any nose I have encountered from a Glenora bottling. Even a delicate degree of spice on hand to maximise the clean barley intensity; the oak used is top notch, showing a delicate trace of bourbon and a gorgeous lime jelly to the butterscotch... wow! **t22.5** melt-in-the-mouth barley reverberates around the palate; **f23** long, a charming light oiliness helping the sweeter elements of the barley to fuse with the warming oak; soft liquorice and Greek honey flourish; **b23** what is there not to enjoy? Some exceptionally good casks involved here. 43%

Glen Breton Battle Of The Glen Aged 15 Years Special Edition db **(94) n23.5 t23.5 f23 b24.** I really did know they were capable of bottling something this good: there isn't a single barrel of this vintage I have not tasted in their warehouse at one time or another during its maturation cycle. This watermark bottling from then is an essentially sweet whisky, tasting all the sweeter as it marks the little distillery's victory over the Goliath that is the Scotch Whisky Association in their rightful battle to retain the right to use the name of their brand. Just sometimes there is evidence there just may be a god... 43% 4200 bottles.

⋯ **Glen Breton Ice Aged 17 Years** aged in Icewine barrels bott 2010 db **(90.5) n22.5** a fascinating mix of inelegance and sharp, fruity focus. More thumbs up than down...; **t24** I am stunned: on delivery alone this is world class whisky without a shadow of doubt: natural elegance such as this comes along only too rarely in whisky. The degree of oil to the malt borders perfection, the intensity and sharpness of the clean apple and pear fruit are exceptional; soft muscovado sugars melt naturally into the buttery mix; **f21.5** such a complicated creature, it is no surprise when the balance collapses under the weight of the bitterness; **b22.5** a different animal to the 10-y-o Icewine version, though having much more to do with the spirit than the casks. Yet never before has this distillery sent me such a box of wonderful delights such as these before. It is as though their victory over the Scotch industry has lifted a cloud of self-doubt. Glenora appears to have come of age. 54.6%

⋯ **Glen Breton Rare Cabot Links Reserve Aged 19 Years** db **(86.5) n21 t22.5 f21 b22.** You know when astronomers build a super-powerful new telescope that gives them a clearer view of when the universe began. This bottling is a bit like that... taking us back to the days of the Glen Breton Big Bang. Lots of dramatic barley to view. But, naturally, all the more basic and primitive elements are there on show, also... 46%

Canadian Blended Whisky

Alberta Premium (95.5) n24 throbbing, pulsing rye on a variety of levels: full and juicy, dull and dusty, firm and flinty. Unique and unmistakable; **t25** my first whisky of the day – and it needs to be. The tastebuds are given such a working over that they need to be fully tuned and fit to take this on. Again it is all about the rye: the first three flavours to pound the mouth are all rye-related. The very first are juicy with a minute sweetness. The second, hanging onto the coattails of the first are Rockies hard and brittle, clattering into the tastebuds with zero yield. Next comes a quick follow through of explosive peppers, but again leaving in their wake a semi-sweet juicy, fruitiness, almost certainly from the malted rye. No other whisky unleashes this combination of grainy punches around the palate. The words beautiful and complex don't even begin to do this whisky justice; **f22.5** dulls down, probably because of the needless caramel added, but there is slightly more depth than before thanks most probably to the malted rye. The spices continue to fizz as the Demerara-tipped vanillas make their mark;

b24 it has just gone 8am and the Vancouver Island sky is one of clear blue. My windows are open to allow in some chilly, early Spring air and, though only the first week of March, an American robin sits in the arbutus tree, resplendent in its now two-toned leaves, calling for a mate, as it has done since 5.15 this morning, his song blending with the lively trill of the house finches and the doleful, maritime anthem of the gull. It seems the natural environment of Alberta Premium, back here to its rye-studded best after a couple I tasted socially in Canada last year appeared comparatively dull and restrained. I am tasting this from Bottle Lott No L93300197 and it is classic, generating all I expect and now demand. A national treasure. *40%*

⸭ **Alberta Premium** bott lott L1317 **(96) n24 t25 f23 b24.** Tasting this three years on from the sample above, there is absolutely nothing to add or subtract (except the finish is fractionally more engrossing): the consistency and brilliance defies belief. *40%*

⸭ **Alberta Premium** bott lott L2150 **(94) n23.5 t24 f23 b23.5.** Fractionally duller than the 2011 bottling sampled above with less emphasis on the crystalline rye and more on cane sugar. Still a treat! *40%*

Alberta Premium 25 Years Old (95) n24 t23 f23 b25. Faultless. Absolutely nothing dominates. Yet every aspect has its moment of conquest and glory. It is neither bitter nor sweet, yet both. It is neither soft nor hard on the palate yet both elements are there. Because of the 100% rye used, this is an entirely new style of whisky to hit the market. No Canadian I know has ever had this uncompromising brilliance, this trueness to style and form. And, frightening to think, it could be improved further by bottling at least 46% and un-chillfiltered. For any whisky lover who ever thought Canadian was incapable of hitting the heights among the world's greats. *40%. Alberta Distillers.*

Alberta Premium 30 Years (88.5) n23 t23.5 f20 b22. It doesn't take much to tip the balance of a whisky this delicate on the nose and delivery. Five extra years in the cask has nudged the oak just a little too far. However, savour the nose and delivery which are to die for. *40%*

⸭ **Alberta Premium Dark Horse (84) n18 t22 f22 b22.** The blurb on the back says it is crafted for the "next generation of whisky connoisseur". Fine. But personally, I'd always shape a whisky for the true connoisseurs of today... I have not spoken to the blending team at Alberta to discuss this and, as the book has to be finished within a week or two, I won't get a chance. But this is the most extraordinary development in Canadian I have seen for a while. The nose is not great: it really does seem as though fruit cordial has been given the lead role. But the taste really does challenge, and I have to say there are many aspects I enjoy. It is as though some peated malt has been added to the mix as the finish does have distinctive smokiness. And the balance has been expertly worked to ensure the sugars don't dominate while the spices are persistent. But if it falls down anywhere, the over reliance on the fruit apart, it is the fact that Alberta makes the best spirit in Canada by a very great distance....yet someone has forgotten to ensure that fact is made clear in the taste and the nose especially. *45%*

Alberta Springs Aged 10 Years (83) n21 t21 f20 b20. Really appears to have had a bit of a flavourectomy. Sweet but all traces of complexity have vanished. *40%* ⊙⊙

Barton's Canadian 36 Months Old (78) n19 t20 f19 b20. Sweet, toffeed, easy-going. *40%*

Bowman's Canadian Whisky (90.5) n22 clean but no shortage of attractive vanilla; **t22** lightly oiled and mouth-clinging. Loads of early chocolate and even a hint of praline; **f23.5** long, distinguished and with the lightly spiced chocolate content heading through the roof; **b23** a delicious, honest Canadian for chocoholics. *40%*

Black Velvet (78) n18 t20 f20 b20. A distinctly off-key nose is compensated for by a rich corn and vanilla kick on the palate. But that famous spice flourish is a distant memory. Another big caramel number. *40%*

Campbell & Cooper Aged a Minimum of 36 Months (84.5) n21.5 t22 f20 b21. Huge flavour profile. An orchard of oranges on the nose and profound vanilla on delivery. *40%*

Canadian Club 100 Proof (89) n21 t23 f22 b23. If you are expecting this to be a high-octane version of the standard CC Premium, you'll be in for a shock. This is a much fruitier dram with an oilier body to absorb the extra strength. An entertaining blend. *50%.*

Canadian Club Premium (92) n23 a comfortable marriage of fruit and drier, almost chalky vanilla; **t22.5** delicate, impressively rounded with just enough firm fruitiness to suggest a semi rye character as well as what now appears to be a ubiquitous sherry-cum-grape note and then a fabulous warming as the spices make an elegant entry; **f23** long, superbly spiced **b23.5** a greatly improved whisky which now finds the fruit fitting into the mix with far more panache than of old. Once a niggardly whisky, often seemingly hell-bent on refusing to enter into any form of complexity: but not now! Great spices in particular. I'm impressed. *40%* ⊙⊙

Canadian Club Aged 6 Years (88.5) n21.5 t22 f22.5 b22.5. Not at all bad for a Canadian some purists turn their nose up at as it's designed for the American market. Just brimming with mouth-watering enormity and style. Dangerously moreish. *40%*

Canadian Club Reserve Aged 10 Years (86) n20 t22 f21.5 b22. Odd cove, this. The nose is less than welcoming and offers a hotchpotch of somewhat discordant notes giving a jumbled message and less than well defined statement of intent. Decent delivery, though, shifting through the gears with some impressive and sultry fruit tying in well with a rare grain onslaught found in Canadian these days. The finish, though, just can't steer away from the rocks of bitterness, alas. Again, as so often appears to be the case with CC, the spices star. 40% ⊙⊙

Canadian Club Classic Aged 12 Years (91.5) n22 fruity, firm, a sprinkle of cinnamon yet a touch closed, even with maximum coaxing; **t24** beautifully coated with honey and grain oils, allowing for a juicy chewiness to gain momentum before delicate spices strike: they don't come much more luxuriant than this; **f21.5** long with a similar copper-honey character to the standard CC. Crushed sultana and sharper raisin; some grains deliver some more fiddly, intrinsic notes. Lots of chalky vanilla confirms the age; a point dropped for the slight furry bitterness at the death; **b23.5** a confident whisky which makes the most of a honeycomb theme. 40%

⊰⊱ **Canadian Club Small Batch Classic 12 Aged 12 Years** batch C12-020 **(75.5) n21 t22.5 f15 b17.** A syrupy whisky which talks a great game on the back label, but fails to deliver in reality. Big fruit, perhaps a little too heavily accented as other avenues of complexity are limited. The bitter, tangy finish is not great at all. 40%

Canadian Club Aged 20 Years (92.5) n24 bread pudding and sherried fruit cake combine. Some real fizzle and entertainment – oh, and some class – make for one of the best Canadian noses around; **t21** a very tame delivery, with soft oils confused by the fruit; pleasant enough but almost a cancelling out of character; **f23.5** readjusts and reinvents itself brilliantly and we are back to the same bread pudding my mum used to make; as those spices settle, some marauding cocoa also goes for it...and then a return to soft corn oil... it's bitter sweet all the way and, as finishes go, this is a bloody long way...!! **b23** in previous years, CC20 has ranked among the worst whiskies I have tasted, not just in Canada, but the world. Their current bottling, though, is not even a distant relation. Sure, it has a big sherry investment. But the sheer elan and clever use of spice make this truly magnificent. Possibly the most pleasant surprise in my latest trawl through all Canada's whiskies. 40%

Canadian Club Sherry Cask batch no. SC-018 **(76) n18 t20 f20 b18.** Twice as strong as you can normally buy Sherry yet somehow has only half the body. As I say, I really don't know what to make of this. Nor do I get the point. 41.3%

Canadian Five Star Rye Whisky (83) n21 t22 f20 b20. An entirely tame, well behaved Canadian which celebrates the inherent sweetness of the species. That said, the immediate impact on the palate is pretty delicious with a quick, flash explosion of something spicy. But it is the deft, satin-soft mouthfeel which may impress most. 40%

Canadian Hunter (85.5) n20.5 t21 f22 b22. Remains truly Canadian in style. The toffee has diminished, allowing far more coffee and cocoa to ensure a delightful middle and finish. 40%

Canadian Mist (78) n19 t20.5 f18.5 b20. Much livelier than previous incarnations despite the inherent, lightly fruited softness. 40%

Canadian Pure Gold (82) n21.5 t20.5 f20 b20. Full-bodied and still a notably lush whisky. The pure gold may have more to do with the caramel than the years in cask but the meat of this whisky still gives you plenty to chew over. I especially enjoy the gradual building of spices. 40%

Canadian Spirit (78) n20 t20 f19 b19. A real toffee-fest with a touch of hard grain around the edges. 40%. Carrington Distillers (Alberta Distillers).

Caribou Crossing Single Barrel (84) n20 t22.5 f20 b21.5. While the nose offers an unholy battle between some apple-fruity rye notes and dry, dusty caramel, there is a real pulsating delivery with the sharper spices helped along the way by the silkiness of the body. Though the caramel offers a toffee-fudge backdrop, a countering dry date sweetness does more than enough to keep it at bay. However, the finish dulls out as the caramel gains the upper hand, though the twitching spices do ensure a light, throbbing beat. An enjoyable Canadian, undoubtedly, I am somewhat perplexed by it. There is no reference to the barrel number so you won't know if you are buying from different casks. Also, if it is single barrel what is the point of the caramel? If it is to make all the casks taste the same, or similar, then why not just blend them together. A badly missed opportunity. 40%. Sazerac.

Centennial 10 Year Limited Edition (88.5) n21.5 t23 f22 b22. Retains its usual honey-flavoured breakfast cereal style, but the complexity has increased. Busy and charming. 40%

Century Reserve 8 Years Old Premium (82) n20 t21 f20 b21. Clean vanilla caramel. 40%

Century Reserve Custom Blend 15 Years Plus (88.5) n21.5 t22 f23 b22. After two days of being ambushed in every direction, or completely steamrollered by Canadian caramel, my tastebuds are in total shock. Caramel kept to an absolute minimum so that it hardly registers at all. Charming and refined drinking. 40%

Century Reserve 21 Years Old (91.5) n23.5 a beautiful mix of banana and soft oak; a teasing spice prickle is offset by a light liquorice and sugar cane juice sweetness: impressively delicate and refined; **t23** the slight hint of rum on the nose is emphatically underscored on delivery: back to sugar cane and the inevitable Highwood distillery spices; **f23** continues on the vanilla-spice theme and, for all the obvious age present, that rum character continues throughout. Lovely strands of honey and even coconut balance the drier elements; **b22** quite beautiful, but a spirit that is as likely to appeal to rum lovers as whisky ones. *40%*

Century Reserve Custom Blend lot no. 1525 **(87) n21.5 t22 f21.5 b22.** An enjoyable whisky which doesn't quite reach its full potential. *40%*

Corby's Canadian 36 Months Old (85) n20 t21 f22 b22. Attractive with fine bitter-sweet balance and I love the late spice kick-back. *40%. Barton. Interesting label: as a keen ornithologist, I had no idea there were parrots in Canada. Must be related to the Norwegian Blue.*

Crown Royal (86) n22 t23.5 f19.5 b21. The Crown has spoken and it has been decreed that this once ultra grainy old whisky is taking its massive move to a silky fruitiness as far as it can go. It was certainly looking that way last time out; on this re-taste (and a few I have unofficially tasted) there is now no room for doubt. If you like grape, especially the sweeter variety, you'll love this. The highpoint is the sublime delivery and starburst of spice. The low point? The buzzy, unhappy finale. The Grain Is Dead. Long Live The Grape! *40%* ⊙ ⊙

Crown Royal Black (85) n22 t23 f18.5 b21.5. Not for the squeamish: a Canadian which goes for it with bold strokes from the off which makes it a whisky worth discovering. The finish needs a rethink, though. *45%* ⊙

Crown Royal Cask No 16 Finished in Cognac Casks (85.5) n21.5 t21 f22 b21. Clean cut and very grapey. The nose is unique in the whisky world: it is one of Cognac. Otherwise struggles to really find its shape and rhythm. A perfect Canadian for those who prefer theirs with an air of grace and refinement but very limited depth. In fact, those who prefer a Cognac. *40%*

Crown Royal Limited Edition (87) n22 t22.5 f20.5 b22. A much happier and productive blend than before with an attractive degree of complexity but the more bitter elements of the finish have been accentuated. *40%* ⊙ ⊙

Crown Royal Special Reserve (96) n24 a clean and attractively spiced affair with cinnamon and the faintest pinch of allspice leading the way: rye at work, one presumes; the fruit is clean and precise with weightier grape overshadowing a green apple freshness; **t24** a spicier element to the usual rye and fruit delivery, much more in keeping with the nose, but that fabulous, contrary mouth-feel of harder grain and softer fruit continues to do the business. The spices build slowly but with an impressive evenness and determination: one of the most outstanding Canadians on the palate of them all; **f24** the finish has been tidied up and with stunning effect: no more sawdust and eye-watering dryness. Both grain and soft fruit ensure a magnificently mouth-watering end to an amazing journey. **b24** complex, well weighted and simply radiant: it is like looking at a perfectly shaped, gossamer clad Deb at a ball. The ryes work astonishingly well here (they appear to be of the malted, ultra-fruity variety) and perhaps to best effect after Alberta Premium, though now it is a hard call between the two. *40%*

Crown Royal XR Extra Rare lot no. L7064 N4 **(93.5) n24 t23 f23 b23.5.** Just about identical to the previous bottle above. The only difference is on the finish where the rye, fortified with spice, decides to hang back and battle it out to the death; the toffee and vanilla make a controlled retreat. Either the same bottling with a slightly different stance after a few years in the bottle, or a different one of extraordinary high consistency. *40%*

Danfield's Limited Edition Aged 21 Years (95) n24 t24 f23.5 b23.5. A quite brilliant first-time whisky. The back label claims this to be small batch, but there is no batch number on the bottle, alas. Or even a visible bottling code. But this is a five star performer and one of this year's whiskies of the world. *40%*

Danfield's Private Reserve (84.5) n20 t21.5 f22 b21. A curious, non-committal whisky which improves on the palate as it goes along. An overdose of caramel (yawn!!) has done it no favours, but there is character enough for it to pulse out some pretty tasty spice. Seamless and silky, for all the toffee there underlying corn-rich clarity is a bit of a turn on. *40%*

8 Seconds Small Batch (86) n20 t22 f22.5 b21.5. Fruity, juicy, luxurious. And perhaps one of the few whiskies on the market anywhere in the world today which could slake a thirst. *40%*

Forty Creek Barrel Select (86.5) n21.5 t22 f21 b21.5. Thank goodness that the sulphur taint I had found on this in recent years has now vanished. A lush, enjoyable easy-goer, this juices up attractively at the start and ends with an almost sophisticated dry pithiness. *40%* ⊙ ⊙

⋯⊱ **Forty Creek Confederation Oak Reserve** lot 1867-B **(94.5) n23.5** much more confidence to the fruit than in the previous bottling: clean and sculpted to fit rather beautifully with the delicate dry coconut and moist golden syrup, muscovado sugar and thinned heather honey; some walnut oil tops off a very attractive experience; **t24** one of Forty Creek's all time great deliveries: you cannot even begin to fault the sublime balance between the corn oil, the sugars and peppers. All this framed by salivating ultra-ripe fruits and a countering vanilla oakiness. Fabulous texture and depth; **f23.5** spiced fruit chocolate pulses like the afterglow of a particularly enjoyable experience...; **b23.5** those who tasted the first batch of this will be intrigued by this follow up. The shape and intensity profile has been re-carved and all now fits together like a jigsaw. *40%*

⋄⋄ **Forty Creek Copper Pot Reserve (91.5)** n23 clean juicy fruit cascades into a spicy hollow; exceptional sweet-dry balance; **t23.5** a big whisky couched in velvet: the delivery bristles and pulses with spiced greengages held on a fabulously firm backbone of what seems like rye (that last statement made me look at the back label...rye is in there!!) with a soothing massage of soft corn oils for the mid-ground; **f22** dry and perhaps a hint of tobacco smoke; the oak shows itself in a sawdusty way, but with a light hint of cocoa and raisin; **b23** one of the beauties of John hall's whiskies at Forty Creek is that they follow no set pattern in the whisky would: they offer flavour profiles really quite different from anything else. That is why they are worth that bit of extra time for your palate to acclimatise. Here you are exceptionally well rewarded... 43%

⋄⋄ **Forty Creek Double Barrel Reserve** lot 247 **(86)** n21.5 t22.5 f20.5 b21.5. The usual juicy ride and plenty to savour early on. But there is something slightly off balance about the finish here. 40%

⋄⋄ **Forty Creek Port Wood Reserve** lot 61 **(95.5)** n24.5 oh my word! Very highest quality Turkish Delight with some pretty top score chocolate; the fruit hangs off the frame full of juice and muscovado sugars. It demands spices...and gets them – with the right pizzazz! **t24** the delivery is pure silk in texture and the most stunning fruit and spice on delivery. Hard to know whether to suck as it melts in the mouth, or chew as the background depth is outrageously nutty, with more cocoa to thicken. It is the astonishing spice that really mesmerises, as it is of almost perfect intensity; **f23** dries into an attractive crushed grape pip dryness, again with the spices lingering; **b24** John P Hall has got his ducks in a row. Magnificent! 45%

Forty Creek Three Grain (76) n19 t20 f18 b19. Not quite as well assembled as some Three grains I have come across over the last few years. There is a lopsidedness to this one: we know the fruit dominates (and I still haven't a clue why, when surely this of all whiskies, just has to be about the grains!) but the bitterness interferes throughout. If there have been sherry casks used here, I would really have a close look at them. 40%

⋄⋄ **Fremont Mischief Whiskey** batch MPJ-0803, bott 6 Oct 11 **(77)** n19 t20 f19 b19. Though this was from the Mischief distillery in Seattle, USA, the whiskey was produced in Canada. Wherever, overly sweet, overly toffeed and bereft of complexity. Like Alberta Springs on a very bad day. 40%

Gibson's Finest Aged 12 Years (77) n18 t20 f19 b20. Unlike the Sterling, going backwards rather than forwards. This is way too syrupy, fruity and toffee impacted. Despite the very good spice, almost closer to a liqueur than a true whisky style. 40% ⊙ ⊙

Gibson's Finest Rare Aged 18 Years (95.5) n24 close your eyes and sniff and you would swear you have a bourbon-rye mix: simultaneously crisp and soft, the sharpness of the rye and apple-style fruitiness is sublime and as enticing as it gets; **t24.5** a perfect transfer onto the palate: spectacularly juicy with all kinds of clean rye and corn notes bobbling around in a gorgeous gentle Demerara sugar backdrop; **f23.5** impressive vanilla and long strands of grain and bitter liquorice; **b23.5** so far ahead of both Sterling and the 12, it is hard to believe they are from the same stable. But make no mistake; this is pure thoroughbred: truly world class. 40%

⋄⋄ **Gibson's Finest 100th Grey Cup Special Edition (87)** n21 the touch of Kentucky on the nose isn't of bourbon but drying tobacco leaf; no shortage of dusty toffee, either; **t23** a string of intense sugar notes – yes, including maple! – makes for a rattling start, with spices pouring in at the first opportunity. The middle is a bit of a No Man's Land...; **f21** dry and bitters as the caramel bites deeper; **b22** when the label tells you there is a hint of maple, they aren't joking... 40%

Gibson's Finest Canadian Whisky Bourbon Cask Rare Reserve (89) n23 t21 f23 b22. A much better version than the first bottling, the depth this time being massively greater. 40%

Gibson's Finest Sterling (86.5) n22 t22.5 f20.5 b21.5. A massively improved Canadian that had me doing the equivalent of a tasting double take: had to look twice at this to check I had the right stuff! Much firmer now in all the right places with the corn making sweeping statements, the golden syrup melting into all the required crevices and spices exploding at the appropriate moments. Just need to sort the heavy toffee and bitter finish out and this would be up in the Canadian Premier League. 40% ⊙ ⊙

Gibson's New Oak (88) n22 t21 f23 b22. Distinctly different from any other Canadian doing the rounds: the oak influence makes a wonderful and clever impact. 40%

Highwood Pure Canadian (84) n20 t21 f22 b21. A decent, ultra-clean Canadian with markedly more character than before. Certainly the caramel has been seriously reduced in effect and the wheat ensures a rather attractive spice buzz while the cane juice sweetness harmonises well. Perhaps most delightful is the wonderful and distinct lack of fruit. 40%

Hiram Walker Special Old (93) n22.5 granite-hard with softer, oilier, more citrusy notes being trampled underfoot by almost impermeable grain; **t24** textbook delivery with the rye offering both yielding juice and granite. Absolutely no let up in the spice development which works outstanding well with the hard skeleton. The sweetness is more upfront now with the honey petering out towards the late middle; just gone up an impressive notch; **f23** drier now with the grain offering rich vanilla though the muscovado sugar signature subtlety remains; the caramel is present but doing a little less damage **b23.5** even with the extra degree of all-round harmony, this remains the most solid, uncompromising Canadian of them all. And I love it! Not least because this is the way Special old has been for a very long time with obviously no intentions of joining the fruity bandwagon. Honest, first class Canadian. *40%*

James Foxe (77.5) **n20 t19.5 f19 b19.** James could do with putting some weight on... *40%*

Lord Calvert (72.5) **n19 t18.5 f17 b18.** Truly eccentric aristocracy, this. Comes from the most noble of homes, Alberta Distillery, and the pedigree of the rye is evident in patches on both nose and delivery. Then marries something very fruity well beneath its class. *40%*

⟐ **Masterson's 10 Year Old Straight Rye Whisky** batch 003 (96.5) **n24** fizzing with fruity finesse, there is little doubting the grain involved here; almost a bubble gum sweetness to the fruit and through the melting softness lurks a note as firm and sharp as a sabre; **t24** just about as mouth-watering as it is spellbinding, the taste buds are immediately immersed in a stellar degree of crisp, sparkling rye notes; vanilla pods pop as it soaks in the juicy, clean rye; **f24** If you want to see an almost perfect degree of spice at work in a whisky, you really can't do better than savour the finish of this gorgeous bottling. Helped along by deft oil, the crystalline sugars and light vanillas just carry on their hypnotic dance; **b24.5** a magnificent whisky without any shadow of doubt. Rye is my favourite whisky type and this displays the style to a degree of excellence which is truly memorable in terms of a commercial bottling. Someone has done an outstanding job in selecting these casks. Interesting, however, that they don't actually state on the bottle that this is Canadian and confuse things a little further by spelling it "whiskey". My understanding is that this is unmalted rye from the outstanding Alberta Distillery in Calgary. What is certain is that this is a true classic of its style. And not so much Masterson's but Masterful. *45%*

McGuinness Silk Tassel (79.5) **n20 t21 f19.5 b19.** Silk or satin? The corn oils offer a delightful sheen but still the caramel is over enthusiastic. *40%*

⟐ **McLoughlin and Steele Blended in the Okanagan Valley** (87.5) **n22** clean vanilla tinged with grapefruit; **t22** more citrus on the juicy delivery. Corn oil fills the mid ground; **f21.5** big, drying vanilla; spice; **b22** as straight as a die: a Canadian Rye... without any discernible rye. *40%*

Wm Morrison Imported Canadian Rye (87.5) **n22 t22 f21.5 b22.** Still a lovely Canadian, though the toffee needs toning down. Not sure what "Full Strength" is doing on the label when bottled at 40%, though... *40%*

Mountain Rock (87) **n22 t20.5 f22.5 b22.** Still a soft Canadian cocking a melt-in-the-mouth snook at its name. But this time the fruit is just over anxious to be heard and a degree of its old stability has been eroded. *40%. Kittling Ridge*

⟐ **Okanagan Spirits Canadian Rye** (88.5) **n23** one of the most delicate and teasing of Canadian noses: a beautiful and quite natural marriage between the grains and vanillas with just the right squeeze of lemon; **t22.5** seriously juicy. Just as light on the nose with a lovely coating of lemon drops. The vanilla really does show at its very cleanest; **f21** vanilla now left alone for a quick finale; **b22** a crisp, quite beautiful whisky with a youthful strain. Sort the thin finish out and we'd have something to really remember! Not, by the way, a whisky distilled at their new distillery. *40%*

Pendleton Let'er Buck (91.5) **n22.5 t23 f22.5 b23.5.** A significantly improved whisky from the ultra-sweet, nigh on syrupy concoction of before. Here the surprisingly complex and sensual grains take star billing, despite the caramel: it almost makes a parody of being Canadian, so unmistakable is the style. For those who affectionately remember Canadian Club from 20-30 years ago, this might bring a moistening of the eye. *40% (80 proof). Hood River Distillers.*

Potter's Crown (83) **n19 t21.5 f21.5 b21.** Silky and about the friendliest and most inoffensive whisky on this planet. The dusty aroma and thick, chewy toffee backbone says it all but still impossible not to enjoy! *40%*

Potter's Special Old a blend of 5 to 11 year old rye whisky (91) **n23.5 t23 f22 b22.5.** More Canadian than a hockey punch-up – and, for all the spice, somewhat more gentle, too. *40%*

Potter's Special Old Rye (85.5) **n21 t23.5 f20 b21.** Not quite the force majeure of a year or two back, the grains are now thinner and starker despite the beautifully striking delivery on the palate. The soft honey tones are an attractive compensation but the austerity on nose and finish takes a little getting used to when remembering previous incarnations. *40%*

Rich and Rare (79) **n20 t20 f20 b19.** Simplistic and soft. One for toffee lovers. *40%*

Rich and Rare Reserve (86.5) **n19.5 t21 f23.5 b22.5.** Actually does what it says on the tin, certainly as to regard the "Rich" bit. But takes off when the finish spices up and even offers some ginger cake on the finale. Lovely stuff. *40%*

Royal Canadian (87.5) **n22 t22.5 f21 b22.** Now there's a whisky which is on the up. *40%*

Royal Canadian Small Batch (88) **n22 t22.5 f21.5 b22.** A big Canadian with a pleasing silk and steel pulse. *40%. Sazerac.*

Royal Reserve (84.5) n19 t22.5 f21.5 b21.5. No question that the delivery is much richer, fresher and entertaining than before with the spices, dovetailing with subtle fruit, ensuring a complexity previously lacking - especially at the death. Frustratingly, the caramel seems to be biting deeper on the nose, which has taken a backward step. A much more enjoyable and satisfying experience, though. *40%*

Royal Reserve Gold (94.5) n24 this was already one of the better Canadian noses. And with this latest bottling the grain complexity has moved up a gear. Bereft of the tacky toffee which dulls so many Canadian whiskies, we have here a joyous mixture of rye and citrus notes beautifully embedded in decent, vanilla-clad oak and the most tantalising of light honey tones; t23.5 a glorious composition of juicy, salivating rye in tandem with a honey-biscuit note gets this off to a stupendous start. It gets better still as the spices lift off and that honey begins to stick to the roof of the mouth; f23 magically light: a dusting of oak gives a nod towards a respectable, aged dryness but then this acts only as a foil to the delicate lime and Fruit Pastille juiciness and late, radiating rye; b24 retains its position as a classy, classy Canadian that is an essay on balance. Don't confuse this with the much duller standard bottling: this has been moulded in recent years into one of the finest – and among its country's consumers - generally most underrated Canadians on the market. *40%*

Sam Barton Aged 5 Years (83.5) n19 t21.5 f22 b21. Exceptionally sweet session whisky with a lovely maple syrup glow and some complexity on the finish. Friendly, hospitable and impossible not to like. *40%. La Martiniquaise, France.*

Schenley Golden Wedding (92) n22 t24 f22 b23. Like a rare, solid marriage, this has improved over time. Always consistent and pleasant, there now appears to be a touch of extra age and maturity which has sent the complexity levels up dramatically. Quite sublime. *40%*

Schenley OFC (90) n22 t22.5 f23 b22.5. Notice anything missing from this whisky? Well the 8-year-old age statement has fallen off the label. But this is still a truly superb whisky which would benefit perhaps from toning down the degree of sweetness, but gets away with it in spectacular fashion thanks to those seductive oils. Not as complex as the magnificent old days, but a whisky that would have you demanding a refill nine time out of ten. *40%*

Seagram's Canadian 83 (86.5) n21 t22 f21.5 b22. A vastly improved blend which has drastically cut the caramel to reveal a melt-in-the-mouth, slightly crisp grain. There are some citrusy edges but the buttery vanilla and pleasing bite all go to make for a chic little number. *40%*

Seagram's VO (91) n22 dried banana skin, a touch of waffle and a complex layering of drier, oaky notes; t23.5 mouth-filling, lush corn oil and a slow, sensual build up of brown sugar and spice; f22.5 back to its oaky promise on the nose as it dries with a mixture of niggly spice and vanilla; b23 with a heavy heart I have to announce the king of rye-enriched Canadian, VO, is dead. Long live the corn-dominant VO. Over the years I have seen the old traditional character ebb away: now I have let go and have no option other than to embrace this whisky for what it has become: infinitely better than a couple of years back; not in the same league as a decade ago. But just taking it on face value, credit where credit is due. This is an enjoyably playful affair, full of vanilla-led good intention, corn and complexity. There is even assertive spice when needed and the most delicately fruity edge...though not rye-style. Thoughtfully blended and with no little skill, I am impressed. And look forward to seeing how this develops in future years. A treat which needs time to discover. *40%* ⊙

Snake River Stampede 8 Years Old dist 12 Dec 99, bott. 18 Jul 08 **(87.5)** n22.5 t22.5 f21 b21.5. A bit concerned when I read in the blurb that they finish this Canadian whisky in sherry butts. But no need; as clean as a perfectly lassoed colt. As silky as a cowboy's kerchief. *40%*

⠿ **Still Waters Special 1+11 Blend** batch 1204, bott 2012 **(92)** n23.5 superb weaving of deep vanilla, heather honey, corn and cocoa oils and muscovado sugars...I must be in Canada..! t23 the most gorgeous texture and complex sugars. Yet, somehow not overly sweet as the drying, chalky vanillas and sharp citrus breaks up the monopoly; f22.5 the vanilla and caramel on its own with the sugars spent leaves a bitter but manageable finale; b23 if the boys at Still Waters distillery end up with a whisky as enjoyable as this when theirs has matured, Canadian whisky will have flourished. *40%. 1200 bottles.*

Tangle Ridge Aged 10 Years (69) n18.5 t19.5 f15 b16. Decidedly less in your face than of old, unless you are thinking custard pies. For all the cleaned up aroma and early injection of spiced sultana, the uncompromisingly grim finish remains its usual messy self. An unpleasant reminder as to why I only taste this when it's Bible time... *40%*

Tesco Canadian Whisky (75) n18 t18 f20 b19. Sweet, clean, uninspiring. *40%*

⠿ **Western Gold Canadian Whisky (91)** n23 a lovely intertwining of delicate, slightly citrusy vanilla and light corn oils. With toffee, of course...; t23 clean, sweet, delicate with outstanding oils from the grain. The thin honey is a treat; f22.5 long and back to citrus vanilla again; b22.5 clean and absolutely classic Canadian: you can't ask for much more, really. *40%*

White Owl (77.5) n19 t19.5 f20 b19. White whisky: in others words, a whisky the same colour as water. To both nose and taste somewhat reminds me of the long gone Manx whisky which was casks of fully matured scotch re-distilled and bottled. Sweet and pleasant. But I doubt if connoisseurs will give two hoots... 40%

Windsor (85.5) n21 t22 f21 b21.5. A whisky you could usually bet your week's wages on for consistency and depth. Here, though, the usual rye fruity, crispness has been dumbed down and though there are enough spices to make this a pleasant affair, the impact of the caramel is a tad too significant. The usual custard sweetness has also changed shape and dry vanilla at the death is the compromise. 40%

Windsor (86) n20 t21 f23 b22. Pleasant but with the majority of edges found on the Canadian edition blunted. Some outstanding, almost attritional, spice towards the middle and finale, though. Soft and desirable throughout: a kind of feminine version of the native bottling. 40%. For US market.

Winn Dixie Canadian Whisky (80) n19 t20 f21 b20. Soft, sweet, toffeed and boasting a little spice...but with minimum fuss. 40%

Wiser's Very Old 18 Years Old (90.5) n24 t23 f21.5 b22. Much better than the last bottling I encountered, which in itself was no slouch. Here, though, the blender has written bolder what he is trying to achieve. 40%

Wiser's De Luxe (86) n20 t22.5 f21.5 b22. Still nothing like the classic, ultra-charming and almost fragile-delicate Wiser's of old. But this present bottling has got its head partly out of the sand by injecting a decently oaked spiciness to the proceedings and one might even fancy detecting shards of fruity- rye brightness beaming through the toffeed clutter. Definitely an impressive turn for the better and the kind of Canadian with a dangerous propensity to grow on you. If they had the nerve to cut the caramel, this could be a cracker... 40%

Wiser's Legacy (95) n24 even by Canadian standards, a little different: coriander and juniper give a slight gin-style edge to this, though waiting in the wings is a subtle, spicy wine quality. The teasing sweetness, not entirely without a bourbon style new-oakiness and hint of rye-fruitiness, has all the intensity of Mona Lisa's smile...; **t24.5** there is a crystalline quality to the nose, and it transfers immediately to the palate. One is reminded of absolutely unblemished First Growth Bordeaux in the way the grape–fruitiness announces itself before progressing into greatness. After that, it takes, thankfully, a very different course except perhaps in the way the spices unfold: first no more than a shadow, then blossoming out into something profound, deep and always in sync with all else that is going on. Cocoa notes arrive early and stay while the grains offer a salivating edge...nothing short of glorious...; **f22.5** serious but high quality and contained oak· dry and toasty but always a light dusting of slightly sweetened vanilla; **b22.5** when my researcher got this bottle for me to taste, she was told by the Wiser's guy that I would love it, as it had been specially designed along the lines of what I considered essential attributes to Canadian whisky. Whether Mr Wiser was serious or not, such a statement both honoured and rankled slightly and made me entirely determined to find every fault with it I could and knock such impertinence down a peg or two. Instead, I was seduced like a 16-year-old virgin schoolboy in the hands of a 30 year-old vixen. An entirely disarming Canadian which is almost a whisky equivalent to the finest of the great French wines in its rich, unfolding style. Complex beyond belief, spiced almost to supernatural perfection, this is one of the great newcomers to world whisky in the last year. It will take a glass of true magnificence to outdo this for Canadian Whisky of the Year. 45%

Wiser's Red Letter (95) n24 t24 f23.5 b23.5. The recent trend with Canadian whisky has been to do away with finesse and cram each bottle with fruit. This returns us to a very old fashioned and traditional Canadian style. And had the rye been upped slightly and the caramel eschewed entirely it might have been a potential world whisky of the year...Even in this form, however, it is certainly good enough to be Canadian Whisky of the Year 2010. 45%

Wiser's Reserve (75) n19 t20 f18 b18. The nose offers curious tobacco while the palate is uneven, with the bitterness out of tandem with the runaway early sweetness. In the confusion the fruit never quite knows which way to turn. A once mighty whisky has fallen. And I now understand it might be the end of the line with the excellent Wiser's Small Batch coming in to replace it. So if you are a reserve fan, buy them up now. 43%

Wiser's Small Batch (90.5) n21.5 much bigger in the fruit department than of yore with the grains struggling to be heard; soft to the point of borderline flat; **t24** that's more like it!! Back online with the huge, salivating, juicy, mouth-enveloping delivery. The spices spark and ark around the palate and for a while the fruits are lost. Layers of grain dominate and the balance between the brown sugar sweetness and the pounding peppers is sublime; **f22** much harder and crisp with the fruit having now fallen by the wayside. Even the spices burn out leaving firm vanilla; **b23** a real oddity with the nose and taste on different planets. The fruity onslaught promised by the drab nose never materialises – thankfully! – and instead we are treated to a rich, grainy explosion. It's the spices, though, that take the plaudits. 43.4%

Wiser's Special Blend (78) n19 t20 f19 b19. A plodding, pleasant whisky with no great desire to offer much beyond caramel. 40%

Japanese Whisky

At Edinburgh Castle in 2010 a fanfare of pipes heralded the launch of the first 70-year-old whisky certainly within living memory. A Speyside scotch single malt, it deservedly brought great acclaim and an enormous degree of publicity. Elsewhere, sneaking in through the back door, came a Japanese single malt bottled by the Whisky Exchange in London as part of their 10th anniversary celebrations. It was 42 years old and from the Karuizawa distillery.

Now Japan tends to get hot... very hot. Certainly a lot hotter than anywhere in Scotland. And though the Winters can sometimes be equally if not more cold than Speyside, I would be quite confident in saying that 42 Japanese Summers is worth at least 70 Scottish in terms of whisky maturation. Ironically, I sat next to WE's owner, Sukhinder Singh, at the Edinburgh event but didn't have time to chat about the Karuizawa. Perhaps the Mortlach edges it in terms of finesse and overall star quality, but for sheer fun the freaky Karuizawa 1967 wins hands down and, for me, and despite its obvious oaky input, was the Japanese Whisky of the Year. I am not the only one praying that this has opened the door for other grandiose Japanese malts to follow.

Yet still there is a great frustration that the myriad types of Japanese whisky is unlikely to be seen outside the mother country, so slow has the expansion of their whisky empire been.

I have met a number of whisky shop owners around the world who will stock only a handful of Japanese simply because they cannot get assurances that what they are being sent does not contain Scotch. Certainly, these mind-blowing single malts which had lorded it with the world's elite were 100% from the land of the rising sun. But until exchanging whiskies within Japanese companies becomes a natural part of their culture it is hard to see how the confidence generated by the excellence of the single malt and grains available as singletons can be extended to the blends.

Part of the problem has been the Japanese custom of refusing to trade with their rivals. Therefore a Japanese whisky, if not made completely from home-distilled spirit, will instead contain a percentage of Scotch rather than whisky from fellow Japanese distillers.

This, ultimately, is doing the industry no favours at all. The practice is partly down to the traditional work ethics of company loyalty and an inherent, and these days false, belief that Scotch whisky is automatically better than Japanese. Back in the late 1990s I planted the first seeds in trying to get rival distillers to discuss with each other the possibility of exchanging whiskies to ensure that their distilleries worked more economically.

In the meantime word is getting round that Japanese whisky is worth finding. It is now not uncommon for me to discuss with whisky lovers at a fair or book signing the merits and differences of Yoichi and Hakushu, two distilleries which are now being correctly recognised for their world-class brilliance. And, increasingly, Yamazaki which has moved away from a comfort zone it operated in for many years and is now offering malts of great magnitude: indeed, it was recently the producer of one of the two

Yamazaki

Osaka

Fukuoka

Yoichi ● **Sapporo**

Sendai ⛩

Shirakawa ⛩

Karuizawa ⛩

Hakushu ⛩   **Hanyu** ⛩

⛩ **Mars Shinshu**   ● **Tokyo**

Gotemba ⛩

Key	
●	**Major Town or City**
⛩	Distillery

Japanese whiskies which was considered as a possible Whisky Bible World Whisky of the Year. And I still get a small thrill when I hear Yoichi's name mentioned around the world: I'm proud to have first brought it to the world's attention way back in 1997 – though these days the distillery, like all others in Japan, has to be a little more careful with their use of sherry.

Mind you, the same didn't have to be said about the Karuizawa 1967. That may have been matured in a sherry butt, but it was filled in the good old days when they were sent from Jerez to Japan still full of the fortified wine, so arrived fresh. Further evidence that there is just no beating the old traditions...

The success of India's Amrut has opened people's minds to the possibility of great whisky being made in lands far from the Scottish glens. Yet still the main problem for whisky lovers is the availability and price of Japanese whisky outside its own borders. The latter is hardly surprising, seeing as the cost of making a litre of spirit in Japan is higher than any other country in the world. But as for availability... even we at the Whisky Bible have problems tracking down many of the great whiskies the country has to offer. It is as though no-one has yet been told there is a huge international market full of people just wanting to discover if the whiskies are as good as I and others have been saying for the last two decades.

Single Malts
CHICHIBU

Golden Horse Chichibu db **(80) n19 t21 f20 b20.** Light, toasty and delicate yet the oak is prominent throughout. Good balancing sweet malt, though. *43%. Toa.*

Golden Horse Chichibu 10 Years Old Single Malt db **(82) n19 t22 f21 b20.** Developing citrus notes lighten the weight as the oak and sweet malt go head to head. *43%. Toa.*

Golden Horse Chichibu Aged 12 Years bott July 08 db **(95.5) n24** a majestic nose: crushed nuts on a big malt plane; diced Slovakian milk chocolate and a bourbon injection of mild honeycomb, hickory and toasty Demerara. Sounds like bourbon, but there is a certain something that is purely Japanese. Meanwhile, a slab of drying dates guarantees immortality, despite a inter-planetary distant, nagging bitterness. Sublime... **t24.5** a fruity delivery intensified by spice and a build up of oils that borders on the obscene. I am salivating and having my mouth coated with intense barley all at the same moment: a near unique experience; the letters at the command of my keyboard can't quite describe the depth of the honey or the subtle layering of sugars; **f23** the malt and vanillas become inseparable while the spices ramp up an extra couple of gears. The delicate sugars and drier oaks absolutely match each other stride for stride. Some very late bitterness, but it hardly matters (actually, it probably does), especially when the honeycomb is making a late comeback. How long can a finish be...? **b24** immaculate, faultless (OK, nearly faultless), whisky. And, rarely for Japanese, bottled at exactly the right age. Had this not been bottled in 2008, a contender for World Whisky of the Year. Guys! You have to get this to me sooner!!! For the record, it kind of took me back to the mid 1970s when I was first studying whisky, for here I felt I was learning about this distillery for the very first time...Oh, and for the best effects: don't bother warming in the glass – just pour...and score... *56%*

Chichibu 14 Years Old Single Malt db **(89) n20** tangerine peel and rice: two years older than the 12-y-o, that hint of bourbon has now become a statement; **t23** brilliantly eclectic arrival on the palate with no organisation at all to the flurry of malt and bourbony oak and tangerine-fruity spices that are whizzing around; **f23** pretty long with firm vanilla and a distinctive oiliness. Something approaching a whiff of smoke adds some extra ballast to the oak; **b23** we are talking mega, in-your-face taste explosions here. A malt with a bourbony attitude that is unquestionably superb. *57%. Toa.*

Chichibu Single Malt 2008 bourbon barrel, bott 2011 db **(89) n22.5** young, but a veritable bouquet of barley; **t23.5** even more youthful, but how can you not fall to your knees and kiss the feet of the intense gristy sugars; **f21.5** bitters out surprisingly for such a babe; **b22.5** lovers of young malty Bunnahabhains will appreciate this doppelganger! Youthful, especially on delivery, but proof –as I have long argued in Japan – that their whisky doesn't have to be of Scottish value ages to excel...A three year old Japanese classic...and how many times have you heard of one of those? *61.8%. For 'Whisky Live Tokyo 2011'.*

Chichibu Peated Single Malt 2008 refill hogshead, bott 2011 db **(84.5) n19 t21 f22 b21.5.** Maybe the right age, just the wrong kind of cask. Love the liquorice on the smoke, though. *62%. For 'Whisky Live Tokyo 2011'.*

Chichibu Single Malt Newborn Heavily Peated cask no. 451, dist 2009, bott 2009 db **(84) n21.5 t22 f20.5 b20.** Chewy, peaty toffee. *61.3%*

⋯⋙ **Ichiro's Malt Chichibu The First** dist 2008, bott 2011 **(88) n22** varying chalky vanilla notes, almost Canadian in style; beautifully dissolved sugars lead into a delicate barley-lemon mix; even a hint of dried tea leaves; **t22.5** much sharper on delivery with the barley again forming a potent link with the citrus to prod through the vanilla and vigorously at the taste buds; **f21.5** just bitters a little as a slightly rougher element of the oak comes into focus; **b22** I remember many years back in a Japanese warehouse telling a distiller and blender there that I thought their whisky was ready at three years old as a single malt. They stared back at me in horror: the Scots brought theirs out at least ten so, as far as they were concerned, that was the right thing to do... Here is proof from this promising new distillery that three years in a decent cask is more than ample. *61.8%. Venture Whisky Co.*

FUJI GOTEMBA 1973. Kirin Distillers.

The Fuji Gotemba 15 Years Old db **(92) n21** diced nuts, especially pistachio with vanilla and a sprinkling of sugar; **t23** mouth watering from the start with a sensational development of sweet malt; **f24** plateaus out with textbook spices binding sweet malt and dry oak. The length is exemplary; **b24** quality malt of great poise. *43%. Kirin.*

The Fuji Gotemba 18 Years Old db **(81) n20 t19 f21 b21.** Jelly-baby fruitiness, complete with powdered sugar. Big, big age apparent. *43%. Kirin.*

Fuji Gotemba 20th Anniversary Pure Malt db **(84) n21 t20 f22 b21.** The nose is a lovely mixture of fruit and mixed oak; the body has a delightful sheen and more fruit with the malt. Handsome stuff. *40%. Kirin.*

HAKUSHU 1973. Suntory.

Hakushu Heavily Peated Aged 9 Years bott 2009 db **(92.5) n22.5** lightly heavily peated with a now lost Port Ellen style gristy sweetness; **t23.5** ultra sweet barley bang on cue and a slow radiation of spice, citrus and sympathetic oak; **f23** drier, oakier but still some sugared lime for balance and freshness. The smoke is distant and barley involved; **b23.5** nothing like as heavily peated as some Hakushus it has been my pleasure to sample over the years. But certainly superbly orchestrated and balanced. 48%

Hakushu Single Malt Whisky Aged 10 Years bott 2009 db **(87.5) n22 t23 f20.5 b22.** Duller than of old. 40%

Hakushu Single Malt Whisky Aged 10 Years bott 2011 db **(88) n22.5** lovely interlocking between citrus, worty grist (some offering delicate smoke) and natural caramels; some walnut oils ramp up the complexity further; **t22** the vaguest smoke imaginable offers extra weight to the juicy barley and cream toffee; **f21.5** simple toffee; **b22** quite youthful and beautiful: a fruitier affair than the last Hakushu 10 I came across. 40%

Hakushu Single Malt Whisky Aged 12 Years db **(91.5) n22.5 t23.5 f22.5 b23.** Just about identical to the 43.3% bottling in every respect. Please see those tasting notes for this little beauty. 43.5%

Hakushu Single Malt Aged 12 Years db **(91) n22 t23 f23 b23.** An even more lightly-peated version of the 40%, with the distillery's fabulous depth on full show. 43.3%

Hakushu Single Malt Whisky Aged 12 Years bott 2011 db **(95.5) n24** light but offering enough to really get the nose twitching: complex oaky tones offering subdued vanilla as a platform for the brighter barley, some of which is offering little more than a soupcon **t23.5** salivating, crisp malt turns towards a sugary, gristy very mildly smoky form; spices engage the vanilla in the middle ground, **f23.5** subtle, teasing spices infiltrate the soft lemon jelly and vanilla sponge cake; **b24.5** a prime example of what makes this such a magnificent distillery. One of the most complex and clever 12 year old malts to be found anywhere in the world this year: a great whisky that could be easily overlooked. 43%

The Hakushu Single Malt Whisky Aged 15 Years Cask Strength db **(95) n24** pure, unmistakable Hakushu: intense, powering, yet clean and refined. Loads of citrus to lighten matters but the local oak ensures enormity; **t23** big, initially oak-threatened but the barley comes flooding back with light oils helping to soften the early scratchiness; first mouthful is dry, the second shows a much truer picture; **t24** now goes into complexity overdrive as all those fruity-barley-oaky- elements continue to jostle for supremacy, only for late spices and gorgeous milky mocha to come in and steal the thunder; **b24** last time round I lamented the disappointing nose. This time perhaps only a degree of over eagerness from the oak has robbed this as a serious Whisky of the Year contender. No matter how you look at it, though, brilliant!! 56%

Hakushu Single Malt Whisky Aged 18 Years bott 2009 db **(86) n20 t23.5 f21 b21.5.** Wow! Where has all this oak come from? Appears to have gone gray overnight...The delivery, though, makes this a malt worth finding because for 20 seconds or so we have absolutely everything in complete harmony, and the degree of barley sweetness is just about perfect. Then all is lost to the duller oak tones again. 43%

Hakushu Single Malt Whisky Aged 18 Years bott 2011 db **(86) n23 t21.5 f20.5 b21.** Never quite finds either the main story or the punch line. Enjoyable but, knowing the capabilities of the distillery, I expected more. Enormous degree of toffee here. The nose, though, is a charmer. 43%

The Hakushu Single Malt Whisky Aged 25 Years db **(93) n23** some blowhard oak is pegged back by an intense barley-fruit mix; thick yet complex; **t24** a wonderful combination of silk and barley sheen juxtaposed with busy but light spice; soft fruits adorn the higher places within the palate while a subtle earthiness rumbles below; **f23** improbably long. Even though some serious extraction has taken place from the oak, the integrity of the barley makes you sigh with pleasure. Now the spices change in nature to soft and playful to warm and rumbling; **b23** a malt which is impossible not to be blown away by. 43%

Hakushu Single Malt Whisky Aged 25 Years bott 2011 db **(91) n23.5** mesmeric dates and crushed walnuts, but little overall sweetness as the oloroso does the job it should. The most vague hint of a treated butt; the overall poise of the aroma is stunning, though; **t23.5** again, the deportment of the delivery is textbook, helped by the lightest smoke drift. Delicate sugars form in slow motion; **f21** bitters out with burnt raisin and a renegade cask; **b23** just one slightly off butt away from total magnificence. 43%

Hakushu 1984 db **(95) n22 t25 f24 b24.** A masterpiece of quite sublime complexity and balance. The sort of experience that gives a meaning to life, the universe and everything... 61%

Hakushu 1988 db **(92) n21** overtly peaty and dense, pleasant but lacking usual Hakushu complexity; **t24** mouthwatering start with massively lively malt and fresh peating hanging on to its coat-tails. Some amazing heather–honey moments that have no right to be there; the peat intensifies then lightens; **f23** lots of rich peat and then intense vanilla; crisp and abrupt at the finale with late bitter chocolate; **b24** like all great whiskies this is one that gangs up on you in a way you are not expecting: the limited complexity on the nose is more than compensated for elsewhere. Superb. If this were an Islay malt the world would be drooling over it. *61%*

Hakushu 1989 Sherry Cask bott 2009 **(88) n22 t22 f22 b22.** A malt drowned in a sea of thick sherry. Enjoyable, though! *62%. Speciality Drinks Ltd bottled for TWE's 10th Anniversary.*

Hakushu Vintage Malt 1990 db **(89) n22** firm barley and firmer oak; **t23** serious intensity on delivery, this time with all the action being enjoyed by the concentrated, grassy barley; **f22** layers of vanilla add balance to the fade; **b22** warming in places with the tastebuds never getting a single moment's peace. *56%. Suntory.*

Scotch Malt Whisky Society Cask 120.05 Aged 17 Years 1st fill barrel, dist Dec 91 **(94) n23** subtly peated in a way Hakushu possibly does best of all; **t24** it's all there: the most deft smoke; firm, eye-watering barley; explodingly over-ripe cherries; an Arbroath Smokie saltiness; oil laced with honey...; **f23.5** remains bullet hard and mercurially smoky to the last departing atom; **b23.5** amazingly, this is a less than perfect cask deployed. But so absurdly good was the spirit filled into it, you barely notice...or care. *59%. 104 bottles.*

Suntory Pure Malt Hakushu Aged 20 Years db **(94) n23** fresh, mildly grapey fruit combined with subtle waves of peat; **t24** the peat is now less subtle: wave upon wave of it bringing with it flotsam of drifting oak and then a very sharp malt tang; **f23** long, sweet spice but the oak forms a chunky alliance with the firm peat. The bitter-sweet compexity almost defies belief; **b24** a hard-to-find malt, but find it you must. Yet another huge nail in the coffin of those who purport Japanese whisky to be automatically inferior to Scotch. *56%*

HANYU

⁙ **Hanyu Final Vintage 2000** cask no. 6309, bott 2010 **(94.5) n23.5** beautifully floral with copious pollen notes, though it doesn't quite make it as far as honey; deep and brooding oak never even contemplates dominance, allowing the slightly burnt fruit equal billing; those floral notes occasionally shift to herbal, even with the vaguest hint of juniper; bizarrely, there is still a residual new-makey youthfulness, too; **t24** busy spice forms a fabulous coating around the now juicy grape: the jaw almost aches from the degree of chewing required to get into the depth of this beauty; **f23.5** dries slightly becoming a little toastier; some wonderful chocolate fruit and nut; **b23.5** a fabulous exhibition in just how a sherry whisky should be: blemish free and exploding from the glass with personality. A fabulous malt made for this kind of strength. *59.7%. sc. Venture Whisky Co.*

Hanyu Single Malt 2000 hogshead refilled into Japanese oak, bott 2011 db **(91.5) n21.5** a bit messy and off key: not from bad distilling, but the oak doesn't appear to know which way to turn; some attractive crystalised sugars; **t24** muscovado sugars melt into a malty morass before sweetening the mocha; anyone who knows such a thing as a coffee Walnut Whip will recognise this...; **f23.5** the coffee vanishes to leave the milky cocoa and muscovado; **b23.5** about as sweet a whisky can go and still be in total control. An after dinner malt if ever there was one... *60.9%. For 'Whisky Live Tokyo 2011'.*

Ichiro's Card "Eight of Clubs" 1998 American oak puncheon finish, bott 2011 **(88.5) n22** a curious bourbon honeycomb effect mixed with drifting smoke. Odd, but rather lovely; **t23** salivating barley on delivery, a small puff of smoke spreads in all directions and then a massive display of sweet caramel; **f21.5** the caramel persists allowing only a few sugars and some smoke to emerge; **b22** vanishes in a cloud of caramel, but has much to say first. *57.5%*

Ichiro's Card "Eight of Diamonds" Spanish oak oloroso finish, dist 1991, bott 2009 **(77.5) n20 t21 f18 b18.5.** Wild cherry with some fizz and bite. But bitter and off key, too. *57.1%*

Ichiro's Card "Five of Clubs" Mizunara hogshead finish, dist 1991, bott 2009 **(84.5) n22 t21.5 f20 b21.** A fruitier number but with a blemish on the finish. *57.4%. Venture Whisky Ltd.*

Ichiro's Card "Four of Diamonds" 2000 PX finish, bott 2011 **(79) n19.5 t22 18 b19.5.** One of the few things harder than diamond is trying to persuade PX casks to work with whisky. Add sulphur into the equation and there is no hope at all. Even when the sulphur is as little as found here. Drinkable, though, against all the odds. *56.9%. Venture Whisky Ltd.*

Ichiro's Card "Four of Spades" 2000 Japanese oak "Mizunara" puncheon finish, dist 2000, bott 2010 **(95) n24** big bourbon character: not just honey and liquorice, but an almost rye-like fruity (cherry) hardness, too; **t24.5** glorious arrival with a manuka and clear honey mix plus a landslide of warming spices. Then it's back to pure bourbon again with the liquorice, molassed and succulent, kicking in; **f23.5** long, at last with an element of maltiness but the butterscotch and vanilla hints at honeycomb, too; **b23.5** I have often heard the Japanese accused of trying to mimic scotch whisky. On this evidence, it's the Kentuckians who should be looking over their shoulder... *58.6%. Venture Whisky Ltd.*

Ichiro's Card "Jack of Hearts" red oak hogshead finish, dist 1991, bott 2010 **(86) n22.5 t22 f20.5 b21.** A knave of a dram. Lulls you into thinking this is going to be a honeyed gem, then mugs you with its rock hard, biting malt. *56.1%. Venture Whisky Ltd.*

Ichiro's Card "King of Clubs" 1988 cognac cask finish, bott 2011 **(83) n21 t22 f20 b20.5.** Cognac casks have the unfortunate habit of tightening and strangling the best out of a whisky...and this petit assassin is no exception. Pleasant in part with the odd strand of peat and molasses escaping. But the bitterness is another disappointment. Anyway, being from cognac cask, the Emperor of Clubs rather than "King", surely... 58%. *Venture Whisky Ltd.*

Ichiro's Card "King of Hearts" PX finish, dist 1986, bott 2009 **(95.5) n23.5** big and fruity: strawberry and figs; more than a trace of smoked oak; some ginger and clove sprinkled in, too; **t24** superb spice delivery, accompanied by soft peat, followed by a salivating salvo of ultra sharp greengages. Finally the barley begins to soak into the middle ground accompanied by that luxurious smoke; **f24** smoked chocolate mousse; **b24** this King of Hearts had some smoky tarts...delicious and complex almost beyond measure! 55.4%

Ichiro's Card "Nine of Spades" 1990 cream sherry butt finish, bott 2010 **(77) n18 t20.5 f18.5 b19.** Creamy for sure. But time for some sulphur-removing raspberries. 52.4%

Ichiro's Card "Queen of Spades" port pipe finish, dist 1990, bott 2009 **(83.5) n22.5 t22 f19 b20.** Lots of toffee; the finish is furry and bitter. 53.1%. *Venture Whisky Ltd.*

Ichiro's Card "Seven of Diamonds" Hanyu 1991 PX finish, bott 2010 **(81.5) n21 t22 f19 b19.5.** Some kind of sulphur note lurks (with intent), but there is also date and walnut in previously undiscovered quantities. Quite literally a bitter sweet experience. 54.8%

Ichiro's Card "Six of Clubs" cream sherry butt finish, dist 2000, bott 2009 **(66) n17 t18 f15 b16.** A sulphurous deuce. 57.9%. *Venture Whisky Ltd.*

Ichiro's Card "Ten of Hearts" Hanyu 2000 Madeira hogshead finish, bott 2011 **(91) n22.5** no off notes from arguably the best wine cask type used in the whisky industry today. A beautiful softness allows barley to flourish amid the grape...; light spices tickle the nose; **t23** sumptuous delivery! Leave in the glass for a while and spices arrive much earlier – and to dramatic effect. Again barley gets a word – no an entire sentence – in before being enveloped by the juicy, warming grape. **f22.5** the spices continue and now enjoy a raisin fudge accompaniment: tops off a gorgeous experience; **b23** thank you, Madeira... 61%

Ichiro's Card "Three of Hearts" Hanyu 2000 Port pipe finish, bott 2010 **(90) n23** spicy plums and warmed marzipan with a Jaffacake type orange filling; **t23.5** fabulous fruit bonbon delivery, with the sugars splitting, allowing the intense fruit to ooze out; soon a big fudge middle arrives, along with coffee-flavoured revels; cream toffees are not in short supply; **f21** a little biting bitterness (not entirely unexpected with a few recognisable noises on the nose and delivery) adds angst to the big caramel; **b22.5** delicious, but an astonishing degree of toffee is created in the process. 61.2%. *Venture Whisky Ltd.*

Ichiro's Card "Two of Hearts" Madeira hogshead finish, dist 1986, bott 2009 **(86) n22 t22 f20 b21.** Big, sweeping, delicious statements: some malty, some bourbon. But, overall, just a shade on the hot and rough and ready side. 56.3%. *Venture Whisky Ltd.*

Ichiro's Card "Two of Spades" Hanyu 1990 Port hogshead finish, bott 2011 **(84.5) n21 t22 f20.5 b21.** Enjoyable. But bizarrely one-dimensional. Another Hanyu lost in a storm of toffee. Just the odd off key note, too. 55.8%. *Venture Whisky Ltd.*

Ichiro's Malt Aged 15 Years 4th bottling **(89.5) n23.5** lively, saline tang to the spicy marmalade; **t23** another, typically Hanyu, sugar-malt juicy salvo; **f21** a degree of tangy buzz; **b22** oozes character and quality. 46%. *Venture Whisky Ltd.*

Ichiro's Malt Aged 20 Years (95.5) n24 a magnificent portrait of complexity. The malt stands proud and clean, offering a mildly crusty light sugariness; the oaks are a model of good manners: vanilla and honey, but in the most modest amounts; here and there the odd molecule of smoke; **t24** a delivery to pray and die for: such spices, such juiciness after so many years: remarkable. The middle ground is taken up by a quite glorious concentrated Malteser candy...but with better milky cocoa than found in the bag; **f23.5** long and brimming with so many layers of barley the head spins. The Malteser story continues; **b24** no this finish; no that finish. Just the distillery allowed to speak in its very own voice. And nothing more eloquent has been heard from it this year. Please, all those owning casks of Hanyu: for heaven's sake take note... 57.5%. *Venture Whisky Ltd.*

Ichiro's Malt Aged 23 Years (92.5) n23 salty; obvious age and some less obvious smoke; **t23.5** beautifully salivating delivery with rich, focussed barley; **f23** long, with a stream of ever-sweetening vanilla; **b23** a fabulous malt you take your time over. 58%

Ichiro's Malt The Final Vintage of Hanyu Aged 10 Years cask no. 6067 **(89.5) n22.5** slight vegetable edge to the thick malt; **t24** wow! That malt is thick! Beefed up with plenty of oak and maple syrup; **f21.5** on the bitter side; **b21.5** if it's a quiet glass of whisky you're after, give this one a miss... 60.8%. *Venture Whisky Ltd.*

One Single Cask Hanyu 1990 cask no. 9305, bott 2009 **(50.5) n23 t23 f22.5 b22.** Huge whisky but borderline OTT oak. The infused sugars do the trick. 53.4%. *Number One Drinks Co.*

One Single Cask Hanyu 1991 Japanese oak, cask no. 370, bott 2009 **(91.5) n22 t23.5 f23 b23.** Unmistakable style: I found myself muttering " ah, local oak!" to myself (tasting close on 800 malts in a couple of months does that to you...) before I spotted the label. Quite beautiful. 57.3%. Number One Drinks Co.

KARUIZAWA 1955. Mercian.

Karuizawa 1967 Vintage sherry cask, bott 2009 db **(96) n24 t24.5 f23.5 b24.** Another engaging, engrossing and, frankly, brilliant malt from this distillery, equalling the oldest I have ever encountered from Karuizawa. If you find it, sell your body, sell your partner's body... anything...just experience it! 58.4%

Karuizawa 1982 sherry, bott 2009 db **(90) n23 t24 f22 b22.** Forget the sherry. Forget the distant, nagging "S" word. Just home in on that astonishing middle: like a million Maltesers dissolving in your mouth all at once...there is nothing else like it in the whisky world. And no other distillery is capable. Alas. 56.1%. Speciality Drinks Ltd bottled for TWE's 10th Anniversary.

⁘ **Karuizawa 1983 Noh Bottling** cask no. 7576, bott 2012 **(90.5) n23** good grief....!!! I think I have nosed something remotely like this only at Ardbeg with the sherry butts closest to the ocean. But even those pale by comparison. So salty, I am not sure I like it...(sniff, sniff...).. actually, I think I do...; **t23** taste this only when sitting in chairs with an arm rest. You need something to drip on to as the salt and fruit seer through you...; luckily, there is just enough molasses to ensure balance, but it takes a while for the shell-shocked taste buds to re-align and spot it; **f22** dry, toasty, burnt fruitcake..where salt appears to have partially replaced the sugar on top...; **b22.5** truly astonishing: an absolute one off. Unquestionably the most sea-salty whisky – malt or otherwise – I have ever tasted in my life. By several thousand fathoms... 57.2%. sc. Number One Drinks Company.

⁘ **Karuizawa 1984** cask no. 3692, bott 2012 **(73.5) n18.5 t20 f17 b19.** Not, sadly, the number one sherry butt... 61.6%. sc. Number One Drinks Company.

Karuizawa 1985 Vintage Single Cask cask no. 7017, bott 2009 db **(78.5) n19 t22.5 f18 b19.** Sherry preserve spread over slightly burnt toast. Pity about that sulphur. 60.8%

Karuizawa Pure Malt Aged 12 Years db **(85) n18 t23 f22 b22.** A recent Gold Medal Winner at the IWSC, but surely not by sporting a fractured nose like this. Thankfully the delivery is quite superb with the emphasis on silky honeycomb. 40%

Karuizawa Pure Malt 15 Years db **(76) n17 t21 f20 b18.** Some vague sulphur notes on the sherry do no favours for what appears to be an otherwise top-quality malt. (Earlier bottlings have been around the 87–88 mark, with the fruit, though clean, not being quite in balance but made up for by an astonishing silkiness with roast chestnut puree and malt). 40%

Karuizawa Single Malt Aged 17 Years db **(87.5) n23 t23 f20 b21.5.** A beautiful malt in so many ways, but one less-than-wonderful sherry butt has robbed this of greatness. How many times has this happened this year...? 40%

Karuizawa Pure Malt Aged 17 Years db **(90) n20** bourbony, big oak and pounding fruit; **t24** enormous stuff: the link between malt and fruit is almost without definition; **f23** amazingly long and silky. Natural vanilla melts in with the almost concentrated malt; **b23** brilliant whisky beautifully made and majestically matured. Neither sweetness nor dryness dominates, always the mark of a quality dram. 40%

Noh Whisky Karuizawa 1976 cask no. 6719, bott 2009 **(91) n22** tight, spiced grape; **t24** enveloping grape dovetailing with thick stratum of malt; impressive early sugars and a mouth feel to die for; the laid back juiciness is a treat; **f22.5** delicate hickory and plenty more rich barley; **b22.5** sticks religiously to the malty house style despite the grape trying to enter from every angle. A beautiful whisky, reminding me what a special year 1976 was for Japan. Happy 35th in April...x. 63%. Number One Drinks Co.

Noh Whisky Karuizawa 1977 cask no. 4592, dist 1977, bott 2010 **(75) n19 t19 f18 b19.** The bizarre dark colour and aggressive sharpness of nose and flavour suggests a small iron nail dropped into the cask at some time in its long life. Pity, for the grape is quite wholesome. 60.7%

KIRIN

Kirin 18 Years Old db **(86.5) n22 t22 f21.5 b21.** Unquestionably over-aged. Even so, still puts up a decent show with juicy citrus trying to add a lighter touch to the uncompromising, ultra dense oak. As entertaining as it is challenging. 43%. Suntory.

KOMAGATAKE

Komagatake 10 Years Old Single Malt db **(78) n19 t20 f19 b20.** A very simple, malty whisky that's chewy and clean with a slight hint of toffee. 40%. Mars.

Komagatake 10 Years Old Sherry Cask db **(67) n16.5 t17 f16.5 b17.** Torpedoed by sulphur. Gruesome. 40%. Mars.

Komagatake 1988 Single Cask sherry cask, cask no. 566, dist 1988, bott 2009 db **(62.5) n15 t16.5 f15 b16.** I can assume only that this has been "finished" in a relatively recent sherry butt. "Finished" is putting it mildly. A sulphur horror show. 46%. Mars.

Komagatake 1989 Single Cask American white oak cask, cask no. 617, dist 1989, bott 2009 db **(88) n23 t22.5 f21 b21.5.** A fine but bitty malt which feels its age at times. 46%. Mars.

Komagatake 1992 Single Cask American white oak cask, cask no. 1144, dist 1992, bott 2009 db **(93.5) n24.5 t23 f22.5 b23.5.** You know when you've had a glass of this: beautiful and no shrinking violet. 46%. Mars.

MIYAGIKYO (see Sendai)

SENDAI 1969. Nikka.

Miyagikyo batch 24H20B db **(89) n22** sweet chestnut and marzipan share the nutty honours; **t23** beautiful delivery, superbly weighted: the malt really has some backbone and some toffee liquorice makes for a chewy middle ground; **f21.5** perhaps a touch too much toffee; **b22** another high quality malt from this improving distillery. 43%

Miyagikyo 10 Years Old batch 06I08C db **(83) n19 t22 f21 b21.** Much better than the sharp nose warns, with some juicy, fruity moments. A little flat, though. 45%

Miyagikyo 12 Years Old batch 08I28A db **(89) n22.5** that familiar gooseberry nose with barley and custard; **t23** juicy and sweetens superbly mainly with gristy barley, though that oaky vanilla lurks nearby; **f21** drier, a hint of bitterness, but that persistent sweet barley compensates; **b22.5** in many ways, absolutely 100% recognisable as the distillery house style; in another this has much more confidence and charisma than of old. 45%

Miyagikyo 15 Years Old batch 02I10D db **(91.5) n23** fruity, as is the expression's style. But now lighter with much more emphasis on a Sauternes-style sultana; **t23.5** pulsing fruit, but the barley is sharp and wonderfully juicy; **f22** vanillas balance the barley and still a residual sweet grape can be found; a mild degree of very late bitterness; **b23** a much lighter, more refined and elegant creature than before. Despite a minor sherry butt blemish, fabulous. 45%

Miyagiko Key Malt Aged 12 Years "Fruity & Rich" db **(90) n22** fruit biscuits with burnt raisin and sugar; **t23** wonderful lift-off of sultana and burnt raisin on a sea of chewy barley. Towards the middle, a brief expression of oak and then much sweeter – and oilier – barley. Fruity; **f22** rich! **b23** a very comfortable whisky, much at home with itself. 55%. Nikka.

Miyagiko Key Malt Aged 12 Years "Soft & Dry" db **(85) n22 t21 f21 b21.** Perhaps needs a degree of sweetness... 55%. Nikka.

Miyagikyo 15 Years Old batch 20C44C db **(84) n20 t21 f22 b21.** Very typically Sendai: light body and limited weight even with all the fruit. Clean and gathers in overall enjoyability, though. 45%

Sendai 12 Years Old code 06C40C db **(89) n17 t22 f27 b21.** To put it politely, the nose is pretty ordinary; but what goes on afterwards is relative bliss with a wonderful, oily, fruity resonance. For those thinking in Scotch terms, this is very Speysidey with the malt intense and chewy. 45%. Nikka.

Sendai Miyagikyo Nikka Single Cask Malt Whisky 1986 dist 16 May 86 bott, 05 Dec 03 db **(88) n22 t20 f24 b22.** Little to do with balance, everything about effect. 63.2%

Sendai Miyagikyo Nikka Single Cask Malt Whisky 1992 dist 22 Apr 92, bott 05 Dec 03 db **(84) n19 t20 f24 b21.** Very strange whisky: I would never have recognised this as Sendai. I don't know if they have used local oak on this but the fruity, off-balance nose and early taste is compensated by an orgy of mouth-watering, softly smoked barley that sends the taste buds into ecstasy. A distinct, at times erratic, whisky that may horrify the purists but really has some perzaz and simply cannot be ignored. 55.3%

SHIRAKAWA

Shirakawa 32 Years Old Single Malt (94) n23 ripe mango meets a riper, rye-encrusted bourbon. We are talking a major aroma here; **t24** the most intense malt you'll ever find explodes and drools all over your tastebuds. To make the flavour bigger still, the oak adds a punchy bourbon quality. Beautiful oils coat the roof of the mouth to amplify the performance; **f23** long, sweet and malty. Some fruitiness does arrive but it is the oak-malt combination that just knocks you out; **b24** just how big can an unpeated malt whisky get? The kind of malt that leaves you in awe, even when you thought you had seen and tasted them all. 55%. Takara.

WHITE OAK DISTILLERY

White Oak Akashi Single Malt Whisky Aged 8 Years bott 2007 db **(74.5) n18.5 t19.5 f17.5 b19.** Always fascinating to find a malt from one of the smaller distilleries in a country. And I look forward to tracking this one down and visiting, something I have yet to do. There is certainly something distinctly small still about his one, with butyric and feintiness causing damage to nose and finish. For all the early malty presence on delivery, some of the off notes are a little on the uncomfortable side. 40%

YAMAZAKI 1923. Suntory.

Yamazaki 1984 bott 2009 db **(94) n24 t24 f22.5 b23.5.** If you like your whisky boringly neutral, lifeless and with nothing to say other than that it has been ruined by sulphur, then this will horrify you. Though there is a little blemish at the very death, there is still no taking away from this being a sublime 25-year-old. When this distillery is on form it makes for compelling whisky and here we have a bottling showing Yamazaki at its brightest. 48%

The Yamazaki Single Malt Whisky Aged 10 Years bott 2011 db **(84) n22 t22 f19 b20.** Plenty to enjoy, especially the intensity of the malt and its happy balance with the oak. But the finish needs a little attention. 40%

The Yamazaki Single Malt Whisky Aged 12 Years bott 2011 db **(90) n23** has retained its sherry trifle character, though now with more custard; **t22** firm delivery: the barley thumps home confidently. It takes the grapes, sugars and a few trailing spices a little while to catch up; **f22.5** the surprising late arrival of oils give the fruit ample time make their mark, especially the sugary banana. The late spices are a treat. **b22.5** A complex and satisfying malt. 43%

The Yamazaki Single Malt Whisky Aged 15 Years Cask Strength db **(94) n23** just a hint that its gone OTT oak-wise, but there is a wisp of smoke to this, too. All in all, wonderful brinkmanship that pays off; **t24** stunning: a massive injection of bourbon-style liquorice and honeycomb plays perfectly against the softer malts. The most controlled of malty explosions... **f23** long, lascivious, the tastebuds are debauched by ingots of honeycomb, molasses and dark sugary notes balanced by the drier oaks; **b24** an extraordinary bottling that far exceeds any previous version I have encountered. Stunning. 56%

The Yamazaki Single Malt Whisky Aged 18 Years bott 2011 db **(89) n23.5** very different from of old: now chocolate encased exotic fruit with kumquat, blood orange and toasted raisin completing the dazzling array; the tannins are almost those found in a fine wine; **t23** lighter delivery than you could possibly expect, the oak backing off leaving delicate barley to go it alone. Soon an ever-increasing number of rich, fresh fruity notes of excellent sweetness; **f20.5** disappointingly furry; **b22** a very slight sulphur flaw takes the edge of what is a remarkably beautiful whisky for most of the time. 43%

The Yamazaki Single Malt Whisky Aged 25 Years db **(87) n23 t22 f20 b22.** It has taken me over an hour to taste this. And still I don't know if I have marked it too high. You'll either love it or hate it – but you'll find nothing else like it..!! 43%

The Yamazaki Sherry Cask Aged 10 Years bott 2009 db **(82.5) n21 t22 f19.5 b20.** Very tight. The grape, initially impressive, is domineering leaving the malt's wings clipped. There are those who will adore this. But, technically and balance-wise, not quite right. 48%

Suntory Pure Malt Yamazaki 25 Years Old db **(91) n23** quite intoxicating marriage between grapey fruitiness and rich oak: supremely spiced and balanced with a wave of pure bourbon following through; **t23** big, big oloroso character then an entrancing molassed, burnt raisin, malty richness; **f22** subtle spices, poppy seed with some late bitter oak; **b23** being matured in Japan, the 25 years doesn't have quite the same value as Scotland. So perhaps in some ways this can lay claim to be one of the most enormously aged, oak-laden whiskies that has somehow kept its grace and star quality. 43%

Suntory Single Malt Yamazaki Aged 12 Years db **(87) n22** delicate, chalky vanilla with a squeeze of kiwifruit and butterscotch; **t23** a wonderfully light touch with fresh house-style mouth-watering barley and transparent fruit setting up the busy middle spice; **f20** pretty dry with oak and toffee; **b22** this was the 2006 bottling which somehow missed entry into the Bible, although tasted. A fruity little babe. 43%

YOICHI 1934. Nikka.

Hokkaido 12 Years Old db **(87) n23 t22 f21 b21.** Full-flavoured malt with absolutely zero yield. Just ricochets around the palate. 43%. Nikka.

Yoichi batch 04H10D **(87.5) n22.5 t22 f21.5 b21.5.** Very drinkable, though you get the feeling it is performing well within itself. 43%

Yoichi batch 04I10D db **(81.5) n21.5 t21.5 f18.5 b20.** A very hard malt: crisp, sweet at first but with limited yield. The apparent sulphur on the finish doesn't help. 43%

Yoichi 10 Years Old batch 08I16C db **(83.5) n21.5 t21 f20.5 b20.5.** Good grief! What has happened to this whisky? Actually, I think I can tell you: too much sherry and caramel makes for a dull malt. Pleasant. Drinkable. But dull. 45%

Yoichi 12 Years Old batch 08I18B db **(75.5) n19 t19 f18.5 b19.** Fruity but flat and sulphury; some smoke perhaps, but all rather hush-hush...and very disappointing, though had you been at the distillery some dozen years ago not entirely surprising. One feared this day might come...and it has. 45%

Yoichi Key Malt Aged 12 Years "Peaty & Salty" db **(95) n23 t25 f23 b24.** Of all the peated whiskies of the world, only Ardbeg can stand shoulder to shoulder with Yoichi when it comes to sheer complexity. Here is an astonishing example of why I rate Yoichi in the best five whiskies in the world. Forget the odd sulphur-tarnished bottling. Get Yoichi in its natural state with perfect balance between oak and malt and it delivers something approaching perfection. And this is just such a bottling. *55%. Nikka.*

Yoichi Key Malt Aged 12 Years "Sherry & Sweet" db **(80) n19 t22 f19 b20.** Sad to report that this should be called "Very Slight Sulphur and Sweet". A real pity because it is obvious that had the Spaniards not molested these butts, they would have been absolutely top-of-the-range. And probably would have scored in the low to mid 90s. I could weep. *55%. Nikka.*

Yoichi Key Malt Aged 12 Years "Woody & Vanillic" db **(83) n21 t22 f20 b20.** Pretty decent whisky. Not sure about creating one that sets out to be woody: that means balance has been sacrificed to concentrate on a particular essence to the whisky that should be used only as a component of complexity. Still, there is enough sweet malt on arrival to make this a dram to be enjoyed. *55%*

Yoichi Single Malt 12 Years Old batch 14F36A db **(91) n22** soft smoke and under-ripe fruit; **t23** profound, chewy barley; lots of small still coppery sharpness and then a gentle awakening of peat; **f23** sweet peats dusted with demerara; it takes some time for the chalky oak to finally have a say; **b23** best when left in the glass for 10-15 minutes: only then does the true story emerge. *45%*

Yoichi 15 Years Old batch 06I08B db **(91.5) n22** surprisingly quiet and well behaved considering the light smokiness drifting about; **t23.5** nutty, chewy and with lots of early toffee. Juices to puckering effect as the barley and phenols strikes home; **f23** sweet and spicy in the right places as the malt begins to find its legs and goes up a notch or two **b23** for an early moment or two possibly one of the most salivating whiskies you'll get your kisser around this year. Wonderfully entertaining yet you still suspect that this is another Yoichi reduced in effect somewhat by either caramel and/or sherry. When it hits its stride, though, becomes a really busy whisky that gets tastebuds in a right lather. But I'm being picky as I know that this is one of the world's top five distilleries and am aware as anyone on this planet of its extraordinary capabilities. Great fun; great whisky – could be better still, but so much better than its siblings... *45%*

Yoichi 20 Years Old db **(95) n23 t23 f25 b24.** I don't know how much they charge for this stuff but either alone or with mates get some for one hell of an experience. What makes it all the more remarkable is that there is a slight sulphury note on the nose: once you taste the stuff that becomes of little consequence *52%. Nikka.*

Yoichi 20 Years Old batch 06I06A db **(87) n22** an enormous statement from the glass. Immediately the odd sulphur note is detected, but the grape and high roast Java (possibly with medium Mycora) comes to its aid. The result is thick and very warehousy; **t22.5** much lighter delivery than nose: the barley actually shows first and juices up. Soon after though, the dark coffee clouds form; spicy in part, but something niggles away... **f20.5** that off key note gains strength amid a mocha recovery; **b22** bitter-sweet experience, both in taste and perception. Not unusual to find sulphur on this guy, but a shame when it alters the course of the malt. *52%*

Yoichi 1987 batch 22G26B **(89.5) n22 t23.5 f21.5 b23** having tasted from quite a number of casks from this year at the distillery itself, I was a bit worried when I saw that sherry butts had been used. However, no great signs of sulphurous ruination here and the marriage of the varying styles of peat and grape has created the desired degree of complexity. *55%*

Nikka Whisky Yoichi (78) n18 t20 f21 b19. Not often I'm lost for words...but this one left me stunned. Nothing like I expected. Not least because it seems either very young. Or not remotely short of feints. Or both. And the whole thing is propped up by caramel. The best bit is the late spice attack...but this is like nothing I would have expected from one of the top five distilleries in the world. *43%*

Nikka Whisky Yoichi 1986 20 Years Old (94) n23 age, the salty sea air of Hokkaido and sweet oak have accounted for the more excessive possibilities of the peat: weighty but restrained; **t24** no holding back here, though, as the delivery is one first of juicy fruit and then silky waves of peat; chunky heavy-duty stuff which, for some reason, appears to float about the palate; the spices shoot on sight; **f23** a sweeter, more sober finale with liquorice and molasses joining forces with the salty oakiness to keep the lid on the smoke; **b24** now this is unambiguous Yoichi :exactly how I have come to know and adore this distillery. *55.0%*

Unspecified Malts

"Hokuto" Suntory Pure Malt Aged 12 Years (93) n22 trademark delicate lightness; fleeting barley chased by soft vanilla; **t24** melt-in-the-mouth malt arrival; hints of honey work well with the loftier barley and earthier oak; **f23** honey on toast with just a little toffee; **b24** another example of Suntory at its most feminine: just so seductive and beautiful. Although a malt, think Lawson's 12-y-o of a decade ago and you have the picture. *40%*

Nikka Whisky From the Barrel (89) n20 carries some weight; good age and subtle malty sugars; **t23** exemplary mouthfeel: delightful oils and nipping spices but the malt remains clean and very sweet; **f22** some dryer oakiness but the malt keeps its balancing sweetness; **b24** a whisky that requires a bit of time and concentration to get the best out of. You will discover something big and exceptionally well balanced. *51.4%. Nikka.*

Nikka Whisky From the Barrel batch 02F26A **(82) n20 t22 f20 b20.** Some attractive honey notes and caramel, but a bit laboured. *51.4%*

Nikka Whisky From the Barrel batch 12F32C db **(91) n22** date and brazil cake; **t24** monumental delivery with soft smoke melting into the most glorious honeycomb known to man; tingly spices and toffee-apple, too; **f22** caramel kicks in slightly but some butterscotch rounds it off wonderfully; **b23** truly great whisky that mostly overcomes the present Japanese curse of big caramel finishes. *51.4%*

Nikka Whisky Single Coffey Malt 12 Years (97) n23.5 forget all about the malt: it's the big bourbony, hickory and honey sweet oak which wins hands down; **t25** hold on to your hats: it's flavour explosion time...on first tasting it's simply too much to comprehend. Only on third or fourth mouthful do you really get an idea. First, the delivery is pretty close to perfection: the soft oils seem to draw every last nuance from the barley; then when it has done that, it manages to mix it with myriad delicate sweet notes radiating from the oak. This includes some of those allied to bourbon, especially chocolate honeycomb and very deep molassed notes usually associated with Demerara Coffey still rum; a unique combination absolutely perfectly displayed; **f24** long...just so long. One mouthful, especially at 55%, last for about six or seven minutes. So impressive here is the delicacy of the fade: after a delivery so large, the finesse is extraordinary. The flavours in effect mirror the earlier delivery. Except now some vanilla does come in to dry things a little; **b24.5** the Scotch Whisky Association would say that this is not single malt whisky because it is made in a Coffey still. When they can get their members to make whisky this stunning on a regular basis via their own pots and casks, then perhaps they should pipe up as their argument might then have a single atom of weight. *55%*

Vatted Malts

All Malt (86) n22 t21 f21 b22. The best example by a mile of an almost unique style of vatted whisky: both malt and "grain" are distilled from entirely malted barley, identical to Kasauli malt whisky in India. Stupendous grace and balance. *40%. Nikka.*

All Malt "Pure & Rich" (89) n22 honeycomb and liquorice with some thumping oak; **t24** beautifully mouthfilling, and "rich" is an understatement. Barley sugar and molten brown sugar combine and then there is a soft gristiness. Big...; **f21** vanilla and caramel with some residual malt; **b22** Not unlike some bottlings of Highland Park with its emphasis on honey. If they could tone down the caramel it'd really be up there. *40%. Nikka.*

All Malt Pure & Rich batch 14F24A **(77) n19 t20 f19 b19.** My former long term Japanese girlfriend, Makie (hope you enjoyed your 30th birthday in April, by the way), used to have a favourite saying, namely: "I am shocked!" Well, I am shocked by this whisky because it is much blander than the previous bottling (04E16D), with all that ultra-delicate and complex honeycomb lost and lovely gristiness removed. For me, one of the biggest surprises – and disappointments - of the 2007 Bible. But proof that, when using something so potentially dangerous as caramel, it is too easy to accidentally cross that fine line between brilliance and blandness. Because, had they gone the other way, we might have had a challenger for World Whisky of the Year. *40%. Nikka.*

Hokuto Pure Malt Aged 12 Years (86) n20 t22 f22 b22. An oaky threat never materialises: excellent mixing. *40%. Suntory.*

Ichiro's Malt Double Distilleries bott 2010 **(86.5) n22.5 t22 f21 b21.** Some imperious barley-rich honey reigns supreme until a bitter wood note bites hard. *46%. Venture Whisky Ltd.*

Ichiro's Malt Mizunara Wood Reserve (76) n19 t21 f18 b19. I have my Reservations about the Wood, too... *46%. Venture Whisky Ltd.*

Malt Club "Pure & Clear" (83) n21 t22 f20 b20. Another improved vatting, much heavier and older than before with bigger spice. *40%. Nikka.*

Mars Maltage Pure Malt 8 Years Old (84) n20 t21 f21 b22. A very level, intense, clean malt with no peaks or troughs, just a steady variance in the degree of sweetness and oak input. Impossible not to have a second glass of. *43%. Mars.*

Nikka Malt 100 The Anniversary Aged 12 Years (73) n18 t19 f18 b18. The depressing and deadly fingerprint of sulphur is all over this. Shame, as the spices excel. *40%*

Nikka Pure Malt Aged 21 Years batch 08I18D db **(89) n23** profound, clean, over-ripe grape with some lovely nip and prickle; weighty with a liquorice bourbony element, too; **t22.5** soft at first then a steady build up of malt and spice. The fruit is never far away; **f21.5** toasty vanilla and a light buzz from the sherry; **b22** by far the best of the set. *43%*

Nikka Pure Malt Aged 17 Years batch 08I30B db **(83) n21 t21 f20 b21.** A very similar shape to the 12-years-old, but older - obviously. Certainly the sherry butts have a big say and don't always do great favours to the high quality spirit. *43%*

Nikka Pure Malt Aged 12 Years batch 10I24C db **(84) n21.5 t21 f20 b21.5**. The nose may be molassed, sticky treacle pudding, but it spices up on the palate. The dull buzz on the finish also tells a tale. *40%*

Pure Malt Black batch 02C58A **(95) n24** an exquisitely crafted nose: studied peat in luxuriant yet deft proportions nestling amid some honeyed malt and oak. The balance between sweet and dry is faultless. There is neither a single off-note nor a ripple of disharmony. The kind of nose you can sink your head into and simply disappear; **t23** for all the evident peat, this is medium-weighted, the subtlety encased in a gentle cloak of oil; **f23** long, silky, fabulously weighted peat running a sweet course through some surging malt and liquorice tones with a bit of salt in there for zip; **b25** well, if anyone can show me a better-balanced whisky than this you know where to get hold of me. You open a bottle of this at your peril: best to do so in the company of friends. Either way, it will be empty before the night is over. *43%. Nikka.*

Pure Malt Black batch 06F54B **(92) n24** great balance to the nose with a careful sprinkling of barley, honey, peat and oak – but never too much of any; **t24** massive, ultra-intense sweet malt with a delicate sub-stratum of smoke; a spiced fruitiness also cranks up the weight and depth; **f21** vanilla kicks in as it thins surprisingly fast; **b23** not the finish of old, but everything else is present and correct for a cracker! *43%. Nikka.*

Pure Malt Red batch 02C30B **(86) n21 t21 f22 b22.** A light malt that appears heavier than it actually is with an almost imperceptible oiliness. *43%. Nikka.*

Pure Malt Red batch 06F54C **(84) n21 t22 f20 b21.** Oak is the pathfinder here, but the oily vanilla-clad barley is light and mouth-watering. *43%. Nikka.*

Pure Malt White batch 02C30C **(92) n23** massive, Islay-style peat with a fresh sea kick thanks to brine amid the barley; **t24** again, the peat-reek hangs firmly on the tastebuds from the word go, the sweetness of the barley tempered by some drying oaky notes suggesting reasonable age. Lots of subtle oils bind the complexity. **f22** liquorice and salt combine to create a powerful malty-oak combo. An oily, kippery smokiness continues to the very end; **b23** a big peaty number displaying the most subtle of hands. *43%. Nikka.*

Pure Malt White batch 06J26 **(91) n22** soft peat interrupted by gentle oak; **t23** biting, nippy malt offering a degree of orangey-citrus fruit amid the building smoke; **f22** sweet vanilla and light smoke that dries towards a salty, tangy, liquorice finish; **b24** a sweet malt, but one with such deft use of peat and oak that one never really notices. Real class. *43%*

Pure Malt White batch 10F46C **(90) n23** the quality of the delicate peat is beyond reproach; some attractive kumquat juices it up nicely; **t23** wonderful balance between silky-soft and nail hard malts with some tasty local oak getting in on the act, **f22** the smoke lessens to allow vanilla and toffee dominance; a sawdusty dryness brings down the curtain; **b22** there is a peculiarly Japanese feel to this delicately peated delight. *43%*

Southern Alps Pure Malt (93) n24 bananas and freshly peeled lemon skin: one of the world's most refreshing and exhilarating whisky noses, **t23** crisp youngish malts, as one might suspect from the nose, mouthwatering and as a clean as an Alpine stream; **f22** some vanilla development and a late slightly creamy flourish but finished with a substantial and startling malty rally boasting a very discreet sweetness; **b24** this is a bottle I have only to look at to start salivating. Sadly, though, I drink sparingly from it as it is a hard whisky to find, even in Japan. Fresh, clean and totally stunning, the term "pure malt" could not be more apposite. Fabulous whisky: a very personal favourite. *40%. Suntory.*

Super Nikka Vatted Pure Malt (76) n20 t19 f19 b18. Decent and chewy but something doesn't quite click with this one. *55.5%. Nikka.*

Taketsuru Pure Malt 12 Years Old (80) n19 t22 f19 b20. For its age, heavier than a sumo wrestler. But perhaps a little more agile over the tastebuds. Lovely silkiness impresses, but lots of toffee. *40%. Nikka.*

Taketsuru Pure Malt 17 Years Old (89) n21 firm oak, but compromises sufficiently to allow several layers of malt to battle through with a touch of peat-coffee; **t22** massive: a toasted, honeyed front gives way to really intense and complex malt notes; **f23** superb. Some late marmalade arrives from somewhere: the toast is slightly burnt but the waves of malty complexity are endless; **b23** not a whisky for the squeamish. This is big stuff – about as big as it gets without peat or rye. No bar shelf or whisky club should be without one. *43%. Nikka.*

Taketsuru Pure Malt 21 Years Old (88) n22 middle-aged bourbon with a heavy, vaguely honeyed malt presence; **t21** the oak remains quite fresh and chewy. Again, the malt is massive; **f22** sweet, oily and more honey arrives; **b23** a much more civilised and gracious offering than the 17 year old: there is certainly nothing linear about the character development from Taketsuru 12 to 21 inclusive. Serious whisky for the serious whisky drinker. *43%. Nikka.*

Zen (84) n19 t22 f22 b21. Sweet, gristy malt; light and clean. *40%. Suntory.*

Japanese Single Grain

Kawasaki Single Grain sherry butt, dist 1982, bott 2011 db **(95.5) n23.5** clean thick grape offering several layers of depth and intensity. Salty and sharp, too. My god, this is very much alive and kicking...; **t24** classic! Faultless grape arm in arm with rich, fruity fudge. Some spices arrive on impact and slowly spread out with the marauding sugars; **f24** chocolate fudge and garibaldi biscuit...carried far on usual oils for a grain...amazing! **b24** my usual reaction to seeing the words "sherry" and "whisky" when in the context of Japanese whisky, is to feel the heart sinking like the sun. Sulphur is a problem that is no stranger to their whiskies. This, however, is a near perfect sherry butt, clean and invigorating. Grain or malt, it makes no difference: excellent spirit plus excellent cask equals (as often as not) magnificence. 65.5%. For 'Whisky Live Tokyo 2011'.

Blends

Ajiwai Kakubin (see Kakubin Ajiwai)

Black Nikka Aged 8 Years (82) n20 t21 f21 b20. Beautifully bourbony, especially on the nose. Lush, silky and great fun. Love it! 40%. Nikka.

The Blend of Nikka (90) n21 a dry, oaky buzz infiltrates some firm grain and sweeter malt; **t23** brilliant! Absolutely outstanding explosion of clean grassy malts thudding into the tastebuds with confidence and precision: mouthwatering and breath-catching; **f22** delightful grain bite to follow the malt; **b24** an adorable blend that makes you sit up and take notice of every enormous mouthful. Classy, complex, charismatic and brilliantly balanced. 45%

Evermore (90) n22 big age, salt and outstanding malt riches to counter the oak; **t23** more massive oak wrapped in a bourbony sweetness with glorious malts and a salty, spicy tang; **f22** long, sweet malt and crisp grains: plenty to chew on and savour; **b23** top-grade, well-aged blended whisky with fabulous depth and complexity that never loses its sweet edge despite the oak. 40%. Kirin.

Ginko (78.5) n20.5 t20 f19 b19. Soft – probably too soft as it could do with some shape and attitude to shrug off the caramel. 46%. Number One Drinks Company.

Golden Horse Busyuu Deluxe (93) n22 some decent signs of age with some classy oak alongside smoke: sexy stuff; **t24** enormous flavour profile simply because it is so fresh: massive malt presence, some of it peaty, bananas and under-ripe grapes; **f23** clean malt and some sharpish grain with a touch of bite, continuing to tantalise the tastebuds for a long time; **b24** whoever blended this has a genuine feel for whisky: a classic in its own right and one of astonishing complexity and textbook balance. 43%. Toa Shuzo. To celebrate the year 2000.

Hibiki (82) n20 t19 f23 b20. The grains here are fresh, forceful and merciless, the malts bouncing off them meekly. Lovely cocoa finale. A blend that brings a tear to the eye. Hard stuff – perfect after a hard day! Love it! 43%. Suntory.

Hibiki Aged 12 Years bott 2011 **(89) n22.5** fruity, full and fat; some Demerara sugars work well with the fruit; **t22** lush and complex with a huge vanilla-butterscotch theme; semi-salivating; **f22** long, fruity and with a touch of oily boiled sugar candy; **b22.5** a sensual whisky full of lightly sugared riches. 43%. Suntory.

Hibiki Aged 17 Years bott 2011 (84.5) n22 t21 f20.5 b21. Big oaks and a clever degree of sweetness. But takes the lazy big toffee option. 43%. Suntory.

Hibiki 50.5 Non Chillfiltered 17 Years Old (84) n22 t22 f20 b20. Pleasant enough in its own right. But against what this particular expression so recently was, hugely disappointing. Last year I lamented the extra use of caramel. This year it has gone through the roof, taking with it all the fineness of complexity that made this blend exceptional. Time for the blending lab to start talking to the bottling hall and sort this out. I want one of the great whiskies back...!! 50.5%. Suntory.

Hibiki Aged 21 Years bott 2011 **(96) n24** cherry fruitcake...with more black cherries than cake. Spiced sherry notes embrace the oak with a voluptuous richness; **t24.5** virtually perfect texture: seemingly silk-like but then a massive outbreak of busy oaky vanilla and juicy barley; the creamy mouth feel supports a mix of maple syrup and muscovado sugars; the middle moves towards a walnut oiliness; **f23.5** long, spicy with a gentle date and walnut fade; **b24** a celebration of blended whisky, irrespective of which country it is from. Of its style, it's hard to raise the bar much higher than this. Stunning. 43%. Suntory.

Hibiki Aged 30 Years (88) n21 less smoky than before, a touch of soap and no shortage of bourbon honeycomb; **t22** sweet delivery with that Kentuckian drawl to the middle; **f22** long, with some extra molasses to the finale; a few extra splinters of oak, too; **b23** still remains a very different animal from most other whiskies you might find: the smoke may have vanished somewhat but the sweet oakiness continues to draw its own unique map. 43%

Hokuto (86) n22 t24 f19 b21. a bemusing blend. At its peak, this is quite superb, cleverly blended whisky. The finish, though, suggests a big caramel input. If the caramel is natural, it should be tempered. If it is added for colouring purposes, then I don't see the point of having the whisky non-chillfiltered in the first place. *50.5%. ncf. Suntory.*

Ichiro's Blend Aged 33 Years (84) n20 t22 f21 b21. Silky and sweet. But the creamy fudge effect appears to wipe out anything important the oak may have to say. Pleasing spices towards the end, though. *48%. Venture Whisky Ltd.*

⋄ **Ichiro's Malt & Grain** bott 2011 **(85) n21 t22 f21 b21.** A clean though curious blend with the grain dominating and forming a jammy-sweet but thin structure. Pleasant throughout. *46%. Venture Whisky Co.*

Imperial (81) n20 t22 f19 b20. Flinty, hard grain softened by malt and vanilla but toffee dulled. *43%. Suntory.*

Kakubin (92) n23 lemon zest and refreshing grain: wonderful; **t23** light, mouthwatering, ultra-juicy with soft barley sub-strata; true melt-in-the-mouth stuff; **f22** long, with charming vanilla but touched by toffee; **b24** absolutely brilliant blend of stunningly refreshing and complex character. One of the most improved brands in the world. *40%. Suntory.*

Kakubin Ajiwai (82) n20 t21 f20 b21. Usual Kakubin hard grain and mouthwatering malt, with this time a hint of warming stem ginger. *40%. Suntory.*

Kakubin Kuro 43° (89) n22 a confusing but sexy mix of what appear to be old oak and burnt toffee; **t23** fabulous weight on arrival with again the oak in the vanguard but controlled by a malty, chewy-toffee arm; **f22** long with soft vanillins and toffee; **b22** big, chewy whisky with ample evidence of old age but such is the intrusion of caramel it's hard to be entirely sure. *43%. Suntory.*

Kakubin New (90) n21 gritty grain with very hard malt to accompany it; **t24** stunning mouth arrival with heaps of mouthwatering young malt and then soft grain and oil. Brilliant stuff; **f21** some beautiful cocoa notes round off the blend perfectly; **b24** seriously divine blending: a refreshing dram of the top order. *40%. Suntory.*

Kirin Whisky Tarujuku 50° (93) n22.5 t24 f23 b23.5. A blend not afraid to make a statement and does so boldly. A sheer joy. *50%. Kirin Distillery Co Ltd.*

Master's Blend Aged 10 Years (87) n21 t23 f22 b21. Chewy, big and satisfying. *40%. Mercian/Karuizawa.*

New Kakubin Suntory *(see Kakubin New)*

Nikka Master Blend Blended Whisky 12 Years Old 70th Anniversary (94) n24 nothing shy or retiring here: big oak, big sherry. A little nervousness with the smoke, maybe; **t23** lush, silky grain arrives and then carries intensely sweet malt and weightier grape; **f24** dries as the oak takes centre stage. But the peripheral fruit malt, gentle smoke and grain combine to offer something not dissimilar to fruit and nut chocolate; **b23** an awesome blend swimming in top quality sherry. Perhaps a fraction too much sweetness on the arrival, but I am nit-picking. A blend for those who like their whiskies to have something to say. And this one just won't shut up. *58%. Nikka.*

The Nikka Whisky Aged 34 Years bott 1999 **(93) n23 t23 f24 b23** A Japanese whisky of antiquity that has not only survived many passing years, but has actually achieved something of stature and sophistication. Over time I have come to appreciate this whisky immensely. It is among the world's greatest blends, no question. *43%. Nikka.*

Nikka Whisky Tsuru Aged 17 Years (94) n23 the usual fruity suspects one associates with a Tsuru blend, especially the apple and oranges. But the grains are now making a bourbony impact, too; **t24** advanced level textbook delivery here because the marriage between fruit, grain and oak is about as well integrated as you might wish for; simperingly soft yet enough rigidity for the malts to really count and the palate to fully appreciate all the complexities offered; **f23** brushed with cocoa, a touch of sultana and some gripping spices, too; only the caramel detracts; **b24** unmistakingly Tsuru in character, very much in line, profile-wise, with the original bottling and if the caramel was cut this could challenge as a world whisky of the year. *43%*

Robert Brown (91) n22.5 t23 f22.5 b23. Just love these clean but full-flavoured blends: a real touch of quality here. *43%. Kirin Brewery Company Ltd.*

Royal 12 Years Old (91) n23 chalky and dry, but malt and oranges – and now some extra juicy grape - add character; just a soupcon of smoke adds the perfect weight; **t23** fabulously complex arrival on the palate with some grainy nip countered by sparkling malt and where once there was smoke there is now ultra clean sherry; **f22** the grains and oak carry on as the spice builds; **b23** a splendidly blended whisky with complexity being the main theme. Beautiful stuff that appears recently to have, with the exception of the nose, traded smoke for grape. *43%*

Royal Aged 15 Years (95) n25 soft ribbons of smoke tie themselves to a kumquat and sherry flag; supremely well weighted and balanced with the grains and malts united by invisible strands; **t24** few whiskies achieve such a beautifully soft and rounded delivery: there is no dominance on arrival as the tastebuds are confronted by a silky marriage of all that is found on the nose, aided and abetted by luxurious grain; **f22** a degree of toffee slightly hinders the fade but the lightness of touch is spellbinding; **b24** unquestionably one of the great blends of the world that can be improved only by a reduction of toffee input. Sensual blending that every true whisky lover must experience: a kind of Japanese Old Parr 18. *43%*

Shirokaku (79) n19 t21 f20 b19. Some over-zealous toffee puts a cap on complexity. Good spices, though. *40%. Suntory.*

Special Reserve 10 Years Old (94) n23 magnificent approach of rich fruit buttressed by firm, clear grain. Some further fruity spices reveal some age is evident; **t24** complex from the off with a tidal tsunami of malt crashing over the tastebuds. The grain holds firm and supports some budding fruit; **f23** a touch of something peaty and pliable begins to take shape with some wonderful malty spices coating the mouth; **b24** a beguiling whisky of near faultless complexity. Blending at its peak. *43%. Suntory.*

Special Reserve Aged 12 Years (89) n21 peaches and cream with a dollop of caramel; **t24** luxurious delivery of perfect weight and softness to body; the barley sweetness works beautifully with the buzz of oak and yielding grains; **f21** caramel-coffee crème from a box of chocs; **b23** a tactile, voluptuous malt that wraps itself like a sated lover around the tastebuds, though the complexity is compromised very slightly by bigger caramel than the 10-y-o. *40%. Suntory.*

Suntory Old (87) n21 dusty and fruity. Attractive nip and balance; **t24** mouthwatering from the off with a rich array of chewy, clean fresh malt: textbook standard, complete with bite; **f20** thins out far quicker than it once did leaving the vanilla to battle it out with toffee; **b22** a delicate and comfortable blend that just appears to have over-simplified itself on the finale. Delicious, but can be much better than this. *40%*

Suntory Old Mild and Smooth (84) n19 t22 f21 b22. Chirpy and lively around the palate, the grains soften the crisp malts wonderfully. *40%*

Suntory Old Rich and Mellow (91) n22 very lightly smoked with healthy maltiness; an extra touch of older oaks in the most recent bottling helps the balance and works wonders; **t23** complex, fat and chewy, no shortage of deep malty tones, including a touch of smoke; **f23** sweeter malts see off the grain, excellent spices; **b23** a pretty malt-rich blend with the grains offering a fat base. Impressive blending. *43%*

Super Nikka (93) n23 excellent crisp, grassy malt base bounces off firm grain. A distant hint of peat, maybe, offers a little weighty extra; **t23** an immediate starburst of rich, mouthwatering and entirely uncompromising malt that almost over-runs the tastebuds; **f23** soft, fabulously intrinsic peaty notes from the Yoichi School give brilliant length and depth. But the cocoa notes from the oak-wrapped grain also offer untold riches; **b24** a very, very fine blend which makes no apology whatsoever for the peaty complexity of Yoichi malt. Now, with less caramel, it's pretty classy stuff. However, Nikka being Nikka you might find the occasional bottling that is entirely devoid of peat, more honeyed and lighter in style (21-22-23-23 Total 89 – no less a quality turn, obviously). Either way, an absolutely brilliant day-to-day, anytime, any place dram. One of the true 24-carat, super nova commonplace blends not just in Japan, but in the world. *43%. Nikka.*

Super Nikka Rare Old batch 02I18D **(90.5) n22 t23 f22.5 b23.** Beautiful whisky which just sings a lilting malty refrain. Strange, though, to find it peatless. *43%. Nikka.*

Torys (76) n18 t19 f20 b19. Lots of toffee in the middle and at the end of this one. The grain used is top class and chewy. *37%. Suntory.*

Torys Whisky Square (80) n19 t20 f21 b20. At first glance very similar to Torys, but very close scrutiny reveals slightly more "new loaf" nose and a better, spicier and less toffeed finale. *37%. Suntory.*

Tsuru (93) n23 apples, cedar, crushed pine nuts, blood oranges and soft malt, all rather chalky and soft – and unusually peatless for Nikka; **t24** fantastic grain bite bringing with it a mouthwateringly clean and fresh attack of sweet and lip-smacking malt; **f22** a continuation of untaxing soft malts and gathering oak, a slight "Malteser" candy quality to it, and then some late sultana fruitiness; **b24** gentle and beautifully structured, genuinely mouthwatering, more-ish and effortlessly noble. If they had the confidence to cut the caramel, this would be even higher up the charts as one of the great blends of the world. And with Japanese whisky becoming far more globally accepted and sought after, now would be a very good time to start. As it is, in my house we pass the ceramic Tsuru bottle as one does the ship's decanter. And it empties very quickly. *43%. Nikka.*

The Whisky (88) n22 t22 f21 b23. A rich, confident and well-balanced dram. *43%. Suntory.*

White (80) n19 t21 f20 b20. Boring nose but explodes on the palate for a fresh, mouth-watering classic blend bite. *40%. Suntory.*

Za (79) n19 t21 f19 b20. Some lively boisterous grain offers a suet-pudding chewiness. A little bitter on the finish. *40%. Suntory.*

European Whisky

The debate about what it means to be European is one that seemingly never ends. By contrast, the discussion on how to define the character of a European whisky is only just beginning.

And as more and more distilleries open throughout mainland Europe, Scandinavia and the British Isles the styles are becoming wider and wider.

Small distillers in mainland Europe, especially those in the Alpine area, share common ground with their US counterparts in often coming into whisky late. Their first love, interest and spirit had been with fruit brandies. It seemed that if something grew in a tree or had a stone when you bit into it, you could be pretty confident that someone in Austria or California was making a clear, eye-watering spirit from it somewhere.

Indeed, when I was writing Jim Murray's Complete Book of Whisky during 1996 and 1997 I travelled to the few mainland Europe distilleries I could find. Even though this was before the days of the internet when research had to be carried out by phone and word of mouth, I visited most – which was few – and missed one or two... which was fewer still.

Today, due mainly to the four solid months it now takes to write the Bible, I can scarcely find the time to go and visit these outposts which stretch from southern Germany to Finland and as far abreast as France to the Czech Republic. It is now not that there is just one or two. But dozens. And I need my good friend Julia Nourney to whizz around capturing samples for me just to try and keep up to date.

It is a fact that there is no one style that we can call European, in the way we might be able to identify a Kentucky bourbon or a Scotch single malt. That is simply because of the diversity of stills – and skills – being deployed to make the spirit. And a no less wide range of grains, or blends of grains, and smoking agents, from peat to wood types, to create the mash.

The distillers who have made major financial investments in equipment and staff appear to be the ones who are enjoying the most consistent results. In the Premier League we have the now firmly established Mackmyra in Sweden and Penderyn in Wales, both of whom use female blenders or distillers. Newly promoted to the highest tier comes St George's in England and just joining them quality-wise, though not quantity, alas, is their British counterpart Hicks and Healey who last year launched their maiden bottling. This eight year old malt has to be the oldest first whisky of any new distillery outside Scotland I can remember in the last 20 years. It is also a distillery which turned European tradition on its head. Throughout mainland Europe you will find small distillers with a serious shortage of the knowledge, money, capacity or will to ferment their own mash. So they will hop along to their local brewery, often old historic ones, and get them to make their wash for them, sans hops.

Hicks and Healey came about quite the other way round. The excellent and historic St Austell Brewery in Cornwall decided to make whisky. So they persuaded a pot-still owning cider brandy maker from within the county to distill their wash for them. With the whisky maturing for eight years in a cellar containing casks of cider brandy, it is little wonder the whisky has a distinct and compelling apple-sharpness to it.

This year also witnessed the first bottling of a fully-fledged whisky from a distillery which promises to be making some impression over the coming years. The Stauning Distillery in Denmark has made a distinctly spicy rye spirit which, in this initial batch, reveals great character even though there is a touch of getting-to-know-you evident between the still and stillman. But other samples of later batches I tasted at the distillery are more relaxed and precise. It will not be long before they are first leaguers.

Another distillery which maintains exceptionally high standards is the Belgian Owl. This is smaller concern than some, but the output of their single malt is consistent, beautifully made, and brimming with personality. It may be true that you can count internationally famous Belgians on one hand, but the whisky-loving world would immediately recognise two fingers of its owl... Some of the most remarkable whisky came from Liechtenstein, the country which was once unable to furnish me – anywhere within its borders – with a decent hotel room but now offers a three-year-old malt which, but for the wideness of its cut, nearly walked off with an award. The Telser distillery has a long history and its move into whisky has been an impressive one: its Telsington IV being the most impressive of all. Perhaps that big, malty, slightly oily and lush style is something of an Alpine trait: another distillery to watch is Interlaken with their Classic, Swiss Highland Single Malt. Which, with a brand name like that, is as likely to stir up the good folk at the Scotch Whisky Association as anything else.

AUSTRIA
ACHENSEE'R EDELBRENNEREI FRANZ KOSTENZER Maurach. Working.

Whisky Alpin Single Malt Rye db **(87.5) n20 t23.5 f21.5 b22.5.** Not until the delivery gets into full stride does the rye ram home. And then it celebrates – in style! 45%

DESTILLERIE GEORG HIEBL Haag. Working.

George Hiebl Mais Whisky 2004 db **(93) n23 t23.5 f23 b23.5.** More bourbon in character than some American bourbons I know...!! Beautifully matured, brilliantly matured and European whisky of the very highest order, Ye..haahhhh!! 43%

DESTILLERIE KAUSL Mühldorf, Wachau. Working.

Wachauer Whisky "G" Single Barrel Gerste (Barley) bott code L6WG db **(90.5) n22 t23 f22.5 b23.** Absolutely charming and well made malt. 40%

DESTILLERIE ROGNER Rappottenstein. Working.

Rogner Waldviertel Whisky 3/3 db **(86.5) n20 t22 f22.5 b22.** Plane sailing once you get past the tight nose. A beautiful display of crisp sugars and come-back-for more grainy juiciness. Lovable stuff, for all its gliches. 41.7%. ncf.

Rogner Waldviertel Rye Whisky No. 13 db **(80) n18.5 t20 f21 b20.5.** If memory serves, the last time I had this guy I was met by an oily tobacco note. It is a unique feature and this reminds me of it. 42.5%. ncf

DESTILLERIE WEUTZ St. Nikolai im Sausal. Working.

Black Peat bott code. L070205/01 db **(73.5) n18.5 t16 f20 b19.** Well...!!! That was different – literally! Apparently the well used for the making of this whisky supplies a water rich in various nutrients. Including iodine and sulphur. Anyone who has taken the waters at Bath will have some kind of idea what we are talking about. The result is something the likes of which I have never before encountered. The delivery is simply bloody awful...but, once you acclimatise, the late middle is quite tolerable, and the finish enjoyable! Possibly the healthiest whisky I have ever tasted! 41.4%. sc.

Franziska bott code. L070206/02 db The 5% elderflower means this is 100% not whisky. But a fascinating and eye-opening way to create a spirit very much in the young Kentucky rye style, especially in the nose. They certainly can do delicious... For the record, the scoring for enjoyment alone: (93) n23.5 t23 f23.5 b23. 48%. Malt refined with 5% elderflower.

St. Nikolaus bott code. L072004/01 db **(86) n20 t22 f22 b22.** Not quite up there with their previous Hot Stone whiskies, but not far off. Certainly enjoys a biscuit style maltiness, which puts me in mind of it slightly. Only really let down by the sweaty armpit nose. 40%. sc.

White Smoke sherry finished, bott code. L062411/01 db **(90) n22.5** confident, biting spices cut their way through the cleanest grape imaginable; salty, as though stuck in a warehouses lashed by a wild Hebridean sea...in land-locked Austria...!! **t22.5** a silk glove but with some sharp claws protruding; the grape is big but isn't allowed to have it its own way as a vague dry oakiness ensures some chewing is to be done; **f22** salty with a huge amount of grape pips and skins having a further drying effect; **b23** at times, seems more like sherry finished in whisky. Not a single off note from the cask (though the same can't quite be said for the actual spirit itself) – a completely sulphur free experience. Wonderful and borderline sophisticated. 40%

REISETBAUER Axberg, Thening. Working.

Reisetbauer Single Malt 7 Years Old Chardonnay and sweet wine cask, bott code LWH 099 db **(85.5) n19 t21 f23.5 b22.** A less than impressive nose is followed by a rocky delivery. But the panning out is truly spectacular as harmony is achieved with a rich honey and nougat mix, helped along the way with pecan nuts and figs. The finish is like a top rank trifle and fruitcake mix. A whisky of two halves. 43%

WHISKY-DESTILLERIE J. HAIDER Roggenreith. Working.

⁖ **Single Malt J.H.** bott code L SM/06 **(91.5) n22** the nougat these days seems to be covered in more and more chocolate...; **t23** wonderful body and a stunning development from basic fine sugars to a much, thicker, ulmo honeyed delicacy; **f23.5** moves into ultra complex mode as the oak now offers varied degrees of weight ands even further deft sugars. The crème brulee works well with the vague nougat; **b23** it must be over a dozen years now since I first went to their distillery. But this is their best batch of whiskies yet... 41%

Original Rye Whisky J.H. L19/05 db **(91.5) n23.5** had I been handed this in Kentucky, my only thought was that it had been a slightly wider cut than normal. But the fresh fruitiness of the grain is textbook; **t23** those oils evident on the nose do an amazing job of harnessing together the richer aspects of this whisky. So the middle ground is back to Kentucky with its liquorice and honeycomb and the cascading caramels. But the feel is entirely different; **f22** long with a fruity toffee fudge fade; **b23** their Original Rye was last year close to bringing home to Austria the Bible's European Whisky of the Year. This is another outstanding bottling. Perhaps not as sharp and mouth-watering as last time, but the marriage between the rye and toffee-honeycomb is a blissful one. Superb yet again! *41%*

⁙ **Original Rye Whisky J.H.** bott code L R/06 **(92.5) n23** unique fruity, juicy, crystalline rye of the highest order. A light spice and cocoa dusting offers balance; **t23.5** big, juicy, a little nougat feinty perhaps, but that is forgiven. The custard sits prettily with the fruit; **f23** retains its crisp juiciness to the end and now the spices roll up for a firecracker farewell...; **b23** this distillery can produce a Kentuckian style rye better than any other distillery outside the US. here is another gorgeous example. *41%*

Pure Rye Malt J.H. L10/05 db **(87.5) n20.5 t22.5 f22.5 b22.** To get the best out this distillery's whisky, it is advisable to either warm the glass or leave for a good 15 minutes or so. This is to burn off the feints which can be apparent. They are here. But the whisky always has the ability to enthral and reveal an inner beauty. I am not sure of it is like a plain-faced woman having a beautiful body, or a gorgeous looker not quite shaping up for Miss World. Oh, and those comments are, above all, for the enjoyment of the young lady who described me as "sexist" to a mutual friend: might as well get hung for a sheep... *41%*

Special Rye Malt "Nougat" J.H. L7/05 db **(72.5) n17 t19 f18 b18.5.** Now this guy is a traditionally feinty beast. This time, though, some butyric pops up. Odd thing, though, the finish possesses a lovely rye "g" spot. *41%*

Special Single Malt Peated J.H. Limited Edition auslese Chardonnay wine cask, bott code. L3/08JU db **(79.5) n19 t20 f21.5 b19.** Technically the best distilled spirit they have ever put into bottle. Virtually no feints or butyric. Just excellent spirit. But, from a flavour perspective, something of a train wreck. The ashy peat and the grape are really not great friends, though they do end up on speaking terms by the finish. Compellingly different. *46%. ncf.*

Special Single Malt Peated J.H. Limited Edition auslese cuvee wine cask, bott code. L2/08LEI db **(84) n19 t20.5 f24 b21.5.** In case the distilling family are wondering. once they enter into this type of whisky, they are marked accordingly. And again we have another malt which begins with no steering wheel as it arrives on the palate, but navigates its way to what must be the equivalent of Austria's chocolate festival for a finish you'll never forget. If you are looking for a whisky with character and something different to say...this might be it. *46%. ncf.*

⁙ **Special Rye Malt Peated J.H. Limited Edition** bott code L 20/08 **(75.5) n18 t19 f19.5 b19.** Well, that was different! Don't think I've seen this rye style from Haider before; pretty certain I have never experienced an ultra-dry whisky offering like this....ever! Let's just say a work in progress... *46%. ncf*

DESTILLERIE WEIDENAUER Kottes. Working.

Waldviertler Single Malt db **(75) n18 t19 f19 b19.** Heavy, lush oily and with a big oak signature. The feel is that the cut taken has been very wide, indeed. *47%*

Waldviertler Dinkelmalz (2008 award label on neck) db **(77.5) n18.5 t21 f19 b19.** A bit rough round the edges from time to time, though the citrus on delivery charms. *42%*

Waldviertler Dinkelmalz (A La carte label on neck) db **(89) n22.5 t23 f21.5 b22.** Now that's far more like what I expect from this usually excellent distillery. *42%*

Waldviertler Dinkel (2008 Silber Medaille label on neck) db **(90) n19.5 t23 f23.5 b24.** The nose apart, the odd feint note here and there can't seriously detract from this majestically attractive whisky and towards the end even helps! Classy, classy whisky...!!! *42%*

Waldviertler Hafer (2007 Silber Medaille label on neck) db **(83.5) n19 t22 f21 b21.5.** A unique flavor profile from these oats. A touch more bitter than usual, perhaps, but there is a superb mouthwatering quality which counters the woody impact. *42%*

Waldviertler Hafer-Malz (2007 Gold Medaille label on neck) db **(91) n22 t22.5 f23 b23.5.** One of those whiskies that just gets better the longer it stays on the palate. Also, a master class in achieving near perfection in the degree of sweetness generated. *42%*

Waldviertler Hafer-Malz (2008 award label on neck) db **(76.5) n20 t19.5 f18 b19.** The big oaks do their best to compensate. But the damage has been done by making the cut here a little too wide and flooding the usual complexity with heavy oils. *42%*

BELGIUM
THE BELGIAN OWL

The Belgian Owl Single Malt Age 3 Years 1st fill bourbon cask, bott code L060111 db **(88.5) n22.5** youthful and zesty, but old enough to enjoy good oak complexity; **t22** again, youthful but the mouth-watering quality of the barley is fabulous; **f22** a lovely spicy fade; **b22** a juicy joy. *46%. nc ncf.*

The Belgian Owl Single Malt Age 4 Years 1st fill bourbon cask, bott code L140211 db **(89.5) n21 t22.5 f23 b23.** Brimming with Belgian vitality: high quality stuff. *46%. nc ncf.*

The Belgian Owl Single Malt Age 4 Years 1st fill bourbon cask, bott code. 270910 db **(94.5) n24** gorgeous marriage between delicate oak and even more delicate barley. Dissolved Lubeck marzipan melts into a lime jam. Youthful, yet almost impossible to see how a four-year-old malt could possibly be more attractive; **t23.5** silky, vaguely juicy maltiness and then any number of complex oaky tones. Again, a light fruitiness threads its way into the picture; **f23** much drier, though both the caramels and oaks remain light; a hint of Belgian chocolate...? **b24** a Belgian treat. *46%. nc ncf.*

The Belgian Owl Single Malt Age 4 Years 1st fill bourbon cask, bott code. L121110 db **(80.5) n19.5 t21 f20 b20.** Surprisingly thin. Seems as though the extra time in the cask has resulted in the overall balance struggling to keep the extra caramels under control. *46%. nc ncf.*

The Belgian Owl Single Malt Age 4 Years 1st fill bourbon cask, bott code. L250511 db **(83) n21 t21 f20 b21.** Soft with mild toffee. But will have benefitted with more time in the cask. *46%. nc ncf.*

The Belgian Owl Single Malt Age 4 Years 1st fill bourbon cask, bott code. L201210 db **(87.5) n22 t22 f21.5 b22.** Beautifully distilled, some exceptionally clean caramel and more oils than might be expected. *46%. nc ncf.*

❖ **The Belgian Owl Single Malt Age 4 Years** 1st fill bourbon cask, bott code. L1707111 db **(89) n23** how bizarre! On nosing this, I was transported back 25 years ago to the Glen Moray distillery when I spent a day going through maturing malt at varying ages. This clean, lemon-fresh barley explosion is a perfect fit for the six-year-old second fill bourbon cask I sampled that day...Just how does the brain do that...?? **t22** now it goes its own way, creating its own path. The barley is sharp yet, though trailed by oils, has the fortitude to offer varying degrees of malty intensity; **f22** long, though the oils remain intense and warming. Eventually the vanilla surfaces; **b22** typically big barley from this excellent distillery, though far more oils from the cut than is the norm. *46%. nc ncf.*

The Belgian Owl Single Malt 48 Months 1st fill bourbon cask no. 4275933 db **(90.5) n22.5** it is as though the big alcohol has burrowed into the oak – like a Burrowing Owl, in fact – and extracted vanilla notes very rarely seen. A delicious sweetness, almost like sugared coffee from a distance, **t23** how many layers can a whisky have? How many waves of flavour can a palate withstand? Plenty of caramel, as you might suspect, and those coffee notes start escalating; **f22** the coffee transforms into mocha. A minor degree of bitterness, but that is well met by any number of delicate sugars; **b23** this is quite probably the most powerful bottled whisky I have encountered anywhere in the world in my entire career. Perhaps what is most remarkable is the beautifully delicate nature of the nose and flavour profile, despite the scary alcohol levels. A unique and, if you have the nerve, wonderful experience. *76.5%. nc ncf sc.*

The Belgian Owl Single Malt Age 55 Months 1st fill bourbon cask no. 4275890 db **(92.2) n22** sweetish marmalade; fudge and vanillas abound; **t23.5** quite faultless delivery: the oils are firm and seem to help the alcohol to fully magnify the superb barley-oak balance. Not a single discordant note, no bitterness, no battling between flavour factions. Just a revelry of delicate flavours presented in a big way; **f23.5** long, with some major toasted fudge and Demerara notes. Also noticeable is a copper sharpness and both a metallic firmness plus a third dimensional sharpness. From somewhere dates and cocoa appear at the very death. The cocoa I understand..but the dates...? **b23.5** fantastic whisky with more twists and turns than a corkscrew. At times like the Hubble telescope looking back to the Belgian Big Bang – the beginning of the dedicated whisky universe in the country. The picking up of extra copper shows it is getting closer to those very first moments at Belgian Owl... *74.3%. nc ncf sc.*

The Belgian Owl Single Malt Age 53 Months 1st fill bourbon cask no. 4275986 db **(90.5) n23** more fudge and Bassetts chocolate liquorice sandwich than Belgian cocoa bonbons; some of the most profound oak yet found from this distillery...; **t23** intense (surprise, surprise) sugars and, also, metallic coppery notes – suggesting small (new?) stills. The barley is also wonderfully intense, clean and precise in its sharpness. Mouth-watering and just so delicious and well weighted; **f22** a late build up of massive natural caramels; **b22.5** enormous whisky, unsurprisingly, as deeply satisfying. *74.1%. nc ncf sc.*

DESTILLERIE RADERMACHER

Lambertus Single Grain Aged 10 Years db **(44) n12 t12 f10 b10.** This is whisky...? Really???!!!!???? Well, that's what it says on the label, and this is a distillery I haven't got round to seeing in action (nor am I now very likely to be invited...). Let's check the label again... Ten years old...blah, blah. Single grain... blah, blah. But, frankly, this tastes like a liqueur rather than a whisky: the fruit flavours do not seem even remotely naturally evolved: synthetic is being kind. But apparently, this is whisky: I have re-checked the label. No mention of additives, so it must be. I am stunned. *40%*

FILLIERS DISTILLERY

Goldly's Belgian Double Still Whisky Aged 10 Years db **(88) n**21.5 **t**23 **f**21.5 **b**22. Having actually discovered this whisky before the distillers – I'll explain one day...!! – I know this could be a lot better. The caramel does great damage to the finish in particular, which should dazzle with its complexity. Even so, a lovely, high-class whisky which should be comfortably in the 90s but falls short. *40%*

CZECH REPUBLIC
Single Malt
RUDOLF JELÍNEK DISTILLERY

Gold Cock Single Malt Aged 12 Years "Green Feathers" bott 27/05/09 db **(89.5) n**22 **t**23.5 **f**22 **b**22. From my first ever malt-related trip to the Czech Republic nearly 20 years ago, it was always a pleasure to get hold of my Gold Cock. I was always told it went down a treat. And this is no exception. Not a particularly big whisky. But since when has size counted? *43%*

STOCK PLZEN - BOZKOV S.R.O.

Hammer Head 1989 db **(88.5) n**22 **t**22.5 **f**22 **b**22. Don't bother looking for complexity: this is one of Europe's maltiest drams...if not the maltiest... *40.7%*

Blends

Gold Cock Aged 3 Years "Red Feathers" bott 22/06/09 **(86) n**22 **t**21 **f**21.5 **b**21.5. Sensual and soft, this is melt-in-the-mouth whisky with a big nod towards the sweet caramels. *40%. Rudolf Jelínek.*

Granette Premium (82) n21 **t**22 **f**19 **b**20. Lighter than the spark of any girl that you will meet in the Czech Republic. Big toffee thrust. *40%*

Printer's Aged 6 Years (86.5) n21.5 **t**22.5 **f**21 **b**21.5. Blended whisky is something often done rather well in the Czech Republic and this brand has managed to maintain its clean, malty integrity and style. Dangerously quaffable. *40%*

DENMARK
STAUNING DISTILLERY Skjern. Working.

Stauning Rye First Impression dist 09 & 10, bott 2011 **(88) n**21.5 **t**22.5 **f**22 **b**22. Not a whisky, as it is too young. But another experience which almost brings a tear to my eye. Even before these guys got their stills underway, I suggested they go for a rye whisky, a grain entirely befitting Denmark. This they have done. Not quite technically perfect, as no first distillation has any right to be. But it still bombards the senses with a major degree of complexity and beauty... and any amount of spice. The fact it is rye is beyond dispute: the grain comes through loud, proud and clear. A few feints have to be disposed of by warming and then the fun, especially with the cinnamon and apple, really begins. Salivating and spicy, it is a quite superb first effort. And having tasted the maturing spirit of a number of later casks there, I can tell you this wonderful whisky distillery-to-be is just clearing its throat... *52.5%. nc ncf. 857 bottles.*

⁙ **Stauning 1st Edition Traditional** dist 2009, bott 2012 **(87) n**21 a greenhorn of an aroma, still wet behind the ears. The pre-pubescent barley does its best to sparkle, but the oils from a wide cut douse its flame a little; **t**23 as is so often the case, the little extra cut can mean a lot of extra flavour on delivery and beyond. And here we have a dazzling combination of intense, gristy barley, nougat-thickened oils, strikingly clear Demerara sugars and the tell-tale coppery-metallic sheen of a new still in action; **f**22 long, thanks to the oils, with the nougat wrapping itself in praline; the sugars take time to fade...; **b**21.5 what a way to enter the world whisky stage! It could have shuffled out with a whisper and shyly hoped no-one would notice its mix of beauty and imperfection. But, no! It goes at you all guns blazing, so by the time your glass is empty, you feel pretty exhausted from the full on experience. I doubt if future bottlings will come at you quite so gung-ho! *63.3%*

⁙ **Stauning 1st Edition Peated** dist 2009, bott 2012 **(94) n**22.5 adore the delicacy of the smoke, the pungency reduced slightly by the lack of salt and the richness of the oil; intriguing chocolate rice pudding background; **t**24 silky on delivery and follow through. Smoked Milky Way candy bar, with the nougat melting in the mouth with the barley and light molasses. Sublime chewiness; **f**24 handles the finish like an old-timer! Some oaky notes arrive with vanilla and butterscotch, but it is the smoke-sugar interplay stretching to such lengths which makes you want to applaud and shake the distillers by the hand...; **b**23.5 I didn't know whether to taste this, the first whisky from Stauning on the first birthday of my first grand-daughter, Islay-Mae, or make this the 999th new whisky I have tasted for 2013 Whisky Bible in recognition that I played a (very!) small part in its foundation....though only by offering encouragement. As fate dictates, both fell on the same day. Ah, this dram before me really is the stuff of history...and though not technically spot on, is the equivalent to half an hour in the gym for the taste buds. A malt of genuine character. Absolutely adore it! *62.8%*

∹ **Stauning Rye Third Solution** dist 2009/2010, bott 2012 **(92) n23 t23.5 f23 b22.5.** No doubting the grain used here: the rye bursts from the glass with massive, sharp fruity intent. Unlike some I have seen made elsewhere, this is very much in the Kentuckian mould and if the cut had been a little more precise, may well even have passed off as such. Not yet whisky, some of the spirit being a little less than the required three years, this bottling sends a very clear message: clean the distillate very slightly and bottle at full age and they will have one of Europe's great whiskies on their hands. This is beautiful stuff which even in this form delights from a multitude of angles. Also, this could well be their trademark whisky as it has the potential to out polish the peated and unpeated barley styles. Are we seeing the formative process of a potential world classic? It wouldn't surprise me. *50.5%*

ENGLAND
HEALEY'S CORNISH CYDER FARM Penhallow. Working.

Hicks & Healey Cornish Single Malt 2004 Cask #29 (94.5) n24.5 quite possibly an aroma I could spend all day getting to know. The interweaving between the soft apples and the softer honeys alone is enough to keep you entertained for a good hour at least. What makes this so special is the shading and texture; this is not a simple canvas on which one side is painted an apple in still life, the other honey. Every hue imaginable appears to be in there; the apples, for instance, appear from crisp green form to sluggish, sweeter brown and bruised. And just to intrigue you further is the slow showing of the spices. Not quite cinnamon, which might have been just too much of a cliché (though in the mix there appears to be a kind of relation), but a dribble of clove oil and linseed. These seem tied in with a burgeoning bourbon characteristic as the red liquorice grows beside the waxed leather. Faultless and almost beautiful beyond words...; **t24** after that astonishing nose it just had to be mouth-watering...and, my word, it is! The spices make an immediate impact, first feisty and then backing off. The delicate fruits refuse to take control and the lightly oiled barley has a bigger role here than on the nose. Again the honey (mainly of the clear, runny English type) waxes and wanes, like on the nose, from one moment being rich and bold, to watery and delicate the next; after a hint of cocoa a few cream caramel notes begin to fill the middle ground; **f22.5** just a hint of oaky bitterness arrives, but the natural caramels are now in the ascendency and offer the desired countering sweetness; late vanilla signs the whisky off; **b23.5** fascinatingly, picking up much more apple here than I did at the distillery, mainly because of the ambient aromas around me there: a great example why all tasting notes I carry out are in controlled environments. Back in January I headed down to the distillery and after going through their casks suggested this one was, like their very finest apples, exactly ripe for picking. The most noticeable thing was that there, in the still house, I picked up only a fraction of the apple I get here in the controlled environment of my tasting room. The distillery makes, above all else, cider brandy, so the aroma is all pervasive. However, my instincts were probably correct, for the apple (doubtless absorbed from the environment of maturing with apple brandy casks, something like the fruit apparent on the whisky of St George's distillery, California) to be found here only contributes positively rather than detracts, especially on the nose...which I have upgraded from excellent then to near faultless now. As new distilleries go, this rates among the best debut bottlings of the last decade. That is not least because most distillers try and launch on three years to get money back as soon as possible. Here they have more than doubled that time and are reaping the benefit...with interest. A dram, then, to keep your nocturnal cinema going on classic mode: "Last night I dreamt I went to Penhallow again." Hang on: twelve syllables... I feel a book coming on... and a film... *61.3%. sc.*

∹ **Hicks & Healey Cornish Whiskey 2004 Cask #32** dist 13 Feb 04, bott Feb 12 db **(96) n24** oh...oh... scrumped apple with rainwater, a sprinkling of cinnamon and barley sugar. The vanilla is no more than cold custard on apple crumble...an aroma unique to Hicks and Healey; **t24.5** a mouth feel to die for: almost a perfect degree of soft oil spreads the sugar-crusted apple to all parts of the palate; a slow honey build thickens further and keeps check on the spices; in mid term the barley at last escapes its apple-rich shadow for a clean, juicy rant: superb! **f23.5** strangely short, leaving a busy spice echo and dry, chalky vanilla; **b24** I picked this one up absent-mindedly, nosed...and was carried to Cornwall. I knew what it was without even opening my eyes. Unmistakable. And just so stunningly beautiful... *60.2%. ncf.*

ST. GEORGE'S Rowdham. Working.

The English Whisky Co. Chapter 6 English Single Malt (unpeated) batch no. 001 **(90) n22.5 t23 f22.5 b22.** We had to wait over 100 years for it to happen. But, at last, another English whisky on the market. Was it worth the wait? On the evidence of this first-ever bottling, then unquestionably. The firm and expert hand of former Laphroaig distillery manager Iain Henderson was on the tiller when this spirit was made three years ago and his fingerprints are all over this precocious and ultra high quality bottling. Adorable clarity to this malt which is, considering its youth, without weakness or blemish and, for its tender years, an uncommonly fine whisky. The 1,000th new whisky for the 2011 Bible. As an Englishman, could there have been any other? *46%. nc ncf.*

The English Whisky Co. Chapter 6 English Single Malt (unpeated) cask no. 163, 165, 171 & 173, dist May 07, bott Jun 10 db **(91) n22 t23 f23.5 b22.5.** Further confirmation that this distillery is on course for true excellence. Here, by comparison to earlier bottlings, the distillate shows some evidence that the stills have been run just a little faster and the cut thinned a little, meaning a laser-sharp crispness to the barley. So reminds me of Glen Grant at this age. *46%*

⠐⠐⠐ **The English Whisky Co. Chapter 6 English Single Malt** ASB casks, cask no. 564 & 567, dist Jun 08, bott Jun 11 db **(90) n23** gorgeously weighted and very happily balanced malt which almost sparkles thanks to crusty honey and marzipan sweetness; **t22.5** again the sugars show first, but are wonderfully subtle thanks, perhaps, to the weight of the swiftly following oils and vanilla; the honey on the nose arrives in the mid term, partnering a growing degree of nougat; **f22** a mild buzz on the finish confirms the suspected wider cut than required...but it is marginal stuff; **b22.5** fascinating to see how the extra year in the barrel has done nothing to diminish the citrus aspect, yet the sugars are better integrated than normal. *46%. ncf. nc*

⠐⠐⠐ **The English Whisky Co. Chapter 6 English Single Malt** ASB casks, cask no. 605, 606, 607 & 608, dist May 08, bott Aug 11 db **(87.5) n22** youthful, as might be expected, but the sharpness does allow the barley to drive home deep and true; for such a light-coloured malt, the oak has a surprising amount to say for itself; **t22** silky delivery really allowing full weight to the ever-intensifying malt; again the oak casts a heavy vanilla shadow; **f21.5** those relatively simplistic barley oak notes work well to the very end; **b22** the citrus notes I was expecting from experience failed to materialise. But there is some attractive compensation. *46%. nc ncf.*

⠐⠐⠐ **The English Whisky Co. Chapter 6 English Single Malt** ASB casks, cask no. 573, 574, 613 & 614, dist May 08, bott Sep 11 db **(92) n23** offers much greater depth than such an age and colour should permit: the secret here is the interweaving of delicate spice among citrusy sugars, and the lack of new make character; **t23.5** mmm...that nibbles the spot perfectly. Slightly oily, a touch of salt from somewhere, but that spice-sugar tandem on the nose translates almost perfectly here. And of course, the barley is hugely intense; **f22** dries, with busy spice still doing its job and even a touch of light cocoa. A squeeze of lemon somehow makes its way through to the end; **b23.5** hugely enjoyable, very well made, excellently matured single malt. As simple as that! *46%. nc ncf.*

⠐⠐⠐ **The English Whisky Co. Chapter 6 English Single Malt** ASB casks, cask no. 586, 587, 588 & 589, dist May 08, bott Sep 11 db **(89) n22** thick barley with a toffee underscore; **t23** gristy sugars suck up some of the more butterscotch oak notes to make, with the oily body, a deliciously chewy experience; **f22** just lovely, clean barley with the vaguest citrus thread; **b22** a fascinating malt to taste alongside the other bottling from this month. Where that is a busy fellow that wears your brains out, this is a straight up and downer which concentrates on doing all the simple things well. *46%. nc ncf.*

⠐⠐⠐ **The English Whisky Co. Chapter 6 English Single Malt** ASB casks, cask no. 478, 479, 480 & 481, dist Aug 08, bott Oct 11 db **(92.5) n24** now back to its most citrusy, with pink grapefruit to the fore; some brilliant muscovado sugars not only sweeten the citrus and ever intensifying barley, but adds subtle weight, too: stunning for a malt so young! **t23** the leading texture on delivery makes you purr: light oils, but not so much that it masks the complex barley tones and the harmony between those sugars and delicate vanillas. The citrus cannot be kept out of things, either; **f22.5** a very slight bitter note – and not the grapefruit – though the barley rolls on and on; **b23** but for one cask betraying the rest with that loose bitterness on the finish and this would have been Liquid Gold.... *46%. nc ncf.*

⠐⠐⠐ **The English Whisky Co. Chapter 6 English Single Malt** ASB casks, cask no. 482, 483, 485 & 486, dist Aug 08, bott Nov 11 db **(85) n21.5 t22 f21 b20.5.** The label says "Not Peated". The nose tells you another story. Unbelievably dense whisky for this distillery with a mix of heavy oil and light phenols. But the oak and sugars don't quite keep apace and balance is compromised. *46%. nc ncf.*

⠐⠐⠐ **The English Whisky Co. Chapter 6 English Single Malt** ASB casks, cask no. 021, 022, 023 & 034, dist Jun 09, bott Jul 12 db **(81) n21 t21 f19 b20.** Always big, malty and chewy. But slightly too many feints for its own good. *46%. nc ncf.*

The English Whisky Co. Chapter 7 Rum Finish ASB & rum cask nos. 024/025, dist Mar 07, bott Oct 10 db **(94) n23.5** a sweet roll call of delicate sugars, including grist; clean and offering just the right amount of balancing spice; **t24** as the nose suggests it might, the whisky simply melts into the palate while the citrusy vitality of the barley generates all the required energy;

f23 just a little cask bitterness for the sugars to contend with, but nothing they can't handle; **b23.5** absolutely exceptional. A near faultless whisky where the youth of the malt and the sweet finesse of the rum casks were born for each other. The kind of light and juicy whisky I, frankly, adore. *46%. nc ncf.*

❖ **The English Whisky Co. Chapter 7 Rum Cask Limited Edition** bott 2011 db **(94) n23.5** lovely interplay between the marmalade and honeyed toast. The sugars are crusty and there is a hint of smoky bacon in the background...a breakfast malt if ever there was one...; **t23.5** as with many rum casks it is the sugar which does the early running, here apparent in both soft and crisp mode, though it is the crisp which appears to have the upper hand. The barley shows its gristy side, but the vanillas are kept in place and seemingly unable to move; the only variables are the citrus notes, which fade and intensify at will; **f23** now almost statue-esque: the flavours, despite the arrival of some light oils, have been set in stone other than delicate spices which tease and mock the unmoving sugars and barley; **b24** tight, disciplined, crisp...I have never had the experience, but this (I have been told) seems just what it is like when bound and whipped by a mistress. Britain's judiciary should be on their way to Norfolk en masse... Absolutely delicious!! *46%. nc ncf sc.*

The English Whisky Co. Chapter 9 English Single Malt (peated) cask no. 102, 115, 124 & 144, dist May 07, bott May 10 db **(93.5) n23 t23.5 f24 b23**. Frankly, it would be churlish to ask any more of a malt whisky of this age. Three years old only, yet going through the gears of complexity like an old 'un. The secret, though, is in the quality of the distillation and the very decent casks used. So exceptional is this, you would almost think that this was created by the guy who made Laphroaig for many a year... *46%*

❖ **The English Whisky Co. Chapter 9 Peated / Smokey** ASB casks, cask no. 565, 566 & 567, dist Dec 07, bott Mar 11 db **(88) n22** lightly smoked kipper with a generous squeeze of lemon juice; **t22** fat, chewy, barley infested and enjoys a slow build-up of phenols; **f22** more citrus and now spiced; **b22** very much like a standard St George's but with a light plume of peaty smoke blowing over the scene... *46%. nc ncf.*

❖ **The English Whisky Co. Chapter 9 Peated / Smokey** ASB casks, cask no. 532, 533, 534 & 535, dist Nov 07, bott Aug 11 db **(86.5) n21.5 t22 f22 b21**. Not sure if this needs a spoon or a knife and fork. Big, thick, intense barley character with the smoke being swept into corners. *46%. nc ncf.*

❖ **The English Whisky Co. Chapter 9 Peated / Smokey** ASB casks, cask no. 0501 & 0489, dist Aug 08, bott Jan 12 db **(95) n23.5** youthful, for sure. But the freshness of that gristy peat and the interplay between clean vanilla pods and delicate muscovado sugars is something else! **t24** one of the best deliveries by any bottling from this distillery yet. I doubt if the weight can be bettered, or the timbre of the delicate peat. Yet more delicate sugar interplay. The oak acts only as a tool for applying weight and a butterscotch buffer between those two main stars and any developing spice; **f23.5** the oils persist and some late citrus thins the barley and smoke with aplomb; **b24** world class whisky with the weight and finesse making all the right noises. For its age, it writes itself in the annals of English whisky folklore. Beyond superb, this wins my Percy Award for things of stunning beauty coming from Norfolk! *46%. nc ncf.*

The English Whisky Co. Chapter 10 Sherry Finish Oloroso sherry hogshead, cask no. 488/489, dist Oct 07, bott Oct 10 db **(91) n23.5** crusty oloroso in its purest dry form; almost a hint of salty crushed olive; of the malt and oak...there is no sign...; **t23** a dry delivery followed – at last –by a trilling infant barley sweet juiciness; the tangy sharpness follows the salty path signposted on the nose; **f22** dry with a soupcon of vanilla doing its level best to add a degree of age; a little spice buzz, but from the grape, I suspect; **b22.5** a spotlessly clean oloroso cask ensures a beautiful malt, though not quite hitting the very highest forms of excellence as the host whisky has not yet formed sufficient muscle to carry the grape without the odd sideways stagger. That said, not a whisky you'd ever say "no" to the offer of a top-up... *46%. nc ncf.*

The English Whisky Co. Chapter 11 "Heavily Peated" ASB cask no. 645/647/648, dist Mar 08, bott May 11 db **(92) n23 t23.5 f22.5 b23**. As the full strength 59.7% version below. Only for wimps. *46%. nc ncf.*

❖ **The English Whisky Co. Chapter 11 Heavily Peated** ASB casks, cask no. 639, 640, 641 & 642, dist Mar 08, bott Nov 11 db **(91.5) n22.5** it may say heavily peated on the label but, perhaps because of the reduction to 46% abv, it actually comes through with a degree of buoyancy; absolutely no coastal influence, as one might expect seeing as it was matured just down the road from land-locked Thetford Forest. But there is still excellent complexity with some gentle hickory notes representing the oak with panache; **t23** much more intense on delivery, but the smoke is soon brushed aside by wave upon wave of dark sugars, starting as muscovado and moving into a more plodding fudge; **f23** long with a touch of butterscotch as the smoke fights back...; **b23** one of the sweetest English whiskies for the last century... *46%. nc ncf.*

The English Whisky Co. Chapter 11 "Heavily Peated" Cask Strength ASB cask no. 645/647/648, dist Mar 08, bott May 11 db **(94) n23.5** although "heavily peated" it is light enough to allow the more citrusy elements of the young barley to ensure a sublime counter lightness. Curiously salty for a land-locked distillery...but just so sexy; **t24** melts in the mouth on impact. No doubting the youth as there is a real greenness to the barley. But it strangely works in its favour because, like on the nose, it generates a sublime counter to the smoke; **f23** just the odd disagreement between the oak and barley, as whiskies of this age have a tendency to do. But once the toy has been put back in the pram, we have a spicy fade which makes your toes curl...; **b23.5** what can you say? A whisky only three years old yet carrying itself with the wisdom of an elder statesman. The pace of the peat is absolutely textbook; the marriage between the smoke and sugars the stuff of dreams. Proof that great – or even intermediate - age is not always the deciding factor. Sometimes, when a distiller has got all his sums right, a whisky can be plucked from the cask at a positively infantile age and still it can have the capacity to knock you off your chair. As this, indeed, does. And if you require proof that adding water to whisky doesn't do a whisky many favours, just try the 46% version... *59.7%. nc ncf.*

⁖ **The English Whisky Co. Chapter 11 Heavily Peated Cask Strength** ASB casks, cask no. 639, 640, 641 & 642, dist Mar 08, bott Nov 11 db **(93) n23** a brooding dram: the kind of malt that appears to have been distilled by Heathcliff on a misty Yorkshire moor rather than by David in Narfark. Thick, peaty embers happy to mix it up with a custardy and maple syrup sweetness; **t23.5** those slightly syrupy sugars spring out of the blocks at a pace. Yet there is a massive follow through of smoke-laden biscuit (actually, German caramelised biscuit, to be precise) as well as one of those jam tarts where you can't work out what the fruit is supposed to be, so dominant is the sugar; **f23** thickens again; mocha sucks in the broiling peat; **b23.5** feels very at home at this strength. impossible not to enjoy! *59.7%. nc ncf.*

The English Whisky Co. Limited Edition "Ibisco Decanter" bourbon cask, dist Nov 06, bott Dec 09 db **(91.5) n22 t24 f23 b22.5**. Quite adorable. Beautifully made whisky from stills small enough to add almost invisible but vital weight. One of the true fun whiskies of the year which further raises the expectations of what this distillery is capable of. *46%*

The English Whisky Co. Royal Marriage db **(86.5) n21 t23 f21.5 b21**. A charming, juicy and superbly made whisky showing the barley in varying weights and textures. But of all their bottlings yet, this is the one which most tellingly reveals its tender years. *46%*

⁖ **Founders Private Cellar** cask no. 0005 db **(94.5) n23.5** purposeful and vibrant, the barley enjoys a rare solidity on the nose for a malt this age, certainly enough to ensure that the encroaching oak has no chance of steering it off course; the sugars are sanguine and pop up only where and when needed, a background honey note is more persistent. **t24** just beautiful! The sugars, relatively shy on the nose, are now more confident, but some of it is from a gristy element which keeps that clean barley at the forefront of every flavour development; the house citrus style here carries a degree of vanilla; **f23** I was waiting for the spices, and at last they arrive – of the bitty, busy variety. A little chocolate honeycomb and butterscotch but the malt also manages to make its way to the finale, carried on a delicate new-makey wave...; **b24** this is the first whisky from this distillery to be bottled at the grand old age of five! And this old timer bears the most eloquent testimony possible to the skills of veteran distiller Iain Henderson: it is a stunner! I drink this to your health, old friend. *60.8%. nc ncf sc.*

⁖ **Founders Private Cellar** peated rum cask, cask no. 0763, bott 19 Sep 11 db **(85.5) n21 t23 f21 b20.5**. An oddball malt: if were a film it would have starred Walter Matthau and Jack Lemon: the disharmony is thoroughly entertaining... I would like to tell you the plot, but that's not easy. This is a cask plucked at a time it wasn't ready: when the barley and oak had zilch accord, when the oils were looking for a comfortable home. But the enormity, especially of the barley, does catch the breath... *60.2%. nc ncf sc.*

⁖ **Founders Private Cellar** peated Sauternes cask, cask no. 0787 db **(87) n22** you almost need a laser to cut through the density of this offering; the grape and smoke have combined with a generous cut to make something almost opaque... **t23** impossible not to love the delivery! After an unhappy delivery, huge marmalade being spread over smoked toast: astonishing! **f20.5** the finish has a few landing problems and struggles to find the city, let alone the runway. Crash lands in a spicy forest...; **b21.5** in Scotland wine casks and peated malt rarely work well together. It's pretty hard going south of the border, too... Does have the odd moment of unfettered brilliance, though. *61.1%. nc ncf sc.*

⁖ **St George's To Commemorate the Diamond Jubilee of Queen Elizabeth II** casks db **(89) n22** thumping young barley on two levels; one crisp and clear, the other covered with an oily sheen; a little stewed pear does no harm at all; **t23** the oils on the nose make no attempt to vanish on delivery: this time they carry both barley and a significant variation on a theme of vanilla; **f22** long, thanks to those oils, with the sugars beginning to formulate. Barley remains clean and dynamic; **b22** should be required drinking at Sandringham. A big, noble malt for a big, noble occasion... *46%. nc ncf. 3,300 bottles.*

FINLAND
PANIMORAVINTOLA BEER HUNTER'S Pori. Working.

Old Buck cask no. 4, dist Mar 04, bott Apr 10 db **(95) n24 t23 f24 b24.** Just read the tasting notes to the second release because, a dose of what almost seems like corn oil and ancient Demerara rum combined apart, oh - and an extra dose of oak, there is barely any difference. I will never, ever forget how I got this sample: I was giving a tasting in Helsinki a few months back to a horseshoe-shaped audience and a chap who had been sitting to my right and joining in with all the fun introduced himself afterwards as I signed a book for him as non other than Mika Heikkinen, the owner and distiller of this glorious whisky. I had not been told he was going to be there. His actual, touchingly humble words were: "You might be disappointed: you may think it rubbish and give it a low score. It just means I have to do better next time." No, I am not disappointed: I am astonished. No, it isn't rubbish: it is, frankly, one of the great whiskies of the year. And if you can do better next time, then you are almost certainly in line for the Bible's World Whisky of the Year award. *70.6%*

TEERENPELI

Teerenpeli Single Malt Whisky Aged 5 Years db **(86) n21.5 t22 f21 b21.5.** No shrinking violet, this impressive first bottling from Teerenpeli. It radiates the chunkier qualities often found with smaller stills, yet still manages to harness the richer barley notes to enjoyable effect. Weighty and a touch oily, the sweet barley which is briefly announced on arrival soon makes way for a more rumbustious combination of oak and higher oils. I look forward to getting there at last to see how it is done...though I think I can already imagine...!! *43%*

FRANCE
Single Malt
DISTILLERIE BERTRAND

Uberach db **(77) n21 t19 f18 b19.** Big, bitter, booming. Gives impression something's happening between smoke and grape... whatever it is, there are no prisoners taken. *42.2%*

DISTILLERIE DES MENHIRS

Eddu Gold db **(93) n22 t23 f24 b24.** Rarely do whiskies turn up in the glass so rich in character to the point of idiosyncrasy. Some purists will recoil from the more assertive elements. I simply rejoice. This is so proud to be different. And exceptionally good, to boot!! *43%*

⁘ **Eddu Grey Rock** db **(80) n19 t20 f21 b20.** Dry. With just a little two much tobacco early on for comfort. *40%*

⁘ **Eddu Grey Rock Brocéliande** db **(86.5) n21.5 t22 f22 b21.** Much fruitier than Eddu Grey Rock, simplistic, but offering a delectable and deft sweetness around the palate. Very good late spice, too. *40%*

⁘ **Eddu Silver** db **(88.5) n21** complex sweet-dry ratio, though still harbouring a touch of tobacco; **t22** beautiful texture on delivery with a silky sheen to the grist as it forms a sweet field in which to play; **f23** long, with the lightest of oily textures ensuring those sugars hit as many outposts as possible. The vanilla really impresses, as does the late milky chocolate; **b22.5** a delightfully balanced malt. *40%*

DISTILLERIE GLANN AR MOR

Glann Ar Mor Aged 3 Years 1st fill bourbon barrel db **(85) n21.5 t22 f20.5 b21.** The slight feints, so typical of European small still whisky, works well in upping the weight, structure and chewability. Juicy barley and cocoa dominate, but tasting after it has sat in an open glass for half an hour works wonders. *46%. Celtic Whisky Compagnie.*

Glann Ar Mor Taol Esa 1 an Gwech 11 db **(72) n18 t19 f17 b18.** is for French. is also for Feinty... *46%. nc ncf sc. Celtic Whisky Compagnie. 336 bottles.*

⁘ **Glann Ar Mor Taol Esa 1an Gwech 12** bourbon barrels db **(83) n20 t21 f21 b21.** Very malty. But never quite gets out of first gear. *46%. nc ncf. 619 bottles.*

Kornog Single Malt Whisky Breton Sant Ivy 2011 db **(94) n23** had I just opened a bottle of Caol Ila, this is pretty much what I would have expected. Telling but not overpowering peat, light oils and big vanillas... **t24** now this is getting scary. The gristy sugars are right out of the Caol Ila repertoire and then, to cap it all, a truck load of lime and sugars. I last saw on a young Port Ellen back in the days when my beard barely sported a greying hair...; **f23.5** long oils and spices while the smoky fug and the sugars just keep on seducing...; **b23.5** the nose, at least, says it was distilled on Islay. To a Frenchman, is that an honour or an insult...? For I have to say, this is the closest to a Scotch whisky I have ever tasted outside those cold, windswept lands.. To be honest, this is better than your average Caol Ila, as the oak is of finer quality. Frankly, this is a never to be forgotten whisky. *578%. nc ncf sc. Celtic Whisky Compagnie. 249 bottles.*

⏺ **Kornog Single Malt Tourbé (Peated) Whisky Breton Sant Erwan 2012** first fill bourbon barrel db **(89) n22.5** delicate smoke struggles to get the better of the liquorice; **t22** sweet, sugar dominant with a trail of phenolic grist; **f22** the oaks edge in, slightly bitter at first but corrected by the sugars; **b22.5** a young peaty whisky which lurks and hides around the palate, one minute seemingly still and silent, then moving in sugary, smoky bursts. *50%. nc ncf sc. 306 bottles.*

⏺ **Kornog Single Malt Tourbé (Peated) Whisky Breton Sant Ivy 2012** first fill bourbon barrel db **(92) n22.5** a very different nose with exceptional sweetness. The liquorice appears blended with lavender and camp coffee and carried weightlessly on the back of lightly smoked treacle...; a kind of low key, sweetened Fisherman's Friend...; **t23** smoky...dries a little...there's that treacle again...; **f23** much more integrated and complex with the vanillas injecting a degree of balancing dryness; **b23.5** with the usual time constraints of writing this book and the number of awful, sulphured whiskies which blight my path, I had kept this back as something to look forward to: last year their 2011 bottling was a masterpiece: out-Islaying Islay This, though, has its own French fingerprint upon it. Sweeter, more diffuse. But, Mon Dieu! A corker nonetheless! *59.9%. nc ncf sc. 260 bottles.*

⏺ **Kornog Single Malt Tourbé (Peated) Whisky Breton Taourc'h Trived 12BC** first fill bourbon barrel db **(95) n24** what a class act! The nose offers a supremely weighted mix of peat and herbs, making the complexity meter almost explode! Added to all this is a distinctly bourbony feel to things with the black liquorice of other bottlings here replaced by the red variety and just a little extra manuka honey; **t23.5** not sure which wins my heart first: the gorgeous texture or the marriage between the clean barley, the dark sugars or the phenols...; **f23.5** spices out like a dream; **b24** no off notes. No bitterness. Complexity on fill volume. I really do have to get to their distillery this year... now, where's that British Airways timetable...? *46%. nc ncf sc. 334 bottles.*

Kornog Taouarc'h Kentan db **(94.5) n24 t24 f23 b23.5.** Not sure there has been this number of perfectly rhapsodic notes coming out of France since Saint Sans was in his pomp... *57.1%*

DISTILLERIE GUILLON
Guillon No. 1 Single Malt de la montagne de Reims db **(87) n22 t21 f22 b22.** Right. I'm impressed. Not exactly faultless, but enough life here really to keep the tastebuds on full alert; By and large well made and truly enjoyable. Well done, Les Chaps! *46%*

DISTILLERIE MEYER
Meyer's Whisky Alsacien Blend Superieur db **(88.5) n23.5 t22.5 f21.5 b22** Impressively clean, barley-thick and confident: a delight. *40%*

DISTILLERIE WARENGHEM
Armorik db **(91) n23 t22 f23 b23.** I admit it; I blanched, when I first nosed this, so vivid was the memory of the last bottling. This, though ,was the most pleasant of surprises. Fabulous stuff: one of the most improved malts in the world. *40%*

Armorik Single Malt 5 Years Old bourbon casks & Breton oak casks, sherry finish, bott 2009 db **(83) n18 t21.5 f22 b21.5.** The standard Armorik is a rewarding whisky to find. This version, though attractively juicy and chewy in part, is a reminder that playing with sherry butts, even good ones, can result in a levelling of the higher points and an ultimately duller whisky. *42%*

⏺ **Armorik Classic** db **(88) n22.5** the oak is confident enough to go head to head with the big barley: complex, lively stuff; **t22** attractive gristy sweetness. Subtle oils spread the Barley intensity; **f21.5** dries towards a powdery vanilla; **b22** quietly sophisticated malt. *46%. ncf.*

⏺ **Armorik Sherry Finish** db **(92) n22.5** delicate, with the fruit nestling rather attractively into the cocoa and firm barley; **t23.5** just love that dry delivery: the few sugars form in slow motion into a marzipan paste with an orange topping; **f23** Lubec at its finest; **b23.5** the first sherry finish today which has not had a sulphur problem...and I'm in my eighth working hour...! Bravo guys! If their Classic was a note on sophistication, then this was an essay. *40%*

Armorik Single Cask sherry butt **(88) n20 t23 f22.5 b22.5.** Now that is seriously enjoyable! An unexpected nougat on the nose but the delivery and flowing richness is a real shock. *55%. sc.*

Breizh Whisky Blended 50% malt/50% grain db **(85.5) n22 t21 f21 b21.5.** A safe, pleasant whisky which happily remains within its sweet, clean and slightly citrusy parameters. *42%*

KAERILIS
⏺ **Kaerilis Rêve d'Azur (Azure Dream) 12** sherry & rum double matured db **(86) n20 t22 f22 b22.** Despite the rum casks, the biggest contributor appears to be the natural caramels gleaned from the casks. A pleasant experience showing some deft toffee and raisin character. *45%. nc ncf sc.*

⋙ **Kaerilis Belle Isle en Rêve (Beautiful Island in a Dream) 14 Ans Âge** dist 1997, cask no. 99 db **(72.5) n18 t19 f18 b18.5.** Sadly, not quite the whisky of my dreams... *52%. nc ncf sc.*

⋙ **Kaerilis Initiales Belle Isle (Beautiful Island) Sêrie Limitêe "Ster Vraz No.9"** db **(83) n21 t21.5 f19 b21.5.** They appear to have found an island with infinite resources of cocoa and nougat. What a lovely whisky these guys would make if only they could get their cuts right. *44%. nc ncf sc.*

⋙ **Kaerilis Le Grand Dérangement (The Great Upheaval)** dist 2000 db **(85.5) n20.5 t22 f21 b22** One of the most honeyed Derangements in history...but still fails to entirely eradicate the feints. *43%. nc ncf sc.*

⋙ **Kaerilis A 'laube du Grand Dérangement (At the Dawn of the Great Upheaval)** dist 2000 db **(83.5) n19 t22.5 f20 b22.** And trust me...they don't come any more Deranged than me... Even so, I am sane enough to recognise what would have been a really excellent malt had only their cuts been just a little more precise. Still, j'adore the citrus and barley intensity. *57%. nc ncf sc.*

WAMBRECHIES DISTILLERY
Wambrechies Single Malt Aged 3 Years db **(78.5) n19 t19 f21 b19.5.** Sweet with a Malteser candy touch. A few feints just dampen the overall effect. There is also an aroma on the nose I kind of recognize, but... *40%*

Wambrechies Single Malt Aged 8 Years db **(83) n20 t21 f21 b21.** There's that aroma again, just like the 3-y-o. Except how it kind of takes me back 30 years to when I hitchhiked across the Sahara. Some of the food I ate with the local families in Morocco and Algeria was among the best I have ever tasted. And here is an aroma I recognize from that time, though I can't say specifically what it is (tomatoes, maybe?). Attractive and unique to whisky, that's for sure. I rather like this malt. There is nothing quite comparable to it. One I need to investigate a whole lot more. *40%*

Blends
P&M Blend Supérieur (82) n21 t21 f20 b20. Bitter and botanical, though no shortage of complexity. *40%. Mavela Distillerie.*

P&M Whisky (89) n22 t23 f22 b22. No mistaking this is from a fruit distillery. Still quite North American, though. *40%*

GERMANY
AV BRENNEREI ANDREAS VALLENDAR Wincheringen. Working.
Threeland Whisky dist 2007, bott code L-Wtr200701 db **(83) n19.5 t22.5 f20 b21.** Whilst pleasant enough in its own right, my eyes opened up at this one, as I remember last year's bottling as being one of the best from anywhere in Europe. That, I recall, was so wonderfully fresh and clean. This one, sadly, is bigger and oilier with evidence that the distiller has included some heads and tails which were excluded last time out. Still malty and mouth watering. But a useful lesson in learning the vital difference between good and great whisky. *46%*

BIRKENHOF-BRENNEREI Nistertal. Working.
Fading Hill 4 1/2 Years American and French oak, cask no. 09 & 11, dist Nov 05, bott Apr 10 db **(74) n18 t20 f17.5 b18.5.** One of those peculiar malts which sends out mixed messages. On one hand, there is a curiously attractive damp hay character and for the more fanciful, orange blossom. On the other, signs, confirmed by the finish, that not all is right or happy. *45.7%. 680 bottles.*

Fading Hill 2005 Meets 2007 cask no. 14 & 19, dist Nov 05 & Oct 07 db **(85.5) n20 t21 f23 b21.5.** Nothing fading about its character: a feinty chap early on but the finish is the best part by a mile: those oils go on forever, bringing some magnificent molten Demerara and cocoa. *45.7%. nc. 690 bottles.*

⋙ **Fading Hill The Fourth** bourbon casks, cask no. 22 & 23, dist Jul 08, bott 14 Mar 12 **(90.5) n22.5** anyone of a certain age will remember this aroma of green Rowntree Fruit Pastels: this is almost identical...; **t22** mouth-watering barley almost with an effervescent quality before the slightly oily vanilla kicks in, then chocolate, then walnut....it's Walnut Whip... good grief..!! **f23** returns to a more fruity depth, with the vanillas and light spice a pleasant accompaniment; **b23** less Fading Hill: more F***ing Hell...!! Can't remember when I was taken down such a scary part of my past before: some of the aromas and flavours are like a time machine...! beautiful stuff. *45.7%. nc ncf.*

BOSCH EDELBRAND Unterlenningen. Working.
Bosch Edelbrand Schwäbischer Whisky lot 9105 db **(83.5) n19 t22.5 f21 b21.** Could really do with making the cut a little more selective: has the promise to become a pretty high

quality whisky. This shows some outstanding depth and honey for some time after the first, impressive delivery. *40%*

BRANNTWEINBRENNEREI WEINBAU ADOLF KELLER Ramsthal.

A.K Whisky bott code L10209 db **(89.5) n22 t23 f22 b22.5**. Hardly faultless from a technical point of view. But if you can't enjoy something as raunchy and ribald as this, you might as well stop drinking whisky. *40%*

A.K Whisky bott code L11110 db **(67) n15 t18 f17 b17**. I think the A.K. stands for the rifle which is required to shoot this ultra fruity, bizarrely scented whisky... 40%

BRENNEREI ANTON BISCHOF Wartmannsroth. Working.

Bischof's Rhöner Whisky bott code L-24 db **(75.5) n17.5 t20 f18 b19**. That unique blend of feints and intense, biscuity grains. Just checked: I see I gave it the same score as last year. Not only unmistakable, but consistently so! *40%*

BRENNEREI DANNENMANN Owen. Working.

Danne's Schwäbischer Whisky dist 2002 db **(89) n22 t23 f22 b22**. An exhausting whisky to try and understand. You crack the code only when you fathom that there are two entirely different songs being played at the same time. 54.6%

Danne's Schwäbischer Whisky dist 2002 db **(78) n19 t21.5 f18.5 b19**. A recognisable style of pungent, full-flavoured central and northern European spirit I have experienced over the many years, though not always associated with whisky. There is both a fruit and vegetable character here but the begrudging and short-lived juicy sweetness is, I assume, the brief bow towards the grain. The finish could almost be a full blown, old-fashioned Swedish or Norwegian aquavit. *43%*

Schwäbischer Whisky vom Bellerhof db **(88) n21 t22 f23 b22**. Easy drinking clean and deliciously sweet malt with that indelible touch of class. *43%*

Schwäbischer Whisky vom Bellerhof db **(88) n23 t22 f21 b22**. An entirely different route to the same high quality whisky...! *4/4%*

BRENNEREI ERICH SIGEL Dettingen. Working.

Original Dettinger Schwäbischer Whisky db **(88) n21.5** sharp: egg custard tart and a supine touch of pine; **t22.5** sugared almonds; body is silky and sweetens gently; **f22** heaps of vanilla and a slow build up of juicy barley notes and spice **b22** softly sophisticated. 40%

BRENNEREI FABER Ferschweiler. Working.

Whisky aus der Eifel Aged 6 Years American oak, dist 2003 db **(91) n23 t23 f22.5 b22.5**. A riveting whisky of uncommonly high quality. 46%

BRENNEREI FRANK RODER Aalen - Wasseralfingen. Working.

Frank's Suebisch Whisky dist 2005 db **(86) n21 t22.5 f21 b21.5**. Impossible not to be charmed by the disarming citrus note. Every aspect of this whisky is low key and delicate. *40%*

BRENNEREI HACK Pinzberg. Working.

Walburgis Franken db **(78) n17 t20 f21 b20**. While the nose puts the 'aahhhh!' in nougat, the sweet walnut-cake nuttiness on delivery and beyond makes some amends. *40%*

BRENNEREI HENRICH Kriftel, Hessia. Working.

⁛ **Gilors Fino Sherry Cask** bott code L12020, dist Apr 09, bott May 12 db **(88.5) n22** an enticing marriage of ulmo honey and nougat candy; the fruit is more orange pith than grape; quite nutty, too; **t22** huge oils, yet the wide cut does not include any unpleasantness. The malt is so intense it outperforms the grape by some distance; **f22.5** despite a little feinty buzz the finale is a beautiful meeting of light sugars – even a hint of honey – with some upstanding vanilla; **b22** the stem of my tasting glass may give way under the weight of this one at any moment...delicious, though! *46%. sc. 471 bottles.*

⁛ **Gilors Port Cask** bott code L12021, dist Apr 09, bott May 12 db **(84.5) n22 t22 f19.5 b21**. One of the heaviest whiskies on the planet, at times seemingly opaque. The distillate began life on the weighty side with a wide cut and the port appears to have plugged any gaps there may have been. The result is a massive, fruity, nutty, tingly concentrated nougat affair for those with strong jaw muscles... *46%. sc. 427 bottles.*

BRENNEREI HÖHLER Aarbergen, Kettenbach. Working.

Whesskey Hessischer aus Caraaroma Malz db **(87) n17.5 t24 f22.5 b23**. What a pity my tasting of this whisky wasn't filmed. Then it would have been recorded me doing this:

nosing...head in hands. Nosing again...shaking head and saying out loud to myself: "either you are going to be a bloody nightmare or something pretty amazing." Tasting it, tasting it for a second time and then, after slumping back in the chair, ejaculating: "you beautiful ugly bastard!" For all the feints and butyric on the dire nose, these somehow (as I suspected) come back to offer on the palate a massive malt. Certainly, no whisky on this planet has a bigger jump in quality from nose to delivery. *62%. nc ncf. Drei Jahre alt Faßtärke.*

Wesskey Hessischen aus Caraaroma Malz und Rauchmalz db **(86.5) n19 t21 f24.5 b22.** These guys specialise in outrageous whiskies which stick two fingers up to you. Again the nose is lacking. And again the whisky fights back with a dazzling exhibition of intense barley and Demerara flavours. The finish is relentless and, full of mocha and barley, a thing of beauty. *57.5%. nc ncf. Drei Jahre alt Faßtärke.*

Wesskey Hessischer aus Rauchmalz dist Jan/Feb 08, bott 25/02/11 db **(85) n19 t21.5 f22.5 b22.** Now there's a weird thing. When I blended some of their Caraaroma and Rauchmalx whiskies together, the nose and flavour profile I created was virtually identical to this. Weirder still, when you put the two poor noses together, they actually improve...two negatives, obviously. Big, chewy, chocolatey stuff. *44%*

Wesskey Hessischer aus Rauchmalz Faßtärke dist Jan/Feb 08, bott 25/02/11 db **(80.5) n18.5 t22 f20 b21.** Big and fruity...like attending a Sultana Fest. With a bar of chocolate as your guest. Some wonderful spices. But, overall, pays the price for a little sloppy distilling with the same faults as seen elsewhere, but this time unable to escape the consequences. *57%. ncf.*

Wesskey Hessischer aus Stammwürze 4 Years Old db **(90) n21 t22.5 f24 b22.5.** There are so many things right with this whisky, but you also get the feeling – even when it as amazing as this - that something is wrong. Either way, bottling like this enliven any evening and give tired taste buds a new lease of life and a will to live... *57%*

Wesskey Hessischer Mais Whisky dist Feb 07, bott Nov 10 db **(84.5) n22 t21.5 f21.5 b19.5.** Well, that was weird. For once they get the nose right. Then it begins to fall apart on the palate... I assume some kind of wine cask, as there is a profound grape and spice presence. But rarely are the cask and spirit on speaking terms. *44%*

BRENNEREI HÖNING Winnweiler, Donnersbergkreis. Working.

∴ **Taranis Single Cask Limited Edition Aged 3 Years** Limousin-Eiche barrel, cask no. 1, dist Sep 08 **(84) n21 t21.5 f20 b21.5.** Anyone for sweetened lemon tea? Pretty refreshing dram – though unusual! *46%. sc. 679 bottles.*

BRENNEREI HÜBNER Stadelhofen, Steinfeld. Working.

Fränkischer Whisky db **(67.5) n15 t17.5 f18 b17.** Well, that was different. Can't really give you tasting notes as such, as I don't really have a reference point as to where to start. Quite simply, a bunch of bizarre aromas and flavours, the vast majority of which I have never encountered before. Another distillery I must seek and visit to find out what all this is about... *40%*

Hubner Los Nr 3 db **(80.5) n20 t22.5 f18 b20.** Overwhelmed by fruit as far as complexity is concerned, but there is a distinctive smoky, salivating theme to this nonetheless. The balance has been trashed and if it were a novel, you'd have to read it three times...and still make no sense of it. A David Lynch film of a whisky...and I love it, though I have no idea why. *40%*

BRENNEREI LOBMÜLLER Talheim. Working.

Schwäbischer Whisky Single Grain cask no. 7 db **(86.5) n20 t22.5 f22 b22.** A friendly, big-hearted, soul full of toffee-chocolate chewiness. Highly enjoyable. *41%*

BRENNEREI MARTIN MEIER Neuravensburg. Working.

Mein 9. Fass db **(84) n19 t21.5 f22 b21.5.** The light spices and dissolving sugars melt beautifully into the malt. Nose apart, this is a ja, nicht ein 9... *42%*

BRENNEREI MARTIN ZIEGLER Baltmannsweiler. Working.

Esslinger Single Malt Aged 8 Years db **(85) n20.5 t22 f21 b21.5.** Malty, nutty, a decent degree of sweetness and toffee marzipan. A well-made malt which you appreciate more as you acclimatise to its compact style. *42%*

BRENNEREI RABEL Owen. Working.

Schwäbischer Whisky db **(76.5) n17 t21.5 f18 b20.** Here's something different. While the nose, or at least the getting it right, is a work in progress, the delivery and body are much more on the ball thanks mainly to a rich treacle and prune element which sees off the thicker distillate. The finish, though, confirms the fault lines. *40%*

BRENNEREI VOLKER THEURER Tübingen-Unterjesingen. Working.

Black Horse Ammertal bott code BL-2010 db **(79)** n18.5 t21 f19 b20.5. The wider cut used in the distilling means this Black Horse has put on a little bit of weight from the BL2008 I tasted in 2010. The light phenols have gone but the sugars have increased. 40%

Sankt Johann Single Barrel Aged 8 Years bott code BL-2010 db **(85)** n19.5 t22 f21.5 b22. Fabulous fun. Once it gets over the drying tobacco nose the inevitable nougat is delivered. But it comes with a milk-creamy mocha which develops in intensity and with just the right doses of treacle to keep the sweetness at desired levels. Good background spices too. A very likeable character, this Saint Johann. 46.5%

BRENNEREI ZAISER Köngen. Working.

Zaiser Schwäbischer Whisky db **(83)** n23 t21.5 f19 b19.5. Surprisingly dry and constricted in development considering the beautiful soft sugars on the nose which also boast excellent clarity. 40%

BRENNEREI ZIEGLER Freudenberg, North Württemberg. Working.

⁘ **Aureum 1865** db **(86.5)** n19 t23 f22.5 b22. Remains one of the most curious, and distinctive, whiskies in Europe. Usually you get little to excite you from the nose, and here you get even less. However, the silky soft delivery goes into its famous caramel overdrive and here even conjures up a classic cream toffee style. Bypass the nose and enjoy a malty, melt-in-the mouth treat, as this is super-drinkable whisky. Sort the nose out and you have one of Germany's finest, for sure. Love it! 43%

DESTILLERIE DREXLER Working.

Drexler Arrach No. 1 Bayerwald Single Cask cask no. 262, dist May 07, bott May 10 db **(88.5)** n21 t23 f22 b22.5. Very good bitter-sweet marriage, but better still is the luxuriant mouth-feel. A well constructed malt. 46%. 210 bottles.

DESTILLERIE HERMANN MÜHLHÄUSER Working.

Mühlhäuser Schwäbischer Whisky aus Korn db **(90.5)** n23 t23 f22 b22.5. Another stunning bottling from this excellent distiller. You have to admire the subtlety of the complexity of this whisky. 41%

Mühlhäuser Schwäbischer Whisky aus Korn db **(90)** n22.5 t23 f22 b22.5. So different! If you are into this, it'll be pastoral perfection. 40%

EDELBRENNEREI PETER HOHMANN Nordheim, Rhön. Working.

Rhöner Grain Whisky Aged 6 Years db **(89)** n21 t22.5 f23 b22.5. Impressively made and matured with a quite lovely marriage between the sugars and spices. 40%

EDELOBST-BRENNEREI ZIEGLER Freudenberg. Working.

AVREUM db **(83)** n21.5 t21 f20 b20.5. A most peculiar, though not unattractive, marriage of marmalade and hops. 43%. 1000 bottles.

FEINBRENNEREI SEVERIN SIMON Alzenau-Michelbach. Working.

Simon's 10 Years Old Bavarian Pure Pot Still db **(86.5)** n21.5 t21.5 f22.5 b21. Not a whiskey to rush. Takes several hours to get to know this chap. When they say Pure Pott Still, I am sure they mean a mixture of malted and unmalted barley. Because that is the only style that offers a whiskey as rock hard as this with virtually no give on the palate. If there is any yield, it comes in a vaguely fruity form but this is a whiskey which sets up an impenetrable barrier and defies you to pass. Fascinating and very different. 40%

FINCH HIGHLAND WHISKY DISTILLERY Nellingen, Alb-Donau. Working.

⁘ **Finch White Label** barrique barrels db **(91)** n23 the grape is clean and quietly intense; the grain sweet and embracing; t22.5 mouth-watering with a delightful fruity-bready combination...almost like grape jelly on a steaming loaf baked that morning; f22 it's all about the grain now, slightly lightened by weak golden syrup; b23 when I borrowed from the local library and read my first books on archaeology and Iron Age man some 45 years ago, I wondered why they grew spelt and tried to imagine what it tasted like. Now I understand. I look forward to someone unearthing the first Iron Age pot still... A Finch which sings most beautifully.... 40%. Spelt and wheat.

⁘ **Finch Destillers Edition** barrique matured/bourbon finish, bott Apr 12 db **(94.5)** n24 could nose this all day: clean, green-graped, greengaged, and just the right degree of honey and red liquorice. Superb! t23.5 a little more aggressive than the nose – but then it couldn't be anything else. a few oils digging in, but again it is that soft honey lead...; f23 the oily bitterness from the cut dissipates as the oak and grains begin to offer extra vanillas...almost like whipped ice cream; **b24** these guys know exactly what they are doing... 40%

GUTSBRENNEREI AGLISHARDT Nellingen. Working.

HFG Dinkelwhisky Single Cask No 2 db **(87.5)** n21.5 t22 f22 b22. good, honest whisky with plenty of charm from the grain. 41.5%

HFG Schwäbischer Whisky db **(72.5)** n18 t19 f17.5 b18. Dry and spicy. But let down by the cask. 40%

HAMMERSCHMIEDE Zorge. Working.

⁘ **The Alrik Smoked Hercynian Single Malt 4 Years Old** PX casks, dist 2008, bott 2012 db **(95)** n24 the busiest of aromas, showing complex weights and the most deft use of dark sugars...ticks away with all the beautiful intricacy of a mechanical Raymond Weil; **t23.5** the delivery offers above average oil, and weighty coconut and molasses for added thickness. The smoke drifts in through the back door, the beech in particular apparent; **f23.5** the PX cask this matured in has done its work and now the barley and vanillas are left to relax... with that most delicate of smokiness which shows only if you are patient enough to wait for it...; **b24** beautiful weight, just-so sweetness, different...and simply adorable. 52.3%. nc ncf. *Smoked with alder and beech.*

⁘ **The Glen Els Elements Air** db **(90.5)** n22.5 surprisingly salty for a malt distilled in such a land-locked country! The delicate barley shows no ill effects for the light citrus which freshens the experience further; **t22** simple, two-toned delivery: both sharp and sweet barley notes vying for supremacy; the oils are soft and lightly sugared; **f23** the rejoining of a slightly salty vanilla thread boosts the complexity considerably. Remains clean and pleasingly sweet to the finish; **b23** a beautifully refined malt. But I just hope that Glen Els is the name of the actual living, breathing distiller, not the brand...otherwise I see the good ol' Scotch Whisky Association finding another reason not to tackle their own problems and instead try to drown at birth a foreign distiller straying into the dangerous field of Scottish nomenclature... 45.9%. 600 bottles.

⁘ **The Glen Els Elements Earth** db **(87.5)** n19.5 if you can imagine: I nose and taste 1200 new whiskies every year for the Bible. How many brand new experiences do I come across every very? Not many. This is one, and despite what appears to be a sulphur flaw there is an extraordinary prune juice poured into intense chocolate mousse. By no means perfect... but wow! **t24** how can a flawed malt offer such brilliance on the palate? Oh my god!! this is the Fruitfest to end them all: the trick is that for all the dates, prunes and raisins on show, it enjoys by rich cocoa accompaniment; **f21** the grizzly, bitter off notes are plain enough, yet still you cannot be anything other than blown away by the softness and ultra complex layering of the remaining fruit... **b23** I'll be honest: this fooled me. On the nose, I detected sulphur. And on the finish, also. So I expected a dud. I was wrong. Good earth for growing grapes... 45.9%. 400 bottles.

⁘ **The Glen Els First Journey** ex-fortified wine European oak, dist 2008, bott 2012 db **(85)** n22 t22 f20 b21. Plenty of soft, yielding grape early on. But become a little too bitter and tight as it progresses. 43%. nc ncf.

⁘ **The Glen Els Madeira Cask** cask no. 25, dist 23 Sep 07, bott 25 Sep 10 db **(76)** n18 t21 f18 b19. A butyric kick to this overcomes even a Madeira cask obviously of a decent quality. 46.5%. sc. 392 bottles.

The Glen Els Single Hercynian Malt dist May 06, bott May 10 db **(86.5)** n22 t22.5 f20.5 b21.5. Loads of baked yam and fresh barley on nose; clean and a touch of the Malteser candy on palate. Thoroughly enjoyable, and doubtless the SWA will love it even more... 51%

⁘ **The Glen Els Tawny Port Cask** cask no. 17, dist 23 Sep 07, bott 7 Oct 10 db **(84.5)** n21 t22.5 f20 b21. Less than impressive distillate saved by an excellent cask. 47.2%. sc. 403 bottles.

⁘ **The Glen Els Unique Distillery Edition** port casks db **(85.5)** n22.5 t21.5 f21.5 b20. You get the feeling that these big wine numbers from Glen Els are something of a work in progress. Its great having a decent spirit. And wonderful to posses superb casks. The trick, as with any whisky, is to create a balance between the two. Despite some pleasant textures here, that balance remains some distance off: the grape is far too much in control. 45.9%. 3,000 bottles.

⁘ **The Glen Els Unique Distillery Edition** sherry casks, dist 2007, bott 2010 db **(81)** n22 t22 f17 b20. Plenty of juicy, fruity spice to enjoy but the finale is somewhat tarnished. 45.9%

⁘ **The Glen Els Unique Single Dulce Negra Malaga** first fill Malaga cask, cask no. 93, dist 17 Jan 08, bott 7 May 12 db **(92)** n22.5 if you are expecting a muscatel-style dessert wine sweetness to this you won't be disappointed. Brimming with sugars, heavily floral and thick with thyme honey, lavender, alovera, pine and tea tree: a one off...! **t23.5** works rather beautifully: clean lightly spiced grape thickens quickly until it moves into an exotic honey zone: a mix between New Zealand beech and manuka leading the way. The spices buzz gently – presumably from the bees – and fits perfectly; a lovely cocoa and hickory flourish in mid-stream; **f22.5** calms, and as the sugars reduce the barley regains a balancing foothold; **b23.5** Glen Els may have got a few of their other wine casks slightly around their necks. But this one has worked astonishingly well. In over 15,000 whiskies tasted in the last decade, I cannot find another whisky as a reference point. Truly unique. *44.4%. nc ncf sc. 384 bottles.*

HELMUT SPERBER Rentweinsdorf. Working.

Sperbers Destillerie Malt Whisky dist 2002 db **(76.5) n17.5 t19 f21 b19.** Great finish with the house cocoa/mocha style. But some of the other characteristics seem other worldly. *46%*

Sperbers Destillerie Malt Whisky dist 2002 db **(77.5) n17.5 t20 f21 b19.** Very similar to the 46% except the sugars are much more eccentric. *59%*

Sperbers Destillerie Single Grain Whisky dist 2002 db **(76) n17 t21 f19 b19.** Once you get past the butyric nose the mouth feel and slow cocoa development is rather lovely. *40%*

KINZIGBRENNEREI MARTIN BROSAMER Biberach. Working.

Kinzigbrennerei Martin Brosamer Single Malt oak cask, dist Apr 05, bott Sep 08 db **(84) n20.5 t21 f21.5 b21.** For all the obvious nougat, the barley is given a clear stage from which to make its sweet speech. *42%. 120 bottles.*

KLEINBRENNEREI FITZKE Herbolzheim-Broggingen. Working.

Schwarzwälder Whisky Emmermalz bott code. L6807 db **(91) n21 t23 f23.5 b23.5.** The ancient grain of emmerkorn is not a usual component of whisky, though as it was used for beer in prehistory it is about time something was done with it in the still. And on this evidence it has been worth waiting for. A magnificently characterful malt. Generally well distilled and beautifully matured, to boot. *43%*

Schwarzwälder Whisky Hafermalz bott code. L6707 db **(70) n17 t18 f17 b18.** Sweet. But way off key. *43%*

Schwarzwälder Whisky Gerstenmalz bott code. L5406 db **(84.5) n18.5 t21.5 f22.5 b22.** Juicy and possessing a plump and shapely body with plenty of spicy and chocolate curves. Especially towards the excellent sugared almond finish. *43%*

Schwarzwälder Whisky Mais bott code. L6305 db **(82.5) n18.5 t21 f22 b21.** Once past the, well...bizarre, nose it is relatively easy going, especially towards the impressive, attractively sticky, end. *43%*

Schwarzwälder Whisky Roggenmalz bott code. L5606 db **(87) n22 t21.5 f22 b21.5.** Hard as nails. *43%*

Schwarzwälder Whisky Weizenmalz bott code. L5706 db **(94) n23 t23 f24 b24.** Superbly made whisky with thumping character despite its fresh and delicate nature. One of Europe's finest, for sure. *43%*

KORNBRENNEREI WAGNER Dauborn. Working.

Golden Ground Grain Whicky Original Dauborner dist 2005 db **(84) n21 t21.5 f21 b20.5.** Lots of latent honey, yet the sum total offers a pretty dry experience. *40%*

Golden Ground Grain Whisky Original Dauborner dist 2005 db **(88) n21 t23 f22 b22.** A little extra feints has worked well for the rich and complex body. *46%*

KOTTMANN'S EDELDESTILLAT-BRENNEREI Bad Ditzenbach. Working.

Schwäbischer Whisky lot no. 120705 **(78.5) n19 t20 f19 b19.5.** Heavy, oily and with much nougat to chew on. *40%*

MÄRKISCHEN SPEZIALITÄTEN BRENNEREI Hagen. Working.

Bonum Bono New Make db **(86) n21 t21.5 f22 b21.5.** Light, citrusy, attractively oiled, juicily malty and lip-smacking. I have also tasted their malt which in several months has upped colour and intensity to superb levels and will be bottled shortly. Can't wait! *55%*

⋰ **Bonum Bono New Make Fassgelagert** db **(85.5) n21.5 t22 f21 b21.** A great deal of citrus early on. But as well as the rich malt there are some bitter-ish, tangy notes creeping in late on. Some serious chewy moments, though. *46%*

NORBERT WINKELMANN Hallerndorf. Working.

Fränkischer Rye Whisky db **(93.5) n24 t24 f22.5 b23.** For the record, the nose is so good to this that I kept it with me one evening after a badly sulphured cask from another distillery had ruined my tasting for the day. The fruity beauty of this was not just balm, but a reminder of just how wonderful whisky should touch you. *42%*

Fränkischer Whiskey Strong Single Malt db **(78) n17.5 t20.5 f20 b20.** A huge whisky, but mainly because the cut has been nothing like so judicial as the rye. *48%*

OBSTBRENNEREI MÜCK Birkenau. Working.

Old Liebersbach Smoking Malt Whisky bott code. L1105 db **(83.5)** n21 t21.5 f21 b20. Good heavens! Don't find many whiskies like this one around the world. Almost a Sugar Fest in part, especially in the earlier stages, then bitters out with an almost shocking suddenness. Fascinating and dramatic, though perhaps not for the purist. *43%*

PRIVATBRENNEREI SONNENSCHEIN Witten-Heven. Demolished.

Sonnenschein 15 db **(79.5)** n19.5 t21 f19 b20. So, it's back!! In its youth, this was a tough whisky to entertain. Many years on and some of the old faults remain, but it has picked up a touch of elegance along the way. *41%*

BRENNEREI REINER MÖSSLEIN Zeilitzheim. Working.

Fränkischer Whisky db **(91)** n23 t23 f22.5 b22.5. Rich, earthy, pungent, full of character and quite adorable. Perhaps an acquired taste for single malt stick-in-the muds, though... *40%*

SEVERIN SIMON Alzenau-Michelbach, Aschaffenburg. Working.

⁙ **Simon's Bavarian Pure Pot Still Whiskey** bott code L0011 db **(84)** n20 t22.5 f20 **b21.5.** Have been looking forward to locking horns with this one again; the last time we met my teeth almost shattered against its rigidity. A different animal this time, with the pine and lemon nose reminding me I have washing up to do. The first minute after delivery is the high point, where for a short while everything comes together for a sweet and tart chewy treat. But the finish carries on with the pine... *40%*

SLYRS Schliersee-Neuhaus. Working.

Slyrs Bavarian Single Malt 2006 lot no. L26752, bott 2009 db **(87.5)** n22 t22 f21.5 b22. A very friendly, malty and well made greeting from Bavaria. *43%*

Slyrs Bavarian Single Malt 2008 lot no. 012341 **(87.5)** n18.5 t23.5 f23 b22.5. I know it sounds strange, but one of my highlights of writing the Whisky Bible is to taste the latest offering from one of the pioneers of European whisky, Slyrs. I have high regard for their whisky, though it has the habit of being cut just a little too wide. Here that has certainly affected the nose. But, for the palate, it ensures rare and beautiful riches. A delight. *43%*

SPREEWALD-BRENNEREI Schlepzig. Working.

Sloupisti 4 Years db **(88.5)** n22 t22 f22 b22.5. Very much grows on you: it is obvious the distillers have worked very hard to get both distillation and maturation right. *40%*

Sloupisti 4 Years (Cask Strength) db **(94)** n23 t24 f23 b24. A mind-blowing fruitfest. Just love the clarity to the flavours. This is such great fun...!! *64.8%*

Spreewälder "Sloupisti" Single Malt No. 1 db **(89.5)** n23 t22.5 f22 b22. Very clean malt which refuses to venture into the realms of bitterness despite the early threat of oak. *40%*

Spreewälder "Sloupisti" Single Malt No. 1 db **(88)** n22.5 t22 f21.5 b22. Usually, whisky is easy to interpret yet I have to admit it: I'm entirely confused. Both labels are identical, except the strength. And they have both been marked as single Malt No 1. Yet the 62.2%, though beautifully made, strikes me as a youngster whilst the weaker version offers some evidence of maturity. Another point: how can the same malt, 50% weaker in strength than its twin, actually have more colour...? Really lovely whisky, but an enigma. *62.2%*

STAATSBRAUEREI ROTHAUS AG Grafenhausen-Rothaus. Working.

Black Forest Single Malt Whisky bourbon cask, dist Dec 07, bott Mar 11 db **(79.5)** n19 t20.5 f20 b20. This is one of the distilleries in Germany I haven't yet visited. So puzzled by what was in my glass, I called my dear friend Julia Nourney who sent me the sample. "Julia. Do they distill from beer, including the hops?" "You asked me exactly the same question last year", she replied. I had forgotten, until she reminded me. Apparently they don't. But it kind of tells a story in itself. *43%*

STEINHAUSER DESTILLERIE Kressbronn, Baden-Württemberg. Working.

⁙ **Brigantia 3 Years Old** bott code L-11/11 db **(83.5)** n21 t22.5 f19 b20.5. The beautiful maltiness of delivery does well until a violent bitterness erupts on the finish. Love the fact that this has turned up in a classic old Cardhu-style bottle from the 1980s, complete with same colour spirit. A bit like an Austin Montego being kitted out like a 1930s Mercedes... although this offers a far better journey than any Montego I travelled in... *43%*

STEINWÄLDER BRENNEREI SCHRAML Erbendorf. Working.

Stonewood 1818 dist 1999 db **(91)** n22.5 t23 f22.5 b23. Consistant throughout with a superb and endearing degree of sweetness. High quality stuff. *45%*

Stonewood 1818 Bavarian Grain Whisky 10 Jahre dist 2000 db **(84)** n19 t22 f21.5 **b21.5.** Comes out all guns blazing spraying juicy citrus in every direction. 45%

UNIVERSITÄT HOHENHEIM Working.

Hohenheim Universität Single Malt (82) n21 t20 f20 b21. The aroma is atractively nutty, marzipan even, and clean; the taste offers gentle oak, adding some weight to an otherwise light, refreshing maltiness. Pleasant if unspectacular. 40%. Made at the university as an experiment. Later sold!

WEINGUT MÖßLEIN Kolitzheim. Working.

Weingut Mößlein Fränkischer Whisky db **(78)** n20 t20.5 f18.5 b19. Doesn't quite gel, sadly. The nose is a strange one: hints of butyric, tobacco and honeycomb... But for all the apparent fruit, never hits its stride. 40%

⚜️ **Weingut Mößlein Fränkischer Whisky 5 Years Old** bott code L01/11 db **(91.5)** n22.5 chocolate cherry and strawberry liqueur; t22 creamy strawberry liqueur filling....with a dash of coffee; **f23** ...with yet more chocolate. But never a moment of over-sweetness. **b23** a joyous whisky but something very odd about it.... 40%

⚜️ **Weingut Mößlein Fränkischer Whisky Single Malt 5 Years Old** bott code L09/11 db **(86.5)** n22 t21 f22.5 b21. Extremely malty. Yet almost monotone in its delivery. Plenty to chew over, nonetheless. 40%

WHISKY DESTILLERIE LIEBL Bad Kötzting. Working.

Coillmór French Oak & Sherry Single Cask dist Nov 07, bott code. LD210 db **(86)** n19 t22 **f23 b22.** Twenty years in this game has given me something of a Pavlovian outlook on some whiskies. So, from vividly nasty experience indelibly lasered into my brain, I automatically shied away from a whisky which had the words "sherry" and "French oak" on the same label: this had the potential of being the double bill from hell. But, ironically, it is the quality of the oak involvement which manages to overcome the worst of some sloppy distilling and ensure, once the nose is out of the way, a joyous riot of fruity juiciness. Impressed! 46%. sc. 1002 bottles.

Coillmór Kastanie Single Cask chestnut cask, cask no. 19, dist 24 Feb 06, bott code. LB0311 db **(91.5)** n22 t23 f23.5 b23. This is a distillery capable of making whisky at both ends of the quality scale. This beautifully intense malt is the best yet produced by the distillery and most definitely Bundeslige...! Hang on! Just noticed it is from a chestnut cask (hence the chestnuts????) Dugger! It ain't whisky, folks! 50.2%. 60 bottles.

⚜️ **Coillmór Peated Single Cask** cask no. 65, dist 14 May 07, bott code LA0312 db **(84)** n21 t22; f20 b21. A clumsy, floral smokiness, as though lavender has been thrown in with the peat. Not too sure about the very late bitterness. 46%. sc. 650 bottles.

⚜️ **Coillmór Peated Single Cask 600th Anniversary Edition** cask no. 91, dist Jan 08, bott code LB0212 db **(87)** n22 one of the driest noses to a peated malt I have experienced worldwide, **t22** a huge wave of oaky caramel perches on top of the juicy barley and semi-acrid peat; **f21** like the nose, it dries until your eyes run; **b22** you have to say that this malt doesn't stand on ceremony: has a lot to say and does so robustly. 43%. sc. 600 bottles.

Coillmór Sherry Single Cask cask no. 84, dist 30/31 Oct 07, bott code. LA0111 db **(76.5)** n18.5 t19 f20 b19. Takes a while for the sweet grape to overcome the heavier oils. 46%. sc.

⚜️ **Coillmór Sherry Single Cask** cask no. 115, bott code LA0212, dist 5 May 08 db **(85.5)** n19 t22 f22.5 b22. Chocolate nougat and juicy raisin. Doesn't win any awards for technicality. But the influence of the grape is a treat. I think some people will be knocked out by this. Love it! 46%. sc. 970 bottles.

WHISKY-DESTILLERIE ROBERT FLEISCHMANN Eggolsheim. Working.

Austrasier Single Cask Grain cask no. 1, dist Jun 98, bott May 11 db **(91)** n22 t22.5 f23.5 **b23.** I really don't know whether the Germans are able to knight someone for their services to whisky. But if they can't they should change the law. Another wonderful piece of high quality whisky fun. 40%. sc.

⚜️ **Austrasier Single Cask Grain** cask no. 1, dist Jun 98, bott Apr 12 db **(95.5)** n23.5 a huge bourbon signature to this with a black and red liquorice mix, along with hickory and prunes; **t24** sensational mouth feel: starts soft but hardens with a firm grainy backbone circled and massaged by soft, fleshy fruity notes, especially those dates which just get juicier and juicier...; **f24** dries slowly as the grain softens and withdraws. Yet it remains spicy, the last twitches in rhythm with the purring sugar; **b24.5** big, thick, pulsing... this is one macho whisky that is sweet enough for the ladies to like. This distillery's finest hour... or two... 40%. nc ncf sc.

Blaue Mause Single Cask Malt cask no. 4, dist Jun 99, bott May 11 db **(88)** n21.5 t22 f22.5 **b22.** An almost perfect exhibition of complex toasted brown sugars. 40%. sc.

❖ **Blaue Maus Single Cask Malt** cask no. 5, dist Jun 98, bott Mar 12 db **(80) n21 t20 f19 b20.** Struggles to gel with the feints churning up a touch too much bitterness. Not the first whisky that has a touch of distant smoke. But is when that smoke appears to have come from a joint. Sure this isn't Dutch whisky...? 40%. nc ncf sc.

Blaue Mause Single Cask Malt 2 Fassfüllung cask no. 1, dist May 98, bott May 11 db **(92.5) n22.5** moist Jamaican ginger cake...; **t24** exceptionally moist Jamaican ginger cake...; **f23** somewhat dried out Jamaican ginger cake; **b23** methinks Blau Mause has sailed recently to Jamaica. 40%. sc.

❖ **Blaue Maus Single Cask Malt 2. Fassfüllung** cask no. 2, dist Jul 96, bott May 12 db **(84.5) n20 t21 f22 b21.5.** The usual nougat nose in evidence as well as the soupy character of this brand's style. But picks up on the finish as the big sugars harmonise with the decent quality oak. 40%. nc ncf sc.

❖ **Blaue Maus Single Cask Malt Fassstärke** cask no. 2, dist Jun 92, bott Apr 12 db **(91) n22** probably has more gin elements than whisky, especially the orange and juniper...; **t23** gin...! No, whisky...No, gin... hang on, the chocolate notes tend to confirm the whisky, as do a procession of dark sugary tones. Everything except the house nougat style; **f23** a little bitterness almost suggests hops, just to confuse matters more...if that was possible..; **b23** suffers a bit of early identity crisis. Whatever it thinks it is, it ends up as a very big experience. 49.3%. nc ncf sc.

Elbe 1 Single Cask Malt cask no. 1, dist Jun 96, bott May 11 db **(81.5) n19 t21 f20.5 b21.** The wall between success and comparative failure can be so thin. This ticks many of the correct boxes. There is vanilla aplenty and a chugging molasses. But something in the distillation is just slightly awry. A must, though, for those looking for an ultra dry dram. 40%. sc.

❖ **Elbe 1 Single Cask Malt** cask no. 1, dist Jun 97, bott Jun 12 db **(91) n22** floral, even with a touch of Indian spice...;...and if anyone can remember those edible silver ball bearing cake decorations... yes, it has that vaguely off-centre aniseed character, too; **t23.5** a beautiful array of muscovado sugars; **f23** superb balance with the gristy sugars and sawdusty vanilla complementing each other; **b23** one of the most restrained, simplistic yet effective malts I have seen from this distillery for a while. 40%. nc ncf sc.

Grüner Hund Single Cask Malt cask no. 3, dist Jul 98, bott May 11 db **(86.5) n21 t22.5 f21.5 b21.5.** Juicy barley assisted by chocolate nougat and molasses. Plenty of heavy oils, too. 40%. sc.

❖ **Grüner Hund Single Cask Malt** cask no. 2, dist May 00, bott Jun 12 db **(84.5) n21 t22.5 f20 b21.** A very even whisky early on with the dark sugars single paced and weighted. Just a touch bitter towards the finish, though. 40%. nc ncf sc.

❖ **Krottentaler Single Cask Malt** cask no. 3, dist Jun 00, bott Jun 12 db **(81) n19 t20 f21 b21.** The sugary grist piles in to overcome the early tobacco. 40%. nc ncf sc.

Old Fahr Single Cask Malt cask no. 2, dist Jun 00, bott May 11 db **(94.5) n23.5 t23.5 f24 b23.5.** An object lesson in excellent whisky making. Robert, you have excelled...! 40%. sc.

❖ **Old Fahr Single Cask Malt** cask no. 5, dist Jun 00, bott Jun 12 db **(89) n22.5** draws upon the light feints to maximise on complexity: Malt Shreddies with a molten Demerara sugar; **t22.5** exactly as the nose suggests, only the Shreddies and sugars have dissolved in spiced custard; **f22** the feints take us to the brink but the chocolate Allsorts and fudge speed to the rescue; **b22** beginning to become one of my favourites from this distillery. Very consistent. 40%. nc ncf sc.

Otto's Uisge Beatha cask no. 1, dist Oct 07, bott May 11 db **(73.5) n17 t19 f18.5 b19.** Incredibly sweet. Incredibly oily. And incredibly out of tune. Sorry, Otto! 40%. sc.

❖ **Otto's Uisge Beatha Fassstärke** cask no. 1, dist Sep 07, bott May 11 db **(79) n18 t20 f21 b20.** Otto: a second chance for glory – and you've blown it again! Much better than the last bottling, with the sugars in better formation. But still too slack and indisciplined. 47.4%. sc.

Schwarzer Pirat Single Malt cask no. 2, dist May 00, bott May 11 db **(87.5) n22 t22 f21.5 b22.** Technically incorrect, but pure entertainment! 40%. sc.

❖ **Schwarzer Pirat Single Cask Malt** cask no. 1, dist Jul 01, bott May 12 db **(82) n22 t21 f19 b19.** Shiver me timbers (and there is timber in this whisky, believe me) this is one pirate that came to a bitter end... 40%. nc ncf sc.

Seute Deern Single Cask Malt cask no. 1, dist Jul 97, bott May 11 db **(85) n20.5 t22 f21 b21.5.** Massively enjoyable whisky. But just one too many hefty oils for greatness. Another showing some classy touches of stem ginger. The sugars are mesmeric. 40%. sc.

❖ **Seute Deem Single Cask Malt** cask no. 2, dist Aug 00, bott Jun 12 db **(94) n23.5** complex and yummy marriage of moist ginger and treacle cakes; **t23** brown sugars secure the softest of textures. Spices up towards the middle as it heads towards a burnt honeycomb; **f23.5** long with the usual oils, but stays on that honeyed theme for a delicate finale; **b24** gets its act together with some of the distiller's softer themes effortlessly uniting. Leave this in the glass for about 15-20 minutes in a warm room for the most beautiful results. 40%. nc ncf sc.

Spinnaker Single Cask Malt cask no. 2, dist Jul 99, bott May 11 db **(93) n22 t23.5 f24 b23.5.** Aha! Spinnaker's back! Seams a couple of years since I last had a new bottling of this German whisky mainstay. A much cleaner version than I remember: none of the normal nougat and better distillation. Quite superb! 40%. sc.

⁙ **Spinnaker Single Cask Malt** cask no. 2, dist Jul 96, bott Jun 12 db **(91) n22** citrus, from Blaue Maus...was ist das...??? **t23.5** wonderfully sweet. A malt which appears to have rolled around in some spilt muscovado sugar and then become stuck in sticky cream toffee; **f22.5** if you wondered where the citrus went, it's back here near the finishing line adding some surprising zest to the busy chocolate fudge fade; **b23** seriously yummy whisky. 40%. nc ncf sc.

LATVIA
LATVIJAS BALZAMS Riga. Working.

L B Lavijas Belzams db **(83) n20 t22 f20 b21.** Soft and yielding on the palate, this is said to be made from Latvian rye, though of all the world's rye whiskies this really does have to be the softest and least fruity. I'll be astonished if there isn't a fair degree of thinning grain in there, too. 40%

LIECHTENSTEIN
TELSER Triesen. Working.

Telsington II 3 Years Old dist 2007 db **(86) n21.5 t22 f21 b21.5.** A firm, big malted fellow with a delicious nuts and treacle sub plot. At its best when left in the glass for a short while, this one doesn't have some high quality grape to help it along like the first-ever bottling. However, a clearer look at the inner working of this whisky makes for a fascinating – and impressive – experience. A few phenols appear to have popped up from somewhere. 42%. sc.

Telsington III 4 Years Old dist 2007 db **(89) n22 t22.5 f22 b22.5.** Very similar to the Telsington II, only has moved on with extra oak. Some of the technical wrinkles have been ironed out with the extra year, though not quite enough to prevent it keeping its craggy character. 42%. sc.

Telsington IV 3 Years Old dist 2008 db **(94) n23.5** complex: a salty, curiously semi-phenolic trait helps embroider shape, texture and relief into the otherwise silky fruits; **t23** one of the best deliveries from mainland Europe this year. possibly the best Truly three dimensional with a juicy fruit character shoulder to shoulder with equally salivating barley and oaky spices. The grape is fabulously clean and offering a spiced dryness of devilish sophistication: whether it is or not, a highest grade Fino style to this; **f23.5** continues along those same beautiful salty, malty, fruity contours, the spices building if anything; **b24** it seemed only right that the 999th new whisky for the 2012 Whisky Bible, a very big number I think you agree, should come from the world's smallest whisky distilling nation. And also because they have the ability to make above average spirit and this, technically, is their best yet. For good measure they have matured it in a first rate cask. The result is a distinguished malt of rare sophistication worthy of the trust I placed in it. 42%. sc.

LUXEMBOURG
DISTILLERIE DIEDENACKER Niederdonven. Working.

⁙ **Diedenacker Number One 2006 Aged 5 Years** Luxembourg white wine French oak barrique, cask no. 2, dist Jan 06, bott Apr 11 db **(90.5) n22.5** as intriguing as it is enchanting: heather honey by the dollop, chocolate nougat and crushed hazelnut...; **t23.5** brilliant complexity soon after the initial quiet delivery. The oils from the still carry a lovely chocolate fudge note and, naturally, spice. But the deployment of the Demerara sugars is superb; **f22** busy vanilla with the oils really digging deep; **b22.5** congratulations to this new distillery – and what a way for Luxembourg to become a whisky nation. A whisky bursting with character and complexity. 42%. nc ncf sc. 450 bottles.

THE NETHERLANDS
ZUIDAM Baarle Nassau. Working.

Zuidam Dutch Rye Aged 5 Years cask no. 446-683, bott no. 81, dist Jan 05, bott Aug 10 **(92.5) n23.5** there is something so sexy and alluring about the nose of a good rye whisky, and this is no exception. Fruity with cinnamon candy spiciness; the oak counters with a bludgeoning heavy-handed liquorice; **t23** no eider down pillow could afford this degree of softness on delivery: the oils from the wide-ish cut work their best and absorb all the fruity grains and natural toffees have to throw at it; juicy, though the grain disappears under the huge caramel. A fruity spiciness begins the fight back, but it takes a while; **f22.5** more settled with the grain showing greater confidence; **b23.5** this bottle stays in my dining room. There is a new classic European to be found. 40%

Zuidam Millstone French Oak cask no. 358-359, bott Jan 00, dist Sep 10 **(74.5) n18 t20 f18.5 b19.** A huge fug of oily toffee. I think it would be a fair assessment to conclude that their distilling skills in 2000 don't quite match their abilities of 2005... 40%. Pure Pot Still.

Zuidam Millstone 5 Years Old cask no. 1129+/m1133, dist Apr 05, bott Jun 10 **(89) n22 t22 f22.5 b22.5.** A thoughtfully made and matured whisky. The evidence is that the still is small and the cut on the wider but fully acceptable side. A joy. 40%. Pure Pot Still.

Zuidam Millstone 8 Years Old cask no. 913t/m915, dist Jan 00, bott Sep 09 **(89) n22 t23 f22 b22.** For their French oak bottling, I had a bit of swipe at the quality of the distillate. I may, however, have been wrong about their ability to make good whisky in 2000. This technically ticks all the boxes with not a single off note – anywhere! 43%. Pure Pot Still.

Zuidam Millstone Peated cask no. 570571, dist Feb 05, bott Sep 10 **(72) n18.5 t17.5 f18 b18.** Zuidam have joined the noble and endless list worldwide who have found making a peaty whisky a little harder than they thought. Perhaps closer to coal tar soap on the nose and wanders in all directions over the palate. Another heroic failure. Heads up: better luck next time, chaps. 40%. Pure Pot Still.

SPAIN

DYC Aged 8 Years (90) n22 t23 f22.5 b22.5. I really am a sucker for clean, cleverly constructed blends like this. So just so enjoyable! 40%

DYC Pure Malt (84.5) n20 t21 f21.5 b21. I admit it's been a few years since I visited the distillery, but from what I then tasted in their warehouses I am surprised that they have not brought out their own single malt to mark the 50th anniversary of the place. This, which contains a percentage of Scotch, I believe, is OK. But no better than what I remember sampling. 40%

DYC Selected Blend (86) n21.5 t22 f21 b21.5. Although still a bantamweight and remains its old refreshing self, has definitely muscled out slightly on nose, delivery and finish...with a distinct hint of smoke. Unquestionably a bigger DYC than before. 40%

MAG'5 (80.5) n19 t21.5 f20 b20. Much more Alonso than Puyol... 40%. Destillerias MG.

SWEDEN
MACKMYRA Gästrikland. Working.

Mackmyra Brukswhisky db **(95.5) n24 t24 f23.5 b24.** One of the most complex and most beautifully structured whiskies of the year. A Mackmyra masterpiece, cementing the distillery among the world's true greats. 41.4%

⋅⋅⋅⋙⋅⋅ **Mackmyra Den Första Utgåvan (The First Edition)** Swedish oak db **(93.5) n23.5** chocolate mint, a delicate thread of muscovado sugar, though typically crisp in that enticing Mackmyra fashion; **t23.5** the delivery is curvaceous, rounded and rolls about the palate with ease. Here and there it radiates a powerful blast of tannin, more often than not breaking down further into stunning cocoa notes; **f23** resumes into mega crisp mode with the barley brittle, but gloved by a soft chocolate sauce on vanilla ice cream...; **b23.5** only Mackmyra combines voluptuousness and severity in such knee-weakening proportions. Like being whipped by a busty blond dominatrix with a thick Scandinavian accent. Or so a judge friend of mine tells me... 46.1%

Mackmyra Moment "Drivved" bott code MM-003 db **(89) n22.5 t22.5 f22 b22.** Young and, after the nose, simplistic, with a limited degree of true complexity. But these Mackmyras are on a different plane to anything they have done before and you cannot be anything other than awestruck. 55.5%

Mackmyra Moment "Jord" bott code MM-004 db **(93) n23** a detached fruitiness, like the sugars from big sultanas; but it's those red liquorice bourbon notes, And spices...mmmm! **t24** huge. Not a prisoner to be seen. I think the weight and oils borde perception. The sugars are also so sublimely well weighted and balanced with the drier vanillas, it is hard to know how you could improve upon this; **f23** the spices up the pace a notch or two, but still those bourbon notes now with a degree of cocoa dryness, which are in complete control; thick cream toffee oozes from the oak...; **b23** anyone with a fondness for bourbon might just have to get a case of this... hard to believe better casks have been used in maturation anywhere in the world this year. 55.1%

Mackmyra Moment "Medvind" bott code MM-001 db **(87) n22.5 t22 f22 b22.** Very few whiskies out there show pre-pubescent youth and a grey beard at the same time... 48.6%

⋅⋅⋅⋙⋅⋅ **Mackmyra Moment "Rimfrost"** db **(95.5) n24** anyone who has walked in a Swedish forest will recognise some of the aromas which massage you: there is something so wonderfully green and natural about this. The slight earthiness suggests recent rainfall on the moss; the sweetness, the clean water freshening the leaves and grasses; a very slight pine and citrus aroma underscores the oak...this is beautiful; **t24** usually when caramels hit the palate, one is overcome by a feeling of frustration with the lazy and relatively talentless blending on show. Not here. The caramels appear to have all the hallmarks of the natural oaks and, rather than fudge up the issue, succeed in helping to allow the complex sugars to have their say without making the event too sickly; naturally, a touch of mocha moves into the middle ground; **f23.5** much more relaxed here. The chocolate notes persist, varying in degrees of creaminess and toffee texture; the blender has done a magnificent job of ensuring complexity from first nose to the very last atom on the finale: a triumph! **b24** I thought that they had got the name "Rimfrost" from sitting on a Stockholm park bench in the middle of a Swedish winter. Apparently not. *53.2%. 1,492 bottles.*

⠆⠆⠆- **Mackmyra Moment "Skog"** db **(95.5) n24** just so intense...yet it appears to allow the aromas out on ration. Elegant, sugar coated, flakes of oaky tannins carry the flag and dates the torch but the slow motion procession of chocolate raisin and physalis is as teasing as it is beautiful...; **t24.5** there is no shyness about the delivery: it is as though all the demure aromas have ganged together and arrived in one orgy of flavour. A molassed mocha leads the way, while dates again hold sway, offering both a chewy toffee version and much juicier sweeter style; it is the astonishing texture and grace in the fragile sugars which really take your breath away, though; **f23** now the vanillas begin to take control barely troubled by the most half-hearted of spicy buzzes; some tart marmalade will not let the taste buds rest entirely; **b24** with a name like "Skog" I wasn't sure if I was supposed to taste this stuff or simply wield the hefty bottle above my head and brain somebody in good Viking tradition. Fortunately I settled for the former...and made the correct choice. Although the latter always remains an open option to anyone who tries to steel this bottle from me. It is by far one of the most beautiful whiskies I have tasted this year... *52.4%. 3,000 bottles.*

⠆⠆⠆- **Mackmyra Moment "Solsken"** db **(92.5) n22.5** a beautiful tapestry of nutty notes, bolstered by delicate spice; **t23.5** a sumptuous delivery with stunning barley and sugars, those dark, molten sugars seemingly leaking from the toasty oakiness which prevails; the lightest thread of ulmo honey towards the middle offers just the right degree of natural vanilla and caramel; **f23** the texture remains the distillery's usual soft yet firm style, with the tannins still apparent and muscovado sugars pulsing along with the crisp, undaunted barley; **b23.5** a treat of a malt. Scandinavian sophistication at its height. *52.6%. 3,000 bottles.*

Mackmyra Moment "Urberg" bott code MM-002 db **(95) n24** probably the most delicate and complex nose from Europe this year: light, yet somehow there is a real weight to the barley; the oak is one of those red-blooded, tannin rich affairs which somehow doesn't come even close to taking control; **t23.5** what a fabulous delivery: all kinds of bourbon traits and characters, like the nose. The barley stands tall and intense; a slow gathering of muscovado sugars; **f23.5** and so it continues; more of the same, with perhaps more vanillas and cocoa and a late tingling spice. **b24.5** beautifully distilled, superbly matured, clever flavour profile, first-rate packaging: the complete deal. Certainly one of the most intense, complex, compelling and simply enjoyable whiskies I have tasted this year. Truly a magic Moment... *55.6%*

Mackmyra Special 05: "Jaktlycka" (Happy Hunting) bott Autumn 2010, bott code MS-005 db **(89) n23 t21 f23 b22.** The youthfulness of the whisky at times causes problems in harmony, as is experienced on delivery. But all else is simply wonderful... *47.2%*

Mackmyra Special 06: "Sommaräng" (Summer Meadow) bott. Summer 2011 bott code MS-006 db **(83.5) n20.5 t21.5 f21 b20.5.** The name of the malt sounds like a Beethoven symphony. But as someone who spends his very rare moments of non-whisky related freedom walking through, up, down and over the countryside of various countries and continents, I can't say this whisky brings to mind the seemingly random but heart-thrilling trilling overhead of the invisible lark; or barley, with its copper shroud glowing against the green sheen of the sprouting grasses, dancing in the fleeting summer breeze. This is too earthy. Too heavy and base. Too one dimensional against the secret hidden textures and pastels of the uplifting summer meadow. An enjoyable malt, for sure. But one for the black moods of winter, with the rain beating its irregular, reassuringly depressing rhythm against the tear-stained window and, as the irrepressible caramels descend, so equally does the darkness of the looming winter equinox. "Winter Wastelands". By the marshes, with the forlorn call of the curlew more like... *46.8%*

⠆⠆⠆- **Mackmyra Special: 07 "Framtidstro" (Hope)** bott Autumn 2011 db **(87.5) n22** salted butter on very fresh toast; some peanut butter, too..? Someone has placed a sprig of lavender on the table; youthful in part; **t23** a gentle dovetailing of oils in differing hues seems to help hoist the sharp, slightly salty barley into a high place; **f20.5** just falls off the pace with a few bitterish notes; **b22** much cleaner, more mezzo-soprano in tone than their previous more base Special. *45.8%*

⠆⠆⠆- **Mackmyra Special: 08 "Handpicked"** bott Spring 2012 db **(88.5) n23.5** wow! Much more of the style Mackmyra is beginning to call its own: intense with a chocolate gait, though here were have grated carrot and dumpling. Once, in Scotland, they would have called this "meaty" (thought the last Scotch blender I described this to told me he was not aware of the phrase...sigh!) Not often a malt gives me a raging appetite...; **t22.5** one of the most silky-soft deliveries ever to issue forth from the Mackmyra bottling hall. Much weightier than the norm, with some major oils from a wider cut than normal. But the way in which the barley and wonderful cocoa notes are caught together is almost mesmerising; **f21** the mildly feinty fault is more evident here, but there is so much to still chew on; **b22** perhaps they should have called it "Henpecked"... for all those guys retreating to a hidden corner of their home with a bottle of this for a quiet moment away from the joys and demands of marital bliss... *46%*

SWITZERLAND
BRAURUEREI LOCHER Appenzell. Working.
⁙ **Edition Austria** old beer cask matured, fresh Merlot cask finish, cask no. 1144/12 db **(87) n23** fabulous nose: almost an essence of chocolate malt, softened by light fruit. A hint of hop...? I hope not...; **t22.5** superb mouth feel with an almost perfect degree of oils; the fruit offers more blood orange than grape; **f20** loses a few marks as a residual hop from the cask adds too bitter a finish; **b21.5** nothing seemingly wrong with the spirit. But hops and whisky simply don't mix. *47.5%. sc. 100 bottles.*

⁙ **Edition Germany** old beer cask matured, fresh Merlot cask finish, cask no. 1101 db **(83.5) n22.5 t21 f20 b20.** So dry, this could have been matured in the Gobi. The residual hops are again unpicking some earlier good work. *48%. sc. 380 bottles.*

⁙ **Edition Lucerne** old beer cask matured, fresh Merlot cask finish, cask no. 1154/12 db **(88.5) n23** the grape, seasoned with a few herbs, is in full cry; **t22.5** the delivery, likewise, gets off to a juicy fruitcake start before a mixture of drier tones begin to inch their way in; **f21** extra residual sugars combat the creeping bitterness; **b22** the best all-rounder from the distillery, but beset with a similar problem to its other offerings. Though doubtless they don't regard this as a problem, but rather their style. Fair enough. *47%. sc. 500 bottles.*

Säntis Malt Swiss Highlander Edition Dreifaltigkeit db **(96.5) n24 t24.5 f24 b24.** This is one of the whiskies of the year, without question. Such is the controlled enormity, the sheer magnitude of what we have here, one cannot help taste the whisky with a blend of pleasure and total awe. *52%*

Säntis Malt Swiss Highlander Edition Säntis oak beer casks db **(88) n22.5 t23 f20.5 b22.** Light, fruity and impressive. *40%*

Säntis Malt Swiss Highlander Edition Sigel oak beer casks db **(91.5) n23.5 t23 f22 b23.** High quality whisky which balances with aplomb. *40%*

BRENNEREI HOLLEN Lauwil. Working.
Hollen Single Malt Aged Over 6 Years matured in red wine casks db **(89) n23 t22.5 f21.5 b22.** Perhaps the fruit is rather too emphatic and, a late show of spice apart, some of the other forms of character development you might wish to see are lacking. Apparently peatless. Possibly, but not entirely convinced. *42%*

Hollen Single Malt Aged Over 6 Years matured in white wine casks db **(90.5) n23 t23.5 f21.5 b22.5.** Many facets to its personality, the nose especially, shows more rum characteristics than malt. A won't-say-no glassful if ever there was one, though, and made and matured to the highest order. Indeed, as I taste and write this, my BlackBerry informs me that Roger Federer is on his way to another Wimbledon title: the similarities in the quiet dignity, elegance and class of both Swiss sportsman and whisky is not such a corny comparison. *42%*

BRENNEREI SCHWAB Oberwil. Working.
Bucheggberger Single Malt cask no. 23, bott no. 10 db **(74) n17 t21 f17 b19.** Decent malty lead, but the intensely bitter finish makes hard work of it. *42%*

BRENNEREI URS LÜTHY Muhen. Working.
Dinkel Whisky pinot noir cask db **(92.5) n23 t24 f22 b23.5.** A big, striking malt which is not afraid to at times make compellingly beautiful statements. *61.5%*

Wyna Whisky Original No. 2 dist Apr 06, bott Apr 09 db **(79) n21 t21 f18 b19.** Fruity, but seriously overcooks the bitterness. *43%. 489 bottles.*

BURGDORFER GASTHAUSBRAUEREI Burgdorf. Working.
Reiner Burgdorfer 5 Years Old cask no. 4 db **(82.5) n18 t22 f21 b21.5.** Recovers from the mildly feinty nose to register some wonderfully lush cocoa notes throughout the coppery, small still development on the palate. *43%*

DESTILLERIE EGNACH Egnach. Silent.
Thursky db **(93) n24** all kinds of big fruit-edged bourbon notes; liquorice and honeydew melon; some lychee and marzipan add wonderfully to the mix; even a slightly rummy style

to this; **t23.5** silky, estery with a controlled sweetness; again there is a lovely bourbon-fruit interaction, perhaps more on the red liquorice honeycomb bourbon style; **f22.5** some oak begins to bite but the honeyed sheen and light mint-cocoa dusting keeps the whisky honest; **b23** such a beautifully even whisky! I am such a sucker for that clean fruity-spice style. Brilliant! 40%

DESTILLERIE HAGEN-RÜHLI Hüttwilen. Working.

Hagen's Best Whisky No. 2 lot no. 00403/04-03-08.08 db **(87) n19 t23.5 f22 b22.5.** Much more Swiss, small still style than previous bottling and although the nose isn't quite the most enticing, the delivery and follow through are a delight. Lovely whisky. 42%

⁘ **Hagen's Best Whisky No. 2** dist 3 May 03, bott 1 Mar 12, bott code L030403 db **(62) n15 t17 f15 b15.** I remember enjoying the Hagen's No 2 a few years back and looked forward to a similar malty blast. Instead, I have just poured myself the Butyric-style Whisky of the Year for 2013. Oh dear, oh dear....! 42%

Hagen's Best Whisky Oak Special lot no. 3031/03.03 -12.07 db **(84) n21 t21.5 f20.5 b21.** A very well made, sweet, uncomplicated malt matured in a thoroughly used bourbon barrel – or so it seems. Not sure if this is a compliment or not, but could easily be mistaken for some kind of Speyside single malt whisky destined for a young blend. 42%

⁘ **Hagen's Best Whisky Oak Special** dist 5 Apr 04, bott 1 Mar 12, bott code L050404 db **(82.5) n19 t21 f22 b21.** When it finally relaxes into its chocolate fix on the finish, then we have at last a malt happy with itself. Until then it never settles. 42%

BRENNEREI-ZENTRUM BAUERNHO Zug. Working

Swissky db **(91) n23 t23 f22 b23.** While retaining a distinct character, this is the cleanest, most refreshing malt yet to come from mainland Europe. Hats off to Edi Bieri for this work of art. Moving stuff. 42%

Swissky Exklusiv Abfüllung L3365 db **(94) n23 t23 f24 b24.** A supremely distilled whisky with the most subtle oak involvement yet. Year after year this distillery bottles truly great single malt, a benchmark for Europe's growing band of small whisky distillers. 40%

ETTER SOEHNE AG Zug. Working.

Johnett db **(89) n22** attractive vanilla and barley mix, with the character of the casks and the stills on public view; citrus drifts in and out; **t22.5** soft, lightly oiled and an ever-increasing build up of quite beautiful and clean barley. Also delicate, nutty sugars, occasionally hinting of praline, sometimes marzipan, one of those malts that prefers to hint rather than state; **f22** a little peach melba on the vanilla and custard tart goes a long way and faithfully sticks to the script;; **b22.5** a sane, beautifully crafted malt which, due to its delicate nature, makes no attempt to hide its few imperfections. An elegant, articulate every day whisky. 42%

HUMBEL SPEZIALITÄTENBRENNEREI Stetten. Working.

Farmer's Club Finest Blended db **(85.5) n22 t22 f20.5 b21.** Clean, well made, astonishingly Scotch-like in its style. In fact, possibly the cleanest whisky made on mainland Europe. Lashings of butterscotch and soft honey; even a coppery sheen while the oak makes delightful conversation. But there appears to be lots of caramel which dulls things down somewhat. 40%

Ourbeer Single Malt db **(84) n21 t20.5 f21.5 b21.** Once more very well made with some entertaining spice. But the caramels have way too much to say for themselves 43%

KOBELT Marbach, St. Gallen. Working.

⁘ **Glen Rhine Whiskey** db **(88) n21** quite a variance between the sweeter and more bitter aromas...hmmm; **t22.5** all the delicate sugars can't arrive quick enough. Light dusting of powdered sugar quickly absorbs the gathering juicy citrus; vanillas spread into the mid ground; **f21.5** the late bitterness arrives on cue... **b22** try and pick your way through this one... can't think of another whisky in the world with that kind of fingerprint. 40%. Corn & barley.

LANGATUN DISTILLERY Langenthal, Kanton Bern. Working.

⁘ **Langatun Old Bear Châteauneuf-du-Pape** cask, dist Apr 08, bott Jan 12, bott code L1201 db **(96) n24** three types of honey detectable: ulmo, orange blossom and heather. Which tends to suggest a fair degree of complexity, especially when you add in a few phenols for good measure; **t24** the texture, the weight, the sugar to oak ratio...it just can't be true. Spices enter the fray, but in tempo to the extraordinary beat of the emerging grape; **f23.5** relatively short and just a little bitter, though an echo of ulmo honey does stay to the last; **b24.5** whisky for the gods... 64%

RUGENBRAU AG Matten bei Interlaken. Working.

⋄ **Century Swiss Highland Single Malt** American oak Oloroso sherry butt, cask no. 24, dist 2 Jul 07, bott Mar 12 db **(87.5) n22** a delicate, slow motion display of vanilla and soft fruit; **t23** distinct early oils from the still make way for a wonderful unravelling of surprisingly intense and juicy barley; **f20.5** a little tangy, alas; **b22** not many whiskies have been matured in ice caverns over the years. Well, none, as far as I know – apart from this one. A curious feature of the malt is how evenly distributed the flavours are, as well as the weight. As slow moving on the nose and palate as a glacier. Wonder if this could have brought the original Alpine Iceman old Frozen Fritz himself, Ötzi, back to life. Well, probably not. But seeing as he was involved in the making of copper, I don't think he would have said no to a second glass. *45%. ncf sc. 1,291 bottles. Matured in ice cavern of Jungfraujoch.*

Interlaken Swiss Highland Single Malt "Classic" oloroso sherry butt db **(95) n23.5** moist raisins on a toasted teacake; **t24** the palate is engulfed by a soft and friendly blanket of light grape. But what really impresses is the structure of the lightly honeyed vanilla, enriched by the walnut oil and Bassett's chocolate liquorice on which the grape is embedded; **f23** plateaus out with those soft oils but the lightest dusting of spice allows the drying of the oak a natural progression; **b24** hugely impressive. I have long said that the finest whiskies made on mainland Europe are to be found in Switzerland. Game, set and match... *46%*

Top Of Europe Swiss Highland Single Malt "Ice Label" bott 2011 **(93.5) n23** a hint of noble rot on this intense grape aroma. The clean wine allows maximum clarity for the clever spices; **t24** mouth-filling, momentarily over thick delivery. Soon, though, it thins sufficiently for the spiced, juicy sultana sugars to pour through. This mingles with a stunning barley; **f23** long with vanilla and caramel forming alongside a mocha richness which envelops the finale **b23.5** I get a lot of stick for heaping praise on European whisky. OK, there is the odd technical flaw in the distillation – though in some ways it works to its advantage. But how many casks do you find like this in Scotland? For sheer quality of its output, this distillery must rate as high as an Alpine peak... *58.9%. sc.*

SPEZIALITÄTENBRENNEREI ZÜRCHER Port. Working.

Zürcher Single Lakeland 3 Years Old dist Jul 06, bott Jul 09 db **(88.5) n21.5 t23 f21.5 b22.5**. This distillery never fails to entertain. Not as technically perfect as usual, but none of the blemishes are seriously damaging and even add a touch of extra character. *42%*

WHISKY CASTLE Elfingen. Working.

Castle One Single Malt Edition Käser cask no. 455, dist Jan 05 db **(86) n19 t22 f23 b22.** Technically, not the best from this distillery with the nose an OTT clash between feints and withering oak . But the extra weight from the extended cut has given the spirit enough muscle to take the weight of the enormous wood influence. The result is demanding, especially at full 68%abv throttle, but ultimately delicious when the Demerara sugars kick in. *68%*

Whisky Castle Sauternes Cask db **(88) n21 t22 f23 b22.** A distillery that has the ability to storm your ramparts. This is no exception. *43%*

Whisky Castle Terroir cask no. 477, dist Sep 06 db **(71.5) n16 t18 f19 b18.5.** Butyric and wildly off target. *43%*

Whisky Castle Vintage cask no. 485, dist Sep 06 db **(90.5) n22 t23 f23 b22.5.** Imagine a whisky angel gently kissing your palate...this is all about very good spirit (with a slightly wide cut) spending time in what appears to be either a high quality virgin cask, or something very close to one. Brimming with character and charisma. *43%*

WALES

PENDERYN Penderyn. Working.

Penderyn bott code 092909 **(93.5) n23 t23.5 f24 b23.** Just couldn't have been more Welsh than any potential offSpring of Catherine Zeta Jones by Tom Jones, conceived while "How Green Is My Valley" was on the DVD player and a Shirley Bassey CD playing in the background. And that after downing three pints of Brains bitter after seeing Swansea City play Cardiff City at the Liberty Stadium, before going home to a plate of cawl while watching Wales beating England at rugby live on BBC Cymru. Yes, it is that unmistakably Penderyn; it is that perfectly, wonderfully and uniquely Welsh. *46%. ncf. Imported by Sazerac Company.*

Penderyn bott code 1131008 (750ml) db **(93.5) n22.5 t23.5 f23.5 b24.** The light cocoa infusion just tops this off perfectly. A truly classic Penderyn; more charm than Tom Jones, hitting just as many pure notes...and just being a fraction of his age *46%. US Market.*

Penderyn Madeira released 7 Jul 10 db **(92) n21.5 t23.5 f23.5 b24.** This bottling is a testament to how far this whisky has moved over the years. There appears to be much more Madeira influence than was once the case, indicating that the malt is being allowed a little longer to mature. This is lush, beguilingly complex whisky of the very top order. *46%. ncf.*

Penderyn Madeira released 4 Aug 10 db **(89) n21 t22.5 f23 b22.5.** Understated, clever and sophisticated. 46%. ncf.

Penderyn Madeira released 9 Sep 10 db **(91) n21.5 t23.5 f23 b23.** Practically a re-run of the July bottling, with the odd tweak here and there. My curiosity spiked, I contacted the Welsh Whisky Company who confirmed they were now, as I was very much suspecting, using a tank to store the vatted casks before bottling... and thus creating a minor solera system. This explains the continuity of style with the slight variation from month to month, rather than the sometimes violent lurches in style from one bottling to the next that had hitherto been the hallmark of Penderyn. Higher quality, for sure...if slightly less excitement and nosing into the unknown for me...! I shall miss its Russian roulette idiosyncrasy... 46%. ncf.

Penderyn Madeira released 4 Oct 10 db **(92.5) n22 t23.5 f23.5 b23.5.** Very much in the same mould as the September release, above, but here the fruit has a warmer, softer, say while the milk chocolate is ramped up a notch or two. A very classy act. 46%. ncf.

Penderyn Madeira released 5 Nov 10 db **(89.5) n21.5 t22 f23.5 b22.5.** Busy on delivery and the creamy development. The finish is dreamy stuff with a wonderful, gradual injection of spice to add a delicate fizz to the usual fruit-chalk interplay. 46%. ncf.

Penderyn Madeira bott code 8 Dec 10 db **(90) n22 t23 f22.5 b22.5.** I believe this saw the light of day only in miniature form. But there is no challenging the size of the whisky: Penderyn in its silkiest mode and allowing the fruit massive scope for flexing its grapy muscle...which it does with style. Big but simply charming. 46%. ncf.

Penderyn Madeira released 1 Jan 11 db **(85.5) n21 t22 f21 b21.5.** Comparatively niggardly on the fruit front while going to town on the drier, pithy notes. Bit like the old days... 46%. ncf.

Penderyn Madeira released 1 Feb 11 db **(94.5) n23.5** light liquorice holds the bourbon flag aloft while the juicy fruit of figs, greengages and grapes whisper volumes; **t23.5** it is hard to remember a standard Penderyn landing being this soft and juicy: a rich custardy sweetness perfectly engulfs the mouth watering fruit, the molten muscovado sugar is simply being wicked, **f23.5** a slow lingering unveiling of that has gone on before, but some spices adding another delicious dimension; **b24** one of the great standard Peneryn bottlings. 46%. ncf.

Penderyn Madeira bott code. Mar 11 db **(92) n22.5 t23 f23.5 b23.** Almost like a chocolate mousse poured over a fruit pudding. And a spicy one at that. Not quite hitting the overall heights of the previous monster bottling. But sensational nonetheless. 46%

Penderyn Madeira bott code. Apr 11 db **(88.5) n21.5 t22 f23 b22.** A much closer relation in style to the Penderyn 41 of March 2011 than the previous standard bottling. Lighter and less lusty with the fruit playing only a bit part by comparison. More room for some of the oakier spices to flourish and help make for a more salivating, feistier and, one might even argue, sophisticated malt. Delicious. 46%

Penderyn Madeira bott code. May 11 db **(87.5) n20.5 t23 f22 b22.** Similar score and enjoyment level as the previous month's bottling, but gets there by taking a different route. Indeed; this really is like the Penderyn 41 with more fruit and oils here and, whether it is the case or not, the impression of greater youth. The spices are a treat. 46%

❄ **Penderyn Madeira** bott code Jun 11 db **(95) n23.5 t23.5 f24 b24.** Concentrates on the fruity side of matters; the nose is a wonderful marriage (did I just put the words" marriage" and "wonderful" in the same sentence?....(shudder)) of rather over-ripe mango and fit-to-burst greengage while the delivery makes maximum gain from the sublime grape and peach lucidity. The finish is aided by the softest oils imaginable which inject the barley this is crying out for. Then a cocoa and raisin fade. It is a whisky that makes you sigh...and for all the right reasons... 46%. ncf.

❄ **Penderyn Madeira** bott Jul 11 db **(91.5) n23 t23 f22.5 b23.** Perhaps if I was asked to pour a Penderyn to display its expected personality in full swing, with little grapey twists here, lightly sugared oaky turns there, this would sum the distillery up almost too well... And not least because of some extra viscosity allowing those sugars to expand as far as they are ever likely to go. 46%. ncf.

❄ **Penderyn Madeira** bott Aug 11 db **(89) n22 t22 f23 b22.** A James Bond of a dram: you could almost make a dry martini from this, so chalky are those oak notes. A little cocoa powder emphasises the point. 46%. ncf.

❄ **Penderyn Madeira** bott Sep 11 db **(91) n23 t23 f22 b23.** You really have to take your hats off to these guys: the consistency is now absolutely top draw and here they appear to have that delicate balance between drier crushed grape pithiness of the Madeira completely in harmony with the sweeter elements of both oak and barley. Here, though, the spices season, entertain and bring alive, something like pepper on a piece of Welsh Rarebit. 46%. ncf.

❄ **Penderyn Madeira** bott Oct 11 db **(94) n23 t23.5 f24 b23.5.** Penderyn with its tie off and top button undone. Relaxed from the moment it hits the palate – or I should say caresses – with a wonderfully soft barley-led fruitiness and then a mercurial display of complex spices and then vanilla-topped mocha. In this form unquestionably one of the easiest-drinking whiskies in the world. the remainder of this bottle won't be going back into my warehouse: this will be sitting in my dining room amid some accomplished others! *46%. ncf.*

⫶ **Penderyn Madeira** bott Nov 11 db **(93) n22.5 t24 f23 b23.5.** Never quite settles like the October bottling, but through choice and design rather than fault. Edgy, dry and at times pretty nutty, with gorgeous walnut oil and chocolate fudge ramping up the complexity on the vanilla and burnt raisin. A malt which fidgets from one part of the palate to the next. But the quality is stunning. We have entered, without doubt, a purple period for Welsh Whisky. It is a bit like the national rugby team of the early 70s and Swansea City of the present: just a joy to behold. *46%. ncf.*

⫶ **Penderyn Madeira** bott Dec 11 db **(89) n22 t22 f23 b22.** Excellent whisky, though seems a come down from the two previous bottlings! Here the oils have become a little snagged with the natural processes, thereby diminishing slightly the complexity. The big, bulging muscovado sugars on delivery, though are rather wonderful. *46%. ncf.*

⫶ **Penderyn Madeira** bott Jan 12 db **(86) n21 t22 f21.5 b21.5.** This one, as pleasant as it is, is just a little too dry and overly spiced to comfortably find a balance and rhythm. *46%. ncf.*

⫶ **Penderyn Madeira** bott Feb 12 db **(92) n21.5 t23 f24 b23.5.** It is as though the gratingly dry character of the previous bottling had been noted and something has been done to make amends. The texture is much softer yet the grape both sturdier and sultana intense. The spices here are as big as any I can remember from this distillery and though they take no prisoners they successfully riddle the malt with complexity. Quite brilliant! *46%. ncf.*

⫶ **Penderyn Madeira** bott Mar 12 db **(91.5) n22.5 t22.5 f23.5 b23.** The even-ness here suggests more casks than normal as we have a white noise on the nose of many of the Penderyn fixtures, though some cancelling others out. There is enough left over, though, to mesmerise. The delivery is also astonishingly well composed with barley and madeira striking an unusual balance of practically going halves in dominance. With the clear, grassy barley actually making this one of the most juicy Penderyns of all time, it is a malt which takes a little time to learn to fly, but when it does, it swoops and rises with elegant abandon. *46%. ncf.*

⫶ **Penderyn Madeira** bott May 12 db **(89.5) n21.5 t23 f22.5 b22.5.** There is a silky theme here that has been missing for a few bottlings. The oils certainly gang up and waylay a few of the more complex notes which weaved their spell in the previous bottling. Still a malt to chew and savour with the barley and spice in perennial battle. *46%. ncf.*

Penderyn 41 db **(91.5) n22** delicate peach and bitter almond; a touch of apricot, too; **t23** the Madeira coats the palate with first a light layer of soft grape, then a heavier one of skin and stone. Against the drier vanillas, the gristy sweetness of the barley is supported by the constant grape; **f24** a charming fade of spiced butterscotch and lightly sweetened cocoa; **b22.5** don't think for one moment it's the reduction of strength that makes this work so well. Rather, it is the outstanding integration of the outlandishly good Madeira casks with the vanilla. At usual strength this would have scored perhaps another couple of points. Oh, the lucky French for whom this was designed... *41%*

Penderyn 41 released 3 Nov 10 db **(88) n21.5 t22 f22.5 b22.5.** Very similar to the November 1910 Release except fewer oils to carry the fruit and a bigger part played by drier, cocoa notes. *41%. ncf.*

Penderyn 41 bott code. Mar 11 db **(84.5) n20 t21 f22 b21.5.** Had me worried at first: the nose and, to a lesser extent, delivery were unusually thin and niggardly. But recovers from the mid ground onwards with its usual fruity charm. *41%*

⫶ **Penderyn 41 Madeira** bott Jun 11 db **(90.5) n22 t23 f22.5 b23** Penderyn at its most demure but also in this case showing it has a few claws, too. Works better at this strength than the Port Wood, probably because there is far more going on between the counter weight of grape and oak . The delivery, though, is the star as early cocoa notes pop up, welded to crunchy muscovado sugars and even a hint of stem ginger. *41%. ncf.*

Penderyn Bourbon Matured Single Cask dist 2000 **(96) n24** although this has spent its entire life in what I assume to be a first fill bourbon cask, one of the sweeter notes here is more likely to be associated with a sauternes cask: that's the one with sticky honey and fruit in equal abundance. Elsewhere we are treated to a plethora of liquorice notes, both of the red and black variety, sandalwood coconut in treacle and, if you have enough hours in the day to devote to such matters...; **t24.5** the delivery is an explosion of sugar and barley but the biggest bang reserved for the immediate spices; a number of vanilla and tannin notes arrive earlier than you might expect, while the oiliness is quite different to what is usually associated with this distillery; **f23.5** thins, by comparison, once the sugars have exhausted themselves. Dries as the oak gains the upper hand, but never so much that the barley is entirely lost or balance is compromised; **b24** Penderyn as rarely seen, even by me. This is as old a Welsh whisky that has been bottled in living memory. And it is one that will live in the memory of this current generation. For I have encountered very few whiskies which revels in a controlled sweetness on so many levels. This is so good, it is frightening. *61.2%*

Penderyn Peated bott code May 10 db **(84) n21 t20 f22 b21.** The smoke at times can barely bother registering. When it does it tends to rail against fruits and oak to create a heated whisky in every sense. Stirring, enjoyable, roughhouse stuff and never for a moment a glass you can relax with. *46%*

⁖ **Penderyn Peated** bott Oct 11 db **(90.5) n22** soft, lilting smoke settles on a sugary landscape; **t23** few malts you find this year will hit the palate creating so much flavour yet so few waves. Really does concentrate on a gristy, sugary quality with success; **f22.5** the sugary fanfare still reverberates; **b23** so few whiskies are quite so well-mannered as this... *46%. ncf.*

⁖ **Penderyn Peated** bott Nov 11 db **(93.5) n23.5** the intensity of the peat is no only for all to see, but enough to hurl you back in your chair: it is not normally like this! There is also, quite curiously, a unique and delicious pea-in-the-pod green-ness (takes me back to the early '60s of shelling the peas from the allotment with my nan), complete with all the earthiness...; **t3** nothing quite so memory-jerking on the delivery...though maybe not quite true...fast forward to the very early 80s and it has the deft, sugary smokiness of some of the Islays of the day; **f23** long, with those sugars making as much as they can from a favourable situation. The peat remains constant and utterly charming; **b24** the nose has rarely been the ace in the deck for Penderyn, but here it strengthens the hand considerably. This is the first Penderyn with some genuine peaty grunt. *46%. ncf.*

⁖ **Penderyn Peated** bott Jan 12 db **(87) n22** the smoke arrives in puffs...; **t22** a drier than normal delivery, though the barley does all it can to pep things up; **f21.5** dries to the point of austerity...; **b21.5** pretty steady stuff. *46%. ncf.*

⁖ **Penderyn Peated** bott May 12 db **(86) n21 t22 f21.5 b21.5.** A curious gin-like juniper quality undermines the peat, though the spices and sugars star. *46%. ncf*

Penderyn Portwood cask no. PT26 db **(81) n18 t22 f21 b20.** Enormous, eye-watering, fruit delivery which all but bludgeons the taste buds into submission. Tightens alarmingly on arrival and then again towards the middle ground and finish. For all its might and magnitude, and occasional lip-smacking deliciousness, at times bitter, grouchy, cramped and, overall, just not in the same league as the previous, legendary, Port Wood Penderyn. Having said all that, so different you just have to try it...!! One for the world's Whisky Clubs: I'd love to be a fly on the fall of the debates around this one... *60.6%*

⁖ **Penderyn Portwood** bott Jan 12 db **(87) n21.5** interesting how bringing the strength down dries the grape to the extent of an added chalkiness; **t22** soft, with a slow unveiling of crystalline sugars and powdery vanillas; **f22** dries even more and heads for a more liquorice and hickory-style harbour...; **b21.5** the breaking down of the oils at this strength also appears to signal a lessening of complexity. Pleasant, though. *42%. ncf.*

⁖ **Penderyn Portwood Swansea City Special** cask no. PT68 db **(96.5) n23.5** an almost mesmeric degree of spice, intertwining with an impressive tapestry of marmalade and blood orange; **t24.5** the delivery is about as rich as it comes, the mouth feel lush but light enough to "see" a degree of barley, albeit fleetingly, as the grape offers up not just a pithy dryness but, to ensure the required balance, a handsome degree of sugar and bewildering spice effect; **f24** not sure anyone does Port wood better than Penderyn, and the finish here confirms with marvellous prose on the palate its beguiling enormity. Those who enjoy spicy chocolate are in for a dram they'll never forget here, though the intensity of the fruitcake is sublime, the cherries bursting its juices all over the palate. **b24.5** on Saturday 30th April 1966 I was taken by my father to see my very first football game: Millwall versus Swansea Town, as they were then known. On 30th April 2011 I celebrated 45 years of agony and ecstasy (though mainly agony!) with my beloved Millwall with a dinner at The Den as we hosted.... would you believe it? Yep, Swansea! The Swans won that day on their march to deserved promotion to the Premier League and it was my honour to be at Wembley to see them overcome Reading in the Play Off Final to book their place among the elite. I have met their Chairman Huw Jenkins on occasion but not yet had the chance to wish him well in his new rarified environment. I toast you and your grand old club, Huw, with this quite stunning, absolutely world class malt, as Welsh now as laverbread, and look forward to the day when the Lions are back among the Swans...Oh, and in the newly acquired knowledge from a discovery I made while tracing back some of my family history over Christmas 2011 that, as fate would have it, my paternal grandmother's family hail in the 19th century from Neath, on the outskirts of Swansea...; that there is not a jot of Scots in me as Murray's previously believed, but a whole load of Welsh! Perhaps goes to explain why I have so long been such a fan of Penderyn! Or, just maybe, this fabulous whisky does... *59.4%. ncf sc.*

Penderyn Sherrywood released 1 Jan 11 db **(94) n23** a hint of salty olives and an almost apologetic, half-hearted move towards something vaguely sweet in the barley and fruit department. Sophisticated hardly covers it...; **t23.5** the wine immediately fills the palate but the oak has a great deal to say. Everything is clean, clearly defined and oozing quality and quiet confidence; **f23.5** more moody swings between salty dry and vaguely sweet – the gap between the two is severe; **b24** drier than the lips of a Welsh Male Voice Choir singing in the Sahara. But a whole lot more harmonious. 46%. ncf.

⁘ **Penderyn Sherrywood** bott Oct 11 db **(89) n22** spotted dog pudding...a whole host of crushed sultanas; **t22** silky, sweet and a slow unravelling of sugars, mainly of muscovado depth; **f22.5** the finish also reveals a lovely suety mix with a grape influence; **b22.5** weird, isn't it. This is a beautiful whisky. But having tasted it straight after the Swansea special Port wood, it is just so tame and docile...!! 46%. ncf.

⁘ **Penderyn Sherrywood** bott Feb 12 db **(94) n22** so dry and chalky...; clean yet relatively non-communicative; **t24** ...yet now so lush and juicy: the nose and delivery have nothing in common whatsoever. Unlikely you could get the bitter-sweet ratio off to such a comfortable degree, or the spices as well defined; the mouth feel, though, is the stuff of dreams; **f24** long with some bitter marmalade resurfacing but this time with intent; the fade is something akin to a sherry trifle mixed in with coffee cake; **b24** fascinating how this sherry works in an entirely different way to the one bottled in October, offering different structure and focus points. But certainly no less quality. I am delighted for Penderyn when I taste this. But I wish some key people from the scotch whisky industry, as well as one or two commentators, would grab hold of this to learn just how a clean, entirely non-sulphured, sherry butt should actually be... if they have the ability to tell the difference (which in some cases I doubt), they will be in for a major shock. Mind you: there are none so blind than those who wish not to see... 46%. ncf.

Penderyn Sherrywood Limited Edition cask no. 546 db **(95) n24** sticky toffee pudding, dates, mildly overcooked Christmas pudding, molasses, unsugared stewed apples...clean, complex and celebrating its own controlled enormity; oh, and those spices...mmmmm!!!! **t24** massive oils coat the mouth to ensure maximum impact with the exploding grape and almost earthy depth. Chocolate fudge, yet no hint of toffee, a fusion of medium roast Java with crisp Nicaraguan cocoa...yet somehow the barley, seemingly roasted, appears to come through into the middle ground to make a telling impact...of its style, it simply doesn't get any better...; **f23** just a mere excellent finish – a bit of a letdown. The sharper more bitter elements of the grape are exposed...luckily enough there is any number of sugar style to make amends...; **b24** this is one of the world great whiskies. Penderyn's consultant, Jim Swan, is responsible for the use and selection of this cask. As was the case with the other single cask selections. It meant an entire four hour tasting afternoon was been spent simply analysing three astonishing casks. If all the world's whiskies were this good I'd never be able to get even close to completing the Bible. The three single casks included here confirm that Penderyn has entered the stratosphere of magnificent whisky. Ignore this distillery entirely at your peril. 50%. ncf sc.

Scotch Malt Whisky Society Cask 128.1 Aged 6 Years 1st fill port barrique, cask no. PT3, dist 2003 **(93.5) n21.5 t24.5 f23.5 b24.** For those single malt fundamentalists who think the SMWS have welshed on their ideals, here is confirming proof: Welsh whisky. But tell me. The drunken nose apart, which has probably robbed it of an award, just which part of this whisky is not fabulous...? 55.6%. sc. 233 bottles.

Scotch Malt Whisky Society Cask 128.2 Aged 7 Years 1st fill Madeira hogshead, cask no. M13, dist 2002 **(86.5) n22.5 t21 f22 b21.** A strange reversal to 128.1. There the nose disintegrates but displays a rare magnificence on the palate while this has a very good nose but doesn't quite find its stride on the palate. Some serious bite, though. 60.5%. 227 bottles

⁘ **Scotch Malt Whisky Society Cask 128.3 Aged 5 Years** first fill barrel, cask no. 600, dist 2006 **(96) n24** if I was a man of leisure, had I nothing to do all day, then I think my hours would be spent nosing this, among other great whisky aromas. This is a show off malt one that on the nose displays a supreme crushed almond (yet without the sugars to make it into marzipan) with the cleanest of crisp barley tones; **t24** the delivery boasts oils never for a moment apparent on the nose and a plethora of sugars ranging from icing to thin Demerara; there are other bourbony fingerprints, too, especially the red liquorice and the hints of honeycomb; **f24** the finish isn't just long; you van grow a beard while waiting for the final sugar notes to disperse. The oils are delicate now, but the barley it carries is super-charged with almost gristy concentrate, while the vanillas take on a custardyness a la rage...; **b24** if this doesn't get Penderyn to bring out a succession of full strength cask whiskies, I don't know what will. This is, without question, world class... 61.3%. sc.

⁘ **Scotch Malt Whisky Society Cask 128.4 Aged 7 Years** first fill port barrique, cask no. 32, dist 2004 **(92) n22** thick fruit, though almost too dense as the lighter barley tones struggle to make themselves heard; **t22.5** heavy duty fruit, with a big blackcurrant (no, not blackberry!) delivery amid some scorching spices; **f24** calms sufficiently to make full use of the plummy sweetness , though the spices could have come from any decent kitchen trying to jack up the intensity of the fruit; late cocoa works rather well; **b23.5** hardly a malt for the faint-hearted, but one many in the Scotch whisky industry, along with 128.3, can take a long hard look at. I'll give you a clue, boys: it is the quality of the casks. That area where the Scotch whisky industry has let us down so badly... 59.4%. sc.

World Whiskies

I have long said that whisky can be made just about anywhere in the world; that it is not writ large in stone that it is the inalienable right for just Scotland, Ireland, Kentucky and Canada to have it all to themselves. And so, it seems, it is increasingly being proved. Perhaps only sandy deserts and fields of ironstone can prevent its make physically and Islam culturally, though even that has not been a barrier to malt whisky being distilled in both Pakistan and Turkey. While not even the world's highest mountains or jungle can prevent the spread of barley and copper pot.

Outside of North America and Europe, whisky's traditional nesting sites, you can head in any direction and find it being made. South America may be well known for its rum, but in the south of Brazil, an area populated by Italian and German settlers many generations back, malt whisky is thriving. In even more lush and tropical climes it can now also be found, with Taiwan and Thailand leading the way.

Japan has long represented Asia with distinction and whisky-making there is in such an advanced state and at a high standard Jim Murray's Whisky Bible has given it its own section. But while neighbouring South Korea has ended its malt distilling venture, further east, and at a very unlikely altitude, Nepal has forged a small industry to team up, geographically, with fellow malt distillers India and Pakistan. The one malt whisky from this region making inroads in world markets is India's Amrut single malt. Actually, inroads is hardly doing them justice. Full-bloodied trailblazing, more like. So good now is their whisky they were, with their fantastically complex brand, Fusion deservedly awarded Jim Murray's Whisky Bible 2010 Third Finest Whisky in the World. That represented a watershed not just for the distillery, but Indian whisky as a whole and in a broader sense the entire world whisky movement: it proved beyond doubt that excellent distilling and maturation wherever you are on this planet will be recognised and rewarded.

Africa is also represented on the whisky stage. There has long been a tradition of blending Scotch malt with South African grain but now there is single malt there, as well. Two malt distilleries, to be precise, with a second being opened at the Drayman's Brewery in Pretoria. I was supposed to have visited it a little while back, but the distiller, obviously not wanting to see me, went to the trouble of falling off his horse and breaking his thigh the actual day before. Wimp.

One relatively new whisky-making region is due immediate further study: Australia. From a distance of 12,000 miles, the waters around Australia's distilleries appear to be muddied. Quality appears to range from the very good to extremely poor. And during the back end of 2004 I managed to discover this first hand when I visited three Tasmanian distilleries and Bakery Hill in Melbourne which perhaps leads the way regarding quality malt whisky made south of the Equator. Certainly green shoots are beginning to sprout at the Tasmania Distillery which has now moved its operation away from its Hobart harbour site to an out of town one close to the airport. The first bottlings of that had been so bad that it will take some time and convincing for those who have already tasted it to go back to it again. However, having been to the warehouse – and having tasted samples from every single cask they have on site – I reported in previous Bibles that it was only a matter of time before those first offerings would be little more than distant – though horrific – memories. Well, as predicted, it is now safe to put your head above the parapet. The last cask strength bottling I tasted was a bloody beaut. For this year's Jim Murray's Whisky Bible 2013, the Sullivans Cove French Oak Port Cask re-wrote the Australian whisky books. Scoring 96.5, it was not just the best I tasted from Taz, but it walked off with the Southern Hemisphere Whisky of the Year Award. Not only that, it made its way to the Whisky Bible World Whisky of the Year taste off conducted among the six best whiskies I tasted this year, hob-nobbing it with the likes of Buffalo Trace, Ardbeg and Ballantine's 17. South Coast chipped in with another stunner, too. Together they represent some of the highlights of world whisky. That is a quite staggering achievement and one which means that I now have no option but to start thumbing through an Atlas and flight timetable to get back over there pronto. The remaining casks of Wilson's malt from New Zealand are disappearing fast and when in New Zealand I discovered the stills from there were not just making rum in Fiji but whisky as well. We are all aware of the delights of island whisky, but a Pacific Island malt? Which leaves Antarctica as the only continent not making whisky, though what some of those scientists get up to for months on end no one knows.

ARGENTINA
Blends
Breeders Choice (84) n21 t22 f21 b20. A sweet blend using Scottish malt and, at the helm, an unusually lush Argentinian grain. *40%*

AUSTRALIA
BAKERY HILL DISTILLERY 1999. Operating.
Bakery Hill Classic Malt cask no. 3009 db **(81) n21 t21.5 f18.5 b20.** Malty and sawdusty. Feints inject some weight and bitters. *46%*

Bakery Hill Classic Malt Cask Strength bourbon cask no. 4510 db **(89) n23 t22.5 f22 b22.** Talk about going back in time: it is 1994 and I am in a warehouse in Dunedin going through the earliest existing casks of Lammerlaw New Zealand malt. The closest thing to it. *60.5%*

Bakery Hill Classic Malt Cask Strength bourbon cask no. 5710 db **(83) n21.5 t21.5 f19.5 b20.5.** One seriously sweet bottling. Plenty of nougat and honey. *60.5%*

Bakery Hill Double Wood bourbon & French oak cask no. 5855 db **(86.5) n22.5 t22.5 f20.5 b21.** Substantial whisky with a delightful chocolate fruit and nut core. *46%*

Bakery Hill Peated Malt bourbon cask no. 6209 db **(88.5) n22** firm, flinty phenols; **t23** crisp barley; crunchy brown sugars alongside the peat; **f21** over-baked caramelised biscuit **b22.5** spic and span, matter of fact malt. *46%*

Bakery Hill Peated Malt Cask Strength French oak cask no. 6009 db **(92.5) n23.5 t24 f22.5 b22.5.** I remember when Talisker had this kind of spice attack. Virtually every phase of this malt works fabulously: a truly wonderful piece of distilling and maturation. *60%*

Bakery Hill Peated Malt Cask Strength bourbon cask no 6810 db **(87) n22.5** the peat is so distant, it could be on the other side of the world...; **t22** the mouth is washed in sweet barley. Some smoke nonchalantly hangs around; **f21** bitter oak; **b21.5** not the kindest cask, but the peat is intriguing. *60%*

BOOIE RANGE DISTILLERY
Booie Range Single Malt db **(72) n14 t20 f19 b19.** Mounts the hurdle of the wildly off-key nose impressively with a distinct, mouth watering barley richness to the palate that really does blossom even on the finish. *40%*

LARK DISTILLERY
The Lark Distillery Single Malt Whisky Cask Strength cask no. LD140, bott Feb 10 db **(80) n19.5 t18.5 f22 b20.** From tip to tail there is a note on this I can't quite put my finger on, or say I much approve of. But there is also a real coppery small still feel to this, bolstered by a late-developing honeycomb and Demerara sheen. *58%*

The Lark Distillery Single Malt Whisky Distillers Selection cask no. LD109, bott Apr 10 db **(86.5) n21.5 t21 f22.5 b21.5.** A chunky affair with some attractive nougat and orange; the star turn is the Rolo candy finale. *46%*

LIMEBURNERS
Limeburners Single Malt Whisky Barrel M23 bott no. 78 db **(90.5) n22.5 t23.5 f22 b22.5.** First time I've tasted anything from this Western Australian mob. Gday fellas! I have to admit, thought it might have been from France at first, as the aroma on nosing blind reminded me of brandy. And not without good reason, it transpires. This no age statement malt spent an unspecified amount of time in American brandy cask before being finished in bourbon casks. Does it work? Yes it does. But now that's torn it lads. You are supposed to start off with a bloody horrible whisky and get better. Now you have gone and made a rod for your own back. Good on you! *61%*

Limeburners Single Malt Whisky Barrel M27 bott no. 47 db **(73) n18 t19 f17 b19.** Malty, but feinty, too. Probably not had the happiest fermentation, either. *43%*

Limeburners Single Malt Whisky Barrel M31 bott no. 293 db **(85.5) n21.5 t22 f21 b21.** Pouting, semi-spiced up sultana fruitcake, complete with a delicate nuttiness; full on in part, yet curiously weightless. *43%. ncf. Great Southern Distilling Co.*

Limeburners Single Malt Whisky M64 Muscat Finish db **(92) n23.5** another big grapey statement from Limeburners. The fruit is thick, clean, sugar-soaked and dripping from the barley; the playful spices on the oak are to die for; **t23** the big alcohol combines perfectly with the seemingly bigger grape and muscular malt. On one hand puckering, on the other, too juicy to be true; **f22.5** a salty finale sits well with the persistent clean grape; **b23** macho malt keeps in touch with its feminine side. Tasty and beautifully made. *61%. ncf.*

Limeburners Single Malt Whisky M67 Sherry Butt Finish db **(86) n21.5 t22 f21 b21.5.** a huge whisky. However, a few cracks which aren't quite papered over despite the magnificent body and chewiness. The main cocoa theme is a corker. *61%. ncf.*

THE NANT DISTILLERY

The Nant Single Malt First Release bott 2010 db **(91.5) n24 t23 f22 b22.5.** Beyond excellent for a first go. The flavours and style could not be more clearly nailed to the mast. I'll be watching this distillery closely. *43%*

The Nant 3 Year Old American oak/Port db **(91.5) n22.5** the aroma of a wine cask hit twice a day by the incoming tide; the odd kumquat sideshow; **t22** delicate evolving of fruit, though the barley remains in control; the oak drives some caramel into the fray, but with excellent understatement; **f23** confirmation of the big salt statement on the nose: some late oils (from the slightly wider cut they managed to get away with) drags some late barley into the picture **b24** beautifully well made whisky. Has the sophistication of a dry martini, but without the olive...yet maintaining the salt. Last year I set out to keep my eyes on these chaps. Not a bad move. *43%*

The Nant 3 Years Old Cask Strength American oak bourbon db **(95.5) n23** several layers of honey and a Sauterenes cask style fruitiness. Where is that coming from...? So big and voluptuous: you don't know whether to go on and drink it or make love to it...; **t24** I'm drinking it: good choice! The malt is obviously young because how else can you get this degree of barley enormity? Juicy, thick and, though carrying a little bit of feint, adorable for its profound richness. Again, some fruit notes wander in from somewhere, and once more they are the kind of orangey-grapey notes one usually associates with Sauterenes. Very odd. **f24** Ridiculously long. You can almost wear your tongue out against the roof of your mouth. Soft muscovado sugars with the lightest touch of honey, liquorice and maple syrup. The vanillas build and then give way to tasty butterscotch; **b24.5** I have really got to get back to Oz to visit these guys. Something majestic is happening here. Whatever it is they are doing, I have to discover first hand...World class. *61.6%*

OLD HOBART DISTILLERY

⁛ **Overeem Port Cask Matured** heavily charred quarter cask finish, cask no. OHD-010, dist 15 Aug 07, bott 15 May 12 db **(89) n23** firm nose allowing the burnt raisin fruitiness to travel only so far; **t23** wonderful dual mouth feel: both firm and yielding, with the grape seemingly present in both; **f21** dries over enthusiastically; **b22** a supreme toastiness works so well with the big fruit. *43%. sc.*

⁛ **Overeem Port Cask Matured Cask Strength** heavily charred quarter cask finish, cask no. OHD-008, dist 15 Aug 07, bott 15 May 12 db **(95) n24** absolutely classic: wonderful juicy date and walnut in a very happy marriage with Dundee cake; **t24.5** lush with an almost piercing saltiness: one of the best wine cask deliveries I have tasted from the southern hemisphere. The fruit not for a moment loses integrity or pace while the sugars, a kind of light Demerara, inject just about perfect sweetness; **f23** dries as the spices begin to pound hard; the fruit becomes subservient to the bourbon-style honeycomb; **b23.5** just get it if you see it: a no brainer! *60%. sc.*

⁛ **Overeem Sherry Cask Matured** medium charred quarter cask finish, cask no. ODG-005, dist 5 Jun 07, bott 1 Jun 12 db **(85.5) n21.5 t22 f21 b21.** No frills. No thrills, either. *43%. sc.*

⁛ **Overeem Sherry Cask Matured Cask Strength** medium charred quarter cask finish, cask no. OHD-003, dist 6 Jun 07, bott 2 Mar 12 db **(91.5) n23** you salty little fruit bomb, you!! **t23** massive viscosity to this voluptuous siren ensuring the intense, spiced grape quite literally sticks around; the oak behaves like a cask three times its age; **f22** the sugars have by now been lost and terse dryness begins to make itself known; **b23.5** must have stolen all the complexity and charisma from cask ODG-005. A treat! *60%. sc.*

SMALL CONCERN DISTILLERY

Cradle Mountain Pure Tasmanian Malt db **(87) n21** curiously vivid bourbon character; sweet vanilla with hints of tangerine and hazelnut. Really very, very attractive; **t22** an almost perfect translation onto the palate: gloriously sweet and gently nutty. The mouthfeel and body is firm and oily at the same time, the barley sparkles as the oak fades. Exceptionally subtle, clean and well made; **f21** pretty long with some cocoa offering a praline effect; **b23** a knock-out malt from a sadly now lost distillery in Tasmania. Faultlessly clean stuff with lots of new oak character but sufficient body to guarantee complexity. *43%*

SOUTHERN COAST DISTILLERS

Southern Coast Single Malt Batch 001 db **(92.5) n23** crisp with varying layers of muscovado sugars; clean (well, a little bit of forgivable wide-ish cut apart, offering haystack barley amongst other delights) yet with a distinct Highland Park style honey and heather; **t24** magnificently crisp, sugar-crusted barley. Some fabulous oils (from that cut) counter the firm, spicy nature; **f22** more spice but with vanilla and cocoa; **b23.5** "a hint of bushfire in the barley" claims the back label. Well, that one's got me stumped; I pride myself in nosing anything and everything, but that particular aroma has passed me by. Perhaps they mean the heather aroma...? Mind you, I did get pretty close to some scary forest fires near Marseilles nearly 30 years ago, but probably not the same thing... Anyway, back to this fabulous first effort. Wow! Could ask for more in a study of crisp brown sugars and sweet cocoa...; 46%

Southern Coast Single Malt Batch 002 db **(96) n24** I am in Guyana. I am tucked into a warm warehouse. And I have my head stuck in a 20- possibly 25-year-old barrel of pre-caramelised pot still rum. Right...? Wow. Magnificent. **t23.5** OK. That coffee flavour. The toffees. The soft oils and broiling sugars. The immeasurable juices. I am still in Guyana. Right? **f24.5** the kind of coffee and confident but fragile elegance you find in a Guyanan pot still; sultanas and burnt raisins run amok; walnut cake and cream...bloody hell...???? What is this...????? **b24** is this the best Australian whisky ever to shamelessly masquerade as Demerara pot still rum? I should think so. Will it ever be beaten? I doubt it. In fact, just how many Demerara rums have I ever tasted of this refinement. One or two, at most. And I have probably tasted more than anyone in the whisky trade living. One of the most astonishing whiskies it has been my honour to taste. Frankly, I am on my knees... 46%

Southern Coast Single Malt Batch 003 db **(79.5) n18 t19 f23 b19.5.** Third time unlucky. Lots of oils and berserk honey. But too feinty, though this went to some finishing school, believe me...! 46%. ncf.

⊰ **Southern Coast Single Malt Batch 004** db **(82.5) n20 t22 f20.5 b20.** An earthy, slightly musty dram with a pleasing essence of ulmo honey but struggles to find structure or balance. 46%

⊰ **Southern Coast Single Malt Batch 005** db **(83.5) n21.5 t22 f20 b20.** Starts off like a Jack Hobbs or Brian Lara or Alec Stewart taking the Aussie quick bowling apart. There is even an unusual, but mightily attractive, sweetened Vegemite hint to this (not as strange as it sounds, actually). But the middle stump is removed by the hefty finish: the cricketing equivalent of an ungainly, head-up hoick to cow corner.... 46%

⊰ **Southern Coast Single Malt Batch 006** db **(95) n24** pot still Demerara rum all the way: a fabulous marriage of heavy sweet notes from molasses to creosote by way of intense liquorice, but all presented with a sophisticated panache..and a cup of Jamaican Blue Mountain coffee...unique in world whisky; **t24** you expect pot still Demerara. and you get it...to a degree. But there is a massive wave of barley here, too, though they have to fight hard to get through the rich oils and intense muscovado sugars; **f23.5** long, with a wonderful marriage of ulmo honey and treacle...oh, and did I mention the Demerara rum...? **b24** when I saw these Southern Coast Whiskies before me, my eyes lit up. Here was my journey to Demerara. Much cheaper and less problem-riddled than any trip I normally make to Guyana.. and with less chance of coming away with my normal stomach complaint. Batches 4 and 5 let me down. But Batch 6.... even the sun has come out for the first time in three days as I nose this... Georgetown, here I come... 46%

TASMAN DISTILLERY

Great Outback Rare Old Australian Single Malt db **(92) n24** I could stick my nose in a glass of this all day. This is sensational: more a question of what we don't have here! The malt is clean, beautifully defined and dovetails with refined, orangey-citrus notes. The oak is near perfection adding only a degree of tempered weight. I don't detect peat, but there is some compensating Blue Mountain coffee; **t24** just so beautifully textured with countless waves of clean, rich malt neither too sweet nor too dry. This is faultless distillate; **f21** lightens considerably with the oak vanilla dominating; **b23** What can you say? An Australian whisky distillery makes a malt to grace the world's stage. But you can't find it outside of Australia. This will have to be rectified. 40%

TASMANIA DISTILLERY

Old Hobart db **(69) n16 t19 f17 b17.** The nose still has some way to go before it can be accepted as a mainstream malt, though there is something more than a little coastal about it this time. However, the arrival on the palate is another matter and I must say I kind of enjoyed its big, oily and increasingly sweet maltiness and crushed sunflower seed nuttiness towards the end. Green (and yellow) shoots are growing. The whisky is unquestionably getting better. 60%

Sullivans Cove db **(61) n13 t15 f17 b16.** Some malt but typically grim, oily and dirty; awesomely weird. 40%. Australia.

Sullivans Cove Bourbon Matured Cask Strength Single Cask barrel no: HH0602, barrel date 21 Feb 01, bott 10 Sep 09 **(81) n18 t24 f20 b19.** An outrageous maltfest, for all its obvious faults. "Distilled with Conviction" the label proudly states, a reference to Tasmania's penal past. But it looks as though the stillman has made his escape as the nose suggests the eye wasn't being kept on the ball as feints abound. Ironically, the resulting extra oils mean the youthful but hugely intense malt simply blows you away. Technically, a nightmare. But you know what? I just love it...!!! (To ramp it up about five or six points, pour into a glass and place in hot water to burn off the higher alcohols. What remains after about five minutes, depending on the temperature of the water, is a much cleaner, more honeyed version). 60%

⁙ **Sullivans Cove Rare Tasmanian Single Cask American** oak bourbon cask, cask no. HH0128, dist 25 Jan 00, bott 21 Sep 11 db **(86) n21 t22.5 f21 b21.5.** A slightly wider cut that normally means a subtle degree of extra oil is floating around, enough to dull the sharper edges of the more complex notes from an obviously top quality cask. As usual from the distillery, though, the sugars make you groan with delight. 47.5%. sc. 246 bottles.

⁙ **Sullivans Cove Rare Tasmanian Single Cask American** oak bourbon cask, cask no. HH0326, dist 30 May 00, bott 12 Jan 12 db **(90.5) n22** orange blossom honey....blossoming! **t23** an oily arm-wrestle between the barley and complex honeys from the cask...; **f22.5** ...it is a tie! And here just a little extra nutty nougat adds depth; **b23** easy going, sweet enough and with sufficient weight to be an anytime kind of a malt. Put it this way: I'd say yes to it anytime, for one...! 47.5%. sc. 256 bottles.

⁙ **Sullivans Cove Rare Tasmanian Single Cask American** oak bourbon cask, cask no. HH0329, dist 2 Jun 00, bott 17 Feb 12 db **(91.5) n23.5** egg custard tart...with a sprinkling of pepper and lime juice; **t23** wow! There goes them there peppers again! The malt positively glows in its own juiciness...and radiating spice all the way; **f22.5** back to the custard and peppers on the nose; **b22.5** complex, in a limited kind of way. But beautifully made and the barley is a delight. 47.5%. 168 bottles.

⁙ **Sullivans Cove Rare Tasmanian Single Cask** American oak bourbon cask, cask no. HH0330, dist 2 Jun 00, bott 17 Feb 12 db **(92) n23** another excellent cask, this time offering some extra natural caramels as well as a bourbony liquorice and spice; **t23.5** top drawer delivery: not just waves of intense malt but bands of muscovado bringing with it thyme honey and drier, countering vanilla; **f22.5** a shade of honey b23 makes muted attempts to head into Kentucky territory. Complex. 47.5%. 238 bottles.

⁙ **Sullivans Cove Rare Tasmanian Single Cask** French oak port cask, cask no. HH0425, dist 8 Aug 00, bott 25 Jan 12 db **(86) n20.5 t23 f21 b21.5.** Huge wine involvement with the chocolatey grape running amuck with a gorgeously soft and rounded assault on the palate. Perhaps, though, could just do with another trick. Still, I'm happy to enjoy the unusual charms offered! 47.5%. sc. 487 bottles.

⁙ **Sullivans Cove Rare Tasmanian Single Cask** French oak port cask, cask no. HH0425, dist 11 Aug 00, bott 21 Sep 11 db **(84) n21 t21 f21 b21.** Pleasant. But straight lines just a little too much thanks to the natural caramels. 47.5%. sc. 453 bottles.

⁙ **Sullivans Cove Rare Tasmanian Single Cask** French oak port cask, cask no. HH0430, dist 15 Aug 00, bott 17 Feb 12 **(77.5) n19 t20 f19 b19.5.** Just never quite gets its act together or feels right. 47.5%. sc. 546 bottles.

⁙ **Sullivans Cove Rare Tasmanian Single Cask** French oak port cask, cask no. HH0509, dist 6 Oct 00, bott 17 Feb 12 **(96.5) n24** busy to the point of being manic. All kinds of toasty, roasty notes, almost vinegary in its bite; coffee roasting in a shop around the corner; **t24** when you get that amount of toast on the nose you half expect a mountain of sugar...and what you get is a complete range; to be more accurate, it is much more honey – especially acacia and heather; **f24** this is ridiculous: now ulmo honey moves in with its caramel and vanilla edged sweetness; yet all the time there are enough drier notes from the oak to ensure balance; **b24.5** although this comes from a wine cask, the dominant forces at work here have much more in common with bourbon style whisky than malt. It is also, unquestionably, one of the world whiskies of the year... 47.5%. sc. 494 bottles.

TIMBOON RAILWAY SHED DISTILLERY

Timboon Single Malt Whisky port cask, dist May 08, bott Jun 10 db **(85) n22.5 t20.5 f21 b21.** Fruity and edgy, almost closer to the botanicals in gin (minus juniper) than single malt. There is a background rumble which is quite unique. Ever seen those war films where the guy manning the radar on the sub detects something, yet despite all his experience cannot quite fathom what it is that ping is telling him? Well that's me with this whisky: I need to get out there to find out what this one is all about. In the meantime, not to be confused with Tim Boon, the England cricket coach who helped plot the downfall of the Aussies in the 2005 Ashes series... 40%

Timboon Single Malt Whisky dist Aug 08, bott May 11 db **(93) n24.5** quite possibly the most complex nose I have come across for a while. Certainly the most fragile. Sometimes I can barely hear what is being said. The orange blossom, bedecked in wisps of thin acacia honey, is stunning; **t23** pastel shades of honey and barley. A little amplification might see off the dogmatic oak; **f22** sawdusty vanilla...and more hints of orange and honey; **b23.5** imagine Tim Boon, the cricketer, going out to face the current England pace attack with one of those foot-long bats used exclusively for players to sign. That, basically, is what we have here with a malt underpowered for the type of job it is capable of doing. Yes, its technique is extraordinary. Certainly, it has moved to the pitch of the barley and is in line with what's coming with rare textbook elegance. But the strength is too feeble to translate into the highest score that it deserves. That said, quality is quality. And this is strictly First Class. *40%*

YALUMBA WINERY

Smith's Angaston Whisky Vintage 1997 Aged 7 Years db **(88) n20** an attractive, if not entirely faultless, combination of barley and fruit sewn together by honey; **t22** an almost implausible silkiness to this: the barley and honey tip-toe over the tastebuds using a touch of oil to help them glide as well; **f23** now we have some serious complexity with the fruits showing a berry-like sharpness, but it's all very effete; **b23** easily one of the most delicate whiskies of the year and one that puts Samuel Smith on the map. Perfect for the hipflask for a night at the ballet. *40%*

Smith's Angaston Whisky Vintage 1998 Aged 8 Years db **(86) n20 t22 f22 b22.** Perhaps conscious that their first offering, a genuine touch of culture that it was, wasn't quite Bruce enough to called Australian, this one's showing bit of aggression. And I mean a bit, as this is no tackle from Lucas Neil. Because after the delivery it's back to the girlie stuff with some admittedly delicious Swiss Roll filling fruitiness. Lovely malt from a distillery I'm going to have to keep my eyes on. *40%*

Vatted Malts

Tasmanian Double Malt Whisky Unpeated (87.5) n22 muscovado sugar and vanilla; **t22** delightfully slick mouth with feel egg yolks and sugar: half way to a cake mix...; **f21.5** powdery oak with a spurt of lemon; **b22** not a chance of getting bored with this guy. A sweet tooth would be useful. *43%. The Nant Distillery.*

BRAZIL
HEUBLEIN DISTILLERY

Durfee Hall Malt Whisky db **(81) n18 t22 f20 b21.** Superbly made whisky; the intensity of the malt is beautifully layered without ever becoming too sweet. Very light bodied and immaculately clean. Good whisky by any standards. *43%*

UNION DISTILLERY

Barrilete db **(72) n18 t19 f18 b17.** Nothing particularly wrong with it technically; it just lacks vitality. Thin but extremely malt intense. *39.1%*

Blends

Cockland Gold Blended Whisky (73) n18 t18 f19 b18. Silky caramel. Traces of malt there, but never quite gets it up. *38%. Fante.*

Drury's Special Reserve (86.5) n21.5 t22 f21 b22. Deceptively attractive, melt-in-the-mouth whisky; at times clean, regulation stuff, but further investigation reveals a honeycomb edge which hits its peak in the middle ground where the spices mix in beautifully. One to seek out and savour when in Brazil. *40%. Campari, Brasil.*

Gold Cup Special Reserve (84.5) n21 t22.5 f20 b21. Ultra soft, easily drinkable and, at times, highly impressive blend which is hampered by a dustiness bestowed upon it by the nagging caramels on both nose and finish. Some lovely early honey does help lift it, though, and there is also attractive Swiss roll jam towards the finish. Yet never quite gets out of third gear despite the most delicate hint of smoke. *39%. Campari, Brasil.*

Gran Par (77) n19.5 t22 f17.5 b18. The delivery is eleven seconds of vaguely malty glory. The remainder is thin and caramelled with no age to live up to the name. And with Par in the title and bagpipes and kilt in the motif, how long before the SWA buys a case of it...? *39%*

Green Valley Special Reserve batch 07/01 **(70) n16 t19 f17 b18.** A softly oiled, gently bitter-sweet blend with a half meaty, half boiled sweet nose. An unusual whisky experience. *38.1%. Muraro & Cia.*

Malte Barrilete Blended Whisky batch 001/03 **(76) n18 t20 f19 b19.** This brand has picked up a distinctive apple-fruitiness in recent years and some extra oak, too. *39.1%.*

Natu Nobilis (81.5) n22.5 t20 f19 b20. The nose boasts a genuinely clean, Speyside-style malt involvement. But to taste is much more non-committal with the soft grain dominating and the grassy notes restricted the occasional foray over the tastebuds. Pleasant, but don't expect a flavor fest. *39%. Pernod Ricard, Brasil.*

Natu Nobilis Celebrity (86) n22.5 t22 f20.5 b21. A classy blend with a decent weight and body, yet never running to fat. Some spice prickle ensures the flavor profile never settles in a neutral zone and the charming, citrus-domiated malt on the nose is immediately found on the juicy delivery. A cut above the standard Natu Nobilis and if the finish could be filled out with extra length and complexity, we'd have an exceptionally impressive blend on our hands. Another blend to seek out whenever in Brazil. *39%. Pernod Ricard, Brasil.*

O Monge batch 02/02 **(69) n17 t18 f17 b17.** Poor nose but it recovers with a malty mouth arrival but the thinness of the grain does few favours. *38.5%. Union Distillery.*

Old Eight Special Reserve (85.5) n20 t21 f22.5 b22. Traditionally reviled by many in Brazil, I can assure you that the big bite followed by calming soft grains is exactly what you need after a day's birding in the jungle. *39%. Campari, Brasil.*

Pitt's (84) n21 t20 f22 b21. The pits certainly aint!! A beautifully malted blend where the barley tries to dominate the exceptionally flinty grain whenever possible. Due to be launched later in 2004, this will be the best Brazil has to offer – though some fine tuning can probably improve the nose and middle even further and up the complexity significantly. I hope, when I visit the distillery early in 2005, I will be able to persuade them to offer a single malt: on this evidence it should, like Pitt's, be an enjoyable experience and perfect company for any World Cup finals. *40%. Busnello Distillery.*

Wall Street (84) n23 t22 f19 b20. Fabulous nose with a sexy citrus-light smoke double bill. And the arrival on the palate excels, too, with a rich texture and confident delivery of malt, again with the smoke dominating. But falls away rather too rapidly as the grains throw the balance out of kilter and ensures too much bitter oak late on. *38%. Pernod Ricard, Brasil.*

INDIA
AMRUT DISTILLERY

Amrut Single Malt batch 27, bott Mar 11 db **(92.5) n23** wow! How weird was that? Put the glass under my nose and...Lammerlaw! I was flown to New Zealand and taken back the best part of 20 years as the aroma showed so many aspects of the malt from that now sadly defunct distillery. Never noticed it on any Amrut before, even when I went through their stocks in the distillery warehouses. Beautifully light with the vanillas dancing on a malty, lightly salty breeze; the bourbon casks are tipping in just-so amounts of hickory; where the Lammerlaw effect comes into its own is with the citrusy haze to the sawdusty oak: a long time since I last encountered that particular timbre **t24** stunning sugars melt effortlessly into the honey-lemon theme; a succession of bourbon-style tones – honeycomb, hickory and liquorice mainly – melt effortlessly into the mix; spices, too...well, it is Indian... **f22.5** light and a little lazy, some spices think about adding to the vanilla, but can't be too fussed; **b23.5** an assured, elegant malt which now strides greatness with nonchalance. *46%. nc ncf.*

Amrut Cask Strength oak barrels, bott no. 01, bott Jul 09 db **(89.5) n23 t22.5 f22 b22.** Another big malty tale from India. But there is a big surge of natural, oily caramels to this one which keeps the complexity levels marginally down. *61.8%*

Amrut Cask Strength batch 5, bott Jun 10 db **(84) n21 t22 f20 b21.** Just a little extra aging here has brought a telling degree of caramel into play, swamping much else. Pleasant, but a reminder of just how fragile the line between greatness and just plain, old-fashioned good. *61.8%. nc ncf.*

Amrut Double Cask ex-bourbon cask no. 2874/2273, bott no. 44, bott Feb 10 db **(96) n23 t24.5 f24 b24.5.** Frankly, a malt I thought I'd never see: how can a whisky survive seven years under the unremitting Bangalore sun? I am proud of the very small part I played in seeing this wonderful whisky see the world: I tasted both casks, containing the oldest whisky Amrut had ever produced, in a cellar at the distillery earlier in the year and passed both not only fit but exceptional. But I made the observation that they would certainly be better still if mixed together as the personalities of both casks very much complimented the other. On the day the younger of the two casks turned seven years old, this they did and bottled it. And just to show how wonderful this whisky is, from now what must surely be from one of the top two or three malt whisky distilleries in the world, simply leave an empty glass of it by your bedside table and smell it first thing in the morning. *46%. 306 bottles.*

Amrut Fusion batch no. 01, bott Mar 09 db **(97) n24** heavy, thickly oaked and complex: some curious barley-sugar notes here shrouded in soft smoke. Big, but seductively gentle, too... **t24** the delivery, though controlled at first, is massive! Then more like con-fusion as that smoke on the nose turns into warming, full blown peat, but it far from gets its own way as a vague sherry trifle note (curious, seeing how there are no sherry butts involved) – the custard presumably is oaky vanilla - hammers home that barley-fruitiness to make for a bit of a free-for-all; but for extra food measure the flavours develop into a really intense chocolate fudge middle which absolutely resonates through the palate; **f24** a slight struggle here as the mouthfeel gets a bit puffy here with the dry peat and oak; enough molassed sweetness to see the malt through to a satisfying end, though. Above all the spices, rather than lying down and accepting their fate, rise up and usher this extraordinary whisky to its exit; **b25** one of the most complex and intriguing new whiskies of 2010 that needs about two days and half a bottle to get even close to fathoming. Not exactly a textbook whisky, with a few edges grinding together like tectonic plates. And there is even odd note, like the fruit and a kind of furry, oaky buzz, which I have never seen before. But that is the point of whiskies like this: to be different, to offer a unique slant. But, ultimately, to entertain and delight. And here it ticks all boxes accordingly. To the extent that this has to be one of the great whiskies found anywhere in the world this year. And the fact it is Indian? Irrelevant: from distillation to maturation this is genius whisky, from whichever continent... *50%*

Amrut Fusion batch 10, bott Mar 11 db **(94.5) n24** playful smoke mingles with Slovakian milk chocolate and crushed almond; for all the brooding oak much lighter than the original bottling but still an essay in complexity; **t24** the sugars are the first to show: the molten stuff on porridge variety. The barley has its big moment four or five flavour-waves in when it turns up the juicy volume; the vanillas grab the middle ground while the smoke hesitates; **f22.5** compared to the first bottling relatively short, though those spices, the remnants of the smoke, continue to buzz - if a little shy about it. Soft, sweetened cocoa marks the fade; **b23.5** superb whisky, though to be plotted on a different map to the now legendary Whisky Bible award-winning Batch 1. This is a much more delicate affair: more hints and shadows rather than statements and substance. Still, though, a fabulous malt whisky in Amrut's best style. *50%. nc.*

Amrut Herald cask no. 2857 db **(92) n23** nutty, north German marzipan smeared with bourbony liquorice; toasty and weighty; **t24** that unique, near perfect Amrut texture on delivery: softly oiled with more than a hint of crème brulee; however, it is the second round of flavours – a spice and molasses mix which really gets the taste buds tingling; **f22** big cream toffee with a dab of lingering spice; **b23** here is the news: Amrut have come up with another fabulous whisky. Actually, the news these days is when they don't... *60.8%. sc. 231 bottles.*

Amrut Intermediate Sherry Matured bott no. 01, bott Jun 10 db **(96.5) n24.5** instead of the usual biscuit aroma, we now get moist cake. And my word: is it fruity and spicy!! Love the freshly waxed oak floor, too. Brain-explodingly complex and multi-layered with one of the most intriguing sherry-style-bourbon-style marriages on the market; **t24** cracking delivery and entirely unique in form. The structure is decidedly oak-based, but acts as no more than a skeleton from which the juicy sultana and spices drape. Salivating, too, as the barley kicks in powerfully. But the liquorice-orangey-honeycomb bourbon theme quietly shapes the flavour profile; the spices pulse and glow; **f23.5** quite a chunk of natural caramel quietens the more exuberant characteristics; long and elegant; **b24.5** how do you get three freshly emptied oloroso butts from Jerez to Bangalore without the casks spoiling, and not use sulphur? Answer: empty two cases of Amrut cask strength whisky into each of the butts before shipping them. Not a single off note. No bitterness whatsoever. And the fruit is left to impart its extraordinary riches on a malt matured also in American oak. Amrut is spoiling us again... *57.1%*

Amrut Peated batch no. 1, bott Sep 08 db **(94) n23** unusually dry peat; not dissimilar to peat reek absorbed by an old leather armchair; a hint of citrus, too; **t24** despite the nose, the immediate sensation is one of being caressed by molassed sugar and then a ratching up of the peat notes. As they get more forceful, so the experience becomes that little bit drier and spicier, though not without the molasses refusing to give way; **f23.5** you can tell the quality of the distillate and the barrels it has been matured in by the crystalline depth to the finish. Everything is clear on the palate and the butterscotch vanillas wrap the phenols for a comfortable and clean finale; **b23.5** absolutely everything you could ask for a peated malt at this strength. The length and complexity are matched only by a train journey through this astonishing country. *46%*

Amrut Peated Cask Strength bott Apr 08 db **(92) n22 t22.5 f24.5 b23.** A touch of youth to this guy but the finish, entirely uncluttered by unnatural caramel or deprived by filtration, confirms a degree of greatness. By the way: if you want to experience something really stunning, try mixing the 2007 and 2008 peated. When you get the proportions right... well, watch out Islay...!! *62.78%*

Amrut Portonova db **(93) n22** a thick pudding of a nose; fruit and caramel have merged into one slightly over-oaked soup; burnt apple pie; **t24** this is essentially a port pipe sandwich...and it shows. The spicy, jammy fruit is interwoven through any amount of caramel while the oaky saltiness gets the taste buds both salivating and puckering until you run dry; **f24** long, massive oak with quite evident traces of the virgin barrels now detectable. And more of a cocoa hue as it progresses. At last some muscovado sugars arrive to supplant the berry fruits; **b23** this is a whisky so big, so blinding that when I first tasted it I was so dazzled I could barely see a thing. It was like coming out of the pitch black into a fierce light. My first instincts, while recoiling, was that there was too much oak at work. Only on acclimatisation did I work out what was going on here...and fall helplessly in love. There is still way too much oak, however you look at it and the nose, which neither improves nor worsens over time confirms that. Indeed, the entire thing is outrageous: I have never come across such a flavour profile before anywhere in the world. But my word: what a statement this makes... Unique. *62.1%*

Amrut Two Continents Limited Edition bott Feb 09 db **(95) n23.5 t24 f23.5 b24.** Here we have a malt distilled in India and matured first on the sub-continent and then Scotland. Let's just say that it is a malt which has travelled exceptionally well...and arrived at greatness. This is exactly how I like my whisky to be. *46%. 786 bottles.*

Amrut Two Continents 2nd Edition bott Jun 11 db **(95) n23.5** suet pudding – spotted dog. Some oils and banana milkshake, too; **t24** voluptuous delivery. A stunning meeting of juicy barley, soft fruits and delicate yet persistent spices; a light oiliness helps the more complex notes glide to all parts of the palate and some muscovado sugars make light of any oaky encroachment; the middle ground heads towards chocolate milkshake; **f23.5** long with the slowest build up of oaks on record. The spices continue to flit and fizz and finally vanilla takes hold; **b24** I didn't expect their 2nd edition of this to get anywhere near the first in quality: it has. Not because of any loss in faith in the distillery – quite the contrary, in fact – but because, if I have learned anything in 20 years reviewing whisky, distillers find it near enough impossible to recreate the sublime. This is a vaguely fruitier effort and all the more fascinating for that. *50%. nc ncf. 892 bottles.*

Amrut 100 Peated Single Malt ex-bourbon/virgin oak barrels db **(92) n23** youthful barley integrates effortlessly with the hickory and smoke: outrageously delicate for a nose so big; **t23** the virgin oak used has injected some major Demerara sugars. The smoke is not quite big enough to keep it all under control, nor the rising tide of vanillins; **f23.5** all kinds of milky mocha notes work well with that soothing smoke; **b22.5** ironically, though one of the older whiskies to come from this distillery, the nose shows a little bit of youth. A quite different style from Amrut's other peated offerings and it was obviously intended. Further proof that this distillery has grown not only in stature but confidence. And with very good reason. *57.1%. nc ncf.*

The Ultimate Amrut 2005 Cask Strength bourbon barrel no. 1641, bott no. 174, dist Dec 05, bott Apr 10 db **(94.5) n23.5** high phenols and proud of it: dank and earthy, bluebells in full bloom; slightly musky with neither the sweet or dry notes enjoying the upper hand; **t24** eye-closingly beautiful: the waves of sweet peat roll uncontainably over the taste buds, the gristy sweetness merge with Demerara sugars and other sub bourbon notes; meanwhile the prickly peat continues its quiet rampage; **f23.5** long, a smoky spice buzz and countless strands of vanilla; **b23.5** it makes no difference whether made and matured in Islay or India, great malt whisky is just that. And this is near faultless. And, what's more, it appears to have a character and personality all its own. *62.8%*

Blackadder Amrut Rum Cask Finish cask BA5/2009, bott Jul 09 **(91.5) n23** thick, almost syrupy; an oak and sugar paste; **t24.5** as massive as expected. Plenty of sugars added to the mocha which punches through to occupy the middle ground; **f21.5** thins out surprisingly; **b22.5** for every action there is an equal and opposite reaction; so sweet to start, so dry on the finish. *62.%. nc ncf. 245 bottles.*

Milroy's of Soho Amrut 2003 cask no. 08/08/30-1, dist Jul 03, bott Jan 09 **(84) n21 t22 f20 b21** Juicy in part and very malty. But this whisky struggles at this kind of age with the oak, especially through the flattening natural caramels, dumbing the beauty down. *46%. 210 bottles.*

JOHN DISTILLERIES

A new single malt distillery in Cuncolim, Goa, which will have three single casks bottled while this book is being printed. Indeed, these cask strength malts are likely be the first bottles sampled for the 2014 edition! I managed to get hold of samples direct from the cask a few days prior to bottling. Each barrel is from the first batch ever produced and turned three years old on 1st August 2012. The scoring I give is therefore of the pre-bottled whisky. **Cask 161** scores a provisional **(94) n22.5 t24.5 f23 b24**, offering sweet malty intensity on its big delivery. **Cask 163** is better still, scoring **(94.5) n24 t24 f23 b23.5**, full of complex vanilla and bourbon notes. Best of all, though, is a real stunner: the massively honeyed **Cask 164** which scores **(96) n24 t24 f24 b24**. A typical Indian beast of a malt having matured way beyond its years. But, coming from coconut-strewn Goa, one with a hint of paradise...

PONDA DISTILLERY

Stillman's Dram Single Malt Whisky Limited Edition bourbon cask no. 11186-90 **(94) n23** beautifully soft peats fuse with lime-led citrus notes. At once delicate and enormous; **t23** softly smoked malts dissolve into honeyed pools on the palate. Sexier and more relaxing than a Goan foot massage; **f24** the way the delicate oak washes gently against the palate, the manner in which the soft peats build to a crescendo - and yet still refuse to overpower – the entrancing waves of muscovado-sweetened coffee, all make for a sublime finale; **b24** well, I thought I had tasted it all with the Amrut cask strength. And then this arrived at my lab…!! I predicted many years back that India would dish out some top grade malt before too long. But I'd be stretching the truth if I said I thought it would ever be this good… 42.8%. McDowell & Co Ltd, India.

Blends

Antiquity blend of rare Scotch and matured Indian malts, bott Feb 06 **(79) n20 t21 f19 b19.** Uncluttered but clever in places with a silky and distinctly malty delivery on the palate; the oak – not noticeable on the nose – dominates the finish intertwined with toffee-caramel. Attractive, but never quite works out which direction it is going. 42.8%. Shaw Wallace Distilleries, India. No added flavours.

⸫ **Antiquity Blue Ultra Premium Whisky** batch 175, bott 16 Sep 11 **(77) n19.5 t20 f18.5 b19.** Busy and nutty, a blend which sets its stall out by depending on a creamy, lush texture. Juicy malt-tinged delivery before spices develop. Bitters out towards the end. 42.8%. United Spirits Ltd.

⸫ **McDowell's Single Malt** batch 33, bott June 11 **(82) n20.5 t21.5 f20 b20.** The malt is hugely intense and offers a degree of gristy juiciness and on the nose something approaching a faint puff of peat. The show is let down by what appears to be very old casks which refuse to offer the support and complexity the decent malt deserves. 42.8%

⸫ **McDowell's Single Malt** batch 33, bott May 11 **(78) n19 t21 f19 b19.** A sharp, salivating malt which works hard to shrug off the tart intrusiveness of some baser cask notes. Silky in part, smoky in others, this malt struggles to find its balance. Curiously, this claims the same batch, 033, as the June bottling. Yet they are like chalk and cheese. This is much darker, too. 42.8%

⸫ **McDowell's No 1 Diet Mate** batch 103, bott 24 Jun 11 **(76.5) n18 t19.5 f19 b20.** A genuinely odd whisky. The nose is scented like a tart's boudoir while the finish is simply tart. The delivery, though, does offer a nimble malt effect while the spices rumble with attractive intent. As a fan of McDowell, I can't say this is quite their finest moment. 42.8%. Blended with Scotch and select Indian malts.

⸫ **Old Oak Aged 12 Years Premium Malt Whisky** batch 76, bott Oct 11 **(72) n19.5 t18 f17.5 b17.** It claims "unique taste". Indeed, it has: a malt whisky totally devoid of any discernable malt flavour. Soft and big on caramel. As a whisky of sorts, OK. As an "Aged 12 Years Premium malt whisky" a bit pathetic. 42.8%. Adinco Distilleries.

Peter Scot Malt Whisky (84) n20 t21 f22 b21. Enjoyable balance between sweetness and oak and entertainingly enlivened by what appears to be some young, juicy malt. 42.8%.

⸫ **Royal Challenge** batch 276, bott 31 Jan 11 **(82) n21.5 t20 f20 b20.5.** The Challenge appears to have been to spread the malts as thinly as possible across the grains yet still make an impact: a kind of malty comb over. The malts used are pretty delicious, though, and makes for a satisfying and attractive blend. 42.8%. A blend of rare Scotch, select grain and mature Indian malts. Mandovi Distilleries for United Spirits Ltd.

⸫ **Royal Stag Barrel Select** batch 212, bott 17 Feb 12 **(75.5) n20.5 t19 f17 b18.** Thin and sweet. But should be shot to put it out of its misery. 42.8% Seagrams. Mix of Scotch malt and India grain spirit.

⸫ **Seagram's Blender's Pride** batch 672 bott 12/12/11 **(85) n21.5 t21 f21 b21.5.** A thoughtful composition of soft sugars and caramels. Excellent texture and, rare for an Indian admix, the finish actually ups in complexity and weight. Good spices and attractive playful smoke on the nose especially. 42.8%. Mix of Scotch malt and India grain spirit.

⸫ **Signature** batch 285, bott 05 Jan 12 **(81.5) n22.5 t22 f17.5 b19.5.** Excellent, rich nose and delivery helped along with a healthy display of peat reek. But more attention has to be paid to the brutally thin finish. 42.8% Mandovi Distilleries for United Spirits Ltd.

NEW ZEALAND
THE SOUTHERN DISTILLING CO LTD

The Coaster Single Malt Whiskey batch no. 2356 **(85) n20 t22 f21 b22.** Distinctly small batch and sma' still with the accent very much on honey. Nosed blind I might have mistaken as Blue Mouse whisky from Germany: certainly European in style. Recovers well from the wobble on the nose and rewards further investigation. 40%

The MacKenzie Blended Malt Whiskey (85) n20 t22 f21 b22. A vaguely spicier, chalkier, mildly less honeyed version of Coaster. Quite banana-laden nose. I have flown over Timeru many times, half way as it is between Christchurch and Dunedin. By the time you read this, there is more than even chance I shall have driven there and visited this distillery. I'll let you know on the website. 40%

WILSON DISTILLERY

Cadenhead's World Whiskies Lammerlaw Aged 10 Years bourbon, bott Sep 07 **(91.5)** n22 t23.5 f23 b23. Stunning bottlings like this can only leave one mourning the loss of this distillery. 48.9%. 198 bottles.

Blends

Kiwi Whisky (37) n2 t12 f11 b12. Strewth! I mean, what can you say? Perhaps the first whisky containing single malt offering virtually no nose at all and the flavour appears to be grain neutral spirit plus lashings of caramel and (so I am told) some Lammerlaw single malt. The word bland has been redefined. As has whisky. 40%. Ever-Rising Enterprises, NZ, for the Asian market.

Wilson's Superior Blend (89) n22 t23 f21 b23. Apparently has a mixed reception in its native New Zealand but I fail to see why: this is unambiguously outstanding blended whisky. On the nose you expect a mouthwatering mouthful and it delivers with aplomb. Despite this being a lower priced blend it is, intriguingly, a marriage of 60% original bottled 10-y-o Lammerlaw and 40% old Wilson's blend, explaining the high malt apparent. Dangerous and delicious and would be better still at a fuller strength...and with less caramel. 37.5%. Continental Wines and Spirits, NZ.

SOUTH AFRICA
JAMES SEDGWICK DISTILLERY

Three Ships 10 Years Old db **(83)** n21 t21 f20 b21. Seems to have changed character, with more emphasis on sherry and natural toffee. The oak offers a thrusting undercurrent. 43%

Three Ships Aged 10 Years Single Malt Limited Edition db **(91)** n22.5 hints of smoke and cocoa, but some course oak has something to say, too; **t22.5** very much like a blend in style: there is bite and a touch of spite. But a soft fruitiness to stem the bleeding; **f23** for a while you think there will be some fruity civility, at times laid on with a red carpet. Then the cat is back, scratching and pawing at you with oaky talons – my word, I love it...! **b23.5** if you are looking for a soft, sophisticated malt whose delicate fingers can sooth your troubled brow, then don't bother with this one. On the other hand, if you are looking for a bit of rough, some entertaining slap and tickle: a slam-bam shag of a whisky - a useful port in a storm - then your boat may just have sailed in... Beware. an evening with this and you'll be secretly coming back for more... 43%

Bain's Cape Mountain Single Grain Whisky db **(85.5)** n21 t22 f21 b21.5. A lively, attractively structured whisky with more attitude than you might expect. Some lovely nip and hint despite the toffee and surprising degree of soft oils. 43%

Blends

Drayman's Solera (86) n19 t22 f23 b22. For a change, the label gets it spot on with its description of chocolate orange: it is there in abundance. If they can get this nose sorted they would be on for an all round impressive dram. As it is, luxuriate in the excellent mouthfeel and gentle interplay between malt and oak. Oh and those chocolate oranges... 43%. Drayman's Distillery. South African/Scotch Whisky.

Harrier (78) n20 t20 f19 b19. Not sure what has happened to this one. Has bittered to a significant degree while the smoke has vanished. A strange, almost synthetic, feel to this now. 43%. South African/Scotch Whisky.

Knights (83) n20.5 t21 f20 b20.5. While the Harrier has crashed, the Knights is now full of promise. Also shows the odd bitter touch but a better all-round richer body not only absorbs the impacts but radiates some malty charm. 43%. South African/Scotch Whisky.

Knights Aged 3 Years (87) n22 bourbony vanillas and toffee; **t22** a superb bite to this with a salivating, sweet and oily follow through; **f22** wonderfully textured vanilla and caramel; **b22** this now appears to be 100% South African whisky if I understand the label correctly: "Distilled Matured and Bottled in South Africa." A vast improvement on when it was Scotch malt and South African grain. Bursting with attitude and vitality. When next in South Africa, this will be my daily dram for sure. Love it. 43%. James Sedgwick Distillery.

Three Ships Bourbon Cask Finish (90) n22 t23 f22.5 b22.5. A soft, even whisky which enjoys its finest moments on delivery. Clean with a pressing, toasty oakiness to the sweeter malt elements. Always a delight. 43%

Three Ships Premium Select Aged 5 Years (93) n23 personality change alert: soft smoke offers an elegant sweetness; **t23.5** the silkiest delivery south of the equator. The grains dominate the mouth feel, but rule with gentle wisdom. The smoke takes a little time to form in any great weight and certainly helps the spices beautifully; **f23** soft enough to melt but with sufficient oils, smoky weight and milk chocolate Maltesers to take the finish into extra time; **b23.5** what a fabulous whisky. The blender has shown a rare degree of craft to make so little smoke do so much. Bravo! 43%. James Sedgwick Distillery.

Three Ships Select (81) n19 t21 f20 b21. Busy and sweet. But I get the feeling that whatever South African malt may be found in Knights does a better job than its Scotch counterpart here. *43%. James Sedgwick Distillery.*

TAIWAN
KAVALAN DISTILLERY

Kavalan db **(91) n23** predominantly fruity: plums and raisins topped by mint; a lovely dried date background; **t23** firm, flinty, juicy delivery with thudding malts soothed and comforted by lighter fruits; the mid ground moves towards a more lush, velvety texture and the first signs an oaky weight; **f22** a light buzz on the tongue points to a less than perfect sherry butt somewhere, but the compactness of the barley against the expansiveness of the delicate fruit remains a source of enjoyment; **b23** a high quality, confident malt which underline's this distillery's enormous potential. *40%*

Kavalan Concertmaster Single Malt Port cask finish db **(87) n22 t23 f20.5 b21.5.** A malt which will split its audience. In Germany, for instance, the light sulphur note will win all kinds of standing ovations; however, to the purist there will be a preference that it was not there. Because this piece has many moments of beauty as the malt and grape mingle and interlink: together they are company, anything else is a crowd. Even so I envisage many an encore for this... *40%*

Kavalan King Car Conductor db **(89.5) n22.5** complex, nutty, salty and vibrant, this conductor has decided to belt this one out, yet leave room for a bit of pathos when necessary...; **t23** a sublime mingling of salty oaks; there is something of the cocktail olive about this; elsewhere clean grapey oaks rule the roost; **f22** sharpens slightly too vividly for comfort but again fruit comes to a crisp rescue; **b22** not quite sure where the salt comes from; this distillery is far enough inland not to be affected. But it is there and does no harm whatsoever. Not quite technically perfect, as at least some of the characteristics are so contra they occasionally jar. But still fabulous whisky and a journey entirely worth embarking on. *46%*

Kavalan Solist Bari̇que db cask no. W080218037 **(90.5) n23** wild hedge fruits over ripening; big salt and vanilla yogurt; dry and creamy...; a little dry note which we might see later...; **t24** the delivery is one of puckering spice and fruit. Juicy, busy, profound. Makes the hairs on your neck stand on end. As they do, a big cocoa middle forms and the raisins appear to roast on your palate; **f21** just wilts slightly with a vaguely over sharp note predicted on the nose; **b22.5** this distillery is, in all the world, my favourite to visit. The drama of the geology in which it is set appears matched only by what one discovers from time to time in their warehouses. It has the potential for true world greatness, though this bottling, for all its magnificence, only nudges rather than grasps at the prospect. *59.2%. nc ncf sc. 237 bottles.*

Kavalan Solist Fino Sherry Cask db cask no. S060814045, bott no. 079/500 **(95) n24.5 t24.5 f22.5 b23.5.** When Dr Jim Swan, the distillery's consultant, told me he thought he'd found a cask which could well be a world-beater, I had mixed feelings. On one hand he'd been right when he'd said the same thing when he found a port pipe for Penderyn which has now entered Welsh whisky folklore. But, on the other, there are many times during the year when those I have long known in the game, including some good friends, have called me after reading my review and asked why I had marked their Great Hope down. Jim, though, has got this one spot on. The natural colour is astonishingly un-fino-esque and the overall experience is one that you come across only too rarely in life – especially with sherry butts. The marriage between the sweeter malt and drier grape notes is a thing of not just beauty, but awe. This is a bottling which will place the King Car Yuan-Shan distillery on the world map of truly great distilleries. Because having an exceptional cask is one thing. You also have to have a spirit excellent enough to maximize the potential of that cask and not be overwhelmed by it. That is exactly what you have here. A great new whisky dynasty has been born... *58.5%. ncf nc.*

Kavalan Solist Fino Sherry Cask db cask no. S060814021 **(97) n24.5** faultless fino: the dry, slightly salty grape offers both a sweet juiciness and a weightier dry pulpiness; delicate, strictly piano but entirely open for key spices to emerge allegro; **t24** the intermezzo is brief and soon we are once more into full blooded spices in which white peppers take the leading role. The malt, astonishingly, can still be heard rumbling among the bases but it is the dry, biting grape and oak which takes the breath away; **f24** the finale, as to be expected, is no half hearted affair; no withering away. This remains sophisticated to the very last, allowing some delicate sugars from the oak to counter and lengthen and add tone; **b24.5** it might be argued that the one and only thing that makes this exceptional is the quality of the cask, rather than the actual malt it contains. Well, let me set the record straight in this one. Earlier this week I made a very rare escape from my tasting room and visited the Royal Albert Hall for the 34th Prom of the 2011 season. The highlight of the evening was Camille Saint-Saens Symphony No 3 – "Organ". Now some critics, when they can find time to extract themselves from their own rear ends, dismiss this as a commoners' piece; something to amuse the plebeian. What they appear to not have is neither the wit nor humanity to understand that Saint-Saens sewed into this work a degree of such subtle shade and emotion, especially in the less dramatic second movement, that it can, when treated correctly, affect those capable of normal warmth and feeling. With so many nerve endings tingling and nowhere to go Saint-Saens seemingly recognised that he required something profound – in this case the organ – to create a backbone. And someone able to use it to maximum effect. And there we had it the other day: the Royal Albert Hall's awe-inspiring organ, and Thomas Trotter to make it come alive: The Solist. And this is what we have here: a perfect fino sherry selected by the maestro Dr Jim Swan. But able to display its full magnificence only because the host spirit is so beautifully composed. Good whisky is, without question, a work of art; great whisky is a tone poem. And here, I beg to insist, is proof. *58.4%. nc ncf sc. 513 bottles.*

⁘ **Ka Va Lan Solist Vinho Barrique** cask W080218011 bott 08 Nov 11 **(93) n23** huge coffee with crushed brown sugars and burnt raisin; **t24** stunning delivery with a controlled intensity and sugary crispness which works so well with the pounding spices. The fruit envelopes the scene offering a softer, complementary structure; **f22.5** much firmer, again with a degree of brittleness. The vanillas are slow coming forward; the spices aren't..; **b23.5** this distillery in a very short time has already planted its flag firmly at the peak of the world's best whiskies. *60%*

Other Brands Available In Taiwan

Eagle Leader Storage Whisky (81.5) n20 t21 f21 b20.5. Attractively smoky with a surprisingly long finish for a whisky which initially appears to lack body. By no means straightforward, but never less than pleasant. *40%*

Golden Hill Single Malt (75) n18 t20 f19 b18. An unwieldy heavyweight. *40%*

Golden Knight All Malt (61) n17 t16 f12 b16. Amazingly thin for a malt with all the weight provided by caramel. *40%*

Golden Shield Storage Whisky (62.5) n17.5 t16 f14 b15. Tarnished gold. Grim. *40%*

Good Deer (in Chinese Characters) *see McAdams Rye Whisky*

Louis Dynasty (66.5) n16 t16 f17.5 b17. A very strange concoction. Certain elements leave much to be desired, offering a most peculiar mouth feel. Yet there is also the odd smoke note which beds down the sweeter, firmer notes. *40%*

McAdams Rye Whisky bott Nov 09 **(85.5) n21 t22 f21.5 b21.5.** Thoroughly delicious stuff absolutely brimming with juicy, crisp grain notes. The body is lightly oiled and shapely while the finish is sweet and attractive. The odd green apple note, too. *40%. Note: Says it's made in Taiwan, but possesses a maple leaf on the label.*

Sea Pirates (77) n18 t21 f19 b19. More Johnny Depp than Errol Flynn. Attractive smoke, though. *40%*

URUGUAY

Dunbar Anejo 5 Años (85.5) n20 t22.5 t21.5 b21.5. A clean, mouth-wateringly attractive mix where the grain nips playfully and the Speyside malts are on best salivating behaviour. Decently blended and boasting a fine spice prickle, too. *40%*

Seagram's Blenders Pride (83) n20.5 t22 f20b20.5. The busy, relatively rich delivery contrasts with the theme of the silky grains and caramel. Easy drinking. *40%*

MISCELLANEOUS

Jaburn & Co Pure Grain & Malt Spirit (53) n14 t13 f13 b13. Tastes like neutral grain and caramel to me. Some shop keepers, I hear, are selling it as whisky though this is not claimed on the label. Trust me: it isn't. *37.5%. Jaburn & Co, Denmark.*

House of Westend Blended Whisky (67) n17 t18 f16 b16. No more than OK if you are being generous; some tobacco-dirty notes around. Doesn't mention country of origin anywhere on the label. *40%. Bernkasteler Burghof, Germany.*

Prince of Wales Welsh Whisky (69) n17 t18 f17 b17. Syrupy aroma is compounded by an almost liqueurish body. Thin in true Scotch substance, probably because it claims to be Welsh but is really Scotch with herbs diffused in a process that took place in Wales. Interestingly, my "liqueur" tasting notes were written before I knew exactly what it was I was tasting, thus proving the point and confirming that, with these additives, this really isn't whisky at all. *40%*

Shepherd's Export Finest Blend (46) n5 t16 f12 b13. A dreadful, illdefined grain-spirit nose is softened on the palate by an early mega-sweet kick. The finish is thin and eventually bitter. Feeble stuff. *37.2%. "A superb blend of Imported Scotch Malt whiskies and Distilled N.Z. grain spirit", claims the label which originally gives the strength as 40%, but has been over-written. Also, the grain, I was told, was from the USA. Southern Grain Spirit, NZ.*

Slàinte

It seems as though you can't have a Bible without a whole lot of begetting. And without all those listed below – vast velodromes full of all the world's whisky people – this Jim Murray's Whisky Bible 2013 would never have been begot at all. A huge amount of blood, sweat and tears go into the production of each edition, more than anyone not directly involved could even begin to comprehend. So, as usual, I must thank my amazing team: James Murray, Ally Telfer, Billy Jeffrey, David Rankin and Dani Dal Molin. Also special thanks to the indefatigable Julia Nourney for again dredging the distilleries of Europe on my behalf. For the North American sections, my heartfelt appreciation goes to the staff and management of the Union Club of British Columbia in Victoria, something of my second home these days, and my dearest friends and supporters of long-standing, Mick and Tammy Secor of the Highland Stillhouse in Oregon City. This tenth edition of the Whisky Bible could also not have been completed without the unstinting support and friendship of Heiko Thieme, Hodie Rondeau and Lawrence Graham, heroes all. Because the list of thank yous had now exceeded two pages, we are starting again with those who have helped in providing help and samples for the 2013 Bible. For all those who have assisted in the previous decade, we remain indebted.

Mitch Abate; Ally Alpine; Duncan Baldwin; Clare Banner; Kirsteen Beeston; Annie Bellis; Menno Bijmolt; Hans Bol; Etienne Bouillon; Birgit Bournemeier; Phil Brandon; Stephen Bremner; Stephanie Bridge; James Brown; Sara Browne; Michael Brzozowski; Alexander Buchholz; Amy Burgess; Bert Cason; Julia Christian; Nick Clark; Dr Martin Collis; Jason Craig; David Croll; Stephen Davies; Alasdair Day; Rob Dietrich; Angela D'Orazio; Jean Donnay; Camille Duhr-Merges; Mariette Duhr-Merges; Gemma Duncan; Ray Edwards; Carsten Ehrlich; Ben Ellefsen; James Espey; Jennifer Eveleigh; Thomas Ewers; Joanna Fearnside; David Fitt; Martyn Flynn; Danny Gandert; Carole Gibson; John Glaser; John Glass; Emily Glynn; Rebecca Groom; Jasmin Haider; Georgina Hall; Scott E Harris; Alistair Hart; Andrew Hart; Donald Hart; Stuart Harvey; Ailsa Hayes; Ross Hendry; Roland Hinterreiter; Bernhard Höning; Emma Hurley; Kai Ivalo; Amelia James; Michael John; Celine Johns; Sebastian Lauinger; Christelle Le Lay; Lars Lindberger; Alistair Longwell; John Maclellan; Dennis Malcolm; Leanne Matthews; Stephen R McCarthy; Angela Mcilrath; Douglas McIvor; Maggie Miller; Euan Mitchell; Paul Mitchell; Henk Mol; Nick Morgan; Maggie Morri; Fabien Mueller; Michael Myers; Andrew Nelstrop; Alex Nicol; Jane Nicol; Soren Norgaard; Tom O'Connor; Casey Overeem; Richard Parker; Sanjay Paul; Amy Preske; Rachel Quinn; Carrie Revell; Kay Riddoch; Massimo Righi; Patrick Roberts; James Robertson; David Roussier; Ronnie Routledge; Jim Rutledge; Caroline Rylance; Paloma Salmeron Planells; John Savage-Onstwedder; Ian Schmidt; Rubyna Sheik; Caley Shoemaker; Jamie Siefken; Sam Simmons; Alastair Sinclair; Sukhinder Singh; Barbara Smith; Gigha Smith; Phil Smith; Cat Spencer; Vicky Stevens; Karen Stewart; Katy Stollery; Henning Svoldgaard; Tom Swift; Chip Tate; Marko Tayburn; Celine Tetu; Sarah Thacker; Hamish Torrie; Richard Urquhart; Stuart Urquhart; CJ Van Dijk; Aurelien Villefranche; Anna Wilson; Nick White; Arthur Winning; Stephen Worrall; Kate Wright; Frank Wu; Tom Wyss; Junko Yaguchi; Ruslan Zamoskovny. And, of course, in warm memory of Mike Smith.

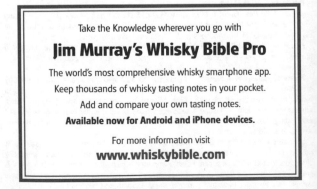